**Fodor's**

# ESSENTIAL JAPAN

# Welcome to Japan

Tradition and modernity share space in this island nation where ancient shrines bump up against skyscrapers. Castles and palaces whisper of history, and bullet trains shuttle you through spectacular landscapes to cities packed with world-class restaurants and shopping. From Tokyo's urban sprawl to the peacefulness of Kyoto, from boisterous Osaka nightlife to Hiroshima's contemplative spirit, Japan's big attractions never fail to dazzle first-time visitors. What keeps people coming back is astoundingly delicious food, a unique culture, and warm hospitality.

## TOP REASONS TO GO

★ **Urban buzz:** Tokyo's skyscrapers, pedestrian throngs, clockwork trains, and nightlife.

★ **Food:** It's all here, from quick noodles to fresh sushi to delicate *kaiseki* cuisine.

★ **Festivals:** You can drop your inhibitions, pick up the sake, and dance in the street.

★ **Mt. Fuji:** The poster mountain for symmetrical, snowcapped peaks looms large.

★ **Shopping:** Craft markets, street stalls, trendy boutiques, flagship department stores.

★ **Serene spaces:** Temples, shrines, and traditional gardens offer room for reflection.

# Contents

**1 EXPERIENCE JAPAN** .............. 9
25 Ultimate Experiences ........... 10
What's Where ..................... 20
What to Eat and Drink in Japan ..... 24
10 Quirky Souvenir Stores in Tokyo .. 26
Traditional Crafts to Buy .......... 28
Japan's Top Temples and Shrines ... 30
Japan with Kids .................. 32
What to Watch and Read .......... 34
Japan Today ..................... 36

**2 TRAVEL SMART** .................. 45
Know Before You Go ............. 46
Getting Here and Around ......... 48
Transportation Planner ........... 56
Essentials ....................... 58
Helpful Japanese Phrases ......... 66
Contacts ......................... 68
Japanese Etiquette ............... 70
Great Itineraries ................. 72
On the Calendar .................. 80
Money-Saving Tips ............... 82

**3 A JAPANESE CULTURE PRIMER** .... 83
Japanese Fine Arts ............... 94
Performing Arts .................. 98
Onsen and Bathing .............. 102
The Ryokan ..................... 106
Japanese Pop Culture ........... 108
Baseball in Japan ............... 110
Japanese Martial Arts .......... 112
Sumo ........................... 114
The Geisha ...................... 116
The Tea Ceremony .............. 118
Japanese Gardens .............. 120
Religion in Japan ............... 122

**4 TOKYO** ........................ 127
Welcome to Tokyo .............. 128
Tokyo's Vending Machines
and Convenience Stores .......... 130
Planning ........................ 132
Imperial Palace (皇居近辺) ....... 138
Marunouchi (丸の内) ............ 142
Nihonbashi (日本橋) ............. 150

Ginza (銀座) .................... 153
Tsukiji (築地) ................... 164
Shiodome (汐留) ................ 165
Aoyama (青山) and
Harajuku (原宿) ................. 169
Shibuya (渋谷) .................. 178
Roppongi (六本木) .............. 187
Shinjuku (新宿) ................. 196
Akihabara (秋葉原) ............. 207
Ueno (上野) .................... 211
Asakusa (浅草) ................. 218
Greater Tokyo ................... 226

**5 SIDE TRIPS FROM TOKYO** ....... 233
Welcome to Side Trips from Tokyo . 234
Planning ........................ 237
Yokohama (横浜) ................ 238
Kamakura (鎌倉) ................ 250
Mt. Fuji (富士山; Fuji-san) ....... 263
Fuji Five Lakes
(富士五湖; Fuji Go-ko) .......... 265
Hakone (箱根) .................. 275
Izu Peninsula
(伊豆半島) ...................... 280
Mt. Takao (高尾山) .............. 289
Nikko (日光) .................... 290

**6 NAGOYA, ISE-SHIMA,
AND THE KII PENINSULA** ....... 303
Welcome to Nagoya,
Ise-Shima, and the Kii Peninsula ... 304
Planning ........................ 307
Nagoya (名古屋) ................ 310
Gifu (岐阜) ..................... 319
Inuyama (犬山) ................. 322
Iga Ueno (伊賀上野) ............ 324
Ise (伊勢) ...................... 324
Kashikojima (賢島) .............. 328
Shingu (新宮) ................... 329
Doro-kyo (瀞峡) ................ 330
Nachi (那智) .................... 330
Shirahama (白浜) ............... 331
Koya-san (高野山) ............... 331

**7 THE JAPAN ALPS AND
THE NORTH CHUBU COAST**...... 335
Welcome to the Japan Alps
and the North Chubu Coast........ 336
Gassho-zukuri Farmhouses........ 338
Planning........................ 341
Karuizawa (軽井沢)............... 343
Kusatsu (草津)................... 344
Nagano (長野).................... 345
Matsumoto (松本)................ 349
Hakuba (白馬).................... 354
Kiso Valley (木曾谷)............. 357
Kamikochi (上高地).............. 358
Takayama (高山)................. 360
Shirakawa-go (白川郷).......... 363
Kanazawa (金沢)................ 364
Noto Peninsula (能登半島)....... 372
Toyama (富山)................... 374
Niigata (新潟)................... 375
Sado Island
(佐渡島; Sado-ga-shima)......... 377

**8 KYOTO** ......................... 381
Welcome to Kyoto................ 382
Planning........................ 384
Eastern Kyoto................... 391
Central Kyoto ................... 417
Southern Kyoto ................. 434
Western Kyoto .................. 438
Arashiyama...................... 443
Northern Kyoto ................. 449

**9 THE KANSAI REGION** ........... 455
Welcome to the Kansai Region..... 456
Nara's Sacred Deer .............. 458
Sake, the Japanese Drink ........ 460
Planning........................ 463
Osaka (大阪市).................. 465
Nara (奈良市) ................... 488
Kobe (神戸市) ................... 502
Himeji (姫路市)................. 520

**Fodor's Features**

Isolation and Engagement:
A History of Japan........................ 39
A Taste of Japan ......................... 85
Shop Tokyo ............................ 159
Peerless Fuji ........................... 266
The Philosopher's Path ................. 398
The Art of Monozukuri.................. 509
A Walk through Hiroshima's
Peace Memorial Park.................. 536
The Henro: Shikoku's 88-
Temple Pilgrimage...................... 569

**10 WESTERN HONSHU** ............ 523
Welcome to Western Honshu...... 524
Planning........................ 526
Okayama (岡山) .................. 528
Kurashiki (倉敷) ................. 530
Hiroshima (広島).................. 532
Miyajima (宮島).................. 544
Iwakuni (岩国市) ................. 547
Hagi (萩) ........................ 548
Tsuwano (津和野) ................ 550
Matsue (松江).................... 553
Izumo Taisha (出雲大社)......... 557

11 **SHIKOKU** . . . . . . . . . . . . . . . . . . . . . **559**
Welcome to Shikoku . . . . . . . . . . . . . 560
Planning . . . . . . . . . . . . . . . . . . . . . . . . 563
Takamatsu (高松) . . . . . . . . . . . . . . . . 565
Naoshima (直島) . . . . . . . . . . . . . . . . . 576
Kotohira (琴平) . . . . . . . . . . . . . . . . . 579
Tokushima (徳島) . . . . . . . . . . . . . . . . 580
Iya Valley and Oboke-Koboke Gorges
(祖谷と大歩危小歩危) . . . . . . . . . . . 583
Kochi (高知) . . . . . . . . . . . . . . . . . . . . 586
Matsuyama (松山) . . . . . . . . . . . . . . . 591
Uchiko (内子) . . . . . . . . . . . . . . . . . . . 596
Uwajima (宇和島市) . . . . . . . . . . . . . . 597
Shimanami Kaido (しまなみ街道) . 598

12 **KYUSHU** . . . . . . . . . . . . . . . . . . . . . . **601**
Welcome to Kyushu . . . . . . . . . . . . . . 602
Planning . . . . . . . . . . . . . . . . . . . . . . . . 605
Fukuoka (福岡) . . . . . . . . . . . . . . . . . 606
Nagasaki (長崎) . . . . . . . . . . . . . . . . 610
Kumamoto (熊本) . . . . . . . . . . . . . . . 616
Mt. Aso (阿蘇山; Aso-san) . . . . . . . 619
Kurokawa Onsen (黒川温泉) . . . . . . 621
Yufuin (湯布院) . . . . . . . . . . . . . . . . . 622
Takachiho (高千穂) . . . . . . . . . . . . . . 625
Kirishima-Kinkowan National Park
(霧島屋久国立公園) . . . . . . . . . . . . 627
Kagoshima (鹿児島) . . . . . . . . . . . . . 628

13 **OKINAWA** . . . . . . . . . . . . . . . . . . . . . **631**
Welcome to Okinawa . . . . . . . . . . . . . 632
Okinawa's World War II Sights . . . . . 634
Planning . . . . . . . . . . . . . . . . . . . . . . . . 637
Okinawa Main Island (沖縄島) . . . . 638
Kerama Islands (慶良間諸島) . . . . . 652
Miyako Islands (宮古諸島) . . . . . . . 653
Yaeyama Islands (八重山諸島) . . . . 657

14 **TOHOKU** . . . . . . . . . . . . . . . . . . . . . . **665**
Welcome to Tohoku . . . . . . . . . . . . . . 666
Planning . . . . . . . . . . . . . . . . . . . . . . . . 669
Sendai (仙台) . . . . . . . . . . . . . . . . . . . 672
Morioka (盛岡) . . . . . . . . . . . . . . . . . 678
Matsushima (松島) . . . . . . . . . . . . . . 682
Yamadera (山寺) . . . . . . . . . . . . . . . . 684
Hiraizumi (平泉) . . . . . . . . . . . . . . . . 685
Yamagata (山形) . . . . . . . . . . . . . . . . 687
Tazawa-ko (田沢湖) . . . . . . . . . . . . . 689
Kakunodate (角館) . . . . . . . . . . . . . . 692
Towada–Hachimantai National Park
(十和田八幡平国立公園) . . . . . . . 694
Hirosaki (弘前) . . . . . . . . . . . . . . . . . 695
Aomori (青森) . . . . . . . . . . . . . . . . . . 698
Akita (秋田) . . . . . . . . . . . . . . . . . . . . 701
Tsuruoka and
Dewa-Sanzan
(鶴岡と出羽三山) . . . . . . . . . . . . . . 704

15 **HOKKAIDO** . . . . . . . . . . . . . . . . . . . . **707**
Welcome to Hokkaido . . . . . . . . . . . . 708
Winter Sports in Hokkaido . . . . . . . . 710
Planning . . . . . . . . . . . . . . . . . . . . . . . . 714
Hakodate (函館) . . . . . . . . . . . . . . . . 718
Sapporo (札幌) . . . . . . . . . . . . . . . . . 722
Teine (サッポロテイネ) . . . . . . . . . . 732
Otaru (小樽) . . . . . . . . . . . . . . . . . . . . 733
Niseko (ニセコ) . . . . . . . . . . . . . . . . . 737
Rusutsu (留寿都村) . . . . . . . . . . . . . . 740
Toyako (洞爺湖) . . . . . . . . . . . . . . . . 741
Noboribetsu Onsen
(登別温泉) . . . . . . . . . . . . . . . . . . . . 743
Shiraoi (白老町) . . . . . . . . . . . . . . . . 744
Daisetsuzan National Park
(大雪山国立公園) . . . . . . . . . . . . . . 744
Furano (富良野市) . . . . . . . . . . . . . . 746

Abashiri (網走) . . . . . . . . . . . . . . . . . . . 747
Shiretoko National Park
(知床国立公園) . . . . . . . . . . . . . . . . . . 749
Akan National Park
(阿寒国立公園) . . . . . . . . . . . . . . . . . . 753
Kushiro-Shitsugen National Park
(釧路湿原国立公園) . . . . . . . . . . . . 756

INDEX . . . . . . . . . . . . . . . . . . . . . . . . . 757

ABOUT OUR WRITERS . . . . . . . . . . 784

## MAPS

Tokyo Metro . . . . . . . . . . . . . . . . . . . . . 134
Imperial Palace,
Marunouchi and Nihonbashi. . 146–147
Ginza and Tsukiji . . . . . . . . . . . . . . . . 154
Shiodome. . . . . . . . . . . . . . . . . . . . . . . . 167
Aoyama and Harajuku . . . . . . . . 172–173
Shibuya . . . . . . . . . . . . . . . . . . . . 180–181
Roppongi . . . . . . . . . . . . . . . . . . . . . . . 192
Shinjuku. . . . . . . . . . . . . . . . . . . . 198–199
Akihabara . . . . . . . . . . . . . . . . . . . . . . 208
Ueno . . . . . . . . . . . . . . . . . . . . . . 214–215
Asakusa. . . . . . . . . . . . . . . . . . . . . . . . 220
Greater Tokyo. . . . . . . . . . . . . . . 228–229
Yokohama . . . . . . . . . . . . . . . . . . 244–245
Kamakura . . . . . . . . . . . . . . . . . . . . . . 254
Fuji-Hakone-Izu National Park . . . . . 264
Nikko. . . . . . . . . . . . . . . . . . . . . . . . . . . 294
Nagoya. . . . . . . . . . . . . . . . . . . . . . . . . 312
Ise . . . . . . . . . . . . . . . . . . . . . . . . . . . . 326
Matsumoto . . . . . . . . . . . . . . . . . . . . . 352
Takayama . . . . . . . . . . . . . . . . . . . . . . 361
Kanazawa . . . . . . . . . . . . . . . . . . . . . . 365

Eastern Kyoto. . . . . . . . . . . . . . . 392–393
Central Kyoto . . . . . . . . . . . . . . . 418–419
Southern Kyoto . . . . . . . . . . . . . . . . . 436
Western Kyoto. . . . . . . . . . . . . . . . . . . 439
Arashiyama. . . . . . . . . . . . . . . . . . . . . . 444
Northern Kyoto . . . . . . . . . . . . . . . . . 450
Osaka, Kita Ward . . . . . . . . . . . 474–475
Osaka, Minami. . . . . . . . . . . . . . 480–481
Nara . . . . . . . . . . . . . . . . . . . . . . 490–491
Kobe . . . . . . . . . . . . . . . . . . . . . . . . . . 505
Hiroshima . . . . . . . . . . . . . . . . . . . . . . 534
Takamatsu. . . . . . . . . . . . . . . . . . . . . . 566
Nagasaki . . . . . . . . . . . . . . . . . . . . . . . 612
Naha . . . . . . . . . . . . . . . . . . . . . . . . . . 641
Miyako Islands. . . . . . . . . . . . . . . . . . . 653
Yaeyama Islands . . . . . . . . . . . . . . . . . 658
Sendai . . . . . . . . . . . . . . . . . . . . . . . . . 676
Hakodate . . . . . . . . . . . . . . . . . . . . . . . 720
Sapporo . . . . . . . . . . . . . . . . . . . . . . . . 723

# Chapter 1

# EXPERIENCE JAPAN

# 25 ULTIMATE EXPERIENCES

Japan offers terrific experiences that should be on every traveler's list. Here are Fodor's top picks for a memorable trip.

## 1 Himeji Castle

Known as the "white heron" for its unique architecture and brilliant white exterior, this is Japan's most famous castle. You'll recognize it from the James Bond movie *You Only Live Twice* and Akira Kurosawa's films. *(Ch. 9)*

## 2 Onsen

The ultimate Japanese relaxation activity is sliding into a steamy bath of geothermally heated water from natural springs called onsen. *(Ch. 4–15)*

## 3 Fish Markets

Fish markets are dotted around in cities and towns all over the country, the Osaka Central Fish Market being one of the biggest and busiest. *(Ch. 9)*

# 4 Mount Fuji

Immortalized by Japanese poets throughout the ages and portrayed by numerous artists, the highest mountain in Japan is the country's most famous icon. *(Ch. 5)*

# 5 Japanese Gardens

Wherever you are in the country, there is a peaceful, well-manicured strolling garden waiting to take you back in time and dial you into reflection mode. *(Ch. 3, 4–15)*

# 6 Kurashiki

In Kurashiki, long, narrow boats that once transported grain now have a cargo of tourists. After a boat ride, visit the Bikan district for its many museums and galleries. *(Ch. 10)*

# 7 Okinawa Beaches

Okinawa is like Thailand without the crowds of tourists—the beaches on these tropical islands are pristine, and it is not uncommon to have one all to yourself. *(Ch. 13)*

# 8 Arashiyama

One of the most photographed places in Kyoto, the groves can be accessed from the main street of Arashiyama, to the north of the entrance to Tenryu-ji temple. *(Ch. 8)*

## 9 Ryokan

Sleeping on a futon on tatami, bathing in the onsen, and eating an elaborate *kaiseki* meal are highlights of staying in a ryokan, a quintessential experience in Japan. *(Ch. 4–15)*

## 10 The "Nation's Kitchen"

Osaka is called "kui-daore no machi," or "the town that loves to eat." Head for the epicurean districts of Ura-Namba, Temma, and Horie to sample the city's culinary favorites. *(Ch. 9)*

## 11 Kabuki

One of Japan's major classical styles of theater, Kabuki traces back to the Edo period and involves elaborate costumes, bold makeup, extravagant wigs, and exaggerated gestures. *(Ch. 2, 3, 4)*

## 12 The Kiso Valley

An ancient 70-km (43-mile) trade route called the Kisoji was developed along this valley during the Edo period (1603–1868) and was the lifeblood for commerce in the region. *(Ch. 7)*

# 13 Nara Park

Here you'll find one of Japan's largest bronze statues of Buddha (Daibutsu), and curious and hungry deer. Purchase deer cookies at the park to feed to them. *(Ch. 9)*

## 14 Temple Stays

The village of Mount Koya in Wakayama Prefecture's misty Kii Mountain Range is a training ground, sanctuary, and home for Shingon Buddhist monks. *(Ch. 6)*

## 15 Karaoke

Get a *nomihodai* (all-you-can-drink) deal where you can order drinks on demand from your room, grab your mics, and sing the night away with your pals. *(Ch. 4)*

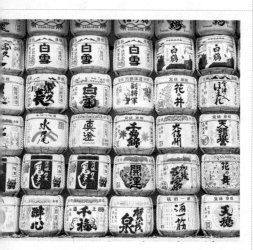

## 16 Sake Breweries

The Nada area in Hyogo produces more sake than any other region; sample the drink and try the many sake-related cosmetics. *(Ch. 9, 11)*

## 17 Sumo Wrestling

Tokyo's Ryogoku district, the center of the sumo world for 200 years, is home to sumo stables (where wrestlers live and train) and the Kokugikan sumo arena. *(Ch. 2, 4, 6, 9)*

## 18 Kumano Kodo

Hike through these ancient pilgrimage routes across the Kii peninsula, endowed with magnificent scenery, remote hot springs, and rich pilgrimage traditions. *(Ch. 6)*

## 19 Peace Memorial Park

Pay respects at Hiroshima's 120,000-square-meter park and Peace Memorial Museum, dedicated to the victims of the 1945 bombing. *(Ch. 10)*

## 20 Sakura-jima Volcano

The active volcano of Sakurajima in southern prefecture of Kagoshima smokes continuously, and minor eruptions often take place multiple times per day. *(Ch. 12)*

## 21 Skiing in Niseko

Averaging around 15-plus meters of snow each season, Niseko in Hokkaido is the most famous ski area in Japan, known for its wide-open powder bowls and tree runs. *(Ch. 15)*

## 22 Itsukushima

Itsukushima Shrine and its "floating" vermillion *torii* gate, which rises out of the ocean at high tide, are some of Japan's most iconic images. *(Ch. 10)*

## 23 Jomon Sugi Tree

Known for being one of the world's oldest trees, Jomon Sugi is estimated to be up to 7,000 years old and is the main attraction on Yakushima. *(Ch. 12)*

## 24 Island-Hopping

The Seto Inland Sea separates Honshu, Shikoku, and Kyushu—three of Japan's four main islands—but is also dotted with pristine little remote islands to be explored. *(Ch. 10, 11, 12)*

# 25 Kyoto Temples and Shrines

One of the historical jewels of Japan, and a past capital city, Kyoto is home to more than 1,600 Buddhist temples and over 400 Shinto shrines. *(Ch. 8)*

# WHAT'S WHERE

**1 Tokyo.** Greater Tokyo is home to more than 10% of Japan's population and would take a lifetime to fully explore. Rather than any coherent center, there is a mosaic of colorful neighborhoods—Shibuya, Asakusa, Ginza, Shinjuku, and dozens more—each with its own atmosphere.

**2 Side Trips from Tokyo.** Both Nikko and Kamakura are a quick train ride away and can provide all your shrine and temple viewings. Hakone offers onsen, outdoor experiences, and spectacular views of Mt. Fuji. Kamakura is home to hiking trails and the 37-foot and nearly 800-year-old Daibutsu—the Great Buddha.

**3 Nagoya, Ise-Shima, and the Kii Peninsula.** Ise Jingu (Grand Shrines of Ise)—the most holy site in Japan's national religion—is found in Ise-Shima National Park. To the south, the Kii Peninsula has magnificent coastal scenery and fishing villages. Inland, the mountain monastery of Koya-san looms mythically with 120 temples.

**4** **The Japan Alps and the North Chubu Coast.** Soaring mountains, slices of old Japan, famed lacquerware and superb hiking, skiing, and onsen soaking are found here. In Kanazawa is Kenroku Garden, one of the three finest in the country.

**5** **Kyoto.** Japan's ancient capital, Kyoto represents 12 centuries worth of history and tradition in its beautiful gardens, castles, museums, and nearly 2,000 temples and shrines—Kinkaku-ji and Kiyomizu-dera top most itineraries. Here you'll also see geisha and sample *kaiseki ryori*, an elegant multicourse meal.

**6** **The Kansai Region.** Nara may not match Kyoto's abundance of sacred sites, but its expansive park and Great Buddha at Todaiji Temple are among Japan's finest. Osaka offers a mix of bright lights, as in the Dotombori entertainment area, and history, such as at Osaka-jo castle. Just minutes by train from Osaka is Kobe, a port city where European and Japanese influences have long mingled.

**7** **Western Honshu.** Mountains divide this region into an urban south and a rural north. Hiroshima is the modern stronghold, where the sobering remnants of the

# WHAT'S WHERE

charred A-Bomb Dome testify to darker times. Offshore at Miyajima, the famous torii shrine gate appears to float on the water. In Okayama, Bizen masters craft the famous local pottery.

**8 Shikoku.** Thanks to its isolation, this southern island has held on to its traditions and staved off the industry that blights parts of Japan. There's great hiking, dramatic scenery, some of the country's freshest seafood, and the can't-miss traditional dancing at the Awa Odori festival in Tokushima.

**9 Kyushu.** Rich in history and heavily reliant on the agriculture industry, lush Kyushu is the southernmost of Japan's four main islands. At Aso National Park you can look into the steaming caldera of Mt. Naka-dake, an active volcano. Resurrected from the second atomic bomb, Nagasaki, long the islands' window to the outside world, is a charming town that cascades over rolling hills offering many spectacular views of the city, mountains, and sea.

**10 Okinawa.** Okinawa is often known as the Hawaii of Japan. Relaxation and water sports are the main attractions of this archipelago, located some 700 km (435 miles) south of Kyushu. A paradise for snorkelers and scuba divers, the islands teem with reefs, canyons, and shelves of coral.

**11 Tohoku.** Mt. Zao draws skiers as well as tourists clamoring for a look at the *juhyo*, snow-covered fir trees that resemble fairy-tale monsters. Sendai is a good base for trips to Mt. Zao and Matsushima, a bay studded with more than 250 pine tree–covered islands. Make time for the traditional town of Kakunodate and Japan's deepest lake, Tazawa-ko.

**12 Hokkaido.** Japan's northernmost island is also its last frontier. Glorious landscapes, hiking, and skiing adventures await. In February, the Sapporo Snow Festival dazzles with huge ice sculptures. To the south are the famous hot springs of Noboribetsu Onsen and Jigokudani (Valley of Hell), a volcanic crater that belches boiling water and sulfurous vapors.

# What to Eat and Drink in Japan

## SUSHI

It goes without saying that you'd be remiss in visiting Japan without sampling sushi, the most well-known genre of Japanese cuisine. While the world's largest fish market has moved from Tsukiji to Toyosu, the Tsukiji neighborhood is still a great place to sample the best, and freshest, sushi in Tokyo.

## JAPANESE WHISKEY

The big whiskey brands in Japan are Yamazaki, Hibiki, Hakushu, Fuji Gotemba, Chichibu, and White Oak. You can visit Fuji Gotemba's distillery at the foot of Mt. Fuji on a day trip from Tokyo. Top whiskey bars in Tokyo include Zoetrope in Shinjuku or Cask Strength in Roppongi.

## SOBA

In addition to being delicious, soba noodles have the added benefit of having more nutritional value (they're more digestible and contain antioxidants) than wheat noodles.

## TEPPANYAKI

Don't call it "hibachi" but do reserve a counter seat at Ginza Fujiya Miyako in Shibuya to watch a skilled chef at work as he prepares duck confit and beautifully marbled miyazaki beef.

## RAMEN

From the miso-based broth of Hokkaido to the milky-in-color pork bone broth of Fukuoka, each region of Japan has developed its own variation on the perennially popular soup. When in Tokyo, head to the Shin-Yokohama Ramen Museum, where you can sample a wide array of ramen from restaurants all over Japan.

## OKONOMIYAKI

"Okonomi" means "whatever you like," and "yaki" means "grilled." *Okonomiyaki* are made with cabbage, flour, eggs, green onions, and usually some type of protein all mixed together and then shaped into a sort of veggie-based, savory pancake. Try all the variations and don't forget the toppings.

## SAKE

*Nihonshu* (sake), also known as Japanese rice wine, is Japan's most famous variety of alcohol. It can be enjoyed hot or cold and paired to your meal. Head to the Japan Sake and Shochu Information Center for 100 varieties.

### CHANKO NABE

*Chanko nabe*—a giant pot of soup made with chicken broth, plenty of good-for-you protein sources, bok choy, and lots of vegetables—is the signature meal of sumo wrestlers actively working on gaining weight as part of their training. It's probably best enjoyed after watching a sumo wrestling demonstration.

### SHABU-SHABU

*Shabu-shabu* is similar to chanko nabe in the sense that it's a "hot pot"–style dish that can include myriad ingredients. But instead of eating your portion from a single bowl, shabu-shabu is cooked one piece at a time.

### YAKITORI

The beauty of *yakitori* is in its simplicity. Skewered chicken is cooked over a charcoal grill and seasoned with a little salt and tare sauce. There's a reason it's a staple of late-night street food and izakayas. For a perfectly calibrated Michelin-starred yakitori experience, visit Birdland in Ginza.

# 10 Quirky Souvenir Stores in Tokyo

### COSPLAY AT COSPATIO
Dressing up is big business in Japan, and serious players come to Cospatio (also known as Cospa), a manufacturer and one of the biggest cosplay stores in Tokyo, for its comprehensive collection of merchandise.

### CAN-CAN AT MR. KANSO
The ordinary becomes a novelty at this series of bars dotted around the city that they stock nothing but canned goods—from sardines to smoked liver. Even the drinks are canned at this quirky, distinctly Japanese hangout.

### NAKANO BROADWAY
Just follow the covered shopping arcade north of Nakano Station to find four floors of shops selling everything from anime and manga figurines to vintage video games.

### GEE!STORE GACHAPON MACHINES
Upstairs from Cospatio, Gee!STORE houses more than 450 gachapon machines—small vending machines where you insert a coin and a figurine pops out. There are literally thousands of types of prizes, which range from anime character toys to cats wearing kimonos to underpants for your smartphone.

### YAMASHIROYA TOY STORE
One minute's walk from Ueno station, Yamashiroya's seven floors of childhood heaven packed with toys, figurines, games, and comics is a bucket-list stop for any kid (or kid at heart). Look for a Pokémon chess set and an entire corner devoted to Totoro.

### KNICKKNACKS AT TOKYU HANDS
From stationery to toilet-seat covers, reflexology slippers to bee-venom face masks, and novelty party supplies to board games, Tokyu Hands has everything you never knew you needed to buy for yourself and everyone on your list.

### OTAKU AT AKIHABARA RADIO KAIKAN
The iconic Akihabara landmark is dedicated to Japanese pop culture, making it an *otaku* (anime, manga, video-game nerd) paradise with 10 floors of shops selling manga, anime, and collectibles such as models and figurines, fanzines, costumes, and accessories.

### EVERYTHING AT DON QUIJOTE

Open 24/7, Don Quijote is a jumble of tall, crowded shelves and sells everything from designer handbags and watches, clothing, and electronics to cheap cosmetics, costumes, and more. It's your one-stop shop for souvenirs including the famed flavored Kit Kats (yes, you *need* every variety).

### WORK WEAR AT MANNEN-YA

This 50-year-old store specializing in Japanese-style construction clothes stocks everything from baggy pants to reinforced shirts to *jika-tabi* (split-toe work shoes). You can also find high-vis helmets, white *cho-cho zubon* (butterfly pants), split-toe socks, and even Hello Kitty merchandise.

### MASKS AT OMOTE

Actors, mask makers, and headwear enthusiasts all frequent this boutique mask store whose selection ranges from noh masks to Venetian-style masks to *hyottoko* (Japanese-style clown masks), with prices starting at a few thousand yen and stretching to the hundreds of thousands.

# Traditional Crafts to Buy

## EDO KIRIKO GLASSWARE

Edo Kiriko glassware is created by carving patterns into the surface of layered colored glass using a diamond-tipped grinder. Ryuichi Kumakura's *kometsunagi*, or rice-chain pattern, is particularly revered and achieved by subtly varying the size of the rice grain shapes he engraves.

## FUROSHIKI WRAPPING CLOTHS

Harajuku may be mecca for the latest in youth fashion, but it's also home to some classic craft shops like Musubi, a charming boutique specializing in traditional *furoshiki* cloths. Used to wrap everything from gifts to bento lunch boxes, these beautifully decorated material squares are the perfect eco-friendly wrapping solution. Around 500 varieties line the shelves in traditional, seasonal, and modern designs made from a variety of fabrics including cotton, silk, and *chirimen* (silk crepe), and using various dying and weaving techniques.

## FINE BAMBOO CRAFTS

Bamboo craft shop Midoriya, established in 1908, is located along the Yanaka Ginza traditional shopping street. Here, three generations of artists have honed their craft. The family-run shop and studio sells bamboo products ranging from the everyday to the exquisite. Traditional *mushikago* insect cages come in a range of shapes and sizes, as well as bamboo bugs and birds to put inside. You'll also find flower baskets, chopsticks, bookmarks, and lunch boxes. *Renkon* (lotus root) coasters are a cheap and trendy takeaway at ¥500.

## VINTAGE FABRIC FASHION

Kukuli is a tiny textiles shop located in the crafty pocket of Kagurazaka, a former geisha hub renowned for its picturesque cobblestone streets. This delightful boutique recycles vintage fabrics and transforms them into trendy fashion pieces. You can buy cloths, tea towels, scarves, and bags made with woven fabric drawn from different regions of the country. These precious and sometimes century-old fabrics are then hand-dyed and redesigned into stylish new products. Alongside the classical motifs of cherry blossom and koi carp, expect to find simple but chic stripes, checks, and geometric patterns.

## TENUGUI HAND TOWELS

*Tenugui* are long multi-purpose traditional hand towels made from dyed cotton cloth. They are considered by many Japanese as a daily necessity and their multiple uses include drying hands after washing them, wiping sweat from your brow on humid summer days, or covering your lap as a napkin during a meal. They have also become a fashion item with people wearing them as headbands, head scarves, and neck scarves.

## JAPANESE-STYLE CLOTHING AND TEXTILES

Opened in the 1990s in the peaceful backstreets of Daikanyama, Okura sells clothing and other textiles based on traditional

Japanese designs and tailoring techniques. "Okura" in Japanese means a storehouse full of old treasures and memories from childhood. The seashells, driftwood, shards of glass, and other materials that are embedded in the ceiling and floor were collected from the beach during the store's construction, and there is a weathered curtain over the entrance. You can find a wide range of items including *aizome* (a traditional Japanese indigo dyeing method) shirts, denims, jackets and sweaters, and the shop stocks men's and women's clothing under their own original brands, including the indigo brand BLUE BLUE JAPAN. The second floor stocks the women's range, where you'll find hairpins, purses, cloths, kimono-motif tops, and all kinds of other things.

## FOLK TOYS AND SOUVENIRS

For traditional souvenirs with a trendy twist, toy shop Atelier Gangu stocks folkcraft toys directly bought from the craftsmen of various regions around Japan as well as the postcards made with papercut art. The postcards depict the folkcraft toys that are no longer available or difficult to find. On its shelves, you will see everything from papier-mâché animals to kites to hand-crafted *maneki-neko* (lucky cats) all made by veteran craftsmen.

## JAPANESE KITCHEN KNIVES

The history of kitchen-supply store Kama-Asa extends all the way back to 1908 when the shop was first opened in Asakusa's Kappabashi (also known as Kitchen Town). The elegant store specializes in handcrafted kitchen knives (roughly 80 different kinds) and Nanbu Tekki iron pans,

woks, and steamers. There is also a selection of knives for left-handed cooks and the friendly staff will engrave a knife for you in Japanese symbols or roman letters at no extra cost.

## TRADITIONAL WASHI PAPER

Founded in 1806, Haibara specializes in making gorgeous letter sets, notebooks, *uchiwa* (round-shaped fans), and envelopes featuring *mizuhiki* knots from traditional *washi* paper. The elegant design of their products can be traced back to the Meiji and late Edo periods when Haibara's founders collaborated with the most renowned painters of that era. They are best known for *gampi* paper made from the outer bark fibers of gampi trees, giving it a smooth texture and silky surface. The shop exterior is a futuristic-looking gray cube just off of Chuo-dori in the Nihonbashi district.

# Japan's Top Temples and Shrines

## TODAI-JI TEMPLE, NARA

Todai-ji is one of the largest wooden structures in the world. Give yourself plenty of time to enjoy the grounds as well as the large wooden gates. Behind the Great Buddha inside Todai-ji's main hall is a hole at the base of a pillar rumored to be the same size as the statue's nostril.

## IZUMO GRAND SHRINE, SHIMANE

Izumo Taisha is something to behold. It is said to be one of the oldest Shinto shrines in Japan. While no one knows when it was originally built, the complex has undoubtedly been rebuilt periodically, as is the case with this type of wooden architectural structures.

## MEIJI SHRINE, TOKYO

Don't be fooled by the forest that surrounds this peaceful spot—it was entirely planted at the beginning of the 20th century, and the shrine established after Emperor Meiji's death. It is a unique layout for a shrine as it was designed by Chuta Ito, who is often called the father of Japanese architecture.

## NEZU SHRINE, TOKYO

Nezu Shrine is perhaps the oldest building in Tokyo, having survived both the 1923 Great Kanto Earthquake as well as World War II. Due to its age from before the division of Shinto and Buddhism, it still shows many of the design elements of a Buddhist temple. The grounds are also home to a hillside of azaleas that bloom in late April or early May.

## ENGAKU-JI TEMPLE, KAMAKURA

If you are headed to Kamakura, it is worth getting off at the Kita-Kamakura stop just before Kamakura Station coming from Tokyo. The Zen temple complex is tucked into a valley and home to gardens, teahouses, places for meditation, carvings in the mountainsides, and even an area for practicing archery. It was established in the late 13th century, and legend has it that white deer came out of a cave to listen to the sermons of its founder.

## SEIGANTO-JI TEMPLE, WAKAYAMA

Perhaps one of Japan's most photogenic temples, Seiganto-ji's three-tiered pagoda sits directly in front of Nachi Falls. The grounds are also connected to the Shinto Kumano Nachi Taisha Shrine, reflecting the two religions' interconnectedness in Japanese history.

### HASE-DERA TEMPLE, KAMAKURA

Many people go to Kamakura to see the Great Buddha, but if you do, don't miss the nearby Hase-dera Temple, which faces the sea and has great panoramic views of both the Pacific and the town of Kamakura. It's also home to beautiful gardens and a unique carved cave you can explore.

### KINKAKU-JI TEMPLE, KYOTO

The spectacular image of Kyoto's Kinkaku-ji's golden pavilion across the water is almost as iconic as Mt Fuji. While you have no doubt seen photos of it, experiencing its beauty is something else.

### RISSHAKU-JI TEMPLE, YAMAGATA

Risshaku-ji is part of the Yamadera temple complex, which is tucked into the mountains between Yamagata City and Sendai in the Tohoku region. The main building is at the base of a series of steps through the forest that will lead you up to beautiful cliff-top views.

### SENSO-JI TEMPLE AND ASAKUSA SHRINE, TOKYO

After passing through the giant Kaminari-mon gate in Tokyo's Asakusa district, you can stroll along the shop-lined path to another grand gate before arriving at the Buddhist Senso-ji Temple. Just to the east of the main temple building, you can also see the smaller Shinto Asakusa Shrine.

# Japan with Kids

## Practicalities

At first glance, Japan might seem busy, bustling, and all business, but it's actually a great destination to explore with kids. Transportation is quick and convenient, hotels and restaurants warmly accommodate children, and there is no shortage of attractions appealing to the younger set. Children in Japan even have their own public holiday (May 5, Children's Day), and allowing your kids to explore the world and experience new things is seen as the hallmark of good parenting.

### ACCOMMODATIONS

Children who don't need their own beds stay free at most Japanese hotels. At ryokan, small children who need neither futons nor meals stay free. There are small extra charges for older children who need their own futon or a special children's meal. Children's meals at some ryokan are kid-friendly feasts in themselves, and although adult meals are large enough to share, if you're traveling with little foodies it can be worth ordering special meals just for them.

### TRANSPORTATION

Children under six usually ride trains in Japan for free (though specifics vary by train company), and children 6–11 are half the adult fare. Japanese trains and station ticket gates are compact, so if you're using a stroller, choose one that folds and can fit through train doors and ticket gates. Most bullet trains and express trains have diaper-changing facilities (おむつ交換台; omutsu kokan-dai); ask the conductor to show you where they are. All rental-car companies can provide rear- or front-facing car seats and booster seats, usually for around ¥1,000 per day. You can ride most public buses with strollers, as long as you use the designated stroller area (usually by the rear doors; look for a stroller logo).

### EATING

Family restaurants in Japan will provide high chairs and booster seats, and Japanese-style restaurants usually have a tatami mat room with low tables that works well for families with small kids. Most restaurants in Japan welcome children and will provide small bowls and cutlery for kids to use. All family-style places have designated no-smoking sections, but some nonfamily restaurants allow smoking throughout the restaurant, so check in advance if this is a concern.

### HEALTH AND SAFETY

Japan is safe, but crowded, and the country's urban crowds can be especially unnerving for kids. In case you're separated in a crowd, it's a good idea to have kids carry a bilingual card with your contact information, hotel information, and basic details such as their name and nationality. Remind kids that if anyone does get lost, they can ask for help at the nearest police box (交番; koban), which is usually close to the train station. Japanese clinics and hospitals offer high-quality care, and many doctors speak at least basic English. If you call or visit a Japanese medical facility, you'll be asked early and often about your child's temperature, so carry a small centigrade thermometer with you just in case.

### OTHER TIPS

Most Japanese department stores and shopping centers have "baby rooms" complete with diaper-changing facilities, private nursing areas, and hot water for infant formula. Some also have diaper vending machines, baby scales, and free stroller rentals.

# In Kyoto

Though a full day touring Kyoto's staid temples and shrines can tire out little ones pretty quickly, there are lots of kid-friendly sights in this traditional city. Of Kyoto's traditional sights, **Nijo Castle,** with its lifelike mannequins reenacting life in this 17th-century shogun palace, is a good option for kids. The hundreds of vermillion gates at **Fushimi Inari Shrine** will also make an impression. Curious eaters will love the **Nishiki Food Market.** Kyoto is flat and its roads run in a grid pattern, making it a good spot for a family bike ride. Most bike-rental companies in Kyoto rent bikes with child seats, and some also offer electric-assist models to ease the strain of pedaling an extra passenger.

# In Tokyo

In Tokyo popular sights for toddlers and school-aged children include **Ueno Zoo,** and **Tokyo Disneyland. Shinjuku Gyoen Gardens** and **Yoyogi Park** are popular family picnic spots. Good options in Tokyo to introduce kids to traditional culture include the **Meiji Shrine** near Harajuku Station or **Senso-ji Temple** in Asakusa. The hands-on "culture experience" programs run by the Yanesen Tourist Information Center are a great chance for older kids to try drumming or take a swordsmanship lesson. Daredevils will enjoy a ride on the Thunder Dolphin, the roller coaster at **Tokyo Dome** that soars and loops around buildings. Kids must be eight or older and 51 inches or taller to ride. There are also gentler rides nearby for younger siblings.

# In Osaka

Osakans love kids and are not shy about it, so traveling with kids in Osaka might involve conversation with friendly strangers. The **Osaka Aquarium Kaiyukan** is one of the world's largest, and is the top kid-friendly attraction in the city. **Osaka Castle** and **Osaka Castle Park** are also great spots to take in the city's history and enjoy a picnic. Near Osaka Station, the **Hep Five Ferris Wheel** offers good views of the city. The rides and attractions at **Universal Studios Japan** are also worth seeing.

# Farther Afield

Although there are fewer English speakers in the Japanese countryside and smaller cities, a slower pace and fewer crowds make traveling in rural areas with kids a relaxing proposition. Kid-friendly attractions in rural Japan include the **Asahiyama Zoo,** Japan's most-visited, in Hokkaido's Asahikawa City (90 minutes from Sapporo).

# What to Watch and Read

### THE YAKUZA

This 1974 film directed by Sydney Pollack is about a retired American detective who returns to Japan after many years in order to help save his friend's daughter who has been kidnapped. The detective had been stationed in Japan during the American occupation after WWII along with one of the other main characters. The film explores the relationships between men and women and the animosity that some people held against their former enemy.

### THE NAKANO THRIFT SHOP

This book by Hiromi Kawakami is a funny journey exploring human interactions and relationships in a thrift store run by the entertaining Mr. Nakano. Hitomi, the woman who works the register, is trying to attract the attention of her coworker but involves other people in her pursuit while a cast of eclectic characters pass through the story.

### NAOMI

Originally titled *Chijin no Ai* (*A Fool's Love*), this book by Junichiro Tanizaki was first published in 1925 and carries the reader on a strange but interesting journey giving insight into how early 20th-century Japan was changing from the perspective of a regular salaryman.

### AN AUTUMN AFTERNOON

The Japanese title of this 1962 film is *Sanma no Aji* (*The Taste of Sanma*, which is a kind of fish commonly eaten in the fall) tells the story of the patriarch of a family realizing the responsibilities that are expected of him. This was the final film of Yasujiro Ozu, who is known for filming as if sitting in *seiza* (on one's knees as is done in polite situations in Japan).

### THE CAT AND THE CITY

Following the story of a stray cat in Tokyo, author Nick Bradley ties together the cat's movement through human spaces and the connections to the people who occupy the fast-changing city. The cat becomes the link between the different characters who are also struggling in the big city and she slowly draws them together.

### DOGS AND DEMONS

Alex Kerr's book tells the stories of a modern Japan and its many crises created by the country's success and overbuilding. The book sheds light on the Japanese sociopolitical system, telling the story of how economic success ultimately causes countless problems, including environmental destruction. This is a look at the underbelly of Japan's success told after the so-called bubble period of excess.

### THE NOBILITY OF FAILURE

This book by Ivan Morris examines the life stories of nine historical figures who faced enormous struggles and, once they realized that there was no hope, accepted their fates to be killed in battle or executed, or took their own lives through ritual suicide. It's a serious book that even addresses the kamikaze pilots of WWII, but is worth a read if you're looking to understand the people of Japan more deeply.

### DEPARTURES (OKURIBITO)

The film *Okuribito*, which means "one who sends away," is a look at death and how societies deal with it but also the urban and rural divide. The story follows a musician who leaves Tokyo and returns to his hometown in Yamagata with his wife. After seeing an ad for a job to help "assisting departures" (and assuming that it must be a travel company), his real struggles begin as he takes a job preparing bodies for cremation. The film, directed by Yojiro Takita, won an Academy Award for Best Foreign Language Film in 2009.

## SPIRITED AWAY (SEN TO CHIHIRO NO KAMIKAKUSHI)

This 2001 fantasy animated film by the acclaimed Hayao Miyazaki tells the story of Chihiro, who finds herself in the world of the *kami* (the gods of Shinto folklore) when she is moving into a new neighborhood. She is only ten years old and has to fend for herself as her parents are turned into pigs. It is a surreal film set in an onsen with a whole slew of fascinating characters passing through and where Chihiro (whose name is taken from her) has to work to free herself and her parents from the spirit world.

## NIP THE BUDS, SHOOT THE KIDS (MEMUSHIRI KOUCHI)

Kenzaburo Oe, winner of the Nobel Prize for literature, wrote this, his first novel, when he was in his early twenties. It tells the harrowing story of young boys trapped in an abandoned village infected by plague and left to fend for themselves in WWII Japan. They have to work together to survive and are joined by other castaways including a Korean boy from a nearby encampment who teaches them to hunt and a deserting soldier who refuses to kill. The cruelty that comes from their situation is clearly not the boys' responsibility, but the fault of adults in charge.

## IQ84

Perhaps better known for his other books like *The Wind-Up Bird Chronicle*, this book by Haruki Murakami was very well received in Japan, but not so well by Western critics. The book follows the story of a woman whose reality is seemingly changing, sending her on a search for what is real. Pronouncing the title in Japanese produces "1-9-8-4" and seems to take place in a parallel 1984.

## TO LIVE (IKIRU)

Akira Kurosawa's 1952 film tells the story of a terminally ill bureaucrat in Tokyo trying to make his last days meaningful. Kurosawa's films are widely celebrated and for good reason (it might be difficult to find a bad one), but this is perhaps his most moving.

## TAMPOPO

Juzu Itami wrote and directed this 1985 comedy that celebrates food and its influence on Japanese society. The offbeat and satirical humor in the story explores human nature, prescriptive habits of the Japanese, class, and feelings of obligation within the backdrop of a ramen shop.

## LIKE FATHER LIKE SON

This 2013 film directed by Hirokazu Koreeda is a thoughtful depiction of contemporary Japanese families that moves beyond its babies-switched-at-birth trope. It won the *Prix du Jury* award at Cannes.

## SHALL WE DANCE?

Directed and written by Masayuki Suo, the 1996 film is a bittersweet comedy about a married businessman who escapes his daily routine by taking ballroom dance lessons. A remake of the film in 2006 starred Richard Gere and Jenifer Lopez.

# Japan Today

## EVER-CHANGING CONTINUITY

The COVID-19 pandemic exposed the good, the bad, and some inner workings of governments all over the world as they struggled to deal with the unknown. For Japan, the public reacted quickly by immediately masking in public. Many credit the practice of mask-wearing to the 1918 influenza pandemic, often called Spanish flu, which hit Japan in two waves killing hundreds of thousands. Since then, wearing masks was normalized and became viewed as a personal responsibility. For the government, however, the pandemic brought a series of scandals and an end to the tenure of the country's longest-serving prime minister—Shinzo Abe. In July 2022, Abe was assassinated while giving a speech in Nara; the assassin had a grudge against the Unification Church, to which the former prime minister had long-standing political ties.

Interestingly, it was perhaps a different crisis—the unprecedented 2011 Tōhoku earthquake and tsunami—that brought Abe to power. The after-effects of that record-breaking 9.0 earthquake are still evident along the northeast coast, and the subsequent disaster at the Fukushima Dai-ichi plant caused everyone to think about energy differently. Only a few of Japan's 48 nuclear power plants have been restarted after all being taken offline due to the public's concern about—at the very least—transparency in the nuclear industry and from government officials. Voters' views on the short-ruling Democratic Party of Japan soured, and they deferred to Abe's Liberal Democratic Party, which has been ruling Japan nearly continuously since 1955, bringing them back to power in 2013.

Abe's party came in with great promises to reinvigorate the economy and get more women into workplaces, but also to amend the constitution to remove the constraints on the nation's Self Defense Forces laid out in Article 9, which only allows Japan's military to defend Japan. Since the war is still within living memory, the push to change the constitution has created some perhaps surprising-looking protests mainly composed of elderly people.

Abe's economic policies and push for more equality in the workplace largely failed. The coronavirus pandemic, however, was the last straw for Abe, and he resigned citing health concerns and leaving his successors to deal with the uncertainty of the pandemic. Many criticized the response, which saw large corporations collecting public funds, a continued push for the 2020 Olympics, vouchers encouraging people to travel and eat out at a time when public health officials were saying to stay home, and even an outbreak of infections among health ministry officials who were partying in Ginza while ignoring their own official advice.

However, since Japanese people value both a concept of *gaman* (enduring the difficult) and an idea of *shikata ga nai* (letting things go), people bore the burden of uncertainty. In fact, broadly speaking, another Japanese tendency is on display here. Japan is known for perfecting crafts and methods through apprenticeships. Through earthquakes, typhoons, and other ways the islands try to kill us, the lack of permanence adds a necessity to innovation. This idea that there is a right way to do things is pervasive and directly connected to the tendency to defer to experts. When faced with a crisis, humans tend to retreat to the known, which is likely why the LDP remained in power—even after so many scandals—since they are the default for many.

As that apprenticeship tradition shows, there is an appreciation for finding the right way to do something. It is this enduring the way things are, yet working within the bounds of what is given, that allows Japan to innovate, but that also keeps things from changing too quickly. While there might be a right way to make ramen, there is freedom to innovate within that framework, leaving foodies with thousands of options.

## JAPANESE SOCIETY AND CULTURAL PRODUCTS

Young people don't seem terribly interested in politics, and you'll likely hear no one talk frankly about political issues. There are other things to keep us entertained. And even if some of Japan's decline is actually visible in the countryside, where many towns are emptying out, the national government spends money on large public projects so that tourists and locals can enjoy clean, well-kept cities and small towns. A happy side-effect of this tendency is that even the hinterlands will have modern performing arts centers and museums worth visiting, so visitors need not limit themselves to large cities.

Manga and anime fans will find endless joy in the streets of Akihabara where events are regularly put on by the giant AKB48 girl band at their café. Their aesthetic is fantastical, like anime characters have come to life. It shows a fondness for the flashy and the new, which is something you can also view

in the eclectic architecture that reflects different eras as things are so often rebuilt. And even though neighboring South Korea has taken a front row seat in pop music from Asia, as K-pop groups like BTS conquer the world, J-pop groups like Arashi are still regionally popular. A fascinating thing to watch is how pop groups have influenced each other over the years. This might allow younger generations to find connections and similarities with their neighbors where older generations saw differences and division.

## FUTURE AND REGIONAL DIVERSITY

On any visit to Japan, you might notice something that you (and most Japanese people) don't necessarily expect, which is the increase of visible minorities. Japan has long attracted students from all over the world, but especially Asia. After graduating, these students sometimes stay, while others return to their home countries creating a kind of soft power that allows for an enduring connection. The future of Japan is likely one of interconnectedness to the outside world—something that has been building for decades.

What's more, low birth rates and a shrinking labor force have almost required the Japanese to begin to accept not only foreign students but also foreign workers, even as talk of immigration remains a way for politicians to dig their own graves. It is not uncommon now to see Southeast and South Asians working at convenience stores or people from Central Asia working at construction sites. For many years, immigrant communities from nearby countries were able to blend in a bit, but these days, it is noticeable, not only in the workers, but also in groups of children you will see in larger cities. This next generation will likely grow up with a very different attitude about immigrants and what it means to be Japanese. Humans love to imagine our cultures and nations as static, but historic evidence shows us that they are nothing of the kind. The Japan you will visit is a snapshot of this moment, and it can change.

But even before considering the increasing diversity coming from outside, it's best to appreciate what exists in the country already. From abroad, Japan is depicted as a monolith. Compared to many places, this is true, but a closer look will show you striking regional differences.

Japanese people also tend to choose to see themselves as a single group, which likely comes from that hard-wired human desire to feel part of something. If you ask a Japanese person about Japan, you'll likely get similar answers about kimono, the cuisine, or the shamisen. However, the terrain of Japan used to isolate groups much more. If you put two people from different regions of Japan together (assuming they can negotiate their dialects enough to communicate), they will talk about how different their regions are in cuisine, language, and customs. And for this reason, it's best for visitors to ask Japanese people about their home regions. This is how you can find out what foods are best to eat or what to experience in an area. People are proud of where they are from and eager to share. When you get a chance, find out what the locals think about their region rather than trying to talk to them about the country. The regions of Japan are islands full of fascinating scenery, friendly people, and delicious food. This impermanent continuity is something we will be enjoying for many years to come.

# ISOLATION AND ENGAGEMENT:
# A HISTORY OF JAPAN   By Robert Morel

A century and a half after opening its shores to outsiders, Japan is still a mystery to many Westerners. Often misunderstood, Japan's history is much deeper than the stereotypes of samurai and geisha, overworked businessmen, and anime. Its long tradition of retaining the old while embracing the new has captivated visitors for centuries.

Much of Japanese history has consisted of the ongoing tension between its seeming isolation from the rest of the world and a desire to be a part of it. During the Edo period, Japan was closed to foreigners for some 250 years. Yet while the country has always had a strong national identity, it has also had a rapacious appetite for all things foreign. Just 50 years after opening its borders, parts of Tokyo looked like London, and Japan had become a colonial power in Asia.

Much earlier, the Japanese imported Buddhism, tea, and their first writing system from China.

In the 19th century, the country incorporated Western architecture, technology, and government. More recently, the Japanese have absorbed Western fashion, music, and pop culture. Nevertheless, the country's history lives on in local traditions, festivals, temples, cities, music, and the arts.

Senso-ji Complex in Tokyo's Asakusa neighborhood

(Top) Horyu-ji Temple, (Bottom) Nihon Shoki, (Right) Large Buddha statue at Todai-ji Temple

## Ancient Japan

10,000 BC–AD 622

The first people in Japan were the hunters and fishers of the Jomon period, known for their pottery. In the following Yayoi period, hunting and fishing gave way to agriculture, as well as the introduction of rice farming and metalworking. Around AD 500 the Yamato tribe consolidated power in what is now the Kansai plain, with Yamato leaders claiming descent from the sun goddess Amaretsu and taking the title of emperor. Prince Shotoku promoted the spread of Buddhism from China and commissioned Horyu-ji Temple in Nara in 607.

■ Horyu-ji Temple (Nara)
■ National Museum (Tokyo)

## Nara Period

710–784

As Japan's first permanent capital and urban center, Nara is often considered the birthplace of Japanese culture. Under the Emperor Shomu, who commissioned the Great Buddha at Todai-ji Temple, Buddhism rose to prominence. The first Japanese written histories, the *Kojiki* and *Nihon Shoki*, were compiled during this period, as was the *Manyoshu*, Japan's first collection of poetry. Since the country was the Eastern terminus of the Silk Road, Japan's royal family amassed an impressive collection of treasures from mainland Asia, many of which are still on display at Todai-ji Temple's Shoso-in.

■ The Great Buddha at Todai-ji Temple (Nara)

## Heian Period

794–1160

Partly to escape intrigues and the rising power of the Nara's Buddhist Priests, in 794 the Emperor Kammu moved the capital to Heian-kyo (now Kyoto). *Heian* translates roughly as "peace and tranquility," and during this time the Imperial court expanded its power throughout Japan. Inside the court, however, life was far from calm. This was a period of great courtly intrigue, and struggles for power between aristocrats, the powerful Fujiwara clan (the most powerful of Japan's four great noble families), and the new military class known as *bushi*. Though some emperors managed to maintain control of the court, the Heian

794–1160: The capital is moved from Nara to Heian-kyo (now Kyoto)

1467–77: The Onin Wars initiate a 100-year period of civil war

| 1100 | 1250 | 1400 | 1550 |

(Right) Zen Garden at the Ryoan-ji Temple, (Top) Noh masks, (Bottom) Kyoto Imperial Palace's wooden orange gates.

period saw the slow rise of the military class, leading to a series of wars that established them as the ruling class until well into the 19th century. Considered Japan's great classical period, this was a time when courtly arts flourished. The new Japanese kana script gave rise to a boom in literature. Compiled in 990, Sei Shonagon's Pillow Book gave a window into courtly life, and Shibuki Murasaki's Tale of Genji is often regarded as the world's first classic novel. Japanese *waka* poetry experienced a revival, breeding the new forms of poetry such as tanka that are still in use today.

■ The Imperial Palace (Kyoto)

## Kamakura Period
1185–1335

As the Imperial Court lost control, the Genpei War (1180–1185) resulted in the defeat of clans loyal to the emperor in Kyoto and the rise of a new government in Kamakura. Yoritomo Minamoto named himself Sei i Tai Shogun and established the Kamakura bakufu, a spartan military government. During this time, Japan repelled two Mongol invasions, thanks to timely typhoons that were later dubbed "kamikaze", or "divine wind." In this militaristic climate, Zen Buddhism, with its focus on self-reliance and discipline, exploded in popularity.

■ Eihiji Temple (Fukushima)
■ Hachimangu Shrine and the Great Buddha (Kamakura)

## Muromachi (Ashikaga) Period
1336–1568

The heyday of the samurai, the Muromachi period was one of near constant civil war. Feudal lords known as *daimyo* consolidated their power in local fiefdoms. Peasant rebellions and piracy were common. Nevertheless, trade flourished. The movement of armies required daimyo to build roads, while improved communications gave birth to many merchant and artisan guilds. Trade with China grew, and in 1543 Portugal began trading with Japan, introducing firearms and Christianity. Noh theater and the tea ceremony were founded, and Kyoto's most famous temples were built in this period.

■ Kinkaku-ji Temple (Kyoto)
■ Ryoan-ji Temple (Kyoto)

(Left) Matsumoto Castle, (Top) three wise monkeys at Toshogu shrine, (Bottom) woodcut of Kabuki actor by Utagawa Toyokuni

## National Unification (Momoyama Period)
### 1568–1600

In 1568 Oda Nobunaga, a lord from Owari in central Japan, marched on Kyoto and took the title of Shogun. He controlled the surrounding territories until his death in 1582, when his successor, Toyotomi Hideyoshi, became the new Shogun. After unifying much of central and western Japan, he attempted unsuccessful invasions of Korea before his death in 1598. In 1600 Tokugawa Ieyasu, a top general, defeated Hideyoshi's successor in the battle of Sekihagara.

- Osaka Castle (Osaka)
- Matsumoto Castle (Matsumoto)

## Edo (Tokugawa) Period
### 1600–1867

The Edo period ushered in 250 years of relative stability and central control. After becoming Shogun, Ieyasu Tokugawa moved the capital to Edo (present-day Tokyo). A system of *daimyo*, lords beholden to the Shogun, was established along with a rigid class system and legal code of conduct. Although Japan cut off trade with the outside world, cities flourished. By the mid-18th century, Edo's population had grown to more than 1 million, and urban centers like Osaka and Kyoto had become densely populated. Despite such rapid growth, urban life in the Edo period was highly organized, with districts managed by neighborhood associations that have persisted (in a modified way) to the present day. Popular entertainment and arts arose to satisfy the thriving merchant and artisan classes. Kabuki, flashy and sensational, overtook Noh theater in popularity, and Japan's famed "floating world" (*ukio*), with its theaters, drinking houses, and geishas emerged. Sumo, long a Shinto tradition, became a professional sport. Much of what both Japanese and foreigners consider "Japanese culture" dates to this period. But by 1853, the Shogun's hold on power was growing tenuous.

- Toshogu (Nikko)
- Katsura Imperial Villa (Kyoto) Muhammad Ali Mosque

(Top) Tokyo University, (Left) wedding in Meiji Shrine, (Bottom) A6M5 fighter plane at Yusyukan museum.

## Meiji Period

1868–1912

The Tokugawa Shogunate's rigid class system and legal code proved to be its undoing. After U.S. Commodore Matthew Perry opened Japan to trade in March 1854, the following years were turbulent. In 1868, the last Shogun, Tokugawa Yoshinobu, ceded power to Emperor Meiji, and Japan began to modernize after 250 years of isolation. Adopting a weak parliamentary system from Germany, rulers moved quickly to develop national industry and universities. Victories over China and Russia also emboldened Japan.

- Tokyo University (Tokyo)
- Heian Shrine (Kyoto)
- Nara National Musuem (Nara)

## Taisho Period

1912–1925

In the early 20th century, urban Japan was beginning to look a lot Europe and North America.

Fashion ranged from traditional *yukata* and kimono to zoot suits and bobbed hair. In 1923 the Great Kanto Earthquake and its resulting fires destroyed Yokohama and much of Tokyo. Although city planners saw this as an opportunity to modernize Tokyo's maze of streets, residents were quick to rebuild, ensuring that many neighborhood maps look much the same today as they did a century ago.

- Asakusa (Tokyo)
- The Shitamachi Museum (Tokyo)
- Meiji Shrine (Tokyo)

## Wartime Japan

1926–1945

Although Japan was was increasingly liberal throughout the 1920s, the economic shocks of the 1930s helped the military gain greater control, resulting in crackdowns on left-leaning groups, the press, and dissidents. In 1931 Japan invaded Manchuria; in 1937 Japan captured Nanking, killing many civilians. Joining the Axis powers in 1936, Japan continued its expansion in Asia and in 1941 attacked Pearl Harbor. After the atomic bombings of Hiroshima and Nagasaki, the Emperor announced Japan's surrender on August 15, 1945.

- Hiroshima Peace Memorial Park (Hiroshima)
- Yasukuni Shrine Museum (Tokyo)

TIMELINE

1964: Tokyo hosts the Summer Olympic games

1989: Emperor Hirohito dies

2006: Shinzo Abe elected as the country's youngest prime minister

2009: Liberal Democratic Party loses power

2019: Emperor Akih abdicates. Reiwa period begins.

1970    1990    2010    2030

(Top) 1964 Summer Olympics, Tokyo, (Bottom) manga comic books, (Right) Shinjuku, Tokyo

## Postwar Japan and the Economic Miracle

**1945–1989**

The initial postwar years were hard on Japan. More than half of Japan's total urban area was in ruins, its industry in shambles, and food shortages common. Kyoto was the only major metropolitan area in the country that escaped widespread damage. Thanks to an educated, dedicated population and smart planning, however, Japan was soon on the road to recovery. A new democratic government was formed and universal suffrage extended to all adult men and women. Japan's famous "Peace Constitution" forbade the country from engaging in warfare. With cooperation from the government, old companies like Matsushita (Panasonic), Mitsubishi, and Toyota began exporting Japanese goods en masse, while upstarts like Honda pushed their way to the top. In 1964 Japan joined the Organization for Economic Cooperation and Development's group of "rich nations" and hosted the Tokyo Olympics. At the same time, anime began gaining popularity at the box office and on TV, with Osamu Tezuka's classic *Tetsuwan Atom* (*Astro Boy*) making a splash when it aired in 1963. In the 1970s and '80s Japan became as well known for its electronics as its cars, with Nintendo, Sony, and Panasonic becoming household names abroad.

- Showa-Kan (Takayama)
- National Stadium (Yoyogi Park)

## From Goods to Culture

**1990–PRESENT**

Unfortunately, much of Japan's rapid growth in the 1980s was unsustainable. By 1991 the bubble had burst, leading to 20 years of limited economic expansion. Japan avoided an economic crisis, and most people continued to lead comfortable, if somewhat simpler, lives. After decades of exporting goods, Japan has—particularly since 2000—become an exporter of culture in the form of animation, video games, and cuisine. Japan, famous for importing ideas, has begun to send its own culture to the world.

- Shinjuku, Harajuku, and Shibuya, (Tokyo)
- Akihabara (Tokyo)
- Manga Museum (Kyoto)

# TRAVEL SMART

Updated by
Robert Morel

★ **CAPITAL:**
Tokyo

👥 **POPULATION:**
125,800,000

💬 **LANGUAGE:**
Japanese

$ **CURRENCY:**
Yen

☎ **COUNTRY CODE:**
81

⚠ **EMERGENCIES:**
Ambulance and Fire: 119;
Police: 110

🚗 **DRIVING:**
On the left

🕐 **TIME:**
13 hours ahead of New York

⚡ **ELECTRICITY:**
100v/50 cycles in Eastern
Japan; 100v/60 cycles in
Western Japan; electrical
plugs have two flat prongs.
US plugs fit into Japanese
sockets.

🌐 **WEB RESOURCES:**
www.japan.travel
www.japan-guide.com
www.hyperdia.com
www.japantimes.co.jp

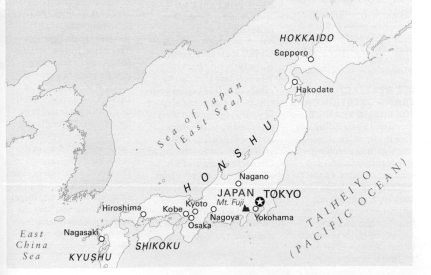

# Know Before You Go

## MASK UP

Wearing masks during flu and allergy seasons was common in Japan even before COVID-19. Masks are generally required in all indoor areas, and it is considered extremely bad form not to wear one when outside anywhere with people around.

## GET A RAIL PASS

If you are traveling to different parts of Japan, consider a JR Rail Pass. This must be purchased *before* coming to Japan (within three months of your visit) and offers great savings on unlimited trips all over the country on almost all JR services for 7, 14, or 21 days. Before you can use your pass in Japan, you will need to activate it by physically visiting a Japan rail office with your passport in hand. Reserve seats on any trains you are planning to take to be certain you will have a seat. This can be done at any JR office (available in most busy stations). If you don't reserve seats, you will be limited to a few cars with unreserved seats and may have to stand.

## GET A PREPAID TRANSPORTATION CARD FOR PUBLIC TRANSIT

If you will be spending any time in any of the larger cities, getting a rechargeable transportation card such as the Suica, PASMO, or ICOCA card means you don't have to figure out which ticket to buy every time you hop on a train. Any of the major transportation cards work on nearly all JR trains and most subways and private rail networks as well as many busses across the country. They are not limited to the city where you buy them. Cards cost ¥500 from station ticket machines (a deposit you can get back if you hand in the card at a station) and can be charged at ticket machines at all stations. You can then tap them on ticket gates and have your fare automatically deducted. They can also be used as payment at many vending machines and convenience stores.

## RENT PORTABLE WI-FI

If you want to guarantee to be connected, the best option is to rent portable Wi-Fi. Japan Wireless and Ninja WiFi rent pocket Wi-Fi routers that can be reserved online before your trip, picked up at the airport or your lodgings and then returned by post before leaving Japan. For free Wi-Fi, look out for the Japan Connected Free Wi-Fi. It offers free access points at stations, landmarks, tourist spots, and other points of interest. While free Wi-Fi is becoming more common it is still far from ubiquitous.

## KNOW HOW TO TAKE A TAXI

Taxis are a good (albeit costly if traveling alone) way to get around Tokyo. Taxis can be found on most corners and can be hailed on the street. Drivers are for the most part courteous, though not necessarily chatty. Unless you're going to a well-known destination such as a major hotel, it's advisable to have a Japanese person write out your destination in Japanese (your hotel concierge can do this for you). Drivers speak varying levels of English so it's best if they can use their car navigation system. Also, don't open or close the doors yourself; the driver does that using a lever by his seat. It's best to pay in cash as few cabs take credit or debit cards. Remember, there is no need to tip.

## THERE'S (ALMOST) NO NEED TO TIP

For the most part, there is no tipping in Japan, regardless of how much you appreciate the service and staff. Instead, learn how to say thank you (*arigato*) in Japanese. There are a few exceptions to this rule: if you hire a private guide or a private driver, it is customary to tip ¥2,000–¥3,000 for a full day with a guide and ¥1,000 for a driver. Tipping is also acceptable at a ryokan, when meals are served in your room. Tip ¥1,000 directly to the server. *Note:* tips in Japan should be handed over in a small envelope; if you forget to pack some, you have the perfect excuse to shop for some cute stationery in Tokyo.

## DOWNLOAD A TRANSLATION APP

While English is understood, it is not widely spoken in Japan so you may want to download a translation app before you travel. Google Translate handles Japanese to English consistently well (with the occasional incomprehensible translation of menus). You can type into it, but it also has a camera function that can translate written text, and with its conversation function you can interpret short phrases. Just remember to download the Japanese language settings before using it. Still, learning a few key phrases will smooth your travels and interactions with locals. Try *konnichiwa* (hello), *arigato* (thank you), and the multipurpose *sumimasen* (excuse me).

## SHIP YOUR LUGGAGE BETWEEN HOTELS

Avoid hauling luggage (and your accumulating souvenirs) around with you on crowded public transport as you travel between hotels by taking advantage of Takkyubin luggage delivery services, a convenient service for sending parcels, luggage, and various other types of goods from door to door nationwide. Delivery can usually be arranged at your hotel and is often same-day (within the same city) or the next day, and costs are moderate. Nothing beats arriving at your hotel to find your bags waiting for you.

## DO NOT EAT ON THE GO

While it is common to see commuters snacking and drinking Starbucks on the go in most major cities, this is highly frowned upon in Japan. It's considered bad manners to eat or drink inside trains, the exception being on the Shinkansen or other long-distance express trains. And you will see signs at markets to eat at the stall rather than to wander with food. Your manners will be rewarded with a clean city and public transportation system and an increased appreciation for your food at mealtimes.

## BE PREPARED FOR A QUAKE

It's not a fun thing to think about when planning a trip, but it's important to remember that Japan experiences frequent earthquakes. Make a note of emergency contact numbers for your embassy. It's also worth taking a minute to check the evacuation route from your hotel room (usually on the door) and reading up on what to do in an earthquake (stay away from windows, take shelter under a sturdy table, and so on). That said, Japan's buildings are meant to stand up to most earthquakes, so the biggest concern is usually things falling off of shelves. Download the NHK World app on your smartphone so that you are updated with any emergency alerts in English. You can also visit ⊕ *www3.nhk.or.jp/nhkworld* for updates in English.

## LEARN A FEW WORDS

You will get by just fine in Tokyo without speaking a word of Japanese, but learning and using a few key phrases is appreciated by locals. Try *konnichiwa* (a more formal hello), *arigato* (thank you), and the multipurpose *domo* (casual hello or thank you). And don't forget *sumimasen* (excuse me) and *gomen nasai* (sorry).

## KNOW WHEN TO SMOKE

Despite tougher laws enacted in 2020, smokers can still light up in smaller restaurants and bars. Establishments that allow smoking will have a small green smoking sign near the door. Non-smoking establishments are becoming more common as the smoking rates decline. Smoking on the street is also prohibited in many places, but there are designated smoking areas in most cities.

## YOU CAN DRINK THE WATER

Tap water is safe to drink throughout Japan so pack a refillable water bottle that you can take with you each day.

# Getting Here and Around

##  Air

Flying time to Japan is 14 hours from New York, 13 hours from Chicago, and 10 hours from Los Angeles.

There are nonstop flights to Tokyo (both Narita and Haneda airports) from many major U.S. airports. Although a few airlines offer nonstop flights to Osaka from the U.S., most travel via Tokyo or another Asian hub city. Fares to Japan usually run around $1,600 (more during peak travel times) but in the off-season there are often good deals to be found.

Japan Airlines (JAL) and United Airlines are the major carriers between North America and Narita Airport in Tokyo; American Airlines, Delta Airlines, and All Nippon Airways (ANA) also link North American cities with Tokyo's Haneda and Narita airports. Most of these airlines also fly into and out of Japan's two other international airports, Kansai International Airport, located south of Osaka, and Centrair, near Nagoya.

Both of Japan's major carriers offer reduced prices for flights within the country, which are real cost- and time-savers if your trip includes destinations such as Kyushu or Hokkaido, though tickets must be booked outside Japan and there are restrictions on use in peak times. JAL offers the Japan Explorer Pass; ANA has a selection of special fares for international visitors.

■TIP➜ **Ask the local tourist board about hotel and local transportation packages that include tickets to major museum exhibits or other special events.**

### AIRPORTS

The major gateway to Japan is Tokyo's Narita Airport (NRT), 80 km (50 miles) northeast of the city. The Haneda Airport International Terminal, which opened in 2010, offers flights to major international cities and is only 20 km (12 miles) south of central Tokyo. The newer Centrair Airport (NGO) near Nagoya opened to take the strain off Narita. International flights also use Kansai International Airport (KIX) outside Osaka to serve the Kansai region, which includes Kobe, Kyoto, Nara, and Osaka. Fares are generally cheapest into Narita, however. A few international flights use Fukuoka Airport, on the island of Kyushu; these include United flights from Guam, JAL from Honolulu, and flights from other Asian destinations. New Chitose Airport, outside Sapporo on the northern island of Hokkaido, handles some international flights, mostly to Asian destinations such as Seoul and Shanghai. Most domestic flights to and from Tokyo are out of Haneda Airport.

Terminals 1 and 2 at Tokyo's Narita Airport are for international flights while Terminal 3 is for low-cost carriers. Terminal 2 has two adjoining wings, north and south. When you arrive, convert your money into yen; you need it for transportation into Tokyo. In both wings ATMs and money-exchange counters are in the wall between the customs inspection area and the arrival lobby. Both terminals have a Japan National Tourism Organization tourist information center, where you can get

| Travel Times from Tokyo | | | |
| --- | --- | --- | --- |
| To | By air | By car or bus | By train |
| Osaka | 1¼ hours | 7–8 hours | 2½ hours |
| Hiroshima | 1½ hours | 10 hours | 5 hours |
| Kyoto | 1¼ hours | 7 hours | 2 hours |
| Fukuoka | 2 hours | 14 hours | 5 hours |
| Sapporo | 1½ hours | 15 hours | 10 hours |
| Naha (Okinawa) | 3 hours | NA | NA |

free maps, brochures, and other visitor information. Directly across from the customs-area exits at both terminals are the ticket counters for airport limousine buses to Tokyo.

If you have a flight delay at Narita, take a local Keisei Line train into Narita town 15 minutes away, where a traditional shopping street and the beautiful Narita-san Shinsho-ji Temple are a peaceful escape from airport noise.

Flying into Haneda provides visitors with quicker access to downtown Tokyo, which is a short monorail ride away. Stop by the currency exchange and tourist information desk in the second-floor arrival lobby before taking a train into the city. There are also numerous jade-uniformed concierge staff on hand to help passengers with any questions.

If you plan to skip Tokyo and center your trip on Kyoto or central or western Honshu, Kansai International Airport (KIX) is the airport to use. Built on reclaimed land in Osaka Bay, it's laid out vertically. The first floor is for international arrivals; the second floor is for domestic departures and arrivals; the third floor has shops and restaurants; and the fourth floor is for international departures. A small tourist information center on the first floor of the passenger terminal building is open daily 9–5. Major carriers are Air Canada, Japan Airlines, and Delta Airlines. The trip from KIX to Kyoto takes 75 minutes by JR train; to Osaka it takes 45–70 minutes.

### GROUND TRANSPORTATION

Known as "the Gateway to Japan," Narita is the easiest airport to use if you are traveling to Tokyo. It takes about 90 minutes—a time very dependent on city traffic—by taxi or bus. The Keisei Skyliner and Japan Railways N'EX are the easiest ways to get into the city. If you are arriving with a Japan Rail Pass and staying in Tokyo for a few days, it is best to pay for the transfer into the city and activate the Rail Pass for travel beyond Tokyo.

Directly across from the customs-area exits at both terminals are the ticket counters for buses to Tokyo. Buses leave from platforms just outside terminal exits, exactly on schedule; the departure time is on the ticket. The Airport Limousine offer shuttle bus service from Narita to Tokyo.

Japan Railways trains stop at Narita Airport terminals 1 and 2. The fastest and most comfortable is the Narita Limited Express (N'EX), which makes 23 runs a day in each direction. Trains from the airport go directly to the central Tokyo Station in just under an hour, then continue to Yokohama and Ofuna. Daily departures begin at 7:44 am; the last train is at 9:44 pm. In addition to regular seats, there is a first-class Green Car and private, four-person compartments. All seats are reserved, and you'll need to reserve one for yourself in advance, as this train fills quickly.

The Keisei Skyliner train runs every 20–30 minutes between the airport terminals and Keisei-Ueno Station. The trip takes around 40 minutes. The first Skyliner leaves Narita for Ueno at 7:28 am, the last at 10:30 pm. From Ueno to Narita the first Skyliner is at 5:58 am, the last at 6:20 pm. There's also an early train from the airport, called the Morning Liner, which leaves at 7:49 am and costs ¥1,400.

# Getting Here and Around

## Travel Times from Tokyo

| From Narita | To | Fares | Times | Notes |
| --- | --- | --- | --- | --- |
| Airport Limousine (buses) | Various hotels in Tokyo and JR Tokyo and Shinjuku train stations | ¥3,100 | Every hr until 9:00 pm | 70–90 mins, can be longer in traffic |
| Airport Limousine (buses) | Tokyo City Air Terminal (TCAT) | ¥2,900 | Every 10–20 min, 6:55 am–11 pm | |
| Narita Limited Express (N'EX) | Central Tokyo Station, then continue to Yokohama and Ofuna | One-way fare ¥3,070; Green Car ¥5,340 | Daily departures begin at 7:40 am; the last train is at 9:44 pm | All seats are reserved |
| Keisei Skyliner train | Keisei-Ueno Station | ¥2,470 | Every 20–30 min, 7:28 am–10:30 pm | All seats are reserved |
| Taxi | Central Tokyo | ¥20,000 or more | | |
| **From Haneda** | **To** | **Fares** | **Times** | **Notes** |
| Tokyo Monorail | Central Tokyo | ¥500 | Every 20 min, 5:13 am–midnight | Trip takes 25–30 min. Connect to other major stations via the Yamanote Line at Hamamatsucho Station |
| Taxi | Central Tokyo | ¥5,000–¥6,000 | | |

### TRANSFERS BETWEEN AIRPORTS

Transfer between Narita and Haneda, the international and domestic airports, is easiest by the Friendly Limousine Bus, which should take 75 minutes and costs ¥3,000. The Keisei Access Express runs between the two airports but requires a transfer at Aoto Station.

 ## Boat

Ferries connect most of the islands of Japan. Some of the more-popular routes are from Tokyo to Tomakomai or Kushiro in Hokkaido; from Tokyo to Shikoku; and from Tokyo or Osaka to Kyushu. You can purchase ferry tickets in advance from travel agencies or before boarding. The ferries are inexpensive and are a pleasant, if slow, way of traveling. Private cabins are available, but it's more fun to travel in the economy class, where everyone sleeps on the carpeted floor in one large room. Passengers eat, drink, and enjoy themselves in a convivial atmosphere.

■ TIP➜ For information on local ferries, see the Essentials sections for individual towns within each chapter.

#  Bus

Japan Railways (JR) offers a number of long-distance buses that are comfortable and inexpensive. You can use Japan Rail Passes on some, but not all, of these buses. Routes and schedules are constantly changing, but tourist information offices will have up-to-date details. It's now possible to travel from Osaka to Tokyo for as little as ¥5,000 one-way. Buses are no-smoking, generally modern, and very comfortable, though overnight journeys still mean sleeping in your seat. Japan Rail Passes are not accepted by private bus companies. City buses outside Tokyo are quite convenient, but be sure of your route and destination, because the bus driver probably won't speak English.

Local buses have a set cost, anywhere from ¥100 to ¥200, depending on the route and municipality, in which case you board at the front of the bus and pay as you get on. On other buses cost is determined by the distance you travel. You take a ticket when you board at the rear door of the bus; it bears the number of the stop at which you boarded. Your fare depends on your destination and is indicated by a board at the front of the bus. Japan Railways also runs buses in some areas that have limited rail service. These buses are covered by the JR Pass, even if some reservation clerks tell you otherwise. Bus schedules can be hard to parse if you don't read Japanese, however, so it's best to ask for help at a tourist information office. The Nihon Bus Association has information about routes and which companies have English information online.

Reservations are not always essential, except at peak holiday times and on the most popular routes, like Tokyo to Osaka.

#  Car

You need an international driving permit (IDP) to drive in Japan. IDPs are available from the American Automobile Association. These international permits, valid only in conjunction with your regular driver's license, are universally recognized; having one may prevent problems with the local authorities. By law, car seats must be installed if the driver is traveling with a child under six.

Major roads in Japan are sufficiently marked in roman type, and on country roads there's usually someone to ask for help. Nevertheless, it's a good idea to have a detailed map with town names written in *kanji* (Japanese characters) and *romaji* (romanized Japanese).

Car travel along the Tokyo–Kyoto–Hiroshima corridor and in other built-up areas of Japan is not as convenient as the trains. Roads are congested, gas is expensive (about ¥160 per liter), and highway tolls are exorbitant (tolls between Tokyo and Kyoto amount to ¥10,550). In major cities, with the exception of main arteries, English signs are few and far between, one-way streets often lead you off the track, and parking is often hard to find.

That said, a car can be the best means for exploring cities outside the metropolitan areas and the rural parts of Japan, especially Kyushu and Hokkaido. Consider taking a train to those areas where exploring the countryside will be most interesting and renting a car locally for a day or even half a day. Book ahead in holiday seasons. Car rental rates in Tokyo begin at ¥6,300 a day and ¥37,800 a week, including tax, for an economy car with unlimited mileage.

# Getting Here and Around

## GASOLINE

Gas stations are plentiful along Japan's toll roads, and prices are fairly uniform across the country. Credit cards are accepted everywhere and are even encouraged—there are discounts for them at some places. Many stations offer both full and self-service and may offer a discount for pumping your own gas. Often you pay after putting in the gas, but there are also machines where you put money in first and then use the receipt to get change back. The staff will offer to take away trash and clean car windows. Tipping is not customary.

## PARKING

There is little on-street parking in Japan. Parking is usually in staffed parking lots or inside large buildings. Expect to pay upward of ¥300 per hour. Parking regulations are strictly enforced, and illegally parked vehicles are towed away. Recovery fees start at ¥30,000 and increase hourly.

## ROAD CONDITIONS

Roads in Japan are often narrower than those in the United States, but they're usually well maintained. Driving in cities can be difficult, as there are many narrow, one-way streets. Japanese drivers stick to the speed limit, but widely ignore bans on mobile phone use and dashboard televisions. Wild boars are not uncommon in rural districts, and have been known to block roads and ram into cars in the mountainous city of Kobe and in Kyushu, especially at night. From December to April northern and mountainous areas are often snowy.

## ROADSIDE EMERGENCIES

Emergency telephones along highways can be used to contact the authorities. A nonprofit service, JHelp.com, offers a free, 24-hour emergency assistance hotline. Car-rental agencies generally offer roadside assistance services.

## RULES OF THE ROAD

In Japan people drive on the left. Speed limits vary, but generally the limit is 80 kph (50 mph) on highways, 40 kph (25 mph) in cities. Penalties for speeding are severe. By law, car seats must be installed if the driver is traveling with a child under six, while the driver and all passengers in cars must wear seat belts at all times. Using a phone while driving is illegal.

Many smaller streets lack sidewalks, so cars, bicycles, and pedestrians share the same space. Fortunately, considering the narrowness of the streets and the volume of traffic, most Japanese drivers are technically skilled. Nevertheless, they may not allow quite as much distance between cars as you're used to. Be prepared for sudden lane changes by other drivers. When waiting at intersections after dark, many drivers, as a courtesy, turn off their main headlights to prevent glare.

Japan has a zero-tolerance policy when it comes to drinking and driving, so it's wisest to avoid alcohol entirely if you plan to drive.

#  Taxi and Rideshare

Taxis are an expensive way of getting around cities in Japan, though nascent deregulation moves are easing the market a little. In many cities, for instance, the first 2 km (1 mile) costs ¥730 and it's ¥90 for every additional 280 meters (400 yards). Between 10 pm and 5 am there is a 20% service charge. If possible, avoid using taxis during rush hours (7:30–9:30 am and 5–7 pm).

# Planning Your Time

Summer brings the rainy season, with particularly heavy rains and stifling humidity in June and July. Avoid July and August, unless you're visiting Hokkaido, where temperatures are more bearable. Fall relieves with clear blue skies and glorious foliage. A few surprise typhoons may occur in early fall, but the storms are usually as quick to leave.

Winter is gray and chilly, with little snow in most areas along the Pacific Ocean side of the country, where temperatures rarely fall below freezing. Hokkaido and the Japan Sea side of the country (facing Korea and Russia) are a different story, with heavy snowfalls in the winter months.

To avoid crowds, be aware of times when most Japanese are vacationing. Usually Japanese vacation on the same holiday dates. As a result, airports, planes, trains, and hotels are booked far in advance. Many businesses, shops, and restaurants are closed during these holidays. Holiday periods include the few days before and after New Year's; Golden Week, which follows Showa Day (April 29); and mid-August at the time of the Obon festivals, when many Japanese return to their ancestral hometowns.

In general, it's easy to hail a cab—simply raise your hand. Japanese taxis have automatic door-opening systems, so do not try to open the taxi door. Stand back when the cab comes to a stop—if you are too close, the door may slam into you. Only the curbside rear door opens. A red light on the dashboard (visible through the front window) indicates an available taxi, and a green light indicates an occupied taxi.

Drivers are for the most part courteous, though not necessarily chatty. Unless you're going to a well-known destination such as a major hotel, it's advisable to have a Japanese person write out your destination in Japanese. Your hotel concierge will do this for you. Remember, there is no need to tip.

Rideshare services are not common in Japan although in some cities the Uber app can be used to hail regular taxis.

##  Train

Riding Japanese trains is one of the pleasures of travel in the country. Efficient and convenient, trains run frequently and on schedule. The Shinkansen (bullet train), one of the fastest trains in the world, connects major cities north and south of Tokyo. It is slightly less expensive than flying, and is in many ways more convenient because train stations are more centrally located than airports. If you have a Japan Rail Pass, it's also extremely affordable.

Other trains, though not as fast as the Shinkansen, are just as convenient and substantially cheaper. There are three types of train services: *futsu* (local service), *tokkyu* (limited express service), and *kyuko* (express service). Both the tokkyu and the kyuko offer a first-class compartment known as the Green Car. Smoking is allowed only in designated carriages on long-distance and

# Getting Here and Around

Shinkansen trains. Local and commuter trains are entirely no-smoking.

Because there are no porters or carts at train stations, it's a good idea to travel light when getting around by train. Savvy travelers often use the *takkyubin* service to send their main luggage ahead to a hotel that they plan to reach later in their wanderings; get the form (and if you need it, assistance) from your hotel concierge). It's also good to know that every train station, however small, has luggage lockers, which cost about ¥400 for 24 hours.

If you plan on traveling by rail, consider a Japan Rail Pass, which offers unlimited travel on Japan Railways (JR) trains. You can purchase one-, two-, or three-week passes. A one-week pass is less expensive than a regular round-trip ticket from Tokyo to Kyoto on the Shinkansen. You must obtain a rail pass voucher prior to departure for Japan (you cannot buy them in Japan), and the pass must be used within three months of purchase. The pass is available only to people with tourist visas, as opposed to business, student, and diplomatic visas.

When you arrive in Japan, you must exchange your voucher for the Japan Rail Pass. You can do this at the Japan Railways desk in the arrivals hall at Narita Airport or at JR stations in major cities. When you make this exchange, you determine the day that you want the rail pass to begin, and, accordingly, when it ends. You do not have to begin travel on the day you make the exchange; instead, pick the starting date to maximize use. The Japan Rail Pass allows you to travel on all JR-operated trains (which cover most destinations in Japan) but not lines owned by other companies.

The JR Pass is also valid on buses operated by Japan Railways. You can make seat reservations without paying a fee on all trains that have reserved-seat coaches, usually long-distance trains. The Japan Rail Pass does not cover the cost of sleeping compartments on overnight trains (called blue trains), nor does it cover the newest and fastest of the Shinkansen trains, the *Nozomi,* which make only one or two stops on longer runs. The pass covers only the *Hikari* Shinkansen, which make a few more stops than the *Nozomi,* and the *Kodama* Shinkansen, which stop at every station along the Shinkansen routes. Nevertheless, it can be used on all the Yamagata, Tohoku, Joetsu, and Hokuriku Shinkansen trains.

Japan Rail Passes are available in coach class and first class, and as the difference in price between the two is relatively small, it's worth the splurge for first class, for real luxury, especially on the Shinkansen. A one-week pass costs ¥33,610 coach class, ¥44,810 first class; a two-week pass costs ¥52,960 coach class, ¥72,310 first class; and a three-week pass costs ¥66,200 coach class, ¥91,670 first class. Children under 11 pay lower rates. The pass pays for itself after one Tokyo–Kyoto round-trip Shinkansen ride. Contact a travel agent or Japan Airlines to purchase the pass.

If you're using a rail pass, there's no need to buy individual tickets, but you should book seats ahead. You can reserve up to two weeks in advance or just minutes before the train departs. There's no penalty if you fail to make a train, and you can reserve again.

Seat reservations for any JR route may be made at any JR station except those in the tiniest villages. The reservation windows or offices, *midori-no-madoguchi,* have green signs in English. If you're traveling without a Japan Rail Pass, there's a surcharge of approximately ¥500 (depending upon distance traveled) for seat reservations, and if you miss the train you'll have to pay for another reservation. All JR trains are no-smoking, although the Shinkansen have a few small, enclosed compartments that allow smoking. Your reservation ticket shows the date and departure time of your train as well as your car and seat number. Notice the markings painted on the platform or on little signs above the platform; ask someone which markings correspond to car numbers. If you don't have a reservation, ask which cars are unreserved. Unreserved tickets can be purchased at regular ticket windows. There are no reservations for local service trains. For traveling short distances, tickets are usually sold at vending machines. A platform ticket is required if you go through the wicket gate onto the platform to meet someone coming off a train. The charge is between ¥130 and ¥170 depending on the station.

Most clerks at train stations know a few basic words of English and can read roman script. They are invariably helpful in plotting your route. The complete railway timetable is a mammoth book written only in Japanese; however, you can get an English-language train schedule from the Japan National Tourism Organization that covers the Shinkansen and a few of the major JR Limited Express trains. JNTO's booklet *The Tourist's Language Handbook* provides helpful information about purchasing tickets in Japan. The Jorudan Route Finder is a good online source for searching train times and prices.

# Transportation Planner

## GETTING AROUND BY TRAIN

Japan (and Tokyo in particular) has one of the world's best train and subway systems: trains are nearly always on time, have clean facilities, and provide a safe environment.

**Shinkansen:** The JR Shinkansen "bullet" trains travel up and down Honshu and into Kyushu. Tokyo Station is Tokyo's main hub, with lines heading north, south, and west. Other Shinkansen lines run to Nagano and Kanazawa, Niigata, Yamagata, and other areas of Tohoku.

**Regional trains:** About 70% of Japan's railways are owned by Japan Railways (JR Group), the other 30% are owned by private companies. Non-JR lines include Tokyu's Toyoko Line between Tokyo's Shibuya and Yokohama to the south. The main line of the Odakyu Company and Keio Inokashira Line use Shinjuku and Shibuya, respectively, as hubs to serve the west of Tokyo. For service to Saitama Prefecture, Tobu offers the Tojo Line, which leaves Tokyo from Ikebukuro Station. The most important JR-owned regional line in Tokyo is the Yamanote Line, which loops around the city, while its Sobu and Chuo lines cross that circle east to west; JR trains also travel to Tokyo Disneyland.

**Subways:** The easiest way to explore Tokyo is via subway. There are two subway companies: Tokyo Metro and Toei. Because these are separate entities, they have separate fares, and it's cheaper to stay with one company. At the outer edges of the subway networks, private companies operate the line. If you're going far afield, be prepared to pay an additional fare.

**Tokyo monorail:** Beginning at Hamamatsu-cho Station, the monorail provides the simplest access to Haneda Airport.

## PURCHASING TICKETS

In Tokyo and other major cities basic fares (train or subway) are between ¥120 and ¥330. Tickets can be purchased from machines that take coins or cash near the gates. Maps above the machines—usually in Japanese and English—give destinations and corresponding fares.

■TIP➜ Get a rechargeable train card to make train travel much smoother as you don't have to figure out the ticket price for every trip. These cards can be used for most trains (and some buses) throughout Japan regardless of the city where you buy it.

The cards have different names depending on the city: in Tokyo, it's **Suica** (from JR machines) or **PASMO** (from subway machines); in Hokkaido, **Kitaca**; in much of the JR West service area, **ICOCA** cards. Tokyo has some one-day passes including the **Tokunai Pass** for unlimited use of JR lines and the **Tokyo Free Kippu,** which covers subways and buses. Purchase tickets for Shinkansen lines and other long-distance regional lines that require a seat reservation at a ticket window.

## JR PASS

The Japan Rail Pass can be used on all JR trains including the Shinkansen bullet trains—except for the fastest Nozomi trains on the Tokaido and Sanyo lines and Mizuho trains on the Kyushu Shinkansen. Hikari or Kodama trains and Sakura or Tsubame trains, however, serve these same respective routes and are included. The pass is also valid on local JR buses and on the JR ferry to Miyajima. Passes must be purchased at an authorized JR outlet outside of Japan before your trip and are available for 7-, 14-, or 21-day periods. Activate them on arrival at a major rail station or Narita Airport. A first-class version allows access to the Shinkansen Lines' special Green Cars.

# HOW TO USE A TICKET MACHINE

Use the map above the ticket machine to determine how much money to put on your ticket. The numbers next to each stop indicate the price from your current station.

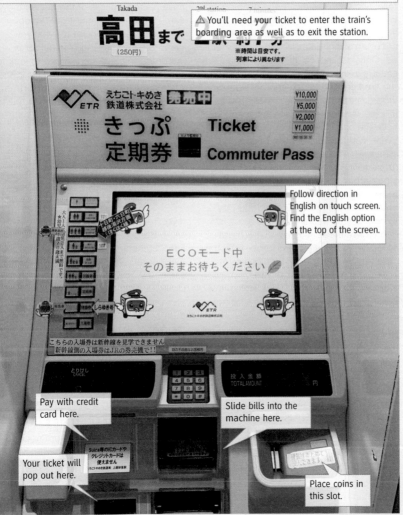

⚠ You'll need your ticket to enter the train's boarding area as well as to exit the station.

Follow direction in English on touch screen. Find the English option at the top of the screen.

Pay with credit card here.

Your ticket will pop out here.

Slide bills into the machine here.

Place coins in this slot.

# Essentials

##  Addresses

The simplest way to decipher a Japanese address is to break it into parts. For example: 6-chome 8-19, Chuo-ku, Fukuoka-shi, Fukuoka-ken. In this address the *chome* indicates a precise area (a block, for example), and the numbers following chome indicate the building within the area. Note that buildings aren't always numbered sequentially; numbers are often assigned as buildings are erected. Only local police officers and mail carriers in Japan seem to be familiar with the area defined by the chome. Sometimes, instead of chome, *machi* (town) is used. Written addresses in Japan also have the opposite order of those in the West, with the city coming before the street. *Ku* refers to a district of a city, *shi* refers to a city name, and *ken* indicates a prefecture, which is roughly equivalent to a state in the United States. It's not unusual for the prefecture and the city to have the same name. There are a few geographic areas in Japan that are not called ken. One is greater Tokyo, which is called Tokyo-to. Other exceptions Kyoto and Osaka, which are followed by the suffix -*fu* (Kyoto-fu, Osaka-fu). Hokkaido, Japan's northernmost island, is also not considered a ken.

Not all addresses conform exactly to the above format. Rural addresses, for example, might use *gun* (county) where city addresses have *ku* (district). Even Japanese people cannot find a building based on the address alone. If you get in a taxi with a written address, do not assume the driver will be able to find your destination. Usually, people provide very detailed instructions or maps to explain their exact locations. It's always good to know the location of your destination in relation to a major building or department store.

## 🍴 Dining

Food, like many other things in Japan, can be expensive. Eating at highly regarded dining rooms is costly; however, you can eat well and reasonably at standard restaurants that may not have signs in English. Many less expensive eateries have plastic replicas of the dishes they serve displayed in their front windows, so you can always point to what you want to eat if the language barrier is insurmountable. A good place to look for moderately priced dining spots is in the restaurant concourse of any department store, usually on the bottom floor.

In general, Japanese standards of hygiene are very high. Tap water is safe, and most hotels have Western-style restrooms, although restaurants may have Japanese-style toilets, with bowls recessed into the floor, over which you must squat.

If you're in a hurry, find a branch of the MOS Burger, Freshness Burger, or First Kitchen chains. They offer familiar hamburgers, but they also have local variations. Yoshinoya is another popular chain, serving grilled salmon, rice, and miso soup for breakfast (until 10), and then hearty portions of rice and beef for the rest of the day.

Convenience store fare is also much tastier than you'd expect. Don't hesitate to grab a quick *onigiri* (rice ball) on the run. Most serve fresh coffee for a fraction of what most coffee shops charge.

### MEALS AND MEALTIMES
Office workers eat lunch from noon to 1 pm, so eat later to avoid crowds. Many restaurants have lunchtime specials until 2:30 pm, and some close their doors between 3 and 5 pm. Note that many restaurants in rural areas close by 9.

Unless otherwise noted, the restaurants listed in this guide are open daily for lunch and dinner.

## PAYING

Beyond major hotels, larger chain restaurants, and smart city dining, credit cards may not be accepted, so check before ordering. Most casual Japanese restaurants will not bring the bill to your table. Instead, get up and pay at the register when you are finished.

## RESERVATIONS

For upmarket, evening dining in major cities ask hotel staff to make reservations—not only will this guarantee a table, but it gives the management time to locate an English menu or staff with some language skills.

#  Embassies and Consulates

The U.S. Embassy is located in Tokyo. There are consulates in Sapporo, Nagoya, Osaka, Fukuoka, and Okinawa.

#  Health & Safety

Japan is a safe, clean country for travelers with drinkable water and no major water- or insect-borne diseases. Condoms are sold widely, but they may not have the brands you're used to. Speak with your physician and/or check the CDC or World Health Organization websites for health alerts, particularly if you're pregnant or traveling with children or have a chronic illness.

## COVID-19

COVID-19 has disrupted travel since March 2020, and travelers should expect sporadic ongoing issues well into 2022 and 2023. Always travel with a mask in case it's required, and keep up to date on the most recent testing and vaccination guidelines for Japan. Many countries require all travelers to be vaccinated against COVID-19, and some still require a PCR or antigen test before travel or upon arrival.

## SPECIFIC ISSUES IN JAPAN

Tap water is safe everywhere in Japan. Medical treatment varies from highly skilled and professional at major hospitals to somewhat less advanced in small neighborhood clinics. At larger hospitals you have a good chance of encountering English-speaking doctors.

Mosquitoes can be a minor irritation during the rainy season, though you are never at risk of contracting anything serious. If you're staying in a ryokan or any place without air-conditioning, anti-mosquito coils or an electric-powered spray will be provided. Dehydration and heatstroke could be concerns if you spend a long time outside during the summer months, but sports drinks are readily available from the nation's ubiquitous vending machines.

## OVER-THE-COUNTER REMEDIES

Medication can only be bought at pharmacies in Japan, but every neighborhood seems to have at least one. Ask for the *yakyoku* (薬局). Pharmacists in Japan are usually able to manage at least a few words of English, and certainly are able to read some, so have a pen and some paper ready, just in case. In Japanese, aspirin is *asupirin* and Tylenol is *Tairenoru*. Following national regulations, Japanese drugs often contain less potent ingredients than foreign brands, so the effects can be disappointing; check advised dosages carefully.

Drugs and medications are widely available at drugstores, although the brand names and use instructions will be in Japanese, so if you're on regular medication, take along enough supplies to cover

# Essentials

the trip. As with any international travel, be sure to bring your prescription or a doctor's note just in case.

##  Immunizations

Visitors to Japan may require valid proof of COVID-19 vaccination and/or a booster; while the need and frequency of boosters is still being discussed in the medical community, it's important to verify the most recent requirements with your physician before you travel.

The CDC recommends travelers to Japan are up to date with their routine vaccinations and Hepatitis A and B vaccinations.

##  Internet

Except for some traditional ryokan and minshiku, nearly all hotels have Wi-Fi. There are some free services that allow tourists to access a number of hotspots around the country. The most useful way to find free public Wi-Fi service in Japan is to check ⊕ *japanfreewifi.com.*

It's also possible to rent a pocket Wi-Fi router so you can use Google Maps to navigate your way around or to use an online translation app, both of which can be very helpful when you are out and about.

Japan Wireless has plans from ¥4,319 for 10 days though it is more expensive per day the shorter the rental. Ninja WiFi has unlimited data rental plans from ¥990 per day regardless of the rental length. For both, it is best to order online before your trip. You can pick up the portable Wi-Fi device at a number of airports or have it sent directly to your hotel.

##  Lodging

Accommodations in Japan range from Japanese-style inns to large Western-style hotels, in all price categories. It's essential to book in advance if you're traveling during peak travel seasons and is recommended at other times.

The *ryokan,* a traditional Japanese inn, provides the most unique experience. Japanese-style interiors include tatami flooring, paper (*shoji*) blinds, a low table for tea service, and pillows. Futons that are rolled out in the evening serve as beds. Stays usually include traditional Japanese morning and evening meals, often with small seafood dishes and regional specialties. Lodges usually offer the use of an *onsen* (hot-spring bath), though many also have in-room showers.

Similar to the ryokan, but less expensive, *minshuku* are Japanese-style bed-and-breakfasts. Usually family-run, these inns feature Japanese-style rooms and meals. Baths (there are usually no in-room bathing options) are part of the shared public areas, which also include toilets.

Business hotels feature Western-style digs in basic, small rooms; these are ideal for one night and are usually close to major transportation hubs. Most major cities have high-end Western-style hotels with ritzy spas, fully equipped gyms, and some of Japan's better restaurants. Many are situated in high-rise buildings and provide fantastic views of the city's skyline.

The boutique hotel arrived late to Japan, but these quirky, trendy properties have taken hold. Earth tones, funky bathrooms, and curvy, chrome fixtures dominate at these hotels, which are priced just above business hotels. On the flip side, hostels are perfect for the budget conscious.

Capsule hotels—generally men-only—are the most spartan accommodations around, providing a chamber that you slide your body into laterally, much like a coffin. There are no frills here, but the price is right. Common areas with televisions and lockers for valuables and luggage come standard.

The often garish love hotel is not really a lodging option but more of a place for couples to relax in private. Most patrons pay for a two-hour stopover (¥4,000), but it is possible to stay overnight (¥8,000). Most have an ostentatious theme, like "Christmas" or "Medieval Europe," reflected in the decor.

Resorts in hot-spring areas, such as Hakone or all over Tohoku, offer quiet luxury, focusing their services and amenities on the relaxation provided by onsen.

A travel agent based in Japan can help you make reservations and other travel arrangements, and this is a particularly useful service since some hotels and ryokan do not have English-language websites.

Jalan, Rakuten Travel, and Nippon Travel Agency offer a wide range of accommodations from big-city luxury to out-of-the-way family guesthouses.

## TEMPLES
You can also arrange accommodations in Buddhist temples, known as shukubo. JNTO has lists of temples that accept guests and you can arrange for your stay here as well. A stay at a temple generally costs ¥3,000 to ¥9,000 per night, including two meals. Some temples offer instruction in meditation or allow you to observe their religious practices, while others simply offer rooms. The Japanese-style accommodations are very simple, and range from beautiful, quiet havens to not-so-comfortable, basic cubicles. For specific information on

temple lodging in the Kii Mountain range in southern Japan, try contacting the Shukubo Temple Lodging Cooperative.

## 💲 Money
The unit of currency in Japan is the yen (¥). There are bills of ¥10,000, ¥5,000, ¥2,000, and ¥1,000. Coins are ¥500, ¥100, ¥50, ¥10, ¥5, and ¥1. Japanese currency floats on the international monetary exchange, so changes can be dramatic.

### ATMS AND BANKS
ATMs at many Japanese banks do not accept foreign-issue debit or credit cards. UFJ and Shinsei banks are members of the Plus network, as are some convenience store cash machines.

The easiest way to withdraw money is at convenience-store ATMs. 7-Eleven stores and 7 Bank ATMs accept most internationally branded cards. ATMs at post offices and major convenience stores accept foreign ATM and debit cards. In more-rural areas, it can be difficult to find suitable ATMs, so it is best to get cash before heading out into the countryside.

PIN codes in Japan are comprised of four digits. In Japanese an ATM is commonly referred to by its English acronym, while a PIN is *ansho bango*. If you need assistance, contact the bank staff by using the phone next to the ATM. Many machines also have English on-screen instructions.

### CREDIT CARDS
Japan still relies predominately on cash, and many smaller businesses (even a few very expensive restaurants) simply don't accept credit cards, even in large cities like Osaka and Tokyo. Hotels and most tourist-related businesses do accept credit cards. MasterCard and Visa are the most widely accepted credit

# Essentials

cards in Japan. When you use a credit card you'll be asked if you intend to pay in one installment as most locals do, say *hai-ikkai* (Yes, one time). Many vendors don't accept American Express.

## 🎒 Packing

Pack light, because porters can be hard to find and storage space in hotel rooms may be tiny.

Although there are no strict dress codes for visiting temples and shrines, you will be out of place in immodest outfits. For sightseeing leave sandals and open-toe shoes behind; you'll need sturdy walking shoes for the gravel pathways that surround temples and fill parks. Make sure to bring comfortable clothing to wear in traditional Japanese restaurants, where you may need to sit on tatami-mat floors. Central and southern Japan are hot and humid June to September, so pack cotton clothing. Winter daytime temperatures in northern Japan hover around freezing, so gloves and hats are necessary, and clip-on shoe spikes can be bought locally.

Japanese do not wear shoes in private homes or in any temples or traditional inns. Having shoes you can quickly slip in and out of is a decided advantage.

All lodgings provide a thermos of hot water and bags of green tea in every room. For coffee you can call room service, buy very sweet coffee in a can from a vending machine, or purchase packets of instant coffee at local convenience stores. If you're staying in a Japanese inn, they probably won't have coffee.

Sunglasses, sunscreen lotions, and hats are readily available, and these days they're not much more expensive in Japan. It's a good idea to carry a couple of plastic bags to protect your camera and clothes during sudden cloudbursts.

## 🌐 Passports and Visas

Hotels in Japan require foreign guests to show passports at check-in, but police are unlikely to ask foreign visitors for on-the-spot identification, although crime crackdowns in nightlife areas of big cities and political tensions with neighboring countries can alter local circumstances in some areas.

Visitors with U.S., Canadian, or U.K. passports do not need to apply for a visa for travel to Japan. However, visitors must have a return (or outbound) ticket to enter the country.

## 💲 Taxes

An 10% national consumption tax is added to all hotel bills. Another 3% local tax is added to the bill if it exceeds ¥15,000. You may save money by paying for your hotel meals separately rather than charging them to your bill.

At luxury hotels, a 10% service charge is added to the bill in place of individual tipping. At more expensive ryokan, where individualized maid service is offered, the service charge is usually 15%. At business hotels and other budget lodgings, no service charge is added to the bill.

There's an across-the-board, nonrefundable 8% consumption tax levied on all sales, which is included in the ticket price. Authorized tax-free shops will knock the tax off purchases over ¥10,000 if you show your passport and a valid tourist visa. A large sign is displayed at such shops.

An 8% tax is also added to all restaurant bills. Another 3% local tax is added to the bill if it exceeds ¥7,500. At more expensive restaurants a 10%–15% service charge is added to the bill. Tipping is not customary.

# 📞 Telephones

Most U.S. mobile phones will work in Japan these days (ask your provider if you will have service in Japan before you travel), but roaming charges can still bo high. For many visitors, the best alternative is to rent a phone from one of the many outlets at Narita, Kansai, and Nagoya airports on arrival. Softbank also sells SIM cards so you can have your own local number in Japan (provided that your phone is unlocked). Most company rental rates start at ¥525 a day.

## CALLING WITHIN JAPAN

There are sometimes public telephones near convenience stores, train and bus stations, and, of course, in hotel lobbies. Phones accept ¥100 coins as well as prepaid telephone cards. Domestic long-distance rates are reduced as much as 50% after 9 pm (40% after 7 pm). Telephone cards, sold in vending machines, hotels, and a variety of stores, are tremendously convenient.

## CALLING OUTSIDE JAPAN

The best way to call abroad is to use an Internet-based service like Facebook Messenger, WhatsApp, or Google Voice. There are still a few telephone cards that can be used to call out of Japan such as the KDDI Super World Card. Each card has different access codes so follow the included instructions. Major U.S. cellular carriers also offer international voice and data plans. Check with your carrier for details.

# 💲 Tipping

Tipping is not common in Japan. It's not necessary to tip in taxis, hair salons, barbershops, bars, or nightclubs. A chauffeur for a hired car usually receives a tip of ¥500 for a half-day excursion and ¥1,000 for a full-day trip. Porters charge fees of ¥250 to ¥300 per bag at railroad stations and ¥200 per piece at airports. It's not customary to tip employees of hotels, even porters, unless a special service has been rendered. In such cases a gratuity of ¥2,000 to ¥3,000 should be placed in an envelope and handed to the staff member discreetly.

# 🧭 Tours

Japan is daunting for first-time visitors, so a package tour is a great way to get into the country and find your feet. But beware of expensive optional tours such as tea ceremonies, theater tours, and night views. Local tourist offices can tell you how to have the same experience without emptying your wallet.

The country can be quite a culture shock, so resist the temptation to book tours that pack in too much sightseeing. Opt for those that include half days of freedom, because just stepping outside the hotel into the local streets is likely to provide some unimagined sights and experiences.

Tokyo and Kyoto feature on almost every tour of Japan, while Hiroshima, Nara, and Nikko are normally the secondary destinations.

## RECOMMENDED COMPANIES
### Alexander & Roberts

GUIDED TOURS | Alexander & Roberts's mix of fully guided and freestyle tours lets travelers choose how much guidance they want during their trip. Although

# Essentials

tours generally focus on the main Tokyo–Kyoto–Hiroshima tourist route, there are optional side trips that take travelers a bit off the beaten track. ☎ 800/221–2216 ⊕ www.alexanderroberts.com ✉ $600 (4-day Kyoto tour)–$6,000 (11-day tour across Japan).

**Explorient Travel Services**

SPECIAL-INTEREST TOURS | Explorient offers private, customizable tours with a focus on luxury travel. Aimed at travelers who want every last detail taken care of, Explorient tours cover both major tourist destinations like Kyoto and Tokyo as well as more out-of-the-way sights such as the inland Sea or Japan's UNESCO World Heritage sites. ☎ 800/785–1233 ⊕ www.explorient.com ✉ $3,500–$6,000.

**Inside Japan Tours**

SPECIAL-INTEREST TOURS | This local company offers self-guided, small group, and private tours, with a focus on unique experiences away from the typical tourist path. ☎ 303/952–0379 ⊕ www.inside-japantours.com.

**Smithsonian Journeys**

SPECIAL-INTEREST TOURS | Smithsonian offers small group tours covering Japan's major tourist sites making them a good choice for travelers looking for the comfort and camaraderie of a group. Although less customizable than private tours, they are generally more affordable. There are also some cruise tours for those interested in traversing the Pacific by boat rather than plane. Tour prices include transportation from the United States. ☎ 855/530–1542 ⊕ www.smithsonianjourneys.org ✉ $6,000.

## SPECIAL-INTEREST TOURS
### CYCLING

Cycling is popular in Japan, but local bike-rental shops may not have frames large enough for non-Japanese cyclists.

For more information on cycling in Japan, see the *Japan Cycling Navigator*.

**Aloha Bike**

SPECIAL-INTEREST TOURS | Aloha Bike's experienced cycling guides take the uncertainty out of cycling across Japan. Although clients need to be fit, Aloha offers a range of tours of varying routes and difficulties. With everything from two-day trips around the Mt. Fuji Five Lakes area, to 11-day treks from coast to coast, it is easy to add a short cycling tour to an otherwise self-planned trip. ☎ 0558/22–1516 ⊕ www.alohabike.com ✉ $400 (2-day tour)–$3,000 (11-day tour).

**Japan Cycling Navigator**

SPECIAL-INTEREST TOURS | A must for travelers planning a self-guided cycling trip, *Japan Cycling Navigator* offers information and on cycling routes throughout the country. ⊕ www.japancycling.org.

### DIVING

Okinawa, Kyushu, and the islands and peninsula south of Tokyo are all popular diving areas. If you are a novice diver, make sure that a dive leader's "English spoken" means real communication skills. Dive Japan has lists of dive services and locations.

**Dive Japan**

SPECIAL-INTEREST TOURS | Although rarely updated, the Dive Japan website is still the best English-language resource for information on dive sites around the country. ⊕ www.divejapan.com.

### ECOTOURS

Whales, monkeys, bears, and cranes—Japan does have fauna and flora to appreciate slowly, but English-language tours are limited. Naturalist Mark Brazil, who writes extensively about wild Japan, leads ecotours through Zegrahm Eco Expeditions.

### One Life Japan

ECOTOURISM | With a range of cycling, hiking, and ecotours, One Life Japan gives travelers an inside look at life in rural Japan. A small, independent outfit, it offers a level of personal interaction and community involvement that larger tours have difficulty matching. Focusing on active, challenging, and sustainable travel, it is a good choice for those looking for an adventure and a look into everyday life far from the big city. ☎ *090/3337–3248* ⊕ *www.onelifejapan. com* 🎫 *$2,000.*

### GOLF

Japan's love affair with golf does not make it any easier for non-Japanese-speaking visitors to reserve a tee time unless introduced by a club member. Golf in Japan, put together by golfing expats, helpfully lists more than 2,000 courses that welcome foreign golfers.

### Golf in Japan

SPECIAL-INTEREST TOURS | For golfers, this website offers extensive information on golf courses and clubs throughout the country, including costs, access, and how to reserve time on the green. ⊕ *www. golf-in-japan.com.*

### HIKING

Japan has well-marked trails, bus/train connections to trailheads, and hidden sights to be discovered. Millions of Japanese are avid and well-equipped hikers. English information is growing, so check local tourist offices for details. Visit Outdoor Japan's website for all outdoor activities. Quest Japan, run by an experienced British hiker, has a range of tours in all seasons.

### Outdoor Japan

ADVENTURE TOURS | Outdoor Japan is the first place to look for information on nearly any kind of outdoor activity, from hiking to snowboarding to kayaking. ⊕ *www. outdoorjapan.com.*

### Quest Japan Tours

ADVENTURE TOURS | Quest Japan offers hiking tours ranging from 10 days to more than two weeks. Not for the inexperienced, these hikes offer a look at some of the country's most stunning mountains and historic trails. ⊕ *questjapan.jp* 🎫 *$2,000.*

### LANGUAGE PROGRAMS

There is no better way to learn the language than to immerse yourself by studying Japanese in Japan, with classes, a homestay, and cultural tours on which to put the newfound skills into action. Japanese Information and Culture Center (JICC) has good links to schools and procedures for study-abroad programs.

### Japan Information and Culture Center (JICC)

SPECIAL-INTEREST TOURS | JICC has a wealth of information about various language programs in Japan. ☎ *202/238– 6900* ⊕ *www.us.emb-japan.go.jp/jicc/.*

## ◉ Visitor Information

The tourist information center (TIC) near Tokyo Station has a wealth of information for visitors, as do the more than 140 tourist information offices around the country certified by JNTO. Look for the sign showing a red question mark and "Information" at train stations and city centers.

# Helpful Japanese Phrases

## BASICS

| | | |
|---|---|---|
| Hello/Good Day | こんにちは。 | kon-ni-chi-wa |
| Yes/no | はい / いいえ | hai / ii-e |
| Please | お願いします | o-ne-gai shi-ma-su |
| Thank you (very much) | ありがとう (ございます) | a-ri-ga-tō (go-zai-ma-su) |
| You're welcome. | どういたしまして。 | dō i-ta-shi-mashi-te |
| I'm sorry (apology) | ごめんなさい。 | go-men na-sai |
| Sorry. (Excuse me.) | すみません。 | su-mi-ma-sen |
| Good morning | おはようございます | o-ha-yō go-zai-ma-su |
| Good evening | こんばんは。 | kom-ban-wa |
| Goodbye | さようなら。 | sa-yō-na-ra |
| Pleased to meet you. | はじめまして。 | pee-ah-chair-ray |
| How are you? | おげんき ですか。 | ko-may-stah |

## NUMBERS

| | | |
|---|---|---|
| half | ハーフ | hā-fu |
| one | 一 / 一つ | i-chi / hi-to-tsu |
| two | 二 / 二つ | ni / fu-ta-tsu |
| three | 三 / 三つ | san / mit-tsu |
| four | 四 / 四つ | yon (shi) / yot-tsu |
| five | 五 / 五つ | go / i-tsu-tsu |
| six | 六 / 六つ | ro-ku / mut-tsu |
| seven | 七 / 七つ | na-na (shi-chi) / na-na-tsu |
| eight | 八 / 八つ | ha-chi / yat-tsu |
| nine | 九 / 九つ | kyū / ko-ko-no-tsu |
| ten | 十 / とう | jū / tō |
| eleven | 十一 | jū i-chi |
| twelve | 十二 | jū ni |
| thirteen | 十三 | jū san |
| fourteen | 十四 | jū yon |
| fifteen | 十五 | jū go |
| sixteen | 十六 | jū ro-ku |
| seventeen | 十七 | jū na-na |
| eighteen | 十八 | jū ha-chi |
| nineteen | 十九 | jū-kyū |
| twenty | 二十 | ni-jū |
| twenty-one | 二十一 | ni-jū i-chi |
| thirty | 三十 | san jū |
| forty | 四十 | yon jū |
| fifty | 五十 | go jū |
| sixty | 六十 | ro-ku jū |
| seventy | 七十 | na-na jū |
| eighty | 八十 | ha-chi jū |
| ninety | 九十 | kyū jū |
| one hundred | 百 | hyaku |
| one thousand | 千 / 一千 | sen / is-sen |
| ten thousand | 一万 | i-chi man |
| one hundred thousand | 十万 | jū man |
| one million | 百万 | hya-ku man |

## COLORS

| | | |
|---|---|---|
| black | 黒 | ku-ro |
| blue | 青 | ao |
| brown | 茶色 | cha-iro |
| green | 緑 | mi-do-ri |
| orange | オレンジ | o-ren-ji |
| purple | 紫 | mu-ra-sa-ki |
| red | 赤 | a-ka |
| white | 白 | shi-ro |
| yellow | 黄色 | ki-iro |

## DAYS OF THE WEEK

| | | |
|---|---|---|
| Sunday | 日曜日 | ni-chi yō-bi |
| Monday | 月曜日 | ge-tsu yō-bi |
| Tuesday | 火曜日 | ka yō-bi |
| Wednesday | 水曜日 | su-i yō-bi |
| Thursday | 木曜日 | mo-ku yō-bi |
| Friday | 金曜日 | kin yō-bi |
| Saturday | 土曜日 | dō yō-bi |

## MONTHS

| | | |
|---|---|---|
| January | 一月 | i-chi ga-tsu |
| February | 二月 | ni ga-tsu |
| March | 三月 | san ga-tsu |
| April | 四月 | shi ga-tsu |
| May | 五月 | go ga-tsu |
| June | 六月 | ro-ku ga-tsu |
| July | 七月 | shi-chi ga-tsu |
| August | 八月 | ha-chi ga-tsu |
| September | 九月 | ku ga-tsu |
| October | 十月 | jū ga-tsu |
| November | 十一月 | jū-i-chi ga-tsu |
| December | 十二月 | jū-ni ga-tsu |

## USEFUL WORDS AND PHRASES

| | | |
|---|---|---|
| Do you understand English? | 英語がわかりますか。 | ei-go ga wa-ka-r ma-su ka |
| I don't understand Japanese. | 日本語がわかりません。 | ni-hon-go ga wa-ka-ri-ma-sen |
| I don't understand. | わかりません。 | wa-ka-ri-ma-sen |
| I don't know. | 知りません。 | shi-ri-ma-sen |
| I understand. | わかりました。 | wa-ka-ri-ma-shi |
| I'm American. | 私はアメリカ人です。 | wa-ta-shi wa a-r ri-ka jin de-su |
| I'm British. | 私はイギリス人です。 | wa-ta-shi wa i-g ri-su jin de-su |
| I'm Australian. | 私はオーストラリア人です。 | wa-ta-shi wa ō-s to-ra-ri-a jin de-s |
| What's your name. | お名前はなんですか。 | o- na-ma-e wa n de-su ka |
| My name is ... | [name] と申します。 | [name] to-mō-shi-ma-su |
| What time is it? | 今何時ですか。 | i-ma nan-ji de-su ka |
| How? | どうやって ですか。 | dō-yat-te de-su k |
| When? | いつ ですか。 | i-tsu de-su ka |

| esterday | 昨日 | ki-nō |
| oday | 今日 | kyō |
| omorrow | 明日 | ashi-ta |
| his morning | けさ | ke-sa |
| his afternoon | 今日の午後 | kyō no go-go |
| onight | 今晩 | kom-ban |
| What? | 何ですか。 | nan de-su ka |
| What is this / hat? | これ / それ は何で すか。 | ko-re / so-re wa nan de-su ka |
| Why? | どうしてですか。 | dō-shi-te de-su ka |
| Who? | どなたですか。 | do-na-ta de-su ka |
| Where is [place thing]? | [place / thing] はどこ ですか。 | [place / thing] wa do-ko de-su ka |
| tation | 駅 | e-ki |
| ubway station | 地下鉄の駅 | chi-ka-te-tsu no e-ki |
| us stop | バス乗り場 | ba-su no-ri-ba |
| irport | 空港 | kū-kō |
| oct office | 郵便局 | yū-bin-kyo-ku |
| ank | 銀行 | gin-kō |
| otel | ホテル | ho-te-ru |
| useum | 博物館 | ha-ku-bu-tsu-kan |
| rt museum / art allery | 美術館 | bi-ju-tsu-kan |
| ospital | 病院 | byō-in |
| levator | エレベーター | e-re-bē-tā |
| Where is the estroom? | トイレはどこですか。 | to-i-re wa do-ko de-su ka |
| ere / there / ver there | ここ / そこ / あそこ | ko-ko / so-ko / a-so-ko |
| eft / right | 左 / 右 | hi-da-ri / mi-gi |
| s it near / far? | 近い / 遠い ですか。 | chi-ka-i / tō-i de-su ka |
| o you have ... | [item] が ありますか。 | [item] ga a-ri-ma-su-ka |
| room | 部屋 | he-ya |
| city map | 市内地図 | shi-nai chi-zu |
| road map | ロードマップ | rō-do map-pu |
| notebook | ノート | nō-to |
| notepad | メモ用紙 | me-mo-yo-shi |
| magazine in nglish | 英語の 雑誌 | ei-go no zas-shi |
| postcard | はがき | ha-ga-ki |
| stamp | 切手 | kit-te |
| ticket | 切符 | kip-pu |
| nvelopes | 封筒 | fū-tō |
| ow much is it? | いくらですか。 | i-ku-ra de-su ka |
| 's expensive / heap | 高い / 安い です。 | ta-ka-i / ya-su-i de-su |
| little / a lot | 少し / たくさん | su-ko-shi / ta-ku-san |
| ore / less | もっと多く / 少なく | mot-to ō-ku/ su-ku-na-ku |
| nough / too any | 十分 / 多すぎる | jū-bun / ō-su-gi-ru |
| feel sick. | 体調が悪い。 | tai-chō ga wa-ru-i |
| all a doctor / mbulance | 医者 / 救急車 を呼んで ください。 | i-sha / kyū-kyū-sha o yon-de ku-da-sai |

| Help! | 助けて! | ta-su-ke-te |
| Stop! | やめて! | ya-me-te |

## DINING OUT

| A bottle of ... / a cup of ... | ... 一本 / ... 一杯 | ... ip-pon / ... ip-pai |
| Two bottles of ... / two cups of ... | ... 二本 / ... 二杯 | ... ni-hon / ... ni-hai |
| Aperitif | 食前酒 | sho-ku-zen shu |
| Beer | ビール | bii-ru |
| Bill / check, please. | お勘定 お願いします。 | o- kan-jō o-ne-ga-i-shi-ma-su |
| Bread | パン | pan |
| Breakfast | 朝食 / 朝ごはん | chō-sho-ku / a-sa go-han |
| Butter | バター | ba-tā |
| Cocktail | カクテル | ka-ku-te-ru |
| Coffee | コーヒー | kō-hī |
| Dinner | 夕食 / 晩ごはん | yū-sho-ku / ban go-han |
| Fork | フォーク | fō-ku |
| I am a vegetarian. | 私は 菜食主義者 / ベ ジタリアンです。 | wa-ta-shi wa saisho-ku shu-gi-sha / be-ji-ta-ri-an de-su |
| I cannot eat [item]. | [item] は食べられま せん。 | [item] wa ta-be-ra-re-ma-sen |
| I'm ready to order. | 注文 お願いします。 | chū-mon o-ne-ga-i-shi-ma-su |
| I'm hungry. | お腹が空いています。 | o-na-ka ga su-i-te i-ma-su |
| I'm thirsty. | 喉が渇いています。 | no-do ga ka-wai-te i-ma-su |
| It's delicious. | 美味しい です。 | oi-shī de-su |
| It doesn't taste good. | 美味しくない です。 | oi-shi ku-nai de-su |
| It's hot. (Be careful, please.) | 暑いです。(気を付けて ください。) | a-tsu-I de-su (ki-o-tsu-ke-te ku-da-sai) |
| Knife | ナイフ | nai-fu |
| Lunch | 昼食 / 昼ごはん | chū-sho-ku / hi-ru go-han |
| Menu | メニュー | me-nyū |
| Napkin | ナプキン | na-pu-kin |
| Pepper | こしょう | ko-shō |
| Plate | 皿 | sa-ra |
| Please give me [item]. | [item] をください。 | [item] o ku-da-sai |
| Salt | 塩 | shi-o |
| Spoon | スプーン | su-pūn |
| Tea (Japanese teas) | お茶 | o-cha |
| Tea (other teas) | 紅茶 | kō-cha |
| Water | 水 | mi-zu |
| Rice wine (sake) | 日本酒 | ni-hon-shu |

# Contacts

##  Air

### AIR PASS INFORMATION

**JAL Japan Explorer Pass**
☏ 800/525–3663 U.S. number ⊕ www.jal.co.jp/aul/en/world/japan_explorer_pass/lp/.

**ANA Special Fares**
☏ 800/235–9262 U.S. number ⊕ www.ana.co.jp/en/in/plan-book/promotions/special-fares.

**Visit Japan Fare**
☏ 800/235–9262 ⊕ www.ana.co.jp/en/us/book-plan/fare/special/visit.html.

### AIPORT INFORMATION

**Centrair Airport (NGO)**
☏ 0569/38–1195 ⊕ www.centrair.jp/en.

**Fukuoka Airport (FUK)**
☏ 092/621–0303 ⊕ www.fukuoka-airport.jp/en.

**Haneda Airport (HND)**
☏ 03/5757–8111 ⊕ tokyo-haneda.com/en.

**Kansai International Airport (KIX)**
☏ 072/455–2500 ⊕ www.kansai-airport.or.jp/en.

**Narita Airport (NRT)**
☏ 0476/34–8000 ⊕ www.narita-airport.jp/en.

**New Chitose Airport (CTS)**
☏ 0123/23–0111 ⊕ www.new-chitose-airport.jp/en.

### GROUND TRANSPORTATION

**Japan Railways**
☏ 050/2016–1603 ⊕ www.jreast.co.jp/e.

**Keisei Railway**
☏ 03/3831–0131 Ueno information counter, 0476/32–8505 Narita Airport counter ⊕ www.keisei.co.jp/keisei/tetudou/skyliner/us.

### TRANSFERS BETWEEN AIRPORTS

**Friendly Airport Limousine**
☏ 03/3665–7232 ⊕ www.limousinebus.co.jp/en.

### AIRLINES

**All Nippon Airways**
☏ 800/235–9262 in U.S., 03/6741–1120 in Japan ⊕ www.ana.co.jp.

**American Airlines**
☏ 800/433–7300 in U.S., 03/3298–7675 in Japan ⊕ www.aa.com.

**Delta Airlines**
☏ 800/221–1212 in U.S., 0570/077–733 in Japan ⊕ www.delta.com.

**Japan Airlines**
☏ 800/525–3663, 050/025–031 in Japan ⊕ www.jal.co.jp.

**United Airlines**
☏ 800/864–8331 in U.S., 03/6732–5011 in Japan ⊕ www.united.com.

##  Boat

**CONTACTS Ferry Sunflower.** ☏ 0120/489-850 ⊕ www.ferry-sunflower.co.jp/en. **Hankyu Ferry.** ☏ 03/6858–5510 ⊕ www.han9f.co.jp. **Meimon Taiyo Ferry.** ☏ 050/3784–9680 ⊕ www.cityline.co.jp.

##  Bus

**CONTACTS Kanto Bus.** ⊕ www.kanto-bus.co.jp/english. **Nihon Bus Association.** ⊕ www.bus.or.jp/eng. **Nishinihon JR Bus.** ☏ 06/6466–9990 ⊕ www.nishinihonjrbus.co.jp/en. **Willer Express.** ☏ 050/5805–0383 ⊕ willerexpress.com.

##  Car

**CAR RENTALS Avis.** ☏ 0210/31–1911 ⊕ www.avis-japan.com. **Budget.** ☏ 0570/054–317 ⊕ www.budgetrentacar.co.jp/en. **Hertz.** ☏ 800/654–3001 ⊕ www.hertz.com. **National Car Rental.** ☏ 800/227–7368 ⊕ www.nationalcar.com.

# 🖥 Embassies and Consulates

**CONTACTS U.S. Consulate Fukuoka.** ✉ *2–5-26 Ohori, Chuo* ☎ *092/751–9331.* **U.S. Consulate General Naha.** ✉ *2–1-1 Toyama, Urasoe* ☎ *098/876–4211.* **U.S. Consulate General Osaka.** ✉ *2–11-5 Nishitenma, Kita-ku* ☎ *06/6315–5900.* **U.S. Consulate General Sapporo.** ✉ *28–3-1 Kitaichijonishi, Chuo-ku* ☎ *011/641–1115.* **U.S. Consulate Nagoya.** ✉ *1–47-1 Nagono, Nakamura-ku* ☎ *052/581–4501.* **U.S Embassy Tokyo.** ✉ *1–10-5 Akasaka, Minato-ku* ☎ *03/3224–5000* ⊕ *jp. usembassy.gov.*

# 🛜 Internet
**WIRELESS HOTSPOT RENTAL Japan Wireless.** ⊕ *www.japan-wireless. com/en.* **Ninja WiFi.** ⊕ *https://ninjawifi.com/en.*

# 🚉 Train
**RAIL PASS CONTACTS Japan Rail Pass.** ⊕ *www. japanrailpass.net.*

**RAIL ROUTE FINDER Jorudan Route Finder.** ⊕ *www. jorudan.co.jp.*

# 📍 Travel Agencies

**CONTACTS IACE Travel.** ☎ *03/5282–1522 in Japan,* 877/489–4223 in North America ⊕ *www. iace-usa.com.* **JTB (Japan Travel Bureau).** ✉ *2–3-11 Higashi-Shinagawa, Shinagawa-ku* ☎ *03/5796–5454 in Japan,* 808/979–0111 in North America ⊕ *www. jtbcorp.jp/en.* **Nippon Travel Agency.** ✉ *Shinbashi Eki-mae Bldg. 1, 2–20-15 Shinbashi, Minato-ku* ☎ *310/768–1870 in U.S., 03/3572–8161 in Japan* ⊕ *www.ntainbound.com.*

# 🛏 Lodging
**TEMPLE LODGING CONTACTS Shukubo Temple Lodging Cooperative.** ☎ *0736/56–2616* ⊕ *www. shukubo.net.*

# ☎ Telephone
**MOBILE PHONE RENTAL CONTACTS JALABC Rental Phone.** ⊕ *www.jalabc. com/english/index3. html.* **Softbank.** ⊕ *www. softbank-rental.jp.*

# 📍 Visitor Information

**TOURIST INFORMATION CENTERS Tourist Information Center (TIC).** ✉ *Shin Tokyo Bldg., 3–3-1 Marunouchi, 1st fl., Chiyoda-ku* ☎ *03/3201–3331* ⊕ *www.jnto.go.jp/eng.*

**ONLINE RESOURCES Web Japan.** ⊕ *web-japan.org.*

**ENGLISH-LANGUAGE MEDIA Asahi Shimbun.** ⊕ *www.asahi.com/ajw.* **The Japan News.** ⊕ *the-japan-news.com.* **Japan Times.** ⊕ *www.japantimes. co.jp.* **Kansai Scene.** ⊕ *www.kansaiscene. com.* **Metropolis.** ⊕ *www. metropolisjapan.com.* **Time Out Tokyo.** ⊕ *www. timeout.jp.*

**TRANSPORTATION CONTACTS Jorudan.** ⊕ *www. jorudan.co.jp.* **Tokyo Metropolitan Government.** ⊕ *www.metro.tokyo. lg.jp/english.* **Urban Rail.** ⊕ *www.urbanrail.net.* **HyperDia.** ⊕ *www.hyperdia.com.*

# Japanese Etiquette

Many Japanese expect foreign visitors to behave differently and are tolerant of faux pas, but they are pleasantly surprised when people acknowledge and observe their customs. The easiest way to ingratiate yourself with the Japanese is to take time to learn and respect Japanese ways.

## GENERAL TIPS

■ Bow upon meeting someone, but don't go over the top. Outside of formal situations a slight nod of the head will suffice.

■ Pointing at someone is considered rude. To make reference to someone or something, gently wave your hand up and down in his or her direction.

■ Direct expression of opinions isn't encouraged. It's more common for people to gently suggest something.

■ Avoid physical contact with people you don't know closely. A slap on the back or hand on the shoulder could be uncomfortable for a Japanese person.

■ Some people will avoid direct eye contact, but they are being polite and not rude. You can follow along and not hold your gaze for too long.

## AT SOMEONE'S HOME

■ Most entertaining is done in restaurants and bars. Don't be offended if you're not invited to someone's home.

■ Should an invitation be extended, a small gift—perhaps a bottle of alcohol or box of sweets, ideally from your country—should be presented.

■ At the entryway, remove your shoes and put on the provided slippers (if any). Remove your slippers if you enter a room with tatami flooring. Before entering the bathroom, remove your house slippers and switch to those found near the bathroom doorway.

■ It's not customary for Japanese businessmen to bring wives along. If you're traveling with your spouse, don't assume that an invitation includes both of you. If you want to bring your spouse, ask in a way that eliminates the need for a direct refusal.

## IN BUSINESS MEETINGS

■ For business meetings, *meishi* (business cards) are highly recommended. Remember to place those you have received in front of you; don't shove them in your pocket or scribble on them. It's also good to have one side of your business card printed in Japanese.

■ Japanese position their employees based upon rank within the company. Don't be surprised if the proceedings seem perfunctory—many major decisions were likely made behind the scenes before the meeting started.

■ Stick to last names and use the honorific -san after the name, as in Tanaka-san (Mr. or Mrs. Tanaka). Also, respect the hierarchy, and as much as possible address yourself to the most senior person in the room.

■ Unfortunately, some Japanese businessmen still don't know how to interact with Western businesswomen. Be patient and, if the need arises, gently remind them that, professionally, you expect to be treated just like anyone else.

## AT LODGINGS AND RYOKAN

■ When you arrive at a minshuku or ryokan, you will usually need to take off your shoes before entering the lobby and change into slippers (although in some places you only need to take your shoes off when entering your room). Remember to remove your slippers before entering your room; never step on the tatami (straw mats) with shoes or slippers.

■ Before entering an onsen, make sure you wash and rinse off entirely before getting into the water. Do not get soap in the tub. Other guests will be using the same bathwater, so it is important to observe this custom. After your bath, change into the *yukata* (cotton robe) provided in your room. Don't worry about walking around in it—other guests will be doing the same. Just don't forget to wear underwear with the *yukata*, as they have a habit of slipping open.

*For tips on ryokan behavior, see the Ryokan Etiquette section in the Japanese Cultural Primer (Chapter 3).*

## AT RESTAURANTS

■ *Oshibori* is a small hot towel provided in Japanese restaurants. This is to wipe your hands but not your face. If you must use it on your face, wipe your face first, then your hands, and never toss it on the table: fold or roll it up.

■ When eating with chopsticks, don't use the part that has entered your mouth to pick up food from communal dishes. Instead, use the end that you've been holding in your hand. If there isn't a special chopstick rest provided, always rest chopsticks on the edge of the tray, bowl, or plate; sticking them upright in your food is reminiscent of how rice is arranged at funerals.

■ There's no taboo against slurping your noodle soup, though women are generally less boisterous about it than men. Pick up the soup bowl and drink directly from it, rather than leaning over the table to sip it. Eat the fish, meat, or vegetables with your chopsticks.

■ When drinking with a friend, never serve yourself. Always pour for the other person, who will in turn pour for you. If you would rather not drink, don't refuse a refill, just sip, keeping your glass at least half full.

■ It's considered gauche to eat as you walk along a public street.

*For tips on dining behavior, see the Dining Etiquette section in the Japanese Cultural Primer (Chapter 3).*

## WHILE SHOPPING

■ After entering a store, the staff will greet you with *irasshaimase,* which is a welcoming phrase. A simple smile is an appropriate acknowledgment. After that, polite requests to view an item or try on a piece of clothing should be followed as anywhere in the West. Bargaining is common at flea markets, but not in regular stores.

■ There's usually a plastic tray at the register for you to place your money or credit card. Your change and receipt, however, will usually be placed in your hand. It should be noted that many small shops do not accept credit cards.

## GIVING GIFTS

■ Gift giving is a year-round national pastime, peaking during summer's *ochugen* and the year-end *oseibo.* Common gifts between friends, family, and associates include elegantly wrapped packages of fruit, noodles, or beer.

■ On Valentine's Day, women give men chocolate, but on White Day in March the roles are reversed. On both of these days it's common to give small gifts to coworkers and friends, not just partners.

■ For weddings and funerals, cash gifts are the norm. Convenience stores carry special envelopes in which the money (always crisp, new bills) should be inserted.

# Great Itineraries

## An Introduction to Japan

The following itinerary covers the barest, surface-scratching minimum in modern Tokyo and glorious Nikko; the temples and shrines of Kamakura, the power center of Japan's first shogunate; the temples of classical Kyoto; and Nara, Japan's first permanent capital. But you really need two weeks to see the biggest highlights.

### DAY 1: ARRIVAL
Flights from the United States tend to land in the late afternoon.

### DAYS 2 AND 3: TOKYO
Visit some of the major Tokyo sights or shops (see Chapter 3). Ginza, Ueno Koen's museums, Tsukiji, the Imperial Palace grounds, and Asakusa are all among the top areas to explore. Arrange to spend your evenings in one or two of the nighttime districts, such as Roppongi or Shinjuku, or try to see a Kabuki, Noh, or Bunraku performance.

### DAYS 4 AND 5: SIDE TRIPS FROM TOKYO
Head to the picturesque Chusen-ji (temple) in Nikko either on your own or with a tour. Also make time to visit Kamakura, perhaps stopping in Yokohama on the way back (see Chapter 4). These trips can all be done conveniently by train.

### DAYS 6, 7, AND 8: THE JAPAN ALPS
Nagano is 90 minutes from Tokyo by bullet train; from there it's 1–2½ hrs to the other destinations by train/bus.

Take the Shinkansen train to Nagano (90 minutes by bullet train) and visit Zenko-ji (temple). Continue by train to Matsumoto (one hour) and visit Karasu-jo (the castle), the Japan Folklore Museum, and the Japan Ukiyo-e Museum. The next day, travel via the mountain village of Kamikochi to Takayama (two hours by bus), one of Japan's best-preserved traditional cities. Finally, on your third day head to the Asa-ichi (morning market); then see other Takayama sights—the farmhouses of Shirakawa-go village or the former samurai-controlled district of Kamisanno-machi—before taking a train via Toyama to Kanazawa in the late afternoon (2½ hours).

### DAYS 9, 10, 11, AND 12: KANAZAWA, KYOTO, AND NARA
Nara is about one hour by train from Kyoto.

Kanazawa has also preserved many of its traditional buildings, and it is one of the country's finest cities. Take in what sights you can, perhaps the Kenroku Garden or the Naga-machi samurai district, before catching the late-afternoon train to Kyoto (a trip of about three hours), where you'll base yourself for a few days. In the morning visit the sights in the eastern district (Higashiyama), and take in the Gion district in the evening. On your second full day in Kyoto, visit more eastern district sights as well as those in the western district. If you are in the city on the 25th of the month, don't miss Kitano Tenman-gu market. On your third day in Kyoto, cover Central Kyoto in the morning, and take a train to Nara in the afternoon to see the elegant temples, the Daibutsu (Great Buddha) of Nara Koen, and the famous deer. Return to Kyoto after dinner.

### DAY 13: OSAKA AND KOBE
Osaka is 30 minutes by train from Kyoto.

In the morning take the train to Osaka, a sprawling city of never-ending urban intrigue. Drop your bags at your hotel (or send them on to Kobe), and hit the consumer electronics shops in the Den Den Town; check out Senri Expo Park, or head to the Osaka Museum of History.

In the afternoon move on to Kobe, which is only 20 minutes by train. It's a port city known for beef and an interest in all things foreign, dating from its days as a trading port. If the Hanshin Tigers are scheduled in the evening, don't miss a chance to catch a game at the historic Koshien Stadium, midway between Kobe and Osaka. Spend the night in either Kobe or Osaka.

## DAY 14: HIMEJI AND KURASHIKI
*Himeji is one hour by train from Osaka; Okayama is one hour by train from Himeji.*

Travel by train to Himeji (one hour) to visit Himeji-jo, its remarkable castle. Continue on to Okayama (one hour) and reach historic Kurashiki by early afternoon. In the historic Bikan area of the city, there are numerous museums.

## DAY 15: HIROSHIMA
*Hiroshima is 70 minutes by train from Kurashiki. Miyajima is one hour from Hiroshima by train and ferry.*

Leave Kurashiki by train in time to reach Hiroshima for lunch. Visit the Peace Memorial Park and then take the train and ferry to Miyajima, with the glorious vermilion *torii* in the bay. If you are up for it, take the one-hour hike up Mt. Misen.

> ### Tips
>
> Not all trains in the Japan Alpine regions are operated by JR, so they may not be included in your JR Rail Pass.
>
> Osaka and Kobe are close together, so if you want access to Osaka's nightlife, you can still stay there and be within each reach of Kobe, Kyoto, and even Nara.
>
> You can fly back to Tokyo from Hiroshima, but flights generally go only to Tokyo Haneda Airport. Since Haneda now has some international flights to the United States, this may be a viable option.

Hiroshima is known for its *okonomiyaki* (a grilled pancake of egg, meat, and cabbage). Give that a try before heading to your hotel for the night.

## DAY 16: TOKYO AND HOME
*Tokyo is four hours from Hiroshima by train.*

Return to Tokyo by Shinkansen train this morning, in time to reach Narita Airport in Tokyo for your flight home.

# Great Itineraries

## An Introduction to Tokyo

### TOKYO IN 3 DAYS

Tokyo is a metropolis that confounds with its complexity: more than 35 million people occupy a greater metropolitan area that includes soaring towers of glass and steel, rolling expressways, numerous temples, parks, and many quiet neighborhoods just off the main streets. Since the end of World War II, the city has constantly reinvented itself. Few things have remained static other than Tokyo's preeminence as Japan's economic center.

### DAY 1: TSUKIJI AND GINZA

Start with an early wander around Tsukiji's outer market to see the bustle before heading into the main market building at 10 am (tourists are allowed in after most of the buying and selling is done, but it's still a fascinating place to see giant frozen tuna and enormous knives you might mistake for a swords). Allow room in your stomach for an early sushi lunch before heading west toward Ginza.

### DAY 2: ASAKUSA AND UENO

Spend the morning at **Senso-ji** and adjacent **Asakusa Jinja** in Asakusa. If you're looking for souvenir gifts—sacred or secular—allow time and tote space for the abundant selection the local vendors along **Nakamise-dori** have to offer. A 10-minute walk west is **Kappabashi,** a street dedicated to outfitting restaurants and bars with dishes, cups, chopsticks, and even plastic food models. From there go to **Ueno** for an afternoon of museums, vistas, and historic sights, and take a break at **Ueno Park.** Keep in mind that in

the evening the crowds in Asakusa are not as intrusive as during the day, and many of the major attractions, including the five-tier pagoda of Senso-ji, are brightly lighted. It's worth it to loop back to get a different view of the area and end the evening with dinner at one of Asakusa's *izakaya* (a drinking den that serves food).

### DAY 3: SHIBUYA AND SHINJUKU

Start off at Shibuya's **Hachiko Square** and the famous "Scramble Crossing" intersection and hit nearby stores like Shibuya 109, which is crammed with teen fashion boutiques. Inside the station building is the once-lost masterpiece by avant-garde artist **Taro Okamoto,** *Myth of Tomorrow,* while towering over the east side of the station is the 34-story Shibuya Hikarie building, one of the latest redevelopments filled with shops, restaurants, and businesses to hit Tokyo. In the afternoon see the Shinto shrine, **Meiji Jingu,** and walk through the nearby Harajuku and **Omotesando** fashion districts. Spend the rest of the afternoon on the west side of **Shinjuku,** Tokyo's 21st-century model city; savor the view from the observation deck of architect Kenzo Tange's monumental **Tokyo Metropolitan Government Office**; and cap off the day visiting **Shinjuku Gyo-en National Garden.** For those seeking a bit of excitement, the red-light district of **Kabuki-cho,** just to the east of **JR Shinjuku Station,** comes alive once the sun goes down; Kabuki-cho and neighboring Golden Gai are full of good places to eat and drink.

## TOKYO IN 5 DAYS

Add these two days onto the three-day itinerary.

### DAY 4: AKIHABARA AND IMPERIAL PALACE

Spend the morning browsing in **Aki-habara,** Tokyo's electronics quarter, and see the nearby Shinto shrine **Kanda Myojin.** In the afternoon, tour the **Imperial Palace** and the grounds surrounding it. The **Chidorigafuchi National Cemetery** has a wonderful park and a boat-rental facility—both great for unwinding. If the **Yomiuri Giants** are in town, catch a game at **Tokyo Dome** in the evening. If not, try a traditional hot spring bath or ride the roller coaster at LaQua amusement park next to Tokyo Dome.

### DAY 5: GET OUT OF TOWN TO KAMAKURA

For a different perspective of Japan, spend a day out of Tokyo. Easily accessible by train is **Kamakura** the 13th-century military capital. The **Great Buddha (Daibutsu)** of **Kotoku-in Temple** in the Hase area of town is but one of many National Treasures of art and architecture in and around Kamakura. An early start will allow you to see most of the important sights in a full day and make it back to Tokyo by late evening. As Kamakura is one of the most popular excursions from Tokyo, avoid the worst of the crowds by going on a weekday, but time it to avoid rush-hour commuting that peaks roughly at 8 am and just after 6 pm.

## Tips

The transit system in Tokyo is amazingly complex. Get a map that clearly defines the subways and rail lines.

The rainy season in June makes sightseeing very unpleasant. If you have a choice, it's best to avoid this time of year.

To reach Tokyo from Narita Airport requires more than an hour by train or bus. A taxi will cost as much as ¥30,000 and take the same amount of time.

No matter what you do, Tokyo will require plenty of walking. Wearing comfortable shoes during all seasons is advisable.

## IF YOU HAVE MORE TIME

With a week or more, you can make Tokyo your base for side trips. After getting your fill of Tokyo, take a train out to **Yokohama,** with its scenic port and Chinatown. A bit farther away but still easily accessible by train is **Nikko,** where the founder of the Tokugawa Shogun dynasty is enshrined. The decadently designed Toshogu Shrine complex is a monument unlike any other in Japan, and the picturesque **Lake Chuzenji** is in forests nearby. Two full days, with an overnight stay, would allow you an ideal, leisurely exploration of both.

# Great Itineraries

## Highlights of Kansai

The following itinerary covers the barest, surface-scratching minimum in modern Tokyo and glorious Nikko; the temples and shrines of Kamakura, the power center of Japan's first shogunate; the temples of classical Kyoto; and Nara, Japan's first permanent capital. But you really need two weeks to see the biggest highlights.

### DAYS 1–3: KYOTO

For many visitors **Kyoto** *is* Japan, and few leave disappointed. Wander in and out of temple precincts like **Ginkaku-ji**, perhaps spot a *maiko* (a geisha in training) strolling about **Gion**, (and dine on *kaiseki ryori*, an elegant culinary event that engages all the senses. Outside the city center, a day trip to hillside **Arashiyama**, the gardens of the Katsura Rikyu, and the temple of Enryaku-ji atop **Hiei-zan** is a must. With nearly 2,000 temples and shrines, exquisite crafts, and serene gardens, Kyoto embodies traditional Japan. For taking some with you, the **Kyoto Handicraft Center** stocks painted screens and traditional wear. Many restaurants serve dishes based on locally sourced ingredients. Embodying this spirit is the seven-hundred-year-old **Nishiki Market**, which includes roughly 100 mom-and-pop shops offering fish and vegetables.

### DAY 4: NARA

In the 8th century, Nara was the capital of Japanese civilization, and many cultural relics of that period, including some of the world's oldest wooden structures (though repaired and rebuilt over the years as necessary), still stand among forested hills and parkland. Be sure to visit Nara's 53-foot-high, 1,300-year-old bronze Daibutsu (Great Buddha) in **Todai-ji** temple and to make friends with the deer of **Nara Koen**. At the **Kofuku-ji** temple, the beautiful three- and five-story pagodas are worth a visit. The **Nara National Museum** has numerous examples of Buddhist scrolls and sculpture.

### DAY 5: KOYA-SAN

More than 100 temples belonging to the Shingon sect of Buddhism stand on one of Japan's holiest mountains, 48 km (30 miles) south of Osaka. Kobo Daishi established the original **Garan** temple complex in AD 816. An exploration of the atmospheric cemetery of **Okuno-in** temple takes you past headstone art and 300-year-old cedar trees. But the temple's primary function is as the mausoleum for Kobo Daishi.

### DAY 6: ISE-JINGU

**Ise-jingu** (Grand Shrines of Ise), with their harmonious architecture and cypress-forest setting, provide one of Japan's most spiritual experiences. The Inner Shrine and Outer Shrine are roughly 6 km (4 miles) apart. In addition, there are 123 affiliated shrines in and around Ise City.

### DAY 7: OSAKA

Although by no means picturesque, **Osaka** provides a taste of urban Japan outside the capital, along with a few traditional sights. The handsome castle **Osaka-jo** nestles among skyscrapers, and the neon of **Dotombori** flashes around the local Kabuki theater. Osakans are passionate about food, and you'll find some of the finest in the country here. The Hanshin Tigers have perhaps the most raucous fans in baseball, and the historic **Koshien Stadium** is the place to see them (and the Tigers) in action (though they play in the **Kyocera Osaka Dome** in August). The **Namba Grand Kagetsu Theatre** is a home to traditional *manzai* (stand-up) comedy and contemporary entertainment. Head to **Den Den Town**, which has shops selling consumer electronics and anime and manga products—much like Akihabara in Tokyo.

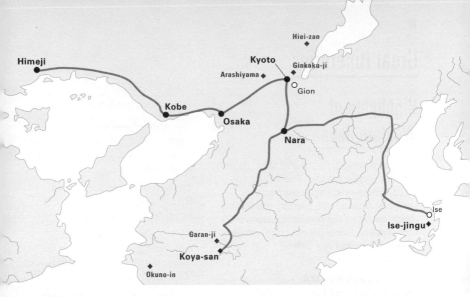

## DAY 8: KOBE

**Kobe** has recovered from the dark day in 1995 when it was struck by an earthquake that killed more than 5,000 people. The **Kobe Earthquake Memorial Museum** is dedicated to the event and its aftermath. Some of the first foreigners to live in Japan after the Meiji Restoration built homes in **Kitano-cho,** near the station, and the area retains a mix of architectural styles. The city will forever be associated with beef, but a trip to its **Chinatown** will reveal numerous Chinese delicacies. At an elevation of 931 meters, **Mt. Rokko** is accessible by cable car and features a museum and garden. On the way up the mountain take a look at Nunobiki Falls, considered one of Japan's most picturesque. The city also has a "life-size" statue for **Tetsujin 28** (Gigantor), the robot in the popular manga and TV series.

## DAY 9: HIMEJI

The city's most famous sight, **Himeji-jo,** also known as the White Egret Castle (Shirasagi-jo), dominates the skyline. The castle takes only a few hours to see, and it's about a 15-minute walk (or a short bus ride) from the train station. Since Himeji is a short (50-minute) train ride from Kobe, it's a pleasant and unhurried

### Tips

Kyoto is known for its traditional inns (ryokan). Book one for at least a night. The bus network is the best way to get around in Kyoto. Buy an all-day pass. Renting a bicycle is also a good choice. In Osaka, people stand on the right side of escalators (with the left being for those walking)—the opposite of the orientation used in Tokyo.

Koya-san and Ise-Jingu are best accessed by non-JR lines. A JR pass will save you money if you travel by Shinkansen beyond Kansai, but if you're flying in and out of Kansai, consider a Surutto pass (Kansai Thru Pass) valid on most companies' trains and buses, or a JR West Kansai pass (which would only cover JR lines).

day-trip destination for those based in Kobe (it's 15 minutes farther if you are based in Kyoto). If you get back early, use the rest of your day to buy last-minute souvenirs.

# Great Itineraries

## Highlights of Western Japan

South and west of Kyoto and Nara, Japan takes on a different feel. The farther you go, the more relaxed people become. Far from Japan's main islands, the stark divide between the tropical beaches of Okinawa and Honshu's concrete metropolises is reflected in a different culture and cuisine.

### DAY 1: MATSUYAMA
Start off in this castle town, Shikoku's largest city and home to several Shingon Buddhist pilgrimage temples and the ancient hot springs of **Dogo Onsen** (*see Chapter 10*).

### DAYS 2 AND 3: IYA VALLEY
The **Iya Valley** may be slightly difficult to access, but it offers untouched, deep canyons, the best river rafting in Japan, and good walking trails. Despite its isolated location, there are some fantastic lodging options here (*see Chapter 10*).

### DAY 4: NAOSHIMA
Adjust to the even slower pace of Naoshima, spending a day at the world-class **Chichu Art Museum,** which integrates artworks into everyday locations, often with inspiring results and the **Benesse House Museum.**

### DAYS 5 AND 6: HIROSHIMA
A quick glance at the busy, attractive city of Hiroshima makes no allusion to the events of August 6, 1945. Only the city's **Peace Memorial Park** (Heiwa Kinen Koen)—with its memorial museum and its **A-Bomb Dome** (Gembaku Domu), a twisted, half-shattered structural ruin—serves as a reminder of the atomic bomb. From Hiroshima, make a quick trip to the island of **Miyajima** to see the floating torii of **Itsukushima Jinja**, a shrine built on stilts above a tidal flat (*see Chapter 9*).

**Tips**

Kurashiki udon noodles are famous around the country. Sample a bowl at least once.

The best way to move around Hiroshima is through the city's streetcar network.

For the crater Nakadake, the sulfurous gas emitted can make breathing difficult. A sign indicates the current levels.

Typhoon season for Okinawa is July through September; a powerful typhoon can wreak havoc on vacation plans.

### DAYS 7 AND 8: YUFUIN AND MT. ASO
One of the locals' favorite pastimes is relaxing in an onsen, and in the artsy spa town of Yufuin on the southernmost island of Kyushu, you can soak in mineral water or bubbling mud. Nearby, five volcanic cones create Japan's largest caldera at **Mt. Aso.** An immense 18 km (11 miles) by 24 km (15 miles), the stark volcanic peak contrasts vividly with the surrounding green hills. One crater, **Naka-dake,** is still active, and reaching it on foot or via cable car affords views of a bubbling, steaming lake.

### DAYS 9 AND 10: OKINAWA
Check out cosmopolitan **Naha,** which gives a feel for how Okinawan culture and cuisine differ from those of "mainland" Japan. Explore the main island's many reminders of its tragic fate during World War II. Take a boat to one of the smaller **Kerama** islands to relax on unspoiled beaches. And to truly appreciate the beauty of the ocean, get into the water—there are plenty of scuba diving and snorkeling centers.

# Highlights of Eastern Japan

With 80% of Japan's surface covered by mountains, the country is a dream for hikers and lovers of the great outdoors. The wilds of Hokkaido, quietly impressive Tohoku, and the vertiginous Japan Alps reward exploration with spectacular scenery and experiences of traditional culture that you are unlikely to have in the urban areas.

## DAYS 1 AND 2: NAGANO

**Nagano** Prefecture, host of the 1998 Winter Olympics, is home to the backbone of the Japan Alps. Visit **Zenko-ji** temple in Nagano City before heading to the hot springs of **Yudanaka Onsen** or **Kusatsu**. In summer, try some day trekking in Hakuba.

## DAY 3: MATSUMOTO

A one-hour train ride from Nagano, Matsumoto is home to the "Black Crow," Matsumoto Castle, as well as the fabulous Ukiyo-e Museum. Spend a day wandering the cafés and craft shops of this samurai town.

## DAYS 4 AND 5: TAKAYAMA

A bus ride over the mountains from Matsumoto brings you to Takayama, with an optional stop in summer at the alpine retreat of **Kamikochi.** You'll find traditional inns, ancient temples, mouthwatering Hida beef, a preserved historical district, and the thatched-roof *gassho-zukuri* farmhouses in the memorable **Hida-no-Sato** folk museum.

## DAY 6: SHIRAKAWAGO AND KANAZAWA

Between Takayama and Kanazawa lie the well-preserved farmhouses of Shirakawa-go, many of which are open to visitors for day visits or overnight stays. Continue on to the modern city of Kanazawa to visit serene **Kenrokuen** gardens

## Tips

In winter, bring warm clothes and snow boots; in summer, be prepared for mosquitoes.

A JR pass will be useful for this itinerary, if you take the Shinkansen from Tokyo to Nagano. Access from Sapporo back to Tokyo can be by air, a lengthy ferry ride from one of the nearby ports, or express train and Shinkansen.

For Hokkaido, take advantage of the abundant seafood, especially the crab; in Nagano, opt for the soba noodles. Don't miss locally brewed sake.

and wander through the Nagamachi samurai district.

## DAYS 7 AND 8: HAGURO-SAN (MT. HAGURO)

This mountain, the most accessible of the Dewa-san range, a trio of sacred mountains in Tohoku, is worth the trip not only for the lovely but rigorous climb (or bus trip) past cedars, waterfalls, and shrines but also for the thatched shrine at the top.

## DAYS 9 AND 10: SAPPORO

A day's ride on the Shinkansen, an overnight ferry from Niigata, or a quick flight on low-cost carrier AirDo gets you to **Sapporo,** a pleasant and accessible city that serves as a good base for exploring the dramatic landscape of Hokkaido. Mountains encircle Sapporo, drawing Japanese and increasing numbers of Australian skiers in winter. Take day trips out to **Toya-ko** or **Shikotsu-ko,** picturesque lakes where you can boat or fish, and to the excellent **Nibutani Ainu Culture Museum** for an insight into the island's original inhabitants.

# On the Calendar

When national holidays fall on Sunday, they are celebrated on the following Monday. Museums and sights are often closed the days after these holidays.

## Winter

### JANUARY 1
**New Year's Day** is the "festival of festivals" for the Japanese. Some women dress in traditional kimonos, and many people visit shrines and hold family reunions. Although the day is solemn, streets are often decorated with pine twigs, plum branches, and bamboo stalks.

### FEBRUARY
During the first half of the month, more than 300 pieces of ice sculpture, some huge, populate the **Sapporo Snow Festival,** bringing some 2 million people to the city to see them.

### FEBRUARY 13–15
The **Namahage Sedo Festival,** in Akita City (Tohoku), enacts in public a ritual from nearby Oga of threatening "good-for-nothings": men in demon masks carrying buckets and huge knives issue dire warnings to loafers.

### FEBRUARY 23
The Imperial Palace in Tokyo, which is usually off-limits to the public, opens its gates on the **emperor's birthday**. The only other day the public can enter the grounds is January 2.

## Spring

### APRIL 29
**Showa Day** is the first day of **Golden Week**—a medley of holidays is when many Japanese take vacations, and hotels, trains, and attractions are booked solid.

### MAY 15
Dating back to the sixth century, the **Aoi Festival,** also known as the Hollyhock Festival, is the first of Kyoto's three most popular celebrations. An "imperial" procession of 300 courtiers starts from the Imperial Palace and makes its way to Shimogamo Shrine to pray for the prosperity of the city. Today's participants are local Kyotoites.

### MID-MAY
Another loud Tokyo blowout, the **Kanda Festival** is all about taking the Kanda shrine's gods out for some fresh air in their *mikoshi* (portable shrines)—not to mention drinking plenty of beer and having a great time on the weekend closest to May 15.

### LATE MAY
The **Sanja Festival,** held on the third weekend of May at Tokyo's Asakusa Jinja, is the city's biggest party. Men, often naked to the waist, carry palanquins through the streets amid revelers. Many of them bear the tattoos of the Yakuza, Japan's Mafia.

## Summer

### JULY 16–17
The **Gion Festival,** which dates back to the ninth century, is perhaps Kyoto's most popular festival. Twenty-nine huge floats sail along downtown streets and make their way to Yasaka Shrine to thank the gods for protection from a pestilence that once ravaged the city.

### JULY 24–25
Osaka's **Tenjin Festival** is a major event, with parades of floats and nighttime fireworks and processions of 100-plus lighted vessels on the city's canals.

**LATE JULY OR EARLY AUGUST**
On Miyajima near Hiroshima, the lunar calendar determines the timing of three stately barges' crossing of the bay to the island's shrine for the **Kangen-sai Festival.**

**AUGUST**
The first week's dreamlike **Neputa Festival,** held in the Tohoku city of Hirosaki, finds nightly processions of floats, populated with illuminated paintings of faces from mythology, through the streets.

**AUGUST 3–7**
The **Nebuta Festival** in northern Tohoku's Aomori noisily celebrates an ancient battle victory with a nighttime parade of illuminated floats.

**AUGUST 5–7**
At Yamagata's **Hanagasa Festival,** in southern Tohoku, celebrants dance through the streets in local costume among floats. Food and drink are on hand for spectators.

**AUGUST 6–8**
Sendai's **Tanabata** celebrates two legendary astrological lovers with a theatrical rendition of their tale, and city residents decorate their streets and houses with colorful paper and bamboo streamers.

**AUGUST 12 15**
At Tokushima's **Awa Odori** festival, streets fill with local residents performing traditional Obon dances. The largest dance festival in Japan, things start off elegant but as the night goes on and drinks get downed, progress to enthusiastic if unpolished street dancing all over the city.

**AUGUST 13–16**
During the **Obon Festival,** a time of Buddhist ceremonies in honor of ancestors, many people take off the entire week to travel to their hometowns—it's best to avoid travel on these days.

**AUGUST 16**
For the **Daimonji Gozan Okuribi,** huge bonfires in the shape of kanji characters illuminate five of the mountains that surround Kyoto. The most famous is the Dai, meaning "big," on the side of Mt. Daimonji in Higashiyama (Kyoto's eastern district). Dress in a cool *yukata* (cotton robe) and walk down to the banks of the Kamo-gawa to view this spectacular summer sight, or catch all five fires from the rooftop of your hotel downtown or a spot in Funaoka-yama or Yoshida-yama parks. There are *Bon* dances to honor the departed as well as the floating of lanterns in Arashiyama (the western district).

# Autumn

**OCTOBER 22**
Kyoto's **Jidai Festival,** the Festival of Eras, features a colorful costume procession of fashions from the 8th through 19th centuries. The procession begins at the Imperial Palace and winds up at Heian Shrine. More than 2,000 Kyotoites voluntarily participate in this festival, which dates back to 1895.

For the **Kurama Fire Festival,** at Kurama Shrine, there is a roaring bonfire and a rowdy portable shrine procession that makes its way through the narrow streets of the small village in the northern suburbs of Kyoto. If you catch a spark, it is believed to bring good luck.

# Winter

**LATE DECEMBER**
City dwellers migrate to the countryside en masse for the **New Year** celebrations. Travel is *not* recommended.

# Money-Saving Tips

## LODGING

Big hotel chains can be expensive, but if you just need a comfortable place to sleep, try a business hotel. Usually near train stations in Japanese cities, these offer basic rooms at reasonable rates, often with weekend discounts. Likewise, if you're thinking of staying in a traditional ryokan, ask about discounts for midweek stays. Booking websites can have good rates, but it is often best to check if possible have a Japanese speaker check the hotel's Japanese website. You can often find the best rates there, often by booking far in advance or at the last minute.

## TRAVEL

Long-distance buses are a surprisingly comfortable way to travel between cities, with many offering slippers, blankets, and private curtained-off sleeper seats. Overnight ferries, with tatami mat sleeping rooms and onboard baths, are also good value. In major cities, one-day subway passes are useful, and in smaller towns renting a bicycle is a budget-friendly way to explore.

## EATING

Cheap eats abound in Japan. There are the usual fast-food chains, but other options include ramen, soba or udon noodle stands, and take-out bento lunches from department store basement food halls. The latter are often marked down after 7 pm. Convenience stores sell bento boxes and quick snacks like *onigiri* (rice balls) or *nikuman* (steamed meat buns). You can always head to a city hall or university cafeteria for a dirt-cheap lunch.

## SHOPPING

Vintage kimonos are surprisingly cheap in Japan. At kimono resellers prices often start at ¥1,000. There are some used kimono shops in Asakusa in Tokyo and many in Kyoto. Antiques markets are a good place for interesting souvenirs. There's an antiques fair at Tokyo Forum on the first and third Sunday of the month, with some exceptions. Visit ⊕ *www.antique-market.jp/english* to confirm dates. There is also a bustling antiques market at Kyoto's Toji temple on the 21st of every month. In department stores and electronics shops, ask about tax-free shopping for foreign visitors.

## SIGHTSEEING

At the country's many publicly funded museums and galleries, admission fees to regular exhibits are usually less than ¥800. Public gardens are also a bargain, usually at less than ¥400 for entry. Though major temples and shrines like Kyoto's Kiyomizu-dera and Kinkakuji charge an entry fee, they're the exception. Most temples and shrines in Japan are free and open to all. Another fun, cheap way to spend a day is visiting some of the hundreds of mini-museums on sometimes very obscure topics that dot this museum-loving nation. Run by volunteers passionate about, say, wooden haircombs or the history of stamps, these tiny museums usually charge less than ¥300 for entry—and you'll often get a private tour as the only guests.

# Chapter 3

# A JAPANESE CULTURE PRIMER

**3**

Updated by
Jay Farris

Something about Japan led you to pick up this book and contemplate a trip. Perhaps it was a meal at your favorite sushi bar back home, the warm tones of an exquisite piece of Japanese pottery, or a Japanese novel or film. Whatever it was that sparked your interest, it's a good bet that something you find in this chapter will make your trip unforgettable.

There is a display of horsemanship called *yabusame* (now to be seen mainly at shrine festivals) in which a mounted archer, in medieval costume, challenges a narrow roped-off course lined at 260-foot intervals with small wooden targets on bamboo posts: the rider has to come down the course at full gallop, drop the reins, nock an arrow, aim and release, and take the reins again—with only seconds to set up again for the next target. Few archers manage a perfect score—but "merely hitting the target is secondary," explains a yabusame official.

Therein lies the key to understanding the fundamentals of Japanese identity as well as its various regional cultures: the passionate attention to form and process. The results are also important, of course; otherwise the forms would be empty gestures. But equally important—perhaps more important—is how you get there. Not for nothing are so many of these disciplines, from the tea ceremony to calligraphy to the martial arts, presented to us as Ways; excellence in any one of them depends on doing it the way it's supposed to be done according to traditions that may be centuries old. Philosophically, this is all about how rules can liberate: spend enough time and effort on the mastery of forms, and one day they leave the realm of conscious thought and become part of you. You are to lose yourself in the Way. Not for nothing, either, are so many elements of Japanese culture rooted in the teachings of Zen Buddhism, about breaking free from the limits of the rational self.

# A TASTE OF JAPAN

By Aidan O'Connor

Get ready for an unparalleled eating adventure: from humble bowls of ramen to elaborate kaiseki feasts, a vast culinary universe awaits visitors to food-obsessed Japan.

Japan's food offerings are united by a few key philosophies. Presentation is paramount—a dedication to visual appeal means that colors and shapes are just as important as aromas, textures, and flavors. Details count—food is prepared with pride and care, and everything from a bowl's shape to a dish's finishing garnish carries meaning. Natural flavors shine through—seasonal ingredients star in minimally processed preparations, with condiments used to enhance flavors rather than mask them.

You'll find these culinary philosophies at all levels, from tiny noodle shops to lively robatayaki grills to elegant sushi restaurants. Here's what you need to know to make the most of your meals. As they say in Japan, *itadakimasho* (let's eat)!

Pressed sushi (*oshizushi*) and Japanese-style fried rice

# THE JAPANESE MEAL

Breakfast (*asa-gohan*, literally "the morning rice") is typically eaten at home and features rice, fried fish, and miso soup. Lunch (*hiru-gohan*), mostly eaten out of the home at school or work, involves a bento lunch box of rice, grilled fish, vegetables, and pickles. The evening meal (*ban-gohan*) has the broadest range, from restaurant meals of sushi to traditional meals cooked at home.

For home-prepared meals, the basic formula consists of one soup and three dishes—a main dish of fish or meat and two vegetable side dishes. These are served together with rice, which is part of every meal. When entertaining guests, more dishes will be served. Classical

Japanese cooking follows the principle of "fives." An ideal meal is thought to use five cooking methods—boiling, grilling, frying, steaming, and serving raw; incorporate five colors—black or purple, white, red or orange, yellow, and green; and feature five tastes—sweet, sour, salty, bitter, and *umami* (the Japanese are credited with discovering umami, or savoriness). Ingredient quality is key, as cooking techniques are intended to coax out an ingredient's maximum natural flavor.

Staple ingredients include seafood, which plays a leading role in Japanese cuisine, with dozens of species available, from familiar choices like *maguro*

## DINING ETIQUETTE

Here are a few tips to help you fit in at the Japanese table:

■ Don't point or gesture with chopsticks.

■ Avoid lingering over communal dishes with your chopsticks while you decide what to take. Do not use the end you have been eating with to remove food from the dish—use the serving chopsticks provided or the thick end of your own chopsticks.

■ When not in use, place your chopsticks on the chopstick rest.

■ Never pass food from your chopsticks to someone else's or leave chopsticks standing in your rice bowl (it resembles incense sticks at a funeral).

■ There is no taboo against slurping your noodle soup, though women are generally less boisterous about it than men.

■ Pick up the soup bowl and drink directly from it. Take the fish or vegetables from it with your chopsticks. Return the lid to the soup bowl when you are finished eating. The rice bowl, too, is to be held in your free hand while you eat from it.

■ When drinking with a friend don't pour your own. Pour for the other person first. He will in turn pour yours.

■ Japanese don't pour sauce on their rice. Sauces are intended for dipping foods into it lightly.

■ It is still considered tacky to eat as you walk along a public street.

Pouring sake into a traditional Japanese cup

(tuna) and *obi* (shrimp) to more exotic selections like *anago* (conger eel) and *fugu* (blowfish). Meat options include chicken, pork, beef, and—in rural areas—venison and wild boar. Then there is a huge variety of vegetables and fungi (both wild and cultivated) such as *renkon* (lotus root), *daikon* (white radish), and matsutake mushrooms. Finally there is the soy bean, eaten whole as edamame, or fermented in tofu or miso.

Condiments range from tangy *shiso* (a member of the mint family) to spicy wasabi and savory soy sauce.

# SUSHI

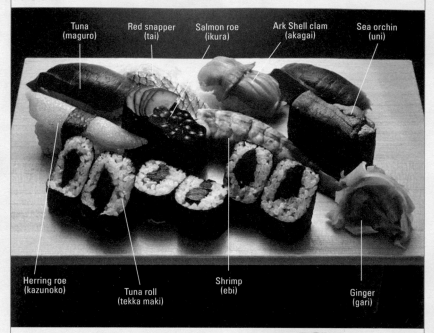

Tuna (maguro) · Red snapper (tai) · Salmon roe (ikura) · Ark Shell clam (akagai) · Sea orchin (uni)

Herring roe (kazunoko) · Tuna roll (tekka maki) · Shrimp (ebi) · Ginger (gari)

Hand-rolled sushi

■ Sushi actually refers to anything, seafood or otherwise, served on or in vinegared rice. It is not raw fish. **Nigiri-zushi** (the sushi best known overseas) is actually a fairly recent development from Tokyo.

■ **Makizushi** is a sushi roll. These can be fat, elaborate rolls or simple sticks.

■ Other types of sushi include **chirashi-zushi** with fish and vegetables scattered artfully into the rice and, in Kyoto and Osaka, **oshizushi** in which preserved mackerel, among other fish, is pressed onto the rice. This is served in slices.

■ **Funazushi**, from around Lake Biwa near Kyoto, is perhaps the oldest type. The fish and rice are buried for six months. The rice is thrown away and the fish is eaten. This technique was historically used as a means of preserving protein. It is an acquired taste.

■ **Kaitenzushi** (conveyor belt sushi) outlets abound and are cheap. However, for the real experience, nothing matches a traditional sushi-ya.

■ Using your hands is acceptable. Dip the fish, not the rice, lightly in the soy.

■ The **beni-shoga** (pickled ginger) is a palate freshener. Nibble sparingly.

■ **Wasabi** may not be served with your sushi, as the chef often dabs a bit on the rice when making your sushi. If you want extra wasabi, ask for it.

■ Customers will often request **omakase** (tasting menu). The chef will then choose and serve the best fish, in the order he deems appropriate.

# RAMEN

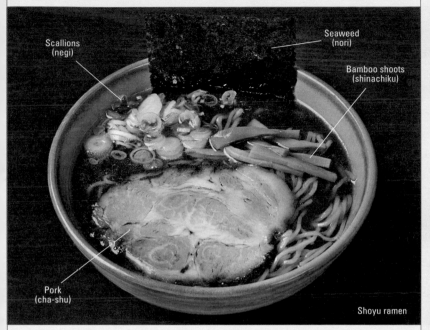

Scallions (negi)

Seaweed (nori)

Bamboo shoots (shinachiku)

Pork (cha-shu)

Shoyu ramen

■ Ramen is practically Japan's national dish. A ramen restaurant is never far away.

■ There are four main types: from the chilly north island of Hokkaido, there is **shio** ramen (salt ramen) and **miso ramen** (ramen in a miso broth). **Shoyu** ramen made with soy sauce is from Tokyo, while **tonkotsu** ramen (ramen in a white pork broth) is from Kyoto. Note that most ramen stocks contain meat or fish.

■ Each area has its own variation—corn and butter ramen in Sapporo; a stock made from pork and dried anchovies in northern Honshu; or Fukuoka's famed **Hakata** ramen with its milky tonkotsu broth and thin noodles with myriad toppings.

■ The reputation of a ramen restaurant depends on its stock, often a closely guarded secret.

■ Ramen is meant to be eaten with gusto. Slurping is normal.

■ Typical toppings include sliced roast pork, bean sprouts, boiled egg, **shinachiku** (fermented bamboo shoots), spring onion, **nori** (dried seaweed) and **kamaboko** (a fishcake made from white fish).

■ Beyond ramen, udon shops and soba shops also offer noodle dishes worth trying.

Miso ramen

Shio ramen

# ROBATAYAKI

Grilled fish (tsukeba)

■ *Robata* means fireside, and the style of cooking is reminiscent of old-fashioned Japanese farmhouse meals cooked over a charcoal fire in an open hearth.

■ Robatayaki restaurants and izakaya taverns serving grilled foods can be found near any busy station.

■ It's easy to order at a robatayaki, because the selection of food to be grilled is lined up at the counter. Fish, meat, vegetables, tofu—take your pick.

■ Some popular choices are *yaki-zakana* (grilled fish), particularly *karei-shio-yaki* (salted and grilled flounder) and *asari saka-mushi* (clams simmered in sake).

■ Try the grilled Japanese *shiitake* (mushrooms), *ao-to* (green peppers), and the *hiyayakko* (chilled tofu sprinkled with bonito flakes, diced green onions, and soy sauce).

Matsutake mushroom

■ *O-tsukuri* (sashimi) and *katsuono tataki* (seared bonito) are very popular. The fish will vary according to the season.

■ Dipping sauces are concocted using soy, *dashi* (soup stock), and a hint of citrus such as yuzu.

■ Many robatayaki pride themselves on their wide selection of sake and shochu.

■ Most Japanese people will finish their meal with a rice dish.

# TEMPURA

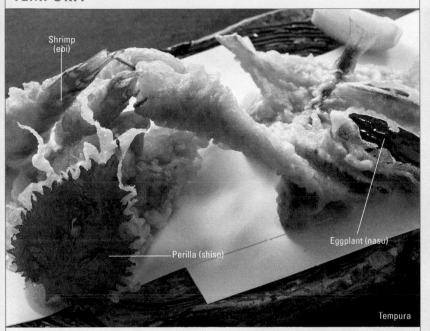

Shrimp (ebi)

Eggplant (nasu)

Perilla (shiso)

Tempura

■ Though tempura features in many busy eateries as part of a meal, it bears little resemblance to the exquisite morsels produced over the course of a full tempura meal at an intimate specialty restaurant.

■ The secret of good tempura lies in the quality of the ingredients, the freshness and temperature of the oil, and the lightness of the batter.

■ Good tempura is light and crispy, not crunchy like fried chicken.

■ Tempura is most often fried in soybean oil, but cottonseed or sesame oil also may be used.

■ Because only the freshest of ingredients will do, the menu changes with the season. Baby corn, green peppers, sweet potato, lotus root, shiitake mushrooms, and shiso leaves are the most common vegetables. In spring expect **sansai** (wild vegetables) picked that morning.

Shrimp Tempura with sweet potatoes

■ Prawns and white fish are also popular tempura items.

■ *Tsuyu* (dipping sauce) is made from dashi seasoned with soy and **mirin** (sweet rice wine). You may see a white mound of grated daikon on your plate. Add that to the tsuyu for a punch of flavor.

■ Alternatively, mixtures of salt and powdered green tea or salt and yuzu may be sprinkled on the tempura.

# BENTO

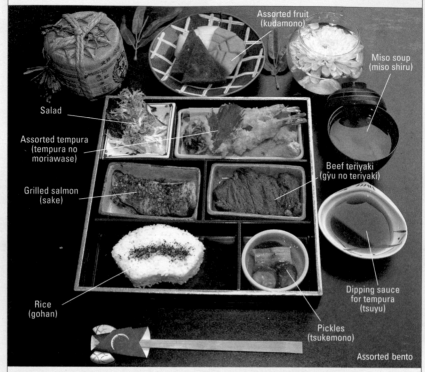

Assorted fruit
(kudamono)

Miso soup
(miso shiru)

Salad

Assorted tempura
(tempura no
moriawase)

Beef teriyaki
(gyū no teriyaki)

Grilled salmon
(sake)

Rice
(gohan)

Dipping sauce
for tempura
(tsuyu)

Pickles
(tsukemono)

Assorted bento

■ Bento boxes, the traditional Japanese box lunch, can be bought everywhere from the basement level of a luxurious department store to a convenience store.

■ A typical bento will contain rice, grilled fish, a selection of vegetable dishes, some pickles, and perhaps a wedge of orange or other fruit.

■ Every region has its *meibutsu,* or speciality dish. These are often showcased in lunch boxes available at stations or local stores.

■ Though the humble bento is usually relatively inexpensive, more ornate and intricate boxes featuring kaiseki dishes or sushi are often bought for special occasions.

Bento lunch box

■ The bento exists in an almost limitless number of variations according to the region and the season.

■ A bento is designed to be taken out and eaten on the move. They are perfect on long-distance train rides or for a picnic in the park.

# BEVERAGES

Sake

■ There are more than 2,000 different brands of sake produced throughout Japan. It is often called rice wine but is actually made by a fermenting process that is more akin to beer-making. The result is a fantastically complex drink with an alcoholic content just above wine (15–17% alcohol). It is the drink of choice with sashimi and traditional Japanese food.

■ There are four main types of sake: *daiginjo, ginjo, junmai,* and *honjozo.* The first two are the most expensive and made from highly polished rice. The latter two, however, also pack flavor and character.

■ Like wine, sake can be sweet (*amakuchi*) or dry (karakuchi). Workaday sake may be drunk warm (*atsukan*) while the higher grades will be served chilled. Sake is the only drink that can be served at any temperature.

■ Another variety is *nama-zake.* This is unpasteurized sake and is prized for its fresh, zingy taste.

■ *Shochu* is a distilled spirit that is often 25% alcohol or more. Like vodka, it can be made from potato, sweet potato, wheat, millet, or rice. It is drunk straight, on the rocks, with water, or in cocktails.

■ Any good izakaya or robatayaki will stock a diverse selection of both sake and shochu, and staff will make recommendations.

■ Beer is, perhaps, the lubricant of choice for most social situations. Japanese beer is of a high standard and tends to be lager. It has a relatively high alcohol content at 5% or more. Recently there has been a boom in microbreweries.

# JAPANESE FINE ARTS

Japanese lacquerware

What raises Japanese handicrafts to the level of fine arts? It is, one could argue, the standards set by the nation's *Ningen kokuho*: its Living National Treasures, who hand down these traditional skills from generation to generation.

Legally speaking, these people are "Holders of Important Intangible Cultural Properties." A law, enacted in 1950, establishes two broad categories of Intangible Property. One comprises the performing arts: Kabuki, Noh, Bunraku puppet theater, and traditional music and dance. The other embraces a wide range of handicrafts, most of them in the various forms and styles of textiles, pottery, lacquerware, papermaking, wood carving, and metalworking—from all over the country. The tiny cohort of individuals and groups who exemplify these traditions at the highest levels receive an annual stipend; the money is intended not so much to support the title holders (Living National Treasures command very healthy sums for their work) as to help them attract and train apprentices, and thus keep the traditions alive.

## CARRYING ON

Official sponsorship has proven itself a necessity in more than a few craft traditions. The weaving of *bashofu*, for example, a fabric from Okinawa, is on its way to becoming a lost art—unless the present Living National Treasure can encourage enough people to carry on with the craft. Papermaking, a cottage industry that once supported some 28,500 households nationwide, now supports only a few hundred.

## LACQUERWARE

Japanese lacquerware has its origins in the Jomon period (10,000–300 BC), and by the Nara period (710–794) most of the techniques we recognize today, such as *maki-e* (literally, "sprinkled picture")—the use of gold or silver powder to underlay the lacquer—had been developed. The Edo period (1603–1868) saw the uses of lacquer extended to vessels and utensils for the newly prosperous merchant class.

The production of lacquerware starts with refining sap from the Japanese sumac (*urushi*). The lacquer is layered on basketry, wood, bamboo, metal, and even paper. The polished black and red surfaces may have inlays of mother-of-pearl or precious metals, creating motifs and designs of exquisite beauty and delicacy. Many regions in Japan are famous for their distinct lacquerware styles, among them Kyoto, Wajima, and Tsugaru. ■ TIP➜ **Tableware with lacquer over plastic bases, rather than wood, are no less beautiful, but far less expensive.**

## PAPERMAKING

*Washi*, Japanese paper, can have a soft translucent quality that seems to belie its amazing strength and durability. It makes a splendid material for calligraphy and brush painting, and it can be fashioned into a wide variety of

Traditional Japanese papermaking

traditional decorative objects. The basic ingredient is the inner bark of the paper mulberry, but leaves, fiber threads, and even gold flake can be added in later stages for a dramatic effect. The raw mulberry branches are first steamed, then bleached in cold water or snow. The fibers are boiled with ash lye, rinsed, beaten into pulp, and soaked in a tank of starchy taro solution. A screen is dipped into the tank, pulled up, and rocked to drain the solution and crosshatch the fibers. The wet sheets of paper are stacked to press out the excess liquid, then dried in the sun.

## CALLIGRAPHY

Calligraphy arrived in Japan around the middle of the 6th century AD with the sacred texts of Buddhism, written in *kanji* (Chinese ideograms). By 800 the *kana* syllabic alphabets of the Japanese language had also developed, and the writing of both kanji and kana with a brush, in india ink, had become an art form—a wedding of meaning and emotion that was (and still is) regarded as a revelation of the writer's individual character. The flow of the line from top to bottom, the balance of shapes and sizes, the thickness of the strokes, the amount of ink on the brush: all contribute to the composition of the work. There are five main styles of calligraphy in Japan. Two are based on

A calligrapher at work

About 30 different styles of porcelain are made in Japan.

the Chinese: *tensho,* typically used for seal carving; and *reisho,* for the copying of sutras. Three are solely Japanese: *kaisho,* the block style often seen in wood carving; and the flowing *sosho* (cursive) and *gyosho* styles. *Sosho* is especially impressive—an expression of freedom and spontaneity that takes years of discipline to achieve; retouching and erasing is impossible.

## CERAMICS

There are some 30 traditional styles of pottery in Japan, from unglazed stoneware to painted porcelain. Since the late 1600s, when Imari and Kakiemon porcelain were exported to Europe, the achievements of Japanese potters have delighted collectors.

Although people have been making pottery in the Japanese archipelago for some 12,000 years, the styles we know today were developed from techniques introduced from the Korean Peninsula and mainland Asia to Japan starting in the 5th century. Some craftspeople discovered deposits of fine kaolin clay in northern Kyushu, and founded the tradition in that region of porcelains like

Arita-yaki, with brilliantly colored enamel decoration over cobalt blue underglaze. Other porcelain wares include Tobe-yaki from Ehime Prefecture, Kutani-yaki from Ishikawa Prefecture, and Kiyomizu-yaki from Kyoto.

These apart, most Japanese pottery is stoneware—which has an earthier appeal, befitting the rougher texture of the clay. Stoneware from Mashiko, where celebrated potter Hamada Shoji (1894–1978) worked, is admired for its rustic brown, black, and white glazes, often applied in abstract patterns. Many regional potters use glazes on stoneware for coloristic effects, like the mottled, crusty Tokoname-yaki, with its red-iron clay. Other styles, among them the rough-surfaced Shigaraki-yaki made near Kyoto; the white or blue-white Hagi-yaki; and Bizen-yaki from Okayama Prefecture, are unglazed: their warm tones and textures are accidents of nature, achieved when the pieces take their colors from the firing process, in sloped, wood-burning through-draft kilns called *anagama* or *nobori-gama,* built on hillsides. The effects depend on the choice of the wood the potter uses, where he places a particular piece in the kiln, and how he manipulates the heat, but the results are never predictable.

Main pottery towns include Hagi, Bizen, and Arita, but you can always find their products in Kyoto and Tokyo. If you do go on a pilgrimage, call ahead to local kilns and tourist organizations to verify that what you want to see will be open and to ask about sales.

**Recommended reading:** *Inside Japanese Ceramics* by Richard L. Wilson.

## TEXTILES

Run your fingers over a Japanese textile, and you touch the fabric of Japanese social history. As the caste system took shape under Buddhist and Confucian influences, it created separate populations of samurai, farmers, artisans, and merchants (in descending order). Rules and conventions emerged—enforced in the Edo period by strict sumptuary laws—about who could wear what and on what occasions. Appearances identified people. One glance at a kimono, and you knew the wearer was a woman of middle age, the wife of a prosperous tradesman, on her way to the wedding of a family connection. Order was maintained. You were what you wore. Courtesans and actors, of course, could dress over-the-top, their roles gave them the license. And little by little, the merchants also found ways around the laws, to dress as befit their growing wealth and power. Evolving styles and techniques of making fabrics gave weavers and dyers and designers new opportunities to show their skills.

Western clothing follows the body line in a sculptural way; the kimono is meant as a one-size-fits-all garment in which gender matters, but size and shape are largely unimportant. Whatever the wearer's height or weight, a kimono is made from one bolt of cloth cut and stitched into panels that provide ample surface for decoration.

Regional styles proliferate. Kyoto's *Nishijin-ori* silk brocade is as sumptuous as a Japanese textile can be. Okinawa produces a variety of stunning fabrics; one, called *bashofu,* is made of plantain-fiber threads, dyed and woven in intricate motifs, and feels like linen. Kyoto's and Tokyo's stencil dyeing techniques yield subtle, elegant geometric patterns and motifs from nature. Kanazawa's *Kaga yuzen* paste-resist dyeing on silk is famous for its flower and bird motifs, in elegant rainbow colors.

The used kimonos you often see in Kyoto or Tokyo flea markets can be bargains. Also look for lighter-weight *yukata* (robes), *obi* (sashes), or handkerchiefs from Arimatsu, near Nagoya, for example. Good introductions to these craft traditions can be seen at Kyoto's Fuzoku Hakubutsukan (Costume Museum) and Nishijin Orimono (Textile Center), and the Edo-period dress collection in Tokyo's National Museum.

Kaga yuzen textiles from Kanazawa exhibit a traditional flower motif.

# PERFORMING ARTS

A highly stylized Noh theater performance

Gorgeous costumes, sword fights and tearful reunions, acrobatics and magical transformations, spectacular makeup and masks, singing and dancing, ghosts and goblins, and star-crossed lovers: traditional Japanese arts are not short on showmanship.

The performing arts all have roots in the trade and exchange with continental Asia. Kabuki makeup as well as *gagaku* ceremonial court music and dance are Chinese-inspired; the four-string *biwa* shares a Silk Road ancestry with the Persian *oud*. Collectively the theater traditions generate work for artisans—weavers and dyers, instrument makers, wood-carvers, and more—who make a special contribution of their own. Common features aside, the differences among them are astonishing. Kabuki is great showbiz, translatable and appreciable pretty much anywhere in the world. Most of an audience that will sit riveted by the graceful, suggestive movements of *buyo* (traditional dance) will fall asleep at a dance-recitation of Noh.

## MASTER PERFORMERS

The performing arts also have National Treasures, but filling the 70 allotted slots is easier than in the fine arts. The worlds of Japanese theater are mainly in the grip of small oligarchies ("schools") where traditions are passed down from father to son. Some of these master performers are 9th- and even 22nd-generation holders of hereditary family stage names and specializations.

# KABUKI

Tradition has it that Kabuki was created around 1600 by an Izumo shrine maiden named Okuni; it was then performed by troupes of women, who were often available as well for prostitution (the authorities soon banned women from the stage as a threat to public order). Eventually Kabuki cleaned up its act and developed a professional role for female impersonators, who train for years to project a seductive, dazzling femininity. By the latter half of the 18th century it had become Everyman's theater par excellence—especially among the townspeople of bustling, hustling Edo. Kabuki had spectacle; it had pathos and tragedy; it had romance and social satire. It had legions of fans, who spent all day at the theater, shouting out the names of their favorite actors at the stirring moments in their favorite plays.

Kabuki flowered especially in the "floating world" of Edo's red-light entertainment district. The theater was a place to see and be seen, to catch the latest trends in music and fashion, where people of all classes came together under one roof—something that happened nearly nowhere else in the city. Strict censorship laws were put in place and just as quickly circumvented by clever playwrights; Kabuki

The Oshika Kabuki troupe

A Kabuki mannequin from the Edo-Tokyo Museum

audiences could watch a *jidai-mono* (historical piece) set in the distant past, where the events and characters made thinly veiled reference to troublesome contemporary events.

The Genroku era (1673–1841) was Kabuki's golden age, when the classic plays of Chikamatsu Monzaemon and Tsuruya Namboku were written, and most of the theatrical conventions and stage techniques we see today were honed to perfection. The *mie*, for example, is a dramatic pose the actor strikes at a certain moment in the play, to establish his character. The use of *kumadori* makeup, derived from Chinese opera and used to symbolize the essential elements of a character's nature, also dates to this period. The exaggerated facial lines of the kumadori, in vivid reds and blues and greens over a white rice-powder base, tell the audience at once that the wearer is a hero or villain, noble or arrogant, passionate or cold. To the Genroku also date revolving stages, trapdoors, and—most important—the *hanamichi*: a long, raised runway from the back of the theater, through the audience, to the main stage, where characters enter, exit, and strike their *mie* poses.

Kabuki traditions are passed down through generations in a small group

The principal character in a Noh play wears a carved, wooden mask.

of families; the roles and great stage names are hereditary. The repertoire does not really grow, but stars like Ichikawa Ennosuke and Bando Tamasaburo have developed unique performance styles that still draw audiences young and old. This ancient art now has a stylish home in the Kengo Kuma–designed Kabuki-za theater in Tokyo's Ginza district, which opened in 2013.

**Recommended reading:** *The Kabuki Guide* by Masakatsu Gunji.

## NOH

Noh is a dramatic tradition far older than Kabuki; it reached a point of formal perfection in the 14th century and survives virtually unchanged from that period. Whereas Kabuki was everyman's theater, Noh developed for the most part under the patronage of the warrior class. It is dignified, ritualized, and symbolic. Many of the plays in the repertoire are drawn from classical literature or tales of the supernatural. The texts are richly poetic, and even the Japanese find them difficult to understand. (Don't despair: the major Noh theaters usually provide synopses of the plays in English.) The action—such as it is—develops at nearly glacial pace.

The principal character in a Noh play wears a carved wooden mask. Such is the skill of the actor, and the mysterious effect of the play, that the mask itself may appear expressionless until the actor "brings it to life," at which point the mask can express a considerable range of emotions. As in Kabuki, the various roles of the Noh repertoire all have specific costumes—robes of silk brocade with intricate patterns that are works of art in themselves. Noh is not a very "accessible" kind of theater: its language is archaic; its conventions are obscure; and its measured, stately pace can put many audiences to sleep.

More accessible is the *kyogen,* a short comic interlude traditionally performed between two Noh plays in a program. The pace is quicker, the costumes (based on actual dress of the medieval period) are simpler, and most *kyogen* do not use masks; the comedy depends on the satiric premise—a clever servant who gets the best of his master, for example—and the lively facial expressions of the actors.

Like Kabuki, Noh has a number of schools, the traditions of which developed as the exclusive property of hereditary families. The major schools have their own theaters in Tokyo and Kyoto, with regular schedules of performances—but if you happen to be in Kyoto on June 1–2, don't miss the Takigi Noh: an outdoor performance given at night, by torchlight, in the precincts of the Heian Shrine. There are other torchlight performances as well in Tokyo, at the Meiji Shrine (early November) and Zojoji Temple (late September), and in Nara at the Kasuga Shrine (May).

## BUNRAKU

The third major form of traditional Japanese drama is Bunraku puppet theater. Itinerant puppeteers were plying their trade in Japan as early as the 10th century; sometime in the late 16th century, a form of narrative ballad called *joruri,* performed to the accompaniment of a three-string banjolike instrument called the *shamisen,* was grafted onto their art, and Bunraku was born. The golden age of Bunraku came some 200 years later, when most of the great plays were written and the puppets themselves evolved to their present form, so expressive and intricate in their movements that they require three people acting in unison to manipulate them.

The puppets are about two-thirds human size and elaborately dressed in period costume; each one is made up of interchangeable parts—a head, shoulder piece, trunk, legs, and arms. The puppeteer called the *omozukai* controls the expression on the puppet's face and its right arm and hand. The *hidarizukai* controls the puppet's left arm and hand along with any props that it is carrying. The *ashizukai* moves the puppet's legs. The most difficult task belongs to the omozukai—a role

it commonly takes some 30 years to master.

Creating the puppet heads is an art in itself, and today there are only a handful of carvers still working. As a rule, the heads are shaped and painted for specific figures—characters of different sex, age, and personality—and fitted with elaborate wigs of human hair in various styles to indicate the puppet's social standing. Able to roll their eyes and lift their eyebrows, the puppets can achieve an amazing range of facial expressions.

The chanters, who provide both the narration of the play and the voices of the puppets, deliver their lines in a kind of high-pitched croak from deep in the throat. The texts they recite are considered to be among the classics of Japanese dramatic literature; the great playwright Chikamatsu Monzaemon (1653–1725) wrote for both Bunraku and Kabuki, and the two dramatic forms often adapted works from each other.

The most important Bunraku troupe is the government-supported National Bunraku Theatre in Osaka, but there are amateur and semiprofessional companies throughout the country.

Bunraku puppets are about two-thirds human size.

# ONSEN AND BATHING

A lakeside rotenburo made from natural rocks

A chain of volcanic islands on the fiery Pacific Rim, Japan has developed a splendid subculture around one of the more manageable manifestations of this powerful resource: the onsen thermal spa.

The benchmark Japanese weekend excursion—be it family outing, company retreat, or romantic getaway—is the hot spring resort. Fissured from end to end with volcanic cracks and crannies, the country positively wheezes with geothermal springs. Hot water gushes and sprays almost everywhere—but most especially in the mountains; there are hot springs in every prefecture, on every offshore island—even in cities often built above the very fault lines themselves.

### YUDEDAKO

The Japanese have a special term for that blissful state of total immersion—*yudedako* (literally, "boiled octopus")—and Japanese people of all ages will journey for miles to attain it. Soaking in hot springs is a step on the road to sound health, good digestion, clear skin, marital harmony—to whatever it is that gives you a general sense of being at one with the universe.

## THE ONSEN EXPERIENCE

An onsen can refer to a particular region or subregion, like Yufuin in Oita Prefecture, Kinugawa in Tochigi, or Hakone in Kanagawa: a resort destination especially well endowed with thermal springs. Or it can mean more specifically a public bathhouse with a spring-fed pool, where you pay an admission fee and soak at your leisure. (At last count, there were some 6,700 of these nationwide.) Or it could mean a lodging—one of two basic varieties—with a spring of its own. One type is the *kanko* hotel: a mega-onsen with multiple baths, in grand pharaonic styles with mosaics and waterfalls, and banquet halls and dinner shows, as well as tatami-floored guest rooms that sleep six—and, inevitably, discos and karaoke bars and souvenir shops. The other type is the onsen of everyone's dreams: the picture-perfect traditional inn, a ryokan of half a dozen rooms, nestled up somewhere in the mountains all by itself, with a spectacular view and a *rotenburo*—an outdoor bath—to enjoy it from.

## THE ROTENBURO

At smaller onsen you can sometimes book a rotenburo, an exquisitely crafted bath with stepping-stones, lanterns, and bamboo screens for a private soak: an hour or so of the purest luxury,

A spa in Shirahama Onsen

especially by moonlight. The rotenburo is a year-round indulgence; the view from the bath might be of a mountainside, white with cherry blossoms in spring; a lakefront doused in the red and gold of maples in autumn; or a winter panorama, with the snow piled high on the pines and hedges that frame the landscape. Whatever the season, you'll need to make reservations well in advance for the best onsen accommodations. Japan has more than 3,000 registered spas; collectively they draw nearly 140 million visitors a year, and hotel space is in high demand.

## WHAT IS AN ONSEN?

By law, an onsen is only an onsen if the water comes out of the ground at a specified minimum temperature, and contains at least one of 19 designated minerals and chemical compounds—which makes for a wide range of choices. There are iron springs with red water; there are silky-smooth alkaline springs; there are springs with radon and sulphur sodium bicarbonate; there are springs with water at a comfortable 100°F (37.8°C), and springs so hot they have bath masters to make sure you stay only for three minutes and not a fatal second longer.

Gakenoyu Onsen in Nagano

Most onsen have single-sex bathing; a few have mixed bathing.

One reason many Westerners are reluctant to go bathing in Japan: Japanese communal bathing is done in the buff—but that shouldn't deter you from the experience. The bath is a great equalizer: in a sense the bath *is* Japan, in its unalloyed egalitarianism. Each bather offers the other an equal degree of respect and regard; people generally do not behave in a way that might spoil the enjoyment of any other bather; nor is anyone embarrassed. It is freeing and you can relax right into it.

## ONSEN ETIQUETTE

Another reason you might have for your reluctance is the worrisome conviction that bathing with a bunch of strangers comes with a raft of rules—rules all those strangers are taught from childhood, but at least one of which you're bound to break, to your everlasting horror and shame. "What if I drop the something into the bath?" is a common fear.

But the pitfalls are not so bad. There certainly are protocols to follow, but it's a short list.

■ While there are still a few spas that keep alive the old custom of *konyoku* (mixed bathing), all of them have separate entrances for men and women, each labeled with Japanese characters.

■ A word of warning: body tattoos, in Japan, are indelibly associated with the yakuza—organized crime families and their minions—and spas commonly refuse entry to tattooed visitors to avoid upsetting their regular clientele. The rule is strictly enforced. Even foreign tourists, who are clearly not involved in Japanese organized crime, can be turned away for their tattoos. If your tattoo is small enough, put a bandage over it. Another option is to only bathe in *kashikiri-buro*, or private baths, which are available at larger onsen and many ryokan. This may also be an appealing option for those who'd rather not bare all in front of multiple strangers.

■ The first room you come to inside is the dressing room. It's often tatami-floored: take your shoes or slippers off in the entryway. The dressing room will have lockers for your keys and valuables, and rows of wicker or plastic baskets on shelves; pick one, and put your clothes in it. If you're staying overnight at an inn with a spa of its own, you'll find a cotton kimono called a *nemaki* in your room—you sleep in it, in lieu of pajamas—and a light quilted jacket called a *hanten*. Night or day, this is standard gear to wear from your room to the spa, anywhere else around the inn, and even for a stroll out of doors. Leave them in the basket.

■ Bring two towels: leave the bigger one in the basket to dry off with, and take the smaller one with you next door to the baths. (You will likely see that this towel to preserve your modesty is the accepted way of moving around in the spa.)

■ The bath area will have rows of washing stations along the walls: countertops with supplies of soap and shampoo, taps, a mirror, shower-head, stool, and bucket. Here's where you get clean—and that means *really* clean. Soap up, shower, scrub off every particle of the day's wear and tear. Leave no trace of soap.

■ You can take the towel with you to the bath, but don't put it in the water. Most people leave theirs on the side or set them folded on top of their heads. (Another item of protocol: spas don't insist on bathing caps, but they do want you to keep your head above water.)

■ Find a pleasant spot; soak in blissful silence if you prefer (but not too long if you're not used to it), or feel free to strike up a conversation with a fellow soaker: *atsui desu ne*—the local equivalent of "It's hot, isn't it?"—is a good start. The Japanese call their friendliest, most relaxing acquaintances *hadaka no o-tsukiai*: naked encounters.

Staying at a mega-onsen? Conviviality reigns in the baths of these establishments, with all sorts of amenities to help it along. At some inns, you can order a small floating table for yourself and your fellow boilers, just big enough for a ceramic flask of sake or two and a suitable number of cups. You get to warm your insides and outsides at the same time.

When you've soaked to your heart's content, dry yourself off with your smaller towel and head back to the dressing room. Depending on the onsen's water, you might want to rinse off before drying off. Grab your larger towel from the basket, wrap it around yourself, and rest a bit until your body temperature drops back to normal. Get dressed and head out to the post-bath rest area to have a cold glass of water and lounge on the tatami mats before heading back out into the world.

You clean yourself thoroughly before setting foot in the onsen.

# THE RYOKAN

A traditional tatami-mat room in a ryokan

You're likely to find Japanese hospitality polished, warm, and professional pretty much anywhere you stay—but nowhere more so than in a ryokan: a traditional inn.

Ryokans are typically one- or two-story wooden buildings where the guest rooms have tatami floors; the bedding—stowed by day in a closet—is rolled out at night. The rooms have hardly any furniture—perhaps one low dining table and cushions on the floor, a chest of drawers with a mirror, and a scroll painting or a flower arrangement in the *tokonoma* (alcove)—but every room in a proper ryokan will have windows with sliding paper screens looking out on an exquisite interior garden or scenery. Rates are per person and include the cost of breakfast and dinner. Some top-of-the-line ryokans might expect first-time guests to have introductions from a known and respected client.

## COSTS

Ryokans of august lineage and exemplary service are expensive: expect to pay ¥40,000 or even ¥60,000 per person per night with two meals. There are plenty of lower-priced ryokan in Japan, which start from ¥10,000 per person, including breakfast and dinner, though these may not have garden views. The Japan National Tourism Organization has a listing of some of the latter.

## RYOKAN ETIQUETTE

Remove your shoes as you step up from the entryway of your ryokan, and change into slippers. An attendant will escort you to your room. (It might take you two or three tries thereafter to find it on your own. Ryokans pride themselves on quiet and privacy, and the rooms are typically laid out in a labyrinth of corridors, where you're seldom aware of the presence of other guests.) Slippers come off at the door; on tatami, only socks/stockings or bare feet are acceptable. Relax first with a cup of green tea, and then head for the bath. In ryokans with thermal pools—not all have them—you can take to the waters at nearly any time and you'll be told of any time restrictions upon checking in. Be mindful of the bathing rules; wash and rinse off thoroughly before you get in the tub for a long hot soak. After your bath, change into a nemaki, the simple cotton kimono you'll find in your room, that doubles as sleepwear—or as standard garb for an informal stroll. These days, ryokans often have private baths, but especially in more venerable establishments (even those with astronomical rates), all facilities may be shared.

Ryokans don't have legions of staff, and will appreciate if you observe their routines and schedules. Guests are

Bedding for a ryokan, which is laid out nightly

expected to arrive in the late afternoon and eat around six. The front doors are sometimes locked at 10, so plan for early evenings. Breakfast is served around eight, and checkout is typically at 10. It might feel rather regimented, but just remember that your only task is to relax.

## FOOD

Not every inn that calls itself a ryokan offers meals. Some offer only breakfast; some have no meals at all. Seek out those that do; it's an important part of the experience. And while some ryokans will allow you to pay a lesser rate and skip dinner, it's worth paying extra for the feast of local specialties in beautiful dishes of all shapes and sizes (sometimes served in your room). When you're finished, your attendant will clear the table and lay out your futon bedding: a mattress filled with cotton wadding and (in winter) a heavy, thick comforter (this often happens when you've stepped out of your room, so don't be surprised). In summer the comforter is replaced with a thinner quilt. In the morning the attendant will clear away the futon and bring in your Japanese-style breakfast: grilled fish, miso soup, pickled vegetables, and rice. If you prefer, the staff will usually be able to come up with coffee and toast, not to mention a fried egg.

A ryokan meal served in myriad little dishes

# JAPANESE POP CULTURE

Pikachu performs at the Pokémon Café

Step onto the streets of Shibuya—or brave the crowds of preening high-school fashionistas populating Harujuku's Takeshita-dori—and you'll get a crash course on Japanese pop culture that extends way beyond familiar exports like Hello Kitty and Godzilla. Japanese pop culture has long been a source of fascination—and sometimes bewilderment—for foreign visitors. New fashion styles, technology, and popular media evolve quickly here, and in something of a vacuum.

That leads to a constant turnover of unique, sometimes wacky trends you won't find anywhere outside Japan. Immerse yourself in the latest fads by walking through neighborhoods like Shibuya, Shimo-Kitazawa, Harujuku, and Akihabara.

## DID YOU KNOW?

There are more than 4 million vending machines in Japan, making it the densest population of machines per capita anywhere in the world. Here automated machines sell everything from hot drinks to live lobsters. Some use facial recognition to verify age for tobacco and beer and even offer indecisive customers age-appropriate drink recommendations.

## KAWAII

*Kawaii*, or "cute," is an aww-inducing aesthetic you'll see all over Tokyo; major airlines plaster depictions of adorable animation characters like Pikachu across the sides of their planes, and even at local police stations it's not unusual for a fluffy, stuffed-animal mascot to be on display. Duck into an arcade photo booth to take *purikura*—pictures that let you choose your own kawaii background—or head to Sanrio Puroland, an entire theme park dedicated to cuteness.

Matriarch of Japanese kawaii, Hello Kitty

## J-POP IDOLS

The age of the pop group is not over in Japan. "Idol" groups are still popular. Over-the-top outfits, sugar-sweet synthesized beats, and love-professing lyrics (with the occasional English word thrown in) dominate the Japanese pop charts. AKB48, one of Tokyo's hottest groups of idols, has hundreds of members, but with a core group of around 48. The AKB in the name refers to Akihabara, which has become a center of pop. AKB48's own theater complex in Akihabara hosts performances or other events regularly. Beloved pop groups like all-male SMAP have been succeeded by younger male groups like Hey! Say! Jump.

## ANIME AND MANGA

Animation (anime) and comic books (manga) are extremely popular with readers both young and old. Comic book addicts, known as *otaku*, claim Tokyo's Akihabara as their home base. Though *otaku* can be translated as "nerd" or "obsessive," the term has been embraced by some. Former prime minister Taro Aso declared himself an otaku and confessed to reading 10 to 20 manga a week.

## VIDEO GAMES

Japan is the cradle of the video game industry, and ever since the early 1970s it's been a dominant force in the gaming market. As companies like Namco gave way to Sega, Nintendo, and Sony, the gaming systems also continued to evolve and become more sophisticated. Like manga and anime, games enjoy a mainstream following. If you're a gamer, you'll be happy to find games that are unreleased in the United States alongside rebooted classics like *The Legend of Zelda* and *Super Mario Bros.*

Distinctive manga style

# BASEBALL IN JAPAN

Mazda Zoom-Zoom Stadium in Hiroshima

Sumo may be the most visible spectator event, but without question, the most popular sport in Japan is baseball. It was first introduced in 1872 by Horace Wilson and has been popular ever since.

Each October two major-league teams in the United States (or one major-league team from the United States and one major-league team from Canada) play the best of seven games to decide the World Series. But judging from the results of the World Baseball Classic (WBC) that Japan has won twice, any true world series of baseball would have to include Japan. Although the Japanese professional-league season is shorter than its American counterpart (around 140 games versus 162 games), the major-league season's brevity is more than made up for by the company-league season, the university circuit, and the spring and summer high school tournaments. In addition there are junior high school and elementary school leagues. Many municipalities and towns even have senior leagues for people over 60 years old. The game is played everywhere: from the southern islands of Okinawa to the northern tip of Hokkaido.

## CATCHING A GAME

Even if you're not a baseball fan, you should try to take in a game on any level for the spectacle. Like the players, the fans come prepared. From team colors and fan paraphernalia to songs and boxed lunches, the Japanese fans have it down. The cheering starts with the first pitch and doesn't end until the last out. Wherever you go to see a game, you will be made to feel welcome and your interest or curiosity will be rewarded.

## BASEBALL-DO

Martial arts in Japan (judo, kendo, kyudo) and many other activities including the tea ceremony (*chado*) and calligraphy (*shodo*) end in the suffix *do* (pronounced "doe," as in the female deer, and meaning "way"). In Japan baseball is also a *do*, an art rather than a sport. Of course, the Japanese watch baseball as they watch any sport, but in terms of their preparation and mental approach to the game, it is a do.

All of Japan's active arts require years of practice to achieve the level of intense concentration and mindlessness that mastery requires. The idea is that if you practice something long enough and hard enough, it will become pure reflex. Then you won't have to think about what to do or when to do it. You will just do it. Major players like Sakamoto, Suzuki, and Nakajima play with a fluidity and grace that is beyond athleticism, exhibiting true mastery of the sport, and the result can be breathtaking.

## SPRING AND SUMMER HIGH SCHOOL TOURNAMENTS

If you're fortunate enough to be in Japan in either March or August, you can attend the high school baseball tournament held annually at Koshien Stadium in Nishinomiya (near Osaka), the mecca of Japanese baseball.

Yokohama's baseball stadium, home to the DeNa BayStars

Players from the Japanese Little League

In what regard is high school baseball held? Well, the pro team that normally plays at Koshien (the Hanshin Tigers) has to hit the road for two weeks in August to make way for the summer tournament. Both high school tournaments last about two weeks. Many of the star high school players go on to be standout players in both Japan and the United States.

## TICKET PRICES

Tickets for a professional baseball game (the season runs from late March to October) are a relatively good buy. At Koshien, home of the Hanshin Tigers, prices range from ¥1,600 for a seat in the outfield to ¥5,000 for a reserved seat on a lower level. When box seats are offered for sale, you can expect to pay around ¥6,000. Prices are similar at Tokyo Dome, where the Yomiuri Giants play.

Tickets for the high school baseball tournaments are even more affordable. Prices range from ¥500 for upper-reserved to ¥1,200 for lower-reserved to ¥1,600 for box seats. Seats in the bleachers are free throughout the tournaments.

A Japanese Culture Primer  BASEBALL IN JAPAN

3

# JAPANESE MARTIAL ARTS

A practice kendo session

Take all that chop-socky stuff in the movies with a grain of salt: the Japanese martial arts are primarily about balance—mental, spiritual, and physical—and only incidentally about attack and self-defense.

Judo and karate are now as much icons of Japan as anime or consumer electronics, and just as enthusiastically embraced abroad. Judo, karate, and aikido, all essentially 20th-century developments, have gone global; it would be hard to name a country anywhere without a network of *dojos* (martial arts academies or training halls) and local organizations, affiliates of the governing bodies in Japan, certifying students and holding competitions. Judo has been an Olympic sport for men since the 1964 games in Tokyo, and for women since 1988. An estimated 50 million people worldwide practice karate, in one or another of the eight different forms recognized by the World Union of Karate-do Federations. Aikido was first introduced abroad in the 1950s; the International Aikido Federation now has affiliates in 44 member nations. Korea and Taiwan have instruction programs in kendo (fencing) that begin at the secondary school level.

## LEVELS

Levels of certification are as much a part of the martial arts as they are in other traditional disciplines—the difference being that marks of rank are clearly visible. Students progress from the 10th *kyu* level to the 1st, and then from 1st *dan* to 8th (or 10th, depending on the system or school). Beginners wear white belts, intermediates wear brown, dan holders wear black or black-and-red.

## KYUDO: THE WAY OF THE BOW

Archery is the oldest of Japan's traditional martial arts, dating from the 12th century, when archers played an important role in the struggles for power among samurai clans. Today it is practiced as a sport and a spiritual discipline. The object is not just to hit the target (no mean feat), but to do so in proper form.

## KENDO: THE WAY OF THE SWORD

Fencing was a mainstay of feudal Japan, but the roots of modern kendo date to the early 18th century, with the introduction of the *shinai*—a practice sword made of bamboo slats—and the distinctive armor (*bogu*) still in use to protect the specific target areas the fencer must strike to earn points in competition. Attacks must be executed with foot stamping and loud spirited shouts called *kiai*.

## JUDO: THE GENTLE WAY

Dr. Kano Jigoro (1860–1938) was the proverbial 90-pound weakling as a teenager; to overcome his frailty, he immersed himself in the martial arts, and over a period of years developed a reformed version of *jujutsu* on "scientific principles," which he finally codified in 1884. The *ju* of judo means "softness" or "gentleness"—because you

use your opponent's strength against them—but this really is a rough-and-tumble contact sport.

## KARATE: THE EMPTY HAND

Odd as it may sound, *karate* (literally: "the empty hand") doesn't quite qualify as a traditional Japanese martial art. Its origins are Chinese, but it was largely developed in the Ryukyu Kingdom (Okinawa before it was annexed), and didn't come to Japan proper until 1922. It lays stress on self-defense, spiritual and mental balance, and *kata*—formal, almost ritual sequences of movement.

## AIKIDO: THE WAY OF HARMONY

The youngest of the Japanese martial arts was developed in the 1920s by Ueshiba Morihei (1883–1969), incorporating elements of both jujutsu and kendo, with much bigger doses of philosophy and spirituality. Aikido techniques consist largely of throws; the first thing a student learns is how to fall safely. After a stylized strike or a punch; the intended receiver counters by getting out of the way and pivoting into a throw or an arm/shoulder pin. The essential idea is to do no damage.

Competitors at a judo tournament

# SUMO

Two wrestlers battle in the ring

This centuries-old national sport of Japan is not to be taken lightly—as anyone who has ever seen a sumo wrestler will testify.

Sheer mass, mind you, isn't necessarily the key to success—though it might seem that way. There are no weight limits or categories in sumo; contenders in the upper ranks average 350 pounds. But Chiyonofuji, one of the all-time great *yokozuna* (grand champions), who tipped the scales at a mere 280 pounds, regularly faced—and defeated—opponents who outweighed him by 200 pounds or more. That said, sumo wrestlers do spend a lot of their time just bulking up, consuming enormous quantities of a high-protein stew called *chanko nabe,* washed down with beer. Akebono, the first foreign-born yokozuna, weighed more than 500 pounds.

## SUMO RULES

The official catalog of sumo techniques includes 82 different ways of pushing, pulling, tripping, tossing, or slapping down your opponent, but the basic rules are exquisitely simple: except for hitting below the belt (which is essentially all a sumo wrestler wears) and striking with a closed fist, almost anything goes. Touch the sand with anything but the soles of your feet, or get forced out of the ring, and you lose.

## SUMO HISTORY

The earliest written references to sumo date back to the year 712; for many centuries it was not a sport, but a Shinto religious rite, associated with Imperial Court ceremonies. Its present form—with the raised clay *dohyo* (platform) and circle of rice straw bales to mark the ring, the ranking system, the referee and judges, the elaborate costumes and purification rituals—was largely developed in the 16th and early 17th centuries.

## THE SUMO WORLD

Sumo is hierarchical and formal. To compete, you must belong to a *heya* (stable) run by a retired wrestler who has purchased that right from the association. The stable master, or *oyakata,* is responsible for bringing in as many new wrestlers as the heya can accommodate, for their training and schooling in the elaborate etiquette of sumo, and for every facet of their daily lives. Youngsters recruited into the sport live in the stable dormitory, doing all the community chores and waiting on their seniors while they learn. When they rise high enough in tournament rankings, they acquire servant-apprentices of their own.

All the stables in the association—now some 43 in number—are in or around

The ceremonial entrance of the tournament participants

Tokyo. Most are clustered on both sides of the Sumida River near the green-roofed Kokugikan (National Sumo Arena), in the areas called Asakusabashi and Ryogoku. Come early in the day, and you can peer through the windows of the heya to watch them practice, or ask your hotel concierge to find a way inside the heya. Some offer opportunities for people to watch the practice.

There are six official sumo tournaments throughout the year: three in Tokyo (January, May, and September); one each in Osaka (March), Nagoya (July), and Fukuoka (November). Wrestlers in the upper divisions fight 15 matches over 15 days. A few weeks before each tournament, a panel of judges and association *toshiyori* (elders) publish a table called a *banzuke,* which divides the 800-plus wrestlers into six ranks and two divisions, East and West, to determine who fights whom. Rankings are based on a wrestler's record in the previous tournament: win a majority of your matches and you go up in the next banzuke; lose a majority and you go down.

If you can't attend one of the Tokyo sumo tournaments, you may want to take a tour of a sumo stable to take in a practice session.

A wrestler in traditional dress outside the arena

# THE GEISHA

A traditional geisha performance in Kanazawa

The geisha—with her white makeup and Cupid's-bow red lip rouge, her hair ornaments, the rich brocade of her kimono—is as much an icon of Japan, instantly recognizable the world over, as Mt. Fuji itself.

*Gei* stands for artistic accomplishment (*sha* simply means "person"), and a geisha must be a person of many talents. As a performer, she should have a lovely voice and a command of traditional dance, and play beautifully on an instrument like the *shamisen*. She must have a finely tuned aesthetic sense, and excel at the art of conversation. In short, she should be the ultimate party hostess and gracious companion. Geisha (or *geiko* in Kyoto dialect) begin their careers at a very young age, when they are accepted into an *okiya*, a sort of guildhall where they live and learn as *maiko* (apprentices). The okiya is a thoroughly matriarchal society; the owner-manager is called *o-kami-san*, who is addressed as *okaasan* (mother), to underscore the fact that the geishas have given up one family for another.

## GEISHA LIFE

The okiya provides the apprentices with room and board, pays for their training and clothing (the latter a staggering expense), and oversees their daily lives. The maiko in turn do household chores; when they have become full-fledged geisha, they contribute a part of their income to the upkeep of the house and its all-female staff of teachers, dressers, and maids.

The world of the geisha reflects Japan's tendency toward mastery and apprenticeships. Sumo's system of heya also show hows traditions of old are not always in line with modern life, yet survive. In the past a young girl from a large family, for example, would likely join another family upon marriage (although boys also might join other households when they marry). An apprentice would join the house of the master for anything from knife-making to woodworking and geisha are no different. Traditionally, this is an opportunity for talented girls to have a job in a world that was much less fluid than modern Japan is today.

## THE GEISHA BUSINESS

There are no free agents in the geisha world; to engage one for a party you need a referral. Geisha work almost exclusively at traditional inns (ryokan), restaurants (*ryotei*), and teahouses (*chaya*); the owners of one will contact an *okiya* with which they have a connection and make the engagement—providing, of course, that you've established yourself as a trustworthy client. That means you will understand and be prepared to pay the bill when it shows up sometime later. Fees for a geisha's or maiko's time are measured in "sticks"—generally, one hour: the time it would take a stick of incense to

Geishas on the streets of Kyoto

Geishas in Kyoto

burn down—and the okiya can really stick it to you. Bills are based on the number of guests at the party and can run as high as ¥25,000 per person or more for a two-hour engagement.

There were as many as 80,000 geisha in the 1920s; today there may be 1,000 left, most of them living and working in the Gion district of Kyoto; in Kanazawa; and in the Shimbashi, Akasaka, and Ginza districts of Tokyo. Fewer and fewer young Japanese women are willing to make the total commitment this closed world demands (even a geisha who opts to live independently will remain affiliated with her okiya for the rest of her career); fewer and fewer Japanese men of means have the taste or inclination to entertain themselves or important guests in this elegant fashion. On the other hand, the profession—while it lasts—does provide considerable job security. A geisha is valued, not solely for her beauty, but for her artistic and social skills—and her absolute discretion (what she might see and hear, for example at a party hosted by a political bigwig for his important business connections, could topple empires).

# THE TEA CEREMONY

A woman in traditional dress prepares tea

The Way of Tea—in Japanese, *Cha-no-yu* or *sado*—is more than a mere ceremony: it is a profound spiritual and meditative ritual. Although you can view it rather inexpensively, the full experience of sado is the meditative experience of losing oneself in the known patterns of serving and drinking.

Tea came to Japan from China in the late 8th century, first as a medicinal plant; it was the Zen monks of the 12th century who started the practice of drinking tea for a refresher between meditation sessions. Rules and customs began to evolve, and they coalesced in the Muromachi period of the 14th and 15th centuries as the earliest form of the Cha-no-yu. The Way of Tea developed an aesthetic of its own, rooted in the Zen sense of discipline, restraint, and simplicity: an aesthetic in which the most valued tea bowls, vessels, and utensils were humble, unadorned—and even imperfect. The choreographed steps were devised to focus the appreciation—in Japanese, called *wabi*—for this subdued and quiet refinement.

## THE TEA PAVILION

Contemplate a Japanese tea pavilion long enough, and you begin to see how much work and thought can go into the design of something so simple. A stone path through a garden, a thatched roof, a low doorway into a single room with a *tokonoma* (alcove) and tatami floor are barely big enough for the tea master and a few guests, and yet are a gateway to the infinite.

The poet-priest Sen no Rikyu (1522–91) is the most revered figure in the history of sado. Three traditional schools of the tea ceremony, the Ura Senke, the Omote Senke, and the Mushakoji Senke—with some variations among them—maintain the forms and aesthetic principles he developed.

A full-scale formal tea ceremony, called a *chaji,* is like a drama in two acts, involving a multicourse *kaiseki* meal, two different kinds of powdered green tea, and an intermission—and can take as long as four hours to perform. Most ceremonies are less formal, confined to the serving of *usucha* ("thin tea") and a confection for an intimate group; these are called *o-chakai.* Both forms demand a strictly determined, stately series of moves to be made by both guests and hosts.

Participants gather first in the *machiai,* a kind of waiting room or shelter in the garden, until they are invited to proceed to the teahouse. They remove their shoes, and enter the teahouse through a low doorway. It is customary to comment on the flower arrangement or scroll in the alcove. The guests sit in *seiza,* their legs tucked under them; the host enters from another small doorway, greets them, and carefully cleans the utensils: bowl, tea scoop,

An outdoor garden tea ceremony

3

A Japanese Culture Primer THE TEA CEREMONY

caddy, ladle, whisk. No matter that they are spotless already; cleaning them is part of the ritual.

When the tea is prepared, it is served first to the principal guest, who turns the bowl in the palm of his hand, drains it in three deep, careful sips, and returns it to the host. The other participants are served in turn. The guests comment on the presentation, and the ceremony is over; when they leave the pavilion, the host bows to them from the door.

Should you be invited to a tea ceremony, you likely won't be expected to have the same mastery of the etiquette as an experienced guest, but the right frame of mind will get you through. Be prepared to sit in seiza for quite a long time. Make conversation that befits the serenity of the moment. (A well-known haiku poetess once said that what she learned most from sado was to think before she spoke.) Above all, pay close attention to the practiced movements of the host, and remember to praise the *wabi*—the understated beauty—of the utensils he or she has chosen.

**Recommended reading:** *The Book of Tea* by Okakura Kakuzo; *Cha-no-Yu: The Japanese Tea Ceremony* by A. L. Sadler.

A bowl of matcha green tea

# JAPANESE GARDENS

The garden of Hogon-in, Kyoto

Oases of calm and contemplation—and philosophical statements in their own right—Japanese gardens are quite unlike the arrangements of flowers, shrubs, and trees you find in the West.

One key to understanding—and more fully enjoying—a Japanese garden is knowing that its design, like all traditional Japanese arts, emerged out of the country's unique mixture of religious and artistic ideas. From Shintoism comes the belief in the divinity or spirit that dwells in natural phenomena like mountains, trees, and stones. The influence of Taoism is reflected in the islands that serve as symbolic heavens for the souls of those who achieve perfect harmony. Buddhist gardens—especially Zen gardens, expressions of the "less is more" aesthetic of the warrior caste—evolved in medieval times as spaces for meditation and the path to enlightenment. The classic example from this period is the *karesansui* (dry landscape) style, a highly abstract composition of meticulously placed rocks and raked sand or gravel, sometimes with a single pruned tree, but with no water at all.

## SHAKEI

*Shakei* (borrowed landscape) is a way of extending the boundaries of the visual space by integrating a nearby attractive view—like a mountain or a sweeping temple roofline, for example—framing and echoing it with plantings of similar shape or color inside the garden itself. A middle ground, usually a hedge or a wall, blocks off any unwanted view and draws the background into the composition.

3

## GARDEN DESIGN

Historically, the first garden designers in Japan were temple priests; the design concepts themselves were originally Chinese. Later, from the 16th century on, the most remarkable Japanese gardens were created by tea masters, who established a genre of their own for settings meant to deepen and refine the tea ceremony experience. Hence the *roji*: a garden path of stepping-stones from the waiting room to the teahouse itself, a transition from the ordinary world outside that prepares participants emotionally and mentally for the ceremony. Gradually gardens moved out of the exclusive realm to which only nobles, wealthy merchants, and poets had access, and the increasingly affluent middle class began to demand professional designers. In the process the elements of the garden became more elaborate, complex, and symbolic.

The "hide-and-reveal" principle, for example, dictates that there should be no point from which all of a garden is visible, that there must always be mystery and incompleteness in its changing perspectives: the garden *unfolds* as you walk from one view to another along the winding path. References to celebrated natural wonders and literary allusions, too, are frequently

Koishikawa Korakuen Garden, Tokyo

used design techniques. Mt. Fuji might be represented by a truncated cone of stones; Ama-no-Hashidate, the famous pine-covered spit of land across Miyazu Bay, near Kyoto, might be rendered by a stone bridge; a lone tree might stand for a mighty forest. Abstract concepts and themes from myths and legends, familiar to many Japanese, are similarly part of the garden vocabulary. The use of boulders in a streambed, for example, can represent life's surmountable difficulties; a pine tree can stand for strength and endurance; islands in a pond can evoke a faraway paradise.

Seasonal change is a highlight of the Japanese garden. The designer in effect choreographs the different plants that come into their glory at different times of year: cherry and plum blossoms and wisteria in spring; hydrangeas, peonies, and water lilies in summer; the spectacular reds and orange of the Japanese maple leaves in autumn. Even in winter the snow clinging to the garden's bare bones makes an impressive sight. In change there is permanence; in permanence there is fluid movement—often represented in the garden with a water element: a pond or a flowing stream, or an abstraction of one in raked gravel or stone.

The gardens of Kinkaku-ji, Kyoto

# RELIGION IN JAPAN

A Shinto shrine near Tokyo

Although both Buddhism and Shinto permeate Japanese society and life, most Japanese are blissfully unconcerned about the distinction between what is Shinto and what is Buddhist. A wedding is often a Shinto ceremony, while a funeral is a Buddhist rite. The religions were separated by edict in 1868.

There's a saying in Japan that you're Shinto at birth (marked with a Shinto ceremony) and Buddhist when you die (honored with a Buddhist funeral). The Japanese take a utilitarian view of religion and use each as suits the occasion. One prays for success in life at a shrine and for the repose of a deceased family member at a temple. There is no thought given to the whys for this—these things simply are. The neighborhood shrine's annual *matsuri* is a time of giving thanks for prosperity and for blessing homes and local businesses. *O-mikoshi,* portable shrines for the gods, are enthusiastically carried around the district by young locals. Shouting and much sake drinking are part of the celebration. But it's a celebration first and foremost.

## RELIGION IN NUMBERS

Although roughly two-thirds of Japanese people identify themselves as Buddhist, most also practice and believe in Shinto, even if they don't identify themselves as Shinto followers per se. The two religions overlap and even complement each other, even though most Japanese people would not consider themselves "religious." The religions are just part of life.

## SHINTO

Shinto (literally, "the way of the *kami* [god]") is a form of animism or nature worship based on myth and rooted to the geography and holy places of the land. It's an ancient belief system, dating back perhaps as far as 500 BC, and is indigenous to Japan. The name is derived from a Chinese word, *shin tao,* coined in the 8th century AD, when divine origins were first ascribed to the royal Yamato family. Fog-enshrouded mountains, pairs of rocks, primeval forests, and geothermal activity are all manifestations of the *kami-sama*

The gates at Futura-san Jinja, Nikko

(honorable gods). For many Japanese the Shinto aspect of their lives is simply the realm of the kami-sama and is not attached to a dogmatic religious framework as it would be in the West.

## BUDDHISM

A Korean king gave a statue of Shaka—the first Buddha, Prince Gautama—to the Yamato Court in AD 538. The Soga clan adopted the foreign faith, using it as a vehicle to change the political order of the day. After battling for control of the country, they established themselves as political rulers, and Buddhism took permanent hold. Simultaneously Japan sent its first ambassadors to China, inaugurating the importation of writing and religion into Japan and the subsequent exchange of ideas in

A statue of Buddha at Todai-ji, Nara

art, construction, language, and other aspects of society with mainland Asia. By the 8th century, Buddhism was well established.

Japanese Buddhism developed in three waves. In the Heian period (794–1185), Esoteric Buddhism was introduced primarily by two priests, both of whom studied in China: Saicho and Kukai. Saicho established a temple on Mt. Hie near Kyoto, making it the most revered mountain in Japan after Mt. Fuji. Kukai established the Shingon sect of Esoteric Buddhism on Mt. Koya, south of Nara. In Japanese temple architecture, Esoteric Buddhism introduced the separation of the temple into an interior for the initiated and an outer layperson's area.

Amidism (Pure Land) was the second wave, introduced by the monk Honen (1133–1212), and it flourished in the late 12th century until the introduction of Zen in 1185. Its adherents saw the world emerging from a period of darkness during which Buddhism had been in decline, and asserted that salvation was offered only to the believers in Amida, a Nyorai (Buddha) or enlightened being. Amidism's promise of salvation and its subsequent versions of heaven and hell earned it the appellation "Devil's Christianity" from

The Senso-ji Complex is the heart and soul of the Asakusa District of Tokyo.

visiting Christian missionaries in the 16th century.

In the Post-Heian period (1185 to the present) the influences of Nichiren and Zen Buddhist philosophies pushed Japanese Buddhism in new directions. Nichiren (1222–82) was a monk who insisted on the primacy of the Lotus Sutra, the supposed last and greatest sutra of Shaka. Zen Buddhism was attractive to the samurai class's ideals of discipline and worldly detachment and thus spread throughout Japan in the 12th century. It was later embraced as a nonintellectual path to enlightenment by those in search of a direct experience of the sublime. More recently Zen has been adopted by a growing number of people in the West as a way to move beyond the subject-object duality that characterizes Western thought.

## SHRINE AND STATE

Although the modern Japanese constitution expressly calls for a separation of church and state, it hasn't always been this way. In fact, twice over the last 150 years, Shinto was the favored

religion and the government used all of its influence to support it.

During the Meiji Restoration (1868), the emperor was made sovereign leader of Japan, and power that had been spread out among the shoguns was consolidated in the Imperial House. Shinto was favored over Buddhism for two reasons. First, according to Shinto, the members of the Imperial Family were direct descendants of the kami who had formed Japan. The second reason was more practical: many of the Buddhist temples were regional power bases that relied upon the shoguns for patronage. Relegating Buddhism to a minor religion with no official support would have a weakening effect on the shoguns, while the government could use Shinto shrines to strengthen its power base.

Indeed, Buddhism was actively suppressed. Temples were closed, priests were harassed, and priceless art was either destroyed or sold. The collections of Japanese art at the Museum of Fine Arts, Boston and the Freer Gallery in

Washington, D.C., were just two of the indirect beneficiaries of this policy.

During the Pacific War (the Japanese term for World War II), Shinto was again used by the military (with the complicity of the Imperial House) to justify an aggressive stance in Asia. (It should be noted that Kokuchukai Buddhism was also used to sanction the invasion of other countries.) The emperor was a god and therefore infallible. Since the Japanese people were essentially one family with the emperor at the head, they were a superior race that was meant to rule the lesser peoples of Asia.

Once ancestor worship was allied with worship of the emperor, the state became something worth dying for. So potent was this mix that General Douglas MacArthur identified state Shinto as one of the first things that had to be dismantled upon the surrender of Japan. The emperor could stay, but shrine and state had to go.

## RELIGIOUS FESTIVALS
Although there are religious festivals and holy days observed throughout the year, the two biggest events in the Japanese religious calendar are New Year's (Oshogatsu) and Obon. New Year's is celebrated from January 1 to 3. Many people visit temples or shrines the night of December 31 to ring in the New Year or in the coming weeks. Temple bells are struck 108 times to symbolize ridding oneself of the 108 human sins. This practice of visiting a temple or shrine for the new year is called *hatsumode*. Food stalls are set up close to the popular places, and the atmosphere is festive and joyous. Many draw fortune slips called *omikuji* to see what kind of a year the oracle has in store for them.

The other major religious event in the Japanese calendar is the Obon holiday, traditionally held from August 13 to 15. Obon is the Japanese festival of the dead when the spirits come back to visit the living. Most people observe the ritual by returning to their hometown or the home of their grandparents. Graves are cleaned and respects are paid to one's ancestors. Family ties are strengthened and renewed.

## VISITING A BUDDHIST TEMPLE
The first thing to do when visiting a temple is to stop at the gate (called *mon* in Japanese), put your hands together and bow. Once inside the gate, you should stop to wash your hands at the stone receptacle usually found immediately upon entering the grounds. Not all temples will have a place for hand washing, but shrines will. Fill one of the ladles with water using your right hand and wash your left hand first. Then refill the ladle with water using your left hand and wash your right hand, being careful to not let the water drip back into the receptacle (the water is considered impure once it touches your hands).

You might also want to light a candle in front of the main altar of the temple and place it inside the glass cabinet. Then put your hands together and bow. You can also light three sticks

Meiji Shrine in Tokyo

The massive *torii* (entrance gates) of the Meiji Shrine are more than 40 feet tall.

of incense (lighting them together is customary) and put them in the large stone or brass stand. This action is also followed with a prayer and a bow.

After praying at the main altar and/or sub-altar, you'll probably want to spend some time walking around the temple grounds. Many have gardens and sculpture worthy of a visit in their own right. Upon leaving many will stop at the gate, turn, put their hands together, and bow to give thanks.

## VISITING A SHINTO SHRINE

Shrines, like temples, have gates, though they are called *torii* and are often painted a bright red-orange, but this varies regionally. There are stained wooden torii, stone, and even metal torii. In terms of their appearance, torii look much like the mathematical symbol for pi. As with the gates of temples, one enters and exits through the torii, bowing on the way in and again on the way out but without clasping the hands.

Inside the shrine grounds, wash your hands as you would at a temple (left hand and then right hand). Then proceed to the main entrance (usually a set of open doors at the top of some stairs), clap twice to alert the kami of your presence, and bow. If there is a bell to ring, that will also summon the kami, as will the sound of money tossed into the box at the shrine's entrance. At a larger shrine there may be special trees, stones, and other holy objects situated throughout the grounds where you can repeat the clapping and praying process. At the beginning of their prayers, people introduce themselves by name and address. Since gods in Japan are local, you are to identify yourself to the god that you are of this place or of some other place and visiting.

After you have finished visiting the shrine, you should turn around at the torii and bow upon leaving.

Chapter 4

# TOKYO

Updated by
Robert Morel

| ⊙ Sights | 🍴 Restaurants | 🛏 Hotels | 🛍 Shopping | 🍸 Nightlife |
|---|---|---|---|---|
| ★★★★★ | ★★★★★ | ★★★★★ | ★★★★★ | ★★★★★ |

# WELCOME TO TOKYO

## TOP REASONS TO GO

★ **Ultimate cityscape:** A skyline of neon-lit streets and vast high-rises awes the senses.

★ **Incredible eats:** From humble ramen to sumptuous sushi, Tokyo is a foodie haven.

★ **Green havens:** Pristine gardens and lush city-center parks soften the urban scene.

★ **Fashion-forward shops:** From Muji to Miyake, Tokyo is a playground for shopaholics.

★ **Contemporary art:** The Mori Art Museum caps a stunningly diverse scene.

★ **Sacred spaces:** Senso-ji Complex and Meiji Shrine offer spiritual retreats.

**1** **Imperial Palace.** The home of the royal family.

**2** **Marunouchi.** Business district adjacent to the Palace.

**3** **Nihonbashi.** Tokyo's central business center.

**4** **Ginza.** High-end stores and restaurants.

**5** **Tsukiji.** The outer market and shops.

**6** **Shiodome.** Plenty of shops, hotels, and restaurants.

**7** **Aoyama and Harajuku.** Adjacent chic neighborhoods with hip shops.

**8** **Shibuya.** Center of fashion, culture, and entertainment for the younger crowd.

**9** **Roppongi.** Mostly museums and shops.

**10** **Shinjuku.** The red-light turned nightlife district Kabuki-cho.

**11** **Akihabara.** Famed for its manga shops, video arcades, and maid cafés.

**12** **Ueno.** Museums and a fine arts university.

**13** **Asakusa.** Home to Senso-ji, Tokyo's most famous temple.

**14** **Greater Tokyo.** Sights outside the immediate city center.

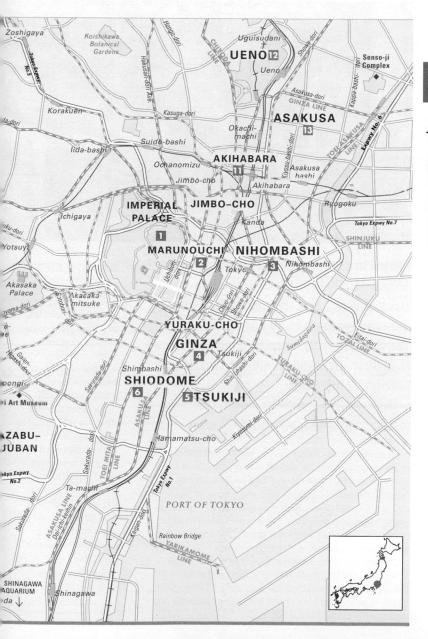

# TOKYO'S VENDING MACHINES AND CONVENIENCE STORES

With a brightly lighted convenience store on practically every corner and a few well-stocked vending machines in between, quick shopping is truly hassle-free in Tokyo—and with items ranging from novel to bizarre, an impulse buy can turn into a journey of discovery.

While vending machines and convenience stores did not originate in Japan, their popularity in the country seems to have no limit. Today Japan has the world's highest density of vending machines per capita, with one machine for every 23 people. Those looking for a wider selection can head to one of the 40,000 or so convenience stores in the country. Canned drinks, both cold and hot, are the main staple of vending machines, but it is not uncommon to find ones with cigarettes, batteries, snacks, ice-cream cones, toiletries, fresh fruit, customized business cards, or even umbrellas. For North Americans used to convenience stores that sell little more than junk food and magazines, the Japanese equivalent can be a source of amazement, boasting everything from postal and courier services and digital photo printing to full hot meals.

### DID YOU KNOW?

Vending machines hold a dizzying array of options from water and fruit juice to sugar-laden coffee, colas, and even alcohol. If you need a healthy snack, Dole installed banana dispensers around Shibuya train station, targeting hurried commuters with no time for breakfast. Need something like a quick change for work? Shinjuku Station even has machines selling white business shirts and ties.

## VENDING MACHINES

If you visit Tokyo during the hot and humid summer months, you'll quickly understand why there is a machine selling cool drinks on every sidewalk. In winter, hot drinks warm both the stomach and hands. Popular drinks include Pocari Sweat, a noncarbonated sports drink with a mild grapefruit taste; Aquarius, a similar drink by Coca-Cola; and Ito En, a variety of cold green tea in plastic bottles. Machines sell beer and other alcoholic beverages, but you may want to avoid *shochu*, alcohol sold in glass jars or paper cartons—not only is it fairly strong at typically 20% ABV, but the variety sold in vending machines is usually of very low, throat-burning quality. Coffee—both hot and cold—comes in small cans. You'll see locals buy one, suck it down, and dispose of the can, all during the two-minute wait for the subway. Hot drinks have a red strip below them on the vending machine and cold drinks are marked with blue. If red Japanese text appears below an item, the machine is sold out. Edible items aren't the only things for sale, as shrines and temples use vending machines to sell *omikuji*, fortunes written on slips of paper.

## CONVENIENCE STORES

The first convenience store opened in Japan in 1973, and like so many other imported concepts, the Japanese have embraced the *konbini*, turning it into something of their own. Beyond the usual products you might expect, Japanese convenience stores also carry *bento* (boxed meals), basic clothing items, and event tickets. Services available include digital photo printing, faxing, and utility bill payments. Convenience stores are actually a great option for a quick meal, including sandwiches, noodle dishes, fresh fruit, and a variety of salads. Peek into the freezer and Häagen-Dazs tempts you with flavors like matcha green tea. Near the cash register are hot food options, including fried chicken and steamed buns stuffed with meat or a sweet bean paste. Step into a 7-Eleven, Lawson, or Family Mart and see familiar brands with a Japanese twist such as salty watermelon Pepsi or soy sauce Pringles.

## TOP BUYS

Japanese Pringles potato chips have come in flavors such as cheese and bacon and seaweed, and new surprising combinations are rolled out every season. Another international brand that often adds a local twist is Kit Kat, which in the past has released matcha green tea, wasabi, and passion fruit versions of its candy bars. New varieties of Kit Kat debut throughout the year, some only available in certain regions. If you are traveling with children, a fun purchase is Ramune, a carbonated drink sold in a glass bottle sealed with a glass marble held in place by the pressure of the gas—push the marble down with your thumb to break the seal. One convenience store treat you cannot leave Japan without trying at least once is *onigiri*, a triangular rice ball containing canned tuna with mayonnaise, pickled plum, or other fillings, and wrapped in sheets of dried seaweed.

From the crush of the morning commute to the evening crowds flowing into shops, restaurants, and bars, Tokyo's image is that of a city that never stops and rarely slows down. It is all too often portrayed as a strange carousel of lights, sounds, and people set on fast-forward, but these days there is a greater focus on cultural development and quality of life.

For a time it seemed that Tokyo was becoming the city of the future—compact urban life surrounded by high-tech skyscrapers, the world's densest rail system, and a 3-D network of highways overlapping and twisting above the city. Nearly thirty years of gradual economic stagnation have cooled that vision, but if Tokyo no longer sees itself as the city of the future, it seems to have settled comfortably into being a city of the present.

Although parts of the city such as Shibuya or Shinjuku's Kabuki-cho continue to overwhelm with a 24-hour cacophony of light, sound, and energy, other neighborhoods are surprisingly relaxed. In Omotesando and Aoyama, people are more likely to be sipping wine or coffee with friends at an outdoor café than downing beer and sake with coworkers in an *izakaya* (a bar that serves food). The people are as varied as their city. Residents of Aoyama may wear European fashion and drive fancy imports, but those residing in Asakusa prefer to be decidedly less flashy.

Even the landscape is varied. The city hosts some of the most unsightly sprawls of concrete housing—extending for miles in all directions—in the world, but offsetting all the concrete and glass is a wealth of green space in the form of parks, temple grounds, and traditional gardens.

Whether you're gazing at the glow of Tokyo's evening lights or the green expanse of its parks, this is a city of astonishing and intriguing beauty. If you're a foodie, artist, design lover, or cultural adventurer, then Tokyo, a city of inspiration and ideas, is for you.

# Planning

## Getting Here and Around

### AIR

The major gateway to Japan is Tokyo's Narita Airport (NRT), 80 km (50 miles) northeast of the city. The Haneda Airport International Terminal also has flights to major international cities and is only 20 km (12 miles) south of central Tokyo. Most domestic flights to and from Tokyo are out of Haneda Airport.

Flying into Haneda provides visitors with quicker access to downtown Tokyo, which is a short monorail ride away. Stop by the currency exchange and tourist information desk in the second-floor arrival lobby before taking a train into the city. There are also numerous jade-uniformed concierge staff on hand to help passengers with any questions.

**AIRPORTS Haneda Airport (HND).**
☎ *03/5757–8111* ⊕ *www.tokyo-air-port-bldg.co.jp/en.* **Narita Airport (NRT).**
☎ *0476/34–8000* ⊕ *www.narita-airport.jp.*

## AIRPORT TRANSFERS

Known as "The Gateway to Japan," Narita is about 90 minutes—dependent on city traffic—by taxi or bus from central Tokyo. The Keisei Skyliner and Japan Railways N'EX are the easiest ways to get into the city.

Japan Railways trains stop at Narita Airport Terminals 1 and 2. The fastest and most comfortable is the Narita Limited Express (N'EX). Trains from the airport go directly to the central Tokyo Station in just about an hour, then continue to Yokohama and Ofuna. Daily departures begin at 7.44 am; the last train is at 9:44 pm. In addition to regular seats, there is a first-class Green Car and private four-person compartments. All seats are reserved, and you need to reserve one for yourself in advance, as this train fills quickly.

**CONTACTS Japan Railways.** ☎ *050/2016–1603 for JR East InfoLine* ⊕ *www.jreast.co.jp/e.* **Keisei Railway.** ☎ *0476/34–6261* ⊕ *www.keisei.co.jp/keisei/tetudou/sky-liner/us.* **TYO-NRT Highway Bus.** ✉ *Tokyo* ⊕ *https://tyo-nrt.com/en.*

## TAXI

Taxis are an expensive way of getting around cities in Japan, although nascent deregulation moves are easing the market a little. In Tokyo the first 2 km (1 mile) costs ¥730 and it's ¥320 for every additional kilometer (½ mile). Between 10 pm and 5 am there is a 20% service charge on top of that. If possible, avoid using taxis during rush hours (7:30–9:30 am and 5–7 pm).

## TRAIN AND SUBWAY

Riding Japanese trains is one of the pleasures of travel in the country. Efficient and convenient, trains run frequently and on schedule. The Shinkansen (bullet train), one of the fastest trains in the world, connects major cities north and south of Tokyo. It is only slightly less expensive than flying, but is in many ways more convenient because train stations are more centrally located than airports (if you have a Japan Rail Pass, it's extremely affordable).

If you plan to travel by rail, get a Japan Rail Pass, which provides unlimited travel on Japan Railways (JR) trains (covering most destinations in Japan) but not on lines owned by other companies. For the Sanyo, Tokaido, and Kyushu Shinkansen lines, the pass is valid on any trains except the Nozomi and Mizuho, which stop infrequently. Nevertheless, it is valid on all trains on the Yamagata, Tohoku, Joetsu, Akita, and Hokuriku Shinkansen lines.

The JR Pass is also valid on some local buses operated by Japan Railways, though not on the long-distance JR highway buses. You can make seat reservations without paying a fee on all trains that have reserved-seat coaches, usually long-distance trains. The Japan Rail Pass does not cover the cost of sleeping compartments on overnight trains (called blue trains).

You can purchase one-, two-, or three-week passes. A one-week pass is about as expensive as a regular round-trip ticket from Tokyo to Kyoto on the Shinkansen. You must obtain a rail pass voucher prior to arrival in Japan (you cannot buy them in Japan), and the pass must be used within three months of purchase. The pass is available only to people with tourist visas, as opposed to business, student, and diplomatic visas.

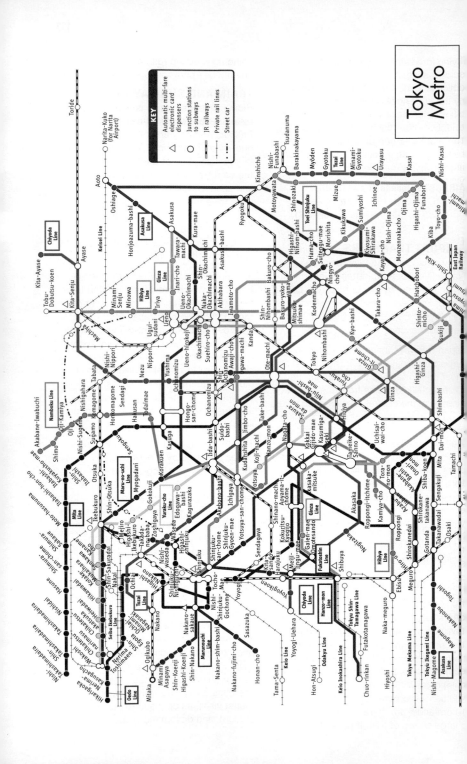

Tokyo Metro

Tokyo Metro and Toei operate separate subway lines in Tokyo, with Tokyo Metro operating the majority of them. The companies charge separate fares—that is, a ticket from one company is not valid on a train operated by the other, so you want to complete a journey on lines operated by one company rather than switching. Some especially useful lines for visitors are the Ginza Line, which moves between Asakusa and Shibuya, and the Oedo and Marunouchi lines, which loop around the city center.

Basic train and subway fares within Tokyo are between ¥170 and ¥360, depending on how far you travel. Purchase tickets from machines that take coins or cash near the gates, or get a Suica or Pasmo prepaid transit card and refill it as needed. Maps above each machine—usually in Japanese and English in central Tokyo—list destinations and fares.

◼ TIP➜ Prepaid Suica or Pasmo transit cards work on all trains, subways, and buses in Tokyo, saving a lot of time and headaches.

# Hotels

Japan may have experienced more than two decades of stagnation following the collapse of the asset-inflated "bubble" economy of the late 1990s, but one wouldn't know it from the steadily increasing number of high-end hotels throughout the metropolis. As land prices subsequently fell, Tokyo's developers seized the chance to construct centrally located skyscrapers. Oftentimes hotels from international brands were installed on the upper floors of these glimmering towers. This boom has complemented the spare-no-expense approach taken by many of the domestic hoteliers a decade earlier, when soaring atriums, elaborate concierge floors, and oceans of marble were all the rage.

Tokyo's present luxury accommodations rival those of any big city in the world.

Lower-profile business and hotels are decent bets for singles or couples who do not need a lot of space; in addition to hostels, exchanges, and rentals, the budget-conscious traveler can opt for ryokan, minshuku, "capsule" hotels, homes, and temples.

A number of boutique hotels have popped up in Tokyo. Modern room furnishings of neutral hues are prevalent, but so are such Japanese touches as paper lanterns and tatami flooring. Reception areas are simple spaces bathed in dim lights and surrounded by earth tone wall panels. Given that these accommodations often contain only a few floors, their locations are likely not easy to find. But when priced at around ¥20,000 a night, they can offer some of the best bargains in a city known for being incredibly expensive.

*Prices in the reviews are the lowest cost of a standard double room in high season. Hotel reviews have been shortened. For full information, visit Fodors.com.*

**4**

**Tokyo** PLANNING

| What It Costs in Yen | | | |
|---|---|---|---|
| $ | $$ | $$$ | $$$$ |
| **HOTELS** | | | |
| under ¥15,000 | ¥15,000– ¥30,000 | ¥30,001– ¥45,000 | over ¥45,000 |

# Nightlife

The sheer diversity of nightlife in Tokyo is breathtaking. Rickety street stands sit yards away from luxury hotels, and wallet-crunching hostess clubs can be found next to cheap and raucous rock bars.

Most bars and clubs in the main entertainment districts have printed price lists, often in English. Drinks generally cost ¥700–¥1,200, although some small exclusive bars and clubs will set you back a lot more. Be wary of establishments without visible price lists. Hostess clubs and small backstreet bars known as "snacks" or "pubs" can be particularly treacherous territory for the unprepared. That drink you've just ordered could set you back a reasonable ¥1,000; you might, on the other hand, have wandered unknowingly into a place that charges you ¥30,000 up front for a whole bottle— and slaps a ¥20,000 cover charge on top. If the bar has hostesses, it's often unclear what the cover charge will be, but as an unfamiliar face, you can bet it will cost you a lot. Ignore the persuasive shills on the streets of Roppongi and Kabuki-cho, who will try to hook you into their establishment. There is, of course, plenty of safe ground: hotel lounges, jazz clubs, and the rapidly expanding Irish pub scene are pretty much the way they are anywhere else.

*Metropolis*, a free English-language weekly magazine, and the *Japan Times* City Guide have up-to-date listings of what's going on in the city; they are available at hotels, book and music stores, some restaurants and cafés, and other locations. The *Japan News* also has entertainment features and listings in the Friday edition.

# Performing Arts

The city is a proving ground for local talent and a magnet for orchestras and concert soloists from all over the world. Tokyo also has modern theater—in somewhat limited choices, to be sure, unless you can follow dialogue in Japanese, but Western repertory companies can always find receptive audiences here for plays in English. And it doesn't take long for a hit show from New York or London to open. Musicals such as *Mamma Mia!* have found enormous popularity here.

Among about 10 professional dance troupes in Japan, the best known are the New National Ballet, which usually performs at the New National Theater, and the K-Ballet Company and the Tokyo Ballet, both of which stage performances at the Bunka Kaikan in Ueno and Orchard Hall of the Bunkamura complex in Shibuya. Tokyo has plenty of venues for opera, and few groups to perform in them, so touring companies like the Metropolitan, the Bolshoi, Sadler's Wells, and the Bayerische Staatsoper find Tokyo a very compelling venue—as well they might when even seats at ¥30,000 or more sell out far in advance.

Tokyo movie theaters screen a broad range of films—everything from big Asian hits to American blockbusters and Oscar nominees. The diversity brought by smaller distributors and an increased appetite for Korean, Middle Eastern, South American, and Aussie cinema have helped develop vibrant small theaters that cater to art-house fans. New multiplexes have also brought new screens to the capital, providing a more comfortable film-going experience than some of the older Japanese theaters.

**TICKETS Ticket Pia.** ✉ *2–18–9 Kaminarimon, Taito-ku, Tokyo* ☎ *0570/02–9111, 03/5774–5200 customer service center* ⊕ *smash-jpn.com/ticket.*

# Restaurants

Tokyo is undoubtedly one of the most exciting dining cities in the world. Seasonal ingredients reign supreme here, and there's an emphasis on freshness. Locals have embraced outside culinary styles with gusto.

Although newer restaurants targeting younger diners strive for authenticity in everything from New York–style bagels to Neapolitan pizza, it is still not uncommon to see menus serving East-meets-West concoctions such as spaghetti topped with cod roe and shredded seaweed. That said, the city's best French and Italian establishments can hold their own on a global scale. Naturally there's also excellent Japanese cuisine available throughout the city, ranging from traditional to nouveau, which can be shockingly expensive.

But not every meal in the city will drain your finances—the current rage is all about *B-kyu gurume* (B-class gourmet), restaurants that fill the gap between nationwide chains and fine cuisine, serving tasty Japanese and Asian food without the extra frills of tablecloths and lacquerware. All department stores and most skyscrapers have at least one floor of restaurants that are accessible, affordable, and reputable.

Asakusa is known for its tempura, and Tsukiji prides itself on its fresh sashimi, which is available in excellent quality throughout the city. Ramen is a passion for many locals, who travel across town or stand in line for an hour in order to sit at the counter of a shop rumored to have the perfect balance of noodles and broth. Even the neighborhood convenience stores will offer colorful salads, sandwiches, and a selection of beer and sake. There have been good and affordable Indian and Chinese restaurants in the city for decades. As a result of increased travel by the Japanese to more exotic locations, Thai, Vietnamese, and Turkish restaurants have popped up around the city.

■ TIP➔ **When in doubt, note that Tokyo's top-rated international hotels also have some of the city's best places to eat and drink.**

*Restaurant reviews are listed in alphabetical order within neighborhood. Prices in the reviews are the average cost of a main course at dinner or, if dinner is not served, at lunch. Restaurant reviews have been shortened. For full information, visit Fodors.com.*

## What It Costs in Yen

| $ | $$ | $$$ | $$$$ |
|---|---|---|---|
| **RESTAURANTS** | | | |
| under ¥1,500 | ¥1,500–¥3,000 | ¥3,001–¥5,000 | over ¥5,000 |

# Shopping

Tokyo is Japan's showcase. The crazy clothing styles, obscure electronics, and new games found here are capable of setting trends for the rest of the country—and perhaps the rest of Asia, and even Europe and America.

Part of the Tokyo shopping experience is simply to observe, and on Saturday especially, in districts like the Ginza and Shinjuku, you will notice that the Japanese approach to shopping can be nothing short of feverish. With brilliantly applied color, balance of form, and superb workmanship, crafts items can be exquisite and well worth the price you'll pay.

In larger stores customers are greeted with a bow. There's a saying in Japan: "o-kyaku-sama wa kami-sama" ("the customer is a god"). And since the competition for your business is fierce, people do take it to heart.

Horror stories abound about prices in Japan—and some of them are true. Yes, European labels can cost a fortune here, but did you really travel all the way to Tokyo to buy an outfit that would be cheaper in the designer mall at home? True, a gift-wrapped melon from a department-store gourmet counter can cost $150. But you can enjoy gawking even if you don't want to spend like that. And if you shop around, you can find plenty of gifts and souvenirs at fair prices.

Credit cards are accepted, although some smaller mom-and-pop shops may still take cash only.

Japan has an across-the-board 10% Value-Added Tax (VAT) imposed on most goods. This tax can be avoided at some duty-free shops in the city (don't forget to bring your passport). It's also waived in the duty-free shops at the international airports, but because these places tend to have higher profit margins, your tax savings there are likely to be offset by the higher markups.

Stores in Tokyo generally open at 10 or 11 am and close at 8 or 9 pm.

# Visitor Information

The Japan National Tourism Organization (JNTO) has an office in Tokyo. The JNTO-affiliated International Tourism Center of Japan also has more than 140 counters and offices nationwide. Look for the sign showing a red question mark and the word "information" at train stations and city centers.

**CONTACT Japan National Tourism Organization.** ✉ *Tokyo* ☎ *03/3201–3331 in Japan, 212/757–5640 in New York, 213/623–1952 in Los Angeles* ⊕ *www. japan.travel/en.*

# When to Go

Spring and fall are the best times to visit. *Sakura* (cherry blossoms) begin blooming in Tokyo by early April, while fall has clear blue skies, albeit punctuated by the occasional typhoon. The short *tsuyu* (rainy season) in June brings humidity and rain that can linger into early July. July and August bring heat, mostly blue skies, and stifling humidity. Winter can be gray and chilly some days, mild and sunny others, with Tokyo and other areas along the coast receiving very little snow. Japanese vacation during three holiday periods: the few days before and after New Year's; Golden Week in early May; and the mid-August week for Obon. Travel's not advised during these times as plane and train tickets book up fast.

# Imperial Palace (皇居近辺)

The Imperial Palace district is the core of Japan's government. It is primarily comprised of the Nagata-cho (surrounding neighborhood), the Imperial Palace (Kokyo-gaien), the Diet (national parliament building), the prime minister's residence (Kantei), and the Supreme Court. The Imperial Palace and the Diet are both important for visitors to see, but the Supreme Court is rather nondescript.

The Imperial Palace was built by the order of Ieyasu Tokugawa, who chose the site for his castle in 1590. The castle had 99 gates (36 in the outer wall), 21 watchtowers (of which 3 are still standing), and 28 armories. The outer defenses stretched from present-day Shimbashi Station to Kanda. Completed in 1640 (and later expanded), it was at the time the largest castle in the world.

The Japanese Imperial Family resides in heavily blockaded sections of the palace grounds. Tours are conducted by reservation only, and restricted to designated outdoor sections, namely, the palace grounds and the East Gardens. While the East Gardens are open to visitors daily, the main grounds are open to the general public only twice a year, on January 2 and December 23 (the emperor's birthday), when thousands of people assemble under the balcony to offer their good wishes to the Imperial Family. The prime minister's residence is only viewable from afar, hidden behind fortified walls and trees.

**Access:** The Imperial Palace is located in the heart of central Tokyo, and the city's other neighborhoods branch out from here. The palace, where the imperial family still resides, is surrounded by a moat that connects through canals to Tokyo Bay and Sumida River (Sumida-gawa) to the east. The best way to

Once the site of the Imperial Palace's innermost defense circles, the East Garden now offers respite in a beautiful setting.

get to the Imperial Palace is by subway. Take the Chiyoda Line to Nijubashimae Station (Exit 6) or the JR lines to Tokyo Station (Marunouchi Central Exit). There are three entrance gates—Ote-mon, Hirakawa-mon, and Kita-hane-bashi-mon. You can also easily get to any of the three from the Ote-machi or Takebashi subway stations.

##  Sights

### Chidorigafuchi National Cemetery
(千鳥ヶ淵戦没者墓苑; *Chidorigafuchi Senbotsusha Boen*)

CEMETERY | High on the edge of the Imperial Palace moat, this cemetery holds the remains of thousands of unknown soldiers and is famous for its springtime cherry blossoms. The adjacent Chidorigafuchi Boathouse rents out rowboats and pedal boats. Only a small part of the palace's outer moat is accessible, but a walk here makes for a refreshing 30 minutes. The entrance to the garden is near Yasukuni Jinja. ⊠ *2 Sanban-cho, Chiyoda-ku, Imperial Palace*

☎ *03/3234–1948* 🚣 *Park free, boat rental from ¥800* 🕐 *Boathouse closed Dec.– Mar.* Ⓜ *Hanzomon and Shinjuku subway lines, Kudanshita Station (Exit 2).*

### ★ Imperial Palace East Gardens
(皇居東御苑; *Kokyo Higashi Gyo-en*)

GARDEN | Formerly part of the grounds of Edo Castle, this garden was claimed for the imperial family after the 1868 Meiji Restoration. Though most of the old castle was torn down or lost to fire, the stone foundations hint at the scale of the country's former seat of power. In the East Gardens you'll find the National Police Agency *dojo* (martial arts hall) and the Ote Rest House; the Museum of the Imperial Collection is next door and features rotating exhibits of imperial household treasures. The Hundred-Man Guardhouse was once defended by four shifts of 100 soldiers each. Past it is the entrance to what was once the *ni-no-ma-ru*, the "second circle" of the fortress. It's now a grove and garden. At the far end is the Suwa Tea Pavilion, an early-19th-century building relocated here from

# Stretch Your Legs

The venue of choice for runners is the **Imperial Palace Outer Garden.** At the west end of the park, Sakurada-mon's (Gate of the Field of Cherry Trees) small courtyard is the traditional starting point for the 5-km (3-mile) run around the palace—though you can join in anywhere along the route. Jogging around the palace is a ritual that begins as early as 6 am and goes on throughout the day, no matter what the weather. Almost everybody runs the course counterclockwise, but now and then you may spot someone going the opposite way.

Looking for a challenge? Japan hosts a number of marathons throughout the year and one of the most famous is the **Tokyo Marathon,** which is held in February. Plan ahead if you're going to sign up, because the registration deadline is at the end of August of the previous year (most of the country's running events require signing up and qualifying far more in advance than their counterparts on other shores). The marathon starts at one of Tokyo's most prominent landmarks, the Tokyo Metropolitan Government Office in Shinjuku-ku, winds its way through the Imperial Palace, past the Tokyo Tower and Asakusa Kaminarimon Gate, and finishes at Tokyo Big Sight Exhibition Center in Koto Ward.

---

another part of the castle grounds. The octagonal tower is the 1966 Tokagakudo Concert Hall. ⊠ *1–1 Chiyoda, Chiyoda-ku, Imperial Palace* ☎ *03/3213–1111* ☜ *Free* Ⓜ *Tozai, Marunouchi, and Chiyoda subway lines, Otemachi Station (Exit C13B).*

### National Diet Building
(国会議事堂; *Kokkai-Gijido*)
GOVERNMENT BUILDING | The Japanese parliament occupies a perfect example of post–World War II Japanese architecture; on a gloomy day it seems as if it might have sprung from the screen of a German Expressionist movie. Started in 1920, construction took 17 years to complete. Guided tours are available most days, but it's best to call ahead to confirm times. The prime minister's residence, Kantei, is across the street; you can try and get a glimpse of it, but it's quite hidden by walls and trees. ⊠ *1–7–1 Nagata-cho, Chiyoda-ku* ☎ *03/5521–7445* ⊕ *www.sangiin.go.jp* ☜ *Free* ⊙ *Closed weekends* Ⓜ *Marunouchi subway line, Kokkai-Gijidomae Station (Exit 2).*

### Ni-ju-bashi Bridge (二重橋)
BRIDGE | Making a graceful arch across the moat, this bridge is surely the most photogenic spot on the grounds of the former Edo Castle. Mere mortals may pass through only on December 23 (the emperor's birthday) and January 2 to pay their respects to the imperial family. The guards in front of their small, octagonal, copper-roof sentry boxes change every hour on the hour—alas, with nothing like the pomp and ceremony at Buckingham Palace. ⊠ *1–7 Chiyoda, Chiyoda-ku* Ⓜ *Chiyoda subway line, Ni-ju-bashi-mae Station (Exit 2).*

### Ote-mon Gate (大手門)
NOTABLE BUILDING | The main entrance to the Imperial Palace East Gardens was in former days the principal gate of Ieyasu Tokugawa's castle. Most of the gate was destroyed in 1945 but was rebuilt in 1967 based on the original plans. The outer part of the gate survived and offers an impressive entrance into the palace's East Gardens. ⊠ *1–1 Chiyoda, Chiyoda-ku* Ⓜ *Tozai, Marunouchi, and Chiyoda subway lines, Ote-machi Station (Exit C10).*

### Yasukuni Shrine

(靖国神社; *Yasukuni Jinja*)

**RELIGIOUS BUILDING** | Founded in 1869, this shrine is dedicated to approximately 2½ million Japanese, Taiwanese, and Koreans who have died since then in war or military service. As the Japanese constitution expressly renounces both militarism and state sponsorship of religion, Yasukuni has been a center of stubborn political debate, particularly since 1978 when a shrine official added the names of several class-A war criminals to the list. Numerous prime ministers have visited the shrine since 1979, causing a political chill between Japan and its close neighbors, Korea and China, who suffered under Japanese colonialism. Despite all this, hundreds of thousands of Japanese come here every year, simply to pray for the repose of friends and relatives they have lost. These pilgrimages are most frenzied on August 15, the anniversary of the conclusion of World War II, when former soldiers and ultra-right-wing groups descend upon the shrine's grounds en masse.

The shrine is not one structure but a complex of buildings that include the Main Hall and the Hall of Worship—both built in the simple, unadorned style of the ancient Shinto shrines at Ise and the Yushukan, a museum of documents and war memorabilia. Also here are a Noh theater and, in the far western corner, a sumo-wrestling ring. Sumo matches are held at Yasukuni in April, during the first of its three annual festivals. You can pick up a pamphlet and simplified map of the shrine, both in English, just inside the grounds.

Refurbished in 2002, the Yushukan presents Japan at its most ambivalent—if not unrepentant—about its more recent militaristic past. Critics charge that the newer exhibits glorify the nation's role in the Pacific War as a noble struggle for independence; certainly there's an agenda here that's hard to reconcile with Japan's firm postwar rejection of militarism as an instrument of national policy. Many Japanese visitors are moved by such displays as the last letters and photographs of young kamikaze pilots, while others find the Yushukan a cautionary, rather than uplifting, experience.

Although some of the exhibits have English labels and notes, the English is not very helpful; most objects, however, speak clearly enough for themselves. Rooms on the second floor house an especially fine collection of medieval swords and armor. Visiting on a Sunday offers a chance to forage at the flea market that runs from morning until sundown. ⌂ *3–1–1 Kudankita, Chiyoda-ku, Imperial Palace* ☎ *03/3261–8326* ⊕ *www.yasukuni.or.jp* ⌁ *Shrine free, Yushukan ¥1,000* Ⓜ *Hanzo-mon and Shinjuku subway lines, Kudanshita Station (Exit 1).*

## 🍴 Restaurants

### Ajanta (アジャンタ)

**$$** | **INDIAN** | In the mid-20th century, the founder of Ajanta came to Tokyo to study electrical engineering. He ended up changing careers and establishing what is today one of the oldest and best Indian restaurants in town. **Known for:** excellent dosa; open late; authentic South Indian cuisine. Ⓢ *Average main: ¥2,000* ⌂ *3–11 Nibancho, Chiyoda-ku* ☎ *03/3264–6955* ⊕ *www.ajanta.com* Ⓜ *Yurakucho Line, Kojimachi Station (Exit 5).*

### Kama-age Udon Sawanoi (釜あげうどん 赤坂澤乃井; *Akasaka Sawanoi*)

**$** | **JAPANESE** | The homemade udon noodles, served in a broth with seafood, vegetables, or chicken, make a perfect light meal or midnight snack. Try the *inaka* (country-style) udon, which has bonito, seaweed flakes, radish shavings, and a raw egg dropped into the hot broth to cook. **Known for:** quick, tasty lunches; lively izakaya-like atmosphere at night; chewy homemade udon noodles. Ⓢ *Average main: ¥1,000* ⌂ *Dear City Akasaka*

*Honkan, 4–2–3 Akasaka, 2nd fl., Mina-to-ku* ☎ *03/3582–2080* ⊕ *akasaka-sawa-noi.com* ⊟ *No credit cards* ⊘ *Closed weekends* Ⓜ *Ginza and Marunouchi subway lines, Akasaka-mitsuke Station (Belle Vie Akasaka Exit).*

### Ninja Tokyo (忍者東京)

$$$$ | **JAPANESE** | **FAMILY** | In keeping with the air of mystery you'd expect from a ninja-theme restaurant, a ninja-costumed waiter leads you through a dark underground maze to your table in an artificial cave. The menu is prix-fixe only, and prices can more than double depending on the set you choose. **Known for:** secret passages; theme restaurant; tableside entertainment. Ⓢ *Average main: ¥10,000* ⊠ *Akasaka Tokyu Plaza, 2–14–3 Nagatacho, Minato-ku* ☎ *03/5157–3936* ⊕ *www.ninja-tokyo.jp* Ⓜ *Ginza and Marunouchi subway lines, Akasaka-mitsuke Station (Tokyu Plaza Exit).*

 ## Hotels

### The Capitol Hotel Tokyu (ザ・キャピトルホテル東急)

$$$$ | **HOTEL** | Everything old is new again: the Capitol, once a boxy 29-floor commercial complex designed by architect Kengo Kuma and run by Hilton, has a long history that includes hosting the Beatles. **Pros:** convenient location; beautiful and spacious pool; no charge for Wi-Fi throughout hotel. **Cons:** government district might not appeal to tourists; the immediate area is very quiet on weekends; pricey. Ⓢ *Rooms from: ¥62,000* ⊠ *2–10–3 Nagatacho, Minato-ku* ☎ *03/3503–0109* ⊕ *www.tokyuhotelsja-pan.com/global/capitol-h* ⤴ *251 rooms* ⦿ *No Meals* Ⓜ *Ginza and Namboku subway lines, Tameike-Sanno Station (Exit 5).*

### Hotel New Otani Tokyo (ホテルニューオータニ東京)

$$$ | **HOTEL** | A bustling complex in the center of Tokyo—restaurants and shopping arcades beneath the sixth-floor lobby swarm with crowds—the New Otani can feel frantic, but its best feature, a spectacular 10-acre Japanese garden, readily visible from the appropriately named Garden Lounge, helps guests find sanctuary. **Pros:** beautiful garden; first-rate concierge; outdoor pool. **Cons:** public areas a bit dated; few sightseeing options within walking distance; complex layout could be off-putting. Ⓢ *Rooms from: ¥39,000* ⊠ *4–1 Kioi-cho, Chiyoda-ku* ☎ *03/3234–5678* ⊕ *www.newotani.co.jp* ⤴ *1479 rooms* ⦿ *No Meals* Ⓜ *Ginza and Marunouchi subway lines, Akasaka-mitsuke Station (Exit 7).*

 ## Shopping

### Yasukuni Jinja Market (靖国神社青空骨董市; *Yasukuni Jinja Aozora Kottou Ichi*)

**ANTIQUES & COLLECTIBLES** | Most Sundays, from sunrise to sunset, antiques hunters can search and explore this flea market, which boasts 30–50 booths run by professional collectors. It's located within the controversial Yasukuni Jinja grounds, so when you're finished shopping, stroll through the shrine that pays respect to dead Japanese soldiers. ⊠ *3–1–1 Kudan-Kita, Chiyoda-ku* ☎ *03/3261–8326* ⊕ *www.yasukuni.or.jp/english/index.html* Ⓜ *Hanzomon and Shinjuku subway lines, Kudanshita Station (Exit 1).*

# Marunouchi (丸の内)

Marunouchi is one of Tokyo's main business districts, making it a good choice for dining and shopping. It is also home to a few notable sights such as Tokyo Station and the Idemitsu Museum of Arts.

**Access:** Marunouchi is best accessed from any of the JR or subway lines that stop at Tokyo Station.

The Tokyo International Forum's glass atrium is the centerpiece of this arts- and culture-oriented building.

# 👁 Sights

## ★ Idemitsu Museum of Arts (出光美術館; *Idemitsu Bijutsukan*)

**ART MUSEUM** | The strength of the collection in these four spacious, well-designed rooms lies in the Tang- and Song-dynasty Chinese porcelain and in the Japanese ceramics—including works by Nonomura Ninsei and Ogata Kenzan. On display are masterpieces of Old Seto, Oribe, Old Kutani, Karatsu, and Kakiemon ware. The museum also houses outstanding examples of Zen painting and calligraphy, wood-block prints, and genre paintings of the Edo period. Of special interest to scholars is the resource collection of shards from virtually every pottery-making culture of the ancient world. The museum is on the ninth floor of the Teikoku Gekijo building, which looks down upon the lavish Imperial Garden. Check ahead on the website to see if reservations are required when you plan to visit. ⊠ *Teigeki Bldg. 9F; 3–1–1 Marunouchi, Chiyoda-ku* ☎ *03/5777–8600* ⊕ *idemitsu-museum.or.jp/en* 🏷 *¥1,200*

🕐 *Closed Mon.* Ⓜ *Yurakucho subway line, Yurakucho Station (Exit B3); Yamanote Line, Yurakucho Station.*

## Tokyo International Forum (東京国際フォーラム; *Tokyo Kokusai Foramu*)

**PLAZA/SQUARE** | This postmodern masterpiece, the work of Uruguay-born American architect Rafael Viñoly, is the first major convention and art center of its kind in Tokyo. Viñoly's design was selected in a 1989 competition that drew nearly 400 entries from 50 countries. The plaza of the Forum is that rarest of Tokyo rarities: civilized open space. There's a long central courtyard with comfortable benches shaded by trees, the setting for an antiques flea market the first and third Sunday of each month. The Forum itself is actually two buildings. Transit fans should take a stroll up the catwalks to the top, which concludes with a view of the Tokyo Station JR lines. ⊠ *3–5–1 Marunouchi, Chiyoda-ku* ☎ *03/5221–9000* ⊕ *www.t-i-forum.co.jp* Ⓜ *Yuraku-cho subway line, Yuraku-cho Station (Exit A-4B).*

**Tokyo Station** (東京駅; *Tokyo Eki*)
**TRAIN/TRAIN STATION** | This work of Kingo Tatsuno, one of Japan's first modern architects, was completed in 1914, with Tatsuno modeling his creation on the railway station of Amsterdam. The building lost its original top story in the air raids of 1945, but was promptly repaired. In the late 1990s, a plan to demolish the station was impeded by public outcry. The highlight is the historic and luxurious Tokyo Station Hotel, on the second and third floors. The area around the station is increasingly popular for dining, shopping, and entertainment. ⊠ *1–9–1 Marunouchi, Chiyoda-ku* Ⓜ *Marunouchi subway line and JR lines.*

## 🍴 Restaurants

★ **Andy's Shin Hinomoto** (新日の基)
$$ | **JAPANESE** | Also known as "Andy's," this izakaya is located directly under the tracks of the Yamanote Line, making the wooden interior shudder each time a train passes overhead. It's a favorite with local and foreign journalists and is actually run by a Brit, Andy, who travels to the seafood market every morning to buy seafood. **Known for:** expansive menu; cozy, lively atmosphere; favorite among Tokyo expats. Ⓢ *Average main: ¥3,000* ⊠ *2–4–4 Yurakucho, Chiyoda-ku* ☎ *03/3214–8021* ⊕ *shin-hinomoto.com* ▭ *No credit cards* ⊗ *Closed Sun. No lunch* Ⓜ *JR Yurakucho Station (Hibiya Exit); Hibiya, Chiyoda, and Mita subway lines, Hibiya Station (Exits A2 and A6).*

**Heichinrou Hibiya** (聘珍樓日比谷店)
$$$$ | **CHINESE** | A short walk from the Imperial Hotel, the Hibiya branch of one of Yokohama's oldest and best Chinese restaurants commands a spectacular view of the Imperial Palace grounds from 28 floors up. Call ahead to reserve a table by the window. **Known for:** lush, classic decor; a popular venue for power lunches; kaisen ryori, a banquet of steamed seafood. Ⓢ *Average main: ¥13,000* ⊠ *Fukoku Seimei Bldg., 2–2–2 Uchisaiwai-cho,* 28th fl., Chiyoda-ku ☎ 03/3508–0555 ⊕ *www.heichin.com* ⊗ *Closed Sun.* Ⓜ *Mita Line, Uchisaiwai-cho Station (Exit A6).*

★ **Robata Honten** (炉端本店)
$$$ | **JAPANESE** | Old, funky, and more than a little cramped, Robata is a bit daunting at first, but fourth-generation chef-owner Takao Inoue holds forth here with an inspired version of Japanese home cooking. He's also a connoisseur of pottery and serves his food on pieces acquired at famous kilns all over the country. **Known for:** no menu; dishes served on unique pottery collection; country-style izakaya. Ⓢ *Average main: ¥5,000* ⊠ *1–3–8 Yurakucho, Chiyoda-ku* ☎ *03/3591–1905* ▭ *No credit cards* ⊗ *Closed some Sun. each month. No lunch* Ⓜ *JR Yuraku-cho Station (Hibiya Exit); Hibiya, Chiyoda, and Mita subway lines, Hibiya Station (Exit A4).*

## 🛏 Hotels

★ **Andaz Tokyo Toranomon Hills** (アンダーズ東京)
$$$$ | **HOTEL** | Set in the revitalized Toranomon district, this Hyatt boutique property occupies the top six floors of one of the city's tallest towers and offers chic guest rooms, considered service, an airy spa, and views, views, views. **Pros:** contemporary design with Japanese aesthetics; stylish rooftop bar; swimming pool overlooks the Imperial palace. **Cons:** long corridors on guestroom floors; high fees to use the pool and gym; finding entrance can be troublesome. Ⓢ *Rooms from: ¥59,000* ⊠ *1–23–4 Toranomon, Minato-ku* ☎ *03/6830–1234* ⊕ *www. hyatt.com/en-US/hotel/japan/andaz-tokyo-toranomon-hills/tyoaz* ⌁ *164 rooms* ⦿| *No Meals* Ⓜ *Ginza subway line, Toranomon Station (Exit 1).*

★ **Aman Tokyo** (アマン東京)
$$$$ | **HOTEL** | Mixing modern design with Japanese aesthetics, the Aman Tokyo is more than a hotel; it is an experience in the center of the city. **Pros:** immaculate

service; blend of Japanese aesthetics and modernity; wonderful views. **Cons:** immediate area is busy on weekdays, dead on weekends; Japanese aesthetic too minimalist for some tastes; nearly double the price of other hotels in its class. $ *Rooms from: ¥90,000* ⌫ *The Otemachi Tower, 1–5–6 Otemachi, Chiyoda-ku* ☎ *03/5224–3333* ⊕ *www. amanresorts.com* ⤴ *84 rooms* |○| *No Meals* Ⓜ *Hanzomon, Chiyoda, Tozai, and Marunouchi subway lines, Otemachi Station (Exits C11 and C8).*

### ★ Four Seasons Hotel Tokyo at Marunouchi (フォーシーズンズホテル丸の内東京)

$$$$ | **HOTEL** | A departure from the typical grand scale of most Four Seasons properties, the Marunouchi branch, set within the glistening Pacific Century Place, has the feel of a boutique hotel. **Pros:** convenient airport access; small number of rooms lends the hotel a boutique feel; helpful, English-speaking staff. **Cons:** the only views are those of nearby Tokyo Station; trains are audible from some rooms; high priced. $ *Rooms from: ¥66,000* ⌫ *Pacific Century Pl., 1–11–1 Marunouchi, Chiyoda-ku* ☎ *03/5222–7222* ⊕ *www.fourseasons.com/marunouchi* ⤴ *57 rooms* |○| *No Meals* Ⓜ *JR Tokyo Station (Yaesu South Exit).*

### Imperial Hotel, Tokyo (帝国ホテル)

$$$$ | **HOTEL** | Though not as fashionable or as spanking new as its neighbor, the Peninsula, the venerable Imperial can't be beat for traditional elegance. **Pros:** an old Japanese hotel with a long history; dining options are varied and superb; large rooms. **Cons:** some rooms have dated interiors; new tower building closest to trains can be noisy; layout can be confusing. $ *Rooms from: ¥48,000* ⌫ *1–1–1 Uchisaiwai-cho, Chiyoda-ku* ☎ *03/3504–1111* ⊕ *www.imperialhotel. co.jp* ⤴ *931 rooms* |○| *No Meals* Ⓜ *Hibiya subway line, Hibiya Station (Exit 5).*

### Marunouchi Hotel (丸ノ内ホテル)

$$ | **HOTEL** | Convenience is one reason to choose the Marunouchi Hotel, occupying the upper 11 floors of the Marunouchi Oazo Building and joining Tokyo Station via an underground walkway. **Pros:** convenient airport access; central location; helpful concierge. **Cons:** rooms are smallish; limited dining choices; designed for business travelers. $ *Rooms from: ¥30,000* ⌫ *1–6–3 Marunouchi, Chiyoda-ku* ☎ *03/3217–1111* ⊕ *www.marunouchi-hotel.co.jp* ⤴ *205 rooms* |○| *No Meals* Ⓜ *JR Tokyo Station (Marunouchi North Exit).*

### ★ Palace Hotel Tokyo (パレスホテル東京)

$$$$ | **HOTEL** | This hotel has a handsome, refined look that sets the stage for a luxury experience. **Pros:** deluxe balcony rooms have excellent views; luxurious yet tasteful design; impeccable service. **Cons:** business-traveler focus; regular deluxe rooms are overvalued; on the pricey side. $ *Rooms from: ¥66,000* ⌫ *1–1–1 Marunouchi, Chiyoda-ku* ☎ *03/3211–5211* ⊕ *www.en.palacehoteltokyo.com* ⤴ *290 rooms* |○| *No Meals* Ⓜ *Chiyoda, Tozai, Hanzomon subway lines, Otemachi Station (Exit C13).*

### The Peninsula Tokyo (ザ・ペニンシュラ東京)

$$$$ | **HOTEL** | From the staff in caps and sharp suits, often assisting guests from a Rolls-Royce shuttling to and from Narita, to the shimmering gold glow emitting from the top floors, the 24-floor Peninsula Tokyo exudes elegance and grace. **Pros:** first-class room interiors; luxurious details; wonderful spa. **Cons:** formal service can feel impersonal; high prices; crowded lobby and public areas can detract from the luxury feel. $ *Rooms from: ¥66,000* ⌫ *1–8–1 Yurakucho, Chiyoda-ku* ☎ *03/6270–2888* ⊕ *www. peninsula.com* ⤴ *314 rooms* |○| *No Meals* Ⓜ *JR Yamanote Line, Yuraku-cho Station (Hibiya-guchi/Hibiya Exit); Mita, Chiyoda, and Hibiya subway lines, Hibiya Station (Exits A6 and A7).*

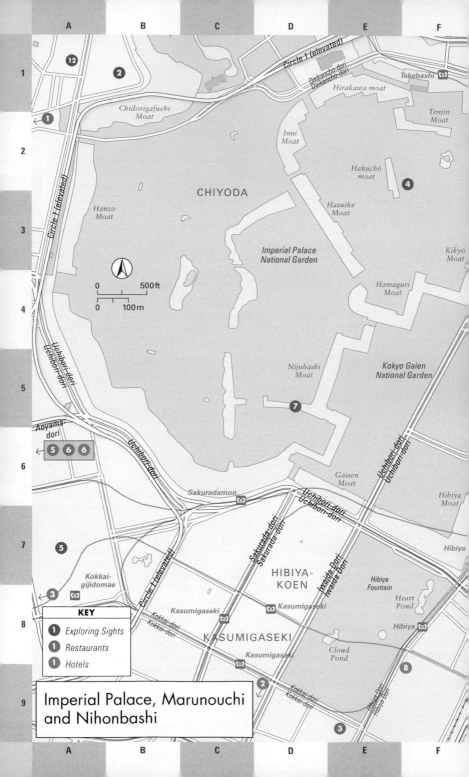

Imperial Palace, Marunouchi and Nihonbashi

## Sights ▼

1 Artizon Museum ..................... **J6**
2 Chidorigafuchi National
  Cemetery ........................... **B1**
3 Idemitsu Museum of Arts......... **G7**
4 Imperial Palace
  East Gardens...................... **F2**
5 National Diet Building............ **A7**
6 Nihonbashi Bridge................. **J3**
7 Ni-ju-bashi Bridge................ **D5**
8 Ote-mon Gate ..................... **G3**
9 Taimeiken Kite Museum .......... **J3**
10 Tokyo International Forum....... **H7**
11 Tokyo Station........................ **I5**
12 Yasukuni Shrine................... **A1**

## Restaurants ▼

1 Ajanta ............................. **A2**
2 Andy's Shin Hinomoto............. **G8**
3 Heichinrou Hibiya.................. **E9**
4 Nihonbashi Yukari ................. **J5**
5 Kama-age Udon Sawanoi ........ **A8**
6 Ninja Tokyo ....................... **A6**
7 Kobata Honten .................... **G8**
8 Signature ......................... **J2**
9 Tapas Molecular Bar ............. **J2**

## Hotels ▼

1 Aman Tokyo ....................... **H3**
2 Andaz Tokyo Toranomon Hills.... **D9**
3 The Capitol Hotel Tokyu.......... **A8**
4 Courtyard by Marriott
  Tokyo Station...................... **J6**
5 Four Seasons Hotel Tokyo at
  Marunouchi ....................... **I6**
6 Hotel New Otani Tokyo........... **A6**
7 Hotel Ryumeikan Tokyo .......... **J4**
8 Imperial Hotel, Tokyo............. **F9**
9 Mandarin Oriental, Tokyo......... **J2**
10 Marunouchi Hotel ................. **I4**
11 Palace Hotel Tokyo ............... **G3**
12 The Peninsula Tokyo ............. **G8**
13 Royal Park Hotel Tokyo .......... **J3**
14 Shangri-La Tokyo ................. **J4**
15 Sumisho Hotel .................... **J3**
16 The Tokyo Station Hotel .......... **I5**

**4**

Tokyo MARUNOUCHI (丸の内)

**Shangri-La Hotel Tokyo**
(シャングリ・ラ ホテル 東京)

$$$$ | **HOTEL** | Boasting high-end luxury, lavish interiors, and superb views of Tokyo Bay and the cityscape from the top 11 floors of Marunouchi Trust Tower Main, Shangri-La Hotel Tokyo's 37-floor building is conveniently located near Tokyo Station. **Pros:** contemporary elegance with an Asian edge; some of Tokyo's most spacious guestrooms; atmospheric Tibetan-inspired Chi Spa. **Cons:** located in a business district; entrance might be hard to find; luxury does not come cheap. [$] *Rooms from: ¥68,000* ✉ *Marunouchi Trust Tower, 1–8–3 Marunouchi, Chiyoda-ku* ☎ *03/6739–7888* 🌐 *www.shangri-la.com* 🛏 *200 rooms* 🍴 *No Meals* [M] *JR Tokyo Station (Yaesu North Exit).*

**The Tokyo Station Hotel**
(東京ステーションホテル)

$$$$ | **HOTEL** | Convenience and nostalgia come together at this hotel, located inside the busy Tokyo train station, a grand building that recently refurbished its redbrick exterior. **Pros:** impeccable service; easy access to shopping; lovely, historic setting. **Cons:** views from some rooms limited; concierge service can be hit or miss; rooms on the small side. [$] *Rooms from: ¥55,000* ✉ *1–9–1 Marunouchi, Chiyoda-ku* ☎ *03/5220–1111* 🌐 *www.tokyostationhotel.jp* 🛏 *150 rooms* 🍴 *No Meals* [M] *JR Line, Tokyo Station (South Exit).*

## Nightlife

### BARS

**Peter**

**BARS** | Like most of Tokyo's high-end hotels, the Peninsula has a high-rise bar. But unlike many staid hotel bars, this 24th-floor spot with a forest of chrome trees, designed by Yabu Pushelberg, is lots of fun. ✉ *Peninsula Tokyo, 1–8–1 Yurakucho, 24th fl., Marunouchi* ☎ *03/6270–2888* 🌐 *www.peninsula.com* [M] *Hibiya and Mita subway lines, Hibiya Station (Exit A6).*

### JAZZ CLUBS

**Cotton Club** (コットンクラブ)

**LIVE MUSIC** | In these intimate and luxurious surroundings you can listen to not only jazz but also a diverse range of music: soul, R&B, J-pop, and world music. The club has such an excellent sound system that musicians such as Ron Carter record here. Fine French cuisine lures music lovers for special nights out and important business entertaining. ✉ *Tokia Bldg., 2–7–3 Marunouchi, 2nd fl., Chiyoda-ku* ☎ *03/3215–1555* 🌐 *bluenotejapan.jp/en/brands/cottonclub* [M] *JR and subway lines, Tokyo Station, directly connected to Tokia Bldg.*

## Performing Arts

### MODERN THEATER

**Takarazuka** (宝塚)

**THEATER** | Japan's all-female theater troupe was founded in the Osaka suburb of Takarazuka in 1913 and has been going strong ever since. Today it has not one but five companies, one of which has a permanent home in Tokyo at the 2,069-seat Takarazuka Theater. Same-day tickets are sold at the box office at either 9:30 am or 10 am for later shows. Advance tickets are available through ticketing agencies and the theater's website. Any remaining tickets are sold at the theater box office. ✉ *1–1–3 Yurakucho, Chiyoda-ku* ☎ *03/5251–2001* 🌐 *kageki.hankyu.co.jp/english/index.html* 🎫 *From ¥3,500* [M] *JR Yamanote Line, Yuraku-cho Station (Hibiya Exit); Hibiya subway line, Hibiya Station (Exit A5); Chiyoda and Mita subway lines, Hibiya Station (Exit A13).*

### FILM

**Toho Cinemas Hibiya**
(TOHO シネマズ日比谷)

**FILM** | With a design that evokes images of the golden days of film, Toho's premier "movie palace" attempts to bring back the days when moviegoing was an experience. With an impressive lobby and one of the largest screens in Tokyo, it is one of the city's best movie theaters.

Arrive a few minutes early to take in the impressive views looking out over Hibiya Park before your show. ⊠ *Tokyo Midtown Hibiya, 1–2 Yurakucho, Chuo-ku* ☎ *050/6868–5068.*

## TRADITIONAL THEATER

### KABUKI

**National Theater of Japan** (国立劇場; *Kokuritsu Gekijo*)

PERFORMANCE VENUE | Architect Hiroyuki Iwamoto's winning entry in the design competition for the National Theater building (1966) is a rendition in concrete of the ancient *azekura* (storehouse) style, invoking the 8th-century Shosoin Imperial Repository in Nara. The large hall seats 1,610 and presents primarily Kabuki theater, ancient court music, and dance. The small hall seats 590 and is used mainly for Bunraku puppet theater and traditional music. Performances are in Japanese, but English-translation headsets are available for many shows. Debut performances, called *kao-mise,* are worth watching to catch the stars of the next generation. Tickets can be reserved until the day of the performance by calling the theater box office between 10 and 6. ⊠ *4–4–1 Hayabusa-cho, Chiyoda-ku* ☎ *03/3265–7411* ⊕ *www.ntj.jac.go.jp/ en* ⓔ *Varies depending on performance* Ⓜ *Hanzo-mon subway line, Hanzo-mon Station (Exit 1).*

# 🛍 Shopping

## BOOKS

**Maruzen** (丸善書店; *Maruzen Shoten*)

BOOKS | FAMILY | In this flagship branch of the Maruzen chain in the Oazo building, there are English titles on the fourth floor as well as art books; the store also hosts occasional art exhibits. ⊠ *1–6–4 Marunouchi, Chiyoda-ku* ☎ *03/5288–8881* Ⓜ *JR Yamanote Line, Tokyo Station (North Exit); Tozai subway line, Otemachi Station (Exit B2C).*

## MALLS AND SHOPPING CENTERS

**Marunouchi Buildings** (丸の内ビル)

SHOPPING CENTER | Bringing some much-needed retail dazzle to the area are these six shopping, office, and dining mega-complexes called Marunocuhi, Shin-marunouchi, Oazu, Iiyo, Brick Square, and Tokia. Highlights include the fifth-floor open terrace on the Marunouchi building, with its view of Tokyo Station, and Bricksquare, which has its own oasislike European garden on the ground floor to rest in between bouts of shopping at the luxury and everyday boutiques. ⊠ *2–4–1 Marunouchi, Chiyoda-ku* ☎ *03/5218–5100* ⊕ *www.marunouchi. com* Ⓜ *Marunouchi subway line, Tokyo Station (Marunouchi Bldg. Exit); JR Yamanote Line, Tokyo Station (Marunouchi Minami-guchi/South Exit).*

**Tokyo Midtown Hibiya** (東京ミッドタウン日比谷)

SHOPPING CENTER | Billed as a luxury entertainment-and-shopping complex, Midtown Hibiya's curvy glass-meets-greenery design is worth a visit for the architecture itself. The complex has six floors of shopping and dining, focusing on high-end and smaller brands. Two floors are devoted to Toho Cinema's premier theater. Outside, the grassy lawn of the sixth-floor garden often hosts events and is a great place to relax outside. ⊠ *1–1–2 Yurakucho, Chiyoda-ku* ☎ *03/5157–1251* ⊕ *www.hibiya. tokyo-midtown.com* Ⓜ *Hibya Station (Exit A11, A12); JR Yurakucho Station (South Exit).*

# Nihonbashi (日本橋)

Tokyo is a city of many centers. The municipal administrative center is in Shinjuku. The national government center is in Kasumigaseki while Nihonbashi is the center of banking and finance.

When Ieyasu Tokugawa had the first bridge constructed at Nihonbashi, he designated it the starting point for the five great roads leading out of his city, the point from which all distances were to be measured. His decree is still in force: the black pole on the present bridge, erected in 1911, is the zero-kilometer marker for all the national highways and is considered the true center of Tokyo.

**Access:** Slightly north of Marunouchi is Nihonbashi, which is also on the Ginza Line and only a few minutes from the bustling Ote-machi Station on the Tozai Line (¥170).

## 👁 Sights

**Artizon Museum** (アーティゾン美術館; *Achizon bijutsukan*)
ART MUSEUM | Formerly the Bridgestone Museum of Art, the Artizon Museum is one of Japan's best private collections of French impressionist art and sculpture and of post-Meiji Japanese painting in Western styles by such artists as Shigeru Aoki and Tsuguji Fujita. The collection, assembled by Bridgestone Tire Company founder Shojiro Ishibashi, also includes works by Rembrandt, Picasso, Utrillo, and Modigliani. The museum also puts on exhibits featuring works from other private collections and museums abroad. ✉ *1–7–2 Kyo-bashi, Chuo-ku* ☎ *03/5777–8600* ⊕ *www.artizon.museum* 💴 *From ¥1,200 depending on exhibition* ⊙ *Closed Mon.* Ⓜ *Ginza subway line, Kyo-bashi Station (Meijiya Exit) or Nihombashi Station (Takashimaya Exit).*

**Nihonbashi Bridge** (日本橋)
BRIDGE | Originally built in 1603, this was the starting point of Edo Japan's five major highways and the point from which all highway distances were measured. Even today one sees signs noting the distance to Nihonbashi. Rebuilt in stone in 1911, the structure's graceful double arch, ornate lamps, and bronze Chinese lions and unicorns are unfortunately marred by an expressway running directly overhead. In the rush to relieve traffic congestion in preparation for the 1964 Olympics, city planners ignored the protestations of residents and preservation groups and pushed ahead with construction. Still, the sight of a modern highway running over the old stone bridge makes for interesting photos and is worth a visit for history buffs. ✉ *1–8 Nihonbashi-muromachi, Chuo-ku* Ⓜ *Tozai and Ginza subway lines, Nihonbashi Station (Exits B5 and B6); Ginza and Hanzomon subway lines, Mitsukoshi-mae Station (Exits B5 and B6).*

**Taimeiken Kite Museum** (たいめいけん凧の博物館; *Tako no Hakubutsukan*)
OTHER MUSEUM | FAMILY | Kite flying is an old tradition in Japan. The collection here includes examples of every shape and variety from all over the country, hand-painted in brilliant colors with figures of birds, geometric patterns, and motifs from Chinese and Japanese mythology. You can call ahead to arrange a kite-making workshop (in Japanese) for groups of children. ✉ *NS Bldg., 1–8–3 Nihonbashi, 2nd fl., Chuo-ku* ☎ *03/3275–2704* ⊕ *www.taimeiken.co.jp/museum.html* 💴 *¥210* Ⓜ *Tozai subway line, Nihonbashi Station (Exit C5); JR Tokyo Station (Yaesu Exit).*

## 🍴 Restaurants

★ **Nihonbashi Yukari** (日本橋ゆかり)
$$$$ | JAPANESE | Anyone looking to experience Japanese haute cuisine in a more relaxed atmosphere should look to this *kappo*-style restaurant, where diners

order and eat at the counter. Third-generation chef—and 2002 Iron Chef champion—Kimio Nonaga displays his artistry in every element of Nihonbashi Yukari's menu. **Known for:** excellent kappo-style lunch sets; chef Nonaga's creative take on Japanese cuisine; affordable for high-end kappo dining. $ *Average main: ¥15,000* ✉ *3–2–14 Nihonbashi, Chuo-ku* ☎ *03/3271–3436* ⊘ *Closed Sun.*

### Signature (シグネチャー)
$$$$ | **FRENCH** | This elegant French restaurant on the 37th floor of the Mandarin Oriental Hotel has wonderful views of the Tokyo skyline as well an open kitchen, where diners can see the masterful chef Nicolas Boujéma and his staff at work. Boujéma has an impressive résumé, having worked in kitchens such as La Tour d'Argent, Le Balzac, and most recently with Pierre Gagnaire. **Known for:** stunning views of the city below; luxurious, modern atmosphere; fine French cuisine with a Japanese flair. $ *Average main: ¥15,000* ✉ *Mandarin Oriental Tokyo, 2–1–1 Nihonbashi, Chuo-ku* ☎ *03/3270–8188* ⊕ *www.mandarinoriental.com/tokyo/dining/signature* Ⓜ *Ginza subway line, Mitsukoshi-mae Station (Exit A7).*

### Tapas Molecular Bar (タパス モレキュラー バー)
$$$$ | **JAPANESE** | Occupying a mysterious place between traditional sushi counter, tapas bar, science lab, and magic show, this award-winning restaurant breaks new ground. In full view of diners, the team of chefs assemble a small parade of bite-size morsels in surprising texture and flavor combinations. **Known for:** exclusive, intimate atmosphere; watching the chefs is almost as good as the food itself; a playful take on fine dining. $ *Average main: ¥16,000* ✉ *Mandarin Oriental Tokyo, 2–1–1 Nihonbashi, Chuo-ku* ☎ *03/3270–8188* ⊕ *www.mandarinoriental.com/tokyo/dining/molecular* ⊘ *No lunch weekdays* Ⓜ *Ginza subway line, Mitsukoshi-mae Station (Exit A7).*

#  Hotels

### Courtyard by Marriott Tokyo Station (コートヤード・バイ・マリオット 東京ステーション)
$$ | **HOTEL** | Situated on the first four floors of the sleek Kyobashi Trust Tower, the Courtyard by Marriott is a convenient option for business travelers. **Pros:** convenient; many nearby dining options; attentive staff. **Cons:** closet space limited; somewhat generic atmosphere; small rooms. $ *Rooms from: ¥20,000* ✉ *2–1–3 Kyobashi, Chuo-ku* ☎ *03/3516-9600* ⊕ *www.cytokyo.com* ⌂ *150 rooms* ⑪ *No Meals* Ⓜ *Ginza subway line, Kyobashi Station (Exit 1); JR lines, Tokyo Station (Yaesu Exit).*

### ★ Hotel Ryumeikan Tokyo (ホテル龍名館東京)
$$ | **HOTEL** | One of the most affordable hotels near Tokyo Station (a mere three-minute walk away), the Ryumeikan is a great option for the business traveler or those making side trips outside the city. **Pros:** great, convenient location; wonderful restaurant; English-speaking staff. **Cons:** rooms can feel small; basic amenities; busy area during the week. $ *Rooms from: ¥24,000* ✉ *1–3–22 Yaesu, Chuo-ku* ☎ *03/3271–0971* ⊕ *www.ryumeikan-tokyo.jp/english* ⌂ *135 rooms* ⑪ *No Meals* Ⓜ *JR Tokyo Station (Yaesu North Exit).*

### ★ Mandarin Oriental, Tokyo (マンダリン オリエンタル 東京)
$$$$ | **HOTEL** | Occupying the top nine floors of the glistening Nihonbashi Mitsui Tower, this hotel is a blend of harmony and outright modernity. **Pros:** wonderful spa and concierge service; nice city views; attractive room interiors. **Cons:** quiet area on the weekends; no pool; pricey. $ *Rooms from: ¥60,000* ✉ *2–1–1 Nihonbashi Muromachi, Chiyoda-ku* ☎ *03/3270–8800* ⊕ *www.mandarinoriental.com/tokyo* ⌂ *178 rooms* ⑪ *No Meals* Ⓜ *Ginza and Hanzomon subway lines, Mitsukoshi-mae Station (Exit A7).*

**Royal Park Hotel Tokyo** (ロイヤルパーク
ホテル)

**$$ | HOTEL |** A passageway connects
this hotel to the Tokyo City Air Terminal,
where you can easily catch a bus to
Narita Airport, making the Royal Park a
great one-night stopover option. **Pros:**
convenient airport access; nice lobby;
warm, friendly service. **Cons:** immediate
area deserted on weekends; beginning to
show its age; not located near downtown. Ⓢ *Rooms from: ¥28,000* ⊠ *2–1–1
Nihonbashi Kakigara-cho, Chuo-ku*
☎ *03/3667–1111* ⊕ *www.rph.co.jp* ⤳ *407
rooms* ⦿ *No Meals* Ⓜ *Hanzo-mon subway line, Suitengu-mae Station (Exit 4).*

**Sumisho Hotel** (住庄ほてる)

**$ | HOTEL |** In a down-to-earth, friendly
neighborhood, this hotel is popular with
budget-minded foreign visitors who prefer
to stay near the small Japanese restaurants and bars of the Ningyo-cho area of
Nihonbashi. **Pros:** nicely priced; friendly
staff; neighborhood restaurants and pubs
have great food for a good price. **Cons:** not
particularly stylish; quiet area on weekends; small rooms and baths. Ⓢ *Rooms
from: ¥11,000* ⊠ *9–14 Nihonbashi-Kobu-
nacho, Chuo-ku* ☎ *03/3661–4603* ⊕ *sum-
isho-hotel.co.jp* ⤳ *83 rooms* ⦿ *No Meals*
Ⓜ *Hibiya and Asakusa subway lines,
Ningyo-cho Station (Exit A5).*

 **Shopping**

## BOOKS

**Yaesu Book Center** (八重洲ブックセンター)

**BOOKS |** English-language paperbacks,
art books, and calendars are available
on the seventh floor of this celebrated
bookstore. ⊠ *2–5–1 Yaesu, Chuo-ku*
☎ *03/3281–1811* Ⓜ *JR Yamanote Line,
Tokyo Station (Yaesu South Exit 5).*

## DEPARTMENT STORES

★ **Mitsukoshi Main Store**
(コレド日本橋; *Mitsukoshi honten*)

**DEPARTMENT STORE |** Founded in 1673 as a
dry-goods store, Mitsukoshi later played
one of the leading roles in introducing

Western merchandise to Japan. It has
retained its image of quality and excellence, with a particularly strong rep-
resentation of Western fashion designers. The store also stocks fine traditional
Japanese goods—don't miss the art gallery and the crafts area on the sixth floor.
With its own subway stop, bronze lions
at the entrance, and an atrium sculpture
of the Japanese goddess Magokoro,
this flagship store merits a visit even if
you're not planning on buying anything.
⊠ *1–4–1 Nihonbashi Muromachi, Chuo-ku*
☎ *03/3241–3311* Ⓜ *Ginza and Hanzo-mon
subway lines, Mitsukoshi-mae Station
(Exits A3 and A5).*

## FOOD

**Yamamoto Seaweed** (山本海苔店;
*Yamamoto Noriten*)

**FOOD |** The Japanese are resourceful in
their uses of products from the sea. Nori,
the paper-thin dried seaweed used to
wrap maki sushi and *onigiri* (rice balls),
is the specialty here. If you plan to bring
some home with you, buy unroasted
nori and toast it yourself at home; the
flavor will be far better than that of the
preroasted sheets. ⊠ *1–6–3 Nihonbashi
Muromachi, Chuo-ku* ☎ *03/3241–0290*
⊕ *www.yamamoto-noriten.co.jp/english*
Ⓜ *Hanzo-mon and Ginza subway lines,
Mitsukoshi-mae Station (Exit A1).*

## MALLS AND SHOPPING CENTERS

**Coredo Nihonbashi** (コレド日本橋)

**MALL |** Unlike other big stores in the
Nihonbashi area, this sparkling mall feels
contemporary thanks to an open layout
and extensive use of glass. Neighboring
it are three more new glittery towers:
Coredo Muromachi 1, 2, and 3, which
fuse traditional housewares stores
with modern fashion boutiques. The
in-house Nihonbashi Tourist Center runs
workshops on everything from dressing
like a Geisha to cooking food. ⊠ *1–4–1
Nihonbashi, Chuo-ku* ☎ *03/3242–0010*
⊕ *mitsui-shopping-park.com/urban* Ⓜ *Ginza, Tozai, and Asakusa subway lines,
Nihonbashi Station (Exit B12).*

**PAPER**

**★ Ozu Washi** (小津和紙)

**STATIONERY** | This shop, which was opened in the 17th century, has one of the largest *washi* showrooms in the city and its own gallery of antique papers. Best to check ahead of time, but they sometimes have classes for just ¥500 on how to make your own washi paper. ✉ *3–6–2 Nihonbashihoncho, Chuo-ku* ☎ *03/3662–1184* 🌐 *www.ozuwashi.net* 🕓 *Closed Sun.* [M] *Ginza and Hanzo-mon subway lines, Mitsukoshi-mae Station (Exit A4).*

**SWORDS AND BLADES**

**Kiya Blades** (木屋本店; *Kiya Honten*)

**OTHER SPECIALTY STORE** | Workers shape and hone blades in one corner of this shop, which carries cutlery, pocketknives, saws, and more. Scissors with handles in the shape of Japanese cranes are among the many unique gift items sold here, and custom-made knives are available, too. Kiya is located in the Coredo Muromachi complex. ✉ *Coredo Muromachi, 2–2–1 Nihonbashi Muromachi, Chuo-ku* ☎ *03/3241–0110* 🌐 *www.kiya-hamono.co.jp* [M] *Ginza subway line, Mitsukoshi-mae Station (Exit A6).*

# Ginza (銀座)

Long known as Tokyo's ritzy shopping district, Ginza was originally the city's banking district, and the district owes its name to the business of moneymaking: in 1912 Ieyasu Tokugawa relocated a plant making silver coins to a patch of reclaimed land east of his castle. The area soon came to be known informally as Ginza (Silver Mint). Today the neighborhood is still home to most of the country's major finance companies, but it's best known as the place where high-end shopping first took root in Japan. Before the turn of the 20th century, Ginza was home to the great mercantile establishments that still define its character. The side streets of Ginza's Sukiya-bashi enclave also have many art galleries, where artists or groups pay for the gallery by the week, publicize their shows themselves, and in some cases even hang their own work.

**Access:** Ginza is east of the Imperial Palace district and East of Tokyo Station. The Ginza and Hibiya subway lines stop at Ginza Station. By walking west from Yuraku-cho Station, Hibiya Park is reachable in 5 min; so is Ginza, in the opposite direction.

## 🍴 Restaurants

**Oshima Ginza** (大志満)

$$$$ | **JAPANESE** | The main draw at Oshima is sampling the *Kaga ryori* cooking of Kanazawa, a small city on the Sea of Japan known for its rich craft traditions. Waitresses dress the part in kimonos of Kanazawa's famous Yuzen dyed silk, and Kutani porcelain and Wajima lacquerware grace the exquisite table settings. **Known for:** excellent seafood from the Sea of Japan; affordable introduction to kaiseki dining; jibuni (duck and potato stew). [$] *Average main: ¥9,000* ✉ *Ginza Core Bldg., 5–8–20 Ginza, 9th fl., Chuo-ku* ☎ *03/3574–8080* 🌐 *www.oshima-site.com* [M] *Ginza, Hibiya, and Marunouchi subway lines, Ginza Station (Exit A5).*

**Rangetsu** (銀座らん月)

$$$$ | **JAPANESE** | Japan enjoys a special reputation for its lovingly raised, tender, marbled domestic beef, and if your budget can bear the weight, Rangetsu serves excellent dishes with this beef as a star ingredient. Try the signature shabu-shabu or sukiyaki course for a primer. **Known for:** over 140 kinds of sake; semiprivate dining rooms; succulent snow crab. [$] *Average main: ¥10,000* ✉ *3–5–8 Ginza, Chuo-ku* ☎ *03/3567–1021* [M] *Marunouchi and Ginza subway lines, Ginza Station (Exits A9 and A10).*

**Sake no Ana** (酒の穴)

$$$ | **JAPANESE** | With roughly 130 varieties of sake from all over Japan available by the carafe, Sake no Ana (literally, "the

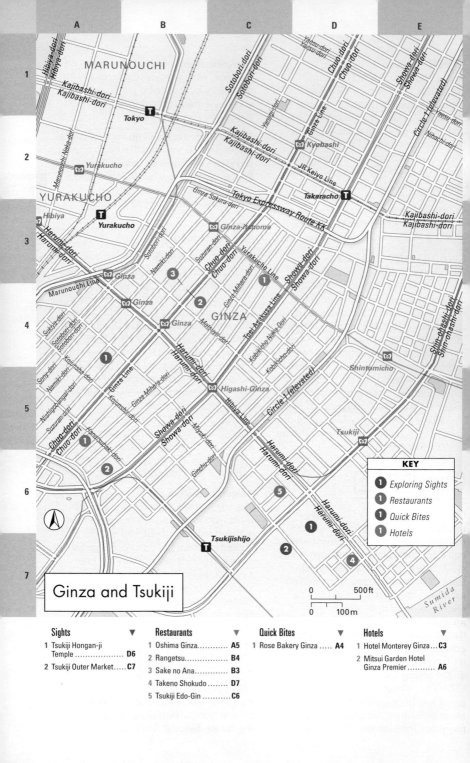

# Ginza and Tsukiji

| Sights ▼ | Restaurants ▼ | Quick Bites ▼ | Hotels ▼ |
|---|---|---|---|
| 1 Tsukiji Hongan-ji Temple .................. **D6** | 1 Oshima Ginza............ **A5** | 1 Rose Bakery Ginza ..... **A4** | 1 Hotel Monterey Ginza... **C3** |
| 2 Tsukiji Outer Market..... **C7** | 2 Rangetsu................ **B4** | | 2 Mitsui Garden Hotel Ginza Premier ........... **A6** |
| | 3 Sake no Ana............. **B3** | | |
| | 4 Takeno Shokudo ........ **D7** | | |
| | 5 Tsukiji Edo-Gin ........... **C6** | | |

# The Power of Tea

Green tea is ubiquitous in Japan; it contains antioxidants twice as powerful as those in red wine that help reduce high blood pressure, lower blood sugar, and fight cancer. A heightened immune system and lower cholesterol are other benefits attributed to green tea.

In Japan pay attention to tea varietals, which are graded by the quality and parts of the plant used, because price and quality runs the spectrum within these categories. For the very best Japanese green tea, take a trip to the Uji region of Kyoto.

*Bancha* **(common tea).** This second-harvest variety ripens between summer and fall, producing leaves larger than those of sencha and a weaker-tasting tea.

*Genmai* **(brown rice tea).** This is a mixture, usually in equal parts, of green tea and roasted brown rice.

*Genmaicha* **(popcorn tea).** This is a blend of bancha and genmai teas.

*Gyokuro* **(jewel dew).** Derived from a grade of green tea called *tencha*

(divine tea), the name comes from the light-green color the tea develops when brewed. Gyokuro is grown in the shade, an essential condition to develop just this type and grade.

*Hojicha* **(panfried tea).** A panfried or oven-roasted green tea.

*Kabusecha* **(covered tea).** Similar to gyokuro, kabusecha leaves are grown in the shade, though for a shorter period, giving it a refined flavor.

*Kukicha* **(stalk tea).** A tea made from stalks by harvesting one bud and three leaves.

*Matcha* **(rubbed tea).** Most often used in the tea ceremony, matcha is a high-quality, hard-to-find powdered green tea. It has a thick, paint-like consistency when mixed with hot water. It is also a popular flavor of ice cream and other sweets in Japan.

*Sencha* **(roasted tea).** This is the green tea you are most likely to try at the local noodle or bento shop. Its leaves are grown under direct sunlight, giving it a different flavor from cousins like gyokuro.

---

sake hole") has its own sake sommelier, Sakamoto-san, who can help diners make a selection. Though most sake-specialty restaurants are open only for dinner, Sake no Ana is also open for lunch. **Known for:** in-house sake sommelier; simple, hearty food; welcoming atmosphere, even for those new to sake. Ⓢ *Average main: ¥5,000* ⊠ *3–5–8 Ginza, Chuo-ku* ☎ *03/3567–1133.*

## ☕ Coffee and Quick Bites

**Rose Bakery Ginza** (ローズベーカリー)
$$ | CAFÉ | Satisfying the need for light, healthy food that is neither raw nor fried,

this airy but rather nondescript bakery and café, which also has branches in Paris and London, serves up a tasty selection of salads, quiches, vegetables, and other deli-style dishes. Although the interior's rows of tables and blank white walls can feel a bit too much like a hip reinterpretation of a school cafeteria, Rose Bakery is a good bet for a quick lunch or pastry while out wandering the Ginza area. **Known for:** flavorful sweets; crisp, fresh salads; lighter fare. Ⓢ *Average main: ¥2,000* ⊠ *6–9–5 Ginza, Ginza Komatsu West Wing 7F, Ginza* ☎ *03/5537–5038* ⊕ *www.rose-bakery.jp* ⊟ *No credit cards.*

## Hotels

**Hotel Monterey Ginza**
(ホテルモントレ銀座)
$ | HOTEL | Yes, the faux-stone exterior that attempts to replicate 20th-century Europe is a bit cheesy, but the Monterey remains a bargain in the middle of Ginza. **Pros:** multiple shopping choices in area; central location; reasonable prices considering the area. **Cons:** rooms are a tad small and a bit outdated; in-hotel dining options are limited; design lacks elegance. *$ Rooms from: ¥12,000 ✉ 2–10–2 Ginza, Chuo-ku ☎ 03/3544–7111 🌐 www.hotelmonterey.co.jp/ginza 224 rooms No Meals M Ginza subway line, Ginza Station (Exit A13).*

**Mitsui Garden Hotel Ginza Premier**
(三井ガーデンホテル銀座プレミア)
$$ | HOTEL | A winning combination—chic and reasonable—this hotel occupies the top of the 38th-floor Nihonbashi Mitsui Tower at the edge of bustling Ginza. **Pros:** affordable; sharp design; convenient location; plenty of nearby shopping. **Cons:** in-hotel restaurant a tad pricey; geared toward business rather than leisure travelers; small rooms. *$ Rooms from: ¥26,000 ✉ 8–13–1 Ginza, Chuo-ku, Chuo-ku ☎ 03/3543–1131 🌐 www.gardenhotels.co.jp 361 rooms No Meals M Ginza subway line, Ginza Station (Exit A3) or JR Shimbashi Station (Ginza Exit).*

## Nightlife

### BARS

**Star Bar Ginza**
BARS | It's often said that Ginza has all the best bars, and Star Bar may be the best of the lot. Owner and bartender Hisashi Kishi is the president of the Japan Bartenders Association, and his attention to detail in the narrow, dark, and calm room is staggering. *✉ 1–5–13 Ginza, B1 fl., Chuo-ku ☎ 03/3535–8005 🌐 starbar.jp/english.shtml M JR Yamanote Line, Yuraku-cho Station (Kyobashi Exit).*

### BEER HALLS AND PUBS

**Ginza Lion** (銀座ライオン)
PUBS | FAMILY | This bar, in business since 1899 and occupying the same stately Chuo-dori location since 1934, is remarkably inexpensive for one of Tokyo's toniest addresses. Ginza shoppers and office workers alike drop by for beer and ballast—anything from Japanese-style fried chicken to spaghetti. *✉ 7–9–20 Ginza, Chuo-ku ☎ 03/3571–2590, 0120/84–8136 for customer service center M Ginza, Hibiya, and Marunouchi subway lines, Ginza Station (Exit A3).*

## Performing Arts

### TRADITIONAL THEATER

### KABUKI

**Kabuki-za Theater** (歌舞伎座)
THEATER | Soon after the Meiji Restoration and its enforced exile in Asakusa, Kabuki began to reestablish itself in this part of the city. The first Kabuki-za was built in 1889, with a European facade. In 1912 the Kabuki-za was taken over by the Shochiku theatrical management company, which replaced the old theater building in 1925; it was damaged during World War II but restored soon thereafter. The most recent iteration of the building retains its classic architecture—until one notices the looming office building coming out of the middle. The interior has been vastly improved, though. Tickets are sold only at the theater's ticket booth. Reservations by phone are recommended. If you want to see what all of the hype is about, this is the place to see a Kabuki show. For a short 15- to 30-minute sampling, get a single-act ticket; the final act usually provides the best spectacle. English Earphone Guides are available for a small fee and provide explanations and comments in English about the performance. *✉ 4–12–15 Ginza, Chuo-ku ☎ 03/3545–6800 🌐 www.kabuki-za.co.jp From ¥3,000 M Hibiya or Asakusa subway line, Higashi-Ginza Station (Exit 3).*

## Shimbashi Enbujo (新橋演舞場)

THEATER | Dating to 1925, this theater was built for the geisha of the Shimbashi quarter to present their spring and autumn performances of traditional music and dance. This is the top spot in Tokyo to see the nation's favorite traditional performing art. The theater is also the home of "Super Kabuki," a faster, jazzier modern version. Seats commonly run ¥3,000–¥16,500, and there's no gallery. ⊠ *6–18–2 Ginza, Chuo-ku* ☎ *03/6745–0888* ⊕ *www.shinbashi-enbujo.co.jp* Ⓜ *Hibiya and Asakusa subway lines, Higashi-Ginza Station (Exit 6).*

## NOH

### Kanze Noh-gakudo (観世能楽堂)

THEATER | This is among the most important of the Noh family schools in Japan, and the current *iemoto* (head) of the school is the 26th in his line. In 2017 Kanze moved to a stylish new theater in Ginza. English-language summaries of the plots are available upon request. ⊠ *Ginza Six Bldg., 6–10–1 Ginza, B3 fl., Chuo-ku* ☎ *03/6274–6579* ⊕ *kanze.net* ⊠ *From ¥6,000 for reserved seats.*

# 🛍 Shopping

## CLOTHING

### ★ Dover Street Market

MIXED CLOTHING | This multistory fashion playhouse is a shrine to exclusives, one-offs, and other hard-to-find pieces from luxury brands all over the world. Curated by Comme des Garçons, the selection may leave all but the most dedicated fashion fans scratching their heads, but the unique interior sculptures and rooftop shrine with Japanese garden alone warrant a visit. ⊠ *6–9–5 Ginza, Chuo-ku* ☎ *03/6228–5080* ⊕ *ginza.doverstreetmarket.com* Ⓜ *Ginza, Hibiya, and Marunouchi subway lines, Ginza Station (Exit A2).*

## Uniqlo (ユニクロ)

MIXED CLOTHING | FAMILY | Customers can wrap themselves in simple, low-priced clothing staples from the company's own brand. This 12-story location is the world's largest, and sells men's, women's, and children's clothing right on the main Ginza drag. ⊠ *6–9–5 Ginza, Chuo-ku* ☎ *03/6252–5181* Ⓜ *Ginza, Hibiya, and Marunouchi subway lines, Ginza Station (Exit A2).*

## DEPARTMENT STORES

### ★ Matsuya (松屋)

DEPARTMENT STORE | On the fourth floor, this gleaming department store houses an excellent selection of Japanese fashion, including Issey Miyake and Yohji Yamamoto. The European-designer boutiques on the second floor are particularly popular with Tokyo's brand-obsessed shoppers. The rooftop terrace is a welcome respite for the weary. ⊠ *3–6–1 Ginza, Chuo-ku* ☎ *03/3567–1211* ⊕ *www.matsuya.com* Ⓜ *Ginza, Marunouchi, and Hibiya subway lines, Ginza Station (Exit A12).*

### Mitsukoshi Ginza (三越銀座)

DEPARTMENT STORE | The Ginza branch of Japan's first department-store chain has been open since 1930 and remains the largest department store in the area, with a sprawling grass-covered terrace on the ninth floor that provides a respite from the shopping bustle. On the third floor is an area called "Le Place" that sells only local designer fashion, and the two basement floors have an impressive selection of delicacies. ⊠ *4–6–16 Ginza, Chuo-ku* ☎ *03/3562–1111* ⊕ *www.mitsukoshi.mistore.jp/ginza.html* Ⓜ *Ginza, Marunouchi, and Hibiya subway lines, Ginza Station (Exits A6, A7, and A8).*

### ★ Muji (無印良品; Mujirushi ryohin)

DEPARTMENT STORE | FAMILY | The new flagship store of this minimalist, design-focused interiors and clothing brand is home to a large selection of furniture, appliances, bedding, and clothes for the whole family. The store also houses a café-bakery, diner, children's play area, and hotel. ⊠ *3–3–5 Ginza, Chuo-ku* ☎ *03/3538–1311* Ⓜ *JR Yamanote Line, Yurakucho subway line, Yurakucho Station (Central Exit); Ginza, Marunouchi, Hibiya subway lines Ginza Station (Exit B4).*

## Wako (和光)

**DEPARTMENT STORE** | This grand old department store is well known for its high-end watches, glassware, and jewelry, as well as having some of the most sophisticated window displays in town. The clock atop the curved 1930s-era building is illuminated at night, making it one of Ginza's more recognized landmarks. ⊠ 4–5–11 Ginza, Chuo-ku ☎ 03/3562–2111 ⊕ www.wako.co.jp Ⓜ Ginza, Marunouchi, and Hibiya subway lines, Ginza Station (Exits A9 and A10).

## ELECTRONICS

### Sukiya Camera (スキヤカメラ)

**CAMERAS & PHOTOGRAPHY** | The cramped Nikon House branch of this two-store operation features so many Nikons—old and new, digital and film—that it could double as a museum to the brand. Plenty of lenses and flashes are available as well. ⊠ 4–3–7 Ginza, Ginza ☎ 03/3561–6000 Ⓜ JR Yamanote Line, Yurakucho Station (Ginza Exit); Ginza, Hibiya, and Marunouchi subway lines, Ginza Station (Exit B10).

## JEWELRY

### Ginza Tanaka (銀座田中)

**JEWELRY & WATCHES** | One of the finest jewelers in Japan was founded in 1892. The store specializes in precious metals and diamond jewelry. It also sells a wide variety of art objects in gold, like those found on Buddhist altars. ⊠ 1–7–7 Ginza, Chuo-ku ☎ 03/5561–0491 ⊕ www.ginza-tanaka.co.jp/en Ⓜ Yurakucho subway line, Ginza 1-chome Station (Exit 7).

### ★ Mikimoto Ginza Main Store (ミキモト銀座本店; Mikimoto Ginza honten)

**JEWELRY & WATCHES** | Kokichi Mikimoto created his technique for cultured pearls in 1893. Since then his name has been associated with the best quality in the industry. Mikimoto's tower in Ginza is a boutique devoted to nature's ready-made gems; the building, like the pearls it holds, dazzles visitors with a facade that resembles Swiss cheese. ⊠ 4–5–5 Ginza, Chuo-ku ☎ 03/3535–4611 ⊕ www.mikimoto.

com Ⓜ Ginza, Hibiya, and Marunouchi subway lines, Ginza Station (Exit C8).

### Tasaki Pearls Ginza Main Store (田崎銀座本店; Tasaki Ginza honten)

**JEWELRY & WATCHES** | Tasaki sells pearls at slightly lower prices than Mikimoto. The brand opened this glittery flagship tower in Ginza that moved them from the old guard into the contemporary big leagues. There's a large collection of pearl and gem items, from costume to bridal and fine jewelry. On the fifth floor is an event space that holds numerous art exhibits. ⊠ 5–7–5 Ginza, Chuo-ku ☎ 03/3289–1111 ⊕ www.tasaki.co.jp Ⓜ Ginza, Hibiya, and Marunouchi subway lines, Ginza Station (Exit A2).

## KIMONOS

### Tansu-ya (たんす屋)

**OTHER SPECIALTY STORE** | This small but pleasant Ginza shop has attractive used kimono, yukata, and other traditional clothing in many fabrics, colors, and patterns. The helpful staff can acquaint you with the somewhat complicated method of putting on the garments. Tax-free locations are scattered throughout the city, including Shibuya, Asakusa, Aoyama, and Shibuya. ⊠ 3–4–5 Ginza, Chuo-ku ☎ 03/3561–8529 ⊕ tansuya.jp Ⓜ Ginza, Hibiya, and Marunouchi subway lines, Ginza Station (Exit A13).

## PAPER

### Itoya (伊東屋)

**CRAFTS** | Completely remodeled in 2015, this huge paper emporium is brimming with locally crafted and imported stationery, much of which is designed to translate traditional motifs onto contemporary office tools. ⊠ 2–7–15 Ginza, Chuo-ku ☎ 03/3561–8311 ⊕ www.ito-ya.co.jp Ⓜ Ginza, Hibiya, and Marunouchi subway lines, Ginza Station (Exit A13).

### Kyukyodo (鳩居堂)

**CRAFTS** | Kyukyodo has been in business since 1663—and in this spacious Ginza location since 1880—selling wonderful handmade Japanese papers, paper

*Continued on page 164*

Shoppers mill around the entrance to Tokyo's Louis Vuitton

 # SHOP TOKYO  By Misha Janette

Tokyo, the most retail-dense city in the world, lures even the most reluctant shoppers with promises of every product imaginable. Travel back in time at department and specialty stores selling traditional ceramics and lacquerware, or leap into the future in Akihabara and other gadget-oriented neighborhoods. Fashionistas watch trends in Harajuku morph before their eyes, while those with more highbrow sensibilities browse the jewelry at stalwarts like Mikimoto.

Each Tokyo neighborhood has its own specialty, style, mood, and type of customer. Local production still thrives in the city's backstreets despite an influx of global chains and mega-corporations. Keep in mind, however, that nearly all of the locally produced goods will cost a pretty penny; the Japanese are meticulous in design and quality, and tend to prefer small-scale production to large output. Here in Tokyo you will find that one-offs and limited-edition items are often the norm rather than the exception.

For clothing, sizing is still the biggest roadblock to really getting the most from Tokyo boutiques. But with the abundance of quirky trends sometimes it's enough just to window-shop.

## WHAT TO BUY

### MANGA

Manga, or Japanese comic books, have had an incredible influence on pop culture around the world. The inherently Japanese-style illustrations are fun to look at, and the simple language is great for studying. Book-Off, a well-known used manga chain, sells comics at rock-bottom prices, sometimes ¥100 each.

### INNERWEAR

The Japanese are known for their electronics, but did you know their textile and fiber industry is also one of the most advanced in the world? The sweat-repelling, heat-conducting, UBAV/UVB-blocking and aloe-vera dispensing underthings available at Tokyo department stores are probably already in every Japanese person's top drawer at home.

### FLAVORED SNACKS

Japan is the land of limited-edition products, and every season brings new, adventurous flavors in finite quantities. All it takes is a trip to the local conve-nience store to find melon- or Sakura-flavored Kit-Kat bars, or sweet Mont Blanc-flavored Pepsi. We dare you to try them.

### PHONE ACCESSORIES

Cell phones and their accoutrement have become a fashion statement all their own. Phone straps, small plastic models that hang from one's phone, are the most popular. They come in all forms, from Asahi beer bottles to Hello Kitty dolls. There are also matching plastic "no peek" sheets that prevent others from spying on your phone's screen.

### HOUSEWARES

Tokyoites appreciate fine design, and this passion is reflected in the exuberance of the city's *zakka* shops—retailers that sell small housewares. The Daikanyama and Aoyama areas positively brim with these stores, but trendy zakka can be found throughout the city. Handmade combs, chopsticks, and towels are other uniquely Japanese treasures to consider picking up while in Tokyo.

### RECORDS

Tokyo's small specialty music stores are a real treat: local music and imports from around the world are usually available on both vinyl and CD. Out-of-print or obscure vinyl editions can run well over ¥10,000, but collectors will find the condition of the jackets to be unmatched.

## SOCKS

As it's customary in Japanese houses to remove one's shoes, socks are more than mere padding between foot and shoe. It's no surprise, then, that the selection of socks goes well beyond black and white. Stripes, polka-dots, Japanese scenery, and monograms are just some of the depictions you'll find at the high-end sock boutiques. The complicated weaving techniques mean they will also cost more than the average cotton pair.

## SAKE SETS

Sake is a big deal here, and the type of sake presented to another can make or break business deals and friendships. Better than just a bottle are the gift sets that include the short sake glasses and oversized bottles in beautiful packaging fit for royalty.

## JEWELRY

Japan has always been known for its craftsmen who possess the ability to create finely detailed work. Jewelry is no exception, especially when cultured pearls are used. Pearls, which have become something of a national symbol, are not inexpensive, but they are much cheaper in Japan than elsewhere.

## WASHLETTE TOILET SEATS

It may seem ludicrous, but the Japanese "washlette" toilet seat is perhaps the best innovation of this millennium. The seats are heated, come with deodorizers, and may even play music to mask any "rude" sounds. Even better, some can be retrofitted to old toilets—just be sure to check your seat measurements before leaving home.

## CHARCOAL

Japanese women have been using charcoal, or *takesumi*, in their beauty routines for centuries, believing it cleans out the pores and moisturizes the skin. Charcoal-infused formulas are used in soaps, cleansers, cremes, and masques, and often are naturally colored pitch-black like squid ink.

## FOLK CRAFTS

Japanese folk crafts, called *mingei*—among them bamboo vases and baskets, fabrics, paper boxes, dolls, and toys—achieve a unique beauty in their simple and sturdy designs. Be aware, however, that simple does not mean cheap. Long hours of labor go into these objects, and every year there are fewer craftspeople left, producing their work in smaller and smaller quantities. Include these items in your budget ahead of time: The best—worth every cent—can be fairly expensive.

## EXPERIENCING JAPANESE DEPATO

The impressive architecture at the Prada flagship matches the designer wares inside.

A visit to a Japanese *depato* (department store) is the perfect Cliff's Notes introduction to Japanese culture. Impeccable service combines with the best luxury brands, gourmet food, and traditional goods—all displayed as enticing eye candy.

These large complexes are found around major train stations and are often owned by the conglomerate rail companies who make their profit when visitors take the train to shop there. The stores themselves commonly have travel agencies, theaters, and art galleries on the premises, as well as reasonably priced and strategically placed restaurants and cafés.

### ARRIVE EARLY

The best way to get the full experience is to arrive just as the store is opening. Err on the early side: Tokyo's department stores are exacting in their opening times. White-gloved ladies and gents bow to waiting customers when the doors open on the hour. Early birds snatch up limited-edition food and goods before they sell out. There's never a dearth of reasons to come: local celebrity appearances, designer Q&A sessions, and fairs.

### ANATOMY OF A DEPATO

The first floors typically house cosmetics, handbags, and shoes, with the next few floors up going to luxury import brands. On many a top floor you'll find gift packages containing Japan's best-loved brands of sake, rice crackers, and other foods. Department stores also typically devote one floor to traditional Japanese crafts, including ceramics, paintings, and lacquerware.

Don't miss the *depachika* (food departments) on the basement levels, where an overwhelming selection of expensive Japanese and Western delicacies are wrapped with the utmost care. More affordable versions come packed deli-style to be taken home for lunch or dinner.

Shibuya's depato attract trendsetters.

## BEST DEPATO FOR...

Most department stores are similar and house the same brands. But some have distinctive characteristics.

**The trendy dresser:** Seibu in Shibuya and Ikebukuro is known for its collection of fashion-forward tenants.

**Emerging designers:** Isetan in Shinjuku oozes style and has ample space on the fourth floor dedicated to up-and-coming designers.

**Gifts:** Shinjuku's Takashimaya is the place to buy souvenirs for discerning friends back home.

**Traditional crafts:** Mitsukoshi in Nihombashi will leave those looking for a bit of Old Japan wide-eyed.

Depato interiors are often dramatic.

## TIPS FOR DEPATO SHOPPING

■ Major department stores accept credit cards and provide shipping services.

■ It's important to remember that, unlike most of the Western world, goods must be purchased in the department where they were found. This goes for nearly every multilevel shop in Japan.

■ Nowadays, most salesclerks speak some English. If you're having communication difficulties, someone will always come to the rescue.

■ On the first floor you'll invariably find a general information booth with maps of the store in English.

■ Some department stores close one or two days a month. To be on the safe side, call ahead.

products, incense, brushes, and other materials for calligraphy. ✉ *5–7–4 Ginza, Chuo-ku* ☎ *03/3571–4429* ⊕ *www. kyukyodo.co.jp* Ⓜ *Ginza, Hibiya, and Marunouchi subway lines, Ginza Station (Exit A2).*

### SWORDS AND KNIVES
#### Token Shibata (刀剣柴田)
**OTHER SPECIALTY STORE** | This tiny, threadbare shop incongruously situated near Ginza's glittering department stores sells expensive well-worn antique swords. They can also sharpen your blade for you. ✉ *5–6–8 Ginza, Chuo-ku* ☎ *03/3573–2801* ⊘ *Closed Sun.* Ⓜ *Ginza, Hibiya, and Marunouchi subway lines, Ginza Station (Exit A1).*

# Tsukiji (築地)

Although the area's most popular attraction—the Tsukiji Wholesale Market (the largest wholesale fish market in the world)—has moved and been replaced by the new Toyosu Fish Market about 2 km (1 mile) to the east, the area still boasts an abundance of market streets and stalls, old sushi restaurants, and one of Tokyo's most famous gardens. Tsukiji is also a reminder of the awesome disaster of the great fire of 1657.

In the space of two days, it killed more than 100,000 people and leveled almost 70% of Ieyasu Tokugawa's new capital. Ieyasu was not a man to be discouraged by mere catastrophe, however; he took it as an opportunity to plan an even bigger and better city, one that would incorporate the marshes east of his castle. Tsukiji, in fact, means "reclaimed land," and a substantial block of land it was, laboriously drained and filled, from present-day Ginza to the bay.

**Access:** The area is best accessed by taking the Hibiya Line to Tsukiji Station.

## ◉ Sights

### Tsukiji Hongan-ji Temple (築地本願寺)
**TEMPLE** | Disaster seemed to follow this temple, which is an outpost of Kyoto's Nishi Hongan-ji. Since it was first located here in 1657, it was destroyed at least five times, and reconstruction in wood was finally abandoned after the Great Kanto Earthquake of 1923. The present stone building dates from 1935. It was designed by Chuta Ito, a pupil of Tokyo Station architect Tatsuno Kingo. Ito's other credits include the Meiji Shrine in Harajuku; he also lobbied for Japan's first law for the preservation of historic buildings. Ito traveled extensively in Asia; the evocations of classical Hindu architecture in the temple's domes and ornaments were his homage to India as the cradle of Buddhism. But with stained-glass windows and a pipe organ as well, the building is nothing if not eclectic. Talks in English are held on the third Saturday of the month at 5:30. ✉ *3–15–1 Tsukiji, Chuo-ku* ☎ *03/3541–1131* ⊕ *www. tsukijihongwanji.jp* ✉ *Free* ⌖ *Daily services at 7 am and 4:30 pm* Ⓜ *Hibiya subway line, Tsukiji Station (Exit 1).*

### ★ Tsukiji Outer Market
(築地場外市場; *Tsukiji jyogai shijo*)
**MARKET** | Enjoying a sushi breakfast at this famous fish market is an integral part of any trip to Tokyo, even now that its famed inner market has been relocated to a nearby island in Tokyo Bay. If you have time for only one market, this is the one to see as the shopkeepers maintain the feeling of the original Tsukiji area. The three square blocks between the former site of Tokyo Central Wholesale Market and Harumi-dori have scores of fishmongers, plus shops and restaurants. Stores sell pickles, tea, crackers and snacks, cutlery (what better place to pick up a professional sushi knife?), baskets, and kitchenware. Hole-in-the-wall sushi bars here have set menus ranging from ¥1,000 to ¥2,500; look for the plastic models of food in glass cases out front. The area includes the row of little

counter restaurants, barely more than street stalls, under the arcade along the east side of Shin-Ohashi-dori, each with its specialty. Come hungry and be sure to stop for *maguro donburi*—a bowl of fresh raw tuna slices served over rice and garnished with bits of dried seaweed. ✉ *Tsukiji 4-chome, Chuo-ku* 🌐 *www.tsukiji.or.jp/english* [M] *Toei Oedo subway line, Tsukiji-shijo Station (Exit A1); Hibiya subway line, Tsukiji Station (Exit 1).*

## 🍴 Restaurants

**Takeno Shokudo** (多け乃食堂)

**$$** | **JAPANESE** | Takeno Shokudo is a neighborhood restaurant that does nothing but the freshest and the best—big portions of it, at very reasonable prices. Sushi and sashimi are the staples, but there's also a wonderful *tendon* bowl with shrimp and eel tempura on rice. À la carte prices are not posted because they vary with the costs that morning in the Toyosu Market. **Known for:** popular with locals; a menu based on what the cooks found in the market that morning; cheap, delicious seafood. [$] *Average main: ¥3,000* ✉ *6–21–2 Tsukiji, Chuo-ku* ☎ *03/3541 8698* 🌐 *tsukijitakeno.owst.jp/en* 💳 *No credit cards* 🕒 *Closed Sun.* [M] *Hibiya subway line, Tsukiji Station (Exit 1); Oedo subway line, Tsukiji-shijo Station (Exit A1).*

**Tsukiji Edo-Gin** (築地江戸銀)

**$$$** | **SUSHI** | In an area that teems with sushi bars, this one maintains its reputation as one of the best. Tsukiji Edo-Gin drapes generous slabs of fish over the vinegared rice rather than perching them demurely on top. **Known for:** sizable portions; one of Tsukiji's best-known sushi restaurants; seafood fresh from the market. [$] *Average main: ¥4,000* ✉ *4–5–1 Tsukiji, Chuo-ku* ☎ *03/3543–4401* 🌐 *www.tsukiji-edogin.co.jp* 💳 *No credit cards* 🕒 *Closed Sun. and early Jan.* [M] *Hibiya subway line, Tsukiji Station (Exit 1); Oedo subway line, Tsukiji-shijo Station (Exit A1).*

## Activities

### TOURS

**Yakatabune Harumiya** (屋形船晴海屋)

**BOAT TOURS** | As during the time of the samurai, cruising in a roof-topped boat, or *yakatabune*, is the perfect means to relax amid bursting fireworks or cherry blossoms. Hosts within the cabin serve multiple courses of tempura and sushi and pour beer, sake and whiskey while the boats cruise past historic bridges and along the riverbanks that make up the bay front. The charm remains intact: guests are treated like royalty and are entertained while floating on the gentle waves of the Sumida or Arakawa River. When the *shoji* (paper blinds) are opened, panoramic views of the illuminated Tokyo nightscape are a sight to behold. Observation decks offer even better viewing opportunities. Boats accommodate groups of 20 to 350, and regular tours run nightly year-round from 7 pm; reserve by email. ✉ *Harumi Josenba, 3-6-1 Harumi, Chuo-ku* ☎ *03/3644–1344* 🌐 *yakatabune-tokyo.com* [M] *Oedo subway line, Kachidoki Station (Exit A3).*

# Shiodome (汐留)

Now a redeveloped business district, Shiodome (literally, "where the tide stops") was once an area of saltwater flats where the Meiji government built the Tokyo terminal in 1872—the original Shimbashi Station—on Japan's first railway line. By 1997, long after the JR had run out of use for the land, an urban renewal plan for the area evolved, and the land was auctioned off. Among the buyers were Nippon Television and Dentsu, the largest advertising agency in Asia.

In 2002, Dentsu consolidated its scattered offices into the centerpiece of the Shiodome project: a 47-story tower and annex designed by Jean Nouvel. With the annex, known as the Caretta Shiodome, Dentsu created an "investment in

Cherry blossoms bloom at Hama Rikyu Garden.

community"—a complex of cultural facilities, shops, and restaurants that has turned Shiodome into one of the most fashionable places in the city.

**Access:** Shiodome is easily accessed by public transport: JR lines and Yurikamome Line at Shimbashi Station, Toei Oedo Line to Shiodome Station, and Asakusa Line and Ginza Line to Shimbashi Station. The connection station to the Yurikamome Monorail, a scenic ride that takes you to Odaiba in approximately 30 minutes, is also here. You can also get around quite easily on foot. There are elevated walkways that connect all the major buildings and subway and train stations.

##  Sights

**Ad Museum Tokyo** (アドミュージアム東京)
OTHER MUSEUM | The Japanese gift for graphic and commercial design comes into historical perspective in these exhibits featuring everything from 18th-century wood-block prints to contemporary fashion photographs and videos. The

museum is maintained by a foundation established in honor of Hideo Yoshida, fourth president of the mammoth Dentsu Advertising Company, and includes a digital library of some 130,000 entries and articles on everything you ever wanted to know about hype. ⊠ *Caretta Shiodome, 1–8–2 Higashi-Shinbashi, B1F–B2F, Minato-ku* ☎ *03/6218–2500* ⊕ *www.admt.jp* ⊠ *Free* ⊗ *Closed Sun. and Mon.* Ⓜ *Toei Oedo subway line, Shiodome Station (Exit 7); JR (Shiodome Exit) and Asakusa and Ginza lines (Exit 4), Shimbashi Station.*

**Hama Rikyu Garden**
(浜離宮庭園; *Hama Rikyu Teien*)
GARDEN | A tiny sanctuary of Japanese tradition and nature that's surrounded by towering glass buildings is a great place to relax or walk off a filling Tsukiji sushi breakfast. The land here was originally owned by the Owari branch of the Tokugawa family from Nagoya, and when a family member became shogun in 1709, his residence was turned into a palace—with pavilions, ornamental gardens,

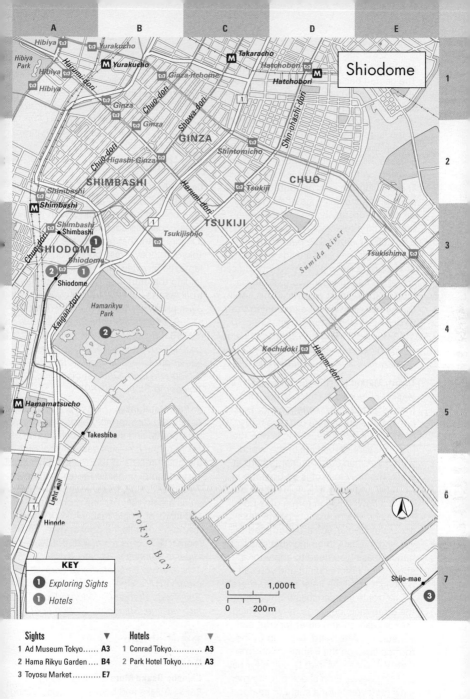

# Shiodome

**Hibiya** · **Yurakucho**
Hibiya Park
Hibiya
Hibiya
**Yurakucho**
**Takaracho** M
Hatchobori M
**Hatchobori**
**Ginza-itchome**
Chuo-dori
Ginza
Ginza
Showa-dori
**GINZA**
Shintomicho
Chuo-Higashi-Ginza
**SHIMBASHI**
Shimbashi
M **Shimbashi**
**CHUO**
Harumi-dori
Tsukiji
Shimbashi
Shimbashi
Shintomicho
**SHIODOME**
Shiodome
**TSUKIJI**
Tsukijishijo
Shiodome
Sumida River
Tsukishima
Kaigan-dori
Hamarikyu Park
Chuo-dori
Kachidoki
Harumi-dori
M **Hamamatsucho**
Takeshiba
Light rail
Hinode
Tokyo Bay
Shijo-mae

## KEY
- ❶ Exploring Sights
- ❶ Hotels

0       1,000 ft
0       200 m

**Sights** ▼
1 Ad Museum Tokyo...... **A3**
2 Hama Rikyu Garden .... **B4**
3 Toyosu Market........... **E7**

**Hotels** ▼
1 Conrad Tokyo............ **A3**
2 Park Hotel Tokyo........ **A3**

pine and cherry groves, and duck ponds. The garden became a public park in 1945, although a good portion of it is fenced off as a nature preserve. None of the original buildings have survived, but on the island in the large pond is a reproduction of the pavilion where former U.S. president Ulysses S. Grant and Mrs. Grant had an audience with Emperior Meiji in 1879. The building can now be rented for parties. The stone linings of the saltwater canal work and some of the bridges underwent a restoration project that was completed in 2009. The path to the left as you enter the garden leads to the "river bus" ferry landing, from which you can cruise up the Sumidagawa to Asakusa. Note that you must pay the admission to the garden even if you're just using the ferry. ✉ *1–1 Hamarikyu–Teien, Chuo-ku* ☎ *03/3541–0200* 🌐 *www.tokyo-park.or.jp/teien/en/hama-rikyu* 🎫 *¥300* Ⓜ *Toei Oedo subway line, Shiodome Station (Exit 8).*

**Toyosu Market** (豊洲市場; *Toyosu Shijo*)
**MARKET** | Opened in October 2018 as the replacement to the legendary Tsukiji Market, the 40-hectare (99 acres) Toyosu Market, like its predecessor, is one the busiest seafood markets in the world, with more than 600 merchants hard at work. The new market is an upgrade in terms of size and modern facilities, but sadly, a downgrade in terms of experience and charm. Visitors get far less access at Toyosu: you are restricted to viewing the early morning auctions from behind glass (you need to apply for a spot online before going) and you can no longer stroll the inner market. There's a fixed route you can follow through the three main buildings, two of which are for seafood, the other for fruit and vegetables. Afterward, head up to the rooftop lawn on the Fisheries Intermediate Wholesale Market Building for bay and city views, then check out the market's restaurants for a sushi or seafood breakfast; some popular Tsukiji restaurants like Sushi Dai have made the move to Toyosu. While this is Toyosu, don't use Toyosu Station as it is a 20-minute walk away; use Shijo-mae Station on the Yurikamome Line. ✉ *6–1 Toyosu, Koto-ku* ☎ *03/3520–8205* 🌐 *www.shijou.metro.tokyo.jp/english/toyosu* 🕒 *Closed Sun.* Ⓜ *Yurikamome Line, Shijo-mae Station.*

## Hotels

**Conrad Tokyo** (コンラッド東京)
**$$$** | **HOTEL** | The Conrad artfully mixes the ultramodern image of Tokyo with traditional Japanese aesthetics, resulting in a luxury hotel that reflects the changing Tokyo of today. **Pros:** modern design; fantastic bay view; fine restaurants. **Cons:** finding the entrance to the elevator is troublesome; charge to use pool and gym; pricey. $ *Rooms from: ¥40,000* ✉ *1–9–1 Higashi-Shinbashi, Minato-ku* ☎ *03/6388–8000* 🌐 *www.conradtokyo.co.jp* *291 rooms* 🍽 *No Meals* Ⓜ *JR Yamanote Line, Shimbashi Station (Shiodome Exit); Oedo subway line, Shiodome Station (Exit 9).*

★ **Park Hotel Tokyo** (パークホテル東京)
**$$** | **HOTEL** | Comfortable beds, large bathrooms, and sweeping panoramas of Tokyo or the bay—it's easy to see why the guest rooms of this reasonably priced "artist" hotel remain a tourist favorite. **Pros:** great value; guest rooms and public areas are stylish; bar has more than 100 kinds of single malt whiskey. **Cons:** few in-room frills; no pool or gym; small rooms. $ *Rooms from: ¥20,000* ✉ *1–7–1 Higashi Shinbashi, Minato-ku* ☎ *03/6252–1111* 🌐 *www.parkhoteltokyo.com* *273 rooms* 🍽 *No Meals* Ⓜ *JR Yamanote Line, Shimbashi Station (Shiodome Exit); Oedo subway line, Shiodome Station (Exit 10).*

## Nightlife

### BARS

**Shinshu Osake Mura** (信州おさけ村)
**BARS** | A sake and beer store specializing in drinks from Nagano prefecture, this standing-room-only place also functions as a very casual bar where you can

sample approximately 50 kinds of sake (pay by the 110-milliliter glass), a dozen craft beers from brewers such as Shiga Kogen, and interesting snacks like spiced cow's tongue. A great option is one of the many reasonably priced three-sake sampler sets. It's tricky to find, being on the first floor of a very dated office building opposite the west exit of Shimbashi Station, but look for the big statue of a *tanuki* (raccoon dog) with extremely large testicles that's outside the building, then go in and turn right. The staff are very friendly and speak enough English to help with the sake choices. Beers are in bottles and cans in the fridge in the tiny backroom; you have to take them to the counter yourself to buy them. ✉ *Shimbashi Ekimae Bldg. 1, 2–20–15 Shinbashi, Minato-ku* ☎ *03/3572–5488* ⊗ *Closed Sun. and Sat. evening* Ⓜ *JR Yamanote Line, Shimbashi Station (West Exit); Ginza subway line, Shimbashi Station (Exit A3).*

# Aoyama (青山) and Harajuku (原宿)

As late as 1960, the area between the Meiji Shrine and the Aoyama Cemetery wasn't a tourist hot spot; the municipal government zoned a chunk of it for low-cost public housing. The few young Japanese people in the area were either hanging around Washington Heights to practice their English or attending the Methodist-founded Aoyama University, and sought entertainment farther south in Shibuya.

When Tokyo won its bid to host the 1964 Olympics, Washington Heights was turned over to the city for the construction of Olympic Village. Aoyama-dori, the avenue through the center of the area, was renovated and the Ginza and Hanzo-mon subway lines were built under it. Suddenly Aoyama became attractive for its Western-style fashion

houses, boutiques, and design studios. By the 1980s the area had become one of the hippest parts of the city. Today the low-cost public housing along Omotesando is long gone, replaced by the glass-and-marble emporia of *the* preeminent fashion houses of Europe: Louis Vuitton, Chanel, Armani, and Prada. Their showrooms here are cash cows of their worldwide empires. Superb shops, restaurants, and amusements in this area target a population of university students, wealthy socialites, young professionals, and people who like to see and be seen.

The heart of Tokyo's youth and street-fashion scene, Harajuku is home to a plethora of stores, boutiques, and cafés. But it isn't only a place for trendy teenagers; Omotesando Dori, the wide, tree-lined avenue stretching from Harajuku to Aoyama, is home to many high-fashion and designer brands. A walk through the neighborhood's winding backstreets also reveals a range of more sophisticated restaurants and cafés. Meanwhile Yoyogi Park and Meiji Shrine offer a respite from Tokyo's crowds and concrete, with a variety of museums and galleries that give a taste of Japanese art and history.

Once a small town on the road from Edo to Kamakura, it was only in the early 20th century that Harajuku started to become a central part of Tokyo. In 1919 the Meiji Shrine was unveiled and Omotesando Dori turned into the bustling boulevard it is today. These two additions brought more visitors, residents, and shops throughout the years. Like much of Tokyo, nearly all of Harajuku was destroyed in the bombings of 1945, with only Meiji Shrine remaining intact. After the war, Harajuku, along with nearby Aoyama, was home to an area called Washington Heights, which housed U.S. military soldiers and several shops catering to these Americans. After the occupation, the area received a boost as the central location of many events in the

1964 Tokyo Olympics. The 2020 Olympics led to a new wave of construction in the area in the hopes of drawing in even more visitors.

**Access:** Harajuku can be accessed from Harajuku Station (JR Yamanote Line) or Meiji JIngu-mae Station (Chiyoda or Fukutoshin subway lines) at the eastern edge of the neighborhood. Omotesando Station (Chiyoda, Ginza, and Hanzomon subway lines) is a 10-minute walk along Omotesando Dori and lies at the border of Harajuku to the east and Aoyama to the west.

# Aoyama

## Sights

**★ Nezu Museum** (根津美術館; *Nezu Bijutsukan*)

**ART MUSEUM** | On view are traditional Japanese and Asian works of art owned by Meiji-period railroad magnate and politician Kaichiro Nezu. For the main building, architect Kengo Kuma designed an arched roof that rises two floors and extends roughly half a block through this upscale Minami Aoyama neighborhood. At any one time, the vast space houses a portion of the 7,400 works of calligraphy, paintings, sculptures, bronzes, and lacquerware that make up the Nezu's collection. The museum is also home to one of Tokyo's finest gardens, featuring 5 acres of ponds, rolling paths, waterfalls, and teahouses. ✉ *6–5–1 Minami-Aoyama, Minato-ku* ☎ *03/3400–2536* 🌐 *www.nezu-muse.or.jp* 🎫 *From ¥1,100* 🕒 *Closed Mon.* [M] *Ginza and Hanzomon subway lines, Omotesando Station (Exit A5).*

## Restaurants

**Darumaya** (だるまや)

**$** | **RAMEN** | The classic bowl of ramen is topped with slices of pork, but Darumaya, in the fashion district of Omotesando, has a slightly different take, topping its noodles with grilled vegetables. In the summertime be sure to order the *hiyashi soba,* a bowl of chilled noodles topped with vegetables and ham in a sesame dressing. **Known for:** refreshing take on ramen; one of few noodle shops in the neighborhood; a quick, affordable lunch in a high-end area. [$] *Average main: ¥950* ✉ *Murayama Bldg., 5–9–5 Minami-Aoyama, 1F, Minato-ku* ☎ *03/3499–6295* 💳 *No credit cards* 🕒 *Closed Sun. and Mon.* [M] *Ginza, Chiyoda, and Hanzomon subway lines, Omotesando Station (Exit B1).*

## Nightlife

### BARS

**Radio** (バー・ラジオ)

**COCKTAIL LOUNGES** | Koji Ozaki is the closest thing Tokyo has to a superstar bartender. This demure septuagenarian, who still works one week per month, has been crafting cocktails for half a century, and he's known for both his perfectionism and creativity. Ozaki designed not only the bar he works behind, but the glasses he serves his creations in (some of the best in the city). All bartenders arrange the bar's flowers. You need to dress up (avoid short pants or flip-flops by all means), and remember, this is a place for quiet relaxation. ✉ *3–10–34 Minami-Aoyama, Aoyama* ☎ *03/3402–2668* 🌐 *www.bar-radio.com* 🕒 *Closed Sun.* [M] *Chiyoda, Ginza, and Hanzomon subway lines, Omotesando Station (Exit A4).*

**Two Rooms**

**COCKTAIL LOUNGES** | Aoyama's dressed-up drinkers hang out on the stylish terrace. Drinks are big, pricey, and modern—think martinis in multiple fresh-fruit flavors such as kiwi. The terrace overlooking the Shinjuku area is particularly comfortable in spring and summer. ✉ *AO Bldg., 3–11–7 Kita-Aoyama, 5th fl., Aoyama* ☎ *03/3498–0002* 🌐 *www.tworooms.jp* [M] *Chiyoda, Ginza, and Hanzomon subway lines, Omotesando Station (Exit B2).*

## JAZZ CLUBS

**Blue Note Tokyo** (ブルーノート東京)

LIVE MUSIC | This premier live jazz venue isn't for everyone: prices are high, sets short, and patrons packed in tight, sometimes sharing a table with strangers. But if you want to catch Pat Metheny and Larry Carlton in a relatively small venue, this is the place. Expect to pay upward of ¥11,000 to see major acts, and ¥6,500 to ¥9,000 for most others. ✉ Raika Bldg., 6–3–16 Minami-Aoyama, Minato-ku, Aoyama ☎ 03/5485–0088 ⊕ www.bluenote.co.jp Ⓜ Chiyoda, Ginza, and Hanzo-mon subway lines, Omotesando Station (Exit A5).

## Performing Arts

### MUSIC

**Kioi Hall** (紀尾井ホール)

CONCERTS | FAMILY | Behind Hotel New Otani stands this relatively small concert venue, which showcases both performances of Western classical music, such as piano and violin recitals, and Japanese works, including shakuhachi flute music. It hosts programs for families to learn how to play such traditional Japanese instruments. ✉ 6–5 Kioicho, Chiyoda-ku ☎ 03/5276-4500 ⊕ www.kioi-hall.or.jp Ⓜ JR, Marunouchi and Nanboku subway lines, Yotsuya Station (Kojimachi Exit); Yurakucho subway line, Kojimachi Station (Exit 2).

## Shopping

### ANTIQUES

**Fuji-Torii** (富士鳥居)

ANTIQUES & COLLECTIBLES | An English-speaking staff, a central Omotesando location, and antiques ranging from ceramics to swords are the big draws at this shop, in business since 1948. In particular Fuji-Torii has an excellent selection of folding screens, lacquerware, painted glassware, and ukiyo-e (woodblock prints). You can also pick up contemporary gifts, such as reading glasses with frames wrapped in traditional fabric. ✉ 6–1–10 Jingumae, Shibuya-ku ☎ 03/3400–2777 ⊕ www.fuji-torii.com ⊙ Closed Tues. and 3rd Mon. of every month Ⓜ Chiyoda and Fukutoshin subway lines, Meiji-Jingumae Station (Exit 4).

**Traditional Crafts Morita** (古民藝もりた; Komingei Morita)

ANTIQUES & COLLECTIBLES | Antiques and new mingei (Japanese folk crafts) are on display alongside a large stock of textiles from throughout Asia. An easy-to-transport gift would be furoshiki, which is rather inexpensive woodblock-printed cloth used as decorative covers in daily life. ✉ 5–12–2 Minami-Aoyama, Minato-ku, Minato-ku ☎ 03/3407–4466 Ⓜ Ginza, Chiyoda, and Hanzomon subway lines, Omotesando Station (Exit B1).

### CERAMICS

**Tatsuya Shoten** (つたや商店)

CERAMICS | Ikebana (flower arrangement) and sado (tea ceremony) goods are the only items sold at this shop, but they come in such stunning variety that a visit is definitely worthwhile. Colorful vases in surprising shapes and traditional ceramic tea sets make unique souvenirs. ✉ 5–10–5 Minami-Aoyama, Minato-ku, Minato-ku ☎ 03/3400–3815 ⊙ Closed 1st and 4th Sun. Ⓜ Ginza, Chiyoda, and Hanzomon subway lines, Omotesando Station (Exit B1).

### CLOTHING

**Bapexclusive Aoyama** (Bapexclusive 青山)

MIXED CLOTHING | Since the late 1990s, no brand has been more coveted by Harajuku scenesters than the BATHING APE label (shortened to BAPE) founded by DJ–fashion designer NIGO. At the height of the craze, hopefuls would line up outside NIGO's well-hidden boutiques and pay ¥7,000 for a T-shirt festooned with a simian visage or Planet of the Apes quote. BAPE has since gone aboveground, with the brand expanding across the globe. You can see what the fuss is all about in this spacious

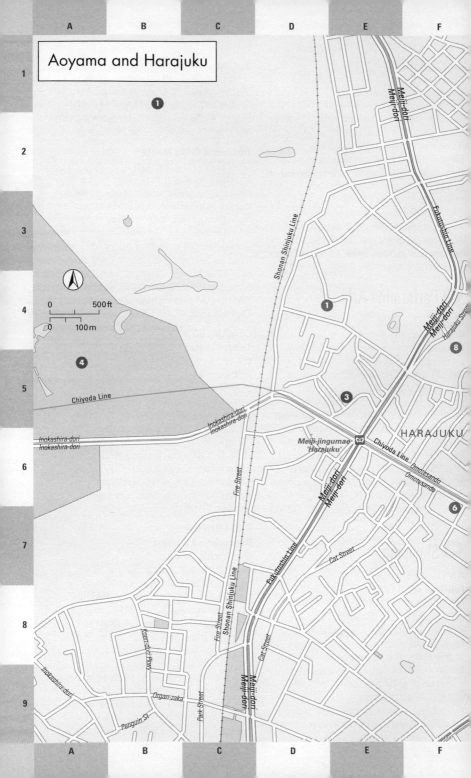

# Aoyama and Harajuku

HARAJUKU

Meiji-jingumae 'Harajuku'

Chiyoda Line
Shonan Shinjuku Line
Fukutoshin Line
Meiji-dori
Inokashira-dori
Harajuku Street
Omotesando
Cat Street
Fire Street
Park Street
Organ-zaka
Penguin St
Kaenzaka Pkwy

0    500 ft
0    100 m

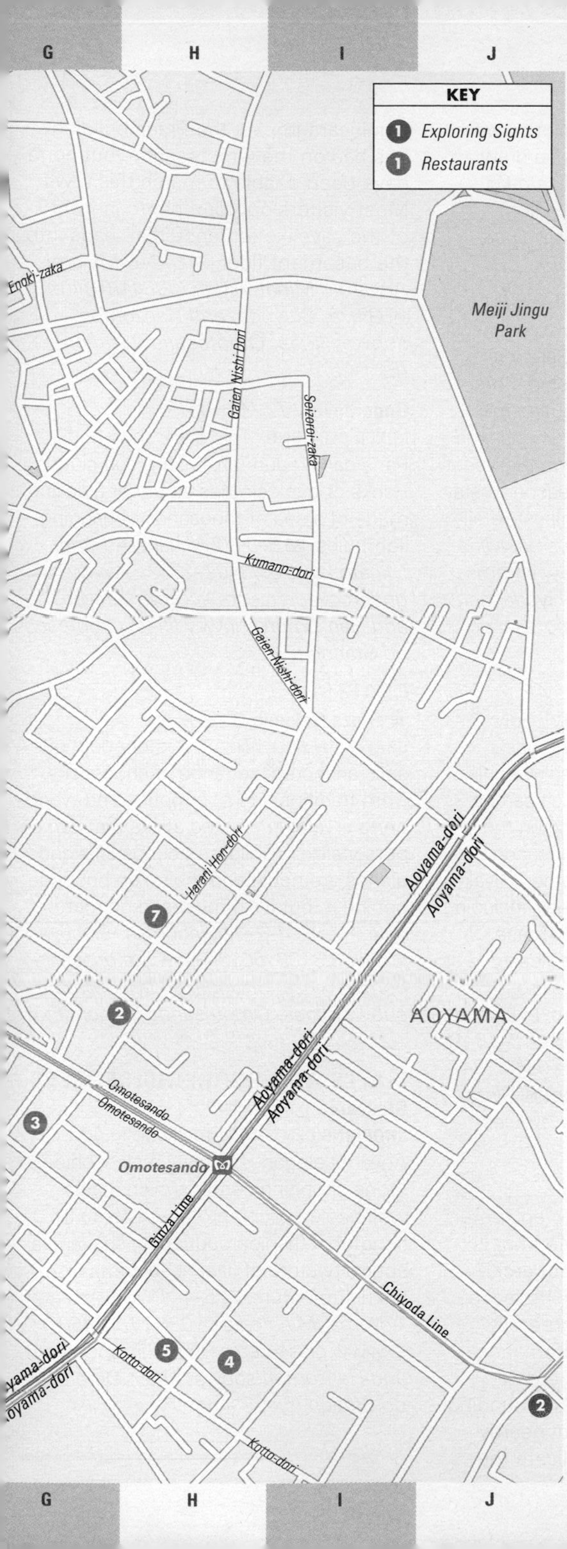

## KEY

1 *Exploring Sights*

1 *Restaurants*

## Sights ▼

1 Meiji Jingu Shrine ................. **B1**
2 Nezu Museum ....................... **J9**
3 Ota Memorial
   Museum of Art ..................... **E5**
4 Yoyogi Park ......................... **A5**

## Restaurants ▼

1 Baird Beer Taproom
   Harajuku ........................... **D4**
2 Barbacoa Churrascaria
   Aoyama ............................. **H7**
3 Brown Rice by
   Neal's Yard Remedies ............. **G7**
4 Cicada ............................... **H9**
5 Darumaya ........................... **H9**
6 Heiroku Sushi
   Shibuya Omotesando .............. **F7**
7 Maisen Aoyama ................... **H6**
8 Sakuratei ........................... **F4**

**4**

**Tokyo** AOYAMA (青山) AND HARAJUKU (原宿)

*Engiki-zaka*

*Meiji Jingu Park*

*Gaien Nishi-Dori*

*Sehoen-zaka*

*Kumano-dori*

*Gaien Nishi-dori*

*Aoyama-dori*

*Aoyama-dori*

*Harajni Hon-dori*

7

2

AOYAMA

*Omotesando*

*Omotesando*

3

*Aoyama-dori*

*Aoyama-dori*

**Omotesando**

*Ginza Line*

*Chiyoda Line*

*oyama-dori*

*Katto-dori*

5

4

*Aoyama-dori*

*Katto-dori*

2

two-story shop with an upstairs conveyor belt of sneakers that is always a draw. ✉ *5–5–8 Minami-Aoyama, Minato-ku* ☎ *03/3407–2145* ⊕ *www.bape.com* Ⓜ *Ginza and Hanzomon subway lines, Omotesando Station (Exit A5).*

### ★ Comme des Garçons (コムデギャルソン)

MIXED CLOTHING | Sinuous low walls snake through Comme des Garçons founder Rei Kawakubo's flagship store, a minimalist labyrinth that houses the designer's signature clothes, shoes, and accessories. Staff members do their best to ignore you, but that's no reason to stay away from one of Tokyo's funkiest retail spaces. ✉ *5–2–1 Minami-Aoyama, Minato-ku* ☎ *03/3406–3951* ⊕ *www.comme-des-garcons.com* Ⓜ *Ginza, Chiyoda, and Hanzomon subway lines, Omotesando Station (Exit A5).*

### ★ Issey Miyake (イッセイミヤケ)

WOMEN'S CLOTHING | The otherworldly creations of internationally renowned brand Issey Miyake are on display at his flagship store in Aoyama, which carries the full Paris line. Keep walking on the same street away from Omotesando Station and also find a string of other Miyake stores just a stone's throw away, including Issey Miyake Men and Pleats Please. At the end of the street is the Reality Lab with a barrage of Miyake's most experimental lines like BaoBao, In-Ei, and incredible origami-like clothing. ✉ *3–18–11 Minami-Aoyama, Minato-ku* ☎ *03/3423–1408* ⊕ *www.isseymiyake.com* Ⓜ *Ginza, Chiyoda, and Hanzomon subway lines, Omotesando Station (Exit A4).*

### ★ Prada

MIXED CLOTHING | This fashion "epicenter," designed by Herzog & de Meuron, is one of the most buzzed-about architectural wonders in the city. Its facade is made up of a mosaic of green glass "bubble" windows: alternating convex and concave panels create distorted reflections of the surrounding area. Many world-renowned, nearby boutiques have tried to replicate the significant impact the Prada building has had on the Omotesando, but none have been unable to match this tower. Most visitors opt for a photo in front of the cavelike entrance that leads into the basement floor. ✉ *5–2–6 Minami-Aoyama, Minato-ku* ☎ *03/6418–0400* Ⓜ *Ginza, Chiyoda, and Hanzomon subway lines, Omotesando Station (Exit A5).*

### Undercover (アンダーカバー)

MIXED CLOTHING | This stark shop houses Paris darling Jun Takahashi's cult clothing. Racks of punk clothes sit under a ceiling made of a sea of thousands of hanging lightbulbs. ✉ *5–3–22 Minami-Aoyama, Minato-ku* ☎ *03/3407–1232* ⊕ *www. undercoverism.com* Ⓜ *Ginza, Chiyoda, and Hanzomon subway lines, Omotesando Station (Exit A5).*

## CRAFTS

### ★ Ginza Natsuno (銀座夏野)

CRAFTS | FAMILY | This two-story boutique sells an incredible range of chopsticks, from traditional to pop motifs, and wooden to crystal-encrusted sticks that can be personalized. Children's chopsticks and dishes are housed in their own boutique behind it, but it's a must-see no matter your age. ✉ *4–2–17 Jingumae, Shibuya-ku* ☎ *03/3403–6033* ⊕ *www.e-ohashi. com* Ⓜ *Ginza, Chiyoda, and Hanzomon subway lines, Omotesando Station (Exit A2).*

## MALLS AND SHOPPING CENTERS

### Glassarea (グラッセリア)

SHOPPING CENTER | Virtually defining Aoyama elegance is this small cobblestone shopping center, which draws well-heeled young professionals to its handful of fashion boutiques, spa, and a specialty store of Japanese crafts from Fukui Prefecture. ✉ *5–4–41 Minami-Aoyama, Minato-ku* ☎ *03/5778–4450* ⊕ *www.glassarea.com* Ⓜ *Ginza, Chiyoda, and Hanzomon subway lines, Omotesando Station (Exit B1).*

### Gyre (ジャイル)

**MALL** | Near the Harajuku end of Omotesando, this mall houses luxury-brand shops such as Chanel and Maison Martin Margiela, three concept shops by Comme des Garçons, and one of only three Museum of Modern Art Design Stores outside New York City. ✉ *5–10–1 Jingumae, Shibuya-ku* ☎ *03/5400–5801* ⊕ *gyre-omotesando.com* Ⓜ *Chiyoda and Fukutoshin subway lines, Meiji-Jingumae Station (Exit 4).*

### Omotesando Hills (表参道ヒルズ)

**SHOPPING CENTER** | Architect Tadao Ando's adventure in concrete is also one of Tokyo's monuments to shopping. Despised and adored with equal zeal, the controversial project demolished the charming yet antiquated Dojunkai Aoyama Apartments along Omotesando Avenue. Six wedge-shape floors include some brand-name heavy hitters (Yves Saint Laurent, Jimmy Choo and Harry Winston) and a wide range of smaller stores whose shelves showcase mid- to high-end shoes and bags. It's worth a stroll to see the latest in Japanese haute couture, and restaurants and cafés can also be found here—but beware of long lines at weekends. ✉ *4–12–10 Jingumae, Shibuya-ku* ☎ *03/3497–0310* ⊕ *www.omotesandohills.com* Ⓜ *Hanzomon, Ginza, and Chiyoda subway lines, Omotesando Station (Exit A2), Chiyoda and Fukutoshin subway lines, Meiji-Jingumae Station (Exit 4).*

# Harajuku

 Sights

### ★ Meiji Jingu Shrine (明治神宮)

**RELIGIOUS BUILDING** | This shrine honors the spirits of Emperor Meiji, who died in 1912, and Empress Shoken. It was established by a resolution of the Imperial Diet the year after the emperor's death to commemorate his role in ending the long isolation of Japan under the Tokugawa Shogunate and setting the country on the road to modernization. Virtually destroyed in an air raid in 1945, it was rebuilt in 1958.

A wonderful spot for photos, the mammoth entrance gates (*torii*), rising 40 feet high, are made from 1,700-year-old cypress trees from Mt. Ari in Taiwan; the crosspieces are 56 feet long. Torii are meant to symbolize the separation of the everyday secular world from the spiritual world of the Shinto shrine. The buildings in the shrine complex, with their curving, green, copper roofs, are also made of cypress wood. The surrounding gardens have some 100,000 flowering shrubs and trees.

An annual festival at the shrine takes place on November 3, Emperor Meiji's birthday, which is a national holiday. On the festival and New Year's Day, as many as 1 million people come to offer prayers and pay their respects. Several other festivals and ceremonial events are held here throughout the year; check by phone or on the shrine website to see what's scheduled during your visit. Even on a normal weekend the shrine draws thousands of visitors, but this seldom disturbs its mood of quiet serenity.

The peaceful Meiji Jingu Gardens (Meiji Jingu Gyoen), where the irises are in full bloom in the latter half of June, is on the left as you walk in from the main gates, before you reach the shrine. Designed by Kengo Kuma, the architect behind Tokyo's new Olympic stadium, the Meiji Jingu Museum displays personal effects and clothes of Emperor and Empress Meiji—perhaps of less interest to foreign visitors than to the Japanese. ✉ *1–1 Yoyogi-kamizonocho, Shibuya-ku* ☎ *03/3379–5511* ⊕ *www.meijijingu.or.jp* ✉ *Shrine free, Meiji Jingu Garden ¥500, museum ¥1,000* Ⓜ *Chiyoda and Fukutoshin subway lines, Meiji-Jingumae Station; JR Yamanote Line, Harajuku Station (Exit 2).*

**Ota Memorial Museum of Art** (太田記念美術館; *Ota Kinen Bijutsukan*)
ART MUSEUM | The gift of former Toho Mutual Life Insurance chairman Seizo Ota, this is probably the city's finest private collection of *ukiyo-e,* traditional Edo-period woodblock prints. Ukiyo-e (pictures of the floating world) flourished in the 18th and 19th centuries. The works on display are selected and changed periodically from the 12,000 prints in the collection, which include some extremely rare work by artists such as Hiroshige, Hokusai, Sharaku, and Utamaro. ⊠ *1–10–10 Jingumae, Shibuya-ku* ☎ *03/3403–0880* ⊕ *www.ukiyoe-ota-muse.jp* 🎟 *From ¥800, depending on exhibit* 🕐 *Closed Mon. and between exhibitions* Ⓜ *Chiyoda and Fukutoshin subway lines, Meiji-Jingu-mae Station (Exit 5); JR Yamanote Line, Harajuku Station (Omotesando Exit).*

**Yoyogi Park** (代々木公園; *Yoyogi Koen*)
CITY PARK | FAMILY | This park is the perfect spot to have a picnic on a sunny day. On Sunday people come to play music, practice martial arts, and ride bicycles on the bike path (rentals are available). From spring through fall there are events, concerts, and festivals most weekends. Although the front half of the park makes for great people-watching, farther along the paths it is easy to find a quiet spot to slip away from the crowds of Harajuku. ⊠ *2–1 Yoyogi-mizonocho, Shibuya-ku* ☎ *03/3469–6081* Ⓜ *Chiyoda and Fukutoshin subway lines, Meiji-Jingumae Station (Exit 2); JR Yamanote Line, Harajuku Station (Omotesando Exit).*

 **Restaurants**

★ **Baird Beer Taproom Harajuku** (ベアードタップルーム原宿)
$$$ | JAPANESE | Founded by American Bryan Baird in 2000, Baird Brewing has become one of the leaders in Japan's now booming craft-beer movement, with a range of year-round brews, such as the hop-heavy Suruga Bay IPA, and creative seasonal beers that use local ingredients such as yuzu citrus and even wasabi. The Harajuku Taproom combines Baird's excellent lineup of microbrews with Japanese *izakaya* (pub) fare like yakitori (grilled chicken skewers), *gyoza* (dumplings), and curry rice. **Known for:** hand-pumped ales on tap; blend of Western and Japanese pub fare; Japanese craft beer. $ *Average main: ¥3,500* ⊠ *No Surrender Bldg., 1–20–13 Jingumae, 2nd fl., Shibuya-ku* ☎ *03/6438–0450* ⊕ *www.bairdbeer.com/taprooms/harajuku* 🕐 *No lunch weekdays* Ⓜ *JR Yamanote Line, Harajuku Station.*

**Barbacoa Churrascaria Aoyama** (バルバッコア青山本店; *Barbacoa Aoyama Honten*)
$$$$ | BRAZILIAN | Carnivores flock here for the all-you-can-eat Brazilian grilled chicken and barbecued beef, which the efficient waiters keep bringing to your table on skewers until you tell them to stop. It comes with a self-serve salad bar and for an extra fee all-you-can-drink beer, wine and other alcohol for two hours. **Known for:** range of wines; excellent salad buffet; meat lover's paradise. $ *Average main: ¥7,500* ⊠ *REIT Omotesando Sq., 4–3–2 Jingumae, Shibuya-ku* ☎ *03/3796–0571* ⊕ *www.barbacoa.jp/aoyama* Ⓜ *Ginza, Chiyoda, and Hanzomon subway lines, Omotesando Station (Exit A2).*

**Brown Rice by Neal's Yard Remedies** (ブラウンライス 食堂)
$$ | VEGETARIAN | Run by Neal's Yard Remedies, this laid-back café has all-natural wooden interiors and natural produce on the menu. If shopping in Harajuku, it's a great place to stop for a healthy Japanese teishoku set, vegetable curry, tofu lemon cake, or other vegan fare. **Known for:** Japanese-style vegan dishes; affordable lunch sets; relaxed atmosphere. $ *Average main: ¥1,700* ⊠ *5–1–8 Jingumae, Shibuya-ku* ☎ *03/5778–5416* ⊕ *www.nealsyard.co.jp/brownrice* Ⓜ *Ginza and Hanzomon subway lines, Omotesando Station (Exit A1).*

★ **Cicada** (シカダ)

$$$ | **MEDITERRANEAN** | Offering up high-end Mediterranean cuisine in an incredibly stylish setting, Cicada's resortlike atmosphere feels a world away from Omotesando's busy shopping streets. In the warmer months, the outdoor patio is especially relaxing. **Known for:** flavorful Mediterranean dishes; stylish bar; terrace dining. [$] *Average main: ¥4,000* ✉ *5–7–28 Minami-Aoyama, Minato-ku* ☎ *03/6434–1255* 🌐 *www.tysons.jp/cicada* [M] *Ginza, Chiyoda, and Hanzomon subway lines, Omotesando Station (Exit B1).*

**Heiroku Sushi Shibuya Omotesando** (平禄寿司)

$$ | **SUSHI** | **FAMILY** | Often, a meal of sushi is a costly indulgence. The rock-bottom alternative is a *kaiten-zushi,* where it is literally served assembly line–style: chefs inside the circular counter place a constant supply of dishes on the revolving belt with plates color-coded for price; just choose whatever takes your fancy as the sushi parades by. **Known for:** fresh, cheap sushi; wide selection of classic and original sushi; essential Japan experience. [$] *Average main: ¥2,000* ✉ *5–8–5 Jingumae, Shibuya-ku* ☎ *03/3498–3968* [M] *Ginza, Chiyoda, and Hanzomon subway lines, Omotesando Station (Exit A1).*

**Maisen Aoyama** (まい泉)

$$$ | **JAPANESE** | Converted from a *sento* (public bathhouse), Maisen still has the old high ceiling (built for ventilation) and the original signs instructing bathers where to change, but now bouquets of seasonal flowers transform the large, airy space into a pleasant dining room. Maisen's specialty is the *tonkatsu* set: tender, juicy, deep-fried pork cutlets served with a tangy sauce, shredded cabbage, miso soup, and rice. **Known for:** hearty lunch sets; succulent deep-fried pork; retro-chic decor. [$] *Average main: ¥3,200* ✉ *4–8–5 Jingumae, Shibuya-ku* ☎ *050/3188-5802* [M] *Ginza, Chiyoda, and Hanzomon subway lines, Omotesando Station (Exit A2).*

## Teenybopper Shoppers

On weekends the heart of Harajuku, particularly the street called Takeshita-dori, belongs to high school and junior high school shoppers, who flock there for the latest trends. Entire industries give themselves convulsions just trying to keep up with adolescent styles. Slip into Harajuku's less-crowded backstreets to find outdoor cafés, designer-ice-cream, and Belgian-waffle stands, and a profusion of stores with names like A BATHING APE and The Virgin Mary—all popular with this younger crowd.

**Sakuratei** (さくら亭)

$$ | **JAPANESE** | At this do-it-yourself restaurant for *okonomiyaki* (a kind of savory pancake made with egg, meat, and vegetables), you choose ingredients and cook them on the *teppan* (grill). Okonomiyaki is generally easy to make, but flipping the pancake to cook the other side can be challenging—potentially messy but still fun. **Known for:** artsy, DIY interior; vegetarian, vegan, and gluten-free options; cooking at your table. [$] *Average main: ¥1,500* ✉ *3–20–1 Jingumae, Shibuya-ku* ☎ *03/3479–0039* 🌐 *www.sakuratei.co.jp* [M] *Chiyoda subway line, Meiji-Jingumae (Harajuku) Station (Exit 5).*

## Shopping

### CLOTHING

★ **Beams** (ビームス)

**MIXED CLOTHING** | Harajuku features a cluster of no fewer than 10 Beams stores that provide Japan's younger folk with extremely hip threads. With branches ranging from street wear to high-end import brands, as well as a record store, uniform gallery, funky "from Tokyo" souvenir shop that sells anime figurines, and one that sells manga alongside designer T-shirts inspired by comic books, shopping here ensures that you or your kids will be properly stocked with the coolest wares from the city. ✉ *3–24–7 Jingumae, Shibuya-ku* ☎ *03/3470–3947* ⊕ *www.beams.co.jp* Ⓜ *JR Harajuku Station (Takeshita-Dori Exit); Chiyoda and Fukutoshin subway lines, Meiji-Jingumae Station (Exit 5).*

### 6% DokiDoki (ロクパーセントドキドキ; *Roku pasento dokidoki*)

**WOMEN'S CLOTHING** | If there's one shop that is the epitome of crazy, *kawaii* (cute) Harajuku fashion, it's this pastel dollhouselike shop on the second floor of a nondescript building. The acid-color tutus and glittery accessories are part of a style called "kawaii anarchy" and may be the most unique shopping experience in Tokyo. The colorful shopgirls alone are an attraction, and if asked nicely, they will happily pose for photos. ✉ *4–28–16 Jingumae, Shibuya-ku* ☎ *03/3479–6116* ⊕ *6dokidoki.com* Ⓜ *Chiyoda and Fuku-toshin subway lines, Meiji-Jingumae Station (Exit 5).*

## MALLS AND SHOPPING CENTERS

### Laforet (ラフォーレ)

**MALL** | The 140 or so stores at this Harajuku mall are where teen trends are born. Although shop genres vary from Gothic Lolita to bohemian chic, they all target fashion-conscious teenagers. Rumor has it that many of the West's top fashion designers still come here to look for inspiration for their next collections. ✉ *1–11–6 Jingumae, Shibuya-ku* ☎ *03/3475–0411* ⊕ *www.laforet.ne.jp/en* Ⓜ *Chiyoda and Fukutoshin subway lines, Meiji-Jingumae Station (Exit 5).*

## TOYS

### ★ Kiddy Land (キデイランド)

**TOYS** | **FAMILY** | The Omotesando landmark commonly regarded as Tokyo's best toy store carries the cutest and most kitschy of everyday goods. This is the leader in making or breaking the popularity of the myriad character goods that Japan spits out seasonally. Like caterpillars with businesspeople faces, some of the items may be odd or surprising, but they're never boring. ✉ *6–1–9 Jingumae, Shibuya-ku* ☎ *03/3409–3431* ⊕ *www.kiddyland.co.jp* Ⓜ *JR Yamanote Line, Harajuku Station (Omotesando Exit); Chiyoda and Fukutoshin subway lines, Meiji-Jingumae Station (Exit 4).*

# Shibuya (渋谷)

One of Tokyo's busiest shopping and entertainment areas, Shibuya is a sometimes overwhelming mix of shops, restaurants, bars, and clubs. Shibuya Scramble is known as one of the world's busiest pedestrian crossings and nearly a tourist sight in its own right. Although most smaller shops tend to be youth-focused, the area's department stores, restaurants, and nightlife draw in people of all ages. Unlike many other parts of Tokyo, Shibuya offers little in way of museums, temples, or traditional culture, but more than makes up for it with its pure energy and atmosphere.

Shibuya gets its name from the samurai family who presided over the area in the 11th century; the family name Shibuya and the land was granted to a Heian period general as a gift for thwarting an attack on the Imperial Palace in Kyoto. For the next six centuries, Shibuya remained a small hamlet of the city. With the opening of Shibuya Station in 1885, the area began to grow, taking off in the 1930s when it became a key terminal linking Tokyo and Yokohama. After being leveled in the war, Shibuya was quickly rebuilt and reestablished its reputation as an entertainment district. In the 1980s and '90s, it was the center of Tokyo's youth and fashion culture as well as the center of the technology industry.

**Access:** Primary access to Shibuya is via the looping JR Yamanote Line, but the Fukutoshin subway line also goes north from Shibuya up through Shinjuku and onto Ikebukuro. Old standbys are the Hanzo-mon and Ginza lines, both of which stop in Omotesando Station (¥170). The Inokashira railway goes toward Kichijoji, home to Inokashira Park, and the Toyoko railway reaches Yokohama in about 30 minutes. Hachiko Exit will be swarmed with people. Just next to it is the "scramble crossing," which leads from the station to the area's concentration of restaurants and shops. Two bus stops provide service to Roppongi to the east and Meguro and Setagaya wards to the west. On Meiji-dori, Harajuku is walkable to the north in 15 minutes, and Ebisu takes about the same going south.

## ◉ Sights

### Myth of Tomorrow
(明日の神話; Asu no Shinwa)
PUBLIC ART | This once-lost mural by avant-garde artist Taro Okamoto has been restored and mounted inside Shibuya Station. Often compared to Picasso's *Guernica*, the 14 colorful panels depict the moment of an atomic bomb detonation. The painting was discovered in 2003 in Mexico City, where in the late '60s it was to be displayed in a hotel but was misplaced following the bankruptcy of the developer. Walk up to the Inokashira Line entrance; the mural is mounted along the hallway that overlooks Hachiko plaza. ⊠ *Shibuya Mark City, 1–12–1 Dogenzaka, Shibuya-ku* Ⓜ *JR Shibuya Station (Hachiko Exit).*

### Statue of Hachiko (ハチ公像; Hachiko zo)
PUBLIC ART | Hachiko is the Japanese version of Lassie; he has even been portrayed in a few heart-wrenching films. Every morning Hachiko's master, a professor at Tokyo University, would take the dog with him as far as Shibuya Station and Hachiko would go back to the station every evening to greet him on his return. In 1925 the professor died of a stroke. Every evening for the next seven years, Hachiko would go to Shibuya and wait there until the last train had pulled out of the station, and as this story of loyalty spread so grew Hachiko's fame. During the dog's lifetime, a handsome bronze statue of Hachiko was installed in front of the station, funded by fans from all over the country. The present version is a replica—the original was melted down for its metal in World War II. This Shibuya landmark is one of the most popular meeting places in the city. Look for the green train car fronting the JR station; the statue is off to the side, where everyone is standing. ⊠ *2–1 Dogenzaka, Shibuya-ku* Ⓜ *JR Shibuya Station (Hachiko Exit).*

### Tokyo Metropolitan Teien Art Museum (東京都庭園美術館; Tokyo-to Teien Bijutsukan)
ART MUSEUM | Once home to Japan's Prince Asaka, this lavish 1930s art deco building hosts a range of fine-arts exhibits throughout the year. With shows ranging from classic paintings to contemporary sculpture, it seems the exhibits are chosen for their ability to harmoniously mix with the building's lush interior. If you visit, be sure to leave time for a stroll through the Teien's Japanese Garden, which is particularly lovely when the leaves change in the fall or during cherry blossom season in April. ⊠ *5–21–9 Shirokanedai, Minato-ku* ☎ *03/3443–0201* ⊕ *www.teien-art-museum.ne.jp* 🎟 *Usually from ¥1,000, but varies by exhibit; garden only ¥200.* ⊗ *Closed Mon.* Ⓜ *JR Yamanote Line or Toei Mita Line, Meguro Station (Central Exit).*

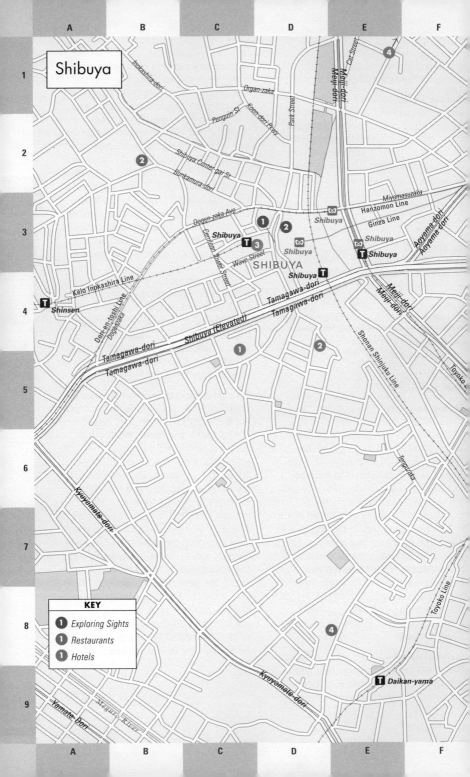

## Sights ▼

1 Myth of Tomorrow ................. **D3**
2 Statue of Hachiko................. **D3**
3 Tokyo Metropolitan
 Teien Art Museum ................. **I9**

## Restaurants ▼

1 Afuri ................................. **I9**
2 Ginza Tempura
 Tenichi Tokyuten .................. **B2**
3 Monsoon Cafe ..................... **I9**
4 Tableaux ............................ **E8**

## Hotels ▼

1 Cerulean Tower Tokyu Hotel ...... **C5**
2 Granbell Hotel Shibuya ........... **D4**
3 Shibuya Excel Hotel Tokyu........ **D3**
4 Trunk Hotel ......................... **E1**

**4**

**Tokyo** SHIBUYA (渋谷)

## What's a Vegetarian to Do? 🍴

Tokyo has had a reputation of being difficult for vegetarians, but as more Japanese opt to forego meat, the number of truly vegetarian and even vegan restaurants is rising. Organic produce has also become more in demand, and many restaurants now serve organic meals that very often are vegetarian. The city's numerous Indian eateries are a safe bet, as are the handful of restaurants that specialize in *shojin ryori*, traditional Zen vegetarian food that emphasizes natural flavors and fresh ingredients without using heavy spices or rich sauces. But you should always inquire when making reservations at these restaurants, as some still use *dashi*, a stock made with smoked skipjack tuna and kelp. The variety and visual beauty of a full-course shojin ryori meal opens new dining dimensions to the vegetarian gourmet. *Goma-dofu*, or sesame-flavored bean curd, for example, is a tasty treat, as is *nasu-dengaku*, grilled eggplant covered with a sweet miso sauce.

Take note that a dish may be described as meat-free even if it contains fish, shrimp, or stock made with meat. Salads and occasionally pastas might come garnished with ham or bacon, so be sure to ask.

If you plan to stay in town long term, check out Alishan (アリサン) (🌐 *store.alishan.jp*), a vegetarian mail-order specialist.

## 🍴 Restaurants

**Afuri**

$ | **RAMEN** | Ramen is the quintessential Japanese fast food: thick Chinese noodles in a bowl of savory broth topped with sliced grilled *chashu* (pork loin). Each neighborhood in Tokyo has its favorite, and in Ebisu the hands-down favorite is Afuri. **Known for:** refreshing shio ramen with yuzu; vegan ramen; quick, affordable meals. [$] *Average main: ¥1,000* ✉ *117 Bldg., 1–1–7 Ebisu, 1st fl., Shibuya-ku* ☎ *03/5795–0750* 💳 *No credit cards* [M] *JR Yamanote Line (Nishi-guchi/West Exit) and Hibiya subway line (Exit 1), Ebisu Station.*

**Ginza Tempura Tenichi Shibuya Tokyuten** (銀座てんぷら天一渋谷東急店)

$$ | **JAPANESE** | Located in Shibuya's Tokyu Department Store, Tenichi is an accessible and relaxed tempura restaurant. The best seats are at the counter, where you can see the chefs work and each piece of tempura will be served piping hot, directly from the oil. **Known for:** friendly service; long lines on weekends; tempura cooked right before your eyes. [$] *Average main: ¥3,000* ✉ *Tokyu Main Building, 2–24–1 Dogenzaka, 8 F, Tokyo* ☎ *03/3477–3891* 🌐 *tenichi.co.jp.*

**Monsoon Cafe** (モンスーンカフェ)

$$ | **ASIAN** | With a dozen locations (including Shinjuku and Omotesando), Monsoon Cafe meets the demand in Tokyo for spicy, primarily Southeast Asian food. Complementing the eclectic pan-Asian food are rattan furniture, brass tableware from Thailand, colorful papier-mâché parrots on gilded stands, Balinese carvings, and ceiling fans. **Known for:** foods from across Asia; relaxed terrace seating; stylish interior. [$] *Average main: ¥2,000* ✉ *15–4 Hachiyama-cho, Shibuya-ku* ☎ *050/5444–9110* 🌐 *monsoon-cafe.jp/daikanyama* [M] *Tokyu Toyoko private rail line, Daikanyama Station (Kita-guchi/North Exit).*

## Tableaux (タブローズ)

**\$\$\$\$** | **ECLECTIC** | This restaurant may lay on more glitz than necessary—the mural in the bar depicts the fall of Pompeii, the banquettes are upholstered in red leather, and the walls are papered in antique gold—but the service is cordial and professional and the food, which is centered on Italian cuisine and U.S. steaks, is superb. The wine list is one of the most varied in town, with more than 200 bottles covering everything from affordable house wines to rarities that will set you back upward of ¥200,000 a bottle. **Known for:** classic high-end European fare; impressive wine list; decor that feels like stepping into a French picture book. $ *Average main: ¥8,000* ✉ *Sunroser Daikanyama Bldg., 11 6 Sarugakucho, 1st fl., Shibuya-ku* ☎ *050/544–5125* ⊕ *www.tableaux.jp* ⊗ *No lunch* 🎩 *Jacket and tie required* Ⓜ *Tokyu Toyoko private rail line, Daikanyama Station (Kita-guchi/North Exit).*

 # Hotels

## Cerulean Tower Tokyu Hotel (セルリアンタワー東急ホテル)

**\$\$\$** | **HOTEL** | Perched on a slope above Shibuya's chaos, the Cerulean Tower has a cavernous yet bustling lobby filled with plenty of attentive, English-speaking staffers. **Pros:** friendly, attentive service; great city views; convenient location. **Cons:** Shibuya is one of Tokyo's more crowded areas; building fronts a very busy street; pricey rates. $ *Rooms from: ¥32,000* ✉ *26–1 Sakuragaokacho, Shibuya-ku* ☎ *03/3476–3000* ⊕ *www.tokyuhotelsjapan.com/global/cerulean-h* ⇨ *411 rooms* ⦿ *No Meals* Ⓜ *JR Shibuya Station (South Exit).*

## Granbell Hotel Shibuya (渋谷グランベルホテル)

**\$\$** | **HOTEL** | Location, location, location— that's the Granbell, and with a minimalist pop-art style to boot. **Pros:** great location; funky, fun design; free Wi-Fi throughout property. **Cons:** neighborhood can be noisy; difficult to find hotel entrance; small rooms. $ *Rooms from: ¥23,000* ✉ *15–17 Sakuragaokacho, Shibuya-ku* ☎ *03/5457–2681* ⊕ *www.granbellhotel.jp/en/shibuya* ⇨ *105 rooms* ⦿ *No Meals* Ⓜ *JR Shibuya Station (West Exit).*

## Shibuya Excel Hotel Tokyu (渋谷エクセルホテル東急)

**\$\$** | **HOTEL** | The key to this unremarkable but very convenient hotel within the towering Mark City complex is access: local shopping and cheap dining options are aplenty, Shinjuku is a five-minute train ride to the north, and the Narita Express departs from nearby Shibuya Station frequently each morning. **Pros:** affordable; convenient location; friendly staff. **Cons:** crowds in the area can be intimidating; few amenities; small, uninspired rooms. $ *Rooms from: ¥27,000* ✉ *1–12–2 Dogenzaka, Shibuya-ku* ☎ *03/5457–0109* ⊕ *www.tokyuhotels.co.jp/shibuya-e* ⇨ *408 rooms* ⦿ *No Meals* Ⓜ *JR Shibuya Station (Hachiko Exit).*

## Trunk Hotel (トランクホテル)

**\$\$\$\$** | **HOTEL** | Located directly between Tokyo's stylish Harajuku, Omotesando, and Shibuya neighborhoods, this boutique hotel brings together local creatives and visitors alike. **Pros:** one of the few unique boutique hotels in Tokyo; excellent location for exploring some of the city's coolest neighborhoods; hotel design, service, and layout foster a sense of community. **Cons:** can be noisy, especially on weekends; expensive for the quality of the rooms; small rooms, even for Tokyo. $ *Rooms from: ¥50,000* ✉ *5–31 Jingumae, Shibuya-ku* ☎ *03/5766–3210* ⊕ *trunk-hotel.com* ⇨ *15 rooms* ⦿ *No Meals* Ⓜ *JR Harajuku; Jingumae (Exit 7); Omotesando (Exit A1); Shibuya (Exit A13).*

#  Nightlife

## BARS

### Akaoni (赤鬼)

**WINE BARS** | The emphasis here is *nama*, unrefined, unpasteurized sake. About 80 kinds from 60 brewing companies are available daily. You may want to sample this unique beverage while in Tokyo, since you won't find it at home: nama is short-lived, too delicate and fresh to transport or export, so it's not widely available overseas. You can accompany your choice with authentic Japanese fare, served here as small bites. Reservations are recommended. ⊠ *2–15–3 Sangenjaya, Shibuya-ku* ☎ *03/3410–9918* ⊕ *www.akaoni39.com* Ⓜ *Denenchofu and Tokyu Setagaya lines, Sangenjaya Station.*

### buri (立喰酒場 buri; *Tachigui Sakaba buri*)

**WINE BARS** | Buri serves up tasty *ji-zake* (local sake) from around Japan in the one-cup style; think sake in a mini mason jar, pairing it with a range of tapas-like servings of sashimi, yakitori, salads, and prosciutto, albeit in a standing-room-only setting. They also have beer on tap. Just a five-minute walk from Ebisu Station, this casual bar fills up quickly on weekends, so it's best to stop in early if you want to grab a table. ⊠ *1–14–1 Ebisu-Nishi, Shibuya-ku* ☎ *03/3496–7744* ⊕ *buri-bar.business.site.*

## DANCE CLUBS

### Shelter

**LIVE MUSIC** | An ever-popular, long-running venue attracts everyone from their late teens to early forties. This is a great place to catch promising local rock bands. Admission runs ¥2,000 to ¥6,000. ⊠ *Senda Bldg., 2–6–10 Kitazawa, B1 fl., Shibuya-ku* ☎ *03/3466–7430* ⊕ *www.loft-prj.co.jp/SHELTER* Ⓜ *Keio Inokashira, Odakyu private rail lines, Shimo-Kitazawa Station (South Exit).*

### Womb

**DANCE CLUBS** | Well-known techno and break-beat DJs make a point of stopping by this Shibuya uberclub on their way through town. The turntable talent, local and international, and four floors of dance and lounge space make Womb Tokyo's most consistently rewarding club experience. Drawing adults from their late twenties to forties, the place gets packed sometimes after 1 in the morning. Entry costs around ¥1,500 to ¥3,500. ⊠ *2–16 Maruyamacho, Shibuya-ku* ☎ *03/5459–0039* ⊕ *www.womb.co.jp* Ⓜ *JR Yamanote Line, Ginza and Hanzomon subway lines, Shibuya Station (Hachiko Exit for JR and Ginza, Exit 3A for Hanzomon).*

## IZAKAYA

### Tatemichiya (立道屋)

**PUBS** | The concrete walls are adorned with rock musicians' autobiographies and posters of the Sex Pistols and Ramones, who also provide the sound track. Artist Yoshitomo Nara has been known to show up here, so if you're lucky, you can drink with him and watch him draw on the walls. ⊠ *B1, 30–8 Sarugakucho, Shibuya-ku* ☎ *03/5459–3431* Ⓜ *Tokyu Toyoko Line, Daikanyama Station.*

## PUBS

### What the Dickens

**PUBS** | This spacious pub in Ebisu feels more authentically British than many of its rivals, thanks partly to a menu of traditional pub grub, including hearty pies. Using aged logs, the second floor feels like a nice tree house. The place hosts regular live music (funk, folk, jazz, rock, reggae—anything goes here) and other events, so it can be very loud, particularly on Friday and Saturday. ⊠ *Roob 6 Bldg., 1–13–3 Ebisu-Nishi, 4th fl., Shibuya-ku* ☎ *03/3780–2099* ⊕ *www.whatthedickens.jp* ⊗ *Closed Mon.* Ⓜ *Hibiya subway line, Ebisu Station (Nishi-guchi/West Exit).*

# Tokyo-Style Nightlife

Tokyo has a variety of nightlife options, so don't limit yourself to your hotel bar in the evenings. Spend some time relaxing the way the locals do at izakaya, karaoke, and live houses—three unique forms of contemporary Japanese entertainment.

## Izakaya

*Izakaya* (literally "drinking places") are Japanese pubs that can be found throughout Tokyo. If you're in the mood for elegant decor and sedate surroundings, look elsewhere; these drinking dens are often noisy, bright, and smoky. But for a taste of authentic Japanese-style socializing, a visit to an izakaya is a must—this is where young people start their nights out, office workers gather on their way home, and students take a break to grab a cheap meal and a drink.

Typically, izakaya have a full lineup of cocktails, a good selection of sake, draft beer, and lots of cheap Japanese and Western food, from sashimi and yakitori to greasy fried chicken; rarely does anything cost more than ¥1,000. Picture menus, which all chain izakaya have, make ordering easy, and because most cocktails retain their Western names, communicating drink preferences shouldn't be difficult.

## Karaoke

In buttoned-down, socially conservative Japan, karaoke is one of the safety valves; almost everyone loosens up when they have a microphone in hand. The phenomenon started in the 1970s when cabaret singer Daisuke Inoue made a coin-operated machine that played his songs on tape so that his fans could sing along. Unfortunately for Inoue, he neglected to patent his creation, thereby failing to cash in as karaoke became one of Japan's favorite pastimes. Nowadays it's the finale of many an office outing, a cheap daytime activity for teens, and a surprisingly popular destination for dates.

Unlike most karaoke bars in the United States, in Japan the singing usually takes place in the seclusion of private rooms that can accommodate groups. Basic hourly charges vary and are almost always higher on weekends, but are usually less than ¥1,000. Most establishments have a large selection of English songs, stay open late, and serve inexpensive food and drink, which you order via a telephone on the wall. Finding a venue around one of the major entertainment hubs is easy—there will be plenty of young touts eager to escort you to their employer. And unlike with most other touts in the city, you won't end up broke by following them.

## Live Houses

Tokyo has numerous small music clubs known as "live houses." These range from the very basic to miniclub venues, and they showcase the best emerging talent on the local scene. Many of the best live houses can be found in the Kichijoji and Koenji areas, although they are tucked away in basements citywide. The music could be gypsy jazz one night and thrash metal the next, so it's worth doing a little research before you turn up. Cover charges vary depending on who's performing but are typically ¥3,000–¥5,000.

#  Performing Arts

## FILM

**Bunkamura** (文化村)

**ARTS CENTERS** | This complex has two movie theaters that tend to screen French and foreign films; a concert, opera, and classic ballet auditorium (Orchard Hall); a performance space (Theater Cocoona, often used for ballet and other dance); a gallery; and a museum. ✉ *2–24–1 Dogenzaka, Shibuya-ku* ☎ *03/3477–9111* ⊕ *www.bunkamura. co.jp* Ⓜ *JR Yamanote Line, Ginza and Hanzomon subway lines, and private rail lines, Shibuya Station (Exit 3A).*

**Eurospace** (ユーロスペース)

**FILM** | One of the best venues for art-house films in Japan screens independent European and Asian hits and small-scale Japanese movies. Directors and actors often appear on the stage, greeting fans on opening days. Occasionally Japanese films run with English subtitles. ✉ *1–5 Maruyamacho, 3rd fl., Shibuya-ku* ☎ *03/3461–0211* ⊕ *www. eurospace.co.jp* Ⓜ *JR Yamanote Line and Ginza and Hanzomon subway lines, Shibuya Station (Hachiko Exit).*

## MUSIC

**NHK Hall** (NHK ホール)

**MUSIC** | The home base for the Japan Broadcasting Corporation's NHK Symphony Orchestra, known as N-Kyo, is probably the auditorium most familiar to Japanese lovers of classical music, as performances here are routinely rebroadcast on the national TV station. ✉ *2–2–1 Jinnan, Shibuya-ku* ☎ *03/3465–1751* ⊕ *www.nhk-sc.or.jp/nhk_hall* Ⓜ *JR Yamanote Line, Harajuku Station (Omote-sando Exit).*

## TRADITIONAL THEATER

### NOH

**National Noh Theater** (国立能楽堂; *Kokuritsu No Gaku Do*)

**THEATER** | **FAMILY** | One of the few public halls to host Noh performances, this theater provides basic English-language summaries of the plots at performances. Individual screens placed in front of each seat also give an English translation. ✉ *4–18–1 Sendagaya, Shibuya-ku* ☎ *03/3423–1331, 03/3230–3000 reservations* ⊕ *www.ntj.jac.go.jp/nou. html* 🎫 *From ¥2,000* Ⓜ *JR Chuo Line, Sendagaya Station (Minami-guchi/South Exit); Oedo subway line, Kokuritsu-Kyogi-jo Station (Exit A4).*

#  Shopping

## BOOKS

★ **Daikanyama T-Site** (代官山 T-Site)

**ART GALLERIES** | This oasis within the metropolis is a calming respite with a leafy garden, trendy terrace eatery, gallery, and, of course, the main business, a shop selling books, music, and videos with a focus on art and design. Almost all 30,000 books here can be taken to the lounge to read, as can a large selection of foreign magazines. Many locals come here to be seen, bringing along their lapdogs dressed in designer duds from the store's pet boutique. ✉ *17–5 Sarugaku-cho, Shibuya-ku* ☎ *03/3770–2525* ⊕ *store. tsite.jp/daikanyama/* Ⓜ *Tokyu Toyoko Line, Daikanyama Station (Central Exit).*

## HOUSEWARES

★ **Tokyu Hands** (東急ハンズ)

**CRAFTS** | **FAMILY** | This chain carries a wide and varied assortment of goods, including hobby and crafts materials, art supplies, and knitting and sewing materials, as well as jewelry, household goods, stationery, even cosmetics. There's a café and exhibit space on the seventh floor with an ever-changing selection of small goods from local artisans for sale. It's not unusual to see Japanese hobbyists spending an entire afternoon browsing in here. ✉ *12–18 Udagawacho, Shibuya-ku* ☎ *03/5489–5111* ⊕ *www.tokyu-hands. co.jp* Ⓜ *JR Yamanote Line and Ginza, Fukutoshin, and Hanzomon subway lines, Shibuya Station (Hachiko Exit for JR, Exits 6 and 7 for subway).*

**Zero First Design** (ゼロファーストデザイン)

HOUSEWARES | Kyu-Yamate-dori at Daikanyama is a well-known hub of interior goods stores, and this one is full of unique and modern pieces from both local and international designers. ⊠ *2–3–1 Aobadai, Shibuya-ku* ☎ *03/5489–6106* ⊕ *01st.com* Ⓜ *Tokyu Toyoko Line, Daikanyama Station (Komazawa-dori Exit).*

## LACQUERWARE

⭐ **Yamada Heiando** (山田平安堂)

CRAFTS | With a spacious, airy layout and lovely lacquerware goods, this fashionable shop is a must for souvenir hunters—and anyone else who appreciates fine design. Rice bowls, sushi trays, bento lunch boxes, *hashioki* (chopstick rests), and jewelry cases come in traditional blacks and reds, as well as patterns both subtle and bold. Prices are fair—many items cost less than ¥10,000—but these are the kinds of goods for which devotees of Japanese craftsmanship would be willing to pay a lot. ⊠ *Hillside Terrace, 18–12 Sarugakucho, G Block #202, Shibuya-ku* ☎ *03/3464–5541* ⊕ *www.heiando1919.com* Ⓜ *Tokyu Toyoko Line, Daikanyama Station (Komazawa-dori Exit).*

## MALLS AND SHOPPING CENTERS

**Parco** (渋谷パルコ)

MALL | These vertical malls filled with small retail shops and boutiques are all within walking distance of one another in the commercial heart of Shibuya. Shops range from a collections of designer brands to an entire floor focused on game and anime goods. The rooftop food garden offers a break from shopping and views over Shibuya. ⊠ *15–1 Udagawa-cho, Shibuya-ku* ☎ *03/3464–5111* ⊕ *www.parco.co.jp* Ⓜ *Ginza, Fukutoshin, and Hanzo-mon subway lines, Shibuya Station (Exits 6 and 7).*

**Shibuya 109**

MALL | This nine-floor outlet is a teenage girl's dream, especially if they follow the *gyaru* tribe, a particularly gaudy and brash fashion genre born in Shibuya. The

place is filled with small stores whose merchandise screams kitsch and trend. Here, the fashionable sales assistants are the stars, and their popularity in this mall can make them media superstars. On weekends, dance concerts and fashion shows are often staged at the front entrance. ⊠ *2–29–1 Dogenzaka, Shibuya-ku* ☎ *03/3477–5111* ⊕ *www.shibuya109.jp* Ⓜ *JR Yamanote Line and Ginza, Fukutoshin, and Hanzomon subway lines, Shibuya Station (Hachiko Exit for JR, Exit 3A for subway lines).*

## MUSIC

**Manhattan Records** (マンハッタンレコード)

MUSIC | Hip-hop, reggae, house, and R&B vinyl can be found here, and a DJ booth pumps out the jams from the center of the room. ⊠ *10–1 Udagawacho, Shibuya-ku* ☎ *03/3477–7166* ⊕ *manhattanrecords.jp* Ⓜ *JR Yamanote Line and Ginza, Fukutoshin, and Hanzomon subway lines, Shibuya Station (Hachiko Exit for JR, Exits 6 and 7 for subway).*

**Tower Records** (タワーレコード)

MUSIC | This huge emporium carries one of the most diverse selections of CDs and DVDs in the world. Take a rest at the café after visiting the second floor, which houses books, with a large selection of English-language publications. ⊠ *1–22–14 Jinnan, Shibuya-ku* ☎ *03/3496–3661* ⊕ *tower.jp/store/kanto/shibuya* Ⓜ *JR Yamanote Line and Ginza, Fukutoshin, and Hanzomon subway lines, Shibuya Station (Hachiko Exit for JR, Exit 7 for subway).*

# Roppongi (六本木)

Roppongi, once known for its clubs, bars, and nightlife, has become one of Tokyo's major shopping, dining, and art districts. The area is abuzz with shoppers, tourists, and office workers throughout the day and evening. As the clock inches closer to the last train, the crowd changes to young clubbers and barhoppers staying out until sunrise.

For many travelers, the lure of the neighborhood is the shopping on offer in ritzy developments like Roppongi Hills and Tokyo Midtown. In addition, though, there's the three points of what's known as Art Triangle Roppongi—the National Art Center, Mori Art Museum, and Suntory Museum of Art. The neighborhood is also home to the Fujifilm Square photo gallery, 21_21 Design Sight, and many art and cultural events.

**Access:** Roppongi is located just east of Shibuya and Aoyama, and south of the Imperial Palace. The best way to get to Roppongi is by subway, and there are two lines that'll take you to Roppongi Station: the Hibiya Line, which takes you right into the complex of Roppongi Hills, or the Oedo Line, with exits convenient to Tokyo Midtown.

#  Sights

★ **Mori Art Museum** (森美術館; *Mori Bijutsukan*)

**ART MUSEUM** | Occupying the 52nd and 53rd floors of Mori Tower, this museum is one of the leading contemporary art showcases in Tokyo. The space is well designed (by American architect Richard Gluckman), intelligently curated, diverse in its media, and hospitable to big crowds. The nine galleries showcase exhibits that rotate every few months and tend to focus on leading contemporary art, architecture, fashion, design, and photography. Tickets include admission to the Roppongi Hills 52nd floor and the City View observation deck. ⊠ *6–10–1 Roppongi, Minato-ku* ☎ *03/5777–8600* ⊕ *mori.art.museum/en* ⊠ *From ¥1,800* Ⓜ *Hibiya subway line, Roppongi Station (Exit 1C).*

**The National Art Center, Tokyo** (国立新美術館; *Kokuritsu Shin Bijutsukan*)

**ART MUSEUM** | Tokyo's largest rotating exhibition space is home to major international modern and contemporary exhibits as well as smaller shows (usually free) and is worth visiting for the architecture alone. Architect Kisho Kurokawa, a cofounder of the influential metabolist movement in 1960, created a stunning facade that shimmers in undulating waves of glass, and the bright exhibition space with its soaring ceilings feels a bit like being inside the set of a utopian sci-fi movie. The building houses seven exhibition areas; a library; a museum shop; a pair of cafés; and a restaurant, Brasserie Paul Bocuse Le Musée, offering fine French dishes. ⊠ *7–22–2 Roppongi, Minato-ku* ☎ *03/5777–8600* ⊕ *www.nact. jp/english* ⊠ *Admission fee varies with exhibit* ⊘ *Closed Tues.* Ⓜ *Toei Oedo and Hibiya lines, Roppongi Station (Exit 7); Chiyoda line, Nogizaka Station (Exit 6).*

**Suntory Museum of Art** (サントリー美術館; *Santori Bijutsukan*)

**ART MUSEUM** | Based on the principle of dividing profits three ways, Suntory, Japan's beverage giant, has committed a third of its profits to what it feels is its corporate and social responsibility to provide the public with art, education, and environmental conservation. The establishment of the Suntory Art Museum in 1961 was just one of the fruits of this initiative, and the museum's current home at Tokyo Midtown Galleria is a beautiful place to view some of Tokyo's finest fine-art exhibitions. Past displays have included everything from works by Picasso and Toulouse-Lautrec to fine kimonos from the Edo period. The museum also runs occasional tea ceremonies; check the website for the monthly schedule. ⊠ *Tokyo Midtown Galleria, 9–7–4 Akasaka, 3rd fl., Minato-ku* ☎ *03/3479–8600* ⊕ *www.suntory. com/sma* ⊠ *From ¥1,300* ⊘ *Closed Tues.*

The National Art Center, Tokyo doesn't have a permanent collection, relying instead on temporary exhibits.

M *Toei Oedo Line, Roppongi Station; Hibiya Line, Roppongi Station (Exit 8).*

## Tokyo Tower (東京タワー)

**VIEWPOINT | FAMILY** | In 1958 Tokyo's fledgling TV networks needed a tall antenna array to transmit signals. Trying to emerge from the devastation of World War II, the nation's capital was also hungry for a landmark—a symbol for the aspirations of a city still without a skyline. The result was the 1,093-foot-high Tokyo Tower, an unabashed knockoff of Paris's Eiffel Tower, complete with great views of the city. The Main Observatory, set at 492 feet above ground, and the Top Deck, up an additional 330 feet, quickly became major tourist attractions. Both observation decks were renovated in 2018 and still draw many visitors a year. On weekends and holidays, ambitious visitors can make the 600-stair climb up to the Main Observatory on foot. ⊠ *4–2–8 Shiba-Koen, Minato-ku* ☎ *03/3433–5111* ⊕ *www.tokyotower.co.jp/en* ✉ *Main Deck only ¥1,200, Main and Top Deck ¥2,800* M *Hibiya subway line, Kamiyacho Station (Exit 1).*

## 21_21 Design Sight

**ART GALLERY** | This low-slung building in the garden at Tokyo Midtown hosts rotating exhibitions focused on cutting-edge art and design. Designed by architect Tadao Ando, the subdued exterior belies the expansive and bright gallery space, where exhibits focus on presenting the world of design in an exciting and accessible light. ⊠ *9–7–6 Akasaka, Minato-ku* ☎ *03/3475–2121* ⊕ *www.2121design-sight.jp/en* ✉ *¥1,200* ⊙ *Closed Tues.* M *Hibiya subway line, Roppongi Station (Exit 6).*

## Did You Know?

The bright orange Eiffel-lookalike, Tokyo Tower, was built in 1958 to symbolize the country's recovery after the destruction of WWII.

## 🍴 Restaurants

**Azure 45**
(アジュール フォーティーファイブ)
$$$$ | **FRENCH** | For his Michelin-starred contemporary French creations, chef de cuisine Shintaro Miyazaki sources the finest Japanese beef, poultry, seafood, and vegetables from around the country. Served on the 45th floor of the Ritz-Carlton, the resulting prix-fixe lunch courses (from ¥5,800) come with a choice of four or five dishes from a changing monthly menu. **Known for:** stunning views; delightful tasting menus; classy atmosphere. [$] *Average main: ¥15,000* ✉ *The Ritz-Carlton, Tokyo, Tokyo Midtown, 9–7–1 Akasaka, Minato-ku* ☎ *03/6434–8711* 🌐 *www.ritzcarlton.com* [M] *Hibiya subway line, Roppongi Station (Exit 4A); Toei Oedo Line, Roppongi Station (Exit 7).*

**Homework's** (ホームワークス)
$$ | **AMERICAN** | Every so often, even on foreign shores, you've got to have a burger. When the urge strikes, the Swiss-and-bacon special at Homework's is an incomparably better choice than anything you can get at one of the global chains. **Known for:** hearty deli sandwiches; relaxed atmosphere; burgers you can sink your teeth into. [$] *Average main: ¥1,500* ✉ *1–5–8 Azabu Juban, Minato-ku* ☎ *03/3405–9884* 🌐 *www.homeworks-1.com* [M] *Namboku and Oedo subway lines, Azabu Juban Station (Exit 4).*

★ **Inakaya East** (田舎家 東店 *Inakaya Higashi ten*)
$$$$ | **JAPANESE** | The style here is *robatayaki*, a dining experience that segues into pure theater. Inside a large U-shape counter, two cooks in traditional garb sit on cushions behind a grill, with a cornucopia of food spread out in front of them: fresh vegetables, seafood, and skewers of beef and chicken. **Known for:** fresh ingredients grilled just right; fun, lively atmosphere; entertaining service. [$] *Average main: ¥10,000* ✉ *3–14–17 Roppongi, Minato-ku* ☎ *03/3408–5040* 🌐 *www.roppongiinakaya.jp* ⏲ *No lunch* [M] *Hibiya subway line, Roppongi Station (Exit 3).*

★ **Kushiyaki Ganchan** (串焼がんちゃん)
$$$ | **JAPANESE** | Smoky, noisy, and cluttered, Ganchan is exactly what the Japanese expect of their yakitori joints—restaurants that specialize in bits of charcoal-broiled chicken and vegetables. The counter here seats barely 15, and you have to squeeze to get to the chairs in back. **Known for:** cozy, down-to-earth atmosphere; fills up on weekends; eclectic decor. [$] *Average main: ¥4,000* ✉ *6–8–23 Roppongi, Minato-ku* ☎ *03/3478–0092* ⏲ *No lunch* [M] *Hibiya subway line, Roppongi Station (Exit 1A).*

**Menya Musashi Kosho** (麺屋武蔵 虎嘯)
$ | **RAMEN** | Serving both ramen and *tsukemen* (noodles with the broth on the side for dipping), this sleek ramen shop is a great stop for a quick and hearty bowl of noodles. The shop's specialty is their fusion broths; a hearty chicken/pork or lighter seafood stock from dried bonito and sardines. **Known for:** ramen in a hip, modern interior; rich, flavorful bowls of noodles; quick and affordable meals. [$] *Average main: ¥1,000* ✉ *4-12-6 Roppongi, Minato-ku* ☎ *03/3497-0634* ▭ *No credit cards.*

**Sankoen** (三幸園)
$$$$ | **KOREAN** | In a neighborhood thick with Korean-barbecue joints, Sankoen stands out as the best of the lot. Korean barbecue is a smoky affair; you cook your own food, usually thin slices of beef and vegetables, on a gas grill at your table. **Known for:** cozy, simple interior; fills up quickly at dinnertime; excellent cuts of meat to grill at your table. [$] *Average main: ¥6,000* ✉ *1–8–7 Azabu Juban, Minato-ku* ☎ *03/3585–6306* ⏲ *Closed Wed.* [M] *Namboku and Oedo subway lines, Azabu Juban Station (Exit 4).*

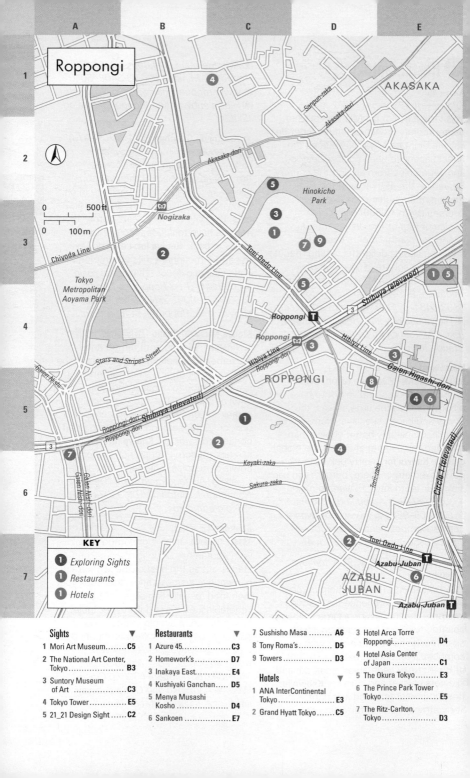

# Roppongi

AKASAKA

Sanpun-zaka

Akasaka-dori

Akasaka-dori

Nogizaka

Chiyoda Line

Tokyo Metropolitan Aoyama Park

Hinokicho Park

Toei Oedo Line

Shibuya (elevated)

Roppongi

Roppongi

Hibiya Line

Hibiya Line

Roppongi-dori

ROPPONGI

Stars and Stripes Street

Gaien Higashi-dori

Gaien Nishi-dori

Roppongi-dori Shibuya (elevated)

Roppongi-dori

Circle T (elevated)

Keyaki-zaka

Sakura-zaka

Torii-zaka

Toei Oedo Line

Azabu-Juban

AZABU-JUBAN

Gaien Nishi-dori Gaien Nishi-dori

Azabu-Juban

**KEY**

- ① Exploring Sights
- ① Restaurants
- ① Hotels

500 ft
100 m

## Sights ▼

1 Mori Art Museum........**C5**
2 The National Art Center, Tokyo .....................**B3**
3 Suntory Museum of Art .....................**C3**
4 Tokyo Tower..............**E5**
5 21_21 Design Sight......**C2**

## Restaurants ▼

1 Azure 45..................**C3**
2 Homework's ............**D7**
3 Inakaya East............**E4**
4 Kushiyaki Ganchan......**D5**
5 Menya Musashi Kosho ...................**D4**
6 Sankoen .................**E7**

7 Sushisho Masa .........**A6**
8 Tony Roma's.............**D5**
9 Towers ..................**D3**

## Hotels ▼

1 ANA InterContinental Tokyo .....................**E3**
2 Grand Hyatt Tokyo .......**C5**

3 Hotel Arca Torre Roppongi.................**D4**
4 Hotel Asia Center of Japan .................**C1**
5 The Okura Tokyo.........**E3**
6 The Prince Park Tower Tokyo .....................**E5**
7 The Ritz-Carlton, Tokyo .....................**D3**

## Sushisho Masa (すし匠 まさ)

**$$$$ | SUSHI** | Diners here need a dose of luck—there are only seven counter seats and reservations fill up fast (ask your hotel concierge to make a reservation for you). You also need a full wallet, as high-end sushi comes at a pretty price. **Known for:** extremely high-quality, fresh fish with rare garnishes; focus on service as well as the food; impeccable attention to detail. $ *Average main: ¥20,000* ✉ *7 Nishi-Azabu Bldg., 4–1–15 Nishi-Azabu, B1 fl., Minato-ku* ☎ *03/3499–9178* ◷ *Closed Mon. No lunch* Ⓜ *Hibiya subway line, Roppongi Station (Exit 1B); Toei Oedo Line, Roppongi Station (Exit 1A).*

## Tony Roma's (トニーローマ)

**$$$ | AMERICAN | FAMILY** | This casual American chain is world-famous for its barbecued ribs. It also serves kid-size (and much larger) portions of burgers, chicken strips, and fried shrimp. **Known for:** large portions of barbecued ribs; friendly service; a taste of the States. $ *Average main: ¥3,500* ✉ *5–4–20 Roppongi, Minato-ku* ☎ *03/3408–2748* ⊕ *tonyromas.jp/en* Ⓜ *Hibiya subway line, Roppongi Station (Exit 3); Toei Oedo Line, Roppongi Station (Exit 3).*

## Towers (タワーズ)

**$$$$ | AMERICAN** | When you're looking for a break from all the ramen, tempura, and yakitori, this restaurant on the 45th floor of the Ritz-Carlton Hotel serves a mix of international flavors that range from American to Southeast Asian to Mediterranean. The prix-fixe lunches include a three-course business lunch (¥6,500), and there are dinners with four and five courses, including one that focuses on produce from Hokkaido (¥13,000). **Known for:** sophisticated fusion dishes; luxurious weekend brunches; views over Tokyo. $ *Average main: ¥13,000* ✉ *Ritz Carlton Hotel, 9–7–1 Akasaka, 45th fl., Minato-ku* ☎ *03/6434–8711* ⊕ *towers.ritzcarltontokyo.com* Ⓜ *Hibiya subway line, Roppongi Station (Exit 4A); Toei Oedo Line, Roppongi Station (Exit 7).*

#  Hotels

## ANA InterContinental Tokyo (ANA インターコンチネンタルホテル東京)

**$$ | HOTEL** | With a central location and modest pricing, the ANA is a great choice for the business traveler, and its ziggurat-atrium points to the heyday of the power lunch: the mid-1980s. **Pros:** great concierge; wonderful city views; spacious lobby. **Cons:** room bathrooms a bit small; few sightseeing options within walking distance; fees for the open-air pool. $ *Rooms from: ¥27,000* ✉ *1–12–33 Akasaka, Minato-ku* ☎ *03/3505–1111* ⊕ *anaintercontinental-tokyo.jp* ⇴ *844 rooms* ⦿ *No Meals* Ⓜ *Ginza and Namboku subway lines, Tameike Sanno Station (Exit 13); Namboku subway line, Roppongi-itchome Station (Exit 3).*

## Grand Hyatt Tokyo (グランドハイアット東京)

**$$$ | HOTEL** | Japanese refinement and a contemporary design come together perfectly at the Grand Hyatt—a tasteful and well-appointed hotel in the middle of Roppongi, one of Tokyo's top entertainment areas. **Pros:** great spa; wide range of restaurants; spacious rooms. **Cons:** easy to get lost in the building's complicated layout; concierge service can be hit-or-miss; rooms lack distinctive character. $ *Rooms from: ¥40,000* ✉ *6–10–3 Roppongi, Minato-ku* ☎ *03/4333–1234* ⊕ *www.hyatt.com/en-US/hotel/japan/grand-hyatt-tokyo/tyogh* ⇴ *387 rooms* ⦿ *No Meals* Ⓜ *Hibiya subway line, Roppongi Station (Exit 1A); Oedo subway line, Roppongi Station (Exit 3).*

## Hotel Arca Torre Roppongi (ホテルアルカトーレ)

**$$ | HOTEL** | Sitting on a coveted location in the heart of one of Tokyo's premier nightlife quarters, this European-inspired hotel is just a few minutes' walk from the Tokyo Midtown and Roppongi Hills shopping-and-entertainment complexes. **Pros:** affordable; convenient access to nightlife; free Wi-Fi. **Cons:** small double rooms;

neighborhood's bars and clubs make the area noisy; no closets. $ *Rooms from: ¥16,000* ⊠ *6–1–23 Roppongi, Minato-ku* ☎ *03/3404–5111* ⊕ *arktower.co.jp/arca-torre* ⇱ *76 rooms* ❍ *No Meals* Ⓜ *Hibiya and Oedo subway lines, Roppongi Station (Exit 3).*

### Hotel Asia Center of Japan (ホテルアジア会館; *Hoteru Ajia Kaikan*)

$ | **HOTEL** | Established in 1957 and renovated in 2015, these budget accommodations have become popular due to their good value and easy access (a 15-minute walk) to the nightlife of Roppongi. **Pros:** affordable; great area for those who love the nightlife; free Wi-Fi. **Cons:** no room service; mostly small rooms; just one restaurant. $ *Rooms from: ¥10,000* ⊠ *8–10–32 Akasaka, Minato-ku* ☎ *03/3402–6111* ⊕ *www.asiacenter.or.jp* ⇱ *173 rooms* ❍ *No Meals* Ⓜ *Ginza and Hanzo-mon subway lines, Aoyama-itchome Station (Exit 4).*

### The Okura Tokyo (オークラ東京)

$$$$ | **HOTEL** | The original Hotel Okura, built before the first Tokyo Olympics, came to be one of Tokyo's most iconic hotels due to its blend of traditional Japanese and modernist design, and now, having been newly rebuilt, it still combines the retro charm of its predecessor with modern luxury. **Pros:** good service; retro-modern design and feel; large rooms. **Cons:** not ideal for families; expensive; retro design not for everyone. $ *Rooms from: ¥57,000* ⊠ *2–10–4 Tora-no-mon, Minato-ku* ☎ *03/3582–0111* ⊕ *theokuratokyo.jp/en* ⇱ *508 rooms* ❍ *No Meals* Ⓜ *Hibiya subway line, Kamiya-cho Station (Exit 4B); Ginza subway line, Tora-no-mon Station (Exit 3).*

### The Prince Park Tower Tokyo (ザ・プリンスパークタワー東京)

$$ | **HOTEL** | **FAMILY** | The surrounding parkland and the absence of any adjacent buildings make the Park Tower a peaceful retreat in the middle of the city. **Pros:** park

nearby; well-stocked convenience store on first floor; fun extras like a bowling alley and pool. **Cons:** extra fee for pool and fitness center; few dining options in immediate area; a tad isolated. $ *Rooms from: ¥30,000* ⊠ *4–8–1 Shiba-koen, Minato-ku* ☎ *03/5400–1111* ⊕ *www.princehotels.com/parktower* ⇱ *603 rooms* ❍ *No Meals* Ⓜ *Oedo subway line, Akabanebashi Station (Akabanebashi Exit).*

### ★ The Ritz-Carlton, Tokyo (ザ・リッツ・カールトン東京)

$$$$ | **HOTEL** | Installed in the top floors of the 53-story Midtown Tower, the Ritz-Carlton provides Tokyo's most luxurious accommodations squarely in the middle of the city. **Pros:** great views of Tokyo; romantic setting; stunning rooms loaded with luxurious goodies. **Cons:** a bit of a walk to the subway; club lounge extras don't live up to the Ritz's reputation; high prices. $ *Rooms from: ¥75,000* ⊠ *9–7–1 Akasaka, Minato-ku* ☎ *03/3423–8000* ⊕ *www.ritzcarlton.com* ⇱ *247 rooms* ❍ *No Meals* Ⓜ *Hibiya subway line, Roppongi Station (Exit 4); Oedo subway line, Roppongi Station (Exit 7).*

##  Nightlife

### BARS

#### Agave (アガヴェ)

**BARS** | In this authentic Mexican cantina, your palate will be tempted by a choice of more than 550 kinds of tequilas and mescals—making this the world's largest selection. Most of the varieties here aren't available anywhere else in Japan, so the steep prices may be worth paying. Foods are mostly Mexican appetizers. ⊠ *DM Bldg., 7–18–11 Roppongi, B1 fl., Minato-ku* ☎ *03/3497–0229* ⊕ *agave.jp* ☽ *Closed Sun.* Ⓜ *Hibiya and Oedo subway lines, Roppongi Station (Exit 3).*

## JAZZ CLUBS

### Billboard Live Tokyo
(ビルボードライブ東京)

LIVE MUSIC | With everything from rock and J-pop to soul and funk, this three-story joint makes one of the best food-and-live music experiences in Tokyo, all with panoramic views of Roppongi. Patrons love this venue partly because they're so close to performers like George Clinton, Dicky Betts, Neneh Cherry, and Howard Jones; they often end up on the stage dancing and singing or shaking hands. Shows usually kick off at 7 and 9:30 pm on weekdays, 6 and 9 pm on Saturday, and 4:30 and 7:30 pm on Sunday. ✉ Tokyo Midtown Garden Terr., 9–7–4 Akasaka, 4th fl., Minato-ku ☎ 03/3405–1133 ⊕ www.billboard-live. com.

## KARAOKE

### Pasela Roppongi (カラオケ パセラ)

THEMED ENTERTAINMENT | This 10-story entertainment complex on the main Roppongi drag of Gaien-Higashi-dori has seven floors of karaoke rooms, some Bali-themed, with more than 10,000 foreign-song titles. Both large and small groups can be accommodated. A Mexican-theme darts bar and a restaurant are also on-site. Rates run ¥700–¥2,000 per hour, and there are also all you can drink deals to keep your tonsils nicely lubricated for singing. ✉ 5–16–3 Roppongi, Minato-ku ☎ 0120/911–086 ⊕ www. pasela.co.jp Ⓜ Hibiya and Oedo subway lines, Roppongi Station (Exit 4A).

# 👜 Shopping

## CERAMICS

### Savoir Vivre (サボア・ヴィーブル)

CERAMICS | In the swanky Axis Building, this store sells contemporary and antique tea sets, cups, bowls, and glassware. ✉ Axis Bldg., 5–17–1 Roppongi, 3rd fl., Minato-ku ☎ 03/3585–7365 ⊕ savoir-vivre.co.jp ⊗ Closed Wed. Ⓜ Hibiya and Oedo subway lines, Roppongi Station (Exit 3).

## CLOTHING

### Restir (リステア)

MIXED CLOTHING | Next to the Midtown Tokyo complex, this is possibly the most exclusive and fashion-forward boutique in the city. Its three floors are made up of a cluster of stores, from luxury stores for men and women to a surf and activewear store, a café, and another store dedicated to high-end lifestyle gadgets like headphones, toy cameras, and stylish mobile peripherals. ✉ 9–6–17 Akasaka, Minato-ku ☎ 03/5413–3708 ⊕ www. restir.com/en Ⓜ Hibiya and Oedo subway lines, Roppongi Station (Exit 8); Chiyoda subway line, Nogizaka Station (Exit 3).

## MALLS AND SHOPPING CENTERS

### Axis (アクシス)

MALL | Classy and cutting-edge furniture, electronics, fabrics, ceramics, and books are sold at this multistory design center on the main Roppongi drag of Gaien-Higashi-dori. Savoir Vivre has an excellent selection of ceramics; Le Garage has accessories for high-end cars. On the fourth floor, the JIDA Design Museum shows the best of what's current in Japanese industrial design. ✉ 5–17–1 Roppongi, Minato-ku ☎ 03/3587–2781 ⊕ www. axisinc.co.jp ⊗ Closed Sun. Ⓜ Hibiya and Oedo subway lines, Roppongi Station (Exit 3); Namboku subway line, Roppongi Itchome Station (Exit 2).

### Roppongi Hills (六本木ヒルズ)

SHOPPING CENTER | FAMILY | You could easily spend a whole day exploring the retail areas of this complex of shops, restaurants, residential and commercial towers, a nine-screen cineplex, the Grand Hyatt Tokyo hotel, and the Mori Art Museum—all wrapped around the TV Asahi studios and sprawled out in five zones located between the Roppongi intersection and Azabu Juban. The shops here emphasize eye-catching design and chichi brands, although finding a particular shop can be a hassle given the building's Escher-like layout. To navigate, go to the information center to retrieve a floor guide with color-coded maps in English. ✉ *6–10–1 Roppongi, Minato-ku* ☎ *03/6406–6000* 🌐 *www.roppongihills.com* Ⓜ *Hibiya and Oedo subway lines, Roppongi Station (Roppongi Hills Exit).*

**Tokyo Midtown** (東京ミッドタウン)
**SHOPPING CENTER** | This huge complex is an architectural statement with sweeping glass roofs and a large walkable garden in the back. The airy, open spaces house exclusive boutiques, hotels, and a concentration of cafés by the world's top pâtissiers on the first few floors. ✉ *9–7–1 Akasaka, Minato-ku* ☎ *03/3475–3100* 🌐 *www.tokyo-midtown.com/en* Ⓜ *Hibiya and Oedo subway lines, Roppongi Station (Exit 8); Chiyoda subway line, Nogizaka Station (Exit 3).*

### SWORDS AND KNIVES
★ **Japan Sword Co.** (日本刀剣; *Nippon Tokken*)
**OTHER SPECIALTY STORE** | Aspiring samurai can learn how to tell their *toshin* (blades) from their *tsuka* (sword handles) with help from the staff at this small shop, which has been open since the Meiji era (1868–1912). Items that range from a circa-1390 samurai sword to inexpensive or decorative reproductions allow you to take a trip back in time. ✉ *3–8–1 Toranomon, Minato-ku* ☎ *03/3434–4321* 🌐 *www.japansword.co.jp* ☯ *Closed Sun.* Ⓜ *Hibiya and Ginza subway lines, Tora-no-mon Station (Exit 2).*

## 🎭 Performing Arts

### MUSIC
**Suntory Hall** (サントリーホール)
**CONCERTS** | This lavishly appointed concert auditorium in the Ark Hills complex has probably the best acoustics in the city, and its great location allows theatergoers to extend their evening out: there's an abundance of great restaurants and bars nearby. ✉ *1–13–1 Akasaka, Minato-ku* ☎ *03/3505–1001* 🌐 *www.suntory.com/culture-sports/suntoryhall* Ⓜ *Ginza subway line, Tameike-Sanno Station (Exit 13);*

*Namboku subway line, Roppongi-Ichome Station (Exit 3).*

# Shinjuku (新宿)

If you love the grittiness and chaos of big cities, you're bound to love Shinjuku. Here all the celebrated virtues of Japanese society—its safety and order, its grace and beauty, its cleanliness and civility—fray at the edges.

To be fair, the area has been on the fringes of respectability for centuries. When Ieyasu, the first Tokugawa shogun, made Edo his capital, Shinjuku was at the junction of two important arteries leading into the city from the west. It became a thriving post station, where travelers would rest and refresh themselves for the last leg of their journey; the appeal of this suburban pit stop was its "teahouses," where the waitresses dispensed a good bit more than sympathy with the tea.

When the Tokugawa dynasty collapsed in 1868, 16-year-old Emperor Meiji moved his capital to Edo, renaming it Tokyo, and modern Shinjuku became the railhead connecting it to Japan's western provinces. It became a haunt for artists, writers, and students; in the 1930s Shinjuku was Tokyo's bohemian quarter. The area was virtually leveled during the firebombings of 1945—a blank slate on which developers could write, as Tokyo surged west after the war.

Now by day the east side of Shinjuku Station is an astonishing concentration of retail stores, vertical malls, and discounters of every stripe and description. By night much of the activity shifts to the nearby quarter of Kabuki-cho. Formerly a gritty red-light district, redevelopment in recent years has turned the area into more of an entertainment and nightlife spot. While there are still some seedy bars and a number of adult-only shops and services, they are overshadowed by the sheer number of the neighborhood's less exotic bars and restaurants.

**Access:** Every day three subways, seven railway lines, and more than 3 million commuters converge on Shinjuku Station, making this the city's busiest and most heavily populated commercial center. The hub at Shinjuku—a vast, interconnected complex of tracks and terminals, department stores and shops—divides the area into two distinctly different sub-cities, Nishi-Shinjuku (West Shinjuku) and Higashi-Shinjuku (East Shinjuku). From Shibuya to the south and Ikebukuro to the north, the JR Yamanote Line is one of the more common ways to reach Shinjuku Station. The Saikyo Line travels the same path but less frequently. The Keio and Odakyu lines serve destinations to the west. Subway lines, like the Marunouchi, Shinjuku, and Toei Oedo, are best used to move to destinations in the center of the city, such as Ote-machi, Kudanshita, and Roppongi. On foot, Kabuki-cho is accessible in minutes to the east. For the forest of office-building skyscrapers, go through the underground passage to the west.

 ## Sights

### Shinjuku Gyoen National Garden
(新宿御苑)

**GARDEN** | This lovely 150-acre park was once the estate of the powerful Naito family of feudal lords, who were among the most trusted retainers of the Tokugawa shoguns. After World War II, the grounds were finally opened to the public. It's a perfect place for leisurely walks: paths wind past ponds and bridges, artificial hills, thoughtfully placed stone lanterns, and more than 3,000 kinds of plants, shrubs, and trees. There are different gardens in Japanese, French, and English styles, as well as a greenhouse (the nation's first, built in 1885) filled with tropical plants. The best times to visit are April, when 75 different species of cherry trees—some 1,500 trees in all—are in bloom, and the first two weeks of November, during the chrysanthemum exhibition. ⊠ *11 Naito-machi, Shinjuku-ku* ☎ *03/3350–0151* ⊠ *¥500* ⊗ *Closed Mon.* Ⓜ *Marunouchi subway line, Shinjuku Gyo-en-mae Station (Exit 1).*

### Tokyo Metropolitan Government Building
(東京都庁; *Tokyo Tocho*)

**VIEWPOINT** | Dominating the western Shinjuku skyline and built at a cost of ¥157 billion, this Kenzo Tange–designed, grandiose, city-hall complex is clearly meant to remind observers that Tokyo's annual budget is bigger than that of the average developing country. The late-20th-century complex consists of a main office building, an annex, the Metropolitan Assembly Building, and a huge central courtyard, often the venue of open-air concerts and exhibitions. The building design has raised some debate: Tokyoites either love it or hate it. On a clear day, from the observation decks on the 45th floors of both towers (663 feet above ground), you can see all the way to Mt. Fuji and to the Boso Peninsula in Chiba Prefecture. Several other skyscrapers in the area have free observation floors—among them the Shinjuku Center Building and the Shinjuku Sumitomo Building—but city hall is the best of the lot. The Metropolitan Government website, incidentally, is an excellent source of information on sightseeing and current events in Tokyo. ⊠ *2–8–1 Nishi-Shinjuku, Shinjuku-ku* ☎ *03/5321–1111* ⊕ *www.metro.tokyo.jp/english/offices/observat.html* ⊠ *Free* ⊗ *South Observation Deck closed 1st and 3rd Tues.; North Observation Deck closed 2nd and 4th Mon.* Ⓜ *ToeiOedo subway line, Tocho-mae Station (Exit A4).*

Sights ▼

1 Shinjuku Gyoen
   National Garden ........ **H6**

2 Tokyo Metropolitan
   Government Office ..... **A5**

Restaurants ▼

1 New York Grill ........... **A7**

2 Ramen Kaijin ............ **F5**

3 Tim Ho Wan Shinjuku
   Southern Terrace ....... **E6**

Hotels ▼

1 Citadines Shinjuku
   Tokyo .................... **J4**

2 Hilton Tokyo ............ **A3**

3 Hotel Century
   Southern Tower ........ **E6**

4 Hyatt Regency Tokyo... **A4**

5 Keio Plaza Hotel
   Tokyo .................... **B4**

6 Park Hyatt Tokyo........ **A7**

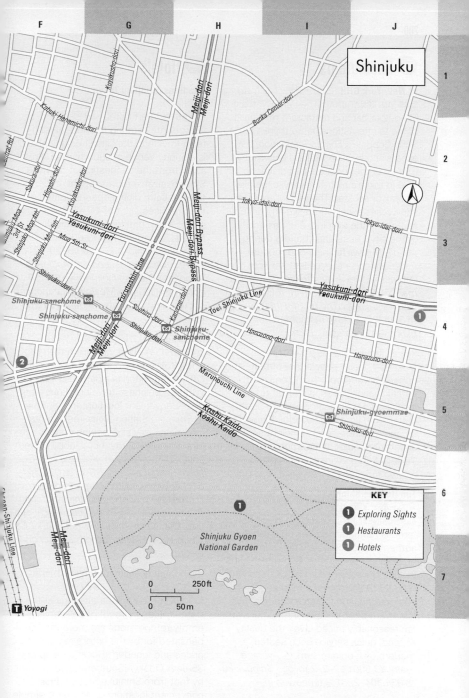

# Shinjuku

Konbuku-dori

Meiji-dori
Meiji-dori

Kabuki-Hanamichi-dori

Bunka Center-dori

Seihei-dori

Sakura-dori

Higashi-dori

Tokyo-idai-dori

Tokyo-idai-dori

Koyatsuno-dori

Shinjuku Moa 4th

3rd St

Shinjuku Moa 4th

Moa 5th St

**Yasukuni-dori**
**Yasukuni-dori**

**Yasukuni-dori**
**Yasukuni-dori**

Furunoshin Line

Shinjuku-dori

Meiji-dori Bypass
Meiji-dori Bypass

❶

**Shinjuku-sanchome** Ⓜ
**Shinjuku-sanchome** Ⓜ

Suehiro-dori

Kaido-dori

Toei Shinjuku Line

❷

Meiji-dori
Meiji-dori

Shinjuku-dori

Ⓜ **Shinjuku-
sanchome**

Hanazono-dori

Hanazono-dori

Marunouchi Line

❶ **Shinjuku-gyoemmae**
Ⓜ

**Koshu Kaido**
**Koshu Kaido**

Shinjuku-dori

Yoyogi-Shinjuku Line

❶

**Shinjuku Gyoen
National Garden**

Meiji-dori
Meiji-dori

| KEY | |
|---|---|
| ❶ | *Exploring Sights* |
| ❶ | *Restaurants* |
| ❶ | *Hotels* |

0 — 250 ft

0 — 50 m

🚉 *Yoyogi*

F G H I J

1 2 3 4 5 6 7

## 🍴 Restaurants

**★ New York Grill** (ニューヨーク グリル)
$$$$ | **INTERNATIONAL** | The Park Hyatt's 52nd-floor bar and restaurant may have come to international fame thanks to Sofia Coppola's *Lost in Translation,* but expats and locals have long known that it's one of the most elegant places to take in Tokyo's nighttime cityscape over a steak or cocktail. The restaurant menu showcases excellent steaks and grilled seafood in the evening, and has one of the city's best lunch buffets during the day. **Known for:** high-end modern American cuisine; excellent service; impressive views over Tokyo. [$] *Average main: ¥20,000* ✉ *Park Hyatt Tokyo, 3–7–1 Nishi-Shinjuku, 52nd fl., Shinjuku-ku* ☎ *03/5322–3458* 🌐 *restaurants.tokyo.park.hyatt.co.jp/en/nyg.html.*

**Ramen Kaijin** (麺屋 海神)
$ | **RAMEN** | Kaijin shows that ramen doesn't have to be rich and heavy to be satisfying. The shop specializes in a clear *shio* (salt) seafood-based broth that is both light and flavorful. **Known for:** unique toppings; quick, efficient service; excellent noodles. [$] *Average main: ¥800* ✉ *3-35-7 Shinjuku, Shinjuku-ku* ☎ *03/3356–5658* 🌐 *menya-kaijin.tokyo.*

**Tim Ho Wan Shinjuku Southern Terrace** (ティム・ホー・ワン)
$$$ | **CHINESE** | This branch of Hong Kong's famous restaurant serves up a variety of authentic and accessible dim sum dishes in a casual atmosphere. Some highlights include the steamed pork spareribs with black bean sauce, deep-fried eggplant with shrimp, and the steamed rice rolls filled with beef, pork, or shrimp. **Known for:** reasonably priced given the quality of food; quick service once seated; a modern take on dim sum. [$] *Average main: ¥3,500* ✉ *2–2–2 Yoyogi, Shibuya-ku* ☎ *03/6304–2861* 🌐 *timhowan.jp.*

## 🛏 Hotels

**Citadines Shinjuku Tokyo** (シタディーン新宿)
$$ | **HOTEL** | Part hotel, part serviced apartments catering to short- or long-term travelers, the Citadines Shinjuku is a sunny venue of superb value. **Pros:** away from the congestion of Shinjuku Station; sizable rooms; bright, cheerful design. **Cons:** dining options limited on the premises; a bit of a walk to Shinjuku's sights and nightlife; a little difficult to find. [$] *Rooms from: ¥19,000* ✉ *1–28–13 Shinjuku, Shinjuku-ku* ☎ *03/5379–7208* 🌐 *www.discoverasr.com/ja/citadines/japan/citadines-shinjuku-tokyo* 🛏 *160 apartments* 🍴 *No Meals* [M] *Marunouchi subway line, Shinjuku Gyoemmae Station (Exit 2).*

**Hilton Tokyo** (ヒルトン東京)
$$ | **HOTEL** | A short walk from the megalithic Tokyo Metropolitan Government Office, the Hilton is a particular favorite of Western business travelers. **Pros:** great gym; convenient location; free shuttle to Shinjuku Station. **Cons:** restaurants are pricey; few sightseeing options immediately nearby; hotel lobby can get busy. [$] *Rooms from: ¥26,000* ✉ *6–6–2 Nishi-Shinjuku, Shinjuku-ku* ☎ *03/3344–5111* 🌐 *www3.hilton.com* 🛏 *811 rooms* 🍴 *No Meals* [M] *Shinjuku Station (Nishi-guchi/West Exit); Marunouchi subway line, Nishi-Shinjuku Station (Exit C8); Oedo subway line, Tocho-mae Station (all exits).*

**Hotel Century Southern Tower** (小田急ホテルセンチュリーサザンタワー)
$$ | **HOTEL** | The sparse offerings at the Century (i.e., no room or bell service, empty refrigerators) are more than compensated for by the hotel's reasonable prices and wonderful location atop the 35-floor Odakyu Southern Tower, minutes by foot from Shinjuku Station. **Pros:** convenient location; great views; simple but tasteful rooms. **Cons:** no room service or pool; small rooms; room amenities are

basic. $ *Rooms from: ¥29,000* ✉ *2–2–1 Yoyogi, Shibuya-ku* ☎ *03/5354–0111* 🌐 *www.southerntower.co.jp* ➘ *375 rooms* |◉| *No Meals* Ⓜ *Shinjuku Station (Minami-guchi/South Exit); Oedo and Shinjuku subway lines, Shinjuku Station (Exit A1).*

### Hyatt Regency Tokyo (ハイアットリージェンシー 東京)

$$ | **HOTEL** | Set amid Shinjuku's skyscrapers, this hotel has the trademark Hyatt atrium-style lobby: seven stories high, with glass elevators soaring upward and three huge chandeliers suspended from above. **Pros:** friendly staff; affordable room rates; spacious rooms. **Cons:** restaurant options are limited outside hotel; starting to show its age; rather generic exteriors and common areas. $ *Rooms from: ¥23,000* ✉ *2–7–2 Nishi-Shinjuku, Shinjuku-ku* ☎ *03/3348–1234* 🌐 *tokyo.regency.hyatt.com* ➘ *744 rooms* |◉| *No Meals* Ⓜ *Marunouchi subway line, Nishi-Shinjuku Station (Exit C8); Oedo subway line, Tocho-mae Station (all exits).*

### Keio Plaza Hotel Tokyo (京工プラザホテル)

$$ | **HOTEL** | Composed of two cereal-box-shape towers, this hotel has a reputation as a business destination that serves its guests with a classic touch. **Pros:** nice pools; affordable nightly rates; convenient location. **Cons:** restaurant options outside hotel limited; crowded if there are conventions or large groups in residence; bland exteriors and common areas. $ *Rooms from: ¥28,000* ✉ *2–2–1 Nishi Shinjuku, Shinjuku-ku* ☎ *03/3344–0111* 🌐 *www.keioplaza.com* ➘ *1436 rooms* |◉| *No Meals* Ⓜ *Shinjuku Station (Nishi-guchi/West Exit).*

### ★ Park Hyatt Tokyo (パークハイアット東京)

$$$$ | **HOTEL** | Sofia Coppola's classic film *Lost in Translation* was a love letter to this hotel, and when the elevator inside the sleek, Kenzo Tange–designed Shinjuku Park Tower whisks you to the atrium lounge with a panorama of Shinjuku through floor-to-ceiling windows, you'll be

smitten as well. **Pros:**; wonderful room interiors; great skyline views; top-class restaurants. **Cons:** somewhat remote; taxi is best way to get to Shinjuku Station; pricey for Shinjuku. $ *Rooms from: ¥56,000* ✉ *3–7–1–2 Nishi-Shinjuku, Shinjuku-ku* ☎ *03/5322–1234* 🌐 *www.hyatt.com* ➘ *177 rooms* |◉| *No Meals* Ⓜ *JR Shinjuku Station (Nishi-guchi/West Exit).*

## 🍸 Nightlife

### BARS

#### Donzoko (どん底)

**BARS** | This venerable bar claims to be Shinjuku's oldest—established in 1951—and has hosted Yukio Mishima and Akira Kurosawa among many other luminaries. It's also one of several bars that claim to have invented the popular *chu-hai* cocktail (*shochu* with juice and soda). The vibrant atmosphere feels more like a pub, and the four floors are almost always packed. ✉ *3–10–2 Shinjuku, Shinjuku-ku* ☎ *03/3354–7749* 🌐 *www.donzoko.co.jp* Ⓜ *Marunouchi and Shinjuku subway lines, Shinjuku san chome Station (Exit C3).*

#### ★ New York Bar (ニューヨーク バー)

**COCKTAIL LOUNGES** | Even before *Lost in Translation* introduced the Park Hyatt's signature lounge to filmgoers worldwide, New York Bar was a local Tokyo favorite. All the style you would expect of one of the city's top hotels combined with superior views of Shinjuku's skyscrapers and neon-lighted streets make this one of the city's premier nighttime venues. The quality of the jazz and service equals that of the view. With the largest selection of U.S. wines in Japan, drinks are priced as you might expect, and there's a cover charge of ¥2,200 after 8 pm (7 pm on Sunday). Local jazz bands play on Sunday. ✉ *Park Hyatt Hotel, 3–7–1 Nishi-Shinjuku, 52nd fl., Shinjuku-ku* ☎ *03/5322–1234* 🌐 *restaurants.tokyo.park.hyatt.co.jp/en/nyb.html* Ⓜ *JR Shinjuku Station (West Exit for the shuttle bus service, South Exit for walk-in).*

# Tokyo's Gay Bars

Gay culture is a little different in Japan than it is in the West. Though Tokyo has a Rainbow Pride event in late April that attracts hundreds of thousands and the gay presence on TV is increasing, most gay life still takes place well under the radar. Even so, there's less prejudice than you might experience elsewhere. People are more likely to be baffled than offended by gay couples, and some hotels may "not compute" that a same-sex couple would like a double bed. But with a little digging you'll find a scene more vibrant than you—or many Tokyoites—might expect. The city's primary LGBTQ+ hub is Ni-chome in the Shinjuku district (take the Shinjuku or Marunouchi subway line to Shinjuku-Sanchome Station; Exit C7). Ni-chome is sometimes likened to its more notorious neighbor Kabuki-cho, and the name is also spoken in hushed tones and accompanied by raised eyebrows. Ni-chome, however, is more subtle in its approach. Gay and gay-friendly establishments can be found sprinkled in other areas, too, among them Shibuya, Asakusa, Ueno, and, surprisingly, Shinbashi, where a cluster of gay bars near Shinbashi Station are cheek-by-jowl with establishments that cater to hard-drinking businessmen out for a night on the town.

## GAY BARS

**Aiiro Cafe** (藍色酒場; *Aiiro Sakaba*)
PUBS | Almost every great gay night out begins at this welcoming street-corner pub with a large red shrine gate, where the patrons spill out onto the street. This is the perfect place to put back a few cocktails, meet new people, and get a feeling for where to go next. The crowd is mixed and very foreigner-friendly. ⊠ *Tenka Bldg., 2–18–1 Shinjuku, Shinjuku-ku* ☎ *03/6273–0740* ⊕ *aliving.net/english.html.*

**Arty Farty** (アーティファーティ)
BARS | Cheap and cheesy, Arty Farty is a fun club, complete with a ministage and stripper pole. Those with aversions to Kylie or Madonna need not bother. The crowd is mixed and foreigner-friendly. ⊠ *Kyutei Bldg., 2–11–7 Shinjuku, 2nd fl., Shinjuku-ku* ☎ *03/5362–9720.*

**Dragon Men**
DANCE CLUBS | Tokyo's swankiest gay lounge, the neon-lit space would look right at home in New York or Paris. ⊠ *Stork Nagasaki, 2–11–4 Shinjuku, Shinjuku-ku* ☎ *03/3341–0606* ⊕ *www.dragonmen69.com* Ⓜ *Marunouchi subway line, Shinjuku-san-chome Station.*

**GB**
BARS | Video monitors at this club show contemporary music hits. On weekends the place is packed with rather quiet and reserved gentlemen, mostly in their thirties and forties, and is also quite popular among foreign residents and visitors—especially before a night out clubbing. ⊠ *Shinjuku Plaza Bldg., 2–12–3 Shinjuku, B1 fl., Shinjuku-ku* ☎ *03/3352–8972* ⊕ *gb-tokyo.com* ☾ *Closed Mon.* Ⓜ *Marunouchi subway line, Shinjuku-san-chome Station.*

**Gold Finger**
BARS | This relaxed bar for "women who love women" is a cozy den of vintage lamps and cafélike ambience. Men are welcome on Friday; Saturday is women-only. ⊠ *Hayashi Bldg., 2-12-11 Shinjuku, Shinjuku-ku* ☎ *03/6383–4649* ⊕ *www.goldfingerparty.com* ☾ *Closed Tues. and Wed.* Ⓜ *Marunouchi subway line, Shinjuku-san-chome Station.*

# All That Tokyo Jazz

The Tokyo jazz scene is one of the world's best, far surpassing that of Paris and New York with its number of venues playing traditional, swing, bossa nova, rhythm and blues, and free jazz. Though popular in Japan before World War II, jazz really took hold of the city after U.S. forces introduced Charlie Parker and Thelonius Monk in the late 1940s. The genre had been banned in wartime Japan as an American vice, but even at the height of the war, fans were able to listen to their favorite artists on Voice of America radio. In the 1960s Japan experienced a boom in all areas of the arts, and jazz was no exception. Since then, the Japanese scene has steadily bloomed, with several local stars—such as Sadao Watanabe in the 1960s and contemporary favorites Keiko Lee and Hiromi Uehara—gaining global attention.

Today there are more than 120 bars and clubs that host live music, plus hundreds that play recorded jazz. Shinjuku, Takadanobaba, and Kichijoji are the city's jazz enclaves. Famous international acts regularly appear at big-name clubs such as the Blue Note, but the smaller, lesser-known joints usually have more atmosphere. With such a large jazz scene, there's an incredible diversity to enjoy, from Louis Armstrong tribute acts to fully improvised free jazz—sometimes on successive nights at the same venue.

If you time your visit right, you can listen to great jazz at one of the city's more than 20 annual festivals dedicated to this adopted musical form. The festivals vary in size and coverage, but two to check out are the Tokyo Jazz Festival and the Asagaya Jazz Street Festival.

## JAZZ BARS

### Jazz Spot Intro (イントロ)

**LIVE MUSIC** | This small basement jazz joint is home to one of the best jazz experiences in Tokyo, with a Saturday "12-hour jam session" that stretches until 5 am. Live sessions run throughout the week except Monday and Friday, when the regulars enjoy listening to the owner's extensive vinyl and CD collection. Italian food is available. ☒ NT Bldg., 2–14–8 Takadanobaba, B1 fl., Shinjuku-ku ☎ 03/3200–4396 ⊕ www.intro.co.jp Ⓜ JR Takadanobaba Station (Waseda Exit).

### Shinjuku Pit Inn (ピットイン)

**LIVE MUSIC** | Most major jazz musicians have played at least once in this classic Tokyo club. The veteran club stages mostly mainstream fare with the odd foray into the avant-garde. The emphasis here is strictly on jazz—and the place resembles a small concert hall. Entry runs ¥1,400–¥5,000. ☒ Accord Shinjuku Bldg., 2–12–4 Shinjuku, B1 fl., Shinjuku-ku ☎ 03/3354–2024 ⊕ pit-inn.com/e Ⓜ Marunouchi subway line, Shinjuku-san-chome Station.

## 🎭 Performing Arts

### MUSIC

**New National Theater and Tokyo Opera City Concert Hall** (新国立劇場; Shin Kokuritsu Gekijo)

**CONCERTS** | With its 1,632-seat main auditorium, this venue nourishes Japan's fledgling efforts to make a name for itself in the world of opera. The Opera City Concert Hall has a massive pipe organ and hosts a free concert on Friday from 11:45 to 12:30, as well as visiting orchestras and performers. Ballet and large-scale operatic productions such

Kabuki-cho, in Shinjuku, is a brightly lit hub for bars, pachinko parlors, and restaurants, as well as tattooed yakuza.

as *Carmen* draw crowds at the New National Theater's Opera House, while the Pit and Playhouse theaters showcase dance and more intimate dramatic works. The complex also includes an art gallery. ⊠ *1–1–1 Honmachi, Shibuya-ku, Shinjuku-ku* ☎ *03/5353–0788, 03/5353–9999 ticket center* ⊕ *www.nntt.jac.go.jp/english* 🎟 *From ¥3,000* Ⓜ *Keio Shin-sen line, Hatsudai Station (Higashi-guchi/East Exit).*

## 🛍 Shopping

### BOOKS

**Books Kinokuniya Tokyo** (紀伊国屋)

BOOKS | This mammoth bookstore, an annex of Takashimaya, devotes most of its sixth floor to English titles, with an excellent selection of travel guides, magazines, and books on Japan. ⊠ *Takashimaya Times Sq., 5–24–2 Sendagaya, Shibuya-ku* ☎ *03/5361–3301* ⊕ *www.kinokuniya.co.jp* Ⓜ *JR Yamanote Line, Shinjuku Station (Minami-guchi/South Exit); Fukutoshin subway line, Shinjuku San-chome Station (Exit E8).*

### CRAFTS

**Bingo-ya** (備後屋)

CRAFTS | This tasteful four-floor shop allows you to complete your souvenir shopping in one place. The store carries traditional handicrafts—including ceramics, toys, lacquerware, Noh masks, fabrics, and lots more—from all over Japan. ⊠ *10–6 Wakamatsucho, Shinjuku-ku* ☎ *03/3202–8778* ⊕ *bingoya.tokyo* ⊙ *Closed Mon. and some weekends* Ⓜ *Oedo subway line, Wakamatsu Kawada Station (Kawada Exit).*

### DEPARTMENT STORES

**Don Quijote** (ドンキホーテ)

DEPARTMENT STORE | This 24-hour discount store has chains all around the country. The generally tight quarters aren't recommended for those with claustrophobia, but bargain hunters love the costumes, odd cosmetics, family-size bags of Japanese snacks, and used luxury handbags and watches. It's all haphazardly stacked from the floor to the ceiling. ⊠ *1–16–5 Kabuki-cho, Shinjuku-ku* ☎ *03/5291–9211* ⊕ *www.donki.com* Ⓜ *Marunouchi, Oedo,*

# The Red Lights of Kabuki-cho

Tokyo has more than its fair share of red-light districts, but the leader of the pack is unquestionably Kabuki-cho, located just north of Shinjuku Station. The land was once a swamp, although its current name refers to an aborted post–World War II effort to bring culture to the area in the form of a landmark Kabuki theater. Until recently, most of the entertainment is of the insalubrious kind, with strip clubs, love hotels, host and hostess clubs, and thinly disguised brothels all luridly advertising their presence. Since the mid-2000s, however, the area has undergone a clean-up to draw in more tourists, similar to the restoration of New York's Times Square in the 1990s.

The area was once home to throngs of Japanese and Chinese gangsters, giving rise to its image domestically as a danger zone. But in truth, Kabuki-cho poses little risk even to the solo traveler. The sheer volume of people in the area each night, combined with a prominent security-camera presence, means that crime stays mostly indoors.

Despite its sordid reputation, Kabuki-cho does have attractions beyond the red lights. There are eateries galore ranging from chain diners to designer restaurants.

and Shinjuku subway lines, JR Yamanote Line, Keio and Odakyu lines, Shinjuku Station (Higashi-guchi/East Exit).

### Isetan (伊勢丹)

DEPARTMENT STORE | Established in 1886, "The Bergdorf's of Tokyo" is known for its high-end fashions both local and foreign, including a selection of larger sizes not found in most Tokyo stores. The second and third floors have champagne bars and snazzy store design that rival the world's best shops, making this one of the most pleasant shopping experiences in Tokyo, or anywhere, for that matter. The basement food court, which includes both traditional and modern prepared cuisine, is one of the city's largest in a department store. ✉ 3–14–1 Shinjuku, Shinjuku-ku ☎ 03/3225–2514 ⊕ isetan.mistore.jp/store/shinjuku Ⓜ JR Yamanote Line, Marunouchi subway line, Shinjuku Station (Higashi-guchi/East Exit for JR, Exits B2, B3, B4, and B5 for subway line).

### ★ Marui 0101 Main Building (0101 マルイ本館)

DEPARTMENT STORE | Easily recognized by its red-and-white "O1" logo, Marui burst onto the department store scene in the 1980s by introducing an in-store credit card—one of the first stores in Japan to do so. The four Marui buildings—Marui Honkan, Marui Annex, Marui One, and Marui Mens—make up the largest department store in the area by a large margin. Women flock to the stores in search of petite clothing, and you can find the largest concentration of Gothic and Lolita clothing in the city at the Annex. ✉ 3–30–13 Shinjuku, Shinjuku-ku ☎ 03/3354–0101 ⊕ www.0101.co.jp/stores/language/en Ⓜ JR Yamanote Line, Shinjuku Station (Higashi-guchi/East Exit); Marunouchi, Shinjuku, and Fukutoshin subway lines, Shinjuku San-chome Station (Exit A1).

**Seibu Ikebukuro** (西武デパート池袋本店)
DEPARTMENT STORE | Even Japanese customers have been known to get lost in this mammoth department store; the main branch is in Ikebukuro, a bustling neighborhood just north of Shinjuku. Seibu has an excellent selection of household goods, from furniture to lacquerware and quirky interior design pieces in its stand-alone Loft shops (which you'll find throughout the city next to Seibu branches, or occasionally in the department store itself). ⊠ *1–28–1 Minami Ikebukuro, Toshima-ku* ☎ *03/3981–8569* ⊕ *www.sogo-seibu.jp/ikebukuro* Ⓜ *JR Yamanote Line, Marunouchi, Fukutoshin, and Yurakucho subway lines, Ikebukuro Station (Minami-guchi/South Exit); Seibu Ikebukuro Line, Seibu Ikebukuro Station (Seibu Department Store Exit); Tobu Tojo Line, Tobu Ikebukuro Station (Minami-guchi/South Exit).*

**Takashimaya** (高島屋)
DEPARTMENT STORE | In Japanese, *taka* means "high"—a fitting word for this store, which is beloved for its superior quality and prestige. Gift givers all over Japan seek out this department store; a present that comes in a Takashimaya bag makes a statement regardless of what's inside. Like most department stores each floor is dedicated to labels with similar price points, but here the north half is for women and south for men, so couples and families can shop on the same floors. The basement-level food court carries every gastronomic delight imaginable, from Japanese crackers and Miyazaki beef to one of the largest gourmet dessert courts in the city. The annexes boast a large-scale Tokyu Hands and Kinokuniya bookstore as well. ⊠ *Takashimaya Times Sq., 5–24–2 Sendagaya, Shibuya-ku* ☎ *03/5361–1111* ⊕ *www.takashimaya.co.jp/shinjuku* Ⓜ *JR Yamanote Line, Shinjuku Station (Minami-guchi/South Exit); Fukutoshin subway line, Shinjuku San-chome Station (Exit E8).*

## ELECTRONICS
**Yodobashi Camera** (ヨドバシカメラ)
ELECTRONICS | This electronics superstore near Shinjuku Station carries a selection comparable to stores in Akihabara. It is made up of a number of annexes, including a watch, hobby, and professional camera building, that together span several blocks. ⊠ *1–11–1 Nishi-Shinjuku, Shinjuku-ku* ☎ *03/3346–1010* ⊕ *www.yodobashi.com* Ⓜ *Marunouchi, Shinjuku, and Oedo subway lines, JR Yamanote Line, Keio and Odakyu lines, Shinjuku Station (Nishi-guchi/West Exit).*

## MUSIC
★ **Disk Union** (ディスクユニオン)
MUSIC | Vinyl junkies rejoice. The Shinjuku flagship of this chain sells Latin, rock, and indie at 33 rpm. Be sure to grab a store flyer that lists all the branches, since each specializes in one music genre. Oh, and for digital folks, CDs are available, too. ⊠ *3–17–5 Shinjuku, Shinjuku-ku* ☎ *03/5919–4565* Ⓜ *Marunouchi, Oedo, and Shinjuku subway lines, JR Yamanote Line, Keio and Odakyu lines, Shinjuku Station (Higashi-guchi/East Exit).*

## PAPER
**Wagami Takamura**
(紙のたかむら; *Kami no Takamura*)
STATIONERY | Specialists in *washi* and other papers printed in traditional Japanese designs, this shop also carries brushes, inkstones, and other tools for calligraphy. At the entrance is a gallery showcasing seasonal traditional stationery and the work of local artists. ⊠ *1–1–2 Higashi-Ikebukuro, Toshima-ku* ☎ *03/3971–7111* ⊕ *www.wagami-takamura.com* Ⓜ *JR Yamanote Line, Marunouchi and Fukutoshin subway lines, Ikebukuro Station (East Exit for JR, Exit 35 for subway).*

# Akihabara (秋葉原)

Akihabara is techno-geek heaven. Also known as Akihabara Electric Town, or just Akiba, this district was once a dizzying collection of small, ultra-specialized electronics and computer shops, but has now become the center of Japan's anime, manga, and computer-focused *otaku* (nerd) culture.

More recently the area has gained mainstream appeal among shoppers and tourists, with large all-in-one electronics shops crowding out many of the smaller and unique stores. Even so, the area has stayed true to its roots. Venture off the main road to see the real Akiba, where "maid cafés" (servers are dressed as maids and treat their customers as "masters and mistresses") mix with computer and hi-fi audio stores filled with dedicated fans searching for computer parts, rare comics, or techno-accessories they can't find anywhere else. For visitors, seeing the subculture and energy of Akiba is as much a draw as the shopping.

**Access:** Akihabara is east of the Imperial Palace, right below Ueno and Asakusa. Akihabara Station is located north of Tokyo Station, on the JR Yamanote, Hibiya, and Tsukuba lines. It's right below Asakusa and Ueno districts. Akihabara is a 20- to 30-minute ride from most hotels in Shinjuku or Minato-ku.

## 👁 Sights

### Nikolai-do Holy Resurrection Cathedral
(ニコライ堂; *Nikolai-do*)
CHURCH | It's curious that a Russian Orthodox cathedral was built in Tokyo's Electric Town, but it's a place to stop for a quick snapshot. Formally, this is the Holy Resurrection Cathedral, derived from its founder, St. Nikolai Kassatkin (1836–1912), a Russian missionary who came to Japan in 1861 and spent the rest of his life here. The building, planned by a Russian engineer and executed by a British architect, was completed in 1891. Heavily damaged in the earthquake of 1923, the cathedral was restored with a dome much more modest than the original. Even so, the cathedral endows this otherwise featureless part of the city with unexpected charm. ✉ *4–1–3 Kanda Surugadai, Chiyoda-ku* ☎ *03/3295–6879* ⊕ *nikolaido.org/en* Ⓜ *Chiyoda subway line, Shin-Ochanomizu Station (Exit B1).*

### Kanda Myojin Shrine (神田明神)
RELIGIOUS BUILDING | This shrine is said to have been founded in AD 730 in a village called Shibasaki, where the Otemachi financial district stands today. The shrine itself was destroyed in the Great Kanto Earthquake of 1923, and the present buildings reproduce in concrete the style of 1616.

You will never be able to see every shrine in the city, and the ones in Akihabara are of minor interest unless you are around for the Kanda Festival—one of Tokyo's three great blowouts—in mid-May. (The other two are the Sanno Festival of Hie Jinja in Nagata-cho and the Sanja Festival of Asakusa Shrine.) Some of the smaller buildings you see as you come up the steps and walk around the Main Hall contain the *mikoshi*—the portable shrines that are featured during the festival. ✉ *2–16–2 Soto-Kanda, Chiyoda-ku* ☎ *03/3254–0753* ⊕ *www.kandamyoujin. or.jp* 🏛 *Museum ¥300* Ⓜ *Ginza subway line, Suehiro-cho Station (Exit 3).*

## 🍴 Restaurants

### Kanda Matsuya (神田まつや)
$ | JAPANESE | Soba, thin buckwheat noodles often served chilled in summer and hot in winter, are available everywhere, even convenience stores. The family-run Matsuya serves authentic soba in a rustic atmosphere. **Known for:** tempura soba; lunchtime crowds; authentic hand-cut noodles. $ *Average main: ¥1,000* ✉ *1–13 Kanda Sudacho,*

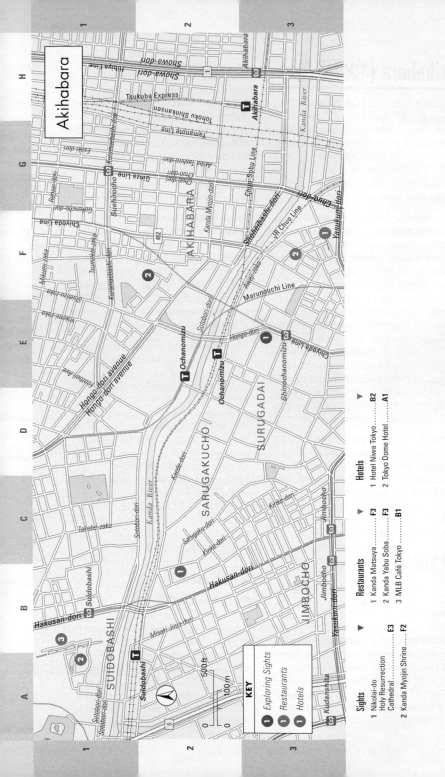

# Akihabara

## KEY

- **1** Exploring Sights
- **1** Restaurants
- **1** Hotels

## Sights

1 Nikolai-do
   Holy Resurrection
   Cathedral ............... **E3**
2 Kanda Myojin Shrine...... **F2**

## Restaurants

1 Kanda Matsuya ........... **F3**
2 Kanda Yabu Soba....... **F3**
3 MLB Café Tokyo .......... **B1**

## Hotels

1 Hotel Niwa Tokyo....... **B2**
2 Tokyo Dome Hotel.......**A1**

Chiyoda-ku ☎ 03/3251–1556 ▭ No credit cards ⊘ Closed Sun. Ⓜ Marunouchi Line, Awajicho Station (Exit A3).

### Kanda Yabu Soba (かんだやぶそば)

$ | **JAPANESE** | The ever-popular Kanda Yabu Soba, located in a recently built but traditional building that replaced the original 130-year-old restaurant after a fire in 2013, is one of the oldest and best places to sit down and savor freshly made soba—be that on tatami or at one of the tables. Soba, thin noodles made from buckwheat flour and quickly dipped into a hot broth or cold dipping sauce, are the lighter cousin of udon. **Known for:** soba sushi rolls; historic atmosphere; excellent rotating seasonal set. Ⓢ Average main: ¥1,000 ✉ 2–10 Kanda Awajicho, Chiyoda-ku ☎ 03/3251–0287 ⊕ www.yabusoba.net ▭ No credit cards ⊘ Closed Wed. Ⓜ JR and Marunouchi lines, Awajicho Station (Exit A3).

### MLB Café Tokyo

$$ | **AMERICAN** | **FAMILY** | Located in the shadow of Tokyo Dome, the primary baseball stadium in Tokyo, this theme restaurant is filled with sports memorabilia and waitstaff dressed in baseball uniforms. With a lineup similar to a Hard Rock Cafe or TGI Friday's it is a good stop for sports-loving kids. **Known for:** sizable burgers; the taste and feel of America as imagined by Japan; a place for baseball fans to catch up on MLB games. Ⓢ Average main: ¥2,000 ✉ 1–3–17 Koraku, Bunkyo-ku ☎ 03/5840–8905 ⊕ www.mlbcafe.jp Ⓜ JR Sobu and Toei Mita subway lines, Suidobashi Station (Exit A5).

##  Hotels

### Hotel Niwa Tokyo (庭のホテル 東京; Niwa no Hoteru Tokyo)

$$ | **HOTEL** | Traditional and contemporary elements come together to make the Niwa Tokyo a prized little boutique hotel in the middle of the city. **Pros:** quiet area; central location; charming Japanese touches. **Cons:** finding entrance is a bit challenging; few major sights within walking distance; small rooms. Ⓢ Rooms from: ¥18,000 ✉ 1–1–16 Misaki-cho, Chiyoda-ku ☎ 03/3293–0028 ⊕ www.hotelniwa.jp ⤴ 238 rooms ⦿ No Meals Ⓜ JR Chuo or Sobu lines, Suido-bashi Station (East Exit); Mita subway line, Suido-bashi Station (Exit A1).

### Tokyo Dome Hotel (東京ドームホテル)

$$ | **HOTEL** | **FAMILY** | Next to the city's most popular sports facility, the Tokyo Dome Hotel has a great location for sports fans at a comfortable price and offers easy train access to most of central Tokyo. **Pros:** convenient location; solid value; great for kids. **Cons:** rooms are a little bland; surrounding area is very crowded during events at Tokyo Dome; being part of an entertainment complex, the immediate surroundings lack local flavor. Ⓢ Rooms from: ¥21,000 ✉ 1–3–61 Koraku, Bunkyo-ku ☎ 03/5805–2111 ⊕ www.tokyodome-hotels.co.jp/e ⤴ 1006 rooms ⦿ No Meals Ⓜ JR lines, Suidobashi Station (East Exit); Namboku and Marunouchi subway lines, Korakuen Station.

## 🛍 Shopping

### CRAFTS

#### 2K540 Aki-Oka Artisan (2k540; アキオカアルチザン)

**CRAFTS** | Located in a renovated area under the train tracks just north of Akihabara Station, this hip collection of 50 some artisanal shops is a great place to hunt for high-end gifts made by local artists and designers. Most shops have a single specialty: paper, ceramics, leather bags, even umbrellas combining traditional techniques with modern design. On weekends some of the shops offer workshops, demonstrations, and other events. ✉ 5-9 Ueno, Taito-ku ☎ 03/6806–0254 ⊘ Closed Wed.

## DOLLS

**Kyugetsu** (九月)

**OTHER SPECIALTY STORE** | In business for more than a century, Kyugetsu sells handcrafted Japanese dolls. Each piece is individually made by one of Kyugetsu's artisans making for a unique—albeit expensive—souvenir. Dolls run from a few hundred to thousands of dollars. ✉ 1-20-4 Yanagibashi, Taito-ku ☎ 03/5687–5176 ⊕ www.kyugetsu.com/e Ⓜ Asakusa subway line, JR Sobu Line, Asakusa-bashi Station (Exit A3).

## ELECTRONICS

**LAOX Akihabara Main Shop** (LAOX 秋葉原本店)

**ELECTRONICS** | One of the big Akihabara department stores, LAOX has several locations and the largest and most comprehensive selection in the district, with four buildings. The seven-story main branch is duty-free, with three floors dedicated to electronic gadgets, such as lightweight vacuum cleaners and eco-friendly humidifiers, that come with English instruction booklets. LAOX has annexes—one exclusively for musical instruments, another for duty-free appliances—and outlets in Ginza, Odaiba, and Narita Airport. This is a good place to find the latest in digital cameras, watches, and games. ■TIP➔ **English-speaking staff members are on call.** ✉ 1–2–9 Soto-Kanda, Chiyoda-ku ☎ 03/3253–7111 ⊕ www.laox.co.jp Ⓜ JR Yamanote Line, Akihabara Station (Electric Town Exit).

**Sofmap** (ソフマップ)

**ELECTRONICS** | One Akihabara retailer that actually benefited from the bursting of Japan's economic bubble in the early 1990s is this electronics chain, once known as a used-PC and software chain with a heavy presence in Tokyo. Now its multiple branches also sell all sorts of new electronics, music, and mobile phones. Most are open daily until 8. ✉ 3–13–12 Soto-Kanda, Chiyoda-ku ☎ 050/3032–9888 ⊕ www.sofmap.com

Ⓜ JR Yamanote Line, Akihabara Station (Electric Town Exit).

**Radio Kaikan** (ラジオ会館)

**ELECTRONICS** | Eight floors featuring a variety of independent vendors selling mini–spy cameras, cell phones disguised as stun guns, manga, plastic models, gadgets, and oddball hobby supplies are sold here. Start browsing from the top floor and work your way down. There are two annexes across the street as well. ✉ 1–15–16 Soto-Kanda, Chiyoda-ku ☎ 03/3251–3711 ⊕ www.akihabara-radiokaikan.co.jp Ⓜ JR Yamanote Line, Akihabara Station (Akihabara Electric Town Exit).

#  Performing Arts

## CONCERTS

**Tokyo Dome** (東京ドーム)

**CONCERTS** | **FAMILY** | A 45,852-seat sports arena, the dome also hosts big-name Japanese pop acts as well as the occasional international star. ✉ 1–3–61 Koraku, Bunkyo-ku ☎ 03/5800–9999 ⊕ www.tokyo-dome.co.jp/e Ⓜ Marunouchi and Namboku subway lines, Koraku-en Station (Exit 2); Mita subway line, Suido-bashi Station (Exit A5); JR Suido-bashi Station (Nishi-guchi/West Exit).

## PERFORMING ARTS CENTERS

**Bunkyo Civic Hall** (文京シビックホール)

**MUSIC** | This three-story, city-run performance hall showcases classical music and ballet, opera, dance, and drama. Visitors might be especially interested in performances of local interest featuring puppets, wind music, and Japanese Kabuki dance. ✉ 1–16–21 Kasuga, Bunkyo-ku ☎ 03/5803–1100, 03/5803–1111 tickets only ⊕ www.b-academy.jp/hall Ⓜ Marunouchi and Namboku subway lines, Kourakuen Station (Exit 5).

# Ueno (上野)

Located in the heart of Ueno, JR Ueno Station is Tokyo's version of the Gare du Nord: the gateway to and from Japan's northeast provinces. Since its completion in 1883, the station has served as a terminus in the great migration to the city by villagers in pursuit of a better life.

Ueno was a place of prominence long before the coming of the railroad. After Ieyasu Tokugawa established his capital here in 1603, 36 subsidiary temples were erected surrounding the Main Hall, and the city of Edo itself expanded to the foot of the hill where the main gate of the Kan ci ji once stood. Some of the most important buildings in the temple complex have survived or have been restored and should not be missed.

Ueno, Asakusa, and Yanaka make up the historical heart of Tokyo. Though the Tokyo Sky Tree transmission tower can be seen from nearly all parts of these neighborhoods, traditional architecture and way of life are preserved here at the northeastern reaches of the city. If you are pressed for time all three areas can be explored in a single day, though if you want to visit Ueno's museums, it is best to devote an entire day to fully appreciate the area.

**Access:** Ueno Station can be accessed by train on the Hibiya Line, Ginza Line, and JR Yamanote Line (Koen Entrance). Be sure to avoid rush hours in the morning (8–9) and evening (6–9) and bring plenty of cash for admission fees to museums and food for the day, as there are few ATMs inside Ueno Park itself. Museums stores accept major credit cards but it is best to be prepared with cash for admission.

## ● Sights

**Ameya Yokocho Market Street** (アメヤ横丁)

MARKET | The sprawling stalls are famous for the traditional prepared foods of the New Year celebrations; during the last few days of December, as many as half a million people crowd into the narrow alleys under the railroad tracks to stock up for the holiday. The market dates to World War II, when not much besides Ueno Station survived the bombings. People would travel from the countryside to sell rice at black-market prices. Before long, there were hundreds of stalls in the black market selling various kinds of *ame* (confections), most made from sweet potatoes, earning the market its name, Ame-ya Yoko-cho (Ameyoko, locally), or "Confectioners' Alley." Shortly before the Korean War, the market was legalized, and soon the stalls were carrying watches, chocolate, ballpoint pens, blue jeans, and T-shirts that had somehow been "liberated" from American PXs. In years to come you'd find Swiss timepieces and fake designor luggage, cosmetics, jewelry, fresh fruit, and fish. Try the raw slices of tuna over rice (*maguro-don*) in one of the small restaurants—cheap, quick, and very good. ⊠ *Ueno 4-chome, Taito-ku* Ⓜ *JR Ueno Station (Hiroko-ji Exit).*

**Kiyomizu Kannon-do Temple** (清水観音堂)

TEMPLE | This National Treasure was a part of Abbot Tenkai's attempt to build a copy of Kyoto's magnificent Kiyomizu-dera in Ueno. His attempt was honorable, but failed to be as impressive as the original. The principal Buddhist image of worship here is the Senju Kannon (Thousand-Armed Goddess of Mercy). Another figure, however, receives greater homage. This is the Kosodate Kannon, who is believed to answer the prayers of women having difficulty conceiving children. If their prayers are answered, they return to Kiyomizu and leave a doll, as both an offering of thanks and a prayer for the child's health. In a ceremony held every September 25, the dolls that have

Ueno Park, with over 1,000 cherry trees, hosts one of the largest cherry blossom festivals in Japan in March and April.

accumulated during the year are burned in a bonfire. ⊠ *1–29 Ueno Koen, Taito-ku* ☎ *03/3821–4749* ✉ *Free* Ⓜ *JR Ueno Station (Koen-guchi/Park Exit).*

### Marishiten Tokudai-ji Temple (摩利支天徳大寺)

TEMPLE | This is a curiosity in a neighborhood of curiosities: a temple on the second floor of a supermarket. Two deities are worshipped here. One is the *bodhisattva* Jizo, and the act of washing this statue is believed to safeguard your health. The other is of the Indian goddess Marici, a daughter of Brahma; she is believed to help worshippers overcome difficulties and succeed in business. ⊠ *4–6–2 Ueno, Taito-ku* Ⓜ *JR Yamanote and Keihin-tohoku lines, Okachi-machi Station (Higashi-guchi/East Exit) or Ueno Station (Hiroko-ji Exit).*

### National Museum of Western Art (国立西洋美術館; *Kokuritsu Seiyo Bijutsukan*)

ART MUSEUM | Along with castings from the original molds of Rodin's *Gate of Hell, The Burghers of Calais,* and *The Thinker,* the wealthy businessman Matsukata Kojiro (1865–1950) acquired some 850 paintings, sketches, and prints by such masters as Renoir, Monet, Gauguin, van Gogh, Delacroix, and Cézanne. Matsukata kept the collection in Europe, but he left it to Japan in his will. The French government sent the artwork to Japan after World War II, and the collection opened to the public in 1959 in a building designed by Swiss-born architect Le Corbusier. Since then, the museum has diversified a bit; more recent acquisitions include works by Reubens, Tintoretto, El Greco, Max Ernst, and Jackson Pollock. The Seiyo is one of the best-organized, most pleasant museums to visit in Tokyo. ⊠ *7–7 Ueno Koen, Taito-ku* ☎ *03/5777–8600* ⊕ *www.nmwa.go.jp* ✉ *¥500; additional fee for special exhibits* ⊙ *Closed Mon.* Ⓜ *JR Ueno Station (Koen-guchi/Park Exit).*

### Shinobazu Pond (不忍池; *Shinobazu-ike*)

BODY OF WATER | FAMILY | When an inlet of Tokyo Bay receded around the 17th century, Shinobazu became a freshwater pond. Abbot Tenkai, founder of Kan-ei-ji on the hill above the pond, had an island made for Benzaiten, the goddess of the arts. Later improvements included a causeway to the island, embankments, and even a racecourse (1884–93). Today the pond is in three sections. The first, a wildlife sanctuary, is home to the city's lotus flowers; this is the only place in Tokyo you can see them bloom from mid-June through August. Some 5,000 wild ducks migrate here from as far away as Siberia, sticking around from September to April. The second section, to the north, belongs to Ueno Zoo; the third, to the west, is a small lake for boating. In July, the Ueno *matsuri* (festival) features food stalls and music events at the pond's edge. At the pond's southwestern corner, there is also a bandshell with various music events throughout the year. ⊠ *5-20 Uenokoen, Taito-ku* ⊠ *Free* Ⓜ *JR Ueno Station (Koen-guchi/Park Exit); Keisei private rail line, Keisei-Ueno Station (Higashi-guchi/East Exit).*

### Shinobazu Pond Bentendo Temple (不忍池 辯天堂; *Shinobazu-ike Bentendo*)
TEMPLE | Perched in the middle of Shinobazu Pond, this temple is dedicated to the goddess Benten, one of the Seven Gods of Good Luck that evolved from a combination of Indian, Chinese, and Japanese mythology. As matron goddess of the arts, she is depicted holding a lutelike musical instrument called a *biwa*. The temple, built by Abbot Tenkai, was destroyed in the bombings of 1945; the present version, with its distinctive octagonal roof, is a faithful copy. You can rent rowboats and pedal boats at a nearby boathouse. ⊠ *2–1 Ueno Koen, Taito-ku* ☎ *03/3828–9502 boathouse* ⊠ *Temple free, boats from ¥700* Ⓜ *JR Ueno Station (Koen-guchi/Park Exit); Keisei private rail line, Keisei-Ueno Station (Ikenohata Exit).*

### Shitamachi Museum (下町風俗資料館; *Shitamachi Fuzoku Shiryokan*)
HISTORY MUSEUM | FAMILY | Japanese society in the days of the Tokugawa shoguns was rigidly stratified. Some 80% of the city's land was allotted to the warrior class, temples, and shrines. The remaining 20%—between Ieyasu's fortifications on the west, and the Sumida-gawa on the east—was known as *Shitamachi*, or "downtown" or the "lower town" (as it expanded, it came to include what today constitutes the Chuo, Taito, Sumida, and Koto wards). It was here that the common, hardworking, free-spending folk, who made up more than half the population, lived. The Shitamachi Museum preserves and exhibits what remained of that way of life as late as 1940.

The two main displays on the first floor are a merchant house and a tenement, intact with all their furnishings. This is a hands-on museum: you can take your shoes off and step up into the rooms. On the second floor are displays of toys, tools, and utensils donated, in most cases, by people who had grown up with them and used them all their lives. There are also photographs and video documentaries of craftspeople at work. Occasionally various traditional skills are demonstrated, and you're welcome to take part. This small but engaging museum makes great use of its space, and there are volunteer English-speaking guides. ⊠ *2–1 Ueno Koen, Taito-ku* ☎ *03/3823–7451* ⊕ *www.taitocity.net/ zaidan/shitamachi* ⊠ *¥300* ☉ *Closed Mon.* Ⓜ *JR Ueno Station (Koen-guchi/Park Exit).*

### Tokyo Metropolitan Art Museum (東京都美術館; *Tokyo-to Bijutsukan*)
ART MUSEUM | By far the most eclectic of Ueno's art museums, the Tokyo Metropolitan hosts large-scale exhibitions ranging from classic masterpieces to modern architecture. The museum's smaller galleries often play home to group exhibitions of painting, photography, calligraphy, sculpture, and nearly any other kind of art one can dream up. Many smaller exhibits are free. ⊠ *8–36 Ueno Koen, Taito-ku* ☎ *03/3823–6921* ⊕ *www. tobikan.jp* ⊠ *Permanent collection free;*

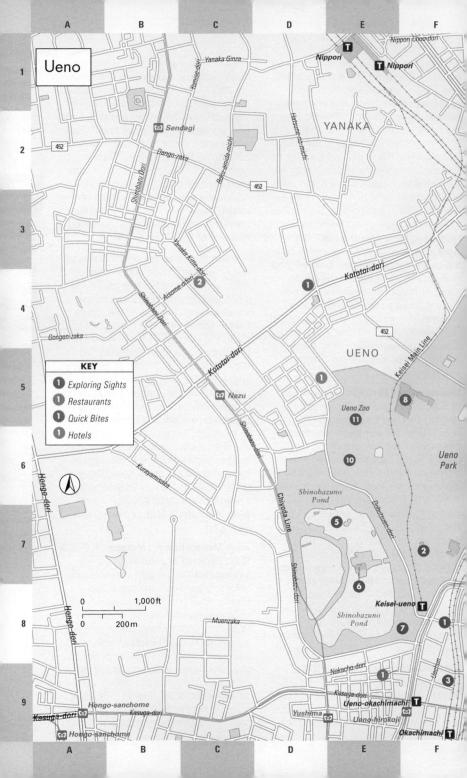

## Sights ▼

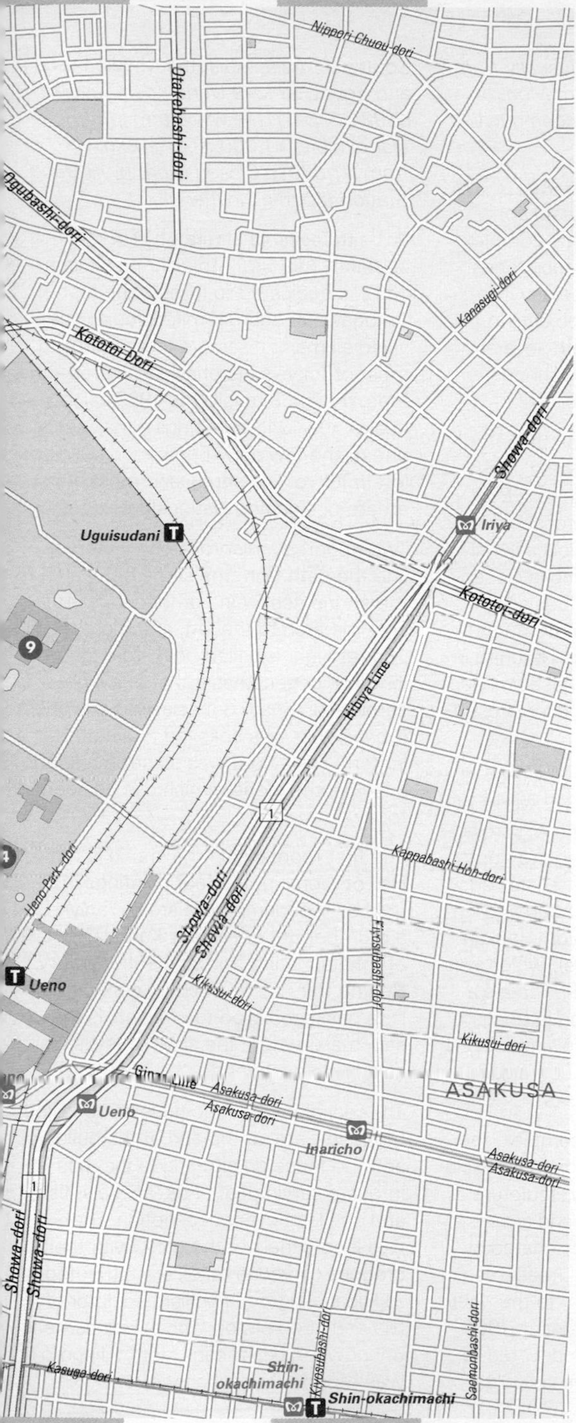

1 Ameya Yokocho
  Street Market ....................... F8
2 Kiyomizu Kannon-do Temple ...... F7
3 Marishiten Tokudai-ji Temple...... F9
4 National Museum
  of Western Art .................... G6
5 Shinobazu Pond.................... E7
6 Shinobazu Pond
  Bentendo Temple.................. E7
7 Shitamachi Museum .............. F8
8 Tokyo Metropolitan
  Art Museum ....................... F5
9 Tokyo National Museum .......... G5
10 Ueno Tosho-gu Shrine ............ E6
11 Ueno Zoo ......................... E5

## Restaurants ▼

1 Tonkatsu Musashino .............. E9

## Quick Bites ▼

1 Kayaba Coffee .................... D4

## Hotels ▼

1 Ryokan Katsutaro................. D5
2 Sawanoya Ryokan................. C4

**4**

Tokyo UENO (上野)

*fees vary for other exhibits (usually from ¥1,000)* ⊘ *Closed 1st and 3rd Mon. of month* Ⓜ *JR Ueno Station (Koen-guchi/Park Exit).*

★ **Tokyo National Museum** (東京国立博物館; *Tokyo Kokuritsu Hakubutsukan*)
**ART MUSEUM** | This four-building complex is one of the world's great repositories of East Asian art and archaeology. The museum has some 87,000 objects in its permanent collection, with several thousand more on loan from shrines, temples, and private owners.

The Western-style building on the left (if you're standing at the main gate), with bronze cupolas, is the Hyokeikan. Built in 1909, it was devoted to archaeological exhibits; aside from the occasional special exhibition, the building is closed today. The larger Heiseikan, behind the Hyokeikan, was built to commemorate the wedding of crown prince Naruhito in 1993 and now houses Japanese archaeological exhibits. The second floor is used for special exhibitions.

In 1878 the 7th-century Horyu-ji (Horyu Temple) in Nara presented 319 works of art in its possession—sculpture, scrolls, masks, and other objects—to the imperial household. These were transferred to the National Museum in 2000 and now reside in the Horyu-ji Homotsukan (Gallery of Horyu-ji Treasures), which was designed by Yoshio Taniguchi. There's a useful guide to the collection in English, and the exhibits are well explained. Don't miss the hall of carved wooden *gigaku* (Buddhist processional) masks.

The central building in the complex, the 1937 Honkan, houses Japanese art exclusively: paintings, calligraphy, sculpture, textiles, ceramics, swords, and armor. Also here are 84 objects designated by the government as National Treasures. The more attractive Toyokan, to the right of the Honkan, was completed in 1968 and recently renovated; it is devoted to the art and antiquities of China, Korea,

Southeast Asia, India, the Middle East, and Egypt. ✉ *13–9 Ueno Koen, Taito-ku* ☎ *03/3822–1111* ⊕ *www.tnm.jp* ⊠ *Regular exhibits ¥1,000, special exhibits from ¥1,600* ⊘ *Closed Mon.* Ⓜ *JR Ueno Station (Koen-guchi/Park Exit).*

★ **Ueno Tosho-gu Shrine** (上野東照宮)
**RELIGIOUS BUILDING** | This shrine, built in 1627, is dedicated to Ieyasu, the first Tokugawa shogun. It miraculously survived all major disasters that destroyed most of Tokyo's historical structures—the fires, the 1868 revolt, the 1923 earthquake, the 1945 bombings—making it one of the few early-Edo-period buildings left in Tokyo. The shrine and most of its art are designated National Treasures.

Two hundred *ishidoro* (stone lanterns) line the path from the stone entry arch to the shrine itself. One of them, just outside the arch to the left, and more than 18 feet high, is called *obaketoro* (ghost lantern). Legend has it that one night a samurai on guard duty slashed at a ghost (*obake*) that was believed to haunt the lantern. His sword was so strong, it left a nick in the stone, which can be seen today.

The first room inside the shrine is the Hall of Worship; the four paintings in gold on wooden panels are by Tan'yu, a member of the famous Kano family of artists, dating from the 15th century. Behind the Hall of Worship, connected by a passage called the *haiden,* is the sanctuary, where the spirit of Ieyasu is said to be enshrined.

The real glory of Tosho-gu is its so-called Chinese Gate, at the end of the building, and the fence on either side that has intricate carvings of birds, animals, fish, and shells of every description. The two long panels of the gate, with their dragons carved in relief, are attributed to Hidari Jingoro, a brilliant sculptor of the early Edo period whose real name is unknown (*hidari* means "left"; Jingoro was reportedly left-handed). ✉ *9–88*

*Ueno Koen, Taito-ku* ☎ *03/3822–3455* 🌐 *www.uenotoshogu.com/en* 🎫 *Shrine free; Peony Garden ¥700* [M] *JR Ueno Station (Koen-guchi/Park Exit).*

**Ueno Zoo** (上野動物園; *Ueno Dobutsuen*)
**ZOO** | **FAMILY** | The two main sections of Japan's first zoo, built in 1882, host an exotic mix of more than 900 species of animals. The giant panda is the biggest draw, but the tigers from Sumatra, gorillas from the lowland swamp areas of western Africa, and numerous monkeys, some from Japan, make a visit to the East Garden worthwhile. The West Garden is highlighted by rhinos, zebras, and hippopotamuses, and a children's area. The process of the zoo's expansion somehow left within its confines the 120-foot, five-story Kan-ei-ji Pagoda. Built in 1631 and rebuilt after a fire in 1639, the building offers traditional Japanese tea ceremony services. ✉ *9–83 Ueno Koen, Taito-ku* ☎ *03/3828–5171* 🌐 *www.tokyo-zoo.net/english/ueno* 🎫 *¥600, free on Mar. 20, May 4, and Oct. 1* 🕒 *Closed Mon.* [M] *JR Ueno Station (Koen-guchi/Park Exit).*

## 🍴 Restaurants

**Tonkatsu Musashino** (とんかつ武蔵野)
**$** | **JAPANESE** | The deep-fried, breaded pork cutlets at this casual restaurant just south of Ueno Park's pond combine generous portions with melt-in-the-mouth tenderness, and for a great price. Set meals here come with enough rice, miso soup, shredded cabbage, and pickles to loosen your belt a notch or two. **Known for:** rich, filling meals; a no-frills local atmosphere. [$] *Average main: ¥1,300* ✉ *2–8–1 Ueno, Taito-ku* ☎ *03/3831–1672* 💳 *No credit cards* [M] *JR Ueno Station.*

## ☕ Coffee and Quick Bites

**Kayaba Coffee** (カヤバ珈琲)
**$** | **CAFÉ** | Standing on the border of Ueno and Yanaka, just a short walk to the west from the National Museum, this historic café is a popular stop for lunch or a light snack. A century old, the café has been stylishly renovated and serves homemade sandwiches, curries, cakes, and *kaki gori*, a traditional treat of flavored shaved ice. **Known for:** popular with local residents; excellent morning sets; retro Japanese drinks and desserts. [$] *Average main: ¥1,000* ✉ *6–1–29 Yanaka, Taito-ku* ☎ *03/3823–3545* 🌐 *taireki.com/en/kayaba.html* 💳 *No credit cards* [M] *JR Nippori Station, JR Ueno Station.*

## 🛏 Hotels

**Ryokan Katsutaro** (旅館勝太郎)
**$** | **B&B/INN** | Established in the 1980s, this small, simple, economical inn is a five-minute walk from the entrance to Ueno Koen (Ueno Park) and a 10-minute walk from the Tokyo National Museum. **Pros:** a traditional and unique Japanese experience; reasonably priced room rates; excellent base for exploring Ueno. **Cons:** small baths; some rooms have shared Japanese baths; no breakfast served. [$] *Rooms from: ¥12,000* ✉ *4–16–8 Ikenohata, Taito ku* ☎ *03/3821 9808* 🛏 *8 rooms* 🍴 *No Meals* [M] *Chiyoda subway line, Nezu Station (Exit 2).*

**Sawanoya Ryokan** (澤の屋旅館)
**$** | **B&B/INN** | The *Shitamachi* sub-area of Ueno is known for its down to-earth friendliness, which you get in full measure at Sawanoya, a popular family business where everybody pitches in to help you plan excursions and book hotels for the next leg of your journey. **Pros:** traditional Japanese experience; affordable rates; friendly management. **Cons:**; many rooms share Japanese baths; a bit of a hike to the subway station; rooms somewhat small. [$] *Rooms from: ¥12,000* ✉ *2–3–11 Yanaka, Taito-ku* ☎ *03/3822–2251* 🌐 *www.sawanoya.com* 🛏 *10 rooms* 🍴 *No Meals* [M] *Chiyoda subway line, Nezu Station (Exit 1).*

##  Performing Arts

### MUSIC

**Tokyo Bunka Kaikan** (東京文化会館)

MUSIC | In the 1960s and '70s this hall was one of the city's premier showcases for classical ballet, orchestral music, and visiting soloists. It still gets major bookings. ✉ *5-45 Uenokoen, Taito-ku* ☎ *03/3828–2111* ⊕ *www.t-bunka.jp/ en* Ⓜ *JR Yamanote Line, Ueno Station (Koen-guchi/Park Exit).*

##  Shopping

### SPECIALITY STORES

**Jusan-ya** (十三や)

SOUVENIRS | A samurai who couldn't support himself as a feudal retainer launched this business selling handmade boxwood combs in 1736. It has been in the same family ever since. Jusan-ya is on Shinobazu-dori, a few doors west of its intersection with Chuo-dori in Ueno. ✉ *2–12–21 Ueno, Taito-ku* ☎ *03/3831–3238* ⊕ *www. kyoto-wel.com/shop/S81004* ⊘ *Closed Sun.* Ⓜ *Ginza subway line, Ueno Hiroko-ji Station (Exit 3); JR Yamanote Line, Ueno Station (Shinobazu Exit).*

# Asakusa (浅草)

Cars make room for the rickshaw drivers, who sometimes outpace the motorized traffic. On the neighborhood's back-streets, neo-French and Italian cafés mix with generations-old soba and tempura shops, while customers in the latest fashions sit with those in traditional kimonos. Kaminari-mon, the gateway to Senso-ji—Tokyo's oldest temple—is a backdrop for artisans and small entrepreneurs, children and grandmothers, hipsters, hucksters, and priests. It is hard not to be swept away by the relaxed energy that pulses through the area. If you have any time to spend in Tokyo, make sure you devote at least a day to exploring Asakusa.

Historically Asakusa has been the city's entertainment hub. Although the main shrine and markets existed from the 14th century, the area blossomed after Ieyasu Tokugawa made Edo his capital in the late 16th century. For the next 300 years, it was the wellspring of almost everything we associate with Japanese culture. During the Edo period it was a pleasure quarter in its own right with stalls selling toys, souvenirs, and sweets; acrobats, jugglers, and strolling musicians; and sake shops and teahouses—where the waitresses often provided more than tea. Then, in 1841, the Kabuki theaters moved to Asakusa. The theaters were here for only a short time, but it was enough to establish Asakusa as *the* entertainment quarter of the city—a reputation it held unchallenged until World War II, when most of the area was destroyed.

After the war, development focused on areas to the west like Shinjuku and Shibuya. In a way this saved Asakusa from becoming yet another neighborhood filled with neon, concrete, and glass, instead mostly keeping to the same style of low buildings and tiny independent shops that existed before the war. Seven decades have certainly changed the neighborhood, but many of the smaller side streets retain the charm and feel of old Tokyo. Although the area has become dramatically more popular in recent years, tourists usually keep to the main streets and line up at the same restaurants around the Senso-ji Temple Complex. Venture a few minutes away from the temple area and the crowds thin out and souvenir shops give way to quiet storefronts selling traditional crafts. Although Senso-ji Temple is well worth seeing, taking the time to wander through the neighborhood gives you a hint of what it may have been like years ago.

**Access:** Asakusa is a border city ward that separates central Tokyo from its suburban areas. It's a unique spiritual and commercial, tourist, and residential area, where locals walk their dogs on the Asakusa Jinja grounds or give offerings and pray at Kannon Temple. Asakusa is just east of Ueno and can be explored in a half day, whether you go straight from Ueno or on a separate excursion. Getting here by subway from Ueno Station (Ginza Line, Ueno Station to Asakusa Station, ¥170) or taxi (approximately ¥1,000) is most convenient. Asakusa is the last stop (eastbound) on the Ginza Line. Another way to get to Asakusa is by river-bus ferry from Hinode Pier, which stops at the southwest corner of Sumida Koen.

## ◉ Sights

### Asakusa Jinja Shrine (浅草神社)
RELIGIOUS BUILDING | Several structures in the famous Senso-ji shrine complex survived the bombings of 1945. The largest, to the right of the Main Hall, is this Shinto shrine to the Hikonuma brothers and their master, Naji-no-Nakamoto—the putative founders of Senso-ji. In Japan, Buddhism and Shintoism have enjoyed a comfortable coexistence since the former arrived from China in the 6th century. The shrine, built in 1649, is also known as Sanja Sama (Shrine of the Three Guardians). Near the entrance to Asakusa Shrine is another survivor of World War II: the original east gate to the temple grounds, Niten-mon, built in 1618 for a shrine to Ieyasu Tokugawa and designated by the government as an Important Cultural Property. ⊠ 2–3–1 Asakusa, Taito-ku ☎ 03/3844–1575 ⊕ www.asakusajinja.jp.

### Dembo-in Temple (伝法院)
GARDEN | Believed to have been made in the 17th century by Kobori Enshu, the genius of Zen landscape design, the garden of Dembo-in is part of the living quarters of the abbot of Senso-ji and the best-kept secret in Asakusa. The garden is usually empty and always utterly serene, an island of privacy in a sea of pilgrims. Spring, when the wisteria blooms, is the ideal time to be here.

A sign in English on Dembo-in-dori—you'll see it about 150 yards west of the intersection with Naka-mise-dori—leads you to the entrance, which is a side door to a large wooden gate. For permission to see the abbot's garden, you must first apply at the temple administration building, between Hozo-mon and the Five-Story Pagoda, in the far corner. ⊠ 2–3–1 Asakusa, Taito-ku ☎ 03/3842–0181 for reservations ☒ Free Ⓜ Ginza subway line, Asakusa Station (Exit 1/ Kaminari-mon Exit).

### Hanayashiki (花やしき)
AMUSEMENT PARK/CARNIVAL | FAMILY
Established in 1853, Tokyo's oldest amusement park has modernized but leans in to its retro atmosphere. Think Coney Island: a haunted house, Ferris wheel, and merry-go-round await the kids who will likely be a little tired of Asakusa's historic areas. ⊠ 2–28–1 Asakusa, Taito-ku ☎ 03/3842–8780 ⊕ www.hanayashiki.net ☒ ¥1,000 (rides from ¥300–¥600 each) Ⓜ Ginza subway line, Asakusa Station (Exit 1/ Kaminari-mon Exit).

### Japanese Sword Museum
(刀剣博物館; Token Hakabutsukan)
OTHER MUSEUM | It's said that in the late 16th century, before Japan closed its doors to the West, the Spanish tried to establish a trade here in weapons made from famous Toledo steel. The Japanese were politely uninterested; they had been making blades of incomparably better quality for more than 600 years. At one time there were some 200 schools of sword making in Japan; swords were prized not only for their effectiveness in battle but for the beauty of the blades and fittings and as symbols of the higher spirituality of the warrior caste. There are few inheritors of this art today and the Sword Museum's mission is to maintain

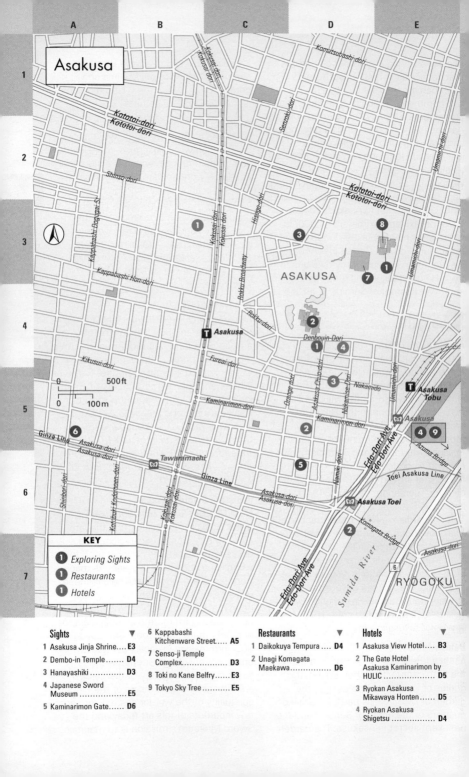

# Asakusa

|   |  A  |  B  |  C  |  D  |  E  |
|---|-----|-----|-----|-----|-----|

**1**

Kototoi-dori
Kototoi-dori

Komatsubashi-dori

Kotsu-dori

Senzoku-dori

**2**

Shinsa-dori

Kototoi-dori
Kototoi-dori

Kappabashi-Dogugai St.

**3**

Kappabashi Hon-dori

Kokusai-dori
Kokusai-dori

Rokku Broadway

Hisago-dori

Umamichi-dori

**ASAKUSA**

8

3

7

1

**4**

T **Asakusa**

Fureai-dori

Kikusui-dori

Denboin-Dori

1

2

4

Asakusa Chuo-dori

3

Nakamise-dori

Nakamido

0   500 ft
0   100 m

**5**

Kaminarimon-dori

Kaminarimon-dori

Orange-dori

2

T **Asakusa Tobu**

4  9  **Asakusa**

Azuma Bridge

Ginza Line

6

Asakusa-dori
Asakusa-dori

Tawaramachi

Ginza Line

**Asakusa**

Namiki-dori

Edo-Dori Ave
Edo-Dori Ave

5

**6**

Shinbori-dori

Katsubu-Kodenmen-dori

Kokusai-dori
Kokusai-dori

Asakusa-dori
Asakusa-dori

Asakusa Toei

Komagata Bridge

Toei Asakusa Line

**7**

Edo-Dori Ave
Edo-Dori Ave

2

6

**RYOGOKU**

Sumida River

Asakusa-dori

---

## KEY
1 *Exploring Sights*
1 *Restaurants*
1 *Hotels*

---

### Sights ▼
1 Asakusa Jinja Shrine.... **E3**
2 Dembo-in Temple ....... **D4**
3 Hanayashiki ............. **D3**
4 Japanese Sword
   Museum .................. **E5**
5 Kaminarimon Gate....... **D6**
6 Kappabashi
   Kitchenware Street..... **A5**
7 Senso-ji Temple
   Complex................. **D3**
8 Toki no Kane Belfry...... **E3**
9 Tokyo Sky Tree .......... **E5**

### Restaurants ▼
1 Daikokuya Tempura .... **D4**
2 Unagi Komagata
   Maekawa................ **D6**

### Hotels ▼
1 Asakusa View Hotel..... **B3**
2 The Gate Hotel
   Asakusa Kaminarimon by
   HULIC ................... **D5**
3 Ryokan Asakusa
   Mikawaya Honten ...... **D5**
4 Ryokan Asakusa
   Shigetsu ................. **D4**

the knowledge and appreciation of sword making. Although the collection has swords made by famous craftsmen such as Nobufusa (a Living National Treasure) and Sanekage (a famous 14th-century sword maker), the focus here is on the swords as objects of beauty. The swords are individually displayed as works of art, giving visitors a chance to appreciate the detail, creativity, and skill involved in crafting each one. In 2018 the museum moved to a larger location in Ryogoku near the Edo-Tokyo Museum. ⊠ *1–12–9 Yokami, Sumida-ku* ☎ *03/6284–1000* ⊕ *www.touken.or.jp* ✉ *¥1,000* ⏱ *Closed Mon.* Ⓜ *JR Sobu line, Ryogoku Station; Toei Subway Oedo Line, Ryogoku Station.*

**Kaminarimon Gate** (雷門)

**HISTORIC SIGHT** | The main entryway to Senso-ji's grounds towers above the ever-present throng of tourists and passing rickshaw drivers. With its huge red-paper lantern hanging in the center, this landmark of Asakusa is picture-perfect. The original gate was destroyed by fire in 1865; the replica you see today was built after World War II. Traditionally, two fearsome guardian gods are installed in the alcoves of Buddhist temple gates to ward off evil spirits. The Thunder God (Kaminari-no-Kami) is on the left with the Wind God (Kaze-no-Kami) on the right. For souvenirs, top at Tokiwa-do, the shop on the west side of the gate for *kaminari okoshi* (thunder crackers), made of rice, millet, sugar, and beans.

Kaminari-mon marks the southern extent of Nakamise-dori, the Street of Inside Shops. The area from Kaminari-mon to the inner gate of the temple was once composed of stalls leased to the townspeople who cleaned and swept the temple grounds. This is now kitsch-souvenir central, with key chains, dolls, and snacks. ⊠ *2–3–1 Asakusa, Taito-ku* Ⓜ *Ginza subway line, Asakusa Station (Exit 1/ Kaminari-mon Exit).*

## The Sanja Festival

The festival, held annually over the third weekend of May, is said to be the biggest, loudest, wildest party in Tokyo. Each of the areas in Asakusa has its own *mikoshi* (a portable shrine), which, on the second day of the festival, is paraded through the streets of Asakusa to the shrine. Many of the "parishioners" take part naked to the waist, or with the sleeves of their tunics rolled up, to expose fantastic red-and-black tattoo patterns that sometimes cover their entire backs and shoulders.

**Kappabashi Kitchenware Street** (かっぱ橋 道具街; *Kappa-bashi Dogu-gai*)

**BUSINESS DISTRICT** | Lined with over 200 shops selling kitchenware and supplies, Kappabashi is shopping heaven for home chefs. The street is worth a visit just to see the vast selection of wares on display—from knives to industrial restaurant supplies to the strikingly realistic plastic food models seen in restaurants.

In the 19th century, according to local legend, a river ran through the present-day Kappabashi district. The surrounding area was poorly drained and was often flooded. A local shopkeeper began a project to improve the drainage, investing all his own money, but met with little success until a troupe of *kappa*—mischievous green water sprites—emerged from the river to help him. A more prosaic explanation for the name of the district points out that the lower-ranking retainers of the local lord used to earn extra money by making straw raincoats, also called *kappa*, that they spread to dry on the bridge. ⊠ *3–18–2 Matsugaya, Taito-ku* Ⓜ *Ginza subway line, Tawara-machi Station (Exit 1).*

Asakusa's heart and soul is the Senso-ji Complex, famous for its 17th-century Shinto shrine, Asakusa Shrine, as well as its garden and the wild Sanja Festival in May.

## ★ Senso-ji Temple Complex (浅草寺)

**TEMPLE** | Even for travelers with little interest in history or temples, this complex in the heart and soul of Asakusa is without a doubt one of Tokyo's must-see sights. Come for its local and historical importance, its garden, its 17th-century Shinto shrine, and Tokyo's most famous festival: the wild Sanja Matsuri in May. The area also offers myriad interesting shops, winding backstreets, and an atmosphere unlike anywhere else in Tokyo.

Established in 645, the bright red Main Hall has long been the center of Asakusa, though what you see today is a faithful replica of the original that burned in the fire raids of 1945. It took 13 years to raise money for the restoration of the beloved Senso-ji, which is much more than a tourist attraction. Kabuki actors still come here before a new season of performances, and sumo wrestlers visit before a tournament to pay their respects. The large lanterns were donated by the geisha associations of Asakusa and nearby

Yanagi-bashi. Most Japanese stop at the huge bronze incense burner, in front of the Main Hall, to bathe their hands and faces in the smoke—it's a charm to ward off illnesses—before climbing the stairs to offer their prayers.

Unlike in many other temples, however, part of the inside has a concrete floor, so you can come and go without removing your shoes. In this area hang Senso-ji's chief claims to artistic importance: a collection of 18th- and 19th-century votive paintings on wood. Plaques of this kind, called *ema,* are still offered to the gods at shrines and temples, but they are commonly simpler and smaller. The worshipper buys a little tablet of wood with the picture already painted on one side and inscribes a prayer on the other. The temple owns more than 50 of these works, which were removed to safety in 1945 to escape the air raids. Only eight of them, depicting scenes from Japanese history and mythology, are on display. A catalog of the collection is on sale in the hall, but the text is in Japanese only.

Lighting is poor in the Main Hall, and the actual works are difficult to see. One thing that visitors cannot see at all is the holy image of Kannon itself, which supposedly lies buried somewhere deep under the temple. Not even the priests of Senso-ji have ever seen it, and there is in fact no conclusive evidence that it actually exists.

Hozo-mon, the gate to the temple courtyard, is also a repository for *sutras* (Buddhist texts) and other treasures of Senso-ji. This gate, too, has its guardian gods; should either god decide to leave his post for a stroll, he can use the enormous pair of sandals hanging on the back wall—the gift of a Yamagata Prefecture village famous for its straw weaving. ⊠ *2–3–1 Asakusa, Taito-ku* ☎ *03/3842– 0181* ⊕ *www.senso-ji.jp* ✉ *Free* Ⓜ *Ginza subway line, Asakusa Station (Exit 1/ Kaminari-mon Exit).*

### Toki no Kane Belfry (時の鐘)

**RELIGIOUS BUILDING** | The tiny hillock Benten-yama, with its shrine to the goddess of good fortune, is the site of this 17th-century belfry. The bell here used to toll the hours for the people of the district, and it was said that you could hear it anywhere within a radius of some 6 km (4 miles). The bell still sounds at 6 am every day, when the temple grounds open. It also rings on New Year's Eve—108 strokes in all, beginning just before midnight, to "ring out" the 108 sins and frailties of humankind and make a clean start for the coming year. Benten-yama and the belfry are at the beginning of the narrow street that parallels Nakamise-dori. ⊠ *2–3 Asakusa, Taito-ku.*

### Tokyo Sky Tree (東京スカイツリー)

**VIEWPOINT** | Opened in 2011 to mixed reviews, this 2,000-plus-foot-tall sky-scraper has become a symbol of the ongoing revival of the eastern side of the city. When it opened, tickets to the observation decks were booked for months in advance and the tower, along with the adjacent Solamachi shopping complex,

continues to draw shoppers and tourists to the area. On a clear day, the views from the 1,155-foot-high Tembo Deck observation area are impressive. For an extra fee, visitors can go to the Tembo Galleria, another 330 feet up. ⊠ *1–1–2 Oshiage, Sumida-ku* ⊕ *www.tokyo-skytree.jp/en* ✉ *Tembo Deck only ¥2,100; Tembo Deck and Tembo Galleria ¥2,700* Ⓜ *Tobu Skytree Line Skytree Station, Tobu Skytree Line Oshiage Station.*

## 🍴 Restaurants

### Daikokuya Tempura (大黒家天麩羅)

**$$ | JAPANESE** | Daikokuya, in the center of Asakusa's historic district, is a point of pilgrimage for both locals and tourists. The specialty here is shrimp tempura, and the menu choices are simple—*tendon* is tempura shrimp served over rice, and the tempura meal includes rice, pickled vegetables, and miso soup. **Known for:** Tokyo-style tempura a cut above the rest; long lines; being an Asakusa landmark. Ⓢ *Average main: ¥2,500* ⊠ *1–38–10 Asakusa, Taito-ku* ☎ *03/3844–1111* ⊕ *www. tempura.co.jp/english* ⊟ *No credit cards* Ⓜ *Ginza and Asakusa subway lines, Asakusa Station.*

### Unagi Komagata Maekawa (鰻駒形前川)

**$$$$ | JAPANESE** | When it comes to preparation, this long-running *unagi* (freshwater eel) restaurant sticks to tradition, claiming to follow a 200-year-old recipe. For its ingredients, however, Maekawa takes a modern turn towards sustainability. **Known for:** sustainably sourced unagi; window seats look out over the river; a classic, no-frills unagi restaurant experience. Ⓢ *Average main: ¥6,000* ⊠ *2–1–29 Komagata, Taito-ku* ☎ *03/3841–6314* ⊕ *www.unagi-maekawa.com.*

## 🛏 Hotels

### Asakusa View Hotel (浅草ビューホテル)

**$$ | HOTEL | FAMILY** | The box-shaped Asakusa View is the largest Western-style hotel in the traditional Asakusa area.

**Pros:** affordable rates; located in a historic temple area; free in-room Wi-Fi. **Cons:** professional but impersonal service; dated rooms; room interiors generally basic. [$] *Rooms from: ¥19,000* ✉ *3–17–1 Nishi-Asakusa, Taito-ku* ☎ *03/3847–1111* 🌐 *www.viewhotels.co.jp/asakusa* 🛏 *326 rooms* 🍴 *No Meals* [M] *Ginza subway line, Tawara-machi Station (Exit 3).*

★ **The Gate Hotel Asakusa Kaminarimon by HULIC** (ザ・ゲートホテル雷門)
**$$** | **HOTEL** | This relative newcomer to the historic Asakusa area presents a certain stylish flair, starting from the entrance, where an elevator whisks you up 13 floors to the beautiful, glass-walled lobby. **Pros:** historic area; surrounded with great dining options; lovely views. **Cons:** not exactly a central location; can be crowded on weekends; rooms small by Western standards. [$] *Rooms from: ¥20,000* ✉ *2–16–11 Kaminarimon, Taito-ku* ☎ *03/5826–3877* 🌐 *www.gate-hotel.jp* 🛏 *137 rooms* 🍴 *No Meals* [M] *Ginza and Asakusa subway lines, Asakusa Station (Exit 2).*

**Ryokan Asakusa Mikawaya Honten** (旅館三河屋本店)
**$** | **B&B/INN** | In the heart of Asakusa, this friendly ryokan with only Japanese-style rooms is just behind the Kaminari-mon, the gateway leading to the Senso-ji complex. **Pros:** affordable accommodations; traditional Japanese experience; interesting shopping in the area. **Cons:** small rooms; friendly staff struggle with English; futons and tatami might not be suitable for those accustomed to Western-style beds. [$] *Rooms from: ¥14,000* ✉ *1–30–12 Asakusa, Taito-ku* ☎ *03/3841–8954* 🌐 *www.asakusamikawaya.com* 🛏 *15 rooms* 🍴 *No Meals* [M] *Ginza subway line, Asakusa Station (Exit 1/Kaminari-mon Exit).*

**Ryokan Asakusa Shigetsu** (旅館浅草 指月)
**$$** | **B&B/INN** | Just off Nakamise-dori and inside the Senso-ji grounds, this small inn, with both Japanese- and Western-style rooms, could not be better located for a visit to the temple. **Pros:** affordable rooms; located in a historic temple area; close to subway station. **Cons:** Western-style rooms are all singles; small rooms; not convenient to central Tokyo. [$] *Rooms from: ¥19,000* ✉ *1–31–11 Asakusa, Taito-ku* ☎ *03/3843–2345* 🌐 *www.shigetsu.com* 🛏 *21 rooms* 🍴 *No Meals* [M] *Ginza subway line, Asakusa Station (Exit 1/Kaminari-mon Exit).*

## Nightlife

### BARS

**Kamiya Bar** (神谷バー)
**BARS** | Tokyo's oldest Western-style bar hasn't had a face-lift for decades (the main building is registered as a tangible cultural property) and that's part of what draws so many drinkers to this bright, noisy venue. The other major attraction is the Denki Bran, a delicious but hang-over-inducing cocktail (comprising gin, red wine, brandy, and curaçao) that was invented here about 100 years ago and is now stocked by bars throughout Japan. ✉ *1–1–1 Asakusa, Taito-ku* ☎ *03/3841–5400* 🕒 *Closed Tues.* [M] *Asakusa and Ginza subway lines, Asakusa Station (Exit 3 and A5).*

**Top of Tree** (天空;)
**COCKTAIL LOUNGES** | **FAMILY** | Perched on the top of the Solamachi complex, this bar-restaurant attracts locals and tourists for overwhelming, breathtaking views of Tokyo Sky Tree. Signature drinks include Amaou-brand strawberry cocktails. The music's mostly jazz, and spacious and cushy seats, with sprawling views of Tokyo through the oversized glass windows and ceiling, make you want to linger. ✉ *Solamachi complex, Tokyo Skytree Town, 1–1–2 Oshiage, 31st fl., Sumida-ku* ☎ *03/5809–7377* 🌐 *www.top-of-tree.jp.*

**World Beer Museum** (世界のビール博物館; *Sekai no Biru Hakubutsukan*)
**BREWPUBS** | As the name suggests, beers from around the world are for sale, including 300 kinds in bottles and 20

more on tap. The large outdoor terrace with low-key downtown views is quiet and pleasant. The English-speaking German staff, when available, can help you choose the right beer. ✉ *Solamachi complex, Tokyo Skytree Town, 1–1–2 Oshiage, 7th fl., Sumida-ku* ☎ *03/5610–2648* ⊕ *www.world-liquor-importers. co.jp/en/index.html.*

# 🛍 Shopping

## FOOD

**Kawahara Shoten** (川原商店)
SOUVENIRS | The brightly colored bulk packages of rice crackers, shrimp-flavored chips, and other Japanese snacks sold here make offbeat gifts. ✉ *3–9–2 Nishi-Asakusa, Taito-ku* ☎ *03/3842–0841* ⊙ *Closed Sun.* Ⓜ *Ginza subway line, Asakusa Station (Exit 1).*

**Tokiwa-do** (常盤堂)
FOOD | Come here to buy some of Tokyo's most famous souvenirs: *kaminari okoshi* (thunder crackers), made of rice, millet, sugar, and beans. The shop is on the west side of Asakusa's Thunder God Gate, the Kaminari-mon entrance to Sen-so-ji, and you can watch as they make them in front of you. ✉ *1–3–2 Asakusa, Taito-ku* ☎ *03/3841–5656* ⊕ *www.tokiwa-do.tokyo* Ⓜ *Ginza subway line, Asakusa Station (Exit 1).*

## SHOPPING STREETS AND ARCADES

**Nakamise Market** (仲見世通り; *Nakamise-dori*)
NEIGHBORHOODS | Although many of the shops have moved from selling traditional crafts to cheap knickknacks (often not made in Japan), it is worth passing down on your way to Senso-ji for the atmosphere. It is just as lively as it was when it was established in the Edo period, although now shops sells cheap sushi key chains and T-shirts alongside traditional hairpieces and silk screens. The entrance is marked by the giant red lantern at the Kaminari-mon, and ends

at the grounds of the Senso-ji Complex. ✉ *Asakusa 1-chome, Taito-ku, Taito-ku* ☎ *03/3844–3350* Ⓜ *Ginza subway line, Asakusa Station (Exit 1).*

**Nishi-Sando Arcade** (西参道商店街; *Nishi-Sando Shoten-gai*)
NEIGHBORHOODS | Kimono and *yukata* (cotton kimono) fabrics, traditional accessories, swords, and festival costumes at very reasonable prices are all for sale at this Asakusa arcade. It runs east of the area's movie theaters, between Roku-ku and the Senso-ji Complex. ✉ *Asakusa 2-chome, Taito-ku, Taito-ku* Ⓜ *Ginza subway line, Asakusa Station (Exit 1).*

## SWORDS AND KNIVES

**Tsubaya Knives** (つば屋包丁店; *Tsubaya Hocho-ten*)
HOUSEWARES | This shop's remarkable selection of high-quality cutlery for professionals is designed for every imaginable use, as the art of food presentation in Japan requires a great variety of cutting implements. The best of these carry the Traditional Craft Association seal: hand-forged tools of tempered blue steel, set in handles banded with deer horn to keep the wood from splitting. Be prepared to pay the premium for these items. A cleaver just for slicing soba can cost as much as ¥50,000. ✉ *3–7–2 Nishi-Asakusa, Taito-ku* ☎ *03/3845–2005* ⊕ *tsubaya.co.jp* Ⓜ *Ginza subway line, Asakusa (Exit 1).*

**Ichiryo-ya Hirakawa** (一両屋平川)
SOUVENIRS | This small, cluttered souvenir shop in the Nishi-Sando arcade carries antique swords and reproductions and has some English-speaking salesclerks. ✉ *2–7–13 Asakusa, Taito-ku* ☎ *03/3843–0052* ⊙ *Closed Thurs.* Ⓜ *Ginza subway line, Asakusa Station (Exit 1) or Tawaramachi Station (Exit 3).*

## TRADITIONAL WARES

**Asakusa Nakaya Honten** (浅草中屋本店)
MIXED CLOTHING | If you want to equip yourself for the neighborhood's annual Sanja Festival in May, this is the place to

come for traditional costumes. Best buys here are *sashiko hanten,* which are thick, woven firemen's jackets; and *happi* coats, cotton tunics printed in bright colors with Japanese characters. Some items are available in children's sizes. ⊠ *2–2–12 Asakusa, Taito-ku* ☎ *03/3841–7877* ⊕ *www.nakaya.co.jp* Ⓜ *Ginza subway line, Asakusa Station (Exit 6).*

### Hyakusuke Cosmetics (百助化粧品店; *Hyakusuke Keishohinten*)

COSMETICS | This is the last place in Tokyo to carry government-approved skin cleanser made from powdered nightingale droppings. Ladies of the Edo period—especially the geisha—swore by the cleanser. These days this 300-year-old-plus cosmetics shop sells little of the nightingale powder, but its theatrical makeup for Kabuki actors, geisha, and traditional weddings—as well as unique items like seaweed shampoo, camellia oil, and handcrafted combs and cosmetic brushes—makes it a worthy addition to your Asakusa shopping itinerary. ⊠ *2–2–14 Asakusa, Taito-ku* ☎ *03/3841–7058* ⊘ *Closed Tues.* Ⓜ *Ginza subway line, Asakusa Station (Exit 6).*

### Soi Interior & Style Design (Soi 器; *Soi Utsuwa*)

CRAFTS | The selection of lacquerware, ceramics, and antiques sold at this Kappabashi shop is modest, but Soi displays the items in a minimalist setting of stone walls and wooden floor planks, with up-tempo jazz in the background. ⊠ *3–25–11 Nishi-Asakusa, Taito-ku* ☎ *03/6802–7732* ⊕ *www.soi-2.jp* Ⓜ *Ginza subway line, Asakusa Station (Exit 6).*

### Tenugui Fuji-ya (てぬぐいふじ屋)

FABRICS | Master textile creator Keiji Kawakami is an expert on the hundreds of traditional towel motifs that have come down from the Edo period: geometric patterns, plants and animals, and scenes from Kabuki plays and festivals. His cotton *tenugui* (pronounced "teh-*noo*-goo-ee") hand towels are collector's items, often framed instead of used as towels. When Kawakami feels he has made enough of one pattern of his own design, he destroys the stencil. The shop is near the corner of Dembo-in Dori, on the street that runs parallel behind Naka-mise dori. ⊠ *2–2–15 Asakusa, Taito-ku, Asakusa* ☎ *03/3841–2283* ⊕ *tenugui-fujiya.jp* ⊘ *Closed Thurs.* Ⓜ *Ginza subway line, Asakusa Station (Exit 1).*

# Greater Tokyo

The size of the city and the diversity of its institutions make it impossible to fit all of Tokyo's interesting sights into neighborhoods. Plenty of worthy places—from Tokyo Disneyland to sumo stables to the old Oji district—fall outside the city's neighborhood repertoire. Yet no guide to Tokyo would be complete without them.

Central Tokyo is routinely described as a concrete haven, yet the Kasai Seaside Park offers numerous flora at the edge of Tokyo Bay. Tokyo has a few traditional areas remaining, but if the sport of sumo tickles your fancy, the largest collection of training stables is in the Ryogoku area. Two things make this working-class *Shitamachi* (downtown) neighborhood worth a special trip: this is the center of the world of sumo wrestling as well as the site of the extraordinary Edo-Tokyo Museum (closed for renovations until 2025). Also outside the city center are some theme parks, like Tokyo Disneyland and Sanrio Puroland, whose numerous kitschy attractions celebrate Japan's love for all that is cute. Creatures from the sea abound at the Shinagawa Aquarium.

**Access:** The areas that lie to the west of Shibuya, south of Shinagawa, north of Ikebukuro, and east of Tokyo Station offer amusement parks, zoos, galleries, and museums. From central Tokyo, the city spreads out like the spokes of a wheel; various railways serve areas in all cardinal directions. For Chiba Prefecture, where Tokyo Disneyland is located, take

Sanrio Puroland is dedicated to one of Japan's most popular exports: Hello Kitty. It's an opulent shrine to cuteness.

Keiyo Line, which originates at Tokyo Station. Use the same line to access Kasai Seaside Park. Multiple JR lines and the Keihin Kyuko Line chug south from Shinagawa Station in the direction of Yokohama and to the Shinagawa Aquarium. The Keio Line, too, starts at Shinjuku Station; Sanrio Puroland is accessible from Tama Center Station on this line. The Namboku Line is a subway line that moves north through Komagome Station on the Yamanote Line before reaching the throwback town of Oji.

##  Sights

**Sanrio Puroland** (サンリオピューロランド)

AMUSEMENT PARK/CARNIVAL | FAMILY | As a theme park dedicated to the world's most famous white cat with no mouth—Hello Kitty, of course—Sanrio Puroland is effectively a shrine to the concept of cuteness. An all-day passport allows for unlimited use of multiple attractions, including three theaters, a boat ride, and the Lady Kitty House—one of many attractions seemingly designed for taking selfies. Pens, packaged snacks, and plush toys are readily available so guests don't leave empty-handed. ✉ *1–31 Ochiai, Tama-shi, Tama* ☎ *042/339–1111* ⊕ *en. puroland.jp* 💴 *¥3,600 weekdays; ¥3,900 weekends and holidays* Ⓜ *Keio Line, Tama Center Station.*

### ★ **Sengaku-ji Temple** (泉岳寺)

TEMPLE | In 1701, a young provincial baron named Asano Takumi-no-Kami attacked and seriously wounded a courtier named Yoshinaka Kira. Asano, for daring to draw his sword in the confines of Edo Castle, was ordered to commit suicide, so his family line was abolished and his fief confiscated. Forty-seven of Asano's loyal retainers vowed revenge; the death of their leader made them *ronin*—masterless samurai. On the night of December 14, 1702, Asano's ronin stormed Kira's villa in Edo, cut off his head, and brought it in triumph to Asano's tomb at Sengaku-ji, the family temple. The ronin were sentenced to commit suicide—which they accepted as the reward, not the price, of their

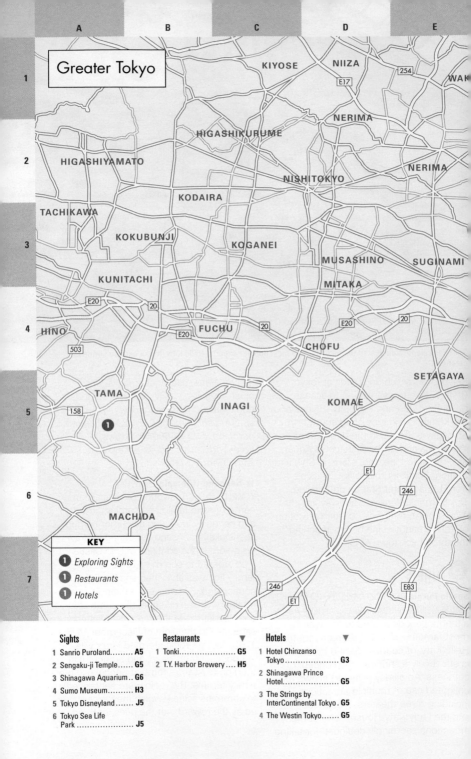

# Greater Tokyo

|   | A | B | C | D | E |
|---|---|---|---|---|---|
| 1 | | | KIYOSE | NIIZA / E17 | 254 / WAK |
| 2 | HIGASHIYAMATO | HIGASHIKURUME | NISHI TOKYO | | NERIMA |
| 3 | TACHIKAWA / KOKUBUNJI | KODAIRA | KOGANEI | MUSASHINO / MITAKA | SUGINAMI |
| 4 | HINO / E20 / 503 | KUNITACHI / 20 / E20 | FUCHU / 20 | CHOFU / E20 / 20 | SETAGAYA |
| 5 | TAMA / 158 / ❶ | INAGI | | KOMAE / E1 | |
| 6 | MACHIDA | | | 246 | |
| 7 | | 246 / E1 | | E83 | |

**KEY**

❶ Exploring Sights
❶ Restaurants
❶ Hotels

**Sights** ▼
1 Sanrio Puroland.......... **A5**
2 Sengaku-ji Temple...... **G5**
3 Shinagawa Aquarium.. **G6**
4 Sumo Museum........... **H3**
5 Tokyo Disneyland........ **J5**
6 Tokyo Sea Life
   Park ...................... **J5**

**Restaurants** ▼
1 Tonki...................... **G5**
2 T.Y. Harbor Brewery .... **H5**

**Hotels** ▼
1 Hotel Chinzanso
   Tokyo .................... **G3**
2 Shinagawa Prince
   Hotel..................... **G5**
3 The Strings by
   InterContinental Tokyo . **G5**
4 The Westin Tokyo....... **G5**

honorable vendetta—and were buried in the temple graveyard with their lord.

Through the centuries this story has become a national epic and the last word on the subject of loyalty and sacrifice, celebrated in every medium from Kabuki to film. The temple still stands, and the graveyard is wreathed in smoke from the bundles of incense that visitors still lay reverently on the tombstones. There is a collection of weapons and other memorabilia from the event in the temple's small museum. One of the items derives from Kira's family's desire to give him a proper burial. The law insisted this could not be done without his head, so they asked for it back. It was entrusted to the temple, and the priests wrote a receipt, which survives even now in the corner of a dusty glass case. "Item," it begins, "One head." ⊠ 2–11–1 Takanawa, Minato-ku ☎ 03/3441–5560 ⊕ www. sengakuji.or.jp 🎫 Temple and grounds free, museum ¥500 Ⓜ Asakusa subway line, Sengakuji Station (Exit A2).

### Shinagawa Aquarium (しながわ水族館 Shinagawa Suizokukan)

**AQUARIUM | FAMILY** | The fun part of this aquarium in southwestern Tokyo is walking through an underwater glass tunnel while some 450 species of fish swim around and above you. There are no pamphlets or explanation panels in English, however, and do your best to avoid weekends, when the dolphin and sea lion shows draw crowds in impossible numbers. Take the local Kyuko Main Line from Shinagawa to Omori Kaigan Station. Turn left as you exit the station and follow the ceramic fish on the sidewalk to the first traffic light; then turn right. ⊠ 3–2–1 Katsushima, Shinagawa-ku ☎ 03/3762–3433 ⊕ www.aquarium.gr.jp 🎫 ¥1,350 ⊘ Often closed Tues. Ⓜ Kyuko Main Line, Omori Kaigan Station.

### Sumo Museum
(相撲博物館; Sumo Hakubutsukan)

**OTHER MUSEUM** | If you can't attend a sumo tournament, visit this museum in the south wing of the arena. There are no explanations in English, but the museum's collection of sumo-related woodblock prints, paintings, and illustrated scrolls includes some outstanding examples of traditional Japanese fine art. ⊠ 1–3–28 Yokoami, Sumida-ku ☎ 03/3622–0366 ⊕ www.sumo. or.jp/KokugikanSumoMuseum 🎫 Free ⊘ Closed weekends.

### Tokyo Disney Resort
(東京ディズニーリゾート)

**AMUSEMENT PARK/CARNIVAL | FAMILY** | Mickey-san and his coterie of Disney characters entertain here at Tokyo Disneyland the same way they do in the California and Florida Disney parks. When the park was built in 1983, it was much smaller than its counterparts in the United States, but the construction in 2001 of the adjacent DisneySea and its seven "Ports of Call," all with different nautical themes and rides, added more than 100 acres to this multifaceted Magic Kingdom.

There are several types of admission tickets. Most people buy the One-Day Passport, which gives you unlimited access to the attractions and shows at one or the other of the two parks. See the park website for other ticketing options. You can buy tickets online from the Tokyo Disney Resort website. ⊠ 1–1 Maihama, Urayasu ☎ 0570/00–8632 ⊕ www. tokyodisneyresort.jp 🎫 From ¥7,900 Ⓜ JR Keiyo Line, Maihama Station.

### Tokyo Sea Life Park (葛西臨海水族園 Kaisai Rinkai Suizoku-en)

**AQUARIUM | FAMILY** | The three-story cylindrical complex of this aquarium houses roughly 600 species of fish and other sea creatures within a dozen areas, including Voyagers of the Sea (Maguro no Kaiyu), with migratory species; Seas of the

World (Sekai no Umi), with species from foreign waters; and the Sea of Tokyo (Tokyo no Umi), devoted to the creatures of the bay and nearby waters. To get here, take the JR Keiyo Line local train from Tokyo Station to Kasai Rinkai Koen Station; the aquarium is a 10-minute walk from the South Exit. ✉ *6–2–3 Rinkai-cho, Edogawa-ku* ☎ *03/3869–5152* 🌐 *www.tokyo-zoo.net/english/kasai* 🎟 *¥700* 🕒 *Closed Wed.* [M] *JR Keiyo Line, Kasai Rinkai Koen Station.*

## 🍴 Restaurants

**Tonki** (とんき)
**$$ | JAPANESE** | A family joint, Tonki is a success that never went conglomerate or added frills to what it does best: deep-fried pork cutlets, soup, raw-cabbage salad, rice, pickles, and tea. That's the standard course, and almost everybody orders it, with good reason—it's utterly delicious. Just listen to customers in line as they put in their usual orders while a server comes around to take it. **Known for:** juicy pork; a line out the door; hearty, affordable meals. [$] *Average main: ¥1,900* ✉ *1–1–2 Shimo-Meguro, Meguro-ku* ☎ *03/3491–9928* 🕒 *Closed Tues. and 3rd Mon. of month. No lunch* [M] *JR Yamanote and Namboku subway lines, Meguro Station (Nishi-guchi/West Exit).*

**T.Y. Harbor Brewery** (T.Y.ハーバーブルワリーレストラン)
**$$$ | ECLECTIC** | A converted warehouse on the waterfront houses this restaurant, known for its grills, California-Asia fusions, and craft beers. Don't miss the wheat ale steamed clams, Thai-style gai yang chicken sate or the Indian spice marinated lamb chops. **Known for:** a selection of craft beers brewed on-site; incorporating Asian elements into classic American fare; outdoor seating overlooking Tokyo Bay. [$] *Average main: ¥4,000* ✉ *2–1–3 Higashi-Shinagawa, Shinagawa-ku* ☎ *03/5479–4555* 🌐 *www.tysons.jp/tyharbor* [M] *Tokyo Monorail or Rinkai Line, Ten-nozu Isle Station (Exit B).*

## 🛏 Hotels

**Hotel Chinzanso Tokyo** (ホテル椿山荘東京)
**$$$$ | HOTEL** | Surrounded by a 17-acre garden, the elegant, European-style Hotel Chinzanso is a sheltered haven in Tokyo's busy metropolis and a former estate of an imperial prince. **Pros:** gorgeous, sprawling grounds; large rooms with huge bathrooms; glamorous pool. **Cons:** isolated location; room interiors a tad dated; limited dining options in immediate area. [$] *Rooms from: ¥57,000* ✉ *2–10–8 Sekiguchi, Bunkyo-ku* ☎ *03/3943–1111* 🌐 *www.hotel-chinzanso-tokyo.com* 🛏 *260 rooms* 🍽 *No Meals* [M] *Yurakucho subway line, Edogawabashi Station (Exit 1A).*

**Shinagawa Prince Hotel** (品川プリンスホテル)
**$$ | HOTEL | FAMILY** | Just a three-minute walk from JR Shinagawa Station, the Prince is a sprawling complex that's part hotel (with four towers) and part entertainment village, featuring everything from an 80-lane bowling alley to tennis courts to an 11-screen movie theater and game centers. **Pros:** affordable rates; multiple entertainment choices, including a bowling alley and an IMAX theater; nice view of Tokyo Bay from lounge. **Cons:** crowded on weekends; rooms can be small; complicated layout. [$] *Rooms from: ¥20,000* ✉ *4–10–30 Takanawa, Minato-ku* ☎ *03/3440–1111* 🌐 *www.princehotels.com/shinagawa* 🛏 *3331 rooms* 🍽 *No Meals* [M] *JR Yamanote Line, Shinagawa Station (Nishi-guchi/West Exit).*

**The Strings by InterContinental Tokyo** (ストリングスホテル東京インターコンチネンタル)
**$$$ | HOTEL** | Beautifully blending modernity with traditional Japanese aesthetics, the Strings is one of Shinagawa's top-tier hotels. **Pros:** great lobby; convenient location; nice view of the Tokyo skyline. **Cons:** finding elevator entrance can be challenging; no pool or spa; expensive restaurants. [$] *Rooms from: ¥35,000*

*✉ 2–16–1 Konan, Minato-ku ☎ 03/5783–1111 🌐 intercontinental-strings.jp 🛏 212 rooms 🍴 No Meals [M] JR Yamanote Line, Shinagawa Station (Konan Exit).*

**The Westin Tokyo**
(ウェスティンホテル東京)
**$$ | HOTEL** | In the Yebisu Garden Place development, the Westin provides easy access to Mitsukoshi department store, the Tokyo Photographic Art Museum, the elegant Ebisu Garden concert hall, and the Joël Robuchon restaurant (in a full-scale reproduction of a Louis XV château). **Pros:** "Heavenly Beds"; large rooms; great concierge. **Cons:** rooms can feel stuffy to some; small gym; walk from station is more than 10 min. [$] *Rooms from: ¥33,000 ✉ 1–4–1 Mita, Meguro-ku ☎ 03/5423–7000 🌐 www.westin-tokyo.co.jp 🛏 438 rooms 🍴 No Meals [M] JR Yamanote Line and Hibiya subway line, Ebisu Station (Higashi-guchi/East Exit).*

# Narita Airport Area

## Hotels

Transportation between Narita Airport and Tokyo proper takes at least 90 minutes given is distance from Tokyo. In heavy traffic, a limousine bus or taxi ride, which could set you back ¥30,000, can stretch to two hours or more. Needless to say, that's not a trip you'll want to take if you have an early flight. A sensible strategy for visitors with early-morning flights home would be to spend the night before at one of the hotels near the airport, all of which have courtesy shuttles to the departure terminals; these hotels are also a boon to visitors en route elsewhere with layovers in Narita. Many of them have soundproof rooms to block out the noise of the airplanes.

**ANA Crowne Plaza Narita**
(ANA クラウンプラザホテル成田)
**$ | HOTEL** | With its brass-and-marble detail in the lobby, this hotel replicates the grand style of other hotels in the ANA chain. **Pros:** convenient location; pleasant staff; airport shuttle. **Cons:** charge to use pool; in-house restaurants are the only dining options in the area; small rooms. [$] *Rooms from: ¥14,000 ✉ 68 Horin-ouchi, Narita ☎ 0476/33–1311 🌐 www.anacrowneplaza-narita.jp 🛏 396 rooms 🍴 No Meals.*

**Hilton Tokyo Narita Airport** (ヒルトン成田)
**$ | HOTEL** | Given its proximity to the airport (a 15-minute free shuttle), this C-shape hotel is a reasonable choice for a one-night visit. **Pros:** reasonably priced rooms; spacious lobby; airport shuttle. **Cons:** common areas a bit worn; in-room Wi-Fi is not free; charge to use the pool and gym. [$] *Rooms from: ¥14,000 ✉ 456 Kosuge, Narita ☎ 0476/33–1121 🌐 www.hilton.com 🛏 548 rooms 🍴 No Meals.*

**Hotel Mystays Premier Narita**
(ホテルマイステイズプレミア成田)
**$ | HOTEL** | This no-frills hotel is perfect for travelers with an early-morning flight out of Narita. **Pros:** views of runway from bar and some rooms; many options to stretch your legs before a flight; excellent value. **Cons:** can get crowded with tour groups; tiny bathrooms; small rooms. [$] *Rooms from: ¥11,000 ✉ 31 Oyama, Narita ☎ 0476/33–1661 🌐 www.mystays.com 🛏 706 rooms 🍴 No Meals.*

**nine hours** (ナインアワーズ)
**$ | HOTEL** | For a layover at Narita, this capsule hotel's location can't be beat—it's actually inside Terminal 2. **Pros:** convenient; reasonably priced; day use and showers available. **Cons:** limited services; can be noisy; tight confines. [$] *Rooms from: ¥5,900 ✉ Narita Airport Terminal 2, 1–1 Furugome, Narita ☎ 0476/33–5109 🌐 ninehours.co.jp/narita 🛏 129 capsules (71 for men, 58 for women) 🍴 No Meals.*

# Chapter 5

# SIDE TRIPS FROM TOKYO

Updated by
Robert Morel

| ◉ Sights | 🍴 Restaurants | 🛏 Hotels | 🛍 Shopping | ☯ Nightlife |
|---|---|---|---|---|
| ★★★★☆ | ★★★☆☆ | ★★★☆☆ | ★★★☆☆ | ★☆☆☆☆ |

# WELCOME TO SIDE TRIPS FROM TOKYO

## TOP REASONS TO GO

★ **Peer at Fuji:**
Climb Japan's tallest mountain or catch a glimpse of it from Fuji-Hakone-Izu National Park.

★ **Escape into rustic Japan:**
The endless modernity of Tokyo seems worlds away in Nikko, where the Tosho-gu area shrines and temples transport you centuries back into the country's past and the Kegon Falls just transport you.

★ **Get into a Zen-like state:**
Kita-Kamakura is home to two preeminent Zen temples, Engaku and Kencho. In Hase, gaze on the Great Buddha or explore inside the giant statue.

★ **Go to China without boarding a plane:** In Yokohama, a port city, sample authentic Chinese goods, spices, and crafts in Chinatown. For a bit of whimsy and a great view, ride Yokohama's Ferris wheel.

**1 Yokohama.** A busy port, Yokohama also has a cultured, relaxed atmosphere and Japan's largest Chinatown.

**2 Kamakura.** A city filled with temples and hiking as well as a bustling town center.

**3 Mount Fuji (Fuji-san).** Japan's tallest and most sacred mountain.

**4 Fuji Five Lakes (Fuji Go-ko).** The five lakes and surrounding mountains offer a quiet getaway and a staging point for visiting Mt. Fuji.

**5 Hakone.** Filled with hot springs and hiking, cafes and museums.

**6 Izu.** From the hot-spring town of Atami's retro vibe to the laid back beach town of Shimoda, visitors come to Izu for the springs, beaches, and costal views.

**7 Mt. Takao.** The most hiked mountain in Japan is an hour's train ride from Shinjuku.

**8 Nikko.** Crowds flock to Nikko to see Tosho-gu, the resting place of Ieyasu Tokugawa.

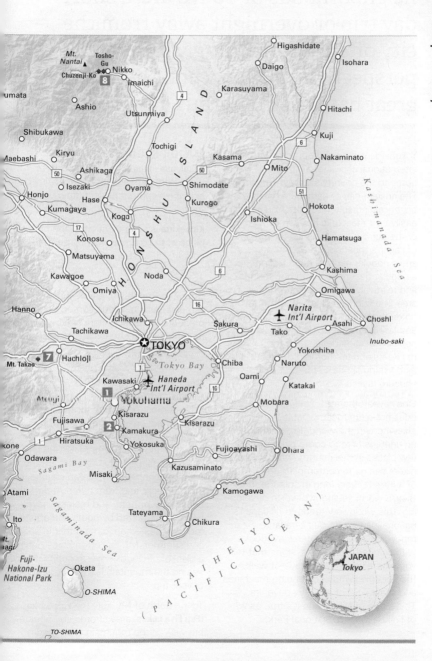

As diverse and exciting as the neighborhoods of Tokyo are, a short day trip or overnight away from the city offers a refreshingly different perspective on Japan, and the city is a great base for numerous day-trips.

Yokohama is a nearby port city with an international character all its own—it's home to the country's largest Chinatown. The ancient city of Kamakura has great historical and cultural sights. You can easily visit the iconic Fuji-san (Mt. Fuji) or the surrounding Fuji Five Lakes, one of Japan's most popular resort areas and a popular national park. Hakone is a popular destination with hot springs and relatively easy access to the Mt. Fuji area. The Izu Peninsula is another favorite hot spring resort areas for both Japanese and foreign travelers. Finally, Nikko, a popular vacation destination for Tokyo residents and the home of Toshogu, the astonishing shrine to the first Tokugawa shogun, Ieyasu.

One caveat: the term "national park" does not quite mean what it does elsewhere in the world. In Japan pristine grandeur is hard to come by; there are few places in this country where intrepid hikers can go to contemplate the beauty of nature for very long in solitude. If a thing's worth seeing, it's worth developing. This worldview tends to fill Japan's national parks with bus caravans, ropeways, gondolas, scenic overlooks with coin-fed telescopes, signs that tell you where you may or may not walk, fried-noodle joints and vending machines, and shacks full of kitschy souvenirs. That's true of Nikko, and it's true as well of Fuji-Hakone-Izu National Park.

## MAJOR REGIONS

**Yokohama** is Japan's largest port. Its waterfront park and its Minato Mirai bayside development project draw visitors from all over.

**Kamakura** is an ancient city—the birthplace of the samurai way of life. The country's first shogun chose this site as the seat of his military government. The warrior elite took much of their ideology from Zen Buddhism, endowing splendid temples. As a religious center, Kamakura presents an extraordinary legacy. Most of its temples and shrines are in settings of remarkable beauty; many are designated National Treasures.

**Mount Fuji,** southwest of Tokyo between Suruga and Sagami bays, is one of Japan's most popular resort areas. The main attraction, of course, is Mt. Fuji, a dormant volcano—it last erupted in 1707—rising to a height of 12,388 feet. The mountain is truly beautiful; utterly captivating in the ways it can change in different light and from different perspectives. Its symmetry and majesty have been immortalized by poets and artists for centuries. Keep in mind that in spring and summer, Mt. Fuji often hides behind a blanket of clouds—worth noting if seeing the mountain is an important part of your trip.

To the north of Mt. Fuji, the **Fuji Go-ko (Fuji Five Lakes)** area affords an unbeatable view of the mountain on clear days

Mt. Fuji is an active volcano that last erupted in 1707.

and makes the best base for a climb to the summit. With its various outdoor activities, such as skating and fishing in winter and boating and hiking in summer, this is a popular resort area for families and business conferences. The five lakes are, from the east, Yamanaka-ko, Kawaguchi-ko, Sai-ko, Shoji-ko, and Motosu-ko. Yamanaka and Kawaguchi are the largest and most developed as resort areas, with Kawaguchi more or less the centerpiece of the group.

**Hakone** has mountains, volcanic landscapes, and lake cruises, plus onsen (hot springs) of its own.

**The Izu Peninsula** is popular for its beaches and scenically rugged coastline.

**Mt. Takao** is actually located within the limits of the metropolitan Tokyo, Mt. Takao is a densely wooded area within an hour of the center of the city and has hiking trails, beautiful scenery, an interesting temple, and a monkey zoo.

**Nikko,** which means "sunlight," is a popular vacation spot for the Japanese, for good reason: its gorgeous sights include a breathtaking waterfall and one of the country's best-known shrines. In addition, Nikko combines the rustic charm of a countryside village (complete with wild monkeys that have the run of the place) with a convenient location not far from Tokyo. Nikko is the site of the Tokugawa Shrine and Nikko Kokuritsu Koen. The centerpiece of the park is Chuzonji ko and the famous Kegon Falls.

# Planning

## Hotels

In both Nikko and the Fuji-Hakone-Izu area, there are modern, Western-style hotels that operate in a fairly standard international style. More common, however, are the traditional ryokan (inns). The main difference between these lodging options is that Western-style hotels are situated in prime tourist locations whereas ryokans stick strictly to Japanese-style rooms and are found in less central locations. The undisputed pleasure of a ryokan is to return to it at the end of a hard day of sightseeing, luxuriate for an hour in a hot bath with your own garden view, put on the *yukata* (cotton kimono) provided for you (remember to close your right side first and then the left), and sit down to a catered private dinner party. There's little point to staying at a Western-style hotel: these places do most of their business with big, boisterous tour groups; the turnover is ruthless; and the cost is way out of proportion to the service they provide.

The price categories listed here are for double occupancy, but you'll find that most normally quote per-person rates, which include breakfast and dinner. Remember to stipulate whether you want a Japanese or Western breakfast. If you don't want dinner at your hotel, it's usually possible to renegotiate the price, but the management will not be happy about it; the two meals are a fixture of their business. The typical ryokan takes great pride in its cuisine, usually with good reason: the evening meal is an elaborate affair of 10 or more different dishes, based on the fresh produce and specialties of the region, served to you in your room on a wonderful variety of trays and tableware designed to celebrate the season.

# Restaurants

The local specialty in Nikko is a soybean-based concoction known as *yuba* (tofu skin); dozens of restaurants in Nikko serve it in a variety of dishes. Other local favorites are soba (buckwheat) and udon (wheat-flour) noodles—both inexpensive, filling, and tasty options for lunch.

Three things about Kamakura make it a good place to dine. It's on the ocean (properly speaking, on Sagami Bay), which means that fresh seafood is everywhere; it's a major tourist stop; and it has long been a prestigious place to

live among Japan's worldly and well-to-do (many successful writers, artists, and intellectuals call Kamakura home). On a day trip from Tokyo, you can feel confident picking a place for lunch almost at random.

Yokohama, as befits a city of more than 3 million people, lacks little in the way of food: from quick-fix lunch counters to elegant dining rooms, you'll find almost every imaginable cuisine. Your best bet is Chinatown—Japan's largest Chinese community—with more than 100 restaurants representing every regional style. If you fancy Italian, Indian, or even Scandinavian, this international port is still guaranteed to provide an eminently satisfying meal.

## RESTAURANT AND HOTEL PRICES

Restaurant prices are the average cost of a main course at dinner, or if dinner is not served, at lunch. Hotel prices are the lowest cost of a standard double room in high season. Restaurant and hotel reviews have been shortened. For full information, visit Fodors.com.

| What It Costs in Yen | | | |
|---|---|---|---|
| $ | $$ | $$$ | $$$$ |
| **RESTAURANTS** | | | |
| under ¥1,500 | ¥1,500–¥3,000 | ¥3,001–¥5,000 | over ¥5,000 |
| **HOTELS** | | | |
| under ¥15,000 | ¥15,000–¥30,000 | ¥30,001–¥45,000 | over ¥45,000 |

# Yokohama (横浜)

*20 km (12½ miles) southwest of Tokyo.*

In 1853, a fleet of four American warships under Commodore Matthew Perry sailed into the bay of Tokyo (then Edo) and presented the reluctant Japanese with the demands of the U.S. government for the opening of diplomatic and commercial relations. The following year Perry returned and first set foot on Japanese soil at Yokohama—then a small fishing village on the mudflats of Tokyo bay.

Two years later New York businessman Townsend Harris became America's first diplomatic representative to Japan. In 1858 he was finally able to negotiate a commercial treaty between the two countries; part of the deal designated four locations—one of them Yokohama— as treaty ports. In 1859 the shogunate created a special settlement in Yokohama for the growing community of merchants, traders, missionaries, and other assorted adventurers drawn to this exotic new land of opportunity.

The foreigners (predominantly Chinese and British, plus a few French, Americans, and Dutch) were confined here to a guarded compound about 5 square km (2 square miles)—placed, in effect, in isolation—but not for long. Within a few short years the shogunal government collapsed, and Japan began to modernize. Western ideas were welcomed, as were Western goods, and the little treaty port became Japan's principal gateway to the outside world. In 1872 Japan's first railway was built, linking Yokohama and Tokyo. In 1889 Yokohama became a city; by then the population had grown to some 120,000. As the city prospered, so did the international community and by the early 1900s Yokohama was the busiest and most modern center of international trade in all of East Asia.

Then Yokohama came tumbling down. On September 1, 1923, the Great Kanto Earthquake devastated the city. The ensuing fires destroyed some 60,000 homes and took more than 40,000 lives. During the six years it took to rebuild the city, many foreign businesses took up quarters elsewhere, primarily in Kobe and Osaka, and did not return.

Over the next 20 years Yokohama continued to grow as an industrial center—until May 29, 1945, when in a span of four hours, some 500 American B-29 bombers leveled nearly half the city and left more than half a million people homeless. When the war ended, what remained became—in effect—the center of the Allied occupation. General Douglas MacArthur set up headquarters here, briefly, before moving to Tokyo; the entire port facility and about a quarter of the city remained in the hands of the U.S. military throughout the 1950s.

By the 1970s Yokohama was once more rising from the debris; in 1978 it surpassed Osaka as the nation's second-largest city, and the population is now inching up to the 3.5-million mark. Boosted by Japan's postwar economic miracle, Yokohama has extended its urban sprawl north to Tokyo and south to Kamakura—in the process creating a whole new subcenter around the Shinkansen Station at Shin-Yokohama.

The development of air travel and the competition from other ports have changed the city's role in Japan's economy. The great liners that once docked at Yokohama's piers are now but a memory, kept alive by a museum ship and the occasional visit of a luxury vessel on a Pacific cruise. Modern Yokohama thrives instead in its industrial, commercial, and service sectors—and a large percentage of its people commute to work in Tokyo. Visit Yokohama for the waterfront and museums.

## GETTING HERE AND AROUND
From Narita Airport, a direct limousine-bus service departs once or twice an hour between 7:05 am and 10:25 pm for Yokohama City Air Terminal (YCAT). YCAT is a five-minute taxi ride from Yokohama Station. JR Narita Express trains going on from Tokyo to Yokohama leave the airport every hour from 7:44 am to 9:44 pm. The fare is ¥4,370 (¥6,640 for the first-class Green Car coaches). Or you can take the limousine-bus service from Narita to Tokyo Station and continue on to Yokohama by train. Either way, the journey from Narita takes two to three hours.

The Airport Limousine Information Desk phone number provides information in English daily from 9 to 6; you can also get timetables on its website. For information in English on Narita Express trains, call the JR Higashi-Nihon Info Line, available daily from 10 to 6.

Most of the things to see in Yokohama are within easy walking distance of a JR or subway station, but this city is so much more negotiable than Tokyo that exploring by bus is a viable alternative. The city map available in the visitor centers in Yokohama shows most major bus routes, and the important stops on the tourist routes are announced in English. The fixed fare is ¥220; one-day passes are also available for ¥600. Contact the Sightseeing Information Office at Yokohama Station (JR, East Exit) for more information and ticket purchases.

One subway line connects Azamino, Shin-Yokohama, Yokohama, Totsuka, and Shonandai. The basic fare is ¥210. One-day passes are also available for ¥830. The Minato Mirai Line, a spur of the Tokyu Toyoko Line, runs from Yokohama Station to all the major points of interest, including Minato Mirai, Chinatown, Yamashita Park, Moto-machi, and Basha-michi. The fare is ¥200–¥220, and one-day unlimited-ride passes are available for ¥530.

There are taxi stands at all the train stations, and you can always flag a cab on the street.

■TIP➜ Vacant taxis show a red light in the windshield.

The basic fare is ¥730 for the first 2 km (1 mile), then ¥90 for every additional 293 meters (0.2 mile). Traffic is heavy in downtown Yokohama, however, and it's often faster to walk.

JR trains from Tokyo Station leave approximately every 10 minutes, depending on the time of day. Take the Yokosuka,

the Tokaido, or the Keihin Tohoku Line to Yokohama Station (the Yokosuka and Tokaido lines take 30 minutes; the Keihin Tohoku Line takes 40 minutes and cost ¥480). From there the Keihin Tohoku Line (Platform 3) goes on to Kannai and Ishikawa-cho, Yokohama's business and downtown areas. If you're going directly to downtown Yokohama from Tokyo, the blue commuter trains of the Keihin Tohoku Line are best.

The private Tokyu Toyoko Line, which runs from Shibuya Station in Tokyo directly to Yokohama Station, is a good alternative if you leave from the western part of Tokyo. ■TIP➜ The term "private" is important because it means that the train does not belong to JR and is not a subway line. If you have a JR Pass, you'll have to buy a separate ticket.

Depending on which Tokyu Toyoko Line you catch—the Limited Express, Semi Express, or Local—the trip takes between 25 and 44 minutes and costs ¥280.

Yokohama Station is the hub that links all the train lines and connects them with the city's subway and bus services. Kannai and Ishikawa-cho are the two downtown stations, both on the Keihin Tohoku Line; trains leave Yokohama Station every two to five minutes from Platform 3. From Sakuragi-cho, Kannai, or Ishikawa-cho, most of Yokohama's points of interest are within easy walking distance; the one notable exception is Sankei-en, which you reach via the JR Keihin Tohoku Line to Negishi Station and then a local bus.

**AIRPORT TRANSPORTATION Airport Limousine Information Desk.** ☎ *03/3665–7220* ⊕ *www.limousinebus.co.jp/en.*

Get a taste of China in Japan with a visit to the restaurants and shops of Yokohama's Chinatown.

# 👁 Sights

Large as Yokohama is, the central area is very negotiable. As with any other port city, much of what it has to offer centers on the waterfront—in this case, on the west side of Tokyo Bay. The downtown area is called Kannai (literally, "within the checkpoint"); this is where the international community was originally confined by the shogunate. Though the center of interest has expanded to include the waterfront and Ishikawa-cho, to the south, Kannai remains the heart of town.

Think of that heart as two adjacent areas. One is the old district of Kannai, bounded by Basha-michi on the northwest and Nippon-odori on the southeast, the Keihin Tohoku Line tracks on the southwest, and the waterfront on the northeast. This area contains the business offices of modern Yokohama. The other area extends southeast from Nippon-odori to the Moto-machi shopping street and the International Cemetery, bordered by Yamashita Koen and the waterfront to

the northeast; in the center is China-town, with Ishikawa-cho Station to the southwest. This is the most interesting part of town for tourists.

■ TIP → **Whether you're coming from Tokyo, Nagoya, or Kamakura, make Ishikawa-cho Station your starting point. Take the South Exit from the station and head in the direction of the waterfront.**

## Bashamichi Street (馬車道)

STREET | Running southwest from Shinko Pier to Kannai is Bashamichi, which literally translates into "Horse-Carriage Street." The street was so named in the 19th century, when it was widened to accommodate the horse-drawn carriages of the city's new European residents. This redbrick thoroughfare and the streets parallel to it have been restored to evoke that past, with faux-antique telephone booths and imitation gas lamps. Here you'll find some of the most elegant coffee shops, patisseries, and boutiques in town. On the block northeast of Kannai Station, as you walk toward the waterfront, is Kannai Hall (look for the red-orange abstract sculpture in front), a handsome venue for chamber music, Noh, classical recitals, and occasional performances by such groups as the Peking Opera. If you're planning to stay late in Yokohama, you might want to check out the listings. ⊠ *Naka-ku* Ⓜ *JR Line, Kannai Station; Minato Mirai Line, Bashamichi Station.*

### Chinatown (中華街; *Chuka-gai*)

NEIGHBORHOOD | Once the largest Chinese settlement in Japan—and easily the city's most popular tourist attraction—Yokohama's Chinatown draws more than 18 million visitors a year. Its narrow streets and alleys are lined with some 350 shops selling foodstuffs, herbal medicines, cookware, toys and ornaments, and clothing and accessories. If China exports it, you'll find it here. Wonderful exotic aromas waft from the spice shops. Even better aromas drift from the quarter's 160-odd restaurants, which serve every major style of Chinese cuisine: this is the best place for lunch in Yokohama. Chinatown is a 10-minute walk southeast of Kannai Station. When you get to Yokohama Stadium, turn left and cut through the municipal park to the top of Nihon-odori. Then take a right, and enter Chinatown through the Gembu-mon (North Gate), which leads to the dazzling red-and-gold, 50-foot-high Zenrin-mon (Good Neighbor Gate). ⊠ *Naka-ku* Ⓜ *JR Line, Ishikawa-cho Station; Minato Mirai Line, Motomachi-Chukagai Station.*

### Cup Noodles Museum Yokohama (カップヌードルミュージアム 横浜)

OTHER MUSEUM | FAMILY | At this hands-on museum, visitors can create their own original instant-ramen flavors and packaging, make fresh noodles by hand, and learn all about what has become one of Japan's biggest culinary exports. Kids can run through the museum's Cup Noodle Park, a playground simulating the noodle-making process, complete with a "noodle net" and "seasoning pool" ball pit. ⊠ *2–3–4 Shinko, Naka-ku*

☎ *045/345–0918* ⊕ *www.cupnoodles-museum.jp/en/yokohama* ⊠ *From ¥500* ⏱ *Closed Tues.*

### Harbor View Park (港の見える丘公園; *Minato-no-Mieru-Oka Koen*)

CITY PARK | The park—a major landmark in this part of the city, known, appropriately enough, as the Bluff (*yamate*)—was once the barracks of the British forces in Yokohama. Come here for spectacular nighttime views of the waterfront, the floodlit gardens of Yamashita Park, and the Bay Bridge. Foreigners were first allowed to build here in 1867, and it has been prime real estate ever since—an enclave of consulates, churches, international schools, private clubs, and palatial Western-style homes. ⊠ *114 Yamatecho, Naka-ku* Ⓜ *JR Line, Ishikawa-cho Station; Minato Mirai Line, Motomachi-Chukagai Station.*

### Hikawa-Maru (氷川丸)

NAUTICAL SIGHT | Moored on the waterfront, more or less in the middle of Yamashita Park, is the Hikawa Maru. The ocean liner was built in 1929 by Yokohama Dock Co. and launched on September 30, 1929. For 31 years, she shuttled passengers between Yokohama and Seattle, Washington, making a total of 238 trips. A tour of the ship evokes the time when Yokohama was a great port of call for the transpacific liners. The ship has a French restaurant, and in summer there's a beer garden on the upper deck. ⊠ *Yamashita-koen, Naka-ku* ☎ *045/641–4362* ⊕ *hikawamaru.nyk.com* ⊠ *¥300* ⏱ *Closed Mon.* Ⓜ *JR Line, Ishikawa-cho Station; Minato Mirai Line, Motomachi-Chukagai Station.*

### Iseyama Kotai Jingu Shrine (伊勢山皇大神宮; *Iseyama Kotai Jingu*)

A branch of the nation's revered Grand Shrines of Ise, this is the most important Shinto shrine in Yokohama—but it's worth a visit only if you've seen most everything else in town. ⊠ *64 Miyazaki-cho, Nishi-ku* ✢ *The shrine is a 10-min walk west of Sakuragi-cho Station* ☎ *045/241–1122*

 Free Ⓜ JR Line, Sakuragi-cho Station; Minato Mirai Line, Minato Mirai Station.

## Kanagawa Prefectural Museum of Cultural History (神奈川県立歴史博物館; Kanagawa Kenritsu Rekishi Hakubutsukan)

HISTORY MUSEUM | One of the few buildings in Yokohama to have survived both the Great Kanto Earthquake of 1923 and World War II, the museum is a few blocks north of Kannai Station on Basha-michi. Most exhibits here have no explanations in English, but the galleries on the third floor showcase some remarkable medieval wooden sculptures (including one of the first Kamakura shogun, Minamoto no Yoritomo), hanging scrolls, portraits, and armor. The exhibits of prehistory and of Yokohama in the early modern period are of much less interest. ⊠ 5–60 Minami Nakadori, Naka-ku ☎ 045/201–0926 ⊕ ch.kanagawa-museum.jp ⊠ From ¥300 ⊗ Closed Mon. Ⓜ JR Line, Kannai Station (Exit 8).

## Landmark Tower (ランドマークタワー)

VIEWPOINT | FAMILY | Although no longer Japan's tallest building—that title now goes to Osaka's Abeno Harukas—this 70-story tower in Yokohama's Minato Mirai is the tallest in Greater Tokyo. The observation deck on the 69th floor has a spectacular view of the city, especially at night; you reach it via a high-speed elevator that carries you up at an ear-popping 45 kph (28 mph). The complex's Dockyard Garden, built in 1896, is a restored dry dock with stepped sides of massive stone blocks. The long, narrow floor of the dock, with its water cascade at one end, makes a wonderful year-round open-air venue for concerts and other events; in summer (July–mid-August), the beer garden installed here is a perfect refuge from the heat. The Yokohama Royal Park Hotel occupies the top 20 stories of the building, and the courtyard on the northeast side connects to Queen's Square, a huge atrium-style vertical mall with dozens of shops (mainly for clothing and accessories) and restaurants. ⊠ 2–2–1

Minatomirai, Nishi-ku ☎ 045/222–5015 ⊕ www.yokohama-landmark.jp ⊠ Elevator to observation deck ¥1,000 Ⓜ JR Line, Sakuragi-cho Station; Minato Mirai Line, Minato Mirai Station.

## Marine Tower (マリンタワー)

VIEWPOINT | For an older generation of Yokohama residents, the 348-foot-high decagonal tower, which opened in 1961, was the city's landmark structure; civic pride prevented them from admitting that it falls lamentably short of an architectural masterpiece. The tower has a navigational beacon at the 338-foot level and purports to be the tallest lighthouse in the world. At the 328-foot level, an observation gallery provides 360-degree views of the harbor and the city, and on clear days in autumn or winter, you can often see Mt. Fuji in the distance. Marine Tower is in the middle of the second block northwest from the end of Yamashita Park, on the left side of the promenade. ⊠ 15 Yamashita-cho, Naka-ku ☎ 045/641–7838 ⊕ www.marinetower.yokohama ⊠ ¥750 Ⓜ JR Line, Ishikawa-cho Station; Minato Mirai Line, Motomachi-Chukagai Station.

## Minato Mirai 21 (みなとみらい21; Minato Mirai Nijyu-ichi)

BUSINESS DISTRICT | If you want to see Yokohama urban development at its most self-assertive, then this is a must. The aim of this project, launched in the mid-1980s, was to turn some three-quarters of a square mile of waterfront property, lying east of the JR Negishi Line railroad tracks between the Yokohama and Sakuragi-cho stations, into a model "city of the future." As a hotel, business, international exhibition, and conference center, it's a smashing success. ⊠ Nishi-ku ⊕ www.minatomirai21.com Ⓜ JR Line, Sakuragi-cho Station; Minato Mirai Line, Minato Mirai Station.

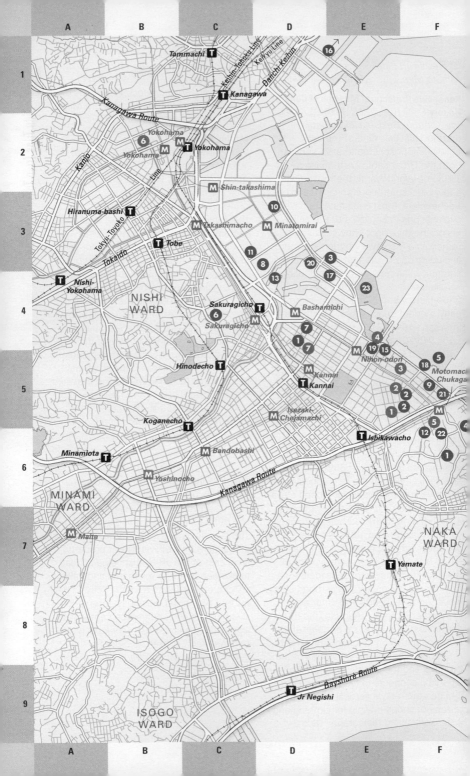

# Yokohama

## Sights ▼

1 Bashamichi Street................. D4
2 Chinatown...................... F5
3 Cup Noodles Museum
   Yokohama..................... E3
4 Harbor View Park.................. F5
5 Hikawa-Maru ...................... F5
6 Iseyama Kotai Jingu Shrine .......C4
7 Kanagawa Prefectural
   Museum of Cultural History ...... D4
8 Landmark Tower.................. D3
9 Marine Tower .................... F5
10 Minato Mirai 21 ................... D3
11 Mitsubishi Minatomirai
   Industrial Museum ................C3
12 Moto-machi...................... F6
13 Nippon Maru Memorial Park..... D4
14 Sankei-en........................ G9
15 Silk Museum .................... E5
16 Soji-ji ......................... E1
17 World Porters .................... E4
18 Yamashita Park .................. F5
19 Yokohama Archives
   of History Museum ............... E4
20 Yokohama Cosmo World.......... D3
21 Yokohama Doll Museum........... F5
22 Yokohama Foreign
   General Cemetery .............. F6
23 Yokohama Red Brick
   Warehouses.................... E4

## Restaurants ▼

1 Kaikin Hanten ................. E5
2 Kaseiro ...................... E5
3 Roma Statione .................. F5
4 Scandia ...................... E4
5 Shunotei Hira................... F5
6 Yokohama Cheese Cafe.......... B2
7 Yokohama Senrya ............... D4

## Quick Bites ▼

1 Enokitei Honten .................. F6
2 Houtenkaku Shinkan .............. F5

*Port of Yokohama*

Bayshore Route

0 ———— 1/2 mi
0 ———— 1/2 km

omoku Jori

14

## KEY

1 *Exploring Sights*
1 *Restaurants*
1 *Quick Bites*

## Mitsubishi Minatomirai Industrial Museum (三菱みなとみらい技術館; *Mitsubishi Minatomirai Gijutsukan*)

SCIENCE MUSEUM | FAMILY | Filling galleries directly across from the Landmark Tower are rocket engines, power plants, a submarine, various gadgets, and displays that simulate piloting helicopters. ⊠ *3–3–1 Minatomirai, Nishi-ku* ☎ *045/200–7351* ⊕ *www.mhi.com/expertise/museum/minatomirai* ⊠ *¥500* ⊙ *Closed Tues.* Ⓜ *JR Line, Sakuragi-cho Station; Minato Mirai Line, Minato Mirai Station.*

## Moto-machi (元町)

STREET | Within a block of Ishikawa-cho Station is the beginning of this street, which follows the course of the Nakamura-gawa (Nakamura River) to the harbor where the Japanese set up shop 100 years ago to serve the foreigners living in Kannai. The street is now lined with smart boutiques and jewelry stores that cater to fashionable young Japanese consumers. ⊠ *Motomachi, Naka-ku* Ⓜ *JR Line, Ishikawa-cho Station; Minato Mirai Line, Motomachi-Chukagai Station.*

## *Nippon Maru* Memorial Park (日本丸メモリアルパーク)

CITY PARK | The centerpiece of the park, which is on the east side of Minato Mirai 21, where the O-okagawa (O-oka River) flows into the bay, is the *Nippon Maru*, a full-rigged three-mast ship popularly called the "Swan of the Pacific." Built in 1930, it served as a training vessel. The Nippon Maru is now retired, but it's an occasional participant in tall-ships festivals and is open for guided tours. Adjacent to the ship is the Yokohama Port Museum, a two-story collection of ship models, displays, and archival materials that celebrate the achievements of the Port of Yokohama from its earliest days to the present. ⊠ *2–1–1 Minatomirai, Nishi-ku* ☎ *045/221–0280* ⊕ *www.nippon-maru.or.jp* ⊠ *¥800* ⊙ *Closed Mon.* Ⓜ *JR Line, Sakuragi-cho Station; Minato Mirai Line, Minato Mirai Station.*

## Bloomin' Season

Walking through Sankei-en is especially delightful in spring, when the flowering trees are at their best: plum blossoms in February and cherry blossoms in early April. In June come the irises, followed by the water lilies. In autumn the trees come back into their own with tinted golden leaves.

## Sankei-en (三渓園)

GARDEN | Opened to the public in 1906, this was once the estate and gardens of Tomitaro Hara (1868–1939), one of Yokohama's wealthiest men, who made his money as a silk merchant before becoming a patron of the arts. On the extensive grounds of the estate he created is a kind of open-air museum of traditional Japanese architecture, some of which was brought here from Kamakura and the western part of the country. Especially noteworthy is Rinshun-kaku, a villa built for the Tokugawa clan in 1649. There's also a tea pavilion, Choshu-kaku, built by the third Tokugawa shogun, Iemitsu. Other buildings include a small temple transported from Kyoto's famed Daitoku-ji and a farmhouse from the Gifu district in the Japan Alps (around Takayama). ⊠ *58–1 Honmoku Sannotani, Naka-ku* ☎ *045/621–0634* ⊕ *www.sankeien.or.jp* ⊠ *Inner garden ¥700* Ⓜ *JR Keihin Tohoku Line to Negishi Station and a local bus (No. 58, 99, or 101) bound for Honmoku; Yokohama Station (East Exit) and take the bus (No. 8 or 148) to Honmoku Sankei-en Mae (the trip takes about 35 min).*

## Silk Museum (シルク博物館; *Shiruku Hakubutsukan*)

OTHER MUSEUM | From the opening of its borders to the beginning of the 20th century, silk was Japan's most sought-after export and nearly all of it went through

Yokohama. The museum, which pays tribute to this period, houses an extensive collection of silk fabrics and an informative exhibit on the silk-making process. People on staff are very happy to answer questions. In the same building, on the first floor, are the main offices of the Yokohama International Tourist Association and the Kanagawa Prefectural Tourist Association. The museum is at the northwestern end of the Yamashita Park promenade, on the second floor of the Silk Center Building. ✉ *1 Yamashita-cho, Naka-ku* ☎ *045/641-0841* ⊕ *www. silkcenter-kbkk.jp/museum* 🎫 *¥500* ⊘ *Closed Mon.* Ⓜ *Minato Mirai Line, Nihon Odori Station (Exit 3).*

## Soji-ji (總持寺)

TEMPLE | One of the two major centers of the Soto sect of Zen Buddhism, Soji-ji, in Yokohama's Tsurumi ward, was founded in 1321. The center was moved here from Ishikawa, on the Noto Peninsula (on the Sea of Japan, north of Kanazawa), after a fire in the 19th century. There's also a Soji-ji monastic complex at Eihei-ji in Fukui Prefecture. The Yokohama Soji-ji is one of the largest and busiest Buddhist institutions in Japan, with more than 200 monks and novices in residence. The 14th-century patron of Soji-ji was the emperor Go-Daigo, who overthrew the Kamakura Shogunate; the emperor is buried here, but his mausoleum is off-limits to visitors. Nevertheless, you can see the Buddha Hall, the Main Hall, and the Treasure House. English tours of the complex are available by reservation. ✉ *2-1-1 Tsurumi, Tsurumi-ku* ⚓ *Take JR Keihin Tohoku Line 2 stops from Sakuragi-cho to Tsurumi. From station, walk 5 min south (back toward Yokohama), passing Tsurumi University on your right. Look out for stone lanterns that mark entrance to temple complex* ☎ *045/581-6021* ⊕ *www.sojiji.jp* 🎫 *¥400 for guided tour* ⊘ *Treasure House closed Mon.*

## World Porters (ワールドポーターズ)

STORE/MALL | This shopping center, on the opposite side of Yokohama Cosmo World, is notable chiefly for its restaurants that overlook the Minato Mirai area. Try arriving at sunset; the spectacular view of twinkling lights and the Landmark Tower, the Ferris wheel, and hotels occasionally include Mt. Fuji in the background. ✉ *2-2-1 Shinko, Naka-ku* ☎ *045/222-2121* ⊕ *www.yim.co.jp* Ⓜ *JR Line, Sakuragi-cho Station; Minato Mirai Line, Minato Mirai Station.*

## Yamashita Park

(山下公園; *Yamashita Koen*)

CITY PARK | This park is perhaps the only positive legacy of the Great Kanto Earthquake of 1923. The debris of the warehouses and other buildings that once stood here were swept away, and the area was made into a 17-acre oasis of green along the waterfront. On spring and summer weekends, the park fills up with families, couples, and groups of friends, making it one of the best people-watching spots in town. The fountain, representing the Guardian of the Water, was presented to Yokohama by San Diego, California, one of its sister cities. ✉ *279 Yamashita-cho, Naka-ku* ⚓ *From Harbor View Park, walk northwest through neighboring French Hill Park and cross walkway over Moto-machi. Turn right on other side and walk 1 block down toward bay to Yamashita-Koen-dori, promenade along park* Ⓜ *JR Line, Ishikawa-cho Station; Minato Mirai Line, Motomachi-Chukagai Station.*

## Yokohama Archives of History Museum

(横浜開港資料館; *Yokohama Kaiko Shiryokan*)

HISTORY MUSEUM | Within the archives, housed in what was once the British Consulate, are some 140,000 items recording the history of Yokohama since the opening of the port to international trade in the mid-19th century. Across the street is a monument to the U.S.–Japanese Friendship Treaty. ✉ *3 Nihonodori,*

*Naka-ku* ✛ *To get here from the Silk Center Building, at the end of the Yamashita Park promenade, walk west to the corner of Nihon-odori; the archives are on the left* ☎ *045/201–2100* ⊕ *www. kaikou.city.yokohama.jp/en* ✉ *¥200* ⊗ *Closed Mon. and Tues.* Ⓜ *Minato Mirai Line, Nihon-odori Station.*

### Yokohama Cosmo World (よこはまコスモワールド)

**AMUSEMENT PARK/CARNIVAL | FAMILY |** This amusement-park complex claims—among its 30 or so rides and attractions—a four story high water-chute ride. The Ferris wheel towers over Yokohama. The park is west of Minato Mirai and Queen's Square, on both sides of the river. ✉ *2–8–1 Shinko, Naka-ku* ☎ *045/641–6591* ⊕ *cosmoworld.jp* ✉ *Park free, rides from ¥400 each* Ⓜ *JR Line, Sakuragi-cho Station; Minato Mirai Line, Minato Mirai Station.*

### Yokohama Doll Museum (横浜人形の家; *Yokohama Ningyo no Ie*)

**OTHER MUSEUM | FAMILY |** This museum houses a collection of roughly 3,500 dolls from all over the world. In Japanese tradition, dolls are less to play with than to display—either in religious folk customs or as the embodiment of some spiritual quality. Japanese visitors to this museum never seem to outgrow their affection for the Western dolls on display here, to which they tend to assign the role of timeless "ambassadors of goodwill" from other cultures. The museum is worth a quick visit, with or without a child in tow. It's just across from the southeast end of Yamashita Park, on the left side of the promenade. ✉ *18 Yamashita-cho, Naka-ku* ☎ *045/671–9361* ⊕ *www.doll-museum. jp* ✉ *¥400* ⊗ *Closed Mon.* Ⓜ *JR Line, Ishikawa-cho Station; Minato Mirai Line, Motomachi-Chukagai Station.*

### Yokohama Foreign General Cemetery (横浜外国人墓地; *Yokohama Gaikokujin Bochi*)

**CEMETERY |** This Yokohama landmark is a reminder of the port city's heritage. It was established in 1854 with a grant of land from the shogunate; the first foreigners to be buried here were Russian sailors assassinated by xenophobes in the early days of the settlement. Most of the 4,500 graves on this hillside are English and American, and about 120 are of the Japanese wives of foreigners; the inscriptions on the crosses and headstones attest to some 40 different nationalities whose citizens lived and died in Yokohama. ✉ *96 Yamate-cho, Naka-ku* ✛ *From Moto-machi Plaza, it's a short walk to north end of cemetery* ⊕ *www. yfgc-japan.com* ✉ *¥200* ⊗ *Closed Mon.* Ⓜ *JR Line, Ishikawa-cho Station; Minato Mirai Line, Motomachi-Chukagai Station.*

### ★ Yokohama Red Brick Warehouses (赤レンガ倉庫; *Aka-Renga Soko*)

**STORE/MALL |** History meets entertainment at Yokohama's Redbrick Warehouses, just a few minutes from World Porters Mall in the Minato Mirai district. Constructed in 1911 to accommodate trade, partially destroyed ten years later in the Kanto earthquake, and then used for military storage in World War II before being taken over by the United States upon Japan's surrender, today these red-brick warehouses are a hipster haven. You'll find unique shops and cafes, restaurants and bars (some with balcony seating), and event spaces. You'll find seasonal fairs and markets and the seafront areas are a perfect picnic spot. ✉ *1–1 Shinko, Naka-ku* ⊕ *www.yokohama-akarenga.jp* Ⓜ *JR Line, Sakuragi-cho Station; Minato Mirai Line, Minato Mirai Station.*

# 🍽 Restaurants

### Kaikin Hanten (華錦飯店)

$$$ | CANTONESE | In contrast to many of the meat-heavy choices in Chinatown, this Cantonese restaurant specializes in fresh, flavorful seafood dishes. Menu highlights include the shrimp-shiso spring rolls, steamed Sakhalin surf clams with garlic, and a rotating selection of fresh fish caught that day. **Known for:** excellent quality at reasonable prices; wide selection of Cantonese dishes; some of Chinatown's freshest seafood. $ *Average main: ¥4,000* ✉ *126–22 Yamashita-cho, Naka-ku* ☎ *050/5485–4599* ⊕ *kakinhanten.gorp.jp.*

### Kaseiro (華正樓)

$$$$ | CHINESE | Chinese food can be hit-or-miss in Japan, but not at Kaseiro. This elegant restaurant, with red carpets and gold-toned walls, is the best of its kind in the city, serving authentic Beijing cuisine, including, of course, Peking duck and shark-fin soup. **Known for:** grand atmosphere; excellent multicourse meals; Yokohama's flagship Chinese restaurant. $ *Average main: ¥10,000* ✉ *186 Yamashita-cho, Chinatown, Naka-ku* ☎ *045/681–2918.*

### Roma Statione (ローマステーション)

$$$ | ITALIAN | Opened more than 40 years ago, this popular venue between Chinatown and Yamashita Park is Yokohama's source for Italian food. The owner, whose father studied cooking in Italy before returning home, is also the head chef and has continued using the original recipes. **Known for:** excellent seafood; extensive Italian wine selection; authentic Italian cuisine. $ *Average main: ¥3,500* ✉ *26 Yamashita-cho, Naka-ku* ☎ *045/681–1818* Ⓜ *Minato Mirai Line, Motomachi-Chukagai Station (Exit 1).*

### Scandia (スカンディヤ)

$$$$ | EUROPEAN | This Scandinavian restaurant near the Silk Center and the business district is known for its smorgasbord. It's popular for business lunches as well as for dinner. **Known for:** good lunch sets; open late; classic Scandinavian cuisine. $ *Average main: ¥6,000* ✉ *1–1 Kaigan-dori, Naka-ku* ☎ *045/201–2262* ⊕ *www.scandia-yokohama.jp.*

### Shunotei Hira (春鶯亭ひら)

$$$$ | JAPANESE | The area of Motomachi is known as the wealthy, posh part of Yokohama; restaurants here tend to be exclusive and expensive, though the service and quality justify the price. This restaurant is an old-style Japanese house complete with a Japanese garden and five private tatami rooms. **Known for:** traditional atmosphere; long dinners; overwhelming 30-course dinners. $ *Average main: ¥13,200* ✉ *1–55 Motomachi, Naka-ku* ☎ *045/662–2215* ⊙ *Closed Mon.*

### Yokohama Cheese Cafe (横浜チーズカフェ)

$$$ | ITALIAN | FAMILY | This is a cozy and inviting casual Italian restaurant, whose interior looks like an Italian country home. There are candles on the tables and an open kitchen where diners can watch the cooks making pizza. **Known for:** rich, creamy fondue; affordable multicourse meals; a cheese lover's paradise. $ *Average main: ¥3,500* ✉ *2–1–10 Kitasaiwai, Nishi-ku* ☎ *045/290–5656* ⊙ *No lunch* Ⓜ *JR Yokohama Station.*

### Yokohama Senrya (瀬里奈 浪漫茶屋; Seryna Romanchaya)

$$$$ | JAPANESE | The hallmarks of this restaurant are *ishiyaki* steak, which is grilled on a hot stone, and *shabu-shabu*—thin slices of beef cooked in boiling water at your table and dipped in one of several sauces; choose from sesame, vinegar, or soy. Fresh vegetables, noodles, and tofu are also dipped into the seasoned broth for a filling yet healthful meal. **Known for:** rustic atmosphere; excellent service; high-grade Wagyu beef. $ *Average main: ¥10,000* ✉ *Shin-Kannai Bldg., 4–45–1 Sumiyoshi-cho, 1st fl., Naka-ku* ☎ *045/681–2727* ⊕ *www.seryna.com/romanjaya/romanjaya.html.*

## Coffee and Quick Bites

**Enokitei Honten** (えの木てい本店)
$$ | **CAFÉ** | Located in one of the area's few remaining historic Western-style houses an Enokitei is a relaxing stop for sweets or a light meal. The interior has the feel of a British-style tea room, with dark wood and antiques, while the garden terrace is surrounded by greenery and flowers much of the year. **Known for:** elegant yet casual atmosphere; afternoon tea; people-watching in the shade. [$] *Average main: ¥1,600* ✉ *89–6 Yamatecho, Naka-ku* ☎ *045/623–2288* 🌐 *www.enokitei.co.jp* 💳 *No credit cards.*

**Houtenkaku Shinkan** (鵬天閣 新館)
$$$ | **SHANGHAINESE** | This no-frills eatery serves up excellent sheng jian bao (Shanghai-style fried dumplings) and other casual Shanghai cuisine all day long. The open kitchen is behind glass so customers can admire the speed with which the chefs cook up this Shanghai staple. **Known for:** authentic Shanghai dumplings; quick and satisfying street food. [$] *Average main: ¥4,000* ✉ *192–15 Yamashita, Naka-ku* ☎ *050/5570–4921* 🌐 *houtenkaku.com/shop-shinkan.*

# Kamakura (鎌倉)

*40 km (25 miles) southwest of Tokyo.*

As a religious center, Kamakura presents an extraordinary legacy. Most of its temples and shrines are in settings of remarkable beauty; many are designated National Treasures. If you have time for just one day trip away from Tokyo, spend it here.

For the aristocrats of the Heian-era Japan (794–1185), life was defined by the Imperial Court in Kyoto. Who in their right mind would venture elsewhere? In Kyoto there was grace and beauty and poignant affairs of the heart; everything beyond was howling wilderness. By the 12th century two clans—the Taira (pronounced "*ta*-ee-ra") and the Minamoto, themselves both offshoots of the imperial line—had come to dominate the affairs of the court and were at each other's throats in a struggle for supremacy. The rivalry between the two clans became an all-out war, and by 1185 the Minamoto were masters of all Japan. Yoritomo no Minamoto forced the Imperial Court to name him shogun; he was now de facto and de jure the military head of state. The emperor was left as a figurehead in Kyoto, and the little fishing village of Kamakura, a superb natural fortress surrounded on three sides by hills and guarded on the fourth by the sea, became—and for 141 years remained—the seat of Japan's first shogunal government.

After 1333, when the center of power returned to Kyoto, Kamakura reverted to being a sleepy backwater town on the edge of the sea. After World War II, it began to develop as a residential area for the well-to-do. Though the religious past is much in evidence, nothing secular survives from the shogunal days; there wasn't much there to begin with. The warriors of Kamakura had little use for courtiers, or their palaces and gardened villas; the shogunate's name for itself, in fact, was the Bakufu—literally, the "tent government."

### GETTING HERE AND AROUND

A bus from Kamakura Station (Sign 5) travels to most of the temples and shrines in the downtown Kamakura area, with stops at most access roads to the temples and shrines. However, you may want to walk out as far as Hokoku-ji and take the bus back; it's easier to recognize the end of the line than any of the stops in between. You can also go by taxi to Hokoku-ji—any cabdriver knows the way—and walk the last leg in reverse.

Bus companies in Kamakura don't conduct guided English tours. Nevertheless, if your time is limited or you don't want to do a lot of walking, the Japanese tours hit the major attractions. These tours depart from Kamakura Station eight times daily, starting at 9 am; the last tour leaves at 1 pm. Purchase tickets at the bus office to the right of the station.

Traveling by train is by far the best way to get to Kamakura. Trains run from Tokyo Station (and Shimbashi Station) every 10 to 15 minutes during the day. The trip takes 56 minutes to Kita-Kamakura and one hour to Kamakura. Take the JR Yokosuka Line from Track 1 downstairs in Tokyo Station (Track 1 upstairs is on a different line and does not go to Kamakura). The cost is ¥820 to Kita-Kamakura, ¥940 to Kamakura (or use your JR Pass). It's now also possible to take a train from Shinjuku, Shibuya, or Ebisu to Kamakura on the Shonan-Shinjuku Line, but these trains depart less frequently than those departing from Tokyo Station. Local train service connects Kita-Kamakura, Kamakura, Hase, and Enoshima.

To return to Tokyo from Enoshima, take a train to Shinjuku on the Odakyu Line. There are 11 express trains daily from here on weekdays between 8:38 am and 8:45 pm; nine trains daily on weekends and national holidays between 8:39 am and 8:46 pm; and even more in summer. The express takes about 70 minutes and costs ¥1,270. Or you can retrace your steps to Kamakura and take the JR Yokosuka Line to Tokyo Station.

## TOURS

JTB Sunrise Tours runs daily English-language trips from Tokyo to Kamakura; these tours are often combined with trips to Hakone. You can book through, and arrange to be picked up at, any of the major hotels. Check to make sure that the tour covers everything you want to see, as many include little more than a passing view of the Great Buddha in Hase. Given how easy it is to get around—most sights are within walking distance of each other, and others are short bus or train rides apart—you're better off seeing Kamakura on your own.

## Timing Tip

If your time is limited, you may want to visit only Engaku Temple and Tokei Temple in Kita-Kamakura before riding the train one stop to Kamakura. If not, follow the main road all the way to Tsuru-ga-oka Hachiman-gu and visit four additional temples en route.

### KSGG Club Volunteer Guides

**GUIDED TOURS** | The KSGG Club Volunteer Guides has a free guide service and regular events. Arrangements must be made in advance through the group's website. ⊕ *volunteerguide-ksgg.jp* ✉ *Free.*

### VISITOR INFORMATION

The Kamakura Station Tourist Information Center has a useful collection of brochures and maps. Visitors heading to Kamakura from Yokohama can plan their excursion at the Kanagawa Prefectural Tourist Association office in the Silk Center, on the Yamashita Park promenade.

**CONTACTS Fujisawa City Tourist Association.** ✉ *2–20–13 Katasekaigan, Fujisawa City* ☎ *0466/22–4141* ⊕ *www.fujisa-wa-kanko.jp.* **Kamakura City Tourist Information Center.** ✉ *1–1–1 Komachi, Kamakura* ☎ *0467/22–3350.* **Kanagawa Prefectural Tourist Association.** ✉ *1 Yamashita-cho, Yokohama* ☎ *045/681–0007* ⊕ *www.kanagawa-kankou.or.jp.*

# Kita–Kamakura

*40 km (25 miles) southwest of Tokyo.*

Hierarchies were important to the Kamakura Shogunate. In the 14th century it established a ranking system called Go-zan (literally, "Five Mountains") for the Zen Buddhist monasteries under its official sponsorship. These are clustered in the Kita-Kamakura district.

## Did You Know?

Engaku Temple belongs to the Rinzai sect of Zen Buddhism. Introduced by China at the beginning of the Kamakura period (1192–1333), Zen was quickly embraced by the emerging warrior class. The samurai especially admired Rinzai's emphasis on the ascetic life as a path to self-transcendence. The monks of Engaku advised the shogunate in matters spiritual, artistic, and political.

# Sights

### Engaku-ji Temple (円覚寺)

TEMPLE | The largest of the Zen monasteries in Kamakura, Engaku-ji (Engaku Temple) was founded in 1282 and ranks second in the Five Mountains hierarchy. Here, prayers were to be offered regularly for the prosperity and well-being of the government; Engaku Temple's special role was to pray for the souls of those who died resisting the Mongol invasions in 1274 and 1281. The temple complex currently holds 18 buildings, but once contained as many as 50. Often damaged in fires and earthquakes, it has been completely restored.

Engaku Temple belongs to the Rinzai sect of Zen Buddhism. The ideas of Zen were introduced to Japan from China at the beginning of the Kamakura period (1192–1333). The samurai especially admired the Rinzai sect, with its emphasis on the ascetic life as a path to self-transcendence. The monks of Engaku Temple played an important role as advisers to the shogunate in matters spiritual, artistic, and political.

Among the National Treasures at Engaku Temple is the Hall of the Holy Relic of Buddha (Shari-den), with its remarkable Chinese-inspired thatched roof. Built in 1282, it was destroyed by fire in 1558 but rebuilt in its original form soon after, in 1563. The hall is said to enshrine a tooth of the Gautama Buddha himself, but it's not on display. In fact, except for the first three days of the New Year, you won't be able to go any farther into the hall than the main gate. Such is the case, alas, with much of the Engaku Temple complex: this is still a functioning monastic center, and many of its most impressive buildings are not open to the public. The accessible National Treasure at Engaku Temple is the Great Bell (Kosho), on the hilltop on the southeast side of the complex. The bell—Kamakura's most famous—was cast in 1301 and stands 8 feet tall. It's rung only on special occasions, such as New Year's Eve. Reaching the bell requires a trek up a long staircase, but once you've made it to the top you can enjoy tea and traditional Japanese sweets at a small outdoor café. The views of the entire temple grounds and surrounding cedar forest from here are tremendous.

The two buildings open to the public at Engaku Temple are the Butsunichi-an, which has a long ceremonial hall where you can enjoy *sado* (Japanese tea ceremony), and the Obai-in. The latter is the mausoleum of the last three regents of the Kamakura Shogunate: Tokimune Hojo, who led the defense of Japan against the Mongol invasions; his son Sadatoki; and his grandson Takatoki. Off to the side of the mausoleum is a quiet garden with apricot trees, which bloom in February. As you exit Kita-Kamakura Station, you'll see the stairway to Engaku Temple just in front of you. ⊠ *409 Yamanouchi, Kamakura* ☎ *0467/22–0478* ⊕ *www.engakuji.or.jp/en* ☞ *¥500.*

### Enno-ji Temple (円応寺)

TEMPLE | In the feudal period, Japan acquired from China a belief in Enma, the lord of hell, who, with his court attendants, judged the souls of the departed and determined their destination in the afterlife. Kamakura's otherwise undistinguished Enno-ji (Enno Temple) houses some remarkable statues of these judges—as grim and merciless a court as you're ever likely to confront. To see them is enough to put you on your best behavior, at least for the rest of your excursion. Enno Temple is a minute's walk or so from Kencho Temple, on the opposite (south) side of the main road to Kamakura. ⊠ *1543 Yamanouchi, Kamakura* ☎ *0467/25–1095* ☞ *¥200.*

### Jochi-ji Temple (浄智寺)

TEMPLE | In the Five Mountains hierarchy, Jochi-ji (Jochi Temple) was ranked fourth. The buildings now in the complex are reconstructions; the Great Kanto

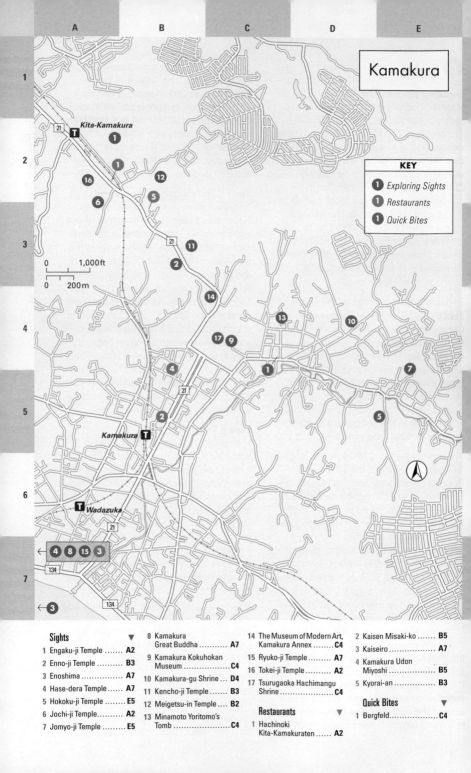

# Kamakura

**KEY**

- **1** *Exploring Sights*
- **1** *Restaurants*
- **1** *Quick Bites*

Kita-Kamakura

Kamakura

Wadazuka

0     1,000ft

0     200m

**Sights** ▼

1 Engaku-ji Temple ....... **A2**
2 Enno-ji Temple .......... **B3**
3 Enoshima ................. **A7**
4 Hase-dera Temple ...... **A7**
5 Hokoku-ji Temple ....... **E5**
6 Jochi-ji Temple.......... **A2**
7 Jomyo-ji Temple ......... **E5**

8 Kamakura
   Great Buddha ........... **A7**
9 Kamakura Kokuhokan
   Museum ................. **C4**
10 Kamakura-gu Shrine ... **D4**
11 Kencho-ji Temple ....... **B3**
12 Meigetsu-in Temple .... **B2**
13 Minamoto Yoritomo's
    Tomb .................... **C4**

14 The Museum of Modern Art,
    Kamakura Annex ........ **C4**
15 Ryuko-ji Temple ......... **A7**
16 Tokei-ji Temple .......... **A2**
17 Tsurugaoka Hachimangu
    Shrine .................... **C4**

**Restaurants** ▼

1 Hachinoki
   Kita-Kamakuraten ...... **A2**

2 Kaisen Misaki-ko ....... **B5**
3 Kaiseiro ................... **A7**
4 Kamakura Udon
   Miyoshi ................... **B5**
5 Kyorai-an ................ **B3**

**Quick Bites** ▼

1 Bergfeld.................. **C4**

Earthquake of 1923 destroyed the originals. The garden here is exquisite. Jochi-ji is on the south side of the railway tracks, a few minutes' walk farther southwest of Tokei-ji in the direction of Kamakura. ✉ *1402 Yamanouchi, Kamakura* ✛ *Turn right off main road (Rte. 21) and cross over small bridge; flight of moss-covered steps leads up to temple* ☎ *0467/22–3943* ⊕ *jochiji.com/en* ✆ *¥200.*

### Kencho-ji Temple (建長寺)

TEMPLE | Founded in 1250, Kencho-ji (Kencho Temple) was the foremost of Kamakura's five great Zen temples, and it lays claim to being the oldest Zen temple in all of Japan. It was modeled on one of the great Chinese monasteries of the time and built for a distinguished Zen master who had just arrived from China. Over the centuries, fires and other disasters have taken their toll on Kencho-ji, and although many buildings have been authentically reconstructed, the temple complex today is half its original size. Near the Main Gate (San-mon) is a bronze bell cast in 1255; it's the temple's most important treasure. The Main Gate and the Lecture Hall (Hatto) are the only two structures to have survived the devastating Great Kanto Earthquake of 1923. Like Engaku-ji, Kencho-ji is a functioning temple of the Rinzai sect, where novices train and laypeople can come to take part in Zen meditation. Nearly hidden at the back of the temple is a long stairway and hiking trail that leads to Zuisen-ji, another of Kamakura's major temples. The hike takes about 90 minutes. ✉ *8 Yamanouchi, Kamakura* ✛ *Entrance to Kencho Temple is about halfway along main road from Kita-Kamakura Station to Tsuru-ga-oka Hachiman-gu, on left* ☎ *0467/22–0981* ⊕ *www.kenchoji.com* ✆ *¥500.*

### Meigetsu-in Temple (明月院)

This temple is also known as Ajisai-dera ("the hydrangea temple"), and when the flowers bloom in June, it becomes one of the most popular places in Kamakura. The gardens transform into a sea of color—pink, white, and blue—and visitors can number in the thousands. A typical Kamakura light rain shouldn't deter you; it only showcases this incredible floral display to its best advantage. Meigetsu-in features Kamakura's largest *yagura* (a tomb cavity enclosing a mural) on which 16 images of Buddha are carved. ✉ *189 Yamanouchi, Kamakura* ✛ *To reach Meigetsu-in from Tokei-ji, walk along Rte. 21 toward Kamakura for about 20 min until you cross railway tracks; take immediate left turn onto narrow side street that doubles back along tracks. This street bends to right and follows course of a little stream called Meigetsu-gawa to temple gate* ☎ *0467/24–3437* ✆ *¥500.*

### Tokei-ji Temple (東慶寺)

A Zen temple of the Rinzai sect, Tokei-ji holds special significance for the study of feminism in medieval Japan. More popularly known as the Enkiri-dera, or Divorce Temple, it was founded in 1285 by the widow of the Hojo regent Tokimune as a refuge for the victims of unhappy marriages. Under the shogunate, a husband of the warrior class could obtain a divorce simply by sending his wife back to her family. Not so for the wife: no matter what cruel and unusual treatment her husband meted out, she was stuck with him. If she ran away, however, and managed to reach Tokei Temple without being caught, she could receive sanctuary at the temple and remain there as a nun. After three years (later reduced to two), she was officially declared divorced. The temple survived as a convent through the Meiji Restoration of 1868. The last abbess died in 1902; her headstone is in the cemetery behind the temple, beneath the plum trees that blossom in February. Tokei Temple was later reestablished as a monastery.

The Matsugaoka Hozo (Treasure House) of Tokei Temple displays several Kamakura-period wooden Buddhas, ink paintings, scrolls, and works of calligraphy, some of which have been designated by the government as Important Cultural Objects. The library, called the Matsugaoka Bunko, was established in memory of the great Zen scholar D. T. Suzuki (1870–1966).

Tokei Temple is on the southwest side of the JR tracks (the side opposite Engaku Temple), less than a five-minute walk south from the station on the main road to Kamakura (Route 21—the Kamakura Kaido), on the right. ✉ *1367 Yamanouchi, Kamakura* ☎ *0467/22–1663* 🌐 *www.tokeiji.com* 🎫 *From ¥200* 🕒 *Matsugaoka Treasure House closed Mon.*

## 🍴 Restaurants

**Hachinoki Kita-Kamakuraten** (鉢の木北鎌倉店)
**$$$ | JAPANESE** | Traditional *shojin ryori* (the vegetarian cuisine of Zen monasteries) is served in this old Japanese house on the Kamakura Kaido (Route 21) near the entrance to Jochi Temple. The seating is mainly in tatami rooms with beautiful antique wood furnishings. **Known for:** peaceful, traditional atmosphere; elegant dining experience; Buddhist-temple cuisine for all budgets. [$] *Average main: ¥3,500* ✉ *350 Yamanouchi, Kamakura* ☎ *0467/23–3723* 🌐 *www.hachinoki.co.jp/english* 🕒 *Closed Wed.*

**Kyorai-an** (去来庵)
**$$ | JAPANESE FUSION** | A traditional Japanese structure houses this restaurant known for its excellent Western-style beef stew along with homemade cheesecake, pastas and local wines. Half the seats are on tatami mats and half are at tables, but all look out on a peaceful patch of greenery. **Known for:** local wines and ingredients; lovely views; classic Japanese-Western cuisine. [$] *Average main: ¥2,500* ✉ *157 Yamanouchi, Kamakura* ✥ *Kyorai-an is on main road from Kita-Kamakura to Kamakura on left side; it's about halfway between Meigetsu Temple and Kencho Temple, up a winding flight of stone steps* ☎ *0467/24–9835* 🌐 *kyoraian.jp* 💳 *No credit cards* 🕒 *Closed Thurs. and Fri.*

# Downtown Kamakura

Downtown Kamakura is a good place to stop for lunch and shopping. Restaurants and shops selling local crafts, especially the carved and lacquered woodwork called Kamakura-bori, abound on Wakamiya Oji and the street parallel to it, Komachi-dori.

When the first Kamakura shogun, Minamoto no Yoritomo, learned he was about to have an heir, he had the tutelary shrine of his family moved to Kamakura from nearby Yui-ga-hama and ordered a stately avenue to be built through the center of his capital from the shrine to the sea. Along this avenue would travel the procession that brought his son—if there were a son—to be presented to the gods. Yoritomo's consort did indeed bear him a son, Yoriie (pronounced "yo-*ree*-ee-eh"), in 1182; Yoriie was brought in great pomp to the shrine and then consecrated to his place in the shogunal succession. Alas, the blessing of the gods did Yoriie little good. He was barely 18 when Yoritomo died, and the regency established by his mother's family, the Hojo, kept him virtually powerless until 1203, when he was banished and eventually assassinated. The Minamoto were never to hold power again, but Yoriie's memory lives on in the street that his father built for him: Wakamiya Oji, "the Avenue of the Young Prince."

## 👁 Sights

**Hokoku-ji Temple** (報国寺)
**TEMPLE** | Visitors to Kamakura tend to overlook this lovely little Zen temple of the Rinzai sect that was built in 1334, but it's worth a look. Over the years it had fallen into disrepair and neglect, until an enterprising priest took over,

cleaned up the gardens, and began promoting the temple for meditation sessions, calligraphy exhibitions, and tea ceremony. Behind the main hall are a thick grove of bamboo and a small tea pavilion—a restful oasis and a fine place to go for *matcha* (green tea). The temple is about 2 km (1 mile) east on Route 204 from the main entrance to Tsuru-ga-oka Hachiman-gu; turn right at the traffic light by the Hokoku Temple Iriguchi bus stop and walk about three minutes south to the gate. ✉ *2–7–4 Jomyo-ji, Kamakura* 🕾 *0467/22–0762* ⊕ *www.hokokuji.or.jp* 🖃 *From ¥300.*

## Jomyo-ji Temple (浄妙寺)

TEMPLE | Founded in 1188, this is one of the Five Mountains Zen monasteries. Though this modest single-story monastery belonging to the Rinzai sect lacks the grandeur and scale of the Engaku and Kencho, it still merits the status of an Important Cultural Property. It is nestled inside an immaculate garden that is particularly beautiful in spring, when the cherry trees bloom. A tea ceremony with Japanese green tea takes place in this lovely setting. The monastery's only distinctive features are its green roof and the statues of Shaka Nyorai and Amida Nyorai, who represent truth and enlightenment, in the main hall. ✉ *3–8–31 Jomyo-ji, Kamakura* ✛ *From Hokoku-ji, cross main street (Rte. 204) that brought you the mile or so from Tsuru-ga-oka Hachiman-gu, and take first narrow street north. The monastery is about 100 yd from corner* 🕾 *0467/22–2818* 🖃 *Jomyo Temple ¥100, tea ceremony ¥500.*

## Kamakura-gu Shrine (鎌倉宮)

RELIGIOUS BUILDING | This Shinto shrine was built after the Meiji Restoration of 1868 and was dedicated to Prince Morinaga (1308–36), the first son of Emperor Go-Daigo. When Go-Daigo overthrew the Kamakura Shogunate and restored Japan to direct imperial rule, Morinaga—who had been in the priesthood—was appointed supreme

commander of his father's forces. The prince lived in turbulent times and died young: when the Ashikaga clan in turn overthrew Go-Daigo's government, Morinaga was taken into exile, held prisoner in a cave behind the present site of Kamakura Shrine, and eventually beheaded. The Homotsu-den (Treasure House), on the northwest corner of the grounds, next to the shrine's administrative office, is of interest mainly for its collection of paintings depicting the life of Prince Morinaga. ✉ *154 Nikaido, Kamakura* ✛ *From Yoritomo's tomb walk to Rte. 204 and turn left; at next traffic light, a narrow street on left leads off at an angle to shrine, about 5-min walk west* 🕾 *0467/22–0318* 🖃 *Shrine free, Treasure House ¥300.*

## Kamakura Kokuhokan Museum (鎌倉国宝館)

ART MUSEUM | This museum was built in 1928 as a repository for many of the most important objects belonging to the shrines and temples in the area; many of these are designated Important Cultural Properties. Located along the east side of the Tsuru-ga-oka Hachiman-gu shrine precincts, the museum has an especially fine collection of devotional and portrait sculpture in wood from the Kamakura and Muromachi periods; the portrait pieces may be among the most expressive and interesting in all of classical Japanese art. ✉ *2–1–1 Yukinoshita, Kamakura* 🕾 *0467/22–0753* ⊕ *www.city.kamakura. kanagawa.jp/kokuhoukan* 🖃 *From ¥700* ☾ *Closed Mon.*

## Minamoto Yoritomo's Tomb (源頼朝の墓; *Minamoto no Yoritomo no Haka*)

TOMB | The man who put Kamakura on the map, so to speak, chose not to leave it when he died: it's only a short walk from Tsuru-ga-oka Hachiman-gu to the tomb of the man responsible for its construction, Minamoto no Yoritomo. If you've already been to Nikko and have seen how a later dynasty of shoguns sought to glorify its own memories, you may be surprised at

# An Ancient Soap Opera

Once a year, during the Spring Festival (early or mid-April, when the cherry trees are in bloom), the Mai-den hall at Tsuru-ga-oka Hachiman-gu is used to stage a heartrending drama about Minamoto no Yoritomo's brother, Yoshitsune. Although Yoritomo was the tactical genius behind the downfall of the Taira clan and the establishment of the Kamakura Shogunate in the late 12th century, it was his dashing half brother who actually defeated the Taira in battle. In so doing, Yoshitsune won the admiration of many, and Yoritomo came to believe that his sibling had ambitions of his own. Despite Yoshitsune's declaration of allegiance, Yoritomo had him exiled and sent assassins to have him killed. Yoshitsune spent his life fleeing from one place to another until, at the age of 30, he was betrayed in his last refuge and took his own life.

Earlier in his exile, Yoshitsune's lover, the dancer Shizuka Gozen, had been captured and brought to Yoritomo and his wife, Masako. They commanded her to dance for them as a kind of penance. Instead she danced for Yoshitsune. Yoritomo was furious, and only Masako's influence kept him from ordering her death. When he discovered, however, that Shizuka was carrying Yoshitsune's child, he ordered that if the child were a boy, he was to be killed. A boy was born. Some versions of the legend have it that the child was slain; others say he was placed in a cradle, like Moses, and cast adrift in the reeds.

the simplicity of Yoritomo's tomb. ⊠ *2–5–2 Nishimikaido, Kamakura* ✛ *Exit Tsuru-ga-oka Hachiman-gu, turn left and then left again, and follow small road up to Yoritomo's tomb* ⊡ *Free.*

### The Museum of Modern Art, Kamakura Annex (神奈川県立近代美術館 鎌倉別館; *Kanagawa Kenritsu Kindai Bijutsukan Kamakura Bekkan*)

**ART MUSEUM** | Just a few minutes' walk from Tsuru-ga-oka Hachiman-gu, this newly refurbished museum houses a collection of Japanese oil paintings and watercolors, woodblock prints, and sculpture. ⊠ *2–8–1 Yukinoshita, Kamakura* ☎ *0467/22–5000* ⊕ *www.moma.pref. kanagawa.jp/en/annex* ⊡ *From ¥700, depending on exhibition* ⊘ *Closed Mon.*

### Tsurugaoka Hachimangu Shrine (鶴岡八幡宮)

**RELIGIOUS BUILDING** | This shrine is dedicated to the legendary emperor Ojin, his wife, and his mother, from whom Minamoto no Yoritomo claimed descent. At the entrance, the small, steeply arched, vermilion Taiko-bashi (Drum Bridge) crosses a stream between two lotus ponds. The ponds were made to Yoritomo's specifications. His wife, Masako, suggested placing islands in each. In the larger Genji Pond, to the right, filled with white lotus flowers, she placed three islands. Genji was another name for clan, and three is an auspicious number. In the smaller Heike Pond, to the left, she put four islands. Heike (pronounced "*heh*-ee-keh") was another name for the rival Taira clan, which the Minamoto had destroyed, and four—homophonous in Japanese with the word for "death"—is very unlucky indeed.

On the far side of the Drum Bridge is the Mai-den. This hall is the setting for a story of the Minamoto celebrated in Noh and Kabuki theater. Beyond the Mai-den, a flight of steps leads to the shrine's Hon-do (Main Hall). To the left of these steps is a ginkgo tree that—according to legend—was witness to a murder that ended the Minamoto line in 1219. From behind this tree, a priest named Kugyo leapt out and beheaded his uncle, the 26-year-old Sanetomo, Yoritomo's second son and the last Minamoto shogun. The priest was quickly apprehended, but Sanetomo's head was never found. As at all other Shinto shrines, the Hon-do is unadorned; the building itself, an 1828 reconstruction, is not particularly noteworthy. ✉ *2–1–31 Yukinoshita, Kamakura* ☎ *0467/22–0315* 🌐 *www.hachimangu.or.jp* 🎫 *Shrine free; Treasure House ¥300.*

## 🍴 Restaurants

**Kaisen Misaki-ko** (海鮮三崎港)
$$ | **SUSHI** | This *kaiten-zushi* (sushi served on a conveyor belt that lets you pick the dishes you want) restaurant serves eye-poppingly large fish portions that hang over the edge of their plates. All the standard sushi creations, including tuna, shrimp, and egg, are prepared here. **Known for:** inexpensive, quality sushi; fast service; friendly, helpful staff and sushi chefs. $ *Average main: ¥1,500* ✉ *1–7–1 Komachi, Kamakura* ☎ *0467/22–6228* 💳 *No credit cards.*

**Kamakura Udon Miyoshi** (鎌倉みよし)
$$ | **JAPANESE** | Serving up some of Kamakura's best handmade udon noodles and tempura, this unpretentious restaurant is a good bet for quick and satisfying lunch. Miyoshi also has a selection of local sakes to pair with your meal. **Known for:** reliability amid the tourist traps in the area; tempura that won't weigh you down; fresh noodles made before your eyes. $ *Average main: ¥1,600* ✉ *1–5–38 Yukinoshita, Kamakura* ☎ *0467/61–4634* 🌐 *www.kamakuraudon.jp* 💳 *No credit cards.*

## ☕ Coffee and Quick Bites

**Bergfeld** (ベルグフェルド)
$ | **BAKERY** | This German bakery serves cakes and cookies that are surprisingly authentic—the baker trained in Germany. There are a few small tables outside, and cozy tables inside where you can enjoy coffee and cakes before resuming your tour. **Known for:** a good break between seeing sights; tasty sandwiches; authentic German pastries and desserts. $ *Average main: ¥700* ✉ *3–9–24 Yukinoshita, Kamakura* ☎ *0467/24–2706* 🌐 *bergfeld-kamakura.com* 💳 *No credit cards* 🕒 *Closed Tues., 1st and 3rd Mon.*

# Hase

On hydrangea-clad hillsides just outside downtown Kamakura are two of the town's main attractions, the Great Buddha and Hase-dera Temple.

## 👁 Sights

**Enoshima** (江ノ島)
**ISLAND** | The Sagami Bay shore in this area has some of the closest beaches to Tokyo, and in the hot, humid summer months it seems as though all of the city's teeming millions pour onto these beaches in search of a vacant patch of rather dirty gray sand. Pass up this mob scene and press on instead to Enoshima. The island is only 4 km (2½ miles) around, with a hill in the middle. Partway up the hill is a shrine where the local fisherfolk used to pray for a bountiful catch—before it became a tourist attraction. Once upon a time it was quite a hike up to the shrine; now there's a series of escalators, flanked by the inevitable stalls selling souvenirs and snacks. The island has several cafés and restaurants, and on clear days some of them have spectacular views of Mt. Fuji and the Izu Peninsula. To reach the causeway from Enoshima Station to the island, walk south from the

Hase-dera, in Kamakura, is dedicated to unborn children. The beautiful temple faces the sea.

station for about 3 km (2 miles), keeping the Katase-gawa (Katase River) on your right. To return to Tokyo from Enoshima, take a train to Shinjuku on the Odakyu line. From the island walk back across the causeway and take the second bridge over the Katase-gawa. Within five minutes you'll come to Katase-Enoshima Station. Or you can retrace your steps to Kamakura and take the JR Yokosuka Line to Tokyo Station. ✉ *Kamakura.*

### ★ Hase-dera Temple (長谷寺)

**TEMPLE** | The only temple in Kamakura facing the sea, this is one of the most beautiful, and saddest, places of pilgrimage in the city. On a landing partway up the stone steps that lead to the temple grounds are hundreds of small stone images of Jizo, one of the *bodhisattvas* in the Buddhist pantheon. Jizo is the savior of children, particularly the souls of the stillborn, aborted, and miscarried; the mothers of these children dress the statues of Jizo in bright red bibs and leave them small offerings of food, heartbreakingly touching acts of prayer.

The Kannon Hall (Kannon-do) at Hase-dera enshrines the largest carved-wood statue in Japan: the votive figure of Juichimen Kannon, the 11-headed goddess of mercy. Standing 30 feet tall, the goddess bears a crown of 10 smaller heads, symbolizing her ability to search out in all directions for those in need of her compassion. No one knows for certain when the figure was carved. According to the temple records, a monk named Tokudo Shonin carved two images of the Juichimen Kannon from a huge laurel tree in 721. One was consecrated to the Hase-dera in present-day Nara Prefecture; the other was thrown into the sea in order to go wherever the sea decided that there were souls in need, and that image washed up on shore near Kamakura. Much later, in 1342, Takauji Ashikaga—the first of the 15 Ashikaga shoguns who followed the Kamakura era—had the statue covered with gold leaf.

The Amida Hall of Hase-dera enshrines the image of a seated Amida Buddha, who presides over the Western Paradise of the Pure Land. Minamoto no Yoritomo ordered the creation of this statue when he reached the age of 42; popular Japanese belief, adopted from China, holds that your 42nd year is particularly unlucky. Yoritomo's act of piety earned him another 11 years—he was 53 when he was thrown by a horse and died of his injuries. The Buddha is popularly known as the *yakuyoke* (good luck) Amida, and many visitors—especially students facing entrance exams—make a point of coming here to pray. To the left of the main halls is a small restaurant where you can buy good-luck candy and admire the view of Kamakura Beach and Sagami Bay. ⊠ *3–11–2 Hase, Kamakura ✛ From Hase Station, walk north about 5 min on main street (Rte. 32) toward Kotoku-in and Great Buddha, and look for signpost to temple on side street to left* ☎ *0467/22–6300* ⊕ *www.hasedera.jp* ⊠ *¥400.*

## ★ Kamakura Great Buddha
(鎌倉大仏; *Kamakura Daibutsu*)

**PUBLIC ART** | The single biggest attraction in Hase is the Great Buddha—sharing the honors with Mt. Fuji, perhaps, as the quintessential picture-postcard image of Japan. The statue of the compassionate Amida Buddha sits cross-legged in the temple courtyard. The 37-foot bronze figure was cast in 1292, three centuries before Europeans reached Japan; the concept of the classical Greek lines in the Buddha's robe must have come over the Silk Route through China during the time of Alexander the Great. The casting was probably first conceived in 1180, by Minamoto no Yoritomo, who wanted a statue to rival the enormous Daibutsu in Nara. Until 1495 the Amida Buddha was housed in a wooden temple, which washed away in a great tidal wave.

It may seem sacrilegious to walk inside the Great Buddha, but for ¥200 you can enter the figure from a doorway in the right side and explore his stomach, with a stairway that leads up to two windows in his back, offering a stunning view of the temple grounds (open until 4:15 pm).

To reach Kotoku-in and the Great Buddha, take the Enoden Line from the west side of JR Kamakura Station three stops to Hase. From the East Exit, turn right and walk north about 10 minutes on the main street (Route 32). ⊠ *4–2–28 Hase, Kamakura* ☎ *0467/22–0703* ⊕ *www.kotoku-in. jp* ⊠ *¥300.*

### Ryuko-ji Temple (龍口寺)

**TEMPLE** | The Kamakura story would not be complete without the tale of Nichiren (1222–82), the monk who founded the only native Japanese sect of Buddhism and is honored here. Nichiren's rejection of both Zen and Jodo (Pure Land) teachings brought him into conflict with the Kamakura Shogunate, and the Hojo regents sent him into exile on the Izu Peninsula in 1261. Later allowed to return, he continued to preach his own interpretation of the Lotus Sutra—and to assert the "blasphemy" of other Buddhist sects, a stance that finally persuaded the Hojo regency, in 1271, to condemn him to death. The execution was to take place on a hill to the south of Hase. As the executioner swung his sword, legend has it that a lightning bolt struck the blade and snapped it in two. Taken aback, the executioner sat down to collect his wits, and a messenger was sent back to Kamakura to report the event. On his way he met another messenger, who was carrying a writ from the Hojo regents commuting Nichiren's sentence to exile on the island of Sado-ga-shima.

Followers of Nichiren built Ryuko Temple in 1337, on the hill where he was to be executed, marking his miraculous deliverance from the headsman. There are other Nichiren temples closer to Kamakura—Myohon-ji and Ankokuron-ji, for example. But Ryuko has not only the typical Nichiren-style main hall, with gold tassels hanging from its roof, but also a beautiful pagoda, built in 1904. ⊠ *3–13–37 Katase, Fujisawa ✛ Take Enoden train line west from Hase to Enoshima—a short, scenic ride that cuts through hills surrounding Kamakura to*

shore. From Enoshima Station walk about 100 yards east, keeping train tracks on your right ☎ 0466/25–7357 ☒ Free.

## 🍴 Restaurants

### Kaiseiro (華正樓)

**$$$$ | CHINESE |** This establishment, in an old Japanese house, serves the best Chinese food in the city. The dining-room windows look out on a small, restful garden. **Known for:** steeped in history; excellent Peking duck and other multicourse meals; elegant atmosphere. ⓢ *Average main: ¥10,000* ☒ *3–1–14 Hase, Kamakura* ☎ *0467/22–0280.*

# Mt. Fuji (富士山; Fuji-san)

*100 km (62 miles) southwest of Tokyo.*

Mt. Fuji is the crown jewel of the national park and an incredibly popular destination for both Japanese and international travelers, but travel time from Tokyo is still longer than to some places that are considerably farther from Tokyo. There are six routes to the summit of the 12,388-foot-high mountain but only two, both accessible by bus, are recommended: from Go-gome (5th Station), on the north side, and from Shin-Go-gome (New 5th Station), on the south.

## GETTING HERE AND AROUND

Take one of the daily buses directly to Go-gome from Tokyo; they run July through August and leave from Shinjuku Station. The journey takes about two hours and 40 minutes from Shinjuku and costs ¥2,600. Reservations are required; book seats through the Fuji Kyuko Highway Bus Reservation Center, the Keio Highway Bus Reservation Center, the Japan Travel Bureau (which should have English-speaking staff), or any major travel agency.

## What Is a Bodhisattva? 👁

A *bodhisattva* is a being that has deferred its own ascendance into Buddhahood to guide the souls of others to salvation. It is considered a deity in Buddhism.

There are no direct trains between Mt. Fuji and Tokyo; as a result, buses are more affordable and convenient. But if you need to return from Mt. Fuji to Tokyo by train, take an hour-long bus ride from Shin-Go-gome to Gotemba (¥1,500). From Gotemba take the JR Tokaido and Gotemba lines to Tokyo Station (¥1,940), or take the JR Asagiri express train from Gotemba to Shinjuku station (¥2,810).

**CONTACTS Fuji Kyuko Highway Bus Reservation Center.** ☎ *0555/73–8181* ⊕ *bus-en. fujikyu.co.jp.* **JTB Sunrise Tours.** サンライズツアー ☒ *Tokyo* ☎ *03/5706–5454* ⊕ *www.sunrise-tours.jp/en.* **Keio Highway Bus Reservation Center.** ☎ *03/5376–2222* ⊕ *highway-buses.jp.*

## 👁 Sights

### ★ Mt. Fuji (富士山; Fuji-san)

**MOUNTAIN |** Rising up out of the surrounding plains, the single, flat-topped peak of Mt. Fuji is a sight to behold. Spending a day—or more commonly an afternoon and the following morning—to hike Mt. Fuji can be a once-in-a-lifetime experience with a fascinating variety of terrain and a stunning view of the sunrise from the peak—provided you go into it with the right expectations. Unlike Japan's more remote mountains like the Japan Alps, Fuji is crowded, and the summer hiking season, when trails are open and accessible (roughly July through September), is short. Timing your hike to see the sunrise can mean that the final stretch

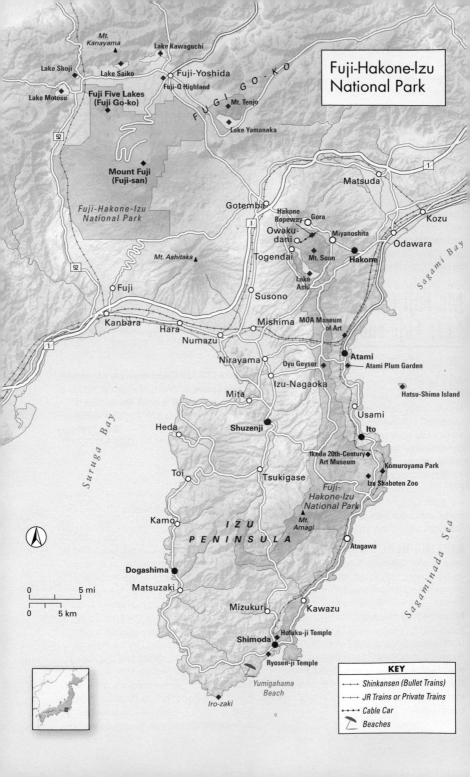

to the summit can feel more like waiting in line than hiking. Still, making the trek to the top and watching the sunrise from Japan's most sacred mountain is a once-in-a-lifetime experience, and there is fun to be had climbing with the crowd.

There are four trails up Fuji, but the most common starting point is the Subaru Line 5th Station (aka Kawaguchiko 5th Station), which is easily accessed by direct buses from Tokyo, Hakone, and many other cities. From here it takes between five to seven hours to reach the summit. The descent takes another three to four hours. There are numerous mountain huts on the way up to sleep for a few hours and adjust to the altitude (¥10,000–¥14,000 per person for a dorm spot, which includes dinner and breakfast), but they fill up quickly during peak times. Spots can be reserved for some huts online, but others require a phone call. The length and altitude require a decent level of fitness but no technical climbing skills. ⊠ *Fuji-Hakone-Izu National Park* ⊕ *www.fujisan-climb.jp* ✉ *¥1,000* ☞ *Outside of hiking season, the weather is highly unpredictable and extremely dangerous, so climbing is strongly discouraged.*

# Fuji Five Lakes (富士五湖; Fuji Go-ko)

*55 km (34 miles) northwest of Hakone.*

To the north of Mt. Fuji, the Fuji Go-ko area affords an unbeatable view of the mountain on clear days and makes the best base for a climb to the summit. With its various outdoor activities, such as skating and fishing in winter and boating and hiking in summer, this is a popular resort area for families and business conferences.

The five lakes are, from the east, Yamanaka-ko, Kawaguchi-ko, Sai-ko, Shoji-ko, and Motosu-ko. Yamanaka and Kawaguchi are the largest and most developed as resort areas, with Kawaguchi more or less the centerpiece of the group.

## GETTING HERE AND AROUND

Direct bus service runs daily from Shinjuku Station in Tokyo to Lake Kawaguchi every hour between 7:10 am and 11:20 pm. Buses go from Kawaguchi-ko Station to Go-gome (the fifth station on the climb up Mt. Fuji) in about an hour; there are eight departures a day until the climbing season (July and August) starts, when there are 15 departures or more, depending on demand.

The transportation hub, as well as one of the major resort areas in the Fuji Five Lakes area, is Kawaguchi-ko. Getting there from Tokyo requires a change of trains at Otsuki. The JR Chuo Line Kaiji and Azusa express trains leave Shinjuku Station for Otsuki on the half hour from 7 am to 8 pm (more frequently in the morning) and take approximately one hour. At Otsuki, change to the private Fuji-Kyuko Line for Kawaguchi-ko, which takes another 50 minutes. The total traveling time is about two hours, and you can use your JR Pass as far as Otsuki; otherwise, the fare is ¥1,490. The Otsuki–Kawaguchi-ko leg costs ¥1,170.

Opened in 2019, the Fuji Kaiyuu train had direct express service from Shinjuku twice daily (three times a day on weekends) Trains run from Shinjuku to Kawaguchi-ko in the morning, with return runs in the afternoon. The journey takes just under two hours and costs ¥4,130 each way. Check the express timetables before you go; you can also call either the JR Higashi-Nihon Info Line or Fuji-kyuuko Kawaguchi-ko Station for train information.

*Continued on page 274*

# PEERLESS FUJI

by Peter MacMillan

Climbing Mt. Fuji

Mount Fuji greets hikers who arrive at its summit just before dawn with the *go-raiko*, or the Honorable Coming of the Light. The reflection of this light shimmers across the sky just before the sun first appears, giving the extraordinary sunrise a mystical feel. Fuji-san's early morning magic is just one of the characteristics of the mountain that has captured the collective imagination of the Japanese, along with its snowy peak, spiritual meaning, and propensity to hide behind clouds. The close-to-perfectly symmetrical cone is an object to conquer physically and to admire from afar.

Japan is more than 70% mountainous, and Fuji is its tallest mountain. It appears in literature, art, and culture from the highest level to the most ordinary in countless ways. In a word, Fuji is ubiquitous.

Since ancient times Mt. Fuji has been an object of worship for both Shinto and Buddhist practitioners. Shrines devoted to Konohana-Sakuya Hime, Mt. Fuji's goddess, dot the trails. So sacred is Fuji that the mountaintop torii gate at the Okumiya of Sengen Taisha Shrine (though at Fuji's foot, the shrine also encompasses the mountain above the 8th station) states that this is the greatest mountain in the world. Typically the gate would provide the shrine's name. Here, the torii defines not the shrine but the sacred space of the mountain.

Rising to 12,385 feet (3,776 meters) Mt. Fuji is an active volcano, but the last eruption was in 1707. Located on the boundaries of Shizuoka and Yamanashi prefectures, the mountain is an easy day trip west of Tokyo, and on clear days you can see the peak from the city. In season, hikers clamber to the peak, but it is gazing upon Fuji that truly inspires awe and wonder. No visit to Japan would be complete without at least a glimpse of this beautiful icon.

(Top left) Mt. Fuji's famous morning light draws visitors, (Top right) the summit is often surrounded by clouds, (Bottom right) the trails are rocky and rugged at times.

# THE SYMBOLISM OF FUJI-SAN

## ARTISTIC FUJI

Mt. Fuji is one of the world's most painted and photographed mountains. But rising above all the visual depictions are Katsushika Hokusai's *Thirty-six Views of Mt. Fuji* and his *One Hundred Views of Mt. Fuji*. The latter is a stunning work and considered his masterpiece. However, the *Thirty-Six Views* is more famous because the images were printed in full color, while the *One Hundred Views* was printed in monochrome black and gray. His *Great Wave off Kanagawa* is one of the most famous prints in the history of art.

Hokusai believed that his depictions would get better and better as he got older, and they did; his *One Hundred Views* was completed when he was 75. He was also obsessed with achieving immortality. In creating the *One Hundred Views of Mt. Fuji*, a mountain always associated with immortality, he hoped to achieve his own. History proved him right.

## LITERARY FUJI

There are thousands of literary works related to Fuji, including traditional and modern poems, haiku, Noh dramas, novels, and plays. In the Man'yoshu, 8th-century poet Yamabe no Akahito famously extolled Fuji: "When I sail out/on the Bay of Tago/every where's white-/Look! Snow's piling up/ on the peak of Fuji." Matsuo Basho, in another well known poem, wrote about not being able to see the mountain: "How lovely and intriguing!/ Covered in drifting fog,/ the day I could not see Fuji." There are many times of the year when Fuji hides behind the clouds, so don't be disappointed if you miss it. Like the great haiku poet, see the mountain in the eye of your heart.

(Top) Katsushika Hokusai's *Red Fuji*,
(Bottom) *Great Wave off Kanagawa*
by Katsushika Hokusai

# SEE FUJI-SAN FROM AFAR

Like the poets and artists who have found inspiration in gazing at Fuji-san, you, too, can catch a glimpse of the snow-capped cone on the horizon. On a clear day, most likely in winter when the air is dry and the clouds lift, the following experiences provide some of the best Fuji views.

## SEE FUJI

**Atop Tokyo.** Visit the Tokyo City View observation promenade on the 52nd floor of the Mori Tower in Roppongi. You can walk all around this circular building and take in the spectacular views of Tokyo and, when the weather is fine, Fuji. While you're here, don't miss the sky-high Mori Art Museum, a contemporary art space on the 52nd and 53rd floors. The evening view of the city is also splendid, but Fuji will be slumbering under the blanket of nightfall.

**From Hakone.** Part of Fuji-Hakone-Izu National Park, the same park Fuji calls home, and an easy day trip from Tokyo, Hakone is a playground of hiking trails, small art museums, an onsen, and more. Head to the beautiful gar-

den at Hakone Detached Palace for scenic views of Fuji-san. Early morning and late evening will provide the best chance for clear skies.

**Speeding out of town.** The classic view of Fuji is from the Shinkansen traveling from Tokyo to Kyoto. Some of the world's fastest transportation technology hums beneath you when, suddenly, the world's most beautiful and sacred mountain appears on the left. This striking combination of the ancient and cutting-edge is at the heart of understanding Japan. Make sure not to fall asleep!

(Top) Shinkansen speeding past Fuji,
(Bottom) Fuji from inside Hakone National Park

# CLIMBING FUJI-SAN
## FROM KAWAGUCHIKO TRAIL

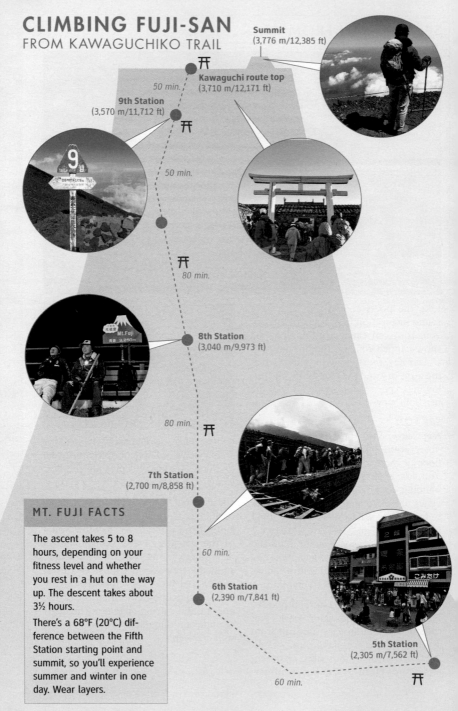

**Summit**
(3,776 m/12,385 ft)

**Kawaguchi route top**
(3,710 m/12,171 ft)

*50 min.*

**9th Station**
(3,570 m/11,712 ft)

*50 min.*

*80 min.*

**8th Station**
(3,040 m/9,973 ft)

*80 min.*

**7th Station**
(2,700 m/8,858 ft)

*60 min.*

**6th Station**
(2,390 m/7,841 ft)

**5th Station**
(2,305 m/7,562 ft)

*60 min.*

## MT. FUJI FACTS

The ascent takes 5 to 8 hours, depending on your fitness level and whether you rest in a hut on the way up. The descent takes about 3½ hours.

There's a 68°F (20°C) difference between the Fifth Station starting point and summit, so you'll experience summer and winter in one day. Wear layers.

A photographer capturing view from Mt. Fuji

Although many Japanese like to climb Mt. Fuji once in their lives, there's a saying in Japanese that only a fool would climb it twice. You, too, can make a once-in-a-lifetime climb during the mountain's official open season from July through August. Unless you're an experienced hiker, do not attempt to make the climb at another time of year.

## TRAIL CONDITIONS

Except for the occasional cobblestone path, the routes are unpaved and at times steep, especially toward the top. Near the end of the climb there are some rope banisters to steady yourself, but for the most part you'll have to rely on your own balance.

Fuji draws huge crowds in season, so expect a lot of company on your hike. The throngs grow thicker in August during the school break and reach their peak during the holiday Obon week in mid-August; it gets so crowded that hikers have to queue up at certain passes. Trails are less crowded overnight. Go during the week and in July for the lightest crowds (though the weather is less reliable). Or accept the crowds and enjoy the friendships that spring up among strangers on the trails.

## TRAILS OVERVIEW

If you're in good health you should be able to climb from the base to the summit. That said, the air is thin, and it can be humbling to struggle for oxygen while some 83-year-old Japanese grandmother blithely leaves you in her dust (it happens).

Most visitors take buses as far as the Fifth Station and hike to the top from there (⇨ See *Mt. Fuji listing in this chapter for more information on buses*). The paved roads end at this halfway point.

Four routes lead to Mt. Fuji's summit—the **Kawaguchiko, Subashiri, Gotemba,** and **Fujinomiya**—and each has a corresponding Fifth Station that serves as the transfer point between bus and foot. Depending on which trail you choose, the ascent takes between 5 and 10 hours. Fujinomiya is closest to the summit; Gotemba is the farthest.

We recommend Kawaguchiko (Fuji-Yoshida) Trail in Yamanashi, as its many first-aid centers and lodging facilities (huts) ensure that you can enjoy the climb. ■TIP➜ Those interested in experiencing Fuji's religious and spiritual aspects should walk this trail from the mountain's foot. Along the way are small shrines that lead to the torii gate at the top, which signifies Fuji's sacred status. While the food and cleanliness standards at mountain huts are subpar, they provide valuable rest spots and even more valuable camaraderie and good will among travelers.

## AT THE TOP

Once you reach the top of Mt. Fuji, you can walk along the ridge of the volcano. A torii gate declares that Fuji is the greatest mountain in the world. It also marks the entrance to the **Fuji-san Honmiya Sengen Taisha Shrine** (at the foot of the mountain near the Kawaguchiko Trail is the shrine's other facility). Inside the shrine, head to the post office where you can mail letters and postcards with a special Mt. Fuji stamp. There's also a chalet at the top for those captivated enough to stay the night.

## NIGHT HIKES

The most spectacular way to hike Mt. Fuji is to time the climb so that you arrive at sunrise. Not only is the light famously enchanting, but the sky is also more likely to be clear, allowing for views back to Tokyo. Those who choose this have a few options. Start from the Kawaguchiko 5th Station on the Kawaguchi Trail around 10 pm (or later, depending on the sunrise time) and hike through the night, arriving at the summit between 4:30 and 5 am, just as the sun begins to rise. A better alternative is to begin in the afternoon or evening and hike to the 7th or 8th Station, spend a few hours resting there, and then depart very early in the morning to see the sun rise. ■TIP→ The trail isn't lit at night, so bring a headlamp to illuminate the way. Avoid carrying flashlights, though, as it is important to keep your hands free in case of a fall

### COMMEMORATE YOUR VISIT

Purchase a walking stick at the base of Mt. Fuji and, as you climb, have it branded at each station. By the time you reach the top you'll have the perfect souvenir to mark your achievement.

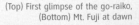

(Top) First glimpse of the go-raiko, (Bottom) Mt. Fuji at dawn

Walking sticks for sale

## TIMING

You can visit this area on a day trip from Tokyo, but unless you want to spend most of it on buses and trains, plan on staying overnight.

## VISITOR INFORMATION

**CONTACT Fuji-Kawaguchiko Tourist Information Center.** ⊠ *364–1 Funatsu, Fujikawaguchiko-machi, Minami-Tsuru-gun* ☎ *0555/72–6700* ⊕ *www.fujisan.ne.jp.*

#  Sights

### Fuji-Q Highland (富士急ハイランド)

**AMUSEMENT PARK/CARNIVAL | FAMILY**
The largest of the recreational facilities at Lake Kawaguchi has an impressive assortment of rides, roller coasters, and other amusements, but it's probably not worth a visit unless you have children in tow. In winter there's superb skating here, with Mt. Fuji for a backdrop. Fuji-kyu Highland is about 15 minutes' walk east from Kawaguchi-ko Station. In addition to the entry fee, there are charges for various attractions, so it's best to get the one-day free pass. ⊠ *5–6–1 Shinnishihara, Fujiyoshida* ☎ *0555/23–2111* ⊕ *www.fujiq. jp/en* ⊠ *1-day free pass ¥6,300.*

### Lake Kawaguchi (河口湖; *Kawaguchi-ko*)

**BODY OF WATER |** A 5- to 10-minute walk from Kawaguchi-ko Station, this is the most developed of the five lakes. It's ringed with weekend retreats and vacation lodges—many of them maintained by companies and universities for their employees. Excursion boats depart from a pier here on 30-minute tours of the lake. The promise, not always fulfilled, is to have two views of Mt. Fuji: one of the mountain itself and the other inverted in its reflection on the water. ⊠ *Kawaguchiko, Fujikawaguchiko.*

### Lake Motosu (本栖湖; *Motosu-ko*)

**BODY OF WATER |** Lake Motosu is the farthest west of the five lakes. It's also the deepest and clearest of the Fuji Go-ko. It takes about 50 minutes to get here by bus. One of the least developed of the lakes, it is a good spot for hiking and nature lovers. ⊠ *Motosuko, Fujikawaguchiko.*

### Lake Saiko (西湖; *Sai-ko*)

**BODY OF WATER |** Between Lakes Shoji and Kawaguchi, Lake Sai is the third-largest lake of the Fuji Go-ko, with only moderate development. From the western shore there is an especially good view of Mt. Fuji. Near Sai-ko there are two natural caves, an ice cave and a wind cave. You can either take a bus or walk to them. ⊠ *Saiko, Fujikawaguchiko.*

### Lake Shoji (精進湖; *Shoji-ko*)

**BODY OF WATER |** Many consider Lake Shoji, the smallest of the lakes, to be the prettiest. There are still remnants of lava flow jutting out from the water, which locals perch upon while fishing. The Shoji Trail leads from Lake Shoji to Mt. Fuji's fifth station through Aoki-ga-hara (Sea of Trees). This forest has an underlying magnetic lava field that makes compasses go haywire. Be prepared with a good trail map before taking this hike. ⊠ *Shojiko, Fujikawaguchiko.*

### Lake Yamanaka (山中湖; *Yamanaka-ko*)

**BODY OF WATER |** The largest lake of the Fuji Go-ko, Yamanaka is 35 minutes by bus to the southeast of Kawaguchi. It's also the closest lake to the popular trail up Mt. Fuji that starts at Go-gome, and many climbers use this resort area as a base. ⊠ *Yamanakoko, Yamanaka-ko-mura.*

### Mt. Tenjo (天上山; *Tenjo-san*)

**MOUNTAIN |** From the shore of Lake Kawaguchi (near the pier), the Kachikachi Ropeway quickly brings you to the top of the 3,622-foot-tall mountain. From the observatory here, the whole of Lake Kawaguchi lies before you, and beyond the lake is a classic view of Mt. Fuji. ⊠ *1163–1 Azagawa, Fujikawaguchiko* ☎ *0555/72–0363 ropeway* ⊕ *www. kachikachiyama-ropeway.com* ⊠ *Round trip ¥900, One way ¥500.*

## Hotels

**Fuji View Hotel** (富士ビューホテル)
$$$ | **HOTEL** | Accommodations are a little threadbare but comfortable and right on the lakefront, and the terrace lounge affords fine views of the lake and of Mt. Fuji beyond. **Pros:** a good value during the week; excellent views from many rooms; convenient shuttle bus to town and the station. **Cons:** can be crowded with tour groups during peak seasons; meals are average; rooms are rather small. [$] *Rooms from: ¥34,000* ✉ *511 Katsuyama, Fujikawaguchiko* ☎ *0555/83–2211* 🌐 *www.fujiview.jp* 🛏 *70 rooms* 🍴 *Free Breakfast.*

**Hotel Mount Fuji** (ホテルマウント富士)
$$$ | **HOTEL** | This is the best resort hotel on Lake Yamanaka, with European-style rooms and all the facilities for a recreational holiday, including on-site game and karaoke rooms and a nature walk on the grounds. **Pros:** comfortable rooms; many activities on the hotel grounds; friendly and helpful staff. **Cons:** convenient location and large banquet halls make it a favorite among tour groups; some guest rooms are dated; one of the more expensive options in the area. [$] *Rooms from: ¥35,000* ✉ *1360–83 Yamanaka, Yamanaka-ko-mura* ☎ *050/3204–4439* 🌐 *www.mtfuji-hotel.com/lp/en* 🛏 *150 rooms* 🍴 *Free Breakfast.*

**Mizno Hotel** (湖のホテル)
$$ | **HOTEL** | Renovated in 2017, the Mizno sports a stylish lodge aesthetic and stunning views of Lake Kawaguchiko and Mt. Fuji. **Pros:** all rooms have views of Mt. Fuji and Lake Kawaguchi; great rooftop bar and terrace; private onsen. **Cons:** much of the appeal of the hotel depends on having good weather; one of the most expensive hotels on the lake; the onsen bath is functional but simple. [$] *Rooms from: ¥30,000* ✉ *187 Azagawa, Fujikawaguchiko* ☎ *0555/72–1234* 🌐 *mzn.jp* 🛏 *27 rooms* 🍴 *Free Breakfast.*

**Roykan Fujitomita** (旅館ふじとみた)
$ | **B&B/INN** | One of the closest lodging options to the Mt. Fuji hiking trails is not much to look at from the outside, but the interior is spacious and homey. **Pros:** spacious rooms; pleasant surrounding grounds; excellent home cooking. **Cons:** rooms are clean but simple; somewhat isolated; very crowded during climbing season. [$] *Rooms from: ¥13,000* ✉ *3235 Shibokusa, Oshinomura, Minami-Tsuru-gun* ☎ *0555/84–3359* 🌐 *www.tim.hi-ho.ne.jp/innfuji* 💳 *No credit cards* 🛏 *9 rooms* 🍴 *Free Breakfast.*

# Hakone (箱根)

*92 km (57 miles) southwest of Tokyo.*

The national park and resort area of Hakone is a popular day trip from Tokyo and a good place for a close-up view of Mt. Fuji (assuming the mountain is not swathed in clouds, as often happens in summer).

**■ TIP→ On summer weekends it often seems as though all of Tokyo has come out to Hakone with you. Expect long lines at cable cars and traffic jams everywhere.**

### DISCOUNTS AND DEALS

Many places in Hakone accept the Hakone Free Pass. It's valid for three days and issued by the privately owned Odakyu Railways. The pass covers the train fare to Hakone and allows you to use any mode of transportation, including the Hakone Tozan Cable Car, the Hakone Ropeway, and the Hakone Cruise Boat. In addition to transportation, Free Pass holders get discounts at museums such as the Hakone Museum of Art, restaurants, and shops. The list of participants is pretty extensive and it always changes, so it's a good idea to check out the website for a complete list of participating companies and terms and conditions.

**CONTACT Odakyu Sightseeing Service Center.** ✉ JR Shinjuku Station, 3–8 Shinjuku, near West Exit, Odawara ☎ 03/5909–0211 ⊕ www.odakyu.jp/english/support.

## GETTING HERE AND AROUND

The typical Hakone route, outlined here, may sound complex, but this is in fact one excursion from Tokyo so well defined that you really can't get lost—no more so, at least, than any of the thousands of Japanese tourists ahead of and behind you. The first leg of the journey is from Odawara or Hakone-Yumoto by train and cable car through the mountains to Togendai, on the north shore of Ashi-no-ko (Lake Ashi). The long way around, from Odawara to Togendai by bus, takes about an hour—in heavy traffic, an hour and a half. The trip over the mountains, on the other hand, takes about two hours. Credit the difference to the Hakone Tozan Tetsu-do Line—possibly the slowest train you'll ever ride. Using three switchbacks to inch its way up the side of the mountain, the train takes 54 minutes to travel the 16 km (10 miles) from Odawara to Gora (38 minutes from Hakone-Yumoto). The steeper it gets, the grander the view.

■ TIP→ **Due to concerns about volcanic activity, sections of the ropeway may be closed and buses will run from Sounzan to Togendai. The Hakone Ropeway's English site is not always up to date, so check with tourist information before you go.**

Trains do not stop at any station en route for any length of time, but they do run frequently enough to allow you to disembark, visit a sight, and catch another train.

Within the Hakone area, buses run every 15 to 30 minutes from Hakone-machi to Hakone-Yumoto Station on the private Odakyu Line (40 minutes, ¥1,000), and Odawara Station (one hour, ¥1,280), where you can take either the Odakyu Romance Car back to Shinjuku Station or a JR Shinkansen to Tokyo Station.

## TIMING

You can cover the best of Hakone in a one-day trip out of Tokyo, but if you want to try the curative powers of the thermal waters or do some hiking, then stay overnight. Two of the best areas are around the old hot-springs resort of Miyanoshita and the western side of Komagatake-san (Mt. Komagatake).

## TOURS

**Hakone Sightseeing Cruise** (箱根海賊船; Hakone Kaizoku-sen)

BOAT TOURS | This ride is free with your Hakone Free Pass; otherwise, buy a ticket at the office in the terminal. A few ships of conventional design ply Lake Ashi; the rest are astonishingly corny Disney knockoffs. One, for example, is rigged like a 17th-century warship. ✉ 181 Hakone, Ashigarashimo District, Hakone ☎ 0460/83–6325 ⊕ www.hakonenavi.jp/international/en ✉ ¥2,220 round-trip (without Hakone Free Pass).

## VISITOR INFORMATION

**CONTACT Hakone Tourist Information Center.** ✉ 706–35 Yumoto, Hakone ☎ 0460/85–5700 ⊕ hakone-japan.com.

# ◉ Sights

**Lake Ashi** (芦ノ湖; Ashino-ko)
VIEWPOINT | From Owaku-dani, the descent by gondola to Togendai on the shore of Lake Ashi takes 25 minutes. There's no reason to linger at Togendai; it's only a terminus for buses to Hakone-Yumoto and Odawara and to the resort villages in the northern part of Hakone. Head straight for the pier, a few minutes' walk down the hill, where boats set out on the lake for Hakone-machi. With still water and good weather, you'll get a breathtaking reflection of the mountains in the waters of the lake as you go. ✉ Motohakone, Hakone.

# The Road to the Shogun

In days gone by, the town of Hakone was on the Tokaido, the main highway between the imperial court in Kyoto and the shogunate in Edo (present-day Tokyo). The road was the only feasible passage through this mountainous country, which made it an ideal place for a checkpoint to control traffic. The Tokugawa Shogunate built the Hakone-machi here in 1618; its most important function was to monitor the *daimyo* (feudal lords) passing through—to keep track, above all, of weapons coming into Edo, and women-folk coming out.

When Ieyasu Tokugawa came to power, Japan had been through nearly 100 years of bloody struggle among rival coalitions of daimyo. Ieyasu emerged supreme because some of his opponents had switched

sides at the last minute, in the Battle of Sekigahara in 1600. The shogun was justifiably paranoid about his "loyal" barons—especially those in the outlying domains—so he required the daimyo to live in Edo for periods of time every two years. When they did return to their own lands, they had to leave their wives behind in Edo, hostages to their good behavior. A noble lady coming through the Hakone Sekisho without an official pass, in short, was a case of treason.

The checkpoint served the Tokugawa dynasty well for 250 years. It was demolished only when the shogunate fell, in the Meiji Restoration of 1868. An exact replica, with an exhibition hall of period costumes and weapons, was built as a tourist attraction in 1965.

## Gora (強羅)

**TOWN** | This small town is at the end of the train line from Odawara and at the lower end of the Hakone Tozan Cable Car. It's a good jumping-off point for hiking and exploring. Ignore the little restaurants and souvenir stands here: get off the train as quickly as you can and make a dash for the cable car at the other end of the station. If you let the rest of the passengers get there before you, and perhaps a tour bus or two, you may stand 45 minutes in line. ⊠ *Gora, Hakone.*

## ★ Hakone Kowakien Yunessun
(箱根小涌園 ユネッサン)

**HOT SPRING** | **FAMILY** | This complex on the hills overlooking Hakone has more than the average onsen. In addition to all the water-based attractions, there is a shopping mall modeled on a European outdoor market, swimsuit rental shop, massage salon, and game center. The park is divided into two main zones, called

Yunessun and Mori no Yu (Forest Bath). In the Yunessun side, you need to wear a swimsuit, and can visit somewhat tacky re-creations of Turkish and ancient Roman baths. You can also take a dip in coffee, green tea, sake, or red wine. It is all a bit corny, but fun. Younger visitors enjoy the waterslides on "Rodeo Mountain." In the more secluded Mori no Yu side, you can go au naturel in a variety of indoor and outdoor, single-sex baths. When signing in at reception, get a waterproof digital wristband that allows you to pay for lockers and drink machines within the complex. ⊠ *1297 Ninotaira Hakone-machi, Hakone* ☎ *0460/82–4126* ⊕ *www.yunessun.com* 🔖 *Yunessun zone ¥2,500, Mori no Yu zone ¥1,500; both for ¥3,500.*

## Hakone Museum of Art
(箱根美術館; *Hakone Bijutsukan*)

**ART MUSEUM** | A sister institution to the MOA Museum of Art in Atami, Hakone Museum of Art is at the second stop of

Passengers floating over the Owaku-dani valley on the Hakone Ropeway can see Fuji looming—on a clear day, of course.

the Hakone Tozan Cable Car. The museum, which consists of two buildings set in a beautiful Japanese garden, houses a modest collection of porcelain and ceramics from China, Korea, and Japan. ✉ *1300 Gora, Hakone* ☎ *0460/82–2623* ⊕ *www.moaart.or.jp/hakone* 🎫 *¥900* 🕐 *Closed Thurs.*

### ★ Hakone Open-Air Museum
(彫刻の森美術館; *Hakone Chokoku-no-mori Bijutsukan*)

ART MUSEUM | Only a few minutes' walk from the Miyanoshita Station (directions are posted in English), the museum houses an astonishing collection of 19th- and 20th-century Western and Japanese sculpture, most of it on display in a spacious, handsome garden. There are works here by Rodin, Moore, Arp, Calder, Giacometti, Takashi Shimizu, and Kotaro Takamura. One section of the garden is devoted to Emilio Greco. Inside are works by Picasso, Léger, and Manzo, among others. ✉ *1121 Ninotaira, Hakone* ☎ *0460/82–1161* ⊕ *www.hakone-oam.or.jp* 🎫 *¥1,600.*

### Hakone Ropeway (箱根ロープウェイ)

TRANSPORTATION | At the cable-car terminus of Soun-zan, a gondola called the Hakone Ropeway swings up over a ridge and crosses the valley called Owaku-dani, also known as "Great Boiling Valley," on its way to Togendai. The landscape here is desolate, with sulfurous billows of steam escaping through holes from some inferno deep in the earth—yet another reminder that Japan is a chain of volcanic islands. At the top of the ridge is one of the two stations where you can leave the gondola. From here, a ¾-km (½-mile) walking course wanders among the sulfur pits in the valley. Just below the station is a restaurant; the food here is not recommended, but on a clear day the view of Mt. Fuji is perfect. Remember that if you get off the gondola at any stage, you will have to wait for someone to make space on a later gondola before you can continue down to Togendai and Ashi-no-ko (but the gondolas come by every minute). ⚠ **Due to concerns about volcanic activity, sections of the ropeway may be closed and buses will run from**

**Sounzan to Togendai. The Hakone Ropeway's English site is not always up-to-date, so check with tourist information before you go.** ✉ *1–15–1 Shiroyama, Odawara* ☎ *0460/32–2205* 🌐 *www.hakonenavi.jp/international/en* 🎫 *¥1,700 round-trip (Sounzan Station to Owakudani Station).*

**Hakone Checkpoint Museum** (箱根関所; *Hakone Sekisho*)
**HISTORIC SIGHT** | This barrier, a checkpoint on the road with a guardhouse and lookout tower, was built in 1618 to inspect incoming and outgoing traffic until it was demolished during the Meiji Restoration of 1868. An exact replica was built as a tourist attraction in 1965 and is only a few minutes' walk from the pier, along the lakeshore in the direction of Moto-Hakone. The hilltop guardhouse offers excellent views of Lake Ashi and the surrounding area. ✉ *1 Hakone-machi, Hakone* ☎ *0460/83–6635* 🌐 *www.hakonesekisyo.jp/english* 🎫 *¥500.*

**Miyanoshita** (宮ノ下)
**RESORT** | The first stop on the train route from Hakone-Yumoto, this is a small but very pleasant and popular resort village. As well as hot springs, this village has antiques shops along its main road and several hiking routes up the ¾-km- (½-mile-) tall Mt. Sengen. If you get to the top, you'll be rewarded with a great view of the gorge. ✉ *Hakone.*

**Mt. Soun** (早雲山; *Soun-zan*)
**MOUNTAIN** | Soun-zan is a good starting point for an afternoon of hiking. From here, trails around Mt. Hakone and Mt. Kamiyama lead towards the lake. Be sure to check with the Tourist Information Office to get a trail map beforehand. ✉ *Hakone.*

## Scrambled or Boiled in Sulfur? 🍴

No, your eyes are not playing tricks on you. Those are in fact local entrepreneurs boiling eggs in the sulfur pits in Owaku-dani. Locals make a passable living selling the eggs, which turn black, to tourists at exorbitant prices. A popular myth suggests that eating one of these eggs can extend your life by seven years.

## 🛏 Hotels

**Fujiya Hotel** (富士屋ホテル)
**$$$$** | **HOTEL** | Built in 1878, and renovated in 2020, this Western-style hotel with modern additions is showing signs of age, but that somehow adds to its charm. **Pros:** wonderful, friendly service; Hakone's most historic hotel; beautiful combination of Western and Japanese architecture. **Cons:** hotel onsen (spa) can't compete with others in the area; price reflects the hotel's historic status rather than its comfort and amenities; often full of noisy tour groups. [$] *Rooms from: ¥65,000* ✉ *359 Miyanoshita, Hakone* ☎ *0460/82–2211* 🌐 *www.fujiyahotel.jp* 🛏 *140 rooms* 🍴 *No Meals*

**Fuji-Hakone Guest House** (富士箱根ゲストハウス)
**$** | **HOTEL** | This small, family run Japanese inn has simple tatami rooms with the bare essentials. **Pros:** friendly staff; inexpensive rates; private onsen baths for guests. **Cons:** accommodations are comfortable but basic; lacks the atmosphere and charm of a traditional ryokan; difficult to access from nearest transportation, especially at night. [$] *Rooms from: ¥12,000* ✉ *912 Sengokuhara*

(103 Moto-Hakone for Moto-Hakone Guest House), Hakone ☎ 0460/84–6577 Fuji-Hakone, 0460/83–7880 Moto-Ha-kone ⊕ fujihakone.com ⤵ 14 rooms ⦿I Free Breakfast.

### The Prince Hakone Lake Ashinoko (箱根プリンスホテル芦ノ湖)

$$$ | HOTEL | You have a choice of hotel rooms or cozy cottages at this resort complex, with the lake in front and the mountains of Koma-ga-take in back. **Pros:** lovely quaint cottages surrounded by nature; views of Mt. Fuji over the lake; spacious guest rooms. **Cons:** popular with groups and business conferences; guest rooms are a bit dated; a bit remote from sightseeing spots. Ⓢ Rooms from: ¥45,000 ⊠ 144 Motohakone, Hakone ☎ 0460/83–1111 ⊕ www.princehotels. com/the_prince_hakone ⤵ 258 rooms ⦿I Free Breakfast.

### Tensui Saryo (天翠茶寮)

$$$$ | B&B/INN | Upon entering this cross between a luxury Western-style hotel and traditional inn, guests remove their shoes and socks, sit at a counter bar with their tired feet resting in the hot-mineral-spring bath under the bar, and enjoy a tea or beer as they check in. **Pros:** four rooms have a private onsen on a terrace; excellent service; easy access from Gora Station. **Cons:** some rooms have limited views; due to its central location, it lacks the seclud-ed ryokan experience; no Japanese food in the restaurant. Ⓢ Rooms from: ¥60,000 ⊠ 1320–276 Gora, Hakone ☎ 0570/062–302 ⊕ www.tensui-saryo. com ⤵ 17 rooms ⦿I Free Breakfast.

# Izu Peninsula (伊豆半島)

Shimoda is 197 km (122 miles) south-west of Tokyo.

Izu is defined by its dramatic rugged coastline, beaches, and onsen (hot springs).

## GETTING HERE AND AROUND

Having your own car makes sense for touring the Izu Peninsula, but only if you're prepared to cope with less-than-ideal road conditions, lots of traffic (especially on holiday weekends), and the paucity of road markers in English. It takes some effort—but exploring the peninsula *is* a lot easier by car than by public transportation. From Tokyo take the Tomei Expressway as far as Oi-mat-suda (about 84 km [52 miles]); then pick up Routes 255 and 135 to Atami (approx-imately 28 km [17 miles]). From Atami drive another 55 km (34 miles) or so down the east coast of the Izu Peninsula to Shimoda.

■ TIP→ One way to save yourself some trouble is to book a car through the Nippon or Toyota rental agency in Tokyo and arrange to pick it up at the Shimoda branch.

You can then simply take a train to Shimoda and use it as a base. From Shi-moda you can drive back up the coast to Kawazu (35 minutes) and then to Shuzen-ji (30 minutes). It is possible to drop off the car in Tokyo, but only at specific branches, so visit your rental-car compa-ny's website or call them in advance.

Trains are by far the easiest and fastest ways to get to the Izu Peninsula and the rest of the Fuji-Hakone-Izu National Park area. The gateway station of Atami is well served by comfortable express trains from Tokyo, on both JR and private railway lines. These in turn connect to local trains and buses that can get you anywhere in the region you want to go. Call the JR Higashi-Nihon Info Line (10–6 daily, except December 31–January 3) for assistance in English.

The *Kodama* Shinkansen from JR Tokyo Station to Atami (¥4,500, 45 minutes) and Mishima (¥4,600, 70 minutes); JR (Japan Railways) passes are valid. The JR local from Atami to Ito takes 25 minutes and costs ¥530. Ito and Atami are also served by the JR Odoriko Super Express (not a Shinkansen train) also departing from Tokyo Station; check the schedule display board for the correct platform. The Tokyo–Ito run takes 1¾ hours and costs ¥4,190; you can also use a JR Pass. The privately owned Izukyu Railways, on which JR Passes are not valid, makes the Ito–Shimoda run in one hour for ¥1,480.

To get to Shuzenji by train, take the private Izu-Hakone Railway from Mishima (¥460, 63 minutes).

**RENTAL-CAR CONTACTS Nippon Rent-a-Car.** ☎ *03/6859–6234* ⊕ *www. nipponrentacar.co.jp.* **Toyota Rent-a-Car.** ☎ *0800/7000–815 toll-free in Japan; English operator available, 92/577 0091 international* ⊕ *rent.toyota.co.jp.*

**TRAIN CONTACTS Izukyu Corpora-tion.** ☎ *0557/53–1115 main office, 0558/22–3202 Izukyu Shimoda Station* ⊕ *www.izukyu.co.jp.* **JR East Info Line.** (*JR Higashi-Nihon Info Line)* ☎ *050/2016–1603 English info line.* **Odakyu Sightseeing Service Center.** ⊠ *Shinjuku Station 1F, Odakyu Railway West Exit* ☎ *03/5909–0211* ⊕ *www.odakyu.jp/english/support.*

## TOURS

If you have limited time and want to see the highlights of Fuji-Hakone-Izu National Park on a day-trip from Tokyo, there are several bus options from JTB Sunrise Tours.

**Dogashima Marine** (堂ヶ島マリン)
**BOAT TOURS** | Once you are on the Izu Peninsula itself, sightseeing excursions by boat are available from several pictur-esque small ports. From Dogashima, you can take the Dogashima Marine short (20 minutes) or long (50 minutes) tours of Izu's rugged west coast. ☎ *0558/52–0013* ⊕ *www.izudougasima-yuransen.com* 🎫 *From ¥1,200.*

**Fuji Kyuko** (富士急行)
**BOAT TOURS** | The Fuji Kyuko company operates a daily ferry to Hatsu-shima from Atami (25 minutes) and another to the island from Ito (23 minutes). ☎ *0557/81–0541* ⊕ *www.fujikyu.co.jp/en* 🎫 *From ¥2,400 round-trip.*

**Izu Cruise** (伊豆クルーズ)
**BOAT TOURS** | Izukyu Marine offers a 40-minute tour by boat from Shimoda to the coastal rock formations at Iro-zaki. ☎ *0558/22–1151* ⊕ *izu-kamori.jp/izu-cruise* 🎫 *From ¥1,400.*

**JTB Sunrise Tours** (サンライズツアー)
**BUS TOURS** | JTB Sunrise Tours operates a tour to Hakone from Tokyo, including a cruise across Lake Ashi and a trip on the gondola over Owaku-dani (including lunch and return to Tokyo by Shinkansen or bus). Sunrise tours depart daily from Tokyo's Hamamatsu-cho Bus Termi-nal and some major hotels. ⊠ *Tokyo* ☎ *03/5796–5454* ⊕ *www.sunrise-tours. jp/en* 🎫 *From ¥12,000.*

## VISITOR INFORMATION

**CONTACTS Atami Information Center.** ⊠ *11–1 Tawarahoncho, Atami* ☎ *0557/81–5297* ⊕ *travel.ataminews.gr.jp/en.* **Shimoda Tourist Association.** (伊豆下田観光ガイド) ⊠ *1–4–27 Shimoda, Shimoda* ☎ *0558/22–1531* ⊕ *www.shimoda-city.com.*

# Atami (熱海)

*100 km (60 miles) southwest of Tokyo Station.*

The gateway to the Izu Peninsula is Atami. Most Japanese travelers make it no farther into the peninsula than this town on Sagami Bay, so Atami itself has a fair number of hotels and traditional inns. Although Atami fell on hard times after the economic bubble burst, it has recently undergone a massive revitalization and is once again a lively tourist town. The city also has frequent firework shows over the bay. They are only 30 minutes long, but the display over the water is stunning nonetheless.

When you arrive, collect a map from the **Atami Information Center** at the train station.

## GETTING HERE AND AROUND

From JR Tokyo Station, take the Tokaido Line to Atami, which is the last stop (one hour, 34 minutes; ¥1,990) or the Kodama Shinkansen (49 minutes, ¥4,270).

##  Sights

### Atami Plum Garden

(熱海梅園; *Atami Bai-en*)

**GARDEN** | The best time to visit the garden is in late January or early February, when its 850 trees bloom. If you do visit, also stop by the small shrine that's in the shadow of an enormous old camphor tree. The shrine is more than 1,000 years old and is popular with people who are asking the gods for help with alcoholism. The tree is more than 2,000 years old and has been designated a National Monument. It's believed that if you walk around the tree once, another year will be added to your life. Atami Bai-en is always open to the public and is 15 minutes by bus from Atami or an eight-minute walk from Kinomiya Station, the next stop south of Atami served by local trains. ⊠ *8–11 Baien-cho, Atami* ☎ *0557/85–2222* ⛩ *¥300 Jan.–early Mar., free the rest of the year.*

### Hatsu-shima Island (初島)

**ISLAND | FAMILY** | If you have the time and the inclination for a beach picnic, it's worth taking the 25-minute high-speed ferry (¥2,500 round-trip) from the pier. There are five departures daily between 7:30 and 5:20 from both Atami and Ito, though the times vary by season. You can easily walk around the island, which is only 4 km (2½ miles) in circumference, in less than two hours. There is also an obstacle course adventure park, great for travelers with kids. Use of the Picnic Garden (daily 10–3) is free. ⊠ *Atami Port, 6–11 Wadahama Minamicho, Atami* ☎ *0557/81–0541 ferry* ⊕ *www.hatsushima.jp.*

### MOA Museum of Art

(MOA美術館; *MOA Bijutsukan*)

**ART MUSEUM** | This museum houses the private collection of the messianic religious leader Mokichi Okada (1882–1955), who founded a movement called the Sekai Kyusei Kyo (Religion for the Salvation of the World). He also acquired more than 3,000 works of art; some are from the Asuka period (sixth and seventh centuries). Among these works are several particularly fine *ukiyo-e* (Edo-era woodblock prints) and ceramics. On a hill above the station and set in a garden full of old plum trees and azaleas, the museum also affords a sweeping view over Atami and the bay. ⊠ *26–2 Momoyama, Atami* ✛ *The easiest way to reach the museum is to take a 5-min taxi ride from the station* ☎ *0557/84–2511* ⊕ *www. moaart.or.jp/en* ⛩ *¥1,600.*

### Oyu Geyser

(大湯間歇泉; *Oyu Kanketsusen*)

**OTHER ATTRACTION** | Located just a 15-minute walk southeast from Atami Station, the geyser used to gush on schedule once every 24 hours but stopped after the Great Kanto Earthquake of 1923. Not happy with this, the local chamber of commerce rigged a pump to raise the geyser every five minutes. ⊠ *4–3 Kamijuku-cho, Atami.*

# Hotels

### Atami Taikanso (熱海大観荘)

$$$ | B&B/INN | The views of the sea must have been the inspiration for Yokoyama Taikan, the Japanese artist who once owned this villa that is now a traditional Japanese inn with exquisite furnishings and individualized service. **Pros:** seaside rooms have beautiful views; luxurious traditional experience; impeccable service. **Cons:** easy to get lost in the complex layout of the hotel; one of Atami's more expensive options; eating dinner may take most of your evening. $ *Rooms from: ¥45,000* ⊠ *7–1 Hayashigaoka-cho, Atami* ☎ *0557/81–8137* ⊕ *www.atami-taikanso.com/en* ⇨ *44 Japanese-style rooms with bath* ⦿ *All-Inclusive.*

### Hotel Micuras (ホテルミクラス)

$$$ | HOTEL | Style, comfort, ocean views, and natural hot springs make this hotel one of Atami's best. **Pros:** stylish, modern; the luxurious infinity-pool onsen looks out over the sea; the view from ocean-facing rooms is superb. **Cons:** rooms are modern but otherwise average; avoid the handful of "Mountain View" rooms, which have no view at all; lacks the history or charm of a traditional inn. $ *Rooms from: ¥40,000* ⊠ *3–19 Higashikaigan-cho, Atami* ☎ *0577/86 111* ⊕ *www.micuras.jp* ⇨ *62 rooms* ⦿ *No Meals.*

# Ito (伊東)

*16 km (10 miles) south of Atami.*

There are some 800 thermal springs in the resort area surrounding Ito. These springs—and the beautiful, rocky, indented coastline nearby—remain the resort's major attractions, although there are plenty of interesting sights here. Some 150 hotels and inns serve the area.

Ito traces its history of associations with the West to 1604, when William Adams (1564–1620), the Englishman whose adventures served as the basis for James Clavell's novel *Shogun,* came ashore.

Four years earlier Adams had beached his disabled Dutch vessel, *De Liefde,* on the shores of the southwestern island of Kyushu and become the first Englishman to set foot on Japan. The authorities, believing that he and his men were Portuguese pirates, put Adams in prison, but he was eventually befriended by the shogun Ieyasu Tokugawa, who brought him to Edo (present-day Tokyo) and granted him an estate. Ieyasu appointed Adams his adviser on foreign affairs. The English castaway taught mathematics, geography, gunnery, and navigation to shogunate officials and in 1604 was ordered to build an 80-ton Western-style ship. Pleased with this venture, Ieyasu ordered the construction of a larger oceangoing vessel. These two ships were built at Ito, where Adams lived from 1605 to 1610.

This history was largely forgotten until British Commonwealth occupation forces began coming to Ito for rest and recuperation after World War II. Adams's memory was revived, and since then the Anjin Festival (the Japanese gave Adams the name *anjin,* which means "pilot") has been held in his honor every August. A monument to the Englishman stands at the mouth of the river.

## GETTING HERE AND AROUND

From JR Tokyo Station or Shinagawa Station, take the Tokaido Line (two hours, 15 minutes; ¥2,310) or the Super Odoriko Express (one hour, 40 minutes; ¥3,890) to Ito Station.

## VISITOR INFORMATION

**CONTACT Ito Onsen Information Center.** (伊東観光協会) *Ito Kanko Kyoukai*) ⊠ *3–12–1 Yukawa, Ito* ☎ *0557/37–6105* ⊕ *itospa.com/en.*

# A Healing Headache

While earthquakes are an annoying, everyday fact of life in Japan, they also provide one of the country's greatest delights: thermal baths. Wherever there are volcanic mountains—and there are a lot— you're sure to find springs of hot water, called onsen, which are rich in all sorts of restorative minerals. Any place where lots of spas have tapped these sources is an *onsen chiiki* (hot-springs resort area). The Izu Peninsula is particularly rich in onsen. It has, in fact, one-fifth of the 2,300-odd officially recognized hot springs in Japan.

Spas take many forms, but the ne plus ultra is that small secluded Japanese mountain inn with a *rotemburo* (an open-air mineral-spring pool). For guests only, these pools are usually in a screened-off nook with a panoramic view. A room in one of these inns on a weekend or in high season should be booked months in advance. (High season is late December to early January, late April to early May, the second and third weeks of August, and the second and third weeks of October.) More typical is the large resort hotel, geared mainly to groups, with one or more large indoor mineral baths of its own. Where whole towns and villages have developed to exploit a local supply of hot water, there will be several of these large hotels, an assortment of smaller inns, and probably a few modest public bathhouses, with no accommodations, where you just pay an entrance fee for a soak of whatever length you wish.

## ⊙ Sights

### Atagawa (熱川)

**RESORT** | South of Ito the coastal scenery is lovely—each sweep around a headland reveals another picturesque sight of a rocky, indented shoreline. There are several spa towns en route to Shimoda. Higashi-Izu (East Izu) has numerous hot-springs resorts, of which Atagawa is the most fashionable. South of Atagawa is Kawazu, a place of relative quiet and solitude, with pools in the forested mountainside and waterfalls plunging through lush greenery. ⊠ *Ito.*

### Ikeda 20th-Century Art Museum (池田20世紀美術館; *Ikeda 20-Seiki Bijutsukan*)

**ART MUSEUM** | The museum, which overlooks Lake Ippeki, houses works by Picasso, Dalí, Chagall, and Matisse, plus a number of woodblock prints. The museum is a 15-minute walk northwest from Izu Shaboten Zoo. ⊠ *614 Totari, Ito* ☎ *0557/45–2211* ⊕ *ikeda20.or.jp/en* ⊡ *¥1,000* ⊘ *Closed Wed.*

### Izu Shaboten Zoo (伊豆シャボテン動物公園; *Izu Shaboten Dobutsukoen*)

**ZOO | FAMILY** | A semi–free-range petting zoo and cactus park may not seem like the best combination, but Izu Shaboten Zoo makes it work. Visitors can feed, pet, or get up close and personal with more than 130 different kinds of animals and 1,500 varieties of cacti. Highlights include the capybara onsen (animals like hot springs too) and "Exciting Monkey House." It's a silly place, but a hit with animal-loving kids. ⊠ *1317–13 Futo, Ito* ⊹ *At the base of Komuro-san (Mt. Komuro), the park is 20 mins south of Ito Station by bus* ☎ *0557/51–1111* ⊕ *izushaboten.com* ⊡ *¥2,400.*

## Komuroyama Park

(小室山公園; *Komuroyama Koen*)

**GARDEN** | Some 3,000 cherry trees of 35 varieties bloom at various times throughout the year. You can take a ski-lift style cable to the top of the mountain, which has a lovely view of the sea below. The park is about 20 minutes south of Ito Station by bus. ✉ *1428 Kawana, Ito* ☎ *0557/37–6105* 🚡 *Free; round-trip lift to mountaintop ¥600.*

 ## Hotels

### Hanafubuki (花吹雪)

**$$$$** | **B&B/INN** | This traditional Japanese inn, which is located in the Jogasaki forest, has modern, comfortable rooms, but still retains classic elements like tatami mats, sliding screen doors, and *chabudai* (low dining tables) with *zabuton* (cushion seating). **Pros:** an authentic Japanese experience; the seven private hot-spring baths are free for guests; excellent dinners. **Cons:** not as quiet as more secluded onsen; regular room rates are high for the area; meals are available to nonguests, so the dining room can be a bit crowded. 💲 *Rooms from: ¥50,000* ✉ *1041 Yawatano Isomichi, Ito* ☎ *0557/54–1550* 🌐 *www.hanafubuki. co.jp* 🛏 *17 rooms* ❗️ *All-Inclusive*

### Yokikan (陽気館)

**$$$** | **B&B/INN** | Overlooking the town of Ito and the sea, Yokikan has been catering to visitors for over a century. **Pros:** views of Ito and the sea from the open-air bath; friendly, welcoming service; simple, understated aesthetic perfect for a relaxing getaway. **Cons:** all rooms are Japanese style (tatami and futon); no private bath in standard rooms; simple, somewhat dated furnishings. 💲 *Rooms from: ¥35,000* ✉ *2–24 Suehiro-cho, Ito* ☎ *0557/37–3101* 🌐 *www.yokikan.co.jp* 🛏 *21 rooms* ❗️ *All-Inclusive.*

# Shimoda (下田)

*35 km (22 miles) south of Ito city.*

Of all the resort towns south of Ito along Izu's eastern coast, none can match the distinction of Shimoda. The town's encounter with the West began when Commodore Matthew Perry anchored his fleet of black ships off the coast here in 1853. To commemorate the event, the three-day Black Ship Festival (Kurofune Matsuri) is held here every year in mid-May. Shimoda was also the site, in 1856, of the first American consulate.

The Shimoda Tourist Office, in front of the station, has the easiest of the local English itineraries to follow. The 2½-km (1½-mile) tour covers most major sights. On request, the tourist office will also help you find local accommodations.

### GETTING HERE AND AROUND

From JR Tokyo Station, take the Odoriko Express direct (¥6,055 ) or the Tokaido Line to Atami, change to the Ito Line, and take it to the final stop, Izukyu Shimoda Station (three hours, 45 minutes; ¥3,260).

### VISITOR INFORMATION

**CONTACT Shimoda Tourist Office.** ✉ *4-27 Itchome, Shimoda* ☎ *0558/22–1531* 🌐 *www.shimoda-city.com.*

## Sights

### Hofuku-ji Temple (宝福寺)

**TEMPLE** | The first American consul to Japan was New York businessman Townsend Harris. Soon after his arrival in Shimoda, Harris asked the Japanese authorities to provide him with a female servant; they sent him a young girl named Okichi Saito, who was engaged to be married. The arrangement brought her a new name, Tojin (the Foreigner's) Okichi, much disgrace, and a tragic end. When Harris sent her away, she tried, but failed, to rejoin her former lover. The shame brought upon her for working and living with a Westerner and the pain of losing the love of her life drove Okichi to drown herself in 1892. Her tale is recounted in Rei Kimura's biographical novel *Butterfly in the Wind* and inspired Puccini's *Madame Butterfly,* although some skeptics say the story is more gossip than fact. Hofuku-ji was Okichi's family temple. The museum annex displays a life-size image of her, and just behind the temple is her grave—where incense is still kept burning in her memory. The grave of her lover, Tsurumatsu, is at Toden-ji, a temple about midway between Hofuku-ji and Shimoda Station. ⊠ *1–18–26 Shimoda, Shimoda* ☎ *0558/22–0960* 🎫 *¥400.*

### Ryosen-ji Temple (了仙寺)

TEMPLE | This is the temple in which the negotiations took place that led to the United States–Japan Treaty of Amity and Commerce of 1858. The Treasure Hall (Homotsu-den) contains more than 300 original artifacts relating to Commodore Perry and the "black ships" that opened Japan to the West. ⊠ *3–12–12 Shimoda, Shimoda* ☎ *0558/22–0657* ⊕ *ryosenji.net/ english* 🎫 *Treasure Hall ¥500.*

### Yumigahama Beach (弓ヶ浜)

BEACH | If you love the sun, make sure you stop at Yumigahama. It's one of the nicest sandy beaches on the whole Izu Peninsula. Although the water is usually warm enough to swim from June, the crowds come out during Japan's beach season in July and August. The bus from Shimoda Station stops here before continuing to Iro-zaki, the last stop on the route. **Amenities:** food and drink (July and August); lifeguards (July and August); toilets; parking (fee). **Best for:** swimming (June–August); solitude (September–June). ⊠ *Shimoda* ✈ *11 km (7 miles) southwest of Shimoda, just south of highway 136.*

# Hotels

### Pension Sakuraya (ペンション桜家)

$ | **B&B/INN** | The best lodgings at this family-run inn just a few minutes' walk from Shimoda's main beach are the Japanese-style corner rooms, which have nice views of the hills surrounding Shimoda. **Pros:** very homey atmosphere; close to the beach; friendly and helpful staff. **Cons:** clean but simple; buses from station can be infrequent; rooms are a bit cramped. Ⓢ *Rooms from: ¥11,000* ⊠ *2584–20 Shirahama, Shimoda* ☎ *0558/23–4470* ⊕ *izu-sakuraya.jp/english* 🛏 *9 rooms* ¶◯¶ *Free Breakfast.*

### Shimoda Prince Hotel (下田プリンスホテル)

$$$ | **HOTEL** | At this modern V-shaped resort hotel that faces the Pacific, the decor is more functional than aesthetic, but a white-sand beach is just steps away, and there's a panoramic view of the ocean from the picture windows in the dining room. **Pros:** an excellent view of the sea; one of the best hotels in town; spacious rooms. **Cons:** lacks the personal charm of smaller establishments; can be very crowded with families during peak summer season; restaurants are on the pricey side. Ⓢ *Rooms from: ¥32,000* ⊠ *1547–1 Shirahama, Shimoda* ☎ *0558/22–2111* ⊕ *www. princehotels.com/shimoda* 🛏 *76 rooms* ¶◯¶ *Free Breakfast.*

### Shimoda Tokyu Hotel (下田東急ホテル)

$$$ | **HOTEL** | Perched just above the bay, the Shimoda Tokyu has impressive views of the Pacific from one side (where rooms cost about 10% more) and mountains from the other. **Pros:** nice views of the ocean; easy access to Shimoda Station and sights; spacious guest rooms. **Cons:** rooms are a bit dated; service can be hit or miss; restaurants are expensive for Tokyo standards. Ⓢ *Rooms from: ¥40,000* ⊠ *5–12–1 Shimoda, Shimoda* ☎ *0558/22–2411* ⊕ *www.tokyuhotels.co.jp/shimoda-h* 🛏 *115 rooms* ¶◯¶ *Free Breakfast.*

# Ryokan Etiquette

Guests are expected to arrive at ryokan in the late afternoon. When you do, put on the slippers that are provided, and a maid will escort you to your room. Remember to remove your slippers before entering your room; never step on the tatami (straw mats) with shoes or slippers. Each room will be simply decorated—one small, low table, cushions on the tatami, and a scroll on the wall—which will probably be *shoji* (sliding paper-paneled walls).

In ryokan with thermal pools, you can take to the waters any time, although the pool doors are usually locked from 11 pm to 6 am. In ryokan without thermal baths or private baths in guest rooms, visits must be staggered. Typically the maid will ask what time you would like to bathe and fit you into a schedule. Make sure you wash and rinse off entirely before getting into the bath. Do not get soap in the tub. Other guests will be using the same bathwater, so it is important to observe this custom. After your bath, change into the yukata provided in your room. Don't worry about walking around in it—other guests will be doing the same.

Dinner is served around 6. At the larger, newer ryokan, meals will be in the dining room; at smaller, more personal ryokan, it is served in your room. When you are finished, a maid will clear away the dishes and lay out your futon. In Japan *futon* means bedding, and this consists of a thin cotton mattress and a heavy, thick comforter, which is replaced with a thinner quilt in summer. The small, hard pillow is filled with grain. Some of the less expensive ryokan (under ¥7,000 per person) have become slightly lackadaisical in changing the quilt cover with each new guest; in as inoffensive a way as possible, feel free to complain—just don't shame the proprietor. Around 8 am, a maid will gently wake you, clear away the futon, and bring in your Japanese-style breakfast, which will probably consist of fish, pickled vegetables, and rice. If this isn't appealing, politely ask if it's possible to have coffee and toast. Checkout is at 10 am.

For a room at a smaller ryokan, make sure you call or email as far in advance as possible for a room—inns are not always willing to accept foreign guests because of language and cultural barriers. It is nearly impossible to get a room in July or August. If you don't speak Japanese, try to have a Japanese speaker reserve a room for you.

# Dogashima (堂ヶ島)

*16 km (10 miles) northeast of Mishima.*

The sea has eroded the coastal rock formations into fantastic shapes near the little port town of Dogashima, including a *tombolo,* or a narrow band of sand, that connects the mainland to a small peninsula with a scenic park.

## GETTING HERE AND AROUND
Dogashima is not directly accessible by train but buses run from Shinjuku and Tokyo Stations. From Tokyo Station, take the JR Shinkansen to Mishima (50 minutes, ¥4,600), change to the Izu Hakone Line to Shuzenji (35 minutes, ¥520), and take the Tokai bus to the Dogashima stop. There is also an express Tokai Bus, Minami Izu Line, which takes you from Shimoda Station to Dogashima (55 minutes).

## TOURS

**Dogashima Marine Sightseeing Boat**
(堂ヶ島マリン遊覧船)

**BOAT TOURS** | Sightseeing boats from Dogashima Pier make 20-minute runs to see the rocks. In an excess of kindness, a recorded loudspeaker—which you can safely ignore—recites the name of every rock you pass on the trip. ☎ 0558/52–0013 ⊕ www.izudougasima-yuransen.com ✍ ¥1,200.

 Hotels

**Dogashima New Ginsui**
(堂ヶ島ニュー銀水)

$$$$ | HOTEL | Perched above the water and a secluded beach, every Japanese-style guest room overlooks the sea. **Pros:** by far the best luxury resort on Izu's west coast; stunning views; concierge. **Cons:** some rooms are a bit dated; can get crowded with families during peak summer season; a bit far from sightseeing spots. $ Rooms from: ¥46,000 ⊠ 2977–1 Nishina, Nishiizu-cho, Kamo-gun ☎ 0558/52–2211 ⊕ www.dougashima-newginsui.jp ⤵ 121 rooms ❢❂❢ All-Inclusive.

# Shuzenji (修善寺)

*25 km (15 miles) south of Mishima by Izu-Hakone Railway.*

Shuzenji—a hot-springs resort in the center of the peninsula, along the valley of the Katsura-gawa (Katsura River)—enjoys a certain historical notoriety as the place where the second Kamakura shogun, Minamoto no Yoriie, was assassinated in the early 13th century. Don't judge the town by the area around the station; most of the hotels and hot springs are 2 km (1 mile) to the west.

## GETTING HERE AND AROUND

The train is by far the easiest way to get to Shuzenji. The JR Tokaido Line runs from Tokyo to Mishima (two hours, 10 minutes; ¥2,310), with a change at Mishima for Shuzenji (35 minutes, ¥520); this is the cheapest option if you don't have a JR Pass. With a JR Pass, a Kodama Shinkansen–Izu Line combination saves an hour. The Tokyo–Mishima Shinkansen leg (50 minutes) costs ¥4,600; the Mishima–Shuzenji Izu Line leg (35 minutes) costs ¥520.

 Hotels

**Goyokan** (五葉館)

$$$ | B&B/INN | This family-run ryokan on Shuzenji's main street has rooms that look out on the Katsura-gawa, plus gorgeous stone-lined (for men) and wood-lined (for women) indoor hot springs. **Pros:** unique, modern take on a ryokan; excellent service; private onsen baths free for guests. **Cons:** decor can be a bit over the top; no bath in rooms; lacks cozy feel of a traditional ryokan. $ Rooms from: ¥40,000 ⊠ 765–2 Shuzenji-cho ☎ 0558/72–2066 ⊕ www.goyokan.co.jp ⤵ 11 rooms ❢❂❢ All-Inclusive.

**Ochiairou** (おちあいろう)

$$$$ | B&B/INN | This traditional ryokan was built in the Showa period, and though it has been renovated and modernized, the main wooden structure remains true to its original design, with spacious and comfortable rooms that look out into the gardens. **Pros:** free pickup from Yugashima bus terminal; lovely garden on the grounds; stunning surroundings. **Cons:** some parts of the hotel show their age; remote; very expensive. $ Rooms from: ¥100,000 ⊠ 1887–1 Yugashima, Izu ☎ 055/885–0014 ⊕ www.ochiairo.co.jp ⤵ 15 rooms ❢❂❢ All-Inclusive.

**Ryokan Sanyoso** (旅館三養荘)

$$$$ | B&B/INN | At the former villa of the Iwasaki family, founders of the Mitsubishi conglomerate, museum-quality antiques furnish the rooms. **Pros:** authentic ryokan and furnishings; Japanese bath available; as luxurious and beautiful a place as you'll find on the Izu Peninsula. **Cons:** not

easy to get to without a car; less intimate than smaller ryokan in the area; most expensive ryokan in the area. $ *Rooms from:* ¥60,000 ⊠ *270 Mamanoue, Izunokuni* ☎ *055/947-1111* ⊕ *www. princehotels.com/sanyo-so* ⤴ *40 rooms* ℺ *All-Inclusive.*

# Mt. Takao (高尾山)

*50 km (31 miles) west of Tokyo.*

There are a total of eight hiking trails within Mori Memorial Forest Park. The three main trails that lead to the top of Mt. Takao begin at Kiyotaka Station, the base station of the funicular railway. There is a large billboard with a map of the mountain and all the trails, and this will help you choose which is best for you.

## ⊙ Sights

★ **Mt. Takao** (高尾山; *Takao-san*)
FOREST | When the concrete skyscrapers of Shinjuku become a bit too much, you can escape to the foot of Mt. Takao and the heavily wooded Meiji Memorial Forest Park that surrounds it in about an hour. Hiking along one of the trails that lead to the top of the 599-meter (1,965-foot) mountain, or enjoying the picturesque view from one of the cable cars that zip up to the peak, it can be difficult to believe that you are still within the limits of the Tokyo metropolitan area. The mountain is associated with *tengu,* one of the best known *yokai* (monster-spirits) of Japanese folklore. This is also the start of the Tokai Nature Trail, which leads all the way to Osaka. The mountain is home to a temple, a monkey zoo, a botanical garden, and a beer hall, but it if you make an early start, it is possible to take in everything in one day, and be back to central Tokyo by nightfall.

The Mt. Takao climb is not nearly as grueling as that of Mt. Fuji, but proper planning is necessary to ensure a safe and pleasant hike. If you intend to take the cable car or the paved trail, wear comfortable sneakers. The unpaved trails, on the other hand, can get quite slippery and hiking boots are essential. It is also a good idea to bring a raincoat in case of sudden showers. The heavily wooded mountain can expose you to extremes of humidity, sunshine, and wind, so dress in layers. Bring plenty of bottled water—there is no running water anywhere on the mountain. Although there are over-priced vending machines and food stalls, your best bet is to pack a lunch. It is mountain-climbing etiquette in Japan to greet people you overtake on the way up or meet coming the opposite direction. Smile and say "konnichiwa." On weekends, the mountain gets unpleasantly overcrowded. On weekdays there are still plenty of hikers but it is a pleasant hike regardless.

By far the most popular way to get to the top of Mt. Takao, Trail 1 starts at Kiyotaka Station, the base station of the cable car, and takes a fairly direct, paved route to the visitor center at the top (3.8 km [2.4 miles], approximately one hour, 40 minutes). The descent is especially stunning at sunset. If you take the cable car, you'll join this trail a third of the way up. Near the start of Trail 1 is a detour to *konpira-dai,* one of several small shrines on the mountain, where there is a clear view of central Tokyo. After returning to Trail 1, continue along as you pass Sanjo Station (the upper station of the chairlift) and Takaosan Station (the cable-car terminal), and you will come to *tenbodai,* an observatory with another view of the Tokyo skyline. If you continue on the trail, pass through Joshinmon Gate and on toward the peak. Or, you detour to Trail 2, a loop (900 yards, 30 minutes) that meets back up with Trail 1 farther up the mountain. Going right on Trail 2 will take you past the *hebitaki,* a picturesque natural waterfall. Going to the left will take you past the Monkey

Zoo and Botanical Garden. The Botanical Garden features wild plants indigenous to the area with explanations mainly in Japanese, and the zoo is home to a few dozen clever monkeys, also native to the mountain (¥400 for entrance to both). If you skip Trail 2 and continue on Trail 1, the next stop is at the octopus cedar, a tree with exposed roots so fantastical, they resemble a giant sea monster. At this point, you will reach the Joshinmon Gate. Continue to the *busharito,* a stone pagoda that literally means "Buddha's bone," and is said to mark one of the spots where pieces of Buddha's remains were spread around the world after his cremation. Just past this is Yakuoin Temple, dedicated to Yakushi Nyorai, the Buddha of Medicine, believed to be built in 744. The 2,500 historical documents surviving in the temple explain Japanese religious beliefs during the Warring States (mid-1400s–1603) and Edo (1603–1868) periods. Trail 1 then continues on to the visitor center at the peak, passing beech, oak, and Japanese nutmeg trees along the way. ✉ *Takao-machi, Tokyo.*

## 🍴 Restaurants

The best thing to do upon reaching the top of Mt. Takao is to eat lunch while enjoying the breathtaking view. On a clear day, you get a nice view of Mt. Fuji, and at the very least you can see the massive urban sprawl of Tokyo. There are food stands selling boxed lunches, rice balls, and other snacks, but it is a good idea to bring your own lunch. The only real restaurant serves only dinner.

**Beer Mountain** (ビアマウント)
$$$ | **INTERNATIONAL** | This beer hall is Mt. Takao's only full-fledged restaurant and serves a prix-fixe two-hour, all-you-can eat, all-you-can drink buffet meal that is a hodgepodge of sausages, pasta, Japanese dishes, and desserts, and there are a number of Japanese beers on tap. Beer Mountain is connected to Takaosan Station, the top station of the Takao Tozan Cable Line. **Known for:** views over the mountains and Western Tokyo; filling post-hike meal; lively outdoor atmosphere. [$] *Average main: ¥3,800* ✉ *2205 Takao-machi, Tokyo* ☎ *042/665–9943* 🌐 *www.takaotozan.co.jp* 🕒 *Closed Oct.–June.*

### Torii

**Symbolizing the boundary between the world of the everyday and a sacred space of the gods, *torii* gates mark the entrance to Shinto shrines. Although they come in various shapes and colors, they all share the same basic design making torii the easiest way to differentiate between a Shinto shrine and Buddhist temple.**

# Nikko (日光)

*130 km (81 miles) north of Tokyo.*

"Think nothing is splendid," asserts an old Japanese proverb, "until you have seen Nikko." Nikko, which means "sunlight," is a popular vacation spot for the Japanese, for good reason: its gorgeous sights include a breathtaking waterfall and one of the country's best-known shrines. In addition, Nikko's Chuzenji area combines the rustic charm of a countryside village (complete with wild monkeys that have the run of the place) with a convenient location not far from Tokyo. If you are just going to see Toshogu Shrine and the surrounding area, Nikko is best as a day-trip from Tokyo as there is little to do in the town proper after dark. The scenic Chuzenji-ko Lake, however, makes for a relaxing overnight stop.

### GETTING HERE AND AROUND

The limited express train of the Tobu Railway has two direct connections from Tokyo to Nikko every morning, starting at 6:30 am from Tobu Asakusa Station, a minute's walk from the last stop on Tokyo's Ginza subway line (one hour, 50 minutes; ¥2,860) with additional trains on weekends, holidays, and in high season. All seats are reserved. Bookings are not accepted over the phone and can be bought only at Asakusa Station. During summer, fall, and weekends, buy tickets a few days in advance. Alternatively, the rapid train takes only a bit longer at half the price and requires no reservations (two hours, 20 minutes; ¥1,390). If you're visiting Nikko on a day trip, note that the last return express train is at 6:51 pm. It is possible to get to Nikko using Japan Railways trains, but will take considerably longer, requires a transfer, and costs more than the Tobu line so it is only recommended if you have extra time and JR Pass. From Ueno Station. Take the Tohoku–Honsen Line limited express to Utsunomiya (about two hours) and transfer to the train for JR Nikko Station (45 minutes). If you're not using the JR Pass, the one-way fare is ¥3,090.

More expensive, but faster, is taking the Shinkansen to Utsunomiya and changing for the JR train to Nikko Station; the one-way fare, including the surcharge for the express, is ¥5,920. The first train leaves Tokyo Station at 6:04 am (or Ueno at 6:10) and takes about 1 hour, 30 minutes to Nikko. To return, take the 9:46 pm train from Nikko to Utsunomiya and catch the last Shinkansen back at 10:38 pm.

It's possible, but unwise, to travel by car from Tokyo to Nikko. The trip takes at least three hours, and merely getting from central Tokyo to the toll-road system can be a nightmare. Coming back, especially on a Saturday or Sunday evening, is even worse.

Buses and taxis can take you from Nikko to the village of Chuzenji and nearby Lake Chuzenji; one-way cab fare from Tobu Nikko Station to Chuzenji is about ¥8,000.

## The Power of the 👁 Japanese Blade

In the corner of the enclosure where the Chinese Gate and Sanctum are found, an antique bronze lantern stands some 7 feet high. Legend has it that the lantern would assume the shape of a goblin at night; the deep nicks in the bronze were inflicted by swordsmen of the Edo period—on guard duty, perhaps, startled into action by a flickering shape in the dark. This proves, if not the existence of goblins, the incredible cutting power of the Japanese blade, a peerlessly forged weapon.

■TIP→ There is no bus service between Tokyo and Nikko.

Local buses leave Tobu Nikko Station for Lake Chuzenji, stopping just above the entrance to Toshogu, approximately every 30 minutes from 6:11 am until 6:55 pm. The fare to Chuzenji is ¥1,250, and the ride takes about 45 minutes. The last return bus from the lake leaves at 8:00 pm, arriving back at Tobu Nikko Station at 8:38 pm.

The town of Nikko is essentially one long avenue—Sugi Namiki (Cryptomeria Avenue)—extending for about 2 km (1 mile) from the railway stations to Toshogu. You can easily walk to most places within town. Tourist inns and shops line the street, and if you have time, you might want to make this a leisurely stroll. The antiques shops along the way may turn up interesting—but expensive—pieces like armor fittings, hibachi, pottery, and dolls. The souvenir shops here sell ample selections of local wood carvings.

One of the experiences you can have in Edo Wonderland is a cruise through the canals on a traditional *yakata* boat.

## VISITOR INFORMATION

You can do a lot of preplanning for your visit to Nikko with a stop at the Japan National Tourist Organization office in Tokyo, where the helpful English-speaking staff will ply you with pamphlets and field your questions about things to see and do. Closer to the source is the Nikko Kyodo Center in Nikko itself, about halfway up the main street of town between the railway stations and Toshogu, on the left; don't expect too much in the way of help in English, but the center does have a good array of English information about local restaurants and shops, registers of inns and hotels, and mapped-out walking tours.

**CONTACT Nikko Kyodo Center.** ⊠ *591 Goko-machi, Nikko* ☎ *0288/54–2496.*

# Toshogu (東照宮)

*120 km (75 miles) north of Tokyo.*

The Toshogu area encompasses three UNESCO World Heritage sites—Toshogu Shrine, Futarasan Shrine, and Rinnoji Temple. These are known as *nisha-ichiji* (two shrines and one temple) and are Nikko's main draw. Signs and maps clearly mark a recommended route that will allow you to see all the major sights, which are within walking distance of each other. You should plan for at least half a day to explore the area around Toshogu Shrine.

## 👁 Sights

### Edo Wonderland
(日光江戸村; *Nikko Edo Mura*)

**MUSEUM VILLAGE | FAMILY |** Edo Wonderland, a living-history theme park a short taxi ride from downtown, re-creates an 18th-century Japanese village. The complex includes sculpted gardens with waterfalls and ponds and 22 vintage buildings, where actors in traditional dress stage martial arts exhibitions, historical theatrical performances, and comedy acts. You can even observe Japanese tea ceremony rituals in gorgeous tatami-floor houses, as well as people dressed as geisha and samurai. Strolling stuffed animal characters and acrobatic ninjas keep kids happy. Nikko Edo Mura has one large restaurant and 15 small food stalls serving period cuisine like *yakisoba* (fried soba) and *dango* (dumplings). ✉ *470–2 Karakura, Nikko* ☎ *0288/77–1777* ⊕ *www.edowonderland.net* 🎫 *¥4,800 unlimited day pass includes rides and shows* ☉ *Closed Wed.*

### Futarasan-jinja Shrine (二荒山神社)
**RELIGIOUS BUILDING |** Nikko's holy ground is far older than the Tokugawa dynasty, in whose honor it was improved upon. Founded in AD 782, Futara-san Jinja (Futura-san Shrine) is a peaceful contrast to the more elaborate Toshogu Shrine. Futarasan has three locations: the Main Shrine at Iosho-gu; the Chugu-shi (Middle Shrine) at Chuzenji-ko; and the Okumiya (Inner Shrine) on top of Mt. Nantai.

The bronze torii at the entrance to the shrine leads to the gilded and elaborately carved Kara-mon (Chinese Gate); beyond it is the Hai-den, the shrine's oratory. The Hai-den, too, is richly carved and decorated, with a dragon-covered ceiling. The Chinese lions on the panels at the rear are by two distinguished painters of the Kano school. From the oratory of the Tai-yu-in a connecting passage leads to the Hon-den (Sanctum)—the present version of which dates from 1619. Designated

## Fortune Gods 👁

Make sure you visit **Gohoten-do**, in the northeast corner of Rinno Temple, behind the Sanbutsu-do. Three of the Seven Gods of Good Fortune, derived from Chinese folk mythology, are enshrined here. These three Buddhist deities are Daikoku-ten and Bishamon-ten, who bring wealth and good harvests, and Benzai-ten, patroness of music and the arts.

a National Treasure, it houses a gilded and lacquered Buddhist altar some 9 feet high, decorated with paintings of animals, birds, and flowers, in which resides the object of all this veneration: a seated wooden figure of Iemitsu himself. ✉ *2307 Sannai, Nikko* ⊹ *Take avenue to left as you're standing before stone torii at Tosho-gu and follow it to end* 🎫 *¥300.*

### Nikko Toshogu Museum (日光東照宮宝物館; *Nikkō Tōshōgū Homotsu-kan*)
**ART MUSEUM |** An unhurried visit to the precincts of Toshogu should definitely include the Treasure House, as it contains a collection of antiquities from its various shrines and temples. From the west gate of Rinno-ji temple, turn left off Omote-sando, just below the pagoda, onto the cedar-lined avenue to Futara-san Jinja. A minute's walk brings you to the museum, on the left. ✉ *2301 Sannai, Nikko* ☎ *0288/54–2558* ⊕ *www.toshogu.or.jp/english/museum* 🎫 *¥1,000.*

### Rinno-ji Temple (輪王寺)
**TEMPLE |** This temple belongs to the Tendai sect of Buddhism, the head temple of which is Enryaku-ji, on Mt. Hiei near Kyoto. The main hall of Rinno Temple, called the Sanbutsu-do, is the largest single building at Toshogu; it enshrines an image of Amida Nyorai, the Buddha of the Western Paradise, flanked on the right by Senju (Thousand-Armed)

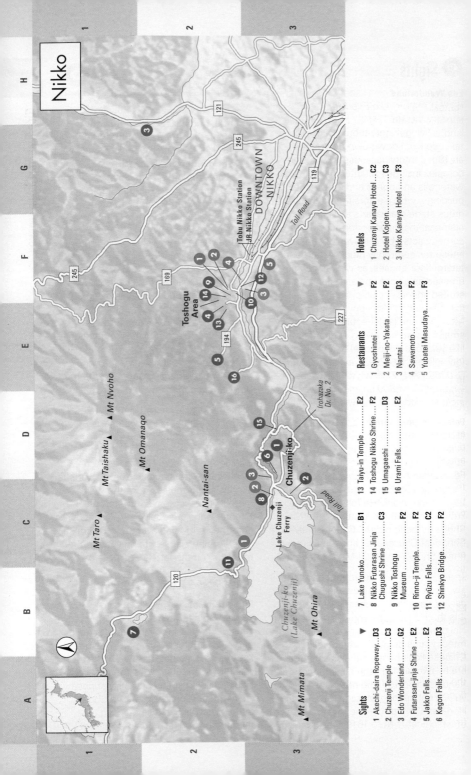

# Nikko

**Toshogu Area**

DOWNTOWN NIKKO

Tobu Nikko Station
JR Nikko Station

Toll Road

Chuzenji-ko

Chuzenji-ko
(Lake Chuzenji)

Lake Chuzenji Ferry

Irohazaka
Dr. No. 2

Toll Road

Mt Mimata ▲

Mt Ohira ▲

Mt Taro ▲

Mt Taishaku ▲     ▲ Mt Nyoho

Mt Omanago ▲

Nantai-san ▲

## Sights ▶

| | |
|---|---|
| 1 Akechi-daira Ropeway | **D3** |
| 2 Chuzenji Temple | **C3** |
| 3 Edo Wonderland | **G2** |
| 4 Futarasan-jinja Shrine | **E2** |
| 5 Jakko Falls | **E2** |
| 6 Kegon Falls | **D3** |
| 7 Lake Yunoko | **B1** |
| 8 Nikko Futarasan Jinja Chugushi Shrine | **C3** |
| 9 Nikko Toshogu Museum | **F2** |
| 10 Rinno-ji Temple | **F2** |
| 11 Ryūzu Falls | **C2** |
| 12 Shinkyo Bridge | **F2** |
| 13 Taiyu-in Temple | **E2** |
| 14 Toshogu Nikko Shrine | **F2** |
| 15 Umagaeshi | **D3** |
| 16 Urami Falls | **E2** |

## Restaurants ▶

| | |
|---|---|
| 1 Gyoshintei | **F2** |
| 2 Meiji-no-Yakata | **F2** |
| 3 Nantai | **D3** |
| 4 Sawamoto | **F2** |
| 5 Yubatei Masudaya | **F3** |

## Hotels ▶

| | |
|---|---|
| 1 Chuzenji Kanaya Hotel | **C2** |
| 2 Hotel Kojoen | **C3** |
| 3 Nikko Kanaya Hotel | **F3** |

# Three Little Monkeys

While in the Sacred Stable of Toshogu Shrine, make sure to look at the second panel from the left. The three monkeys, commonly known as "Hear no evil, Speak no evil, See no evil" have become something of a Nikko trademark; the image has been reproduced on plaques, bags, and souvenirs. Although the phrase's true origins are uncertain, scholars and legend suggest it originated from this shrine as a visual interpretation of the religious phrase, "If we do not hear, see, or speak evil, we ourselves shall be spared all evil." As for the monkeys, it's been said that a Chinese Buddhist monk introduced the image to Japan in the 8th century.

Kannon, the goddess of mercy, and on the left by Bato-Kannon, regarded as the protector of animals. These three images are lacquered in gold and date from the early part of the 17th century. The original Sanbutsu-do is said to have been built in 848 by the priest Ennin (794–864), also known as Jikaku-Daishi. The present building dates from 1648.

In the southwest corner of the Rinno Temple compound, behind the abbot's residence, is an especially fine Japanese garden called Shoyo-en, created in 1815 and thoughtfully designed to present a different perspective of its rocks, ponds, and flowering plants from every turn on its path. To the right of the entrance to the garden is the Homotsu-den (Treasure Hall) of Rinno Temple, a museum with a collection of some 6,000 works of lacquerware, painting, and Buddhist sculpture. The museum is rather small, and only a few of the pieces in the collection—many of them designated National Treasures and Important Cultural Properties—are on display at any given time. ✉ *2300 Sannai, Nikko* ☎ *0288/54–0531* ⊕ *www.rinnoji.or.jp* ✉ *¥1,000.*

### Shinkyo Bridge (神橋)

BRIDGE | Built in 1636 for shoguns and imperial messengers visiting the shrine, the original bridge was destroyed in a flood; the present red-lacquer wooden structure dates to 1907. Buses leaving from either railway station at Nikko go straight up the main street to the bridge, opposite the first of the main entrances to Toshogu. The Sacred Bridge is just to the left of a modern bridge, where the road curves and crosses the Daiya-gawa (Daiya River). ✉ *2307 Sannai, Nikko* ✉ *¥300 to stand on the bridge, free to view.*

### Taiyu-in Temple (大猷院廟)

TEMPLE | This grandiose building is the resting place of the third Tokugawa shogun, Iemitsu (1604–51), who imposed a policy of national isolation on Japan that was to last more than 200 years. Iemitsu, one suspects, had it in mind to upstage his illustrious grandfather; he marked the approach to his own tomb with no fewer than six different decorative gates. The first is another Nio-mon—a Gate of the Deva Kings—like the one at Toshogu. The dragon painted on the ceiling is by Yasunobu Kano. A flight of stone steps leads from here to the second gate, the Niton mon, a two-story structure protected front and back by carved and painted images of guardian gods. Beyond it, two more flights of steps lead to the middle courtyard. As you climb the last steps to Iemitsu's shrine, you'll pass a bell tower on the right and a drum tower on the left; directly ahead is the third gate, the remarkable Yasha-mon, so named for the figures of *yasha* (she-demons) in the four niches. This structure is also known as the Peony Gate (Botan-mon) for the carvings that decorate it.

Toshogu honors Ieyasu Tokugawa, the first shogun and founder of Tokyo.

As you exit the shrine, on the west side, you come to the fifth gate: the Koka-mon, built in the style of the late Ming dynasty of China. The gate is normally closed, but from here another flight of stone steps leads to the sixth and last gate—the cast copper Inuki-mon, inscribed with characters in Sanskrit—and Iemitsu's tomb. ⊠ *2300 Sannai, Nikko* ⬛ *¥550*.

★ **Toshogu Nikko Shrine** (東照宮)
RELIGIOUS BUILDING | With its riot of colors and carvings, inlaid pillars, red-lacquer corridors, and extensive use of gold leaf, this 17th-century shrine to Ieyasu Tokugawa is one of the most elaborately decorated shrines in Japan.

The Hon-den (Main Hall) of Toshogu is the ultimate purpose of the shrine. You approach it from the rows of lockers at the far end of the enclosure; here you remove and store your shoes, step up into the shrine, and follow a winding corridor to the Oratory (Hai-den)—the ante-room, resplendent in its lacquered pillars, carved friezes, and coffered ceilings bedecked with dragons. Over the lintels are paintings by Tosa Mitsuoki (1617–91) of the 36 great poets of the Heian period, with their poems in the calligraphy of Emperor Go-Mizunoo. Deeper yet, at the back of the Oratory, is the Inner Chamber (Nai-jin)—repository of the Sacred Mirror that represents the spirit of the deity enshrined here. The hall is enclosed by a wall of painted and carved panel screens; opposite the right-hand corner of the wall, facing the shrine, is the Kito-den, a hall where annual prayers were once offered for the peace of the nation.

Behind the Inner Chamber is the Inner-most Chamber (Nai-Nai-jin). No visitors come this far. Here, in the very heart of Toshogu, is the gold-lacquer shrine where the spirit of Ieyasu resides—along with two other deities, whom the Tokuga-was later decided were fit companions. One was Toyotomi Hideyoshi, Ieyasu's mentor and liege lord in the long wars of unification at the end of the 16th century. The other was Minamoto no Yoritomo, brilliant military tactician and founder

# Ieyasu's Legacy

In 1600 Ieyasu Tokugawa (1543–1616) won a battle at a place in the mountains of south-central Japan called Seki-ga-hara that left him the undisputed ruler of the archipelago. He died 16 years later, but the Tokugawa Shogunate would last another 252 years.

The founder of such a dynasty required a fitting resting place. Ieyasu (ee-eh-ya-su) had provided for one in his will: a mausoleum at Nikko, in a forest of tall cedars, where a religious center had been founded more than eight centuries earlier. The year after his death, in accordance with Buddhist custom, he was given a kaimyo—an honorific name to bear in the afterlife. Thenceforth he was Tosho-Daigongen: the Great Incarnation Who Illuminates the East. The Imperial Court at Kyoto declared him a god, and his remains were taken in a procession of great pomp and ceremony to be enshrined at Nikko.

The dynasty he left behind was enormously rich. Ieyasu's personal fief, on the Kanto Plain, was worth 2½ million koku of rice. One koku, in monetary terms, was equivalent to the cost of keeping one retainer in the necessities of life for a year. The shogunate itself, however, was still an uncertainty. It had only recently taken control after more than a century of civil war. The founder's tomb had a political purpose: to inspire awe and to make manifest the power of the Tokugawas. It was Ieyasu's legacy, a statement of his family's right to rule.

Toshogu was built by his grandson, the third shogun, Iemitsu (it was Iemitsu who established the policy of national isolation, which closed the doors of Japan to the outside world for more than 200 years). The mausoleum and shrine required the labor of 15,000 people for two years (1634–36). Craftsmen and artists of the first rank were assembled from all over the country. Every surface was carved and painted and lacquered in the most intricate detail imaginable. Toshogu shimmers with the reflections of 2,489,000 sheets of gold leaf. Roof beams and rafter ends with dragon heads, lions, and elephants in bas-relief; friezes of phoenixes, wild ducks, and monkeys; inlaid pillars and red-lacquer corridors: Toshogu is everything a 17th-century warlord would consider gorgeous, and the inspiration is very Chinese.

of the earlier (12th-century) Kamakura Shogunate (Ieyasu claimed Yoritomo for an ancestor).

Between the Goma-do and the Kagura-den (a hall where ceremonial dances are performed to honor the gods) is a passage to the Sakashita-mon (Gate at the Foot of the Hill). Above the gateway is another famous symbol of Toshogu, the Sleeping Cat—a small panel said to have been carved by Hidari Jingoro (Jingoro the Left-handed), a late-16th-century master carpenter and sculptor credited with important contributions to numerous Tokugawa-period temples, shrines, and palaces. Climb the flight of 200 stone steps through a forest of cryptomeria to arrive at Ieyasu's tomb–worth it for the view of the Yomei-mon and Kara-mon from above.

The centerpiece of Toshogu is the Yomei-mon (Gate of Sunlight), at the top of the second flight of stone steps. A designated National Treasure, it's also called the

Higurashi-mon (Twilight Gate)—implying that you could gape at its richness of detail all day, until sunset. And rich it is indeed: 36 feet high and dazzling white, the gate has 12 columns, beams, and roof brackets carved with dragons, lions, clouds, peonies, Chinese sages, and demigods, painted vivid hues of red, blue, green, and gold. On one of the central columns, there are two carved tigers; the natural grain of the wood is used to bring out the "fur." As you enter the Yomei-mon, there are galleries running east and west for some 700 feet; their paneled fences are also carved and painted with nature motifs.

The portable shrines that appear in the Toshogu Festival, held yearly on May 17–18, are kept in the Shinyo-sha, a storeroom to the left as you come through the Twilight Gate into the heart of the shrine. The paintings on the ceiling, of *tennin* (Buddhist angels) playing harps, are by Tan-yu Kano (1602–74).

Mere mortals may not pass through the Chinese Gate (Kara-mon), which is the "official" entrance to the Toshogu inner shrine. Like its counterpart, the Yomei-mon, on the opposite side of the courtyard, the Kara-mon is a National Treasure—and, like the Yomei-mon, is carved and painted in elaborate detail with dragons and other auspicious figures. ✉ *2301 Sannai, Nikko* ☎ *0288/54–0560* 🎫 *¥1,300.*

## 🍴 Restaurants

**Gyoshintei** (尭心亭)
**$$$** | **JAPANESE FUSION** | This is the only restaurant in Nikko devoted to *shojin ryori,* the Buddhist-temple vegetarian fare that evolved centuries ago into haute cuisine. Gyoshintei is decorated in the style of a *ryotei* (traditional restaurant), with all-tatami seating. **Known for:** serene setting; traditional atmosphere; Buddhist-temple cuisine. [$] *Average main: ¥4,200* ✉ *2339–1 Sannai, Nikko* ☎ *0288/53–3751* 🌐 *www.meiji-yakata.com/en/gyoshin/menu.html* 🕒 *Closed Thurs.*

**Yubatei Masudaya** (ゆば亭ますだや)
**$$$** | **JAPANESE** | Masudaya started out as a sake maker more than a century ago, but for four generations now, it has been the town's best-known restaurant. The specialty is *yuba* (tofu skin), which the chefs transform, with the help of local vegetables and fresh fish, into sumptuous high cuisine. **Known for:** relaxing environment; a perfect place to try yuba tofu cuisine; fresh local ingredients. [$] *Average main: ¥4,290* ✉ *439–2 Ishiya-machi, Nikko* ☎ *0288/54–2151* 🌐 *www.nikko-yuba.com* 🕒 *Closed Thurs. No dinner.*

**Meiji-no-Yakata** (明治の館)
**$$$** | **EUROPEAN** | Not far from the east entrance to Rinno-ji temple, Meiji-no-Yakata is an elegant 19th-century Western-style stone house, originally built as a summer retreat for an American diplomat. The food, too, is Western-style: specialties of the house include fresh rainbow trout from Lake Chuzenji, roast lamb with pepper sauce, and melt-in-your-mouth filet mignon made from local Tochigi beef. **Known for:** excellent

### Did You Know? 👁

Under the policy of national seclusion, only the Dutch retained trading privileges with Japan. Even then, they were confined to the tiny artificial island of Dejima, in the port of Nagasaki. They regularly sent tokens of their esteem to the shogunate to keep their precarious monopoly, including the two bronze items found in the Sacred Stable, which were sent in 1636. The 200-year-plus monopoly was dissolved when Japan decided to open its borders to other Western countries in 1858.

desserts; lovely outdoor seating; classic high-end Japanese–Western cuisine. $ *Average main: ¥4,000* ⊠ *2339–1 Sannai, Nikko* ☎ *0288/53–3751* ⊕ *www. meiji-yakata.com/en/meiji.*

### Sawamoto (澤本)

$$$ | JAPANESE | Charcoal-broiled *unagi* (eel) is an acquired taste, and there's no better place in Nikko to acquire it than at this small and unpretentious place with only five plain-wood tables. Service can be lukewarm, but Sawamoto is reliable for a light lunch or very early dinner of unagi on a bed of rice, served in an elegant lacquered box. **Known for:** 90 years of history; simple, comfortable atmosphere; simple, beautifully prepared unagi. $ *Average main: ¥4,000* ⊠ *1037–1 Kamihatsuishi-machi, Nikko* ☎ *0288/54– 0163* ☽ *No dinner.*

##  Hotels

### Nikko Kanaya Hotel (日光金谷ホテル)

$$$ | RESORT | This family-run operation is a little worn around the edges after a century of operation, but it still has the best location in town—across the street from Tosho-gu—and the main building is a delightful, rambling Victorian structure that has hosted royalty and other important personages from around the world. **Pros:** spacious; helpful staff; perfect location for sightseeing in Nikko. **Cons:** very touristy; daytime visitors browse through the old building and its gift shops; some annex rooms lack the historic charm of the main building; rooms rather pricey. $ *Rooms from: ¥44,000* ⊠ *1300 Kami Hatsuishi-machi, Nikko* ☎ *0288/54–0001* ⊕ *www.kanayahotel.co.jp* ⤳ *70 rooms* ❑ *Free Breakfast.*

# Chuzenji-ko (中禅寺湖)

*120 km (75 miles) north of Tokyo.*

More than 3,900 feet above sea level, at the base of the volcano known as Nan-tai-san, is Chuzenji-ko (Lake Chuzenji), renowned for its clean waters and fresh air. People come to boat and fish on the lake and to enjoy the surrounding scenic woodlands, waterfalls, and hills.

## TOURS

### Lake Chuzenji Ferry (中禅寺湖機船 *Chuzenjiko Kisen*)

BOAT TOURS | Explore Lake Chuzenji on chartered 60-minute boat rides. ⊠ *2478- 21 Chugushi, Nikko* ☎ *0288/55–0360* ⊕ *chuzenjiko-cruise.com/index.html* ⤳ *¥050.*

##  Sights

### Akechi-daira Ropeway (明智平ロープウェイ)

VIEWPOINT | If you want to avoid the hairpin turns, try the ropeway that runs from Akechi-daira Station directly to the Akechi-daira lookout. It takes three minutes and the panoramic views of Nikko and Kegon Falls are priceless. ⊠ *703 Hosomachi, Nikko* ☎ *0288/55–0331* ⤳ *¥1,000 round trip.*

### Chuzenji Temple (中禅寺)

TEMPLE | A subtemple of Rinno Temple, at Tosho-gu, the principal object of worship here is the Tachi-ki Kannon, a 17-foot-tall standing statue of the Buddhist goddess of mercy, said to have been carved more than 1,000 years ago by the priest Shodo from the living trunk of a single Judas tree. The bus trip from Nikko to the national park area ends at Chuzenji village, which shares its name with the temple established here in 784. ⊠ *2578 Chugushi, Nikko* ⊕ *1½ km (1 mile) south of Chugu-shi village along eastern shore*

## Did You Know?

The 320-foot-high Kegon Falls draws visitors from all over Japan and the world. The spectacular sight near Lake Chuzenji is also home to 12 other waterfalls. Behind and next to Kegon, these falls drip out of cracks in the volcano, Nantai-san. Try to spot a few of them once you've taken in Kegon's grandeur.

*of lake* ☎ 0288/55-0013 ⊕ *www.rinnoji. or.jp/temple/chuzenji* 🖼 ¥500.

## Jakko Falls (寂光滝; *Jakko-no-taki*)

**WILDLIFE REFUGE** | Falling water is one of the special charms of the Nikko National Park area; people going by bus or car from Toshogu to Lake Chuzenji often stop off en route to see these falls, which descend in a series of seven terraced stages, forming a sheet of water about 100 feet high. About 1 km (½ mile) from the shrine precincts, at the Tamozawa bus stop, a narrow road to the right leads to an uphill walk of some 3 km (2 miles) to the falls. ⊠ *Nikko.*

## ★ Kegon Falls (華厳滝; *Kegon-no-taki*)

**WATERFALL** | More than anything else, the country's most famous falls are what draw the crowds of Japanese visitors to Chuzenji. Fed by the eastward flow of the lake, the falls drop 318 feet into a rugged gorge; an elevator takes you to an observation platform at the bottom. The volume of water over the falls is carefully regulated, but it's especially impressive after a summer rain or a typhoon. In winter the falls do not freeze completely but form a beautiful cascade of icicles. The elevator is just a few minutes' walk east from the bus stop at Chuzenji village, downhill and off to the right at the far end of the parking lot. ⊠ *2479-2 Chugushi, Nikko* ☎ 0288/55-0030 🖼 *Elevator ¥570.*

## Lake Yunoko (湯ノ湖; *Yuno-ko*)

**BODY OF WATER** | Located on the northern shore of peaceful Yunoko (Lake Yuno), a series of isolated hot springs were once a popular destination for 14th-century aristocrats. Today the area is still known for its hot springs—being able to soak in an onsen all year long, even when temperatures drop below zero, will always be a major plus—but they are now controlled by separate resorts. Besides the healing and relaxing effects of the baths, visitors come for the hiking trails, fishing, camping, skiing, bird-watching, and mountain-climbing opportunities. Try to avoid the fall season, as it's peak

visitor time and there are always delays. ⊠ *Yumoto, Nikko* ⊹ *You can get to the Yumoto onsen by taking the Tobu operated buses, which leave Tobu Nikko and JR Nikko stations. There are one or two services an hour, depending on the time of the day. A one-way trip from central Nikko takes about 80 minutes and costs ¥1,950.*

## Nikko Futarasan Jinja Chugushi Shrine (二荒山神社中宮祠)

**RELIGIOUS BUILDING** | A subshrine of the Futarasan Shrine at Toshogu, this is the major religious center on the north side of Lake Chuzenji, about 1½ km (1 miles) west of the village. The Homotsu-den (Treasure House) contains an interesting historical collection, including swords, lacquerware, and medieval shrine palanquins. ⊠ *2484 Chugushi, Nikko* ☎ 0288/55-0017 🖼 *Homotsu Den ¥300; Shrine free.*

## Ryuzu Falls (竜頭滝; *Ryuzu-no-taki*)

**WATERFALL** | If you've budgeted a second day for Nikko, you might want to consider a walk around the lake. A paved road along the north shore extends for about 8 km (5 miles), one-third of the whole distance, as far as the "beach" at Shobu-ga-hama. Here, where the road branches off to the north for Senjogahara, are the lovely cascades of Ryuzu no Taki, literally Dragon's Head Falls. To the left is a steep footpath that continues around the lake to Senju-ga-hama and then to a campsite at Asegata. The path is well marked but can get rough in places. From Asegata it's less than an hour's walk back to Chuzenji village. ⊠ *Nikko.*

## Umagaeshi (馬返し)

**VIEWPOINT** | In the old days, the road became too rough for horse riding, so riders had to alight and proceed on foot; the lake is 4,165 feet above sea level. From Umagaeshi the bus climbs a one-way toll road up the pass; the old road has been widened and is used for the traffic coming down. The two roads are full of steep hairpin turns, and on a clear day the view up and down the valley is magnificent—especially from the halfway point at Akechi-daira (Akechi Plain), from which you can see the summit of Nantai-san (Mt. Nantai), reaching 8,149 feet. Hiking season lasts from May through mid-October; if you push it, you can make the ascent in about four hours. Wild monkeys make their homes in these mountains, and they've learned the convenience of mooching from visitors along the route. Be careful—they have a way of not taking no for an answer. Do not give in to the temptation to give them food—they will never leave you alone if you do. ✉ *Nikko* ↔ *About 10 km (6 miles) from Tobu Station in Nikko, or 8 km (5 miles) from Toshogu.*

**Urami Falls** (裏見滝; *Urami-no-taki*)
**WATERFALL** | A poetic description says it all and still holds true: "The water," wrote the great 17th-century poet Basho, "seemed to take a flying leap and drop a hundred feet from the top of a cave into a green pool surrounded by a thousand rocks. One was supposed to inch one's way into the cave and enjoy the falls from behind." The falls and the gorge are striking—but you should make the climb only if you have good hiking shoes and are willing to get wet in the process. ✉ *Nikko* ↔ *The steep climb to cave begins at Arasawa bus stop, with a turn to right off Chuzenji road.*

## 🍴 Restaurants

**Nantai** (なんたい)
**$$** | **JAPANESE** | The low tables, antiques, and pillows scattered on tatami flooring make visitors feel like they're dining in a traditional Japanese living room. Try the Nikko specialty, *yuba* (tofu skin), which comes with the *nabe* (hot pot) for dinner. **Known for:** cozy atmosphere; local specialties from Chuzen-ji; home-style hot-pot cuisine. [$] *Average main: ¥3,000* ✉ *2478–8 Chugushi, Nikko* ☎ *080/7091–3200* 🕒 *Closed Thurs.*

## 🛏 Hotels

**Chuzenji Kanaya Hotel** (中禅寺金谷ホテル)
**$$$** | **RESORT** | Pastel colors decorate the simple, tasteful rooms of this outpost of the Nikko Kanaya on the road from the village to Shobu-ga-hama, and floor-to-ceiling windows overlook the lake or grounds. **Pros:** relaxing resort feel; spacious rooms; excellent food. **Cons:** no outside dining options nearby after dark; not easy to access without a car; the most expensive hotel in the area. [$] *Rooms from: ¥42,000* ✉ *2482 Chugushi, Nikko* ☎ *0288/51–0001* 🌐 *www.kanayahotel.co.jp/eng* 🛏 *60 rooms* 🍴 *Free Breakfast.*

**Hotel Kojoen** (湖上苑)
**$$** | **B&B/INN** | Located at the entrance to Lake Chuzenji, Hotel Kojoen is an excellent middle ground between the area's larger luxury hotels and bare-bones pensions. **Pros:** easy access; relaxing; excellent meals. **Cons:** outdoor hot spring crowded during peak times; rooms are on the small side; Western-style rooms are clean but dated. [$] *Rooms from: ¥25,000* ✉ *2478 Chugushi, Nikko* ☎ *0288/55–0500* 🌐 *www.kojoen.com* 🛏 *10 rooms.*

# Chapter 6

# NAGOYA, ISE-SHIMA, AND THE KII PENINSULA

Updated by
Rob Goss

| ⊙ Sights | 🍴 Restaurants | 🛏 Hotels | 🛍 Shopping | 🍸 Nightlife |
|---|---|---|---|---|
| ★★★☆☆ | ★★★★☆ | ★★★☆☆ | ★★☆☆☆ | ★★★☆☆ |

# WELCOME TO NAGOYA, ISE-SHIMA, AND THE KII PENINSULA

## TOP REASONS TO GO

★ **The shrines:** The Grand Shrines of Ise, rebuilt every two decades for the last 1,500 years, are the most sacred in Japan.

★ **Shopping:** Nagoya's Noritake is one of the world's largest porcelain makers. Seto, Tajimi, and Tokoname produce ceramics, Arimatsu tie-dyed fabrics, Gifu paper lanterns and umbrellas, and Seki knives and samurai swords.

★ **Japan at play:** See the sumo tournament in July, watch a Chunichi Dragons baseball game or take in a Grampus soccer match.

★ **Fish from the bird's mouth:** In *ukai,* cormorants snatch *ayu* (sweetfish) from the water, but rings around the birds' necks prevent them from swallowing their catch, which is taken by fishermen.

★ **Japan's modernization:** Meiji-mura holds more than 60 original Meiji-era buildings (1868–1912)—including the foyer of Frank Lloyd Wright's Imperial Hotel—that were reconstructed here.

**1 Nagoya.** A manufacturing, business, and cultural hub.

**2 Gifu.** To the north are cormorant fishing and craft centers.

**3 Inuyama.** Home to Japan's oldest castle, Inuyama-jo.

**4 Iga Ueno.** The castle town of Iga-Ueno is the birthplace of the Iga school of ninjutsu.

**5 Ise.** Ise's grand shrines, Ise Jingu, are the most sacred in Japan.

**6 Kashikojima.** The largest island in Ago Bay.

**7 Shingu.** Home to Hayatama-taisha, one of three grand shrines linked by trails.

**8 Doro-kyo.** This stunning gorge is defined by jagged ravines and aquamarine waters.

**9 Nachi.** Draws are a grand shrine and waterfall.

**10 Shirahama.** Resort town known for its white-sand beach and ancient hot-spring baths.

**11 Koya-san.** Dotted by 117 temples, this is a spiritual retreat. Stay overnight in a temple.

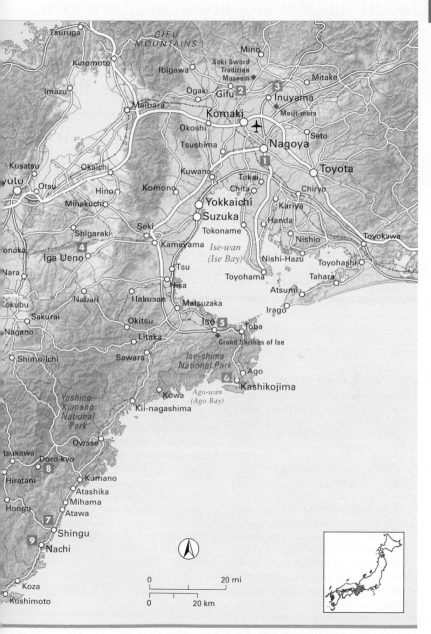

Nagoya punches well above its weight. The present-day industries of Japan's fourth-largest city are a corollary to its *monozukuri* (art of making things) culture. This is manifested in the efficiency of Toyota's production lines, but traditional crafts including ceramics, tie-dyeing, and knife making are still very much alive. The Greater Nagoya area's GDP accounts for just over 10% of the country's total GDP, but this economic prowess is matched by a capacity to pleasantly surprise any visitor.

Nagoya purrs along contentedly, burdened neither by a second-city complex nor by hordes of tourists, and despite a population of 2.5 million it has an agreeable small-town atmosphere. A substantial immigrant population, by Japanese standards, includes many South Americans working in local factories and provides international flavor to the city's food and entertainment choices.

On arrival you will first notice the twin white skyscrapers sprouting from the ultramodern station, almost a city in itself. An extensive network of underground shopping malls stretches out in all directions below the wide, clean streets around Nagoya Station and in downtown Sakae. Aboveground are huge department stores and international fashion boutiques. The even taller building opposite the station, the multipurpose 42-story Midland Square, houses the headquarters of the sales division of auto-making giant Toyota, the driving force of the local economy.

Within two hours' drive of the city are the revered Grand Shrines of Ise, Japan's most important Shinto site, and to the south are the quiet fishing villages of Ise-Shima National Park. Southwest of Nagoya, on the untamed Kii Peninsula, steep-walled gorges, ancient pilgrimage trails, and forested headlands give way to pristine bays, and fine sandy beaches await in Shirahama. Inland is the remarkable mountain temple town of Koya-san. Add to this some memorable *matsuri* (festivals), and this corner of Japan becomes far more than just another stop on the Shinkansen train.

## MAJOR REGIONS

**Nagoya** is Japan's manufacturing center, and as such has never had quite the same allure for travelers as culturally rich Kyoto or Tokyo. But as well as being an ideal jumping-off point to explore central Japan, there are plenty of reasons to delve under Nagoya's commercial skin. With the ancient Atsuta Shrine and (rebuilt) Nagoya Castle, the city offers glimpses into feudal Japan, while the manufacturing culture extends to an array of fine local crafts. The lively nightlife and Nagoya's culinary traditions can both stand up to anywhere else in Japan.

Old Japan resonates in the foothills of the Hida Sanmyaku (飛騨山脈; Hida Mountains) of **South Gifu-ken,** just north of Nagoya. Ancient customs and crafts, such as cormorant fishing and umbrella, lantern, pottery, and sword making, are still practiced, and the nation's oldest castle, Inuyama-jo, has seen it all for almost 500 years. **Gifu** is the main center of *ukai* (cormorant fishing). **Inuyama** also offers the fishing experience, and it boasts a superior castle and, in Meiji-mura, an outstanding museum. **Iga Ueno** is famous as a center of ninjutsu training.

Hanging like a fin underneath central Honshu, Ise-Shima is a scenic and sacred counterweight to Japan's overbuilt industrial corridor. **Ise-Shima National Park,** which holds the supremely venerated shrines of Ise Jingu, extends east from Ise to Toba (the center of the pearl industry), and south to the indented coastline and pine-clad islands near **Kashikojima.** The bottom hook of the peninsula, around to Goza via Daio, has some of the prettiest coves on the Ago Bay, each one home to oyster nets and small groups of fishing boats.

Beyond Ise-Shima, the **Kii Peninsula** has magnificent marine scenery, coastal fishing villages, beach resorts, and the temple mountain of Koya-san. Wakayama Prefecture, which constitutes much of the Kii Peninsula, has a population of only

1 million, and life here moves at a relaxed pace. From Shingu you can reach all three great shrines of the Kumano Kodo pilgrimage route. Nearby Yoshino-Kumano National Park has pristine gorges, holy mountains, and another ancient Buddhist site at Yoshino-san, where gorgeous hillside sakura flower in early April.

Wakayama Prefecture is also home to the town of **Koya-san,** the mountain-side base of Shingon Buddhism. Founded by the monk Kobo Daishi (aka Kukai) in the ninth century, Koya today extends to 117 temples, many of which offer temple lodgings where travelers can try seasonal *shojin-ryori* vegetarian cuisine and join monks for their morning rituals. The UNESCO-designated sites here include Shingon's head temple, Kongobuji, which is best known for its Zen rock garden and priceless screen-door paintings.

# Planning

## Getting Here and Around

In Nagoya subways are the easiest way to get around. Outside the city the extensive rail network will take you to most places of interest, although buses may be necessary on the remote Kii Peninsula.

### AIR

Nagoya's compact, user-friendly Chubu Centrair International Airport (referred to locally as just "Centrair") serves overseas flights and is a hub for domestic travel. Many major airlines have offices in downtown Nagoya, 45 km (28 miles) northeast of the airport, including Japan Airlines (JAL) and All Nippon Airways (ANA), both of which fly from Nagoya to most major Japanese cities. The Meitetsu μSky Limited Express train makes the 28-minute run between Centrair and Nagoya Station for ¥1,250. This price includes a "first-class" seat-reservation fee.

## AIRLINE CONTACTS All Nippon Airways.
☎ *0570/029–767 in Japan (Mileage Club Members only), 0570/029–222 in Japan (non-Mileage Club members)* ⊕ *www. ana.co.jp.* **Japan Airlines.** ☎ *0120/747–222* ⊕ *www.jal.com.*

## AIRPORT CONTACTS Chubu Centrair International Airport.
✉ *1–1 Centrair, Tokoname* ☎ *0569/38–1195 daily 6:40 am–10 pm* ⊕ *www.centrair.jp.* **Meitetsu Airport Limited Express.** ☎ *052/582–5151 weekdays 8–7, weekends 8–6* ⊕ *www.meitetsu.co.jp.*

## BUS
Highway buses operated by JR and Meitetsu connect Nagoya with major cities, including Tokyo and Kyoto. The fare is half that of the Shinkansen trains, but the journey takes three times longer.

City buses crisscross Nagoya, mostly running either north–south or east–west. The basic fare is ¥210—pay when you get on the bus. A one-day bus pass costs ¥620; a one-day pass for the Me-guru loop bus, which stops at many of Nagoya's attractions, is ¥500; and a combination bus-subway pass costs ¥870.

Detailed information on bus travel can be collected at the tourist information office in the center of Nagoya Station, and day passes and combination passes are available at ticket machines in bus terminals and subway stations.

## BUS CONTACTS JR Tokai Bus.
☎ *0570/048–939* ⊕ *www.jrtbinm.co.jp.* **Meitetsu Highway Bus.** ☎ *052/582–0489* ⊕ *www.meitetsu-bus.co.jp.* **Nagoya City Transportation Bureau.** ☎ *052/522–0111* ⊕ *www.kotsu.city.nagoya.jp.*

## CAR
The journey on the two-lane expressway from Tokyo to Nagoya takes about 5 hours; from Kyoto allow 2½ hours. Major highways also connect Nagoya to Nagano, Takayama, Kanazawa, and Nara. Japanese highways are jam-prone, with holiday season traffic jams out of Tokyo sometimes reaching 100 km (60 miles) in length. Signposting is confusing, so be sure to get a car with satellite navigation or a good road map.

Wide main streets make Nagoya relatively easy to navigate. Road signs in the city often point to places out of town, however, so a detailed map is advised.

## TRAIN
Frequent bullet trains run between Tokyo and Nagoya. The ride takes 1 hour, 58 minutes on the *Hikari* Shinkansen and 2½ hours on the slower *Kodama* Shinkansen. The trip west to Kyoto takes 40 to 50 minutes, and Shin-Osaka is about 1 hour. JR Passes are not accepted on the faster *Nozomi* Shinkansen, which does the journey from Tokyo in 1 hour, 35 minutes. Less-expensive Limited Express trains proceed from Nagoya into and across the Japan Alps—to Takayama, Toyama, Matsumoto, and Nagano.

# Hotels

Nagoya's lodging ranges from ryokan (traditional Japanese inns) and efficient business hotels to large luxury palaces. At Koya-san, temple accommodation is a fascinating experience. Furnishings in temples ranges from ryokan-like luxury to spartan but sufficient, and the food is strictly vegetarian. You will probably be invited to attend the early-morning prayer service and fire ceremonies—an experience well worth getting up for. In addition to holidays, hotels can be busy in October and November owing to conferences held in Nagoya and autumn foliage outside the city. The large hotels in downtown Nagoya have English-speaking staff, but (if you haven't booked hotels in advance) it's advisable to ask at the tourist information center to make reservations for you outside the city.

# Festivals

Nagoya and the surrounding cities host a wide variety of *matsuri* (festivals) throughout the year. Running the gamut from chaotic to tranquil and beautiful to bizarre, these events bring the culture and traditions of the area to life in ways that castles, museums, and temples cannot. The tourist information center or Nagoya International Center can provide lists of upcoming festivals, which are free.

## February
**Hadaka (Naked) Festival.** For 1,250 years, thousands of men aged 25 and 42 (unlucky ages in Japan) have braved the winter cold wearing nothing but *fundoshi* (loincloths). Their goal, in an event that regularly results in serious injury to participants, is to touch the *shin otoko* (the one truly "naked man") and transmit their bad spirits to him before he reaches Konomiya shrine and submits to cleansing rituals. Eagerness to achieve this task often leads to stampedes, but the crowds of more than 100,000 are well protected from harm. The festival is held at varying dates in February, on January 13 of the lunar year—contact Nagoya City Tourist Information Center in JR Nagoya Station for details. Konomiya Station is 15 minutes north of Nagoya on the Meitetsu Gifu Line, and the shrine is a 10-minute walk from the station.

## March
**Honen Festival.** The 1,500-year-old Tagata-jinja in Komaki is home to one of Japan's male fertility festivals. On March 15 large crowds gather to watch and take pictures of a 6-foot, 885-pound *owasegata* (phallus) being carried between two shrines and offered to the *kami* (god) for peace and a good harvest. The festival starts at 10 am and climaxes with face-size "lucky" rice cakes being tossed into the crowd just before 4 pm. Visitors who get hungry before then will find plenty of street stalls selling phallic-shape snacks, including chocolate-coated bananas. The closest station is Tagata-jinja-mae on the Meitetsu Komaki Line. Change at Inuyama if you are traveling from Nagoya. The train takes one hour.

## July
**Owari Tsushima Tenno Festival.** The main feature of this charming, low-key event is five wood-and-straw boats decorated with 365 paper lanterns (for the days of the year) arranged into a circular shape and 12 more (representing the months) hanging from a mast. The 500-year-old festival occurs over two days on the fourth weekend in July. Haunting traditional music accompanies the boats as they drift around the river and the lanterns and fireworks reflect in the water. Tsushima is 25 minutes west of Nagoya on the Meitetsu Bisai Line. Follow the crowds west from the station for about 15 minutes to the shrine and festival area.

## August
**Domannaka.** More than 20,000 dancers in troupes of up to 150 each arrive from all over Japan to take over Nagoya's public spaces. Started in 1999, this energetic festival has rapidly gained popularity. It mixes hip-hop beats with spiced-up traditional dance moves and colorful costumes. Domannaka, or Domatsuri to give its local nickname, takes place over a weekend in late August.

# Restaurants

Restaurants in Nagoya and on the peninsulas are slightly less expensive than in Tokyo. Your cheapest options are the noodle shops, *donburi* (rice bowl) chains, and *kaiten* (revolving) sushi and curry houses. Nagoya's coffee shops are also known for their cheaper-than-usual morning sets, where for not much more than the price of a regular cup of coffee you will also get some toast, a sandwich, or a small portion of bacon and eggs. Franchised restaurants often have English alongside Japanese on their menus, but don't expect the staff to know more than a few words.

## RESTAURANT AND HOTEL PRICES

Restaurant prices are the average cost of a main course at dinner or, if dinner is not served, at lunch. Hotel prices are the lowest cost of a standard double room in high season. Restaurant and hotel reviews have been shortened. For full information, visit Fodors.com. *For a short course on accommodations in Japan, see Accommodations in Travel Smart.*

| What It Costs in Yen | | | |
|---|---|---|---|
| $ | $$ | $$$ | $$$$ |
| **RESTAURANTS** | | | |
| under ¥1,500 | ¥1,500– ¥3,000 | ¥3,001– ¥5,000 | over ¥5,000 |
| **HOTELS** | | | |
| under ¥12,000 | ¥12,000– ¥18,000 | ¥18,001– ¥22,000 | over ¥22,000 |

# Visitor Information

The **Nagoya International Center** is a worthwhile stop on any Nagoya itinerary. Multilingual staff have a wealth of information on Nagoya and the surrounding area, and the center publishes a monthly newsletter, *Nagoya Calendar,* which gives up-to-date advice, information, and event listings in English. It is one stop from JR Nagoya Station on the Sakura-dori subway line or a seven-minute walk through the underground walkway that follows the line.

**CONTACT Nagoya International Center.** ✉ *1–47–1 Nagono, Nakamura-ku* ☎ *052/581–0100* ⊕ *www.nic-nagoya.or.jp/en.*

# When to Go

Spring is the most popular season, especially early April when cherry trees bloom. Nagoya gets extremely hot and humid in July and August, but in autumn the trees turn color under blue skies. Sea breezes make coastal areas bearable in summer. Cold winds blow into Nagoya from the ski grounds to the north in winter, but Wakayama Prefecture remains mild. The weather can be changeable along the coastline of Ise-Shima, and the area is occasionally hit hard by typhoons in the July to October storm season. If you're heading inland on the Kii Peninsula be prepared for hilly terrain.

# Nagoya (名古屋)

*366 km (227 miles) west of Tokyo, 190 km (118 miles) east of Osaka, 148 km (92 miles) east of Kyoto.*

In 1612 Shogun Ieyasu Tokugawa established Nagoya by permitting his ninth son to build a castle here. Industry and merchant houses sprang up in the shadow of this magnificent fortress, as did pleasure quarters for samurai. Supported by taxing the rich harvests of the surrounding Nobi plain, the Tokugawa family used the castle as its power center for the next 250 years.

After the Meiji Restoration in 1868, when Japan began trade with the West in earnest, Nagoya developed rapidly. When the harbor opened to international shipping in 1907, Nagoya's industrial growth accelerated, and by the 1930s it was supporting Japanese expansionism in China with munitions and aircraft. This choice of industry was Nagoya's downfall; very little of the city was left standing after World War II.

Less than two months after the war, ambitious and extensive reconstruction plans were laid, and Nagoya began its remarkable comeback as an industrial metropolis. Planners laid down a grid system, with wide avenues intersecting at right angles. Hisaya-odori, a broad avenue with a park in its 328-foot-wide median, bisects the city. At Nagoya's center is an imposing 590-foot-high television tower (useful for getting your bearings). Nagoya Castle is north of the tower, Atsuta Shrine a way off to the south, Higashiyama Park east, and the JR Station west. The Sakae subway station serves as the center of the downtown commercial area. Today Nagoya is home to 2.3 million people living in a 326-square-km (126-square-mile) area.

## GETTING HERE AND AROUND
### BUS
The golden **Nagoya Sightseeing Route Bus,** known to locals as the Me-guru, provides cheap tours of the city. The service runs Tuesday through Sunday on a loop from Nagoya Station, via Toyota Commemorative Museum of Industry and Technology, Noritake Garden, Nagoya-jo, the Tokugawa Art Museum, and Sakae. A single ticket is ¥210, while a hop-on, hop-off ticket for the day, which can be bought on the bus, costs ¥500 and includes discounts of 10% to 20% on most major attractions. The buses run once or twice hourly on weekdays, two or three times per week on weekends, but don't run on Monday when many attractions are closed.

**CONTACT Nagoya Sightseeing Route Bus.** ☎ 052/521–8990 ⊕ www.nagoya-info.jp/en/useful/meguru.

### TAXI
Taxis are parked at all major stations and hotels. Elsewhere it is still far easier to wave one down on the street than to call one of the Japanese-speaking reservation numbers. The initial fare is typically ¥450 for the first kilometer, then ¥80 for each additional 231 meters. A ride from Nagoya Station to Nagoya-jo costs about ¥1,500. For English-speaking taxi service and charters, try MK Taxi.

**CONTACT MK Taxi Nagoya.** ✉ Nagoya ☎ 052/912–5489 ⊕ www.mktaxi-japan.com/taxi.

### SUBWAY
All Nagoya's stations have bilingual maps, and many trains have English announcements. The Higashiyama Line snakes from the west into JR Nagoya Station and then goes due east, cutting through the city center at Sakae. The Meijo Line runs in a loop, passing through the city center at downtown Sakae. A spur line, the Meito, connects Kanayama to Nagoya Port. The Tsurumai Line runs north–south through the city, then shoots east from Osu Kannon to cross the city center. A fourth line, the Sakura-dori, cuts through the city center from the JR Station, paralleling the east–west section of the Higashiyama Line. The basic fare is ¥200. A one-day pass for Nagoya's subways costs ¥760, while a combination bus-subway pass is ¥870 on weekdays and ¥620 (Weekend Eco Pass) on weekends or national holidays. All the passes can be bought at station ticket machines.

Nagoya's subway system is user-friendly, with signs and announcements in English, and it can get you to almost all places of interest in the city.

The JR trains are the easiest for jumping on and off, but they do not serve all destinations. Meitetsu and Kintetsu stations are sometimes lacking in English signage, though Meitetsu prints a handy English-language guide to their network with instructions on how to purchase

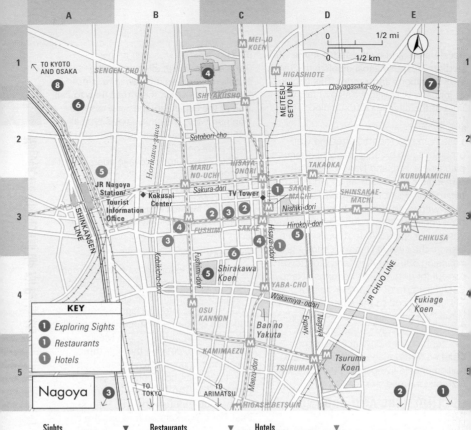

## Nagoya

**KEY**
- 1 Exploring Sights
- 1 Restaurants
- 1 Hotels

**Sights** ▼

1 Arimatsu-Narumi
  Tie-Dyeing Museum..... **E5**
2 Atsuta Shrine............ **E5**
3 Legoland Japan
  Resort.................... **A5**
4 Nagoya Castle .......... **C1**
5 Nagoya City
  Science Museum........ **C4**
6 Noritake Garden ........ **A2**
7 Tokugawa Art
  Museum ................. **E1**
8 Toyota Commemorative
  Museum of Industry
  and Technology ......... **A1**

**Restaurants** ▼

1 Craftbeer Keg
  Nagoya................... **C3**
2 Ibasho.................... **C3**
3 Kisoji Nishikiten......... **C3**
4 Mokumoku Kaze
  no Budo.................. **C3**
5 Sekai no
  Yama-chan Honten..... **D3**
6 Yamamotoya
  Sohonke ................. **C3**

**Hotels** ▼

1 the b nagoya ............ **C3**
2 Dormy Inn Premium
  Nagoya Sakae .......... **C3**
3 Hilton Nagoya.......... **B3**
4 Nagoya Kanko Hotel ... **B3**
5 Nine Hours
  Nagoya station......... **A2**

tickets. You can pick up a copy at Meitetsu Nagoya Station or Chubu Centrair International Airport.

**JR Nagoya Station** is like a small city, with a variety of shops in, under, and around the station complex, including a narrow basement alley called Nagoya Umaimon-dori (名古屋うまいもん通り) that has a dozen restaurants specializing in regional flavors. The main **Nagoya City Tourist Information Center** is in the station's central concourse. English-speaking staff can supply sightseeing information, subway maps, and details of upcoming events. Smaller information centers are in three other parts of the city—Sakae, Kanayama, and Nagoya Port.

**CONTACT JR Nagoya Station.** ⊠ *1–1–4 Meieki, Nagoya* ☎ *050/3772–3910 daily 6 am–midnight* ⊕ *www.jr-central.co.jp.*

### VISITOR INFORMATION

**CONTACTS Nagoya City Tourist Information Center.** ⊠ *1–4–1 Meieki, Nagoya Station, Nakamura-ku* ☎ *052/541–4301.* **Nagoya Port Tourist Information Center.** ⊠ *1–9 Minato-cho, Minato-ku ⊕ In Garden Wharf next to Nagoya-ko subway station* ☎ *052/654–7000.* **Sakae Tourist Information Center.** ⊠ *Oasis 21 Bus Station and Shopping Center, 1–1–1 Higashi-sakura, Higashi-ku* ☎ *052/963–5252.*

## ⊙ Sights

### Arimatsu-Narumi Tie-Dyeing Museum
(有松・鳴海絞会館; *Arimatsu-Narumi Shibori Kaikan*)

**OTHER MUSEUM** | Traditional *shibori* (tie-dyed cotton) has been produced in this area for more than 400 years. Here you can learn about the history of the dyeing technique and see demonstrations of the production process. The museum sells samples of the cloth, which features striking white designs on the deepest indigo, as well as clothing, tablecloths, and other items. You can also try making your own tie-dyed souvenirs at one of the regular workshops, which require

a reservation and have an extra cost. Arimatsu Station is 25 minutes south of Nagoya on the Meitetsu Nagoya Line. ⊠ *3008 Arimatsu, Midori-ku* ☎ *052/621–0111* ⊕ *www.shibori-kaikan.com/en* ☑ *¥300; workshops from ¥1,800.*

### Atsuta Shrine (熱田神宮; *Atsuta Jingu*)
**TEMPLE** | A shrine has stood at the site of Atsuta Jingu for 1,700 years. After Ise, this is the country's most important Shinto shrine. The Treasure House (宝物館; Homotsukan) is reputed to house one of the emperor's three imperial regalia—the Grass-Mowing Sword (Kusanagi-no-Tsurugi)—and although it is never on public display, there are many other worthy artifacts to see. Nestled among 1,000 year old trees, making it easy to spot from the train, the shrine is an oasis of tradition in the midst of modern industrialism. Dozens of major festivals and religious events are held here each year. From Meitetsu Nagoya Station take the Meitetsu Nagoya Line south to Jingumae Station. The shrine is across the road from the West Exit. ⊠ *1–1–1 Jingu, Atsuta-ku* ☎ *052/671–4151* ⊕ *www.atsutajingu.or.jp* ☑ *Shrine free, Treasure House ¥500* ☉ *Treasure House closed last Wed. and Thurs. each month.*

### Legoland Japan Resort
(レゴランドジャパン)

**AMUSEMENT PARK/CARNIVAL** | **FAMILY** | When Legoland Japan opened in the Nagoya port area in 2017 it gave the region something to rival the Universal Studios Japan amusement park in Osaka and Disney Resorts just outside Tokyo. Aimed at kids aged 2 to 12 (and their families), the park brings together more than 40 rides spread across seven zones, including the medieval-themed Knights Kingdom and its Dragon roller coaster and water fights in the Pirate Shores zone. As you might expect from Lego, there are also plenty of models to check out—10,000 in all using a total of 17 million Lego bricks. ⊠ *2–2–1 Kinjo Futa, Minato-ku*

# Coming Soon: Ghibli Park

Building on the success of the Ghibli Museum in Tokyo, legendary animators Studio Ghibli, the people behind films such as *My Neighbor Totoro* and *Spirited Away*, have announced a new theme park in Aichi Earth Expo Memorial Park, about 15 km (9 miles) east of Nagoya. Ghibli Park will consist of five zones, three opening in November 2022 and the remaining two slated for autumn 2023. As of this writing, published details are scant, but the breadcrumbs that have been released have Ghibli's legions of fans salivating. Visitors in the first year can check out exhibits on Ghibli films in the Ghibli's Grand Warehouse Zone, then head to the Hill of Youth Zone for the World Emporium, the antique shop from the Ghibli film *Whisper of the Heart*. Full details are yet to be announced for the Dondoko Forest Zone that also opens in November 2022, and the subsequent Valley of Witches and Mononoke Forest Zones. Look out for more at ⊕ *ghibli-park.jp/en.*

☏ *050/5840–0505* ⊕ *www.legoland.jp/en* 🎫 *¥4,600 for a day pass.*

**Nagoya Castle** (名古屋城; *Nagoya-jo*)
CASTLE/PALACE | The main keep of this Nagoya landmark, a 1950s ferro-concrete reconstruction of the 1612 original, was closed in May 2018 to be pulled down and replaced by a fully wooden reconstruction by December 2022. Or that was the plan. As of March 2022, the old keep is still standing, but nobody can enter. However, the castle ground's are still more than worth a visit for the painstakingly rebuilt Honmaru Palace, which was unveiled in 2018. Made mostly of *hinoki* (Japanese cypress), it is richly decorated with elaborate wall and screen-door paintings, intricate wood carvings, decorative metal fittings, and fine lacquering. It's a modern-day masterpiece of traditional Japanese crafting. Check out the ceilings as you get deeper into the palace, as their design becomes increasingly more complex to reflect the higher status of those allowed into the inner sanctums. Nagoya Castle's east gate is one block north of the Shiyakusho (市役所; City Hall) subway station. If you get hungry while there, just across from the castle's east entrance is a new cluster of a dozen or so restaurants and cafes, collectively called Kinshachi Yokocho. ✉ *1–1 Honmaru, Nishi-ku* ☏ *052/231–1700* ⊕ *www.nagoyajo.city. nagoya.jp* 🎫 *¥500.*

**Nagoya City Science Museum** (名古屋市科学館; *Nagoya-shi Kagakukan*)
OTHER MUSEUM | FAMILY | Given a major makeover in 2011, the seven-story Nagoya City Science Museum is packed with fun, hands-on attractions designed to teach kids of all ages about science. The highlights are a planetarium—Japan's biggest—and several visually impressive "labs" where you can experience a tornado, learn about electricity, or feel the Arctic cold. ✉ *2–17–1 Sakae, Naka-ku* ☏ *052/201–4486* ⊕ *www.ncsm.city.nagoya.jp/en* 🎫 *Museum only ¥400, museum and planetarium ¥800* 🕐 *Closed Mon. and 3rd Fri.*

**Noritake Garden**
(ノリタケの森; *Noritake-no-Mori*)
FACTORY | Delicate colors and intricate hand-painted designs characterize the china of Noritake, one of the world's largest manufacturers of porcelain. Its garden complex includes a craft center—effectively a mini-factory where workers demonstrate the 15-step manufacturing process from modeling to glazing to hand painting. You can even paint a design and

Honmaru Palace within Nagoya Castle is known for its elaborate screen-door paintings.

transfer it to a piece of china, or decorate a porcelain dinosaur. China-painting workshops run from 10 to 4, but the cost does not include the price of shipping your piece once it has been fired (only plates can be shipped overseas). The upper floors house a small museum displaying "Old Noritake" works with art nouveau and art deco influences. A free Welcome Center shows the diverse industrial applications of ceramics, from circuit boards to racing helmets. There's the odd bargain to be found in the outlet section of the company shop. Noritake Garden is a 15-minute walk north of JR Nagoya Station or five minutes from Exit 2 of the Kamejima subway station, and can easily be combined with a trip to the nearby Toyota Commemorative Museum. ⊠ 3–1–36 Noritake-Shinmachi, Nishi-ku ☎ 052/561–7114 ⊕ www.noritake.co.jp/ eng/mori ⊠ Garden free; ¥500 Craft Center; ¥800 including Toyota Commemorative Museum; ¥2,000 to ¥3,500 china-painting workshops ⊙ Closed Mon.

**Tokugawa Art Museum** (徳川美術館; Tokugawa Bijutsukan)

HISTORY MUSEUM | The seldom-displayed 12th-century hand scrolls of The Tale of Genji, widely recognized as the world's first novel, are housed here. Even when the scrolls are not available, beautiful relics of the lifestyle of the aristocratic samurai class—including swords and armor, tea-ceremony artifacts, Noh masks, clothing, and furnishings—fascinate visitors. If you're visiting specifically to see the scrolls, check out the Hosa Library rooms, which house an incredible collection of other ancient scrolls and texts (some 110,000 in all), some dating to the 8th century. If you've got time, it's worth paying an additional ¥150 for entry to the adjacent Tokugawaen (徳川園), an attractive Japanese garden modeled in the Edo style. Tokugawa Art Museum is a 10-minute walk south of Exit 3 of Ozone Station, which is on the Meijo subway line and the JR Chuo Line. It's also served by the Me-guru bus, which gives a ¥200 discount on admission for bus pass holders. ⊠ 1017 Tokugawa-cho,

*Higashi-ku* ☎ *052/935–6262* 🌐 *www.tokugawa-art-museum.jp/en* 🎟 *¥1,400* 🕓 *Closed Mon., and late Dec.–Jan. 3.*

**Toyota Commemorative Museum of Industry and Technology** (トヨタ産業技術記念館; *Sangyo-gijutsu Kinenkan*)
**OTHER MUSEUM** | **FAMILY** | Housed in the distinctive brick buildings of the company's original factory, this museum is dedicated to the rise of Nagoya's most famous company. Toyota's textile-industry origins are explored in the first of two immense halls, with an amazing selection of looms illustrating the evolution of spinning and weaving technologies over the last 200 years. The second, even larger hall focuses on the company's move into auto manufacturing, with exhibits including the Model AA, Toyota's first mass-production automobile. In the Technoland zone, kids can try out a wind tunnel, play with water and air jets, operate a virtual weaving machine, and test out mini electric cars. The museum is a 20-minute walk north of JR Nagoya Station or three minutes from JR Sako Station. ✉ *4–1–35 Noritake-Shinmachi, Nishi-ku* ☎ *052/551–6115* 🌐 *www.tcmit.org* 🎟 *¥500; ¥800 includes Noritake Garden* 🕓 *Closed Mon.*

## 🍴 Restaurants

Nagoya Station and Sakae have the highest concentrations of restaurants in the area.

**Craftbeer Keg Nagoya** (ケグ名古屋)
**$$$** | **ECLECTIC** | The focus of this laid-back eatery near Hisaya Odori Station is craft beer, with 13 taps pouring a frequently changing lineup of well-handled microbrews, mostly from Japan, such as excellent Ise Kadoya brews from Ise. To go with the beer, there's a menu that includes wild boar sausages, lamb and garlic dumplings, and pizza. **Known for:** good pizzas; meat dishes that pair well with beer; Japanese craft brews. [$] *Average main: ¥5,000* ✉ *1–10–13 Higashisakura, Higashi-ku* ☎ *052/971–8211* 🌐 *kegnagoya.owst.jp.*

**Ibasho** (いば昇)
**$$$** | **JAPANESE** | This fabulous old wooden restaurant specializes in grilled eel (*unagi*), which fills the restaurant with a mouthwatering, charcoal-grill aroma. Some of the seating is at low tables on raised tatami-mat flooring, though there are also tables and chairs overlooking a small Japanese garden. **Known for:** charming rustic interiors; English menu; hitsumabushi, a Nagoya specialty featuring chopped eel smothered in miso sauce and served on rice. [$] *Average main: ¥3,200* ✉ *3–13–22 Nishiki, Naka-ku* ☎ *052/951–1166* 🌐 *www.ibashou.jp* 💳 *No credit cards* 🕓 *Closed Sun., and the 2nd and 3rd Mon. of each month.*

**Kisoji Nishikiten** (木曽路 錦店)
**$$$$** | **JAPANESE** | Come here for *shabu-shabu*—thinly sliced beef and vegetables that you boil in broth in the center of your table and then dip into various sauces before eating. The set courses aren't cheap, but the quality makes this restaurant worth a splurge. **Known for:** traditional service; good sukiyaki and sashimi sets; Matsusaka beef shabu-shabu. [$] *Average main: ¥9,000* ✉ *3–20–15 Nishiki, Naka-ku* ☎ *052/951–3755* 🌐 *www.kisoji.co.jp/kisoji/english.*

**Mokumoku Kaze no Budo** (モクモク風の葡萄)
**$$** | **JAPANESE** | In a perfect world, all school and office canteens would be a bit more like this rustic restaurant in La Chic mall in Sakae. For a reasonable set price, you get all you can eat from a generously stocked buffet, which explains why it is always busy and lively. **Known for:** locally sourced produce; all-you-can-drink options; healthy dishes. [$] *Average main: ¥2,500* ✉ *La Chic, 3–6–1 Sakae, 7th fl., Naka-ku* ☎ *052/241–0909.*

### Sekai no Yama-chan Honten (世界の山ちゃん 本店)

$$ | **JAPANESE** | Peppery *tebasaki* (deep-fried chicken wings) are the specialty at the main branch of Nagoya's best-known izakaya chain, though you can also order sashimi, fried noodles and other favorites. The prices are affordable, and it always attracts a lively crowd. **Known for:** Taiwan yakisoba (fried noodles); Nagoya classics; deep-fried chicken wings. $ *Average main: ¥2,500* ⊠ *4–9–6 Sakae, Naka-ku* ☎ *052/242–1342* ⊕ *www. yamachan.co.jp* ⊗ *No lunch.*

### Yamamotoya Sohonke (山本屋総本家)

$ | **JAPANESE** | *Misonikomi udon* (noodles in a miso-based broth with green onions and mushrooms) dominates the menu at this simple restaurant. A big, steaming bowl of this hearty, cold-chasing specialty is usually filling enough, though you can pay a little extra to top it off with something like a raw egg, or opt for a side dish like yakitori chicken. **Known for:** nice, near-rustic interiors; friendly service; misonokomi udon noodles, a regional favorite. $ *Average main: ¥1,100* ⊠ *3–12–19 Sakae, Naka-ku* ☎ *052/241–5617* ⊕ *yamamotoya.co.jp* ⊟ *No credit cards* ⊗ *Closed Tues. and Wed.*

## 🛏 Hotels

Nagoya's hotels are concentrated in three major areas: the district around JR Nagoya Station, downtown Fushimi and Sakae, and the Nagoya Castle area.

### the b nagoya (ザ・ビー名古屋)

$ | **HOTEL** | The Nagoya branch of this business hotel chain combines an excellent central location in Sakae (on Hisaya-odori) with good value rates. **Pros:** good discounts booking online; good rates on singles for solo travelers; great location. **Cons:** rooms will be too compact for some; not many facilities; can get a bit noisy. $ *Rooms from: ¥6,200* ⊠ *4–15–23 Sakae, Naka-ku* ☎ *052/264–1732* ⊕ *en.*

theb-hotels.com/theb/nagoya ⊅ *219 rooms* ⦿ *Free Breakfast.*

### Dormy Inn Premium Nagoya Sakae (ドーミーインPREMIUM名古屋栄)

$ | **HOTEL** | This dependable, budget business hotel's Nagoya outlet features all the usual Dormy touches aimed to please weary business travelers, including communal hot-spring baths, free late-night ramen, complimentary ice bars after bathing, and all-you-can drink coffee in the lobby. **Pros:** decent breakfast for an extra fee; great value for what you get; on-site hot-spring baths. **Cons:** rooms are small; rooms have showers but no baths; can be noisy. $ *Rooms from: ¥11,400* ⊠ *2–20–1 Nishiki, Naka-ku* ☎ *052/231–5480* ⊕ *www.hotespa.net/ hotels/nagoyasakae* ⦿ *No Meals.*

### Hilton Nagoya (ヒルトン名古屋)

$$$$ | **HOTEL** | This large business hotel always gets good guest reviews for service and location, and it's a reliable option in Nagoya. **Pros:** attentive and flexible staff; convenient location; excellent restaurants. **Cons:** typical upper-end business-hotel atmosphere with no unique character; local business-hotel brands are cheaper; can fill up with conference guests. $ *Rooms from: ¥29,925* ⊠ *1–3–3 Sakae, Naka-ku* ☎ *052/212–1111* ⊕ *www.hilton.com* ⊅ *460 rooms* ⦿ *Free Breakfast.*

### ★ Nagoya Kanko Hotel (名古屋観光ホテル)

$$$$ | **HOTEL** | The imperial family and visiting baseball teams are among those served by the city's oldest hotel, which is also a haunt for celebrities in search of a little privacy. **Pros:** exceptional service; great selection of dining options; great central location. **Cons:** restaurants and bars are expensive; can fill up quickly when big conferences are on; old-fashioned elegance won't be to everyone's taste. $ *Rooms from: ¥25,000* ⊠ *1–19–30 Nishiki, Naka-ku* ☎ *052/231–7711* ⊕ *www.nagoyakankohotel.co.jp* ⊅ *342 rooms* ⦿ *No Meals.*

**Nine Hours Nagoya Station** (ナインアワーズ名古屋駅; *Nain awazu nagoya-eki*)
**$ | HOTEL** | Two minutes from Nagoya Station, Nine Hours is a modern take on the capsule hotel, designed for short stays on a tight budget. **Pros:** unlike most capsule hotels, multi-night stays are possible; great value for backpackers or solo travelers; convenient location. **Cons:** can be noisy; almost no amenities or facilities; the sleeping pods aren't for the claustrophobic. [$] *Rooms from: ¥3,100* ✉ *2–42–2 Meieki, Nakamura-ku* ☎ *052/526–1665* 🌐 *ninehours.co.jp/nagoya-station* 🛏 *156 sleeping pods* 🍴 *No Meals.*

## Nightlife

Sakae has a high concentration of bars and clubs appealing to pleasure seekers of all stripes. For clubs, expect to pay between ¥1,000 and ¥3,000 for admission (usually including a couple of drinks).

**Caravan**
**BARS** | On Hirokoji-dori, opposite the reverse side of the Nagoya Kanko Hotel, this second-floor bar with friendly, young staff specializes in craft gin and craft beers (in cans and bottles) from around the world. They also cook decent pizzas, and have sports on screens around the bar. ✉ *1–4–10 Sakae, Naka-ku* ☎ *052/265–9372.*

**iD Café**
**DANCE CLUBS** | A young crowd gathers at this wild, five-floor club, where the music ranges from techno and trance to reggae and hip-hop. Admission varies by day and gender (men pay more) and includes one to four free drinks (men get more of those). ✉ *Mitsukoshi Bldg., 3–1–15 Sakae, Naka-ku* ☎ *052/251–0382* 🌐 *www.idcafe.info.*

**Marumikanko Building** (丸美観光ビル)
**LIVE MUSIC** | Two of the city's best clubs can be found in this building, two blocks south of Hirokoji-dori: Club JB's and Sound Bar MiRAi. ✉ *4–3–15 Sakae, Naka-ku* ☎ *052/684–8077.*

## Activities

In Nagoya you will find Japanese sports fans just as entertaining as the action on the field. Ask at the tourist information center about upcoming events and where to buy tickets.

### BASEBALL

**Chunichi Dragons**
**BASEBALL & SOFTBALL** | The Chunichi Dragons play home games at the 40,500-capacity Nagoya Dome. Two leagues of six teams make up Japanese professional baseball, and the Dragons have won the Central League pennant eight times and the Japan Series twice. In recent years the team is in a groove, reaching the Japan Series in 2004 and 2006 before finally winning it—for the first time since 1954—in 2007. They came close again in 2010 and 2011, losing both Japan Series in game seven, but since then have reached the post-season just once. Fans here are a bit different—they sing well-drilled songs for each of the batters on their own team, but sit in stony silence when the opposing team is at bat. The season runs from late March to October, and other than when a big team such as the Yomiuri Giants or Hanshin Tigers is in town, tickets are usually available at the stadium, but they can be bought in advance at local 7-Eleven, Lawson, and Family Mart convenience stores. ✉ *Nagoya Dome, 1–1–1 Daikominami, Higashi-ku* 🌐 *dragons.jp* 🎫 *¥1,600–¥7,200.*

### SOCCER

**Nagoya Grampus**
**SOCCER** | The remarkably loyal fans who turn up in the thousands to cheer on Nagoya Grampus finally had something to cheer about in 2010, as the team romped to a first J-League Division One title. Until then, Grampus had a reputation as perennial underachievers, always seeming to hang around midtable in J-League 1—despite having had star players such as Gary Lineker and Dragan

Stojkovic (now the head coach)—and managing a couple of Emperor's Cup wins in the 1990s. But despite being runners-up in 2011, midtable mediocrity has once again returned, with the only highlight a sole triumph in the not-so-glittering J-League Cup in 2021. From March to December they currently play home games at the futuristic 40,000-seat Toyota Stadium, 40 kilometers southeast of Nagoya in Toyota city. In previous seasons, they've also played in the more conveniently located 27,000-seat Paloma Mizuho Stadium in Nagoya. ✉ *Toyota Stadium, 7–2 Sengokucho, Toyota City* ⊕ *nagoya-grampus.jp* ✆ *¥2,800–¥8,600* ☞ *Tickets can sometimes be bought at the stadium, but it's safer to buy in advance via the the J-League website: www.jleague.jp/en/ticket.*

## SUMO

**Nagoya Grand Sumo Tournament** (大相撲名古屋場所; *Oozumou Nagoya Basho*)
**LOCAL SPORTS** | Over 15 days in mid-July Nagoya's Aichi Prefectural Gymnasium (aka Dolphin's Arena) hosts one of the three *honbasho* sumo tournaments held outside Tokyo each year. The arena holds 8,000 people, and you are almost guaranteed a good view of the *dohyo* (ring). Tickets, which start at ¥3,000, are often available on the day of the tournament, but it's better to book ahead. The venue is a two-minute walk from Exit 7 of the Shiyakusho subway station. ✉ *Aichi Prefectural Gymnasium, 1–1 Ninomaru, Naka-ku* ☎ *052/971–2516* ⊕ *www.sumo.or.jp.*

# Gifu (岐阜)

*30 km (18 miles) northwest of Nagoya.*

The city center spreads several blocks north from the JR and Meitetsu stations. Extensive rebuilding after World War II didn't create the prettiest place, but there is plenty going on. *Wagasa* (oiled paper umbrellas) are handmade in small family-owned shops, and *chochin* (paper

lanterns) and lacquered *uchiwa* fans are also produced locally. If you are interested in seeing these items being made, ask at the tourist information center for workshops that allow visitors.

However, Gifu's main attraction is its 1,300-year tradition of *ukai* fishing, which uses specially trained live cormorants to catch fish in the river. It's a sight to behold. While they are fishing, the birds' necks are banded so that they cannot swallow the fish they catch. Between May 11 and October 15, you can watch cormorant fishing from the banks of the river just east of Nagara Bridge at around 7:30 pm each evening. Or you can buy a ticket on one of about 130 boats to see the process up close. There's no fishing on the autumn full moon or on rare occasions when the water is deemed to be dangerously high.

## GETTING HERE AND AROUND

Gifu is a 20-minute ride on the JR Tokaido Line (¥470) or 30-minute ride on the Meitetsu Nagoya Line (¥570) from Nagoya. Gifu Park, in and around which most of the main attractions are centered, is 15 minutes (¥220) by bus (No. N32, N41, N80, or N86) or 30 minutes on foot north from JR Gifu Station.

A city tourist information office is on the second floor of the train station, just outside the ticket gates.

## TOURS

**Gifu City Cormorant Fishing Observation Boat Office** (岐阜市鵜飼観覧船事務所; *Gifu-shi Ukai Kanransen Jimusho*)
**BOAT TOURS** | During the season, you can buy a ticket on one of about 130 boats, each carrying between 15 and 50 spectators to watch the cormorant fishing up close. Allow two hours for an *ukai* outing—about 90 minutes to eat and drink (bring your own food if you haven't arranged for dinner) and a half-hour to watch the fishing. The boat trips depart at 6:15, 6:45, and 7:15 nightly; reservations, made through the Gifu City Cormorant

Fishing Observation Boat Office or the tourist information center, are essential. ✉ *2–1 Minato-machi, Gifu-shi* ☎ *058/262–0104* ⊕ *www.ukai-gifucity.jp/ukai/e* 🎫 *From ¥3,500.*

## VISITOR INFORMATION

**CONTACT Gifu Tourist Information Office.** ✉ *JR Gifu Station, 1–10–1 Hashimoto-cho, Gifu-shi* ☎ *058/262–4415* ⊕ *www.gifucvb.or.jp/en.*

# ◉ Sights

**Gifu City Museum of History** (岐阜市歴史博物館; *Gifu-shi Rekishi Hakubutsukan*) **HISTORY MUSEUM | FAMILY** | In Gifu Park, five minutes south of the cable-car station, sits this well-presented hands-on-museum, with exhibits covering Gifu from the prehistoric age through to feudal and pre-modern Japan. On the second floor you can dress up in traditional clothing and play old Japanese games such as *bansugoroku* (similar to backgammon). ✉ *2–18–1 Omiya-cho, Gifu-shi* ☎ *058/265–0010* ⊕ *www.rekihaku.gifu.gifu.jp/en* 🎫 *¥310* ⊙ *Closed Mon.*

**Gifu Castle** (岐阜城; *Gifu-jo*) **CASTLE/PALACE** | This castle, perched dramatically on top of Mt. Kinka, overlooks the city center and Nagara River. It's most striking when illuminated at night, backdropped by the mountain that changes color in fall. The current building dates from 1956 (the 16th-century structure was destroyed by an 1891 earthquake) and looks like a Japanese city office from the same era, though the view of Gifu from Mt. Kinka is worth the hike. A cable-car ride up from Gifu Park (¥1,100 round-trip) gets you to the castle in 10 minutes, or you can walk the 2.3-km (1½-mile) path to the 1,079-foot summit in about an hour. Take Bus N32, N41, N80, or N86 to Gifu Park (15 minutes, ¥220). ✉ *Kinkanzan, Gifu-shi* ☎ *058/263–4853* 🎫 *¥200.*

**Nagara River Ukai Museum** (長良川うかいミュージアム; *Nagaragawa Ukai Myujiamu*) **OTHER MUSEUM** | Learn about the history of *ukai* fishing, in which fishermen use live cormorants to catch river fish, and the lives of the odd-looking birds at the center of it, at this smart museum alongside the Nagara River. It's near the Ryokan Sugiyama, a six-minute walk from the Ukai-ya bus stop. ✉ *51–2 Nagara, Gifu-shi* ☎ *058/210–1555* ⊕ *ukaimuseum.jp* 🎫 *¥500* ⊙ *Closed Tues. and mid-Oct.–Apr.*

**Nawa Insect Museum** (名和昆虫博物館; *Nawa Konchu Hakubutsukan*) **SCIENCE MUSEUM | FAMILY** | Located in Gifu Park, this small museum houses disturbingly large beetles, colorful butterflies, and other bugs. ✉ *2–18 Omiya-cho, Gifu-shi* ☎ *058/263–0038* 🎫 *¥600* ⊙ *Closed Tues.–Thurs.*

**Seki Traditional Swordsmith Museum** (関鍛冶伝承館; *Seki Kaji Denshokan*) **HISTORY MUSEUM** | Seki has a 700-year-old sword-manufacturing heritage, and you'll appreciate the artistry and skill of Japanese sword smiths at this museum. Three types of metal are used to form blades, which are forged multiple times and then beaten into shape with a hammer. Demonstrations are held on the first Sunday of each month, except in October, when special displays occur during the Seki Cutlery Festival in the middle of the month. Seki is 30 minutes northeast of Gifu via the Meitetsu Minomachi Line. ✉ *9–1 Minamikasuga-cho, Sekimachi* ☎ *0575/23–3825* 🎫 *¥300* ⊙ *Closed Tues.*

**Shoho-ji Temple** (正法寺) **TEMPLE** | This small temple is rather run-down, but it houses Japan's third-largest Buddha, which you can often view with no other visitors in sight. This imposing incarnation of Shaka Nyorai (Great Buddha) is 45 feet tall and constructed of pasted-together paper *sutra* (prayers) coated with clay and stucco and then lacquered and gilded; it took 38 years

Nighttime cormorant fishing (called ukai) is a top attraction in Gifu.

to complete. From Gifu Park, walk two blocks south. ✉ *8 Daibutsu-cho, Gifu-shi* ☎ *058/264–2760* 🌐 *www.gifu daibutsu.com* 🎫 *¥200.*

## 🍴 Restaurants

**U no Iori U** (鵜の庵 鵜)

**$$** | **JAPANESE** | Cormorants strut around the Japanese garden outside this café owned by a family that upholds the 1,300-year-old *ukai* tradition. It's a block and a half west of Ryokan Sugiyama. **Known for:** relaxing place for coffee with garden views; close to many of Gifu's main attractions; locally caught, fresh sweetfish rice porridge called ayu-zosui. [$] *Average main: ¥1,500* ✉ *94–10 Naka-Ukai, Nagara, Gifu-shi* ☎ *058/232–2839* 💳 *No credit cards* 🕒 *Closed 2nd and 4th Sun.; 1st, 3rd, and 5th Mon. No dinner.*

## 🛏 Hotels

**Hotel Resol Gifu** (ホテルリソル岐阜)

**$** | **HOTEL** | Situated one block north of JR Gifu Station, this conveniently located hotel comes with larger-than-average Western-style rooms and some of the best views in Gifu. **Pros:** spacious rooms by local standards; lovely views; close to station. **Cons:** rather bland modern interiors; sterile atmosphere; often booked up well in advance. [$] *Rooms from: ¥11,800* ✉ *5–8 Nagazumi-cho, Gifu-shi* ☎ *058/262–9269* 🌐 *www.resol-gifu.com/en* 🛏 *119 rooms* 🍴 *Free Breakfast.*

**Ryokan Sugiyama** (旅館すぎ山)

**$$$$** | **B&B/INN** | Across the Nagara River from Gifu Castle, Ryokan Sugiyama is a tasteful blend of traditional and modern, offering large rooms with tatami floors and elegant shoji doors—ask for one overlooking the river. **Pros:** good food included in room rates; ideally positioned for ukai watchers; rooftop hot-spring bath with great views. **Cons:** not much to do at night nearby; needs booking well in advance in ukai season; pricey. $ *Rooms from: ¥25,300* ✉ *73–1 Nagara, Gifu-shi* ☎ *058/231–0161* ⊕ *www.gifu-sugiyama. com* �', 45 rooms ❙⊘❙ *All-Inclusive*.

# Inuyama (犬山)

*22 km (14 miles) east of Gifu, 32 km (20 miles) north of Nagoya.*

Inuyama sits along the Kiso River, on the border between Aichi and Gifu prefectures. A historically strategic site, the city changed hands several times during the Edo period. You can see cormorant fishing here from June 1 to October 15; tickets can be purchased at major hotels.

## GETTING HERE AND AROUND

Access Inuyama on the Meitetsu Kakami-gahara Line via Gifu or on the Meitetsu Inuyama Line via Nagoya.

## TOURS

A good way to see the Kiso-gawa is on a small riverboat. To take the 40-minute daytime tour, take the very brief trip on the Meitetsu Inuyama Line from Inuyama to Inuyama Koen. During the ukai fishing season, you could also do an evening boat trip to watch this traditional form of fishing up close. Kisogawa Ukai offers both these tours. The tourist information office in the station can give you more information on traveling the river and fishing.

### Kisogawa Ukai (木曽川鵜飼)

BOAT TOURS | The company offers daytime trips between March 20 and November 18, and evening ukai tours from June 1 to October 15. ☎ *0574/28–2727* ⊕ *www. kisogawa-ukai.jp* ➔ *Daytime boat tours ¥1,000, evening ukai tours from ¥3,000.*

## VISITOR INFORMATION

CONTACT **Inuyama Tourist Information Office.** ✉ *Inuyama Station, 14 Inuyama-fu-jimi-cho, Inuyama* ☎ *0568/61–6000* ⊕ *inuyama.gr.jp.*

# 👁 Sights

**Inuyama Castle** (犬山城; *Inuyama-jo*)
CASTLE/PALACE | Inuyama's most famous sight is Inuyama Castle, also known as Hakutei-jo (White Emperor Castle). Built in 1537, it is the oldest of the 12 original castles in Japan. The exceedingly pretty castle stands amid carefully tended grounds on a bluff overlooking the Kiso River. Climb up the creaky staircases to the top floor for a great view of the river, city, and surrounding hills. The gift shops and small section of old town at the foot of the castle hill are good for browsing. From Inuyama-Yuen Eki, walk southwest along the river for 10 minutes. ✉ *65–2 Kita-koken, Inuyama* ☎ *0568/61–1711* ⊕ *inuyama-castle.jp* ➔ *¥550.*

**Jo-an Teahouse**
(如庵茶室; *Joan Chashitsu*)
GARDEN | In the traditional Uraku-en garden, which reopened in March 2022 after several years of renovations, sits the Jo-an Teahouse. Originally constructed in Kyoto in 1618, the teahouse was moved to its present site in 1971. Admission to the garden is pricey, so it's worth paying an extra fee to be served green tea in the traditional style. Uraku-en is less than ½ km (¼ mile) from Inuyama-jo. ✉ *1 Gomon-saki, Inuyama* ☎ *0568/61–4608* ⊕ *www.meitetsu.co.jp/urakuen* ➔ *¥1,000 garden; tea ¥600 extra.*

★ **Meiji-mura Museum** (博物館明治村; *Hakubutsukan Meiji-mura*)
MUSEUM VILLAGE | Considered one of Japan's best museums, Meiji-mura has more than 60 buildings originally constructed during the Meiji era (1868–1912), when Japan ended its policy of isolationism and swiftly industrialized. The best way to experience the exhibits is to wander about, stopping at things that catch your eye. There's an English pamphlet to help guide you. If you get tired of walking, hop on a tram originally from Kyoto, a steam train from Yoko-hama, and an old village bus; a single

pass gives you access to all three for an additional fee. Among the exhibits are a surprisingly beautiful octagonal wood prison from Kanazawa, a Kabuki theater from Osaka that hosts occasional performances, and the former homes of renowned writers Soseki Natsume and Lafcadio Hearn. The lobby of legendary American architect Frank Lloyd Wright's Imperial Hotel, where Charlie Chaplin and Marilyn Monroe were once guests, is arguably the highlight. It opened on the day of the Great Kanto Earthquake in 1923, 11 years after the death of Emperor Meiji, and though it is not strictly a Meiji-era building, its sense of grandeur and history are truly unique. Buses run from Inuyama Station to Meiji-mura two to three times an hour from 9 to 4. The ride takes 20 minutes and costs ¥430. ✉ *1 Uchiyama, Inuyama* ☎ *0568/67–0314* 🌐 *www.meijimura.com* 🎟 *¥2,000; ¥1,300 for tram, train, and bus.*

## Restaurants

**Tofu Cafe Urashima** (豆腐かふぇ浦嶌)
$$ | **JAPANESE** | Coffee and sweets are on the menu alongside tofu-based lunches at this mellow but popular café about a 10-minute walk southeast of the castle. Try the Tamatebako Kaiseki lunch set, which comes in an attractive lacquerware box and (alongside pickles, vegetable side dishes, and miso soup) features tofu that's been grilled on skewers and accented with a sweet-savory soy-based sauce. **Known for:** no meat dishes; good coffee and desserts for those not looking for a full meal; reasonable priced lunch sets. [$] *Average main: ¥1,650* ✉ *726–2 Higashikoken, Inuyama* ☎ *0568/27–5678* 💳 *No credit cards* 🕒 *Closed Tues.*

## Hotels

**Hotel μ Style** (ホテルミュースタイル)
$$ | **HOTEL** | Opened in 2021, this bright and airy hotel next to Inuyama Station offers simple, but smart Western-style rooms. **Pros:** great access to Inuyama's main station; lots of cultural activities available; communal hot-spring baths. **Cons:** located in a bland part of Inuyama; might feel too tourist-focused for some; a 15-minute walk from Inuyama Castle. [$] *Rooms from: ¥16,500* ✉ *16–2 Inuyama-fujimi-cho, Inuyama* ☎ *0568/54–3111* 🌐 *www.m-inuyama-h.co.jp* 🛏 *118 rooms* 🍴 *Free Breakfast.*

## Activities

### HIKING

**Mount Tsugao** (継鹿尾山; *Tsugao-san*)
**HIKING & WALKING** | To get here, start on the riverside trail at the base of Inuyama Castle. Follow the paved trail east past the best-avoided Monkey Park, then north to Jakko Temple (built in AD 654), where the maples blaze in fall. Along the route are good views of the foothills stretching north from the banks of the Kiso-gawa. You can climb Tsugao-san or continue northeast to Obora Pond and southeast to Zenjino Station, where you can catch the Meitetsu Hiromi Line two stops back to Inuyama Station. The train passes through Zenjino at least three times an hour. From Inuyama-jo to Zenjino Station is an 8-km (5-mile) hike. Allow 2½ hours from the castle to the top of Tsugao-san; add another hour if you continue to Zenjino via Obora Pond. ✉ *Inuyama.*

# Iga Ueno (伊賀上野)

*95 km (59 miles) southwest of Nagoya, 67 km (42 miles) southeast of Kyoto, 39 km (24 miles) east of Nara, 88 km (55 miles) east of Osaka.*

This small city halfway between Nagoya and Nara has some interesting claims to fame. Noted haiku poet Matsuo Basho was born here in the 1640s, and it was home to one of Japan's leading ninja schools. Some locals even suggest Basho was himself a ninja.

### GETTING HERE AND AROUND
Iga Ueno is accessible from Nagoya, Kyoto, Nara, and Osaka on JR lines.

## ◉ Sights

**Iga-Ryu Ninja Museum** (伊賀流忍者博物館; *Iga Ryu Ninja Hakubutsukan*)
OTHER MUSEUM | FAMILY | The Iga-Ryu school of ninjutsu was one of the top two training centers for Japan's ancient spies and assassins in the 14th century. At the ninja residence, a guide in traditional dress explains how they were always prepared for attack. The hidden doors and secret passages are ingenious. Energetic demonstrations of ninja weapons like throwing stars, swords, daggers, and sickles are fun, and afterwards you can try out the throwing star. If you want to walk around the museum and town dressed up as a ninja, staff can point you to shops where you can rent all the gear. One special exhibit gives you some background on ninja history and techniques, while another displays the disguises and encryption used here, as well as the inventive tools that enabled them to walk on water and scale sheer walls. The museum is in Ueno Park, a 10-minute walk up the hill from Uenoshi Station. ⊠ *Ueno Park, 117–13–1 Ueno Marunouchi, Iga Ueno* 🕾 *0595/23–0311* ⊕ *www.iganinja.jp/en* 🎫 *¥800; weapons demonstration ¥500; throwing stars lesson ¥300.*

**Iga Ueno Castle** (伊賀上野城; *Iga Ueno-jo*)
CASTLE/PALACE | This castle stands today because of one man's determination and wealth. The first castle built here was destroyed by a rainstorm in 1612, before it was completed. More than 300 years later, local resident Katsu Kawasaki financed a replica that sits atop vertiginous 98-foot stone walls—be careful when it's windy. Kawasaki also paid for the Basho Memorial Museum, built in memory of Japan's famous wandering poet, Matsuo Basho, which stands near the castle in Ueno Park. ⊠ *106 Ueno-marunouchi, Iga Ueno* 🕾 *0595/21–3148* ⊕ *igaueno-castle.jp* 🎫 *¥600.*

# Ise (伊勢)

*107 km (66 miles) south of Nagoya, 158 km (98 miles) southeast of Kyoto, 127 km (79 miles) east of Nara, 143 km (89 miles) east of Osaka.*

When you step off the train, you may feel that Ise is a drab city, but hidden in two forests of towering cedar trees are the most important Shinto shrines in Japan. Indeed, the city's income comes mainly from the pilgrims who visit Geku (外宮) and Naiku (内宮), the Outer and Inner shrines, respectively. Near the Inner Shrine you'll find an array of shops in the Oharai-machi neighborhood hawking souvenirs to the busloads of tourists and plenty of places to eat such local specialties as deep-fried oysters, skewers of Matsusaka beef, *Ise udon* (udon noodles with a thick broth) and *akafuku* (sweet rice cakes). The busiest times at Ise Jingu are during the Grand Festival in mid-October every year, when crowds gather to see the pageantry, and on New Year's Eve and Day, when hundreds of thousands come to pray for good fortune.

### GETTING HERE AND AROUND
Ise can be reached from Kyoto, Nara, and Osaka by the JR and Kintetsu lines, with the latter's Limited Express service from

The Grand Shrine of Ise is rebuilt every 20 years, in accordance with the Shinto tradition.

Nagoya being the fastest option. The city has two stations five minutes apart, Ise-Shi (JR and Kintetsu) and Uji-Yamada (Kintetsu only). From either station it's a 10-minute walk through town to the Outer Shrine. A frequent shuttle bus makes the 6-km (4-mile) trip between Geku and Naiku; a bus also goes directly from the Inner Shrine to Uji-Yamada Station.

## VISITOR INFORMATION

**CONTACT Geku-mae Tourist Information Center.** (外宮前観光案内所; *Geku-mae Kankou Annaijyo*) ✉ *14–6 Honmachi, Ise* ✛ *Directly across from the Outer Shrine* ☎ *0596/63–6262* ⊕ *en.ise-kanko.jp.*

 Sights

### ★ Grand Shrines of Ise
(伊勢神宮; *Ise Jingu*)
RELIGIOUS BUILDING | These shrines are rebuilt every 20 years, in accordance with Shinto tradition. To begin a new generational cycle, exact replicas of the previous halls are erected with new wood,

using the same centuries-old methods, on adjacent sites. The old buildings are then dismantled. The main halls you see now—the 62nd set—were completed in 2013 at an estimated cost of more than ¥5.5 billion. For the Japanese, importance is found in the form of the buildings; the vintage of the materials is of little concern. You cannot enter any of the buildings, but the tantalizing glimpses of the main halls that you catch while walking the grounds add to the mystique of the site. Both Grand Shrines exhibit a natural harmony that the more-contrived buildings in later Japanese architecture do not.

Deep in a park of ancient Japanese cedars, Geku, dating from AD 477, is dedicated to Toyouke Omikami, goddess of agriculture. Its buildings are simple, predating the 6th-century Chinese and Korean influence. It's made from unpainted *hinoki* (cypress), with a closely cropped thatched roof. You can see very little of the exterior of Geku—only its roof and glimpses of its walls—and none

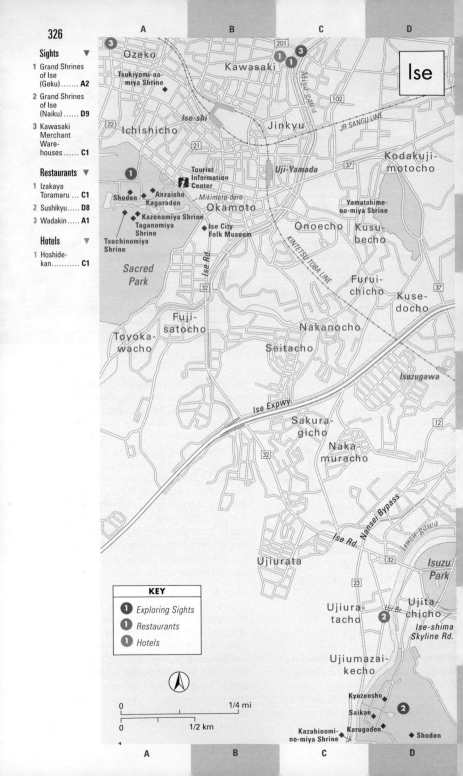

**Sights** ▼

1 Grand Shrines
of Ise
(Geku) ....... **A2**

2 Grand Shrines
of Ise
(Naiku) ...... **D9**

3 Kawasaki
Merchant
Ware-
houses ...... **C1**

**Restaurants** ▼

1 Izakaya
Toramaru ... **C1**

2 Sushikyu ..... **D8**

3 Wadakin ..... **A1**

**Hotels** ▼

1 Hoshide-
kan ........... **C1**

**Ise**

Ozeko
Tsukiyomi-no-
miya Shrine
Kawasaki
Ise-shi
Jinkyu
Ichishicho
Kodakuji-
motocho
Tourist
Information
Center
Uji-Yamada
Mikimoto-dori
Shoden
Anzaisho
Kaguraden
Okamoto
Yamatohime-
no-miya Shrine
Kazenomiya Shrine
Taganomiya
Shrine
Ise City
Folk Museum
Onoecho
Kusu-
becho
Tsuchinomiya
Shrine
Furui-
chicho
Kuse-
docho
Sacred
Park
Fuji-
satocho
Nakanocho
Toyoka-
wacho
Seitacho
Isuzugawa
Ise Expwy
Sakura-
gicho
Naka-
muracho
Ujiurata
Isuzu
Park
KEY
Exploring Sights
Restaurants
Hotels
Uji Br.
Ujita-
chicho
Ujiura-
tacho
Ise-shima
Skyline Rd.
Ujiumazai-
kecho
Kyozensho
Saikan
Karugaden
Shoden
Kazahinomi-
no-miya Shrine

0                1/4 mi
0                1/2 km

# The Pearl Divers

At Toba, before Kokichi Mikimoto (1858–1954) perfected a method for cultivating pearls here in 1893. *Ama*, or female divers (women were believed to have bigger lungs), would dive all day, bringing up a thousand oysters, but they wouldn't necessarily find a valuable pearl. Pearl oysters are now farmed, and the famous female divers are a dying breed. On the outlying islands, however, women do still dive for abalone, octopus, and edible seaweed.

The quickest way to get from Ise to Toba is a 17-minute ride on the JR Line for ¥330. Pick up English-language maps from the Toba Tourist Information Center, just outside the station.

**Toba Tourist Information Center.** Outside Exit 1 of Kintetsu Toba Station, you'll find an English map of the main attractions. ☎ 0599/25–2844 ⊕ *www. toba.gr.jp.*

**Mikimoto Pearl Museum** (ミキモト真珠博物館; Mikimoto Shinju no Hakubutsukan.) This museum on Pearl Island, 500 yards southeast from Toba Station, explores the history of pearl diving in Japan. ✉ *1–7–1 Toba, Toba* ☎ *0599/25 2028* ⊕ *www.mikimoto pearl museum.co.jp* 🎫 *¥1,650.*

of the interior. Four fences surround the shrine, and only the Imperial Family and their envoys may enter. Geku is a five-minute walk southwest of Ise-Shi Station or a 10-minute walk west of Uji-Yamada Station.

The even more venerated Naiku is 6 km (4 miles) southeast of Geku. Naiku is said to be where the Yata-no-Kagami (Sacred Mirror) is kept, one of the three sacred treasures of the imperial regalia. The shrine, reputed to date from 4 BC, also houses the spirit of the sun goddess Amaterasu, who Japanese mythology says was born of the left eye of Izanagi, one of the first two gods to inhabit the earth. According to legend, Amaterasu was the great-great-grandmother of the first mortal emperor of Japan, Jimmu. Thus, she is revered as the country's ancestral goddess-mother and guardian deity. The Inner Shrine's architecture is simple. If you did not know its origin, you might call it classically modern. The use of unpainted cypress causes Naiku to blend into the ancient forest encircling it.

To get to Naiku, take Bus 51 or 55 from Uji-Yamada Station or in front of Geku to the Naiku-mae bus stop, which is right in front of the shrine. The ride takes about 20 minutes and costs ¥440. ✉ *Ise Jingu Naiku, 1 Ujitachi-cho, Ise* ⊕ *www.isejin-gu.or.jp/en* 🎫 *Free.*

### Kawasaki Merchant Warehouses
(河崎商人蔵; *Kawasaki Shoningura*)
**HISTORIC DISTRICT** | Near the Hoshide-kan inn, four blocks of historic buildings alongside the Setagawa River form the Kawasaki area, once a transportation and trade hub that at its peak was home to 100 warehouses and stores supplying Ise. Many of these renovated buildings now house galleries, cafés, and restaurants—like Izakaya Toramaru—while others function as simple stores, as they have done for generations. It's a charming neighborhood to stroll for an hour or two. The tourist information center has a map of the area listing all the businesses, or you can grab a copy from the Hoshide-kan. ✉ *Kawasaki, Ise* 🎫 *Free.*

## 🍴 Restaurants

### Izakaya Toramaru (虎丸)

**$$$ | JAPANESE |** This traditional restaurant in a replica warehouse in the Kawasaki area does not open unless there is a delivery of fresh fish, which indicates how seriously the cooks take their food. As well as a wide variety of fresh fish dishes, there are also plenty of meat and izakaya staples on the menu, all served in haphazardly shaped pottery dishes. **Known for:** expertly prepared sashimi; welcoming atmosphere; good selection of sake and shochu. Ⓢ *Average main: ¥5,000 ✉ 2–13–6 Kawasaki, Ise ☎ 0596/22–9298 ▭ No credit cards* ⊗ *Closed Tues. No lunch.*

### Sushikyu (すし久)

**$$ | SUSHI |** In the old Oharai-machi neighborhood a few minutes' walk from the entrance to the Naiku, Sushikyu has been serving a regional specialty called *tekone-zushi* for generations. The *donburi* (rice bowl), topped with raw slices of bonito marinated in soy sauce and with dried seaweed and wasabi added to taste, was originally a fisherman's dish quickly prepared at sea. **Known for:** filling lunch sets centered on the tekone-zushi; second-floor window seats with nice river views; charming 120-year-old building. Ⓢ *Average main: ¥1,900 ✉ 20 Ujinakanokiricho, Ise ☎ 0596/27–0229* ⊗ *No dinner.*

### Wadakin (和田金)

**$$$$ | JAPANESE |** If you love beef, make a pilgrimage to Matsusaka, one express train stop north of Ise. Wadakin claims to be the originator of Matsusaka beef's fame; the cattle are raised with loving care on the restaurant's farm out in the countryside. **Known for:** also serves the Matsusaka-gyu in sukiyaki; it's extremely popular, so reservations are a must; the chef's steak dinner course. Ⓢ *Average main: ¥16,000 ✉ 1878 Naka-machi ☎ 0598/21–1188 ⊕ e-wadakin.co.jp* ⊗ *Closed 4th Tues. of month.*

## 🛏 Hotels

### Hoshide–kan (星出館)

**$ | B&B/INN |** Almost a century old, this traditional inn has wood-decorated tatami rooms and narrow, squeaking corridors. **Pros:** inn rents bicycles; good location; charming building. **Cons:** at the mercy of the elements in summer and winter; shared bathing facilities; area is quiet after dark. Ⓢ *Rooms from: ¥11,800 ✉ 2–15–2 Kawasaki, Ise ☎ 0596/28–2377 ⊕ www.hoshidekan.jp ⤳ 10 rooms* ⦿⃝ *No Meals.*

# Kashikojima (賢島)

*25 km (16 miles) south of Toba, 145 km (90 miles) south of Nagoya.*

The jagged coastline at Ago-wan (Ago Bay), with calm waters and countless hidden coves, presents a dramatic final view of the Ise Peninsula. The best approach to Kashikojima is to catch a bus to Goza, the tip of the headland, and ride a ferry back across the bay. From the boat you'll get a close-up look at the hundreds of floating wooden rafts from which the pearl-bearing oysters are suspended.

### GETTING HERE AND AROUND

Kashikojima can be reached on the Kintetsu Line from Toba (40 minutes, ¥480) or Nagoya (just over two hours, ¥3,680) or by bus from Toba. It's possible to follow the coast from Kashikojima to the Kii Peninsula, but there is no train, and in many places the road cuts inland, making the journey long and tedious. From Kashikojima you are better off taking the Kintetsu Line back to Toba to change to the JR Sangu Line and travel to Taki, where you can take the JR Kisei Line south to the Kii Peninsula.

## Sights

**Daio** (大王)

**TOWN** | Tucked behind a promontory, this fishing village is an interesting stop on the journey around the headland. At a small fish market you can sample fresh squid, mackerel, and other seafood. Standing above the village is Daiozaki todai (大王崎灯台), a 72-feet tall lighthouse built in 1927 that's open to visitors daily from 9 to 4. To reach this towering white structure, walk up the narrow street lined with fish stalls and pearl souvenir shops at the back of the harbor. ✉ *Kashikojima* 🌐 *www.daiozaki.com* 🎫 *Lighthouse ¥300.*

## Hotels

**Shima Kanko Hotel** (志摩観光ホテル)

**$$$$** | **HOTEL** | Originally opened in the 1950s and then reopened in 2016 after a major renovation ahead of hosting the Ise-Shima G7 summit, the Shima Kanko is Ise-Shima's premier Western-style luxury hotel, with a very refined look and feel throughout its two zones: the spacious Classic and the Bay Suites. **Pros:** impeccable service; meals can be included; superb views of the bay, especially at sunset. **Cons:** can feel overly formal; room interiors will be too conservative for some; restaurants and bars priced at a premium. [$] *Rooms from: ¥34,000* ✉ *731 Shinmei, Kashikojima* ☎ *0599/43–1211* 🌐 *global.miyakohotels.ne.jp/shima* 🛏 *164 rooms* 🍴 *Free Breakfast.*

**Ishiyama-so** (石山荘)

**$** | **B&B/INN** | On tiny Yokoyama Island, this small inn has painted its name in large letters on the red roof. **Pros:** idyllic setting; friendly owners; doesn't get much more remote than this. **Cons:** limited dining options; no private baths; no frills. [$] *Rooms from: ¥7,000* ✉ *Ago-cho, Yokoyama-jima* ☎ *0599/52–1527* 💳 *No credit cards* 🛏 *6 rooms* 🍴 *Free Breakfast.*

# Shingu (新宮)

*138 km (86 miles) southwest of Taki, 231 km (144 miles) southwest of Nagoya.*

Shingu is home to one of the three great Kumano Sanzan shrines, which sits at the mouth of the Kumano River.

### GETTING HERE AND AROUND

You can reach Shingu by JR Limited Express from Taki, Shirahama or Nagoya. The Shingu Tourist Association Information Center is to the left as you exit the station.

### VISITOR INFORMATION

**CONTACT Shingu Tourist Association Information Center.** ✉ *Shingu Station, 2–1–11 Jofuku, Shingu* ☎ *0735/22–2840* 🌐 *www.shinguu.jp.*

## Sights

One of the few north–south roads penetrating the Kii Peninsula begins in town and continues inland to Nara by way of Doro-kyo (Doro Gorge). A drive on this winding, steep, narrow road, especially on a bus, warrants motion-sickness pills. The mossy canyon walls outside your window and the rushing water far below inspire wonder, but frequent sharp curves provide plenty of anxiety. Continue north on the road past Doro-kyo to reach one of the three great Kumano Sanzan shrines, **Hongu-taisha Shrine** (本宮大社), which has attractive wooden architecture and a thatched roof.

**Hayatama Shrine** (速玉大社; *Hayatama-taisha*)

**RELIGIOUS BUILDING** | Although the buildings here are modern re-creations, this great shrine is said to have been located here since at least the 12th century, and is steeped in much Shinto mythology. A sacred stone found here was said to have once carried three Shinto deities to Earth. ✉ *1 Shingu, Shingu* 🌐 *kumano-hayatama.jp* 🎫 *Free.*

**Hongu Shrine** (本宮大社; *Hongu-taisha*)
**RELIGIOUS BUILDING** | Of the three Kumano Sanzan grand shrines, Hongu-taisha is the most revered, being the head shrine of some 3,000 Kumano shrines nationwide. It's also the one hidden deepest in the Kii Peninsula's interior. With its understated wooden structures and thatched roofs, it blends in perfectly with the giant cedars that surround it. What would have once been an arduous trek through mountain and forest is now a straightforward trip on public transport (though people still walk the pilgrimage trails). To get there from Shingu, take a bus 80 minutes to the Hongu-taisha-mae bus stop. If you are staying over in Shingu, this is easily done as a day-trip. ✉ *Hongu-machi, Tanabe-shi, Shingu* 🌐 *www.hongutaisha.jp* 🎫 *Shrine free, Treasure Hall ¥300.*

## Hotels

**Shingu UI Hotel** (新宮ユーアイホテル)
**$$** | **HOTEL** | Shingu isn't blessed with great accommodation, but this business hotel with fair-size Western- and Japanese-style rooms is a reasonable option if you're staying overnight. **Pros:** convenient base for day-trippers; decent service; good range of rooms. **Cons:** showing its age; lacking atmosphere; perfunctory decor. $ *Rooms from: ¥13,900* ✉ *3–12 Inosawa, Shingu* ☎ *0735/22–6611* 🌐 *www.ui-hotel.co.jp* 🛏 *84 rooms* 🍴 *Free Breakfast.*

# Doro-kyo (瀞峡)

*20 km (12 miles) north of Shingu.*

The wide ocean views of the coastal journey to Shingu give way to gorges and mountainsides of a deep, mossy green when you pass through the tunnel five minutes north of the city. Up the Kumano River, the walls of the steep-sided Doro-kyo gorge rise above you. Farther up, sheer 150-foot cliffs tower over the Kumano-gawa. Try a two-hour boat tour of the gorge with Kumano Kanko, details of which are available at the Shingu Tourist Association Information Center.

### GETTING HERE AND AROUND

All Doro-kyo tours depart and end at Shiko, which is a 35-minute bus ride from Shingu.

### TOURS

**Kumano Kanko**
**BOAT TOURS** | This company offers two-hour jet boat tours of Doro-kyo Gorge departing from Shiko several times a day starting at 9:30 am year-round. The final tour departs at 2:30 pm. You can save a bit of money by packaging your bus ride to Shiko with the jet boat tour ticket. ✉ *272 Hitari, Shingu* 🌐 *kumanokanko.nankai-nanki.jp/en/dorokyo* 🎫 *From ¥3,500.*

# Nachi (那智)

*13 km (8 miles) southwest of Shingu.*

Reputed to be 1,400 years old, this is perhaps the most impressive of the Kumano Sanzan shrines.

### GETTING HERE AND AROUND

Nachi can be reached by hourly JR services via Shingu. The trip takes 20 minutes and costs ¥240. From Nachi Station, a 16-minute bus ride (¥490) gets you to the shrine and waterfall.

## Sights

**Nachi Shrine** (那智大社; *Nachi-taisha*)
**RELIGIOUS BUILDING** | The shrine overlooks Nachi-no-taki (那智の滝), the highest waterfall in Japan, which drops 430 feet into a rocky river. At the bus stop near the falls, a large *torii* (gate) marks the start of a short path that leads to a paved clearing near the foot of the falls. A 15-minute climb up the mossy stone path opposite the souvenir shops is the temple and its small museum. You can

ride an elevator to the top of the bright-red pagoda for an on-high view of the waterfall. Next to the shrine is the 1587 Buddhist temple Seiganto-ji (青岸渡寺), starting point for a 33-temple Kannon pilgrimage through western Honshu. Many visitors walk here via the cobbled Daimonzaka slope (大門坂), found one bus stop before Nachi Falls, for a brief taste of the ancient Kumano Kodo pilgrimage trails. ⊠ 1 Nachi-san, Nachikatsuura ⊕ kumanonachitaisha.or.jp ⊠ Shrine free, elevator ¥300, museum ¥200.

# Shirahama (白浜)

*82 km (51 miles) west of Nachi, 178 km (111 miles) south of Osaka.*

Rounding the peninsula 54 km (34 miles) northwest of Shio-no-misaki, Shirahama is a small headland famous for its pure white-sand beach, which, confusingly, is called Shirarahama. If you're wondering why it looks and feels so different from the other beaches, it's because 750,000 cubic meters of this sand was imported from Australia to battle erosion in the 1990s. Hot springs are dotted along the beach and around the cape. The climate, which allows beach days even in winter, makes Shirahama an inviting base for exploring the area. Although it can be intolerably busy in July and August, it is otherwise pretty laid-back. JR trains from Nachi, Shingu, and Osaka run to Shirahama. A 17-minute bus ride from the train station gets you to the beachside town.

## ◉ Sights

### Sakino-yu Hot Spring
(埼の湯温泉; *Sakino-yu Onsen*)
HOT SPRING | Soak in this open-air hollow among the wave-beaten rocks facing the Pacific Ocean, where it's said that emperors Saimei (594–661) and Mommu (683–707) once bathed. It's at the south end of the main beach, below Hotel

Seamore. ⊠ *Shirahama* ⊠ ¥500, ¥200 towel rental.

### Shirara-yu Hot Spring
(白良湯温泉; *Shirara-yu Onsen*)
HOT SPRING | At the north end of the beach, locals come and go all day to bathe and chat. The baths overlook the beach and ocean from the second floor of this old wooden building, and on the first floor is an open lounge area. You can rent towels, but bring your own toiletries. ⊠ *Shirahama* ⊠ ¥420, ¥200 towel rental ⊙ Closed Thurs.

# Koya-san (高野山)

*63 km (39 miles) east of Wakayama, 64 km (40 miles) southeast of Osaka.*

This UNESCO World Heritage site is the headquarters of the Shingon sect of Buddhism, founded by Kukai, also known as Kobo Daishi, in AD 816.

## GETTING HERE AND AROUND
If you approach Koya-san by cutting across Yoshino-Kumano National Park by bus from Shingu or Hongu on Route 168, get off the bus at Gojo (five hours, ¥4,600 from Shingu; 3½ hours, ¥3,250 from Hongu), and backtrack one station on the JR Line to Hashimoto; then take the Nankai Line. If you are coming from Osaka, take the Nankai Line from Namba Station, which sometimes requires a change of train at Hashimoto Station.

By rail, the last leg of the trip is a five-minute cable-car ride (¥500) from Gokuraku-bashi Station. JR Passes are not valid for the cable car. The lift deposits you at the top of 3,000-foot Koya-san, where you can pick up a map and hop on a bus to the main attractions, which are about 2½ km (1½ miles) from the station and 4 km (2½ miles) from each other on opposite sides of town. Two buses leave the station when the cable car arrives, which is every 20 or 30 minutes. One goes to Okuno-in Cemetery, on the east

Koya-san is a UNESCO World Heritage site and the headquarters of the Shingon sect of Buddhism.

end of the main road, and the other goes to the Dai-mon, to the west. The main Koya-san Tourist Association office, at the intersection in the center of town, can be reached by either bus for ¥300. The staff here can arrange volunteer English-speaking guides to take visitors to Koya-san's main sights, and they also have audio guides (¥500) and maps available that are handy for self-guided tours of the town.

## VISITOR INFORMATION

**CONTACT Koyasan Temple Lodging Association.** ⊠ *600 Koya-san, Koya* ☎ *0736/56–2616* ⊕ *shukubo.net.*

 Sights

### Dai-mon Gate (大門)

**NOTABLE BUILDING** | Every year, a million visitors pass through Koya-san's Great Gate to enter the sprawling complex of 117 temples and monasteries. Traveling

to Koya-san takes you through mountain wilderness, but the town itself is sheltered and self-contained. The main buildings are imposing, while the minor temples are in a wide range of styles and colors, each offering small-scale beauty in its decor or garden. Monks, pilgrims, and tourists mingle in the main street, the sneaker-wearing, motorcycle-riding monks often appearing the least pious of all. ⊠ *249 Koya-san, Koya* ⊠ *Free.*

### Kongobu-ji Temple (金剛峯寺)

On the southwestern side of Koya-san, Kongobu-ji is the chief temple of Shingon Buddhism. It was first built in 1592 as the family temple of Hideyoshi Toyotomi, and rebuilt in 1861 to become the main temple of the Koya-san community. The screen-door artwork and Banryutei landscaped rock garden, the largest in Japan, are both well worth the admission fee. ⊠ *132 Koya-san, Koya* ⊠ *¥1,000.*

### ★ Okuno-in Cemetery (奥之院)

CEMETERY | If time is limited, head for this memorial park first. Many Japanese make pilgrimages to the mausoleum of Kobo Daishi or pay their respects to their ancestors buried here. Arrive early in the morning, before the groups take over, or even better, at dusk, when it gets wonderfully spooky.

Exploring this cemetery is like peeking into a lost and mysterious realm. Incense hangs in the air, and you can almost feel the millions of prayers said here clinging to the gnarled branches of 300-year-old cedar trees reaching into the sky. The old-growth forest is a rarity in Japan, and among the trees are buried some of the country's most prominent families, their graves marked by mossy pagodas and red-robed bodhisattvas.

You can reach Okuno-in by way of the 2½-km (1½-mile) main walkway, which is lined with more than 100,000 tombs, monuments, and statues. The lane enters the cemetery at Ichi-no-hashi; follow the main street straight east from the town center for 15 minutes to find this small bridge at the edge of the forest.

The path from Okuno-in-mae ends at the refined Toro-do (Lantern Hall), named after its 11,000 lanterns. Two fires burn in this hall; one has reportedly been alight since 1016, the other since 1088. Behind the hall is the mausoleum of Kobo Daishi. The hall and the mausoleum altar are extremely beautiful, with subtle lighting and soft gold coloring. ✉ *550 Koya-san, Koya* ✉ *Free*.

### Reihokan Treasure Hall (霊宝館)

OTHER MUSEUM | Chosen from the museum's 78,000-piece collection, you'll find more than 5,000 well-preserved Buddhist relics on display here, some dating back 1,000 years. The New Gallery houses themed exhibitions of sculpture, painting, and artifacts. The Main Gallery has a permanent exhibition of Buddha and bodhisattva figures and calligraphic scrolls. The museum sits across the road from the Danjo Garan. ✉ *306 Koya-san, Koya* ☎ *0736/56–2029* ⊕ *www.reihokan. or.jp/en* ✉ *¥1,300*.

### Sacred Precinct (壇上伽藍; *Danjo Garan*)

The most striking of Danjo Garan's outsized halls is the 147-feet tall Kompon-daito (Great Stupa). This red pagoda with an interior of brightly colored beams contains five large seated gold Buddhas. Last rebuilt in 1937, the two-story structure has an unusual style and rich vermilion color. From Kongobu-ji, walk down the temple's main stairs and take the road to the right of the parking lot in front of you, in less than five minutes you will reach Danjo Garan itself. ✉ *152 Koya-san, Koya* ✉ *¥500 to enter the Kompon-daito*.

 ## Hotels

Koya-san has no modern hotels; however, 52 of the temples offer Japanese-style accommodations—tatami floors, futon mattresses, and traditional Japanese shared baths. You eat the same food as the priests. Dinner and breakfast is *shojin ryori*, vegetarian cuisine that uses locally made tofu and seasonal vegetables. Prices start from ¥9,500 per person, including breakfast and dinner. All the temples are open to foreign guests, but only half will cater to non-Japanese speakers. An advance reservation is strongly advisable, especially in October and November, when crowds come for the autumn leaves, and the August holidays. Arrangements can be made through Koya-san Shukubo Association, the Nankai Railway Company office in Namba Station (Osaka), and in some cases directly with the temples.

**Eko-in Temple** (恵光院)

$$$ | **B&B/INN** | This friendly temple, close to Okuno-in, is where you can take part in morning prayers and observe the morning fire ceremony. **Pros:** good vegetarian food included; very welcoming to foreigners; can book directly online in English. **Cons:** no room-only rates; shared bathing facilities; the smallest rooms are cramped. [$] *Rooms from: ¥22,000* ✉ *497 Koya-san, Koya* ☎ *0736/56–2514* 🌐 *www.ekoin.jp/en* 🛏 *36 rooms* 🍴 *All-Inclusive.*

# Chapter 7

# THE JAPAN ALPS AND THE NORTH CHUBU COAST

Updated by
Rob Goss

| ◉ Sights | 🍴 Restaurants | 🛏 Hotels | 🛍 Shopping | 🍸 Nightlife |
|----------|---------------|----------|-------------|-------------|
| ★★★★☆ | ★★★☆☆ | ★★★☆☆ | ★★☆☆☆ | ★★☆☆☆ |

# WELCOME TO THE JAPAN ALPS AND THE NORTH CHUBU COAST

## TOP REASONS TO GO

★ **Onsen:** The salty, calcium-rich waters of coastal thermal spas and iron- and sulfur-heavy springs in the mountains make your skin smooth, your bones strong, and set your mind at ease.

★ **Hiking:** The Japan Alps offer staggering views and a serious workout. Trails wind through peaks and ridges, and summer brings wildflowers to the highland slopes and valleys.

★ **Skiing:** The resorts around Nagano attract outdoor enthusiasts, particularly on weekends. Shiga Kogen, near Yudanaka, and Happo-one, near Hakuba, are among the best areas.

★ **Feudal Japan:** Visit the former samurai quarters in Kanazawa's Naga-machi section. Matsumoto Castle evokes the history of a strictly hierarchical society.

★ **Folk art:** Kanazawa is renowned for dyed silk and pottery, while Matsumoto has excellent wood craftsmanship. Lacquer is a specialty of the Noto Peninsula.

**1** **Karuizawa.** Laidback summer retreat.

**2** **Kusatsu.** Hot springs and traditional relaxation.

**3** **Nagano.** Zenko-ji Temple and snow monkeys.

**4** **Matsumoto.** Feudal-era castle.

**5** **Hakuba.** Top winter-sports destination.

**6** **Kiso Valley.** This wooded valley with picturesque villages.

**7** **Kamikochi.** Gateway to mountain hikes.

**8** **Takayama.** Historic districts, excellent cuisine, and famous festivals.

**9** **Shirakawa-go.** UNESCO-designated, steeply thatched gassho-zukuri houses.

**10** **Kanazawa.** Old samurai and geisha districts.

**11** **Noto Peninsula (Noto-hanto).** An unhurried look at rural Japan.

**12** **Toyama.** Starting point of the scenic Kurobe Gorge Railway.

**13** **Niigata.** Famed for its rice, sake, and fresh seafood.

**14** **Sado Island (Sado-ga-shima).** A windswept island known for its natural beauty and gentle ways.

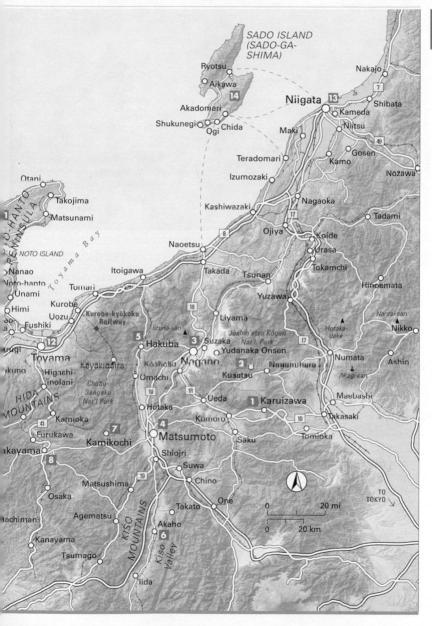

# GASSHO-ZUKURI FARMHOUSES

A Doboruku Matsuri procession

It's tempting to think of traditional domestic architecture in Japan, with its paper windows and tatami mats and sliding screens as insubstantial. The moment you see a *gassho-zukuri* farmhouse, that temptation will disappear.

The term gassho-zukuri in Japanese means "praying hands structure." As hands come together, fingertips touching, in Buddhist observance, so lie the sloping, gable roofs of these remarkable farmhouses. Featuring watertight layers of reed thatching 3 feet thick or more, over massive wooden beams, the roofs are set at a steep 60-degree angle to keep the snow from piling up. The mountain forests of Gifu and Toyama prefectures in the Japan Alps, where most of these houses survive, get some of the heaviest snowfalls in Japan—12 feet of it, from November through March, is not uncommon—and no less a roof would do. The houses, four and sometimes five stories high, are usually built on a north–south axis, so the angle offers the least resistance to the winter wind. They are a masterfully practical architectural adaptation to challenging weather conditions, but they also have a certain beauty.

## STRONGLY BUILT

Gassho-zukuri houses represent one of the crowning achievements of traditional Japanese carpentry. Astonishingly these houses were built without nails, pegs, or brackets. Complex joinery, ropes, and strips of hazel wood hold the beams together, the joints tightened with small wedges, typically with no diagonal bracing. They are flexible enough to withstand winter storms and even earthquakes.

## A PRACTICAL HOUSE

Like most traditional farmhouses, the gassho-zukuri was a living and working space for multiple generations of an immediate and extended family and their hired help under the one pitched roof. Sleeping quarters were on the first and second floors; in the medieval period, the ground floor was also used for the making of niter (for gunpowder) in summer—as tribute paid to the feudal lord in lieu of taxes—and *washi* (Japanese paper) in winter. The triangular top stories were reserved for silkworm cultivation. Stables were connected to the living space, so no one had to go outdoors during the winter months—except, alas, to the outhouse.

A snowy winter in Shirokawa-go

In the center of the huge open room on the main floor was—and still is—the *irori,* a charcoal fire pit with a huge wooden pot hook suspended over it for cooking. In winter it was the only source of heat in the house; the higher your standing in the family, the closer you got to sit by the fire. The hearth sent billows of smoke upward to cure meats and dry food set on a metal grill suspended from the ceiling; the rising heat also kept the precious silkworms warm. Centuries of smoke would darken the walls and beams of the house, giving them as well a protective coating against insects, but the smoke takes

its toll on the thatching, which has to be replaced every 30 or 40 years. When there's a roof to be done, the whole community pitches in, laying some 20 truckloads of new reeds in two or three days.

### SEEING THE GASSHO-ZUKURI TODAY

At one time, it was estimated that there were more than 1,800 of these extraordinary farmhouses in the mountain villages of central Japan, between the castle towns of Nagoya and Kanazawa, many dating back to the 17th century. Today only some 150 remain, the largest number of them in three villages—Ainokura, Ogi-machi and Suganuma—in the deeply rural Shirakawa-go and Gokayama regions on the border of Toyama and Gitu prefectures, which together were declared a UNESCO World Heritage site in 1995. Access to them is by no means easy, but since the 1990s these villages have become increasingly popular tourist destinations, especially for domestic travelers; many of the houses in Ogimachi have been converted to min-shuku (guesthouses) to accommodate visitors to this area. Another group of gassho-zukuri farmhouses can be found in Hida no Sato (Hida Folk Village), an open-air historical museum in the Gifu city of Takayama.

Gassho-zukuri farmhouses in Shirakawa-go

Until the 20th century brought highways and railways to central Japan, villages in this alpine region were largely isolated from the rest of the country. Unique traditions still linger in this region of snow-topped mountains, coastal cliffs, open-air hot springs, and superb hiking and skiing.

Come here for traditional architecture in towns like Tsumago and Magome, or to wander around thatch-roofed farmhouses in rural Gokayama and Shirakawa-go. Visit Buddhist temples such as Nagano's Zenko-ji, and Kanazawa's Nichiren Myoryu-ji (locally called Ninja-dera, or the temple of the Ninja).

Central Japan is justly famous for its festivals. Takayama's biannual town festival in April and October draws crowds from all over the country. Sado Island parties for days on end during its annual Earth Celebration in August, hosted by taiko drum group Kodo, and the tiny town of Nanao on the Noto Peninsula hosts the riotous Seihakusai Dekayama festival in May. When they're not dancing in the streets, local craftspeople produce some of Japan's best ceramics, pottery, dyed silk, wood carvings, and lacquerware.

Escape summer city heat by trekking in the Japan Alps or strolling through the car-free alpine village of Kamikochi. When the winter snows start to fall, ski fields in Nagano and Niigata offer endless fresh powder, and the many hot springs and sake breweries in the region are a weary snowbunny's dream.

Food lovers should head to the Hokuriku coastline, where Ishikawa, Toyama, and Niigata prefectures meet the Sea of Japan. The cold winters and abundant rainfall make this one of Japan's major rice-producing regions, and where there's rice there's sake. The locally brewed sake pairs perfectly with sashimi straight from the ocean.

## MAJOR REGIONS

The **Japan Alps** cover a region known as Shinshu, between the north and south coasts of the Chubu area. There are 10 peaks above 9,800 feet that attract both skiers and hikers, but the region also has many parks and forests for less-strenuous nature exploring. Roads and railways through the Japan Alps follow the valleys, greatly lengthening trips such as the three-hour Matsumoto–Takayama ride, and trains may be infrequent and end as early as 7 pm. Buses are not as convenient as trains, but some scenic routes are recommended.

The center of culture and commerce in the Hokuriku region, **Kanazawa** ranks among Japan's best-loved cities, like a smaller and less touristed version of Kyoto. To the east are snowcapped mountains, including the revered (and hikeable) Haku-san. To the north stretches the clawlike peninsula of the **Noto-hanto,** where lush rolling hills and rice fields meet scenic coastlines. Farther north along the North Chubu Coast of the Sea of Japan are the hardworking industrial capitals of **Toyama** and **Niigata.** Offshore from the North Chubu Coast is the secluded **Sado Island,** worth the sometimes choppy ferry ride for its rugged coastline, terraced rice fields, Noh traditions, and slow way of life.

South of Toyama, in Gifu Prefecture, is the city of **Takayama,** known for its historic districts and morning markets, as well as being a good jumping off point for trips to the UNESCO-designated village of **Shirakawa-go** and mountain hikes in **Kamikochi.** East of Takayama, **Matsumoto** in Nagano Prefecture is home to a magnificent 16th-century castle, while elsewhere in **Nagano** you find winter sports areas, such as Hakuba, and the hot-spring town of Yudanaka.

# Planning

## Getting Here and Around

Travel in the Alps is largely restricted to the valleys and river gorges that run north and south. The only east–west route is through the mountains, between Matsumoto and Takayama. It's easier to go along the coast and through the foothills of Fukui, Ishikawa, Toyama, and Niigata, except in winter when Fukui gets hit with furious blizzards. In Noto-hanto, buses and trains can be relied on for trips to key places.

### AIR

The major airport in the area is Komatsu Airport in Kanazawa, although there are daily flights from Fukuoka, Osaka, and Sapporo to Shinshu-Matsumoto Airport and from Tokyo and Sapporo to Toyama Kitokito Airport for those wanting to reach the Alps quickly. Toyama also has routes to and from Dalian, Seoul, Shanghai, and Taipei. Since the opening of Noto Satoyama Airport in Wajima, you can reach the Noto Peninsula in one hour from Tokyo. Chubu International Airport (Centrair) near Nagoya has frequent domestic and international flights.

### BUS AND TRAIN

Whether to take the bus or the train isn't usually a choice, because there is often only one form of public transportation to the place you're going. Not all train lines in Nagano Prefecture are JR, so budget in additional charges if you are traveling on a JR pass.

Shinkansen service has effectively shortened the distance to the Alps and north Chubu coast from the east: using the Hokuriku Shinkansen the trip takes about 90 minutes from Tokyo to Nagano and 2½ hours from Tokyo to Kanazawa. Unless you are coming from Niigata, you will need to approach Takayama from the south, taking the Shinkansen from Kyoto or Tokyo to Nagoya Station and changing there to a JR express train. From Kyoto, the JR Thunderbird express connects to Kanazawa in just over two hours.

### CAR

To really explore the area, rent a car in Kanazawa or Toyama to make the loop of the Noto Peninsula at your own pace. Another good driving route is between Kanazawa and Takayama via Shirakawa-go.

An economy-size car costs about ¥8,000 per day or ¥50,000 per week. Reserve the car in a city like Kanazawa, Nagano, or Matsumoto, or before you leave Tokyo, Nagoya, or Kyoto—not many people speak English in rural Japan. In most cases, you are expected to return the car with a full tank of gas. Tollways are convenient but expensive and less scenic than the many beautiful national roads in the region.

In winter certain roads through the central Japan Alps are closed, and the road into Kamikochi is inaccessible from November through April.

# Hotels

Accommodations run the gamut from Japanese-style inns to large, modern hotels. Ryokan and minshuku (guest-houses) serve traditional Japanese food, and usually highlight regional specialties. Hotels in the bigger cities have a variety of Western and Japanese restaurants. Japanese inns mostly include two meals in the room rate. In summer it's advisable to book as far in advance as possible.

Most hotels have high-speed Internet connections in the rooms or an Internet terminal for guest use, but ryokan rarely do. Hotel lobbies and areas around train and bus stations often have free Wi-Fi access.

# Planning Your Time

Even a quick loop of the major towns and destinations—the Alps, the Noto Penin-sula, the Chubu Coast, and Sado Island—takes more than a week. To enjoy the unique scenery and culture of the region, it is best to choose two or three cities as sightseeing hubs. In the Alps region, frequent trains run north and south through the mountain valleys, while cut-ting across the mountains east to west, and visiting smaller towns requires more planning. Local tourist offices can supply you with detailed bus and train informa-tion for the surrounding area.

# Restaurants

Traditional Japanese *ryotei* specialize in seasonal delicacies while casual eateries serve delicious home-style cooking and regional dishes. Western fare is easy to come by, especially in larger cities like Kanazawa, which is famed for the local Kaga cuisine.

## RESTAURANT AND HOTEL PRICES

Restaurant and hotel reviews have been shortened. For full information, visit Fodors.com. Restaurant prices are the average cost of a main course at dinner or, if dinner is not served, at lunch. Hotel prices are the lowest cost of a standard double room in high season.

| What It Costs in Yen | | | |
|---|---|---|---|
| $ | $$ | $$$ | $$$$ |
| **RESTAURANTS** | | | |
| under ¥1,500 | ¥1,500–¥3,000 | ¥3,001–¥5,000 | over ¥5,000 |
| **HOTELS** | | | |
| under ¥12,000 | ¥12,000–¥18,000 | ¥18,001–¥22,000 | over ¥22,000 |

# Visitor Information

Offices of the JR Travel Information Center and Japan Travel Bureau are at major train stations. They can help you book local tours, hotel reservations, and travel tickets. You shouldn't assume English will be spoken, but someone usually speaks sufficiently well for your basic needs. Where public transportation is infrequent, such as the Noto-hanto and Sado-ga-shima, local tours are available; however, the guides usually speak only Japanese or limited English.

# When to Go

Temperatures vary widely from the coastal areas to the mountains. Hikers should bring warm clothes even in sum-mer. Cherry-blossom season in April is beautiful; May, June, and September are when transportation is safe and reliable and not too crowded. At the height of summer, from mid-July to the end of August, the Alps and coastal regions are the prime getaway for those fleeing the stagnant heat of urban Japan—expect throngs of tourists and lofty prices. The skiing season peaks over Christmas and New Year's. Winter's heavy snows make driving around the Alps difficult or impossible, and only a few buses and trains run per day. It's fine if you're sticking to the major cities, but unless you've got skiing to do, and a direct train to get there, winter is not ideal for exploring the countryside.

## LOCAL FESTIVALS

Takayama's spring and fall festivals (April 14 and 15 and October 9 and 10) transform the usually quiet town into a rowdy, colorful party, culminating in a musical parade of intricately carved and decorated *yatai* (floats) and *karakuri* marionettes. Flags and draperies adorn local houses, and at night the yatai are hung with lanterns. Book rooms well ahead and expect inflated prices. April's Sanno Matsuri is slightly bigger than October's Hachi-man Matsuri.

During Kanazawa's **Hyaku-man-goku Matsuri** (early June) parades of people dressed in ancient Kaga costumes march through the city to the sound of folk music. Torchlit Noh theater performances, ladder-top acrobatics by Kaga firemen, and singing and dancing in parks create a contagious atmosphere of merrymaking.

Of the many festivals on the Noto-hanto, the most impressive are Nanao's **Seihakusai Dekayama festival,** a 400-year old tradition during which a trio of 30-ton wooden *dekayama* (towering mountain) floats are hauled around the city streets by locals, held May 3–5, and Issaki Hoto Matsuri, held the first Saturday of August.

# Karuizawa (軽井沢)

*170 km (105 miles) northwest of Tokyo, 72 km (45 miles) southeast of Nagano.*

When Archdeacon A. C. Shaw, an English prelate, built his summer villa here in 1886 at the foot of Mt. Asama in southeastern Nagano Prefecture, he sparked the interest of fashionable, affluent Tokyoites, who soon made it their preferred summer destination. Some became patrons of the arts, which led to the opening of galleries and art museums. Pamphlets on current exhibitions are at the tourist office.

Emperor Akihito met the Empress Michiko on a tennis court here in the 1950s. Two decades later John Lennon and Yoko Ono lolled at her family's *besso* (summer house) and the Mampei Hotel. In the Karuizawa Prince Shopping Plaza, near the Karuizawa train station, more than 500 branches of trendy boutiques sell the same goods as their flagship stores in Tokyo, often at substantially discounted prices.

## GETTING HERE AND AROUND

Coming from Tokyo, Karuizawa is a nice stop en route to the hot-spring towns of Kusatsu and Yudanaka or Matsumoto and Kamikochi. The town itself is easy to explore by foot, taxi, or bicycle. Naka-Karuizawa Station, one stop (five minutes) away on the Shinano Tetsudo Line, is a gateway to Shiraito and Ryugaeshi waterfalls, the Yacho wild bird sanctuary, and hiking trails.

■TIP→ **Karuizawa is very crowded from mid-July to late August, so book your accommodations well in advance.**

**VISITOR INFORMATION**

**CONTACT Karuizawa Tourist Information Center.** ✉ *JR Karuizawa Station, Karuizawa-eki* ☎ *0267/42–2491* 🌐 *www.karuizawa-kankokyokai.jp.*

## Sights

**Karuizawa Wild Bird Forest** (軽井沢野鳥の森; *Karuizawa Yacho-no-mori*)

**FOREST** | This sanctuary is home to some 80 bird species, including the Japanese white-eye. You can watch from two observation huts along a 2½-km (1½-mile) forest course. To get here from Karuizawa Station, take a free shuttle bus bound for the "Hoshino area," or take the local Seibu Koden bus. Get off at the Tombo no Yu stop and walk about one minute to the park. You can wander around on your own (free), or book a two-hour guided ecotour in English for a charge. **■ TIP→ Try to book at least a week in advance for English tours.** ✉ *Nagakura Hoshino, Karuizawa-cho* ☎ *0267/45–7777* 🌐 *picchio.co.jp* 🎫 *Free; ecotour ¥2,500.*

**Mt. Asama Overlook** (碓氷峠から見た浅間山; *Usuitoge kara mita asamayama*)

**VOLCANO** | This active volcano of more than 8,000 feet threatens to put an end to the whole "Highlands Ginza" below. For a view of the glorious Asama-san in its entirety, head to the observation platform at Usui-toge (Usui Pass). You can also see neighboring Myogi-san, as well as the whole Yatsugatake, a range of eight volcanic peaks. Walk northeast along shop-filled Karuizawa Ginza street to the end, past Nite-bashi, and follow the trail through an evergreen forest to the pass. A lovely view justifies the 1½-hour walk. From late April to late November, buses (¥500) leave almost hourly if you want a ride back. ✉ *Mt. Asama.*

**Shiraito and Ryugaeshi Waterfalls** (白糸の滝と竜返しの滝; *Shiraito-no-taki and Ryugaeshi-no-taki*)

**WATERFALL** | Hiking paths get crowded during the tourist season, but these waterfalls make a good afternoon excursion in the off-season. To get to the trailhead at Mine-no-Chaya, take the bus from Karuizawa Station. The ride takes about 25 minutes and costs ¥710. From the trailhead it's about a one-hour hike to Shiraito for the 3-meter-high, 70-meter-wide falls. You can take the bus back to Karuizawa Station from here or continue on to the not-so-impressive Ryugaeshi falls (90 minutes). From these falls it's a 15-minute walk to the bus stop and a 20-minute bus ride back to Karuizawa. ✉ *Shiraito-no-taki* 🎫 *Free.*

## Restaurants

**Kastanie** (カスターニエ)

**$$** | **MEDITERRANEAN** | **FAMILY** | The tiled bar and wooden tables are as inviting as the staff of this family-friendly restaurant a few blocks north of Karuizawa Station. The menu is centered on rotisserie chicken, served alongside healthy salads and other dishes using local, seasonal produce. **Known for:** small selection of local craft beers; well-made pizza; herb-seasoned rotisserie chicken. [$] *Average main: ¥3,000* ✉ *23–2 Karuizawa Higashi* ☎ *0267/42–3081* 🌐 *www.kastanie.co.jp/en* 🕒 *Closed Mon.*

# Kusatsu (草津)

*42 km (26 miles) north of Karuizawa.*

The highly touted hot springs at Kusatsu contain sulfur, iron, aluminum, and even trace amounts of arsenic. Every minute the *yu-batake* (hot-spring field) gushes over 1,000 gallons of near-boiling water, which is cooled in seven long wooden boxes and sent to more than 100 guesthouses in the village. The hot-spring field is beautifully lighted at night.

### GETTING HERE AND AROUND

Just inside the border of Gunma Prefecture, the springs can be reached by Seibu Kanko bus year-round from Karuizawa (1¼ hrs). Buses depart from the north side of Karuizawa Station.

### VISITOR INFORMATION

**CONTACT Kusatsu Information Center.** ✉ *28 Kusatsu-machi* ☎ *0279/88–0800* 🌐 *www.kusatsu-onsen.ne.jp.*

## Sights

**Netsu-no-yu Bath** (熱乃湯; *Netsu-no-yu*)
**HOT SPRING** | This is the often unbearably hot public bath next door to the *yu-batake* (hot springs field) that is popularly known as a "fever bath." You can't actually bathe here, but you can watch one of six daily *yumomi* shows in which locals in colorful traditional garb churn the waters with long wooden planks until they reach a comfortable temperature. You can also sign up for a Yumomi Experience and try churning the waters yourself. It's about 20 minutes of churning and fairly tiring, but you'll be enthusiastically encouraged by local yumomi pros. ✉ *414 Kusatsu-cho* ☎ *0279/88–3613* 🎟 *Yumomi Show ¥600, Yumomi Experience ¥250.*

**Sai-no-Kawara Open-Air Bath** (西の河原露天風呂; *Sai-no-Kawara Rotenburo*)
**HOT SPRING** | For a soak in the open air, try this expansive bath at the western end of Kusatsu village, which has pleasing scenery by day and lots of stars by night. Known for its milky waters, the bath can hold up to 100 people at a time. It's a 15-minute walk west from the Kusatsu bus terminal. ✉ *521–3 Kusatsu-machi* ☎ *0279/88–6167* 🌐 *www.sainokawara.com/en* 🎟 *¥600.*

## Hotels

**Kusatsu Hotel** (草津ホテル)
**$$$$** | **HOTEL** | Built in 1913, but with a smart, new annex added in 2020, the Kusatsu Hotel is a blend of classic and contemporary ryokan. **Pros:** charming old building; selection of natural hot-spring baths; only a five-minute walk from the Yubatake and town center. **Cons:** a few of the Japanese-style rooms have no bath; might feel too formal for some; prices skyrocket during peak seasons. [$] *Rooms from: ¥27,200* ✉ *479 Kusatsu* ☎ *0279/88-5011* 🌐 *www.kusatsuhotel.com* 🛏 *43 rooms* 🍴 *No Meals.*

# Nagano (長野)

*245 km (152 miles) northwest of Tokyo, 72 km (45 miles) northwest of Karuizawa, 249 km (155 miles) northeast of Nagoya.*

Nagano Prefecture is called the "Roof of Japan," home to the northern, central, and southern Japan Alps and six national parks that offer year-round recreational activities. Active volcanoes include Mt. Asama on the border between Nagano and Gunma prefectures and Mt. Ontake in Nagano Prefecture, which is a destination for religious pilgrims.

Rimmed by mountains, the city of Nagano began life as a temple town with the founding of Zenko-ji in the 7th century. In time for the 1998 Winter Olympics, a new Shinkansen line was built connecting Tokyo and Nagano, and new highways were added to handle the car and bus traffic. Suddenly, with Nagano City as a transport hub, the fairly inaccessible Alps region in the wider area of Nagano Prefecture was opened to visitors. Tourism in the region peaks in winter when the fresh powder on Nagano Prefecture's ski hills and its abundant natural hot spring baths draw crowds, but a second boom follows in summer when the mountains open for alpine hiking. For most people visiting Nagano Prefecture, Nagano City isn't the main draw, but it is worthwhile to spend a night before then moving on to natural attractions nearby.

Zenko-ji is a nonsectarian Buddhist temple that accepts believers of all faiths.

## GETTING HERE AND AROUND

Nagano is 99 minutes from Tokyo Station by Shinkansen, 31 minutes from Karuiza-wa by Shinkansen, and three hours from Nagoya by the JR Wide View Shinano express. It's a convenient base for visiting some of the surrounding onsen and mountains, though you can easily see the main sights around Zenko-ji Temple in half a day.

## VISITOR INFORMATION

You'll find tourist information offices in Kusatsu, Nagano, and Yamanouchi.

**CONTACTS Nagano City Tourist Information Office.** ✉ *Nagano Station, 1038–4, Nagano* ☎ *026/226–5626* ⊕ *www.go-nagano.net.* **Yamanouchi Information Center.** ✉ *3352–1 Hirao, Yamanouchi-machi* ☎ *0269/33–2138* ⊕ *www.info-yamanouchi.net.*

 Sights

### Zenko-ji Temple (善光寺)

**TEMPLE** | Nagano's unusual temple is the final destination each year for millions of religious pilgrims. Since the 7th century, this nonsectarian Buddhist temple has accepted believers of all faiths and admitted women when other temples forbade it. Each morning the head priest (Tendai sect) and head priestess (Jodo sect) hold a joint service to pray for the prosperity of the assembled pilgrims (usually on tour packages). Visitors rub the worn wooden statue of the ancient doctor Binzuru (Pindola Bharadvaja in Sanskrit) for relief of aches and pains. After the service, descend into the pitch-black tunnel in the basement to find the iron latch on the wall; seizing it is said to bring enlightenment.

The temple is a 3-km (2-mile) walk from the station or, from 8:35 onwards, you could take the Gururin-go or retro Binzuru-go buses from the station (¥150, 10 minutes). They run every 15 minutes. Those buses aren't running in time for the morning service, however, which starts from 5:30 to 7 am, depending on the season, so you might want to ask your hotel to reserve a taxi for that.

# On the Menu

Every microregion in Japan's alpine region has its specialties and unique style of preparing seafood from the Sea of Japan. Vitamin-rich seaweed such as *wakame* or *kombu* is a common ingredient, sometimes served in miso soup with tiny *shijimi* clams.

In **Toyama**, spring brings tiny purple-hued baby firefly squid (*hotaru-ika*) to the menu, which are boiled in soy sauce or sake and eaten whole with a tart mustard-miso sauce. Try the seasonal *ama-ebi* (sweet shrimp) and *masu-zushi* (thinly sliced trout sushi pressed flat). In winter crabs abound, including the red, long-legged *beni-zuwaigani*.

**Fukui** has huge *echizen-gani* crabs. When boiled with salt and dipped in rice vinegar, they're pure heaven. In both Fukui and Ishikawa, restaurants serve *echizen-soba* (homemade buckwheat noodles with mountain vegetables) with a *dashi* stock and grazed *daikon* radish; either for dipping or mixed in with the noodles.

The seafood-based *Kaga-ryori* (Kaga cuisine) is common to **Kanazawa and Noto-hanto.** *Tai* (sea bream) is topped with mountain-fern brackens, greens, and mushrooms. At Wajima's early-morning fish market near the tip of Noto-hanto and at Kanazawa's *Omi-cho* market you have your choice of everything from abalone to seaweed, and plenty of restaurants nearby serve seafood dishes with it.

In **Niigata Prefecture** try *noppei-jiru*, a hot (or cold) soup with *sato-imo* (a type of sweet potato) as its base, and mushrooms, salmon, and other local ingredients. It goes well with hot rice and grilled fish. *Wappa-meshi* is steamed rice garnished with local ingredients, like wild vegetables, chicken, fish, and shellfish. In autumn try *kiku-no-ohitashi*, a side dish of chrysanthemum petals marinated in vinegar. Niigata has outstanding fish in winter—*buri* (yellowtail), flatfish, sole, oysters, abalone, and shrimp. A local specialty is *namban ebi*, raw shrimp dipped in soy sauce and wasabi. It's butter-tender and especially sweet on Sado-ga-shima. Also on Sado-ga-shima, take advantage of the excellent wakame dishes and *sazae-no-tsuboyaki* (wreath shellfish) broiled in their shells with a soy or miso sauce.

The area around **Matsumoto** is known for its wasabi and chilled *zarusoba* (buckwheat noodles). Eel steamed inside rice wrapped in bamboo leaves is also popular, as is the local take on deep-fried chicken, the garlicky *sanzoku-yaki*. For those without culinary inhibitions, there's also *inago*, locust simmered in sugar and soy sauce.

*Sansai soba* (buckwheat noodles with mountain vegetables) and *sansai-ryori* (wild vegetables and mushrooms in soups or tempura) are specialties in the mountainous areas of **Takayama and Nagano.** Local river fish like *ayu* (smelt) or *iwana* (char) are grilled on a spit with *shoyu* (soy sauce) or salt. *Hoba miso* is a dark, slightly sweet type of miso roasted on a large magnolia leaf.

Nagano is also famous for *ba-sashi* (raw horse meat), *sakura nabe* (horse-meat stew, cooked in an earthenware pot), and boiled baby bees. The former two are still very popular; as for the latter, even locals admit they're something of an acquired taste.

✉ *4–9–1 Motoyoshi, Nagano* ☎ *026/234–3591* 🌐 *www.zenkoji.jp* 🎫 *¥500 for the inner sanctuary.*

## 🍴 Restaurants

**Fujiya Gohonjin** (ザ フジヤ ゴホンジン)
$$$$ | **ITALIAN** | This stately building just outside the gates of Zenko-ji combines a bar, lounge, café, and fantastic Italian restaurant. The rather formal modern dining room offers prix-fixe or à la carte options featuring high-quality local ingredients, while the bar and lounge serve up light meals in stately surroundings and the café is a little more relaxed. **Known for:** extensive wine and champagne list in the main restaurant; good pasta; herb-grilled meat and seafood. [$] *Average main: ¥6,500* ✉ *80 Daimon-cho, Nagano* ☎ *026/232–1241* 🌐 *www.thefujiyagohonjin.com.*

## 🛏 Hotels

**Sotetsu Fresa Inn Nagano Zenkoji-guchi** (相鉄フレッサイン長野善光寺口)
$ | **HOTEL** | A coffee table and two easy chairs are squeezed into each compact Western-style room here, which is all you need if you're en route to other Alps destinations. **Pros:** convenient location next to the station; friendly staff; well-maintained property. **Cons:** nondescript decor; not much atmosphere; small rooms. [$] *Rooms from: ¥9,690* ✉ *1356 Suehiro-cho, Nagano* ☎ *026/480–2031* 🌐 *sotetsu-hotels.com* 🛏 *143 rooms* 🍴 *Free Breakfast.*

# Side Trip to Yudanaka Onsen and Shibu Onsen

*Yudanaka Onsen is 32 km (20 miles) northeast of Nagano; Shibu Onsen is 2 km (1¼ miles) from Yudanaka Onsen.*

Northeast of Nagano, these historic hot-spring towns in close proximity to each other are the gateway to the Shiga Kogen Plateau ski area, known for its alpine skiing and snowboarding. Yudanaka and Shibu are worthwhile destinations, where you can soak in a public baths on a daytrip or stay at a traditional inn and take things more slowly. You can even spot monkeys taking a bath at their favorite hot spring. Both towns are considerably developed, but Shibu has managed to preserve the atmosphere of a traditional hot-spring town.

### GETTING HERE AND AROUND

Yudanaka is the last stop on the Nagano Dentetsu Line's Yukemuri Express service; the trip from Nagano takes 45 minutes and costs ¥1,590. From the Yudanako station, it's a quick five-minute trip by bus (¥210) to Shibu onsen; alternatively, you could take a taxi or even walk in about 30 minutes.

## 👁 Sights

**Jigoku-dani Monkey Park** (地獄谷野猿公苑; *Jigoku-dani Yaen Koen*)
**HOT SPRING** | When snow is on the ground, the Japanese white macaques (Asian monkeys) that make their home here are a big draw, as are their bathing habits. To be on the safe side, don't feed or touch them—or look them in the eye. The train goes as far as Yudanaka; from there, take a taxi or bus to Kanbayashi Onsen, from which it is a 30- to 40-minute walk. There is also a direct bus to Kanbayashi Onsen from Nagano Station. Although winter is the best time to see the bathing apes, there are usually some in the onsen in other seasons. Wear good shoes as the path can get muddy, and leave heavy luggage at your hotel or in your car. ✉ *6845 Yamanouchi-machi, Shimotakai-gun, Yamanouchi-machi* ☎ *0269/33–4379* 🌐 *www.jigokudani-yaenkoen.co.jp* 🎫 *¥800.*

**Shibu Onsen's Nine Baths**
(九湯めぐり; *Kyu-to Meguri*)
**HOT SPRING** | As well as hot-spring baths within ryokan, Shibu has nine baths scattered around town, each of which is said to bring a different benefit to bathers, from soothing intestinal issues to treating neuralgia. Legend has it that bathing in all nine results in longevity and protection from evil. Bath number 9 (called O-yu) is open to day-trippers (buy a ticket at the local tourist office), but if you stay at an inn in Shibu, you'll be given a key that unlocks all nine baths, so you can don your in-room yukata gown and hop from bath to bath. ✉ *Shibu Onsen Visitor Center, 2112–1 Hirao, Yamanouchi-machi* 🌐 *www.shibuonsen.net/english* 🎫 *Free for ryokan guests; ¥500 for bath number 9 for non-ryokan guests* ☞ *Baths open 6 am to 10 pm.*

## Hotels

**Ryokan Kanaguya** (旅館金具屋)
**$$$$** | **B&B/INN** | Before it was upstaged by the bathing monkeys, Kanaguya Ryokan, the town's oldest and grandest traditional inn, was Shibu Onsen's main draw. **Pros:** attentive service; historical building; roof top outdoor bath. **Cons:** no credit cards accepted; limited English ability; few rooms with attached baths. [$] *Rooms from: ¥39,600* ✉ *2202 Hirao, Shibu Onsen, Yamanouchi-machi* ☎ *0269/33–3131* 🌐 *www.kanaguya.com* 🛏 *29 rooms (19 with shared bath)* 🍴 *All-Inclusive* ☞ *Reservations for non-Japanese need to be made through the agent listed on their website.*

**Uotoshi Ryokan** (魚敏旅館)
**$$** | **B&B/INN** | This small ryokan in the steamy village of Yudanaka has a *hinoki* (cypress) bathtub that's continually fed by the hot springs. **Pros:** the chance to try your hand at Japanese archery is a rare treat; quirky owners offer genuine local hospitality; room with dinner and breakfast packages available for a few thousand yen extra. **Cons:** no rooms with bath; can fill up with school tours in March and summer; bigger inns with more facilities available in town. [$] *Rooms from: ¥13,200* ✉ *2563 Sano, Yamanouchi-machi, Yamanouchi-machi* ☎ *0269/33–1215* 🌐 *www.avis.ne.jp/~miyasaka* 🛏 *8 rooms* 🍴 *Free Breakfast.*

# Matsumoto (松本)

*64 km (40 miles) southwest of Nagano, 245 km (152 miles) northwest of Tokyo, 200 km (125 miles) northeast of Nagoya.*

Snowcapped peaks surround the old castle town of Matsumoto, where the air is cool and dry on the alpine plateau. More interesting and picturesque than Nagano and less touristy than Takayama, this gateway to the northern Alps is one of the best bases for exploring the area. Full of good cafés and restaurants, Matsumoto is also a center for traditional crafts—including *tensan,* or fabric woven from silk taken from wild silkworms; Matsumoto *shiki,* or lacquerware; and Azumino glass. Old merchant houses stand along Nakamachi Street, south of the castle. Several influential educators, lawyers, and writers from this city have impacted Japan's sociopolitical system in the past.

Though it only takes a day to visit the main sights in town, Matsumoto's restaurants, cafés, and relaxed atmosphere make it a hard place to leave. It is worth staying a night or two to visit the outlying museums and hot springs. Matsumoto is also a good base to visit Kamikochi to the west, or the post towns of Magome and Tsumago to the south.

### GETTING HERE AND AROUND

Fuji Dream Airlines (FDA), code-sharing with Japan Airlines, has daily flights to Matsumoto from Fukuoka, Kobe, Osaka, and Sapporo. Trains are also available: Matsumoto is 50 minutes from Nagano and 2¼ hours from Nagoya on the JR Wide View Shinano express, and 2¾ hours from Tokyo's Shinjuku Station on

Matsumoto-jo is also called "Crow Castle" because of its black walls.

the JR Azusa express. By bus it's 2½ hours east of Takayama.

**CONTACT Fuji Dream Airlines.** ☎ *0570/55–0489* ⊕ *www.fujidream.co.jp.*

## VISITOR INFORMATION

Matsumoto is compact, so grab a map at the tourist information center at the JR Station and head for the old part of town near the Chitose-bashi Bridge at the end of Hon-machi-dori. Alternatively Matsumoto's Town Sneaker shuttle bus (¥200 flat fee in most sections, ¥150 in some; day pass ¥500) stops at the main sights, and the tourist office can direct you to one of the many locations renting bicycles.

**CONTACT Matsumoto Tourist Information Center.** ⊠ *Matsumoto Station, 1–1–1 Fukashi, Matsumoto* ☎ *0263/32–2814* ⊕ *visitmatsumoto.com.*

 **Sights**

### OLD TOWN

**Matsumoto Castle** (松本城; *Matsumoto-jo*)

**CASTLE/PALACE** | Nicknamed "Crow Castle" for its black walls, this local landmark began as a small fortress with moats in 1504. It was remodeled into its current three-turreted form between 1592 and 1614, just as Japan became a consolidated nation under a central government. The civil wars ended and the peaceful Edo period (1603–1868) began, rendering medieval castles obsolete. Its late construction explains why the 95-foot-tall *tenshukaku* (inner tower) is the oldest surviving tower in Japan—no battles were ever fought here. Exhibits on each floor break up the challenging climb up very steep stairs. If you hunker down to look through rectangular openings (broad enough to scan for potential enemies) on the sixth floor, you'll have a gorgeous view of the surrounding mountains. In the southeast corner of the castle grounds, the Matsumoto City Museum (closed until autumn

2023 for renovations) exhibits samurai clothing and centuries-old agricultural implements.

At the end of July there is a *taiko* (Japanese drum) festival, and on November 3 the Matsumoto Castle Festival features a samurai parade, martial arts displays, and outdoor tea ceremonies. In late January an ice-sculpture exhibition is held in the museum's park. The castle is a 15-minute walk from the station. ⊠ *4–1 Marunouchi, Matsumoto* ☎ *0263/32–2902* ⊕ *www. matsumoto-castle.jp* 🎫 *¥700*.

### Matsumoto City Museum of Art (松本市美術館 *Matsumotoshi Bijutsukan*)

ART MUSEUM | The red polka dots on the facade of this museum, east of the Nakamachi district, are a very firm nod to arguably the most famous person to come from Matsumoto: artist Yayoi Kusama. Part of the permanent collection focuses of Kusama's avant-garde art and art installations, and includes a version of the iconic yellow and black pumpkin sculpture installed on Naoshima Island. There are also exhibits of calligraphy, painting and sculpture from other Matsumoto-born artists. ⊠ *4–2–22 Chuo, Matsumoto* ☎ *0263/39–7400* ⊕ *matsumoto-artmuse.jp/en* 🎫 *¥410* ☾ *Closed Mon.*

### Nakamachi District (中町)

HISTORIC DISTRICT | In the Edo era (1603–1868) Nakamachi was Matsumoto's central district, through which passed a key highway connecting the region to Kyoto, Nagoya, and Zenko-ji Temple in Nagano. Today, the main street here is still lined with old wooden buildings and white-painted *kura* (warehouses) that house craft stores, galleries, and hip cafes. It's a lovely place for a stroll. Running parallel, just across the Metoba River, Nawate Street has a similarly retro vibe, though that comes alive more at night because of its cluster of restaurants and bars. Nakamachi is a five-minute walk south of the castle or 10 minutes east of Matsumoto Station. The Town

Sneaker bus also stops there. ⊠ *3–3–17 Chuo, Matsumoto* ⊕ *nakamachi.org/en* ☾ *Many of the stores close Wed.*

## WEST OF THE STATION

Two of the city's best museums are west of the JR Station, both served by the Ukiyoe-hakubutsukan / Rekishi-no-sato stop about 20 minutes from Matsumoto Station on the Town Sneaker bus.

### Matsumoto History Village (松本歴史の里; *Matsumoto Rekishi no Sato*)

MUSEUM VILLAGE | Next to the Ukiyo-e Museum is Japan's oldest wooden courthouse. Displays pertain to the history of law enforcement from the feudal period to the modern era. ⊠ *2196–01 Shimadachi, Matsumoto* ☎ *0263/47–4515* 🎫 *¥410* ☾ *Closed Mon.*

### Japan Wood-Block Print Museum (日本浮世絵博物館; *Nihon Ukiyoe Hakubutsukan*)

ART MUSEUM | The museum is devoted to the lively, colorful, and widely popular *ukiyo-e* woodblock prints of Edo-period artists. Highlights include Hiroshige's scenes of the Tokaido (the main trading route through Honshu in feudal Japan), Hokusai's views of Mt. Fuji, and Sharaku's Kabuki actors. Based on the enormous holdings of the wealthy Sakai family, the museum's 100,000 pieces (displays rotate every three months) include some of Japan's finest prints and represent the largest collection of its kind in the world. ⊠ *2206–1 Shimadachi, Matsumoto* ☎ *0263/47–4440* ⊕ *www. japan-ukiyoe-museum.com* 🎫 *¥1,000* ☾ *Closed Mon.*

## AROUND MATSUMOTO (松本の周辺)

The local train to the Daio horseradish farm and the Rokuzan Art Museum journeys through vibrant green fields, apple orchards, and miles of rice paddies.

### Daio Wasabi Farm (大王わさび農場; *Daio Wasabi Nojo*)

FARM/RANCH | At the country's largest wasabi farm, the green horseradish

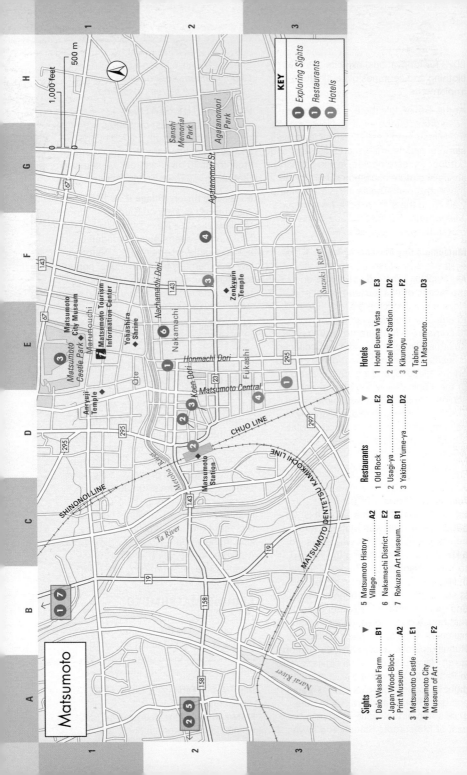

# Matsumoto

500 m
1,000 feet

**KEY**

1 Exploring Sights

1 Restaurants

1 Hotels

**Sights** ▶
1 Daio Wasabi Farm......**B1**
2 Japan Wood-Block
 Print Museum......**A2**
3 Matsumoto Castle......**E1**
4 Matsumoto City
 Museum of Art......**F2**
5 Matsumoto History
 Village......**A2**
6 Nakamachi District......**E2**
7 Rokuzan Art Museum......**B1**

**Restaurants** ▶
1 Old Rock......**E2**
2 Usagi-ya......**D2**
3 Yakitori Yume-ya......**D2**

**Hotels** ▶
1 Hotel Buena Vista......**E3**
2 Hotel New Station......**D2**
3 Kikunoyu......**F2**
4 Tabino
 Lit Matsumoto......**D3**

Matsumoto Castle Park
Matsumoto City Museum
Marunouchi
Matsumoto Tourism Information Center
Yohashira Shrine
Anryuji Temple
Ote
Koen-Dori
Nakamachi
Honmachi Dori
Nakamachi Dori
Fukashi
Matsumoto Central
Zenkyuin Temple
Matsumoto Station
Agatanomori St.
Sanshi Memorial Park
Agatanomori Park
Suzuki River
Metoba River
Ta River
Narai River
SHINONOI LINE
CHUO LINE
MATSUMOTO DENTETSU KAMIKOCHI LINE

143
67
143
143
295
23
295
295
297
19
158
158
19
67

roots are cultivated in flat gravel beds irrigated by melted snow from the Alps. The chilly mineral water is ideal for the durable wasabi. The on-site shop sells the farm's products, which range from wasabi cheese to wasabi chocolate and wasabi ice cream (sounds bad, tastes pretty good), while the several cafes and restaurant's also serve wasabi-focused fare. The closest train station is Hotaka, 26 minutes (¥330) north along the JR Oito Line from Matsumoto Station. To reach the farm from Hotaka Station, take a 40-minute walk along a path (the station attendant will direct you), rent a bike, or hop in a taxi for about ¥1,300. ✉ *3640 Hotaka, Azumino* ☎ *0263/82–8118* 🌐 *www.daiowasabi.co.jp* 🎫 *Free.*

**Rokuzan Art Museum** (碌山美術館; *Rokuzan Bijutsukan*)

**ART MUSEUM** | This museum displays the work of Rokuzan Ogiwara, a sculptor who was influenced by Auguste Rodin and pioneered modern sculptural styles in Japan. He is especially known for his female figures in repose and male figures in heroic poses. This ivy-covered brick building with a stunning bell tower is in Hotaka, 26 minutes (¥330) north of Matsumoto Station on the JR Oito Line. From Hotaka Station it's a 10-minute walk to the museum. ✉ *5095–1 Hotaka, Azumino* ☎ *0263/82–2094* 🌐 *www.rokuzan.jp* 🎫 *¥700* 🕑 *Closed Mon. and the day following a public holiday Nov.–Apr.*

## 🍴 Restaurants

**Old Rock** (オールドロック)

**$$** | **ECLECTIC** | Two blocks before the Chitose-bashi Bridge, this Japanese version of a traditional British pub serves fish-and-chips and pizza along with local Matsumoto beer and rotating craft brews from elsewhere. It's close to Parco department store, between the station and castle. **Known for:** local craft beer; decent fish-and-chips; pizza. [$] *Average main: ¥1,500* ✉ *2–3–20 Chuo, Matsumoto* ☎ *0263/38–0069* 🌐 *pub-old-rock.com* 🕑 *Closed Wed. No lunch.*

**Usagi-ya** (卯屋)

**$$** | **JAPANESE** | This bustling izakaya across the street from the annex of Hotel Iidaya on the station's east side serves up izakaya staples plus regional specialties like *basashi* (raw horse meat), *sansoku-yaki* (a kind of fried chicken) and rabbit (*usagi* means "rabbit"). There's no English menu, so keep an eye out for what others are eating and point to whatever looks good. **Known for:** local oddity inago (simmered grasshoppers); range of sake and shochu; excellent sashimi of Shinshu salmon. [$] *Average main: ¥3,000* ✉ *1–2–12 Chuo, Matsumoto* ☎ *0263/36–2544* 💳 *No credit cards* 🕑 *Closed Sun.*

**Yakitori Yume-ya** (焼き鳥夢屋)

**$$** | **JAPANESE** | With a retro vibe, Yume-ya specializes in old-style *yakitori* (skewered, grilled meat and vegetables). Cozy up to the narrow counter for food and drinks, or sit outside during the warmer months. **Known for:** particularly good negima (chicken and leek) skewers; snacks like edamame and chilled tofu; deer liver pate. [$] *Average main: ¥2,000* ✉ *Showa Yokocho, 1–13–11 Chuo, Matsumoto* ☎ *0263/33–8430* 💳 *No credit cards* 🕑 *Closed Sun.*

## 🛏 Hotels

**Hotel Buena Vista** (ホテルブエナビスタ)

**$$** | **HOTEL** | One step up from a standard Japanese business hotel, the Buena Vista has a glowing marble lobby and facilities that include a coffeehouse, café-bar, and three restaurants. **Pros:** large rooms by local standards; good location; upper floors have great views. **Cons:** decor that borders on being a garish relic of the 1980s; can be busy with conventions and weddings; buffet dinner is pricey. [$] *Rooms from: ¥12,600* ✉ *1–2–1 Hon-jo, Matsumoto* ☎ *0263/37–0111* 🌐 *www.buena-vista.co.jp* 🛏 *200 rooms* 🍴 *No Meals.*

## Hotel New Station
### (ホテルニューステーション)
$ | **HOTEL** | Although business hotels are often cold, this one warms things up with a cheerful staff and a lively restaurant that serves freshwater *iwana* (char)—an area specialty. **Pros:** inexpensive rates, especially off-peak; excellent staff; near the station. **Cons:** dated interior design; can get noisy; small rooms. $ *Rooms from: ¥9,980* ⊠ *1–1–11 Chuo, Matsumoto* ☎ *0263/35–3850* ⊕ *www. hotel-ns.com* ⮡ *95 rooms* ⑩ *Free Breakfast.*

## Kikunoyu (菊の湯)
$$$$ | **B&B/INN** | Built in the traditional *honmune-zukuri* style, this hot-springs lodging has a characteristic peaked roof, ornamental woodwork above the front gable, and bow windows. **Pros:** rates include breakfast and dinner; excellent hot-springs baths; staff speak some English. **Cons:** not all rooms have a bath (those without, however, are substantially cheaper); will feel overly formal to some; not a good base for other sightseeing. $ *Rooms from: ¥44,000* ⊠ *1–29–7 Asama-onsen, Matsumoto* ☎ *0263/46–2300* ⊕ *www.kikunoyu.com* ⮡ *17 rooms* ⑩ *All-Inclusive.*

## Tabino Lit Matsumoto
### (たびのホテルlit松本)
$ | **HOTEL** | A few minutes south of Matsumoto Station, near the Hotel Buena Vista, the Tabino added a smart budget option to Matsumoto when it opened in the summer of 2021. **Pros:** friendly staff; great value; on-site hot spring baths. **Cons:** a long walk to the main sights; not much English spoken; not many in-room amenities. $ *Rooms from: ¥11,700* ⊠ *1–4–5 Fukashi, Matsumoto* ☎ *0263/39–5050* ⊕ *matsumoto.tabi-no-hotel.jp* ⮡ *176 rooms* ⑩ *No Meals.*

 Nightlife

## Eonta (エオンタ)
**BARS** | This jazz bar has been popular with locals since the 1970s. Sit at the bar or on the corner sofas and choose from the extensive list of cocktails. Eonta is in a quasi-dilapidated two-story building a few blocks southeast of the castle. ⊠ *4–9–7 Ote, Matsumoto* ☎ *0263/33–0505* ⊗ *Closed Wed.*

## Matsumoto Brewery Taproom Media Garden
### (松本ブルワリーTAPルーム本町店)
**BREWPUBS** | Founded in 2016, the Matsumoto Brewery makes a great selection of pale ales, bitters, and stouts, which you can try, along with guest beers, at this taproom in the sleek Media Garden complex, halfway between the station and Nakamachi. They also have a smaller taproom in an old *kura* in Nakamachi (closed Tues.), although that closes by 7 pm. ⊠ *2–20–2 Chuo, Matsumoto* ⊕ *matsu-brew.com/aboutus/#taproom* ⊗ *Closed Wed.* ⮡ *Open until 10 pm.*

# Hakuba (白馬)

*64 km (40 miles) north of Matsumoto, 48 km (30 miles) northwest of Nagano.*

In the northwestern part of Nagano Prefecture, Hakuba Village lies beneath the magnificent Hakuba mountain range, the best of the northern Japan Alps. Hakuba means "white horse," because the main peak, Mt. Shirouma-dake (9,617 feet), resembles a horse. This is a well-developed, all-year resort area for trekking, skiing, and climbing around the 9,500-foot mountains among rare alpine flora, insects, and wildlife. Gondola and chairlifts carry you up to ridges with panoramic views. Olympic alpine runs and ski jumps await winter sports fans, and summer visitors can still find snow, especially in the Grand Snowy Gorge.

Because the main attractions of Hakuba are hiking and skiing in the mountains,

Hakuba Village, at the foot of the Hakuba mountain range, is green in spring and summer and a major skiing center in winter.

plan to stay at least two days to take advantage of the surroundings. The ski season in Hakuba runs from late November to the first week of May. The hiking season runs from late June until the end of September, and the trails can be especially crowded in August. In July the mountains are covered in fields of wildflowers, making for a spectacular sight.

## GETTING HERE AND AROUND

Both the JR Limited Express (one hour, ¥2,190) and the JR Oito Line (1¾ hours, ¥1,170) run from Matsumoto to Hakuba. From Nagano the bus will take about an hour.

## VISITOR INFORMATION

The Hakuba Village Office of Tourism, to the right as you exit the train station, provides basic maps (mostly in Japanese). Near the Alpico bus terminal and Happo bus stop is the Happo-one Tourism Association, which can help you reserve a hotel room (for the peak summer and winter seasons, you should book in advance). Run by a Canadian and Japanese couple, Evergreen Outdoor

Center offers a variety of outdoor tours year-round. It is also a good place to get information on outdoor activities in the Hakuba area.

**CONTACTS Evergreen Outdoor Center.** ⊠ *Kokusai Lodge, 4377 Hokujou, Hakuba* ☎ *0261/72–5150* ⊕ *www.evergreen-hakuba.com.* **Hakuba Village Office of Tourism.** ⊠ *6329–1 Hokujou, Hakuba* ☎ *0261/72–5000* ⊕ *www.hakubavalley.jp.* **Happo-one Tourism Association.** ⊠ *5734  1 Hokujou, Hakuba-mura* ☎ *0261/72–3066* ⊕ *www.happo-one.jp.*

 **Sights**

### Happo-one Ski Resort (八方尾根スキー場; *Happo-one Sukii-jyo*)

SPORTS VENUE | Hakuba itself is one of Japan's best ski destinations, famous for powder snow, clear weather, and miles of tracks. The Happo-one (*one* pronounced "oh-ney") resort is the best in town, and hosted several events for the 1998 Nagano Winter Olympics. Almost all the runs here are intermediate level, with the rest split between beginner and advanced, the latter including the two runs (Olympic I and Olympic II) that were used in 1998 for the men's and women's downhill events. Japan's first parallel jumping hills were also constructed here with critical points of 393 feet and 295 feet, and each has a scaffold structure for the in-run and landing slope. All runs deliver breathtaking views if the mist doesn't roll in.

Happo-one also has some great summer hiking, though the high elevation means that even in summer a sweater or light jacket may be needed. You can reach the hiking area via three connecting gondolas, collectively called the Happo Alpen Line (five minutes to Happo Gondola Station, then eight minutes to Usagidaira, then an additional 10 minutes by alpine lift). From here the jewel-like Happo Pond is a 6-km (4-mile) hike. For more-ambitious hikers, three more hours gets you to the top of Mt. Karamatsu-dake.

To get from the center of town to Happo-one, it's a five-minute, 3-km (2-mile) bus ride from Hakuba to Happo Information Center, and then a 15-minute walk through the resort of Swiss-like chalets and hotels to the gondola station. Facilities: 13 trails, 494 acres; 3,513-foot vertical drop; 22 lifts ✉ *5734–1 Hokujou, Hakuba* ☎ *0261/72–3066* 🌐 *www.happo-one.jp* 🎫 *One-day ski pass ¥5,500, summer Happo Alpen Line ticket (one-way) ¥3,000.*

**Mt. Shirouma** (白馬岳; *Shirouma-dake*)
**MOUNTAIN** | Hiking at the bottom of Daisekkei (Big Snow) Gorge, which extends for 3½ km (2 miles), requires warm clothes even in midsummer, when temperatures can dip below freezing. More than 100 types of alpine flowers grace the nearby fields in summer. From the trailhead at Sarukura Village (reached by a 30-minute, ¥1,000 bus ride from Hakuba Station), the hike through the forest takes 1 hour 45 minutes. If you're lucky, you may spot a snow grouse, a protected species in Japan. For climbers who want to scale Mt. Shirouma, which takes six hours to the top (two huts are on the way for overnight stays), proper equipment is necessary. ✉ *Shirouma Mountain* 🌐 *www.hakuba-sanso.co.jp.*

**Tsugaike Nature Garden** (栂池自然園; *Tsugaike Shizen-en*)
**NATURE PRESERVE** | This marshland, almost 6,000 feet above sea level, dazzles with a wide variety of rare alpine flora from early June to late October and is graced with gold and crimson leaves from September to October. It's a three-hour walk to take in the entire park. If the weather turns bad, there's always the climbing wall in the visitor center to try. The best way to get here is to take a bus (25 minutes) from Otari Station, two stops from Hakuba, and then a gondola up to the alpine park. ✉ *Chikuniotsu, Kita-Azumi-gun, Otari-mura* ☎ *0261/82–2233* 🌐 *sizenen.otarimura.com* 🎫 *Park entry ¥320. Gondola (with park entry) ¥3,700 return.*

**Yari Onsen** (鑓温泉)
**HOT SPRING** | The trail from Sarukura to Yarigatake—a hike of four hours—leads to the area's highest outdoor hot spring, Yari Onsen. It's part of a lodge that also has camping grounds (with gear rentals), but you can payto use the onsen. The lodge is open from mid-July to the end of September. Sarukura is a 40-minute bus ride from Hakuba Station. Crampons can be rented in Hakuba Village. ✉ *Hakuba* ☎ *0261/72–2002* 🌐 *www.hakuba-sanso.co.jp* 🎫 *¥500.*

## 🛏 Hotels

**The Happo** (ザ・八方)
**$$$** | **HOTEL** | A few hundred meters from the Happo-one Resort, this sleek hotel is one of Hakuba's newest, having opened in December 2021. **Pros:** convenient location for skiing; family friendly; contemporary luxury. **Cons:** limited on-site dining options; aimed mostly at a younger crowd; cheaper options nearby. [$] *Rooms*

Traditional houses have been restored along Magome's sloping streets.

*from: ¥19,600* ✉ *5090–1 Hokujou, Hakuba* ☎ *0261/75–5511* ⊕ *www.the-happo.com* ➲ *30 rooms* ❖ *Free Breakfast.*

**Pension Noichigo** (ペンション野いちご)
**$$** | **B&B/INN** | A five-minute walk (or ski) from the Happo-one lift, the family-run Noichigo feels more like a European guesthouse than a Japanese inn. **Pros:** excellent location for hiking and skiing; drawing classes on-site; friendly, knowledgeable owners. **Cons:** not much to do in the neighborhood after dark; showing its age; fewer amenities than larger hotels. ⓢ *Rooms from: ¥14,000* ✉ *4869 Hokujou, Wadano* ☎ *0261/72–4707* ⊕ *www.janis.or.jp/users/noichigo* ➲ *6 rooms* ❖ *No Meals.*

# Kiso Valley (木曾谷)

*89 km (55 miles) south of Matsumoto.*

This deep and narrow valley is cut by the Kiso River and walled in by the central Alps to the east and the northern Alps to the west. In the Edo era (1603–1868), the Kiso Valley (or *Kisoji*) thrived as a result of being on the Nakasendo (central highway), the inland route that connected Kyoto and Edo (present-day Tokyo).

After the Tokaido highway was built along the Pacific coast and the Chuo train line was constructed to connect Nagoya and Niigata, Kisoji's 11 once-bustling post villages, where travelers and traders once stopped to refresh themselves and share news, became ghost towns. Two villages, Tsumago and Magome, have benefited from efforts to retain the memory of these old settlements. Traditional houses have been restored along the sloping stone streets and power lines have been buried underground. Walking through these historical areas, you can almost imagine life centuries ago, when the rustic shops were stocked with supplies for travelers instead of the traditional crafts now offered for sale.

## GETTING HERE AND AROUND

The central valley town of Nagiso is two hours south of Matsumoto on the JR Chuo Line (¥1,520). Tsumago is a 10-minute bus ride (¥300) from JR Nagiso Station. Magome is closer to JR Nakatsugawa Station, which is 12 minutes south on the same line. Both towns are served by buses from the Nagiso and Nakatsugawa stations, so you can take a bus to one village and return from the other. Local buses between Magome and Tsumago are infrequent. A taxi costs about ¥3,000. To get to Takayama, take the JR Chuo Line from Nakatsugawa or Nagiso to Tajimi, change to a local JR Takayama Line train to Mina-Ota, then an express train to Takayama (total four hours). There are also infrequent buses from Nakatsugawa to the hot spring town of Gero, 40 minutes from Takayama by express train. There are also direct highway buses from Magome to Tokyo's Shinjuku Station (4½ hours, ¥5,070).

### VISITOR INFORMATION

The staff at Magome Tourist Information Office—in the village center along the old post road—can help you reserve a hotel room, though as with any hotel booking in Japan, it is highly recommended to reserve in advance. The Tsumago Tourist Information Office, in the center of town, has the same services as the Magome tourist office.

**CONTACTS Magome Tourist Information Office.** ✉ *4300–1 Magome, Nakatsugawa* ☎ *0573/69–2336* 🌐 *kiso-magome.com.* **Tsumago Tourist Information Office.** ✉ *2159–2 Nagiso-machi, Kiso-gun* ☎ *0264/57–3123* 🌐 *tsumago.jp.*

## 🛏 Hotels

**Hatago Matsushiro-ya** (旅籠松代屋)
$$$ | **B&B/INN** | This small ryokan has welcomed guests since 1804 with a strictly traditional experience: 10 large tatami rooms share a single bath and four clean but old-fashioned pit toilets, and the walls are sliding paper screens. **Pros:** traditional setting; beautiful building; option of booking room only or room and meals. **Cons:** paper walls mean little privacy; building is somewhat exposed to the elements; no private bath or toilets. [$] *Rooms from: ¥21,600* ✉ *807 Azuma-Terashita, Tsumago, Minami-Nagiso-machi, Kiso-gun* ☎ *0264/57–3022* 💳 *No credit cards* 🕒 *Closed Wed.* 🛏 *10 rooms* 🍴 *All-Inclusive.*

**Onyado Daikichi** (御宿大吉)
$$ | **B&B/INN** | The windows in all six tatami rooms of this minshuku face the wooded valley, and although you can opt for a room-only stay, it's only an extra couple of thousand yen to book dinner and breakfast too, which is a good idea with nowhere to eat nearby. **Pros:** lovely views; traditional setting; tasty food. **Cons:** no nearby restaurants; the food might be too adventurous for some; no baths en suite. [$] *Rooms from: ¥13,000* ✉ *Nagiso-machi, Tsumago, Kiso-gun* ☎ *0264/57–2595* 🌐 *www17.plala.or.jp/daikiti* 💳 *No credit cards* 🛏 *6 rooms* 🍴 *All-Inclusive.*

# Kamikochi (上高地)

*48 km (30 miles) west of Matsumoto, 64 km (40 miles) east of Takayama.*

The incomparably scenic route from Matsumoto to Takayama winds over the mountains and through Chubu-Sangaku National Park (Chubu-Sangaku Kokuritsu Koen) via Kamikochi. Entry to the village is only possible after mid-April, when plows have removed the almost 30 feet of winter snow, and continues until the snow returns in mid-November. If you spend the night in Kamikochi, which is surrounded by virgin forests of birch, larch, and hemlock, consider renting a rowboat at Taisho Pond (Taisho-ike) for the spectacular view of the snow-covered peaks.

Unless you plan to do some serious hiking, Kamikochi is best done as a day-trip from Takayama or Matsumoto.

### GETTING HERE AND AROUND

No cars are allowed in Kamikochi. Take the Matsumoto Dentetsu Line from Matsumoto Station to Shin-Shimashima, the last stop. The ride takes 30 minutes and departs once or twice an hour. At Shin-Shimashima Station, cross the road for the one-hour bus journey to Nakano-yu and Kamikochi (¥2,710 for a bus-and-train combo ticket). There are also buses from Matsumoto to Kamikochi, departing almost hourly each day when the road is open (mid-April–November; ¥2,570), as well as direct highway buses from Nagano, Tokyo (Tokyo, Shibuya and Shinjuku stations), Kyoto, and Osaka run by the Alpico bus company. To get here from Takayama, take a bus to Hirayu Onsen (one hour; ¥1,600) and change to another bus for Kamikochi (25 minutes; ¥1,180). There are some direct buses in summer from Takayama.

### VISITOR INFORMATION

Up-to-date bus and road information is available at the Matsumoto and Takayama tourist offices. Kamikochi is where the trails for some of the most famed alpine ascents begin; favorite peaks are Mt. Yariga-take and Mt. Hotaka-dake. Most maps are in Japanese, but some English information is available from tourist information offices. Planning in advance is essential; climbs range from a few days to a week, and the trails can be crowded in summer. The Kamikochi Resort Hotel Association's English-language website is a good source of information on hotels, transport, trekking, and other activities.

**CONTACT Kamikochi Resort Hotel Association.** ✉ *Kamikochi* 🌐 *www.kamikochi.org.*

## Hotels

Hotels and ryokan here close from mid-November to mid-April.

★ **Imperial Hotel** (上高地帝国ホテル; *Kamikochi Teikoku Hoteru*)
**$$$$ | HOTEL** | This rustic alpine lodge is owned by Tokyo's legendary Imperial Hotel, and the service is so exemplary because the staff are borrowed from that establishment for the summer. **Pros:** luxurious accommodations; professional staff; beautiful architecture. **Cons:** better-value dining elsewhere; might feel too formal for some; rooms more expensive than other lodgings in the area. [$] *Rooms from: ¥49,335* ✉ *Azumi-kamikochi, Matsumoto* ☎ *0263/95–2001* 🌐 *www.imperialhotel.co.jp* 🕒 *Closed mid-Nov.–mid-Apr.* 🛏 *74 rooms* 🍴 *Free Breakfast.*

**Taisho-ike Hotel** (大正池ホテル)
**$$$$ | HOTEL** | This small mountain resort is perched on the rim of the brilliant-blue Taisho Pond. **Pros:** lovely views; comfortable Western-style rooms; onsen baths. **Cons:** bit of a walk from the center of Kamikochi; plain decor throughout; Japanese-style rooms are on the small side. [$] *Rooms from: ¥24,750* ✉ *Azumi-kamikochi, Matsumoto* ☎ *0263/95–2301* 🌐 *www.taisyoike.co.jp* 🛏 *27 rooms* 🍴 *No Meals.*

## Activities

### HIKING

As you approach Kamikochi, the valley opens onto a row of towering mountains: Oku-Hotaka-san is the highest, at 10,466 feet. Mae-Hotaka-san, at 10,138 feet, is on the left. To the right is 9,544-foot Nishi-Hotaka-san. The icy waters of the Azusa-gawa flow from the small Taisho Pond at the southeast entrance to the basin.

There are many hiking trails in the river valley around Kamikochi. One easy three-hour walk east starts at **Kappabashi** (河童橋), a small suspension bridge over the crystal clear Azusa-gawa, a few minutes northeast of the bus terminal. Along the way is a stone sculpture of the British explorer Reverend Walter Weston, the first foreigner to ascend these mountains. Continuing on the south side of the river, the trail cuts through a pasture to rejoin the river at Myoshin Bridge. Cross here to reach Myoshin-ike (Myoshin Pond). At the edge of the pond sits the small Hotaka Jinja Kappabashi (Water Sprite Bridge). To see the beautiful **Taisho-ike** (大正池), head southeast from Kappabashi for a 20-minute walk. You can rent a boat from in front of the Taisho-ike Hotel (¥1,000 per half-hour).

# Takayama (高山)

*267 km (166 miles) north of Nagoya, 80 km (50 miles) north of Matsumoto.*

Originally called Hida, Takayama is a tranquil town whose rustic charms are the result of hundreds of years of peaceful isolation in the Hida Mountains. In the compact downtown, shops and restaurants mingle with museums and inns along rows of traditional wood-lattice buildings. In keeping with Japanese tradition, a peculiar-looking ball of cedar leaves (a *sugidama*) suspended outside a storefront indicates a drinking establishment or brewery. Nicknamed "Little Kyoto," Takayama has fewer crowds and wider streets, not to mention fresh mountain air and gorgeous scenery.

Takayama's hugely popular festivals, spring's Sanno Matsuri (April 14 and 15) and the slightly smaller autumn Hachiman Matsuri (October 9 and 10), draw hundreds of thousands of spectators for parades of floats. Hotels are booked solid during Matsuri time, so if you plan to join the festivities, make reservations several months in advance.

## GETTING HERE AND AROUND
Takayama has four daily connections north to Toyama by the JR Wide View Hida express train, which takes 90 minutes and costs ¥2,980. You can transfer to the Hokuriku Shinkansen at Toyama Station to go back to Tokyo, or west to Kanazawa and the Noto-hanto. It's easy to get to Takayama by bus from Matsumoto for ¥3,500. Buses also run

from Takayama to Kamikochi (¥2,650) and Shirakawa-go (¥2,600).

Laid out in a compact grid, Takayama can be explored on foot or bicycle. Several shops rent bikes; ask at the tourist information office for details.

## VISITOR INFORMATION
The Hida Tourist Information Office, in front of the JR Station, is open from April to November, daily 8:30–7; and from December to March, daily 8:30–5:30. The English-speaking staff provide maps and helps with accommodations, both in town and in the surrounding mountains.

**CONTACT Hida Tourist Information Office.** ✉ *Eki-mae, Takayama* ☎ *0577/32–5328* ⊕ *www.hida.jp/english.*

#  Sights

### ★ Hida Folk Village
(飛騨の里; *Hida no Sato*)
MUSEUM VILLAGE | These traditional farmhouses, dating from the Edo period, were transplanted from all over the region. Many of the houses are A-frames with thatch roofs called gassho-zukuri (praying hands). A dozen of the buildings are "private houses" displaying folk artifacts like tableware and weaving tools. Another five houses are folk-craft workshops, with demonstrations of *ichii ittobori* (wood carving), *Hida-nuri* (Hida lacquering), and other traditional regional arts, as well as hands-on crafting experiences. It's possible to walk here from Takayama Station, or take a 10-minute bus ride. ✉ *1–590 Kami-Okamoto-cho, Gifu, Takayama* ☎ *0577/34–4711* ⊕ *www. hidanosato-tpo.jp/english12.htm* 🎫 *¥700.*

### Kokubun-ji Temple (国分寺)
TEMPLE | The city's oldest temple, dating from 1588, houses many objects of art in its treasure house, including a precious sword used by the Heike clan. In the Main Hall (built in 1615) sits a figure of Yakushi Nyorai, a Buddha who eases those struggling with illness. In front of

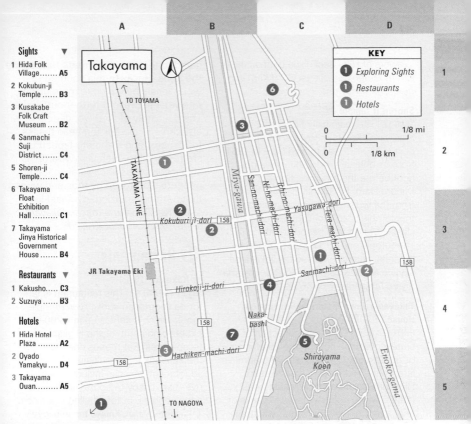

## Sights ▼

1 Hida Folk
Village....... **A5**

2 Kokubun-ji
Temple ..... **B3**

3 Kusakabe
Folk Craft
Museum .... **B2**

4 Sanmachi
Suji
District ...... **C4**

5 Shoren-ji
Temple....... **C4**

6 Takayama
Float
Exhibition
Hall .......... **C1**

7 Takayama
Jinya Historical
Government
House ....... **B4**

## Restaurants ▼

1 Kakusho..... **C3**

2 Suzuya ...... **B3**

## Hotels ▼

1 Hida Hotel
Plaza ........ **A2**

2 Oyado
Yamakyu .... **D4**

3 Takayama
Ouan......... **A5**

the three-story pagoda is a wooden statue of another esoteric Buddhist figure, Kannon Bosatsu, who vowed to hear the voices of all people and immediately grant salvation to those who suffer. The ginkgo tree standing beside the pagoda is believed to be more than 1,250 years old. ⊠ 1–83 Sowa-machi, Takayama ☎ 0577/32–1395 ⊠ ¥300 for the treasure house.

## Kusakabe Folk Craft Museum (日下部民芸館; Kusakabe Mingeikan)

**HISTORIC HOME** | This museum is in a house from the 1880s that belonged to the Kusakabe family—wealthy traders of the Edo period. This national treasure served as a residence and warehouse, where the handsome interior, with heavy, polished beams and an earthy barren floor, provides an appropriate setting for Hida folk crafts such as lacquered bowls and wood carvings, as well as trappings of family wealth that include a bridal palanquin. ⊠ 1–52 Ojin-machi, Takayama ☎ 0577/32–0072 ⊕ www.kusakabe-min-geikan.com ⊠ ¥500 ⊘ Closed Tues.

## Sanmachi Suji District (三町筋)

**HISTORIC DISTRICT** | A 10-minute walk east of Takayama Station, this charming, old street in the heart of Takayama's historic quarter is lined with wooden Edo-era merchant homes and stores, as well as the occasional tall *kura* warehouse built to house Takayama's priceless festival floats. Be warned that it can get extremely crowded with tourists, but it's still worth a stroll. You'll find old sake breweries here, like Funasaka at the street's southern end, where you can sample local brews. As well as craft stores and cafes, there are also plenty of small stores selling snacks, such as skewers of Hida beef, Hida beef sushi, or sweet *dango* dumplings. ✉ *20 Kamisan-no-machi, Takayama.*

**Shoren-ji Temple** (照蓮寺)

**TEMPLE** | The main hall of Shoren-ji in Shiroyama Koen (Shiroyama Park) was built in 1504. It was moved here in 1961 from its original site in Shirakawa-go, right before the area was flooded by the Miboro Dam. Beautifully carved, allegedly from the wood of a single cedar tree, this temple is an excellent example of classic Muromachi-period architecture. The temple sits on a hill surrounded by gardens, and you can see the Takayama skyline and the park below. ✉ *Shiroyama Koen, Takayama* ☎ *0577/32–2052.*

**Takayama Jinya Historical Government House** (高山陣屋)

**HISTORIC HOME** | This rare collection of stately buildings housed the 25 officials of the Tokugawa Shogunate who administered the Hida region for 176 years. Highlights include an original storehouse (1606), which held city taxes in sacks of rice, a torture chamber (curiously translated as the "law court"), and samurai barracks. Free, guided tours in English are available on request and take 30 to 50 minutes. Fruit, vegetables, and local crafts are sold at the nearby Jinya-mae Asa-ichi morning market, open until noon. From the JR Station, head east on Hirokoji-dori for a few blocks to the old section of town. Before the bridge, which crosses the small Miya-gawa, turn right, pass another bridge, and the Takayama Jinya is on your right. ✉ *1–5 Hachiken-machi, Takayama* ☎ *0577/32–0643* 🎟 *¥440.*

**Takayama Float Exhibition Hall** (高山祭屋台会館; *Takayama Matsuri Yatai Kaikan*)

**HISTORY MUSEUM** | This community center displays four of the 17th- and 18th-century *yatai* (festival floats) used in Takayama's famous Sanno and Hachiman festivals. More than two centuries ago Japan was ravaged by the bubonic plague, and yatai were built and paraded through the streets to appease the gods. Because this seemed to work, locals built bigger, more elaborate yatai to prevent further outbreaks. The delicately etched wooden panels, carved wooden lion-head masks for dances, and elaborate tapestries are remarkable. Technical wizardry is also involved, as each yatai contains puppets, controlled by rods and wires, that perform amazing, gymnast-like feats. ✉ *178 Sakura-machi, Takayama* ☎ *0577/32–5100* 🎟 *¥1,000.*

## 🍴 Restaurants

**★ Kakusho** (角正)

**$$$$ | JAPANESE** | This restaurant is famous for its vegetarian *shojin ryori* (temple food), which it serves up in a 200-year-old building south of the Higashiyama temple area. Set menus change with the seasons and aren't always fully vegetarian; they can include salt-grilled river fish, crispy tempura, handmade soba noodles, or tofu chilled in ice-cold Takayama water. **Known for:** in a lovely Edo-period house; garden views; shojin ryori. [$] *Average main: ¥13,000* ✉ *2–98 Babacho-dori, Takayama* ☎ *0577/32–0174* 🌐 *www.kakusyo.com* 💳 *No credit cards* ☞ *Reservations recommended.*

**Suzuya** (寿々や)

**$$ | JAPANESE** | This restaurant's recipes have been passed down over several generations—the house specialty is the superb and inexpensive *sansai-ryori*, as well as more expensive dishes using highly rated Hida beef. Suzuya is in a traditional Hida-style house, and the wood-beamed dining room has an intimate feel. **Known for:** Hida beef; rustic atmosphere; healthy sansai ryori set meals. [$] *Average main: ¥3,000* ✉ *24 Hanakawa-cho, Takayama* ☎ *0577/32–2484* 🌐 *suzuyatakayama.ec-net.jp* 🕒 *Closed Tues.*

# ⊟ Hotels

## Hida Hotel Plaza (ひだホテルプラザ)

$$$$ | HOTEL | The best international-style hotel in town, the Hida Hotel Plaza exudes a old-style atmosphere. **Pros:** luxurious furnishings; central location; rooftop hot spring. **Cons:** can be crowded during events; Western-style rooms drab compared to the Japanese rooms; lacks the personal touch of many area ryokan and inns. $ *Rooms from: ¥30,800* ⊠ *2–60 Hanaoka-cho, Takayama* ☎ *0577/33–4600* ⊕ *www.hida-hotelplaza. co.jp* ⤳ *226 rooms* ⦿ *Free Breakfast.*

## Oyado Yamakyu (お宿山久)

$$$ | B&B/INN | Antiques-filled nooks with chairs and coffee tables become cozy lounges in this old Tera-machi minshuku. **Pros:** warm atmosphere; excellent food; relaxing communal bath. **Cons:** no private baths; not a wide range of amenities and facilities; early-to-bed curfew means less freedom. $ *Rooms from: ¥19,800* ⊠ *58 Tensho-ji-machi, Takayama* ☎ *0577/32– 3756* ⊕ *www.takayama-yamakyu.com* ⤳ *18 rooms* ⦿ *Free Breakfast.*

## Takayama Ouan (高山桜庵)

$$ | HOTEL | A several-minute walk south of Takayama Station, the Ouan is a business hotel with ryokan (traditional inn) touches. **Pros:** several free private hot-spring baths available; friendly staff; free Wi-Fi. **Cons:** not much in the immediate vicinity; not many facilities; breakfast not worth the extra fee. $ *Rooms from: ¥13,400* ⊠ *4–313 Hanasato-machi, Takayama* ☎ *0577/37–2230* ⊕ *www.hotespa. net/hotels/takayama* ⤳ *167 rooms* ⦿ *No Meals.*

# ☖ Nightlife

Nightlife in sleepy Takayama revolves around locally produced beer and sake. Try one of the many small Japanese-style bars, or *izakaya,* that line the streets to the north of Kokubunji Street.

## Dekonaru Yokocho (でこなる横丁)

GATHERING PLACES | Located in the Ichiban-gai bar and restaurant district, this cluster of a dozen covered food stalls, each with counters that barely seat six or seven people, is a great place to try Hida-gyu beef, Takayama ramen, yakitori, and other dishes that pair well with Takayama's sake. You'll probably end up chatting with locals too. ⊠ *4–2 Asahi-machi, Takayama* ⊕ *dekonaru.com.*

# Shirakawa-go (白川郷)

*50 km (31 miles) northwest of Takayama.*

It's speculated that the Shirakawa-go area—and particularly Ogi-machi, an Edo-period village deep within—was originally populated by survivors of the powerful Taira family, who were nearly killed off in the 12th century by the rival Genji family. The majority of the residents living here still inhabit gassho-zukuri houses. Their shape and materials enable the houses to withstand the heavy regional snow, and in summer the straw keeps the houses cool. Household activities center on the *irori* (open hearth), which sends smoke up through the timbers and thatch roof. Meats and fish are preserved (usually on a metal shelf suspended above the hearth) by the ascending smoke, which also prevents insects and vermin from taking up residence in the straw.

Shirakawa-go makes for a good day trip from Kanazawa or Takayama, or as a stop on the way to either. Several of the old houses are now minshuku, making Ogi-machi village a relaxing place to stay overnight.

## GETTING HERE AND AROUND

It's more convenient to drive to Shirakawa-go and Ogi-machi, but it's possible to get there by public transportation. Four buses depart from Nagoya's Meitetsu

Bus Center between 8 and 9:20 am daily, taking three hours and costing ¥3,000 to ¥4,000, depending on the season. There are also eight buses a day between Shirakawa-go and Kanazawa (1 hour 15 minutes; ¥2,000). Some routes require advance seat reservations, which you can do at tourist offices. From Takayama, buses travel year-round four to six times a day, taking 50 minutes and costing ¥2,600 one-way, ¥4,600 round-trip.

## VISITOR INFORMATION

Many old houses in Ogi-machi village function as minshuku. To stay in one, make rservations through the Shiraka-wa-go Tourist Office, open daily 9–5. It's next to the bus terminal.

**CONTACT Shirakawa-go Tourist Association.** ✉ *1086 Ogi-machi, Shirakawa-mura, Ogi-machi* ☎ *0576/96–1013* ⊕ *shiraka-wa-go.gr.jp/en.*

 **Sights**

★ **Gassho-zukuri Minkaen Outdoor Museum** (白川郷掌造り民家園; *Shirakawa-go Gassho-zukuri Minkaen*)

MUSEUM VILLAGE | Opposite Ogi-machi, on the banks of the Sho-gawa, this open-air museum has 26 traditional gassho-zukuri farmhouses. The houses were transplanted from four villages that fell prey to the Miboro Dam, built upriver in 1972. Over the years a colony of artisans has established itself in the village. From mid-April to mid-October, you can watch them creating folk crafts like weaving, pottery, woodwork, and hand-dyeing in a few of the preserved houses, and try some crafts for yourself. Many of the products are for sale. In winter, stop by the "rest station" gassho-zukuri to warm up with tea by an irori hearth. Keep in mind that individual houses do close irregularly. ✉ *2499 Ogi-machi, Shirakawa mura, Ono-gun, Ogi-machi* ☎ *0576/96–1231* ⊕ *www. shirakawago-minkaen.jp/english* 💴 *¥600* 🕑 *Closed Thurs., Dec.–Mar.*

# Kanazawa (金沢)

*259 km (160 miles) northeast of Kyoto, 244 km (151 miles) north of Nagoya, 104 km (64 miles) northwest of Takayama, 305 km (190 miles) southwest of Niigata.*

Twenty-first-century Kanazawa presents an extraordinary union of unblemished Old Japan and a modern, trendsetting city. More than 300 years of history have been preserved in the earthen walls and flowing canals of Naga-machi, the former samurai quarter west of downtown; the cluster of Buddhist temples in Tera-machi on the southern bank of the Sai-gawa River; and the wooden facades of the Higashi Chaya former geisha district, located north of the Asano-gawa River. Modern art, fashion, music, and international dining thrive in the downtown core of Korinbo, and in the shopping districts of Tate-machi and Kata-machi. The Sea of Japan provides both great seafood and a somewhat dreary climate. Fortunately, cold, gray, and wet weather is offset by friendly people and only adds to the sad, romantic air of the city.

In the feudal times of the Edo period, the prime rice-growing areas around Kanazawa (known then as the province of Kaga) made the ruling Maeda clan the second-wealthiest in the country. Harvests came in at more than *hyaku-man-goku* (1 million *koku,* the Edo-period unit of measurement based on how much rice would feed one person for a year). This wealth funded various cultural pursuits such as silk dyeing, ceramics, and the production of gold-leaf and lacquerware products.

This prosperity did not pass unnoticed. The fear of attack by the Edo daimyo inspired the Maeda lords to construct one of the country's most massive castles amid a mazelike network of narrow, winding lanes that made the approach difficult and an invasion nearly impossible. These defensive tactics paid off, and Kanazawa enjoyed 300 years

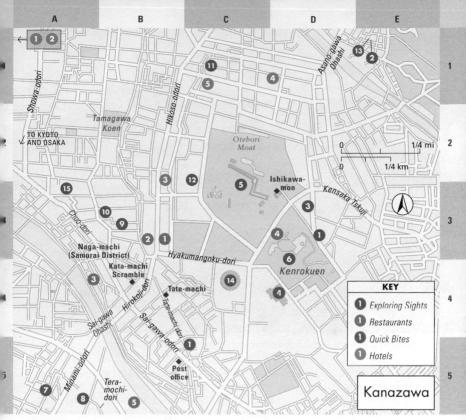

Kanazawa

**KEY**
- ① Exploring Sights
- ① Restaurants
- ① Quick Bites
- ① Hotels

**Sights** ▼
1 Gyokusen Garden....... **D3**
2 Higashi Chaya District .. **E1**
3 Ishikawa Local
  Products Center ........ **D3**
4 Ishikawa Prefectural
  Museum of Art.......... **D4**
5 Kanazawa Castle Park.. **C3**
6 Kenroku Garden ........ **D3**
7 Kutani Pottery Kiln...... **A5**
8 Myoryu-ji Temple ....... **A5**
9 Naga-machi
  Samurai District......... **B3**
10 Nomura-ke
  Samurai Residence..... **B3**
11 Omi-cho Market ......... **C1**
12 Oyama Shrine ........... **C2**
13 Shima Teahouse ........ **E1**
14 21st Century Museum
  of Contemporary Art..... **C4**
15 Workshop of
  Kaga-Yuzen.............. **A3**

**Restaurants** ▼
1 Fumuroya ............... **B3**
2 Kincharyo............... **B3**
3 Legian.................... **A4**
4 Miyoshian ............... **D3**
5 Ryotei Suginoi .......... **B5**

**Quick Bites** ▼
1 Noda-ya Tea Shop....... **C5**

**Hotels** ▼
1 Hotel Nikko
  Kanazawa .............. **A1**
2 Hyatt Centric
  Kanazawa .............. **A1**
3 Kanazawa
  New Grand Hotel ....... **B2**
4 Nakayasu Ryokan ...... **D1**
5 Ryokan Asadaya ........ **C1**

The intimate Gyokusen Garden is one of the most impressive sights in Kanazawa.

of peace and prosperity. Nevertheless, seven fires over the centuries reduced the once-mighty Kanazawa-jo to just the remaining castle walls and a single, impressive gate.

Between sightseeing, shopping, and sampling Kanazawa's many restaurants and cafés, it is worth staying here a couple of nights. Though the atmosphere of the city changes with each season, it is an excellent place to visit any time of the year.

## GETTING HERE AND AROUND

By train, Kanazawa is 2½ hours from Tokyo, 2¼ hours from Kyoto; three hours from Nagoya; two hours from Takayama (requiring a change to the Shinkansen at Toyama); and three hours from Niigata. The 2½-hour bus between Kanazawa and Takayama, which makes a stop in Shirakawa-go, is also an option; there are four daily, and the cost is ¥3,600 one-way.

Ideal for tourists, the city's loop bus departs in both directions every 15 minutes from 8:30 am to 6 pm from Gate 0 of Kanazawa Station's East Exit, and takes you to the major tourist sites. Stops are announced in English and displayed on a digital board at the front of the bus. A single ride costs ¥200; the day pass is ¥600. You can purchase the pass from the Hokutetsu bus ticket office in front of Kanazawa Station.

Kanazawa is a good place to rent a car to explore the Noto-hanto and other parts of the Sea of Japan coast. The area around the station is where you'll find all the major car-rental companies.

## VISITOR INFORMATION

The Kanazawa Tourist Information Center has two desks at the train station and English-speaking staff who can help you find accommodations or arrange tours with volunteer guides.

**CONTACT Kanazawa Tourist Information Center.** ⊠ *1–1–1 Kinoshinbo-machi, Kanazawa* ☎ *076/232–6200* ⊕ *visitkanazawa.jp.*

# ◉ Sights

## ★ Gyokusen Garden (玉泉園)

**GARDEN** | This tiny garden was built by Kim Yeocheol, who later became Naokata Wakita when he married into the ruling Kanazawa family. Yeocheol was the son of a Korean captive brought to Japan in the late 16th century. He became a wealthy merchant, using his fortune to build this quiet getaway. The garden's intimate tranquility stems from the imaginative and subtle arrangement of moss, maple trees, and small stepping stones by the pond. Two waterfalls that gracefully form the Chinese character for *mizu* (water) feed the pond. The garden is markedly different from the bold strokes of Kenroku Garden. You can have tea and sweets here for ¥1,500 (admission included). ✉ *8–3 Kosho-machi, Kanazawa* 📞 *076/221–0181* 💴 *¥700* 🕐 *Closed Tues.–Thurs.*

## Higashi Chaya District

(ひがし茶屋街; *Higashi Chaya Machi*)

**HISTORIC SIGHT** | This high-class entertainment district of Edo-period Kanazawa was near the Asano-gawa. Now the pleasures are limited to viewing quaint old geisha houses recognizable by their wood-slat facades and latticed windows. Many have become tearooms, restaurants, local craft (and souvenir) stores, or minshuku. Take the JR bus from Kanazawa Station (¥200) to Hachira-cho, just before the Asano-gawa Ohashi. Cross the bridge and walk northeast into the quarter. ✉ *Higashi no Kurawa, Kanazawa.*

## Ishikawa Local Products Center

(石川県観光物産館; *Ishikawa-ken Kanko Bussankan*)

**STORE/MALL** | **FAMILY** | Near Gyokusen Garden, the center serves as a place where you can both buy traditional crafts from the region and see demonstrations of Yuzen dyeing, pottery, and lacquerware production. You can also try your hand at etching a personal glass seal, decorating items with delicate gold leaf, making Japanese sweets, and other crafts at regularly scheduled workshops. ✉ *2–20 Kenroku-cho, Kanazawa* 📞 *076/222–7788* 🌐 *www.kanazawa-kankou.jp/en* 💴 *Free; hands-on experiences from ¥700* 🕐 *Closed Tues. Dec.–Feb.*

## Ishikawa Prefectural Museum of Art

(石川県立美術館; *Ishikawa Kenritsu Bijutsukan*)

**ART MUSEUM** | Come here to see the country's best permanent collection of *Kutani-yaki* (colorful overglaze-painted porcelain), dyed fabrics, and old Japanese paintings. ✉ *2–1 Dewa-machi, southwest of Kenrokuen, Kanazawa* 📞 *076/231–7580* 🌐 *www.ishibi.pref.ishikawa. jp/e_home* 💴 *¥370* 🕐 *Closed between exhibtions (2–3 days 10 times a year).*

## Kanazawa Castle Park

(金沢城公園; *Kanazawa-jo Koen*)

**CASTLE/PALACE** | Though most of the castle is a reproduction, the original Ishikawa-mon (Ishikawa Gate) remains intact—its thick mossy stone base is topped with curving black eaves and white-lead roof tiles. The tiles could be melted down and molded into ammunition in case of a prolonged siege. To reach the castle, take any bus (¥200) from Gate 11 at the bus terminal outside the JR Station, or walk 30 minutes. ✉ *1–1 Marunouchi, Kanazawa* 📞 *076/234–3800* 🌐 *www. pref.ishikawa.jp/siro-niwa/kanazawajou/e* 💴 *Free.*

## ★ Kenroku Garden (兼六園)

**GARDEN** | Across the street from the Kanazawa Castle is the largest of the three most famous landscaped gardens in the country (the other two are Mito's Kairaku Garden and Okayama's Koraku Garden). The Maeda lord Tsunanori began construction of Kenrokuen in 1676, and by the early 1880s it had become 25 sprawling acres of skillfully wrought bridges and fountains, ponds, and waterfalls. The garden changes with the seasons: spring brings cherry blossoms; brilliant azaleas foretell the arrival of summer; autumn paints the maples deep yellow and red; and in winter the pine trees are strung with long ropes, tied from trunk to bough, for protection against heavy snowfalls. Kenrokuen means "Garden of Six Qualities." The garden was so named because it exhibited the six superior characteristics judged necessary by the Chinese Sung Dynasty for the perfect garden: spaciousness, artistic merit, majesty, abundant water, extensive views, and seclusion. Despite the promise of its last attribute, the gardens attract a mad stampede of visitors—herded by megaphone—during cherry-blossom season (mid-April) and Golden Week (late April and early May). Early morning is the most sensible time for a visit, when the grounds are a little more peaceful and relaxing. ⊠ *1 Kenroku-cho, Kanazawa* ☎ *076/234–3800* ⊕ *www.pref.ishikawa.jp/siro-niwa/ken-rokuen/en* ⊠ *¥320.*

### Kutani Pottery Kiln
(九谷光仙窯; *Kutani Kosen Gama*)
FACTORY | You can watch artisans making the local Kutani pottery, which is noted for its vibrant color schemes, at this spot dating from 1870. If you fancy doing something hands-on, there are also pottery workshops here (apply at least two days in advance) and ceramic painting experiences; unfortunately, the workshop fees don't include the shipping costs of anything you make. ⊠ *5–3–3 No-machi, Kanazawa* ☎ *076/241–0902* ⊕ *kutanikosen.com/en* ⊠ *Free; pottery workshops ¥5,500.*

### ★ Myoryu-ji Temple (妙立寺)
TEMPLE | On the south side of the Sai-gawa is the intriguing and mysterious Myoryu-ji. Its popular name, Ninja-dera (Temple of the Ninja), suggests it was a clandestine training center for martial-arts masters who crept around in the dead of night armed with *shuriken* (star-shape blades). In fact, the temple was built to provide an escape route for the daimyo in case of invasion. Ninja-dera was built by Toshitsune in 1643, when the Tokugawa

Shogunate was stealthily knocking off local warlords and eliminating competition. At first glance, it appears a modest yet handsome two-story structure. Inside, however, you find 29 staircases, seven levels, myriad secret passageways and trapdoors, a tunnel to the castle hidden beneath the well in the kitchen, and even a *seppuku* room, where the lord could perform an emergency ritual suicide. Unfortunately (or fortunately, considering all the booby traps), visitors are not permitted to explore the hidden lair alone. You must join a Japanese-language tour (hourly on weekdays and twice hourly on weekends) and follow along with your English pamphlet. Reservations by phone are necessary, but can usually be made on the day of your visit. ⊠ *1–2–12 No-machi, Kanazawa* ☎ *076/241–0888* ⊕ *www.myouryuji.or.jp* ⊠ *¥1,000* ⌂ *Access by reservation only. Call (simple English is ok) before going.*

### Naga-machi Samurai District (長町)
HISTORIC SIGHT | Behind the modern Korinbo Tokyu Square shopping center, Seseragi-dori leads to the samurai district where the Maeda clan lived. Narrow, snaking streets are lined with golden adobe walls footed with large stones and topped with black tiles. Stop by the Nomura-ke Samurai Residence to get a look inside one of the area's historic mansions. ⊠ *Naga-machi, Kanazawa.*

### Nomura-ke Samurai Residence (武家屋敷跡 野村家; *Buke Yashiki Ato Nomura-ke*)
HISTORIC HOME | This elegant house in Naga-machi was rebuilt more than 100 years ago by an industrialist named Nomura. Visit the Jodan-no-ma drawing room made of cypress, with elaborate designs in rosewood and ebony. Then pass through the sliding doors to a wooden veranda. Rest your feet here, and take in the stunning little garden with weathered lanterns among pine and maple trees, and various shrubs and bonsai. Stepping stones lead to a pond dotted with moss-covered rocks

and brilliant orange-flecked carp. In the upstairs tearoom you can enjoy a bird's-eye view of the gardens and a cup of *matcha* (green tea) for ¥300. ⊠ *1–3–32 Naga-machi, Kanazawa* ☎ *076/221–3553* ⊕ *www.nomurake.com* ⊠ ¥550.

### Omi-cho Market
(近江町市場; *Omi-cho Ichiba*)
MARKET | This market in the center of the downtown was established almost 300 years ago. Today, the 170 or so vendors here run the gamut from fishmongers selling highly prized crab and seafood from the Sea of Japan, to sake stores, grocers and restaurants. The place is full of energy and color. Most stores are open from 9 am to 5:30 pm, although the restaurants in the second floor stay open later. ⊠ *50 Kami Omi-cho, Kanazawa* ⊕ *ohmicho-ichiba.com* ⊠ *Free*.

### Oyama Shrine (尾山神社; *Oyama Jinja*)
RELIGIOUS BUILDING | Built in 1599, Oyama Jinja was dedicated to Lord Toshiie Maeda, the founder of the Maeda clan. The shrine's unusual three-story gate, Shin-mon, was completed in 1875. Previously located atop Mt. Utatsu, the square arch and its stained-glass windows were believed to once function as a lighthouse, guiding ships in from the Sea of Japan to the Kanaiwa Port, 6 km (4 miles) northwest. You're free to walk around the shrine. ⊠ *11–1 Oyama-cho, Kanazawa* ☎ *076/231–7210* ⊕ *www.oyama-jinja.or.jp* ⊠ *Free*.

### Shima Teahouse
(お茶屋志摩; *Ochaya Shima*)
HISTORIC HOME | Constructed in the early 19th century, this elegant former geisha house, listed as a National Important Cultural Asset, is now a museum of Kanazawa geisha culture. While there, stop off in the tea room for matcha and sweets. That costs an extra ¥500 to ¥700 on top of admission, depending on the type of sweet. ⊠ *1–13–21 Higashi-yama, Kanazawa* ☎ *076/252–5675* ⊕ *www.ochaya-shima.com* ⊠ ¥500.

### 21st Century Museum of Contemporary Art
(21世紀美術館; *21 Seiki Bijutsukan*)
ART MUSEUM | This circular building was created to entwine a museum's architecture with the art exhibits, and for exhibition designers to take cues from the architecture. Transparent walls and scattered galleries encourage visitors to choose their own route. Previous exhibitions have included a Gerhard Richter retrospective, a video installation by Mathew Barney, and the work of Japanese photographer Araki Nobuyoshi. The building itself is a sight worth seeing, and the free, public terraces and plazas are a perfect place to stroll and relax. It's south of Kanazawa Park, next to city hall. ⊠ *1–2–1 Hirosaka, Kanazawa* ☎ *076/220–2800* ⊕ *www.kanazawa21. jp/en* ⊠ *Varies by exhibition; sometimes free* ☉ *Closed Mon*.

### Workshop of Kaga-Yuzen (長町友禅館; *Naga-machi Yuzenkan*)
FACTORY | A few houses have been carefully restored in the Naga-machi samurai district, including the Naga-machi Yuzenkan, where you can buy silk products and watch demonstrations of Yuzen silk painting—a centuries-old technique in which intricate floral designs with delicate white outlines are meticulously painted onto silk used for kimonos. You can also sign up for a wide range of experiences, from dressing up in kimono to creating your own designs on silk. ⊠ *2–6–16 Naga-machi, Kanazawa* ☎ *076/264–2811* ⊕ *kagayuzen-club.co.jp/ en* ⊠ ¥350 ☉ *Closed Tues. and Wed., and Dec.–Feb.*

## 🍴 Restaurants

### Fumuroya (不室屋)
$$ | JAPANESE | This shop specializes in *fu*, or wheat gluten. Its adjacent restaurant offers *kaiseki*-like lunch sets that change monthly but are centered on the wheat gluten and in-season vegetables like shiitake mushrooms. **Known for:** healthy set lunches; aromatic matcha and sweet

sets; traditional setting with low tables on tatami flooring. $ *Average main: ¥2,500* ✉ *1–1–1 Korinbo, Kanazawa* ☎ *076/220–1452* ⊕ *www.fumuroya.co.jp* ⏰ *Closed Wed. No dinner.*

### Kincharyo (加賀料理 金茶寮)

$$$$ | JAPANESE | As the seasons change, so do the menu options at this *kaiseki ryori*–focused showplace in the Kanazawa Tokyu Hotel. In spring your meal may include *hotaru-ika* (firefly squid) and *iidako* (baby octopus) no larger than your thumbnail, in fall expect matsutake mushrooms to make an appearance. **Known for:** affordable prix-fixe kaiseki dinner; good sake pairings; lunch bento boxes. $ *Average main: ¥10,000* ✉ *Kanazawa Tokyu Hotel, 2–1–1 Korinbo, 3rd fl., Kanazawa* ☎ *076/263–5511* ⊕ *kinchar-you.co.jp.*

### Legian (レギャン)

$$ | INDONESIAN | You might be surprised to find a funky Balinese eatery alongside the Sai-gawa River, but the nasi goreng, satay and other familiar dishes all taste like the real deal. From Kata-machi Scramble (the area's central intersection), turn right just before Sai-gawa Bridge, and follow the narrow lane along the river. **Known for:** fun ice-cream flavors like purple yam; Indonesian beer; good nasi goreng (fried rice). $ *Average main: ¥2,000* ✉ *2–31–30 Kata-machi, Kanazawa* ☎ *076/262–6510* ▭ *No credit cards* ⏰ *No lunch.*

### Miyoshian (三芳庵)

$$ | JAPANESE | At this place in the renowned Kenroku Garden, excellent fish and vegetable dishes have been carefully prepared for nearly one hundred years. The prices are still reasonable, and the garden views from the tatami are an added bonus. **Known for:** annex that serves matcha tea with Japanese sweets; formal dinner courses by reservation only and limited to 10 people daily; good value, healthy lunch sets. $ *Average main: ¥2,000* ✉ *1–1 Kenroku-cho, Kanazawa* ☎ *076/221–0127* ⊕ *miyoshian.net* ▭ *No credit cards* ⏰ *Closed Wed.*

### Ryotei Suginoi (料亭 杉の井)

$$$$ | JAPANESE | On the south bank of the Sai-gawa River close to the Sakura-bashi Bridge, this Michelin two-star restaurant serves Kaga specialties. Dinner in a private room overlooking the garden is a splurge but worth it. **Known for:** refined levels of service (so children under 10 are not allowed); reservations needed at least three days ahead; food served on fine Kutani china and Oribe pottery. $ *Average main: ¥13,000* ✉ *3–11 Kyokawa-machi, Kanazawa* ☎ *076/243–2288* ⊕ *kanazawa-suginoi.co.jp* ☞ *No children under 10 allowed.*

##  Coffee and Quick Bites

### Noda-ya Tea Shop (野田屋茶店; *Noda-ya Chaten*)

$ | CAFÉ | Slip into this little shop, in business since 1859, for a scoop of delicious *sofuto kurimu* (soft-serve ice cream) or a cup of tea. You can relax in the small garden in the rear or on benches out front. **Known for:** pretty garden; tea-flavored ice cream; range of teas and matcha floats. $ *Average main: ¥500* ✉ *3 Tate-machi, Kanazawa* ☎ *076/221–0982* ▭ *No credit cards.*

## Hotels

### Hotel Nikko Kanazawa (ホテル日航金沢)

$$$ | HOTEL | This 30-story hotel's exotic lobby is more reminiscent of Singapore than Japan, with tropical plants, cherry-oak slatted doors, and colonial-style furniture. **Pros:** near the train station; spacious rooms; great views. **Cons:** better value dining options elsewhere; too conservative for some; it's a long walk to Kata-machi's sights and nightlife. $ *Rooms from: ¥20,090* ✉ *2–15–1 Hon-machi, Kanazawa* ☎ *076/234–1111* ⊕ *www.hnkanazawa.jp* ⮡ *254 rooms* ⏹ *No Meals.*

**Hyatt Centric Kanazawa** (ハイアット セントリック 金沢)
**$$$ | HOTEL** | Opened next to Kanazawa Station in 2020, the Hyatt Centric delivers stylish rooms and common areas, but with deliberately trimmed back facilities in an attempt to keep fees down. **Pros:** friendly, multilingual staff; 24-hour fitness center; fresh, fashionable design and vibe. **Cons:** station area is removed from the main sights and nightlife; minimal facilities, by design, which won't appeal to everyone; not geared towards families. $ *Rooms from: ¥19,100* ✉ *1–5–2 Hirooka, Kanazawa* ☎ *076/256–1234* 🌐 *www.hyatt.com* 🛏 *253 rooms* 🍴 *No Meals.*

**Kanazawa New Grand Hotel** (金沢ニューグランドホテル)
**$$$$ | HOTEL** | Stepping into this hotel's sleek black-and-cream marble lobby is a refreshing break from the dreary concrete of the city's main drag. **Pros:** free Wi-Fi; lovely views; restaurant serves excellent French cuisine. **Cons:** rooms could use an update, especially given the price; can be busy with weddings; few interesting places in the immediate vicinity. $ *Rooms from: ¥28,000* ✉ *4–1 Minami-cho, Kanazawa* ☎ *076/233–1311* 🌐 *www.new-grand.co.jp* 🛏 *104 rooms* 🍴 *No Meals.*

**Nakayasu Ryokan** (中安旅館)
**$$ | B&B/INN** | Just north of Kenroku Garden, this family-run ryokan dates from 1920, going out of their way to welcome foreign travelers and providing sound travel advice on Kanazawa and the surrounding region. **Pros:** dinner and breakfast use local ingredients; spotless rooms; free bicycles. **Cons:** tired-looking lobby; few amenities and facilities; some rooms have shared baths. $ *Rooms from: ¥14,200* ✉ *1–10–31 Owari-cho, Kanazawa* ☎ *076/2321–3128* 🌐 *nakayasu-ryokan.co.jp* 💳 *No credit cards* 🛏 *21 rooms* 🍴 *All-Inclusive.*

**Ryokan Asadaya** (旅館浅田屋)
**$$$$ | B&B/INN** | Established during the Meiji Restoration (1867), this small ryokan is the most lavish lodging in Kanazawa, and guests come from all over Japan as much for the food (breakfast and dinner are included in the rate) as for the stay. **Pros:** historic property; elegant furnishings; great meals. **Cons:** a bit far from downtown; no credit cards accepted despite the high cost; extraordinarily expensive. $ *Rooms from: ¥96,800* ✉ *23 Jikken-machi, Kanazawa* ☎ *076/232–2228* 🌐 *www.asadaya.co.jp* 💳 *No credit cards* 🛏 *5 rooms* 🍴 *All-Inclusive.*

## 🍸 Nightlife

All-night fun can be found in the center of town.

**■ TIP→ Be warned: many bars and night spots don't take credit cards.**

**Oriental Brewing** (オリエンタルブルーイング)
**BREWPUBS** | Kanazawa's first craft brewer when it launched in 2016, Oriental Brewing has three small pubs in the city, one in Higashiyama, one by the station, and this one in Korinbo. The eight taps here always include a mix of domestic guest brews and Oriental's own creations—things like wheat beer with spicy *sansho* pepper and stout using locally roasted tea—all served in 350 ml glasses. Come 4 to 6, Monday to Friday for the ¥500 happy hour. ✉ *2–4–26 Korinbo, Kanazawa* ☎ *076/256–0776* 🌐 *www.orientalbrewing.com.*

**Pole-Pole** (ポレポレ)
**LIVE MUSIC** | Pronounced "po-ray po-ray," this reggae bar is run by the same jolly owner as the restaurant Legian, which sits next door. If you want to sit, arrive before midnight. The two dark, cramped rooms get so full that the crowd spills out into the hallway. Pole-Pole is open until 2 am on weeknights and until 5 am on weekends. ✉ *2–31–30 Kata-machi, Kanazawa* ☎ *076/260–1138.*

# Noto Peninsula (能登半島)

*Nanao is 72 km (45 miles) northeast of Kanazawa; Wajima is 113 km (70 miles) northeast of Kanazawa; Matsunami is 132 km (82 miles) northeast of Kanazawa.*

Thought to be named after an *Ainu* (indigenous Japanese) word for "nose," the Noto-hanto, a quasi-national park, juts out into the Sea of Japan and shelters the bays of both Nanao and Toyama. Steep, densely forested hills line the eroded west coast, which is wind- and wave-blasted in winter and ruggedly beautiful in other seasons. The eastern shoreline is lapped by calmer waters and has stunning views of Tate-yama (Mt. Tate), the Hida Mountains, and even of some of Nagano's alpine peaks more than 105 km (70 miles) away.

A quick sightseeing circuit of the Noto-hanto, from Hakui to Nanao, can be done in six to eight hours, but to absorb the peninsula's remarkable scenery, stay two or three days, stopping in Wajima and at one of the minshuku along the coast; arrangements can be made through tourist information offices in Kanazawa, Nanao, or Wajima.

This region is well known for its festivals. Seihakusai Dekayama festival, a 400-year-old tradition held May 3–5 in Nanao, is essentially three days of nonstop partying. Huge (26-foot) 10-ton floats resembling ships called *dekayama* (big mountains) are paraded through the streets. At midnight the floats become miniature Kabuki stages for dance performances by costumed children.

## GETTING HERE AND AROUND

You can fly to Noto-Satoyama Airport from Tokyo (two daily flights with ANA) and take the Furusato Taxi shuttle bus to nearby towns. There is semi-regular bus service around the peninsula, but the best way to get around is by car. Driving from Kanazawa is easiest, but you can also take the train to Wakura Station and pick up a rental car from Nissan Rent-a-Car there. You can also combine train and bus trips or guided tours, which can be arranged in Kanazawa.

**RENTAL CAR CONTACT Nissan Rent-a-Car.** ⊠ *4–22 Yube, Ishisaki-machi, Nanao* ☎ *0767/62–0323* ⊕ *nissan-rentacar.com.*

**VISITOR INFORMATION Wajima Tourist Information Center.** ⊠ *20–1–131 Kawai-machi, Wajima* ☎ *0768/22–1503.*

 **Sights**

**Mitsuke Island** (見附島; *Mitsuke-jima*)
ISLAND | Just south of the village of Suzu is a dramatic offshore rock formation called Mitsuke-jima, a huge wedge of rock topped with lush vegetation, connected to the shore with a pebbly path popular with lovers, who can ring a bell here to wish for everlasting love. Locals, however, also have a very unromantic name for it; "Gunkan-jima" (Battleship Island), because it resembles a warship sailing to attack. ⊠ *Mitsuke-Jima, Suzu.*

**Myojo-ji Temple** (妙成寺)
TEMPLE | This seldom-visited but well-tended temple complex sits a few miles north of the town of Hakui on the bus route from Kanazawa. The temple, founded in 1294 and belonging to the Nichiren sect of Buddhism, has a five-story pagoda dating from the 1600s. A large, colorful Buddha statue sits inside a squat wooden building. The influence of mainland Asia is visible in the gargantuan, wooden guardian deities. It's a 10-minute walk to the temple from the nearest bus stop. ⊠ *1 Yo Taki-dani-machi, Hakui* ☎ *0767/27–1226* ⊕ *myojoji-noto.jp* 🎫 *¥500.*

**Noto Seacoast** (能登金剛海岸; *Noto Kongo Kaigan*)
SCENIC DRIVE | Although inland buses will get you around faster, the coastal route

is recommended for its scenic value. The 16-km (10-mile) stretch between Fuku-ura and Sekinohana, known as the Noto Seacoast, has fantastic wind- and wave-eroded rocks, from craggy towers to partly submerged checkerboard-pattern platforms. Among the best is Gan-mon, a rock cut through the center by water. Gan-mon is about 45 minutes north of Hakui and is a stop on tour-bus routes. The Wajima Tourist Information Center can give you details of boat tours, if you want to see the coast from the water. ⊠ *Noto Seacoast.*

### Soji-ji Soin Temple (總持寺相院)

TEMPLE | The Zen temple complex at Monzen once served as the Soto sect's headquarters. Though a fire destroyed most of the buildings in 1818 and the sect moved its headquarters to Yokohama in 1911, this is still an important training temple. Strolling paths traverse the lush grounds, where you can see some spectacular red maples and an elaborately carved gate. It's possible to stay here for ¥7,000 if you have a serious interest in Zen Buddhism (be advised that room doors don't lock). To get here, take a bus to the Soji-ji Soin Mae bus stop. ⊠ *1–18–1 Monzen, Monzen-cho* ☎ *0768/42–0005* ⊕ *noto-soin.jp* ☜ *¥500.*

### Takaoka City (高岡)

TOWN | The southern gateway to the Noto Peninsula, thanks to being a shinkansen stop, Takaoka is mostly known for its traditions of copper, bronze, and iron smithing, and remains a major bell-casting center. No wonder it has one of Japan's three oldest Daibutsu (Great Buddha) statues. The Takaoka Daibutsu is made entirely of bronze. A short walk from the station is Zuiryu-ji, a delightful Zen temple. A sprawling park, Kojo-koen, is particularly stunning in autumn, with its red-and-silver maples. With Yamacho-suji and Kanayamachi, the city also has a pair of historic, merchant districts dotted with old buildings. ⊠ *Toyama.*

### Wajima Lacquerware Museum
(輪島塗会館; *Wajima Nuri Kaikan*)

OTHER MUSEUM | To observe the traditional lacquerware manufacturing process, visit Wajima Lacquerware Museum. The production of a single piece involves more than 20 steps, from wood preparation and linen reinforcement to the application of layers of lacquer, carefully dried and polished between coats. The facility is in the center of town on the north side of Route 249, near the New Bridge. ⊠ *24–55 Kawai-machi, Wajima* ☎ *0768/22–2155* ☜ *¥300.*

### Wajima Morning Market
(輪島朝市; *Wajima Asaichi*)

MARKET | At the tip of the peninsula, the fishing village of Wajima is known for its gorgeous lacquerware. A good place to purchase some fine pieces is the Wajima Morning Market, held from 8 am to noon daily except for the second and fourth Wednesday of each month. You can also buy seafood, fruit, vegetables, and local crafts from elderly women wearing indigo *monpei* (field pants). Almost anyone can point you in the right direction. ⊠ *Asa-ichi dori, Kawai-machi, Wajima* ☎ *0768/22–7653.*

##  Restaurants

### Heart and Beer (日本海俱楽部)

$$ | ECLECTIC | A terrific brewery and log-cabin-style restaurant is five minutes by taxi from Matsunami Station (on the Noto Line). It's operated by two beer masters from Eastern Europe in conjunction with an association that helps people with disabilities. **Known for:** spit-roasted chicken; rustic setting (and cash-only); European-style microbrews. Ⓢ *Average main: ¥3,000* ⊠ *92 Aza Tatekabe, Uchi-ura-machi* ☎ *0768/72–8181* ▭ *No credit cards* ☉ *Closed Wed.*

### Shin-puku (神ぷく)

$$$ | JAPANESE | Various sashimi and sushi combinations are reasonably priced at this small but beautiful sushi bar close

to the post office in Wajima. With the post office on your right, walk two blocks down Route 249. **Known for:** seafood donburi; local sake; good-value sushi sets, though cash-only. $ *Average main: ¥4,000 ⊠ 5–41–23 Kawai-machi, Wajima ☎ 0768/22–8133* ▭ *No credit cards.*

##  Hotels

### Fukasan (深三)

$$ | **B&B/INN** | Near the morning market and the harbor, this two-story wooden minshuku is furnished with locally made crafts and can be booked without meals or with; if you opt to pay just a couple of thousand yen extra for the latter, the usual menu is local seafood, vegetables, and Noto Peninsula rice. **Pros:** near morning market; traditional atmosphere; friendly staff. **Cons:** need to check in by 5 pm; no baths en suite; fewer amenities than a larger hotel. $ *Rooms from: ¥13,500 ⊠ 4–4 Kawai-machi, Wajima ☎ 0768/22–9933* ⊕ *fukasan.jp* ▭ *No credit cards* ⊅ *4 rooms* ⦿ *No Meals.*

### Mawaki Po-re Po-re (真脇ポーレポーレ)

$$$$ | **B&B/INN** | Built into a hillock, this little hotel has great views of the sea and surrounding hills; breakfast and dinner are included in the rates; and the staff are kind. **Pros:** great views; quiet atmosphere; close to mineral baths. **Cons:** not much English spoken; Western-style rooms not as smart as the Japanese rooms; somewhat out of the way. $ *Rooms from: ¥35,200 ⊠ 19–110 Mawaki, Noto-cho, Hosu-gun ☎ 0768/62–4700* ⊅ *11 rooms* ⦿ *All-Inclusive.*

### Shunran no Sato (春欄の里)

$$$$ | **B&B/INN** | **FAMILY** | Close to 50 traditional houses in this farming village at the end of the peninsula have been turned into minshuku like Shunran-no-Sato, giving you the chance to experience rural life, including meals (included in the rate) that are as local as you can get—the rice is harvested from paddies outside the houses. **Pros:** only accepts one group of guests a day, so you'll have it to yourself; some English spoken; rare chance to experience rural life. **Cons:** no hotel-style amenities; not much else in the area; access difficult without a car. $ *Rooms from: ¥27,500 ⊠ 16–9 Miya-chi, Noto-cho, Hosu-gun ☎ 0768/76–0021* ⊕ *www.shunran-no-sato.com* ⊅ *1 room (up to 3 guests)* ⦿ *All-Inclusive.*

# Toyama (富山)

*18 km (11 miles) southeast of Takaoka, 61 km (38 miles) east of Kanazawa, 282 km (175 miles) north of Kyoto.*

Busy, industrial Toyama is beautified by Toyama-joshi Koen (Toyama Castle Park), a spread of greenery with a reconstructed version of the original 1532 castle. Toyama Bay is the habitat of the glowing *hotaru ika*, or "firefly squid." Their spawning grounds stretch for 15 km (9 miles) along the coast from Uozu to the right bank of Toyama City's Jouganji River and about 1½ km (¾ mile) from shore. From March until June, their spawning season, the females gather close to the seabed and come to the surface from dusk until midnight. From the early morning until dawn, the sea magically glows from the squids' photophores, blue-white light-producing organs that attract their prey. This phenomenon has been designated a Special Natural Monument. Sightseeing boats provide close-up views.

## GETTING HERE AND AROUND

All Nippon Airways has three flights daily between Tokyo and Toyama. Toyama is 19 minutes from Takaoka and one hour from Kanazawa by JR Limited Express, and three and four hours north of Kyoto and Nagoya, respectively, by JR. Toyama has a network of streetcars that can take you to most destinations within town.

**VISITOR INFORMATION Toyama Tourist Information Office.** ⊠ *Toyama Station, 1–230 Merin-cho ☎ 076/431–3255* ⊕ *foreign.info-toyama.com/en.*

The Kurobe Gorge Railway operates from April through November through the deepest valley in Japan.

## 👁 Sights

**Kurobe Gorge Railway** (黒部峡谷鉄道;
*Kurobe Keikoku Tetsudo*)

**TRAIN/TRAIN STATION** | Running from spring
to fall along the deepest valley in Japan,
the open-air Kurobe Gorge Railway takes
you on an 80-minute ride past gushing
springs and waterfalls. You might even
see wild monkeys or a *serow*, a type of
mountain goat. One of the best views
is from the 128-foot-high bridge called
Atobiki-kyo, while the best time of year
is mid-October to early November for
the tremendous fall foliage. Bring a
windbreaker, even in summer, as it can
be a cold and damp ride, or spend an
extra ¥530 to upgrade to a more sheltered first-class seat. Kuronagi Onsen,
Kanetsuri Onsen, and Meiken Onsen are
three of the hot springs along the trolley
route. You can get off at any of them
and enjoy a soak. ⊠ *11 Kurobe Keiko-
ku-guchi, Kurobeshin* ☎ *0765/62–1011
for reservations only* ⊕ *www.kurotetu.
co.jp/en* 🎫 *¥1,980 one-way* ⏱ *Closed
Dec.–mid-Apr.*

# Niigata (新潟)

*250 km (155 miles) northeast of Toyama,
335 km (205 miles) north of Tokyo.*

The coast between Kurobe and Niigata
is flat and not so interesting. Two towns
along the way, Naoetsu and Teradomari,
serve as ferry ports to Ogi and Akadomari,
respectively, on Sado Island. From Niigata
ferries go to Sado and even Hokkaido. In
the skiing season people fly into Niigata
before traveling by train to the northern
Alps for quick access to ski resorts.

## GETTING HERE AND AROUND

Niigata is four hours by bus from Toyama,
and two hours, 15 minutes from Tokyo by
Shinkansen. Niigata serves as a transfer
point en route to Sado Island, but has
enough to see and do to justify spending
a night in the city.

## VISITOR INFORMATION

There is a tourist information center at
the Bandai-guchi exit of Niigata Station,
where staff can provide English maps

and information on sights in the city, including restaurant information. If you are traveling on to Sado Island, Niigata Kotsu Information Center is found to the left of the Ryotsu bus terminal, just after getting off the ferry.

**CONTACT Niigata Station Bandai Exit Tourist Information Center.** ✉ *Niigata Station, 1–1–1 Hanazono, Chuo-ku* ☎ *025/241–7914* ⊕ *www.nvcb.or.jp.*

## 👁 Sights

### Imayo Tsukasa Sake Brewery (今代司酒造; *Imayo Tsukasa Shuzou*)

**BREWERY** | Originally established as an inn and sake shop in 1767, but brewing since the Meiji period, Imayo Tsukasa is one of the ninety or so sake brewers that have made Niigata famous for *nihonshu* (sake). They run 30-minute tours of the brewery every day (hourly from 9 to 4 on weekends, and 1 to 4 on weekdays), where staff explain the sake brewing process. That's followed by a tasting session, where you can sample multiple brews. Better yet, it's free, and there is an English speaker available for each 2 pm tour. You need to book in advance, online or by phone, but that can be done same day. It's a 15-minute walk east of Niigata Station. ✉ *1–1 Kagamigaoka, Chuo-ku* ☎ *025/245–3231* ⊕ *imayotsukasa.co.jp/en.*

### Northern Culture Museum (北方文化博物館; *Hoppo Bunka Hakubutsukan*)

**HISTORIC HOME** | On the banks of the Agano River on the Kanbara Plain, the museum is a 40-minute bus ride from Niigata Station. This former estate was established in the Edo period by the Ito family, which, by the 1930s, was the largest landowner in the Kaetsu area, with 8,352 acres of paddy fields, 2,500 acres of forest, and 78 overseers who controlled no fewer than 2,800 tenants. Ito Mansion, built in 1887, was their home for generations until the Land Reform Act of 1946. With its valuable art collection

it became this museum, which has 65 rooms, as well as three restaurants and a coffee shop.

Its five teahouses are in different parts of the garden (two of them built later), and numerous natural rocks—mostly from Kyoto—are artistically arranged around the pond. At Niigata ask the tourist information office to point you in the direction of the right bus, which takes 40 minutes. A taxi takes 20 minutes. ✉ *2–15–25 Somi, Niigata* ☎ *025/385–2001* ⊕ *hoppou-bunka.com/english* 🎫 *¥800.*

### Saitou Family Villa (旧齋藤家別邸; *Kyu Saitou-ke Bettei*)

**HISTORIC HOME** | The Saitou family was one of Niigata's most successful merchant families in the Meiji period. Their old villa, built in 1917, is a charming two-story wooden building with a pretty landscaped garden that is especially stunning when the leaves change color in the fall. Once you've explored the building and strolled the garden, stop for *matcha* tea and sweets in the tatami-floored tearoom that looks out into the grounds. To get there, take the Niigata loop bus to the Hoppo Bunka Hakubutsukan Niigata Bunkan-mae stop, from where it's a two-minute walk. ✉ *567 Nishi Ohatamachi, Chuo-ku* ☎ *025/210–8350* ⊕ *saitouke.jp* 🎫 *¥300; tea and sweets ¥500* 🕐 *Closed Mon.*

### Ponshukan (ぽんしゅ館)

**STORE/MALL** | This sake shop in the malls connected to Niigata Station is best known for its tasting room, where you can sample little cups of sake from each of Niigata's 90 or so breweries, all self-served from a wall of 100 shiny, silver vending machines. For a small fee, you'll be given a sake cup and five coins for the vending machines. You can also try pairing each sake with a selection of regional salts. Afterwards, the shop itself has an interesting range of sake-related souvenirs, from the actual drinks to moisturizing masks and soap made with sake lees, plus regional snacks and deli foods.

✉ Niigata Station, 1–96–47 Hanazono, Chuo-ku ☎ 025/240–7090 ⊕ www.pon-shukan.com/en ✐ ¥500 sake tasting.

## 🍽 Restaurants

### Inaka-ya (田舎家)

$$$ | **JAPANESE** | Seasonal seafood and regional specialties dominate the menu here, with dishes like *wappa-meshi* (rice steamed in a wooden box with toppings of salmon, chicken, or crab) making for an inexpensive and excellent lunch and, depending on the season, more elaborate dinner courses including *yanagi karei hitohoshi-yaki* (grilled flounder), *nodo-guro shioyaki* (grilled blackthroat seaperch), and *buri teriyaki* (yellowtail). Inaka-ya, which closes between lunch and dinner from 2:30 to 5, is found in the heart of Furu-machi, the local eating and drinking district. **Known for:** grilled sweetfish from June to September; excellent sashimi assortments; rock oysters from May to August. $ *Average main: ¥5,000* ✉ 1457 Kyuban-cho, Furu-machi-dori, Niigata ☎ 025/223–1266 ⊕ inakayaniigata.owst.jp.

### Marui (丸伊)

$$$ | **SUSHI** | Here you'll find all kinds of fresh fish, some of which are found only in the Sea of Japan. For easy ordering, opt for a set course and ask for a Niigata sake to go with it; nowhere in Japan does sake better. **Known for:** superb selection of locally made sake; blackthroat seaperch (nodo-guro), as sashimi or grilled, which is always good in Niigata; dinner sets featuring sushi and grilled fish from ¥5,000. $ *Average main: ¥5,000* ✉ 8–1411 Higashibori-dori, Niigata ☎ 025/228–0101.

## 🛏 Hotels

### Hotel Mets Niigata (ホテルメッツ新潟)

$$ | **HOTEL** | This sleek hotel offers spotless, if cramped, rooms at reasonable rates. **Pros:** great location; connected to the train station; close to shopping and dining. **Cons:** station area can be noisy at night; better value (albeit for less) at budget business hotel chains; rooms are small. $ *Rooms from: ¥15,000* ✉ 1–96–47 Hanazono, Niigata ☎ 025/246–2100 ⊕ www.hotelmets.jp/niigata ➫ 197 rooms ⦿ Free Breakfast.

### Okura Hotel Niigata (ホテルオークラ新潟)

$$$ | **HOTEL** | On the Shinano River, about 1½ km (1 mile) from the station, the Okura offers views of the water from many of its rooms. **Pros:** city views; excellent service; good location. **Cons:** conservative decor; can be crowded with wedding and conference guests; pricey for what you get. $ *Rooms from: ¥19,000* ✉ 6–53 Kawabata-cho, Niigata ☎ 025/224–6111 ⊕ www.okura-niigata.co.jp ➫ 265 rooms ⦿ Free Breakfast.

# Sado Island (佐渡島; Sado-ga-shima)

*84 km (52 miles) west of Niigata.*

Sado is known as much for its unblemished natural beauty as for its melancholy history. Revolutionary intellectuals, such as the Buddhist monk Nichiren, were banished to Sado to endure harsh exile as punishment for treason. When gold was discovered on Sado during the Edo period (1603–1868), the homeless and poverty-stricken were sent to Sado to work as forced laborers in the mines. This long history of hardship has left a tradition of soulful ballads and folk dances. Even the bamboo grown on the island is said to be the best for making *shakuhachi,* the flutes that accompany the mournful music.

May through September is the best time to visit Sado. In January and February, the weather is bitterly cold, and at other times storms can prevent sea and air crossings. Although the island is Japan's fifth-largest, it's still relatively small, at 857 square km (331 square miles). Two parallel mountain chains running along the northern and southern coasts are split by a wide plain, and it is here that the island's cities are found. Despite the more than 1 million tourists who visit the island each year (more than 20 times the number of inhabitants), the pace is slow.

Sado's usual port of entry is **Ryotsu** (両津), the island's largest township. The town's center runs between Kamo-ko (Kamo Lake) and the coast, with most of the hotels and ryokan on the shore of the lake. Kamo-ko is connected to the sea by a small inlet running through the middle of town. Ryotsu's Ebisu quarter has the island's largest concentration of restaurants and bars. Give yourself at least two days to take advantage of the beauty of Sado Island. For music lovers, the Kodo Earth Celebration in mid-August is not to be missed.

## GETTING HERE AND AROUND

Sado Kisen Ferries' main route, from Niigata to Ryotsu, has both regular ferry and hydrofoil services. The ferry journey takes 2½ hours, with three to five crossings a day; the one-way fare is ¥2,810 to ¥16,360, depending on what class you choose. The jetfoil (¥6,900 one-way) takes one hour, with five crossings each way daily in summer, three in winter. Bus No. 17 or 18, leaving from in front of the JR Niigata Station, takes 15 minutes (¥210) to reach the dock.

From May to October, there is also a jetfoil running twice daily between the town of Ogi, on Sado, and Naoetsu, a smaller city two hours by express train south of Niigata. One-way fares start from ¥7,110.

Frequent bus service is available between major towns on Sado-ga-shima. The scenic 60-minute bus ride from Ryotsu to Aikawa departs every 30 minutes and costs ¥840. Or you could get a one-, two- or three-day bus pass covering the entire island (¥1,500 to ¥3,000). There is also a sightseeing taxi offering three, four, or five-hour tours of the island for a flat rate.

From late April to late November, Sado Bus also operates several sightseeing bus routes taking in the island's best sights. Day tickets cost ¥3,600 to ¥9,900, depending on the route. It's an efficient way to see the island, but these buses have a magnetic attraction to souvenir shops. You can make bus-tour reservations directly with the Niigata Kotsu Sado Sightseeing Bus Center.If you have an international driver's license, a more flexible option is to rent a car from one of the rental firms in Ryotsu. You can reserve a car online in English with Nippon Rent-A-Car, which has a branch near the port. Twelve-hour rates vary from ¥5,940 to ¥9,130 in peak season, depending on car size.

**CAR RENTAL Nippon Rent-A-Car.** ⊠ *226–3 Ryotsu-ebisu, Sado* ☎ *0259/23–4020* ⊕ *www.nrgroup-global.com/en.*

**FERRY Sado Kisen Ferries.** ⊠ *353 Ryotsu Minato, Sado* ☎ *0570/200–310* ⊕ *www. sadokisen.co.jp.*

**TOURS Niigata Kotsu Sado Sightseeing Bus Center.** ⊠ *80 Kawaharada Suwamachi, Sado* ☎ *0259/52–3200.*

**VISITOR INFORMATION Sado Tourism Association.** ⊠ *Ryotsu Port, Terminal Bldg., 353 Ryotsu-minato, Sado* ☎ *0259/27– 5000* ⊕ *www.visitsado.com/en.*

# Sights

The simplest way to explore Sado is to take the bus from Ryotsu west to Aikawa, or rent a car from Ryotsu. Before gold was discovered here in 1601, it was a town of 10,000 people. The population swelled to 125,000 before the gold was exhausted. Now it's just over 50,000.

### Ogi (小木)

**TOWN** | This tiny port town on Sado's southwest coast is famous for *taraibune*, tublike boats used for fishing. You can be paddled around the harbor in one by old ladies in traditional attire for a small fee. Taraibune can also be found in the village

The main attraction in Ogi, on Sado Island, is a trip on a traditional fishing boat.

of Shukunegi on the Sawasaki coast, where the water is dotted with rocky islets and the shore is covered with rock lilies in summer. ⊠ *Ogi Machi, Sado* ✉ *¥600 for 10-min taraibune trip.*

## Osado Skyline Drive (大佐渡スカイライン)
SCENIC DRIVE | The island's most scenic route is the roughly 30-km (19-mile) Osa-do Skyline Drive, which snakes across the mountains from Ryotsu to Aikawa. If you aren't using a rental car, you must take either a tour bus from Ryotsu or a taxi from Aikawa to Chiguse, where you can catch a bus for the return trip. (You can do the route in reverse as well.) It's particularly beautiful in autumn foliage season. ⊠ *Sado Skyline Rd., Sado.*

## Sado Gold Mine (佐渡金山; *Sado Kinzan*)
MINE | This mine was once the most pro-ductive in Japan, producing gold, silver, and copper for the Tokugawa shogunate. After closing in the late 1980s, it has been preserved as a historical museum. Part of the mine's 325 km (250 miles) of underground tunnels, some running as deep as 1,969 feet, are open to the

public. For a steep fee, you could don Mixed Reality glasses for a 30-minute walk in the Dohyu Tunnel, to see how Edo-period slaves worked the mine in appalling conditions. A cheaper option is to pay for tech-free access to parts of the Dohyu and Sohdayu tunnels. The mine is a tough 40-minute uphill walk or a five-minute taxi ride (about ¥900) from the bus stop at Aikawa. Three daily Nana-Ura Kaigan buses let you off at the Sado-Kinzan-mae bus stop. ⊠ *1305 Shimo-Aikawa, Sado* ☎ *0259/74–2389* ⊕ *www.sado-kinzan.com* ✉ *¥1,400; ¥3,000 VR Experience.*

## Senkaku Bay (尖閣湾; *Senkaku-wan*)
Glass-bottomed boats operate sightseeing cruises around Senakaku Bay, offering views of the fantastic, sea-eroded rock for-mations and 60-foot cliffs. You get off the boat at Senkaku-wan Ageshima Yuen (Sen-kaku Bay Ageshima Island Park), where you can picnic, stroll, and gaze at the varied rock formations offshore. From the park, return by bus from the pier to Aikawa. To reach the bay, take a 15-minute bus ride

from Aikawa to Senkaku-wan Ageshima Yuen Mae bus stop, where you catch boats for the 40-minute sightseeing cruise. The one-way cruise boat runs mid-March to late November. It's also possible to enter the park without taking a cruise. Once there, you could also try several hands-on activities, including fishing with a bamboo rod (¥550, 30 minutes) and preparing dried squid (¥1,500, 40 minutes). ✉ *Senka-ku-wan Ageshima Yuen* ☎ *0259/75–2311* 🚢 *Boats ¥1,100; park entry ¥550.*

### Shukunegi (宿根木)

**TOWN** | Once known for building small wooden ships to traverse the waters between Sado and Honshu, laid-back Shukunegi is a great place to see traditional buildings that date back more than a century. From Ogi, you can reach Shukunegi by bus or by bike. If renting a bike in Ogi, ask for an electric assist model to help power you up the steep hills between the two towns. ✉ *Shukunegi.*

##  Restaurants

### Uoharu (魚春)

$$ | **JAPANESE** | A short drive from the ferry terminal in Ogi, this three-story building has a fish shop on the ground level and a casual seafood restaurant upstairs serving superfresh seasonal fish. The restaurant owners sometimes take unscheduled days off, so call in advance to make sure they're open. **Known for:** sashimi set meals; grilled sazae (turban shell); donburi (bowls of rice topped with a mix of seafood). $ *Average main: ¥2,000* ✉ *415–1 Ogi-machi* ☎ *0259/86–2085* 🚫 *No credit cards* 🕒 *Closed the 1st and 15th of each month.*

### Itamae no Mise Takeya (板前の店 竹屋)

$$ | **JAPANESE** | In business for more than half a century, this small restaurant in Aikawa specializes in seafood, with excellent sashimi and simmered dishes, but also a local favorite called *ikagoro*; squid (innards and all) mixed with sliced onions, mushrooms, and miso paste, before being

sauteed. If you are staying without a meal plan at the Hotel Mancho or Hotel Oosado, both just down the coast from Aikawa, this is a good value option for a local dinner. **Known for:** local sake; sashimi; ikagoro (sauteed squid with onions, mushrooms, and miso). $ *Average main: ¥3,000* ✉ *1–5–3 Aikawa, Sado* ☎ *0259/74–3328* 🚫 *No credit cards* 🕒 *Lunch only on Sun.*

##  Hotels

You can make hotel reservations at the information counters of Sado Kisen ship company at Niigata Port or Ryotsu Port, though many hotels are also listed on well-known booking sites (sometimes with better rates).

### Hotel Mancho (ホテル万長)

$$$$ | **HOTEL** | Arguably the best hotel on the island's west coast, the Mancho caters mostly to Japanese tourists. **Pros:** excellent views in clear weather; friendly staff; nice onsen baths. **Cons:** dismal views on rainy days; quiet area if you want to go out at night; need to taxi into Aikawa; no English spoken. $ *Rooms from: ¥26,400* ✉ *58 Orito, Sado* ☎ *0259/74–3221* 🛏 *82 rooms* 🍴 *Free Breakfast.*

### Hotel Oosado (ホテル大佐渡)

$$$$ | **RESORT** | Perched on a cliff overlooking the Sea of Japan, this resort offers ocean views, an open-air hot-spring pool, and comfortable Japanese- or Western-style rooms. **Pros:** delicious meals; ocean views; peaceful location. **Cons:** Western-style rooms are uninspiring; no nightlife nearby; not much sightseeing nearby. $ *Rooms from: ¥49,700* ✉ *288–2 Kabuse Aikawa, Sado* ☎ *0259/74–3300* ⊕ *hotel-oosado.jp* 🛏 *74 rooms* 🍴 *All-Inclusive.*

# Chapter 8

# KYOTO

Updated by
Tom Fay

| 👁 Sights | 🍽 Restaurants | 🛏 Hotels | 🛍 Shopping | 🍸 Nightlife |
|---|---|---|---|---|
| ★★★★★ | ★★★★★ | ★★★★☆ | ★★★☆☆ | ★★★☆☆ |

# WELCOME TO KYOTO

## TOP REASONS TO GO

★ **Architecture:** Despite modernization, about 27,000 traditional houses still grace the Kyoto cityscape. The preservation districts include Sannen-zaka, Gion Shinbashi, the sake brewing district in Fushimi, and the canal street leading to Kamigamo Jinja.

★ **Gardens:** Chinese-influenced gardens symbolize paradise on Earth. The *karesansui* (rock gardens) of Zen temples signify the quest for wholeness; the most famous of these is at Ryoan-ji.

★ **Crafts:** There's no shortage of art and antiques shops; secondhand kimonos are a bargain; and ceramics, lacquerware, and woven bamboo make great souvenirs.

★ **Living culture:** With their opulent kimonos, hair ornaments, and artistic skills, the professional dancers and performers known as geisha are revered as an embodiment of Japanese culture.

★ **Festivals:** Kyoto is known for its elaborate festivals.

Central Kyoto is fairly compact and easily navigable. Its grid layout, originally modeled on Xi'an, in China, makes this Japan's most rational urban space. Karasuma-dori bisects Kyoto Station in the middle of the city. East of the Kamogawa River, Higashiyama holds many popular sights, all connected by the congested Higashi-oji-dori.

**1 Eastern Kyoto.** Higashiyama, as Eastern Kyoto is known, abounds with temples and shrines. The Gion shopping and entertainment neighborhood is also here.

**2 Central Kyoto.** Here are most hotels, the business district, and the Kiyamachi entertainment area. The Karasuma subway line runs north–south through central Kyoto.

**3 Southern Kyoto.** The area south of Kyoto Station contains several gems, including the unforgettable Fushimi-Inari Taisha shrine. The tea-producing city of Uji shares a border with Kyoto.

**4 Western Kyoto.** Though not as dense with sights as eastern Kyoto, this neighborhood includes many temples and gardens.

**5 Arashiyama.** Just outside the city, the exquisite Katsura Imperial Villa, the lovely Tenryu-ji Temple, and beautiful riverside parks are in Arashiyama.

**6 Northern Kyoto.** Far from the city center, the main attractions of Northern Kyoto are the Buddhist enclave Enryaku-ji atop Mt. Hiei and the charming countryside of Ohara.

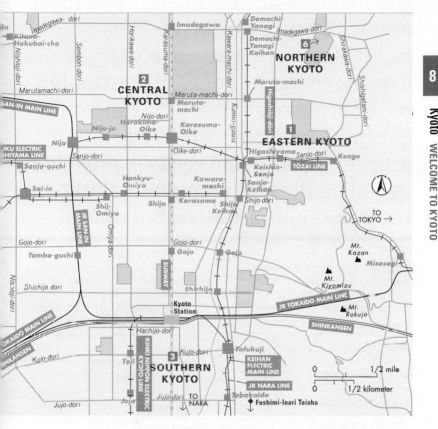

The astonishing number of temples, shrines, and palaces that adorn the city make Kyoto's architecture its most famous feature worldwide. Japan's capital for more than 1,000 years, Kyoto was the center not only of politics, but religion, philosophy, art, culture, and cuisine. All of Japan's refined cultural arts blossomed from seeds planted here, including the tea ceremony, Kabuki theater, Zen, and Tantric Buddhism.

Breathtaking sights are everywhere, though some places truly stand out, among them Kyoto's great temples, such as Kiyomizu-dera in the city's eastern mountains, and the forest-cloaked Fushimi-Inari Taisha, a shrine pathway through a miles-long chain of towering vermilion gates. Visitors also flock to cultural hubs like the Museum of Traditional Crafts, which showcases the city's artisanal legacy, and Sanjusangen-do Temple, with its 1,000 golden statues of Kannon, the Japanese Goddess of Mercy.

Kyoto residents have a fierce sense of propriety about nearly everything, ranging from good table manners to family pedigree. This subtle yet strict code has some notorious consequences for locals—who are not considered true Kyotoites unless they can trace their lineage back four generations—but certain benefits for visitors. Wear out your welcome in a Kyoto home, and they are likely to offer you tea as a signal that your time is up. The refined and symbolic Kyoto mindset, however, insists that nothing made here should be

of less than exquisite craftsmanship and stellar design. This philosophy means that whether browsing for gifts in a handkerchief shop, sightseeing at a local temple, or sitting down to a 12-course dinner, whatever you encounter is likely to be top-notch. As a visitor here you're a guest of the city, and Kyoto will make sure you leave with wonderful memories.

## Planning

With hundreds of temples and shrines and several former imperial and shogun residences, Kyoto offers a lot to see. Don't run yourself ragged trying to take in everything—even many locals have trouble finding the time to experience all the history and culture here. Balance a morning at temples or museums with an afternoon in traditional shops, and a morning at the market with the rest of the day in Arashiyama or at one of the imperial villas. Visit at least one of the mountaintop temple complexes such as Enryaku-ji on Hiei-zan, Daigo-ji, or Ohara. Remember that you must apply in advance (anywhere from one to several days) to visit attractions that require permits such as the Imperial Palace, the imperial villas Katsura Rikyu and Shuga-ku-in, and Koinzan Saiho-ji.

# Getting Here and Around

Kyoto has an excellent public transportation system, so getting around the city is a snap. Buses are frequent and reliable, though the thick crowds can make riding them somewhat claustrophobic. JR trains and five private light-rails and subways service the city, and are especially useful for reaching outlying sights and making day trips to nearby cities.

## AIR

International and some domestic flights land at Kansai International Airport, near Osaka. Osaka's Itami Airport handles all regional flights. To get to downtown Kyoto from Kansai Airport, the quickest rail option is the JR Haruka Limited Express (75 minutes; ¥3,430 reserved, ¥2,900 unreserved). From Itami, buses depart approximately every 20 minutes between 8:10 am and 9:15 pm (approx. 55 minutes; ¥1,340). MK Taxi offers shuttle buses from both Kansai (¥3,500) and Itami (¥3,000); reserve in advance.

## BUS

Buses in Kyoto are quick, reliable, and punctual. Buses 100 and 101 connect all the major sightseeing spots. Pick up route maps at the Kyoto Tourist Information Center.

Within the city the fare is ¥230, which you pay when getting off the bus; outside the city limits the fare varies according to distance. Several special transportation passes are available: A one-day bus pass (*ichinichi basu ken*) for City Bus users costs ¥700 and may be purchased on the bus or at transportation kiosks. Another, more comprehensive day pass includes use of City Bus, Kyoto Bus, and the subway. It is called the Subway & Bus One-Day Pass (*Chikatetsu basu ichinichi ken*) and costs ¥1,100 for adults and ¥550 for children. These passes as well as maps of bus and subway lines are available in Kyoto Station at kiosks and ticket vendors marked *Kōtsū Annai* (Transport Information); at the tourist information center mentioned above; at the Shijō Karasuma, Ōike-Karasuma, and Keihan subway stations; at Kitaōji Bus and Subway Terminal; and at major hotels. Integrated-circuit (IC) cards that resemble a credit card: Pasmo; Suica; ICOCA; PiTaPa, can now be used on most local trains and buses in Kyoto. ICOCA and PiTaPa are most often available in Kyoto and Osaka making travel much easier. One purchases them at a station or convenience store by putting ¥500 into a designated IC machine. Along with the initial charge, one inserts enough money to cover a day or two, recharging when needed. The maximum that can be charged is ¥20,000. To use the card, just tap the screen at the turnstile when entering a station or getting off a bus, and the remaining amount will be shown on the screen. The card shows no identification so if you misplace or lose it you lose the remaining amount. If you are taking the bus (¥230) more than three times a day, the ¥700 one-day bus pass is more economical than an IC card which charges full fare each use.

■**TIP→ Trips to Uji, Ohara, and other outlying areas are not included in the one-day all-you-can-ride pass.**

## SUBWAY

Kyoto has a 28-station subway system. The Karasuma Line runs north to south from Kokusai Kaikan to Takeda. The Tozai Line runs between Uzumasa Tenjingawa in the west and Roku-jizo in the east. Purchase tickets at the vending machines in stations before boarding. Fares begin at ¥210 and increase with distance traveled. Service runs from 5:30 am to 11:30 pm. First and last train times are posted at the entrance of each station.

## TAXI

Taxis are readily available in Kyoto. Fares for smaller-size cabs start at ¥640 for the first 2 km (1 mile), with ¥100 added for each additional 500 meters (1,640 feet). Many taxi companies provide guided tours of the city, priced per hour or per route. MK Taxi runs tours starting at ¥28,520 for three hours. There are fixed fares for some sightseeing services that start and end at Kyoto Station. A seven-hour tour of the city's major sights will cost from around ¥30,000 with a number of the 17 taxi companies, including Yasaka Taxi.

**CONTACTS Keihan Taxi.** ✉ *Kyoto* ☎ *075/622–4000.* **MK Taxi.** ✉ *Kyoto* ☎ *075/778–4141* ⊕ *www.mktaxi-japan. com.* **Yasaka Taxi.** ✉ *Kyoto* ☎ *075/842– 1214* ⊕ *www.yasakataxi.jp.*

## TRAIN

Frequent Shinkansen trains run between Tokyo and Kyoto, taking 2 hours 10 minutes. The one-way reserved fare is ¥14,170. JR train service between Osaka and Kyoto costs ¥570 and takes 30 minutes. Keihan and Hankyu lines express trains take 40 minutes and cost between ¥400 and ¥480. They depart every 15 minutes from Osaka's Yodoyabashi and Osaka-Umeda stations.

For travel to Kyoto's northern reaches, change from the Keihan subway line to the Eizan Railway by transferring at Imadegawa-dori/Demachi-Yanagi Station. The Eizan has two lines, the Kurama Line, running north to Kurama, and the Eizan Line, running northeast to Yase. The Hankyu Line, which, within Kyoto, runs west as far as the Katsura Imperial Villa, connects with the subway at Karasuma Station. From Shijo-Omiya Station, the Keifuku Arashiyama Line runs to western Kyoto. JR also runs to western Kyoto on the San-in Main Line.

# Hotels

No other Japanese city can compete with Kyoto for style and grace. For the ultimate experience of Kyoto hospitality, stay in a ryokan, a traditional Japanese inn. Though often costly, a night in a ryokan guarantees you beautiful traditional Japanese surroundings, excellent service, and two elegant meals (breakfast and dinner) in most cases. But you don't have to limit yourself to the traditional. Kyoto is a tourist city, so accommodations range from luxurious hotels to small guesthouses. Service in this city is impeccable. The information desks are well stocked, and concierges or guest-relations managers are often available in the lobby to respond to your needs.

*Hotel prices are the lowest cost of a standard double room in high season. Hotel reviews have been shortened. For full information, visit Fodors.com.*

| What It Costs in Yen | | | |
| --- | --- | --- | --- |
| **$** | **$$** | **$$$** | **$$$$** |
| **LODGING FOR TWO** | | | |
| under ¥12,000 | ¥12,000– ¥18,000 | ¥18,001– ¥22,000 | over ¥22,000 |

# Nightlife

Though Kyoto's nightlife is more sedate than Osaka's, the areas around the old geisha quarters downtown thrive with nightclubs and bars. The Kiyamachi area along the small canal near Ponto-cho in central Kyoto is packed full of bars, restaurants, and a few dance clubs and is as close to a consolidated nightlife area as you'll get in Kyoto. It's full of small watering holes with red lanterns (indicating inexpensive places) or small neon signs in front. It's also fun to walk around the Gion in eastern Kyoto and Ponto-cho in central Kyoto to try to catch a glimpse of a geisha or maiko stealing down an alleyway on her way to or from an appointment.

# Performing Arts

Kyoto is known for its traditional performances—particularly dance and Noh theater. All dialogue is in Japanese, but sometimes there are synopses available. From time to time international musicians play the intimate venues. The most convenient source for information is your hotel concierge or guest-relations manager, who may even have a few tickets on hand. For further information on Kyoto's arts scene, check the music and theater sections of the quarterly magazine *Kansai Scene,* free at some English-friendly bookshops, hotels, and bars; you can also find information on the website (⊕ *www.kansaiscene. com).* Another source is the *Kyoto Visitor's Guide,* which devotes a few pages to "This Month's Theater." Look at the festival listings for temple and shrine performances. It's available free from the Kyoto Tourist Information Center on the ninth floor of the Kyoto Station Building; the staff can also provide you with information.

## NOH

Kyoto is the home of Japan's most ancient form of traditional theater, Noh, which is more ritualistic and sophisticated than Kabuki. Some understanding of the plot of each play is necessary to enjoy a performance, an acquired taste that is generally slow-moving and solemnly chanted. The carved masks used by the main actors express a whole range of emotions, though the mask itself may appear expressionless until the actor "brings it to life." Noh performances are held year-round and tickets range in price from ¥3,000 to ¥13,000. Particularly memorable are outdoor Noh performances, especially **Takigi Noh,** held outdoors by firelight on the nights of June 1 and 2 in the precincts of the Heian Jingu. For more information about performances, contact the Kyoto Tourist Information Center.

## KABUKI

Kabuki developed in the Edo period as a theatrical art with lavish costumes and sets and dynamic all-male performances. Though Kabuki is faster-paced than Noh, a single performance can easily take half a day. Devotees pack bentos to eat while watching shows. Kyoto hosts traveling Kabuki performances periodically; most of the troupes are based in Tokyo. Especially anticipated in Kyoto is the annual monthlong **Kaomise** (Face Showing) Kabuki festival in December, featuring top Kabuki stars and introducing up-and-coming artists. Tickets cost between ¥5,500 and ¥27,000 and should be booked weeks in advance.

## SEASONAL DANCE

In spring and autumn, *geiko* and *maiko* perform dances and songs that pay tribute to the seasonal splendor. Spring dances are held in four of the districts, and are referred to as **Miyako Odori, Kamogawa Odori, Kyo Odori,** and **Kitano Odori.** In autumn these troupes as well as Gion Odori bring the total to five major performances. Stage settings are spectacular.

# Planning Your Time

It would take several days minimum just to take in Kyoto's highlights, more if you want to bask in the serenity of the city's temples and gardens. You could easily spend a day each in Ohara and Arashiyama and walking along the Philosopher's Path. Nijo Castle takes about an hour to visit because its grounds are so large; otherwise, a half hour to 45 minutes at most sights is enough for most people. Walking around the old Imperial Palace and park is a nice one-hour stroll. The main part of Gion is easily done in half an hour because so much of its architecture can only be seen from the outside and not toured.

# Restaurants

Attuned to subtle seasonal changes, Kyoto cuisine emphasizes freshness and contrast. From the finest *ryotei* (high-class Japanese restaurants) to the smallest *izakaya* (pub), the distinctive elements of gracious hospitality, subtle flavors, and attention to decor create an experience that engages all the senses. Both elaborate establishments and casual shops usually offer set menus at lunchtime, at a considerably lower price than at dinner. Although the finest traditional *kaiseki ryori* (the elaborate, multicourse meal) is often costly, this experience is highly recommended at least once during your visit to Japan.

If you find yourself with an unintelligible menu, ask for the *omakase,* or chef's recommendation; you can specify your budget in some instances. The custom of dining early, from 6 pm until 8 pm, still endures in very traditional restaurants, but many restaurants are open until 10 or 11 pm. If possible, let the hotel staff make reservations for you. For more formal restaurants try to book at least two days in advance; bookings are often not accepted for the following day if called in after 4 pm. Keep in mind that not all restaurants accept credit cards.

*Restaurant prices are the average cost of a main course at dinner or, if dinner is not served, at lunch. Restaurant reviews have been shortened. For full information, visit Fodors.com.*

| What It Costs in Yen | | | |
|---|---|---|---|
| $ | $$ | $$$ | $$$$ |
| **AT DINNER** | | | |
| under ¥1,500 | ¥1,500– ¥3,000 | ¥3,001– ¥5,000 | over ¥5,000 |

# Shopping

Most shops slide their doors open at 10, and many shopkeepers partake of the morning ritual of sweeping and watering the entrance to welcome the first customers. Traditional shops lock up at 6 or 7 in the evening. Stores often close sporadically once or twice a month (closings are irregular), so it helps to call in advance if you're making a special trip. On weekends, downtown can be very crowded.

A shopkeeper's traditional greeting to a customer is *o-ideyasu* (Kyoto-ben, or Kyoto dialect, for "honored to have you here"), voiced in the lilting Kyoto intonations with the required bowing of the head. When a customer makes a purchase, the shopkeeper will respond with *o-okini* ("thank you" in Kyoto-ben), a smile, and a bow. Take notice of the careful effort and adroitness with which purchases are wrapped; it's an art in itself.

Kyoto's *depato* (department stores) are small in comparison to their mammoth counterparts in Tokyo and Osaka. They still carry a wide range of goods and are great places for one-stop souvenir shopping. Wandering around the basement food halls is a good way to build up an appetite. Prices drop dramatically during end-of-season sales.

Kyoto has several popular seasonal fairs, from local area pottery sales to the national antiques fairs, usually held in May, June, and October. Several temple markets take place in Kyoto each month. These are great places to pick up bargain kimonos or unusual souvenirs. They're also some of the best spots for people-watching.

## KYOTO SHOPPING DISTRICTS

Kyoto is compact and relatively easy to navigate. Major shops line both sides of **Shijo-dori,** which runs east–west, and **Kawaramachi-dori,** which runs north–south. Concentrate on Shijo-dori between Yasaka Jinja and Karasuma Station as well as Kawaramachi-dori between Sanjo-dori and Shijo-dori. Some of modern Kyoto's shopping districts are near Kyoto Station in central Kyoto. **Porta** (ポルタ), under Kyoto Station, a sprawling subterranean arcade, contains more than 200 shops and restaurants. **Aeon Mall** (イオンモール) on the south side of Kyoto Station has the feel of a large Western mall.

Roads leading to **Kiyomizu-dera** run uphill, yet you may hardly notice the steepness for all of the alluring shops that line the way. Be sure to peek in for unique gifts. Food shops offer sample morsels, and tea shops serve complimentary cups of tea. **Shin-Kyogoku**, a covered arcade running between Teramachi-dori and Kawaramachi-dori, is another general-purpose shopping area with many souvenir shops.

# Tours

### Doi Taxi Tours

GUIDED TOURS | Former U.S. president Bill Clinton is among the past customers of the extremely popular Mr. Doi, whose English is nearly perfect. Mr. Doi will take care of everything as you travel with him in comfort and style in his car. Contact him directly or have your hotel concierge do so. ✉ *Kyoto* ☎ *090/9596–5546* ⊕ *www.kyoto-doitaxi.com* 🕸 *From ¥7,000.*

### Esprit Travel

GUIDED TOURS | This respected U.S.-based outfit creates deluxe culture-oriented group and private package tours that include encounters with artists, craftspeople, landscape designers, and other artisans and contributors to Japanese culture. On these tours you might visit places not generally open to the public. Custom private packages start at $700 per person per night, with a seven-night

minimum. ✉ *Kyoto* ☎ *800/377–7481* ⊕ *www.esprittravel.com* 🕸 *From $6,000.*

### Kyoto Sights and Nights

GUIDED TOURS | Peter MacIntosh of Kyoto Sights and Nights is a seasoned guide whose late-afternoon 90-minute walking tour of the geisha areas provides insight into the mysterious world of the female entertainers known as geisha. ✉ *Kyoto* ☎ *090/5169–1654* ⊕ *www.kyotosightsandnights.com/walking.html* 🕸 *From ¥3,000.*

### WaRaiDo Guide Networks

GUIDED TOURS | The five-hour Backstreet Walking Tour (an all-English daytime tour) is this company's flagship offering. The walk, which starts at Kyoto JR Station, takes in a temple, Shinto shrines, former geisha areas, and artisans' workshops, with a final stop for dessert and tea. The company's guides also conduct a 100-minute nighttime tour of the Gion geisha district. ✉ *Kyoto* ☎ *075/366–6238* ⊕ *www.waraido.com/tours* 🕸 *Daytime tour ¥2,000, nighttime tour ¥1,200* Ⓜ *Kyoto JR Station.*

### Windows to Japan

GUIDED TOURS | A Kyoto-based company, Windows crafts custom tours to places all over the country based on clients' interests and wishes. The tours aim to provide a "window" into Japanese culture and society. ✉ *Quest Oike 2F, 15–1 Yamanouchi-Miyawaki-cho, Ukyo-ku, Kyoto* ☎ *075/748–0286* ⊕ *www.windows-tojapan.com* 🕸 *Call for prices.*

# Visitor Information

One of the city's best resources, the Kyoto Tourist Information Center, is on the second floor of Kyoto Station. Heading away from the tracks, take the escalator up one flight; the information desk is next to the entrance of Isetan Department Store. The office publishes pamphlets with five self-guided walking tours, including maps. The tours range in

# A Brief History of Kyoto

Although Kyoto was Japan's capital for more than 10 centuries, the real center of political power was often elsewhere, be it Kamakura (1192–1333) or Edo (1603–1868). Until 710 Japan's capital moved with the accession of each new emperor. When it was decided that this expense was too great, Nara was chosen as the permanent capital. This experiment lasted 74 years, during which Buddhists rallied for, and achieved, tremendous political power. In an effort to thwart them, Emperor Kammu moved the capital to Nagaoka for a decade and then, in 794, to Kyoto.

Until the end of the 12th century, the city flourished under imperial rule. The city's nobility, known as "cloud dwellers," cultivated an extraordinary culture of refinement called *miyabi*. But when imperial power waned, the city saw the rise of the samurai class, employed to protect the noble families' interests. Ensuing clashes between various clans led to the Gempei War (1180–85), from which the samurai emerged victorious. The *bushido*, or warrior spirit, found a counterpart in the minimalism of Zen Buddhism's austerity. The past luxury of miyabi was replaced with Zen's respect for frugality and discipline.

This period also brought devastating civil wars. Because the various feuding clans needed the emperor's support to claim legitimacy, Kyoto, as imperial capital, became the stage for bitter struggles. The Onin Civil War (1467–77) was particularly devastating for Kyoto. Two feudal lords, Yamana and Hosokawa, disputed who should succeed the reigning shogun. Yamana camped in the western part of the city with 90,000 troops, and Hosokawa settled in the eastern part with 100,000 troops. Central Kyoto was the battlefield, and many of the city's buildings were destroyed.

Ieyasu Tokugawa, founder of the Tokugawa shogunate, eventually moved the country's political center to Edo. Kyoto remained the imperial capital, and the first three Tokugawa shoguns paid homage to the city by restoring old temples and building new villas in the early 1700s. Much of what you see in Kyoto dates from this period. When Emperor Meiji was restored to power in the late 1860s his capital and Imperial Court were moved to Tokyo. Commerce flourished, though, and Kyoto continued as the center of traditional culture.

length from about 40 to 80 minutes. The office is open daily 8:30 to 7 year-round, and there's Wi-Fi access. To get the lay of the land, pick up an up-to-date bus map, a tourist map, and a copy of the free monthly *Kyoto Visitor's Guide,* which contains invaluable information on restaurants, hotels, and festivals and fairs.

The tourist information center (open daily 8:30–5) inside Hankyu Kyoto-Kawaramachi Station also offers maps and much information in English, Korean and Chinese.

Visitors require special permission from the Imperial Household Agency to visit three sights in Kyoto: Kyoto Imperial Palace, Katsura Imperial Villa, and Shugaku-in Imperial Villa. It's best to obtain permission at least a few days in advance, but the permission to visit the Imperial Palace can often be obtained for a same-day visit by going to each place where, at 11 am, entry slips will be given on a first-come, first-served basis (I.D. required), or by going to the agency's office in the northwest corner of the Imperial Palace's park. You can also apply online (⊕ *sankan. kunaicho.go.jp/english*). The office is closed Monday; if Monday is a national holiday, then it's closed Tuesday.

A good general-information resource for tourists, the Kyoto International Community House has a library on-site and can arrange home visits and lessons in calligraphy, the tea ceremony, and Japanese.

**CONTACTS Imperial Household Agency.** ✉ *3 Kyoto Gyoen-nai, Kamigyo-ku* ✛ *5-min walk from Karasuma-Imadegawa subway station* ☎ *075/221–1215* ⊕ *sankan.kunaicho.go.jp/english*. **Kyoto International Community House.** ✉ *2-1 Toriicho, Awata-guchi, Sakyo-ku* ✛ *7-min walk from Keage subway* ☎ *075/752–3010* ⊕ *www.kcif.or.jp/web/en*. **Kyoto Tourist Information Center.** ✉ *JR Kyoto Station, Karasuma-dori, Shimogyo-ku* ✛ *Upper level, next to Isetan Department Store entrance* ☎ *075/343–0548*. **Kyoto Visitor's Guide.** ✉ *Kyoto* ⊕ *www.kvg-kyoto.com*.

# When to Go

Cherry-blossom time in spring (usually the first week of April) and the glorious autumn foliage in early November are remarkable, though the city can become extremely crowded and very expensive. Except for the depths of winter, the rainy season in June, and the peak of summer heat in late July and August, Kyoto's climate is mild enough to make sightseeing pleasant the rest of the year. In the high season (April, May, and from September to November) the large numbers of visitors can make accommodations scarce.

# Eastern Kyoto

East of the Kamogawa River, in the neighborhoods known as Higashiyama (literally, Eastern Mountain) and Okazaki, are some of Kyoto's most dazzling shrines and temples, stretching from solemn Sanjusangen-do in the south to the elegant Ginkaku-ji in the north. The cobbled streets of the Gion district are mysterious during the day, and even more so at night.

**Access:** Subway lines crisscross eastern Kyoto, making them a great way to get around. Maps detailing the extensive bus network are available at tourist information centers. Buses run on major roads like Shichijo-dori, Shijo-dori, and Higashi-oji-dori. But the best way to explore these neighborhoods is on foot. Starting from anywhere, you can't walk 10 minutes in any direction without encountering a landmark.

## ◉ Sights

### Anraku-ji Temple (安楽寺)

**TEMPLE** | This small temple in the foothills of Higashiyama dates back to the 12th century, when the priest Honen began to preach a novel means of salvation accessible to anyone, the recitation of the name of Amida Buddha (*nenbutsu*). Two of Honen's disciples, Anraku and Juren, preached this new, at the time heretical, faith in the countryside outside the usual surveillance. Two ladies in the Imperial Court, Matsumushi and Suzumushi, who were also said to be concubines of Emperor Go-Toba (1180–1239), inspired by the teachings, became nuns. Convinced that the monks had seduced the two ladies, the emperor had the monks seized and beheaded. The court ladies then took their own lives in response, and Honen was exiled as a heretic. When he was finally permitted to return to Kyoto in 1212, the now elderly priest had Anraku-ji built to honor his faithful disciples and their two converts. The tombs of all four are on the temple grounds. The shrine is open in spring to showcase its gorgeous azaleas and in autumn for its vivid maples. ✉ *Shishigatani, 21 Goshonodan-cho, Sakyo-ku* ✛ *From Kyoto Station take Bus 5 to Shinyodo-mae bus stop, from there it is a 10-min walk* ☎ *075/771–5360* ⊕ *anraku-ji-kyoto.com* 🎫 *¥500*.

**AKYO-KU**

Shirakawa-dori

Shishigadani-dori

**OKAZAKI**

arutamachi-dori

yoto
y Zoo

Shirakawa-dori

**Keage
Station**

TOZAI LINE

**GASHIYAMA**

Himukai-Daijingu
Shrine

0        2,000 feet
0    500 m

Mt.
Kazan

Misasagi

Mt.
Kiyomizu

**Kyotodaigaku
Kasan Observatory**

**Seikanji
Temple**

TOKAIDO MAIN LINE

**KEY**

1 *Exploring Sights*
1 *Restaurants*
1 *Quick Bites*
1 *Hotels*

## Sights ▼

1 Anraku-ji Temple........ **A1**
2 Chion-in Temple.......... **F6**
3 Chishaku-in Temple ..... **E9**
4 Choraku-ji Temple ....... **F6**
5 Eikan-do (Zenrin-ji)
   Temple ................... **H4**
6 Ginkaku-ji Temple........**I1**
7 Hakusa Son-so
   Garden.................... **H1**
8 Heian Jingu Shrine ..... **F3**
9 Honen-in Temple..........**I2**
10 Kawai Kanjiro
   Memorial House ......... **E8**
11 Kiyomizu-dera
   Temple ................... **F7**
12 Kodai-ji Temple........... **F7**
13 Kyoto Museum of
   Crafts and Design........ **F4**
14 Kyoto National
   Museum ................. **D9**
15 Kyoto University
   Museum ................. **E1**
16 Miroku-in Temple ....... **H1**
17 Murayama Park......... **A9**
18 Murin-an Garden ....... **G4**
19 Nanzen-ji Temple ....... **H4**
20 National Museum
   of Modern Art, Kyoto.... **F4**
21 Otoyo Shrine ............ **H3**
22 Sanjusangen-do Hall... **D9**
23 Sannon-zaka
   and Ninen-zaka .......... **F8**
24 Sen-oku Hakuko Kan
   Museum ................. **H3**
25 Shoren-in Temple........ **F5**
26 Yasaka Shrine............ **E6**

## Restaurants ▼

1 Gahojin Kappa .......... **D6**
2 Izama..................... **A5**
3 Kikunoi ................... **F6**
4 Kisaki Yudofu............ **H2**
5 Nanzenji Junsei
   Restaurant............... **G4**
6 Nanzenji Sando
   Kikusui ................... **G5**
7 Omen Ginkaku-ji ....... **H1**
8 Ramen Miyako Gion..... **E6**
9 Yagenbori ............... **E6**

## Quick Bites ▼

1 Bunnosuke Chaya ....... **E7**
2 Zen Café ................. **D6**

## Hotels ▼

1 Four Seasons
   Hotel Kyoto .............. **E9**
2 Hotel Ethnography
   Gion Furumonzen ....... **E5**
3 Hyatt Regency Kyoto    **D9**
4 Kyomachiya-Ryokan-
   Sakura Honganji ........ **A8**
5 The Ritz-Carlton,
   Kyoto ..................... **D4**
6 The Westin Miyako
   Kyoto ..................... **G5**
7 Yachiyo................... **G5**

## Chion-in Temple (知恩院)

TEMPLE | The headquarters of the Jodo sect of Buddhism, Chion-in is impressive enough to have been cast in the film *The Last Samurai* as a stand-in for Edo Castle. Everything here is on a massive scale. The imposing tiered gateway is the largest in the country, and the bell inside the temple grounds, cast in 1633, is the heaviest in Japan, requiring 17 monks to ring it. If you're in Kyoto over New Year's, you can hear it being struck 108 times to release believers from the 108 worldly desires of the old year. The bell may not be struck again until the previous sound has ceased, so it takes more than an hour to ring in the new year. The event is nationally televised.

The extensive temple buildings contain many artworks, along with simpler pleasures such as the exposed *uguisu-bari* (nightingale floor)—floor planks that "chirp" when trod upon, alerting residents of potential intruders. There are two halls, the greater and lesser, connected via corridors with gardens between.

The temple is adjacent to Maruyama Park. As with most Kyoto temples, Chion-in's history includes a litany of fires and earthquakes. Most of the buildings you see date from the early 1600s. ⊠ *400 Rinka-cho, Higashiyama-ku* ✛ *From Kyoto Station take Bus 206 to Gion stop* ☎ *075/531–2111* ⊕ *www.chion-in.or.jp/en* 🎫 *¥500.*

## Chishaku-in Temple (智積院)

TEMPLE | The lush garden of Chishaku-in and paintings by Tohaku Hasegawa and his son Kyuzo make a visit to this temple a memorable experience. A small museum exhibits works by father and son that are among the finest of the Momoyama period (1573–1615). The elder Hasegawa (1539–1610) painted exclusively for Zen temples in his later years, with masterpieces ranging from lyrical monochrome ink creations to bolder, more colorful works such as the gold-backed images

of cherry, maple, pine, and plum trees exhibited here, and ones of autumn grasses. A mountain in China reputedly inspired the design of the temple's hilly garden, whose pond was sculpted to look like a river. The pond is stocked with colorful carp. Equally colorful when they're in bloom are the mounds of sculpted camellia and azalea bushes. ⊠ *964 Higashi-kawaramachi, Higashi-oji Nanajo-sagaru, Higashiyama-ku* ✛ *From Kyoto Station take Bus 206 or 208 to Higashiyama-Shichijo stop; temple is at southern junction of Shichijo-dori and Higashi-oji-dori* ⊕ *www.chisan.or.jp* 🎫 *¥500.*

## Choraku-ji Temple (長楽寺)

TEMPLE | A procession of stone lanterns lines the steep stairway to this tiny temple founded in the early 9th century by Emperor Kammu with the priest Saicho. In 1185, after the Minamoto clan's defeat of the Taira clan in the Genpei War, the last survivor found refuge here, a circumstance depicted in the epic *The Tale of the Heike*. Within the temple, note the 11-headed statue of Kannon, evocative of the deity's Indian origins. Another structure houses precious items: ancient scrolls, remnants of a child emperor's clothing, and Buddhist images. ⊠ *Maruyama Park, 626 Maruyama-cho, Higashiyama-ku* ✛ *Far eastern section of park* ☎ *075/561-0589* ⊕ *www.chorakuji.or.jp* 🎫 *¥500.*

## Eikan-do (Zenrin-ji) Temple (永観堂禅林寺)

TEMPLE | Next to the Nanzen-ji temple complex, Eikan-do (also known as Zen-rin-ji) was built after the original temple, dating from 855, was destroyed in the 15th century. Visitors come throughout the year to see the image of Amida Buddha statue, which represents the time when Eikan paused in his prayers and the Buddha turned his head to encourage him to continue. The temple draws the most visitors in autumn, when people come to see the colorful foliage, and in November, when there's an excellent

Ginkaku-ji (Temple of the Silver Pavilion) was built in the late 15th century as a retirement villa for Shogun Yoshimasa Ashikaga.

display of painted doors. ✉ *48 Eikan-do-cho, Higashiyama-ku* ⚓ *South end of Philosopher's Walk* ☎ *075/761–0007* 🌐 *www.eikando.or.jp* 🎟 *Nov. ¥1,000; Dec.–Oct. ¥600.*

### ★ Ginkaku-ji Temple (銀閣寺)

**TEMPLE** | A UNESCO World Heritage site, Ginkaku-ji (the Temple of the Silver Pavilion) was intended to impress the courtly world with its opulence, but the current structure is actually an exercise in elegance and restraint. Yoshimasa Ashikaga spent years constructing his retirement villa in a conspicuous homage to his grandfather's Golden Pavilion on the west side of town. The shogun wanted the large hall here to be wrapped in silver leaf, but during construction in the 1470s a tumultuous war and government unrest left the clan bereft of funds. Today an elaborate entryway of stone, bamboo, and hedge lead into a modest compound of buildings giving way to extensive gardens. The Silver Pavilion, which stares down at its reflection in the water, sits among the rolling moss-covered hillsides, dark pools, and an enormous dry garden, called the Sea of Sand. ✉ *1 Ginkaku-ji-cho, Sakyo-ku* ⚓ *From Kyoto Station take Bus 5, 17 or 100 to Ginkaku-ji-michi stop* ☎ *075/771–5725* 🌐 *www.shokoku-ji.jp/en/ginkakuji* 🎟 *¥500.*

### Hakusa Son-so Garden (白砂村荘)

**GARDEN** | A century-old villa (the name means "inn of white sand") with a large stroll garden, this was once the home of the painter Kansetsu Hashimoto (1883–1945). Combining influences from various Japanese periods and drawing inspiration from Chinese imagery, Hashimoto created a unique style of painting. A new museum contains many of Hashimoto's sketches and paintings, as well as works by his Chinese and Japanese contemporaries and an enthralling collection of Greek and Persian pottery. An exquisite stone garden and a teahouse are also open to the public. If you book at least two days in advance, it's possible to experience a complete tea ceremony. Adjacent to the estate is the Noa Noa café, which serves light casual fare

## Did You Know?

Kyoto's Gion district is the city's geisha district (and has been since the 16th century). You can still see geisha in traditional dress traveling to their appointments in the early evening.

# The Geisha of Gion

Japan's traditional and modern worlds intersect where Shijo-dori crosses Hanami-koji-dori in the district of Gion. To the south, stone streets lead past wood-fronted teahouses displaying red paper lanterns; on the north side of Shijo-dori are high-rises filled with bars. Eastward is Yasaka Jinja's commanding orange-and-white arched gate; westward are the city's best department stores.

Gion remains Kyoto's center for high culture such as Kabuki theater, but perhaps more famous to foreign visitors is the world of the geisha, referred to as *geiko* in Kyoto, brought into the spotlight in recent decades by the novel and subsequent film

*Memoirs of a Geisha*. Wandering around Hanami-koji-dori at dinner time you might see *maiko-san* and *geiko-san*, the modern equivalents of apprentice and senior geisha, on their way to appointments at exclusive teahouses behind curtained doorways.

The practiced gait of these women and their gorgeous apparel marks them as the most refined and talented in the traditional performing arts. The spring and autumn dance revues entertain hundreds of admirers. Several restaurants and inns can arrange for private parties to have a maiko-san or geiko-san sing and dance while you dine.

from ¥1,500. ✉ *37 Ishibashi-cho, east of Imadegawa and Ginkaku-ji intersection, Higashiyama-ku* ⚎ *From Kyoto Station take Bus 5 or 100 to Ginkaku-ji-michi stop and walk east along canal* ☎ *075/751–0446* ⊕ *www.hakusasonso.jp* ⚑ *¥1,300.*

## Heian Jingu Shrine (平安神宮)

RELIGIOUS BUILDING | The massive vermilion *torii* gate of Heian Jingu is one of Kyoto's best-known symbols. Built in the 1890s to commemorate the 1,100th anniversary of Kyoto's founding, Heian Jingu pays homage to the two emperors who bookend the city's era of national prominence: Kammu, who brought the imperial throne here in 794, and Komei, whose reign ending in 1866 saw the sun set on Kyoto's days as the capital. An assertion of Kyoto's unfaded splendor, Heian Jingu was built as a slightly smaller replica of the Imperial Palace, destroyed in 1227. The architecture reveals China's strong influence on the early Japanese court. The gate, the biggest in Japan, is particularly impressive, as are the

three elaborate gardens behind the main shrine, conceived by the master designer Ogawa Jihei, which draw on Kyoto's landscaping origins. The complex makes a wonderful backdrop for several annual events, most famously the brazier-lighted plays of Takigi Noh Drama every June 1 and 2, and the Jidai Costume Festival on October 22. ✉ *Okazakinishi Tenno-cho, Sakyo-ku* ⚎ *3-min walk from Bus 5, 32, or 100 to Heian Jingu stop; 7-min walk from Tozai subway station of Higashiyama; 10-min walk from Keihan train station at Sanjo-dori* ☎ *075/761–0221* ⊕ *www.heianjingu.or.jp* ⚑ *Gardens ¥600.*

### Honen-in Temple (法然院)

TEMPLE | South of Ginkaku Temple on the Philosopher's Path lie the serene grounds of a once rural temple. Tall spindly bush camellia and slender maple trees form a canopy over the long entry path. Inside the temple's thatched gateway, two long regular mounds of sand are formed into shapes symbolizing the changing seasons. While strolling through the verdant

*Continued on page 404*

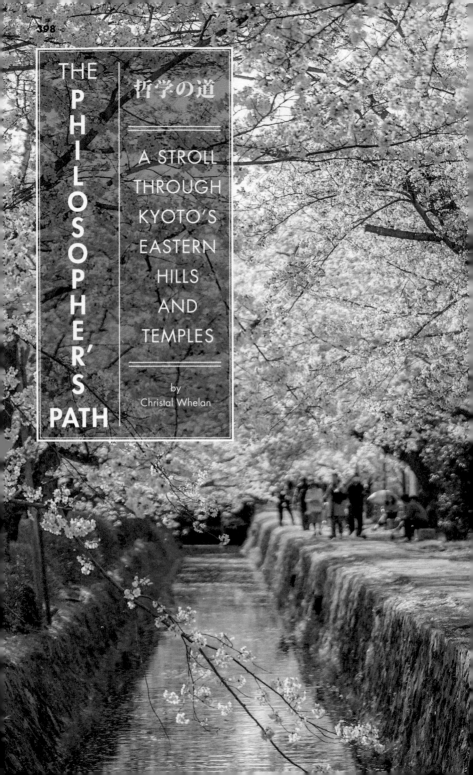

# THE PHILOSOPHER'S PATH

哲学の道

## A STROLL THROUGH KYOTO'S EASTERN HILLS AND TEMPLES

by
Christal Whelan

"If my heart can become pure and simple, like that of a child, I think there probably can be no greater happiness."  —Kitaro Nishida

Tucked away in the lush foothills of the Eastern Mountains of Kyoto, the Philosopher's Path winds along a canal lined with cherry trees and through a quiet residential neighborhood. With notable Buddhist temples, imperial tombs, Shinto shrines, and quaint shops, the route has become one of the city's most popular walking courses.

Although it traverses an area rich in antiquity, the Philosopher's Path is a modern promenade, receiving its name in the early Showa era (1926–1989) after its counterpart in Heidelberg. Later, the path became associated with the legacy of the philosopher Kitaro Nishida (1870–1945), renowned for his synthesis of Eastern and Western thought, who walked the path daily. Today many follow in Nishida's foot-steps along the canal and likewise bear witness to the drama of the changing seasons. Flanked by two bridges—the Nyakaou-ji and Ginkaku-ji—and a Zen temple at both ends, this mile offers a perfect balance of Japanese history, culture, cuisine, art, and devotion to nature all within a single walk.

(Opposite) The Philosopher's Path;
(Top) A tea house on the Philosopher's Path

Ginkaku-ji

*If you decide to follow this route from south to north, simply reverse the walk.*

Begin your morning at **Ginkaku-ji**, the Silver Pavilion. Although it was once the aesthetic and cultural center of a nation, fires over the years have ravaged the complex and left only two original buildings, both now National Treasures—the Kannon-den and the Toku-do. These graceful structures are thatched with layers of thin cypress shingles. On the apex of the Kannon-den a bronze phoenix stands perched prophetically, and the paper windows shimmer with reflections from the rippling pond below. Exquisite dry sand and classical stroll gardens are by Soami, a master landscape designer of the medieval period. The road away from Gin-

kaju-ji, down an incline, leads to the Philosopher's Path on the left. If you're in need of some fortification, detour a few hundred meters away to the pert **Noa Noa** café which serves coffee drinks, pizzas, and sturdier pasta dishes.

Heading south, the outdoor chapel at **Shounzan Mirokuin** is dedicated to the bodhisattva Jizo, who protects children and those in dire straits. This temple belongs to Shugendo, a fusion of mountain veneration, Shinto, and Japanese Tantric Buddhism (here, Tendai). Normally closed, the temple opens to the public on August 28, from 1 to 3 pm, when the ascetic practitioners called *yamabushi* hold a religious procession that culminates in a *saito-goma*, or outdoor fire ceremony.

Follow the path markers and cross the bridge to **Honen-in Temple.** The thatched entrance gate and the temple grounds are the highlights here since the temple interior is closed to the public most of the year. To the right of

the entry is a building used for contemporary year-round art exhibitions. Honen-in, built in the late 17th century, is named for the founder of the Jodo sect of Buddhism, who chose the site during the 13th century, when he also arranged to have the temple of **Anraku-ji**, to the south, constructed to honor four believers who died tragically.

The temple hosts the popular *kabocha kuyo*, a service conducted since 1790 in honor of pumpkin-squash (July 25, 9–3).

The nearby **Otoyo Jinja** is an ancient Shinto shrine that serves as the guardian for the people living in the nearby neighborhoods. Otoyo holds

Sen-oku Museum

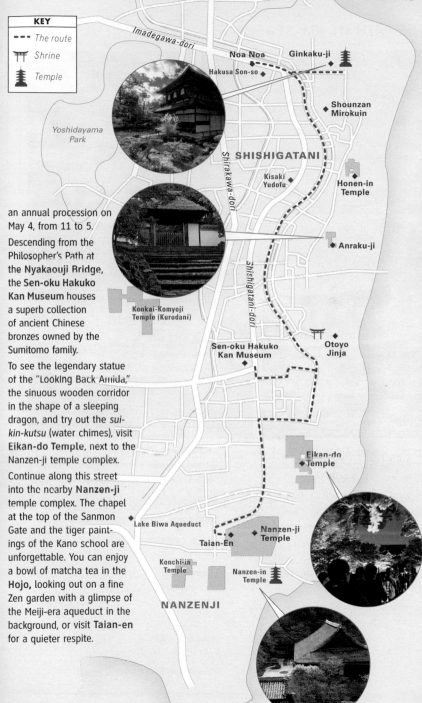

**KEY**

- - - *The route*

⛩ *Shrine*

🏯 *Temple*

Imadegawa-dori

Noa Noa

Hakusa Son-so

Ginkaku-ji

Yoshidayama Park

Shounzan Mirokuin

Shirakawa-dori

SHISHIGATANI

Kisaki Yudofu

Honen-in Temple

an annual procession on May 4, from 11 to 5.

Descending from the Philosopher's Path at the **Nyakaouji Bridge**, the **Sen-oku Hakuko Kan Museum** houses a superb collection of ancient Chinese bronzes owned by the Sumitomo family.

To see the legendary statue of the "Looking Back Amida," the sinuous wooden corridor in the shape of a sleeping dragon, and try out the *suikin-kutsu* (water chimes), visit **Eikan-do Temple**, next to the Nanzen-ji temple complex.

Continue along this street into the nearby **Nanzen-ji** temple complex. The chapel at the top of the Sanmon Gate and the tiger paintings of the Kano school are unforgettable. You can enjoy a bowl of matcha tea in the **Hojo,** looking out on a fine Zen garden with a glimpse of the Meiji-era aqueduct in the background, or visit **Taian-en** for a quieter respite.

Anraku-ji

Shishigatani-dori

Konkai-Komyoji Temple (Kurodani)

Sen-oku Hakuko Kan Museum

Otoyo Jinja

Eikan-do Temple

Lake Biwa Aqueduct

Nanzen-ji Temple

Taian-En

Konchi-in Temple

Nanzen-in Temple

NANZENJI

# THE PATH IN ALL SEASONS

In the **spring**, the eruption of cherry blossoms transforms the Philosopher's Path into a heavenly pink.

With the **summer** comes fireflies, flourishes of hydrangea, bird song, cicada cries, and murmur of water tumbling over rocks.

The **autumn** gives way to a palette of yellows, oranges, and the deep red of the Japanese maple.

In **winter** snows blanket the Philosopher's Path.

## SEASONAL EVENTS

**Go-san Okuribi** (Sending off ceremony on five mountains): August 16

**Kabocha Kuyo** (Anraku-ji): July 25, 9–3

**Saito goma** (Mirokuin): August 28, 1–3

**Otoyo gyoretsu** (Otoyo Jinja): May 4, 11–5

**Eikando** (Light Up): Nov. 6–30, 5:30–9, evening autumn foliage viewing

(Top left) Spring cherry blossoms;
(Top right) summer strolling;
(Bottom left) Ginkaku-ji in winter;
(Bottom right) the fall Eikando festival

## PRACTICAL INFO

A dry landscape garden, or *karesansui*, at Honen-in temple

### GETTING THERE

You can begin your walk at either end of the pathway—Ginkaku-ji or Nanzen-ji. If you choose Nanzen-ji, take the subway (Tozai line) from Sanjo-Keikan and get off at Keage, or catch Bus 5 from Kyoto Station to Nazen-ji Eikando-mae. From either, it is a 10-minute walk. To start from Ginkaku-ji, catch Bus 17, 5, or 100 and get off at Ginkaku-ji-mae. An easy walk up Imadegawa to Ginkaku-ji-michi leads into the temple.

### TIMING

With no stops along the way, the entire course takes just under an hour. But if you stop at the suggested points of interest, allow three hours or more. You can begin at any time, but should bear in mind that Gingaku-ji closes at 4:30 or 5 depending on the season. A visit to Ginkaku-ji is probably best done as early as possible (it opens at 8:30 am) to beat the crowds at one of Kyoto's most frequented temples.

### FUEL UP

If you begin the walk at Gingaku-ji, then you will wind up at Taian-en for either lunch or dinner, depending on what hour you set out. The trip from north to south allows you to end up sipping from a frothy bowl of green tea in Nanzen-ji's **Hojo,** or Abbots' Quarters, or sitting down to a traditional bento lunch or a multi-course meal at Taian-en. A trip in the reverse (from Nanzen-ji to Ginkaku-ji) can conclude with dinner at either **Kisaki Yudofu,** or for a more sumptuous *kaiseki* feast, try the teahouse at the **Hakusa Sonso** (down the hill from Ginkaju-ji) in its garden (reservations required).

### SHUIN-CHO

From whichever end you do start, be sure to pick up a *shuin-cho* at your starting temple (¥1,500). These small, cloth-covered books have thick, blank sheets for collecting ink stamps and calligraphic signatures from each temple you visit. There is a nominal fee for these signatures, but they're worth every yen for such an authentic souvenir of Japan's ancient capital.

garden, you may notice the tombs of several notables, including novelist Junichiro Tanizaki (1886–1965), economist Hajime Kawakami (1879–1946), and artist Heihachiro Fukuda (1892–1974).

The temple, built in 1680, is on a site chosen in the 13th century by Honen, founder of the populist Jodo sect of Buddhism. This is a training temple. Year-round, monks place 25 flowers before the Amida Buddha statue in the main hall, representing the 25 bodhisattvas who accompany the Buddha to receive the souls of the newly deceased. ✉ *Shishigatani-Goshonodan-cho, Sakyo-ku* ✢ *From Kyoto Station take Bus 5 to Shodoji bus stop, then walk east for 10 min. It's also a 10-min walk from Ginka-ku-ji Temple* ☎ *075/771–2420* ⊕ *www. honen-in.jp* ✉ *Free.*

### Kawai Kanjiro Memorial House (河井寛次郎記念館; *Kawai Kanjiro Kinenkan*)

**HISTORIC HOME** | The house and workshop of prolific potter Kanjiro Kawai (1890–1966) has been transformed into a museum showcasing his distinctive works. The asymmetrical vases, bowls, and pots on display represent only a fraction of his output of this leading light of the *Mingei* (folk art) movement of the 1920s. Besides the intriguing workshop and enormous kiln preserved in an inner courtyard, there is residence itself, an old country farmhouse Kaiwai had moved to this location. A little hard to find, this compound is along a small street one block west of Higashi-oji-dori and two blocks south of Gojo-dori. ✉ *569 Kanei-cho, Gojo-zaka, Higashiyama-ku* ✢ *20-min walk from Kyoto Station, or take Bus 100 or 206 to Gojo-zaka, walk west on Gojo-dori, and take first left* ☎ *075/561–3585* ⊕ *www.kanjiro.jp* ✉ *¥900.*

### ★ Kiyomizu-dera Temple (清水寺)

**TEMPLE** | Pilgrims have climbed Higashi-yama's stone-inlaid streets to this historic mountainside temple, a UNESCO World Heritage site, for centuries. Kiyomizu-de-ra's tremendous gates and pagodas are marvels to behold. The main hall's huge veranda, jutting out over the forested valley, is one of the city's quintessential images. Immense timbers support the large deck and gracefully angular cypress-shingle roof. Finding the courage to set out on a daring new adventure is often likened to "taking a leap from the veranda of Kiyomizu."

The temple was founded in AD 780, but the buildings you see today date from 1633. Two huge temple guardians man the gateway, and the first sight is of people trying to lift the heavy iron staves and geta clogs, supposedly used by the warrior Benkei. The interior of the temple has been darkened by the ages. Visitors may pass along the area behind the main altar, a metaphoric journey into the soul; in the dark passageway below the temple, quietly follow a chain of thick wooden beads to an ancient tablet carved with the Sanskrit rune for heart. Away from the main hall, the quirky Jishu Shrine is dedicated to Okuni Nushi-no-mikoto, a deity considered to be a powerful matchmaker. Many young people visit the shrine to seek help in finding their life partners. They try to walk between two stones placed 59 feet apart, with their eyes closed. It's said that love will materialize for anyone who can walk in a straight line between the two.

Farther down the path, the Sound of Feathers waterfall funnels down in three perfect streams before a raised platform. You can catch some of its water by using one of the long-handled silver cups; drinking from the falls supposedly helps with health, longevity, and academic success. If you need more to fortify you, enjoy some noodles, shaved iced, hot tea, or cold beer (depending on the season) from one of the old stalls below the trellised balcony. ✉ *1 Kiyomizu, Higashiyama-ku* ✢ *Take Bus 100 or 206 to Gojo-zaka or Kiyomizu-michi, then walk uphill 10 min* ☎ *075/551–1234* ⊕ *www. kiyomizudera.or.jp* ✉ *¥400.*

# The Warlord Who Unified Japan

Toyotomi Hideyoshi (1536–98) ranks among Japan's most fascinating leaders. During the late 16th century, the country was strife-ridden, with various warriors fighting for supremacy. Nobunaga Oda partially succeeded, but he was ambushed and died. Hideyoshi, his foot soldier, completed the job. Hideyoshi's tastes for the arts brought him into contact with the famous tea master Sen no Rikyu. Both men practiced that art diligently, transforming it to one of the most subtle and sophisticated forms of entertainment in Japan. The son of a commoner, of tiny stature with the uncomely appearance of a monkey—his nickname was "Sarusan" (Mr. Monkey)—Hideyoshi was responsible for realigning the streets of Kyoto, surrounding the city with an earthen embankment to defend it, and later, constructing a castle in Fushimi. He spent extravagantly building temples, shrines, and palaces. In his declining years, he attempted to conquer Korea and beyond with unfortunate results, but his accomplishments, including bringing peace to Japan after decades of civil war, overshadow his late-in-life missteps.

## Kodai-ji Temple (高台寺)

TEMPLE | On a quiet stone-inlaid street in the Eastern Hills district, Kodai-ji is a jewel of a Momoyama-era temple complex. A koi pond figures in the beautifully tended garden, whose teahouses sit elegantly on higher ground. Many of the splendid paintings and friezes inside the temple buildings were relocated from Fushimi Castle, parts of which were used to construct Kodai-ji in the early 1600s, most notably the sinuous covered walkway. A back-lacquered altar filled with tiny images is a masterpiece of that craft.

The temple was a memorial to Toyotomi Hideyoshi (1537–98), a powerful warrior and political leader, commissioned by his wife Nene (1548–1624). The road in front of the temple is called Nene-no-michi in her honor. On the hills overlooking the main temple, which dates to 1912, are teahouses designed by a pupil of the tea master Sen-no-Rikyu; they are identifiable by their umbrella-shaped bamboo ceilings, thatched roofs, and large circular windows. Evening illumination in April, November, and December is popular among locals and visitors. ⊠ *Shimogawara-cho, Higashiyama-ku* ⊹ *From Kyoto Station, take Bus 206 (Bus 207 from Shijo-Kawaramachi Station) to Higashiyama-Yasui stop and walk east 5 min* ☎ *075/561–9966* ⊕ *www.kodaiji. com/e_index.html* ⊠ *¥600.*

## Kyoto Museum of Crafts and Design

(京都伝統産業ミュージアム;
*Kyoto Dento Sangyo Myujiamu)*

ART MUSEUM | This museum on the Miyako Messe exhibition hall's basement level is devoted to the finely made crafts for which Kyoto is famous. Bamboo tea utensils, lacquerware, Buddhist imagery, and fine silk textiles, including kimonos, are among the traditional craft objects on display. Artisans are invited to create their works at the museum to help visitors comprehend the remarkable skill required to master a craft, and well-made videos further illustrate the point. At the museum's shop, you can purchase pieces similar to those on display. ⊠ *B1F Miyako Messe Kyoto Exhibition Center, 9-1 Seishoji-cho, Okazaki, Sakyo-ku* ⊹ *Museum is on south side of Nijodori, opposite ROHM Theatre Kyoto* ☎ *075/762–2670* ⊕ *www.kmtc.jp* ⊠ *Free.*

## Kyoto National Museum
(京都国立博物館;
*Kokuritsu Hakubutsukan*)
HISTORY MUSEUM | The national museum is one of three established in the late 19th century (the others are in Tokyo and Nara) to preserve Japanese antiquities and traditional culture. The original 1897 redbrick French Renaissance–style building presently is not in use. In 2014 an angular limestone, steel, and glass structure designed by Yoshio Taniguchi became the much-praised home of the permanent collection. The architect's other commissions include the Gallery of Horyuji Treasures at the Tokyo National Museum, Tokyo Sea Life Park, and the 2004 redesign of New York City's Museum of Modern Art.

Calligraphy, textiles and costumes, lacquerware, metalwork, and sculpture are exhibited on the first floor. Paintings are on the second floor, the strengths being religious and secular Japanese painting, works from China, and medieval ink and Momoyama-Edo painting. Archaeological relics and ceramics fill the third floor. The labels are in English and Japanese, and audio guides are available for a fee. ⊠ *527 Chaya-machi, at corner of Shichijo-dori and Higashi-oji-dori, Higashiyama-ku* ⊹ *From Kyoto Station take Bus 206 or 208 to Sanjusangen-do-mae stop* ☎ *075/525–2473* ⊕ *www.kyohaku.go.jp* ✉ *¥700 (admission varies with exhibitions), ¥500 for audio guide.*

## Kyoto University Museum (京都大学総合博物館; *Kyoto Daigaku Sogohakubutsukan*)
HISTORY MUSEUM | FAMILY | The university's small natural history museum displays ancient stone coffins, fossils, and many other artifacts. A two-story exhibition is devoted to the school's Primate Research Institute, world-famous for its investigations of human and nonhuman primates. ⊠ *Sakyo Ku, Yoshida Cho, beside university campus, east side of Higashi-oji, south of Imadegawa-dori, Kyoto* ⊹ *3-min walk from Imadegawa and*

*Higashi-oji bus stops* ☎ *075/753–3272* ⊕ *www.museum.kyoto-u.ac.jp* ✉ *¥400.*

## Maruyama Park
(円山公園; *Maruyama Koen*)
CITY PARK | A gift to the city in 1886, this well-attended park lies just north of the also popular Yasaka Shrine. Crowds flow through, locals stop to people-watch, vendors supply visitors with beverages, and musicians occasionally entertain passersby. Visitation spikes as the new year dawns, when many people gather to hear the gigantic bell of Chion-in rung at midnight; and during cherry-blossom season, when the sky turns pink with those overhead boughs. ⊠ *Higashiyama-ku* ⊹ *From Kyoto Station take Bus 206 to Higashiyama stop at Shijo-dori.*

## Miroku-in Temple (弥勒院)
TEMPLE | Set on the mountainside of Philosopher's Walk is the small shrine of Shiawase no Jizo (Joyful Jizo), with an image of the Buddhist figure holding a child on his left arm and a pilgrim's staff in his right hand. Similar images of the protector of children and the guardian of travelers can be found throughout the city, often clothed by devotees in colored bibs and caps. Jizo is beloved by Kyoto's citizens—fresh bouquets of flowers are dutifully set in the shrines twice a month. The image of *Dainichi Nyorai*, or the Cosmic Buddha, in the building beside the Jizo shrine, is attended to by mountain priests who announce their presence by blowing a conch shell, one of which rests on a low table, and by wearing deerskin aprons, much like the deerskin draped over another low table. ⊠ *29 Jodoji Minamida-cho, Sakyo-ku* ⊹ *From Kyoto Station take Bus 5 or 17 to either Ginkakuji-michi or Ginkakuji-mae bus stops, it is then a 3-min walk south down the Philosopher's Path* ☎ *075/771–2277* ⊕ *www7b.biglobe.ne.jp/~mirokuin/index.html* ✉ *Free.*

## Murin-an Garden (無鄰菴)
GARDEN | Ogawa Jihei (1860–1932), a leading landscape architect of the Meiji period, departed from tradition in

# Five Kyoto Gardens Not to Miss

To know Kyoto is to know its gardens, which at their best express an admirable quest for beauty, harmony, and discreet joy. Below are five exquisite examples not to be missed.

## Daitoku-ji

This Zen temple complex shelters some of Kyoto's finest contemplative gardens, most notably the rock-and-gravel garden at the subtemple Daisen-in.

## Heian Jingu Shrine

In conceiving the stroll garden at this late-19th-century shrine honoring Kyoto's founding, designer Ogawa Jihei took inspiration from some of the city's original 1,200-year-old gardens.

## Koinzan Saiho-ji

More than a hundred varieties of moss carpet the one-of-a-kind two-level garden at this appropriately named landmark, the Moss Temple.

## Konchi-in

Of all the gardens in Japan, the one at this subtemple of Nanzen-ji most closely resembles the designs of Kobori Enshu, a famous 17th-century landscape gardener.

## Ryoan-ji

The world's most renowned Zen dry rock garden continues to intrigue scholars and visitors alike for the subtle message of its meticulous design.

developing this late-19th-century garden whose rolling expanses of English-style lawn represent the first use of this type of ground cover within a Japanese garden. The blending of Western and Japanese influences can also be detected in some of the architecture and interiors of this estate, once part of Nanzen-ji, that was commissioned by Arimoto Yamagata, twice Japan's prime minister in the late 19th century. The paths of Murin-an, a small but classic Meiji stroll garden, meander along converging streams and past a three-tier waterfall. The garden's southern section is almost always in shadow, creating wonderful contrasts. ✉ *31 Nanzenji-Kusakawa-cho, Sakyo-ku* ✢ *From Kyoto Station take Bus 5 or 86 to either Jingumichi or Okazaki-koen Bijut-sukan Heian Jingu-mae. Or it's a 7-min walk from Keage Station on the Tozai subway line* ☎ *075/771–3909* ⊕ *www.murin-an.jp* ✑ *¥600.*

**Nanzen-ji Temple** (南禅寺)

**TEMPLE** | Several magnificent temples share this corner of the forested foothills between Heian Jingu and Ginkaku-ji, but with its historic gatehouse the most prominent is Nanzen-ji. A short distance away are Nanzen-in, a subtemple noted for its garden's serene beauty, and Kochi-in, a subtemple, which also has a noteworthy garden.

As happened with Ginkaku-ji, the villa of Nanzen-ji was turned into a temple upon the death of its owner, Emperor Kameyama (1249–1305). By the 14th century this had become the most powerful Zen temple in Japan, which spurred the Tendai monks to destroy it. During the 15th-century Onin Civil War the buildings were again demolished. Some were reconstructed during the 16th century.

Nanzen-ji has again become one of Kyoto's most important Rinzai Zen temple complexes, and monks are still trained here. Entrance is through the enormous

1628 Sanmon (Triple Gate), the classic "gateless" gate of Zen Buddhism that symbolizes entrance into the most sacred part of the temple precincts. After ascending, visitors have a view of the city beyond and the statue of Goemon Ishikawa. In 1594 this Robin Hood–style outlaw tried but failed to kill the *daimyo* (feudal lord) Toyotomi Hideyoshi. He hid in this gate until his capture, after which he was boiled to death in a cauldron of oil, thus lending his name to the old traditional rounded iron bathtubs once popular in Japan. His story is still enacted in many Kabuki plays.

On your way to see the major subtemples and gardens within the complex, don't overlook Nanzen-ji's other attractions. The Hojo (Abbots' Quarters) is a National Treasure. Inside, screens with impressive 16th-century paintings divide the chambers. Eitoku Kano (1543–90) painted these wall panels of the Twenty-Four Paragons of Filial Piety and Hermits. Outside, Enshu Kobori (1579–1647) is responsible for what's commonly known as the Leaping Tiger Garden, an excellent example of a dry rock-and-sand garden. The large rocks are grouped with clipped azaleas, maples, pines, and moss, all positioned against a plain white well behind the raked gravel expanse. The greenery effectively connects the garden with the lush forested hillside beyond. Visible in the complex's southeastern section is an arched redbrick aqueduct from the 1890s, with the waters of Lake Biwa, in the next prefecture, still flowing along it. The canopy of trees here, which keeps this favorite picture-taking spot cool, stands as a reminder of the city's awakening to new technology that changed residents' lives. Boring through the mountain allowed supplies as well as water to flow more easily into the city.

**Nanzen-in** (南禅院). This sub temples' east-facing garden has recently been renovated into a contemplative one with a pathway of diamond-shaped stones resting on moss-covered ground. Farther back is a large stroll garden with bridges over the tree-shaded, koi-stocked pond. A small building back here with a curving Chinese-style roof is a memorial to Emperor Kameyama.

**Konchi-in** (金地院). Recognized by aficionados around the world as one of Japan's finest gardens, Konchi-in was first established in the 15th century. It was moved inside Nanzen-ji's temple complex in 1605 and landscaped by designer Enshu Kobori several decades later. The elaborate black-lacquered gate, reminiscent of Nikko, is a shrine dedicated to Tokugawa Ieyasu, the shogun whose clan ruled Japan for centuries. The garden is one of Japan's finest examples of a classic tortoise-and-crane design, representing longevity and wisdom. It's also the most authentic example of Kobori's work. Konchi-in is before Nanzen-ji's main entrance, slightly southwest of the Sanmon Gate. ✉ *Nanzenji, Sakyo-ku* ✚ *From Kyoto Station take Bus 5 to Nanzenji Eikando-michi bus stop, from there it is a 10-min walk southeast. Alternatively, it is a 10-min walk from Keage Station on the Tozai subway line* ☎ *075/771–0365 Nanzen-ji Main Number, 075/771–3511 Konchi-in* ⊕ *www.nanzenji.or.jp* ✉ *Nanzen-in subtemple ¥400, Abbotts' Quarters ¥600, Konchi-in subtemple ¥500, Sanmon Gate ¥600.*

**National Museum of Modern Art, Kyoto** (京都国立近代美術館; *Kyoto Kokuritsu Kindai Bijutsukan*)
**ART MUSEUM** | Architect Fumihiko Maki, whose recent commissions include the Aga Khan Museum in Toronto (2014) and 4 World Trade Center in New York City (2013), designed Museum of Modern Art's 1986 steel, glass, and reinforced concrete structure. The museum is known for its collection of modern Japanese paintings, with an emphasis on the artistic movements in the Kansai region. The museum's other important holdings

include ceramic treasures by Kanjiro Kawai, Rosanjin Kitaoji, Shoji Hamada, and others. ✉ *Enshoji-cho, on west side of Jingu-michi, south of Heian Jingu, Sakyo-ku ✛ Take Bus 5 or 100 to Kyoto Kaikan Bijustsukan-mae ☎ 075/761–4111 ⊕ www.momak.go.jp 💴 Admission fee changes with exhibition.*

**Otoyo Shrine** (大豊神社; *Otoyo Jinja*)
**RELIGIOUS BUILDING** | Dating from 887, this very small shrine is best known for its "guardian rats." Most shrines have pairs of Koma-inu, mythical dogs, but Otoyo is unique in this regard, and very popular during the Year of the Rat. As with the canine twosomes, one rat's mouth is open, and the other's closed. The main halls enshrine Sukunahikona-no-mikoto, the Japanese god of medicine; Emperor Ojin, Japan's 15th emperor; and Sugawara Michizane (845–903), a Heian-era poet and politician. The grounds are resplendent with several varieties of camellia. Otoyo Jinja is considered the guardian shrine for people who live in the adjacent neighborhoods of Shishigatani, Honenin, and Nanzenji. ✉ *Shishigatani, Miyanomae-machi Kanyuchi, Sakyo-ku ✛ Just off the southern end of the Philosopher's Path. From Kawaramachi Sanjo Station take Bus 32 to Miyanomaecho bus stop, then walk 2 min east ☎ 075/771–1351 💴 Free.*

★ **Sanjusangen-do Hall** (三十三間堂)
**HISTORIC SIGHT** | This 400-foot-long hall preserves 1,001 golden, graceful Buddhist images, one of the world's most magnificent collections of wooden statuary. Enthroned in the hall's center is a seated thousand-armed Kannon (enlightened being) crowned with 10 tiny heads. Tankei, a noted sculptor of the Kamakura period (1192–1333), carved the statue. In the corridor behind it are 30 other images, carved by the members of the same school of sculptors, that include the mythological birdlike beings called Garuda, the holy man Basusenin, and the gods of wind and thunder. The

name of the hall refers to the 33 spaces between the 34 pillars that make up its length. ✉ *657 Sanjusangen-do Mawari-cho, Higashiyama-ku ✛ From Kyoto Station, take Bus 206, 208, or 100 to Sanjusangen-do-mae stop; temple is to southeast of Hyatt Regency ⊕ sanjusangendo.jp 💴 ¥600.*

**Sannen-zaka and Ninen-zaka** (三年坂と二年坂)
**STREET** | With their ancient stone paths and traditional wooden buildings, these two winding streets are the finest extant examples of Old Kyoto—the area is one of four historic preservation districts in the city. Shops along the way sell crafts such as pottery, dolls, and bamboo baskets. ✉ *Higashiyama-ku ✛ 7-min walk uphill from bus stop at Higashi-oji and Gojo.*

**Sen-oku Hakuko Kan Museum** (泉屋博古館)
**HISTORY MUSEUM** | The very fine Sen-oku Hakuko Kan museum exhibits ancient Chinese bronzes collected over three decades by Kichizaemon Sumitomo (1865–1926), the 15th head of the family behind the 400-year-old Sumitomo Corporation. Following the collapse of the Qing dynasty in 1912, many of China's treasures appeared in foreign markets, enabling Kichizaemon to amass the largest collection outside China. The museum's strongest suits are objects crafted during the Shang and Zhou periods (1600–221 BC), though the holdings include more recent items such as ritual implements, musical instruments, mirrors, bells, and calligraphy. The museum closes in winter and when new exhibitions are being installed, so call or check website before coming. ✉ *24 Miyanomae-cho, Shishigatani, Sakyo-ku ✛ Take Bus 5, 93, 203, or 204 to Higashi-Tenno-cho stop and walk 5 min ☎ 075/771–6411 ⊕ www.sen-oku.or.jp/kyoto 💴 ¥800.*

**Shoren-in Temple** (青蓮院)
**TEMPLE** | Large 800-year-old camphor trees flank the entrance path to this

Tendai sect temple. Although the present main hall dates from 1895, its interior sliding doors and screens are the work of the 16th-century painter Motonobu Kano, known for combining Chinese ink techniques and Japanese ornamental styles, and more recently, the vivid blue-and-gold lotus paintings of Kimura Hideki, a Kyoto artist, are displayed. The painting of a blue Fudo Myo-o, a Buddhist deity, is a copy of the 900-year-old National Treasure now kept in the Kyoto National Museum. Shoren-in served as a temporary Imperial Palace during the 18th century. Its stroll gardens and delicate interior architecture represent fine examples of staggered *tokonoma* (alcove) shelves and covered corridors leading to other buildings. In fall and spring the temple is lighted up from 6 to 10 pm. ✉ *69-1 Sanjobo-cho, Awataguchi, Higashiyama-ku* ✥ *From Kyoto Station take Bus 5, 86, 100 or 206 to the Higashiyama-Sanjo stop* ☎ *075/561–2345* 🌐 *www.shorenin.com/english* 🎟 *¥500.*

**Yasaka Shrine** (八坂神社; *Yasaka Jinja*)
**RELIGIOUS BUILDING** | Stone stairs lead up through the vermilion-and-white gate of Kyoto's central shrine, which plays an essential role in the city's fiscal good fortune. In addition to the good-luck charms people flock here to buy, you will see the names of the city's biggest stores and companies marking the lanterns hanging from the main hall's eaves, each of the corporate sponsors seeking financial favor as well. The shrine, just off Higashi-oji-dori, was built in the 7th century above an underground lake to ensure that the god who resided in the east—the blue water dragon—received the fresh water needed to ensure healthy Earth energy. The original enshrined Shinto deity, Susano-no-mikoto, later came to be associated with the Buddhist spirit Gozu Ten-no, a protector against pestilence and the god of prosperity. Also known as the Gion Shrine, Yasaka hosts the Gion Festival, a monthlong event that takes place in July. The festival started in AD 869 as a religious ritual to rid the city of a terrible plague that originated in Kyoto and swiftly spread all over Japan. The grounds of Yasaka Shrine are filled with revelers during cherry-blossom season, usually in early April. ✉ *625 Gion-machi, Kitagawa, Higashiyama-ku* ✥ *From Kyoto Station take Bus 206 or 100 to Gion bus stop; shrine is 1-min walk east from stops on Higashi-oji and Shijo-dori* 🌐 *www.yasaka-jinja.or.jp* 🎟 *Free.*

## 🍴 Restaurants

**Gahojin Kappa** (我逢人かっぱ)
$ | **JAPANESE** | In contrast to the expensive restaurants favored by tourists, residents seek out just-plain-folks places like this fun one. It's a late-night izakaya specializing in *robata-yaki*, which is to say it's a casual bar-restaurant with a charcoal grill and great selection of meat, poultry, and vegetable dishes. **Known for:** casual atmosphere; large à la carte selection; popular with tourists and locals. [$] *Average main: ¥390* ✉ *Sueyoshi-cho, Nawate-dori Shijo-agaru, Higashiyama-ku* ☎ *075/531–1112* 💳 *No credit cards* 🕒 *Closed Mon. No lunch.*

**Izama** (居様)
$$ | **JAPANESE** | Patrons enter this restaurant through a dark-blue curtain on the east side of Shinmachi-dori. The design inside is pure contemporary, minimalist, and sleek. **Known for:** fancy but affordable; modern decor; Kyoto vegetables. [$] *Average main: ¥2,800* ✉ *Mitsui Garden Hotel-Shinmachi, Rokkaku-dori Nakagyo-ku, east side of Shinmachi-dori, Kyoto* ☎ *075/251–2500* 🌐 *kyoto-izama-web.com.*

★ **Kikunoi** (菊乃井)
$$$$ | **JAPANESE** | The care lavished on every aspect of dining is unparalleled here, thanks to the conscientious attention of Kikunoi's owner, Yoshihiro Murata, a world-renowned chef and authority on Kyoto cuisine. A lifetime study of French and Japanese cooking, a commitment to using the finest local

## On the Menu

Compared with the style of cooking elsewhere in Japan, *Kyoto-ryori* (Kyoto cuisine) is lighter and more delicate, stressing the natural flavor of seasonal ingredients over enhancement with heavy sauces and broths. *O-banzai* (Kyoto home cooking) is served at many restaurants at reasonable prices. The freshness and quality of the ingredients is paramount, and chefs carefully handpick only the best. *Sosaku ryori* (creative cuisine) is becoming popular as chefs find inspiration in other cultures while retaining light and subtle flavors.

Kyoto is also the home of *shojin ryori*, the Zen vegetarian-style cooking best sampled on the grounds of one of the city's Zen temples, such as Tenryu-ji in Arashiyama. Local delicacies like *fu* (glutinous wheat cakes) and *yuba* (soy-milk skimmings) have found their way into the mainstream of Kyoto ryori, but were originally devised to provide protein in the traditional Buddhist diet.

For a reasonably priced alternative to the *kaiseki ryori* (the elaborate, multicourse, often expensive meal), the *kaiseki bento* (box lunch) served by many ryotei is a good place to start. Box lunches are so popular in Kyoto that restaurants compete to make their bento unique, exquisite, and delicious.

ingredients, and a playful creative sense make every meal hum with flavor. **Known for:** innovative cooking; elegant service; French-influenced Japanese cuisine. $ *Average main: ¥15,500* ✉ *Yasaka-toriimae-sagaru, Shimokawara-dori, 459 Shimokawara-cho, Higashiyama-ku* ☎ *075/561–0015* 🌐 *kikunoi.jp.*

**Kisaki Yudofu** (京湯どうふ 琵さ起)
$$ | **JAPANESE** | Tempura and tofu hot pots cooked at the table are staples at this attractive two-story restaurant along the tree-lined Philosopher's Path. Try the *Kisaki nabe*, which includes pork, chicken, beef, chrysanthemum leaf, shiitake mushrooms, and spinach. **Known for:** fine tofu cuisine; peaceful surroundings; friendly service. $ *Average main: ¥2,500* ✉ *19–173 Minamida-cho, Jodoji, Sakyo-ku* ☎ *075/751–7406* 🌐 *kyoto-kisaki.com/english.html* 🕒 *Closed Wed.*

**Nanzenji Junsei Restaurant** (南禅寺順正)
$$$ | **JAPANESE** | A short walk west of Nanzen-ji's middle gate, Junsei specializes in *yudofu* (simmered tofu) served in the traditional Kyoto kaiseki style. The beautiful Edo-period building sits among wonderful sculpted gardens; entrance is slightly set back from the road, through a small gate with two lanterns hanging on either side. **Known for:** traditional cuisine; beautiful setting; peaceful atmosphere. $ *Average main: ¥4,000* ✉ *60 Nanzen-ji, Sakyo-ku, Kyoto* ☎ *075/761–2311* 🌐 *to-fu.co.jp.*

**Nanzenji Sando Kikusui** (南禅寺参道菊水)
$$$$ | **JAPANESE** | Near Nanzen-ji Temple, Kikusui serves elegant kaiseki ryori (traditional cuisine) with an aristocratic flair. Dine on tatami mats at low tables or at table-and-chair seating, all overlooking an elegant Japanese garden. **Known for:** classic menu; intimate seating; beautiful setting. $ *Average main: ¥12,000* ✉ *31 Fukui-cho, Nanzen-ji, Sakyo-ku* ☎ *075/771–4101* 🌐 *kyoto-kikusui.com.*

**Omen Ginkaku-ji** (おめん銀閣寺本店; *Omen Ginkakuji Honten*)
$$ | **JAPANESE** | The country-style exterior of this popular noodle shop near the Philosopher's Path echoes the hearty fare served within. *Men* means noodles; the

*O* is honorific, appropriately so. **Known for:** English menu with vegan options; variety of noodle dishes; rustic interior. $ *Average main: ¥1,950* ✉ *74 Ishi-bashi-cho, Jodoji, Sakyo-ku* ✛ *North side of Shishigatani-dori a little east of Ginkaku-ji-michi* ☎ *075/771–8994* ⊕ *omen.co.jp* ⊘ *Closed Thurs.*

### Ramen Miyako Gion (らぁーめん京)

$ | **JAPANESE** | After a long day of sightseeing there is nothing better than a hearty bowl of ramen, and this place is one of the best in Kyoto. Great choice of rich broths (pork, chicken, soy sauce, salt, miso), reasonably priced, plus there's an English menu. **Known for:** friendly service; flavorsome bowls of ramen noodles; authentic and affordable. $ *Average main: ¥1,100* ✉ *303 Gion-machi Kitagawa, Higashiyama-ku* ☎ *075/541–1385* ⊕ *www.ramen-miyako.com* ▭ *No credit cards.*

### Yagenbori (やげんぼり)

$$$$ | **JAPANESE** | Enjoy fine traditional fare inside this distinctive red and wooden-latticed *machiya*-style townhouse in the heart of Gion. If you snag one of the counter seats, then the chefs prepare everything right in front of you. **Known for:** large selection of à la carte dishes; cozy interior; excellent service. $ *Average main: ¥11,000* ✉ *570–122 Gionmachi Minamigawa, Higashiyama-ku* ☎ *075/525–3332* ⊕ *yagenbori.co.jp* ⊘ *Closed Tues.*

## ☕ Coffee and Quick Bites

### Bunnosuke Chaya (文の助茶屋)

$ | **JAPANESE** | On the road to Kiyomizu-dera, a wooden archway plastered with *senja-fuda* (name cards pilgrims affix on the entryways to shrines and temples) is the entry to this charming courtyard teahouse that opened in 1910. The specialties here are *amazake*, a sweet, nonalcoholic sake often served hot with a touch of ginger, and *warabimochi* rice cakes. **Known for:** traditional sweets and desserts; authentic and historic setting; relaxing atmosphere. $ *Average main: ¥500* ✉ *373 Yasaka Uemachi Shimogawara-dori, Higashi-iru, Higashiyama-ku* ☎ *075/561–1972* ▭ *No credit cards* ⊘ *Closed weekdays.*

### Zen Café

$$ | **DESSERTS** | Nestling right in the heart of Kyoto's traditional *geisha* district, this café serves up traditional Japanese sweets and desserts in a stylish minimalist setting. Living up to its name, the quiet and cosy space is styled like a modern art gallery, and is a great place to sip on a green tea or coffee while sampling delicate and seasonal treats such as *kuzumochi* (a jelly-like *mochi* cake). **Known for:** Japanese sweets; contemporary vibe; polite and friendly service. $ *Average main: ¥2,500* ✉ *570–210 Gion-machi, Minamigawa, Hanamachi, Higashiyama-ku* ☎ *075/533–8686* ⊕ *www.kagizen.co.jp* ⊘ *Closed Mon.*

## 🛏 Hotels

### Four Seasons Hotel Kyoto (フォーシーズンズホテル京都)

$$$$ | **HOTEL** | Nestled in the foothills of the Eastern Mountains, the Four Seasons is a seven-minute walk from the Kyoto National Museum and some of Kyoto's popular temples. **Pros:** secluded yet near major sightseeing; well-equipped fitness center; excellent restaurants. **Cons:** 5-minute walk uphill from the nearest bus stop; not within walking distance of downtown; expensive. $ *Rooms from: ¥65,000* ✉ *445–3 Myoho-in Maeka-wa-cho, Higashiyama-ku* ☎ *075/541–8288* ⊕ *www.fourseasons.com/kyoto* ⇥ *123 rooms* ☷ *No Meals.*

### Hotel Ethnography Gion Furumonzen (ホテルエスノグラフィー)

$$ | **HOTEL** | Murals, art objects, and custom-made furniture by local artists enliven every room and even the public hallways of this boutique in the heart of Gion; two Kyoto hotels (Gion

Shinmonzen is the other) are within a block of each other on the antiques shop–lined streets of Furumonzen and Shinmonzen, respectively. **Pros:** multilingual staff; wall murals and art on walls; planned events for guests. **Cons:** small rooms; no shops or fitness center; breakfast provided only upon request. [$] *Rooms from: ¥15,000* ✉ *350 Miyoshi-cho, Higashiyama-ku* ☎ *075/746–4109* 🌐 *www.hotel-ethnography.com* 🛏 *18 rooms* 🍴 *No Meals.*

**★ Hyatt Regency Kyoto**
(ハイアットリージェンシー京都)
**$$$$ | HOTEL |** Directly opposite the Kyoto National Museum and next to the famous Sanjusangen-do Temple, this is one of Kyoto's premier hotels, offering spacious tasteful rooms. **Pros:** peaceful location; multilingual staff; extravagant breakfast. **Cons:** far from downtown Kyoto; no pool; plain facade. [$] *Rooms from: ¥25,000* ✉ *644–2 Sanjusangen-do-mawari, Higashiyama-ku* ☎ *075/541–1234* 🌐 *kyoto.regency.hyatt.com* 🛏 *189 rooms* 🍴 *No Meals.*

**★ The Ritz-Carlton, Kyoto**
(ザ・リッツ・カールトン京都)
**$$$$ | HOTEL |** Along the scenic Kamo River with views of the Eastern Mountains, the Ritz-Carlton provides world-class luxury in a Japanese milieu, with subtle lighting, artistic ornamentation, and a renovated century-old estate used for dining. **Pros:** fabulous views from river-facing rooms; world-class service; luxurious decor. **Cons:** very expensive; non-river views are nothing special; you won't want to leave. [$] *Rooms from: ¥70,000* ✉ *Kamogawa Nijo-Ohashi Hotori, Nagagyo ku, Kyoto* ☎ *075/746–5555* 🌐 *www.ritzcarlton.com/kyoto* 🛏 *134 rooms* 🍴 *No Meals.*

**The Westin Miyako Hotel**
(ウェスティン都ホテル京都)
**$$$ | HOTEL | FAMILY |** At the foot of the Philosopher's Path and near the temple and shrine-filled Okazaki area, the renovated Westin Miyako is only minutes from major attractions. **Pros:** quiet area; helpful concierge; free transfer from Kyoto Station. **Cons:** pool has limited hours; some facilities dated; not within walking distance of downtown. [$] *Rooms from: ¥20,000* ✉ *Sanjo-Keage, Higashiyama-ku* ☎ *075/771–7111* 🌐 *www.marriott.com* 🛏 *320 rooms* 🍴 *No Meals.*

**Yachiyo** (八千代)
**$$$$ | B&B/INN |** This ryokan feels very "Japanese," and what it lacks in big-hotel amenities it makes up for in atmosphere, albeit with some limitations, including some shared-bath rooms, that may not appeal to all travelers. **Pros:** rooms with garden views; quiet surroundings; Western-breakfast option. **Cons:** staff's English language skills are spotty; public areas and some rooms look careworn; not all rooms have garden views. [$] *Rooms from: ¥24,000* ✉ *34 Nanzen-ji-Fukuchi-cho, Sakyo-ku* ☎ *075/771–4148* 🌐 *www.ryokan-yachiyo.com* 🛏 *25 rooms (20 with bath)* 🍴 *Free Breakfast.*

## 🍸 Nightlife

### MUSIC

**Club Metro** (クラブメトロ)
**LIVE MUSIC |** Popular Metro frequently hosts famous DJs from Tokyo and abroad. The range of music played—experimental dance, hip-hop, reggae, disco, salsa, and more—is very broad. ✉ *Ebisu Bldg., 82 Shimotsutsumi-cho, Marutamachi-sagaru, Kawabata-dori, Sakyo-ku* ✥ *Near Keihan Station* ☎ *075/752–2787* 🌐 *www.metro.ne.jp.*

## 🎫 Performing Arts

### CONCERTS

**Kyoto Concert Hall**
(京都コンサートホール)
**CONCERTS |** The architect Isozaki Arata designed this complex that has a huge round glass facade and a spiral entrance walkway up to the 1,839-seat Main Hall, the home of the Kyoto Symphony Orchestra. Visiting orchestras and

artists, including excellent ones unknown outside Asia, also perform here and in the 514-seat Ensemble Hall. Ask your concierge for a schedule. There's a restaurant on the ground floor. ⊠ *1–26 Hangi-cho, Shimogamo, Sakyo-ku* ✛ *5-min walk from Kitayama subway station* ☎ *075/711–2980* ⊕ *www.kyoto-concerthall.org* ⊠ *From ¥5,000.*

**Rohm Theater Kyoto** (ロームシアター京都)

THEATER | Located in the Okazaki area, this concert and performance venue was formerly known as Kyoto Kaikan. It reopened in 2016 with more seating and new facilities. ⊠ *13 Okazakisaishoji-cho, Sakyo-ku* ☎ *075/771–6051* ⊕ *rohmtheatrekyoto.jp/en.*

## SEASONAL DANCES AND TRADITIONAL PERFORMANCES

★ **Gion Corner Theater** (ギオンコーナー)

THEATER | This theater's 50-minute performances sample five traditional disciplines: *gagaku* (court music), *kyomai* (Kyoto-style dance), *Bunraku* (puppet theater), *kyogen* (comic drama), and *koto* (Japanese harp). The theater is old, the seats aren't comfortable, and this is definitely a tourist trap, but it's also only place to see these performing arts most of year. The admission price is a bargain considering the number of talented artists involved. ⊠ *Yasaka Hall, 570-2 Gion-machi Minamigawa, Higashi-yama-ku* ✛ *5-min walk from Shijo-Gion bus stop or Hankyu Kawaramachi or Keihan Shijo train station* ☎ *075/561–1119* ⊕ *www.kyoto-gioncorner.com/global/ en.html* ⊠ *¥3,150* ⊙ *Mar.–Nov., nightly at 6 and 7; Dec.–Feb., Fri., weekends, and holidays at 6 and 7.*

## KABUKI

**Minami-za** (南座)

THEATER | The renovated Minami-za theater, the oldest in Japan, hosts Kabuki performances most of the year. Even the mounted posters announcing the plays here are beautifully rendered. The typical Kabuki performance can last up to four hours; there are two shows daily. Box

lunches are the choice meal during a play so that one does not miss anything. Front downstairs seats are often occupied by the "who's who" of the world of maiko and geiko. ⊠ *Shijo Kamogawa, Higashi-yama-ku* ✛ *Southeast side of Shijo and Kawabata-dori* ☎ *075/561–1155* ⊕ *www. kabukiweb.net/theatres/minamiza.*

## NOH

**Kanze Kaikan Noh Theater** (観世会館)

THEATER | This is one of Kyoto's oldest Noh schools. The libretto is all in Japanese, with only some information in English. ⊠ *44 Enshoji-cho, Okazaki, Sakyo-ku* ☎ *075/771–6114* ⊕ *www.kyoto-kanze.jp* ⊠ *¥2,000–¥6,000.*

#  Shopping

## ART AND ANTIQUES

If you are looking for antiques in eastern Kyoto, **Nawate-dori,** in the Higashiyama-ku neighborhood between Shijo-dori and Sanjo-dori, is noted for fine antique textiles, ceramics, and paintings.

**Shinmonzen-dori,** also in Higashiyama-ku, is an unpretentious little street of two-story wooden buildings between Higashi-oji-dori and Hanami-koji-dori, just north of Gion. About a dozen and a half shops here specialize in scrolls, *netsuke* (small carved figures to attach to Japanese clothing), lacquerware, bronze, woodblock prints, paintings, and antiques. Shop with confidence, because shopkeepers are trustworthy and goods are authentic. Pick up a copy of the pamphlet *Shinmonzen Street Shopping Guide* from your hotel or from the Kyoto Tourist Information Center to learn more about them.

## CERAMICS

**Asahi-do** (朝日堂)

CERAMICS | In the heart of the pottery district near Kiyomizu-dera, Asahi-do specializes in Kyoto-style hand-painted porcelain. It offers the widest selection of any pottery store in the area, and can arrange overseas shipping. ⊠ *1–280*

Kiyomizu, Higashiyama-ku ☎ 075/531–2181 ⊕ www.asahido.co.jp.

## CRAFTS

### Kurochiku

(くろちく倭美坐; *Kurochiku Wabiza*)

**CRAFTS** | Fine traditional crafts, including reasonably priced dolls, ceramics, lacquerware, prints, incense, textiles, and bonsai, can be found at this center. ✉ Gion Kurochiku Bldg., 275 Gion-machi Kitagawa, Higashiyama-ku ✦ *From Kyoto Station, take any bus that stops at Gion on Shijo-dori* ☎ 075/541–1196 ⊕ www.kurochiku.co.jp.

### Kyoto Handicraft Center

(京都ハンディクラフトセンター)

**CRAFTS** | This center has served visitors and residents for decades with its huge selection of crafts and art, both new and old. Various vendors sell dolls, kimonos, pottery, swords, woodblock prints, and pearls, and you'll find one of the best collections of English-language books on Japan. The prices are reasonable in this duty-free commercial center that's also great just for browsing. Regular demonstrations of traditional craft techniques and hands-on workshops (reservation required before 5 pm) make this place tourist-oriented, though not a tourist trap. Everything is of high quality. ✉ 17 Entomi-cho, Shogo-in, north side of Marutamachi-dori, north of Heian Jingu, Sakyo-ku ✦ *From Kyoto Station take Bus 206 to Kumano Jinja-mae, or Bus 31, 201, or 203 from Shijo-Kawaramachi Station* ☎ 075/761–8001 ⊕ www.kyotohandicraftcenter.com/?lang=en.

## DOLLS

*Ningyo* were first used in Japan in the purification rites associated with the Doll Festival, an annual family-oriented event on March 3. Kyoto ningyo are made with fine detail and embellishment.

# Shuincho

The *shuincho* is a booklet usually no larger than 4 by 6 inches, usually covered with brocade, composed of blank sheets of heavyweight paper that continuously fold out. You can find them at gift stores or at temples for as little as ¥1,000. Use them to collect ink stamps from places you visit while in Japan. Stamps and stamp pads are ubiquitous in Japan—at sites, train stations, and some restaurants. Most stamps are given for free; at temples monks will write calligraphy over the stamp for a small fee.

### Ando Japanese Doll Shop

(安藤人形店; *Ando Ningyo-ten*)

**ANTIQUES & COLLECTIBLES** | The Ando brothers, Tadao and Tadahiko, handmake dolls for the Imperial Court and individual families. The finest silk brocades adorn these *Hina* and *Ichimatsu* dolls, which have earned high praise and many awards over the years. ✉ Kamigyo Ku, Aburanokoji, Marutamachi-dori, agaru, Kyoto ✦ *Take Bus 9 to Horikawa/Marutamachi stop and walk 3 min* ☎ 075/231–7466 ⊕ www.ando-doll.com/english.

## HOUSEWARES

### Eirakuya (永楽屋)

**HOUSEWARES** | The *tenugui* hand towels sold by this shop have served many purposes through the centuries. In designs today that range from traditional to playful, the towels make wonderful scarves, napkins, bottle holders, and other items depending on how you twist and shape them. The colors and designs are so vibrant and eye-catching that framing one and hanging it as art is another possibility. This Eirakuya store is one of several in the city. ✉ 242 Gion-cho, Higashi-iri, Yamatoji, Higashiyama-ku, Nakagyo-ku ☎ 075/532–1125 ⊕ www.eirakuya.jp.

# Kyoto Crafts

Temples, shrines, and gardens can't be taken home with you. You can, however, pack up a few *omiyage* (mementos) for which this city is famous. The ancient craftspeople of Kyoto served the Imperial Court for more than 1,000 years, and the prefix *kyo* before a craft is synonymous with fine craftsmanship.

## Dolls

*Kyo-ningyo*, exquisite display dolls, have been made in Kyoto since the 9th century. Constructed of wood coated with white shell paste and clothed in elaborate, miniature patterned-silk brocades, Kyoto dolls are considered the finest in Japan. Kyoto is also known for ceramic dolls and *kyo-gangu*, its local varieties of folk toys.

## Fans

*Kyo-sensu* are embellished folding fans used as accoutrements in Noh theater, tea ceremonies, and Japanese dance. They also have a practical use—to keep you cool. Unlike other Japanese crafts, which have their origin in Tang Dynasty China, the folding fan originated in Kyoto.

## Lacquerware

*Kyo-shikki* refers to Kyoto lacquerware, which also has its roots in the 9th century. The making of lacquerware, adopted from the Chinese, is a delicate process requiring patience and skill. Finished lacquerware products range from furniture to spoons and bowls, which are carved from cypress, cedar, or horse-chestnut wood. These pieces have a brilliant luster; some designs are decorated with gold leaf and inlaid mother-of-pearl.

## Ceramics

*Kyo-yaki* is the general term applied to ceramics made in local kilns; the most popular ware is from Kyoto's Kiyomizu district. Often colorfully hand-painted in blue, red, and green on white, these elegantly shaped teacups, bowls, and vases are thrown on potters' wheels located in the Kiyomizu district and in Kiyomizu-danchi in Yamashina. Streets leading up to Kiyomizu-dera—Chawan-zaka, Sannen-zaka, and Ninen-zaka—are sprinkled with kyo-yaki shops.

## Silk

*Nishijin-ori* is the weaving of silk. *Nishijin* refers to a Kyoto district producing the best silk textiles in all Japan, which are used to make kimonos. *Kyo-yuzen* is a paste-resist silk-dyeing technique developed by 17th-century dyer Yuzen Miyazaki. Fantastic designs are created on plain white silk pieces through the process of either *tegaki yuzen* (hand-painting) or *kata yuzen* (stenciling).

## LACQUERWARE

**Zohiko Lacquerware** (象彦京都寺町店)
**ANTIQUES & COLLECTIBLES** | Kyoto's oldest and most renowned maker of lustrous lacquerware trays, tea ceremony utensils, calligraphy, boxes and other lacquer products was established in 1661. The showroom on Teramachi-dori has both contemporary and traditional specimens. ✉ *Nakagyo-ku, Teramachi-dori, Nijo agaru, nishi-gawa, Kyoto ✛ West side of Teramachi-dori, north of Nijo-dori; 10-min walk from Karasuma Oike subway station, 3-min walk from Kawaramachi Nijo bus stop ☎ 075/229–6625 ⊕ www.zohiko. co.jp/shop.*

## TEMPLE MARKETS

### Chion-ji Hyakumanben-san Handicraft Market (百万遍さんの手づくり市; Hyakumanben-san Tezukuri-ichi)

MARKET | A market specializing in hand-made goods and crafts is held here on the 15th of each month. Dolls, small carved wooden statues, fabric, ceramics, costume jewelry, and many other items are sold. Baked goods and other foods are available. ✉ *Imadegawa and Higashi-ioji-dori, northeast corner, opposite Kyoto University campus, Higashiyama-ku* ✤ *Take Bus 206 from Kyoto Station to Hyakumanben stop.*

# Central Kyoto

The two major sights in central Kyoto are the opulent Nijo Castle and the more modest Imperial Palace. Visiting the latter requires permission, and you must join a guided tour. Central Kyoto is a big shopping destination: west of the Kamogawa to Karasuma-dori and on the north–south axis between Shijo-dori and Oike-dori, there are department stores, specialty shops, and restaurants. The walk (from 20 to 30 minutes) down Sanjo-dori from the south end of Nijo Castle to eastern Kyoto is loaded with tea- and coffee-houses, international cuisine, high-end boutiques, and museums.

**Access:** Buses and several subway lines service all of central Kyoto's sights, but taxis may be a cost-neutral and easy way for groups of three or four to get around the central and eastern parts of the city. Farther-away areas like Arashiyama and Fushimi are best accessed by train.

## ◉ Sights

### East Hongan-ji Temple
(東本願寺; Higashi-Hongan-ji)

TEMPLE | The high walls, immense wooden gates, and enormous roof of the Otani headquarters of the Jodo Shinshu sect of Buddhism are sufficiently impressive to convince some newcomers they're looking at the Imperial Palace. In the current complex, largely an 1895 reconstruction, the cavernous Hondo (Main Hall), also called the Amida-do, the second-largest wooden structure in Japan, dwarfs everything else. During the temple's construction, female devotees offered their hair, which was woven into strong, thick ropes used to set heavy timbers into place. A coiled length of one of these *kezuna* is within a glass case in a passageway between the Amida-do and the Daishi-do, a double-roof structure notable for its graceful curving lines. ✉ *Karasuma Shichijo-agaru, Shimogyo-ku* ✤ *From Kyoto Station walk 5 min north on Karasuma-dori* ☎ *075/371-9181* ⊕ *www.higashihonganji.or.jp* 🎫 *Free.*

### Kyoto Aquarium
(京都水族館; Kyoto Suizokukan)

AQUARIUM | FAMILY | Inspired by the multitude of rivers that flow into the Kyoto basin, this landlocked city opened an aquarium to display Kyoto's native salamander, a large specimen that dwells deep in forest streams. Holding 500 tons of water, the main pool is truly one of a kind. A horseshoe-shape pool gives you the illusion that you're swimming with sea lions. The penguins and dolphin stadium are also popular. ✉ *Umekoji Park, 35–1 Kankijicho, Shimogyo-ku* ✤ *15-min walk west of Kyoto Station* ☎ *075/354-3130* ⊕ *www.kyoto-aquarium.com/en/index.html* 🎫 *¥2,200.*

### Kyoto Imperial Palace
(京都御所; Kyoto Gosho)

CASTLE/PALACE | Although it tops many tourists' list of must-see sights, the former Imperial Palace often leaves them disappointed because visitors may not enter any of the buildings on the subdued hour-long tour. The original building burned down in 1788, as did some of its replacements. The present structure dates from 1855. The garden, however, is a revelation, the work of a century of master landscapers. Its noteworthy

## KEY

1 Exploring Sights
1 Restaurants
1 Quick Bites
1 Hotels

KYOTO UNIVERSITY

*amachi*

*Higashiyama*

HIGASHIYAMA

ON

0 ————— 2,000 feet
0 ————— 500 m

TOKAIDO MAIN LINE

### Sights ▼

1 East Hongan-ji Temple .. **C8**
2 Kyoto Aquarium ......... **B9**
3 Kyoto Imperial Palace... **E1**
4 Kyoto International
Manga Museum ........ **D4**
5 Kyoto Railway
Museum ................. **A9**
6 Kyoto Seishu
Netsuke Art Museum .. **B6**
7 Kyoto Station ............ **D9**
8 Nijo Castle ............... **B3**
9 Nijo Encampment ....... **B4**
10 Nishijin-ori Textile
Center .................... **C1**
11 Raku Museum ............ **C1**
12 Toji Temple .............. **B9**
13 West Hongan-ji
Temple ................... **C8**

### Restaurants ▼

1 Baan Rim Naam ........ **F8**
2 Ca' Del Viale ............ **A4**
3 Cafe Bibliotic HELLO! ... **E3**
4 Ganko Nijyoen .......... **F4**
5 Giro Giro Hitoshina ..... **F7**
6 Indépendants ........... **E5**
7 Kerala ................... **F4**
8 Korean Kitchen
Anpan ................... **D5**
9 Mankamero ............ **B2**
10 Manzaratei Nishiki ..... **D5**
11 Mishima-tei .............. **F5**
12 Omen Nippon .......... **F5**
13 Ponto-cho Robin ........ **F5**
14 Ponto-cho Suishin ...... **D9**
15 Restaurant Ugawa ...... **F3**
16 Shinsen-en Heihachi .. **B4**
17 Yoshikawa Inn
Restaurant ............... **E4**
18 Zezekan Pocchiri ....... **D5**

### Quick Bites ▼

1 Maeda Coffee Meirin .. **D5**

### Hotels ▼

1 ANA Crowne Plaza
Hotel Kyoto ............. **C4**
2 Hiiragiya ................. **E4**
3 Hotel Granvia Kyoto .... **D9**
4 Hotel Kanra ............. **D8**
5 K's House Kyoto ......... **E8**
6 Kinmata .................. **E5**
7 Kyoto Brighton Hotel ... **D1**
8 Kyoto Garden Palace ... **D1**
9 Matsubaya Inn .......... **D8**
10 Miyako Hotel
Kyoto Hachijo .......... **D9**
11 Nishiyama Ryokan ...... **E4**
12 Rihga Royal Hotel
Kyoto .................... **C9**
13 The Screen .............. **E3**
14 Tawaraya Ryokan ....... **E4**
15 Yoshikawa ............... **E4**

8

Kyoto CENTRAL KYOTO

facets include the stone shoreline of the pond, the graceful bridges, and the magnificent trees and flower selection.

To see the palace, you must receive permission from the Imperial Household Agency. You can usually arrange a same-day visit by showing your passport at the office, in the park's northwest corner, but you can also apply there earlier or make a request online. Guided tours in English begin inside the imperial park at the Seishomon entrance. ⊠ *Kunaicho, Kyoto Gyoen-nai, Kamigyo-ku* ⊹ *For Imperial Household Agency, 5-min walk southeast from Imadegawa/Karasuma subway station* ☎ *075/211–1215* ⊕ *sankan.kunaicho. go.jp* ▱ *Free.*

### Kyoto International Manga Museum
(京都国際マンガミュージアム; *Kyoto Kokusai Manga Museum*)
ART MUSEUM | Many famous artists have signed the walls at this bilingual museum that claims to have the world's largest collection of manga materials. Most international visitors likely associate manga with Tokyo, but Kyoto is a significant hub for the stylized comic books thanks to its rich traditions and universities specializing in the visual arts. The main permanent installation answers the question "What is manga?" and temporary exhibitions probe topics such as depictions of war in the comics. The museum's approximately 300,000 artifacts include items from outside Japan and early examples of the genre. The shelves of the Wall of Manga hold 50,000 publications you can peruse on site. ⊠ *Karasuma-Oike, Nakagyo-ku* ⊹ *Karasuma or Tozai subway to Karasuma Oike Station, or Kyoto Bus 61, 62, or 63, or Kyoto City Bus 15, 51, or 65 to Karasuma Oike stop* ☎ *075/254–7414* ⊕ *www.kyotomm.jp* ▱ *¥900* ⊗ *Closed Tue. and Wed.*

### Kyoto Railway Museum (京都鉄道博物館; *Kyoto Tetsudo Hakubutsukan*)
OTHER MUSEUM | For train enthusiasts, the sleek architecture reflects Japan's Shinkansen Bullet train. Inside, 53 trains including 20 locomotives are on display. One attraction even allows the visitor to "drive" a bullet train via a stimulated video screen. ⊠ *Kankiji-cho, Shimogyo-ku* ⊹ *A short 2-min walk from Umekoji-Kyotonishi Station, or a 20-min walk west of Kyoto Station* ⊕ *www.kyotorailwaymuseum.jp* ▱ *¥1,200* ⊗ *Closed Wed.*

### Kyoto Seishu Netsuke Art Museum
(清宗根付館; *Seishu Netsuke-kan*)
ART MUSEUM | *Netsuke* are miniature carvings of wood, ivory, and stone traditionally used as toggles of tobacco cases or just as ornamentation. This museum is within an former samurai's estate. The architecture and garden alone make this a worthwhile visit, but the collection of netsuke is fascinating as well. ⊠ *Nakagyo-ku, 46 Mibukayougosho-cho, Kyoto* ⊹ *5-min walk south from Shijo Mibu bus stop, 10-min walk from Hankyu subway Shijo Omiya Station* ☎ *075/802–7000* ⊕ *www.netsukekan.jp/en* ▱ *¥1,000.*

### Kyoto Station (京都駅; *Kyoto-eki*)
TRAIN/TRAIN STATION | This massive steel-and-glass train station, hailed by some as an architectural masterpiece and derided by many Kyotoites for failing to convey their beloved city's genteel spirit, is more than just the city's central point of arrival and departure: the station, designed by Tokyoite Hiroshi Hara and completed in 1997, houses dozens of shops and restaurants and offers great views of the city from the 12th floor. If you have the time, ride the escalators from the concourse floor up to the open roof, a journey Hara says he choreographed to replicate ascending from a valley floor. Excellent ramen shops cluster on the 10th level. ⊠ *137 Karasuma-dori Shiokoji-sagaru, Shimogyo-ku* ⊕ *www.kyoto-station-building.co.jp.*

### Nijo Encampment (二条陣屋; *Nijo Jinya*)
HISTORIC HOME | A short walk south of Nijo-jo, this 17th-century merchant house saw later service as an inn for traveling *daimyo* (feudal lords). A warren of rooms, Nijo Jinya is crammed with built-in

Nijo-jo was constructed in 1603 as the residence of Ieyasu Tokugawa, the founder of the shogunate.

safeguards against attack, including hidden staircases, secret passageways, and hallways too narrow to allow the wielding of a sword. The house is again a family residence, so visitation is limited to one-hour tours that require reserva tions at least a day ahead. The tours are in Japanese, but you can arrange for an interpreter on the house's website. ✉ *137 Sanbo Omiya-cho, 2 blocks south of Nijo Castle, Nakagyo-ku* ✛ *Take Bus 9, 12, 50, or 101 to Horikawa Oike and walk west 5 min* ☎ *075/841–0972* ⊕ *nijyojinya. net/English.html* ✐ *¥1,000.*

★ **Nijo Castle** (二条城; *Nijō-jo*)

**CASTLE/PALACE** | Another of Kyoto's World Heritage sites, this castle whose construction began in 1603 is a grandiose and unequivocal statement of power by Ieyasu, the first Tokugawa shogun. In the early Edo period, the shogun stripped all power from Kyoto's Imperial Court by consolidating a new military and political center at his far-off fortress in Tokyo. Nijo-jo's moat and towering walls are intimidating enough, but once inside, a

second moat and defensive wall assert the power of the warlord. What seems a second line of defense has less to do with defending the castle than reinforcing the structure's social statement: access to the inner sanctum depended on a visitor's status within the shogunate's hierarchy. Once inside, a guest was as much a hostage as a guest, a point surely driven home by the castle's ingenious nightingale floors, which "chirp" as people walk across them, revealing their movements. If you look under the balcony while strolling the garden, you can observe how the mechanism behind this architectural feature works.

The Tokugawa shoguns were rarely in Kyoto. Ieyasu stayed in the castle three times, and the second shogun stayed twice, including the time in 1626 when Emperor Gomizuno-o was granted an audience. After that, for the next 224 years, no Tokugawa shogun visited Kyoto, and the castle fell into disrepair. Only when the Tokugawa shogunate was under pressure from a failing economy did the 14th shogun, Tokugawa Iemochi (1846–66), come to Kyoto to confer with the emperor. The 15th and last Tokugawa shogun, Yoshinobu, famously returned power to the emperor in 1867, the central event of the Meiji Restoration. Since 1939, the castle has belonged to the city of Kyoto, and considerable restoration has taken place.

You can explore Nijo-jo at your own pace, and handy audio guides provide explanations of what you are seeing. Entry is through the impressive Kara-mon gate, whose sharp angles were intended to slow an attack. The path from the Kara-mon leads to the Ni-no-maru Palace, whose five buildings are divided into various smaller chambers. The costumed mannequins inside the central hall are displayed as their real-life counterparts might have reacted at the moment of the Tokugawa shogunate's demise. Following this, governmental power returned to the reigning emperor. The impressive garden was created by landscape designer Enshu Kobori shortly before Emperor Gomizuno-o's visit in 1626. Crane- and tortoise-shape islands symbolize strength and longevity. ⊠ *Horikawa Nishi-iru, Nijo-dori, Nakagyo-ku* ⊹ *3-min walk from Karasuma Oike subway station, or take Bus 9, 12, 50, or 101 to Nijo-jo-mae* ☎ *075/841–0096* ⊕ *nijo-jocastle.city. kyoto.lg.jp* ⊠ *¥620.*

### Nishijin-ori Textile Center
(西陣織会館; *Nishijin-ori Kaikan*)
FACTORY | The sound of looms and spinning machines adds a subtle rhythm to the narrow streets of the Nishijin district, a longtime center of weaving and dyeing in northwestern Kyoto. The textile center here was established to showcase the skills of the local artisans. In hands-on lessons you can weave your own garment: for ¥2,200 you'll learn something and get a great souvenir. Reserve ahead and you can try on various different kimonos, rent one for a night on the town, or even buy one (¥10,000). On the second floor are weavers at work and items for sale, and artisans work at their crafts on the third floor. Several times a day, kimono-clad models appear in the latest seasonal designs during 15-minute shows. ⊠ *Horikawai-Imadegawa-Minami-Iru, Kamigyo-ku* ⊹ *Take Bus 9, 12, 51, 59, 101, 201 or 203 to Horikawa-Imadegawa stop* ☎ *075/451–9231* ⊕ *www. nishijin.or.jp* ⊠ *Free.*

### Raku Museum
(樂美術館; *Raku Bijutsukan*)
OTHER MUSEUM | Serious collectors of tea-ceremony utensils are likely to have a raku bowl in their collections. The Raku Museum displays more than 1,000 bowls and containers of subtle beauty embodying the Japanese aesthetic terms of *wabi* and *sabi*, which refer to "understated elegance" and "mature beauty." *Raku* refers to a low-temperature firing technique that yields a ceramic that is soft to the touch. Raku is the family name with a long history of creating pleasing tea utensils for the shogun's use. ⊠ *84 Aburakoji, Nakadachi-uri agaru, east of Horikawa-dori, 3 blocks south of Imadegawa-dori, Kamigyo-ku* ⊹ *Take Karasuma subway to Imadegawa Station or Bus 9 or 12 to Ichi-jo-modori-bashi* ☎ *075/414– 0304* ⊕ *www.raku-yaki.or.jp/e/museum* ⊠ *Around ¥900 (fee varies, depending on exhibition).*

### To-ji Temple (東寺)
TEMPLE | Famous for its towering pagoda, the most prominent one visible when entering the city, the temple of To-ji was established by imperial edict in AD 796 and called the East Temple. Farther west was Sai-ji, the West Temple, but receiving no special patronage it was long ago destroyed. To-ji, on the other hand, was assigned to the priest Kukai (AD 774– 835), also known as Kobo Daishi, a major figure in Japanese Buddhism whose accomplishments include founding the Shingon sect in the early 9th century and establishing the 88-temple pilgrimage on the island of Shikoku.

Fires and battles during the 16th century destroyed the temple buildings, but many were rebuilt, including in 1603 the Kon-do (Main Hall), which blends Chinese and Japanese elements. The one building that has managed to survive the ravages of war since it was built in 1491 is the Ko-do (Lecture Hall). Inside this hall are 15 original statues of Buddhist gods, forming a mandala, that are considered masterpieces of the Heian era (AD 750–1150). There's a daily morning service at 6 am in the Daishi-do with devotional chanting.

On the 21st of each month, a market known locally as Kobo-san (after Kobo Daishi) is held. Used and old kimonos, fans, furniture, potted plants, oriental medicine, kitchen utensils, and many other items can be found at bargain prices. A little patience and a pencil and paper to write down your desired price will make the venture an enjoyable one. A smaller antiques market is held on the first Sunday of the month. ✉ *1 Kujo-cho, Minami-ku, Kyoto* ✣ *15-min walk southwest of Kyoto Station, or take Kintetsu subway additional one stop; Bus 207 also serves To-ji* ☎ *075/691–3325* 🌐 *www.toji.or.jp/en* 🎫 *¥500 main buildings, other parts free.*

**West Hongan-ji Temple**
(西本願寺; *Nishi-Hongan-ji*)
**TEMPLE** | The interior of this enormous World Heritage site has 1,000 tatami mats in its main hall, and as the headquarters for the Jodo Shinshu sect of Buddhism has a similar number of followers. The compound contains many fine examples of 16th-century Momoyama architecture. Among the most renowned of these is a gate on the south side. Elaborately carved in fascinating detail, it is called Higureshi-no-mon (All the Day Long Gate) because one could stand and look at its depictions of mythical and real animals, birds, and flowers for hours.

Founded in 1272, the sect gained great popularity by appealing to the masses in making paradise accessible by reciting a simple incantation. As with all Jodo Shinshu temples, the main altar is the image of Amida Buddha, surrounded by vases of graceful gold-painted lotus and a canopy of hanging gold ornaments, all of which seem to glow in the darkened hall. Some of the Buddhist images belonging to this temple are now housed in the Ryukoku Museum, across the street on the east side of Horikawa. A re-creation of the murals in Chinese cave paintings have been replicated via photographs in the museum.

Several buildings can be entered if permission is granted that takes from a week to a month to obtain (visit website for details). One of them, the Hiunkaku Pavilion, a graceful three-story structure built in 1587, was once the residence of the warlord Toyotomi Hideyoshi and was moved here. The morning service, which takes place daily at 6 am, provides a good opportunity to observe or participate. ✉ *Gakurin-cho, Higashi-nakasuji, Rokujo-sagaru, on Horikawa-dori, a block north of Shichijo-dori, Shimogyo-ku* ✣ *5-min walk north of Kyoto Station* ☎ *075/371–5181* 🌐 *www.hongwanji.or.jp/english* 🎫 *Free.*

## 🍴 Restaurants

**Baan Rim Naam** (バーン・リムナーム)
$ | **THAI** | The two well-trained Thai chefs here prepare several dozen of their country's dishes at very reasonable prices. Spicy green papaya salad, hot-and-sour prawn soup with rice noodles, and green curry with chicken are all on the menu—there's a version in English—and vegetarian dishes are served. **Known for:** riverside setting; traditional Thai cuisine; extensive menu. [$] *Average main: ¥1,200* ✉ *Kiyamachi-dori, Higashi-iru, Shijo Minami, Kyoto* ✣ *2 blocks south of Shijo-dori on east (river) side of Kiyamachi-dori* ☎ *075/352–3823* 🌐 *www.rimnaam.com/english_page.html* 🕒 *Closed Mon.*

## Ca' Del Viale (カ・デル ヴィアーレ)

$$ | ITALIAN | The signature dish at this well-regarded trattoria is handmade pasta topped with a flavorful tomato sauce. Carefully selected organic vegetables and fine Italian ham are among the antipasti stars. **Known for:** outdoor terrace; authentic Italian food; skilled and knowledgeable chefs. $ *Average main: ¥2,800* ⊠ *Senbon, Sanjo Nishi-iru, Kitagawa Nakagyo-ku, Nakagyo-ku* ☎ *075/812–2366* ⊕ *www.watanabechef.com/ca-del-viale* ⊙ *Closed Mon.*

## Café Bibliotic HELLO! (カフェビブリオテックハロー)

$$ | CAFÉ | Leafy banana trees visible from several blocks away mark this airy two-story town-house café that's especially popular at night with young people. Lunch options that include sandwiches, rice dishes, and curries change regularly. **Known for:** casual atmosphere; reasonably priced menu; stylish and cozy. $ *Average main: ¥1,500* ⊠ *Nijo-dori Yanaginobana, Higashi-iru, 650 Haremeicho, Nakagyo-ku* ✛ *North side of Nijo-dori, east of Yanaginobanba-dori* ☎ *075/231–8625* ⊕ *cafe-hello.jp* ⊟ *No credit cards* ⊙ *Closed Mon.*

## Ganko Nijyoen (がんこ高瀬川二条苑)

$$ | JAPANESE | The estate of a former prime minister has been turned into a kaiseki (multicourse-meal) restaurant, and the stroll garden by landscape artist Ogawa Jihei ensures wonderful views by day or night. The century-old traditional structure, between the Kamo and Takase rivers, suits the delicate tasting courses served by kimono-clad women. **Known for:** traditional cuisine; some Maiko performances; garden setting. $ *Average main: ¥3,000* ⊠ *Kiyamachi-dori, Nijo sagaru, Nakagyo-ku* ✛ *On Kiyamachi-dori just south of Nijo-dori* ☎ *075/223–3456* ⊕ *gu-takasegawa.gorp.jp.*

## ★ Giro Giro Hitoshina (枝魯枝魯ひとしな)

$$$ | JAPANESE | Popular Giro Giro has a lively atmosphere, excellent food, and great Takase-gawa River location. Sit at the counter to watch the busy chefs, many of whom have studied at the owner's Paris location, or grab a table upstairs. **Known for:** innovative dishes; convivial atmosphere; ever-changing menu. $ *Average main: ¥4,500* ⊠ *420–7 Nanba-cho, Nishi Kiya-machi-dori, Higashigawa, Matsubarashita, Shimogyo-ku* ☎ *075/343–7070* ⊙ *No lunch.*

## Indépendants (アンデパンダン)

$ | CAFÉ | A great backpacker hangout, this café is especially popular midday, when a devoted clientele of students and artists comes for the cheap, bountiful plate lunches (including curries, salads, and soups), friendly service, live music, and convivial atmosphere. The setting is the former Mainichi Newspaper Building, with its brick-and-plaster basement, colorful mosaic tiles, and exposed masonry. **Known for:** excellent desserts; vintage and stylish interior; hip atmosphere. $ *Average main: ¥980* ⊠ *1928 Bldg., Sanjo-dori and Gokomachi-dori, Nakagyo-ku* ✛ *Southeast corner, 1 block west of Teramachi shopping arcade* ☎ *075/255–4312* ⊕ *cafe-independants. com.*

## Kerala (ケララ)

$$$ | INDIAN | Imported spices and very fresh vegetables are the secrets to this second-floor Indian restaurant's success. Dishes may not be as spicy as you would expect, but the spinach, lamb, and chickpea curries—also the tandoori chicken—are deeply flavorful. **Known for:** hearty Indian food; casual atmosphere; welcoming and kind staff. $ *Average main: ¥3,500* ⊠ *Kawaramachi-dori Sanjo-agaru Nishigawa, Nakagyo-ku* ☎ *075/251–0141.*

## Korean Kitchen Anpan (韓国料理 内房アンパン; *Kankoku Ryori Anpan*)

$ | KOREAN | Authentic and delicious Korean food in the heart of Kyoto. While the presentation and surroundings won't win any prizes, the basic no-frills vibe fits well with the general punchiness of the flavors. **Known for:** central location; hearty homestyle dishes; great service. $ *Average main: ¥1,400* ⊠ *37 Kamanza-cho,*

*Sanjo-dori, Nakagyo-ku* ☎ *075/223–1928* 🌐 *kyotoanpan.web.fc2.com* 🕑 *Closed Sun.*

★ **Mankamero** (萬亀楼)

$$$$ | **JAPANESE** | Since 1722 Mankamero's specialty has been *yusoku ryori*, cuisine intended for members of the Imperial Court. Every step of the meal is incredibly elaborate, down to the ceremonially dressed chef who prepares your dishes using specially made utensils. **Known for:** lively service; imperial cuisine; historic ambience. [$] *Average main: ¥20,000* ✉ *387 Ebisu-cho, Kamigyo-ku* ☎ *075/441–5020* 🌐 *mankamerou.com.*

**Manzaratei Nishiki** (まんざら亭)

$$$ | **JAPANESE** | The unpretentious vibe, the sense of adventure, and the superb cuisine—Japanese-based, with European and other Asian influences—have made Manzaratei a local favorite. Depending on the season, the ample menu includes handmade soba, oven-roasted chicken, or spring rolls with citrusy *ponzu* dressing. **Known for:** innovative cuisine; outdoor dining; friendly atmosphere. [$] *Average main: ¥3,500* ✉ *Karasuma Nishiki-koji, 317 Nishi-iru, Nakagyo Ku, Uradeyama-cho* ✣ *A block north of Shijo-dori and Karasuma-dori intersection* ☎ *075/257–5748* 🌐 *manzara.co.jp/nishiki/cuisine.html* 🕑 *No lunch.*

**Mishima-tei** (三嶋亭)

$$$$ | **JAPANESE** | Five generations of chefs have preserved the delicious *sukiyaki* recipe prepared since 1873 at this restaurant that was among the nation's first to serve beef. A kimono-clad attendant will serve and assist with the dishes cooked at your table. **Known for:** excellent beef; gracious service; vintage vibe. [$] *Average main: ¥8,000* ✉ *405 Sakuranomachi, Teramachi, Sanjo-sagaru, Higashi-iru, Nakagyo-ku* ✣ *South of Sanjo-dori at southeast entrance to Teramachi arcade* ☎ *075/221–0003* 🌐 *mishima-tei.co.jp* 🕑 *Closed Wed.*

**Omen Nippon** (おめん 四条先斗町店)

$$ | **JAPANESE** | This branch of the famed soba noodle shop is convenient to the downtown shopping area, just across the river from Gion. It's a perfect place to drop in for a lunch of udon noodle soup with a liberal sprinkling of sesame seeds. **Known for:** large selection of noodle dishes; casual setting; great service. [$] *Average main: ¥1,500* ✉ *171–1 Kashiwaya-cho, Nakagyo-ku* ✣ *North side of Shiji-dori a little west of Ponto-cho* ☎ *075/253–0377* 🌐 *www.omen.co.jp* 🕑 *Closed Thurs.*

**Ponto-cho Robin** (先斗町魯ビン)

$$$$ | **JAPANESE** | An adventurous menu sets this restaurant inside a 150-year-old town house apart from its competition. The chef here goes to the market daily and improvises based on what's fresh. **Known for:** river views; popular hot-pot dish; stylish presentation. [$] *Average main: ¥7,000* ✉ *137–4 Wakamatsu-cho, Ponto-cho, Nakagyo-ku* ☎ *075/222–8200 direct line, 050/3628–2022 reservation line* 🌐 *www.robin-kyoto.com.*

**Ponto-cho Suishin** (先斗町すいしん)

$ | **JAPANESE** | Nestled along the atmospheric Pontocho Alley, this establishment's black-and-white latticed storefront with a lantern above the door conceals a vegetable lover's paradise. The dining area is raised with sunken seating, allowing customers to view the busy chefs in the open kitchen. **Known for:** local produce; comfortable setting; reasonable prices. [$] *Average main: ¥1,400* ✉ *181 Zaimoku-cho, Ponto-cho, Nakagyo-ku* ☎ *075/221–8596* 🌐 *suishinhonten.gorp.jp.*

**Restaurant Ogawa** (レストラン おがわ)

$$$$ | **FRENCH** | The best in Kyoto-style nouvelle cuisine is served in this intimate spot in the center of town. Dishes depend on the chef's whims as much as on what's in season, but the menu might include buttery, risotto-like rice pilaf topped with delicate sea urchin; duck meat and foie gras in bite-size

portions; and hors d'oeuvres such as oyster gratin, crab-and-scallop stew, and wild mushroom tempura. **Known for:** take-all-you-want dessert tray; chef grants special requests with notice; French and Japanese fusion dishes. $ *Average main: ¥10,260 ⊠ Joy Building 2F, 362 Nijo, Kawaramachi-dori, Nakagyo-ku, Nakagyo-ku ☎ 075/256–2203 ⊕ r-ogawa.com ☾ Closed Tues.*

### Yoshikawa Inn Restaurant (吉川)

$$$$ | **JAPANESE** | Adjacent to an inn of the same name, Yoshikawa serves multi-course kaiseki ryori lunches and dinners. The beautifully presented meal includes soup, vegetables, grilled or baked fish, and a light, crisp tempura that is the house specialty. **Known for:** steeped in tradition; beautiful garden setting; exquisite servings of tempura. $ *Average main: ¥12,500 ⊠ Tomino-koji, Oike-sagaru, Nakagyo-ku ☎ 075/221–5544 ⊕ kyoto-yoshikawa.co.jp/en ☾ Closed Sun.*

### Zezekan Pocchiri (膳處漢 ぽっちり)

$$ | **CHINESE** | A Taisho-era kimono business office and home was meticulously renovated into this restaurant whose Chinese cuisine is prepared as though it were Japanese. The streetside former office is furnished with Chinese tables and chairs and tatami rooms with low tables and cushion seating; some of the areas have views of the well-groomed inner-courtyard garden. **Known for:** Chinese and Japanese fusion dishes; ornate decor; beautiful courtyard. $ *Average main: ¥3,000 ⊠ Nishiki-koji, Muromachi-Nishi-iru, 283–2 Tenjinyama-cho, Nakagyo-ku ☎ 075/257–5766.*

## ☕ Coffee and Quick Bites

### Maeda Coffee Meirin (前田珈琲 明倫店)

$ | **CAFÉ** | The lively café occupies a classroom in a former elementary school the city converted into an arts center. Maeda serves simple fare, an assortment of beverages, and some innovative desserts. **Known for:** arty vibe; housed in former classroom; light fare. $ *Average main: ¥950 ⊠ 546–2 Kyoto Arts Center, Yamabushiyama-cho, Nakagyo Ku, Kyoto ✛ 5-min walk from Karasuma-Shijo intersection ☎ 075/221–2224 ⊕ www.maedacoffee.com/shopinfo/meirin ⊟ No credit cards.*

##  Hotels

### ANA Crowne Plaza Hotel Kyoto (ANAクラウンプラザホテル京都)

$$ | **HOTEL** | Some of the rooms at this Western-style chain property have great views of Nijo Castle, which sits directly across the street, but though reasonably well appointed, they and the public areas are strictly standard issue and hardly atmospheric. **Pros:** popular rooftop beer garden; English-speaking concierge; Nijo Castle views. **Cons:** dated room decor; gym and sauna cost extra; Western chain-property feel. $ *Rooms from: ¥18,000 ⊠ Nijo-jo-mae, Horikawa-dori, Nakagyo-ku, Nakagyo-ku ☎ 075/231–1155 ⊕ www.anacpkyoto.com ⇲ 303 rooms ⦿ No Meals.*

### ★ Hiiragiya Ryokan (柊家旅館)

$$$$ | **B&B/INN** | Founded in 1818 to accommodate provincial lords visiting the capital, this elegant inn is well known for its restrained and subtle beauty. **Pros:** excellent location; multilingual staff; holly-infused soaps and bath oils. **Cons:** fairly expensive; on a busy street; inflexible meal plans. $ *Rooms from: ¥40,000 ⊠ Nakahakusan-cho, Fuyacho-Anekoji-agaru, Nakagyo-ku ☎ 075/221–1136 ⊕ www.hiiragiya.co.jp ⇲ 28 rooms ⦿ All-Inclusive.*

### ★ Hotel Granvia Kyoto (ホテルグランヴィア京都)

$$$$ | **HOTEL** | **FAMILY** | Located at Kyoto Station, the hotel is noteworthy for its good service and fusion of ultramodern design and traditional Japanese style. **Pros:** good location; interesting architecture; amenities-laden. **Cons:** slightly dated in places; main entrance is up a narrow

escalator; charge for pool and gym. [$] *Rooms from: ¥25,000 ✉ Kyoto Station, Karasuma-dori, Shimogyo-ku ☎ 075/344–8888 🌐 www.granviakyoto.com 🛏 535 rooms 🍴 No Meals.*

**Hotel Kanra** (ホテルカンラ京都)
**$$$$** | **HOTEL** | This chic downtown pied-à-terre successfully combines traditional ryokan elements—sliding paper screens, tatami rooms—with some unexpected boutique-hotel touches like the contemporary room design and the lobby aromas that change with the season (citrus when it's cool outside, mint when it's warm). **Pros:**; excellent restaurant with reasonable prices; near subway; on-site electric-bicycle rental. **Cons:** on a busy street; not close to the best restaurants and shopping; smallest rooms may be too snug for some. [$] *Rooms from: ¥30,000 ✉ Shimogyo ku, Rokujo-sagaru, Kyoto ✣ 2-min walk from Gojo subway station ☎ 075/344–3815 🌐 www.uds-hotels.com/en/kanra/kyoto 🛏 29 rooms 🍴 No Meals.*

**K's House Kyoto** (ケイズハウス京都)
**$** | **HOTEL** | Although this hostel is best known as a backpacker getaway, the modern architecture, smart facilities, multilingual staff, and central location make it a great find. **Pros:** bike rentals; affordable all-you can eat buffet; chance to meet fellow travelers. **Cons:** spartan decor; most rooms lack private baths; small rooms. [$] *Rooms from: ¥4600 ✉ 418 Nayacho, Shichijo-agaru, Dotemachi-dori, Shimogyo-ku ☎ 075/342–2444 🌐 kshouse.jp/kyoto-e/index.html 🛏 140 rooms 🍴 No Meals.*

**Kinmata** (斤又)
**$$$$** | **B&B/INN** | Only a few hundred feet from Kyoto's main street of Shijo-dori, the Kinmata has retained its historic character and appeal despite the garish evolution of the surrounding area: stepping into the incense-tinged entranceway to your quiet tatami room slows the pulse and calms the spirit. **Pros:** antique furnishings; great location; welcoming atmosphere. **Cons:** shared bath requires patrons to reserve a bathing time; books up fast (it's best to e-mail to reserve a room); unofficial midnight curfew. [$] *Rooms from: ¥45,000 ✉ Gokomachi Shijo Agaru, Nakagyo-ku ☎ 075/221–1039 ✉ kaiseki@kinmata.com 🌐 www.kinmata.com 🛏 7 rooms with shared bath 🍴 Free Breakfast.*

★ **Kyoto Brighton Hotel**
(京都ブライトンホテル)
**$$$** | **HOTEL** | **FAMILY** | One of the city's best hotels, the Kyoto Brighton has an elegant design, and its staff display a thorough dedication to gracious, efficient hospitality. **Pros:** conscientious staff; free concerts on summer evenings; noteworthy restaurants. **Cons:** area may be too quiet for some; a bit far from Kyoto Station; expensive. [$] *Rooms from: ¥20,000 ✉ Nakadachiuri, Shin-machi-dori, Kamigyo-ku ☎ 075/441–4411 🌐 kyoto.brightonhotels.co.jp 🛏 185 rooms 🍴 No Meals.*

**Kyoto Garden Palace**
(京都ガーデンパレス)
**$$$** | **HOTEL** | Situated just across the road from the Imperial Palace and gardens, the Kyoto Garden Palace is a classically-styled yet unfussy hotel, offering excellent Japanese hospitality plus quiet, clean and comfortable rooms. **Pros:** reasonably priced; great food in the restaurants; exceptional customer service. **Cons:** not so near the station; old-fashioned amenities; rooms can be slightly stuffy. [$] *Rooms from: ¥22,000 ✉ 605 Tatsumae-cho, Shimochojamachi Agaru, Karasuma-dori, Kamigyo-ku ☎ 075/411–0111 🌐 hotelgp-kyoto.com 🛏 99 rooms 🍴 No Meals.*

**Matsubaya Ryokan** (松葉家旅館)
**$$** | **B&B/INN** | This unpretentious ryokan welcomed its first guest, a monk from the nearby Higashi-Hongan-ji Temple, in 1884. **Pros:** friendly staff; plenty of restaurants and convenience stores nearby; tasty breakfast. **Cons:** thin walls; staff speak little English; bland

rooms. $ Rooms from: ¥17,000 ☒ Ka-mijuzuya-machi-dori, Higashi Nito-in, Nishi-iru, Shimogyo-ku ☎ 075/351–3727 ⊕ www.matsubayainn.com ⇄ 8 rooms (7 with bath) ˚⦾˚ No Meals.

### Miyako Hotel Kyoto Hachijo
(都ホテル京都八条)
**$$ | HOTEL | FAMILY |** Directly south of Kyoto Station, this refurbished hotel is more convenient than glamorous. **Pros:** next to Kyoto Station; quiet and convenient; pleasant staff. **Cons:** lacks luxury touches; some rooms showing their age; slightly stuffy decor. $ Rooms from: ¥12,000 ☒ 17 Nishi-Kujoin-cho, Minami-ku ☎ 075/661–7111 ⊕ global.miyakohotels.ne.jp/kyo-to-hachijo ⇄ 988 rooms ˚⦾˚ No Meals.

### Nishiyama Ryokan (西山旅館)
**$$ | B&B/INN |** In a neighborhood with many traditional buildings, this ryo-kan that's an easy distance from the city center has a welcoming staff and serves delightful kaiseki (multicourse) meals. **Pros:** helpful concierge and welcoming staff; flexible meal plans; good food. **Cons:** some rooms have tiny bathrooms; a little expensive for what it is; basic hotel feel. $ Rooms from: ¥17,000 ☒ Gokomachi-dori, Nijo-sagaru, Nakagyo-ku ☎ 075/222–1166 ⊕ www.ryokan-kyoto.com ⇄ 30 rooms ˚⦾˚ Free Breakfast.

### Rihga Royal Hotel Kyoto
(リーガロイヤルホテル京都)
**$$$ | HOTEL | FAMILY |** One of Kyoto's major hotels, recognized for its excellent service and restaurants, the Rihga Royal is a five-minute walk from Kyoto Station, mak-ing it an especially fine choice for those with early train connections. **Pros:** close to Kyoto Station; clean and contemporary feel; excellent restaurants. **Cons:** walls are a little thin; near a busy and noisy inter-section; extra charge for pool and sauna. $ Rooms from: ¥20,000 ☒ 1 Taimatsucho, Shiokoji-sagaru, Higashi Horikawa-dori, Shimogyo-ku ☎ 075/341–1121, 800/877–7107 in U.S. ⊕ www.rihgaroyalkyoto.com ⇄ 494 rooms ˚⦾˚ No Meals.

### The Screen (ホテル ザ・スクリーン)
**$$$ | HOTEL |** Its chic interiors have enabled this boutique hotel near the Imperial Palace to gain a foothold in this competitive market with individu-ally designed suites, each the unique creation of a different renowned local or international interior designer. **Pros:** super stylish; close to shops; most guests feel pampered here. **Cons:** minimalist style does not appeal to everyone; not much English spoken; a bit of a walk from the station. $ Rooms from: ¥20,000 ☒ 640–1 Shimogoryomae-cho, Nakagyo-ku ☎ 075/252–1113 ⊕ www.screen-hotel.jp ⇄ 13 suites ˚⦾˚ No Meals.

### ★ Tawaraya Ryokan (俵屋)
**$$$$ | B&B/INN |** Founded by the Okazaki family more than 300 years ago and now run by the 11th generation, this hotel is justly celebrated for its hospitality, sumptuous but subdued decor, impecca-ble service, and splendid gardens. **Pros:** excellent reputation; impeccable service; superb antiques. **Cons:** must reserve dinner a day in advance; no online reser-vations; extremely expensive. $ Rooms from: ¥50,000 ☒ Fuyacho-Aneyako-ji-agaru, Nakahakusan-cho, Nakagyo-ku ☎ 075/211–5566 ⇄ 18 rooms ˚⦾˚ Free Breakfast.

### ★ Yoshikawa (吉川)
**$$$$ | B&B/INN |** This mid-century yet traditional inn is within walking distance of the downtown shopping area and has authentic sukiya-zukuri style (teahouse architecture): the rooms have views of the landscaped garden. **Pros:** indoor gar-den; fine food; driver available. **Cons:** not the most beautiful part of Kyoto; fixed meal times; expensive. $ Rooms from: ¥30,000 ☒ Tomino-koji, Oike-sagaru, Nakagyo-ku ☎ 075/221–5544 ⊕ kyoto-yo-shikawa.co.jp/en ⇄ 9 rooms ˚⦾˚ Free Breakfast.

**Nightlife**

## BARS
### A-Bar (エイバー)

**PUBS** | This wood-paneled one-room izakaya pub doesn't look like much, but it regularly fills up with expats and locals. Visitors and regulars sit around the communal tables to swap stories and adventures. Watch out for flying bottle caps, though—the staff have a knack for popping open beer bottles with chopsticks. ✉ *Reiho Bulding, Nishi Kiyamachi-dori, Shijo-agaru, 2nd fl., Nakagyo-ku* ✛ *1 block west of Kiyamachi-dori* ☎ *075/213–2129.*

### Yoramu (よらむ)

**WINE BARS** | An Israeli sake aficionado named Yoram stocks an extensive selection of the delicate rice wine, from unfiltered to aged, fruity to dry, all available by the glass. A tasting set of three kinds of sake starts at ¥1,200. The dishes on the menu have all been chosen to complement the libations. By day this cozy bar is a soba shop run by Yoram's partner. ✉ *Nakagyo-Ku, Higashinotoin, Nijo-dori, Higashi-iru, Nakagyo-ku* ✛ *South of Nijo-dori, east of Higashino-toin-dori* ☎ *075/213–1512* ⊕ *sakebar-yoramu.com* ⊘ *Closed Sun.–Tues.*

## LIVE MUSIC
### Bonds Rosary

**LIVE MUSIC** | Performances almost nightly with Japanese and non-Japanese musicians. Seat charge is ¥600, but the cover charge changes with the acts. The venue is on the 3rd floor of the Ohto Building (also read as Kamo-higashi Building), a few buildings north of Shijo-dori on the west side of Yamato-oji-dori. Doors open at 6:30 and performances start at 7:30. ✉ *Ohto Bldg., 234 Nijuikkencho Nawate-dori, 3rd fl., Higashiyama-ku* ☎ *075/285–2859* ⊕ *bondsrosary.com.*

### Indépendants (アンデパンダン)

**LIVE MUSIC** | Trestle tables line the graffiti-covered walls of this basement café-bar that hosts indie rock, jazz, and blues musicians. It's a good place to tap into Kyoto's underground music scene. In the evening you can order simple plates to accompany your beer or wine. ✉ *1928 Bldg., Sanjo-dori and Gokomachi-dori, Nakagyo-ku* ✛ *Southeast corner, 1 block west of Teramachi shopping arcade* ☎ *075/255–4312* ⊕ *www.cafe-independants.com.*

### Taku Taku (ライブハウス磔磔)

**LIVE MUSIC** | An enduring live-music venue that generally presents rock and blues acts, Taku Taku occasionally hosts well-known Japanese performers. You can find it in an old *kura,* or storehouse, in the backstreets southwest of the Takashimaya department store. ✉ *Tominokoji-dori, Bukkoji-sagaru, Shimogyo-ku* ☎ *075/351–1321* ⊕ *www.geisya.or.jp/~takutaku.*

### UrBANGUILD

**LIVE MUSIC** | The atmosphere is very "New York experimental theater" at this multidisciplinary venue for music, dance, video, and other performances about 20 nights a month. Events are from ¥2,000 and the cover charge includes a drink; you can also order snacks and light meals. ✉ *New Kyoto Bldg., Nakagyo Ku, Kiyamachi, Sanjo Shita, 3rd fl., Kyoto* ✛ *East side of Kiyamachi, 2 blocks south of Sanjo-dori; 5-min walk from bus stops on Kawaramachi Shijo or Sanjo* ☎ *075/212–1125* ⊕ *www.urbanguild.net.*

## 🎭 Performing Arts

## NOH
### Kongo Noh Theater
(金剛能楽堂; *Kongo Nogaku-do*)

**THEATER** | This theater presenting performances of the Kongo school of Noh drama was moved to this location on the former estate of an aristocrat. The architecture is completely modern, but the garden—there's a view of it from the lobby—is completely traditional. English translations of the librettos are often available. ✉ *Karasuma-dori, Ichijo-sagaru, Kamigyo-ku* ✛ *Just south of Imadegawa* *subway stop* ☎ *075/441–7222* ⊕ *www.kongou-net.com* 🎟 *¥2,500–¥7,000.*

## SEASONAL DANCE AND TRADITIONAL PERFORMANCES

**Ponto-cho Kabukirenjo Theater** (先斗町歌舞伎練場)

THEATER | The maiko and geiko of the Ponto-cho district perform at this theater in spring and fall. Occasionally other dance performances are scheduled here. ✉ *Ponto-cho, Sanjo-sagaru, Nakagyo-ku* ☎ *075/221–2025* ⊕ *en.kamogawa-odori.com/kaburenjou* 🎟 *¥2,000–¥6,000.*

 # Shopping

## ART AND ANTIQUES

Teramachi-dori (寺町通り), between Oike-dori and Marutamachi-dori in Nakagyo-ku, is known for antiques of all kinds and tea-ceremony utensils.

**Gallery Utsuwa-kan** (ギャラリー器館)

ART GALLERIES | Kyoto's hottest place to see contemporary arts and crafts—mostly ceramics but also glass—displays works on four floors. Though young, the artists represented already have established reputations. The gallery, whose name means "containers," is in just south of Daitoku-ji Temple. Packaging and shipping can be arranged. ✉ *20–17 Murasakino Higashino Cho, Kyoto Kita Ku, Kyoto* ⊕ *Bus 204, 205, or 206 to Diatoku-ji-mae stop, or 1-min walk from temple* ☎ *075/493–4521* ⊕ *www.g-utsu-wakan.com.*

## DEPARTMENT STORES

**Daimaru Department Store** (大丸)

DEPARTMENT STORE | This large department store is known for high-quality merchandise—cosmetics, clothing, furniture, kitchenwares, and other products that appeal to more expensive and conservative tastes. International shipping is available. An exhibition hall and several galleries are worth checking out, as are sections displaying traditional crafts. In the basement are prepared foods, breads, cakes, wine, and other edibles.

✉ *Shijo-Karasuma, Shimogyo-ku* ⊕ *1-min walk from Karasuma Station (Hankyu-Kyoto train), 2-min walk from Shijo Station (Karasuma subway)* ☎ *075/211–8111* ⊕ *www.daimaru.co.jp/kyoto.*

**Fujii Daimaru Department Store** (藤井大丸)

DEPARTMENT STORE | This store focuses on trendy fashions but caters to all ages. Many locals favor the basement food market for its reasonable prices and wine selection. ✉ *Shijo-Teramachi, Shimogyo-ku* ⊕ *2-min walk from Kawaramachi Station (Hankyu-Kyoto train), 5-min walk from Shijo Station (Karasuma subway)* ☎ *075/211–8181* ⊕ *www.fujiidaimaru.co.jp.*

**Isetan** (伊勢丹)

DEPARTMENT STORE | The 13-story Isetan, in the Kyoto Station Building, is a branch of its Tokyo-based cousin. The feel here is slightly less exclusive than in Tokyo. The store sells high-quality goods and has a well-attended exhibition hall. Many of the restaurants have city views. ✉ *Kyoto Station Bldg., Karasuma-dori, Shimogyo-ku* ⊕ *Kyoto Station Karasuma subway* ☎ *075/352–1111* ⊕ *www.mistore.jp/store/kyoto.html.*

**Takashimaya Department Store** (高島屋)

DEPARTMENT STORE | Another of Kyoto's favorite department stores, Takashimaya specializes in luxury goods and designer fashions. You'll find an accommodating, English-speaking staff and a convenient money-exchange counter. The top floor has bargain merchandise, and another floor is filled with restaurants to revive the shop weary. The exhibition hall and galleries are also worth a visit, as is the basement gourmet food market. ✉ *Shijo-Kawaramachi, Shimogyo-ku* ☎ *075/221–8811* ⊕ *www.takashimaya.co.jp/kyoto.*

## FOLK CRAFTS

**Kuraya Hashimoto** (蔵屋はしもと)

OTHER SPECIALTY STORE | One of Kyoto's best collections of antique and newly forged swords is fittingly located on a

corner south of Nijo Castle. Authentic swords are not for sale, but sword paraphernalia and related items are on display. ✉ *Nishihorikawa-dori, southeast corner of Nijo-jo, Nakagyo-ku* ☎ *075/811–4645* ⊕ *www.kurayahashimoto.com.*

### Ryushido (龍枝堂)

STATIONERY | One-room Ryushido sells exquisite paper products for calligraphers: paper of varying thicknesses, writing brushes, ink sticks, ink stones, and paperweights. The shop has a classic, artisanal feel. ✉ *Nijo-agaru, Tera-machi-dori, Kamigyo-ku* ☎ *075/252–4120.*

### Yamato Mingei-ten (やまと民芸店)

CRAFTS | The ceramics, glass, basketry, lacquerware, and other objects sold here are made with such artistry that only their utilitarian nature nudges them into the craft, as opposed to fine art, category. The owner keeps the prices reasonable so these beautiful things will be appreciated and used daily. ✉ *Kawaramachi-dori, Takoyakushi-agaru, Nakagyo-ku* ☎ *075/221–2641* ⊕ *yamatomingeiten.jimdofree.com.*

## INCENSE

### Kyukyodo (鳩居堂)

CRAFTS | In an attractive traditional building, this shop has been in business for 330 years, specializing in stationery, brushes for calligraphy, and incense, some of which (aloeswood) is more expensive than gold. ✉ *Nakagyo-ku, Teramachi-dori, Oike sagaru, opposite Nishi-Hongan-ji-mae, Shimogyo-ku* ✣ *In covered shopping arcade of Teramachi* ☎ *075/231–0510* ⊕ *www.kyukyodo.co.jp.*

## KIMONOS AND ACCESSORIES

Shimmering new silk kimonos can cost more than ¥1,000,000—they are art objects, as well as couture—while equally stunning old silk kimonos can cost less than ¥3,000. You can find used kimonos at some local end-of-the-month temple markets.

### Aizen Kobo (愛染工房)

OTHER SPECIALTY STORE | Fine handwoven and hand-dyed indigo textiles are this shop's specialty. The indigo plant is grown only in one place in Japan nowadays, and Aizen Kobo makes exclusive use of that product crafting cloth and garments in this rich deep-blue color. The owner dyes the cloth and his wife, Hisako Utsuki, designs. ✉ *Omiya Nishi-iru, Nakasuji-dori, Kamigyo-ku* ☎ *075/441–0355* ⊕ *www.aizenkobo.jp.*

### Fuuka Kimono (風香)

MIXED CLOTHING | Tucked away on a quiet side-street, this small store offers kimono and yukata rentals for men and women at very reasonable prices, with a decent selection of items available for purchase too. The friendly English-speaking staff are knowledgable and patient, and will ensure that you are wearing everything correctly. ✉ *Koya Building 3F, 302 Aya-horikawa-cho, Shimogyo-ku* ☎ *075/802–0511* ⊕ *www.fuukakimono-store.com* ⊘ *Closed weekends.*

### Kasagen (かさ源)

OTHER SPECIALTY STORE | A thing of beauty more than utility in Japan, traditional umbrellas provide protection from the scorching sun and pelting rain. Since 1861, Kasagen has produced beautiful oiled-paper umbrellas that are guaranteed to last for years. ✉ *112 Shinyodo-mae-cho, Kamigyo-ku, Higashiyama-ku* ☎ *075/203–0134* ⊕ *kasagen.jp.*

### Miyawaki Baisen-an (宮脇賣扇庵)

CRAFTS | The famous fan shop Miyawaki Baisen-an has been in business since 1823, delighting customers not only with its fine collection of lacquered, scented, painted, and paper fans, but also with the old-world atmosphere of the shop itself. ✉ *Tominokoji Higashi-iru, Rokkaku-dori, Nakagyo-ku* ☎ *075/221–0181* ⊕ *www.baisenan.co.jp.*

## MARKETS
### Nishiki-koji (錦小路)
MARKET | Kyoto's central food market is located elsewhere, but restaurateurs and housewives visit this long, narrow street to select fresh produce and other foods. In recent years, the covered arcade has started to include souvenir shops in addition to tempting edibles. Ogling is fine. At some places you might be offered samples. If that happens, don't be shy—have a taste. ⊠ *Nishiki-koji-dori, Nakagyo-ku.*

### Tokyu Hands (東急ハンズ)
HOUSEWARES | This popular store, part of a national chain, has four floors of uniquely designed items you didn't know you needed until you saw them—from kitchen utensils to bath products, brush-pens, and traditional products. ⊠ *Kyoto* ✛ *On the south side of Shijo-dori, one block east of Karasuma-dori* ☎ *075/254–3109* ⊕ *kyoto.tokyu-hands.co.jp.*

## TEMPLE MARKETS
### Kitano Tenman-gu (北野天満宮)
SOUVENIRS | On the 25th of each month, the streets around the shrine grounds overflow with all sorts of goods: used clothing and kimonos, food, plants, furniture, Buddhist images, dolls—just about everything you can imagine. Bargaining with a smile often brings good results. ⊠ *Imakoji-agaru, Onmae-dori, Kamigyo-ku.*

### To-ji (東寺)
SOUVENIRS | One of the two largest temple markets takes place on the 21st of each month. Vendors arrive early and set up by 7 or 8 am. Hundreds of stalls display fans, kimonos, antiques, potted plants, herbs, and newly designed clothing. Bring a pencil and paper to help you bargain down the price. The temple also hosts a smaller antiques market on the first Sunday of the month. ⊠ *1 Kujo-cho, Minami-ku.*

# Southern Kyoto

The most interesting southern Kyoto sights are three religious structures: Byodo-in, Fushimi-Inari Taisha, and Tofuku-ji. A UNESCO World Heritage site, Byodo-in is a 40-minute train ride south of Kyoto in Uji, whose other religious sites include Kosho-ji, a quiet Zen temple, and Ujiga-mijinja, another World Heritage site. Uji is one of Japan's major tea-producing districts, as evident by all the tea shops lining the streets. Stop in and sample this fine green tea brewed at a temperature guaranteed to enhance its flavor. The tourist information center has maps in English. Both Fushimi-Inari Taisha and the Temple Daigo-ji in southern Kyoto are on mountains with trails to explore.

**Access:** The temples and shrines in southern Kyoto are far from one another, so traveling time can eat into your day. If you visit Tofuku-ji, consider combining it with a visit to Fushimi-Inari Taisha, farther south. Uji City can easily take the thorough traveler an entire day, too. To get to Uji, take the JR Nara Line or the Keihan Line to Uji Station.

##  Sights

### ★ Byodo-in Temple (平等院)
TEMPLE | In 1083 the Fujiwara no Yorimichi, a member of a very powerful clan, built this villa, a UNESCO World Heritage site whose image graces the face of ¥10 coins. The main building, the Amida-do, is known as the Phoenix Hall, owing to the sweep of its curved roofline. A large statue of Amida Buddha, compassionate and benevolent, sits in repose as he views those below him. Small mounted images of *bosatsu* (enlightened beings) drift through clouds, playing instruments and dancing, an 11th-century image of paradise. The landscaped garden and pond reflect Amida's paradise. A video in the museum takes viewers back a millennium to demonstrate what the original bright

colors would have looked like. Other small images of the 52 small wooden *kuyo* or reverent bosatsu have been put on display here. ✉ *116 Ujirenge, Uji* ✆ *12-min walk east toward river from Uji Station* ☎ *0774/21–2861* ⊕ *www.byodoin.or.jp* 🎟 *¥600; additional ¥300 for Phoenix Hall.*

## Daigo-ji Temple (醍醐寺)

TEMPLE | Goju-no-to, the five-story main pagoda of the Daigo-ji Temple complex, dates from AD 951 and is reputed to be the oldest existing structure in Kyoto. Daigo-ji, which includes many subtemples, was founded in AD 874 in the Eastern Mountains foothills in what is now the southeastern suburb of Yamashina Ward. Many of the smaller temples, along with the pagoda, can be found on the lower, entry level, with more up a long stone stairway that takes 45 minutes to ascend.

By the late 16th century the Daigo-ji enclave had begun to decline in importance, and its buildings showed signs of neglect. The warlord Toyotomi Hideyoshi paid a visit when the cherry trees were in bloom, and their beauty so delighted him that he ordered the complex restored. Among the notable subtemples is Sanbo-in, a 1598 reconstruction commissioned by Hideyoshi of a temple built here in 1115. The present structure has a Momoyama-period thatched roof; displayed inside are colorful, gold-leaf paintings of Chinese village scenes. The adjacent multistone garden combines elements of a *chisen-kaiyu* (stroll garden with a pond) and a *karesansui* (dry garden). Visitors cannot stroll the main garden, but a newer one to the left of the entrance can be entered.

Daigo-ji holds the Daigo-ichi, a monthly bazaar held on the 29th, with food and clothing stalls that line the temple walkways. ✉ *22 Higashi Oji-cho, Fushimi-ku* ✆ *Take Tozai subway to Daigo Station and walk 10 min* ☎ *075/571–0002* ⊕ *www. daigoji.or.jp/guide_fee_e.html* 🎟 *¥800 for lower level; ¥500 for upper level.*

# Hidden Christians ◉

Japan's so-called Hidden Christians are descended from early converts to Christianity as introduced to Japan in 1549 by the Spanish Jesuit missionary Francis Xavier. Christianity initially flourished under the warlord Oda Nobunaga, but after his death the edicts of 1614 and 1640 outlawed the religion. Churches were burned, Christians were executed (or exiled), and a system to ferret out remaining Christians was instituted. An estimated 150,000 Christians went underground at this time, only beginning to reemerge in the Meiji period.

## ★ Fushimi Inari Shrine

(伏見稲荷大社; *Fushimi-Inari Taisha*)
RELIGIOUS BUILDING | This shrine's thousands of red gates may well be the quintessential image of Japan. The gates line the path up the mountainside, parted at irregular intervals by shrines, altars, mausoleums, and hundreds of foxes in stone and bronze. This is the central headquarters for 40,000 shrines nationally that pay tribute to Inari, the god of rice, sake, and prosperity. As Japan's economic focus shifted from agriculture to other businesses, Inari was adopted as the patron deity of any kind of entrepreneurial venture—the gates in the path are donated by businesses from around the country seeking a blessing. Walking the whole circuit takes about two hours, a bit longer if you stop at the shops selling snacks along the way. Hikers can continue up the path and follow it along the Higashiyama Range and into central Kyoto. ✉ *68 Fukakusa Yabu-no-uchi-cho, Fushimi-ku* ✆ *Take JR Nara Line to Inari Station or Keihan Railway to Fushimi-Inari Station* 🎟 *Free.*

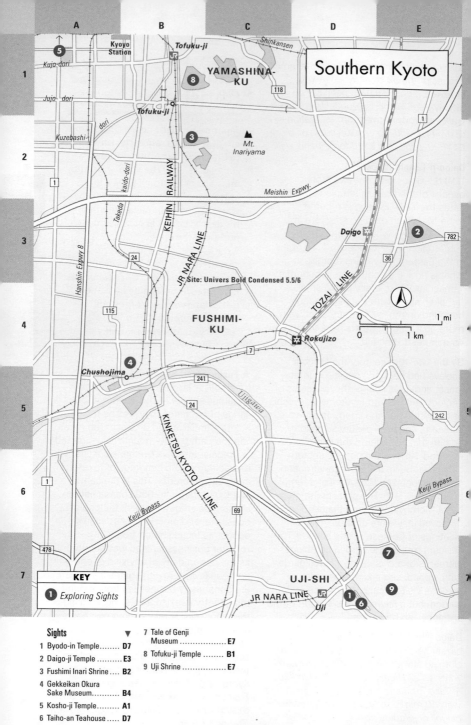

Southern Kyoto

A
B
C
D
E

1
Kujo-dori
Kyoyo Station
Tofuku-ji
YAMASHINA-KU
Shinkansen
118

2
Jujo-dori
Tofuku-ji
Kuzebashi-
dori
3
Mt. Inariyama
Meishin Expwy.

3
kaido-dori
Takeda
KEIHIN RAILWAY
JR NARA LINE
24
115
Site: Univers Bold Condensed 5.5/6
Daigo
2
782
36
TOZAI LINE

4
Hanshin Expwy 8
FUSHIMI-KU
7
Rokujizo
0        1 mi
0        1 km

5
Chushojima
4
KINKETSU KYOTO LINE
241
24
Ujigawa
242

6
1
Keiji Bypass
69
Keiji Bypass

7
478
KEY
1 Exploring Sights
UJI-SHI
JR NARA LINE
Uji
1
6
9
7

Sights ▼

1 Byodo-in Temple........ D7
2 Daigo-ji Temple .......... E3
3 Fushimi Inari Shrine .... B2
4 Gekkeikan Okura
   Sake Museum........... B4
5 Kosho-ji Temple......... A1
6 Taiho-an Teahouse ..... D7
7 Tale of Genji
   Museum .................. E7
8 Tofuku-ji Temple ........ B1
9 Uji Shrine ................. E7

## Gekkeikan Okura Sake Museum (月桂冠大倉記念館; *Gekkeikan Okura Kinenkan*)

**BREWERY** | Not far from the Fushimi-Inari Shrine lies a district of high-walled sake breweries and warehouses, some dating to the early Edo period—Gekkeikan, founded in 1637, is one of the oldest and best known. Its museum displays many artifacts connected to the brewing process. The admission fee includes a tasting and small bottle of sake or plum wine. Fushimi is noted for its pure springs. If your water bottle is empty, fill it up at the on-site well. ⊠ *247 Minamihama-cho, Fushimi-ku* ✚ *5-min walk from Keihan Line's Chushojima Station, 10-min walk from Kintetsu Kyoto Line's Momoyama Goryo-mae Station* ☎ *075/623–2056* ⊕ *www.gekkeikan.co.jp* ⊠ *¥600.*

## Kosho-ji Temple (興聖寺)

**TEMPLE** | One of the few Soto sect Zen temples in Kyoto, Kosho-ji was founded in the 13th century in Kyoto, where it remained until it burned down four centuries later. The temple was rebuilt in Uji in the 17th century from timber provided by the Tokugawa shogunate, and it has remained unchanged ever since. The Chinese influence is evident in the architecture and dolphin finials gracing the roof. Kosho-ji, across the river from Byodo-in and upriver from Uji-gami Shrine, is popular in spring for its azaleas and in autumn for its maple trees. Walk a ways on the loop trail to the right of the temple for a view of Uji City. ⊠ *2–7–1 Yamada, Uji* ☎ *0774/21-2040* ⊕ *uji-koush-ouji.jp* ⊠ *Free.*

## Taiho-an Teahouse (対鳳庵)

**VIEWPOINT** | Uji is renowned throughout Japan for its excellent tea, and this teahouse along the picturesque banks of the Uji River is a fine place to enjoy a cup of the green variety with a seasonal Japanese sweet. To experience a full tea ceremony, you must book it in advance. ⊠ *1-5 Ujitogawa, Uji* ☎ *0774/23–3334.*

## Tale of Genji Museum (源氏物語ミュージアム; *Genji Monogatari Myujiamu*)

**HISTORY MUSEUM** | *The Tale of Genji* is an 11th-century literary masterpiece that depicts the life of an imperial prince. The final chapters, set in the Uji region, are commonly referred to as the Uji-Jujo, or the Ten Uji Chapters. The museum offers a glimpse into this classic epic through life-size displays, colorful murals, and interesting related videos, as well as temporary seasonal exhibits. ⊠ *45–26 Uji-Higashiuchi, Uji* ✚ *Take Keihan-Uji train to Uji Station and walk east 8 mins* ☎ *774/39–9300* ⊠ *¥600.*

## Tofuku-ji Temple (東福寺)

**TEMPLE** | The immense Sanmon Gate at the west entrance of Tofuku-ji, a Rinzai Zen temple, is the oldest gate in Japan and one of three approaches to this medieval complex of 24 temples. Modeled after its counterpart at Todai-ji, in Nara, the 72-foot-high gate was destroyed several times over the years by fire. The gate was disassembled and reconstructed in 1978. Entry is not permitted through the gate, but you can observe it up close.

Tofuku-ji was established in 1236 and ranks, along with Myoshin-ji and Daitoku-ji, among the most important temples in Kyoto. Arranged around the main hall are four contrasting gardens (separate admission), both dry gravel and landscaped, including a stroll garden. The Heavenly Way Bridge that spans a maple-filled ravine is one of Kyoto's most popular autumn viewing spots. The gardens in the Hojo (abbot's quarters), completed in 1939, were the first large-scale commission of Shigemori Mirei, a famous garden designer. ⊠ *15–777 Hon-machi, Higashiyama-ku* ✚ *Take Bus 88 or 208 from Kyoto Station to Tofuku-ji stop and walk 12 min, or JR Nara or Keihan train to Tofuku-ji Station and walk southeast 15 min* ☎ *075/561–0087* ⊕ *www.tofukuji.jp* ⊠ *¥600 temple; ¥500 gardens.*

Kinkaku-ji was burned down in 1950 and was rebuilt in 1955; its top two stories were covered in gold leaf.

**Uji Shrine** (宇治神社; *Uji Jinja*)

RELIGIOUS BUILDING | Across the river from Byodo-in, this small Shinto shrine is known for its rabbit motifs. It can be reached by walking along the Sawarabi-no-michi, a picturesque winding road which also leads a little further on to the larger Ujigami Jinja, said to be the oldest remaining Shinto shrine in Japan. ⊠ *1 Yamada, Uji* ⊹ *A 10-min walk from Keihan Uji Station, or a 15-min walk from JR Uji Station* ☏ *0774/21-3041* ⊕ *www.uji-jinja. com* ⊡ *Free.*

# Western Kyoto

Western Kyoto's most iconic sights are the opulent golden temple at Kinkaku-ji and the dazzling rock garden at Ryoan-ji, but the city's western precincts are filled with remarkable religious architecture. The sprawling temple complexes Daitoku-ji and Myoshin-ji are well worth a visit, as is the blossom-covered Kitano Tenman-gu, which hosts a fabulous market each month.

**Access:** The sights in the northern and western parts of this area can be reached easily using city buses. For the Katsura Imperial Villa, rail is best; and to reach Koinzan Saiho-ji, you can take Kyoto Bus 73 from Kyoto Station.

 Sights

**Daitoku-ji Temple** (大徳寺)

TEMPLE | This major temple complex of the Rinzai sect of Zen Buddhism dates from 1319, but fires during the Onin Civil War destroyed it in 1468. Most buildings now here were erected under the patronage of the warlord Toyotomi Hideyoshi in the late 16th century. The four subtemples below are open to visitors much of the year, and several others are open during the spring and autumn.

**Daisen-in** is best known for its Muromachi-era garden, attributed to Soko Kogaku (1465–1548). The rock-and-gravel garden

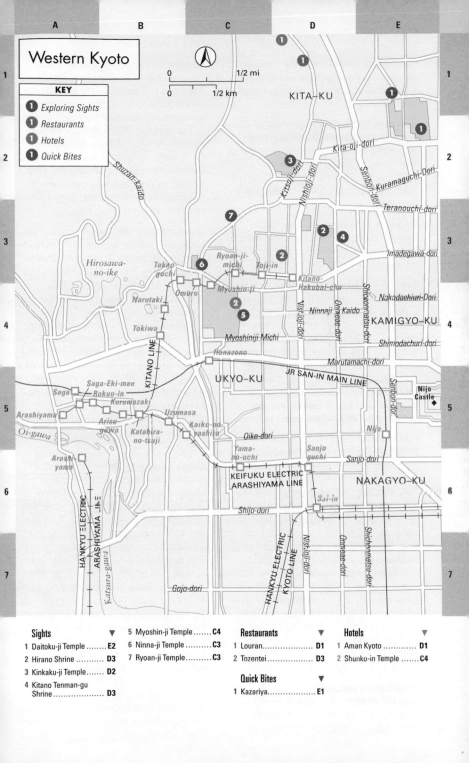

# Western Kyoto

**KEY**

1 Exploring Sights
1 Restaurants
1 Hotels
1 Quick Bites

KITA-KU

Kita-oji-dori

Kuramaguchi-Dori

Teranouchi-dori

Imadegawa-dori

Hirosawa-no-ike

Taka-guchi

Ryoan-ji-michi

Toji-in

Kitano-Hakubai-cho

Nakadachiuri-Dori

KAMIGYO-KU

Omuro

Myoshin-ji

Narutaki

Ninnaji Kaido

Shimodachiuri-dori

Tokiwa

Myoshinji Michi

Marutamachi-dori

Hanazono

UKYO-KU

JR SAN-IN MAIN LINE

Nijo Castle

Saga-Eki-mae

Rokuo-in

Saga

Kurumazaki

Uzumasa

Nijo

Arashiyama

Arisu-gawa

Katahira-no-tsuji

Kaiko-no-yashiro

Oike-dori

Oi-gawa

Yama-no-uchi

Sanjo-guchi

Sanjo-dori

Arashi-yama

Saiin

NAKAGYO-KU

KEIFUKU ELECTRIC ARASHIYAMA LINE

Shijo-dori

Gojo-dori

**Sights** ▼

1 Daitoku-ji Temple ........ **E2**
2 Hirano Shrine ........... **D3**
3 Kinkaku-ji Temple ....... **D2**
4 Kitano Tenman-gu Shrine .................. **D3**
5 Myoshin-ji Temple ....... **C4**
6 Ninna-ji Temple ......... **C3**
7 Ryoan-ji Temple ......... **C3**

**Restaurants** ▼

1 Louran .................... **D1**
2 Tozentei ................. **D3**

**Quick Bites** ▼

1 Kazariya .................. **E1**

**Hotels** ▼

1 Aman Kyoto ............. **D1**
2 Shunko-in Temple ....... **C4**

depicts the flow of life in the movement of a river, swirling around rocks, over a waterfall, and finally into an ocean of nothingness.

**Ryogen-in** has five small gardens of gravel, stone, and moss. The Ah-Un garden includes a stone with ripples emanating from it, symbolizing the cycle of life, from the "ah" sound said at birth to the "un" said at death, encompassing all in between.

**Koto-in** is famous for its long, maple tree–lined approach and the single stone lantern central to the main moss-carpeted garden.

**Zuiho-in** has Hidden Christian roots. Its rock garden suggests an abstract cross; a statue of Mary is supposedly buried under the stone lantern in an adjacent garden. ⊠ *53 Murasakino Daitokuji-cho, Kita-ku* ⊹ *Take Karasuma subway to Kita-oji Station and walk west 15 min, or take Bus 12, 204, 206, and others west on Kitaoji-dori to Daitokuji-mae stop* ☎ *075/491–0019* ✆ *Free to grounds; subtemples ¥350–¥500 each.*

**Hirano Shrine** (平野神社; *Hirano Jinja*)
RELIGIOUS BUILDING | The gorgeous cherry blossoms at this modest shrine near Kinkaku-ji have been the focus of an annual spring festival since AD 985. The pale-pink petals contrast with vermilion lanterns lining the lanes of the Heian-style complex. The shrine was brought here from Nagaoka, the country's capital after Nara and before Kyoto. The four buildings open for touring date from the 17th century. Installed next to a 400-year-old camphor tree is a huge magnetic boulder from Iwate Prefecture, chosen for the power it is said to contain. ⊠ *1 Miyamo-to-cho, Hirano, Kita-ku* ⊹ *Take Bus 50 or 205 to Kinugasako-mae* ☎ *075/461–4450* ⊕ *www.hiranojinja.com* ✆ *Free.*

★ **Kinkaku-ji Temple** (金閣寺)
TEMPLE | Possibly the world's most ostentatious retirement cottage, the magnificent gold-sheathed Kinkaku-ji

(Temple of the Golden Pavilion) was commissioned by Shogun Yoshimitsu Ashikaga (1358–1409). He erected the villa in 1393 in anticipation of the time when he would retire from active politics to manage the affairs of state through the new shogun, his 10-year-old son. On Yoshimitsu's death his son followed his father's wishes and converted the villa into a temple. The grounds were designed in a stroll-garden style favored by 11th-century aristocrats.

The current temple was reconstructed in the 1950s after a monk set fire to the standing structure. The monk's internal conflict is the focus of Yukio Mishima's 1956 famous novel *Temple of the Golden Pavilion,* published the year after construction had finished. Corresponding to Yoshimitsu's original vision, the top two stories are coated with gold leaf, a spectacular sight when reflected in the pond's still waters. Kinkaku-ji is one of 17 Kyoto-area locations collectively designated a UNESCO World Heritage site. ⊠ *1 Kinkaku-ji-cho, Kita-ku* ⊹ *Take Bus 12, 59, 101, 102, 204, or 205 to Kinkaku-ji-mae* ☎ *075/461-0013* ⊕ *www.shokoku-ji.jp/ kinkakuji* ✆ *¥400.*

**Kitano Tenman-gu Shrine** (北野天満宮)
RELIGIOUS BUILDING | A Shinto shrine of major importance to the city, Kitano Tenman-gu is famous for the hundreds of plum trees on its grounds. Built in AD 947 to honor Sugawara no Michizane, a celebrated scholar and politician, this was the first shrine in Japan where a person was enshrined as a deity. It is also well-known to students, who come to ask the gods' help in passing exams. On the 25th of every month, Tenjin-san, streets around the shrine turn into a huge market. Treasures, old and new, food, bonsai, gadgets, and other items delight throngs of shoppers. ⊠ *Imako-ji-agaru, Onmae-dori, Kamigyo-ku* ⊹ *Take Bus 50, 101, or 203 to Kitano Tenman-gu-mae* ⊕ *kitanotenmangu.or.jp* ✆ *Free, Treasure House ¥800.*

## Did You Know?

The famous Ryoan-ji is a dry garden that consists of just 15 rocks arranged in three groupings and surrounded by gravel. In Buddhist philosophy the number 15 signifies completeness, but only 14 rocks are visible from any particular viewpoint in the garden.

## Myoshin-ji Temple (妙心寺)

**TEMPLE** | A Zen temple complex with 47 subtemples, Myoshin-ji contains many valuable treasures. One of them, a painting of a coiling, writhing dragon by Tan'yu (1602–74), a major artist of the Kano school of painting, graces the ceiling of the main temple's Hatto lecture hall. The dragon, a revered animal in Asia, symbolizes might and success. You can apply at the hall for a 20-minute tour of it and the temple's bathhouse, where after scraping off the grime loosened by the heat and steam, monks rinsed off with buckets of water that flowed down the slanted floors.

Japan's oldest bell is in daily use in Myoshin-ji, having tolled out the hour for meditation since 698. Shunko-in, one of the 47 subtemples, has a Hidden Christian bell. Made in Portugal in 1577, the bell was placed in Nanban-ji Church, Kyoto's first Christian church. Established in 1576, the church was the center of Catholic missionary activity until eligious persecution brought about its destruction in 1587. ✉ *1 Hanazono Myoshinji-cho, Ukyo-ku* ✛ *From Sanjo-Keihan Station take Bus 62, 63, 65 or 66 to Myoshin-ji-mae stop, or JR Sagano train to Hanazono* ☎ *075/461–5226* ⊕ *www.myoshinji. or.jp/english* ✉ *¥700.*

## Ninna-ji Temple (仁和寺)

**TEMPLE** | Immense images of temple guardians are enclosed on both sides of the massive gate here. With a five-tier pagoda at its center, Ninna-ji has grounds filled with late-blooming cherry trees that attract crowds every May. Emperor Omuro's palace stood on this site in the late 9th century, but the buildings you see today were constructed in the 17th century. The Hondo (Main Hall), moved here from the Imperial Palace, is the home of the Omura School of Ikebana. A miniature version of Shikoku island's 88-temple pilgrimage wends it way up the mountain behind the complex. The walk takes about an hour. Ninna-ji,

a UNESCO World Heritage site, is a 10-minute walk west of Ryoan-ji and a 5-minute walk northwest of Myoshin-ji's north gate. ✉ *33 Ouchi Omuro, Ukyo-ku* ✛ *Take Bus 26 or 59 to Omuro-ninna-ji, or JR Sagano train to Hanazono-cho* ☎ *075/461–1155* ⊕ *www.ninnaji.jp/en* ✉ *¥500.*

## ★ Ryoan-ji Temple (龍安寺)

**GARDEN** | The arrangement of stones amid the raked sand of this temple's rock garden is appropriately solemn for a National Treasure and UNESCO World Heritage site. The simple composition, a photograph in many schoolchildren's textbooks, can be viewed as a contemplative oasis or a riddle to challenge the mind. From any single vantage point, only 14 of the 15 stones can be seen. In the Buddhist tradition the number 15 signifies completion, and the garden's message is interpreted by many to be that completion is not possible in this world. As mystical as the experience is for some visitors, first-timers may find themselves mystified at the garden's fame. This is a setting that changes with every viewing, reflecting the maturity of the onlooker as years pass. The stroll garden beyond the temple building remains much as it was originally designed in the 11th century. ✉ *13 Goryoshita-cho, Ryoan-ji, Ukyo-ku* ✛ *Take Bus 50 or 55 to Ritsumeikan-daigaku-mae stop, Bus 59 to Ryoan-ji-mae stop, or Keifuku Kitano train to Ryoan-jimichi* ☎ *075/463–2216* ⊕ *www.ryoanji. jp/smph/eng* ✉ *¥500.*

# 🍴 Restaurants

## Louran (楼蘭)

**$$** | **CHINESE FUSION** | Exquisite Chinese fare is presented French-style at a wooded resort in Kyoto's northwestern quadrant. The chefs focus on the cuisines of four regions—Szechuan, Guangdong, Shanghai, and Beijing—and the meals are served graciously in dining areas decorated with black carved Chinese furnishings. **Known for:** fantastic service; beautiful grounds; eclectic dishes. $ *Average main: ¥2,100* ✉ *Shozan Resort Kyoto, Kita Ku, Gentaku Ishi cho 27, Kyoto* ✛ *15-min taxi ride from Kitaoji subway station or 20-min walk from Gentaku-mae bus stop on Kitaoji* ☎ *075/491–5101* ⊕ *sho-zan.co.jp/restaurant/louran.html.*

### Tozentei (陶然亭)

$$$$ | **JAPANESE** | Nestled among the backstreets of northwest Kyoto, Tozentei emphasizes to-the-letter traditional Japanese cooking. The meals here, made with only local produce, are old-school enough to please a shogun. **Known for:** innovative dishes; beautiful tableware; vintage atmosphere. $ *Average main: ¥10,000* ✉ *31–1 Komatsubara Minami-machi, Kita-ku* ☎ *075/461–7866.*

## ☕ Coffee and Quick Bites

### Kazariya (かざりや)

$ | **JAPANESE** | Kazariya has been serving tea and *aburi mochi*—charcoal-grilled and skewered rice-flour cakes dipped in sweet miso sauce—for centuries. You can enjoy the treats under the eaves of 17th-century houses as you watch visitors proceeding to and from the Imamiya Shrine. **Known for:** rustic setting; traditional snacks; relaxation spot. $ *Average main: ¥500* ✉ *96 Murasakino Imamiya-cho, Kita-ku* ☎ *075/491–9402* 🚫 *No credit cards* ⊗ *Closed most Wed.*

## 🛏 Hotels

### ★ Aman Kyoto (アマン京都)

$$$$ | **HOTEL** | Tucked away in the hills not far from the Golden Pavilion, Aman Kyoto is one of the city's finest establishments, surrounded by an expansive forest garden of green moss-covered lawns and cobbled stone footpaths. **Pros:** rooms and facilities ooze with high-end class; stunning natural garden setting; outstandingly friendly and bespoke service. **Cons:** quite expensive; a bit out of the way of shops and other amenities; difficult to access by train and bus. $ *Rooms from: ¥150,000*

✉ *1 Okitayama, Washimine-cho, Kita-ku* ☎ *075/496–1333* ⊕ *amankyoto.com* 🚲 *26 rooms* ⦿ *Free Breakfast.*

### Shunko-in Temple (春光院)

$ | **B&B/INN** | Visiting Kyoto's temples conveys a sense of the city's spiritual side, but staying in one is a more intimate way of experiencing an aspect of monastic life. **Pros:** insider tour; chance to meet interesting people; plenty of atmosphere. **Cons:** basic facilities; books up fast; no meal service. $ *Rooms from: ¥5,500* ✉ *42 Myoshinji-cho, Hanazono, Ukyo-ku* ☎ *075/462–5488* ⊕ *shunkoin.com* 🚫 *No credit cards* 🚲 *6 rooms, 2 with bath* ⦿ *No Meals.*

# Arashiyama

Beyond the city is the semirural hillside area of Arashiyama, which lies along and above the banks of the Oi-gawa (the local name for the Katsura-gawa as it courses through this area). The pleasure of Arashiyama, the westernmost part of Kyoto, is the same as it has been for centuries. The gentle foothills of the mountains, covered with cherry and maple trees, are splendid. The sights are spaced apart, connected by a pathway that meanders along the hillside, through fields and a peaceful bamboo grove, and past several craft shops and restaurants. It's no wonder that the aristocracy of feudal Japan came here to escape famine, riots, and political intrigue.

**Access:** The easiest ways to get to Arashiyama are by the JR San-in Main Line from Kyoto Station to Saga Station, or via the Keifuku Electric Railway to Arashiyama Station, which is just south of Saga Station. You can also take the scenic truck train, a fine way to view the river gorge.

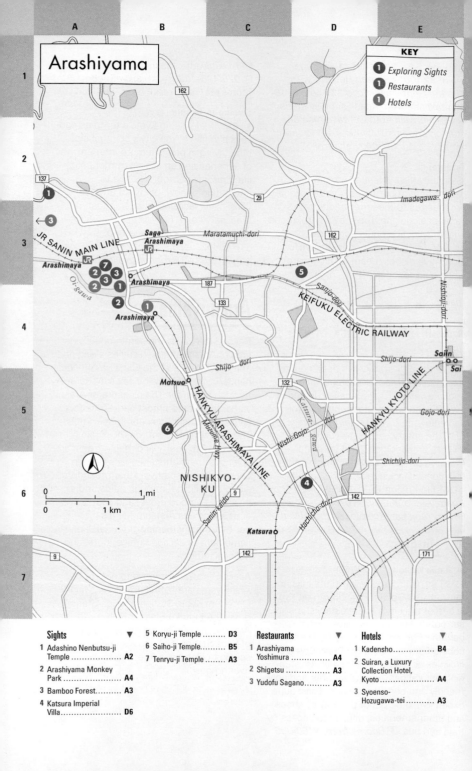

# Arashiyama

**KEY**
- ① Exploring Sights
- ① Restaurants
- ① Hotels

## Sights ▼

1 Adashino Nenbutsu-ji
Temple .................. **A2**

2 Arashiyama Monkey
Park ...................... **A4**

3 Bamboo Forest.......... **A3**

4 Katsura Imperial
Villa....................... **D6**

5 Koryu-ji Temple ......... **D3**

6 Saiho-ji Temple.......... **B5**

7 Tenryu-ji Temple ........ **A3**

## Restaurants ▼

1 Arashiyama
Yoshimura ................ **A4**

2 Shigetsu ................. **A3**

3 Yudofu Sagano.......... **A3**

## Hotels ▼

1 Kadensho................. **B4**

2 Suiran, a Luxury
Collection Hotel,
Kyoto ..................... **A4**

3 Syoenso-
Hozugawa-tei ........... **A3**

#  Sights

## ★ Adashino Nembutsu-ji Temple
(化野念仏寺)

**TEMPLE** | The most unusual feature of this temple is its cemetery, where about 8,000 stone images stand, a solemn sea of silent mourners. The statues honor the many nameless dead who fell victim to the tumult of pre-Edo Japan and were abandoned in the outskirts of the city, burned here in mass pyres. On August 23 and 24, a ceremony called Sento-kuyo is held here, with more than 1,000 candles lighted for the peaceful repose of these spirits. Whatever time of year you visit, the quiet repose of the multitude of images will make a lasting impression. The temple's main hall, built in 1712, contains an arresting statue of Amida Buddha carved by the Kamakura-era sculptor Tankei. ⊠ *17 Adashino-cho, Saga-toriimoto, Ukyo-ku* ⊹ *Take Bus 72 from Kyoto Station to Arashiyama Toriimoto, or walk 20 min from Saga Arashiyama JR Station* ☎ *075/861–2221* ⊕ *www.nenbutsuji.jp* ⊠ *¥500.*

## Arashiyama Monkey Park
(嵐山モンキーパーク)

**ZOO | FAMILY** | The tables are turned at this primate reserve where humans enter a cage-like hut while the resident monkeys roam free—except when clinging to the cage's fencing to grab peanuts offered by visitors. Outside the hut humans and monkeys are free to mingle, and there great views out over the city. Scientists at Kyoto University's Primate Research Institute track the movement of these macaques, the most northern monkeys in the world. The hike to the hill-top hut takes 20 minutes up a steep paved path. Look for entrance at the southern end of the Togetsukyo Bridge. ⊠ *Genrokuyama-cho, 8 Arashiyama, Nishikyo-ku* ⊕ *www.monkeypark.jp* ⊠ *¥550.*

## Bamboo Forest
(竹林の小径; *Chikurin-no-komichi*)

**FOREST** | A narrow path through dense patches of bamboo—thick, with straight, smooth green stems—gives most who pass through it a feeling of composure and tranquillity. The wind, clacking the stems and rustling the leaves, provides the sound track. Though bamboo has treelike qualities, it is actually a grass that grows throughout the country. Its springtime shoots are a culinary treat. ⊠ *Ukyo-ku* ⊹ *Short walk from Saga-Arashiyama train station on road to Okochi Sansoa.*

## ★ Katsura Imperial Villa
(桂離宮; *Katsura Rikyu*)

**HISTORIC HOME** | Considered the epitome of beauty, culture, landscape, and architecture, the Imperial Villa is highly regarded here and abroad. The landscape architect Enshu Kobori (1579–1647) employed aesthetic gardening concepts founded on *shin-gyo-so* (formal, semiformal, informal) principles that imbue every pathway with a special beauty. Kobori incorporated horticultural references to famous Japanese literature, including *The Tale of Genji*, and natural sites.

Built in the 17th century for Prince Toshihito, brother of Emperor Go-yozei, Katsura is in southwestern Kyoto near the western bank of the Katsura River. Bridges constructed from earth, stone, and wood connect five islets in the pond, some moss-covered, softened by the ages yet as fresh as rain.

The villa is fairly remote from other historical sites. Allow several hours for a visit, for which you must secure permission from the Imperial Household Agency in Kyoto, by filling out and submitting a form on the agency's website, or by assembling at 11 am at the site to gain admission if space allows. ⊠ *Katsura Rikyu Shimizu-cho, Ukyo-ku* ☎ *075/211–1215* ⊕ *sankan.kunaicho.go.jp/english/guide/katsura.html* ⊠ *Free.*

The Katsura Imperial Villa includes Japan's oldest-surviving stroll garden, which dates to the 17th century.

### ★ Koryu-ji Temple (広隆寺)

**TEMPLE** | One of Kyoto's oldest temples, Koryu-ji was founded in AD 622 by Kawakatsu Hata in memory of Prince Shotoku (AD 572–621). Shotoku ruled during an era before the founding of Kyoto. When the capital was to be moved from Nara, the Hata clan was living in this area and invited the present emperor to build a new capital on their lands. Prince Shotoku was the first powerful advocate of Buddhism after it was introduced to Japan in AD 552 and based his government on its dictates.

In the Hatto (Lecture Hall) of the main temple stand three statues, each a National Treasure. The central statue, a seated Buddha, is flanked by the figures of the Thousand-armed Kannon and Fukukenjaku-Kannon. In the Taishi-do (Prince Hall) is a wooden statue of Prince Shotoku, thought to have been carved by him personally. Another statue of Shotoku here is believed to depict him at age 16, when it was carved.

The most famous of the Buddhist images in the Reiho-den (Treasure House) is the statue of Miroku Bosatsu, who, according to Buddhist belief, is destined to appear on Earth in the far-off future to save those unable to achieve enlightenment. Japan's first registered National Treasure, this exquisite wooden statue is thought to date from the 6th or 7th century. This may be the most captivating, ethereal Buddhist image in Kyoto. The epitome of serenity, the image's gentle face is one of the finest examples of 6th-century wooden carving in the world. Other images represent a progression of the carving techniques for which Japan is renowned. ⊠ *Hachioka-cho, Uzumasa, Ukyo-ku* ✛ *From Kyoto Station take JR San-in Main Line train to Hanazono Station and board Bus 61. From Shijo-Omiya Station in central Kyoto, take Keifuku Electric Arashiyama train to Uzumasa Station. From central or western Kyoto, take Bus 61, 62, or 63 to Uzumasa-koryu-ji-mae stop* ☎ *075/861–1461* ⊠ *¥800.*

## ★ Saiho-ji Temple (西芳寺)

GARDEN | Also known as Kokedera or the "Moss Temple," the monks who run this temple and garden complex require visitors to perform a task upon arrival to prepare them to appreciate fully the alternative realm they are entering. After sitting quietly, you're given an inkstone, a brush, and a sheet of tracing paper covering a *shakyo*, or sutra, you are encouraged to trace. The exercise complete, you may enter the grounds, with a calm and perhaps awakened spirit, and stroll at your leisure.

The inspiration for the temple's name becomes apparent as you observe the gently swirling greens and blues the 120 varieties of moss create throughout the garden. Designed by the monk Suso Soseki (1275–1351), the garden was a forerunner of later contemplative Zen gardens. This garden, designed on two levels surrounding a pond shaped like the Chinese character for heart, represents Jodo, the western paradise of Buddhism. Permission is required to visit Koinzan Saiho-ji. The simplest ways to arrange a visit are to ask your hotel's concierge, contact the Kyoto Tourist Information Center, or apply directly by mail. It's best to apply at least a month ahead, however, as the limited spaces fill up quickly. ✉ 66 Jingatani-cho, Matsuo, Nishikyo-ku ✦ From Arashiyama or Kyoto Stations take City Bus 63 or 73 to the last stop Kokedera-Suzumushidera ☎ 075/391–3631 ⊕ saihoji-kokedera.com ✑ ¥3,000.

## ★ Tenryu-ji Temple (天龍寺)

TEMPLE | Meaning "Temple of the Heavenly Dragon," this sacred spot is well named. In the 14th century, Emperor Go-Daigo, who had brought an end to the Kamakura shogunate, was forced from his throne by Takauji Ashikaga. After Go-Daigo died, Takauji had twinges of conscience. That's when Priest Muso Soseki had a dream in which a golden dragon rose from the nearby Oi-gawa. He told the shogun about his dream and interpreted it to mean the spirit of Go-Daigo was not at peace. Worried about this ill omen, Takauji completed Tenryu-ji in 1339 on the same spot where Go-Daigo had his favorite villa. Apparently the late emperor's spirit was appeased. Construction took several years and was partly financed by a trading mission to China, which brought back treasures of the Ming dynasty.

In the Hatto (Lecture Hall), where today's monks meditate, a huge "cloud dragon" is painted on the ceiling. The temple was often ravaged by fire, and the current buildings are as recent as 1900; the painting of the dragon was rendered by Shonen Suzuki, a 20th-century artist.

The Sogenchi garden, which dates from the 14th century, is one of Kyoto's most noteworthy gardens. Muso Soseki, an influential Zen monk and garden designer, created the garden to resemble Mt. Horai in China, the mythological home of the Immortals. It is famed for its arrangement of vertical stones embanking the large pond and as one of the first gardens to use "borrowed scenery," incorporating the mountains in the distance into the design of the garden. Now a UNESCO World Heritage site, the temple and its grounds are well attended by many admirers. There is also an excellent vegetarian Zen cuisine restaurant, Shigetsu, at the southern end of the temple grounds. ✉ 68 Susuki-no-bamba-cho, Saga-Tenryu-ji, Ukyo-ku ✦ From Kyoto Station take JR San-in Main Line train to Saga Station and walk west 12 mins. From Shijo-Omiya Station in central Kyoto take Keifuku Dentetsu-Arashiyama train to Arashiyama Station and walk west 5 mins. Or take Bus 61, 72, or 83 to Arashiyama Tenryu-ji-mae stop ☎ 075/881–1235 ⊕ www.tenryuji.com/en ✑ Garden only ¥500; garden and buildings ¥800; cloud-dragon painting ¥500.

## 🍴 Restaurants

**Arashiyama Yoshimura** (嵐山よしむら)
$$ | **JAPANESE** | This old-style soba noodle shop two blocks south of Tenryu-ji Temple sits right in the thick of things and has a splendid view of the river. Feel free to relax on a cushion and face the river while you recharge before visiting your next temple. **Known for:** delicious tempura; river views; tasty soba noodles. [$] *Average main: ¥1,500* ✉ *Sagatenryuji, 3 Susukinobabacho, Ukyo-ku* ☎ *075/863–5700* 🌐 *yoshimura-gr.com* ⏲ *No dinner.*

★ **Shigetsu** (篩月)
$$$ | **JAPANESE** | If you visit Tenryu-ji at lunchtime, consider dining at Shigetsu, within the temple precinct. The *tenzo,* a monk trained to prepare Zen cuisine, creates a multicourse meal that achieves the harmony of the six basic flavors—bitter, sour, sweet, salty, light, and hot—attributes necessary to balance body and mind. **Known for:** wonderful hospitality; advance reservations (made online) required; vegetarian and vegan dishes. [$] *Average main: ¥5,500* ✉ *Tenryu-ji Temple, 68 Susuki-no-bamba-cho, Ukyo-ku* ✥ *From Kyoto Station take JR San-in Main Line train to Saga Station and walk west 12 mins. From Shijo-Omiya Station in central Kyoto take Keifuku Dentetsu-Arashiyama train to Arashiyama Station and walk west 5 mins. Or take Bus 61, 72, or 83 to Arashiyama Tenryu-ji-mae stop* ☎ *075/882–9725* 🌐 *www.tenryuji.com/en/shigetsu* ⏲ *No dinner.*

**Yudofu Sagano** (湯豆腐 嵯峨野)
$$$ | **JAPANESE** | Amid Arashiyama's lush bamboo forests, this quiet retreat offers a fine example of hot-pot tofu *yudofu* cooking. The set meal includes delicacies such as *abura-age* (fried tofu with black sesame seeds), tempura vegetables and shrimp, and Kyoto's famous Morita tofu. **Known for:** large variety of tofu dishes; beautiful garden setting; refined atmosphere. [$] *Average main: ¥5,000* ✉ *45 Susuki-no-bamba-cho, Saga, Tenryu-ji, Ukyo-ku* ☎ *075/871–6946* 🌐 *kyoto-sagano.jp.*

## 🛏 Hotels

**Kadensho** (花伝抄)
$$$$ | **HOTEL** | If the beauty of Arashiyama inspires you to spend the night in the area, consider this resort whose draws include its kimono-clad staff, modern amenities, multicourse meals, and spacious hot springs short walk from the monkey park. **Pros:** good food; public and private onsen; modern interior. **Cons:** must wait to use private onsen during peak season; neighborhood shops close by 7 pm; staff don't speak much English. [$] *Rooms from: ¥35,000* ✉ *5–4 Arashiyama Nishiichikawa-cho, Nishikyo-ku* ☎ *075/863–0489* 🛏 *100 rooms* 🍴 *Free Breakfast.*

**Suiran, a Luxury Collection Hotel, Kyoto** (翠嵐 ラグジュアリーコレクションホテル 京都)
$$$$ | **HOTEL** | The original wooden structure of an industrialist's traditional estate was renovated into the river-view dining room of this woodsy hotel, one of Kyoto's most upscale properties. **Pros:** private hot-spring baths; quiet, restful setting; exquisite dining facilities. **Cons:** tiny gym, no pool; may feel too isolated for some guests; expensive. [$] *Rooms from: ¥60,000* ✉ *12 Susukino-baba-cho, Saga-Tenryuji, Ukyo-ku, Kyoto* ☎ *075/872–0101* 🌐 *www.suihotels.com/suiran-kyoto* 🛏 *39 rooms* 🍴 *No Meals.*

**Syoenso-Hozugawa-tei** (松園荘保津川亭)
$$$$ | **RESORT** | Some rooms at this hillside hot-springs resort outside Kyoto proper have their own *rotemburo* (outdoor hot tub) overlooking a private garden, but gender-separated communal baths are available to all guests. **Pros:** healthful hot springs; some rooms have private baths; mountain views. **Cons:** expensive; little English spoken; far from city center. [$] *Rooms from: ¥26,000* ✉ *Yunohana-onsen, 1–4 Hiedanocho, Ashinoyama,*

*Kameoka* ☎ *0771/22–0903* ⊕ *www. syoenso.com* 🛏 *56 rooms.*

# Northern Kyoto

The mountain, Hiei-zan, and the Ohara region are the focal points in the northern suburbs of Kyoto. For several centuries Ohara was a sleepy Kyoto backwater surrounded by mountains. Although it's catching up with the times, it retains a feeling of Old Japan. Hiei-zan is a fount of Kyoto history. On its flanks the priest Saicho founded Enryaku-ji in the 8th century and with it the vital Tendai sect of Buddhism. It's an essential Kyoto sight, and walking on forested slopes among its 70-odd temples is a good reason to make the trek to Hiei-zan.

**Access:** The sights in northern Kyoto are spread out and must be reached by a combination of train, bus, and cable car. It's best to make this a day trip to allow some time to explore Ohara and Hiei-zan. If you're booked on a tour to the Shuga-ku-in Imperial Villa on the same day, then you'll probably only have time to explore one or the other.

## ◉ Sights

### ★ Enryaku-ji Temple (延暦寺)

**TEMPLE** | This temple complex, a UNESCO World Heritage site, is as majestic as the mountain where it is located. Mt. Hiei has a long and entangled history with the capital, an involved and intriguing involvement with the court and the stronghold of warrior monks it became. More than a millennium ago, the priest Dengyo-Daishi (767–822), also known as Saicho, was given imperial permission to build a temple to protect the city against misfortune it was believed would emanate from the northeast. The temple grew in wealth and power and became a training place for monks-turned-warriors to force the Imperial Court to accede to its leaders' demands. The power accrued over the

centuries lasting until Nobunaga Oda, the general who helped unify Japan and ended more than a century of civil strife, destroyed the complex in 1571.

The current temple is divided into three complexes—Todo, Saito, and Yoka-wa—that date from the 17th century. The Kompon Chu-do hall in Todo has a massive copper roof in the *irimoya-zukuri* layered style. Its dark, cavernous interior conveys the mysticism for which the Tendai sect is known. Giant pillars and a coffered ceiling shelter the central altar, which is surrounded by religious images. You can kneel with worshippers on a dais above the shadowy recess containing the smaller altars, an arrangement that looks upon the enshrined deities. The interior, darkened by the smoke of centuries of lighted candles, conveys a sense of spirituality even among nonbelievers. Each of the ornate oil lanterns hanging before the altar represents a stage of enlightenment. Near the main hall, a mausoleum contains the remains of Saicho.

Saito is a 25-minute walk from Todo along a stairway lined with stone lanterns. The ancient wooden temple in the Yokawa complex has been replaced with a concrete structure, dimming some of its allure, though like Todo and Saito it remains remarkable for its longevity and active religious rites. The mountain-top temple complex can be accessed from either the west (Kyoto side) or the east (Shiga/Lake Biwa side). ✉ *Enryaku-ji, 4220 Sakamoto-hon-machi, Otsu* ✚ *To access cable car to base of temple from the east side, take JR Kosei train to Hieizan-Sakamoto Station, Keihan train to Sakamoto-Hieizanguchi Station, or for the west side Eiden/Eizan train from Demachi-Yanagi Station to Yase-Hieizanguchi Station; Kyoto Buses 16, 17, and 19 also run to Yase-Hieizanguchi* ☎ *077/578–0001* ⊕ *www.hieizan.or.jp* 🎫 *¥1,000, Eizan cable car ¥800, Sakamoto cable car ¥870* ⊗ *Eizan cable car closed in winter.*

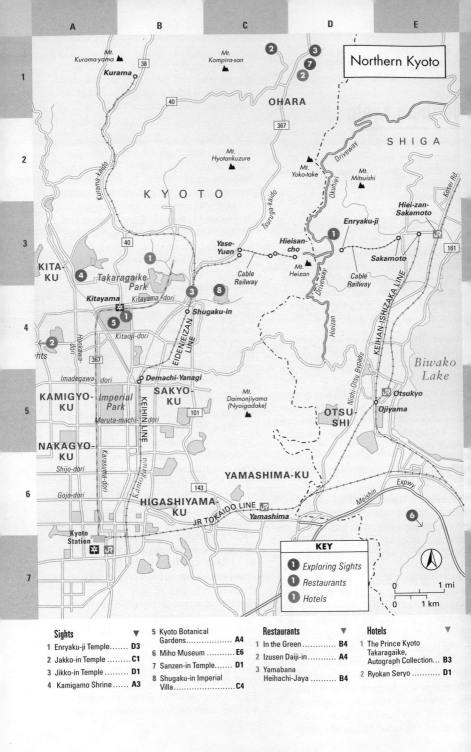

Northern Kyoto

A | B | C | D | E

1 — Mt. Kurama-yama, Kurama, Mt. Kompira-san, OHARA
2 — Mt. Hyotankuzure, K Y O T O, Mt. Yoko-take, SHIGA, Mt. Mitsuishi, Hiei-zan-Sakamoto
3 — KITA-KU, Takaragaike Park, Kitayama, Yase-Yuen, Hieisan-cho, Mt. Heizan, Enryaku-ji, Sakamoto, Cable Railway
4 — Shugaku-in, EIDEN/EIZAN LINE, Biwako Lake
5 — Demachi-Yanagi, KAMIGYO-KU, Imperial Park, SAKYO-KU, Mt. Daimonjiyama (Nyoigadake), OTSU-SHI, Otsukyo, Ojiyama, NAKAGYO-KU
6 — Shijo-dori, Gojo-dori, HIGASHIYAMA-KU, YAMASHIMA-KU, JR TOKAIDO LINE, Yamashima, Meishin Expwy
7 — Kyoto Station

**KEY**

- ① Exploring Sights
- ① Restaurants
- ① Hotels

0   1 mi
0   1 km

## Sights ▼
1 Enryaku-ji Temple....... **D3**
2 Jakko-in Temple ......... **C1**
3 Jikko-in Temple ......... **D1**
4 Kamigamo Shrine ...... **A3**
5 Kyoto Botanical Gardens.................. **A4**
6 Miho Museum ............ **E6**
7 Sanzen-in Temple....... **D1**
8 Shugaku-in Imperial Villa....................... **C4**

## Restaurants ▼
1 In the Green ............. **B4**
2 Izusen Daiji-in ........... **A4**
3 Yamabana Heihachi-Jaya .......... **B4**

## Hotels ▼
1 The Prince Kyoto Takaragaike, Autograph Collection... **B3**
2 Ryokan Seryo ............ **D1**

The Saio-dai, an unmarried woman, represents the emperor in the Aoi Matsuri (Hollyhock Festival), which takes place in mid-May.

### Jakko-in Temple (寂光院)

TEMPLE | The small and beloved nunnery was completely rebuilt in 2005 after a devastating fire, but its history is almost as old as the city. Rival clans had their final battle in 1185, taking the lives of all except Kenreimon-in, the 29-year-old mother of eight-year-old Emperor Antoku. Kenreimon-in returned to the capital and eventually this remote place to spend her days in prayer. Years passed until a visit by a retired emperor who was moved to write a poem about her harsh existence as embodied by the gnarled remains of a cherry tree on the ground. Jakko-in is on the west, or opposite side of the valley from Sanzen-in. The steep stairway approaching the nunnery evokes the solitude Kenreimon-in and the other nuns who lived here endured. ⊠ *676 Oharakusao-cho, Sakyo-ku* ✛ *From Kyoto Station take Kyoto Line Bus 17 or 18 (90-min ride), or subway to Kokusai Station and board Kyoto Bus 6, 17, or 19; walk is about 20 min* ☎ *075/744–3341* ⊕ *www.jakkoin.jp* 🎫 *¥600.*

### Jikko-in Temple (実光院)

TEMPLE | Smaller than other nearby temples, this one is less visited and quieter. A gong has been placed its humble-looking entrance for visitors to strike before stepping down inside. The garden for viewing is small and delicate; there's a larger stroll garden as well. Within the Main Hall are 36 portraits of Chinese poets by members of the Kano School. Near Sanzen-in, Jikko-in is easily combined with a visit to that temple. ⊠ *187 Ohara Shorinin-cho, Sakyo-ku* ✛ *From Kyoto Station take Kyoto Line Bus 17 or 19 for 90 mins to Ohara stop and walk northeast 7 mins* ☎ *075/744–2537* ⊕ *jikkoin.com* 🎫 *¥800 for entrance and a bowl of green tea.*

### Kamigamo Shrine
(上賀茂神社; *Kamigamo Jinja*)

RELIGIOUS BUILDING | The approach at one of Kyoto's oldest and most stately shrines takes visitors along a path in the middle of an expanse of lawn and through the red torii gate. That same path is the scene of horse racing on May 5 and the approach of the imperial messenger of the Hollyhock Festival on May 15 as he reports the events of the court to the resident gods.

At this favorite place for weddings, visitors may be pleasantly surprised to see one taking place in the inner shrine. The grounds are vast, with smaller shrines and a stream into which believers write their wishes on pieces of kimono-shape paper and set them afloat. In recent years, the shrine has become the setting for a torch-lit Noh drama play on the evening of July 1. On other days, families spread out their picnic blankets on the lawn or in shadier spots and enjoy the day. ✉ *339 Motoyama, Kamigamo, Kita-ku* ✛ *Bus 9 to Kamigamojinja-mae or Kamigamo Misono-bashi stop, or from Kyoto Station take Karasuma subway to Kitayama Station and walk north 25 mins* ☏ *075/781–0011* ⊕ *www.kamigamojinja.jp/english* ✍ *Free.*

## Kyoto Botanical Gardens (京都府立植物園; *Kyoto Furitsu Shokubutsuen*)

GARDEN | Japan's oldest public botanical garden has been welcoming visitors since 1924 and features a huge variety of plants and flowers from around the world, including Japan's famous bonsai. The sprawling gardens are filled with seasonal blooms, so colorful displays are guaranteed throughout the year. It also happens to be one of the best places in the city to catch cherry blossoms in the spring or the stunning tones of autumn in the fall. The showpiece conservatory is home to over 4,000 kinds of flora, divided into tropical collections, desert environs and an alpine temperate zone. ✉ *Hangi-cho, Shimogamo, Sakyo-ku* ✛ *Take a train to Kitayama Station on the Karasuma Subway Line* ☏ *075/701-0141* ⊕ *www.pref.kyoto.jp/en/02-02-10.html* ✍ *¥200, Conservatory ¥250.*

## Miho Museum (ミホミュージアム; *Miho Bijutsukan*)

ART MUSEUM | The phenomenal architecture and impressive collection of Japanese tea-ceremony artifacts and antiquities from the West, China, and the Middle East make a visit to this museum in Shiga Prefecture well worth the hour-long journey from Kyoto. Three-quarters of the museum, which opened in 1997, is underground, with skylights illuminating the displays. The grounds are extensively and beautifully landscaped and well incorporated into architect I. M. Pei's design. The Japanese collection is housed in a wing separate from the antiquities. ✉ *300 Momodani, Shiga-ken, Shigarakicho-kinose* ✛ *From Kyoto Station take any train on the JR Biwako Line to Ishiyama Station, then Teisan Line bus for 50 mins* ☏ *0748/82–3411* ⊕ *www.miho.jp* ✍ *¥1,300.*

## Sanzen-in Temple (三千院)

TEMPLE | In the rural village of Ohara, northeast of the city, this Tendai sect temple was founded by the priest Dengyo-Daishi (767–822), also known as Saicho. The approach is up steep stone steps and onto the temple grounds. Tall cypress trees admit spots of sunlight onto the moss-and fern ground cover. The most famous building, constructed in AD 985, houses a huge image of Amida Buddha. On either side are images of Seishi and Kannon. The convex ceiling is painted with scenes of paradise, but with the passing of the centuries, these paintings of the descent of Amida, accompanied by 25 bodhisattvas, to welcome the believer are fading. Famed for its maples, the temple draws its largest crowds in autumn, but the grounds north of the main buildings have been planted with hundreds of hydrangea bushes, in bloom throughout June. ✉ *540 Ohara Raigoin-cho, Sakyo-ku* ✛ *From Kyoto Station take Kyoto Line Bus 17 north, or subway to Kokusai Station and board Bus 1 or 17* ☏ *075/744–2531* ⊕ *www.sanzenin.or.jp* ✍ *¥700.*

Sanzen-in, a temple of the Tendai Buddhist sect, faces east, not south, as is the case with most Buddhist temples.

**Shugaku-in Imperial Villa**
(修学院離宮; *Shugaku-in Rikyu*)
**CASTLE/PALACE** | The Imperial Villa was in active use until about 100 years ago when it became part of the Imperial Household Agency, thereby requiring permission to enter. The extensive hillside grounds are split into lower, middle and upper levels and are masterpieces of gardening. The maples and cherries are especially pretty in their seasons, but year-round the Imperial retreat is an essay in the respect the Japanese have for nature. The goal wasn't to have gold and diamonds decorating their lives, but well-trimmed pine trees, painted wooden doors, and stone-strewn pathways.

You can apply for permission to visit the villa online or at the Kyoto office of the Imperial Household Agency—if you haven't applied before your arrival in Kyoto, your hotel concierge can also assist you. Visitors are asked to arrive, identification ready, 10 minutes prior to the appointed tour time. Although the approximately 80-minute tours are in Japanese, free English-language audio guides are available. Be aware that the route involves some steep inclines. ✉ *Yabusoe Shugaku-in, Sakyo-ku* ✥ *From Kyoto Station take Bus 5 (about 1 hr) to Shugakuin-rikyu-michi stop and walk east 15 min, or Keifuku Eizan train from Demachi-Yanagi Station to Shugakuin Station and walk northeast 20 min* ☎ *075/211–1215* 🌐 *sankan.kunaicho.go.jp* 🎫 *Free.*

## 🍴 Restaurants

**In the Green** (イン ザ グリーン)
**$ | CAFE** | This combination trattoria, pizzeria, and café in a contemporary glass, metal, and wood space borders the northern side of the Kyoto Botanical Gardens. Both the location and the food make it popular, so it is wise to make a reservation by phone or in person and see the gardens first. **Known for:** daily-changing menu; simple meat and fish dishes; oven-baked pizza. [$] *Average main: ¥1,300* ✉ *In the Green, Shokubutsuen Kitayama-mon, Sakyo-ku, Kyoto*

✢ *3-min walk from Kitayama subway station* ☎ *075/706–8740* 🌐 *www.inthegreen.jp.*

**Izusen Daiji-in** (泉仙大慈院)
$$$ | **JAPANESE** | Vegetarian cuisine plays a part in all major Kyoto temples, and one of the most scenic restaurants in which to sample it is in the southwestern section of Daitoku-ji. The monastic shojin ryori cuisine here is served in luminous red-lacquer bowls at low tables in the temple garden (beware the mosquitoes in summer) or inside if the weather is inclement. **Known for:** red-lacquer tableware; vegetarian dishes; relaxing setting. [$] *Average main: ¥3,800* ✉ *4 Daitoku-ji-cho, Murasakino, Kita-ku* ☎ *075/491–6665 inside Izusen* 🌐 *kyoto-izusen.com.*

**Yamabana Heihachi-Jaya** (山ばな 平八茶屋)
$$$$ | **JAPANESE** | Along one of the centuries-old exit roads from the city into the mountains, this roadside inn is beloved for its multicourse kaiseki ryori dinners, duck hot pots, boar stew, and boxed lunches with mountain potatoes and barley rice. There were seven roads that led out of the city, and wayside inns such as Yamabana Heihachi-Jaya provided travelers with food and respite before the long trek ahead. **Known for:** classic dishes; historic setting; river views. [$] *Average main: ¥15,000* ✉ *8–1 Kawagishi-cho, Yamabana, Sakyo-ku* ☎ *075/781–5008* 🌐 *www.heihachi.co.jp/english* ⏲ *Closed Wed.*

## Hotels

**The Prince Kyoto Takaragaike, Autograph Collection** (プリンス京都宝ヶ池)
$$ | **HOTEL** | **FAMILY** | Directly across from the Kyoto International Conference Hall, nestled in a forest setting, the Grand Prince Takaragaike will make you feel like visiting royalty. **Pros:** excellent breakfast; responsive staff; spacious rooms. **Cons:** dated decor; expensive meals; in far-northern part of the city. [$] *Rooms from: ¥17,500* ✉ *Takaraga-ike, 1092–2 Hataedacho, Iwakura, Sakyo-ku* ☎ *075/712–1111* 🌐 *www.marriott.com* 🛏 *309 rooms* 🍴 *Free Breakfast.*

**Ryokan Seryo** (旅館芹生)
$$$$ | **B&B/INN** | A bit of a miniature miracle, the Ryokan Seryo is in the semirural village of Ohara, near the Sanzen-in Temple. **Pros:** peaceful atmosphere; great food; rejuvenating hot springs. **Cons:** far from downtown; communal hot spring is open to the public during business hours; service can feel a little cold. [$] *Rooms from: ¥47,000* ✉ *22 Shorinin-cho, Ohara, Sakyo-ku* ☎ *075/744–2301* 🌐 *www.seryo.co.jp* 🛏 *8 rooms* 🍴 *All-Inclusive.*

# Chapter 9

# THE KANSAI REGION

Updated by
Tom Fay

| 👁 Sights | 🍴 Restaurants | 🛏 Hotels | 🛍 Shopping | 🍸 Nightlife |
|-----------|---------------|----------|------------|-------------|
| ★★★★☆ | ★★★★☆ | ★★★★☆ | ★★★★★ | ★★★★☆ |

# WELCOME TO THE KANSAI REGION

## TOP REASONS TO GO

★ **Architecture:** Skyscrapers share Osaka's skyline with 4th-century burial mounds; Nara's wealth of temples, pagodas, and shrines is outstanding.

★ **Food:** Osaka has been known as "Japan's Kitchen" since the 17th century. Highly marbleized Kobe beef is world-famous.

★ **Nada no Sake:** The sake breweries of Nada, in western Kobe, use mineral-rich water and Yamada Nishiki rice, grown near Mt. Rokko.

★ **Shopping:** Locals in old wooden shops sell Nara's famous crafts: *sumi* (ink sticks) for calligraphy, *Narasarashi* (fine handwoven, sun-bleached linen), and *akahadayaki* pottery.

★ **Todai-ji Temple Complex:** The complex in Nara includes the Daibutsu-den and its Great Buddha. The 8th-century San-gatsu-do houses Tenpyo-era statues.

★ **Himeji Castle:** The towering white castle is one of the few surviving structures from Japan's feudal period.

Osaka sits between Kobe to the west and Nara to the east and has the Kansai region's main international airport, which serves all three cities. Travel to either Kobe or Nara from Osaka takes about 30 minutes, and it's about an hour from Kobe to Nara, and vice versa. Kyoto is the other major tourist destination in the Kansai region, and it is covered separately.

**1 Osaka.** The people's eccentric friendliness in Japan's third-largest city plays against its rough-and-tumble urban background.

**2 Nara.** Visitors come for Nara's expansive parks and temples only to be enchanted by its rustic side streets and quiet sense of history.

**3 Kobe.** The city's relaxed cosmopolitan vibe blends into the waterfalls and onsen (thermal spas) of Arima.

**4 Himeji.** One of the few surviving feudal-era edifices that survive in modern-day Japan.

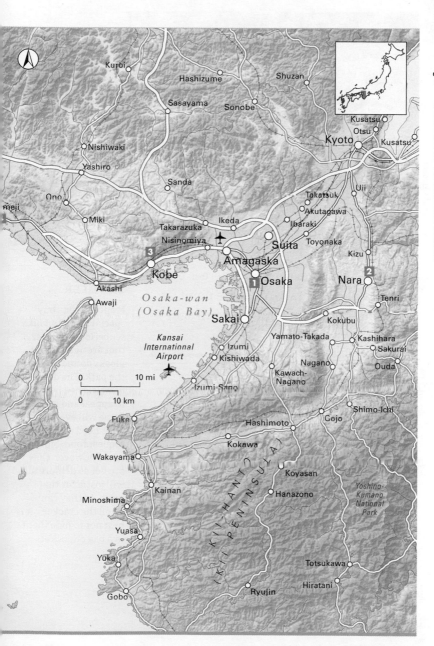

# NARA'S SACRED DEER

Nara's sacred sika deer

Of all the attractions in Nara, there is one that no visitor can miss. At some point, as you wander between temples, you'll spot the city's sacred deer.

Nara's deer have been part of the landscape of the city for as long as any of the temples, and they rival Todai-ji (with its Daibutsu, the famed statue of Buddha) as the favorite attraction for many tourists. Red and flecked with white in summer, their coats turn gray in winter; today there are some 1,300 deer freely roaming around Nara Park and the surrounding hills. After such a long time cohabiting with humans they are familiar with us. And they are used to deference: traffic stops when they decide to cross the road, and they are likely to make their interest in being hand-fed known as soon as they approach you.

### FEEDING THE DEER

Many tourists buy special biscuits, *shika senbei* (deer crackers), that are available at kiosks dotted around the park. The deer have learned how to appeal and cajole. Some will even bow their head meekly to request food. More often, however, they are not so demure and will jostle for that treat. As they can smell the crackers, it is best not to hide them in a bag or pocket.

Visitors should be wary of mothers in May and June, when they will be fiercely protective of their fawns. Likewise, young males can be unpredictable in the rutting season in fall.

## THE LEGEND OF THE DEER

Legend has it that in AD 768 a white deer carried the deity Takemikazuchi-no-Mikoto, one of the first four deities of Kasuga Taisha, from a distant province called Hitachi (now known as Ibaraki, north of Tokyo) all the way to Nara. As a reward, the deer was hailed as divine—and would be forever untouchable. Ever since, the deer inhabiting the Kasuga hills, now part of Nara Park, were considered messengers of the gods and have been both protected and revered. It was only after World War II that the animals were stripped of their divine status, though they are no less cherished and are designated as natural treasures by the government. One hapless, would-be poacher found this out in 2010, when he tried to bag some illicit venison but ended up with a stretch in jail.

## SHIKA NO TSUNOKIRI

Partly to protect visitors, but chiefly to stop the deer from hurting each other, there is an antler-cutting ceremony each October. The *shika no tsunokiri* has changed little in 300 years.

Deer nibbling the grass in Nara Koen

Feeding the deer

The bucks are chased into a special enclosure near Kasuga Taisha by *seko* (beaters) in traditional garb. The seko use *juji* (nets made of bamboo with rope), which they hurl at the animals, hook the antlers, and then pull the bucks in. A Shinto priest next gives each animal some purified water before sawing off its antlers. All males over four years face the same indignation. The fully grown antlers do not have nerves or veins, so no lasting harm is done, but the bucks do not undergo the ordeal easily.

## SENTO-KUN

So popular are the deer with tourists that when Nara recently celebrated 1,300 years since its founding and was looking for a character that would embody everything about the city, the winning entry was *Sento-kun*. Looking suspiciously like an impish Buddha with antlers, he did not go down well with some of the city's more conservative figures who thought him disrespectful. Sento-kun has, however, proved enormously popular with visitors ever since and, if nothing else, is confirmation that Nara's deer are as big a draw as any of the magnificent temples or shrines.

# SAKE, THE JAPANESE DRINK

Toasting with sake

Sake, or *nihonshu*, is the essential Japanese drink. Ranging in taste from fruity and bright to rich and mellow, there is a nihonshu for virtually every palate. Many sake breweries offer free tours and tastings to tourists.

Sake is brewed throughout Japan, and brewery tours are common. If you are in Kansai, you may want to visit one of the breweries in Nada, which accounts for more than a quarter of Japan's sake production. Thanks to a near-perfect combination of rice, water, brewing techniques, and its location next to the port of Kobe, Nada has been Japan's premier sake-brewing region since the 18th century. Many breweries offer tours in both Japanese and English, followed by free tastings and a chance to buy the hard-to-find sake produced there. Unfortunately, few breweries allow guests to enter the actual brewing area. To visit a brewery, call ahead for reservations since tours may only be available on certain days. If you don't have time for a brewery visit, most souvenir shops sell local sake. Just ask for *ji-zake* (local sake).

## KOBE SHU-SHIN-KAN BREWERY

Kobe Shu-shin-kan Brewery (☎ 078/841–1121), in business since 1751, is one of the few that opens its brew house to tours. Sake is brewed from October to March, but the rest of the year you can still see the facilities and learn about the process. To book a tour call the day before. There's also a shop (daily 10–6) and restaurant.

# Important Sake Terms

Like wine, nihonshu is nuanced and complex. It is officially separated into different grades depending on how much of the rice grain remains after polishing. Since the glutinous, low-protein inner cores of rice kernels produce the best sake, more polishing results in better sake.

## DAI-GINJOSHU (大吟醸酒)

The highest grade of sake, *dai-ginjoshu* rice is polished so that only 50% of the grain remains. These sake are usually complex, light, and crisp. If you only try one nihonshu in Japan, make sure it is a dai-ginjoshu.

## GINJOSHU (吟醸酒)

The second-highest level sake, *ginjoshu* uses rice with 60% of the grain remaining. Ginjoshu usually has a clear, crisp flavor and slightly fruity bouquet.

## HONJOZOSHU (本醸造酒)

*Honjozushu* rice is polished so that less than 70% of the grain remains. These sake are less complex than ginjoshu and dai-ginjoshu, but still light and fragrant. Quite affordable, they are an excellent companion to most Japanese food.

## FUTSUSHU (普通酒)

Literally "normal sake," *futsushu* is the table wine of nihonshu. Some varieties

Assorted sake bottles

are quite tasty, while others are best avoided. Most hot sake, or *atsukan,* is this variety.

## JUNMAISHU (純米酒)

*Junmaishu* ("pure rice") indicates a sake that has been brewed using only white rice, pure water, and the fermenting agent *koji*. Not one of the four official grades of nihonshu, there are junmai honjozoshu (often called simply junmaishu), junmai ginjoshu, and junmai dai-ginjoshu. Junmai sake often has a mellow, smooth flavor.

## NAMAZAKE (生酒)

Bottled without aging, these unpasteurized sakes are known for their refreshing crispness. *Namazake* is only available for a short time after being brewed and must be refrigerated. While breweries release namazake at different times, spring is the most popular season.

## NIGORIZAKE (にごり酒)

*Nigorizake* is only slightly filtered, giving it a cloudy white appearance. Nigori sake has a heavier, sweeter taste than other sake.

## NIHONSHUDO (日本酒度)

This indicates whether a sake is sweet or dry. Dry sake has a positive number while sweet sake has a negative. For those new to nihonshudo, sake in the +/-5 range is some of the most popular.

Sake served in a wooden *masu*

Stretching from Mie Prefecture in the east to Hyogo Prefecture in the west, the Kansai region is both a snapshot of archetypal Japan and a showcase for the country's diversity. As home to Japan's capitals for nearly a millennium, Kansai is the undisputed seat of Japanese culture and tradition.

It is the birthplace of Japan's traditional theater styles—Noh, Kabuki, and Bunraku—as well as the tea ceremony, Japanese Buddhism, and *ikebana* (flower arrangement). Thanks to Kobe and Osaka, it was also the heart of Japanese trade and industry until Tokyo surpassed it in the 1970s.

After the Kanto region around Tokyo, Kansai is Japan's most populous and economically important area. Most major companies have offices in Kansai and a few, like Panasonic and Nintendo, still have their headquarters in the region. Though much of the shipping and manufacturing industry has moved overseas, the cities of Kansai have responded by investing heavily in science, research, and technology businesses.

Because of its size and location, the geography of Kansai is as varied as the culture. The Kii mountain range in southern Mie and Nara prefectures quickly gives way to the stunning rural coastline of Wakayama. Most of the region's population is concentrated around the four cities of Osaka, Kyoto, Kobe, and Nara, all in southern Kansai. Northern Kansai, including Lake Biwa and the Sea of Japan coast, is quite rural. Thanks to the tempering effect of the inland sea, the climate of Kansai is generally mild, though summers are renowned for their humidity.

Kansai deserves its reputation as the culinary center of Japan. Whether it be delicate temple food in Kyoto and Nara, hearty Osaka fare, or Kobe's cosmopolitan fusion of Japanese and Western cuisines, no other region has such a range of local specialties. Kyoto may be the Kansai's main draw, but to sample the diversity of Japan's cities, make time to see Osaka, Kobe, and Nara. Within an hour's train ride, each city has its own unique culture, cuisine, and attractions. No other region of Japan produces such urban variety in such a small area.

Osaka's urban energy complements its offbeat fashions and reputation as Japan's culinary capital. For urban explorers, the side streets of Amerika-mura, Minami-horie, or Shin-Sekai offer countless surprises. Anime fans can visit Den Den Town for the latest games, anime goods, and "maid" cafés (where waitresses dress in French parlor-maid uniforms).

In Kobe's East-meets-West cosmopolitan mix, travelers can wander Chinatown and have tea in a 19th-century European mansion before taking a cable car up Mt.

Rokko for the romantic night view or a stay at Arima Onsen. For foodies, the city is home to Kobe beef and Japan's largest concentration of sake distilleries.

Nara is home to Japan's most famous UNESCO World Heritage site, where visitors can feed (or fend off) Nara Park's gregarious deer and see the stunning Todai-ji and Horyu-ji temples. The charming old houses of Nara-machi have become restaurants, galleries, and cafés—the perfect places to find souvenirs and sample local specialties like *nara-zuke* (vegetables pickled in sake).

Each city may not be for everyone, but to skip all three is to miss out on a chance to see some of Japan's most unique urban landscapes.

# Planning

## Getting Here and Around

### AIR

Many international carriers fly into Kansai International Airport (KIX) south of Osaka, which handles all of the Kansai region's international flights as well as connecting domestic flights to major Japanese cities. The airport, constructed on reclaimed land in Osaka Bay, is easy to navigate and is an interesting sight in its own right. Exiting customs on the first floor, you will find English-language tourist information and direct access to the limousine buses that run to many downtown hotels and destinations (roughly 60 minutes, depending on the destination). Japan Airlines (JAL) and All Nippon Airways (ANA) have ongoing domestic flights to many major cities—Tokyo is about 60 minutes away, Sapporo about 2 hours, and Naha (Okinawa) about 2 hours 30 minutes. Peach Aviation, a Kansai-based discount carrier, offers inexpensive flights to many cities.

About half of domestic flights use Itami Airport, roughly 30 minutes northwest of Osaka, and it is closer to all three of Kansai's major cities. Travel to Kobe from Itami Airport takes about 40 minutes, 55 minutes to Nara.

**AIRLINES Air Canada.** ☎ *010-800/6699–2222* ⊕ *www.aircanada.com.* **All Nippon Airways.** ☎ *0570/029–709* ⊕ *www.ana.co.jp.* **Delta Airlines.** ☎ *0570/077–733* ⊕ *www.delta.com.* **Japan Airlines.** ☎ *0570/025–121* ⊕ *www.jal.com.* **Peach Aviation.** ☎ *03/6731–9241* ⊕ *www.flypeach.com.*

**AIRPORTS Kansai International Airport.** ✉ *1-Banchi, Senshu-kuko Kita, Izumisano* ☎ *07/2455–2500* ⊕ *www.kansai-airport.or.jp/en.* **Usaka International Airport.** (*Itami Airport*) ✉ *Ōsaka* ☎ *06/6856–6781* ⊕ *www.osaka-airport.co.jp.*

### AIRPORT TRANSFERS

From Kansai Airport, Osaka is about 30 to 70 minutes away by bus or train, Kobe about 90 minutes by train, and Nara about 90 minutes by train.

To get to Osaka, the Haruka Express is free if you have a Japan Railpass and takes about 60 minutes.

### BUS

There are a number of highway buses to Osaka from most cities in Japan, and from Osaka it's an easy trip to either Kobe or Nara. There are many bus companies, but JR Bus is one of the most popular.

**CONTACT JR West Bus.** ✉ *1–3–23 Hokko, Konohana-ku* ☎ *057/000–2424* ⊕ *www.nishinihonjrbus.co.jp/en.*

### TRAIN

Hikari Shinkansen trains from Tokyo Station to Shin-Osaka Station take about 3 hours and cost ¥14,400; the trip to Kobe from Tokyo takes 3¼ hours and costs ¥14,950. The Nozomi Shinkansen trains cost a bit more and are about 30 minutes faster, but you can't use a JR Pass on these trains.

Nara can be reached from either Osaka or Kobe, but there are no direct trains from Tokyo. From Kintetsu's Osaka Namba Station, Nara is 38 minutes by Ordinary Express train (¥570), which leaves every 20 minutes. The JR Line rapid train from Tenno-ji Station takes 33 minutes and costs ¥470; from JR Namba it costs ¥570 and takes 50 minutes; from Osaka Station it takes 50 minutes and costs ¥810.

From Kobe, take the JR Tokaido Line rapid train from San-no-miya Station to Osaka (around 25 minutes) and transfer to one of the trains listed here.

The Kansai Thru Pass offers unlimited travel on many private railways, subways, and buses and discounts at more than 350 tourist sights in Kansai. It can be a good choice for people doing a lot of sightseeing in all three cities, but at ¥4,380 for two days (¥5,400 for three) it is not a good value for visitors with JR Passes or those who plan to stay mostly in one city. Passes can be purchased at the main tourist information centers in Osaka and Nara.

**CONTACT Kansai Thru Pass.** ⊕ *www.surut-to.com/tickets/kansai_thru_english.html.*

# Hotels

Hotels in Kansai are slightly cheaper than those in Tokyo. Business hotels and international hotels comprise most of the lodging offerings in the larger cities, while ryokan (traditional inns) are common in more-rural destinations like Arima Onsen. Because of Kyoto's popularity during Golden Week (beginning of May), cherry-blossom season (mid-March to early April), and its autumn foliage (October and November), hotels in the surrounding cities are often booked solid. If you are traveling during one of these times, reserve a room early. Large international-chain hotels have English-speaking staff, but it's advisable to ask a tourist information center to make reservations for you outside the city.

# Planning Your Time

For many tourists, Osaka is a day trip, but it is also an excellent base for exploring the surrounding Kansai region—Kyoto, Nara, and Kobe are each 30 minutes away by train. Osaka is also the most convenient jumping-off point for a trip to the mountainside monasteries of Koya-san, two hours away on the Nankai private rail line.

Most visitors miss the best that Nara has to offer on a hurried day trip from Kyoto, Osaka, or Kobe. If time is an issue, the city is compact and well connected enough to explore all the temples and shrines in Nara Koen and spend a full morning or afternoon shopping and walking the streets of Nara-machi in one day. Spending a night in Nara gives you a chance to see a more traditional side of Kansai and to hit the main temples before the crowds arrive. Staying in Kobe means a chance to see the city's famous night panorama from the top of Mt. Rokko and a relaxing dinner at one of the many excellent restaurants overlooking the harbor.

The big attractions of Kobe can be covered in a day or two. Hit the Great Hanshin-Awaji Earthquake Museum and the Kobe City Museum in the morning. Follow this with a stroll around Kitano-cho and a café stop, and wind down the day at Harborland for dinner. On a second day head up Rokko-san and to the resort town of Arima, where you can soak in mineral hot springs and wander the quaint streets.

# Restaurants

Thanks to its history and unique culture, the Kansai region offers an unparalleled variety of Japanese cuisine. In addition to the local specialties of Osaka, Kobe, and Nara, Kansai has the same inexpensive chain restaurants as Tokyo and a good variety of international food.

## RESTAURANT AND HOTEL PRICES

Restaurant prices are the average cost of a main course at dinner or, if dinner is not served, at lunch. Hotel prices are the lowest cost of a standard double room in high season. Restaurant and hotel reviews have been shortened. For full information, visit Fodors.com.

| What It Costs in Yen | | | |
|---|---|---|---|
| $ | $$ | $$$ | $$$$ |
| **RESTAURANTS** | | | |
| under ¥1,500 | ¥1,500– ¥3,000 | ¥3,001– ¥5,000 | over ¥5,000 |
| **HOTELS** | | | |
| under ¥12,000 | ¥12,000– ¥18,000 | ¥18,001– ¥22,000 | over ¥22,000 |

## Visitor Information

There's a regional visitor information center in Kansai International Airport. Each city has its own visitor information center as well.

**CONTACT Kansai Tourist Information Center.** ✉ 1F Terminal 1 Bldg., Kansai International Airport, 1 Senshu-kuko Kita, Osaka ☎ 072/456-6160 ⊕ www.tourist-information-center.jp/kansai/en/kix.

## When to Go

Spring (March to May) and fall (September to November) are the best times to visit the Kansai region. The cherry blossoms flower mid-March to early April, and the autumn leaves are brightest around mid-November. Summer (mid-June to August) is very hot and sticky, but winters are usually dry, sunny, and cold. There's an erratic rainy season, mostly in June and July.

# Osaka (大阪市)

From Minami's neon-lighted Dotombori and historic Tenno-ji to the high-rises and underground shopping labyrinths of Kita, Osaka pulses with its own unique rhythm. Home to some of Japan's best food, most unique fashions, and warmest locals, Osaka rewards spontaneous exploration of random side streets or chats with a stranger.

Excluded from the formal circles of power and aristocratic culture in 16th-century Edo (Tokyo), Osaka took advantage of its position as Japan's trading center, developing its own art forms such as Bunraku puppet theater and Rakugo comic storytelling. It was in Osaka that feudal Japan's famed Floating World—the dining, theater, and pleasure district—was at its strongest and most inventive. Wealthy merchants and common laborers alike squandered fortunes on culinary delights, turning Osaka into "Japan's Kitchen," a moniker the city still has today. Though the city suffered a blow when the Meiji government canceled all of the samurai class's outstanding debts to the merchants, it was quick to recover. At the turn of the 20th century, it had become Japan's largest and most prosperous city, a center of commerce and manufacturing.

Today Osaka remains Japan's iconoclastic metropolis, refusing to fit Tokyo's norms and expectations. Unlike the hordes of Tokyo, Osakans are fiercely independent. As a contrast to the neon and concrete surroundings, the people of Osaka are known as Japan's friendliest and most outgoing. Ask someone on the street for directions in Tokyo and you are lucky to get so much as a glance. Ask someone in Osaka and you get a conversation.

The main areas of the city, Kita (north) and Minami (south), are divided by two rivers: the Dojima-gawa and the Tosabori-gawa. Between Kita and Minami is

Naka-no-shima, an island and the municipal center of Osaka.

Kita (north of Chuo Dori) is Osaka's economic hub and contains Osaka's largest stations: JR Osaka and Hankyu Umeda. The area is crammed with shops, department stores, and restaurants. Nearby are a nightlife district, Kita-shinchi; Naka-no-shima and the Museum of Oriental Ceramics (under renovation through 2023); Osaka-jo (Osaka Castle); and Osaka Koen (Osaka Park).

Restaurants, bars, department stores, and boutiques attract Osaka's youth to Minami (south Chuo Dori); theatergoers head to the National Bunraku Theatre and electronics lovers to Den Den Town. For a glimpse of old Osaka, visit Tenno-ji Temple and Shin Sekai. The main stations are Namba, Shin-sai-bashi, Namba Nankai, and Tenno-ji. There's easy access to the Municipal Museum of Fine Art and Sumiyoshi Taisha (Sumiyoshi Grand Shrine).

The bay area, to the west of the city center, is home to the Osaka Aquarium and Universal Studios Japan. The Shinkansen stops at Shin-Osaka, three stops (about five minutes) north of Osaka Station on the Mido-suji subway line. To the north of Shin-Osaka is Senri Expo Park.

## GETTING HERE AND AROUND
### AIRPORT TRANSFERS

Frequent trains run from Kansai International Airport to Tenno-ji and Shin Osaka (JR Kansai Airport Express Haruka, 30 and 45 minutes), JR Kyobashi Station (Kansai Airport Rapid, 70 minutes), and the Nankai Namba Station (Nankai Rapid Limited Express, 30 minutes).

Buses from Itami Airport operate at intervals of 15 minutes to one hour (depending on your destination), daily 6 am to 9 pm, and take passengers to seven locations in Osaka: Shin-Osaka Station, Umeda, Namba (near the Nikko and Holiday Inn hotels), Ue-hon-machi, Abeno, Sakai-higashi, and Osaka Business Park (near the Hotel New Otani). Buses take

25 to 50 minutes, depending on the destination, and cost ¥510 to ¥650.

### SUBWAY

Osaka's subway system (called the 'Metro') is extensive and efficient, running from early morning until nearly midnight at intervals of three to five minutes. Fares are between ¥180 and ¥400 and are determined by the distance traveled. Mido-suji is the main line, which runs north–south and has stations at Shin-Osaka, Umeda (next to Osaka Station), Shin-sai-bashi, Namba, and Tenno-ji. The Osaka 1-Day Pass (¥800 weekdays, ¥600 on weekends) provides unlimited municipal transportation on subways and city buses—at the commuter ticket machines in major subway stations and at the Japan Travel Bureau office in Osaka Station.

The JR Loop Line (Kanjo-sen) circles the city above ground and intersects with all subway lines. Fares range from ¥130 to ¥200, or you can use your JR Pass; these trains are not included in the day-pass price.

If you plan to do a lot of sightseeing, the Osaka Amazing pass is an excellent deal. For ¥2,800 (one day) or ¥3,600 (two days) you get unlimited travel on all non-JR trains and buses, a coupon book, and free admission to many of Osaka's most popular sights like Osaka Castle, the Museum of Oriental Ceramics (under renovation through 2023), and the Osaka City Museum of Fine Arts.

### TAXI

You'll have no problem hailing taxis on the street or at taxi stands. (A red light in the lower left corner of the windshield indicates availability.) The problem is Osaka's heavy traffic. Fares are metered at ¥660 for the first 2 km (1 mile), plus ¥80 for each additional 300 meters. Few taxi drivers speak English, so it's advisable to have your destination written in Japanese characters to show to the driver. You don't need to tip, and many

# Venice of the East

Despite changes in its political fortunes, Osaka developed as a trade center during the emerging Japanese (Yamato) nation, a role its waterways had destined it to play. Exchange wasn't limited to commerce. Buddhism and Chinese characters filtered into the fledgling Japanese society through Osaka to Nara, and from Nara to the rest of the country.

## A Merchant City

By 1590 Hideyoshi Toyotomi (1536–98), the first *daimyo* (warlord) to unite Japan, had completed construction of Osaka Castle to protect his realm against the unruly clans of Kyoto. He designated Osaka a merchant city to consolidate his position. After Toyotomi died, Ieyasu Tokugawa's (1543–1616) forces defeated the Toyotomi legacy at the Battle of Sekigahara in 1600. Osaka's strategic importance was again short-lived, as Tokugawa moved the capital to Edo (now Tokyo) in 1603. Osaka grew rich supplying the new capital with rice, soy sauce, and sake as Edo transformed its agricultural land into city suburbs. All copper produced in Japan was exported through Osaka, and the National Rice Exchange was headquartered in Dojima, near Kita-shinchi: "70% of the nation's wealth comes from Osaka" was the catch-phrase of the era. Some of Japan's business dynasties were founded during the economic boom of the 17th century, and they prevail today— Sumitomo, Konoike, and Mitsui among them.

## "Manchester of the East"

By the end of the Genroku era (1688–1704) Osaka's barons were patronizing Bunraku puppetry and Kamigata Kabuki (comic Kabuki). Chikamatsu Monzaemon (1653–1724), writer of *The Forty-Seven Ronin*, penned the tragedies, which quickly became classics. Ihara Saikaku (1642–93) immortalized the city's merchants in the risqué *Life of an Amorous Man* and *The Great Mirror of Male Love*. When Tokyo became the official capital of Japan in 1868 there were fears that the "Venice of the East" would suffer. But expansion of the spinning and textile industries assured prosperity, and earned Osaka a new epithet— "Manchester of the East."

## Japan's Main Port

As a consequence of the Great Kanto Earthquake in 1923, Osaka became Japan's main port and by 1926 the country's largest city. Chemical and heavy industries grew during World War I, and were prime targets for American bombers during World War II. Much of Osaka was flattened, and more than a third of the prefecture's 4.8 million people were left homeless. During the postwar years many Osaka companies moved their headquarters to Tokyo. Even so, Osaka was rebuilt and went on to host Asia's first World Expo in 1970. It has since fashioned itself as a city of cutting-edge technology, trendsetting, and a unique way of life. The Osaka City Government plans to revive the "Water City" appellation for Osaka, but for now the heritage of the city's waterways lives on in its place-names: *bashi* (bridge), *horie* (canal), and *semba* (dockyard).

taxis now accept credit cards. Late at night, generally after midnight, there's a 20% surcharge. Expect to pay ¥1,500 for trips between Osaka Station and Shin-sai-bashi/Namba. For short distances, walking is recommended.

## TRAIN

Shin-Osaka Station, on the north side of the Yodogawa River, is linked to the city center by the JR Kyoto Line and the Mido-suji subway line. On either line the ride, which takes 6 to 20 minutes depending on your midcity destination, costs ¥180 to ¥230. A taxi from Shin-Osaka Station to central Osaka costs ¥1,500 to ¥2,700.

## HOTELS

Osaka is known more as a business center than as a tourist destination, so hotel facilities are usually excellent, but their features are rarely distinctive, except at the high end of the scale. The city has modern accommodations for almost every taste. Choose accommodations based on location rather than amenities. Note that most hotels offer special rates much lower than the listed rack rates.

## NIGHTLIFE

Osaka has a lively nightlife scene, though it often revolves around eating and drinking. The Kita (North) area surrounds JR Umeda Station; and the Minami (South) area is between the Shin-sai-bashi and Namba districts and includes part of Chuo-ku (Central Ward). Many Japanese refer to Minami as being "for kids," but there are plenty of good restaurants and drinking spots for more-seasoned bon vivants. Osaka's hip young things hang out in Amerika-mura, in the southern part of Chuo-ku, with its innumerable bars and clubs. Kita draws a slightly more adult crowd, including businesspeople.

## RESTAURANTS

You can find a particularly broad range of Japanese food in Osaka, from the local snack foods, *okonomiyaki* (a thick pancake filled with cabbage and other ingredients) and *takoyaki* (tasty, grilled octopus in batter), to full *kaiseki* restaurants. The seafood from the Seto Inland Sea is always fresh, as is the tender beef used at the many Korean barbecue restaurants in Osaka's Korea Town, Tsuruhashi, located just outside the west exit of Tsuruhashi Station. It is also easy to find a variety of international cuisines throughout town.

Under Osaka Station is the Shin-Umeda Shokudogai—a maze of narrow alleys lined with *izakaya* (lively after-work drinking haunts). The beer and hot snacks comfort many an overworked person on the commute home.

For some lively dining, head to Dotombori-dori and Soemon-cho (pronounced "*so*-eh-mon cho"), two areas along Dotombori River packed with restaurants and bars. Kimono-clad *mama-sans* serve the city's expense-accounters at Kitashinchi, in south Kita-ku, the city's most exclusive dining quarter.

## SHOPPING

As with everything else in Osaka, the city rewards shoppers with a sense of adventure. Though Osaka is full of shopping complexes, towering department stores, and brand-name shops, you must step away from the main streets and explore neighborhood shops and boutiques to find the best deals, newest electronics, and cutting-edge fashions. Osaka's miles of labyrinthine underground shopping complexes offer an escape from summer heat and are an experience in and of themselves. The network of tunnels and shops in underground Umeda is the most impressive (and confusing). Fortunately, signs and maps are plentiful and the information-desk staff speak English.

At one time famous for its traditional crafts—particularly *karaki-sashimono* (ornately carved furniture), fine Naniwa Suzu-ki pewterware, and *uchihamono* (Sakai cutlery)—Osaka lost much of its traditional industry during World War II. The simplest way to find Osakan crafts is to visit one of the major department stores.

There are specialized wholesale areas throughout the city, and many have a few retail shops as well. One such area is **Doguya-suji,** just east of Nankai Namba Station and the Takashimaya department store. This street is lined with shops selling nothing but kitchen goods—all sorts of pots, pans, utensils, and glassware are piled to the rafters. Though most customers are in the restaurant trade, laypeople shop here, too. Feel free to wander around: there's no obligation to buy. A trip here could be combined with a visit to nearby **Den Den Town,** known for its electronic goods. Also in this neighborhood, east of the main entrance to Doguya-suji, is **Kuromon Ichiba,** the famous market district where chefs select the treats—fruits, vegetables, meat, and much more—cooked at the city's restaurants that evening.

Though it is being slowly invaded by chain stores, Osaka's famed **Amerika-mura** is still a good place to find hip fashions. For original boutiques and cutting-edge styles, head to the streets of **Minami-semba** and **Minami-horie** to the west.

## SIGHTS

Most of Osaka's museums are closed Monday. One exception is Senri Expo Park, which closes (along with its museums) Wednesday. Museums stay open on Monday national holidays, closing the following day instead. Likewise, Senri Expo Park stays open on Wednesday holidays, closing Thursday instead.

## VISITOR INFORMATION

The main visitor information center is inside JR Osaka Station on the ground floor. The Shin-Osaka center is at the JR local line exit at Shin-Osaka Station. The Namba center is on the first floor of Nankai Namba Station. They are all open

daily 9 to 8 and closed December 31 to January 3.

**CONTACTS Namba Tourist Information Center.** ☒ *5–1–60 Namba, Chuo-ku* ☎ *06/6131–4550.* **Osaka Tourist Information Center.** ☒ *3–1–1 Umeda, JR Osaka Station, 1F, Kita-ku* ☎ *06/6131–4550.* **Shin-Osaka Tourist Information Center.** ☒ *JR Shin-Osaka Station, 3F, 5–16–1 Nishinakajima, Yodo-gawa-ku* ☎ *06/6131–4450.*

# Kita (北区)

Culture by day and glamour by night: Kita (north of Chuo Dori) is the place to come for the museums of Naka-no-shima, the city's deluxe department stores, and the chance to lose yourself (intentionally or not) in one of Japan's largest underground shopping labyrinths. At night take in the view from the Umeda Sky Building or the Ferris wheel at the HEP Five department store before you explore Osaka's upscale entertainment district, Kita-shinichi. The Museum of Oriental Ceramics is closed for most of 2022 and 2023 for a major renovation.

## ◉ Sights

### Hattori Ryokuchi Park (服部緑地)

MUSEUM VILLAGE | Come for the park's open-air Museum of Old Japanese Farmhouses (Nihon Minka Shuraku Hakubutsukan), and wander about full-size traditional rural buildings such as the giant *gassho-zukuri* (thatched-roof) farmhouse from Gifu Prefecture. The park also has horseback-riding facilities, tennis courts, and an open-air stage that hosts concerts and other events in summer. There's even an outdoor Kabuki theater. An English-language pamphlet is available. Take the Mido-suji subway line from Umeda to Ryokuchi Koen Station; the park is a 10-minute walk away. ☒ *1–1 Hattori Ryokuchi, Toyonaka* ☎ *06/6862–4945 park office, 06/6862–3137 museum* ⊕ *hattori.*

Osaka's aquarium is one of the best in Japan and also one of the world's largest.

osaka-park.or.jp ✉ Park free, museum ¥500 ⊘ Museum closed Mon.

**Japan Folk Crafts Museum Osaka** (大阪日本民芸館; *Osaka Nihon Mingeikan*)
ART MUSEUM | The exhibits of "beauty from day-to-day life" at this museum in Senri Expo Park explore the diversity and intricacy of Japanese handicrafts from Hokkaido to Okinawa. The cloth, wood, and bamboo items in simple displays evoke Japan's traditional past and make quite a contrast to Osaka's modernity. ✉ Senri Expo Park, 10–5 Bampaku Koen, Suita ☎ 06/6877–1971 ⊕ www.mingei-kan-osaka.or.jp/en/info ✉ ¥710 ⊘ Closed Wed.

**National Museum of Ethnology**
(国立民族学博物館;
*Kokuritsu Minzokugaku Hakubutsukan*)
HISTORY MUSEUM | The National Museum of Ethnology has informative displays about the Ainu (the original inhabitants of Hokkaido) and other cultures from around the world. Information sheets explaining the sections of the museum are available and supplement the English-language

brochure included with admission. The museum is on the east side of the main road that runs north–south through Senri Expo Park. ✉ Senri Expo Park, Suita ☎ 06/6876–2151 ⊕ www.minpaku.ac.jp/en ✉ ¥580 ⊘ Closed Wed.

★ **Osaka Aquarium Kaiyukan** (大阪水族館海遊館; *Osaka Suizokukan Kaiyukan*)
AQUARIUM | FAMILY | This eye-catching red, gray, and blue building is Japan's best aquarium outside of Okinawa and one of the world's largest. More than 11,000 tons of water hold a multitude of sea creatures, including whale sharks, king penguins, giant spider crabs, jellyfish, and sea otters. You can stroll through 15 different environments, including the rivers and streams of Japanese and Ecuadoran forests, the icy waters around Antarctica, the dark depths of the Sea of Japan, and the volcanically active Pacific Ring of Fire. The surrounding Tempozan Harbor Village also contains a contemporary culture museum, a giant ferris wheel, cruises around Osaka Bay on a reproduction of the Santa María, and

# Top Reasons to Go to Osaka

**The World of Tomorrow:** Dotombori buzzes with energy in the heart of Osaka's frenzied neonscape. Domestic robots and space-shuttle parts bring high-tech to the narrow streets.

**Japan's Kitchen:** Osaka has been *nihon no daidokoro* (the country's kitchen) since the 17th century. Now the cuisine borrows from all over the world.

**Party 'til the Rising Sun:** See next season's fashions previewed in Shin-sai-bashi, get down in a club, or belt out hits in a subterranean karaoke bar.

**Osaka Aquarium:** The Osaka Kaiyu-kan is an epic voyage through the depths of the marine world. The king penguins are enchanting, and the whale shark is a wonder of the sea.

**Architecture:** Skyscrapers share Osaka's 1,500-year-old skyline with 4th-century burial mounds. Minimalist master Tadao Ando redefines the Japanese cityscape from his office in downtown Osaka.

---

various shops and restaurants. There are often street performances outside on weekends. To get here, take the Chuo subway line to Osaka-ko Station; the aquarium is a five-minute walk northwest from the station. ⊠ *1–1–10 Kaigan-dori, Minato-ku* ☎ *06/6576–5501* ⊕ *www. kaiyukan.com/language/eng* 🕮 *¥2,400* Ⓜ *Osakako Station.*

★ **Osaka Castle** (大阪城; *Osaka-jo*)
**CASTLE/PALACE** | Osaka's most visible tourist attraction and symbol, Osaka Castle exemplifies the city's ability to change with the times. Originally built in the 1580s, what you see today is a five-story reconstruction completed in 1931. Instead of leaving a collection of steep wooden staircases and empty rooms, Osaka turned its castle into an elevator-equipped museum celebrating the history of its creator, Hideyoshi Toyotomi, the chief imperial minister to unite Japan.

For those more interested in aesthetics than artifacts, the eighth-floor *donjon* (tower) offers a stunning view of the urban landscape. Watching the sun set behind the skyscrapers is reason enough for a visit. The surrounding park makes for a relaxing break from the energy of

the city as well. From Osaka-jo Koen-mae Station, it's about a 10-minute uphill walk to the castle. You can also take the Tani-machi subway line from Higashi-Umeda Station (just southeast of Osaka Station) to Tanimachi 4-chome Station, from there it's a 15-minute walk. ⊠ *1–1 Osaka-jo, Chuo-ku* ☎ *06/6941–3044* ⊕ *www.osaka-castle.net* 🕮 *¥600.*

**Osaka Expo Park**
(万博記念公園; *Banpaku Kinen Koen*)
**GARDEN** | Originally the site of Expo '70, the garden-filled Senri Expo Park still draws visitors thanks to the presence of the National Museum of Ethnology, the Japan Folk Art Museum, and the enormous statue by Taro Okamoto called *Tower of the Sun.* Located outside the city center, the park offers an interesting look at how Osaka has blossomed in the postwar years in the Expo '70 Pavilion. ⊠ *Senri Expo Park, Suita* ☎ *06/6877–7387* ⊕ *www.expo70-park.jp* 🕮 *Gardens ¥260 each; Expo '70 Pavilion ¥210* 🕐 *Closed Wed.* Ⓜ *Osaka Monorail Line, Banpaku Kinen Koen Station.*

Osaka-jo, originally built in the 1580s and reconstructed in 1931, is on a hill above the Osaka-jo Koen-mae Station.

★ **Osaka Museum of History** (大阪歴史博物館; *Osaka Rekishi Hakubutsukan*)
**HISTORY MUSEUM | FAMILY |** Informative as it is enjoyable, the Osaka Museum of History immerses you in the city's history from pre-feudal times to the early 20th century. Full of life-size displays and hands-on activities, the museum does an excellent job of offering attractions for both children and adults. There are two paths through the exhibits, a Highlight Course (to get a hint of Osaka's past in less than an hour) and the Complete Course (for a fuller experience). The museum makes an excellent stop on the way to Osaka Castle. ✉ *4–1–30 Otemae, Osaka ✛ Chuo-ku* ☎ *06/6946–5728* ⊕ *www.mus-his.city.osaka.jp* 🖅 *¥600* 🕐 *Closed Tues.* Ⓜ *Tanimachi 4-chome Station (exit 9 or 2).*

**Tenman-gu Shrine** (天満宮)
**RELIGIOUS BUILDING |** This 10th-century shrine is the main site of the annual Tenjin Matsuri, held July 24 and 25, one of the largest and most enthusiastically celebrated festivals in Japan. Dozens of floats are paraded through the streets, and more than 100 vessels, lighted by lanterns, sail along the canals amid fireworks. The shrine is dedicated to Sugawara no Michizane, the Japanese patron of scholars. Sugawara was out of favor at court when he died in 903. Two years later plague and drought swept Japan—Sugawara was exacting revenge from the grave. To appease Sugawara's spirit he was deified as Tenjin-sama. He is enshrined at Tenman-gu. On the 5th, 15th, and 25th of each month students throughout Japan visit Tenman-gu shrines to pray for academic success. ✉ *2–1–8 Tenshinbashi, Kita-ku* ☎ *06/6353–0025* ⊕ *osakatemmangu.or.jp* 🖅 *Free* Ⓜ *JR Tozai Line Osaka Tenmangu Station or Tanimachi Subway Line Minami Mori Machi Station.*

**Universal Studios Japan** (ユニバーサルスタジオジャパン)
**AMUSEMENT PARK/CARNIVAL | FAMILY** The 140-acre Universal Studios Japan combines the most popular rides and shows from Universal's Hollywood and

# On the Menu

Osakans are passionate about food. In fact, they coined the word *kuidaore*— to eat until you drop. They expect restaurants to use the freshest ingredients. For centuries the nearby Seto Inland Sea has allowed easy access to fresh seafood. Osakans continue to have discriminating palates and demand their money's worth.

Osakan cuisine is flavored with a soy sauce lighter in color and milder in flavor than the soy used in Tokyo. One local delicacy is *okonomiyaki*, something between a pancake and an omelet, filled with cabbage, mountain yams, pork, shrimp, and other ingredients. *Osaka-zushi* (Osaka-style sushi), made in wooden molds, has a distinctive square shape. *Unagi* (eel) remains a popular local dish; grilled unagi is eaten in summer for quick energy. *Fugu* (blowfish), served boiled or raw, is a winter delicacy. Osaka is

also the home of *kappo-ryori*, intimate, counter-only eateries that serve only the freshest seasonal foods in a relaxed atmosphere.

The thick, white noodles known as *udon* are a Japanese staple, but Osakans are particularly fond of *kitsune* udon, a local dish (now popular throughout Japan) in which the noodles are served with fried tofu known as *abura-age*. Another Osaka invention is *takoyaki*, griddle dumplings with octopus, green onions, and ginger smothered in a delicious sauce. Sold by street vendors in Dotombori, these tasty snacks also appear at every festival and street market in Kansai. And for heavier fare, Osaka is famous for *kushi katsu*, skewered, deep-fried meat and vegetables. If you don't want to fall over, try to leave the table *hara-hachi bunme*, meaning "80% full."

Florida movie-studio theme parks with special attractions designed specifically for Japan. Popular attractions include those based on Harry Potter, Spider-Man, and the most recently opened Super Nintendo World. The Japan-only Snoopy attraction appeals to the local infatuation with all things cute, as do the daily Hello Kitty parades. Restaurants and food outlets abound throughout the park, and the road from JR Universal City Station is lined with the likes of Hard Rock Cafe and Bubba Gump Shrimp, local fast-food chain MOS Burger, and Ganko Sushi. Due to high demand on weekends and during holiday periods, tickets should be bought online in advance. Express passes (to skip the lines for some attractions) can be purchased for an additional fee. ⊠ *2–1–33 Sakurajima, Konohana-ku* ⊹ *Take the JR Yumesaki (also called the JR Sakurajima) Line from Osaka to*

*Universal City Station (may require a change at Nishikujo)* ☎ *0570/200–606* ⊕ *www.usj.co.jp* ⊠ *From ¥8,400.*

 **Restaurants**

### Akashiya (明石屋)

**$$ | JAPANESE |** It may look like a hole-in-the-wall from the outside, but this tiny cash-only restaurant serves up some of Osaka's finest *akashi-yaki*, a much fluffier and more delicate take on the city's famous grilled octopus. The staff are friendly and helpful. **Known for:** broad range of local sake; cozy, rustic atmosphere; melt-in-your-mouth akashi-yaki. ⓢ *Average main: ¥2,200* ⊠ *Kita Shinichi Bldg., 1–3–23 Dojima, 1st fl., Kita-ku* ☎ *06/6341–3910* ▬ *No credit cards* ⊗ *Closed Sun. No lunch.*

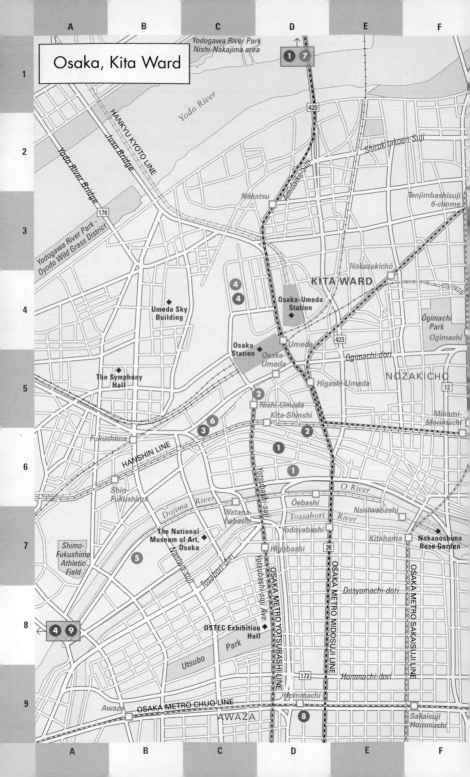

## Sights ▼

1 Hattori Ryokuchi Park............. D1
2 Japan Folk Crafts
  Museum Osaka .................... I1
3 National Museum
  of Ethnology ..................... I1
4 Osaka Aquarium Kaiyukan ....... A8
5 Osaka Castle ....................... I8
6 Osaka Expo Park................... I1
7 Osaka Museum of History ........ H9
8 Tenman-gu Shrine................. D9
9 Universal Studios Japan.......... A8

## Restaurants ▼

1 Akashiya.......................... D6
2 Batten Yokato .................... D6
3 La Baie........................... C6
4 Shunkoku Shunsai................. C4

## Hotels ▼

1 ANA Crowne Plaza Osaka........ D6
2 Hilton Osaka..................... C5
3 Hotel New Otani Osaka ........... J7
4 InterContinental Osaka .......... C4
5 Rihga Royal Hotel Osaka......... B7
6 The Ritz-Carlton, Osaka ........... C5
7 Shin-Osaka
  Washington Hotel Plaza .......... D1

### Batten Yokato (バッテンよかとぉ)

**$$ | JAPANESE |** In the basement of Kita-Shinichi's Aspa (Takagawa Umeda) Building, the hip, low-ceilinged Batten Yokato serves a wide selection of very good *yakitori* (skewered meat and vegetables) in a fun, cozy atmosphere. Sitting at the long bar, you can watch the cooks work and call out requests. **Known for:** yakitori grilled to perfection; specially sourced Hakata chicken; entertaining open kitchen. $ *Average main: ¥3,000* ✉ *Takagawa Umeda Bldg., 1–11–24 Kita-shinichi, 1st fl., Kita-ku, Chuo-ku* ☎ *06/4799–7447* ⊘ *Closed Sun. No lunch.*

### ★ La Baie (ラ・ベ)

**$$$$ | FRENCH |** The city's premier hotel restaurant serves extremely good French food. The elegant yet relaxed atmosphere, seasonal menus, and extensive wine list make La Baie an excellent choice when you're in the mood for European-style fare. **Known for:** dining room feels like 19th century Europe; excellent table-side service; impressive list of French wines. $ *Average main: ¥15,000* ✉ *The Ritz-Carlton Osaka, 2–5–25 Umeda, Kita-ku* ☎ *06/6343–7020* ⊕ *labaie.ritzcarltonosaka.com* ⊘ *Closed Mon. and Tues.*

### Shunkoku Shunsai (旬穀旬菜)

**$$ | ASIAN FUSION |** Shunkoku Shunsai (literally "seasonal grains, seasonal vegetables") is a tasty change from the heavier Osaka cuisine. The healthy French-Japanese fusion dishes are fresh and light but filling, and the ¥1,155 lunch sets are a good value. **Known for:** fresh produce grown just across the street; healthy set meals; refreshing salads. $ *Average main: ¥3,000* ✉ *Grand Front Osaka North Bldg., 3–1 Ofuku-cho, 6th fl., Kita-ku* ☎ *06/6359–3072* ▭ *No credit cards* ⊘ *No dinner Mon.*

##  Hotels

### ANA Crowne Plaza Osaka (ANAクラウンプラザホテル大阪)

**$$$$ | HOTEL |** One of Osaka's most venerable deluxe hotels, the Crowne Plaza overlooks Naka-no-shima Park. **Pros:** centrally located; interesting architecture; cozy rooms. **Cons:** regular rooms are on the small side; service is efficient but a bit too businesslike; at least a 10-minute walk from heart of the Kita area. $ *Rooms from: ¥25,000* ✉ *1–3–1 Dojima-hama, Kita-ku* ☎ *06/6347–1112* ⊕ *www.anacrowneplaza-osaka.jp* ⊷ *493 rooms* ⊘ *No Meals.*

### Hilton Osaka (ヒルトン大阪)

**$$$$ | HOTEL |** Glitz and glitter lure expense-accounters to the Hilton Osaka, in the heart of the business district, a typical Western-style hotel with endless marble and brass. **Pros:** deluxe and executive floors have stylish rooms; good spa and indoor swimming pool; across from JR Osaka Station. **Cons:** service is hit or miss; restaurants and breakfast are just average; little sets it apart from less expensive hotels. $ *Rooms from: ¥50,000* ✉ *1–8–8 Umeda, Kita-ku* ☎ *06/6347–7111* ⊕ *www.hilton.com* ⊷ *525 rooms* ⊘ *No Meals.*

### Hotel New Otani Osaka (ホテルニューオータニ大阪)

**$$$$ | HOTEL |** Indoor and outdoor pools, a rooftop garden, tennis courts, and a sparkling marble atrium make this hotel a popular choice for both Japanese and Western travelers. **Pros:** rooms facing the castle have beautiful views; large rooms; many amenities. **Cons:** outdoor pool only open in July and August; rooms without castle views are average; not as centrally located as other hotels. $ *Rooms from: ¥35,000* ✉ *1–4–1 Shiromi, Chuo-ku* ☎ *06/6941–1111* ⊕ *www.newotani.co.jp/en/osaka* ⊷ *578 rooms* ⊘ *No Meals.*

### ★ InterContinental Osaka
(インターコンチネンタルホテル大阪)

$$$$ | HOTEL | Since it opened in 2013, the InterContinental Osaka has been regarded as one of the city's top luxury hotels. **Pros:** excellent location next to Umeda Station; lovely views; everything's completely up-to-date. **Cons:** although good, service is not always at a five-star level; navigating the Osaka Station complex to get to the hotel can be confusing; one of the most expensive hotels in the area. $ *Rooms from: ¥40,000* ⊠ *3–60 Ofuka-cho, Kita-ku* ☎ *06/6374–5700* ⊕ *www.ihg.com* ⇨ *272 rooms* ❑ *No Meals.*

### Rihga Royal Hotel Osaka
(リーガロイヤルホテル大阪)

$$$$ | HOTEL | Built in the 1930s, the well-established Rihga Royal is where the royal family stays when visiting Osaka. **Pros:** the scale is impressive; amenities abound; imperial visits set it apart from similar hotels. **Cons:** regular rooms are small; hotel is clean but dated; less-than-convenient location requires taking the shuttle bus. $ *Rooms from: ¥32,000* ⊠ *5–3–68 Naka-no-shima, Kita-ku* ☎ *06/6448–1121* ⊕ *www.rihga.com* ⇨ *1,033 rooms* ❑ *No Meals.*

### ★ The Ritz-Carlton, Osaka
(リッツカールトン大阪)

$$$$ | HOTEL | More intimate than the city's other luxury hotels, the Ritz-Carlton combines a homey atmosphere and European elegance. **Pros:** luxurious to the last detail; high-tech touches; stunning views. **Cons:** the Old Europe decor isn't for everyone; breakfast is a letdown for this class of hotel; rates hit the stratosphere. $ *Rooms from: ¥45,000* ⊠ *2–5–25 Umeda, Kita-ku* ☎ *06/6343–7000* ⊕ *www.ritzcarlton.com* ⇨ *292 rooms* ❑ *No Meals.*

### Shin-Osaka Washington Hotel Plaza
(新大阪ワシントンホテルプラザ)

$$ | HOTEL | Part of a no-nonsense chain of business hotels, the Shin-Osaka Washington Hotel Plaza is the smartest of its kind. **Pros:** great location if you have an early train to catch; good value; nice Chinese restaurant. **Cons:** tiny rooms; many staff members have limited English; not very close to any sights or nightlife. $ *Rooms from: ¥15,000* ⊠ *5–5–15 Nishi-Nakajima, Yodo-gawa-ku* ☎ *06/6303–8111* ⊕ *washington.jp/shinosaka/en* ⇨ *490 rooms* ❑ *No Meals.*

##  Nightlife

### BARS
**Bar K** (バー・ケイ)

BARS | With subdued, dark wood interiors and relaxed ambience, Bar K is the best place in Osaka to sample a range of Japanese whiskeys. The knowledgeable bartenders also mix excellent cocktails. ⊠ *1–3–3 Sonezaki-shinichi, Kita-ku* ☎ *06/6343–1167* ⊕ *bar-k.jp* ☺ *Closed Sun.*

### JAZZ
**Mr. Kelly's** (ミスターケリーズ)

LIVE MUSIC | This club on the ground floor of the Hotel Vista Prima Donna regularly features a jazz trio and a vocalist. Well-known acts also stop by for performances. The cover charge starts at ¥3,500. ⊠ *Hotel Mystays, 2–4–1 Sonezaki Shinchi, 1st fl., Kita-ku* ☎ *06/6342–5821* ⊕ *www.misterkellys.co.jp* ☺ *Closed Sun.*

### ROCK AND ALTERNATIVE
**Club Quattro** (クラブクアトロ)

LIVE MUSIC | Up-and-coming Japanese rock bands and popular Western bands play at this popular venue. The sound system is excellent. ⊠ *Plaza Umeda, 8–17 Taiyujicho, 10th fl., Kita-ku* ☎ *06/6311–8111* ⊕ *www.club-quattro.com/en/umeda*

##  Shopping

### DEPARTMENT STORES
**Hanshin Hyakkaten** (阪神百貨店)

DEPARTMENT STORE | The food hall in the basement of Hanshin department store is the city's best. ⊠ *1–13–13 Umeda, Kita-ku* ☎ *06/6345–1201* ⊕ *www.hanshin-dept.jp.*

**Hankyu Hyakkaten** (阪急百貨店)

DEPARTMENT STORE | Headquartered in Osaka, Hankyu has 15 floors of shopping. Across the street is Hankyu Men's Osaka, which claims to have the country's largest selection of men's clothing. ⊠ *8–7 Kakuta-cho, Kita-ku* ☎ *06/6361–1381* ⊕ *www.hankyu-dept.co.jp/fl/english/honten.*

**HEP Five** (ヘップファイブ)

DEPARTMENT STORE | If you want to take a break from shopping, head to the roof of HEP Five, where you can take in great night views of the city from the enormous Ferris wheel for just ¥600. ⊠ *5–15 Kakuda-cho, Kita-ku* ☎ *06/6313–0501* ⊕ *www.hepfive.jp.*

### ELECTRONICS

Although some Japanese electronic goods may be cheaper in the United States than in Japan, many electronics products are released on the Japanese market 6 to 12 months before they reach the West. The reason to buy in Japan is to find something you won't find elsewhere, not to find a bargain.

**Yodobashi Camera** (ヨドバシカメラ)

ELECTRONICS | Don't be put off by the name: this enormous electronics department store sells far more than just cameras. On the north side of JR Osaka Station, the store is impossible to miss. ⊠ *1–1 Ofuka-cho, Kita-ku* ☎ *06/4802–1010* ⊕ *www.yodobashi.com.*

### SHOPPING COMPLEXES AND MALLS

Hilton Plaza West and East have international brands like Max Mara, Dunhill, Chanel, and Ferragamo. Herbis Ent Plaza is a local high-end shopping complex connected to the Hilton Plaza West complex. These three shopping complexes are opposite Osaka Station.

**Grand Front Osaka** (グランフロント大阪)

SHOPPING CENTER | Opened in 2013, this stylish shopping complex sits just outside Umeda Station. With more than 266 shops, restaurants, and galleries as well as the InterContinental Hotel, this all-in-one complex is set to fulfill just about any shopping needs. It is a pleasant space to wander around, and the seats on the upper floors are relaxing spots to chill and people-watch. ⊠ *3–60 Ofukacho, Kita-ku* ☎ *06/6372–6300* ⊕ *www.grand-front-osaka.jp.*

**NU Chayamachi** (NU茶屋町)

SHOPPING CENTER | To the east of the Hankyu Grand Building is NU Chayamachi—a collection of small boutiques, both local and foreign, and some good cafés. ⊠ *10–12 Chayamachi, Kita-ku* ☎ *06/6373–7371* ⊕ *nu-chayamachi.com.*

 ## Activities

### BASEBALL

**Hanshin Tigers** (阪神タイガース)

BASEBALL & SOFTBALL | The Orix Buffaloes are the local team, but it is the Hanshin Tigers from Nishinomiya, between Kobe and Osaka, that prompt excited fans to jump into the Dotombori River. The Tigers are based in historic Koshien Stadium near Kobe, but they play at the Saka Dome (Kyocera Domu Osaka) for the season opener and during the month of August. The Osaka Dome looks like a spaceship and has pleasing-to-the-eye curved edges in a city dominated by gray cubes. Tickets cost as little as ¥1,600. Buy them at the gate, at Lawson convenience stores, or online. The dome is next to Osaka Domu-mae Chiyozaki subway station on the Nagahori Tsurumi-ryokuchi Line. ⊠ *1–8–2 Koshien-cho, Nishinomiya* ⊕ *hanshintigers.jp.*

### SOCCER

**Gamba Osaka** (ガンバ大阪)

SOCCER | The Gamba Osaka soccer team play at the Suita City Football Stadium (also known as the Panasonic Stadium Suita), located in the north part of the city. Access is via the Osaka Monorail to Bampaku-kinen-koen Station. Tickets start at ¥1,500 for adults, and the season runs from March to November. ⊠ *3–3*

*Senri Bampaku Koen, Suita* ☎ *06/6875–8111* ⊕ *www.gamba-osaka.net/en.*

# Minami (ミナミ)

Tradition by day and neon by night, Minami is the place to come for Osaka history: Japan's oldest temple, a breathtaking collection of Japanese art in the Osaka City Museum of Fine Arts, and a mausoleum bigger than the pyramids. And then youth culture takes over: this is where future fashionistas forge the haute couture of tomorrow. Amid all this modernity are glimpses of an older Osaka in sights like Shin Sekai and Tenno-ji Temple.

 ## Sights

### Amerika-mura (アメリカ村)

**NEIGHBORHOOD** | Though it takes its name from the original shops that sold cheap American fashions and accessories, Amerika-mura (meaning "America Village"), or Ame-mura (pronounced "*ah*-meh *moo*-ra") as it's more often called, is now a bustling district full of trendy clothing stores, record stores, bars, cafés, and clubs that cater to teenagers and young adults. Shops are densely packed, and it's virtually impossible to walk these streets on weekends. To see the variety of styles and fashions prevalent among urban youth, Ame-Mura is *the* place to go in Osaka. ⊠ *West side of Mido-suji, 6 blocks south of Shin-sai-bashi Station, Chuo-ku.*

### ★ Dotonbori (道頓堀)

**NEIGHBORHOOD** | If you only have one night in Osaka, the neighborhood of Dotonbori (named after the canal and adjacent street of the same name) is the place to go. Once Osaka's old theater district, Dotonbori is now a lively pedestrian zone centered around the Ebisu-bashi Bridge, which lies under the neon lights of the Glico 'Running Man' sign, one of Osaka's main landmarks and popular hangout spot. Nearby streets are filled with restaurants, shops, and the shouts of countless touts, each proclaiming (usually falsely) that their restaurant is the only one worth visiting. Sadly, many of the restaurants on the main street are being replaced by drugstores catering to overseas tourists, but the side streets in the area are a culinary treasure-trove. Stroll along the riverfront walkways to avoid the crowds, or slip into Hozenji Yokocho Alley, two blocks south of Dotonbori-dori, to splash water on the moss-covered statues at Hozenji Shrine or dine in any of the excellent restaurants hidden away on this quiet street. ⊠ *Dotonbori-dori, Chuo-ku.*

### Isshin-ji Temple (一心寺)

**TEMPLE** | The ultramodern gate and fierce guardian statues of Isshin-ji Temple are a stark contrast to the nearby Shitenno-ji Temple. Dating back to 1185, the temple is now known for its Okotsubutsu—a Buddha statue made of the cremated remains of more than 200,000 people laid to rest at Isshin-ji. Far from morbid, the statue is meant to reaffirm one's respect for the deceased and to turn them into an object of everyday worship. An Okutsubutsu is made every 10 years, the first in 1887. Though 12 Okutsubutsu have been made, due to a direct hit to the temple during World War II, only the six crafted after the war remain. ⊠ *2–8–69 Osaka, Tenno-ji-ku* ⊕ *Sakaisuji Subway Line Ebisu-cho Station, Osaka JR Loop Line Tennoji Station* ☎ *06/6771–0444* ⊕ *isshinji.or.jp* 🎫 *Free.*

### Keitaku-en Garden (慶沢園)

**GARDEN** | Jihei Ogawa, master gardener of the late Meiji period, spent 10 years working the late Lord Sumitomo's circular garden into a masterpiece. The woods surrounding the pond are a riot of color in spring, when the cherry blossoms and azaleas bloom. Keitaku-en is adjacent to Shiritsu Bijutsukan in Tenno-ji Koen. ⊠ *108 Chausuyama-cho, Tenno-ji-ku* ☎ *06/6761–1770* 🎫 *¥150* ⊗ *Closed Mon.*

# Osaka, Minami

CHUO WARD

Tanimachiyon-chome

Osaka Museum
of History

Osaka Castle
Park

UEMACHI

Tanimachi
6-chome

TSURUMI-RYOKUCHI LINE

102

National
Bunraku Theatre

Sennichimae-dori

Tanimachi-
chome

OSAKA METRO TANIMACHI LINE

Osaka Uehommachi
Station

TENNOJI WARD

Shitennōji-mae
Yūhigaoka

0        1/4 mi

0        1/4 km

Tennōji

Teradachō

OSAKA LOOP LINE

Osaka-Abenobashi
Station

## KEY

1 Sights
1 Restaurants
1 Quick Bites
1 Hotels

## Sights ▼

1  Amerika-Mura ..................... **E3**
2  Dotonbori ........................... **E4**
3  Isshin-ji Temple ................... **G8**
4  Keitaku-en Garden ............... **G9**
5  Mido-suji Boulevard............... **E1**
6  Nipponbashi Den Den Town....... **F6**
7  Osaka City Museum
   of Fine Arts ........................ **G9**
8  Shin Sekai .......................... **F8**
9  Shitennoji Temple.................. **H7**
10 Sumiyoshi Taisha
   Grand Shrine ....................... **E9**
11 Tenno-ji Park ...................... **G8**
12 Tomb of Emperor Nintoku.......... **E9**
13 Tsutenkaku Tower ................. **F8**

## Restaurants ▼

1  Hana Goyomi........................ **E5**
2  Kani Doraku Dotombori Honten... **E4**
3  Kigawa.............................. **F4**
4  Mizuno .............................. **F4**
5  Taqueria La Fonda ................. **H1**

## Quick Bites ▼

1  Planet3rd ........................... **E3**
2  Yaekatsu ............................ **F9**

## Hotels ▼

1  Cross Hotel Osaka.................. **E4**
2  Hoarton Hotel
   Shinsaibashi Nagahori Dori ..... **D3**
3  Hotel Nikko Osaka.................. **E3**
4  Osaka Marriott Miyako Hotel .... **H9**
5  The St. Regis Osaka ............... **E1**
6  Sheraton Miyako
   Hotel Osaka ........................ **J5**
7  Swissôtel Nankai Osaka........... **E5**
8  Toyoko Inn
   Shinsaibashi Nishi................. **D3**

**Mido-suji Boulevard** (御堂筋)

STREET | Osaka's Champs Élysées, this ginko-tree-lined boulevard is Osaka's most elegant thoroughfare and home to its greatest concentration of department stores. To the east of Mido-suji is the Shin-sai-bashi-suji arcade, one of Osaka's best shopping and entertainment streets. If you're in town on the second Sunday in October, catch the annual Mido-suji Parade, with its colorful procession of floats and musicians. ⊠ *Chuo-ku* ✛ *The Shin-sai-bashi stop (Exit 7) on Mido-suji subway line is in heart of city's shopping districts.*

**Nipponbashi Den Den Town**
(でんでんタウン)

NEIGHBORHOOD | All the latest video games, computers, cameras, phones, build-your-own-robot kits, and other gadgets are on display here. Even if you are not in the market for electronics, a stroll through Den Den Town provides an interesting look at Japan's anime, video game, and computer subcultures. "Den Den" is derived from the word *denki,* which means "electricity." ⊠ *2 blocks east of Namba Station, Naniwa-ku.*

**Osaka City Museum of Fine Arts** (大阪市立 美術館; *Osaka Shiritsu Bijutsukan*)

ART MUSEUM | The building isn't too impressive, but the exceptional collection of 12th- to 14th-century classical Japanese art on the second floor is. Other collections include the works of Edo-period artist Korin Ogata, more than 3,000 examples of modern lacquerware, and a collection of Chinese paintings and artifacts. Temporary exhibitions often feature famous international works and artists. Take the Loop Line or the Mido-suji subway line to Tenno-ji Station, or the Tani-machi subway to Shitenno-ji-mae. ⊠ *1–82 Chausuyama-cho, Tenno-ji-ku* ☎ *06/6771–4874* ⊕ *www.osaka-art-museum.jp/en* ☑ *¥300* ⊙ *Closed Mon.*

★ **Shin Sekai** (新世界)

NEIGHBORHOOD | Stepping into Shin Sekai is a chance to see the Osaka of a generation ago. Built in 1912, the neighborhood was meant to emulate New York and Paris (complete with its own Eiffel Tower). After the war the area fell into neglect and became one of the few dangerous areas in Osaka. Over the past few decades, Shin Sekai has cleaned up its act while retaining its retro feel. On weekends everyone lines up to try *kushi katsu,* or batter-fried meat and vegetables on skewers. Near Tennoji Park and Shitennoji Temple, it's an excellent afternoon or early-evening stop. After dinner visit Tsutenkaku Tower for lovely night views of Osaka. ⊠ *Ebisu-Higashi* ✛ *The easiest way to get to Shin Sekai is from Exit 2 of Dobutsuen-mae subway on Mido-suji Line. Cross street in direction of towering pachinko parlor, and walk through Jan Jan Yokocho, the covered shopping street that leads to Shin Sekai* ☑ *Free.*

**Shitennoji Temple** (四天王寺)

TEMPLE | Tenno-ji, as this temple is popularly known, is one of the most important historic sights in Osaka and the oldest temple in Japan. Founded in 593, it's been destroyed by fire many times. The last reconstruction of this Five-Storied Pagoda in 1965 has maintained the original design and adhered to the traditional mathematical alignment. What has managed to survive from earlier times is the 1294 stone *torii* (gate) that stands at the main entrance. (Interestingly enough, these are rarely used at Buddhist temples.)

The founder, Umayado no Mikoto (573–621), posthumously known as Prince Shotoku (Shotoku Taishi), is considered one of early Japan's most enlightened rulers. He was made regent over his aunt, Suiko, and set about instituting reforms and establishing Buddhism as the state religion. Buddhism had been introduced to Japan from China and Korea in the early 500s, but it was seen as a threat to the aristocracy, who claimed prestige and power based up their godlike ancestry. On the 21st of every month, the temple hosts a flea market that sells antiques and baubles; go in the morning for a feeling of Old Japan. ⊠ *1–11–18 Shitenno-ji, Tenno-ji-ku* ⊹ *Three train lines will take you near Shitenno-ji. The Tani-machi-suji subway line's Shitenno-ji-mae Station is closest to temple and temple park. Loop Line's Tenno-ji Station is several blocks south of temple. Mido-suji subway line also has a Tenno-ji stop, next to JR Station* ☎ *06/6771–0066* ⊕ *www.shitennoji.or.jp* 💲 *Temple ¥300; Garden ¥300; Treasure Hall ¥500.*

## Sumiyoshi Taisha Grand Shrine (住吉大社)

RELIGIOUS BUILDING | In a city of mariners it's no surprise that locals revere Sumiyoshi Taisha, dedicated to the guardian deity of sailors. According to legend, the shrine was founded by Empress Jingu in 211 to express her gratitude for her safe return from a voyage to Korea. Sumiyoshi Taisha is one of three shrines built prior to the arrival of Buddhism in Japan (the other two are Ise Jingu in Mie Prefecture and Izumo Taisha in Tottori Prefecture). According to Shinto custom, shrines were torn down and rebuilt at set intervals to the exact specifications of the original. Sumiyoshi was last replaced in 1810. Sumiyoshi is also famous for its *taiko-bashi* (arched bridge), given by Yodo-gimi, the consort of Hideyoshi Toyotomi, who bore him a son.

Every June 14 starting at 1 pm, a colorful rice-planting festival takes place here with traditional folk performances and processions. Sumiyoshi Matsuri, a large and lively festival, is held from July 30 to August 1. A crowd of rowdy young men carries a 2-ton portable shrine from Sumiyoshi Taisha to Yamato-gawa and back; this is followed by an all-night street bazaar. To reach the shrine, take the 20-minute ride south on the Nankai Main Line from Nankai Namba Station to Sumiyoshi Koen Station. ⊠ *2–9–89 Sumiyoshi, Sumiyoshi-ku* ☎ *06/6672–0753* ⊕ *www.sumiyoshitaisha.net* 💲 *Free.*

## ★ Tenno-ji Park
(天王寺公園; *Tennoji Koen*)

CITY PARK | The best place to get away from the noise and concrete of the city, this park contains not only the Osaka Museum of Fine Art and the garden of Keitaku-en, but also Tenno-ji Zoo. At the northern end of the park is a prehistoric burial mound, Chausuyama Kofun, which was the site of Tokugawa Ieyasu's camp during the siege of Osaka-jo in 1614–15. Visit in the morning or evening when the park is at its quietest. Leading up to the park entrance is the newly renovated Tenshiba—an area of terrace cafés and shops looking out on a grassy lawn, popular with couples and families. On weekends it often hosts various events. ⊠ *6–74 Chausuyama-cho, Tenno-ji-ku* ⊕ *tennoji-park.jp* 💲 *Free* Ⓜ *Osaka JR Loop Line Tennoji Station.*

## Tomb of Emperor Nintoku
(大仙陵古墳; *Daisenryo Kofun*)

RUINS | The 4th-century mausoleum of Emperor Nintoku is the largest of the Mozu Kofun, 49 burial mounds located in the city of Sakai, southeast of Osaka. This is the largest tomb in Japan, and covers an even bigger area than that of the pyramids of Egypt—archaeologists calculate that the central mound of this site occupies 1.3 million square feet. Construction took more than 20 years and required a total workforce of about 800,000 laborers. It was declared a UNESCO World Heritage site in 2019. Surrounding the emperor's keyhole-shaped burial place are three moats and pine, cedar, and cypress trees. You can walk around the outer moat in about an hour to get an idea of the size of the mausoleum and the grounds. The free 21st-floor observatory in the Sakai City Hall complex offers an aerial view of the tomb. ⊠ *7–1 Daisen-cho, Sakai-shi* ⊹ *Sakai is 14.5 km (9 miles) south of Osaka, a 10- to 20-minute train ride* ☎ *072/955–1115* 🎟 *Free* [M] *JR Hanwa Line Mozu Station.*

**Tsutenkaku Tower** (通天閣)
**OBSERVATORY** | Nearly every major city in Japan has its tower, and while they all offer lovely views, most are not much to look at themselves. But Shin Sekai's Tsutenkaku breaks this trend with its decidedly unique appearance. Built in 1912 with the rest of Shin Sekai, the original tower merged Paris's Arc de Triomphe and Eiffel Tower into a single design. Though the original was damaged after a fire and then dismantled to supply iron for Japan's war effort, it was redesigned and rebuilt in 1956. On the face of the tower is Japan's largest clock (changing color by the minute); the top displays different-color LED lights to indicate the weather. Charmingly gaudy, Tsutenkaku is considered one of the symbols of Osaka, and looks most striking when lit-up in neon colors at night. The 91-meter (299-foot) high observation deck provides a good view of the city and a chance to meet Billiken, Shin Sekai's deity of "things as they ought to be." ✉ *1–18–6 Ebisu Higashi, Tenno-ji-ku* ☎ *06/6641–9555* 🌐 *www.tsutenkaku.co.jp* 🎟 *¥900.*

## 🍴 Restaurants

**Hana Goyomi** (花暦)
**$$$$** | **JAPANESE** | Dining at the Swissôtel's flagship restaurant is an elegant escape from the crowds of Osaka. The seasonal kaiseki dinners are presented with exquisite attention to detail, bringing out the flavor of each ingredient. **Known for:** a relaxed escape from the bustle of Osaka; impeccable service; seasonal set menus. [$] *Average main: ¥10,000* ✉ *Swissôtel Nankai Osaka, 5–1–60 Namba, Chuo-ku* ☎ *06/6646–5127* 🌐 *www.swissotel.com/hotels/nankai-osaka.*

**Kani Doraku Dotombori Honten** (かに道楽)
**$$$** | **SEAFOOD** | The most famous restaurant on Dotombori-dori—the enormous mechanical crab is a local landmark—Kani Doraku has fine crab dishes at reasonable prices. The lunch set menu includes large portions of crab; dinner is more expensive ¥6,000. **Known for:** mountains of crab; take-out crab legs; one of Osaka's best-known restaurants. [$] *Average main: ¥5,000* ✉ *1–6–18 Dotombori, Chuo-ku* ☎ *06/6211–8975* 🌐 *douraku.co.jp/kansai/honten.*

**Kigawa** (喜川)
**$$$$** | **JAPANESE** | There's no better place to try Osaka's *kappo-ryori* (a more intimate, less formal version of *kaiseki-ryori*) than the restaurant that started the trend. Chef and owner Osamu Ueno scours the markets daily to find the best ingredients for dinner each evening. **Known for:** refined setting; flavorful multicourse meals; meticulous attention to detail. [$] *Average main: ¥15,000* ✉ *1–7–7 Dotonbori, Chuo-ku* ☎ *06/6211–3030* ⏲ *Closed Mon.*

★ **Mizuno** (美津の)
**$$** | **JAPANESE** | If there is one food Osaka is known for, it is okonomiyaki, a savory pancake that can be filled with vegetables, meat, or seafood. Mizuno, opened in 1945, is one of the city's best and oldest places to try this hearty specialty. **Known for:** locally sourced ingredients; long lines, but worth the wait; hearty and delicious Osaka fare. [$] *Average main: ¥1,500* ✉ *1–4–15 Dotombori, Chuo-ku* ☎ *06/6212–6360* 🌐 *www.mizuno-osaka.com.*

**Taqueria La Fonda** (タケリア ラ フォンダ)
**$** | **MEXICAN** | Serving up some of the best Tex-Mex food in the city, this tiny taqueria is an excellent stop for travelers in need of some comfort food. The owner makes his own salsas and tortillas, and offers up some unique dishes like cactus tacos in addition to the standard Tex-Mex fare. **Known for:** friendly, at-home feel; fills up quickly at dinnertime; Osaka's most authentic Mexican food. [$] *Average main: ¥1,000* ✉ *2–2–14 Tokui-cho, Chuo-ku* ☎ *06/6943–5657* 💳 *No credit cards.*

## Coffee and Quick Bites

**Planet 3rd Café** (プラネットサード)

$$ | **CAFÉ** | A hip hangout on the fringe of Amerika-mura, Planet 3rd is perfect for a quick snack or a full meal. The food is tasty—consisting mostly of sandwiches, curries, and sweets—and the atmosphere is cool and laid back. **Known for:** good breakfast sets from 7 am; vegetarian, dairy-free, and vegan options; tasty café fare. [$] *Average main: ¥1,500* ✉ *1–5–24 Nishi-Shin-sai-bashi, Chuo-ku* ☎ *06/6282–5277* 🌐 *www.cafecompany.co.jp/brands/planet3rd* 💳 *No credit cards.*

**Yaekatsu** (八重勝)

$$ | **JAPANESE** | For a real taste of Osaka, line up for *kushi katsu* (skewered meats and vegetables) outside Shin Sekai's Yaekatsu. This no-frills, counter-only restaurant has the reputation of being one of Osaka's oldest and best places to get kushi katsu. **Known for:** retro atmosphere; long lines on weekends; some of the most authentic kushi katsu in Japan. [$] *Average main: ¥2,000* ✉ *3–4–13 Ebisu-higashi, Naniwa-ku* ☎ *06/6643–6332* 💳 *No credit cards* 🕒 *Closed Thurs.*

## Hotels

**Cross Hotel Osaka** (クロスホテル大阪)

$$$$ | **HOTEL** | One of Osaka's most stylishly modern and hip hotels, Cross is perfectly located for exploring the south side of Osaka. **Pros:** excellent bathrooms with large tubs; right in the center of Minami's dining, shopping, and nightlife; friendly, energetic staff. **Cons:** pricey for a midrange hotel; breakfasts are a bit hit-or-miss; between night-owl guests and the highway below, it can be somewhat noisy. [$] *Rooms from: ¥30,000* ✉ *2–5–15 Shin-sai-bashi-suji, Chuo-ku* ☎ *06/6213–8281* 🌐 *crosshotel.com/osaka* 🛏 *229 rooms* 🍴 *No Meals* [M] *Midosuji Subway line Namba Station (Exit 24).*

**Hearton Hotel Shinsaibashi Nagahori Dori** (ハートンホテル心斎橋)

$ | **HOTEL** | For travelers on a budget, the Hearton Hotel Shin-sai-bashi offers a good location and very reasonable rates. **Pros:** good location for shopping and nightlife; inexpensive rates; friendly and helpful staff. **Cons:** not many amenities; English is limited; simple rooms. [$] *Rooms from: ¥10,000* ✉ *1–5–24 Nishi-Shin-sai-bashi, Chuo-ku* ☎ *06/6251–3711* 🌐 *www.hearton.co.jp/en/shinsaibashi* 🛏 *302 rooms* 🍴 *No Meals.*

**Hotel Nikko Osaka** (ホテル日航大阪)

$$$$ | **HOTEL** | A striking white tower in the colorful Shin-sai-bashi district, the Nikko is within easy reach of shopping meccas like Amerika-mura. **Pros:** excellent location near shopping and nightlife; premium rooms are spacious with views over the city; friendly, efficient service. **Cons:** regular rooms are dated; can get crowded with tour groups; a good value much of the year, but overpriced during peak seasons. [$] *Rooms from: ¥30,000* ✉ *1–33 Nishi-Shin-sai-bashi, Chuo-ku* ✣ *From Exit 8 at Shin-sai-bashi Station on the Mido-suji Line, you walk directly into the hotel.* ☎ *06/6244–1111* 🌐 *www.hno.co.jp* 🛏 *603 rooms* 🍴 *No Meals.*

★ **Osaka Marriott Miyako Hotel** (大阪マリオット都ホテル)

$$$$ | **HOTEL** | One of the city's newest luxury hotels looks out over the city from Osaka's tallest building and has some of the best nighttime views of any hotel in the region. **Pros:** being directly above Tenno-ji Station gives it easy access to many of Kansai's sights; floor-to-ceiling windows; outstanding views over the city. **Cons:** service is not always up to five-star standards; bar and lounge have high cover charges and are often crowded; not walking distance from the center of Osaka's shopping and nightlife. [$] *Rooms from: ¥42,000* ✉ *1–1–43 Abeno-suji, Abeno-ku* ☎ *06/6628–6111* 🌐 *www.marriott.com/hotels/*

The Shinsaibashi district, where the Osaka Marriott Miyako Hotel is located, is also one of Osaka's busiest shopping areas.

*travel/osamc-osaka-marriott-miyako-hotel* 🛏 *360 rooms* 🍴 *No Meals.*

**Sheraton Miyako Hotel Osaka**
(シェラトン都ホテル大阪)
**$$$** | **HOTEL** | An excellent base for exploring Osaka, the Miyako is also handy when you plan on taking day trips to Kyoto and Nara—the Kintetsu Ue-hon-machi Station next door offers quick access to both cities. **Pros:** excellent location for visiting other Kansai cities; discounts for booking online; airport shuttle available. **Cons:** the main sights and nightlife require a cab ride; can get crowded with tour groups; less luxurious than some of its rivals. [$] *Rooms from: ¥20,000* ✉ *6–1–55 Uehonmachi, Tenno-ji-ku* ☎ *06/6773–1111* 🌐 *www.miyakohotels.ne.jp/osaka* 🛏 *577 rooms* 🍴 *No Meals.*

**The St. Regis Osaka**
(セントレジスホテル大阪)
**$$$$** | **HOTEL** | One of Osaka's top luxury hotels, the St. Regis offers an oasis of comfort just a short walk from the lights and excitement of Shin-sai-bashi and Namba, and a short train ride from many of the city's major sights. **Pros:** butler service; luxurious interiors; real attention to detail. **Cons:** Honmachi Station is not a convenient base for visiting other places in Kansai; for the class of hotel, breakfast is merely okay; very expensive, especially by Osaka standards. [$] *Rooms from: ¥70,000* ✉ *3–6–12 Honmachi, Chuo-ku* ☎ *06/6258–3333* 🌐 *www.marriott.com* 🛏 *160 rooms* 🍴 *No Meals* [M] *Honmachi Station (Chuo, Midosuji, or Yotsubashi Subway lines).*

**★ Swissôtel Nankai Osaka**
(スイスホテル南海大阪)
**$$$$** | **HOTEL** | European-style furnishings and mellow contemporary art make the standard rooms at this high-end hotel some of the best in the city. **Pros:** best location in Osaka; higher-end rooms are luxurious; at Nankai Namba Station. **Cons:** not very accommodating for families with kids; basic rooms are somewhat dated; one of the most expensive hotels in the area. [$] *Rooms from: ¥50,000* ✉ *5–1–60 Namba, Chuo-ku* ☎ *06/6646–1111*

⊕ *www.swissotel.com/hotels/nankai-osaka* 🔁 *546 rooms* ⦿⦿ *No Meals.*

### Toyoko Inn Shinsaibashi Nishi (東横イン心斎橋西)

**$** | **HOTEL** | Close to the laid-back cafés of Minami, the Toyoko Inn is a comfortable business hotel with rates that won't empty your wallet. **Pros:** excellent value for the area; helpful staff; located near the Minami hot spots. **Cons:** few amenities; clean but dated facilities; small rooms. ⓢ *Rooms from: ¥9,000* ✉ *1–9–22 Kita-horie, Nishi-ku* ☎ *06/6536–1045* ⊕ *www.toyoko-inn.com* 🔁 *144 rooms* ⦿⦿ *Free Breakfast.*

##  Nightlife

### BARS

#### Café Absinthe (カフェアブサン)

**CAFÉS** | After browsing the fashions in Minami's boutiques, pop into Café Absinthe in neighboring Kita-horie for Mediterranean food and good music. Live performances usually start at around 9. The music and the crowd are very international and very laid-back. ✉ *1 2 27 Kita-horie, Nishi-ku* ☎ *06/6534–6635* ⊘ *Closed Tues.*

## 🎭 Performing Arts

### BUNRAKU

#### National Bunraku Theatre (国立文楽劇場; *Kokuritsu Bunraku Gekijo*)

**THEATER** | Theater fans won't want to miss the chance to see a performance at Osaka's National Bunraku Theatre. Bunraku is not your average puppet show: the 3-foot-tall puppets each require a trio of handlers, and the stories, mostly originating in Osaka, contain all the drama and tension (if not the sword fights) of a good samurai drama. The National Bunraku Theatre is Japan's premier place to watch this 300-year-old art form. An Earphone Guide (¥650 rental) explains the action in English as the play unfolds. Performances are usually twice daily (late morning and late afternoon) on weekends; tickets

can be bought via the website. There is also a free museum inside. ✉ *1–12–10 Nippon-bashi, Chuo-ku* ☎ *06/6212–2531* ⊕ *www.ntj.jac.go.jp* 🎫 *From ¥2,300* Ⓜ *Sennichimae or Sakai-suji Subway Line Nipponbashi Station (Exit 7).*

##  Shopping

### DEPARTMENT STORES

All major Japanese *depato* (department stores) are represented in Osaka. They're open 10 to 7, but usually close one day a month, on a Wednesday or Thursday.

#### Daimaru (大丸)

**DEPARTMENT STORE** | The department stores in Osaka are "gourmet palaces," each with several floors of restaurants. Daimaru, an Osaka landmark, has one of the best selections. ✉ *1–7–1 Shinsai-bashi-suji, Chuo-ku* ☎ *06/6271–1231* ⊕ *www.daimaru.co.jp.e.md.hp.transer. com/umedamise.*

#### Kintetsu Department Store Main Store (近鉄百貨店本店; *Kintetsu Hyakkaten Honten*)

**DEPARTMENT STORE** | Occupying 16 floors at the base of Abeno Harukas, Osaka's tallest building, this is one of the largest department stores in Japan. In addition to the usual shops and restaurants, there are numerous stores specializing in souvenirs of all kinds, and the useful Foreign Customer's Salon helps with tax-free shopping and overseas shipping. ✉ *1–1–43 Abenosuji, Abeno-ku, Osaka* ☎ *06/6624–1111* ⊕ *abenoharukas.d-kintetsu.co.jp/special/foreign/index.html* Ⓜ *JR Tennoji Station or Kintetsu Abenobashi Station.*

#### Takashimaya (高島屋)

**DEPARTMENT STORE** | One of the largest Japanese department store chains, Takashimaya has an impressive presence in Osaka. ✉ *5–1–5 Namba, Chuo-ku* ☎ *06/6631–1101* ⊕ *www.takashimaya. co.jp/osaka/index.html.*

##  Activities

### SUMO

#### Edion Arena Osaka
(エディオンアリーナ大阪)

**LOCAL SPORTS** | The sumo scene has become a hotbed of international rivalry as Bulgarians, Estonians, and some Mongolians with attitude have been edging the local talent out of the *basho* (ring). From the second Sunday through the fourth Sunday in March, one of Japan's six sumo tournaments takes place in Osaka at the arena formerly known as the Osaka Prefectural Gymnasium. Most seats, known as *masu-seki,* are prebooked before the tournament begins, but standing-room tickets (¥1,000) and a limited number of seats (¥2,500) are available on the day of the event. Tickets go on sale from around 7:45 am and often sell out fast. The stadium is a 10-minute walk from Namba Station. ✉ *3–4–36 Namba-naka, Naniwa-ku* ☎ *06/6631–0121* ⊕ *www. sumo.or.jp/en.*

# Nara (奈良市)

Nara is a place of synthesis, where Chinese art, religion, and architecture fused with Japanese language and Shinto traditions. The city was established in AD 710 and was then known as Heijo-Kyo (citadel of peace). Fujiwara-no-Fuhito, father-in-law of Emperor Mommu, was responsible for the city's creation. His grandson, the future Emperor Shomu, later graced the new capital with its wealth of temples, pagodas, and shrines.

Buddhism had come to Japan in the 6th century. Along with *kanji* (Chinese characters) and tea, it spread throughout the archipelago. Emperor Shomu hoped that making the new capital the center of Buddhism would unite the country and secure his position as head of an emergent nation state. The grandest of the Buddhist temples built in Nara during this era was Todai-ji, which Emperor Shomu intended as a nexus for all the temples of his realm. But after 84 years the citadel of peace fell victim to the very intrigue that the emperor had tried to suppress. In AD 794, the capital moved to Kyoto and Nara lost prominence, as did the Kegon sect that still manages Todai-ji today.

Now Nara is a provincial city whose most obvious role is a historical one, and Todai-ji is a monument rather than a political stronghold. Nara is a site of renewal and reinvention that has overcome typhoons, fires, and wars to remain a city of superlatives. Its position in the national consciousness as the birthplace of modern Japanese culture is well secured.

With relatively flat roads, an abundance of greenery, and most of the major sights located within Nara Koen, by far the best way to see Nara is on foot. Even the quaint, traditional streets of Nara-machi are a 10-minute walk from Nara's two central stations. For people with less time, most of the main sites can be reached by bicycle, except for those along the eastern edge of the park, such as the San-gatsu-do, the Ni-gatsu-do, and Kasuga Taisha.

Almost at the center of the Japanese archipelago, Nara is on the Yamato plain, with Osaka to the west and Kyoto to the north. Much of what you'll come to Nara to see is in picturesque Nara Koen (Nara Park), which is a short distance east of the two main stations.

It was created out of wasteland in 1880 and sits west of the Kasuga Mountain and the cleared slopes of Wakakusa-yama, on the edge of a dense forest. The park is home to some 1,200 tame deer, the focus of much local lore and legend. The commercial shopping district is south of Kintetsu Nara Station, while Sanjo-dori, west of Nara Koen and Nara-machi, has the two main tourist shopping areas. Horyu-ji, Yakushi-ji, and

Toshodai-ji, the major temples of western Nara, are all on one bus route or can be reached by JR train.

Nara-machi was the "new" area of Nara at the beginning of the Edo period (1603–1868). Today its lanes and alleys are still lined by old wooden houses with latticed windows and whitewashed walls. Many of these old houses have been converted into galleries, museums, and shops.

In Western Nara, Horyu-ji Temple has the oldest wooden structures in the world and is considered the apotheosis of classical Japanese architecture. Toshodai-ji Temple is where Ganjin, the first Buddhist monk to come to Japan from China, taught Japanese monks and legitimized the spread of Buddhism throughout the country.

## GETTING HERE AND AROUND
### AIRPORT TRANSFERS
The hourly airport limousine bus from KIX takes 90 minutes and costs ¥2,100. From Itami, buses leave every hour or two, take 90 minutes, and cost ¥1,510.

**CONTACTS Osaka Airport Transport.** ✉ 2–17–3 Hotarugaike Nishimachi, Toyonaka, Osaka ☎ 06/6844–1124 ⊕ www.okkbus.co.jp/en. **Kansai Airport Transportation.** ✉ 2-12 Rinku Orai Kita, Izumisano ☎ 072/461-1374 ⊕ www.kate.co.jp/en.

### BUS
Two local bus routes circle the main sites (Todai-ji, Kasuga Taisha, and Shin-Yakushi-ji) in the central and eastern parts of the city: Bus 1 runs counterclockwise, and Bus 2 runs clockwise. Both stop at JR Nara Station and Kintetsu Nara Station and have a flat fare of ¥210. The city also offers one- and two-day bus passes ranging from ¥500 to ¥1,500 depending on area.

Bus 97 heads west to Horyu-ji (with stops at Toshodai-ji and Yakushi-ji), takes about one hour, and costs ¥770; you can catch it in front of either station. Pick up a bus map at the Nara City Tourist Information Center.

### TAXI
For small groups, short taxi rides within Nara cost only slightly more than buses. Expect to pay about ¥1,000 to get to Kasuga Taisha from either of the main train stations.

### TRAIN
From Kyoto, the best option is the private Kintetsu Railway's trains, which run directly to Kintetsu Nara Station (50 minutes, ¥640). The express takes 40 minutes and costs ¥1,160 (change at Yamato-Saidai-ji). JR trains from Kyoto run to JR Nara Station; express trains take 45 minutes, locals take 70 minutes. All JR trains cost ¥720 without a JR Pass.

To get to Horyu-ji Temple in western Nara, take a JR Main Line train from JR Nara Station. The ride to Horyu-ji Station takes 11 minutes and costs ¥220.

### HOTELS
Nara has accommodations in every style and price range. Since most people treat the city as a day-trip destination, at night the quiet streets are the domain of Nara's residents. Hotels in central Nara around the main railway stations are a little noisier than those closer to Nara Koen and in Nara-machi. In spring and autumn and at peak holiday periods, rooms are hard to find on weekend nights. Book well in advance if you plan to travel to Nara during these times.

### RESTAURANTS
It's a sin to visit Nara and not have a *kaiseki* dinner (an aesthetically arranged 7- to 12-course set meal using the freshest ingredients) if you can afford the splurge. It's usually an evening meal, but most kaiseki restaurants serve mini-kaiseki at lunchtime for day-trippers that are considerably more affordable. Most traditional restaurants are small and have set courses. Nara retires early, and restaurants close around 10 pm, taking last orders around 9 pm. Small restaurants and *izakaya* (after-work drinking haunts that serve an array of small dishes and drinks) are dispersed

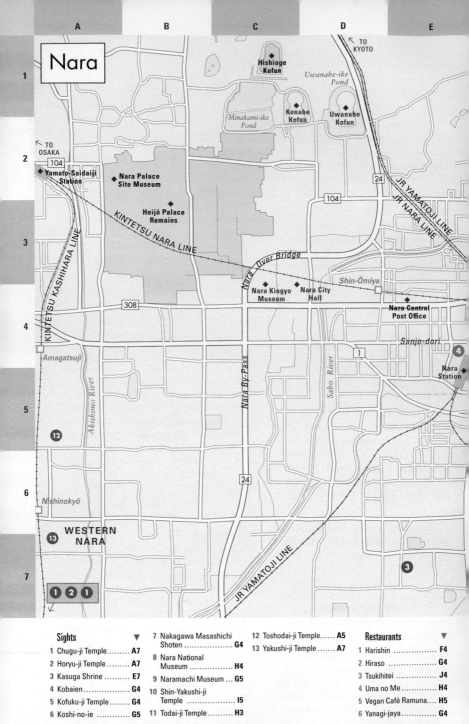

# Nara

**Sights** ▼

1 Chugu-ji Temple......... **A7**
2 Horyu-ji Temple ......... **A7**
3 Kasuga Shrine .......... **E7**
4 Kobaien .................. **G4**
5 Kofuku-ji Temple ........ **G4**
6 Koshi-no-ie ............. **G5**

7 Nakagawa Masashichi
  Shoten .................... **G4**
8 Nara National
  Museum ................. **H4**
9 Naramachi Museum ... **G5**
10 Shin-Yakushi-ji
  Temple ................... **I5**
11 Todai-ji Temple.......... **H3**

12 Toshodai-ji Temple...... **A5**
13 Yakushi-ji Temple ....... **A7**

**Restaurants** ▼

1 Harishin .................. **F4**
2 Hiraso .................... **G4**
3 Tsukihitei ................ **J4**
4 Uma no Me .............. **H4**
5 Vegan Café Ramuna.... **H5**
6 Yanagi-jaya .............. **G4**

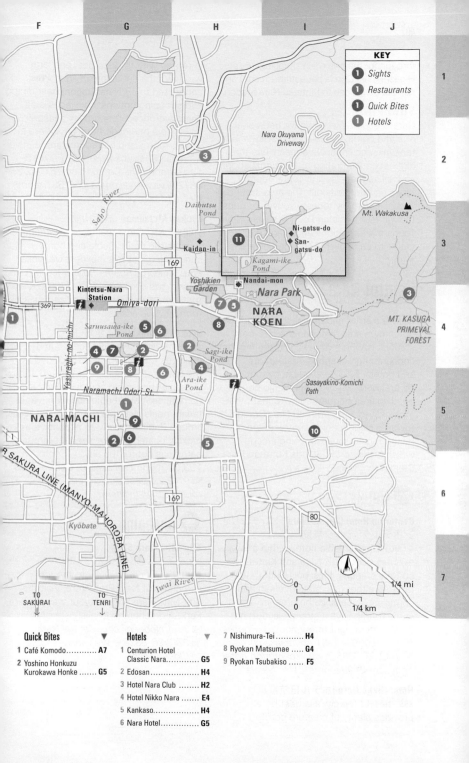

KEY
1 Sights
1 Restaurants
1 Quick Bites
1 Hotels

Nara Okuyama
Driveway

Saho River

Daibutsu
Pond

Mt. Wakakusa

169

Kaidan-in

Ni-gatsu-do
San-
gatsu-do

11

Kagami-ike
Pond

Kintetsu-Nara
Station

369    Omiya-dori

Yoshikien
Garden

Nandai-mon

Nara Park

7   5

NARA
KOEN

3

Saruusawa-ike
Pond

5   6

8

MT. KASUGA
PRIMEVAL
FOREST

Yasuragi-no-mithi

4   7     2

9

8

2

6

Sagi-ike
Pond

Sasayakino-Komichi
Path

Naramachi Odori St.

Ara-ike
Pond

1

NARA-MACHI

1

9

2   6

5

10

169

80

Kyōbate

Iwai River

TO
SAKURAI

TO
TENRI

0              1/4 mi

0              1/4 km

**Quick Bites** ▼
1 Café Komodo............. **A7**
2 Yoshino Honkuzu
  Kurokawa Honke ....... **G5**

**Hotels** ▼
1 Centurion Hotel
  Classic Nara............. **G5**
2 Edosan.................... **H4**
3 Hotel Nara Club ........ **H2**
4 Hotel Nikko Nara ....... **E4**
5 Kankaso................... **H4**
6 Nara Hotel............... **G5**

7 Nishimura-Tei ........... **H4**
8 Ryokan Matsumae ..... **G4**
9 Ryokan Tsubakiso ...... **F5**

throughout the two main shopping streets, Higashi-muki Dori (a pedestrian arcade) and Konishi-dori, close to Kintetsu Nara Station.

## SHOPPING

Nara is especially known for traditional arts and crafts, including *akahadayaki* pottery, ink, and linen. Nara-machi has the highest concentration of traditional shops as well as those selling contemporary takes on the traditional. The area around Todai-ji has many touristy souvenir shops, though few that stand out. The Nara City Tourism Information Office can supply you with an English-language guide and map.

# Central Nara

Nara is a small and compact city, and the downtown area between the two train stations is where you will find the highest concentration of shops, restaurants, and hotels. Easily explorable by foot, central Nara's main street, Sanjo-dori, is a bustling area frequented by tourists that runs east to west from JR Nara Station towards Nara Koen; it is intersected by the Higashimuki shopping arcade, which leads north towards Kintetsu-Nara Station.

##  Hotels

### Centurion Hotel Classic Nara (センチュリオンホテルクラシック奈良)

$ | **HOTEL** | Affordable hotel within a few minutes walk of JR Nara and Kintetsu-Nara stations. **Pros:** polite staff; not far from either train station; clean and comfortable. **Cons:** bathrooms are small; some rooms have a strange layout; not much natural light throughout. $ *Rooms from: ¥9,000* ⊠ *1–51 Aburasaka-cho* ☎ *0742/93–5066* ⊕ *www.centurion-hotel. com/nara* ⤴ *90 rooms* ¶◎¶ *No Meals.*

### Hotel Nikko Nara (ホテル日航奈良)

$$$ | **HOTEL** | The city's largest hotel provides plenty of creature comforts in rooms with thick carpets and large windows that let in lots of light. **Pros:** connected to JR Nara Station; near dining and shopping options; courteous staff. **Cons:** overpriced during peak seasons; feels like a midrange hotel anywhere in Japan; rooms and bathrooms are relatively small. $ *Rooms from: ¥21,000* ⊠ *8–1 Sanjo-honmachi, Central Nara* ☎ *0742/35–6812* ⊕ *www.nikkonara.jp* ⤴ *331 rooms* ¶◎¶ *No Meals.*

### Ryokan Matsumae (旅館松前)

$ | **B&B/INN** | Get a real taste of Japanese living in the comfortable and homely surroundings of this inexpensive ryokan. **Pros:**. **Cons:**. $ *Rooms from: ¥10,000* ⊠ *5 Imamikado-cho* ☎ *0742/22–3686* ⊕ *www. matsumae.co.jp* ⊟ *No credit cards* ⤴ *15 rooms* ¶◎¶ *No Meals.*

### Ryokan Tsubakiso (旅館椿荘)

$$$$ | **B&B/INN** | Friendly service and delicious meals, which are included in the basic rates, make for a relaxed stay in this quiet mix of old and new. **Pros:** lovely garden; central yet quiet location; vegetarian meals available upon request. **Cons:** limited English; nearly as expensive as ryokan located in Nara Koen; communal bathing is not for the shy. $ *Rooms from: ¥33,000* ⊠ *35 Tsubaki-cho, Central Nara* ☎ *0742/22–5330* ⊟ *No credit cards* ⤴ *7 rooms* ¶◎¶ *All-Inclusive.*

##  Shopping

### Kite-Mite Nara Shop (きてみてならショップ)

**CRAFTS** | For an overview of the arts and crafts of Nara Prefecture, visit the Kite-Mite Nara Shop on your way to Nara Park. A brochure in English is available. ⊠ *38–1 Noborioji-cho, Central Nara* ☎ *0742/26–8828* ⊕ *www.nara-shop.jp* ⊙ *Closed Mon.*

# Nara Koen (奈良公園)

Nara Koen has the city's popular tourist sights. Even so, it is wide enough to accommodate thousands of giggling schoolchildren and other Japanese tourists, yet still feel spacious and quiet. Be warned that it is home to many divine messengers of god: the sika deer seen just about everywhere. While habituated to humans, they like and expect to be hand-fed.

## ◉ Sights

### ★ Kasuga Shrine

(春日大社; *Kasuga Taisha*)

**RELIGIOUS BUILDING** | Famous for the more than 2,000 stone *mantoro* (lanterns) that line its pathways, Kasuga Taisha is a monument to the Shinto tradition of worshipping nature. The lighting of the lanterns on three days of the year attracts large crowds that whisper with reverential excitement. February 3 is the Mantoro Festival, celebrating the beginning of spring, and August 14 and 15 are the Chugen Mantoro Festival, when the living show respect to their ancestors by lighting their way back to Earth for their annual visit.

Kasuga Taisha was founded in AD 768 and for centuries, according to Shinto custom, the shrine was reconstructed every 20 years on its original design—not merely to renew the materials but also to purify the site. It's said that Kasuga Taisha has been rebuilt more than 50 times, its current incarnation dates from 1893. After you pass through the orange *torii* (gate), the first wooden structure you'll see is the Hai-den (Offering Hall); to its left is the Naorai-den (Entertainment Hall). To the left of Naorai-den are the four Hon-den (Main Shrines). Designated as National Treasures, they are painted vermilion and green—a striking contrast to the dark wooden exterior of most Nara temples. To get to Kasuga Taisha from Nara Koen,

# Deer Issues

Nara's symbolic deer have the run of the place, and you may read about how they will bow respectfully when given a treat. In truth, they can be a bit aggressive when pursuing handouts from tourists (especially first thing in the morning, when they are still hungry, nibbling at bags and clothing). The deer also have little respect for traffic laws, so keep an eye open when out on the roads. Any deer that still have their antlers are capable of injuring humans if they feel threatened, so please act sensibly.

walk east past the Five-Storied Pagoda until you reach a torii. This path will lead you to the shrine. ✉ *160 Kasuga-no-cho, Nara Koen, Nara Koen* ☎ *0742/22–7788* ⊕ *www.kasugataisha.or.jp/en/about_en* ✉ *Free; main sanctuary ¥500; museum ¥500; gardens ¥500.*

### Kōfuku-ji Temple (興福寺)

**TEMPLE** | The Kofuku-ji Temple's Five-Storied Pagoda dominates the skyline. Built in 1426, it's an exact replica of the original pagoda that Empress Komyo built here in AD 730, which burned to the ground. At 164 feet, it is the second tallest in Japan, a few centimeters shorter than the pagoda at To-ji Temple in Kyoto. To the southwest of the Five-Storied Pagoda, down a flight of steps, is the Three-Story Pagoda. Built in 1114, it is renowned for its graceful lines and fine proportions.

Although the Five-Storied Pagoda is Kofuku-ji's most eye-catching building, the main attraction is the first-rate collection of Buddhist statues in the Tokondo (Eastern Golden Hall). A reconstruction dating from the 15th century, the hall was built to speed the recovery of the ailing Empress Gensho. It is dominated

# Fire Festivals and Light-Ups in Nara

## January

**Wakakusa-yama Yaki (Grass-Burning Festival).** On the night before the second Monday in January, 15 priests set Wakakusa-yama's dry grass afire while fireworks illuminate Kofuku-ji's Five-Storied Pagoda in one of Japan's most photographed rituals. This rite is believed to commemorate the resolution of a boundary dispute between the monks and priests of Todai-ji and Kofuku-ji. The fireworks start at 5:50 and the grass fire is lighted at 6.

## February

**Mantoro (Lantern Festival).** On February 3 the 2,000 stone and 1,000 bronze lanterns at Kasuga Taisha are lighted to mark the traditional end of winter called *setsubun*. It takes place between 6 and 8:30 pm.

## March

**Shuni-e Omizutori (Water-Drawing Festival).** From March 1 to 14 priests circle the upper gallery of the Ni-gatsu-do (Second Month Hall) wielding 21-foot-long *taimatsu* (bamboo torches) weighing more than 160 pounds, while sparks fall on those below. Catching the embers burns out sins and wards off evil. This festival is more than 1,200 years old, a rite of repentance to the Eleven-Headed Kannon, an incarnation of the Goddess of Mercy. These evening events happen March 1 to 11 and 13, 7 to 7:20; March 12, 7:30 to 8:15; March 14, for five minutes from 6:30 to 6:35.

## July–October

**Light-up Promenade.** Sights including Yakushi-ji, Kofuku-ji, and Todai-ji are illuminated at night in July, August, September from 7 to 10, and October from 6 to 10.

## August

**Toka-e.** From August 1 to 15 Nara Koen is aglow with more than 7,000 candles from 7 to 9:45 pm.

**Chugen Mantoro (Midyear Lantern Festival).** For more than 800 years the thousands of lanterns at Kasuga Taisha have been lighted to guide ancestors back to Earth on their annual pilgrimage, in Obon on August 14 to 15 from 7 to 9:30 pm.

by a statue of Yakushi Nyorai (Physician of the Soul) and is flanked by the Four Heavenly Kings and the Twelve Heavenly Generals. In contrast to the highly stylized and enlightened Yakushi Nyorai, the seated figure on the left is a statue of a mortal, Yuima Koji. A lay devotee of Buddhism, Yuima was respected for his eloquence but perhaps more revered for his belief that enlightenment could be accomplished through meditation even while mortal passions were indulged. Although Kofuku-ji Temple is no longer a religious mecca, you may see older Japanese writing on *ema* (votive plaques) left by pilgrims to ensure the happiness and safety of their families. The exquisite incense and the patina of the gold leaf on the drapery of the Yakushi Nyorai create a reflective experience.

The concrete-and-steel Kokuhokan (National Treasure House), north of Kofuku-ji, houses the largest and most varied collection of National Treasure sculpture and other works of art. The most famous is a statue of Ashura, one of the Buddha's eight protectors, with three heads and six arms.

Although parts of the temple are under construction through 2023, most of the complex will remain open. ✉ *48 Noborioji-cho, Nara Koen* ☎ *0742/22–7755* ⊕ *www.kohfukuji.com* ✉ *Eastern Golden Hall ¥300, National Treasure House ¥700; Central Golden Hall ¥500.*

## Nara National Museum (奈良国立博物館; *Nara Kokuritsu Hakubutsukan*)

**ART MUSEUM** | One of the earliest examples of Western-style Meiji architecture, the Nara National Museum was completed in 1889 to much controversy over its decidedly non-Japanese design. True to Nara's reputation as the seat of Japanese culture, the museum houses sculpture from China, Korea, and Japan, though its collection focuses mainly on the Nara and Heian periods. The West Wing has paintings, calligraphy, ceramics, and archaeological artifacts from Japan, some dating back to the 10th-century BC. The East Wing is used for temporary exhibitions. During the driest days of November, the Shoso-in Repository, behind the Todai-ji, displays some of its magnificent collection. ✉ *50 Noborioji-cho, Nara Koen* ☎ *0742/22–7771* ⊕ *www.narahaku.go.jp* ✉ *¥700* ⊗ *Closed Mon.*

## Shin-Yakushi-ji Temple (新薬師寺)

**TEMPLE** | This temple was founded in 747 by Empress Komyo (701–760) in gratitude for the recovery of her sick husband, Emperor Shomu. Only the Main Hall, which houses many fine objects from the Nara period, remains. In the center of the hall is a wooden statue of Yakushi Nyorai, the Physician of the Soul. Surrounding this statue are 12 clay images of the Twelve Divine Generals who protected Yakushi. Eleven of these figures are originals. The generals stand in threatening poses, bearing spears, swords, and other weapons, and wear terrifying expressions. ✉ *1352 Takabatake-cho, Nara Koen* ☎ *0742/22–3736* ⊕ *www.shinyakushiji.or.jp* ✉ *¥600.*

## ★ Todai-ji Temple (東大寺)

**TEMPLE** | Completed in AD 752, this temple complex was conceived by Emperor Shomu in the 8th century as the seat of authority for Buddhist Japan. An earthquake damaged it in AD 855, and in 1180 the temple was burned to the ground. Its reconstruction met a similar fate during the 16th-century civil wars. Only the most central buildings in the once sprawling complex exist today. Among the structures, the Daibutsu-den is the grandest, with huge beams that seemingly converge upward toward infinity.

The Hall of the Great Buddha (大仏殿; Daibutsu-den) is a rare example of monumentality in the land of the diminutive bonsai. The current Daibutsu-den was restored in 1709 at two-thirds its original scale. At 157 feet tall and 187 feet wide, it is the largest wooden structure in the world.

Inside the Daibutsu-den is the Daibutsu, a 53-foot bronze statue of the Buddha. His hand alone is the size of six tatami mats. The Daibutsu was originally commissioned by Emperor Shomu in AD 743 and completed six years later. A statue of this scale had never been cast before in Japan, and it was meant to serve as a symbol to unite the country. The Daibutsu was dedicated in AD 752 in a grand ceremony attended by the then-retired Emperor Shomu, the Imperial Court, and 10,000 priests and nuns. The current Daibutsu is an amalgamation of work done in three eras: the 8th, 12th, and 17th centuries.

A peaceful pebble garden in the courtyard of Kaidan-in belies the ferocious expressions of the Four Heavenly Guardian clay statues inside. Depicted in full armor and wielding weapons, they are an arresting sight. The current *kaidan-in,* a building where monks are ordained, dates from 1731. The Kaidan-in is in northwestern Nara Koen, west of the Daibutsu-den.

Todai-ji's Daibatsu-den houses a 53-foot statue of the Buddha.

The soaring Nandai-mon (Great Southern Gate), the entrance to the temple complex, is supported by 18 large wooden pillars, each 62 feet high and nearly 3 ⅓ feet in diameter. The original gate was destroyed in a typhoon in 962 and rebuilt in 1199. Two outer niches on either side of the gate contain fearsome wooden figures of Deva kings, who guard the great Buddha within. They are the work of master sculptor Unkei, of the Kamakura period (1185–1335). In the inner niches are a pair of stone *koma-inu* (Korean dogs), mythical guardians that ward off evil.

Named for a ritual that begins in February and culminates in the spectacular sparks and flames of the Omizu-tori festival in March, the Ni-gatsu-do (Second Month Temple) was founded in 752. It houses important images of the Buddha that are, alas, not on display. Still, its hilltop location and veranda afford a commanding view of Nara Koen. Behind the Ni-gatsu-do is a lovely rest area, where free water and cold tea are available daily from 9 to 4. Although no food is sold, it's a quiet spot to enjoy a picnic.

The San-gatsu-do (Third Month Temple), founded in 733, is the oldest original building in the Todai-ji complex. It takes its name from the *sutra* (Buddhist scripture) reading ceremonies held here in the third month of the ancient lunar calendar (present-day February to April). You can sit on benches covered with tatami mats and appreciate the 8th-century treasures that crowd the small room. The principal display is the lacquer statue of Fukukensaku Kannon, the goddess of mercy, whose diadem is encrusted with thousands of pearls and gemstones. The two clay *bosatsu* (bodhisattva) statues on either side of her, the Gakko (Moonlight) and the Nikko (Sunlight), are fine examples of the Tenpyo period (Nara period), the height of classical Japanese sculpture. The English pamphlet included with admission details all the statues in the San-gatsu-do.

The important temples and structures are close together; allow about three hours to see everything, allowing for time to feed the deer. ✉ *406–1 Zoushi-chou, Nara Koen* ✥ *To get to Todai-ji, board Bus 2 from JR Station or Kintetsu Nara Station and exit at Daibutsu-den. Cross street to path that leads to temple. You can also walk from Kintetsu Nara Station in about 15 mins by heading east on Noborioji-dori. In Nara Koen, turn left onto pedestrians-only street that leads to Todai-ji. A taxi from JR or Kintetsu Nara station costs about ¥1,000* ☎ *0742/22–5511* 🌐 *www.todaiji.or.jp* 🎫 *¥600.*

## 🍴 Restaurants

**Tsukihitei** (月日亭)
$$$$ | **JAPANESE** | Deep in the forest behind Kasuga Taisha, Tsukihitei has the perfect setting for a traditional kaiseki meal. From the walk up a wooded path to the tranquillity of your own tatami room, everything here is conducive to experiencing the beautiful presentation and delicate flavors—as Helen Keller did when she dined here in 1948. **Known for:** beautifully prepares traditional kaiseki courses; reservations required; serene natural surroundings. [$] *Average main: ¥25,000* ✉ *158 Kasugano-cho, Nara Koen* ☎ *0742/26–2021* 🌐 *www.nara-ryoutei.com/tsukihitei.*

**Uma no Me** (馬の目)
$$$ | **JAPANESE** | In a little 1920s farmhouse just north of Ara-ike pond in Nara Koen this delightful restaurant with dark beams and pottery-lined walls serves delicious home-style cooking. Everything is prepared from scratch. **Known for:** cozy, at-home feeling; excellent lunch courses; simple, traditional fare focusing on the flavors of individual ingredients. [$] *Average main: ¥3,500* ✉ *1158 Takabatake-cho, Nara Koen* ☎ *0742/23–7784* 💳 *No credit cards* 🕒 *Closed Thurs.*

**Vegan Café Ramuna** (楽夢菜)
$ | **VEGETARIAN** | Tucked away on a side-street a few minutes walk from Nara Koen, this cozy little vegan café offers a wide selection of vegan dishes, from ramen or Japanese curry, to bento boxes and burgers. Every dish is made and served with real care and heart by the woman who runs the place, and the warm homely atmosphere, not to mention the delicious food, makes this one of the best vegan restaurants in the entire region. **Known for:** the best vegan food in Nara; only open on Saturday (for lunch only); exceptionally kind and friendly owner. [$] *Average main: ¥1,000* ✉ *1028–5 Takabatake-cho* ☎ *0742/42–9395* 🌐 *www.ramuna.jp* 💳 *No credit cards* 🕒 *Closed Sun.–Fri. No dinner.*

**Yanagi-jaya** (柳茶屋)
$$ | **JAPANESE** | Specializing in Japanese sweets and elegant bento box meals, Yanagi-jaya's secluded tatami rooms and peacful garden transports diners to a bygone age. It can be found among the trees on a street corner, just a short walk east along the path from Kofuku-ji's Five-Storied Pagoda. **Known for:** offering a sampling of Nara cuisine at a reasonable price; lovely views; Nara's famous warabi-mochi, a delicate sweet. [$] *Average main: ¥3,000* ✉ *4–48 Noborioji-cho, Nara Koen* ☎ *0742/22–7560* 🌐 *www.narachameshi.com* 💳 *No credit cards* 🕒 *Closed Mon. No dinner.*

## ☕ Coffee and Quick Bites

**Yoshino Honkuzu Kurokawa Honke** (吉野本葛黒川本家)
$$ | **ASIAN** | Part of a business established since 1615, this store serves a multitude of dishes made using *kuzu*, a starchy edible plant traditionally used in cooking throughout the Nara region. The affordable set menus include savory and sweet dishes, and the chilled *kuzu-mochi* desserts and ice-cream are a refreshing treat on a hot day. **Known for:** traditional Nara-style Japanese sweets; close to some of Nara's main attractions; reasonable prices. [$] *Average main: ¥2,000* ✉ *16 Kasugano-cho* ☎ *0742/20–0610* 🌐 *www.yoshinokuzu.com.*

##  Hotels

### Edosan (江戸三)

**$$$$ | B&B/INN |** Individual cottages, some with thatched roofs in the greenery of Nara Park, make Edosan one of Nara's most peaceful and unique lodgings. **Pros:** perfect location in Nara Park; closest neighbors are the deer; great in-room dining. **Cons:** English not spoken; most cottages do not have a private bath; traffic from nearby road. $ *Rooms from: ¥43,000 ⊠ 1167 Takabatake-cho, Nara Koen ☎ 0742/26–2662 ⊕ www.edosan.jp ⤴ 10 cottages ❍ Free Breakfast.*

### Hotel Nara Club (奈良倶楽部)

**$$ | B&B/INN |** On a street of old houses with traditional gardens, this small hotel is reminiscent of a European pension. **Pros:** peaceful location; not far from main sights; home-cooked meals using local produce. **Cons:** cozy, but lacks the elegance of a traditional ryokan; rooms are cozy but basic; long walk from train stations. $ *Rooms from: ¥14,000 ⊠ 21 Kitamikado-cho, Nara Koen ☎ 0742/22–3450 ⊕ www.naraclub.com ▭ No credit cards ⤴ 8 rooms ❍ Free Breakfast.*

### ★ Kankaso (観鹿荘)

**$$$$ | B&B/INN |** At once exquisitely refined and delightfully friendly, Kankaso exemplifies the best of Japanese hospitality, and a delicious kaiseki dinner is included, as is breakfast. **Pros:** long history of serving foreign guests; traditional architecture; convenient to Nara Koen. **Cons:** due to the traditional architecture, it can be chilly in winter; common areas are clean but worn down; little English spoken. $ *Rooms from: ¥42,000 ⊠ 10 Kasugano-cho, Nara Koen ☎ 0742/26–1128 ⊕ www.kankaso.jp ⤴ 9 rooms ❍ All-Inclusive.*

### ★ Nara Hotel (奈良ホテル)

**$$$$ | HOTEL |** Built in 1909, this hotel is a beautiful synthesis of Japanese and Western architecture. **Pros:** very spacious rooms; top-class service; imperial atmosphere. **Cons:** historic charm to some can feel dated to others; getting to the hotel requires a hike up the hill or short taxi ride; nothing here comes cheap. $ *Rooms from: ¥30,000 ⊠ 1096 Takabatake-cho, Nara Koen ☎ 0742/26–3300 ⊕ www.narahotel.co.jp ⤴ 132 rooms ❍ No Meals.*

# Naramachi (奈良町)

Naramachi is a maze of lanes and alleys lined with old warehouses and *machiya* (traditional wooden houses) that have been converted into galleries, shops, and cafés. A lot of locals still live here, so the smell of grilled mackerel at lunchtime or roasted tea in the afternoon wafts through the air. Many of the old shops deal in Nara's renowned arts and crafts, such as *akahadayaki* pottery, ink, and linen. In recent years Naramachi has also become home to younger artisans with a contemporary take on the city's traditional crafts. A free map, available from any Nara City Tourism Information Office, guides you to the main shops, museums, and galleries, as do English signposts.

Remember that stores can close irregularly. From the southwest corner of Sarusawa-ike, with the pond notice board on your left, walk straight until you come to a main road, on the other side of which is the center of Nara-machi.

## ◉ Sights

### Kobaien (古梅園)

**FACTORY |** Nara accounts for about 90% of Japan's sumi ink production, and for 400 years Kobaien has made fine ink sticks for calligraphy and ink painting. More recently, some types of sumi ink have been used for tattooing. From November to April the shop also offers ink-making workshops for ¥4,000. ⊠ *7 Tsubai-cho, Nara-machi ☎ 0742/23–2965 ⊕ www.kobaien.jp ⊗ Closed weekends.*

## Koshi-no-ie (格子の家)

**HISTORIC HOME** | This well-to-do merchant's house has been thoroughly restored, making it a quick trip through the Edo period. English pamphlets are available. ⊠ *44 Gango-ji-cho, Nara-machi* ☎ *0742/23–4820* 🎟 *Free* ⊗ *Closed Mon.*

## Naramachi Museum

(奈良町資料館; *Naramachi Shiryokan*)
**HISTORY MUSEUM** | So just what are those red cloth animals on pieces of rope outside houses in Nara? Called *migawarizaru* (substitute monkeys), they are hung on the eaves of houses to ward off illness and accidents. There is a monkey for every member of a household ready to suffer illness and accidents in place of its owner. The migawarizaru are just one of the many traditions that have lived on in Nara-machi. The Nara-machi Shiryokan displays many other artifacts relating to the history of this neighborhood. ⊠ *14–2 Nishi Shinya-cho, Nara-machi* ☎ *0742/22–5509* ⊕ *naramachi.co.jp* 🎟 *Free.*

 Restaurants

## Harishin (はり新)

$$ | **JAPANESE** | This eatery's *kamitsumichi* bento box, with a selection of sashimi, fried shrimp, tofu, vegetables, and homemade plum liqueur, is a bargain. Harishin is traditional and quite rustic. **Known for:** traditional, Naramachi atmosphere; fresh, local foods; relaxing setting. $ *Average main: ¥3,190* ⊠ *15 Nakashinya-cho, Nara-machi* ☎ *0742/22–2669* ⊕ *harishin.com* ▭ *No credit cards* ⊗ *Closed Mon.*

## Hiraso (平宗)

$$ | **SUSHI** | At Hiraso you can try *kakino-ha-zushi*, sushi wrapped in persimmon leaves. What's more, you can take it away in a nicely wrapped wooden box for a satisfying lunch in Nara Park. **Known for:** unique, affordable lunches; cozy atmosphere; the best place to get food for a picnic in the park. $ *Average main: ¥2,500* ⊠ *30–1 Imamikado-cho,*

*Nara-machi* ☎ *0742/22–0866* ⊕ *kakinoha. co.jp/naramise* ⊗ *Closed Mon.*

 Hotels

## Nishimura-Tei (西村邸)

$$ | **B&B/INN** | Of all the traditional-style guesthouses in Naramachi, this refurbished property is one of the most stylish and authentic. **Pros:** in the heart of a peaceful and historic district; clean, quiet and stylish; owner is kind and helpful. **Cons:** very limited number of rooms; shared shower facilities; online booking may be difficult for non-Japanese speakers. $ *Rooms from: ¥13,000* ⊠ *20 Hanazono-cho* ⊕ *www.nishimuratei.com* ⇥ *3 rooms* ☉ *Free Breakfast.*

🛍 Shopping

## Kai (界)

**CRAFTS** | Rooted in tradition, Kai houses a collection of shops with new takes on traditional Japanese arts and crafts. In addition to a café and gallery, Kai also serves as work and gallery space for various local artisans. With artists producing everything from paintings to wood carvings to glass jewelry, this is an excellent stop for unique souvenirs. ⊠ *12–1 Wakido-cho, Nara-machi* ☎ *0742/24–3056* ⊕ *www.kai.st* ⊗ *Closed Mon.*

## Nakagawa Masashichi Shoten

(中川政七商店)
**CRAFTS** | Hidden on a narrow backstreet, this stylish and recently refurbished store sells various souvenirs and Nara specialties, including handwoven, sun-bleached linens which are a local specialty known as Nara *sarashi*. You can enjoy green tea and Japanese sweets while admiring views of the garden at the on-site café. ⊠ *31–1 Ganrin-in-cho, Nara-machi* ☎ *0742/22–2188* ⊕ *www. nakagawa-masashichi.jp.*

Horyu-ji's wooden buildings are among the world's oldest.

# Western Nara
# (奈良西部)

Horyu-ji is home to some of the oldest wooden buildings in the world. Just east of Horyu-ji is Chugu-ji, with one of the finest sculptures in Japan, the 7th-century Miroku Bodhisattva. A short bus ride back toward Nara brings you to Yakushi-ji and Toshodai-ji temples, both religious and political centers during the Nara period.

Western Nara is over 13 km (8 miles, a 24-minute train ride) from Nara station. To visit all four temples in one day, go to Horyu-ji by the JR Main Line first (Chugu-ji is a 10-minute walk from Horyu-ji) and proceed to Toshodai-ji and Yakushi-ji by bus. From there, the easiest way back to Nara is by bus or taxi, or you can also take a Kintetsu Line train.

## ⊙ Sights

### Chugu-ji Temple (中宮寺)

TEMPLE | This temple was originally the home of Prince Shotoku's mother in the 6th century and is now a Buddhist nunnery. It houses an amazing wooden statue of the Miroku Bodhisattva, the Buddha of the Future. His gentle countenance has been a famous image of hope since it was carved, sometime in the Asuka period (AD 552–645). ⊠ *1–1–2 Horyu-j Kita, Ikaruga-cho, Ikoma-gun, Western Nara* ⊹ *Chugu-ji is a few minutes' walk north of Horyu-ji's Yumedono* ☏ *0745/75–2106* ⊕ *www.chuguji.jp* ⊠ *¥600.*

### ★ Horyu-ji Temple (法隆寺)

TEMPLE | This temple is the jewel in the crown of classical Japanese architecture. In the morning, elderly locals on their way to work pray in front of the temple with intensity. Founded in AD 607 by Prince Shotoku (AD 573–621), Horyu-ji's original wooden buildings are among the world's oldest. The first gate you pass

# Bringing Buddhism to Japan

Toshodai-ji Temple was built in AD 751 for Ganjin, a Chinese priest who traveled to Japan at the invitation of Emperor Shomu. At that time, Japanese monks had never received formal instruction from a Buddhist monk. The invitation was extended by two Japanese monks who had traveled to China in search of a Buddhist willing to undertake the arduous and perilous journey to Japan.

It seemed that Ganjin would never make it to Japan. On his first journey some of his disciples betrayed him. His second journey resulted in a shipwreck. During the third trip his ship was blown off course, and on his fourth trip government officials refused him permission to leave China. Before his next attempt, he contracted an eye disease that left him blind. He persevered, nonetheless, and finally reached Japan in AD 750. Ganjin shared his knowledge of Buddhism with his adopted country and served as a teacher to many Japanese abbots as well as Emperor Shomu. He is also remembered for bringing the first sampling of sugar to Japan. Every June 6, to commemorate his birthday, the Miei-do (Founder's Hall) in the back of the temple grounds displays a lacquer statue of Ganjin that dates from AD 763.

through is the Nandai-mon, which was rebuilt in 1438 and is thus a relatively young 500 years old. The second gate, Chu-mon (Middle Gate), is the 607 original. Unlike most Japanese gates, which are supported by two pillars at the ends, central pillars support this gate. Note their entasis, or swelling at the center, an architectural feature from ancient Greece that traveled as far as Japan. Such columns are found in Japan only in the 7th-century structures of Nara.

After passing through the gates, you enter the temple's western precincts. The first building on the right is the Kon-do (Main Hall), a two-story reproduction of the original 7th-century hall, which displays Buddhist images and objects from as far back as the Asuka period (AD 552–645). The Five-Storied Pagoda to its left was disassembled in World War II to protect it from air raids, after which it was reconstructed with the same materials used in AD 607. Behind the pagoda is the Daiko-do (Lecture Hall), destroyed by fire and rebuilt in AD 990. Inside is a statue of Yakushi Nyorai (Physician of the Soul) carved from a camphor tree.

From the Daiko-do walk past the Kon-do and Chu-mon; then turn left and walk past the pond on your right. You come to two concrete buildings known as the Daihozo-den (Great Treasure Hall), which display statues, sculptures, ancient Buddhist religious articles, and brocades. Of particular interest is a miniature shrine that belonged to Lady Tachibana, mother of Empress Komyo. The shrine is about 2½ feet high; the Buddha inside is about 20 inches tall. The Todai-mon (Great East Gate) opens onto Horyu-ji's eastern grounds. The octagonal Yumedono (Hall of Dreams) was so named because Prince Shotoku used to meditate in it. ⊠ *1-1 Horyuji Sannai, Ikaruga-cho, Ikoma-gun, Western Nara* ✛ *The temple is a short shuttle ride or a 15-min walk from Horyu-ji Station. Alternatively, Bus 52, 60, or 97 to Horyu-ji is a 50-minute ride from the JR Nara Station or Kintetsu Nara Station (¥760). The Horyu-ji-mae bus stop is in front of the temple* ☎ *0745/75–2555* ⊕ *www.horyuji.or.jp* 🎟 *¥1,500.*

### Toshodai-ji Temple (唐招提寺)

TEMPLE | The main entrance to Toshodai-ji Temple, which was built in AD 751, is called the Path of History, since in Nara's imperial days dignitaries and priests trod this route; today it is lined with clay-walled houses, tranquil gardens, and the occasional shop selling crafts.

At the temple's entrance entasis pillars support the Nandai-mon (Great South Gate). Beyond the Nandai-mon is the Kon-do (Main Hall), a superb example of classical Nara architecture. It was restored in 2009. Inside the hall is a lacquer statue of Vairocana Buddha, the same incarnation of Buddha that is enshrined at Todai-ji. The halo surrounding him was originally covered with 1,000 Buddhas; now there are 864. In back of the Kon-do sits the Daiko-do (Lecture Hall), formerly an assembly hall of the Nara Imperial Court, the only remaining example of Nara palace architecture. ✉ *13–46 Gojo-cho, Western Nara* ✛ *Toshodai-ji is a 10-min walk from the rear gate of Yakushi-ji along the Path of History. From central Nara or Horyu-ji, take Bus 52 or 97 to the stop in front of Toshodai-ji* ☎ *0742/33–7900* ⊕ *toshodaiji. jp* 🖅 *¥1,000.*

### Yakushi-ji Temple (薬師寺)

TEMPLE | The two pagodas that tower over Yakushi Temple are an analogy of past and present Japan. Yakushi-ji's East Pagoda dates from 1285, and has such an interesting asymmetrical shape that it inspired Boston Museum of Fine Arts curator Ernest Fenollosa (1853–1908), an early Western specialist in Japanese art, to remark that it was as beautiful as "frozen music." Its simple, dark brown beams with white ends contrast starkly with its flashier, vermilion-painted 20th-century neighbor, the West Tower, built in 1981. For many, the new goes against the "imperfect, impermanent, and incomplete" principles of the old *wabi-sabi* aesthetic; but we think the contrast thrusts Yakushi-ji right into the 21st-century. Officially named one of the Seven Great Temples of Nara, Yakushi-ji was founded in 680 and moved to its current location in 718. ✉ *457 Nishino-kyo-cho, Western Nara* ✛ *From central Nara take either the Kintetsu Line train, changing at Yamato-Saidai-ji to Nishino-kyo, or Bus 52 or 97 to Yakushi-ji; from Horyu-ji or Chugu-ji, take Bus 97 to Yak-ushi-ji-mae.* ☎ *0742/33–6001* ⊕ *yakushiji. or.jp* 🖅 *¥1,100.*

## ☕ Coffee and Quick Bites

### Café Komodo (カフェこもど)

$ | JAPANESE | Located on a quiet back-street just a short walk south of Horyu-ji's Great Eastern Gate, this low-key yet stylish café offers delicious lunch sets, including very local specialties such as *tatsuta-age* (a type of fried chicken) and deep-fried *ofu* (steamed wheat gluten). The café also has its own woodwork studio and shop, with a number of robot-themed wooden toys on display. **Known for:** unusual delicacies; friendly vibe and peaceful atmosphere; fresh local produce. $ *Average main: ¥1,200* ✉ *Horyuji 2-chome 1–25, Ikaruga-cho, Ikoma, Nara, Nara-shi* ☎ *0745/75–0305* 🚫 *No credit cards* 🕐 *Closed Thurs.*

# Kobe (神戸市)

Kobe resonates with a cool, hip vibe, a condition of its internationalism and its position between mountains and sea. With more than 42,000 foreigners living in the city, representing more than 132 countries, Kobe may be Japan's most diverse city. It has great international cuisine, from Indonesian to French. It also has some of the best Japanese cuisine, especially the famous Kobe beef.

Kobe's diversity is largely attributable to its harbor. The port was a major center for trade with China dating back to the Nara period (AD 710–794). Kobe's prominence increased briefly for six months in the 12th century when the capital was moved from Kyoto to Fukuhara, now western Kobe. Japan acquiesced to opening five ports, and on January 1, 1868, international ships sailed into Kobe's harbor. American and European sailors and traders soon settled in Kobe, and their culture and technology spread throughout the city. Cinema and jazz made their debut in Kobe, and that legacy is ongoing. Many original residences have survived, and the European structures contrast strikingly with the old Japanese buildings and modern high-rises.

Prior to 1995, Kobe was Japan's busiest port. But on January 17, 1995, an earthquake with a magnitude of 7.2 hit the Kobe area, killing more than 6,400 people, injuring almost 40,000, and destroying more than 100,000 homes. Communication lines were destroyed, damaged roads prevented escape and relief, and fires raged throughout the city. Kobe made a remarkable and quick recovery.

The city now pulses with the activity of a modern, industrialized city. The colorful skyline reflects off the night water, adding to Kobe's reputation as a city for lovers. Don't come to Kobe looking for traditional Japan; appreciate its urban energy, savor its international cuisine, and take advantage of its shopping.

Kobe lies along the Seto Inland Sea in the center of Honshu, a little west of Osaka and several hours east of Hiroshima. Smaller than Tokyo and Osaka, Kobe is more accessible and less formidable. It is large enough, however, to keep you occupied with new attractions and events no matter how frequently you visit.

Divided into approximately 10 distinctive neighborhoods, the city extends from the business-oriented region near the harbor to the lower slopes of Mt. Rokko. Penned in by natural boundaries, Kobe expanded its territory with man-made islands in the harbor.

Rokko Island is home to numerous foreign companies and a number of shopping plazas, and is where foreigners now tend to settle. Port Island features conference centers and an amusement park. Port Island is linked with downtown by a fully computerized monorail—with no human conductor—that extends south to the Kobe airport.

Downtown, San-no-miya Station, in the city center, marks the heart of Kobe's entertainment and nightlife area. Every night passersby linger to hear musicians in a small park just north of the station. Moto-machi's stores are to the west, and most of the business district lies south of San-no-miya.

In Kitano-cho, Kobe's original European and American settlers built elegant residences, now known as *ijinkan*, on the city's northern slopes. Many of the preserved ijinkan have been turned into museums. Small boutiques, international cafés, and a few antiques shops seduce visitors to meander along Kitano-zaka and Pearl Street.

North of Kobe, the impressive Nunobiki Falls are surprisingly accessible from downtown, just behind the Shin-Kobe Station. Rokko-san (*san* means "mountain") is a little farther out, providing great views and cool mountain air. Arima Onsen, on the other side of Rokko-san, is one of Japan's oldest hot-springs destinations.

## GETTING HERE AND AROUND
### AIRPORT TRANSFERS

From Kansai International Airport, ignore the train and take the comfortable limousine bus (70 minutes, ¥2,000), which drops you off in front of San-no-miya Station.

From Osaka Itami Airport, buses to San-no-miya Station leave from a stand between the airport's two terminals approximately every 20 minutes from 7:45 am to 9:10 pm. The trip takes about 40 minutes (¥1,070).

Kobe Airport handles mainly domestic flights, is 20 minutes from JR San-no-miya Station via the Portliner (¥340 one-way).

**AIRPORT CONTACT Kobe Airport.** ⊠ *1 Kobekuko, Chuo-ku* ☎ *078/304–7777* ⊕ *www.kairport.co.jp.*

## SUBWAY

Kobe's main subway line runs from Tanigami in the far north of the city, and passes through Shin-Kobe and San-no-miya stations before continuing west to the outskirts of town. Another line runs along the coast from San-no-miya and links up with the main line at Shin-Nagata Station. Fares start at ¥200 and are determined by destination. The San-no-miya–Shin-Kobe trip costs ¥210.

The Portliner was the first digitally driven monorail in the world, and departs from San-no-miya Station every six minutes from 6:05 am until 11:40 pm on its loop to and around Port Island. The ride affords a close-up view of Kobe Harbor.

## TRAIN

The Shinkansen (bullet train) stops at the Shin-Kobe Station, just north of San-no-miya. The two are connected by the Seishin-Yamate Line that extends north from San-no-miya Station to the Shin-Kobe Station. Shin-Kobe also connects to Arima.

The trip between Osaka Station and Kobe's San-no-miya Station takes 24 minutes on the JR Kobe Line rapid train, which leaves at 15-minute intervals throughout the day; without a JR Pass the fare is ¥410. The Hankyu and Hanshin private lines run between Osaka and Kobe for ¥320.

The City Loop bus starts at San-no-miya and circles through Meriken Park, Harborland, and Kitano before returning to San-no-miya. Taxis are easy to find at San-no-miya Station, but can also be found at any *noriba*, or taxi stand.

Purchase tickets from a vending machine; you surrender them on passing through the turnstile at your destination station. Fares depend on your destination.

Three rail lines, JR, Hankyu, and Hanshin, cut straight through the city from one side to the other, and converge at San-no-miya Station. Most of the city is a 10-minute walk from a train station, making trains the most convenient way to get around.

## HOTELS

Kobe is an industrialized city that caters to business travelers. There are many comfortable, well-situated business hotels, almost all of which have rooms with basics like air-conditioning, private bath, and TV.

## NIGHTLIFE

Kobe's compactness is an advantage— virtually all the best bars are within walking distance of each other. Kobe is regarded as the center of Japan's thriving jazz scene.

## RESTAURANTS

Kobe is the place to find international cuisine, especially dishes from Europe and Southeast Asia. Excellent restaurants are found practically anywhere but are especially prevalent north of San-no-miya Station and in the Kitano area. For a quick snack, stop by one of the city's delicious bakeries.

## SHOPPING

Kobe's historic shopping area is known as **Moto-machi.** It extends west for 2 km (1 mile) from JR Moto-machi Station. Much of the district is under a covered arcade, which starts opposite the Daimaru department store and runs just north of Nankin-machi. Moto-machi is more of a functional shopping area, selling housewares (including antiques), imported foods, and electronics, with restaurants scattered between.

Nearly connected to the Moto-machi arcade, the **San-no-miya Center Gai** arcade extends from the Hankyu department

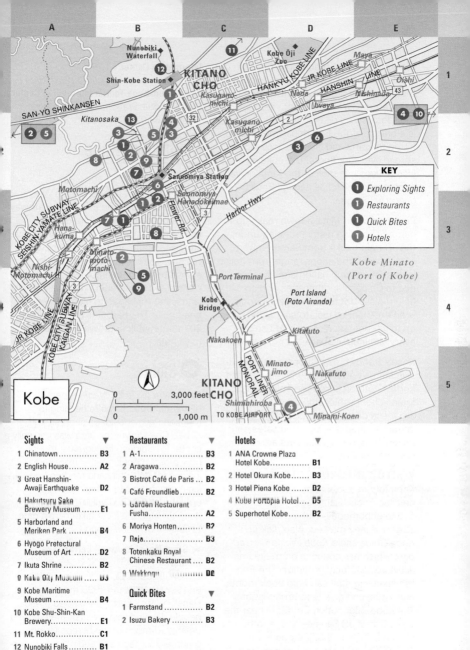

## Kobe

3,000 feet
1,000 m
TO KOBE AIRPORT

## Sights ▼

1 Chinatown ............... B3
2 English House ........... A2
3 Great Hanshin-
   Awaji Earthquake ...... D2
4 Hakutsuru Saka
   Brewery Museum ....... E1
5 Harborland and
   Meriken Park ........... B4
6 Hyogo Prefectural
   Museum of Art ......... D2
7 Ikuta Shrine ............. B2
8 Kobe City Museum ..... B3
9 Kobe Maritime
   Museum ................. B4
10 Kobe Shu-Shin-Kan
   Brewery.................. E1
11 Mt. Rokko ................ C1
12 Nunobiki Falls ........... B1
13 Weathercock House ... B2

## Restaurants ▼

1 A-1....................... B3
2 Aragawa ................. B2
3 Bistrot Café de Paris ... B2
4 Café Freundlieb ......... B2
5 Garden Restaurant
   Fusha.................... A2
6 Moriya Honten .......... B2
7 Raja..................... B3
8 Totenkaku Royal
   Chinese Restaurant .... B2
9 Wakkoqu ............... B2

## Quick Bites ▼

1 Farmstand ............... B2
2 Isuzu Bakery ............ B3

## Hotels ▼

1 ANA Crowne Plaza
   Hotel Kobe.............. B1
2 Hotel Okura Kobe....... B3
3 Hotel Piena Kobe ....... D2
4 Kobe Portopia Hotel.... D5
5 Superhotel Kobe........ B2

store to the Moto-machi area for 1 km (½ mile). Because it's next to San-no-miya Station, this is a good stop for a bite to eat. Center Gai has a hipper vibe than the Moto-machi district. Next to Hankyu is a branch of the Loft department store, home to crafts and lifestyle accessories spread over four floors. The building also houses a branch of the Kinokuniya bookstore, which has a small English-language selection.

**Piazza Kobe** and **Motoko Town** make up the narrow shopping district running under the JR train tracks from San-no-miya to Moto-machi. The shops range from Italian leather shoes and handmade accessories to Chinese apothecaries and small electronics. Not for the claustrophobic, it is an excellent chance to see Japan living up to its reputation of making use of every last inch of space.

Kobe's trendy crowd shops in the exclusive stores on **Tor Road,** which stretches north–south on a tree-lined slope into Kitano-cho. Fashionable boutiques selling Japanese designer brands and imported goods alternate with chic cafés and restaurants. The side streets are fun to poke about.

### VISITOR INFORMATION
Kobe Tourist Information Center offers detailed English-language maps of all the neighborhoods, with attractions and streets clearly marked. Also pick up a *Kobe Guide* and a *Kobe Welcome Coupon,* which has coupons on museums, activities, and transportation. The English-speaking staff can help book rooms, find tours, and give recommendations. The Kobe Information Center is near the West Exit of JR San-no-miya; another branch is at the JR Shin-Kobe Station. The JTB Travel Gate can arrange for hotel reservations, train tickets, package tours, and more throughout the country.

**VISITOR INFORMATION JTB Travel Gate.** ⊠ *JR San-no-miya Station, 5–1–305 Kotono-cho, Kobe* ☎ *078/231–4118.* **Kobe Information Center.** ⊠ *JR San-no-miya Station, 8 Kumoi-dori, Chuo-ku* ☎ *078/241–1050.* **Shin-Kobe Tourist Information Center.** ⊠ *Shin-Kobe Station, 1–3–1 Kanocho, Chuo-ku* ☎ *078/241–9550.*

# Downtown Kobe

In 1868, after nearly 200 years of isolation, Kobe's port opened to the West, and Kobe became an important gateway for cultural exchange. Confined to a small area by its natural boundaries, the city has kept its industrial harbor within the city limits. The harbor's shipping cranes project incongruously against the city's sleek skyscrapers, but the overall landscape manages to blend together beautifully. The harbor is approximately a 20-minute walk southwest of the San-no-miya area.

## ◉ Sights

**Chinatown** (南京町; *Nankin-machi*)
NEIGHBORHOOD | If you're heading to Meriken Park, consider a short stop in Kobe's Chinatown. The area was originally a center for Chinese immigrants, though it is now mostly popular with Japanese tourists looking for souvenirs and food. To find Nankin-machi from Moto-machi Station, walk on the port side and enter the neighborhood through the large fake-marble gate. ⊠ *Sakaemachi-dori, Chuo-ku.*

★ **Great Hanshin-Awaji Earthquake Memorial** (人と防災未来センター; *Hito to Bousai Shourai Center*)
HISTORY MUSEUM | In 1995 the Great Hanshin-Awaji Earthquake killed 6,433 people, leveled vast areas of the city, and destroyed much of the harbor. Using documentary footage and audio, an introductory film shows the frightening destruction of this modern city. A re-created postquake display and high-tech exhibits convey the sorrows and memories of the event. This excellent museum has English pamphlets and electronic guides, and

English-speaking volunteers are on hand. It's a 10-minute walk from the South Exit of JR Nada Station, one stop east of JR San-no-miya Station. ✉ *1–5–2 Wakinohama Kaigan-dori, Chuo-ku* ☎ *078/262–5050* ⊕ *www.dri.ne.jp* ✉ *¥600* ⊙ *Closed Mon.*

## Hakutsuru Sake Brewery Museum (白鶴酒造資料館; *Hakutsuru Shuzo Shiryokan*)
BREWERY | Nada, one of Kobe's westernmost neighborhoods, is home to a number of museums and breweries—many offering free sake tasting. The most popular is the Hakutsuru Sake Brewery Museum, where at the door you'll find a sake barrel of immense proportions. Traditional tools and devices and life-size figures of traditionally clad brewers demonstrate the sake-brewing process. There are also videos in English. The tour ends with free tastings. It's a five-minute walk south from Hanshin Sumiyoshi Station. Brewery Museum tours are by reservation only, so be sure to call ahead at least a couple days in advance. ✉ *4–5–5 Sumiyoshiminami-machi, Higashinada-ku* ☎ *078/822–8907* ⊕ *www.hakutsuru.co.jp/english/culture/museum.html* ✉ *Free* ⚠ *Reservations essential.*

## Harborland and Meriken Park (ハーバーランドとメリケンパーク)
MARINA/PIER | No trip to Kobe is complete without a waterside visit. Within Meriken Park broken slabs of thick concrete and crooked lightposts are preserved as part of the Port of Kobe Earthquake Memorial Park. Across the grassy park the Kobe Maritime Museum's roofline of white metal poles, designed like the billowing sails of a tall ship, contrast beautifully with the crimson Port Tower. The top of the tower provides a 360-degree view of Kobe. A walkway connects to Harborland's outdoor shopping mall. Eat dinner at any of the restaurants on the waterfront and enjoy the stunning nighttime view. Nearby, a small Ferris wheel rotates lazily, the colors of its flashing lights bouncing off the sides of nearby ships. Meriken Park and Harborland are a 10-minute walk south of Moto-machi Station. ✉ *1 Kawazaki-cho, Chuo-ku* ⊕ *www.harborland.co.jp.*

## ★ Hyogo Prefectural Museum of Art (兵庫県立美術館; *Hyogo Kenritsu Bijutsukan*)
ART MUSEUM | This striking concrete edifice was designed by acclaimed architect Tadao Ando. Working primarily with concrete, Ando is known for his use of light and water, blending indoors and outdoors and utilizing flowing geometric paths. The permanent exhibit here features art from prominent 20th-century Japanese painters Ryohei Koiso and Heizo Kanayama, Kobe natives who specialized in Western techniques. The museum rotates its vast collection, displaying fantastic modern works from Japanese artists as well as sculptures by Henry Moore and Auguste Rodin. It also hosts international touring shows. It's a 10-minute walk from the South Exit of JR Nada Station, one stop east of JR San-no-miya Station. ✉ *1–1–1 Wakinohama Kaigan-dori, Chuo-ku* ☎ *078/262–0901* ⊕ *www.artm.pref.hyogo.jp* ✉ *¥500* ⊙ *Closed Mon.*

## Ikuta Shrine (生田神社; *Ikuta Jinja*)
RELIGIOUS BUILDING | Legend has it that this shrine was founded by Empress Jingu in the 3rd century, making it one of Japan's oldest. An impressive orange *torii* (gate), rebuilt after the 1995 earthquake, stands amid the bustle of modern Kobe, welcoming tourists and religious observers alike. Every year two Noh plays, *Ebira* and *Ikuta Atsumori*, at Ikuta's Autumn Festival retell parts of the 12th-century Genpei War. It's just a six-minute walk northwest of San-no-miya Station. ✉ *1–2–1 Shimoyamate-dori, Chuo-ku* ☎ *078/321–3851* ⊕ *ikutajinja.or.jp* ✉ *Free.*

## Kobe City Museum (神戸市立博物館; *Kobe Shiritsu Hakubutsukan*)
HISTORY MUSEUM | This museum specializes in work from the 16th and 17th centuries, focusing on reciprocal cultural influences between East and West. The

first floor has a variety of displays on the West's impact on Japan in the second half of the 17th century. Other exhibits document the influence of Western hairstyles for women and the arrival of electric and gas lamps. The museum also has an impressive collection of woodcuts, maps, and archaeological artifacts, as well as Namban-style art, namely prints, silkscreens, and paintings from the late 16th to 17th century, usually depicting foreigners in Japanese settings. The historical exhibits are fascinating, but it is the artwork from this period that is the real draw.

From San-no-miya Station, walk south on Flower Road to Higashi-Yuenchi Koen. Walk through the park to the Kobe Minato post office, across the street on the west side. Then head east along the street in front of the post office toward the Oriental Hotel. Turn left at the corner in front of the hotel, and the City Museum is in the old Bank of Tokyo building at the end of the block. ✉ *24 Kyomachi, Chuo-ku* ☎ *078/391–0035* 🌐 *www.kobecitymuseum.jp* 🎫 *¥300* 🕒 *Closed Mon.*

**Kobe Maritime Museum** (神戸海洋博物館; *Kobe Kaiyo Hakubutsukan*)
**OTHER MUSEUM** | The Kobe Maritime Museum is the stunning building with a billowing roofline of metal sails. It showcases detailed ship models, opening with a 27-foot model of the HMS *Rodney,* the British flagship that led a 12-ship flotilla into Kobe Harbor on January 1, 1868. A model of the *Oshoro Maru,* one of Japan's earliest sailing ships, is adorned with pearls, rubies, gold, and silver. There are also displays of modern tankers. Kawasaki Good Times World is also inside the museum. High-tech displays and interactive models showcase the Kawasaki company's history. You can ride a helicopter flight simulator and see a robot work at a Rubik's Cube. Admission is included in the fee for the museum. ✉ *2–2 Hatoba-cho, Chuo-ku* ☎ *078/327–8983* 🌐 *www.kobe-maritime-museum.com* 🎫 *¥900* 🕒 *Closed Mon.*

**Kobe Shu-Shin-Kan Brewery** (酒心館)
**BREWERY** | This is one of the few sake breweries open to tours (from January to November), which should be booked at least two days before to ensure an English-speaking guide. All of the signposting is in Japanese, but there's a fine shop. ✉ *1–8–17 Mikagetsukamachi, Higashinada-ku* ☎ *078/841–1121* ✉ *info@shushinkan.co.jp (for reservations)* 🌐 *enjoyfukuju.com* 🎫 *Free* ✍ *Reservations essential.*

## 🍴 Restaurants

**A-1**
**$$$$** | **STEAKHOUSE** | With a relaxed atmosphere, A-1 is known for serving thick slices of Kobe beef. The *teppanyaki* steak (broiled on a hot plate) is cooked in a marinade of spices, wine, and soy and served with charcoal-grilled vegetables and crisp garlic potatoes. **Known for:** where the locals go for a good steak; reservations recommended; the best deal on Kobe beef in town. [$] *Average main: ¥5,200* ✉ *Lighthouse Bldg., 2–2–9 Shimoyamate-dori, 1st fl., Chuo-ku* ☎ *078/331–8676* 🌐 *kobe-a-1.com.*

★ **Aragawa** (あらがわ)
**$$$$** | **STEAKHOUSE** | Japan's first steak house is famed for its superb, hand-fed Kobe beef from a single farm in the nearby city of Sanda. The melt-in-your-mouth *sumiyaki* (charcoal-broiled) steak is worth its weight in yen and is only served with mustard and pepper. (Don't even think about asking for other condiments.) The dining room's dark-wood paneling and lovely chandelier give it a European air. **Known for:** decadent multicourse meals; one of the most famous steak houses in Japan; the finest Kobe beef steaks around. [$] *Average main: ¥36,000* ✉ *2–15–18 Nakayamate-dori, Chuo-ku*

*Continued on page 515*

# THE ART OF MONOZUKURI
## TRADITIONAL JAPANESE CRAFTS

By Jared Lubarsky

The Japanese take pride in their *monozukuri*: their gift for making things. And well they should, with traditions of craftsmanship centuries old to draw on, an itch for perfection, a loving respect for materials, and a profound aesthetic sense of what can be done with them.

There are really two craft traditions in Japan. In the first are the one-of-a-kind works of art—inlaid furniture and furnishings with designs in gold and mother-of-pearl, brocaded textiles, Tea Ceremony utensils, and so on—made by master artisans for wealthy patrons. These days, the descendants of these masters swell the ranks of Japan's *ningen koku-ho*, the official roster of Living National Treasures, who keep their crafts alive and set the standards of excellence. In the other are the humble charms of the *mingei* (folk craft) tradition: work in clay and bamboo, lacquer and native wood, iron and hand-forged steel—things made by nameless craftsmen for everyday use. Over the centuries the two traditions have enriched each other, and together they put Japanese craft work up among the best presents you can bring home from anywhere.

(Top left) Kiyomizu pottery, ningyo doll, Darumas; (bottom) kokeshi doll

# JAPANESE CERAMICS

Shopping for imari porcelain

Mashiko ware

If one Japanese folk tradition can be said to have contributed more than any other to Japan's collective cultural heritage, it must be pottery—admired by collectors and craftspeople all over the world. The tradition dates back more than 2,000 years, though pottery-making began to flourish as a real art form in the 16th century. Most Japanese pottery, apart from some porcelain and earthenware, is stoneware—formed into a wonderful variety of vases, cups, bowls, and platters and fired in climbing kilns on the slopes of hills.

Just visiting the regions where distinctive styles have developed would make a great *wanderjahr* in Japan. The village of Arita in Kyushu is famous for **imari** porcelain, with patterns of flowers and birds in bright enamel colors over blue and red underglazes. The folk pottery of **Mashiko**, in Tochigi Prefecture (northeast of Tokyo and southeast of Nikko), is admired for its rough textures and simple, warm colors. **Hagi** ware, from Western Honshu, is known for the rugged and rustic shapes of its Tea Ceremony bowls and cups. The red-brown **Bizen** ware from Okayama prefecture (also in Western Honshu)— one of the six remaining pottery centers of medieval Japan—is unglazed; every piece takes its unique colors and tones from the wood ash in the kiln. But you may also be interested in **Kyo-yaki** ceramics and porcelain from Kyoto, **Akahadayaki** pottery from Nara, or the **Jo-yachi** (glazed) pottery of Okinawa.

Hagi ware

Imari-Arita ware

Mashiko ware

Tobe ware

Kokutani ware

Bizen ware

Suzu ware

Matsushiro ware

Kutani ware

**WHERE TO FIND:** Most department stores in cities all over Japan have several different kinds of ceramics, though you'll find more regional specialties in the areas where they are produced. At first glance, Japanese ceramics may seem priced for a prince's table, but keep an eye out for seasonal sales; you can often find affordable pieces you will want to keep forever.

## TOKYO SOURCE

Almost everyone passes through Tokyo on a trip to Japan. If you want to get an overview of traditional crafts or buy some souvenirs, the **Japan Traditional Craft Center** (✉ 8-1-22 Akasaka, Minato-ku, Tokyo 107-0052 1F ☎ 03/5785-1301 ⊕ www.kougeihin.jp) is open daily 11–7 and sells crafts from all over the country, in most of the important categories from paper to tools to pottery, under its own seal of approval.

# TYPES OF JAPANESE CRAFTS

Although you'll find regional craft specialties all over Japan, in every mega-metropolis and small village, the best overall selection of stores will be found in Tokyo, Kyoto, and Nara. But you can save money by looking for regional crafts closer to the source.

Hina ningyo dolls

Furoshiki

## DOLLS

Traditional dolls, meant primarily for display and not as playthings, come in many different styles. **Kokeshi** dolls, which date from the Edo period, are long cylinders of wood with painted features. **Daruma** are papier-mâché dolls painted red, round as Humpty-Dumpties, representing a Buddhist priest who legend says meditated in the lotus position for so long that his arms and legs atrophied. **Hakata** dolls, from Kyushu, are ceramic figurines in traditional costume, such as geisha, samurai, or festival dancers. **Kyo-ningyo**, from Kyoto, are made of wood coated with white shell paste and then clothed in elaborate costumes.

**WHERE TO FIND:** Buy Kyo-ningyo in Kyoto, Hakata in Kyushu (especially in Fukuoka). Kokeshi come from the Tohoku region. Daruma can be purchased at temples all over Japan, but they come from Takasaki, north of Tokyo.

Kokeshi

## PRINTED FABRICS

Stencil-dyed fabrics were an important element of the Edo (old Tokyo) craft tradition, and survive in a range of motifs and intricate geometric designs—especially for light summer kimonos, room dividers, and cushion covers. *Furoshiki*—large cotton squares for wrapping, storing, and carrying things—make great wall hangings, as do the smaller cotton hand towels called *tenugui*, which are used as towels or as a head-covering in Kendo (Japanese sword-fighting).

**WHERE TO FIND:** Furoshiki and tenugui can be found all over Japan, but some stores specialize in them.

Tenugui

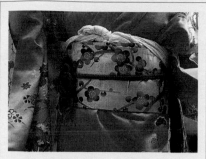

## KIMONOS

Most Japanese women, unless they work in traditional restaurants, nowadays only wear kimonos rented for special occasions like weddings and coming-of-age ceremonies. A new one, in brocaded silk, can cost ¥1 million ($11,000) or more. Reluctant to pay that much for a bathrobe or a conversation piece? You might settle for a secondhand version—about ¥10,000 ($82) in a flea market, for one in decent condition—or look instead for cotton summer kimonos, called *yukata*, in a wide variety of colorful designs; you can buy one new for ¥7,000–¥10,000.

**WHERE TO FIND:** Kimonos are sold all over Japan, but you might want to look in Kyoto's Temple Markets for a reasonably priced, used kimono. Kyushu is also known for reasonably priced kimonos.

Wajima nuri, lacquerware

## LACQUERWARE

For its history, diversity, and fine workmanship, lacquerware rivals ceramics as the traditional Japanese craft nonpareil. One warning: lacquerware thrives on humidity. Cheaper pieces usually have plastic rather than wood underneath, and because these won't shrink and crack in dry climates, they make safer—but no less attractive—buys.

**WHERE TO FIND:** Lacquerware can be found all over Japan, but it is a specialty of the Noto Peninsula (particularly Wajima). It's also very widely made in Kyushu.

Kimonos

Shopping for Lacquerware in Wajima

Washi (Sugihara paper)

## PAPER

What packs light and flat in your suitcase, won't break, doesn't cost much, and makes a great gift? The answer is *washi* (handmade paper, usually of mulberry fibers), which the Japanese craft in a myriad of colors, textures, and designs and fashion into an astonishing number of useful and decorative objects. Look for stationery, greeting cards, single sheets in color and classical motifs for gift wrapping and origami, and washi-covered jewelry boxes.

**WHERE TO FIND:** There are washi manufacturers all over Japan, but some of the most famous types are **Mino Washi** calligraphy paper from Gifu (*see Nagoya, Ise-Shima, and the Kii Peninsula*); **Tosa Washi** from Kochi (*see Shikoku*); and **Yama Washi** from Fukuoka (Kyushu).

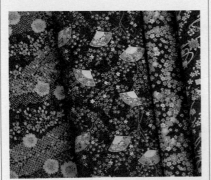

Patterned Washi

## SWORDS AND KNIVES

Supple and incredibly strong, hand-forged steel was for centuries the stuff of samurai swords and armor. Genuine antique swords seldom come on the market now (imitations sold as flashy souvenirs are not really worth considering), and when they do they fetch daunting prices. But the same craftsmanship is still applied to a range of kitchen knives and cleavers, comparable in both quality and price to the best Western brands.

A set of japanese knife in a shop in Tokyo

**WHERE TO FIND:** You can find Japanese knives in any big-city department store, or look for them on the side streets of Kappabashi, the restaurant wholesale supply district in Tokyo. But the center for Japanese knife- and sword-making is the city of Seki, a few miles northeast of Gifu (*see Nagoya, Ise-Shima, and the Kii Peninsula*).

Tanto Japanese sword

☎ 078/221–8547 🌐 *www.aragawa.co.jp*
🕒 *Closed Sun.*

**Bistrot Café de Paris**
(ビストロカフェドパリ)
$$ | **FRENCH** | This lively café offers above average French cuisine that you can enjoy on an outdoor terrace—a true rarity in Japan. The menu covers all the bases, ranging from couscous to bouillabaisse. **Known for:** delightful service; quality and fairly affordable lunch sets; some of the best terrace seating in Kobe. [$] *Average main: ¥2,000* ✉ *1–7–21 Yamamoto-dori, Chuo-ku* ☎ *078/241–9448* 🌐 *cafe-de-paris.jp.*

**Café Freundlieb** (カフェ フロインドリーブ)
$$ | **CAFÉ** | Housed in the former Kobe Union Church, this café exemplifies Kobe's relaxed beauty. High ceilings, arched windows, and white walls give the dining room a bright, airy feel. **Known for:** excellent baked goods; good sandwiches and salads for a light lunch; beautiful decor. [$] *Average main: ¥1,500* ✉ *4–6–15 Ikuta-cho, Chuo-ku* ☎ *078/231–6051* 🌐 *freundlieb.jp* 💳 *No credit cards* 🕒 *Closed Wed.*

**Garden Restaurant Fusha**
(ガーデンレストラン 風舎)
$$$ | **EUROPEAN** | Perfect for a romantic dinner overlooking the lights of Kobe, Fusha serves up delicious French-inspired European dishes in a relaxing, country-chic setting. The restaurant requires a 20-minute taxi ride from Shin-Kobe or Sannomiya Station, but offers a stunning nighttime view of the city and harbor from the candlelit outdoor tables. **Known for:** romantic dinners; European-style multicourse dinners; panoramic views of the city below. [$] *Average main: ¥5,000* ✉ *Kikusui Golf Club, 1 Karasuharacho, Kobe* ✥ *The restaurant is difficult to get to on your own. It is best to get a taxi from Sannomiya or Shin-Kobe Station* ☎ *078/511–2400* 🌐 *r.goope.jp/fusya* 🕒 *Closed Tues. and Mon. twice monthly.*

## Reared on Beer 🍴

Around the world, Kobe beef is legendary for its succulence and taste. Cows receive daily massages, and in summer they ingest a diet of sake and beer mash. They are descended from an ancient line of *Wagyu* (Japanese cows) known to be genetically predisposed to higher marbling. True Kobe beef comes from only 262 farms in the Tajima region of Hyogo Prefecture (of which Kobe is the capital), each of which raise an average of five animals. The best beef restaurants are mostly in the central Chuo ku district, and Kobe beef is on the menu at the top hotels.

**Moriya Honten** (モーリヤ本店)
$$$$ | **STEAKHOUSE** | Moriya's flagship restaurant stands where the business began in 1885 as a butcher shop. Now this cozy restaurant serves excellent grade A5 Kobe Wagyu (the highest rank of Japanese beef) at reasonable prices. **Known for:** convenient location; friendly, personalized service; one of the wider selections of steak cuts in town. [$] *Average main: ¥8,000* ✉ *2–1–17 Shimoyamate-dori, Chuo-ku* ☎ *078/391–4603* 🌐 *www.mouriya.co.jp/en/head/index.html.*

**Raja** (ラジャ)
$$ | **INDIAN** | The mellow atmosphere at Raja is matched by the delicious Indian food. The restaurant is now in its second generation; the friendly owner-chef is the son of the reputed first Indian chef in Kobe. **Known for:** juicy, flavorful tandoori; affordable lunch sets; rich, creamy curries. [$] *Average main: ¥1,500* ✉ *Sanotatsu Bldg., 2–7–4 Sakaemachi-dori, 1st fl., Chuo-ku* ☎ *078/332–5253* 🌐 *raja-kobe.com* 💳 *No credit cards* 🕒 *Closed Mon.*

**Totenkaku Royal Chinese Restaurant** (東天閣)
$$$$ | **CHINESE** | This place has been famous since 1945 for its Peking duck, flown in fresh from China (it's not cheap). Built at the turn of the 20th century, Totenkaku is in one of Kobe's historic homes. **Known for:** historic atmosphere; Kobe's premier Chinese restaurant; elegant private dining rooms. [$] *Average main: ¥10,000* ✉ *3–14–18 Yamamoto-dori, Chuo-ku* ☎ *078/231–1351* 🌐 *kobe-totenkaku.com.*

★ **Wakkoqu** (和黒)
$$$$ | **STEAKHOUSE** | At this elegant dining room, the excellent Kobe beef is sliced thin and cooked before you on a teppanyaki grill along with fresh vegetables and served with pepper, mustard, and soy sauce for dipping. Wakkoqu uses meat from three-year-old cows that have never been bred, which is said to be the reason for its unbelievable tenderness. **Known for:** delicious lunch sets that don't break the bank; meals cooked right in front of you; excellent service. [$] *Average main: ¥6,000* ✉ *Hillside Terrace Bldg., 1–22–13 Naka-yamate-dori, 1st fl., Chuo-ku* ☎ *078/222–0678* 🌐 *wakkoqu.com.*

## Coffee and Quick Bites

**Farmstand** (ファームスタンド)
$ | **CAFÉ** | A collaboration between a local development group and Kobe farmers, Farmstand serves fresh deli-plates and café fare. Meals are mostly vegetarian, and in the afternoon it is a great place for coffee and dessert. **Known for:** fresh, organic meals; flavorful desserts; supports local small farms. [$] *Average main: ¥1,000* ✉ *1–7–15 Yamato-dori, Chuo-ku* ☎ *080/2570–8194* 🌐 *eatlocalkobe.org/farmstand* 💳 *No credit cards* 🕒 *No dinner.*

**Isuzu Bakery** (イスズベーカリ)
$ | **BAKERY** | Kobe has many excellent bakeries, but this one, a Kobe institution since 1946 with a branch just west of San-no-miya Station, is notable for its fine selection of Japanese-style pastries and breads. Among its most popular items are the *kare-pan* (curry bread); crispy donut-like snacks filled with a mild curry sauce. **Known for:** delicious Japanese-style breads; fresh and affordable. [$] *Average main: ¥700* ✉ *2-chome 1–14 Kitanaga-sadori, Kobe* ☎ *078/333–4180* 🌐 *www.isuzu-bakery.jp.*

## Hotels

★ **ANA Crowne Plaza Hotel Kobe** (ANAクラウンプラザ神戸)
$$$$ | **HOTEL** | One of the tallest buildings in Kobe, this hotel stands out at night when its brightly lighted tower points heavenward. **Pros:** nice views of the city; connected to Shin-Kobe Station; efficient and knowledgable staff. **Cons:** some guest rooms are a bit dated; bathrooms are on the small side; one of the city's pricier options. [$] *Rooms from: ¥30,000* ✉ *1-chome 1 Kitano-cho, Chuo-ku* ☎ *078/291–1121* 🌐 *www.anacrowneplaza-kobe.jp/en* 🛏 *592 rooms* 🍴 *No Meals.*

**Hotel Okura Kobe** (ホテルオークラ神戸)
$$$$ | **HOTEL** | Rising 35 stories over Meriken Park, this is one of the city's best lodgings. **Pros:** high level of customer service; choice of Western or Japanese rooms; great views. **Cons:** Western rooms are somewhat dated; a bit of a hike to most of the city's sights; the extras are pricey. [$] *Rooms from: ¥35,000* ✉ *Meriken Koen, 2–1 Hatoba-cho, Chuo-ku* ☎ *078/333–0111* 🌐 *www.kobe.hotelokura.co.jp* 🛏 *474 rooms* 🍴 *No Meals.*

**Hotel Piena Kobe** (ホテルピエナ神戸)
$$ | **HOTEL** | With its excellent staff, comfortable rooms, and award-winning breakfasts, Hotel Piena is a step above other midrange business hotels in downtown Kobe. **Pros:** excellent location for sightseeing in Kobe; award-winning breakfasts; the staff go out of their way to be helpful. **Cons:** though spotless, the rooms feel a bit dated; noise from the highway is audible in rooms on lower floors; rooms are

The Crowne Plaza Kobe is one of the tallest buildings in town.

smaller than higher-end hotels. $ *Rooms from: ¥15,000* ⊠ *4–20–5 Ninomiya-cho, Chuo-ku* ☎ *078/241–1010* ⊕ *www.piena. co.jp* ⟿ *90 rooms* ⦿ *No Meals* Ⓜ *San-nomiya Station or Shin-Kobe Station.*

**Kobe Portopia Hotel** (ポートピアホテル)
**$$$$ | HOTEL |** A huge hotel with every imaginable amenity, the sleek Portopia Hotel rises high above the city. **Pros:** lots of facilities; sweeping views; close to the airport. **Cons:** not convenient for downtown sightseeing; can get crowded with conference and tour groups; a little dated. $ *Rooms from: ¥35,000* ⊠ *6–10–1 Minatojima Naka machi, Chuo-ku* ☎ *078/302–1111* ⊕ *www.portopia.co.jp* ⟿ *745 rooms* ⦿ *No Meals.*

**Superhotel Kobe** (スーパーホテル神戸)
**$ | HOTEL |** This budget-friendly business hotel is cheap and cheerful; it's also in a convenient downtown location. **Pros:** bargain prices; central location; great value. **Cons:** narrow beds; few amenities; small rooms. $ *Rooms from: ¥8,000* ⊠ *2–1–11 Kano-cho, Chuo-ku* ☎ *078/261–9000* ⊕ *www.superhoteljapan.com/en/s-hotels/ kobe* ⟿ *87 rooms* ⦿ *Free Breakfast.*

##  Nightlife

**The Cave Kobe** (ケイヴ神戸)
**LIVE MUSIC |** Located in a basement below the streets of downtown Kobe, this friendly bar is a shrine to all things associated with the Beatles. The owner is a massive fan, and the bar is a recreation of the legendary Cavern Club in Liverpool, where the "Fab Four" first made their name. There are regular performances by Beatles tribute acts, making it is a great place to listen to some live music and discover more about Japan's ongoing obsession with this band. ⊠ *1-chome 5–9 Nakayamatedori, Kobe* ☎ *090/1024–4999* ⊕ *cavekobe.wixsite.com/cavekobe* ☉ *Closed Mon.*

**Sone** (ソネ)
**LIVE MUSIC |** The city's most famous jazz club has been run by the Sone family since 1961. There are three sets of live music every night, starting at 6:30, and

the action often centers on a jazz trio with a guest vocalist. Spacious and relaxed, the place serves pizza, pasta, and salads. There's a cover charge of ¥1,320 (occasionally a bit more depending on the band). ⊠ *1–24–10 Nakayamate-dori, Chuo-ku* ☎ *078/221–2055* ⊕ *kobe-sone.com.*

**Starboard** (スターボード)

BREWPUBS | Although the craft-brewing craze may have run its course in the States, it is still going full steam ahead in Japan. Starboard's relaxed pub atmosphere is a great place to try some of Kobe's local beers. There is also an all-you-can-drink course for ¥2,500. ⊠ *2–7–12 Kitanagasa-dori, Chuo-ku* ☎ *78/392–3265.*

## Shopping

### DOLLS

**Sakae-ya Doll Store** (栄屋人形材料店; *Sakae-ya Ninngyo Zairyou-ten*)

CRAFTS | This store sells traditional Japanese dolls, from *kimekomi* (animals representing the zodiac calendar) to the samurai and kimono-clad ladies. There are also good examples of *oshie* (three-dimensional pictures made of silk). The tiny shop is packed with cloth for doll making, cupboards for hiding doll-making supplies, and, of course, dolls. ⊠ *5–8–5 Motomachi-dori, Chuo-ku* ☎ *078/341–1307* ⊗ *Closed Sun., Mon., and Wed.*

### JEWELRY, CERAMICS, AND LACQUERWARE

★ **Antique Nanae** (奈々重)

ANTIQUES & COLLECTIBLES | This darling and inexpensive antiques shop in Kitano-cho has a large collection of high-quality *yukata* (lightweight summer kimonos) that you can try on. There's also a good selection of ceramics and lacquerware. Nanae, the owner, enjoys explaining the history behind the pieces. ⊠ *Kurata Bldg.,*

## Disappearing Dolls

The *Arima ningyo fude* (Arima doll brush) makes a nice souvenir. Made for calligraphy, the brushes have handles wrapped in colorful silk thread, and a little doll pops out of the handle when writing. The doll disappears when the brush is laid down. Made for more than 1,300 years, the dolls symbolize the birth of Prince Arima, who (legend has it) was born after his father Emperor Kotoku visited Arima Springs. The brushes are handmade locally, and their beautiful designs make them popular gift items.

*2–14–26 Yamamoto-dori, 1st fl., Chuo-ku* ☎ *078/222–8565* ⊕ *www.antiquenanae.com* ⊗ *Closed Wed.*

**Kinoshita Pearl** (木下真珠; *Kinoshita Shinju*)

JEWELRY & WATCHES | Established in 1938, this small boutique offers unique designs and quality service. Although the shop offers many classic designs, it has a range of more modern pearl jewelry as well. ⊠ *1–1–7 Yamamoto-dori, Chuo-ku* ☎ *078/230–2870* ⊕ *www.kinoshita-pearl-kobe.jp* ⊗ *Closed Wed.*

### MALLS

**Santica Town** (さんちかタウン)

MALL | Santica Town is an underground shopping mall with 120 shops and 30 restaurants. It extends for several blocks beneath Flower Road south from San-no-miya Station. It's closed the third Wednesday of the month. ⊠ *1–10–1 San-no-miya, Chuo-ku* ⊕ *www.santica.com.*

# Kitano-cho

Wealthy foreigners, including Americans, English, and Germans, settled in the Kitano area in the late 19th century, bringing Western-style domestic architecture. Their homes are referred to in Kobe as *ijinkan*, and the district is extremely popular with Japanese tourists, who enjoy the rare opportunity to see old-fashioned Western houses. Some residences are still inhabited by Westerners, but more than a dozen 19th-century ijinkan in Kitano-cho are open to the public. A few of them are worth exploring, but seeing them all can be repetitive. The curious mélange of Japanese and Western Victorian and Gothic architecture makes for a good neighborhood walk. The streets are littered with small boutiques, cafés, and a few antiques shops.

To get to Kitano-cho, walk 15 minutes north along Kitano-zaka-dori from San-no-miya Station or 10 minutes west along Kitano-dori from Shin-Kobe Station. Yamamoto-dori (nicknamed Ijinkan-dori) is Kitano's main east–west street, and the ijinkan are on the small side streets ascending the hill. Tourist information centers offer detailed area maps with all attractions marked in English.

## ◉ Sights

**English House** (英国館; *Eikoku-kan*)
HISTORIC HOME | This typically old-fashioned Western house was constructed in 1907 by an Englishman named Baker and served as a makeshift hospital during World War II. Now it's a house museum by day and an English pub by night. Antique baroque and Victorian furnishings dominate the interior, there are several downstairs bars, and a bottle of champagne rests in the bathtub. A classic black Jaguar in the driveway and an enormous moose head on the wall

complete the English atmosphere. ✉ 2–3–16 Kitano-cho, Chuo-ku ☎ 0120/888–581 ⊕ kobe-ijinkan.net/england ☜ ¥750.

**Weathercock House**
(風見鶏の館; *Kazamidori no Yakata*)
HISTORIC HOME | More elaborate than any other Kobe ijinkan, this one, built by a German trader in 1910, stands out strikingly in red brick at the north end of Kitano-cho. The interior reflects various traditional German architectural styles, including that of a medieval castle. Its architecture makes this the most famous ijinkan, but the interiors are spartan, with few additional attractions. ✉ 3–13–3 Kitano-cho, Chuo-ku ☎ 078/242–3223 ⊕ kobe-kazamidori.com ☜ ¥500.

# North of Kobe

Thanks to Kobe's mountain backdrop, hiking is a popular local pastime. From Shin-Kobe Station it's a short climb to the Nunobiki Falls. For a good mountain day hike, try going up Rokko-san; from Hankyu Kobe Line Rokko Station you can take a bus or taxi to Rokko Cable-Shita cable-car station (*shita* means "down," or "bottom"). From there you can either hike all the way up the mountain or take the cable car partway. You may see wild boar—harmless unless provoked—in the forested mountains.

## ◉ Sights

★ **Mt. Rokko** (六甲山; *Rokko-san*)
VIEWPOINT | Three cable cars scale Mt. Rokko, providing spectacular views of lush forests. If you think it's beautiful during the day, time your trip so you'll descend after dusk, when you can see the city lights twinkle against the black sea.

You can do this trip in a half day, but you may want a full day to explore the area. To get to Rokko-san, take the Hankyu Kobe Line from Hankyu San-no-miya Station to Hankyu Rokko Station (¥190). From there take a taxi or a bus to Rokko Cable-Shita Station. A funicular railway travels up the mountain to Rokko-sanjo Station (¥600). The spread-out summit area is home to various attractions including a viewing terrace, tea rooms, a botanical garden and even a snow park in the winter; the Rokko Sanjo Bus runs regularly between the various facilities (¥210 to ¥260).

The Japanese were already enjoying the thermal waters at Arima Onsen (有馬温泉) before the 7th century. Arima is on the north slope of Rokko-san and consists of a maze of tiny streets and traditional houses. Some 30 ryokan use the curative powers of the water to attract guests. Although the water gushes up freely from springs, some ryokan charge as much as ¥10,000 for use of their baths. Go instead to the public bath, Kin-no-Yu, in the center of the village near the bus terminal. Here ¥650 gets you a soak in the steaming waters. Kin-no-Yu is open daily 8 am to 10 pm (closed the second and fourth Tuesday of the month). Take the subway north from JR Shin-Kobe Station, transferring at Tanigami and ending at Arima Onsen (¥680). ⌧ *Arima-cho, Kita-ku.*

**Nunobiki Falls**

(布引の滝; *Nunobiki no Taki*)

**WATERFALL** | In the hustle and bustle of this modern city, you wouldn't think that one of Japan's most impressive waterfalls would be just behind the train station. Nunobiki Falls has four gushing cascades in the forests of Mt. Rokko. References to their beauty have appeared in Japanese literature since the 10th century. They are a 20-minute walk from Shin-Kobe Station. After the falls you can pick up the Shin-Kobe Ropeway, which stops just above the falls before continuing on to the Nunobiki Herb Park. The stopping point provides a beautiful view of the city, especially at night. The signs leading you to the falls are in Japanese, but the ANA Crowne Plaza Hotel can provide English-language hiking maps. ⌧ *Chuo-ku* ✛ *The path begins just to the west of the ANA Crowne Plaza Hotel.*

# Himeji (姫路市)

*50 km (33 miles) west of Kobe.*

Situated nearly halfway between Kobe and Okayama on the shores of the Seto Inland Sea, Himeji is a small city famous for its magnificent castle, Himeji-jo. The castle is arguably the finest and grandest example of classical Japanese castle design, and was one of the first designated UNESCO World Heritage Sites in the country.

Himeji-jo is, in fact, one of Japan's great survivors. It avoided demolition in the Meiji Period when the government set about dismantling many Japanese castles; it never saw any serious warfare or battles; it survived WWII bombings and the Great Hanshin Earthquake of 1995, and perhaps most remarkably of all for a large wooden structure, it never burned to the ground in a fire. As the most impressive of Japan's twelve remaining original castles (the vast majority of castles in Japan have been either destroyed or rebuilt), Himeji-jo is a cultural icon and Japan's most visited castle, and following an extensive refurbishment completed in 2015, it has now been fully restored to its earlier feudal brilliance.

Himeji-jo, about 50 km (31 miles) west of Kobe, can be reached in about 40 minutes by train.

The city of Himeji is the second largest urban area in Hyogo Prefecture (after Kobe) and so it has a good selection of shops, restaurants and other attractions, although if truth be told, the vast majority of visitors never stray much further than the short stretch between the station and the castle.

Himeji makes for a great day or half-day trip from Kobe, Kyoto or Osaka, or even as a quick stop-off if traveling onward to Hiroshima and western Japan.

## GETTING HERE AND AROUND
Himeji is most easily accessed via the JR Special Rapid (Sanyo Line), which will deposit you in JR Himeji Station after 40 minutes of travel time from Kobe. The shinkansen takes just 16 minutes from Shin-Kobe or 30 minutes from Shin-Osaka.

##  Sights

★ **Himeji Castle** (姫路城; *Himeji-jo*)
CASTLE/PALACE | Also known as Shirasa-gi-jo (White Egret Castle), Himeji Castle is visible as soon as you exit the train station. Universally beloved, it dazzles the city from atop a nearby hill. A visit to Himeji-jo could well be one of the high points of your trip to Japan, especially if you can manage to see the brilliantly lighted castle soaring above cherry blossoms or pine branches at night. Thanks to frequent rail service, it should be easy to hop off, visit the castle, and jump on another train two hours later.

Himeji-jo is regarded as medieval Japan's crowning achievement of castle design and construction. It arrived at its present state of perfection after many transformations, however. It was first a fortress in the year 1333 and was transformed into a castle in 1346. Radically enlarged by Terumasa Ikeda in the period 1601–10, it has remained essentially the same ever since, surviving numerous wars and—perhaps even more miraculously—never once falling victim to the scourge of fire.

The five-story, six-floor main *donjon* (stronghold) stands more than 100 feet high and is built into a 50-foot-high stone foundation. Surrounding this main donjon are three smaller ones; all four are connected by covered passageways. Attackers would have had to cross three moats, penetrate the outer walls, and then withstand withering attack from the four towers. It was an impregnable fortress then, and its grace and grand proportions still inspire awe. Filmmaker Akira Kurosawa used Himeji-jo's exterior and the castle's grounds in his brilliant 1985 movie *Ran*.

Free guided tours in English are usually available from volunteer guides, though they cannot be booked in advance; ask when you buy your entry ticket. Tours usually take 90 minutes. ✉ *68 Honmachi, Himeji* ⚓ *From the central north exit of JR Himeji Station, the castle is a 15- to 20-min walk or a 5-min bus ride; also, bicycles are available free at the tourist office next door. The bus departs from the station plaza, on your left as you exit* ☎ *079/285–1146* ⊕ *www.himejicastle.jp/en* 🎫 *¥1,000.*

Chapter 10

# WESTERN HONSHU

Updated by
Chris Willson

● **Sights**
★★★★★

⑪ **Restaurants**
★★★★☆

🛏 **Hotels**
★★★★☆

● **Shopping**
★★★☆☆

🍸 **Nightlife**
★★★☆☆

# WELCOME TO WESTERN HONSHU

## TOP REASONS TO GO

★ **Photogenic icons:** The O-torii gate of Itsukushima Shrine on Miyajima Island, the graceful arches of Kintaikyo Bridge, Okayama's Crow Castle, and Korakuen Garden.

★ **Fabulous seafood:** Oysters (*kaki*) in Hiroshima; *anago* (conger eel) in Miyajima; *uni-don* (sea urchin over rice) in Hagi; *mamakari* (a sardinelike fish) in Kurashiki; and little black *shijimi* clams in Matsue.

★ **Lessons of the past:** Although the Atomic Bomb Dome in Hiroshima is held in great reverence, the city has embraced the future with its energetic multinational vibe.

★ **Landscape and history:** The stunning nature of the San-in region, along with the historic buildings of Matsue and Tsuwano, is unlike anywhere else in Japan.

Western Honshu is bisected by a chain of picturesque, rugged mountains called the Chugoku San-chi. These mountains run east–west, making north–south travel limited.

**1 Okayama.** The impressive Crow Castle, and Korakuen Garden, one of Japan's finest.

**2 Kurashiki.** A picture-postcard historical district with riverside ryokan.

**3 Hiroshima.** Memorials to the horrors of the past, while embracing the present and building for the future.

**4 Miyajima.** Itsukushima Shrine, inquisitive deer, and Japan's most famous torii gate.

**5 Iwakuni.** The stunning wooden bridge Kintaikyo spans the Nishiki River.

**6 Hagi.** Charming castle town on the coast with samurai residences.

**7 Tsuwano.** Picturesque hamlet, home to Taiko-dani Inari Shrine.

**8 Matsue.** Seafood paradise, galleries, gardens and the 500-year-old Matsue castle.

**9 Izumo Taisha.** One of Japan's oldest and most venerable Shinto shrines.

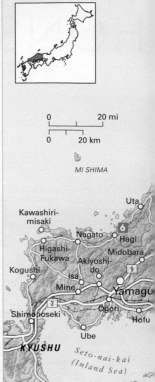

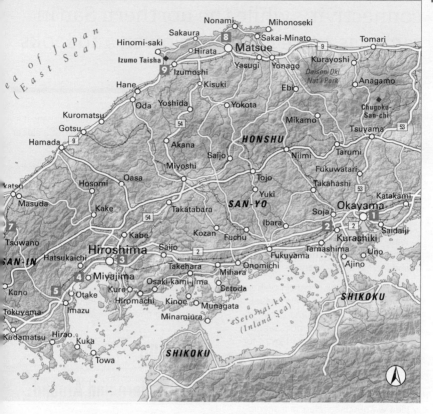

Sea of Japan
(East Sea)

Nonami
Sakaura
Mihonoseki
Hinomi-saki
Hirata
Sakai-Minato
Tomari
Izumo Taisha
9 Izumoshi
Matsue
9
Yasugi
Yonago
Kurayoshi
Hane
Kisuki
Daisen-Oki
Nat'l Park
Anagamo
Oda
Yoshida
Yokota
Ebi
Chugoku-
San-chi
Kuromatsu
Mikamo
Tsuyama
53
Gotsu
HONSHU
Hamada
9
Akana
Saijo
Niimi
Tarumi
Miyoshi
Fukuwatari
katsu
Hosomi
Oasa
Tojo
Takahashi
Katakami
Masuda
Kake
Takatabara
SAN-YO
Yuki
53
Okayama
1
7
Kozan
Fuchu
Ibara
Soja
2
2
Saidaiji
Tsuwano
Kabe
Saijo
Tamashima
Kurashiki
SAN-IN
Hatsukaichi
Hiroshima
3
2
Fukuyama
Uno
Ajino
Kano
4
Miyajima
Takehara
Mihara
Onomichi
Otake
Kure
Osaki-kami-jima
Setoda
SHIKOKU
Imazu
5
Hiromachi
Kinoe
Munagata
Kudamatsu
Hirao
Kuka
Minamiura
Seto-nai-kai
(Inland Sea)
Towa
SHIKOKU

The two regions of western Honshu have distinctly different personalities. The southern Sanyo region embraces modern connectivity, while the northern San'in region is more isolated, slower, and looks to the past.

Although the southern coast, or Sanyo, has basically gone along with Japan's full-steam-ahead efforts to set the pace for the developed world, you can still encounter pockets of dramatic old-world charm among the modern and shockingly new. The San'in coast, on the other hand, has largely escaped the scourge of over-development, yet you may be surprised to learn that everything you'd want in a city can be found up there, concentrated in and around lovely Matsue.

Happily, neither coast is short on history, religious significance, scenic beauty, or culinary delights. Hiroshima survived one of history's most horrible events to become a lively, famously friendly, for-ward-looking city. Kurashiki has a remark-ably preserved old-style district that can whisk you back to Edo times with a stroll down willow-draped canals and stylish-ly tiled warehouses. Hagi is a scenic bayside town that for 500 years has been the center of *Hagi-yaki* ceramics, coveted light-color and smooth-texture earthen-ware glazed with mysteriously translu-cent milky colors.

### MAJOR REGIONS
Sanyo means "sunny side of the moun-tain range," and the southern **Sanyo Region** along the Inland Sea is celebrated for its mild, clear climate. Although it's highly developed, to say the least, and you can't see or appreciate much of its

beauty from the train or the highway, it's wonderfully easy to stop and get a closer look at it.

If you're looking for adventure in a "real Japan" setting, the **San'in Region** is the place. Though the endless narrow ridges of steep mountains can make access from the south difficult, slow, and expensive, this hard fact of geography has kept the entire north stretch of west-ern Honshu delightfully isolated. Any effort to explore it pays off in dividends of great scenery, precious local crafts, tasty seafood, rich history, and genuinely welcoming people.

# Planning

## Getting Here and Around

### AIR
Hiroshima Airport and Okayama Airport both provide easy direct access to the Sanyo region. Yonago Kitaro Airport, near Matsue, is the most convenient airport for the San'in region. If you have a Japan rail pass with free access to the Shinkansen, you should also consider flying into Fukuoka Airport from where you can get to Shin-Yamaguchi Station in less than an hour.

## BOAT AND FERRY

Hiroshima is a ferry hub. Setonaikai Kisen runs up to eight boats daily to Miyajima (¥1,900 one-way) as well as regular and high-speed ferries to Matsuyama (regular ¥4,500; high-speed ¥7,800).

**CONTACT Setonaikai Kisen.** ⊠ *1–12–23 Ujinakaigan, Minami-ku* ☎ *082/253–1212* ⊕ *www.setonaikaikisen.co.jp/language/en.*

## BUS

You won't likely need highway buses, except for making the one-hour run between JR Shin-Yamaguchi and Hagi (knocking three hours off the train-travel time). Two companies operate bus routes: JR and Bocho bus lines. Japan Rail Passes are only valid for use on the JR buses.

**CONTACT Bocho Bus Center.** ⊕ *www.bochobus.co.jp.*

## CAR

All the major cities and most of the towns listed here will have at least a basic choice of car-rental outlets. Shinkansen trains are the best way to get around the southern coast, but for the northern Sanyo region renting a car can be a good option. Before renting, check that they have a vehicle available with GPS that can be switched to English.

## TRAIN

By far the easiest way to travel to western Honshu and along its southern coast is by the Shinkansen. The Kodama Shinkansen begins at Shin-Osaka and stops include Shin-Kobe, Himeji, Okayama, Ohin-Kurashiki, Hiroshima, Shin-Iwakuni, and Shin-Yamaguchi before reaching its destination at Hakata Station in Fukuoka. The Hikari Shinkansen is faster with fewer stops. The Nozomi Shinkansen that runs from Tokyo to Hakata is the fastest train in Japan, and stops at even fewer stations, but is not covered by the Japan Rail Pass.

JR express trains run along the Sanyo and San'in coasts, making a loop beginning and ending in Kyoto. Crossing from one coast to the other in western Honshu requires traveling fairly slowly through the mountains.

It is always advisable to reserve seats on the popular routes between big cities and to holiday destinations during peak season. Most train stations now have tourist offices with English speakers that can help with booking.

## Hotels

Accommodations cover a broad spectrum, from pensions and *minshuku* (private residences that rent rooms) to large, modern resort hotels that have little character but all the facilities you'd expect of an international chain. Large city and resort hotels have Western and Japanese restaurants. In summer or on holiday weekends hotel reservations are necessary. Unless otherwise noted, rooms have private baths, air-conditioning, and basic TV service.

*For a short course on accommodations in Japan, see Lodging in the Travel Smart chapter.*

## Restaurants

Western Honshu is one of the best regions to sample local Japanese seafood, with regional specialties from the Sea of Japan and Inland Sea. The oysters in Hiroshima, sea eel on Miyajima, and sashimi and sushi on the San'in coast are all superb. Matsue's location means that a variety of both freshwater and saltwater fish are available. Most reasonably priced restaurants have a visual display of the menu in the window, if not photos on the menu pages. If you cannot order in Japanese and no English is spoken, you can always lead the waiter to the window display and point. If you're adventurous, it is always fun to ask, "*Osusume?*" which means "What do you recommend?"

## RESTAURANT AND HOTEL PRICES

Restaurant prices are the average cost of a main course at dinner or, if dinner is not served, at lunch. Hotel prices are the lowest cost of a standard double room in high season. Restaurant and hotel reviews have been shortened. For full information, visit Fodors.com.

### What It Costs in Yen

| $ | $$ | $$$ | $$$$ |
|---|---|---|---|
| **RESTAURANTS** | | | |
| under ¥1,500 | ¥1,500–¥3,000 | ¥3,001–¥5,000 | over ¥5,000 |
| **HOTELS** | | | |
| under ¥12,000 | ¥12,000–¥18,000 | ¥18,001–¥22,000 | over ¥22,000 |

# Visitor Information

Most major towns and nowadays even the small ones have tourist information centers that offer free maps and brochures. They can also help you secure accommodation. They are most commonly located within the main train station complex.

# When to Go

Sanyo is the sunniest region in Japan, and almost any time is a good time to visit. The northern coast, or San'in, does get a strong dose of winter, but the reward is a wonderfully long, delightful spring. Like most of Japan, western Honshu gets oppressively muggy by midsummer, but the wind off the Sea of Japan cools the San'in coast. Summer festivals and autumn colors are spectacular throughout the region, and these always attract many tourists; reserve well ahead if you are traveling then.

# Okayama (岡山)

*672 km (418 miles) west of Tokyo, 188 km (117 miles) southeast of Matsue.*

The city of Okayama claims to have the most sunny days in Japan, and the disposition of the locals tends to reflect this. A beautiful black castle is set across the Asahi River from Korakuen, one of Japan's top three gardens. It's location on the main east-west Shinkansen train route means it easily accessible.

## GETTING HERE AND AROUND

The JR Shinkansen will speed you from Tokyo to Okayama in three hours, 14 minutes (¥16,600), Hiroshima (40 mins, ¥5,610), Shin-Osaka (49 minutes ¥5,610). From Matsue you can reach the city in two hours, 34 minutes by JR Ltd. Exp. Yakumo (¥5,610).

Hop on one of the frequent streetcars plying Momotaro-dori, the main boulevard heading east from the Okayama Station (¥100) to get around town. To get to the castle, park, and museums ride three stops east and walk southeast. For ¥580 you can buy a combined park-castle admission ticket.

Okayama is also an attractive base for visiting the historic charms of Kurashiki—only a 20-minute local JR train hop to the west (11 minutes by express train).

Should you need a map of Okayama or city information, head to the tourist information office in the underground shopping center to the right of the JR Station's East Exit.

## VISITOR INFORMATION

**CONTACT Okayama City Tourist Information Center.** ⊠ *JR Station 2F, South Exit, 1–1 Ekimoto-machi, Okayama* ☎ *086/222–2912.*

The Korakuen Garden in Okayama was built in the early 18th century.

# ◉ Sights

## ★ Korakuen Garden

(岡山後楽園; *Okayama Korakuen*)
GARDEN | FAMILY | Korakuen is a "Special Place of Scenic Beauty" (as designated by the government), and one of Japan's finest gardens. It has charming tea arbors, green lawns, ponds, and hills that were created at the turn of the 18th century on the banks of the Asahi River. Maple, apricot, and cherry trees give the 32-acre park plenty of flowers and shade. The riverside setting, with Okayama Castle in the background, is delightful. The garden's popularity increases in peak season (April to August), but this is one of the country's largest gardens, so you won't feel hemmed in by crowds. From Okayama Station, it is a 20-minute walk, or you can jump on the city tram for three stops to Shiroshita Station, and then it's a five-minute walk. ⊠ *1–5 Korakuen, Okayama* ☏ *086/272–1148* ⊕ *okayama-korakuen.jp* 🎫 *¥410.*

## Okayama Castle (岡山城; *Okayama-jo*)

CASTLE/PALACE | FAMILY | Painted a shadowy shade of black and set off dramatically by lead tiles and contrasting white vertical-slat shutters, Okayama's castle is known locally as *U-jo* (Crow Castle). Though it was built in the 16th century, only the "moon-viewing" outlying tower survived World War II. A replica was painstakingly constructed in 1966. The middle floors now house objects that represent the region's history, including a collection of armor and swords and a palanquin you can climb into to have your photo taken. Unlike many other castles with great views, this one has an elevator to take you up the six floors. A five-minute walk across the bridge brings you from the South Exit of Korakuen to the castle. Boats are available for rent on the river below from Hekisuien. Okayama Castle was under renovation until end of 2022. ⊠ *2–3–1 Marunouchi, Kita, Okayama* ☏ *086/225–2096* ⊕ *okayama-kanko. net/ujo* 🎫 *¥300.*

**Okayama Orient Museum**
(岡山市立オリエント美術館;
*Okayama Shiritsu Oriento Bijutsukan*)
**HISTORY MUSEUM** | On display at any time are at least 2,000 items from an impressive collection. Special exhibitions vary, but they generally show how Middle Eastern art reached ancient Japan via the Silk Road. The collections include items ranging from Persian glass goblets to ornate mirrors to early stringed instruments. Located not far from the castle and Korakuen Garden, it is a 15-minute walk from Okayama Station. ✉ *9–32 Tenjin-cho, Okayama* ☎ *086/232–3636* 🌐 *www.orientmuseum.jp* 🎫 *¥310* 🕒 *Closed Mon.*

## Coffee and Quick Bites

**Hekisuien** (碧水園)
**$** | **JAPANESE** | Set riverside with fantastic views of Okayama Castle, this small cafe and restaurant is the perfect place to grab lunch or coffee when exploring the castle and Korakuen Garden. You can also rent a swan boat to paddle around on the Asahi River after your meal. **Known for:** lunch with a view of the castle; bamboo shoot udon; Okayama pork bowl. [$] *Average main: ¥1,000* ✉ *1–6 Korakuen, Okayama* ✣ *Located right next to the South Gate of Korakuen Garden* ☎ *086/272–1605* 🌐 *hekisuien.jp* 🕒 *No dinner.*

## Hotels

**Hotel Granvia Okayama**
(ホテルグランヴィア岡山)
**$$$** | **HOTEL** | Bright-white marble and richly stained wood dominate the lobby at this large, luxurious hotel, a comfortable base for exploring the area. **Pros:** most convenient location for the train; elegant rooms; nice cafe. **Cons:** it is a 25-minute walk to the castle and gardens; beds are on the hard side; pool and other amenities cost extra. [$] *Rooms from: ¥20,570* ✉ *1–5 Ekimoto-machi, Kita-ku, Okayama* ☎ *086/234–7000* 🌐 *www.granvia-oka.co.jp* 🛏 *329 rooms* 🍴 *No Meals.*

# Kurashiki (倉敷)

*749 km (465 miles) west of Tokyo, 196 km (122 miles) west of Shin-Osaka, 17 km (10 miles) west of Okayama.*

From the 17th through the 19th century, this vital shipping port supplied Osaka with cotton, textiles, sugar, reeds, and rice. Today Kurashiki thrives on income from tourism. If your views were limited to what you see just outside the station, you'd be forgiven for thinking Kurashiki is just another modern Japanese city dominated by concrete. However, walking 10 minutes southeast of the station brings you to Bikan Chiku, a neighborhood of tree-lined canals, bridges, shops, restaurants, ryokan, and museums.

You can see most of Kurashiki's sights in a day, but it's worth staying longer, perhaps in a splendid old ryokan, to fully appreciate the time-machine aspect of the place. The Bikan district is artfully lit up at night, and a stroll down the willow-draped canals after a sumptuous meal can be an unforgettably romantic journey. The town also makes a convenient base for trips to Hiroshima (one hour, ¥6,550), Okayama (11 minutes, ¥1,620) and Himeji (49 minutes, ¥4,190). Note that virtually the entire town shuts down on Monday.

### GETTING HERE AND AROUND

Kurashiki is three hours, 50 minutes west of Tokyo or one hour west of Shin-Osaka by the Shinkansen and San-yo Line. In town you can stroll leisurely through the streets taking in the scenery.

Kurashiki Tourist Information Office, outside the South Exit of the train station, has a knowledgeable staff who provide useful maps and information. There's a branch in the Bikan district a block past the Ohara Art Museum. It sells ¥500 tickets for the 20-minute canal-boat tours (summer only).

## VISITOR INFORMATION

**CONTACT Kurashiki Tourist Information Office.** ✉ *West Bldg., 1–7–2 Achi, 2nd fl., Kurashiki* ☎ *086/424–1770.*

 Sights

### Kurashiki Museum of Folkcraft

(倉敷民芸館; *Kurashiki Mingei-kan*)

**HISTORY MUSEUM** | Founded in 1936, the Museum of Folkcraft highlights the beauty of traditional objects used in everyday life. Housed in a series of 18th-century storefronts, the atmosphere perfectly suits the many wooden, ceramic, and lacquerware objects on display. There are no detailed descriptions in English, but the elegance of the pieces on display speaks for itself. ✉ *1–4 11 Chuo, Kurashiki* ☎ *086/422–1637* ⊕ *kurashiki-mingeikan. com* ✉ *¥1,000* ⊗ *Closed Mon.*

### Ohara Art Museum

(大原美術館; *Ohara Bijutsukan*)

**ART MUSEUM** | In 1930, noted art collector and founder Magosaburo Ohara built this Parthenon-style building to house a collection of Western art with works by El Greco, Corot, Manet, Monet, Rodin, Gauguin, Picasso, Toulouse-Lautrec, and many others. They were shrewdly acquired for him by his friend Kojima Torajiro, a talented artist whom he dispatched to Europe for purchases. The museum is wonderfully compact and can be appreciated in a single morning or an afternoon. Two wings exhibit Japanese paintings, tapestries, woodblock prints, and pottery—including works by Shoji Hamada and Bernard Leach—as well as modern and ancient Asian art, much of it also brought home from trips made by Torajiro at Ohara's behest. The adjoining Kogei-kan (crafts hall) displays a selection of ceramic and textile art and is housed in a beautiful Edo-period storehouse. ✉ *1–1–15 Chuo, Kurashiki* ☎ *086/422–0005* ⊕ *www.ohara. or.jp* ✉ *¥1,500* ⊗ *Closed Mon.*

## 🍴 Restaurants

### Hamayoshi (浜吉)

**$$ | JAPANESE** | Three tables and a counter make up this intimate restaurant specializing in fish from the Seto Nai-kai. Sushi is one option; another is *mamakari,* a kind of vinegary sashimi sliced from a small fish caught in the Inland Sea. **Known for:** intimate dining; seafood delicacies; mantis shrimp sashimi. $ *Average main: ¥3,000* ✉ *2–19–30 Achi, Kurashiki* ☎ *086/421–3430* ⊗ *Closed Mon.*

### KuShuKuShu (9494) (クシュクシュ)

**$$ | JAPANESE** | You'll be happy to find this lively little izakaya, a Kurashiki favorite for more than 20 years. Cool music and loud laughter can be heard from here when everything else on the street is locked up tight. **Known for:** lively in the evenings; classic izakaya fare; cash only. $ *Average main: ¥1,800* ✉ *2–16–41 Achi, Kurashiki* ☎ *086/421–0949* ▭ *No credit cards* ⊗ *Closed Tues.*

### Restaurant Kiyutei (レストラン亀遊亭)

**$$ | FUSION** | Best known for its steaks, this attractive Kurashiki-style restaurant has been in business since 1909. Kiyutei sits right at the end of the tree-lined Kurashiki River; the entrance is behind a gate across the street from the entrance to the Ohara Art Museum. **Known for:** affordable lunch sets; crowded on weekends; classic Japanese-Western fusion dishes. $ *Average main: ¥3,000* ✉ *1–2–20 Chuo, Kurashiki* ☎ *086/422–5140* ⊕ *www.kiyutei.jp* ⊗ *Closed Wed.*

## 🛏 Hotels

### Kurashiki Kokusai Hotel (倉敷国際ホテル)

**$$$$ | HOTEL** | The town's oldest Western-style hotel welcomes guests with a black-tile lobby and dramatic Japanese wood-block prints. **Pros:** location is near the good stuff; welcoming atmosphere; capable staff. **Cons:** some rooms need updating; rooms are on the small side; not riverside like the ryokan. $ *Rooms*

*from: ¥50,400* ✉ *1–1–44 Chuo, Kurashiki* ☎ *086/422–5141* 🌐 *www.kurashiki-kokusai-hotel.co.jp* 🛏 *105 rooms* 🍴 *No Meals.*

★ **Ryokan Kurashiki** (旅館くらしき)
$$$$ | **B&B/INN** | If you're going to splurge for a luxury ryokan, this is the place. **Pros:** the feel of a luxury hotel; excellent food; lots of antiques and period pieces. **Cons:** Kurashiki's most expensive lodging; the lavish dinner can take most of the evening; not the "pure" ryokan experience as all rooms have western style beds. [$] *Rooms from: ¥94,300* ✉ *4–1 Hon-machi, Kurashiki* ☎ *086/422–0730* 🌐 *www.ryokan-kurashiki.jp* 🛏 *8 rooms* 🍴 *All-Inclusive.*

**Ryori-Ryokan Tsurugata** (料理旅館鶴形)
$$$$ | **B&B/INN** | Treat yourself to a stay—or perhaps just a fantastic dinner—at this charming ryokan built in 1774. **Pros:** a great value; steeped in tradition; some rooms have private baths. **Cons:** a slower pace than most Westerners expect; service can be somewhat inflexible; books up quickly. [$] *Rooms from: ¥40,000* ✉ *1–3–15 Chuo, Kurashiki* ☎ *086/424–1635* 🌐 *www.turugata.jp* 🛏 *11 rooms* 🍴 *All-Inclusive.*

**Toyoko Inn Kurashiki Station South Exit** (東横イン倉敷駅南口; *Toyoko Inn Kurashiki-eki Minami-guchi*)
$ | **HOTEL** | This reasonably priced hotel is one of Kurashiki's most popular, as it offers basic, reliably comfortable rooms at a great value. **Pros:** great location; free breakfast; free Internet. **Cons:** tiny rooms; rooms are clean but spartan; not directly in the old town. [$] *Rooms from: ¥7,500* ✉ *2–10–20 Achi, Kurashiki* ☎ *086/430–1045* 🌐 *www.toyoko-inn.com* 🛏 *154 rooms* 🍴 *Free Breakfast.*

# Hiroshima (広島)

*342 km (213 miles) west of Shin-Osaka, 864 km (537 miles) from Tokyo.*

On August 6, 1945, at 8:15 am, a massive chunk of metal known as *Little Boy* fell from an American plane, and the sky ignited and glowed for an instant. In that brief moment, however, it became as hot as the surface of the sun in Hiroshima, until then a rather ordinary workaday city in wartime Japan. Half the city was leveled by the resulting blast, and the rest was set ablaze. Rain impregnated with radioactive fallout then fell, killing many that the fire and 1,000-mph shock wave had not. By the end of this mind-boggling disaster, more than 140,000 people died.

Modern Hiroshima's Peace Memorial Park (平和記念公園; *Heiwa Kinen Koen*) is at the northern point of the triangle formed by two of Hiroshima's rivers, the Ota-gawa (also called Hon-kawa) and Motoyasu-gawa. Monuments to that day abound in the park, but one site bears witness to that enormous release of atomic energy: the A-Bomb Dome. Its gloomy shadows are now surrounded by a vibrant, rebuilt city. As if to show just how earnestly Hiroshima has redefined itself, only a short walk to the east is Nagarekawa-cho, the city's most raucous nightlife district.

## GETTING HERE AND AROUND

The streetcar (tram) is an easy form of transport in Hiroshima. Enter the middle door and take a ticket from the automatic dispenser. Pay the driver at the front door when you leave. All fares within city limits are ¥190. A one-day pass is ¥700, available for purchase at the platform outside JR Hiroshima Station. There are nine streetcar lines; four depart from the JR Station. Stops are announced by a recording, and each stop has a sign in *romaji* (romanized Japanese) posted on the platform.

Buses also joust with the traffic on Hiroshima's hectic streets. Information in English can be gathered at any of the Hiroshima tourist information offices. The Hiroshima Bus Company's red-and-white Bus 24 gets from Hiroshima Station to the Peace Memorial Park (¥190).

Taxis can be hailed throughout the city. Look for cabs that have the light (空車) illuminated, indicating they are ready to pick up passengers. The fare for the first 1½ km (1 mile) is ¥660, then around ¥250 for every kilometer.

Two excellent, English-speaking tourist information offices are in JR Hiroshima Station, both on the first floor at the southern and northern exits. The main tourist office, the Rest House in Peace Memorial Park, sits between the river and the Children's Peace Monument.

## VISITOR INFORMATION

**CONTACTS Hiroshima City Tourist Information Center.** ✉ *JR Hiroshima Station, Shinkansen Exit, 2–37 Matsubara-cho, 2nd fl., Minami-ku* ☎ *082/263–5120.* **Rest House in Peace Memorial Park.** ✉ *1–1 Nakajima-cho, Naka-ku* ☎ *082/247–6738.*

 # Sights

## ★ Atomic Bomb Dome

(原爆ドーム; *Gembaku Domu*)
**MONUMENT** | This ruin is a poignant symbol of man's self-destructiveness. It was the city's old Industrial Promotion Hall, and it stands in stark contrast to the new Hiroshima, which hums along close by. Despite being directly below the bomb blast, the building did not collapse into rubble like the rest of the city. Eerie, twisted, and charred, the iron-and-concrete dome has stood darkly brooding next to the river, basically untouched since that horrible morning. The sad old building's foreboding, derelict appearance can be emotionally overwhelming. The site is just outside the official northeast

boundary of Peace Memorial Park. Take Tram 2 or 6 from Hiroshima Station to the Gembaku-Domu-mae stop. ✉ *North of Heiwa Kinen Koen, Hiroshima.*

## Children's Peace Monument

(原爆の子像; *Genbaku-no-ko-zo*)
**MONUMENT** | Many consider this the most profound memorial in Peace Memorial Park. The figure is of Sadako, a 10-year-old girl who developed leukemia as a result of exposure to the atomic radiation that lingered long after the blast. She believed that if she could fold 1,000 paper *senbazuru* (cranes)—a Japanese symbol of good fortune and longevity—her illness would be cured. Her story has become a folktale of sorts, and it inspired a nationwide paper crane folding effort among schoolchildren that continues to this day. The colorful chains of paper cranes—delivered daily from schools all over the world—are visually and emotionally striking. ✉ *Heiwa Kinen Koen, Hiroshima.*

## 5 Days Children's Museum (こども文化科学館; *5-Days Kodomo Bunka Kagakukan*)
The city's hands-on children's museum is a good diversion for the kids. The joyful noise of excited children alleviates the somber mood of Peace Memorial Park. Kids get a kick out of conducting their own science experiments. To get here, leave the Peace Memorial Park via Aioi-bashi at the North Entrance and walk north and east, keeping the river on your left. Admission is free to the main part of the museum. If you wish to also see the planetarium, there's a fee for high-schoolers and adults. ✉ *5–83 Moto-machi, Naka-ku* ☎ *082/222–5346* ⊕ *www.pyonta.city.hiroshima.jp* ➽ *Free; planetarium ¥510 (adults)* ◷ *Closed Mon.*

## Flame of Peace

(平和の灯; *Heiwa no Tomoshibi*)
**MONUMENT** | Behind the Memorial Cenotaph, this flame will be extinguished only when all atomic weapons are banished. In the meantime, every August 6, the citizens of Hiroshima float paper lanterns

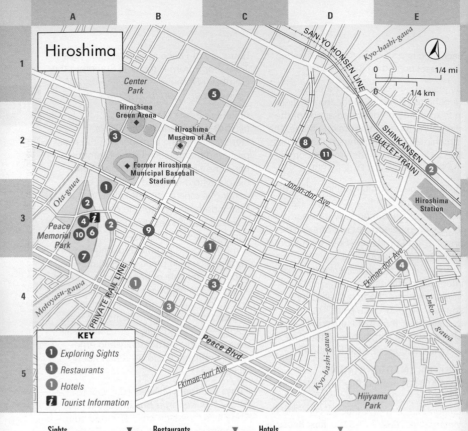

# Hiroshima

## Sights ▼

1 Atomic Bomb Dome .... **A3**

2 Children's Peace
  Monument .............. **A3**

3 5 Days
  Children's Museum ..... **A2**

4 Flame of Peace ......... **A3**

5 Hiroshima Castle ......... **C1**

6 Hiroshima National
  Peace Memorial Hall
  for the Atomic Bomb
  Victims .................. **A3**

7 Hiroshima Peace
  Memorial Museum ..... **A3**

8 Hiroshima Prefectural
  Art Museum ............. **D2**

9 Hiroshima Shopping
  Street .................... **B3**

10 Memorial Cenotaph .... **A3**

11 Shukkeien Garden ...... **D2**

## Restaurants ▼

1 Kamameshi Suishin
  Honten .................. **C3**

2 Kanawa Oyster Boat ... **A3**

3 Okonomimura ........... **C4**

## Hotels ▼

1 ANA Crowne Plaza
  Hotel Hiroshima ......... **B4**

2 Hotel Granvia
  Hiroshima ................ **E2**

3 Mitsui Garden Hotel
  Hiroshima ................ **B4**

4 Toyoko Inn Hiroshima
  Ekimae Ohashi
  Minami .................... **E4**

# Visiting Peace Memorial Park

## History

Before the atomic bomb, the area now home to Peace Park was known as the Nakajima District. Nakajima was a lively, urban center populated by around 6,500 residents. In 1949 it was decided that this area—decimated on account of being so near the bomb's hypocenter—would be reborn as a monument for peace. The park was designed by Kenzo Tange, after his design won in an international architecture competition.

## The Route

The park and surrounding monuments are not structured on a grid. Visitors are welcome to make their own trail and wander off the main paths to explore. The park can be experienced in as little as an hour, with a trip to the Cenotaph, Flame of Peace, and adjoining A-Bomb Dome area, but visitors with more time should take the opportunity to walk a meandering circle around the museum. Visiting the area's nearly 60 monuments can easily fill an afternoon. The park is particularly vivid in the summer, when the oleander flowers—a gift from sister-city Honolulu—are in full bloom.

## Getting Here

Riding the streetcar from JR Hiroshima Station is an easy way to reach Peace Park. Take Tram 1 bound for Hiroshima Port via Kamiya-cho, disembarking at Chuden-Mae. From Chuden-Mae, it's a 5-minute walk to the front of the Hiroshima Peace Memorial Museum. Riding Tram 2 or 6 will also take you to the Genbakudomu-mae stop (in front of the A-Bomb Dome). Within the city, streetcar fares are a flat ¥190, payable when you get off.

## Visitor Center

The Hiroshima Peace Memorial Museum has maps and information for English speakers. International Conference Center Hiroshima, located opposite the museum in the same building, also offers assistance, in addition to English-language newspapers and magazines.

## What's Nearby

The park is surrounded by a bustling commercial area, with no shortage of restaurants. Indeed, many visitors are surprised to find a regular commercial center so close to Peace Memorial Park. There are also a few tourist-friendly eateries along the riverside, including Kakifune Kawana, a floating restaurant that boasts some of the best oysters in town.

down the city's rivers for the repose of the souls of the atomic-bomb victims. ✉ *Heiwa Kinen Koen, Hiroshima*.

**Hiroshima Castle** (広島城; *Hiroshima-jo*) CASTLE/PALACE | Hiroshima Castle was originally built by Terumoto Mori on the Ota-gawa delta in 1589. He named the surrounding flatlands *Hiro-Shima*, meaning "wide island," and it stuck. The Imperial Japanese Army used the castle as headquarters in World War II, and with its significant depot of munitions it was one of the targets of the bomb. It was destroyed in the blast. In 1958 the five-story *donjon* (main tower) was rebuilt to its original specifications. Unlike many castles in Japan, it has lots of brown wood paneling that gives

*Continued on page 542*

*Hiroshima is a city on which an atomic bomb was dropped.*
*Hiroshima is a city with many memorials for the lives lost.*
*Hiroshima is a city which continually seeks peace.*

Part of a translated poem at the entrance to Hiroshima's Peace Museum

A WALK THROUGH HIROSHIMA'S
# PEACE MEMORIAL
# PARK

By Paige Ferrari

Paper lanterns float on the Motoyasu River during Hiroshima's annual Peace Ceremony.

Peace Park is both the physical and emotional center of Hiroshima. Some of the monuments here, such as the Memorial Cenotaph, have become internationally recognizable icons for peace. Others are lesser-known, but nonetheless powerful, monuments dedicated to specific groups and individuals who lost their lives on August 6, 1945. After a visit to the museum, walking through the park provides time for reflection. Like Hiroshima itself, the park honors an unhappy history while presenting an optimistic view for the future. Atomic bomb survivors—known as *Hibakusha*—and rowdy, yellow-capped groups of school kids alike visit the park throughout the year to remember the past. Though the details of the atomic bomb's impact are grim, the overwhelming message is one of hope and peace. Visitors of all backgrounds and nationalities should feel welcome here.

# STARTING FROM THE PEACE MUSEUM

As you exit the ❶ **Peace Museum** and stand under the elevated section, walk straight along the path towards the iconic A-Bomb Dome.

Framing the dome is the ❷ **Memorial Cenotaph.** The dome is shaped like a traditional Japanese house and records the names of 260,000 who ultimately perished from the initial bombing or, later, from its effects. The epitaph is translated: "Let all souls here rest in peace, for we shall not repeat the evil." Each year on August 6, thousands gather here to remember the events of past.

Continuing along the main path, which runs to the left of the Cenotaph, you'll pass by the ❸ **Pond for Peace.** Its water is intended as a symbolic offering for the victims who were unable to quench their thirst after the bomb's detonation and subsequent black rain.

At the end of the pond burns the ❹ **Flame of Peace,** first lit during the 1964 Tokyo Olympics. The structure itself resembles a pair of cupped hands. Hiroshima residents will tell you that this flame is not an eternal one. It will be extinguished the day the world is free of all nuclear weapons.

Ahead and on your left is what many visitors find to be Peace Park's most moving offering, the ❺ **Children's Peace Monument.** The statue and the cases of paper cranes behind it are dedicated to all the children who died in the blast and from radiation-related sicknesses after, including Sadako Sasaki, whose determination to fold 1,000 paper cranes before she succumbed to leukemia at age 12, is one of Hiroshima's most heartbreaking and enduring stories. Brightly colored paper cranes, on display in a series of glass

cases behind the monument, are brought from around the world but especially by groups of Japanese elementary school students.

Break off the path and walk to your left. Here, in a wooded region at the edge of the park, you'll find a cluster of specific monuments. These include the ❻ **Monument for the Korean A-Bomb Victims,** the ❼ **A-bombed Gravestone,** and the ❽ **Atomic Memorial Mound.** The mound is a particularly solemn place. Constructed on the 10-year anniversary of the bombing, it was an area once used as a crematorium and now holds the ashes of roughly 70,000 victims.

Walking towards the tip of the park, you'll come upon the ❾ **Peace Bell,** built in 1964. A map of the world without borders is carved on the bell, and all visitors are welcome to strike the bell. The bell's sound is intended to remind all who hear it of the reverberations of nuclear power. Nearby, at the narrow tip of the park near the Aioi-bashi bridge, stands the ❿ **Peace Clock Tower.** Built in 1967, the clock chimes each morning at 8:15, the moment the bomb was dropped.

Walk across the ⓫ **Aioi-bashi Bridge.** This bridge, with its characteristic T-shape, was selected as the target for the bombing. On the opposite side of the bridge you can walk around the ⓬ **A-Bomb Dome,** once the city's Industrial Promotions Hall.

To visit the bomb's nearby hypocenter, walk past the A-Bomb Dome as if you're returning to the museum. To your left, across a small street outside the park perimeter, you'll see a black temple and a white temple standing side by side, bisected by a small street. In front of the white building is a statue with a shadow permanently burned into the pedestal, a product of thermal radiation. Walk down the street between these buildings for a block, then walk half a block to your right to find yourself standing in front of what used to be ⓭ **Shima Hospital,** the bomb's hypocenter. A small

(above) A couple honors the victims of the atomic bombing at the Peace Memorial Park.

Genbaku-
Domu-mae

Aioi-bashi
Br.

11

12

10

9

13

14

Motoyasu-bashi
Br.

Hiroshima Monument
for the A-Bomb Victims

5

8

7

15

4

6

3

16

2

17

18

1

Peace Boulevard

Heiwa-ohashi
Br.

plaque shows what the area looked like directly after the blast, but otherwise there is little to distinguish it from the surrounding commercial area.

Find your way back to the trail in front of the A-Bomb Dome. Walking back towards the museum you'll come upon the **14 Memorial Tower for Mobilized Students** on your left. On the day of the bombing, children as young as 12 were working outside, demolishing buildings in order to create fire-breaks that would minimize the damage from potential air attacks. Of the 8,400 students working that day, nearly 6,400 died.

As you cross the Motoyasu Bridge back onto the main park grounds, ahead on your right you'll see the **15 Rest House** and tourist information center. Walking back towards the museum's main building, the modern-looking building ahead of you is the **16 Hiroshima National Peace Memorial Hall for the Atomic Bomb Victims,** opened in 2002. Inside you can hear survivor stories and visit the research library, which houses over 100,000 memoirs written by survivors. The basement of the center provides a breathtaking artist's rendition of a 360-degree view from the hypocenter.

Walking more towards the museum itself, you'll find the **17 Monument dedicated to Sankichi Toge,** who was 28 at the time of the bombings. After the war, Toge protested nuclear weapons through his poetry, including the one that is on the monument. A lock of Sankichi's hair and his pen are buried on the monument, the Japanese side of which faces towards his home.

Directly in front of the museum's snack and gift store, you'll find a small, cordoned-off **18 Chinese Parasol Tree.** This tree is also an A-bomb survivor. Despite being scorched in the blast, new leaves started to bud and develop the next year. Today, it is a symbol for the tenacity of life and rebirth.

This is a good space to end your walk, although you should feel free to cross Heiwa Dori (Peace Boulevard) to take in some of the smaller, scattered monuments, or simply take some time to rest and reflect.

## TOTAL DESTRUCTION

A-Bomb Dome today

Looking at bustling Hiroshima today, there is little evidence of the almost total destruction that visited the city on August 6, 1945. The first atomic bomb was dropped on Japan at 8:15 am and exploded approximately 1,900 feet above the city, centered on the Shima Hospital (the actual target, the Aioi-bashi Bridge, was missed). The intial blast radius was approximately 1 square mile, and the fireball resulting from the explosion engulfed approximately 4.4 square miles; fires eventually destroyed about 69% of the buildings of Hiroshima. In the initial blast, 70,000 to 80,000 people were killed immediately, with as many as 180,000 more killed eventually by injuries sustained in the bombing or by radiation and its after-effects. The destruction in the city was almost complete in the blast- and fire-ravaged areas, and very few structures survived. The city's Industrial Promotions Hall (now better known as the **A-Bomb Dome**) was less than 500 feet from ground zero and was one of the few structures in the immediate blast radius to survive. Compared to the destruction in Nagasaki three days later, the number of dead and the amount of destruction in Hiroshima was considerably more because the city is built on a flat river plain.

Atomic bomb mushroom clouds over Hiroshima

Viewing the A-Bomb Dome in the bomb's immediate aftermath

Ground Zero before the bombing shows a busy city; each circle is approximately ⅓ mi.

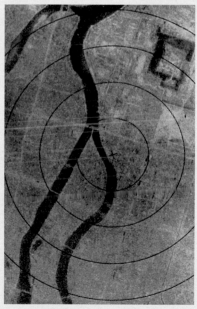

Ground Zero after the bombing (same scale). Note the almost complete lack of standing structures.

it a warm appearance, and it stands in intriguing contrast to the modern city that has evolved around it. The modern interior feels anything but castlelike, but has exhibits from Japan's feudal Edo period (17th through 19th centuries). It's a 15-minute walk north from the A-Bomb Dome. ✉ *21–1 Moto-machi, Naka-ku* ☎ *082/221–7512* 🎟 *¥370.*

### Hiroshima National Peace Memorial Hall for the Atomic Bomb Victims
(国立広島原爆死没者追悼平和祈念館; *Kokuritsu Hiroshima Genbakushibotsu-sha Tsuito Heiwa Kinen-kan*)

**HISTORY MUSEUM** | The memorial recounts the stories of known victims of the atomic devastation. In addition to the extensive archives of names, a collection of personal photos lends immediacy to one of the most shocking moments in history. A spiraling ramp leads downward to the Hall of Remembrance, a sobering 360-degree panorama of Hiroshima after the war. It is only up close that one sees that the photorealistic view is actually a collage of 140,000 black and white tiles, the number of people estimated to have died in the blast and in the months following. Heartbreaking firsthand accounts and memoirs of survivors are available for viewing. ✉ *1–6 Nakajima-cho, Naka-ku* ☎ *082/543–6271* ⊕ *www.hiro-tsuitoki-nenkan.go.jp* 🎟 *Free.*

### ★ Hiroshima Peace Memorial Museum
(広島平和記念資料館; *Heiwa Kinen Shiryokan*)

**HISTORY MUSEUM** | Displays of models, charred fragments of clothing, melted ceramic tiles, lunch boxes, watches, and shocking photographs tell Hiroshima's story of death and destruction. A visit here may be too intense for some (especially children), but to appreciate the horror of the bombing and the hope that made Hiroshima into the city it is today, this museum is highly recommended. The heat-ray-photographed human shadow permanently imprinted on granite steps can take you well beyond sadness,

and the Dalí-esque watch forever stopped at 8:15 is chilling. Most exhibits have brief explanations in English, and more-detailed information is on the audio tour, which you can rent separately. ✉ *1–2 Nakajima-cho, Naka-ku* ☎ *082/241–4004* ⊕ *hpmmuseum.jp* 🎟 *¥200.*

### Hiroshima Prefectural Art Museum
(広島県立美術館; *Hiroshima Kenritsu Bijutsukan*)

**ART MUSEUM** | Next to the Shukkei Garden, this museum is a visual treat. Standouts include two particularly surrealistic pieces: a typically fantastical piece by Salvador Dalí called *Dream of Venus*; and Ikuo Hirayama's much closer-to-home *Holocaust at Hiroshima*. Hirayama, who became one of Japan's most acclaimed artists, was a junior-high-school student at the time the A-bomb was dropped. The museum also holds excellent rotating exhibitions of art from classic to contemporary. ✉ *2–22 Kaminobori-cho, Naka-ku* ☎ *082/221–6246* ⊕ *www.hpam.jp* 🎟 *¥510.*

### Hondori Shopping Street (本通り)

**STREET** | Around Hiroshima's central district are hundreds of shops. Take the tram that runs from the main station to stop T-31, or simply walk east across the north bridge out of Peace Park. The big department stores—Sogo, Fukuya, Tenmaya, and Mitsukoshi—are at the east end of the arcade near the Hatchobori streetcar stop. Many restaurants—including a big, gorgeous Andersen's, a popular bakery chain (one block down on the right from T-31)—are also found here. ✉ *Hondori, Hon-dori.*

### Memorial Cenotaph (原爆死没者慰霊碑; *Gembaku Shibotsusha Irei-hi*)

**MONUMENT** | Designed by Japanese architect Kenzo Tange, the cenotaph resembles the primitive A-frame houses of Japan's earliest inhabitants. Buried inside is a chest containing the names of those who died in the destruction and aftermath of the atomic bomb. On the exterior is the inscription, "Rest in peace, for the error shall not be repeated." Looking through the Cenotaph at the Flame of Peace at night, after the sun has set and crowds have gone home, is an eerily beautiful experience. The cenotaph stands before the north side of the Heiwa Kinen Shiryokan. ⊠ *Heiwa Kinen Koen, Hiroshima.*

## Shukkeien Garden (縮景園)

GARDEN | Designed in 1630 by Lord Naga-akira Asano (the name means "shrunken scenery garden"), Shukkeien Garden resembles one once found around a famed lake in Hangzhou, China, which the *daimyo* (lord) wanted to re-create for leisurely strolls. The water is dotted with tiny rocky islets sprouting gnarled pine trees. Small bridges cross above lots of colorful carp, a fish venerated for its long and vigorous life. Shukkeien Garden sits east of Hiroshima Castle on the banks of the Kyobashi-gawa River. From JR Hiroshima Station take streetcar 1, 2, or 6 then transfer to the Hakush-ima Line at Hatchobori, and get off at Shukkeien-mae. ⊠ *2–11 Kaminobori-cho, Naka-ku* ☎ *082/221–3620* ⊕ *shukkeien. jp* ⊠ *¥260.*

##  Restaurants

The main place for shopping and dining is around Hondori Shopping Street. Near Hiroshima Station you'll find various malls with food courts, and there are numerous places to grab a bite in the station complex itself. During cherry blossom season in particular you'll see locals and visitors enjoying a picnic near Hiroshima Castle or along the riverside.

## Kamameshi Suishin Honten (釜飯酔心本店)

$$ | JAPANESE | Famous for its *kama-meshi,* or rice casseroles, this restaurant serves the freshest fish from the Seto Nai-kai—*fugu,* or puffer fish, oysters, and eel, to name but a few. If you prefer your fish cooked, try the rock-fish grilled with soy sauce. **Known for:** local Hiroshima cuisine; fresh seafood;

welcoming atmosphere. $ *Average main: ¥1,600* ⊠ *6–7 Tate-machi, Naka-ku* ☎ *082/247–4411.*

## Kanawa Oyster Boat (かき船かなわ; *Kaki-fune Kanawa*)

$$$$ | SEAFOOD | Hiroshima is known for its oysters, and Kanawa, on a barge moored on the Motoyasu-gawa, gets its oysters from a particularly salty area of the Inland Sea. It's believed that these waters impart the firm flesh and sweet, robust taste that loyal customers love to splurge on. **Known for:** specially sourced Hiroshima oysters year-round; views of the river; excellent set menus. $ *Average main: ¥13,000* ⊠ *1-chome Jisaki, Otemachi, Naka-ku* ☎ *082/241–7416* ⊕ *www.kanawa.co.jp.*

## Okonomimura (お好み村)

$ | JAPANESE | The Okonomimura Building contains around 20 shops that all serve *okonomiyaki* (literally, "as you like it grilled"). Okonomiyaki is best described as an everything omelet, topped with bits of shrimp, pork, squid, or chicken, cabbage, and bean sprouts. **Known for:** lively—bordering on chaotic—atmosphere; long lines around dinnertime; cash only. $ *Average main: ¥850* ⊠ *Shintenchi Plaza, 5–13 Shintenchi, 2nd–4th fl., Naka-ku* ☎ *082/241–2210* ⊕ *www.okonomi-mura.jp/foreign/english.html* ⊟ *No credit cards.*

## 🛏 Hotels

### ANA Crowne Plaza Hotel Hiroshima (ANAクラウンプラザホテル広島)

$$$$ | HOTEL | This reliable and popular hotel puts you close to the Peace Park and the nightlife of Nagarekawa. **Pros:** spacious double rooms; free Internet access; handy location for Peace Memorial Park. **Cons:** one of the city's pricier hotels; single rooms are small; distance from train station. $ *Rooms from: ¥33,500* ⊠ *7–20 Naka-machi, Naka-ku* ☎ *082/241–1111* ⊕ *www.ihg.com* ⊐ *410 rooms* ⊠ *Free Breakfast.*

**Hotel Granvia Hiroshima** (ホテルグランヴィア広島)
$$$ | **HOTEL** | Connected by walkways to Hiroshima's JR Station, this conveniently located hotel is welcoming to weary travelers. **Pros:** handy when you're catching a train; helpful staff; free Wi-Fi. **Cons:** limited English of some staff; lower floors can be a bit noisy; far from shopping district and sightseeing. [$] *Rooms from: ¥23,610* ✉ *1–5 Matsubara-cho, Minami-ku* ☎ *082/262–1111* 🌐 *www.hgh.co.jp/english* 🛏 *404 rooms* 🍴 *No Meals.*

**Mitsui Garden Hotel Hiroshima** (三井ガーデンホテル広島)
$$$$ | **HOTEL** | This modern and comfortable hotel is an excellent base for exploring the area around Peace Memorial Park as well as the city's restaurants and nightlife. **Pros:** excellent value; convenient location; a slight step up from most Japanese business hotels. **Cons:** a bit of a hike from JR Hiroshima Station; rooms are comfortable but basic; single rooms are tiny. [$] *Rooms from: ¥22,230* ✉ *9–12 Nakamachi, Naka-ku* ☎ *082/240–1131* 🌐 *www.gardenhotels.co.jp/hiroshima/eng* 🛏 *281 rooms* 🍴 *No Meals.*

**Toyoko Inn Hiroshima Ekimae Ohashi Minami** (東横INN広島駅前大橋南)
$ | **HOTEL** | Just a short walk from JR Hiroshima Station, this functional Japanese business hotel is identical to the nearly 300 other hotels in the chain. **Pros:** value for money; proximity to the train station; free breakfast. **Cons:** far from the main shopping and sightseeing areas; compact sparse rooms; check in from 4 pm (3 pm if club member). [$] *Rooms from: ¥8,000* ✉ *1–1–1 Matoba-cho, Minami-ku* ☎ *082/568–1045* 🌐 *www.toyoko-inn.com/eng* 🛏 *150 rooms* 🍴 *Free Breakfast.*

# Miyajima (宮島)

*27 km (16 miles) southeast of Hiroshima.*

Miyajima's majestic orange O-torii, or "big gate," is made of several stout, rot-resistant camphor-tree trunks, and is famed for the illusion it gives of "floating" over the water. The torii gate is one of Japan's most enduring scenic attractions, but some of the time it actually presides over brownish tidal sand flats, so you will want to time your visit for when the tide is in. Ferry offices and hotels can give you a tidal forecast—don't forget to ask.

Behind the torii gate is the elegant Itsukushima Jinja shrine. For a few hundred yen you can walk the labyrinthine wooden boardwalks out over the tidal basin and pick your spots to snap those perfect photos.

To get to the shrine and to see the torii, go right from the pier on the path that leads through the village, which is crowded with restaurants, hotels, and souvenir shops. As you pass through the park, expect to be greeted by herds of fearless deer. Don't show or let them smell any food, or else you'll become too popular; they do have little horns, and they are known to eat most anything within reach.

## GETTING HERE AND AROUND

The easiest, least expensive way to get to Miyajima is to take the train on the JR Sanyo Line from Hiroshima Station to Miyajimaguchi Station. From Miyajimaguchi Station, a three-minute walk takes you to the pier where ferries depart for Miyajima. The train takes about 25 minutes (¥420) and departs from Hiroshima every 15–20 minutes. There are two boats, but the JR Rail Pass is only valid on the JR-operated boat (¥360 round-trip without a Rail Pass). If you are staying close to the Peace Memorial Park rather than Hiroshima Station, another option to

Miyajima's O-torii sits at the entrance to a cove and is in the water at high tide.

get to Miyajima is by the smaller shuttle boat that runs from the Peace Memorial Park (right next to the tourist information center) to the Miyajima Port. It's more expensive at ¥2,200 one way, but you won't have to first make your way to the train station on the other side of town.

Allow a minimum of three hours for the major sights of Miyajima, and a full day if you also plan to hike up the mountain. Bicycle rentals are available at the Miyajima ferry terminal, offering a quick way to scoot around the island. A more adventurous option is to explore the coast of Miyajima by kayak.

Inside the ferry terminal (common to both lines) is the English-speaking Miyajima Tourist Association.

## VISITOR INFORMATION

**CONTACT Miyajima Tourist Association.** ⊠ *1162–18 Miyajima, Miyajima* ☎ *0829/44–2011* ⊕ *www.miyajima.or.jp.*

##  Sights

**Five-Storied Pagoda** (五重塔; *Go-ju-no-to*)
NOTABLE BUILDING | Hokoku Shrine (also known as the Toyokuni Shrine) is a complex of buildings overlooking Itsukshima Shrine and the O-torii Gate. The Senjokaku Pavilion is a large wooden hall, and beside it is the shrine's major landmark, the 28-meter-high Five-Storied Pagoda. At night, the pagoda is beautifully illuminated. ⊠ *1–1 Miyajima-cho, Hatsukaichi, Miyajima* ✛ *At end of Miyajima's main shopping street on way to Itsukushima Shrine.*

**Itsukushima Shrine**
(厳島神社; *Itsukushima Jinja*)
RELIGIOUS BUILDING | This shrine was founded in AD 593 and dedicated to the three daughters of Susano-o-no-Mikoto, the Shinto god of the moon—also of the oceans, moon-tugged as they are. It has been continually repaired and rebuilt, and the present structure is a 16th-century copy of 12th-century buildings. The orange woodwork next to the glaring white walls is attractive,

especially when complemented by a blue sky and sea. The deck has the best frontal views of the torii gate. ✉ *1–1 Miyajima-cho, Miyajima* ☎ *0829/44–2020* 🎟 *¥300.*

**Momijidani Park**
(紅葉谷公園; *Momijidani Koen*)
**VIEWPOINT** | Many people spend only half a day on Miyajima, but if you have more time, take a stroll through the park that is inland from Itsukushima Shrine. It is most famous for the colorful maple leaves *(momiji)* in the fall. Continuing on from the park you can take a cable car or hike to the summit of Mt. Misen. From the cable car upper terminus to the top of the mountain is still a short hike, but from there you can look out over Seto Island Sea and all the way to Hiroshima. If you walk all the way up the mountain rather than using the cable car, it takes around 90 minutes depending on your fitness level and how hot and humid the day is. Iwaso Ryokan is located in the park amongst the maple trees. ✉ *Miyajima* ✥ *From Itsukushima Shrine, follow narrow street along river inland. Momijidani park is about a 5-min walk. Keep following street another 5 mins to get to cable-car* 🎟 *Free; cable car ¥1,800 round-trip.*

**O-torii Gate** (大鳥居)
**RELIGIOUS BUILDING** | Miyajima's O-torii gate stands nearly 50 feet tall at the entrance to the cove where the ancient Shinto shrine is. This, the 18th version, was built in 1875, and has become one of the nation's most recognizable symbols. Hotels and ferry operators have tide charts so you can maximize your photo opportunities. At low tide, though, you can walk over the sand flats to admire the gate up close. From June 2019 to December 2022 the torii gate was covered in scaffolding for structural repairs.

If you stay overnight on the island, and if the weather cooperates, you're guaranteed to get some photos to die for, because the gate is lighted up in spectacular fashion at night. The nearby five-story pagoda and the shrine are also illuminated. ✉ *1–1 Miyajimacho, Hatsukaichi, Miyajima.*

## 🛏 Hotels

**Iwaso Ryokan** (岩惣)
**$$$$** | **B&B/INN** | For traditional elegance, it's easy to like this venerable Japanese inn. **Pros:** charm to spare; great views; delicious 12-course meals. **Cons:** you'll feel like royalty—until you get the bill; the hot spring may be a bit too hot and stuffy for some; not all rooms have private baths. [$] *Rooms from: ¥50,000* ✉ *345 Miyajima-cho, Miyajima* ☎ *0829/44–2233* 🌐 *www.iwaso.com* 🛏 *38 rooms* 🍴 *All-Inclusive.*

**Ryokan Jukeiso** (聚景荘)
**$$$$** | **B&B/INN** | This charming hillside ryokan has been around for more than a century, and it owes its longevity to its having the best views on the island. **Pros:** great views, inside and out; quiet hillside retreat; unobtrusive service. **Cons:** staying on Miyajima is more expensive than hotels on the mainland; lacks the intimacy of more traditional-style ryokan; steep stairs and slopes may be tough for some. [$] *Rooms from: ¥60,000* ✉ *50 Miyajima-cho, Miyajima* ☎ *0829/44–0300* 🌐 *miyajima-jukeiso.com* 🛏 *13 rooms* 🍴 *All-Inclusive.*

## 🏃 Activities

### KAYAKING

**Miyajima Sea Kayak** (宮島シーカヤック)
**CANOEING & ROWING** | Exploring the coast of Miyajima by sea kayak, and paddling near the giant torii gate makes for an unforgettable experience at an already magical place. Haru-san runs excellent tours that start at 90 minutes and go up to six hours. The best time for kayaking will depend on the tides, so you'll need to book in advance, and see when Haru-san recommends. ✉ *Miyajima* ☎ *070/7565–4932* 🌐 *www.miyajima-seakayak.com* 🎟 *From ¥5,000 (for a 90-minute tour).*

# Yamaguchi: Gateway to the San'in Region

Yamaguchi (山口) is a small town, but one where you're likely to experience a disarming level of hospitality. It's also a logical base for striking out for territory hinterlands like Hagi and Tsuwano, especially if accommodations are fully booked in those romantic hideaways. The Shinkansen at nearby Shin-Yamaguchi will get you there, and—if you have the time to look around—the English-speaking tourist information office will happily provide you with a map. For overnight stays, the Sunroute Kokusai Hotel Yamaguchi is a basic, affordable option, about a 10-minute walk from the station.

You're likely to make new friends if you duck in for a bite at favorite local restaurants or one of the many sushi bars or soba shops located in the covered shopping mall about a five-minute walk up the street from JR Yamaguchi Station.

If you're more interested in resting your travel-weary body than grabbing a meal, pop your bags in a coin locker and head one train stop over to the Yuda Onsen, where the healing sulfur baths will leave you feeling rejuvenated and ready for the next leg of your journey.

# Iwakuni (岩国市)

*365 km (227 miles) west of Shin-Osaka, 41 km (26 miles) south west from Hiroshima.*

A short train ride southwest from Hiroshima, Iwakuni City is a worthwhile day trip primarily due to Kintaikyo, arguably Japan's most famous (and most beautiful) bridge. The city's castle provides panoramic views over the area and is accessible by a ropeway. During the first week of April the cherry trees that line the river and roads of Iwakuni are covered in blossom, making this one of Japan's top sakura viewing spots.

## GETTING HERE AND AROUND

Hiroshima Station to Iwakuni Station takes 49 minutes (¥770) on the JR Sanyo line. Then it is a 20-minute bus west to Kintaikyo Bridge. A better option (particularly if you have a rail pass) is to take the Kodama Shinkansen from Hiroshima Station to Shin-Iwakuni Station which is just 14 minutes (¥1,640). Be aware that the faster Nozomi Shinkansen do not stop at Shin-Iwakuni.

From Shin-Iwakuni Station you can take a 15-minute bus ride east to Kintaikyo Bridge, or rent a bicycle from in front of the train station and for most of the ride you'll follow the river to the bridge.

The base of the ropeway that takes you up to the castle is just a 10-minute walk from the bridge.

## ◉ Sights

**Iwakuni Castle** (岩国城; *Iwakuni-jo*)
CASTLE/PALACE | On a day trip to Iwakuni City it is also worth checking out Iwakuni Castle, which is perched atop Mt. Shiroyama. It is accessed by a ropeway that starts just a 10-minute walk from Kintaikyo Bridge. Although the original castle was destroyed, this 1962 replica still provides fine views out over Iwakuni City and the Seto Island Sea beyond. ✉ *3-chome Yokoyama, Iwakuni* ☎ *0827/41–1477* ⊕ *kankou.iwakuni-city. net/itn/iwakuni-castle* 🎫 *Ropeway ¥560 round-trip, castle ¥270; combo ticket for bridge, ropeway, and castle ¥970.*

### Kintaikyo Bridge (錦帯橋)

BRIDGE | One of the world's most famous wooden bridges. Originally built in 1673, Kintaikyo Bridge spans the Nishiki River with five consecutive arches set atop four stone and two wooden piers. After being washed away by floods in 1950, it was rebuilt in 1953 and remains a Japanese National Treasure. Visiting the bridge is particularly popular when viewing cherry blossom in the spring, or viewing the changing colors of the leaves in the fall. You must pay a fee to cross the bridge (there's a small booth at either end of the bridge). A set discount ticket that covers the bridge, the ropeway, and Iwakuni Castle is also available. ⊠ Iwakuni ⌧ ¥310 for bridge; ¥970 for combo ticket for ropeway, bridge, and Iwakuni Castle

# Hagi (萩)

*117 km (73 miles) north of Yamaguchi.*

Hagi is virtually surrounded by two branches of the Abu-gawa—the river's south channel, Hashimoto-gawa, and the river's northeast fork, Matsumoto-gawa. Rising in great semicircles behind the sleepy town are symmetrical waves of shadowy mountains, while before it stretches a sparkling blue sea.

Hagi is rich with history, and, owing to its remoteness, retains the atmosphere of a traditional castle town—though, unfortunately, its castle was a casualty of the Meiji Restoration. Turning away from feudalism to support the new order, the city was of critical importance in the 1865 to 1867 movement to restore power to the emperor. Japan's first prime minister, Hirobumi Ito (1841–1909), was a Hagi native.

Hagi is also famous for *Hagi-yaki*, a type of earthenware with soft colors and milky, translucent glazes ranging from beige to pink. The esteemed local ceramics industry began in the 16th century when a Mori general brought home captive Korean potters (perhaps his consolation for a failed invasion) to create pottery for their new masters. The visually soothing Hagi-yaki is second only to Raku-yaki as the most coveted pottery in Japan, and it does not come cheaply, except during the annual price-friendly Hagi-yaki Festival every May 1–5.

## GETTING HERE AND AROUND

Access to Hagi from anywhere on the southern coast of Honshu is easiest using a combination of Shinkansen train to Shin-Yamaguchi Station, and then the express bus "Super Hagi" from Shin-Yamaguchi Station to Hagi. The express bus takes around 60 minutes and costs ¥1,600.

As the town is flat, the ideal way to explore Hagi is by bicycle, and you can rent a bike for between ¥800 and ¥1,000 per day near the stations or shopping arcades. A local bus system (red bus) loops around town for ¥100 a ride or ¥500 for a full day.

City information is available from English-speaking staff at the Hagi City Tourism Association next to JR Hagi Station. There is also an information office at JR Higashi Hagi Station.

## VISITOR INFORMATION

CONTACT **Hagi City Tourism Association.** ⊠ 3537–3 Tsubaki, Hagi ☎ 0838/25–1750 ⊕ www.hagishi.com/en.

 ## Sights

If you've just arrived by bus, you won't be impressed by the run-down buildings around the Hagi Bus Center. That's okay—there's no need to linger here. Head three short blocks north, then left onto Tamachi Mall, and then west through the quaint older sections of town for 15 minutes to see the park and castle ruins. If you need to make a tourist info stop first, the Tourist Bureau is two doors down from the bus depot.

**Akiyoshido Cave** (秋芳洞; *Akiyoshi-do*)
CAVE | This otherworldly limestone cavern, one of Japan's largest, lies halfway between Hagi and Yamaguchi. Although the cavern is roughly 6 miles long, only a bit less than a mile is open to the public. The path is easily accessible and lighted just enough for you to marvel at the size, but dim enough to retain a sense of wonder and mystery. Although droves of tour groups can ruin the atmosphere on weekend mornings, they have mostly cleared out by the afternoon.

The Akiyoshi Plain above the cave is a beautiful limestone karst, and makes for a pleasant spring or autumn hike. The observatory (accessible by elevator from the cave) offers impressive views in every season. If you plan to cross from the San'in to the Sanyo region, stopping a couple of hours at Akiyoshido Cave is highly recommended. Buses run from Shin-Yamaguchi Station to Akiyoshido Cave in around 45 minutes. ⊠ *Hirotani Shuhocho Akiyoshi, Akiyoshidai National Park* ☎ *0837/62–0899* ⊕ *en.karusuto.com/spot/akiyoshido* ☜ *¥1,300.*

**Hagi Tamachi Shopping Arcade**
(田町商店街; *Tamachi Shoten-gai*)
PEDESTRIAN MALL | This is the busiest street in Hagi, with some 130 shops selling local products from Yamaguchi Prefecture. The shopping mood is addictive, the wares gorgeous, and the shopkeepers friendly, so your money can go quickly. The arcade is halfway between Hagi Station and Higashi-Hagi Station. ⊠ *Central Hagi.*

**Horiuchi** (堀内)
HISTORIC DISTRICT | This is the old samurai section of town. From Shizuki Koen, cross the canal (on the middle bridge) to the east side, and head toward downtown. The tomb of Tenju-in is a memorial to Terumoto Mori, who in the early 16th century founded the tenacious clan that ruled the Choshu area for 13 generations. Next you come to the Outer Gate of Mori; the Toida Masuda House Walls are

on your right as you head south. Dating from the 18th century, these are the longest mud walls in the area. At the next chance, turn right and head west to the ancient, wooden Fukuhara Gate. ⊠ *Hagi.*

**Senshunraku Jōzan Pottery Studio**
(千春楽城山)
FACTORY | Stop in at this pottery studio near Shizuki Koen, perhaps the best place to browse through and purchase magnificent pottery. Usually you are welcome to enter the studios and see the kilns across the street every day. Classes for a chance to make your own may be available. Bicycles can be rented here as well. ⊠ *37–1 Horiuchi, Horiuchi* ☎ *0838/25–1666.*

**Shizuki Park** (指月公園 *Shizuki Koen*)
CITY PARK | Hagi's westernmost end is bounded on three sides by the sea. This large, lovely park contains the ruins of Hagi Castle and Hana-no-e Teahouse. Hagi Castle was one of many castles destroyed by the Meiji government around 1874 for being an embarrassing symbol of backward ways. The dramatic seaside location, with its stupendous mountain backdrop, must have made the castle a truly superb sight in its day, but alas, we can only imagine, since the walls and moats are all that remain.

The Hana-no-e Teahouse is a bare-bones oasis of Zen, set amid meditative gardens and judiciously pruned greenery. The attendants make the classic, slightly bitter *matcha* tea (¥500) for you while you reflect on the transient nature of life—or consider where you'd like to go next.

Mori House, south of the park, is a long narrow building once home to samurai foot soldiers in the late 18th century. The rooms are sparse and placed one next to the other. This arrangement allowed the soldiers to leap into rank-and-file assembly just outside at a moment's notice. ⊠ *1–1 Horiuchi, Hagi* ☎ *0838/25–1826* ☜ *¥220, includes admission to Hagi*

*Castle Ruins Area, Hana-no-e Teahouse, and Mori House.*

##  Restaurants

### ★ Kappo Chiyo (割烹千代)

$$$$ | JAPANESE | Imagine a *kappo* (fine dining) course that includes squid and scallops cooked before you with butter on a sizzling-hot river stone and such goodies as *fugu*—served as sashimi or cooked tempura-style—stuffed with foie gras. Zingy homemade pickles reset your palate for each successive treat. **Known for:** the highest-quality local ingredients; lavish multicourse dinners; elegant atmosphere. $ *Average main: ¥11,000* ⊠ *20–4 Imafuruhagi-machi, Hagi* ☎ *0838/22–1128* ⊕ *chiyo.in* ⏱ *Closed Mon. No dinner Sun.*

### Sobaho Fujitaya (蕎麦舗ふじたや)

$ | JAPANESE | Colorful local characters come to this casual restaurant for beer and sake and *seiro-soba* (thin buckwheat noodles served in steaming-hot baskets) and hot tempura served on fragrant handmade cypress trays. The restaurant is usually open by 11 am (or when the noodles are ready), but it closes at 6 (or when all the noodles are gone), so only a very early dinner is possible here. **Known for:** a local favorite; seiro-soba; simple, delicious lunches. $ *Average main: ¥1,000* ⊠ *59 Kumagaya-cho, Hagi* ☎ *0838/22–1086* ⊟ *No credit cards* ⏱ *Closed Wed. and Fri. No dinner.*

##  Hotels

### Hokumon Yashiki (北門屋敷)

$$$$ | B&B/INN | An elegant ryokan built upon the ruins of an old Mori clan estate, the luxurious Hokumon Yashiki pampers you in a style the ruling elite were surely accustomed to in the good old days. **Pros:** unique interior design melds traditional Japanese style with European elements; top-notch hospitality; one of the most conspicuously traditional inns in the world. **Cons:** the bath is not a natural hot spring; quiet, but lacks the serenity of more rural ryokan; one of the most expensive lodgings in Hagi. $ *Rooms from: ¥66,000* ⊠ *210 Horiuchi, Hagi* ☎ *0838/22–7521* ⊕ *www.hokumon.co.jp* ⇘ *38 rooms* ⏹️ *All-Inclusive.*

### Resort Hotel Mihagi (リゾートホテル美萩)

$$$$ | HOTEL | Considering its view over the sea, spacious rooms, and proximity to Hagi's old town, Mihagi is a great option. **Pros:** huge rooms; relaxing atmosphere; a short walk from most of Hagi's sights. **Cons:** the hotel is a hike from the station—take a taxi; Western-style rooms are clean, but have dated design; price depends on type of evening meal selected. $ *Rooms from: ¥57,200* ⊠ *485 Horiuchi, Horiuchi* ☎ *0838/21–7121* ⊕ *resorthotel-mihagi.com* ⇘ *39 rooms* ⏹️ *All-Inclusive.*

# Tsuwano (津和野)

*93 km (58 miles) northeast of Hagi, 50 km (31 miles) northeast of Yamaguchi, 63 km (39 miles) northeast of Shin-Yamaguchi.*

This hauntingly beautiful town, tucked into a narrow north–south valley at the foot of conical Aono-yama and its attendant dormant volcanic mountain friends, may be the most picturesque hamlet in all Japan. If you catch it on a clear day, the view from the old castle ruins simply takes your breath away. Even when it's cloudy, the mist hangs romantically among the trees and ridges. The stucco-and-tile walls harken back to ancient times, like those in Hagi and Kurashiki, and the clear, carp-filled streams running beside the streets can induce even tired, jaded travelers to take a leisurely stroll or bike ride backward through time.

It's easy to see why Tsuwano has come to be known as "Little Kyoto," and it's easier still to imagine how a gifted spirit and intellect could soar here. The towering Japanese literary figure Ogai Mori, novelist and poet, was born (in 1862) and lived here, until, at the age of 12, he went off and enrolled at Tokyo University's preparatory program in medicine.

## GETTING HERE AND AROUND

Tsuwano is most conveniently reached by train: it's two hours, 40 minutes northeast of Hagi by JR (¥1,690) with a change at Masuda. From Yamaguchi City you can get the Ltd. Express and it's just 47 minutes (¥2,190). If you've just arrived on the Shinkansen at Shin-Yamaguchi Station, it's the same Ltd. Express train for 60 minutes (¥2,370). If you're traveling from Matsue City the Ltd. Express train will get you to Tsuwano in two hours 40 minutes (¥5,610).

In Tsuwano all sights are within easy walking distance. You can also rent a bicycle from one of the four shops near the station plaza (two hours ¥500; all day ¥800).

## VISITOR INFORMATION

The tourist information office is inside the photograph gallery to the right of the railway station. It has free brochures, and staff members will help you reserve accommodations. As with most places in town, little English is spoken here.

**CONTACT Tsuwano International Information Center.** ⊠ *71–2 Ushiroda, Tsuwano* ☎ *0856/72–1771.*

 **Sights**

### Former Residence of Ogai Mori
(森鴎外旧宅; *Mori Ogai Kyutaku*)
HISTORIC HOME | While spartan, the house is worth a visit to commemorate the achievements of this gifted genius who called Tsuwano his home. Ogai Mori (1862–1922), son of the head physician to the daimyo of Shimane, became a doctor at the young age of 19 and, in spite of courting trouble for his outspoken criticism of Japan's backward ways, went on to become the author of such acclaimed novels as *The Wild Geese* and *Vita Sexualis*. He was also a prominent

figure in the fledgling government behind the Meiji Restoration. From Tsuwano Station it's a 12-block walk south along the main road, or take the bus and get off at Ogai Kyukyo-mae. ⊠ *1–230 Machida, Kanoashi-gun, Tsuwano* ☎ *0856/72–3210* 💴 *¥600.*

### Roadside Station Tsuwano Onsen
(なごみの里; *Nagomi-no-Sato*)
HOT SPRING | Tsuwano puts its geothermal gifts to good use at the spa at this hot spring. Inside and out, the tubs have great views of the surrounding gumdrop-shape volcanic peaks. It's west of everything else in town, across the river from the Washibara Hachiman-gu (a shrine where traditional horseback archery contests are held the second Sunday of April every year), but still not too far to get to by rented bike. ⊠ *256 Washibara, Tsuwano* ☎ *0856/72–4122* 🌐 *nagomi-nosato.com* 💴 *¥610* 🕓 *Closed Thurs.*

### Taikodani Inari-jinja Shrine (太鼓谷稲成神社; *Taikodani Inari-jinja*)
RELIGIOUS BUILDING | This is one of the five most revered Inari shrines in Japan. Inari shrines are connected with the fox, a Shinto symbol of luck and cleverness. People come to pray for good fortune in business and health. A series of 1,174 red wooden gates are suspended above steps that climb up the western side of the valley to the shrine, and the journey is a nice hike with a jaw-dropping view of the valley waiting for you at the top. From the station, follow the streamside Tono-machi-dori past the Katoriku Kyokai (Catholic church), but before crossing the river turn right onto the small lane. The lane leads to the tunnel-like approach through the gates to the structure high on a cliffside. You can also take a bus that approaches by a back road; the Tsuwano Tourist Information Office can help with this. Yasaka Jinja is another shrine on the site, where every July 20 and 27 sees the famous Sagi-mai Shinji (i.e., Heron Dance) Festival. ⊠ *409 Ushiroda,*

Dancers dress as white egrets in Tsuwano's Sagi-mai Shinji (Heron Dance) festival.

Tsuwano ☎ 0856/72–0219 ⊕ taikodani. jp 🖙 Free.

### Tsuwano Castle Ruins (津和野城跡; *Tsuwano Shiroato*)

RUINS | The local castle was another casualty of the Meiji Restoration in the late 19th century, but from the derelict ruins there is an awesome panoramic view of the dormant volcanic cone of Aono-yama to the east and the entire valley stretching out below. To get here you can hike a marked trail that leads from Taikodani Inari-Jinja Shrine or take a chairlift from below the Taikodani Inari-Jinja Shrine for ¥700 round-trip. The chairlift takes only 5 minutes, and from the top it's about a 20-minute moderate hike to the castle foundations. ⊠ 477–20 Ushiroda, Tsuwano.

##  Restaurants

### Aoki Sushi (あおき寿司)

$$ | SUSHI | An old-fashioned sushi restaurant with a few tables on tatami mats and a long bar counter with stools, the rustic restaurant has a cheerful staff and reasonable prices. It's also within easy walking distance of Tsuwano Station. **Known for:** friendly atmosphere; cash-only and usually open until 10 pm (late for Tsuwano); affordable, quality sushi. $ *Average main:* ¥1,600 ⊠ 78–10 Ushiroda, Kanoashi-gun, Tsuwano ☎ 0856/72–0444 ▭ *No credit cards* ☉ *Closed Tues.*

### ★ Yuuki (遊亀)

$$ | JAPANESE | *Unagi* (freshwater eel) and delectable mountain vegetables maintain Yuki's highly venerated reputation. The kitchen also serves river smelt and other specialties, and in summer they prepare *ayu* (sweetfish) dishes. **Known for:** unagi; cash-only and rustic atmosphere; ayu (sweetfish) dishes in summer. $ *Average main:* ¥3,000 ⊠ 271–4 Ushiroda, Tsuwano ☎ 0856/72–0162 ⊕ yuuki-tsuwano. com ▭ *No credit cards.*

**Hotels**

**Wakasagi-no-Yado** (民宿若さぎの宿)

**$$ | B&B/INN |** Despite knowing little English, the family that runs this small but satisfactory inn is eager to help overseas tourists and will meet you at Tsuwano Station, an eight-minute walk away. **Pros:** nice location; heartwarming hospitality; bicycles for rent. **Cons:** no private bathrooms; very simple accommodations; small, spartan rooms. $ *Rooms from:* *¥15,840* ⊠ *Mori-mura ro-21, Tsuwano* ☎ *0856/72–1146* ▭ *No credit cards* ⊘ *Usually closed for several weeks around the end of the year.* ⇨ *7 rooms* ⦿*❘ Free Breakfast.*

# Matsue (松江)

*194 km (121 miles) northeast of Tsuwano, 172 km (107 miles) northwest of Kurashiki.*

Matsue is a city blessed with so much overwhelming beauty and good food that you will wonder what to look at, what to eat, and what to do first. It's where the Shinji-ko Lake empties into the Naka-umi Lagoon, which connects directly with the Sea of Japan. This makes Matsue a seafood lover's paradise; specialties include both kinds of eel, all kinds of shrimp, shellfish, carp, sea bass, smelt, whitebait, and the famous black shijimi clams from Shinji-ko Lake. The water also provides the city with a lovely network of canals.

Matsue also attracts and holds onto some of the country's most welcoming and interesting people, both foreign and native. This remote realm is a traveler's favorite, and once you've come here you'll surely be back—it's that kind of place. In the 1890s the famed journalist-novelist Lafcadio Hearn came here and promptly fell in love, first with the place, and then with a local woman—a samurai's daughter, no less. In true journalistic fashion he proceeded to let the entire world know about it.

## GETTING HERE AND AROUND

The JR Super Oki Express travels to Matsue from Tsuwano in 2 hours, 40 minutes ¥5,610). From Kurashiki it is 2 hours, 23 minutes on the Ltd. Express Yakumo (¥5,280). From Okayama it is one stop further; two hours 34 minutes (¥5,610).

Most sights in Matsue are within walking distance of each other. Where they are not, the buses fill in. The bus station faces the train station. The Horikawa Pleasure Boat circles the area around the castle. The unlimited-ride one-day pass (¥1,500) is a relaxing way to see the town and passes by many of the main sights.

## VISITOR INFORMATION

The Matsue Tourist Information Office is outside JR Matsue Station and open daily 9–6. You can collect free maps and brochures and use the internet. Many of Matsue's tourist attractions have discounted prices for foreigners; you'll need to show your passport or foreigner's registration card at the entrance.

**CONTACTS Matsue International Tourist Information Center.** ⊠ *665 Asahi-machi, Matsue* ☎ *0852/21–4034* ⊕ *www.visit-matsue.com.*

**Sights**

### ★ Adachi Museum of Art (足立美術館; *Adachi Bijutsukan*)

**ART MUSEUM** | Located outside of Matsue City in neighboring Yasugi, The Adachi Museum of Art is well worth the trip. The gardens around the museum are some of the most breathtaking in all of Japan. The path around the gardens reveals new delights around every corner. Adding to their beauty is the borrowed landscape backdrop of low hills and forests beyond. The museum interior has a large selection of 19th- and 20th-century Japanese masters as well as temporary exhibitions throughout the year. The museum runs free shuttle buses every 30 minutes from Yasugi Station which take 20 minutes. Yasugi Station is 27 minutes east of Matsue Station on the local train (¥420). Try to time your arrival close to the museum opening hour of 9 am to avoid group tours, which start arriving around 10:30. ⊠ *320 Furukawa-Cho, Yasugi* ☎ *0854/28–7111* ⊕ *www.adachi-museum.or.jp* ⌨ *¥2,300 (¥2,000 for foreign visitors).*

### Lafcadio Hearn Memorial Museum (小泉八雲記念館; *Koizumi Yakumo Kinenkan*)

**HISTORY MUSEUM** | The museum has a good collection of the author's manuscripts and other artifacts related to his life in Japan. One room also holds small rotating art and culture exhibitions related to Matsue. It's adjacent to Koizumi Yakumo Kyukyo, Hearn's former residence in Matsue. Two minutes from the Memorial Hall is the Hearn Kyukyo bus stop, where a bus goes back to the center of town and the station. ⊠ *322 Okudani-cho, Matsue* ☎ *0852/21–2147* ⊕ *www.hearn-museum-matsue.jp* ⌨ *¥410.*

### Lafcadio Hearn's Former Residence (小泉八雲旧居; *Koizumi Yakumo Kyukyo*)

**HISTORIC HOME** | The celebrated writer's house has remained unchanged since he left Matsue in 1891. Born of an Irish father and a Greek mother, Lafcadio Hearn (1850–1904) spent his early years in Europe and moved to the United States to become a journalist. In 1890 he traveled to Yokohama, Japan, and made his way to Matsue, where he began teaching. There he met and married a samurai's daughter named Setsu Koizumi. He later took posts in Kumamoto, Kobe, and Tokyo. Disdainful of the materialism of the West, he was destined to be a lifelong Japanophile and resident. He became a Japanese citizen, taking the name Yakumo Koizumi. His most famous works were *Glimpses of Unfamiliar Japan* (1894) and *Japan: An Attempt at Interpretation* (1904). The house's simple elegance makes it worth a quick stop even for those unfamiliar with Hearn. ⊠ *315 Kitahori-cho, Matsue* ☎ *0852/23–0714* ⌨ *¥310.*

### Lake Shinji (宍道湖; *Shinji-ko*)

**BODY OF WATER** | When dusk rolls around, you'll want to position yourself well. You won't get a better sunset than the one seen every night over the town's lake. As locals do, you can watch it from Shinji-ko Ohashi, the town's westernmost bridge, but the best spot is south of the bridge, along the road, down near water level in Shirakata Koen, the narrow lakeside park just west of the NHK Building. This is a great place to kick back and enjoy some tasty local microbrews and sushi. A popular *yuhi* (sunset) spot is the patio of the Prefectural Art Museum, visible and adjacent to the park above. ⊠ *1–21 Nadamachi, Matsue.*

### Matsue Castle (松江城; *Matsue-jo*)

**CASTLE/PALACE** | Start a tour of Matsue at the enchanting and shadowy castle and walk in the castle park, Shiroyama Koen, under aromatic pines. Constructed of exactly such wood, the castle was completed in 1611. Not only did it survive the Meiji upheavals intact, but it was, amazingly, never ransacked during the civil

Matsue-jo is one of the most striking buildings in the region; it has been standing since its construction in 1611.

war–type turbulence of the Tokugawa Shogunate. Perhaps it's the properties of the wood, or the angles, or the mysterious tricks of light and shadows, but this castle truly feels *alive* and is a must-see sight of the region.

Built by the daimyo of Izumo, Yoshiharu Horio, for protection, Matsue-jo's *donjon* (main tower), at 98 feet, is the second tallest among originals still standing in Japan. Crouching as it does below and behind the surrounding lofty pines, Matsue-jo is slightly spooky, even in daytime. This is a fabulously preserved walk-in time capsule, with six interior levels belied by a tricky facade that suggests only five. The lower floors display an appropriately macabre collection of samurai swords and armor. The long climb to the castle's uppermost floor is definitely worth it for the view encompasses the city, Lake Shinji, the Shimane Peninsula, and—if weather conditions permit—the distant mystical snowy peak of Daisen.

The castle and park are 2 km (1¼ miles) northwest from Matsue Station. ⊠ *1–5*

*Tono-machi, Matsue* ☎ *0852/21–4030* ⊕ *www.matsue-castle.jp* ✉ *¥680 (Foreign visitors ¥470).*

### Matsue History Museum
(松江歴史館; *Matsue Rekishi-kan*)
**HISTORY MUSEUM** | Situated right beside the moat of Matsue Castle, this small museum gives visitors a good overview of Matsue's 400-year history. In addition to a diorama of the old castle town and scenes of daily life (including models of typical Edo-era meals), the photographs of Matsue in the Meji-era offer a rare chance to see what a provincial capital in Japan looked like at the beginning of the 20th century. English audio guides are available free of charge. The adjoining café, Kissa Kiharu, offers workshops such as making Japanese confectionery or incense among other traditional crafts. It is also a good place to relax and have coffee while looking out over the museum's Japanese garden. ⊠ *279 Tonomachi, Matsue* ☎ *0852/32–1607* ⊕ *matsu-reki.jp* ✉ *¥510* ⊙ *Closed Mon.*

### Meimei-an Tea House (明々庵)

**RESTAURANT** | Built in 1779, this is one of Japan's best-preserved tea houses. Located next to the former samurai residence, the teahouse offers views of Matsue Castle and for a small fee you can have a cup of green tea and locally made sweets. To get here, leave Shiroyama Koen, the castle park, at its East Exit and follow the moat going north; at the top of the park a road leads to the right, northwest of the castle. The teahouse is a short climb up this road. Before you enter, turn around for one of the best views of Matsue's hilltop castle. ⊠ *278 Kitahori-cho, Matsue* ☎ *0852/21–9863* ⊠ *¥410, ¥820 with a cup of green tea.*

### Shiomi Samurai Residence (武家屋敷; *Buke Yashiki*)

**HISTORIC HOME** | Built in 1730, this house belonged to the well-to-do Shiomi family, chief retainers to the daimyo. Note the separate servant quarters, a shed for the palanquin, and slats in the walls to allow cooling breezes to flow through the rooms. A few rooms have somewhat kitschy dioramas recreating scenes from household life, but they do give an idea of how Matsue samurai lived in the late Edo period. Buke Yashiki is on the main road at the base of the side street on which Meimei-an Teahouse is located (keep the castle moat on your left). ⊠ *305 Kitahori-cho, Matsue* ☎ *0852/22–2243* ⊕ *www.matsue-bukeyashiki.jp* ⊠ *¥310.*

## 🍴 Restaurants

### ★ Kawakyo (川京)

**$$$** | **JAPANESE** | This intimate, counter-only restaurant is the best place to try local sake and a set meal, including the seven famous delicacies from Shinji-ko and Matsue's coast. The staff are outgoing, as are the regular crowd. **Known for:** a friendly, family-run restaurant; reservations recommended; the best place to sample local Matsue cuisine. $ *Average main: ¥4,290* ⊠ *65 Suetsugu Hon-machi, Matsue* ⊹ *Kawakyo is in the block just east of the middle (Matsue Ohashi) bridge, a block north of the river* ☎ *0852/22–1312* ⊟ *No credit cards* ⊘ *Closed Sun. No lunch.*

### Okuizumo Ohashi (奥出雲大橋)

$ | **JAPANESE** | If you're pressed for time but want to grab a decent lunch, try some *warigo soba*, a local buckwheat-noodle specialty. Ohashi has a filling, healthful set lunch. **Known for:** tasty, affordable lunch sets; warigo soba; tempura sets. $ *Average main: ¥1,000* ⊠ *3–5–26 Nishitsuda, Matsue* ☎ *0852/26–6551* ⊟ *No credit cards* ⊘ *Closed Thurs.*

### Yakumo-an (八雲庵)

$ | **JAPANESE** | Surrounded by a colorful garden, the dining area at this traditional house is the best place to try the *sanshoku warigo soba*, a local specialty where three soba dishes are served in lacquerware with each dish having a different topping (quail egg, grated yam, grated radish). Located near the Buke Yashiki and Lafcadio Hearn House, it offers a relaxing break after a morning of sightseeing. **Known for:** beautiful location; warigo soba; kamo nanban soba. $ *Average main: ¥1,000* ⊠ *308 Kitahori-cho, Matsue* ⊹ *North of castle* ☎ *0852/22–2400* ⊕ *yakumoan.jp* ⊟ *No credit cards* ⊘ *No dinner.*

## 🛏 Hotels

### Naniwa Issui (なにわ一水)

**$$$$** | **B&B/INN** | A swanky ryokan near the Matsue Shinji-ko Onsen Station (for easy access to the shrine of Izumo Taisha), Naniwa Issui is envied for its amazing views out over the big lake and for its hot spring. **Pros:** beautiful views over Lake Shinju; private balcony tubs put you in the lap of luxury; the public bath is small for a hotel this size. **Cons:** quite expensive for Matsue; noise from the road below carries up to rooms on lower floors; 10-minute walk to bus stop. $ *Rooms from: ¥38,000* ✉ *63 Chidori-cho, Matsue* ☎ *0852/21–4132* 🌐 *www.naniwa-i.com* 🛏 *23 rooms* 🍴 *All-Inclusive.*

**Ryokan Terazuya** (旅館寺津屋)
**$** | **B&B/INN** | The same family has maintained a tradition of heartwarming hospitality at this charming riverside ryokan since 1893, but it's a strictly cash-only operation. **Pros:** high level of hospitality; train station pickup service; great dinner (as add-on). **Cons:** noise from the street and nearby Shirakata Shrine; guests have to be back in the ryokan by 10 pm; no private baths. $ *Rooms from: ¥10,400* ✉ *60–3 Tenjin-machi, Matsue* ☎ *0852/21–3480* 🌐 *www.mable.ne.jp/~terazuya/english* 💳 *No credit cards* 🛏 *6 rooms* 🍴 *No Meals.*

# Izumo Taisha (出雲大社)

*37 km (23 miles) west of Matsue.*

One of the oldest of Japan's Shinto shrines, Izumo Taisha has been of tremendous cultural significance—second only to the great shrine at Ise Jingu—since the 6th century. The main building was last rebuilt in 1744. In ancient days it was the largest wooden building in the country, but since the 13th century, each time it was rebuilt, it was scaled to half its former size, and it is now *only* 78 feet tall.

### GETTING HERE AND AROUND

The shrine is most easily seen on a day trip from Matsue, and the easiest way is to go from Matsue Shinji-ko Onsen Station. Buses run often between it and Matsue Station. It takes one hour on the Ichibata Dentetsu (electric railway; ¥820) from Matsue Shinji-ko Onsen Station. After about 50 minutes you'll need to change trains at Kawato Station for the final 10-minute leg to Izumo Taisha-mae Station. You can also get there by taking the JR train from Matsue Station to JR Izumo Station, then transferring to the Ichibata Bus for a 30-minute ride (¥510) to the Izumo Taisha Seimon stop.

## Sights

★ **Izumo Taisha Shrine** (出雲大社)
**RELIGIOUS BUILDING** | Nature has arrayed a shrine of its own to compliment the ornate but somehow subdued structures: a lofty ridge of forested peaks rises behind, a boulevard of fragrant ancient pines lines the approach, and lush green lawns flank both sides. Pilgrims come here primarily to pray for success in courtship and marriage.

The *honden* (main building) dates from 1744 and most of the other were buildings from 1688 onward. The architectural style, with its saddled crests and ornamental roof fixtures resembling crossed swords, is said to be unique to the Izumo region, but some similarities with the main Shinto shrine on the Kii Peninsula can be noted. The taisha is dedicated to a male god, Okuninushi, the creator of the land and god of marriage and fortune. Instead of clapping twice, as at other shrines, you should clap four times—twice for yourself, and twice for your current or future partner. According to folklore, if you successfully throw a ¥5 coin so that it sticks up into the sacred hanging strands of the enormously thick 5-ton, 25 foot-long twisted straw rope, or *shimenawa*, suspended above the entrance to the main building, you will be doubly assured of good luck in marriage. It is almost impossible to do without some kind of cheating—which may say something about the difficulties of marriage.

Two rectangular buildings on either side of the compound are believed to house the visiting millions of Shinto gods during the 10th lunar month of each year. In the rest of Japan the lunar October is referred to as "Kannazuki" (month without gods), while in Izumo, October is called "Kamiarizuki" (month with gods). The shrine is a five-minute walk north, to the right along the main street, from Izumo Taisha-mae Station. ✉ 195 Taishocho Kizukihigashi, Izumo, Matsue ☎ 0853/53–3100 ☜ Free.

# Chapter 11

# SHIKOKU

Updated by
Rob Goss

⊙ Sights  🍴 Restaurants  🛏 Hotels  🛍 Shopping  🍸 Nightlife
★★★★☆   ★★★☆☆      ★★★☆☆   ★☆☆☆☆    ★☆☆☆☆

# WELCOME TO SHIKOKU

## TOP REASONS TO GO

★ **Get out in nature:** Discover Shikoku's natural charms by rafting, hiking, walking, or swimming. Best of all, bicycle across the Seto Inland Sea on a series of island-hopping bridges.

★ **Local classes:** Try a martial art, make soba noodles, dye fabrics, and learn a two-step in time for the summer dances.

★ **Frequent festivals:** Festivals mark every weekend between April and October leading up to the biggest dance festivals in the nation—Yosakoi and Awa Odori.

★ **Friendly hosts:** Encounter Shikoku's legendary hospitality firsthand in the region's ryokan and restaurants.

★ **The "real" Japan:** With its time-forgotten towns like Uchiko, unique landmarks like Dogo Onsen and Konpira-san Shrine, and acres of rice, Shikoku may well be the closest a tourist can get to the "real" Japan.

**1 Takamatsu.** Home to one of Japan's finest gardens and the gateway to Naoshima.

**2 Naoshima.** Once-sleepy island that is now home to contemporary galleries and art installations.

**3 Kotohira.** Near Konpira-san, a mountain-side shrine reached by more than 700 steps.

**4 Tokushima.** Raucous Awa-Odori summer dance festival; also near the whirlpools of Naruto.

**5 Iya Valley and Okoboke-Koboke Gorges.** A mixture of magical scenery, quaint villages, and white-water rafting.

**6 Kochi.** Immensely good seafood, lively markets, and a notable castle and temple.

**7 Matsuyama.** Japan's oldest hot-spring baths and a most unusual temple.

**8 Uchiko.** Charming farming town with a long tradition of candle-making.

**9 Uwajima.** A shrine that doubles as a sex museum and home to "bull sumo" fights.

**10 Shimanami Kaido.** This 70-km (43-mile) scenic biking route connects Hiroshima Prefecture to Shikoku.

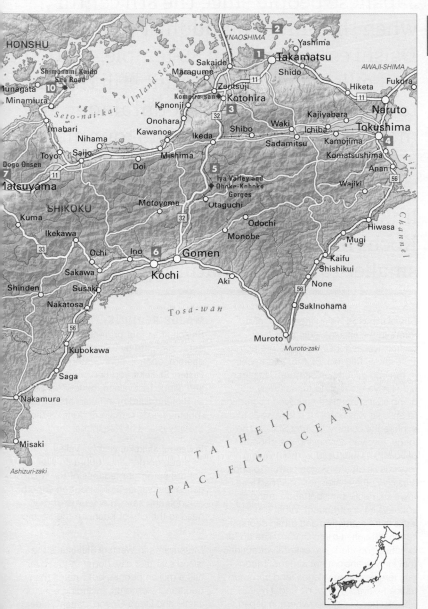

HONSHU

NAOSHIMA

Yashima

Shimanami Kaido
Sea Road

Sakaide
Maragume

Takamatsu

Shido

AWAJI-SHIMA

Funagata
Minamiura

Zentsuji

Hiketa

Fukura

Kompira-san
Kanonji

Kotohira

Naruto

Seto-nai-kai

(Inland Sea)

Onohara

Kajiyabara

Imabari

Kawanoe

Shibo

Ikeda

Waki

Ichiba

Tokushima

Nihama

Mishima

Sadamitsu

Kamojima

Toyo

Saijo

Doi

Komatsushima

Dogo Onsen

Matsuyama

SHIKOKU

Motoyama

Iya Valley and
Oboke-Koboke
Gorges

Utaguchi

Anan

Wajiki

Kuma

Odochi

Hiwasa

Ikekawa

Monobe

Mugi

Ochi

Ino

Gomen

Kaifu
Shishikui

Sakawa

Kochi

Aki

None

Shinden

Susaki

Nakatosa

Tosa-wan

Sakinohama

Kubokawa

Muroto

Muroto-zaki

Saga

Nakamura

Misaki

Ashizuri-zaki

TAIHEIYO

(PACIFIC OCEAN)

Kii Channel

The smallest of Japan's four main islands, Shikoku has been a travel destination for Japanese people since the 8th century, when the Shingon Buddhist priest Kobo Daishi established an 88-temple, 1,200-km (745-mile) pilgrimage circuit still traveled to this day. Shikoku is mountainous and mostly rural, but three of its four main cities—Matsuyama, Tokushima, and Takamatsu—have good transportation links to Honshu. They and the fourth, Kochi, are gateways to the island's smaller towns and natural getaways.

*Shikoku* means "four kingdoms" and refers to the ancient regions of Awa, Sanuki, Iyo, and Tosa, now the prefectures Tokushima, Kagawa, Ehime, and Kochi. In the Edo period non-samurai Japanese didn't have the right to travel freely, so going on a shogunate-approved pilgrimage to Shikoku was one of the few ways to explore the country. Visiting Shikoku no longer involves convincing the shogun of your piety, but because Shikoku's rewards lie off the beaten path, exploring it involves the challenges of a road less traveled. Public transportation in the countryside is infrequent. What the island lacks in infrastructure and urban sophistication, though, it more than makes up for in natural wonders and cultural attractions that include ancient hot springs, mountain temples, farm villages, and summer dance festivals. You won't find a match for Shikoku hospitality elsewhere in Japan.

## MAJOR REGIONS

Shikoku has four prefectures, but is easiest to navigate by thinking in terms of its eastern, central, and western areas. In **Eastern Shikoku,** you find giant whirlpools and dance festivals in Tokushima, as well as Ritsurin Garden in Takamatsu, the mountain-side temple of Konpira-san, and the arty island of Naoshima.

In **Central Shikoku,** visit Iya Valley, with its steep gorges and mountain villages. For the summer madness of the Yosakoi dance festival, or a night out on superb seafood and sake at any time of year, head to the city of Kochi on the Pacific coast.

Matsuyama in **Western Shikoku** is the island's largest city, home to just over half a million people, but retains many traditional elements, including a hilltop castle and Dogo Onsen, Japan's oldest hot spring. It's also a great base for exploring Shikoku's western side. South from there is the old town of Uchiko and the quirky attractions of Uwajima; site of a sex museum and sumo bulls. Looking north, the Shimanami Kaido is one of Japan's best cycling routes.

# Planning

# Getting Here and Around

Depending on your route, you'll likely arrive in one of three cities. Coming by train from Kansai, you're most likely to arrive in Takamatsu. Coming by ferry from Hiroshima or Osaka, you'll arrive in Matsuyama. If you take a bus from Kansai or an overnight ferry from Tokyo, Tokushima will be your first stop. All those arrival points also have small airports for domestic flights, as does Kochi. Driving is a fantastic way to explore the countryside, and renting a car can save you time and sometimes even a little money, but be ready for challenging mountain roads. Traveling by train and bus is simpler, though service in rural areas can be infrequent and irregular. Missing a train doesn't always mean just waiting a bit for the next one: it might not arrive for hours.

## AIR

All Nippon Airways and Japan Airlines provide domestic flights to and from Takamatsu, Kochi, Matsuyama, and Tokushima. Some low-cost airlines fly to Shikoku as well, but the routes change frequently and have been heavily disrupted by the pandemic; as of early 2022 cheap domestic routes included flights from Tokyo (Narita Airport) to Kochi on Fuji Dream Airlines and from Nagoya to Kochi on JetStar Airlines. International low-cost flights also run between Matsuyama and Takamatsu and major cities in Asia.

**CONTACTS Fuji Dream Airlines.** ⊕ *www. fujidream.co.jp/en.* **JetStar Japan.** ⊕ *www. jetstar.com/jp/en.*

## BOAT

Shikoku receives ferries from Tokyo, Osaka, Kobe, western Honshu, and Kyushu. Except for overnight ferries, reservations are rarely necessary if you don't have a vehicle, though it's a good idea to make one during the busy travel seasons of Golden Week (early May) and Obon (mid-August). Popular routes are Tokushima to Tokyo (19 hours), Toyo (near Matsuyama) to Kobe/Osaka (8 hours overnight), Matsuyama to Hiroshima (three hours by slow boat or 70 minutes by hydrofoil), Yawatahama (west of Matsuyama) to Beppu (three hours), Takamatsu to Kobe (4½ hours), and Tokushima to Wakayama (two hours).

## BUS

Short-haul and overnight buses connect Shikoku's four major cities to each other and to cities on Honshu—useful when no direct train route exists. Buses also provide access to far-flung coastal and mountain regions.

## CAR

Shikoku's narrow roads present challenges, but having your own transportation provides a priceless escape into the island's mountainous interior and secluded small towns. At airports and major stations you'll find a variety of nationwide rental companies who offer online reservations in English, including Nissan Rent-a-Car, Toyota Rent-a-Car, and (by JR stations) JR Eki Rent-a-Car. You must have an international driving permit. Tourist information centers have good maps illustrating Shikoku's major roads and highways, and getting around is straightforward.

Fishing towns and rice-farming villages are all over the island. Although driving on expressways will save you a little time, if you stick to them you'll never see what life is like outside Shikoku's cities. Try the rewarding, easily navigable numbered prefectural routes. As a bonus, you'll also save on the exorbitant tolls.

■ TIP➜ **If you're planning to drive through the mountains, consider renting a "kei-car."**

These smaller vehicles, identifiable by their yellow license plates, are a bit slow on the expressways but are perfect for navigating narrow mountain roads.

### TRAIN

Getting to Shikoku by train usually requires transferring in Okayama to a Shi-koku-bound express train. Another option is the JR Sunrise Seto sleeper train from Tokyo to Takamatsu; a fun experience, although getting tickets means visiting a Midori no Madoguchi ticket office at a major JR station well in advance. Shikoku is belted by a single-rail track with branches into the interior. Because there is just a single track in most places, expect irregular schedules and long waits for local trains as express ones hurtle by. The Japan Rail Pass is good on all normal and express trains. Some train lines on Shikoku (mostly in rural Kochi) are not owned by Japan Railways, so you will have to pay a small extra fee to use your Japan Rail Pass on these lines.

There are Japan Rail Pass alternatives. A ¥16,440 Shikoku Free Kippu ticket is good for three days of unlimited train use. In the month of your birthday you can purchase a ¥9,680 Birthday Ticket good for three days of unlimited travel for you and up to three companions. The best deal, however, is for non-Japanese passport holders only: the All Shikoku Rail Pass, which comes in 3-, 4-, 5-, and 7-day versions, costing ¥9,500 to ¥13,500, and including both JR and private lines. Shi-koku is the rare place in Japan where a Japan Rail Pass may not save you money; price out your trip carefully to determine if the pass is worth it.

**CONTACT Japan Rail Shikoku.** ⊕ *www. jr-shikoku.co.jp/global/en.*

# Hotels

Accommodations on Shikoku range from ryokan and minshuku (guest houses) in old homes to international hotels and lavish onsen (thermal spa) resorts. Large city and resort hotels serve Western and Japanese food. Reservations are essential during major festivals and Japanese holiday periods, and are recommended at any time of year when traveling outside major cities.

*For a short course on accommodations in Japan, see Lodging in the Travel Smart chapter.*

# Planning Your Time

A few days are enough to sample Shiko-ku's main pleasures, but a week on the island will allow you to discover some hidden treasures. If your time is limited, tour a major city and a rural area—Tokus-hima and the Iya Valley, for instance, or Takamatsu and Naoshima, or Matsuyama and the Shimanami Kaido. If you have a week, add a trip to Kochi and another rural area. Express trains circle Shikoku, and the drive between most points on the island usually takes no more than four hours, so it might seem possible to cram a lot into your time. But Shikoku runs a bit slower than mainland Japan. Ease into the same leisurely pace as the locals and take the time to linger at rural temples, chat with Buddhist pilgrims, and enjoy long lunches in the surprisingly sophisticated restaurants.

# Restaurants

Eating in Shikoku can be a surprisingly cosmopolitan experience. Matsuyama offers the widest variety of cuisines, everything from French to Indian. Takamatsu is another foodie haven, with many bistros, cafés, and izakaya pubs in and around the shopping arcades.

Kochi and Tokushima have fewer foreign restaurants, but small Japanese eateries here serve local specialties. In the main cities many restaurants stay open late, but in smaller towns most places close by 8 pm.

## RESTAURANT AND HOTEL PRICES

Restaurant prices are per person for a main course, set meal, or equivalent combinations of smaller dishes. Hotel prices are for a double room with private bath, excluding service and tax. Restaurant and hotel reviews have been shortened. For full information, visit Fodors.com.

### What It Costs in Yen

|  | $ | $$ | $$$ | $$$$ |
|---|---|---|---|---|
| **RESTAURANTS** | | | | |
|  | under ¥1,500 | ¥1,500–¥3,000 | ¥3,001–¥5,000 | over ¥5,000 |
| **HOTELS** | | | | |
|  | under ¥12,000 | ¥12,000–¥18,000 | ¥18,001–¥22,000 | over ¥22,000 |

## Tours

### Shikoku Tours

GUIDED TOURS | If you would prefer a guided experience, Matsuyama-based Shikoku Tours can arrange various tours in English all over the island. These include everything from four-hour tasting tours of the Shikoku pilgrimage to several-day, small-group excursions in the Iya Valley and week-long cycling tours from the Shimanami Kaido down to southern Kochi. ⊠ Matsuyama ⊕ www.shikokutours.com ✉ 4-hour tours from ¥12,000 per person; week-long tours from ¥298,000 per person.

## Visitor Information

Tourist information centers in Shikoku's main cities might have the only skilled English speakers you'll meet on the island. They can help you with advice, travel reservations, and maps. Foreign tourists are still relatively rare on Shikoku, so be specific about what you're interested in, and ask a lot of questions. The website of Tourism Shikoku, based in Takamatsu, has advice and itineraries for the entire island.

CONTACT **Tourism Shikoku.** ⊠ Takamatsu ⊕ shikoku-tourism.com/en.

## When to Go

Shikoku's unspoiled scenery offers some perfect locations in which to bask in the fleeting glories of springtime cherry blossoms and autumn foliage without the usual Honshu crowds. Summer is festival time throughout the country, but Shikoku has the best of the bunch in two epic dance festivals: Yosakoi in Kochi, held from August 9 to 12, and Tokushima's Awa Odori, held from August 12 to 15. Winter is mild on the island, but the roads into Iya can ice up, and the early autumn typhoons that batter Kochi and southern Ehime can disrupt transportation.

## Takamatsu (高松)

*71 km (44 miles) south of Okayama and 70 km (43 miles) northwest of Tokushima.*

If you're coming to Shikoku by train, your first stop will likely be Takamatsu, the capital of Kagawa Prefecture. Takamatsu combines urban verve with a relaxed down-home atmosphere. There is something Parisian in the air here: the locals' unwavering devotion to taking things slow, the city's wide sunlit boulevards, funky shops, and cafés, and the prefectural government's dedication to funding the arts make Takamatsu the perfect place to slow down, look around, and adjust to Shikoku time.

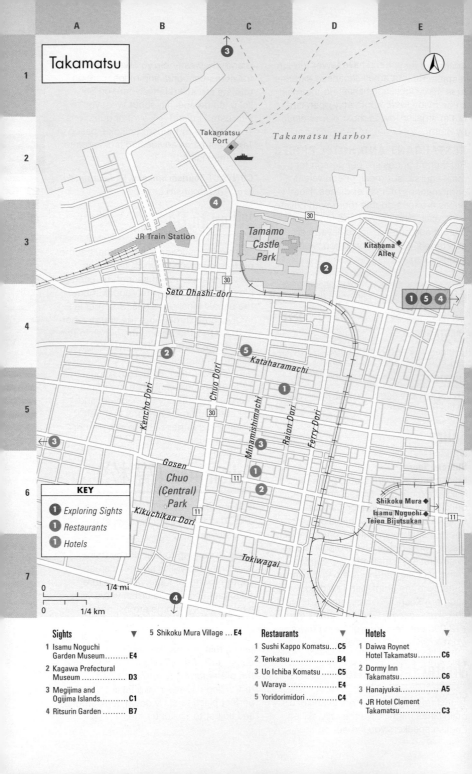

# Takamatsu

**Sights** ▼

5 Shikoku Mura Village ... **E4**

1 Isamu Noguchi Garden Museum......... **E4**

2 Kagawa Prefectural Museum ................. **D3**

3 Megijima and Ogijima Islands............ **C1**

4 Ritsurin Garden ......... **B7**

**Restaurants** ▼

1 Sushi Kappo Komatsu... **C5**

2 Tenkatsu ................. **B4**

3 Uo Ichiba Komatsu ...... **C5**

4 Waraya ................... **E4**

5 Yoridorimidori ............ **C4**

**Hotels** ▼

1 Daiwa Roynet Hotel Takamatsu......... **C6**

2 Dormy Inn Takamatsu................ **C6**

3 Hanajyukai.............. **A5**

4 JR Hotel Clement Takamatsu................ **C3**

## GETTING HERE AND AROUND

It takes 55 minutes to get to Takamatsu from Okayama by JR's Marine Liner limited express train, 2½ hours from Matsuyama on JR's Ishizuchi limited express, and 1¼ hours from Tokushima on JR's Uzushio service. Buses also run between Takamatsu and Shikoku's other major cities, as well as to and from Tokyo (11 hours), Nagoya (7 hours), Osaka (3½ hours) and elsewhere on Honshu. Ferries from Kobe arrive in about 4 hours.

You're most likely to set off exploring from Takamatsu's northern tip, where the JR Station, bus platforms, and ferry port bracket a wide piazza around the JR Hotel Clement. At the northwest corner of the grassy Tamamo Castle park, continue straight along the park's edge toward the Kagawa Prefectural Museum and Kitahama Alley, or turn left down broad Chuo-dori to hit the city. Ten minutes on foot will bring you to the covered Hyogo-machi shopping arcade and within easy striking distance of other city sights. Takamatsu's biggest draw, Ritsurin Garden, is a 20-minute walk south.

The east-lying districts Yashima and Mure are home to two captivating attractions: the historical preserve Shikoku Mura Museum and the Isamu Noguchi Garden Museum, a superb sculpture park. Just outside the main city, both sights are easy to access by car or local train.

## VISITOR INFORMATION

The small tourist information office in front of the JR Station's ticket gates is the place to get maps, timetables, and travel advice about Takamatsu and other Shikoku destinations. Some staffers speak English quite well. Ask about current hotel and other discounts for visitors. For local events try I-PAL Kagawa, a cultural exchange office in the central Chuo Park.

**CONTACTS I-PAL Kagawa.** ⊠ 1–11–63 Bancho, Takamatsu ⊕ en.i-pal.or.jp. **Takamatsu Tourist Information Office.** ⊠ JR Takamatsu Station, 1 Hamano-cho, Takamatsu ⊕ www.art-takamatsu.com/en.

#  Sights

### ★ Isamu Noguchi Garden Museum
(イサム・ノグチ庭園美術館; *Isamu Noguchi Teien Bijutsukan*)

**ART MUSEUM** | A wonderland of indoor and outdoor sculpture both playful and profound, this facility occupies the former studio and grounds of the Japanese-American sculptor Isamu Noguchi (1904–88). The modernist artist, whose large-scale sculptures grace buildings, parks, and gardens around the world, was also known for his furniture (most notably the Noguchi table), lamps, and landscape architecture. The artist's sensitivity and expressiveness are in evidence everywhere on this site that exhibits his works in stone and other media.

Officially, visitation requires reservation by fax or email at least 10 days in advance, but if you call the museum you might be able to gain entrance on shorter notice. One advantage to early booking, though, is that you'll have a better chance of having an English speaker accompany you as you tour. ⊠ 3519 Mure, Mure-cho, Takamatsu ⊕ 10-min taxi ride from JR Yashima Station, or 2 stops farther on Kotoden Shido Line to Kotoden Yakuri Station and take a 5-min taxi or walk 20 min 🕾 087/870–1500 ⊕ www.isamunoguchi.or.jp 🕮 ¥2,200 ⊗ Closed Mon., Wed., Fri., and Sun. ⌂ Reservations required.

### Kagawa Prefectural Museum
(香川県立ミュージアム; *Kagawa Kenritsu Myuujiamu*)

**HISTORY MUSEUM** | **FAMILY** | Just east of the castle park, this museum contains exhibits about Kagawa's history and art. A third-floor exhibit chronicles regional history from ancient to modern times; the second floor displays art from the museum's permanent collection and presents special exhibitions; and the ground floor has an art-books library and a hands-on area where kids can play with traditional Japanese toys. Free English audio guides are available, but you needn't know a lick of Japanese to enjoy walking inside a Neolithic hut, sitting in a 19th-century schoolroom, or crawling with a magnifying glass on the giant photo-to map of Kagawa. ✉ *5–5 Tamamo-cho, Takamatsu* ☎ *087/822–0002* ⊕ *www. pref.kagawa.lg.jp/kmuseum/kmuseum* 🖻 *¥410* ☾ *Closed Mon.*

### ★ Ritsurin Garden
(栗林公園; *Ritsurin-koen*)

**GARDEN | FAMILY** | Built by a feudal lord in the 17th century, this garden became public property after the 19th-century Meiji Restoration and is now a registered National Treasure. With 75 total acres, 16 of them landscaped, Ritsurin contains close to 1,000 sculpted pine trees, six carp-filled ponds, and two wooden teahouses where samurai used to gather to perform tea ceremonies and compose haiku. Give yourself at least two hours to stroll through the garden, and don't miss Kikugetsu-tei teahouse, which serves green tea and snacks daily from 9 to 4:30, with lunch also available in spring and autumn (reservation only). There is also a rustic kiosk serving simple udon lunches, tempura, and chestnut ice cream, as well as offering kimono rental (¥3,500 for two hours) if you fancy a stroll in traditional finery. The garden is especially peaceful in the early morning or late afternoon. English maps are provided at the entrance. Audio guides cost ¥200, but if you book at least a week in advance you might be able to engage a free volunteer guide who speaks English. ✉ *1–20–16 Ritsurin-cho, Takamatsu* ✛ *10-min taxi ride from Takamatsu Station, 3-min walk from JR Ritsurinkoen Kitaguchi Station, 10-min walk from Kotoden Ritsurin Koen Station* ☎ *087/833–7411* ⊕ *www.my-kagawa.jp/en/ritsurin* 🖻 *¥410.*

## Cheap Bicycles

In Takamatsu, take advantage of the cheap bicycle rental available at an underground garage near the JR Station and at six other locations around the city. For ¥200 a day, the whole city will open up to you. Explore out-of-the-way spots like the two skinny piers and cute lighthouses off the sun port north of the station, perfect for watching the sunset. Bikes can be returned to any rental station—a real convenience.

### Shikoku Mura Village
(四国村ミュージアム)

**MUSEUM VILLAGE** | An open-air museum east of central Takamatsu, Shikoku Mura consists of traditional houses that have been relocated from around Shikoku. The park does a fabulous job of illustrating how life on Shikoku has changed throughout the centuries. You can enter Shikoku Mura by crossing a rickety vine bridge, or play it safe and use the sidewalk detour. The route through the park is clearly marked, and the information boards in English are thoughtful and thorough. The highlights include a village Kabuki theater relocated from Shodoshima Island, thatched-roof farmhouses from mountain villages, fishermen's huts, sugarcane-pressing sheds, and lighthouse-keepers' residences.

The prolific Osaka-born architect Tadao Ando designed the concrete-and-glass Shikoku Mura Gallery on-site. On a hill above the sugarcane-pressing shed, it looks as if shipped here from central Tokyo. Works by Renoir, Picasso, and Pierre Bonnard are displayed inside, but the showstopper is the outdoor water garden. ✉ *91 Yashima-Naka-machi, Takamatsu* ✛ *Take Kotoden Shido Line to Kotoden-Yashima Station and walk*

*Continued on page 574*

# THE HENRO: SHIKOKU'S 88-TEMPLE PILGRIMAGE

By Annamarie Sasagawa

On the mountainous island of Shikoku, 88 sacred temples have welcomed Buddhist pilgrims for over 1,000 years. Leave your everyday world behind, and walk in the footsteps of tradition on Shikoku's ancient pilgrimage trail.

Shikoku's 88-temple Pilgrimage is an 870-mile Buddhist pilgrimage route encircling the island of Shikoku. The pilgrimage dates from the 9th century and is the longest of Japan's ancient pilgrimage trails.

Unlike Europe's Camino de Santiago de Campostela pilgrimage, in which pilgrims travel toward a sacred destination, all 88 temples on the Shikoku circuit are considered equally sacred; thus, there is no start- or end-point. A pilgrim completes the journey by traveling full-circle.

Although eight of the 88 temples belong to other sects of Buddhism, the Shikoku pilgrimage is a Shingon Buddhist tradition. It's unique among Japan's Buddhist pilgrimage routes in its devotion to Kobo Daishi, the founder of Shingon Buddhism. Each temple on the route, no matter which Buddhist deity it enshrines, also houses a small building dedicated to the spirit of this ancient monk.

(Top left) Chikurin-ji
(Top right) Byodo-ji
(Bottom right) Kumatani-ji

# KOCHI ONE-DAY LOOP: TEMPLES 31-33

Most tourists—even those with plenty of time to spare—won't be able to travel the entire circuit. But if you have been drawn to Shikoku, you will certainly want to get a taste of the pilgrimage experience even if you don't have two full months to hike the whole route. You won't be alone; many Westerners want to partake and can be seen hiking along with the other foot pilgrims (who are in short supply these days since most go on group bus tours). You don't need to don full pilgrim garb to get a taste of this experience, but you may want to buy a *Shuin-cho* (calligraphy book) to gather stamps from the various temples if you haven't already purchased one (these are available at all the larger temples). Kochi is a particularly good place to visit a few temples since there are three within reasonable walking distance. Try this one-day, 15-mile

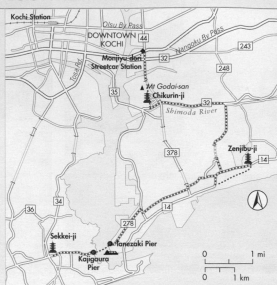

walk that takes you to the three pilgrimage temples within Kochi's city limits: **Chikurin-ji**, **Zenjibi-ji**, and **Sekkei-ji**. Allow a full day (approximately 9 hours) to complete this loop. You'll find some small shops and vending machines along the way where you can get

snacks and drinks, but be sure to pack a lunch.

From Kochi Station, take the streetcar to Monjiyu-dori station, changing at Hari-maya Bashi. (20 minutes, ¥190). Walk south from the station and cross the canal. The big hill in front of you is Mt. Godai-san.

Chikurin-ji

Chikurin-ji

Zenjibu-ji

Sekkei-ji

Turn left after the bridge, and keep an eye out for small white signs with red arrows and a stenciled silhouette of a pilgrim. Follow these signs past a shrine and up Mt. Gogai-san to **Chikurin-ji** (#31).

After visiting Chikurin-ji, follow the trail south down Mt. Godai-san. It's a steep descent. When you get to the bottom, cross the Shimoda River and turn left. Again,

look for signs that mark the pilgrim trail. After about an hour on this trail, go through the tunnel on your left. After the tunnel, you'll see a pond and **Zenjibu-ji** (#32), atop a small hill. Zenjibu-ji was also founded in 724 (on some road signs it's also called Mine-ji).

Walk southwest from Zenjibu-ji along the coast for about 90 minutes. When you reach the end of the pen-

insula, take the free small ferry across. **Sekkei-ji** (#33), is about 1 mi west of the ferry stop on the other side. It's a Rinzai Zen temple that was founded in AD 815.

Nagahama Shucho-jo bus stop is a 3-minute walk from Sekkei-ji. Buses run from here back to Kochi station (25 minutes, ¥440).

## WHO WAS KOBO DAISHI?

Kukai, or Kobo Daishi—as he is more widely known by the honorific title bestowed after his death—was a Buddhist priest, founder of Shingon Buddhism, an esoteric form of Buddhism that focuses on rituals instead of abstract meditation. He was a scholar, calligrapher, pilgrim, and all-round adventurer.

Born to an aristocratic family in Kagawa prefecture on Shikoku in ad 774, he went to Nara in 791 to study Confucian classics, where he became interested in Buddhism. In 804, he used his family connections to join an expedition to China, where he studied esoteric Buddhism in Xi'an for two years with the Chinese master Hui-kuo.

Statue of Kobo Daishi

After returning to Japan, he became the head priest of Nara's Todai-ji temple in 810. In 819, he founded the monastery town of Koya-san high in the mountains of Wakayama prefecture. For the next 16 years, Kobo Daishi traveled between Koya-san, the courts and universities of Kyoto, and pilgrimage sites around Japan. In 835, he died—or according to Shingon Buddhist tradition did not die but rather left this world to enter eternal meditation in a cave in Koya-san, where he's still believed to be.

Kobo Daishi felt a lifelong tension between academic learning and the lessons of travel that resonates with many Japanese today.

# HISTORY OF THE PILGRIMAGE

## THE PILGRIMAGE BEGINS

The cost and difficulty of travel kept the numbers of pilgrims low until the Tokugawa era (1603–1868). Shogun **Ieyasu Tokugawa**'s rise to power in 1603 brought political stability to Japan after a century of civil war. Increased prosperity among peasants and better roads made travel possible for many who could never travel before.

Keen to prevent rural rebellion, however, the shogun quickly forbade commoners from traveling freely. The only way for a peasant to travel legally was by obtaining permission to make a pilgrimage. Shikoku was a popular destination for these "passport pilgrims." The pilgrims surged in numbers, quickly turning Shikoku's sleepy temple towns into rather lively places, and so they have remained.

## A LULL IN FOOT TRAFFIC

The fun stopped when Japan entered the Meiji era (1868–1912). In the face of growing European influence in Asia, Japan's new imperial government scrambled to transform the nation into a modern power. As part of this modernization effort, Japan's ruling elite promoted a return to "pure" Japanese values, favoring Shinto, Japan's indigenous religion, over Buddhism, an import from mainland Asia.

During this period of anti-Buddhist sentiment, pilgrim numbers dropped, and six of the pilgrimage's 88 temples were destroyed, damaged, or relocated. World War II left Japan's citizens with little extra money to donate to the temples or pilgrims.

## THE MODERN PILGRIMAGE

As Japan's economic recovery took hold, pilgrims once again began to arrive on Shikoku. Rising incomes and the time pressures of urban life soon created a market among would-be pilgrims for faster ways to complete the circuit. The first pilgrimage bus tours began in the 1950s, and the majority of pilgrims have traveled by car or bus ever since.

(Top left) Yakuo-ji
(Top middle) Ieyasu Tokugawa
(Top right) Gokuraku-ji
(Top bottom) Nagao-ji

# WALKING THE PILGRIMAGE

Pilgrims walking along a Shikoku beach

It takes about two months to walk the entire 870-mile pilgrimage circuit. All 88 temples now have road access, so it's possible to do the pilgrimage by car or motorcycle in just under two weeks. By bicycle, the circuit takes about a month.

**WHEN TO GO:** Spring (mid-March to mid-April), brings cherry blossoms and mild weather to Shikoku and is the most popular pilgrimage season. Autumn (early October to mid-November) is also a good time to go. The rainy season (June) is best avoided; winter can be quite cold, summer hot and humid.

**WHERE TO START:** Although the temples are numbered, you don't have to start at #1. Start wherever is convenient and complete the circle, ideally in a clockwise fashion. However, a superstition among pilgrims says that if you travel counterclockwise (*gyaku-uchi*) you're more likely to encounter Kobo Daishi en route.

**WHERE TO STAY:** About a third of the 88 temples provide accommodation and meals to pilgrims for about ¥6,000 per person, but space at temple lodgings (*shukubo*) fills up fast with bus tour groups. Some temples also provide free basic accommodation in wooden sheds called *tsuyado*, which are not much more than a roof over your head. You must bring your own blankets and food. In villages near smaller temples, you'll find many *minshuku* at about the same cost as temple lodging. English isn't widely spoken on Shikoku, so some Japanese skills will make things smoother.

**GEAR:** To walk the pilgrimage, you'll need sturdy shoes, raingear, a warm jacket, a bilingual map, mobile phone, and enough cash to survive between major cities.

If you want to look like a Japanese pilgrim, you'll need some extra gear. A white pilgrim's overcoat (*oizuru*) indicates to the world that you're on a spiritual journey and are prepared to die en route. Black Chinese characters on a pilgrim's *oizuru* read "two people walking together" and remind lonely pilgrims that Kobo Daishi is walking with them.

You'll also need a conical straw hat, a sutra book, an embroidered stole, a set of Buddhist rosary beads, a bell, a wooden staff, and a Shuin-cho in which to collect seals from each temple (the book is not unlike the Spanish *credencial* used by pilgrims on the Camino de Santiago de Compostela) and is also available in places like Kyoto and Nara. Larger temples on Shikoku sell all these accessories, and they make good souvenirs, though they aren't at all necessary to do the walk.

**TOURS:** Bus tours are given in Japanese only, but the Japan-based tour operator Walk Japan (⊕ *www.walkjapan.com*) offers customized guided tours to some pilgrimage temples.

*10 min, or JR Kotoku Line to Yashima Station and walk 15 min* ☎ *087/843–3111* 🌐 *www.shikokumura.or.jp* 🎫 *¥1,600* 🕒 *Closed Tues.*

**Megijima and Ogijima Islands** (女木島と男木島)
**ISLAND** | **FAMILY** | While Naoshima is the most popular of the Seto Inland Sea islands to visit from Takamatsu (thanks to its collection of galleries and outdoor art), there are smaller islands well worth a look. In recent years, art installations and the Setouchi Trienniale contemporary art festival have expanded to both Megijima and Ogijima, just without the polish (or price) of Naoshima's major venues. Beyond the low-key art, walking around Megijima gives the opportunity to slowly take in the laidback island life enjoyed by the 170 or so islanders, as well as to explore old smuggling caves once said to be home to ogres or just chill on Megijima's scenic beach. Over on Ogijima, population 160, you can stroll through the island's old village and on to its photogenic lighthouse, before checking out even more art installations. It all makes for a very mellow day out.

Megijima and Ogijima can easily be visited together in a day, and will leave a much smaller dent in your budget than gallery hopping on Naoshima. A Shiyujima Kaiun ferry service runs at least six times daily from Takamatsu to Megijima (20 minutes) and then on to Ogijima (another 20 minutes). ✉ *Takamatsu.*

## 🍴 Restaurants

Dozens of great restaurants and stores are scattered along the central Marugame-machi arcade and the side streets lacing it to Raion-dori arcade. The city's late bedtime makes it easy to move from a meal to a nightlife spot before finding a second stop for a bite later on.

**Sushi Kappo Komatsu** (寿司割烹小松)
**$$$$** | **JAPANESE** | Specializing in fish from the Seto Inland Sea, this intimate sushi restaurant is the place to mingle with food-loving locals or enjoy an intimate dinner for two. The ingredients are top-quality, and everyone here wants to make sure you enjoy your experience. **Known for:** traditional atmosphere; aesthetic experience; amazing sushi. [$] *Average main: ¥7,000* ✉ *Raion-dori arcade, 10–16 Gobo-machi, Takamatsu* ☎ *087/826–3812* 🕒 *Closed Sun. No lunch Mon.–Thurs.*

**Tenkatsu** (天勝)
**$$$** | **JAPANESE** | Find your favorite fish in the pool at Tenkatsu, and it will be on your plate a few minutes later. You can sit close to the action at the big black countertop, or dine on tatami with sunken *horigotatsu* tables. **Known for:** large variety of seafood; hot pots; local favorites like honetsukidori chicken. [$] *Average main: ¥4,000* ✉ *7–8 Hyogo-machi, Takamatsu* ☎ *087/821–5380.*

**Uo Ichiba Komatsu** (魚市場小松)
**$$$** | **JAPANESE** | **FAMILY** | The simmering energy of a cantina thrives in this three-story izakaya, where tanks full of eels and fish wait to be selected for your plate, and the chefs do a dazzling job preparing them. The other Japanese fare is also top-notch. **Known for:** amazing seafood; lively atmosphere; good selection of local sake. [$] *Average main: ¥4,500* ✉ *7–1 Furubaba-cho, Takamatsu* ☎ *087/826–2056* 🕒 *Closed Sun. No lunch.*

**Waraya** (わら家)
**$** | **JAPANESE** | Locals take fierce pride in Kagawa's culinary specialty, *sanuki-udon* noodles, traveling distances that defy common sense to sample the ones served at this restored riverside house at the base of Shikoku Mura. Stop here for lunch and enjoy the rustic waterwheel.

**Known for:** udon noodles; rustic setting; shrimp tempura toppings. [$] *Average main: ¥700* ✉ *91 Yashima-Naka-machi, Takamatsu* ☎ *087/843–3115* 🌐 *www.wara-ya.co.jp* 💳 *No credit cards.*

**Yoridorimidori** (寄鳥味鳥)
$$ | **JAPANESE** | In Hyogo-machi, the northern part of Takamatsu's warren of arcades, Yoridorimidori is one of those places locals tell you to go to try Takamatsu soul food. It doesn't disappoint. **Known for:** honetsukidori chicken; local sake; lively atmosphere. [$] *Average main: ¥3,000* ✉ *1–24 Hyogo-machi, Takamatsu* ☎ *087/822–8247* 💳 *No credit cards* 🕒 *Closed Mon. No lunch.*

## Hotels

**Daiwa Roynet Hotel Takamatsu** (ダイワロイネットホテル高松)
$$ | **HOTEL** | A reliable and well-maintained business hotel chain next to the Marugame-machi shopping arcade, the Roynet has helpful staff and great access to Takamatsu's main drinking and dining areas. **Pros:** central location for restaurants and bars; helpful staff; good value. **Cons:** a long walk from the station and ferry; small rooms; short on local flavor. [$] *Rooms from: ¥14,500* ✉ *8–23 Marugame-cho, Takamatsu* ☎ *087/811–7855* 🌐 *www.daiwaroynet.jp/en/takamatsu* 🛏 *175 rooms* 🍴 *No Meals.*

**Dormy Inn Takamatsu** (ドーミーイン高松)
$ | **HOTEL** | With its central location, smart decor, and great amenities, this branch of a national chain seems almost too good to be true in this price range. **Pros:** great value; convenient location for nightlife; rooftop bath. **Cons:** a long walk (or taxi) from the ferry or main station; small rooms; biggest rooms are twins. [$] *Rooms from: ¥11,600* ✉ *1–10–10 Kawara-machi, Takamatsu* ☎ *087/832–5489* 🌐 *www.hotespa.net/hotels/takamatsu* 🛏 *151 rooms* 🍴 *No Meals.*

**Hanajyukai** (花樹海)
$$$ | **B&B/INN** | A top choice for a luxury ryokan experience, Hanajyukai overlooks city and sea from a flower-covered mountainside. **Pros:** great service; city views; natural hot-spring baths. **Cons:** expensive (but excellent) add-on meal plans; might feel too formal for some; away from downtown. [$] *Rooms from: ¥19,800* ✉ *3–5–10 Nishitakara-cho, Takamatsu* ☎ *087/861–5580* 🌐 *www.hanajyukai.jp* 🛏 *45 rooms* 🍴 *No Meals.*

**JR Hotel Clement Takamatsu** (JRホテルクレメント高松)
$$$$ | **HOTEL** | If you're inclined to indulge in Western-style comfort, this hotel next to Takamatsu Station is a good choice. **Pros:** convenient location for buses, ferries and trains; spacious rooms; great views. **Cons:** a bit of a walk for nightlife; uninspiring decor; overpriced dining options. [$] *Rooms from: ¥22,819* ✉ *1–1 Hamano-cho, Takamatsu* ☎ *087/811–1111* 🌐 *www.jrclement.co.jp/takamatsu* 🛏 *300 rooms* 🍴 *No Meals.*

## Shopping

**Kitahama Alley** (北浜アリー)
**SHOPPING CENTER** | The former warehouse district of Kitahama Alley escaped the wrecking ball, and thanks to a cohort of young entrepreneurs it now contains funky shops, craft workspaces, cafés, and a large gallery space. The challenge is finding the place: the salt-blasted wooden and metal buildings look so derelict you might pass by without realizing it. Kitahama Alley is a 10-minute walk from Takamatsu Station. Follow the coastline east past Tamamo Park until a canal cuts back toward the city. You'll see the warehouses on your right. Poke into stores like Depot, which sells funky fashion and home items, and Peeka-Booya, whose baby clothes are likely more fashionable than anything in your own wardrobe. For a quick bite, try

the quiche and cake at 206 Tsu Ma Mu. ✉ 4–14 Kitahama-cho, Takamatsu ⊕ en. kitahama-alley.com.

# Naoshima (直島)

*20 km (12 miles) by ferry northeast of Takamatsu.*

In past centuries, pirate attacks were the biggest surprise you might encounter on the Seto Inland Sea. Now, it's the world-class art museums of Naoshima. This tiny island in the Inland Sea between Taka-matsu and Okayama hosts four major contemporary art museums as well as an installation art project and numerous other arty sights. Several surrounding islands have also gotten into the action, including Teshima, Inujima, Shodoshima, Megijima, and Ogijima, all of which participate in the Setouchi Triennale international art festival. If you're a contemporary art fan, don't miss out on the cultural activities here. If contemporary art isn't your thing, Naoshima probably won't convert you, especially with the high admission fees to many of the venues.

It's possible to see Naoshima's major sights in one (very long) day, but staying on the island overnight allows a more leisurely pace. After the day-trippers leave on the late-afternoon ferry, Naoshima feels like a different place altogether. Just be aware that many art venues here close on Mondays.

## GETTING HERE AND AROUND

You can reach Naoshima by taking a short ferry ride from Takamatsu in Kagawa Prefecture or Uno in Okayama Prefecture. The trip from Takamatsu to Naoshima's Miyanoura Port takes 30 minutes on the passenger-only ferry and 50 minutes on the car ferry. From Uno Port, a few hundred meters from Uno Station, the passenger-only ferry and car ferry take 15 and 20 minutes, respectively, to reach Miyanoura. There are also ferries to and between Naoshima's neighboring islands, though the smaller islands might have only one or two departures a day.

Trains from Okayama to Uno Station take 50 minutes. Direct trains don't run between 8 am and 3 pm, but you can take a Kojima-bound local train and make a simple change at Chaya-machi to one headed to Uno. A bus to Uno Port leaves every half-hour from Okayama Station (one hour).

Get around Naoshima by bicycle, on the town bus, or in the island's one and only taxi. The town bus costs ¥100 per ride and goes to all major sights. Regular bikes are available at Miyanoura Port, but you'll want a battery-assisted model to get you up the hill to Chichu Art Museum and the Benesse House Museum. TVC Service Rent-a-cycle across from Miyanoura Port is a good option—they will also store luggage. If you rented a bike in Takamatsu, you can bring it on the ferry (¥310 each way). If you have an international driver's license, you can rent a scooter from TVC to zip around the island, but it's best to reserve this at least a day in advance.

Aside from the villages of Miyanoura and Honmura, which can be covered on foot in about 10 minutes, Naoshima's only other major sights are its art museums and installations.

**CONTACT TVC Service Rent-a-cycle.** ✉ 2249–6 Miyanoura, Naoshima-cho, Kagawa-gun ☎ 087/892–3212.

## VISITOR INFORMATION

**CONTACT Naoshima Visitor Information Center.** ✉ Miyanoura Port, 2249–40 Miyanoura, Naoshima-cho, Kagawa-gun ☎ 087/892–2299 ⊕ naoshima.net/en.

The majority of the Chichu Art Museum is underground.

 Sights

## Art House Project
(ベネッセアートサイト 家プロジェクト;
*Benesse Ato Saito Ie Purojekuto*)
**MUSEUM VILLAGE** | The artists of the Art House Project have transformed seven structures or sites in the Honmura district that were abandoned as islanders departed to seek work in the city. Art, memory, and everyday life blend together as you wander through the seven "houses" (including a shrine and a former temple) while villagers around you go about their business. If you have time for only one site, make it *Minamidera*, designed by architect Tadao Ando to hold an artwork by James Turrell. ⊠ *771 Honmura, Naoshima-cho, Kagawa-gun* ☎ *087/892–3223 for Benesse House* ⊕ *www. benesse-artsite.jp/en/art/arthouse.html* ✉ *¥420 for single-site ticket except Kinza (¥520); ¥1,050 for 6 sites except Kinza* ⚬ *Kinza is reservation only.*

## Benesse House Museum
(ベネッセハウス ミュージアム)
**ART GALLERY** | Site-specific installations can be seen from the road leading to this top-class contemporary art museum. Inside, full-length windows illuminate a rotating collection of installation pieces in natural sunlight. The latest addition, about a 10-minute walk away (opposite the Lee Ufan Museum) but covered by the Benesse House Museum ticket, is the stunning Valley Gallery, a Tadao Ando-designed venue that as of March 2022 is the permanent indoor and outdoor home of Yayoi Kusama's sprawling *Narcissus Garden* installation. The museum is open later than others on the island, so if you only have a day here, save this museum for the evening. ⊠ *Gotanchi, Naoshima-cho, Kagawa-gun* ☎ *087/892–3223* ⊕ *www.benesse-artsite.jp/en* ✉ *¥1,300.*

## Chichu Art Museum
(地中美術館; *Chichu Bijutsukan*)
**ART GALLERY** | *Chichu* means "inside the earth," and this museum built into a hillside overlooking Naoshima's south

coast lives up to its name. Designed by the internationally recognized architect Tadao Ando, the museum is a work of art in itself. The Chichu exhibits works by Claude Monet, Walter de Maria, James Turrell, and other major artists in natural light. The Monet gallery, which features five paintings from Monet's *Water Lilies* series, is breathtaking. Buy tickets at the office 50 yards down the road; during busy periods, you may have to wait to enter. ✉ *3449–1 Naoshima-cho, Kagawa-gun* ☎ *087/892–3755* 🌐 *benesse-artsite.jp/en/art/chichu.html* 🎫 *¥2,100* 🕒 *Closed Mon.*

**Lee Ufan Museum**
(李禹煥美術館; *Ri Ufan Bijutsukan*)
**ART GALLERY** | Yet another Tadao Ando creation, this museum devoted to Lee Ufan, a much-honored painter and sculptor who was born in Korea but then spent much of his career based in Japan, aims to encourage a "slightly out-of-the-ordinary encounter with art, architecture, and nature." Opinions vary about how atypical the experience is, but it's definitely not a passive one. Wear comfortable shoes that are easy to remove; you'll be standing a lot and removing your shoes in parts of the museum. ✉ *1390 Azakura-ura, Naoshima-cho, Kagawa-gun* ☎ *087/840–8285* 🌐 *benesse-artsite.jp/en/art/lee-ufan.html* 🎫 *¥1,030* 🕒 *Closed Mon.*

**Hiroshi Sugimoto Gallery: Time Corridors**
(杉本博司ギャラリー 時の回廊; *Sugimoto Hiroshi Gyarari Toki no Kairo*)
**ART GALLERY** | Opened as an extension to the Benesse House complex in 2022, to coincide with Benesse's 30th anniversary on Nasohima, Time Corridors was designed by Tadao Ando (in typically stark concrete style) to house the largely black and white, abstract photography of Hiroshi Sugimoto. Also here, however, is Sugimoto's striking "Mondrian" glass teahouse installation, set in the middle of a water feature outside the lowly lit museum. You can slowly view the latter from the comfort of the museum's tea room, where tea and a sweet are served as part of the admission fee. As the gallery is only open from 11 am to 3 pm daily and allows a limited number of visitors at a time, it's best to reserve a visiting time in advance. ✉ *Gotanchi, Naoshima-cho, Kagawa-gun* 🌐 *benesse-artsite.jp/art/sugimoto-gallery.html* 🎫 *¥1,500.*

**Naoshima Bath I ♥ Yu** (直島銭湯 I♥湯)
**HOT SPRING** | Two minutes on foot from Miyanoura Port is Japan's funkiest public bath (*yu* means "hot water"). Created by artist Shinro Ohtake, the bathhouse contains, among other things, an aircraft cockpit, the bottom of a ship, and an elephant statue sourced from a museum of erotica. Towels, shampoo, and soap are for sale inside; the pools themselves are gender-segregated. ✉ *2252–2 Miyanoura, Naoshima-cho, Kagawa-gun* ☎ *087/892–2626* 🌐 *benesse-artsite.jp/en/art/naoshimasento.html* 🎫 *¥660* 🕒 *Closed Mon.*

## 🍴 Restaurants

Naoshima cafés keep relaxed island hours, usually staying open until sundown, which is fine for day-trippers, but you need to plan ahead if your lodging doesn't provide dinner.

**Aisunao** (あいすなお)
**$** | **JAPANESE** | **FAMILY** | Aisunao is centrally located and famous for its healthy and predominantly vegetarian lunches. Situated in a traditional Japanese guesthouse, diners sit on raised tatami mats overlooking a garden. **Known for:** healthy food; tranquil experience; vegetarian lunch. [$] *Average main: ¥1,000* ✉ *765 Honmura, Naoshima-cho, Kagawa-gun* ☎ *087/892–3830* 💳 *No credit cards* 🕒 *Closed Mon.*

**Café Salon Nakaoku** (カフェサロン中奥)
**$$** | **ECLECTIC** | Sandwiches, rice omelets, and Italian dishes are among the eclectic fare served at this café inside a traditional house. This is a good spot for a meal, or just coffee and cake. **Known for:** authentic setting; great homemade cakes; pasta. [$] *Average main: ¥2,000* ✉ *1167*

*Honmura, Naoshima-cho, Kagawa-gun* ☎ *087/892–3887* ⊟ *No credit cards* ⊗ *Closed Tues.*

### Museum Restaurant Issen (ミュージアムレストラン 一扇)

**$$$$** | **JAPANESE** | Located in the Benesse House Museum, Restaurant Issen serves traditional kaiseki food in beautifully curated surroundings and with impeccable service. A highly aesthetic experience, and one of the most elegant dining options on the island. **Known for:** kaiseki cuisine; seasonal and local ingredients; Warhol work on the walls. $ *Average main: ¥9,680* ⊠ *Benesse House Museum, Kagawa-gun* ☎ *087/892–3223* ⊕ *benesse-artsite.jp/en/stay/benessehouse/restaurant.html.*

### Shima-Shoku-Do Miyanda (島食Doみやんだ)

**$** | **JAPANESE** | Connected to a small gallery a few doors down from the I ♥ Yu baths in Miyanoura, this rickety looking restaurant serves up traditional, simple *teishoku* set meals for lunch and dinner. With the classic combo of rice, miso soup, and pickles, expect super-fresh sashimi and other seafood options. **Known for:** fresh sashimi and other seafood; terraced seating; filling teishoku set meals. $ *Average main: ¥1,300* ⊠ *2268–2 Miyanoura, Naoshima-cho, Kagawa-gun* ☎ *087/813–4400* ⊟ *No credit cards* ⊗ *Closed Mon.*

## 🛏 Hotels

Accommodations on Naoshima are mostly basic guesthouses, minshuku with shared facilities, and the luxury rooms at Benesse House. There aren't many mid-range options. Places fill up quickly on weekends and during holidays, so book as far in advance as possible.

### ★ Hotel Benesse House (ベネッセハウス)

**$$$$** | **HOTEL** | It's hard to say what part of a stay at the Hotel Benesse House is the most memorable: the gorgeous views of the Seto Inland Sea, special access to the artworks at the Benesse Museum, or the Tadao Ando architecture and the luxurious yet minimalist decor of the hotel rooms. **Pros:** access to art in and around the hotel; peaceful surroundings; stunning views. **Cons:** might feel too hushed for some; not convenient to other island dining options; restaurants are expensive. $ *Rooms from: ¥32,670* ⊠ *Gotanji, Naoshima-cho, Kagawa-gun* ☎ *087/892–3223* ⊕ *benesse-artsite.jp/en/stay/benessehouse* ⇨ *65 rooms* ⊗ *No Meals.*

### Ryokan Shioya (旅館志おや)

**$$** | **B&B/INN** | **FAMILY** | Just a three-minute walk from Miyanoura ferry terminal you'll find Ryokan Shioya—a hidden little gem where the hostess, Yukiko-san, carefully attends to her guests and makes great food. **Pros:** classic and authentic Japanese rooms; great homecooked food included; centrally located and easy access. **Cons:** not much English spoken; thin walls, so rooms are a bit chilly in winter; no online booking available. $ *Rooms from: ¥16,000* ⊠ *2222 Miyanoura, Naoshima-cho, Kagawa-gun* ☎ *087/892–3050* ⊟ *No credit cards* ⇨ *5 rooms* ⊗ *All-Inclusive.*

# Kotohira (琴平)

*45 km (28 miles) southwest of Takamatsu.*

Kotohira's draw is the Konpira Shrine, a mountaintop temple to the Shinto deity who protects seafarers. Though it's a long climb up a flight of stone steps, the shrine and its views of the Inland Sea are worth it. Other than the shrine, there's not much else in town. An evening stroll along its canal-lined streets can be pleasant, but if you have limited time on Shikoku you'll want to stay elsewhere.

## GETTING HERE AND AROUND

Kotohira is one hour from Takamatsu by trains run by JR (¥870) or Kotoden (¥630). JR's Shimanto Limited Express also runs there in 42 mins (¥1,400). Each company has its own station. Before heading to the shrine, pick up a map at the information center between the two stations.

**VISITOR INFORMATION**
**CONTACT Kotohira Tourist Information Center.** ⊠ *869-5 Enai, Kotohira* ☎ *087/775-3500* ⊕ *kotohira-kankou.com/en.*

 Sights

### Kinryo Sake Museum and Brewery (金陵の郷; *Kinryo no Sato*)

**BREWERY** | After climbing up to the Konpira Shrine, you may want some refreshment, or at least a diversion. When you get back to the bottom of all those steps, congratulate yourself with a stop and free tasting at this sake museum and brewery marked by an enormous sake bottle hanging to the left of the temple stairs. You can't miss it. ⊠ *623 Kotohira-cho, Kotohira* ☎ *0877/73–4133* ⊕ *www.nishino-kinryo.co.jp/en/museum* ⊑ *Free.*

### Konpira Shrine (金刀比羅宮; *Kotohira-gu*)

**RELIGIOUS BUILDING** | According to legend, this shrine, which is also known as Kotohira-gu, was founded in the 1st century. It's stood on top of Mt. Zozu ever since, protecting sailors and seafarers. Visiting requires some effort; you'll have to climb 785 steps to the impressive main shrine and 583 more to the final lookout. It's also possible to travel by taxi to the upper gate, or even hire two sturdy locals to carry you up in a straw basket (look for them at the base of the mountain). The first half of the climb is crowded with souvenir shops, but after that the setting is more peaceful. You'll glimpse the ocean as you climb, and the noise of the town gives way to the sounds of rustling trees and birdsong. The Treasure House, on your right after you pass through the stone gate, displays masks used in Noh and Kabuki theater. The Shoin, sometimes closed for maintenance, is an Edo-period

hall with artifacts and screens painted by Okyo Maruyama (1733–95), celebrated in his day and now for his realistic style. ⊠ *892–1 Kotohira-cho, Kotohira* ☎ *0877/75–2121* ⊑ *Shrine free, ¥800 for Treasure House, ¥800 for Shoin.*

# Tokushima (徳島)

*70 km (43 miles) southeast of Takamatsu and 160 km (100 miles) northeast of Kochi.*

Tokushima means "virtuous island"—ironic, considering the local residents' fondness for drinking, dancing, and hard partying. The city's annual **Awa Odori** dance festival is Japan's biggest, but there's fun to be had year-round in Tokushima and the surrounding area. Most visitors stay near the city center or in Naruto, a nearby peninsula famous for giant whirlpools that churn and thunder in the rocky straits below the cliffs. Nearby, the ambitious Otsuka Museum attracts huge crowds for its bizarre and breathtaking archive of the world's art. In surrounding towns and villages you can try your hand at local crafts like indigo-dyeing papermaking as they've been done for centuries. Back in the city proper, you'll learn to dance the Awa Odori, either in a special performance hall or with the million others dancing in the streets every summer during the Awa Odori Festival. Tokushima's major sights can be covered in a well-planned day or two, giving you plenty of time to move on to the mountains and gorges of Iya.

### GETTING HERE AND AROUND

Tokushima is accessible by JR train: 1¼ hours from Takamatsu; 2 hours from Okayama (usually with a transfer at Takamatsu); about 2½ hours from Kochi (via Awa Ikeda); 3 hours, 20 minutes from Shin-Osaka (via Okayama); and 3 hours, 40 minutes from Matsuyama (via Takamatsu). Buses are also an option. Highway buses depart from Takamatsu

(1½ hours); Kobe (2 hours); Kochi (2 hours, 40 minutes); and Matsuyama (3 hours, 20 minutes), as well as Kyoto (3¼ hours) and Osaka (2½ hours). Overnight buses also travel here from Tokyo (10 hours), and there are ferries from Tokyo (19 hours) and Wakayama (2 hours).

Buses leave Tokushima for Naruto Park (61 minutes) and Naruto Sightseeing Port (55 minutes) on the hour between 9 and 4, costing ¥720; the return has more varied times, so check the schedule. The boat quay at Naruto Kanko-ko (sightseeing port) is about a 15-minute walk from Uzu-no-michi, while the Otsuka Museum is 1 km (½ mile) away (there's a bus stop there too). There are also trains from Tokushima to Naruto Station (39 minutes, ¥390); catch a bus or taxi from there to the coast. If you opt to bus it and find yourself with time to kill waiting in Naruto, don't worry, there's a free, piping hot (and spring-fed) footbath at the the bus stop in front of Naruto Station. After that, also take a minute to pick up the local bus schedule in English from the information center at Naruto Station, as that will help you time your hops between sights on the once to twice hourly local buses.

Going by car from Tokushima takes roughly a half hour. Major car-rental companies such as Toyota Rent a Car and Nissan Rent a Car have offices near Tokushima Station. It's always a good idea to book ahead, and you can often score discounts by booking a few weeks in advance. During busy travel seasons reservations are essential.

■ TIP → **Tokushima's best sights are far from the city center. Consider renting a car rather than relying on public transportation.**

**CONTACTS Nissan Rent a Car.** ⊠ *1–10 Minamidekijima-cho, Tokushima* ☎ *088/625–1612* ⊕ *nissan-rentacar.com/english.* **Toyota Rent a Car.** ⊠ *1–18 Nakano-cho, Tokushima* ☎ *088/652–0100* ⊕ *rent.toyota.co.jp/eng.*

## TOURS

### Naruto Sightseeing Boats

(鳴門観光汽船; *Naruto Kankou Kisen*)
**BOAT TOURS | FAMILY |** This well-regarded company offers half-hour tours of the Naruto Whirlpools on two ships: the *Wonder Naruto* (¥1,800, daily departures every 40 minutes from 9 to 4:20) and the *Aqua Eddy* (¥2,400, daily departures every half hour from 9:15 to 4:15). Reservations are required for the *Aqua Eddy*. You can book online or by phone. Both ships depart from the small pier in the sightseeing port (Naruto Kanko-ko), at the southwest end of Naruto Park. ⊠ *Naruto Park, Kameura Kanko-ko, Tokushima* ☎ *088/687–0101* ⊕ *www.uzusio.com* ☑ *From ¥1,800.*

Outside of Awa-Odori season, Tokushima isn't the most exciting of places to stay. Like many regional cities, it has plenty of partially-shuttered shopping streets and other scars of a stuttering regional economy. If you do stay a night, however, take advantage of the half-hour river tours running from Ryokoku-bashi near the Toyoko Inn. They're operated by volunteers from the Shin-Machi River Preservation Society. On weekdays from September through June, the tours run every 40 minutes from 1 pm to 3:40 pm. In July and August, tours run from 5 pm to 7:40 pm. The tours are free, but you can drop change in the donation box, if you'd like to help the volunteers with the efforts to preserve Tokushima's old waterways.

## VISITOR INFORMATION

Before hitting town, head up by glass elevator to the Clement Tower Station Building's sixth floor. Here you'll find the TOPIA tourist information center. The center's fluent English speakers provide bus and train schedules, tide calendars (necessary for seeing the whirlpools at their best), and a good battle plan for tackling it all. TOPIA staff members can also advise you about travel to other Shikoku destinations.

**CONTACT TOPIA.** ✉ *Clement Plaza 6th fl., 1–61 Terashima-Honcho Nishi, Tokushima* ☎ *088/656–3303* ⊕ *www.topia.ne.jp/ english.*

 Sights

### Awa Odori Kaikan (阿波おどり会館)

**PERFORMANCE VENUE | FAMILY |** If you miss summer's Awa Odori dance festival, you can still get a dose at this museum and theater. *Odori* means "dance," and silk-robed professionals perform the famous local step here nightly. But shine your shoes: when the troupe leader starts talking to the audience, he's looking for volunteers. Thankfully, it's an easy dance. You might get a prize for participating, and one special award goes to the biggest fool on the floor—this honor is a staple of the festival, and it's not always the foreigners who win. The best show is at 8 pm. Arrive early and browse the gift shop or treat yourself to a ropeway ride up the mountain for a lovely city view. The third floor of the building is a small museum dedicated to the Awa Odori Festival. ✉ *2–20 Shin-machi-bashi, Tokushima* ☎ *088/611–1611* ⊕ *awaodori-kaikan. jp/en* ✉ *Museum ¥300, afternoon dance ¥800, evening dance ¥1,000, Bizan ropeway ¥1,030 (return).*

### Hall of Awa Japanese Handmade Paper
(阿波和紙伝統会館;
*Awa Washi Dento Kaikan*)

**OTHER MUSEUM |** Trek out to this paper museum, also known as Awa Washi Kaikan, to make your own postcards and browse the phenomenal gift shop, which stocks everything from sheets of softer-than-silk wrapping paper to peerless parasols. The trip here by train takes 55 minutes to Awa-Yamakawa Station (or 33 minutes by the infrequent limited express), then you walk 15 minutes to the hall. It's easier to rent a car and make the one-hour drive, especially if you are continuing on to the Iya Valley. ✉ *141 Kawahigashi, Yamakawa-cho, Tokushima* ☎ *0883/42–6120* ⊕ *awagami.com/pages/ hall-of-awa-japanese-paper-museum* ✉ *Museum ¥300, papermaking from ¥500* ⊗ *Closed Mon.*

### Naruto Whirlpools
(鳴門の渦潮; *Naruto no Uzushio*)

**BODY OF WATER |** You can hear the thunderous roar of the giant tidal whirlpools at Naruto Kaikyo (the Naruto Straits) long before you see them. When they come into sight, the contrast between peaceful sky and furious, frothing sea is striking. The whirlpools are formed when the changing tides force a huge volume of water through the narrow, rocky bottleneck. A glass-bottom promenade called Uzu-no-michi overlooks the pools from 45 meters (148 feet) up, though even safely behind glass it's sweat-inducing if you don't like heights, especially when the promenade vibrates as trains rattle over the bridge above. The view, however, is even better from the deck of a tour boat. A few companies with different-size vessels offer rides that cost between ¥1,500 and ¥2,500, but all of them are exhilarating. Two of the best boats are the *Wonder Naruto* and the smaller *Aqua Eddy*, both run by Naruto Kankou Kisen. The tide table on the promenade's website shows when the pools will be at their best. ✉ *Naruto Park, Tokushima* ☎ *088/683–6262* ⊕ *www.uzunomichi. com* ✉ *¥510 for promenade.*

### Otsuka Museum of Art (大塚国際美術館;
*Otsuka Kokusai Bijutsukan*)

**ART MUSEUM |** About 1 km (½ mile) before buses from Naruto and Tokushima reach Naruto Park, they stop at this impressive and bewildering ceramic art museum. Its founders commissioned more than 1,000 faithful reproductions of Western-art masterpieces on ceramic panels, the concept being that while Picasso's painting *Guernica* or Michelangelo's Sistine Chapel ceiling may fade with time, ceramic reproductions of them will live on forever. Exhibits are arranged by era, from antiquity to modern times, and it's all there, from a Pompeian banquet scene to Rembrandt's self-portraits to Warhol's *Marilyn x 100.* Cumulatively, the artworks are a bit overwhelming, though certainly not forgettable. You won't forget the price either. The lofty admission price isn't for someone with a mere passing interest in art. ✉ *65–1 Fukuike, Naruto-cho* ☎ *088/687–3737* 🌐 *o-museum.or.jp* 🎫 *¥3,300* 🕓 *Closed Mon.*

## 🍴 Restaurants

Tokushima has a decent selection of places to eat and drink at night, predominantly in the form of izakayas.

**Domannaka** (どまん中)
$$$ | **JAPANESE** | This modern izakaya-style Japanese restaurant on the same small street as the Agnes Hotel (near Tokushima Station) specializes in skewers of flame-grilled chicken, beef, pork, and seafood. The vast menu also includes hot-pot stews, fresh seafood dishes, and tempura items, and there's plenty of local sake to wash it all down. **Known for:** great chicken skewers; excellent selection of sake; beautiful atmosphere. [$] *Average main: ¥4,000* ✉ *1–47 Terashima Honcho Nishi, Tokushima* ☎ *088/623–3293* 🌐 *www.wa-domannaka.jp/en* 💳 *No credit cards* 🕓 *Closed Sun. except when Mon. is a public holiday, then closed Mon. No lunch.*

## 🛏 Hotels

For convenience and comfort, look at the cluster of newer hotels by the train station.

**Agnes Hotel** (アグネスホテル)
$$ | **HOTEL** | A level-up on the typical business hotel, the Agnes has a more sophisticated feel than similarly priced options in town. **Pros:** two minutes away from the train station; English-speaking manager; terrific pastries at the cafe. **Cons:** limited facilities; spartan decor; no doubles, just singles and twins. [$] *Rooms from: ¥13,000* ✉ *1–28 Terashima Honcho Nishi, Tokushima* ☎ *088/626–2222* 🌐 *www.agneshotel.jp/en* 🔑 *61 rooms* 🍴 *No Meals.*

**Hotel Sunroute** (ホテルサンルート徳島)
$$ | **HOTEL** | Smart but affordable, this hotel offers great city access—it's across from the JR Station—and a good range of facilities and amenities. **Pros:** nice on-site public baths and spa; excellent location; used to international clientele. **Cons:** can fill with tour groups; can be noisy; bland room decor. [$] *Rooms from: ¥12,200* ✉ *1–5–1 Moto-machi, Tokushima* ☎ *088/653–8111* 🌐 *www.sunroute-tokushima.com/en* 🔑 *177 rooms* 🍴 *Free Breakfast.*

**Toyoko Inn Tokushima Station** (東横イン徳島駅; *Toyoko In Tokushima Eki*)
$ | **HOTEL** | Comfortable facilities and easy city access make for a pleasing stay at this budget chain hotel. **Pros:** two-minute walk from train station; close to dining options; cheap rates. **Cons:** minimal facilities; bland decor; rooms could be bigger. [$] *Rooms from: ¥7,600* ✉ *1–5 Ryogoku Hon-cho, Tokushima* ☎ *088/657–1045* 🌐 *www.toyoko-inn.com* 🔑 *139 rooms* 🍴 *Free Breakfast.*

# Iya Valley and Oboke-Koboke Gorges (祖谷と大歩危小歩危)

*32 km (20 miles) south of Awa Ikeda, 105 km (65 miles) west of Tokushima, 135 km (84 miles) east of Matsuyama.*

In the Iya Valley, mountain villages cling to the side of improbably steep hills while turquoise rivers rush through the ravines below. This remote region was once so isolated that it became the retreat of choice for Heike clan warriors after they lost an epic battle to their Minamoto rivals in the 12th century. To get to Iya now, you don't have to string your own vine bridges across ravines

## Iya Valley Experiences

If a day or two spent rafting, canyoning, and bridge walking (with a night at a hot-springs resort) leaves you wanting more, venture farther into the Iya Valley. Mt. Tsurugi, the *fufu-bashi* (so-called husband-and-wife vine bridges), and a handful of onsen-hotels and craft workshops await. Getting here isn't overly complicated—follow signs toward Higashi-Iya and Tsurugi-san—but the narrow mountain roads are challenging, and just to be sure you'll want someone to mark the way on a map. You can also take a Yonkoh bus from West Iya to Kubo, transfer to a smaller bus bound for Mt. Tsurugi, and get off at the Kazura-bashi bus stop. Buses are infrequent, so check the schedule carefully to avoid getting stranded in the hills. The *taiken*, or "experiences," offered by local artisans are unique activities. Making delicious buckwheat *soba* noodles is rewarding, especially because this region is famous for its hearty strand of buckwheat, but making tofu or hiring a local guide to climb Tsurugi-san with you is great fun, too. Staffers at Miyoshi City Office of Tourism in front of Awa Ikeda Station have details about the crafts workshops, as does the downloadable map and brochure on their website (⊕ *miyoshi-tourism.jp/en*).

like the Heike did, although some of the bridges remain. If you want to feel as though you've escaped modern Japan for a hidden world, you can't do better than here.

After some local government mergers in 2006, the villages in the Iya Valley were combined to become Miyoshi City. Don't be fooled by the "city" moniker, though—Miyoshi City is actually a collection of rural villages administered from the small riverside town of Awa Ikeda, 32 km (20 miles) north of the Iya Valley.

Next to Iya, the Yoshino River roars through Okobe and Koboke gorges, where you'll find some of Japan's best white-water rafting. Try your hand at making delicious Iya soba or local crafts, or trek deeper into the valley to hike to the swordlike summit of Mt. Tsurugi.

### GETTING HERE AND AROUND

Access Iya by taking the Nanpu express train from Awa Ikeda (20 mins), Kochi (51 minutes), or Okayama (1¾ hours) to Oboke Station, in the foothills of the Iya Valley. From Tokushima take the Tsurugisan express to Awa Ikeda (1¼ hours), then transfer. From Takamatsu the Shimanto express train also connects to Awa Ikeda (1¼ hours). One benefit of coming via Awa Ikeda is that you can stop by the tourist information center by the station. Once you've reached Oboke, Yonkoh buses run to many of the main sights, including the vine bridges, but with infrequent services. If you're comfortable driving on narrow mountain roads, a car offers the best way to see the valley. The closest rental-car offices are in Awa Ikeda and Oboke (just one in each), but renting in Tokushima and driving into the valley via Route 438/439 over Mt. Tsurugi makes sense because of the beautiful scenery, as does renting in Kochi and driving in via Route 32, which follows the Yoshino River, before connecting with Route 439.

■ TIP➜ Rent the smallest car possible. Mountain roads are narrow, and corners are tight!

The Iya Valley's most famous attractions are its *kazura-bashi* (vine bridges).

## VISITOR INFORMATION

Miyoshi City Office of Tourism has an excellent English website with information and downloadable maps for the Iya Valley.

**CONTACT Miyoshi City Office of Tourism.** ✉ *In front of Awa Ikeda Station, 1810–18 Sarada, Ikeda-cho, Miyoshi City* ☎ *0883/76–0877* ⊕ *miyoshi-tourism.jp/en.*

##  Sights

### Chiiori House (篠庵)

HISTORIC HOME | Alex Kerr, an American artist and writer, stumbled across this dilapidated traditional farmhouse in the 1970s while traveling in Iya. He bought it and began the painstaking work of restoring its thatched roof and heavy wooden beams. Named Chiiori House, it is now the cornerstone of the activities of the Chiiori Trust, a nonprofit foundation working to preserve the region's traditional beauty while revitalizing its rural communities. You can visit the restored (thatch roof and all) Chiiori House for the day or spend the night. Reserve ahead to do either. ✉ *209 Tsurui, Higashi-Iya* ☎ *0883/88–5290* ⊕ *chiiori.org* ✉ *¥500 to visit, accommodation fee varies by number of guests, but is ¥19,250 per person for groups of 2 to 3.*

### Vine Bridges (かずら橋; *Kazura-Bashi*)

HISTORIC SIGHT | Iya's most famous feature is its trio of *kazura-bashi* (vine bridges) spanning its gorges. The most popular—referred to by most signs, maps, and locals simply as "Kazura-bashi"—is 20 minutes by car from Oboke Station. A less-visited pair are closer to Mt. Tsurugi. The bridges date back 800 years, to the aftermath of the momentous Gempei War, when the defeated Heike clan fled to these valleys after losing to the rival Minamoto clan. If the refugees were attacked, they could cut the vines at a moment's notice. These days, thin steel wires reinforce the precarious planks, and fresh vines are restrung every three years, but it still feels death-defying to cross the boards over the rivers. To visit Kazura-bashi, follow signs to it from

Route 32 or Route 45. If you're driving, park in the cheaper lots up the hill. The tall waterfall down the path is free, but you'll pay to cross the bridge. ✉ *Nishi-Iya Sanzon Village, Miyoshi City* ☎ *0883/76–0877 Miyoshi City Tourism* 💳 *¥550 to cross bridge.*

##  Hotels

### ★ Chiiori House (篏庵)

**$$$$** | **B&B/INN** | If a search for absolute serenity is what brought you to Iya, head straight for Chiiori House. **Pros:** breath-taking views; unforgettable atmosphere; adding dinner is possible. **Cons:** access is by winding mountain road; can be cold in winter; bring your own breakfast. 💲 *Rooms from: ¥38,500* ✉ *209 Tsurui, Higashi-Iya* ☎ *0883/88–5290* ⊕ *www. chiiori-stay.jp* ⤴ *1 house* ⃒◎⃒ *No Meals.*

### Iya no Yado Kazuraya (祖谷の宿 かずらや)

**$$$$** | **B&B/INN** | This traditional inn just up the road from Kazura-bashi has spacious rooms, an outdoor hot-spring bath, and unobstructed views of the valley, but the home-style feast you're served at dinner and breakfast are what you'll write home about. **Pros:** traditional cooking; family hospitality; rustic setting. **Cons:** nothing to do nearby after dark; limited facilities beyond the ryokan basics; limited English spoken. 💲 *Rooms from: ¥31,000* ✉ *78 Kantei, Nishi-Iya Yamamura, Miyoshi City* ☎ *0883/87–2831* ⊕ *iyanoyado-kazuraya. com* 🚫 *No credit cards* ⤴ *18 rooms* ⃒◎⃒ *All-Inclusive.*

### ★ Iya Onsen (祖谷温泉)

**$$$$** | **B&B/INN** | Perched on the edge of a steep ravine above the Iya River, this upscale hot-springs inn provides absolute luxury in the middle of nowhere. **Pros:** can book online in English; traditional cuisine; stunning outdoor riverside bath. **Cons:** not a great option for kids; quite formal; not much sightseeing nearby. 💲 *Rooms from: ¥39,140* ✉ *367–28 Matsuo Matsumoto, Miyoshi-shi*

☎ *0883/75–2311* ⊕ *www.iyaonsen.co.jp/ en* ⤴ *20 rooms* ⃒◎⃒ *All-Inclusive.*

### ★ Togenkyo Iya Farmhouses (桃源郷祖谷 の山里; *Togenkyo Iya no Satoyama*)

**$$$$** | **HOUSE** | Staying at this group of eight farmhouses in the mountains of eastern Iya is the perfect way to experience traditional life here. **Pros:** traditional architecture; tasteful facilities; lots of privacy. **Cons:** will need to bring drinks and snacks; extra effort to arrange meals; access by winding mountain lane can be a challenge. 💲 *Rooms from: ¥24,600* ✉ *96–3 Wada, Higashi-Iya* ☎ *0883/88–2540* ⊕ *www.tougenkyo-iya. jp* ⤴ *8 houses.*

## 🏃 Activities

### WHITE-WATER RAFTING

### ★ Happy Raft (ハッピーラフト)

**WHITE-WATER RAFTING** | Rafting down the wild Yoshino River's rocky gorges is one of this region's great thrills, and this company is your best bet for well-trained bilingual guides and friendly service. Half- or full-day trips can be arranged, equipment included. You can also try a combination rafting-and-canyoning trip. The staff are a great resource for travel tips about the area. Everything can be booked online in English. ✉ *221–1 Ikadagi, Otoyo-cho, Nagaoka-gun* ✛ *7½ km (4½ miles) south of Oboke Station on Rte. 32* ☎ *0887/75–0500* ⊕ *en.happyraft.com* 💳 *From ¥7,500 for a half-day trip* ⏱ *No tours Dec.–Mar.*

# Kochi (高知)

*130 km (81 miles) southwest of Takamatsu, 160 km (100 miles) southwest of Tokushima, 155 km (96 miles) southeast of Matsuyama, 110 km (68 miles) northeast of Nakamura, near the southern Ehime border.*

Kochi has earned a reputation for being different. The locals are rough-talking, boisterous, and social, and their spirited

White-water rafting is a popular activity in the Iya Valley.

city has an attitude that will dispel any stereotypes of Japanese shyness. The famous Yosakoi Dance Festival, one of Japan's most popular summer events, is an explosion of parades and performances that fills the city for days, but any time of year Kochi has a fun-loving energy about it.

## GETTING HERE AND AROUND

By train Kochi is 2½ hours from Tokushima (via Awa Ikeda), about 2¼ hours from Takamatsu (with a change at Tadotsu or Utazu), and 4 hours from Matsuyama (via Tadotsu). By bus it is 2½ hours from Matsuyama, 2¼ hours from Takamatsu, and 3 hours from Tokushima.

Half of the city's top attractions are within striking distance of Harimaya-bashi; a bridge that is a 10-minute walk south of the train station. Getting around by bicycle is a great option; the tourist office outside the train station provides free bikes for day use.

Streetcars from the station travel just about everywhere for ¥200 (with fares rising once the streetcar goes further afield), and the tram lines are easily navigable. Yosakoi Gururin buses travel the city center; access farther-flung sights like Katsurahama Beach, Chikurin-ji Temple, and the Makino Botanical Garden by the My Yu bus. You can board these in front of Kochi Station. It's worth spending ¥1,000 (half-price if you show a non-Japanese passport) for a one-day bus pass that also covers the streetcar's ¥200 basic fare zone.

## VISITOR INFORMATION

The main Kochi Tourist Information Center, in the Obiya machi shopping arcade by Hirome Market, has English-speaking staff and plenty of useful pamphlets. Make sure to grab the excellent English-language city and prefecture map. There's also a small tourist information booth in the Tosa Terrace outside the station.

**CONTACT Kochi Tourist Information Center.**
✉ *Obiya-machi Shotengai, 2–1–25 Obiya-machi, Kochi* ☎ *088/856–8670* ⊕ *visitkochijapan.com/en.*

# Downtown

##  Sights

**Harimaya Bridge** (はりまや橋; *Harimaya-bashi*)

**BRIDGE** | This arched red bridge is at the center of Kochi's best-known story, a tragic tale about a Buddhist priest caught buying a hairpin for a lover on this very spot. Several shops nearby sell hairpins these days, and you can go shopping for bargains in the area's twisting, tunneled arcades, and side streets. Locals come out to dine, drink, and chat in parks and at outdoor cafés around here until the wee hours. When the stores and bars finally close, there's always a ramen cart or two doing business on the sidewalk, so pull up a stool and dig in. Kochi people won't pay you much mind until you start talking to them, but many are affable and easy to engage. ✉ *Harimaya-bashi, Kochi.*

**Kochi Castle** (高知城; *Kochi-jo*)

**CASTLE/PALACE** | West of downtown's markets and arcades you'll find barrel-chested Kochi Castle, whose feel is more rough-hewn and lived-in than that of other Japanese castles; maybe not surprising, as much of it remains intact from the 1600s. The view from the topmost watchtower is splendid, and walking up the enormous steps or through the receiving chambers, which today are filled with historical exhibits, is like being transported to the Edo period. ✉ *1–2–1 Marunouchi, Kochi* ☎ *088/824–5701* ⊕ *kochipark.jp/kochijyo* 🎫 *¥420.*

**Yokoyama Memorial Manga Museum** (横山隆一記念まんが館; *Yokoyama Ryuichi Kinen Manga Kan*)

**OTHER MUSEUM** | **FAMILY** | Spread over three floors, this playful modern facility celebrates the life and work of Japan's first great cartoonist, hometown boy Ryuichi Yokoyama. His most popular character, Fuku-chan, is still widely loved, as the crowds of schoolkids reading comics in the museum's free manga library will attest. The cartoons inspire and delight, and no language skill is required to enjoy most of the visual humor. Look through World War II propaganda cartoons (from the Japanese point of view), interactive print stations, dioramas, model railroads, and tons of comic strips. ✉ *Kochi City Culture Plaza, 2–1 Kutanda, Kochi* ⊹ *7-min walk east of Harimaya Bridge* ☎ *088/883–5029* ⊕ *www.kfca.jp/manga-kan* 🎫 *¥410* ⊙ *Closed Mon.*

## 🍴 Restaurants

**Myojin-Maru** (明神丸)

**$** | **JAPANESE** | This ever-popular place in Hirome Market has perfected *katsuo tataki,* the regional fish specialty and the only item on the menu other than beer and rice. Fresh cuts of skipjack tuna are seared to perfection by a cook perilously close to being engulfed by the flames that he's feeding with big handfuls of straw. **Known for:** cozy and relaxed atmosphere; local favorite; amazing skipjack tuna (katsuo tataki). $ *Average main: ¥1,150* ✉ *Hirome-ichiba Market, 2–3–1 Obiya-machi, Kochi* ☎ *088/820–5101.*

**Tosa Ryori Tsukasa** (土佐料理司)

**$$$** | **JAPANESE** | Meals here range from simple lunchtime bento boxes to the lavish fish platters that are a Kochi specialty. The staff will recommend the local favorite *katsuo* (skipjack tuna)—in Japanese it's *sasuga Kochi,* "just as you'd expect in Kochi"—but consider the *shabu-shabu* meat and vegetable combinations, which your servers will teach you to cook on a special table in your private tatami room. **Known for:** great hot pots; excellent lunch sets; amazing katsuo (local fish). $ *Average main: ¥5,000* ✉ *1–2–15 Harimaya-cho, Kochi* ☎ *088/873–4351.*

## Coffee and Quick Bites

**Faust** (ファウスト)
$ | **EUROPEAN** | This delightful café-restaurant sits just off the main drag between Harimaya-bashi and the castle. Choose a table by the window and people-watch on the cobbled lane, or head indoors to the quirky third-floor dining area. **Known for:** delicious cakes; great coffee; cheap breakfast sets.
*$ Average main: ¥900 ✉ 1–2–22 Hon-machi, Kochi ☎ 088/873–4111 💳 No credit cards.*

## Hotels

**Jyoseikan** (城西館)
$$$$ | **HOTEL** | "Fit for a king" is often an exaggeration, but in this case it's true Jyoseikan is where the emperor stays when the royal family comes to Kochi. **Pros:** generously sized Japanese-style rooms; excellent service; close to the castle and market. **Cons:** Western-style twins are nothing special; a very formal experience; not all staffers speak English.
*$ Rooms from: ¥35,200 ✉ 2–5–34 Kami-machi, Kochi ☎ 088/875–0111 🌐 en.jyosei-kan.co.jp 🛏 62 rooms 🍴 All-Inclusive.*

**Richmond Hotel Kochi**
(リッチモンドホテル高知)
$ | **HOTEL** | Pristine rooms, excellent rates, and a prime location near nightlife and shopping make this hotel a superb midrange choice. **Pros:** unbeatable location; spotless facilities; accommodating staff. **Cons:** basic facilities; can be a noisy area; regular-class rooms cramped.
*$ Rooms from: ¥9400 ✉ Obiyamachi shopping arcade, 1-9-4 Obiyamachi, Kochi ☎ 088/820–1122 🌐 richmondhotel.jp/en/kochi 🛏 234 rooms 🍴 No Meals.*

**7Days Hotel** (セブンデイズホテル)
$ | **HOTEL** | The 7Days and its slightly plusher annex 7Days Plus are budget business hotels done right. **Pros:** very low rates; connecting rooms for families; good breakfast. **Cons:** business hotels can be noisy at night; away from entertainment; won't win any design awards.
*$ Rooms from: ¥7,400 ✉ 2–13–6 and 2–13–17 Harimaya-cho, Kochi ☎ 088/884–7100, 088/884–7111 🌐 www.7dayshotel.com 🛏 170 rooms 🍴 No Meals.*

## Shopping

**Hirome Market** (ひろめ市場; *Hirome-ichiba*)
**MARKET** | The best place to mingle with locals is at the Hirome Market. A few stores at the busy market sell interesting pottery, jewelry, and souvenirs, but everyone's really here for the food. Serving everything from sushi to ramen and fried chicken to curry, the dozens of tiny eateries and food counters have so many delicious dishes that you couldn't try them all in a year. If your chosen spot doesn't have a picture menu, you can always point to someone else's plate across the broad wooden tables. The market is at the western end of the main arcade, close to the castle, about 15 minutes by foot from JR Kochi Station. Look for the mass of bicycles parked around a squat ramen stand beside the entrance, a big orange-and-green sign above the hangar-bay door, and a large crowd of well-fed locals. *✉ 2–3–1 Obiya-machi, Kochi ☎ 088/822–5287 🌐 hirome.co.jp.*

**Sunday Market** (日曜市; *Nichiyo-ichi*)
**MARKET** | Dating back to the late 17th century, this popular weekly market offers a mile of fruits and vegetables, flowers, snacks, and a smattering of crafts. It's not a great place for souvenir shopping, but why not try some *yuzu-an* in a pastry pocket? This Kochi specialty replaces the red beans often found in desserts with a paste made from the sour yellow yuzu citrus grown in the prefecture. Nichiyo-ichi runs along broad, palm-lined Otetsuji-dori Street from Harimaya Bridge right up to the gates of Kochi Castle. The 300 or so stalls operate from roughly 6 am to 3 pm. *✉ Otetsuji-dori, Kochi ⏲ Closed Mon.–Sat.*

# Outside the City Center

## ◉ Sights

### Chikurin-ji Temple (竹林寺)

TEMPLE | Buddhist pilgrims had been communing with nature in the garden of this austere mountaintop temple long before the giant ferns moved in next door at the Makino Botanical Garden. The garden, a registered National Treasure, dates from the 13th century. Its simple arrangement of ponds, rocks, and pine trees provides a soothing contrast to the vibrant foliage next door. The setting is particularly peaceful in the late afternoon. Linger at the temple a while, and you're likely to encounter white-clad Shingon Buddhist pilgrims visiting on their way around the island. ✉ 3577 Godaisan, Kochi ☎ 088/882–3085 ⊕ www.chikurinji. com ⨝ ¥400 for garden.

### Katsurahama Beach (桂浜)

BEACH | The prefecture may be known for its great surfing and swimming beaches, but rocky Katsurahama Beach has other attractions. It's best known for its giant statue of the 19th-century political reformer Sakamoto Ryoma, Kochi's local-born hero, staring grimly out to sea from his big black pedestal. The view from a cliff-top shrine is great (moon-watching from this spot is depicted in many prints), and for history buffs there is a museum to Sakamoto Ryoma nearby. Get here by Kochi Kenkotsu bus (40 minutes) or My Yu bus (50 minutes) from Kochi Station. ✉ 778 Urado, Kochi.

### ★ Makino Botanical Garden (牧野植物園; Makino Shokubutsuen)

GARDEN | FAMILY | Planted in honor of Kochi botanist Tomitaro Makino, this Eden-like valley of flowers and trees lies hidden atop Mt. Godaisan. Different trails for each season show off the best nature has to offer. Hours can disappear as you walk through the azaleas, camellias, chrysanthemums, and thousands of other plants in this huge and lovingly tended landscape. Don't miss the giant ferns, so big you can actually sit in them. You're encouraged to leave the paths and explore on your own—as Makino wrote, "to commune with nature we need to make ourselves free and jump into her." You'll find more of his quotes, recollections, philosophy, and drawings in a fascinating museum inside the park. ✉ 4200–6 Godaisan, Kochi ☎ 088/882–2601 ⊕ www.makino.or.jp ⨝ ¥730.

### Muroto Cape (室戸岬; Muroto Misaki)

NATURE SIGHT | A surreal coastline awaits you at far-off Muroto. The road east from Kochi follows a rugged shoreline cut by inlets and indentations along a landscape out of Dr. Seuss, where the Pacific "Black Current" (kuroshio) has shaped enormous terraces going down to the sea. A concrete promenade lets you walk the farthest tip of sea-sculpted land, where detailed signs in English explain local geography and history.

Muroto Cape is a 2½-hour drive along the coast road. To get here by public transportation, take a 1¼-hour train ride to Nahari Station on the private Tosa-Kuroshio Gomen-Nahari Line (¥1,340), and a one-hour bus ride from there (¥1,200). The Muroto UNESCO Global Geopark website lists model courses for exploring the area. ✉ Muroto-misakicho ⊕ www.muroto-geo. jp/en.

### Sakamoto Ryoma Memorial Museum (坂本龍馬記念館; Sakamoto Ryoma Kinenkan)

HISTORY MUSEUM | During the turbulent times before the Meiji Restoration, Sakamoto Ryoma was a radical and a revolutionary. The political changes he instigated were enough to get him killed, as you'll learn in this museum jutting fabulously over the sand and surf near Katsurahama Beach. After seeing the blood-splashed screen from the room where he was assassinated, you'll finally know who the cowboyish samurai plastered on every street corner in Kochi is. ✉ 830 Urado-Shiroyama, Kochi ✛ 35-min ride on Kochi Kenkotsu bus to Ryoma Kinenkan

stop ☎ 088/841–0001 ⊕ ryoma-kinenkan.
jp/country/en 🖭 ¥700.

# Matsuyama (松山)

*160 km (100 miles) southwest of
Takamatsu, 120 km (75 miles) west of
Awa Ikeda, 195 km (120 miles) west of
Tokushima, 155 km (96 miles) northwest
of Kochi.*

Shikoku's largest city, Matsuyama prides
itself on a great history, friendly disposition, fantastic cultural attractions, and
a love for fine food and haiku. You'll be
quickly captivated by the sights and feel
of the city, and you can join in the fun.
Bathe at Dogo Onsen—Japan's oldest
hot spring—hit the fashion avenue downtown, or go restaurant crawling through
the best spots on the island. Denizens
say it's *sumi-yasui* (easy living) here, and
you'll find Matsuyama one of the most
rewarding stops along your route.

Though a large and not particularly
well-organized city, Matsuyama is easy
to navigate and is served by a good
tram network. For visitors the action is
concentrated around a few locations, the
main one being the enormous central
landmark, Matsuyama Castle.

## GETTING HERE AND AROUND
### BOAT
Except for the Orange Ferry services
from Osaka and Kobe, which dock in
towns east of Matsuyama, all ferries to
Matsuyama arrive at Matsuyama Kanko
Ko Terminal. Get from here to central
Matsuyama by taking a taxi (about
¥3,000, 20 minutes) or direct Iyotetsu
bus (¥750, 20 minutes from the JR station, but there are also other stops in the
city center). There are also direct buses
from Kanko Ko Terminal to Dogo Onsen
(¥940, 45 minutes).

**From Hiroshima:** The Setonaikai Kisen and
Ishizaki Kisen companies run hydrofoils
from Hiroshima Port nine times a day

each (70 minutes, ¥7,800 one-way).
Their slow ferries from Hiroshima makes
10 trips a day each (2½ hours, ¥4,500
one-way).

**From Kansai:** The Orange Ferry runs
overnight boats from Osaka to Toyo, and
from Kobe to Niihama. Toyo and Niihama
are east of Matsuyama. On both routes,
private single rooms start from ¥7,200,
and a private cabin for two starts at
¥11,300. The Osaka-Toyo route also has
smart Japanese-style private rooms and
suites. Buses operated by either JR or
Iyotetsu Bus Company connect Toyo Port
with Matsuyama, and both ports are also
near JR stations.

**From Kyushu:** Uwajima Unyu runs ferries
between Beppu and Uwajima (three
hours, from ¥3,650). Uwajima is 80
minutes by JR train from Matsuyama.
Orange Ferry runs boats between
Usuki and Yawatahama (2½ hours, from
¥2,750). Yawatahama is 45 minutes by JR
train from Matsuyama. Kokudo Kyushu
Ferry operates between Saganoseki and
Misaki (70 minutes, from ¥1,090). Misaki
is three hours by bus from Matsuyama.

**CONTACTS Ishizaki Kisen.** ☎ 089/953–
1003 ⊕ www.ishizakikisen.co.jp/
language/en. **Kokudo Kyushu Ferry.**
☎ 050/3184–1944 ⊕ www.koku94.
jp. **Orange Ferry.** ☎ 0898/64–4121
⊕ www.orange-ferry.co.jp. **Setonaikai
Kisen.** ☎ 082/253–1212 in Hiroshima,
089/953–1003 in Matsuyama ⊕ setonai-
kaikisen.co.jp/language/en. **Uwajima Unyu.**
☎ 0894/22–2100 ⊕ www.uwajimaunyu.
co.jp/english.

### TRAIN
By train Matsuyama is about 2½ hours
from Takamatsu, about 3½ hours from
Tokushima (via Takamatsu), 4 hours from
Kochi (via Tadotsu), and 6½ hours from
Tokyo (via Okayama). By bus it is about
2½ hours to Kochi and 3¼ hours to Tok-
ushima. There are two main train stations
in the city, JR Matsuyama Station and
Matsuyama Shieki Station. JR trains

and buses arrive at the JR Matsuyama Station, which is a bit far from the city center. Iyotetsu trains go to the more central Matsuyama Shieki Station. Trams and local buses serve both.

### TRAM

The best way to get around Matsuyama is by the Shinai Densha tram. Rides cost ¥170 per person, paid when you exit. A day-pass costs ¥700 and can be bought at stations or from the tram driver. Tram 5 runs from the JR Station to Dogo Onsen, and most of the city's best spots are along the way. The stop in the center of Matsuyama is Okaido-mae on Ichiban-cho street. If the urge to write a haiku hits you on the tram, you are in luck. With Matsuyama having been the birthplace of Masaoka Shiki and several other famous haiku poets, most trams today have little post boxes on them, specifically for people to post haiku to the city's annual competition (in English is fine). There's a special form next to the boxes, and with haiku in English you don't have to conform to the traditional format of three sentences of five, seven and five syllables. Anything short and sweet can work.

If you're traveling with kids, don't miss a ride on the special Botchan steam trams that putter around the city. Botchan trains run between Shieki and Dogo Onsen six times a day, and twice a day between the JR station and Dogo Onsen. A one-way trip is ¥1,300.

### VISITOR INFORMATION

There are tourist information offices at the JR train station, castle cable car station, Dogo, and in Mitsukoshi department store. English maps are available even if an English speaker is not. The peerless desk staff at the Ehime Prefectural International Center (EPIC) provides advice about events, transportation, hotel reservations, and even bicycles (rentable for a refundable ¥1,000 deposit; ¥3,000 deposit if you also borrow a helmet). EPIC is next to the Kenmin Bunka Kaikan, or People's Cultural Hall, off Tram 5's Minami-machi stop.

**CONTACTS Ehime Prefectural International Center.** (*EPIC*) ⊠ *1–1 Dogo Ichiman, Matsuyama* ☎ *089/917–5678* ⊕ *www.epic. or.jp.* **Matsuyama City Tourist Information Office.** ⊠ *Matsuyama Station, 1–14–1 Minamiedo, Matsuyama* ☎ *089/931–3914* ⊕ *en.matsuyama-sightseeing.com.*

##  Sights

### Dogo Onsen Bathhouse (道後温泉本館; *Dogo Onsen Honkan*)

**HOT SPRING** | Tell people you're heading to Matsuyama, and Dogo Onsen will be the first place they recommend. These hot springs have been the city's top attraction for the last millennium. Japan's oldest written text mentions it as a favorite of gods, emperors, and peasants alike, and it's still in daily use by locals and visitors. The main wooden building at present-day Dogo dates from 1894 and looks like a fairy tale castle; albeit one with scaffolding until exterior and interior renovations are completed (expected sometime in 2022).

At this writing, you can access only the Kami-no-Yu baths, but once renovation work is complete, you'll once again (for additional fees) be able to try all the other baths there and enjoy tea and sweets after a good soak. As an alternative, there's always the swanky Asuka-no-Yu annex that opened nearby in 2017. Built in a traditional style, it offers an experience similar to Dogo Onsen, with several baths, tatami chill-out areas, the chance to don a lightweight *yukata* robe, and refreshments. All baths at both facilities are separated by gender. Remember proper onsen etiquette: wash and rinse yourself (and your towel) before getting into the bath (without your towel). ⊠ *5–6 Yuno-machi, Dogo, Matsuyama* ☎ *089/921–5141* ⊕ *dogo.jp/en* ⊠ *From ¥420 for Kami-no-Yu baths, from ¥610 for Asuka-no-Yu annex.*

Dogo Onsen, Japan's oldest hot spring, is the biggest draw in Matsuyama.

### Ehime Museum of Art (愛媛県立美術館; *Ehime Kenritsu Bijutsukan*)

ART MUSEUM | The permanent collection of this museum occupying a modern city-center building isn't that big, but the selection of recent Japanese art is terrific, and the temporary exhibits are extensive. The galleries often host exhibits of works by local artists. ⊠ *Horinouchi, Matsuyama* ☏ *089/932–0010* ⊕ *www.ehime-art.jp* ⊠ *¥330* ⊙ *Closed Mon.*

### ★ Ishite-ji Temple (石手寺)

TEMPLE | A 15-minute walk from Dogo Onsen, Ishite Temple is Shingon Buddhism at play. Half serene pilgrimage destination, half ancient Buddhist-themed fun park, the temple is more than worth a visit. As sprawling and elegantly unkempt as the city around it, it contains surprises that are, like the temple cats, too numerous to count.

Enter the temple by way of a stone road that's flanked by wooden stalls with vendors selling calligraphy brushes, *omiyage*-paper fortunes, and pilgrimage

gear. Just inside the colossal temple gate you'll see a table for folding origami cranes; make one and it will be added to the heavy, colorful bunches hanging around the pillars. Past the cranes lies the main hall of worship, where you're likely to see a pilgrim or two chanting a sutra. In the surrounding area you'll also see painted panels, golden statues, a giant mandala on the stairway to the main shrine, a wooden *kami* (spirit) with a sword you can heft, and a huge bronze bell to ring (¥100).

It's serene and memorable, but the real fun at Ishite-ji Temple starts in a long, dark cave to the left of the main worship hall. It feels impossibly long, and when you finally emerge on the other side—past startling wooden statues and 88 stone Buddhas—you'll be confronted by a 100-foot statue of the priest Kobo Daishi striding across the mountains. The mountain behind the temple also holds a few surprises: a scrambling rock pathway leads up the mountain, where two spooky caves are yours to explore (even most locals don't know about them). ✉ *2–9–21 Ishite, Matsuyama* ☎ *089/977–0870* 🎫 *Free.*

**Itami Juzo Memorial Museum** (伊丹十三記念館; *Itami Juzo Kinenkan*)

**OTHER MUSEUM** | The late Juzo Itami (1933–97) is regarded as one of Japan's most innovative and captivating film directors, known for his affectionate and absurdist portraits of Japanese life. Each film starred his wife Nobuko Miyamoto and an off-the-wall supporting character, sometimes played by Itami himself. The director's best-known films include *Tampopo* (1985), centering on a bedraggled ramen-shop owner trying to make the perfect soup, and *Ososhiki* (*The Funeral*, 1984), the story of an idiosyncratic family coming together for a funeral. If you haven't seen these films, they're musts for any visitor to Japan; if you have, then you'll love the museum, curated by Miyamoto herself, showcasing video clips and objects from Itami's life. ✉ *1–6–10 Higashi Ishii, Matsuyama* ✣ *From Shieki Station, ¥1,200 taxi ride or take Tobe-bound bus 20 mins to Amayama-bashi Bridge stop, then backtrack 2 min on foot to museum* ☎ *089/969–1313* 🌐 *itami-kinenkan.jp/en/index.html* 🎫 *¥800* 🕒 *Closed Tues.*

**Matsuyama Castle** (松山城; *Matsuyama-jo*)

**CASTLE/PALACE** | Mighty Matsuyama Castle stands on a 433-feet mountain in the middle of town, and the views of the city from here are stunning. Dating from 1603, it's one of the cooler castles in Japan. Inside you can watch footage of the post–World War II reconstruction; the shaping and joining of wood and the stamping out of straw wattle for the walls is astonishing. There is no concrete, no rebar, and only enough nails to hold down the floorboards. Dark-wood passageways carry the smell of old smoke from the numerous fires the castle has endured.

To get to the castle, walk uphill about 30 or 40 minutes or ride the ropeway partway up and continue on foot about 15 minutes to the castle. The station is on Ropeway Street, just north of the Okaido shopping arcade. If you have time, also visit the Ninomaru garden just west of the castle. ✉ *1 Marunouchi, Matsuyama* ☎ *089/921–4873* 🎫 *Castle ¥520, ropeway ¥520, garden ¥200.*

## 🍴 Restaurants

Matsuyama has many great restaurants. The two best streets to follow both run parallel to the main arcade. For the first, head into Okaido from the Starbucks, and go left at the first stoplight (this is Niban-cho), then take your first right to find foodie heaven. No spot on the strip is terribly expensive, and each place has a lot of character and great food. A few blocks farther east, the main artery of Yasaka-dori has many great places to eat and drink lining both sides.

**Amitie** (アミティエ)

$$$ | **BISTRO** | Weekend lunch and the prix-fixe dinners are outstanding—and a good value—at this special place serving French- and Italian-inspired bistro-style cuisine. The food and presentation are excellent without being snooty, and the softly worn wooden interior is funky yet not crass or grimy. **Known for:** funky atmosphere; delicious fish dishes; rich meat dishes. [$] *Average main: ¥4,000* ✉ *6–23 Minami Horibata-cho, Matsuyama* ✣ *Near Bijutsukan-mae tram stop, across moat from Ehime Museum of Art* ☎ *089/998–2811* 🕒 *Closed Tues. No lunch weekdays.*

**Dogo Bakushukan** (道後麦酒館)

$$ | **JAPANESE** | Brew pub meets izakaya at this rustic joint by the Dogo Onsen Bathhouse. You'll find plenty of meaty and fishing izakaya staples on the extensive menu to make a good lunch or dinner. **Known for:** excellent seafood; grilled meats; German-style beers. [$] *Average*

main: ¥3,000 ✉ 20–13 Dogoyuno-machi, Dogo ☎ 089/945-6866 🌐 www.dogobeer.jp/bakusyukan-restaurant.

## Coffee and Quick Bites

**Un Petit Peu** (アン・プチ・プー)

$ | **CAFÉ** | Delicious handmade custards and crepes and a two-story dining area with corner views of Matsuyama's busy night scene make this coffee-and-pastry shop a perfect part of any evening out. Extremely popular and open into the wee hours, it's a great place to meet Matsuyamans. **Known for:** local favorite; delicious desserts; late-night eats. [$] *Average main: ¥800 ✉ 1–10–9 Niban-cho, Matsuyama ☎ 089/931–8550 🕓 Closed Sun. No lunch*

## Hotels

**ANA Crowne Plaza Matsuyama** (ANAクラウンプラザホテル松山)

$ | **HOTEL** | Downtown's biggest international hotel, the ANA has some great city views and a good range of facilities, including a fitness center, several restaurants, and a sky bar. **Pros:** next to city center; easy access to sights; good value doubles. **Cons:** breakfast cheaper in cafes nearby; fairly sterile atmosphere; somewhat generic rooms. [$] *Rooms from: ¥10,350 ✉ 3–2–1 Ichiban-cho, Matsuyama ☎ 089/933–5511 🌐 www.anacpmatsuyama.com/english 🛏 330 rooms 🍴 No Meals.*

**Hotel Checkin Matsuyama** (チェックイン松山)

$ | **HOTEL** | At the epicenter of dining and nightlife in downtown Matsuyama, this reasonably priced hotel has a hard-to-beat address. **Pros:** prime city location; family size rooms; hotel bath draws water from Dogo Onsen. **Cons:** dated rooms and limited facilities; breakfast area can be crowded; lower floors get some street noise. [$] *Rooms from: ¥7,500 ✉ 2–7–3 Sanban-cho, Matsuyama ☎ 089/998–7000 🌐 www.checkin.co.jp/matsuyama 🛏 269 rooms 🍴 No Meals.*

**Hotel Dogo Yaya** (ホテル道後やや)

$$ | **HOTEL** | Guest rooms at this more affordable alternative to Yume Kura are compact but have a modern Japanese aesthetic, and the service here is remarkable. **Pros:** close to Dogo Onsen; fashionable facilities; great breakfasts. **Cons:** rooms are small; some rooms have small windows; staff speak only basic English. [$] *Rooms from: ¥17,000 ✉ 6–1 Dogo Tako-cho, Dogo ☎ 089/907–1181 🌐 www.yayahotel.jp 🛏 68 rooms 🍴 Free Breakfast.*

**Hotel Patio Dogo** (ホテルパティオドウゴ)

$$ | **HOTEL** | From the outside, you might think you've booked a drab business hotel, but inside everything is surprisingly smart and contemporary. **Pros:** nice bathrooms; spacious "deluxe" rooms; excellent location. **Cons:** better value options elsewhere in Matsuyama; limited facilities compared to bigger Western-style hotels; standard doubles and singles are cramped. [$] *Rooms from: ¥17,000 ✉ 20–12 Dogoyuno-machi, Dogo ☎ 089/941–4128 🌐 www.patio-dogo.co.jp 🛏 101 rooms 🍴 No Meals.*

**Yume Kura** (夢蔵)

$$$$ | **B&B/INN** | A splurge but absolutely worth it, this high class ryokan behind the Dogo Onsen bathhouse delivers the royal treatment. **Pros:** great location; elegant decor; incredible service. **Cons:** no in-room dinner service; meals are not optional; no double beds. [$] *Rooms from: ¥60,000 ✉ 4–5 Dogo Yutsuki-cho, Dogo ☎ 089/931–1180 🌐 www.yume-kura.jp 🛏 7 rooms 🍴 All-Inclusive.*

## Nightlife

**Hoyaken** (ホヤケン)

**BARS** | In recent years Matsuyama has been promoting its haiku poetry heritage in conjunction with the city's nightlife; namely, promoting bars where you can go to drink and, if the urge takes you, write haiku poems. Located near the castle (on Sanban-cho street), Hoyaken is one of those bars, run by a husband and wife who are haiku and sake aficionados. Grab a counter seat, pick up a pencil and paper, and get creative with the minimum amount of words, all while sipping on some of the best regional sake Ehime Prefecture has to offer. You might even be given a haiku penname by the owners. If you aren't sure about how to write a haiku, there are explanations on hand in English, plus booklets full of seasonal words to inspire you. For a list of more haiku-slash-drinking venues, check out the Matsuyama Haiku Bar website. ⊠ 2–5–17 Sanban-cho, Matsuyama ⊕ matsuyamahaiku.jp/haitomatsuyama/eng/bar ⊙ Closed Sun.

### Moonglow (ムーングロウ)

**PIANO BARS** | This cozy piano bar near the Okaido shopping arcade has been hosting local and visiting jazz musicians since the 1980s. The music is as good as you'd encounter in any of Japan's major cities, and it's all the more delightful when paired with one of the bar's quirky cocktails. ⊠ 3–2–15 Sanbancho, Matsuyama ⊹ On Chifune-machi St., 3 buildings north of 114 Bank ☎ 089/931–3294 ⊕ www.bekkoame.ne.jp/~moon-g69 ⊙ Closed Sun.

## 🛍 Shopping

Matsuyama is arguably the fashion capital of Shikoku (though Takamatsu might disagree), and a stroll down its main shopping arcades, **Okaido** and **Gintengai,** is perfect for both window shopping and fashionista watching. Okaido begins at the Starbucks on Ichiban-cho and goes south for a kilometer until turning right into the Gintengai; Gintengai empties out by a large Takashimaya department store and the city bus and tram terminal, Shieki Station.

Okaido, Gintengai, and Shieki complete a square adjacent to the Matsuyama

Castle's moat. Inside is **Chifune-machi,** bursting with clothing stores, cafés, and other shops. You won't stumble on any hidden temples or ancient ruins, but there's plenty of good shopping.

# Uchiko (内子)

*50 km (30 miles) south of Matsuyama.*

This small farming town in the mountains south of Matsuyama was a major producer of Japanese paper and wax until the early 20th century. Now it's a peaceful mountain town of old merchant houses, candle and umbrella workshops, and an impressive turn-of-the-20th-century Kabuki theater. In the mid-20th century, it became famous as the hometown of the novelist Oe Kenzaburo, the second Japanese writer to win the Nobel Prize in literature. If you want a quiet night away in the kind of traditional setting Oe would have enjoyed here, stay at one of Uchiko's refurbished old townhouses.

### GETTING HERE AND AROUND

Uchiko is small enough to cover on foot, and strolling through this old town is the best way to experience it. From Uchiko Station, follow a wooden sign pointing left to the old shopping street Yokaichi, where the only change for centuries has been the height of plants against the beige-orange walls. You won't need more than a morning to poke through the fun shops full of good, cheap souvenirs: straw pinwheels, tea leaves, sour *tsukemono* pickles, and local sake.

## 👁 Sights

### ★ Japanese Wax Museum and Kamihaga Residence (木蠟資料館 上芳我邸; *Mokuro Shiryokan Kamihaga-tei*)

**OTHER MUSEUM** | The former residence of the Kamihaga family, which established the city's wax industry, is now a well-maintained museum. Exhibits here explain the rise and fall of this once-thriving industry. Comprehensive English signage and hands-on exhibits teach you more than you thought there was to know about the changing fortunes of this wax town. ✉ *2696 Uchiko, Uchiko* ☎ *0893/44–2771* 🎟 *¥500.*

**Uchiko-za Kabuki Theater** (内子座)
**HISTORIC SIGHT** | This wooden theater opened its doors in 1916, when the city was flush with cash. It has been putting on traditional Kabuki and Bunraku performances ever since. When no performances are scheduled, you can view the interior's revolving stage and trapdoors. ✉ *2102 Uchiko, Uchiko* ☎ *0893/44–2840* 🎟 *¥400.*

**Uchiko Townhouse Museum** (町家資料館; *Machiya Shiryokan*)
**HISTORIC HOME** | Just northeast of Omori's Wax Workshop, this museum is an 18th-century town house that once belonged to a wealthy family and is now open to the public. ✉ *3023 Uchiko, Uchiko* ☎ *0893/44–5212* 🎟 *Free.*

## 🛏 Hotels

**Ori** (織)
**$$$$** | **B&B/INN** | A charming old townhouse in the heart of Uchiko, defined by its dark wooden beams and tatami mat floors, Ori is only available to one group of up to eight people per night in three rooms, but still staffed with several locals who will happily help guests immerse themselves into the community. **Pros:** a charming old building with modern touches; friendly staff who will help you make the best of your time in Uchiko; extremely private. **Cons:** no dinner options; pricey unless traveling in a large group; not much nightlife nearby. [$] *Rooms from: ¥55,000* ✉ *3013 Uchiko, Uchiko* 🌐 *comminca-stays.com/accommodation/ori* 🛏 *1 house* 🍴 *Free Breakfast* ☞ *¥50,000 base rate, plus ¥2,500 per person.*

## 🛍 Shopping

**Omori's Wax Workshop** (大森和蠟燭屋; *Omori Wa Rosokuya*)
**CRAFTS** | The highlight of Yokaichi Street is this shop where an elderly gentleman and his sons make distinctive candles by hand. The smaller ones are inexpensive, but the larger are surprisingly costly. This is the largest candle shop in the shopping arcade. ✉ *2214 Uchiko, Uchiko* ☎ *0893/43–0385* 🌐 *omoriwarosoku.jp.*

# Uwajima (宇和島市)

*90 km (56 miles) south of Matsuyama, 130 km (80 miles) west of Kochi.*

A quiet fishing town south of Matsuyama on the Uwa Sea, Uwajima has two unusual claims to fame, its sumo-style bullfights and a sex museum that's part of a Shinto fertility shrine. The town is also the site of one of the 12 original castles remaining in Japan, the modest Uwajima-jo. There are accommodations here, but the best of Uwajima can be done easily in a day trip from Matsuyama or Uchiko, so there seems little reason to spend more time here.

### GETTING HERE AND AROUND

The best way to get around Uwajima is by bicycle; you can rent bikes from several places around the station, including Eki Rent-a-Car and Inugai, from ¥100 per hour, depending on the type of bike.

### VISITOR INFORMATION

There's a tourist information booth inside the train station, but the main Uwajima Tourist Information office is in the ferry terminal about a 10-minute walk west.

**CONTACT Uwajima Tourist Information.** ✉ *1–318–16 Benten-cho, Uwajima* ☎ *089/522–3934* 🌐 *uwajima-tourism.org.*

## 👁 Sights

**Taga Shrine** (多賀神社; *Taga Jinja*)
**RELIGIOUS BUILDING** | Visitors flock to this Shinto fertility shrine not far from the train station, though not necessarily to pray: Uwajima's infamous sex museum is located here. You can tell when you've arrived—no, that sculpture is not a giant squid. Just beyond it is the museum, called Deko Boko Jindou (literally, a shrine honoring "things that poke out, things that go in"). The three-floor collection is astonishing. It's best to leave the kids at the castle for this one, as they won't be admitted. ⊠ *1340 Fujie, Uwajima* ☎ *089/522–3444* 🎫 *¥800.*

**Uwajima Castle** (宇和島城; *Uwajima-jo*)
**CASTLE/PALACE** | Built at the end of the 16th century, Uwajima-jo is one of the 12 castles remaining intact from the Edo era. Compared to Shikoku's Matsuyama Castle, the three-story main keep here is a very modest affair, but still worth a look for the samurai exhibits on display and the top-floor view back over Uwajima. ⊠ *1 Marunouchi, Uwajima* ☎ *0895/22–2832* ⊕ *www.city.uwajima.ehime.jp/site/uwajima-jo* 🎫 *¥200.*

# Shimanami Kaido (しまなみ街道)

*45 km (28 miles) north of Matsuyama.*

Beginning in Imabari, this 70-km (44-mile) road-and-bridge route connects Imabari and Onomichi and offers some of Japan's most pleasant cycling.

## GETTING HERE AND AROUND
Rental bikes, regular, tandem, and electric, are available from Sunrise Itoyama, also a budget lodging that's a good place to stop for the night if you've followed the route from Onomichi to Imabari.

**CONTACT Sunrise Itoyama Rental Bike Terminal.** ⊠ *2–8–1 Sunaba-cho,*

## The Demon Bull

So-called demon bulls (*ushi-oni*) are common in Shikoku and Kansai folklore. Fearsome creatures with the bodies of bulls and the heads of demons, they will set a curse on the family of anyone who injures or angers them. Uwajima residents in particular have been traditionally wary of demon bulls and, just in case, still hold the *Warei Tasai Uwajima Ushi-oni* festival to pacify them. The event, from July 22 to 24 every year, includes fireworks, parades, concerts, and bullfighting.

*Imabari* ☎ *089/841–3196* ⊕ *www.sunrise-itoyama.jp.*

## VISITOR INFORMATION
The shop employees in Imabari don't speak much English, so if you have communication problems go through the ICIEA, Imabari's helpful international-exchange association.

**CONTACT Imabari City International Exchange Association.** (*ICIEA*) ⊠ *Imabari City Hall, 2–5–1 Minamidaimon-cho, Imabari* ☎ *089/834–5763* ⊕ *iciea.jp/e_index.html.*

## 👁 Sights

**Hakata Salt Company Omishima Factory** (伯方塩 大三島工場; *Hakata Shio Omishima Kojo*)
**FACTORY** | For centuries Hakata Island has been famous for its high-quality salt, and the Hakata Salt Company offers daily, free, self-guided tours of its factory on Omishima Island that take about 30 minutes to complete, though they were suspended during the pandemic and expected to resume sometime in 2022. As you stroll along a marked visitor's path

The Tatara Ohashi Bridge is part of the Shimanami Kaido, a road-and-bridge network that connects Shikoku with western Honshu.

through the factory, you'll see workers turn seawater into table salt, package it, and ship it all over Japan. There's also plenty of information, though most only in Japanese, about the history of salt. If the factory touring has you craving something salty, try the salt ice cream sold on-site. If that's not enough, you can also take a dip in the salt baths at the Mare Grassia bath complex next door. ✉ 32 Utena, Omishima ☎ 0897/82–0660 ⊕ www.hakatanoshio.co.jp/factory/index. php ☞ Check website to see if tours have resumed post-pandemic.

### Mare Grassia Omishima Baths
(マーレグラッシア大三島)

**HOT SPRING** | This public bath complex is like your average friendly Japanese town bathhouse, except for one thing: the extremely salty water. One or two of the baths in the multi-bath bathing area are salted with Hakata salt from the factory next door. Islanders believe salt baths help draw out impurities and beautify your skin, but if self-pickling is not your thing you can always take a dip in the non-saltwater indoor or outdoor baths. ✉ 5902 Miyaura, Omishima ☎ 0897/82–0100 ☞ ¥510 ⊙ Closed Wed.

### Oyamazumi Shrine
(大山祇神社; Oyamazumi Jinja)

**RELIGIOUS BUILDING** | Omishima, three islands over from Imabari, is home to this expansive shrine. Founded in the 6th century, it honors the Shinto god of mountains, sea, and war. In the 8th century, victorious warriors started leaving their weaponry here after battle as thanks for divine favor. The museum on the shrine's grounds holds more than two-thirds of the nation's designated National Treasures in swords, spears, breastplates, and helmets. ✉ 3327 Miyaura, Omishima ☎ 0897/82–0032 ☞ ¥1,000.

### ★ Shimanami Kaido Cycling Route
(しまなみ海道)

**SCENIC DRIVE | FAMILY** | By far the most scenic way to travel between Shikoku and western Honshu is the Shimanami Kaido, a 70-km (44-mile) expressway built with bicyclists in mind. The route, a series of roads and six long bridges, connects Imabari, just north of Matsuyama, with Onomichi, just east of Hiroshima, by way of islands in the Seto Inland Sea. Most of the islands were accessible only by ferry until the expressway was completed in 1999. By the early 2000s, the Shimanami Kaido was already one of western Japan's most popular cycling routes.

A bicycle trip across this road-and-bridge network takes in fishing villages, tangerine orchards, pearl farms, seaweed pastures, and long stretches of sparkling sea. A separate cycling track runs along each bridge, so you don't have to deal with car traffic for most of the ride. Cycling paths are clearly marked on the islands, and maps are readily available. The cycling isn't strenuous, so don't get discouraged by that first big corkscrew pathway up from Imabari to the Kurushima Ohashi Bridge. After that it's clear sailing.

Biking to Onomichi takes about six to eight hours. If you decide you've had enough cycling along the way, you can leave your rental bike at any of 15 stations and complete your journey by ferry or bus. The well-informed staff members at the stations have all the schedules. Your hotel can even send your luggage ahead. The best starting point for planning a ride is the Shimanami Japan tourism website, which has a downloadable cycling guide in English. 🌐 *shimanami-cycle.or.jp/cycling/en.html.*

## 🛏 Hotels

**Azumi Setoda**

$$$$ | **HOTEL** | In a small port town on Ikuchi Island, where the Shimanami Kaido enters the outskirts of Onomichi, this luxury ryokan has repurposed a 140-year-old merchant's estate to create an inviting spot to end your bike tour. **Pros:** traditional, peaceful setting; immersive activities available; superb service. **Cons:** not much in the area; need to backtrack a little if staying after finishing the Shimanami Kaido cycling route; central Onomichi has far cheaper options. [$] *Rooms from: ¥80,000* ✉ *269 Setodacho, Onomichi* ☎ *0845/23–7911* 🌐 *azumi.co/setoda/en* 🛏 *22 rooms* 🍴 *All-Inclusive.*

# Chapter 12

# KYUSHU

12

Updated by
Chris Willson

 Sights
★★★☆☆

 Restaurants
★★★★☆

 Hotels
★★★★☆

 Shopping
★★★☆☆

 Nightlife
★★★☆☆

# WELCOME TO KYUSHU

## TOP REASONS TO GO

★ **Diverse cities:** Fukuoka has vibrant nightlife, Nagasaki exudes old-world charm, Kumamoto's castle dominates the city, and Kagoshima's palm trees calm travelers.

★ **Gastronomy:** Find the sought-after Hakata ramen in Fukuoka. Nagasaki has *champon* (seafood and vegetable noodle soup), and Kagoshima has *kurobuta tonkatsu* (breaded pork cutlet).

★ **Volcanoes and hot springs:** Mt. Aso is notoriously active, as is the volcanic island Sakurajima, across the bay from Kagoshima City. Hot springs are found throughout Kyushu.

★ **Getting into the wild:** With its lava flows, outlying islands, rugged mountains, and national parks, Kyushu is an adventurer's dream. Most trails require only good shoes, water, and some time.

★ **Remote access:** Bullet trains now extend all the way to Kagoshima, and in another hour, you can be on the hot sand of Ibusuki's beaches.

Kyushu lies west and south of Honshu, with Fukuoka in the north, Nagasaki on the west coast, and the central city of Kumamoto. Mt. Aso, Takachiho, and Kagoshima make good side trips.

**1 Fukuoka.** Dining, shopping, and nightlife.

**2 Nagasaki.** You'll see the spirit of entrepreneurship that helped the city revive after World War II.

**3 Kumamoto.** A fantastic 17th-century castle and the idyllic Suizenji Jojuen Garden.

**4 Mt. Aso.** Aso National Park with its active volcanoes inside the world's largest caldera.

**5 Kurokawa Onsen.** Small riverside town focused exclusively on onsen bathing.

**6 Yufuin.** Hot spring resort beneath Mt. Yufu.

**7 Takachiho.** An iconic gorge, exceptional ryokan, and traditional kagura performances.

**8 Kirishima-Kinkowan National Park.** Volcanoes, lakes, shrines, and excellent onsen.

**9 Kagoshima.** Hot sand baths and beaches at the southern reaches of the prefecture.

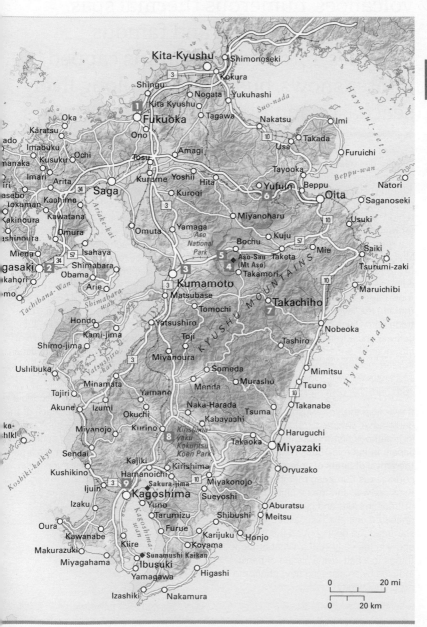

Kyushu's landscape couldn't be more varied, with active yet accessible volcanoes, numerous thermal spas, endless fields of rice and famous potatoes, forested mountains capped by winter snows, busy harbors along lively seacoasts, and pleasant seaside retreats.

Kyushu has been inhabited and favored for human settlement for more than 10,000 years, and ruins and artifacts thousands of years old suggest that the region was the most important gateway for human contact between Japan and the rest of Asia. The most rapid anthropological changes occurred from about 300 BC to AD 300, when rice became widely cultivated and complex pottery and tools began to appear, thus conveniently framing the Yayoi period. Continuous trade with China brought prosperity and culture, and advanced ceramics were introduced—and then produced—by Korean masters who were employed and enslaved by the local fiefdoms of the 16th and 17th centuries.

It was also through Kyushu that Western knowledge, weapons, religion, and cooking methods first made their way into Japan. In the mid-1500s Nagasaki saw the arrival of fleets of enterprising and courageous European merchants and missionaries, and the resulting frenzy of trade in ideas and goods continued unabated until the Tokugawa Shogunate slammed the door shut on the whole show in the early 1600s. What brought things to a halt was a plague of panic induced by an alarming new phenomenon: Christianity.

The Portuguese and other Catholics not afraid to preach to the natives were expelled and permanently barred. The Dutch, however, were considered more money-minded, and therefore less threatening, and were permitted to stay—under scrutiny and isolation. They were housed within the enclave of Dejima, a man-made island in Nagasaki Harbor, where they were encouraged to keep bringing in coveted goods but were constantly guarded and watched. For the next 200 years, this profitable little arrangement would be the only form of contact the West would have with Japan until the arrival of Perry's forceful "Black Ship."

Today Kyushu is a fascinating mix of old and new, nature and culture. Much of the remote and rugged interior—such as that surrounding Mt. Aso's fuming cone—is still an isolated wilderness, yet the amenities of modern life are well supplied in cities and coastal resorts.

# Planning

## Getting Here and Around

For most major destinations in Kyushu, access is easiest by train. Express trains run between Fukuoka and Nagasaki, while bullet trains connect Fukuoka with Kumamoto and Kagoshima. From Kumamoto, renting a car is the best way to explore the Mt. Aso region, Kurokawa, Yufuin, Takachiho, and the Kirishima-Kinkowan National Park. Frequent and inexpensive ferries ply the bays and ports, linking Kyushu with offshore islands. During holiday seasons you'll want to reserve seats on express trains and book rental vehicles in advance.

### AIR

Air routes link Kyushu's major cities with Tokyo and Osaka. Fukuoka, Nagasaki, and Kagoshima have the most frequent and useful daily connections and offer some international flights. When using domestic carriers like ANA you need not enter and return from the same city: it's easy to fly into Fukuoka and out of Kagoshima, for example.

**CONTACTS All Nippon Airways.** (*ANA*) ☏ *03/6741–6685* ⊕ *www.ana.co.jp.* **Japan Airlines.** ☏ *0570/025–121* ⊕ *www.jal. co.jp/en.* **Skymark Airlines.** ☏ *0570/039- 283* ⊕ *www.skymark.co.jp/en.*

### BUS

Buses make useful connections around Kyushu, and if you don't have a JR Rail Pass they are often much cheaper than the trains. The bus between Nagasaki and Kumamoto is half the price and takes about the same time; plus you don't have to make any changes or wait for connections as you do with trains. A highway bus makes a trip between Kumamoto to Yufuin, either direct or with a stopover at the Mt. Aso crater. The Kyushu bus network portal website is the best way to check on bus times and prices and to make reservations.

**CONTACTS Kyushu Express Bus.** ⊕ *kyush- ubusbooking.com.* **Kyushu Bus Network Portal.** ⊕ *atbus-de.com.*

### CAR

Renting a car is a good idea in Kyushu if you have lots of time and you will be exploring the more out-of-the-way places such as Mt. Aso, Kirishima-Kinkowan National Park, or Takachiho. All the major rental outfits have offices in the big cities near the JR stations or airports.

### TRAIN

High-speed bullet trains link Fukuoka with Kagoshima. Express trains making the popular runs between Fukuoka and Nagasaki or Fukuoka and Yufuin (via Oita) are jammed on weekends and holidays, so book at least a day ahead.

## Hotels

You can find the usual American hotel chains, with all the familiar extras, in places like Fukuoka and Nagasaki. The rural areas surrounding Aso and Kagoshima have snug little inns with views of the surrounding peaks. In Yufuin nearly all hotels and ryokan (guesthouses) offer soothing thermal mineral water baths. Unless otherwise noted, all hotel rooms have private baths. Reservations are essential during the long national holidays, particularly Golden Week (from late April to early May), Obon (mid-August), and New Year's (the first week of January) when Japanese tourists flock to the island.

## Planning Your Time

Fukuoka is a great base for exploring the northern part of Kyushu. Spend a day orienting yourself and seeing Fukuoka's sights, then take day trips to Nagasaki, Kumamoto, and Yufuin. If you have more time, it's worth getting off the beaten track to see the volcano Mt. Aso, and on to Takachiho. After a day in Kagoshima, you could spend a couple of days exploring the beautiful mountainous area of Kirishima, or jump on a ferry to the island of Yakushima.

# Restaurants

Fresh fish is served everywhere on Kyushu, and there is a lot of meat as well. Local specialties abound and are often reasonably priced. In the bigger cities like Fukuoka, Nagasaki, Kumamoto, and Kagoshima—and along the stylish new streets of Yufuin—you'll find plenty of Western-style restaurants.

## RESTAURANT AND HOTEL PRICES

Restaurant prices are the average cost of a main course at dinner or, if dinner is not served, at lunch. Hotel prices are the lowest cost of a standard double room in high season. Restaurant and hotel reviews have been shortened. For full information, visit Fodors.com.

| What It Costs in Yen | | | |
|---|---|---|---|
| $ | $$ | $$$ | $$$$ |
| **RESTAURANTS** | | | |
| under ¥1,500 | ¥1,500– ¥3,000 | ¥3,001– ¥5,000 | over ¥5,000 |
| **HOTELS** | | | |
| under ¥12,000 | ¥12,000– ¥18,000 | ¥18,001– ¥22,000 | over ¥22,000 |

# Visitor Information

Every major city has tourist information offices near shopping, sightseeing, and eating areas, and one or more near the high-speed train exit of each JR train station. An English speaker is usually on duty during peak travel hours. The bigger hotels generally have front-desk employees who speak and understand some English; they are good sources for information on local sights and restaurants.

# When to Go

In early spring it's pleasantly warm, and the greenery is at its best. May and June usher in heavy rains, and July and August are intensely muggy. September is summery, but watch for typhoons, which can blow in at any time until late October. Autumn colors appear in late October or early November, particularly in the north. In January and February the mountains of central Kyushu receive a little snowfall, and that's when the Siberian cranes show up for the gentle winter the region enjoys.

# Fukuoka (福岡)

*1,175 km (730 miles) west of Tokyo, 622 km (386 miles) west of Shin-Osaka.*

Fukuoka is an excellent base to begin exploring Kyushu. To get a sense of the city, walk along the meandering Naka-gawa River. The stunning Canal City shopping complex, a 15-minute walk west of Hakata Station, is full of great people-watching, shops, and dining. You'll find a bit of everything, from global coffee and fast-food outlets to famous local ramen.

For night owls, there's plenty happening in the west-central downtown alleys in an area known as Tenjin at truly astounding hours. Friday nights only begin at midnight, usually with a huge and hearty bowl of *tonkotsu* (pork-bone soup) ramen—often referred to as "Hakata ramen"—a rich, tasty staple that locals seem to depend on for their legendary all-night stamina.

The Naka-gawa River divides the city. Everything west of the river is known as Fukuoka, while everything east—including the train station—is referred to as Hakata, so trains might say to or from Hakata rather than Fukuoka. But don't be confused: Hakata is just a *ku,* or district, of the whole place, which is still Fukuoka.

## GETTING HERE AND AROUND

Fukuoka Airport is Kyushu's main airport. It's just two stops away—only six minutes—from Fukuoka's Hakata train station on the Kuko subway line. All Nippon Airways (ANA), Japan Airlines (JAL), and Skymark Airlines (SKY), fly from Tokyo's Haneda Airport. ANA, Jetstar and Peach also fly from Tokyo's Narita Airport. Domestic flights also arrive from Sapporo, Nagoya, Osaka, Naha, and Ishigaki.

Expressway buses makes the 2½-hour trip between Fukuoka and Nagasaki. Buses also make the four-hour trip between Fukuoka and Kagoshima. JR Shinkansen trains travel from Tokyo (six hours) via Osaka and Hiroshima to Fukuoka's Hakata Station. The unreserved regular fare is ¥22,220 and trains depart every 30 minutes. Regular JR Express trains also ply this route, but are much slower.

After World War II Fukuoka was rebuilt with wide, tree-lined avenues arranged on an easy-to-navigate Western-style grid. The subway system connects the downtown attractions with a convenient extension to the international airport. The two major transportation hubs are Hakata Station and Tenjin Station. Tenjin, in the heart of downtown Fukuoka, is the terminal for both subway lines. The Kuko Line runs to Hakata Station and on to Fukuoka Airport, and the Hakozaki Line runs out toward the bay. From Fukuoka Airport to Hakata Station, the fare is ¥260. A One-Day Pass for the subway costs ¥640.

Most city buses leave from **Hakata Bus Terminal** across the street from Hakata Station, and from Tenjin Bus Center. A Downtown Fukuoka One-Day Pass costs ¥1000.

**AIRPORT INFORMATION Fukuoka Airport.**
☎ *092/621–6059 domestic, 092/621–0303 international* ⊕ *www.fukuoka-airport.jp/en.*

**BUS CONTACT Nishitetsu Bus Reservations Call Center.** ☎ *092/734–2727* ⊕ *www.atbus-de.com.*

**BUS DEPOTS Hakata Bus Terminal.**
✉ *Hakata-eki Chuo-gai, Fukuoka* ⊕ *www.h-bt.jp/en.* **Tenjin Bus Center.** ✉ *2–1–1 Tenjin, Fukuoka* ☎ *0570/00–1010 Nishitetsu Customer Service* ⊕ *www.nishitetsu.jp/en.*

## VISITOR INFORMATION

The staff members of the Fukuoka City Tourist Information Center dispense up-to-date information about hotels, sights, restaurants, and rental cars, and have pamphlets about area attractions and businesses. Sign-language assistance is also provided.

**CONTACT Fukuoka City Tourist Information Center.** ✉ *Hakata Station, 1–1 Hakataeki-Chuo-gai, Fukuoka* ☎ *092/431–3003* ⊕ *yokanavi.com/on.*

 **Sights**

**Ohori Park** (大濠公園; *Ohori Koen*)
**CITY PARK | FAMILY |** The lake in this park was once part of an impressive moat surrounding Fukuoka's castle. A leisurely 2-km (1-mile) path follows its perimeter. In early April the pink-and-white flowers of the park's 2,600 cherry trees present a dazzling display. Within the park is the Fukuoka City Art Museum (⊕ *www.fukuoka-art-museum.jp*), which houses a few notable works by Dalí, Miró, Chagall, and Warhol. It reopened after a major renewal in March 2019. Across from it is a traditional Japanese garden. Stop for a quick bite or a luxurious meal at Boathouse Ohori Park on the edge of the lake. ✉ *1–6 Ohorikoen, Chuo* ⊹ *10 min subway ride from Hakata Station to Ohori Park Station* ☎ *092/741–8377 Japanese Garden* ⊕ *www.ohoriteien.jp* ⊠ *Park free, museum ¥200, garden ¥250.*

**Shofukuji Temple** (聖福寺)
**TEMPLE |** The monk Eisai (1141–1215) returned from a long stint in China to introduce Zen Buddhism to Japan and planted the first tea-bush seeds. Nowadays most tea is grown in other regions such as Shizuoka, but you can still buy

the green tea from this region, with its legendary hue and flavor, in stores as far away as Tokyo. Eisai also established Shofukuji Temple, Japan's first Zen temple, which the inscription on the main gate by Emperor Gotoba commemorates. In Zen tradition, the grounds and structure reflect the calm, austere nature of this deeply meditative philosophy. The bronze bell in the belfry was designated an Important Cultural Property. ✉ *6–1 Gokusho-machi, Hakata-ekimae* ✥ *15-min walk northwest from Hakata Station, or 5-min walk north of Gion Station* ☎ *092/291–0775* 🎫 *Free.*

## 🍴 Restaurants

**Ichi-ran** (一蘭)
**$ | JAPANESE** | Folks in Fukuoka wait in long lines for these rectangular black boxes of extra-thin noodles swimming in pork-bone broth and topped with tasty *char-shu* (slices of roasted pork), *negi* (green onions), and sprinkles of *togarashi* (red pepper). Fill out an order form (available in English) to indicate exactly how you like it, then buy a ticket from the machine outside the door and place your ticket and order form on the counter. **Known for:** within Canal City; chewy noodles; customizable dishes. [$] *Average main: ¥930* ✉ *Canal City Hakata, 1–2–22 Sumiyoshi, 1st fl., Hakata-ekimae* ☎ *092/263–2201* 🌐 *www.ichiran.co.jp/english* 💳 *No credit cards.*

**Sonu Sonu Vegan Cafe & Restaurant** (ソヌソヌ)
**$ | VEGETARIAN** | Keema curry, pizzas, burgers, and burrito bowls are staples at this trendy vegan café in Tenjin. Also a great place to get coffee and a slice of cake when you're taking a break from the shops of west Fukuoka. **Known for:** fantastic vegan burgers; modern minimalist design of café; friendly bilingual staff. [$] *Average main: ¥1,200* ✉ *3–6–29 1F Tenjin, Chuo* ☎ *070/2299–7338.*

## 🛏 Hotels

**Canal City Fukuoka Washington Hotel** (キャナルシティ・福岡ワシントンホテル)
**$$$$ | HOTEL** | Much classier than other members of this hotel chain, the Washington has guest rooms with views of the city or the sci-fi half-dome of Canal City. **Pros:** great value; comfortable rooms; prime window-shopping location. **Cons:** street noise; bathroom fittings look timeworn; staff speak limited English. [$] *Rooms from: ¥23,120* ✉ *1–2–20 Sumiyoshi, Hakata-ekimae* ☎ *092/282–8800, 092/282–0757* 🌐 *www.washington-hotels.jp/fukuoka* 🛏 *423 rooms* 🍴 *No Meals.*

**Grand Hyatt Fukuoka** (グランド・ハイアット・福岡)
**$$$$ | HOTEL** | Far and away the best hotel in town, the sophisticated Grand Hyatt overlooks the Canal City shopping and entertainment complex. **Pros:** convenient access to shopping and the Naka River; exemplary service; excellent restaurants and bars. **Cons:** could use better soundproofing; location within a mall may not suit everyone; extra charges for spa and pool unless you're a suite guest. [$] *Rooms from: ¥48,400* ✉ *1–2–82 Sumiyoshi, Canal City, Fukuoka* ☎ *092/282–1234* 🌐 *www.hyatt.com* 🛏 *372 rooms* 🍴 *No Meals.*

**Hakata Excel Hotel Tokyu** (博多エクセルホテル東急)
**$$ | HOTEL** | Overlooking the Naka River, this upscale Western-style hotel is a short walk from Canal City. **Pros:** views of the Naka River; wide selection of rooms; speedy Wi-Fi. **Cons:** noise from the street below; cheaper rooms can be small; seedy "entertainment district" close by. [$] *Rooms from: ¥14,400* ✉ *4–6–7 Nakasu, Fukuoka* ☎ *092/262–0109* 🌐 *www.tokyuhotelsjapan.com/global/hakata-e* 🛏 *308 rooms* 🍴 *No Meals.*

**Toyoko Inn Hakata Nishi-nakasu**
(東横イン博多西中洲)

**$ | HOTEL |** There are more than 250 Toyoko Inn business hotels scattered around Japan, and this branch offers budget-minded travelers cramped but clean accommodations, reasonable rates, and a central location near Canal City. **Pros:** near the Naka River; free breakfast; easy online booking. **Cons:** 4 pm check-in; some noise from the busy road; rooms are cramped and bland. $ *Rooms from: ¥10,807* ⊠ *1–16 Nishinakasu, Chuo* ☎ *092/739–1045, 092/739–1046* ⊕ *www. toyoko-inn.com/e_hotel/00044/index.html* ➯ *260 rooms* ⦿ *Free Breakfast.*

## ⛾ Nightlife

Fukuoka seems forever in the throes of an ongoing party—perhaps in a heroic endeavor to put off the inevitable hangover—but the surest places for memorable nightlife action are the Nakasu and Tenjin areas, which run along the Naka River. Nakasu is on the east side of the river; Tenjin is on the west. There are plenty of bars and restaurants, but the locals recommend that you, grab some ramen, yakitori, or tempura from one of the *yatai* street vendors that set up their tiny riverside restaurants close to sunset and stay open until around 2 am. The red-light district of Nakasu, a block in from the river, has many snack bars and soaplands and is best avoided.

## 🛍 Shopping

Fukuoka is known for two traditional folk crafts: Hakata *ningyo* (dolls) and Hakata *obi* (kimono sashes). Made of fired clay, hand-painted with bright colors and distinctive expressions, Hakata ningyo represent children, samurais, and geisha. The obi are made of a local silk that has a slightly coarse texture; bags and purses made of this silk make excellent souvenirs.

Kyushu has a rich ceramics tradition. The shops and kilns of Arita, Karatsu, and Imari and other towns of Saga Prefecture, in particular, continue to produce fine pottery, especially a delicate-looking but surprisingly tough type of porcelain. The earthenware of Karatsu, particularly the fine tea ceremony wares, are much admired by ceramics collectors within and outside Japan.

**Canal City Hakata** (キャナルシティ博多)

**MALL | FAMILY |** Canal City is the modern shopping and entertainment hub for Fukuoka. Located next to the Nakasu River, the group of curvy bright red buildings surround a central courtyard where there is an hourly fountain show. The mall is filled with Japanese and international brands, the restaurant selection diverse, and there's a cinema complex with IMAX screens on the top floors. It is flanked on the river side by the Grand Hyatt Fukuoka hotel, and on the Hakata side by the Canal City Fukuoka Washington Hotel. It's a 15-minute walk from Hakata Station or Tenjin Station, or a seven-minute walk from the Gion subway station. ⊠ *1–2, Sumiyoshi, Fukuoka* ☎ *92/282–2525* ⊕ *canalcity.co.jp/english.*

**Iwataya** (岩田屋)

**DEPARTMENT STORE |** The fifth floor of the new section of this department store carries the city's most complete selection of local merchandise, including Hakata dolls, silk, and ceramics. Also check out the impressive selection of kimono, obi, and the more inexpensive summer yukata. Iwataya fills two buildings on either side of the street with an above-ground walkway connecting the two sections. If you can't find what you need here, there are several more high-end department stores nearby including Mitsukoshi, Daimaru, Parco, and Vioro. ⊠ *2–5–35 Tenjin, Fukuoka* ⊹ *Take Tenjin subway station Exit W-5 and walk two blocks* ☎ *092/721–1111* ⊕ *www.i.iwataya-mitsukoshi.co.jp.*

**12**

**Kyushu FUKUOKA** (福岡)

# Nagasaki (長崎)

*154 km (96 miles) southwest of Fukuoka (Hakata Station).*

Blessed with a breathtaking location, Nagasaki is strung together on a long series of hillocks in a scenic valley that follows the arms of the Urakami River down into a gentle harbor. Unlike Hiroshima, the city was left with no suitably intact reminders of the atomic bombing, and perhaps for this reason, there were apparently no compunctions about rebuilding the town right up to the edge of a tiny ground-zero circle with a stark steel monument at its center. Although almost all buildings are relatively new, Nagasaki's international history shows through, from lively and compact Chinatown to the European-style mansions and Catholic churches on the hillsides.

The city isn't small, but it occupies a long winding valley, so you can experience it in manageable increments. Similarities with San Francisco are frequently noted. The comparison is not far off, though the posters advertising whale-bacon and manga remind you of where you are. Most of the interesting sights, restaurants, and shopping areas are south of Nagasaki Station, but the Peace Park and the Atomic Bomb Museum are to the north, 10 to 15 minutes by streetcar or taxi.

## GETTING HERE AND AROUND

The trip from Nagasaki Airport to Nagasaki City takes approximately 45 minutes by bus or car. A regular shuttle bus travels between Nagasaki Airport and Nagasaki Station and costs ¥1,000. All Nippon Airways and Japan Airlines fly daily from Haneda Airport in Tokyo to Nagasaki Airport (1¾ hours). There are also direct flights to Nagasaki from Okinawa, Nagoya, Kobe, and Osaka.

Highway buses run from Fukuoka's Tenjin Bus Center, Hakata Bus Terminal, and Fukuoka Airport to Nagasaki Bus Terminal; the trip takes 2 hours, 30 minutes and costs ¥2,620. Highway buses can get you to Unzen, a string of hot springs on the Shimabara Peninsula, in 1 hour, 40 minutes (¥1,850), and direct to Kumamoto in 3 hours for ¥3,700.

From Fukuoka's Hakata Station, the JR Kamome Express train costs ¥4,270 and takes around two hours.

Nagasaki is small enough to cover on foot, and the streetcar system is the most convenient mode of transportation. Stops are posted in English, and lines extend to every attraction in town. You can purchase a one-day streetcar pass (¥600) at tourist offices and major hotels. If you don't have a pass, pay ¥140 as you get off the streetcar. If you wish to transfer from one streetcar to another at the Shinchi Chinatown stop or the Civic Hall stop, get a *norikae kippu* (transfer ticket) from the driver. Local buses are not as convenient, and the routes, timetables, and fares are complicated.

One-hour cruises of Nagasaki Harbor depart from Nagasaki-ko (Nagasaki Port) at noon and 4 pm; the cost is ¥2,000.

**AIRPORT INFORMATION Nagasaki Airport.** ✉ *Mishima-machi, Omura* ☎ *095/752–5555* ⊕ *nagasaki-airport.jp/en.*

**BUS DEPOT Nagasaki Ken-ei Bus Terminal.** ✉ *3–1 Daikoku-machi, Nagasaki* ☎ *095/826–6221* ⊕ *keneibus.jp.*

**TRAIN STATION Nagasaki Train Station.** ✉ *1–60 Onoue-machi, Nagasaki* ☎ *095/822–0063* ⊕ *www.jrkyushu.co.jp.*

## TOURS

### Nagasaki Port Pleasure Cruises

**BOAT TOURS** | Dating back to when it brought in wealth and culture from across the seas, Nagasaki's greatest asset has always been its port. A short pleasure cruise around the harbor is a relaxing way to see the heart and soul of the city. ✉ *Ferry Terminal, Nagasaki* ☎ *095/824–0088* 🎫 *From ¥2,000.*

Glover Garden has a large koi pond.

## VISITOR INFORMATION
**CONTACT Nagasaki Tourist Information Center.** ✉ *Nagasaki Train Station, 1–1 Onoue-machi, Nagasaki* ☎ *095/823–3631.*

##  Sights

**Confucius Shrine and Museum** (孔子廟; *Koshi-byo*)

**HISTORY MUSEUM** | This bright-red shrine was built in 1893 by the Chinese residents of Nagasaki. The small Historical Museum of China displays artifacts on loan from Beijing's Palace Museum of Historical Treasures and National Museum of Chinese History. ✉ *10–36 Oura-machi, Nagasaki* ✛ *Take streetcar to Ishi-bashi stop and follow signs leading to shrine* ☎ *095/824–4022* 🎫 *¥660.*

**Dejima** (出島)

**HISTORIC DISTRICT** | When the government deported foreigners from Japan in the mid-17th century, Dutch traders were the only Westerners allowed to remain—but they were relegated to, and confined on, this artificial island in Nagasaki Harbor.

Here you can see a 450-year-old mix of Dutch housing styles that is popular among Japanese tourists. ✉ *6–3 Dejima-machi, Nagasaki* ✛ *Take Tram 1 to the Dejima stop* ☎ *095/821–7200* ⊕ *nagasakidejima.jp/english* 🎫 *¥520.*

**Dutch Slope** (オランダ坂; *Oranda-saka*)

**STREET** | This cobblestone incline is a good place to wander on the way to Chinatown and Glover Garden. Dutch residents built the wooden houses here in the late 19th century. Many become shops and tearooms in summer. To get here, follow the street on the southeastern side of the Confucius Shrine. ✉ *2 Higashiyamatemachi, Nagasaki.*

★ **Glover Garden** (グラバー園; *Guraba-en*)

**MUSEUM VILLAGE** | This garden contains an impressive assortment of 19th-century Western houses. Greco-Roman porticoes and arches, wooden verandas, and other random elements of European architecture adorn the structures, which are often crowned with Japanese-style roofs. The main attraction is the 1863 mansion of Thomas Glover, a prominent

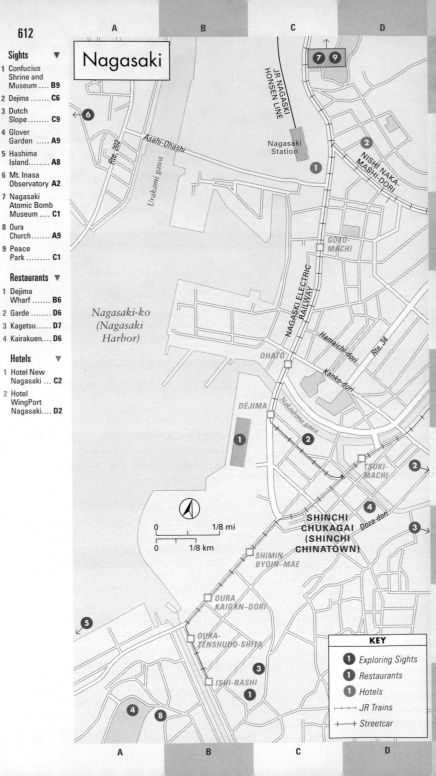

## Sights ▼

1 Confucius Shrine and Museum .... **B9**
2 Dejima ....... **C6**
3 Dutch Slope ........ **C9**
4 Glover Garden ..... **A9**
5 Hashima Island........ **A8**
6 Mt. Inasa Observatory **A2**
7 Nagasaki Atomic Bomb Museum .... **C1**
8 Oura Church ....... **A9**
9 Peace Park ......... **C1**

## Restaurants ▼

1 Dejima Wharf ....... **B6**
2 Garde ........ **D6**
3 Kagetsu ...... **D7**
4 Kairakuen.... **D6**

## Hotels ▼

1 Hotel New Nagasaki ... **C2**
2 Hotel WingPort Nagasaki.... **D2**

Nagasaki

JR NAGASAKI HONSEN LINE

Nagasaki Station

NISHI NAKA-MASHI-DORI

Rte. 202

Asahi-Ohashi

Urakami gawa

GOTO-MACHI

NAGASAKI ELECTRIC RAILWAY

Nagasaki-ko
(Nagasaki Harbor)

Hamaichi-dori

Rte. 34

OHATO

Kanko-dori

DEJIMA

Nakashima gawa

TSUKI-MACHI

SHINCHI CHUKAGAI (SHINCHI CHINATOWN)

Doza-dori

SHIMIN BYOIN-MAE

OURA KAIGAN-DORI

OURA-TENSHUDO-SHITA

ISHI-BASHI

0    1/8 mi
0    1/8 km

### KEY

1 Exploring Sights
1 Restaurants
1 Hotels
+—+ JR Trains
+—+ Streetcar

# August 9, 1945

On August 9, 1945, three days after the blast at Hiroshima, Nagasaki fell victim to a second atomic bomb because of bad weather. The plane, named Bockscar, was supposed to drop the Fat Man, a new and experimental plutonium bomb, on the war industry complexes in Kokura. A delay in hooking up with Bockscar's B-29 escorts meant that when they reached Kokura, bad weather had rolled in and blocked their view. So they headed over to the secondary target, Nagasaki and its vital shipyards, and dropped the bomb there.

More powerful than the uranium bomb dropped on Hiroshima, the Fat Man's core of plutonium, surrounded by TNT, imploded. The runaway fission chain reaction released the heat- and light-wave radiation of a small sun over the target, which in turn delivered a blast pressure of tons per square inch. Virtually nothing within miles of the blast was left standing, or even recognizable. Nagasaki's hilly topography and conformity to undulating river valley floors had made it a less desirable target, but it did help save a number of residential areas from total destruction. Meanwhile, 6.7 square km (2.59 square miles) were obliterated, 74,884 people were killed in the blast or died shortly thereafter, and another 74,909 were injured. The effects of radioactivity caused the deaths of an estimated 70,000 others within five years.

Scottish merchant who introduced steam locomotives and industrial coal mining to Japan. Escalators whisk you up the steep hillside to the gardens, where you can admire the views of Nagasaki and the harbor. ⊠ 8–1 Minami Yamate-machi, Nagasaki ✚ Take Tram 5 to Oura Tenshu-do-shita and follow signs ☎ 095/822–8223 ⊕ www.glover-garden.jp 💲 ¥620.

### Hashima Island (軍艦島; Gunkanjima)

ISLAND | This small island of Hashima, 12 miles southwest from the Nagasaki Port, was a coal mine with bleak concrete apartment blocks for 5,000 workers. From the sea, the industrial development made the island appear like a giant battleship. In 1974, when the mine closed, the entire island was abandoned. From April 2009 the island became open to the public. Yamasa Shipping offers Gunkanjima Landing & Cruise twice-daily at 9 and 1. Gunkanjima was featured in the James Bond movie Skyfall, where it appeared as the headquarters of Bond's nemesis Raoul Silva. ⊠ Takashimamachi, Nagasaki ⊕ www.yamasa-kaiun.net/en 💲 ¥4,510 for ferry and entry.

### Mt. Inasa Observatory (稲佐山公園展望台; Inasayama Koen Tenbodai)

VIEWPOINT | One of Japan's famous romantic night views, the Mt. Inasa Observation Platform provides panoramic views of Nagasaki City, the local mountains and the coastline. Accessible by the 1-km (½-mile) Nagasaki Ropeway with departures every 15 minutes. ⊠ 8–1 Fuchimachi, Nagasaki ☎ 095/861–3640 ⊕ www.inasayama.com/ropeway 💲 Observatory free; ropeway ¥730 one-way, ¥1,250 round-trip.

### Nagasaki Atomic Bomb Museum (長崎原爆資料館; Genbaku Shiryokan)

HISTORY MUSEUM | The spiral staircase of this museum takes you down into a dark, thought-provoking collection of video loops, dioramas, and exhibits that demonstrate the devastating effects of the bomb detonated in Nagasaki. English audio tours are available, though what

This statue of a godlike man with outstretched arms sits at the center of Nagasaki's Heiwa Koen.

you see is already a lot to handle. The continuous, unblinking film footage is absolutely nauseating at several points, and a melted and blasted wall clock, as surreal as any Dalí painting, sears its way into your consciousness. ☒ 7–8 Hirano-machi, Nagasaki ☎ 095/844–1231 ⊕ nabmuseum.jp ☒ ¥200 (optional audio guide ¥157).

**Oura Church** (大浦天主堂; *Oura Tenshudo*)
CHURCH | This church below the entrance to Glover Garden survived the bomb that leveled much of the city. It was constructed in 1865 to commemorate the death of 26 Christians crucified in 1597, victims of Toyotomi Hideyoshi's gruesome message of religious intolerance. It's the oldest Gothic-style building in Japan. ☒ 5–3 Minami Yamate-machi, Nagasaki ✛ 5-min walk from Oura Tenshu-do-shita tram stop ☎ 095/823–2628 ⊕ nagasaki-oura-church.jp ☒ ¥1,000.

**Peace Park** (平和公園; *Heiwa Koen*)
MONUMENT | Nagasaki's Peace Park was built on the grounds of an old prison that was destroyed in the atomic blast. In the middle is a large statue of a godlike man sitting with one arm stretched to the sky and one to the land. A short distance down the hill, Hypocenter Koen marks the bomb's hypocenter. A solitary pillar was erected to mark the exact epicenter. Curiously little distance separates the pillar from anything else. In contrast to the looming Hiroshima Bomb Dome, when you come upon this spot you might not immediately recognize its significance. ☒ 9 Matsuyamamachi, Nagasaki ✛ From Nagasaki Station take Tram 1 or 3 to Matsuya-machi stop ⊕ www.nagasakipeace.jp ☒ Free.

## 🍴 Restaurants

**Dejima Wharf** (出島ワーフ)
$ | ECLECTIC | Warm evenings draw crowds to the outdoor terraces of this trendy two-story wooden complex on the pier next to Nagasaki Port. Just a short walk from the historic buildings at Dejima, you'll find a sprawl of tantalizing seafood restaurants—the oysters come highly recommended—along with Italian, Chinese, and steak restaurants. **Known**

**for:** a range of restaurants; harbor views; fresh seafood. $ *Average main: ¥1,100* ✉ *Dejima Wharf, 1–1–109 Dejimamachi, Nagasaki* ⊕ *dejimawharf.com/en* ▭ *No credit cards.*

### Garde (ガルダ)

$ | **ITALIAN** | Crispy thin-crust pizza and tasty pasta dishes are the mainstays at this Italian restaurant in the Shian-bashi entertainment quarter east of Chinatown. From the Shian-bashi tram stop, head two blocks north into the arcade and one block west. **Known for:** eat in or take out; reasonable prices; local institution. $ *Average main: ¥1,350* ✉ *1–20 Kajiya-machi, Nagasaki* ☎ *095/826–1302* ▭ *No credit cards* ⊗ *Closed Tues.*

### Kagetsu (花月)

$$$$ | **JAPANESE** | Billing itself as "one of the most important historical restaurants of Japan," this quiet hilltop retreat is Nagasaki's most prestigious dining room with fine cuisine that matches its reputation. The interior wooden beams date to 1618. **Known for:** geisha can be booked in advance to perform during meals (extra fees); kaiseki (multicourse meals); well-priced lunchtime bento boxes. $ *Average main: ¥19,800* ✉ *2–1 Maruyama-cho, Nagasaki* ✛ *About 656 ft. south of Shian-bashi tram stop* ☎ *095/822–0191* ⊕ *www.ryoutei-kagetsu.co.jp.*

### Kairakuen (会楽園)

$ | **CHINESE** | This ornate Chinese restaurant is a local favorite, and it's easy to see, smell, and taste why. Kairakuen serves the best *chanpon*—Nagasaki's signature dish of Chinese-style noodles, vegetables, and pork-based broth—in town. **Known for:** variety of dishes; reasonable prices; large bowls of champon. $ *Average main: ¥1,320* ✉ *10–16 Shinchi-machi, Nagasaki* ✛ *Take tram to Shinchi Chinatown and walk two blocks southeast along river* ☎ *095/822–4261* ⊕ *www.kairakuen.tv.*

##  Hotels

### Hotel New Nagasaki (ホテルニュー長崎)

$$$$ | **HOTEL** | Glossy marble and massive slabs of granite dominate this popular and upscale hotel. **Pros:** you can't get closer to the station; great shopping next door; spacious rooms. **Cons:** limited number of English-speaking staff; breakfast not included; too busy for solitude seekers. $ *Rooms from: ¥32,000* ✉ *14–5 Daikoku-machi, Nagasaki* ☎ *095/826–8000, 095/823–2000* ⊕ *www.newnaga.com* ⤳ *153 rooms* ❏ *No Meals.*

### Hotel WingPort Nagasaki (ホテルウイング・ポート長崎)

$$$ | **HOTEL** | A business center, rental laptops, and in-room Internet connections attract corporate travelers to this hotel whose guest quarters are simple, functional, and a good value. **Pros:** spacious rooms; close to train station and FamilyMart; good value. **Cons:** small rooms; spartan furnishings; light sleepers beware—noises travel well here. $ *Rooms from: ¥19,000* ✉ *9–2 Daikoku-machi, Nagasaki* ☎ *095/833–2800, 095/833–2801* ⊕ *www.wingport.com/en* ⤳ *200 rooms* ❏ *No Meals.*

## 🛍 Shopping

*Castella* sponge cake, the popular souvenir of Nagasaki, was introduced by the Portuguese in the mid-16th century. The original recipe called for just eggs, flour, and sugar, but it's been tinkered with over time. Every sweet shop and souvenir store in town has its own specially flavored recipe, but you're advised to stick with the plain old version—a delightful treat with coffee or tea.

### SHOPPING AREAS

As the sun sets, everyone converges at **Amu Plaza Nagasaki** (アミュプラザ長崎), which towers over Nagasaki Station. The newest shops and restaurants can be found here, along with a multiscreen movie complex. Amu Plaza is thoroughly modern, and a striking contrast to the city's old-fashioned style.

Not far from Dejima, **Hamano-machi** (浜町) is the major shopping district in downtown Nagasaki. This covered arcade stretches over four blocks and contains numerous department stores, cake shops, cafés, pharmacies, and fashion boutiques.

### Fukusaya (福砂屋)

**FOOD** | *Castella* is a simple brick-shaped sponge cake first brought to Nagasaki by the Portuguese. The bakery Fukusaya has been in business since the Meiji period, so when you say "castella" in Nagasaki, most people think of this shop's cakes and their distinctive yellow packaging. There's a branch on the first floor of Amu Plaza Nagasaki, next to Nagasaki Station. ✉ *Onouemachi 1–1, Nagasaki* ☎ *095/808–2938* ⊕ *www.fukusaya.co.jp.*

# Kumamoto (熊本)

*118 km (73 miles) south of Fukuoka (Hakata).*

Kumamoto is nearly midway along the curve of the west coast of Kyushu. From here you can go west to Nagasaki, north to Fukuoka, east to Aso-san, and south to Kagoshima.

The city has many sights, including the nationally famous Suizen-ji Garden, but the most renowned is Kumamoto Castle, a structure once deemed impregnable. Kiyomasa Kato ushered in the 17th century with the construction of a mighty fortress that was even bigger than the current replica, and he and his son held sway here until the 1630s. The Hosokawa clan then took over, and for the next few centuries Kumamoto was a center of the Tokugawa governmental authority.

In 1877 the real "Last Samurai," Saigo Takamori, brought his army of rebels here to battle untested Meiji government conscripts holed up inside. Things were looking grim for the rebels. Then Takamori ordered his starving men to butcher their horses for raw and ready food. Strengthened, they breached the castle 53 days into the siege. It may have been the first time raw horseflesh (*ba-sashi*) was eaten in Japan, but locals continue to devour it to help their stamina.

It is possible to see the homes of a number of notable residents, including the writers Lafcadio Hearn and Soseki Natsume, both of whom lived here for brief periods while teaching English.

The town's attractions are to the northeast, squeezed in between the Tsuboi and Shira rivers. Most of what constitutes downtown huddles around the old castle up there.

On April 14th, 2016, a strong earthquake (magnitude 6.5) shook Kumamoto; it was followed by a second stronger earthquake (magnitude 7.3) on April 16th, 2016. Fifty people were killed during the earthquakes, and more than 3,000 residents were injured. The total number of fatalities is now written at 225 to include those who died later of indirect causes such as illnesses that worsened due to evacuation. Damage was done to many of the city's buildings including Kumamoto Castle. The city is in a period of renewal made possible by the strength and resilience of its residents. It remains an excellent place to visit, and access to parts of the castle and historical buildings will increase as reconstruction continues.

## GETTING HERE AND AROUND

The Kyushu-Sanko bus makes the one-hour run from Kumamoto Airport to JR Kumamoto Station for ¥800. Flights on ANA, JAL, and Sky Net Asia connect Tokyo's Haneda Airport with Kumamoto Airport (1¾ hours). ANA and JAL fly the hour-long route from Osaka's Itami Airport.

The Nagasaki Ken-ei Bus (from Nagasaki Ken-ei Bus Terminal) costs ¥4,200 and takes around four hours to get to

Kumamoto Sakuramachi Bus Terminal. Kyushu-Sanko buses leaving from Kumamoto Sakuramachi Bus Terminal take 3½ hours to get to Kagoshima (¥3,770). There's also a Kyushu Sanko bus route linking the onsen (thermal baths) paradise of Yufuin and Kumamoto in 4½ hours for ¥4,200.

Shinkansen trains from Fukuoka's Hakata Station stop at Kumamoto Station and take 35 to 50 minutes (¥4,700); the two hour, 20 minute trip from Nagasaki (¥7,080) includes a change at Shin-Tosu. Getting from Kumamoto to Kagoshima-Chuo on the bullet train takes just 47 minutes (¥6,540).

This is one spread-out city, and buses get stuck in all the traffic, so your best bet is to hop a streetcar. Tram lines (A and B) connect the major areas of the city. The fare is a flat ¥170; pay as you get off. From the Kumamoto Eki-mae streetcar stop in front of the train station, it's a 10-minute ride to downtown. One-day *waku waku* travel passes, good for use on streetcars and city buses, are available for ¥500 from the city tourist information office. There is also a Castle Loop Bus that connects a string of sights around the castle with a stop across from the main train station and runs every 30 minutes from 8:30 am to 9 pm daily. Tickets (¥160 single stop, or ¥400 for the day) can be bought at the tourist office in the station or at the Kumamoto Sakuramachi Bus Terminal near the castle.

**AIRPORT INFORMATION Aso Kumamoto Airport.** ⊠ *1802–2 Oyatsu, Mashiki-machi, Kumamoto* ☎ *096/232–2311* ⊕ *www. kumamoto-airport.co.jp/en.*

**BUS DEPOT Kumamoto Sakuramachi Bus Terminal.** ⊠ *Kumamoto* ☎ *096/354–1111* ⊕ *sakuramachi-kumamoto.jp/bus.*

**TRAIN STATION Kumamoto Station.** ⊠ *3–15–1 Kasuga, Kumamoto* ☎ *050/3786–1717.*

## VISITOR INFORMATION

Staff at the Kumamoto Station Tourist Information Center provide maps and information in English. The online Kumamoto Nagomi Tourism Site has good descriptions of major sights in the prefecture and useful information about ATM locations, emergency procedures, events, etiquette in public baths, and other topics. The Kumamoto Guide website provides tourism information for Kumamoto City. Contact tourism information to check which sights are open to the public following the 2016 Kumamoto earthquake.

**CONTACTS Kumamoto Nagomi Tourism Site.** ⊠ *Kumamoto Prefecture Tourism Federation, Kumamoto* ☎ *096/382–2660* ⊕ *kumanago.jp/en.* **Kumamoto Station Tourist Information.** ⊠ *JR Kumamoto Station, 3–15–1 Kasuga, Kumamoto* ☎ *096/327–9500.*

 # Sights

★ **Kumamoto Castle**
(熊本城; *Kumamoto-jo*)
**CASTLE/PALACE** | The towering, ominous castle was completed in 1607, having been designed and built by Kiyomasa Kato (1562–1611), the area's feudal lord or *daimyo*. Gracefully curved, white-edged roofs rest atop the mysterious black keep. Look for slanted windows perfect for unleashing rock falls, one of many clever features to prevent intrusion. The top floor of the reconstructed castle commands an excellent view of Kumamoto, and exhibits include samurai weapons and armor arrayed to evoke images of the fearless warriors charging into battle. Kumamoto Castle was damaged by the earthquakes in April 2016. The restoration of the Tenshukaku Tower was completed in 2021, with other reconstruction continuing. Elevated views of the castle can be seen from the Kumamoto Castle Hotel and City Hall. ⊠ *1–1 Honmaru, Kumamoto-shi, Kumamoto* ⊕ *Take Tram A to Kumamoto*

*Castle/City Hall stop* ☎ *096/352–5900* 🌐 *kumamoto-guide.jp/kumamoto-castle/en/admission* 🎫 *¥800.*

**Suizenji Jojuen Garden** (水前寺成趣園)
**GARDEN** | Created in the mid-17th century, the garden was originally part of the sprawling villa of the ruling Hosokawa family. The garden is dotted with impeccably trimmed bushes and trees. Beside a pond surrounded by a network of stone bridges, an undulating knoll of lush green grass represents Japan—there's even a Mt. Fuji-like cone. For a few hundred yen you can sit on the tatami of the Kokindenju teahouse, sip green tea, and quietly contemplate the gardens. Also on the grounds is Izumi Jinja (Izumi Shrine), which houses the tombs of several eminent Hosokawa clan members. ✉ *8–1 Suizenji-koen, Kumamoto* ✥ *Take Tram A or B east from Kumamoto Castle to Suizenji Park stop* ☎ *096/383–0074* 🌐 *www.suizenji.or.jp* 🎫 *¥400.*

## 🍴 Restaurants

**Aoyagi** (青柳)
**$$** | **JAPANESE** | The extensive menu here includes regional favorites in addition to sushi and tofu dishes. You can relax in a booth or sit at the counter and admire the skilled chefs. **Known for:** tempura-style karashi renkon (lotus root stuffed with fiery chile and mustard powder); near Kumamoto Castle tram stop; basashi. [$] *Average main: ¥2,500* ✉ *1–2–10 Shimotori, Kumamoto* ☎ *096/353–0311* 🌐 *aoyagi.ne.jp.*

★ **Tour De Château** (トゥールド シャトー)
**$$$** | **FRENCH** | This romantic restaurant on the 11th floor of the Kumamoto Hotel Castle has stunning sunset views of Kumamoto Castle. During the day the restaurant is used for wedding receptions, but at night (when there are not events) it opens to the public for dinner. **Known for:** French-Japanese fusion dishes; elegant service; stunning views. [$] *Average main: ¥5,000* ✉ *Kumamoto Hotel Castle, 4–2 Jotomachi, 11th fl., Kumamoto* ☎ *096/326–3311* 🌐 *www.hotel-castle.co.jp/en* ⏲ *No lunch* ☞ *Often booked for weddings and events, so check in advance for availability.*

## 🛏 Hotels

**Kumamoto Hotel Castle**
(熊本ホテルキャッスル)
**$$** | **HOTEL** | Across from and named for the city's best-loved landmark, this hotel has great views and provides excellent service. **Pros:** great staff; eye-catching location; excellent restaurant. **Cons:** not all rooms have castle views; some room furnishings showing their age; may be fully booked by wedding parties. [$] *Rooms from: ¥17,000* ✉ *4–2 Jotomachi, Kumamoto* ☎ *096/326–3311, 096/326–3324* 🌐 *www.hotel-castle.co.jp/en* 🛏 *179 rooms* 🍴 *No Meals.*

**The New Hotel Kumamoto**
(ザ・ニュー ホテル 熊本)
**$$** | **HOTEL** | It's not as over-the-top as its big-city counterparts, but this hotel is endowed with the same crisp service and all the right amenities. **Pros:** convenient for the train station; friendly staff; clean rooms. **Cons:** no room service; noise from the train station; far from castle and city restaurants. [$] *Rooms from: ¥16,000* ✉ *1–13–1 Kasuga, Kumamoto* ☎ *096/326–1111, 096/326–0800* 🌐 *www.thenewkumamoto.jp/eng* 🛏 *123 rooms* 🍴 *No Meals.*

**Toyoko Inn Kumamoto Sakuramachi Bus Terminal Mae**
(東横INN熊本桜町バスターミナル前)
**$** | **HOTEL** | Inexpensive but functional accommodations, a complimentary Japanese breakfast—*onigiri* (rice balls wrapped in seaweed), miso soup, and coffee—and free Internet access in the lobby are among the pluses of a stay at this member of one of the country's largest hotel chains. **Pros:** free breakfast; inexpensive; laundry facilities. **Cons:** small rooms; sometimes noisy; 4 pm check-in.

Ⓢ *Rooms from: ¥10,200* ✉ *1–24 Koyai-ma-machi, Kumamoto* ☎ *096/322–1045, 096/322–2045* ⊕ *www.toyoko-inn.com* ➥ *152 rooms* ◯◯ *Free Breakfast.*

# 🛍 Shopping

Kumamoto's most famous product is *Higo zogan,* or Higo inlay. A unique form of metalwork originally employed in the decoration of swords, scabbards, and gunstocks of the Hosokawa clan, it consists of black steel delicately inlaid with silver and gold. It is now used to make fashionable jewelry that does not come cheap; a simple pendant can run ¥8,000, and prices for large pieces reach ¥700,000 and more. Other local products include gold paper lanterns, dolls, tops, and fine cutlery.

### Kumamoto Prefectural Traditional Crafts Center (熊本県伝統工芸館 *Kumamoto ken Dento Kogei-kan*)

**CRAFTS** | This is the best place to buy regional handicrafts. It's in a brick building across from the Akazu-mon entrance to the castle. Along with Higo zogan, check out the *kiji-uma* (literally, "pheasant horses"), a traditional toy for boys, or the *hana-te-bako* (flower-covered boxes), a traditional present for girls. On the second floor there is a Special Permanent Exhibition Room (¥210). ✉ *3–35 Chiba-jo-machi, Kumamoto* ☎ *096/324–4930* ⊕ *kumamoto-kougeikan.jp* ⊘ *Closed Mon.*

# Mt. Aso (阿蘇山; Aso-san)

*49.7 km (31 miles) northeast of Kumamoto.*

The Aso-Kuju National Park comprises one of the world's largest caldera—128 km (80 miles) in circumference, from 18 km to 24 km (11 to 15 miles) wide in places—formed after a massive lava-dome collapse some 100,000 years ago. Inside the crater are seven settlements, not to mention herds of cows and horses. The emerald-green grasses that nourish them thrive in the fertile volcanic soil. The crater area contains five volcanic cones; one is the still-active Nakadake, which sticks up out of the side of the taller Taka-dake just east of the crater's center. Trekking in the Aso-Kuju National Park depends on the level of volcanic activity.

## GETTING HERE AND AROUND

Train services between Kumamoto and Aso had been affected by the Kumamoto earthquake but is now running. However the train line south of Aso is closed from Nakamatsu Station to Tateno Station until August 2023. Highway buses make frequent runs from Kumamoto Sakuramachi Bus Terminal to Aso Station. Twice a day the Kyushu bus continues from Aso Station to Kurokawa then Yufuin, and once a day all the way to Beppu. Local buses run from Aso Station up to Kusaneri. The bus stop is next to the Aso Volcano Museum and the Visitors Center (30 minutes, ¥650).

The Aso Nishi Cable Car once took visitors up to Kako Nishi (West Crater) but the service was permanently stopped after an eruption in 2016. When there is limited volcanic activity a shuttle bus runs from the Kusaneri area up to the crater edge, or visitors can walk. On October 20th, 2021, Mt. Aso erupted once again and at time of writing the area around the crater is currently closed to visitors.

Aso-san makes an excellent stopover on the way from Kumamoto to Kurokawa (northeast) or Takachiho (southeast). The JR line running east from JR Aso Station to Oita (and then to Yufuin, Usa, or even Fukuoka) is still running.

If you start early, you can make Aso-san a day trip from Kumamoto. If you want to spend more time in the park, stay overnight in one of the mountain pensions clustered south of Mt Aso. Another option would be to rent a car

This churning, bubbling lake is found in the crater of Naka-dake in Mt. Aso National Park.

in Fukuoka, Kumamoto, or Kagoshima and explore the Aso-Kuju National Park, Kurokawa, Yufuin, Takachiho, and Kirishima-Kinkowan National Park at your own pace.

**BUS CONTACT Kyushu-Sanko Buses.**
☎ *096/354–4845* ⊕ *kyushubusbooking. com.*

**TRAIN STATION JR Aso Station.** ✉ *1444–2 Kurokawa, Aso* ☎ *0967/34–0101.*

## VISITOR INFORMATION

Stop by the Aso Tourist Information Office next to the train station to get your bearings and check conditions. When the volcano is producing higher than normal amounts of toxic gases, park officials close the crater-edge area.

**CONTACT Aso Tourist Information Office.** ✉ *Inside JR Aso Station, 1440–2 Kurokawa, Aso* ☎ *0967/34–1600.*

##  Sights

**Aso Volcano Museum** (阿蘇火山博物館; *Aso Kazan Hakubutsukan*)
The Aso Volcano Museum on the 2nd and 3rd floor of the building is showing its age, and only a small percentage of the exhibits have English descriptions. However, the video presentation in the five-screen multipurpose hall has subtitles and is an interesting introduction to vulcanology and the various giant calderas around the world. On the first floor a new visitors center and café has a lot of fascinating information in English and Japanese. The museum and visitor center is beside the Kusasenri parking lot and rest area. ✉ *1930 Akamizu* ☎ *0967/34–2111* ⊕ *www.asomuse.jp* 💳 *¥860.*

**Kusasenri-ga-hama** (草千里ヶ浜)
**NATURE SIGHT** | During summer, in this bowl-shaped meadow you'll find cows and horses grazing around a marshy pond on the lush grass. In early March the old grasses are burned, leaving the landscape

looking desolate, but it allows fresh and tasty green grass to vigorously grow back. Depending on volcanic conditions, and if you have time, hike along an easy trail that goes 5½ km (3½ miles) around the base of Kijima-dake. It takes an hour or so, and provides excellent views of the otherworldly terrain. You could also march the 3 km (2 miles) straight across the rugged lava plain to the foot of Naka-dake. For several other trails in the area, pick up the "Aso Trekking Route Map" at the information center in JR Aso Station. In summer it is possible to sit on a horse and be led for a slow walk around the grassy meadow. It is a popular option for those who have never ridden a horse before. ✉ *Akamizu, Aso.*

**Naka-dake** (中岳)

**VOLCANO** | For many visitors, the smoldering crater of Mt. Aso's Naka-dake is the highlight of a visit to the Aso-Kuju National Park. Inside the crater, a churning ash-gray lake bubbles and spits scalding, reeking steam. The Nakadake cable car was closed following an eruption for 2016. A shuttle bus from the parking area to the crater runs when there is limited volcanic activity, but this service was halted after the October 2021 eruption. If rumbling turns to shaking, and steam and smoke turn to sizable ash fall, there are bunker-like concrete shelters located across the area. ✉ *808–5 Kurokawa, Aso* ☎ *0967/34–0411.*

## Hotels

In the Aso-Kuju National Park caldera, south of Mt. Aso, you'll find numerous small hotels such as Pension Angelica. These are a particularly good option is you are traveling by car onwards to Takachiho on Route 325. If your next destination after the Aso-Kuju National Park is following Route 11 (aka the Yamanami Highway) to Kurokawa or Yufuin, look for accommodation to the north of Mt. Aso such as El Patio Ranch.

**Pension Angelica**
(ペンションアンジェリカ)

**$$$$** | **B&B/INN** | The main appeal of this manor in the woods is the hospitality of the Tatsuji family. **Pros:** heartwarming hosts; excellent food; fresh air and quiet. **Cons:** other side of the Mt. Aso than the main town; hard beds; access to and from the hotel easiest by car. [$] *Rooms from: ¥26,400* ✉ *1800 Shirakawa, Minami-aso-mura, Aso* ☎ *0967/62–2223* 🛏 *7 rooms* 🍴 *All-Inclusive.*

**El Patio Ranch**
(エルパティオ牧場; *Eru Patio Bokujo*)

**$$$$** | **HOTEL** | **FAMILY** | The Aso-Kuju National Park is famous for horses and cows, and at the El Patio Ranch you can live your cowboy or cowgirl dreams as you walk, trot, or canter around the local area. **Pros:** view the horses from your room; friendly staff; guests get discounted horse riding. **Cons:** limited dining options; functional rather than luxurious rooms; requires car access. [$] *Rooms from: ¥25,300* ✉ *2305–1 Ichinomiyamachi Sanno, Aso* ☎ *0967/22–3861* 🌐 *epr-r.com* 🛏 *6 rooms* 🍴 *No Meals.*

# Kurokawa Onsen (黒川温泉)

*32 km (20 miles) north from Aso Station; 50 km (31 miles) southwest of Yufuin.*

In northern Kyushu, Beppu is the busiest (and arguably the most overdeveloped) onsen town. Yufuin has a mixture of onsen, local crafts, and café, but is still a tourist hub. Kurokawa Onsen is much quieter and focused almost solely on getting into hot water.

The key "sights" are the numerous ryokan in Kurokawa Onsen, and each has its own hot spring bath(s) that is free for its guests. However, most of Kurokawa's ryokan also allow nonguests to use their onsen for a small charge. At times, an onsen pass is available that lets you bathe at a selection of onsen for one price.

For most visitors, Kurokawa Onsen is about relaxation. Have a soak, a nice long meal, a few beers, then head to bed. Most onsen are divided into male and female baths. Usually, you can't enter onsen if you have any tattoos. Follow proper etiquette and remember to wash thoroughly in the showers before you enter the onsen pool.

### GETTING HERE AND AROUND

Kurokawa is most easily accessed by car. If you've rented a vehicle, it is a great place to stop when traveling between Yufuin and Aso along the beautiful Yamanami Highway. The Yamanami Highway is one of the most scenic routes in Japan, so on weekends you'll see many Japanese out for a leisurely drive or cruising through the mountainous landscape on motorbikes, and bicycles.

Highway buses reach Kurokawa from Fukuoka's Hakata Station (3 hours, ¥3,470). The Kyushu Odan Bus from Kumamoto Station stops in Aso then Kurokawa, Yufuin, with the terminus at Beppu. Kumamoto Station to Kurokawa is three hours, ¥2,800. Kurokawa to Yufuin is 90 minutes, ¥2,200.

As accommodation in Kurokawa is almost exclusively onsen ryokan with inclusive evening meals at set times, make sure you arrive with ample time.

 Hotels

There are many ryokan in Kurokawa Onsen, but most hosts speak only limited English and will have strict arrival times so that dinner can be served at the appropriate hour. The evening meal is usually part of the price, so eating outside of your ryokan can be difficult due to limited options in town. In general, Japanese ryokan are getting more used to working with guests who have dietary needs, including vegetarians, however

you'll need to let them know the specifics in advance.

### Yumerindo (夢龍胆)

$$$$ | B&B/INN | Soak the stresses of the world away as you sit naked in the outdoor pool of the Yumerindo ryokan, eat a multicourse Japanese meal, and retire to your futon for a good night's sleep. **Pros:** traditional kaiseki multicourse dinner; relaxing onsen; flexible with dietary requirements. **Cons:** limited English; must book dinner and breakfast; some furnishings timeworn. $ Rooms from: ¥36,000 ✉ 6430–1 Manganji, Minamioguni, Aso ☎ 967/44–0321 ⊕ www.yumerindo.com/index.html ↪ 23 rooms ⦙◯⦙ All-Inclusive.

# Yufuin (湯布院)

*135 km (84 miles) southeast of Hakata/Fukuoka.*

Southwest of the majestic twin peaks of Mt. Yufu, this tranquil village resembles a checkered quilt. Forests nestle up to clusters of galleries, eclectic cafés, local crafts shops, and rustic lodgings. Most of the year, Yufuin is a relatively peaceful area, but things heat up in July and August with the arrival of national music and film festivals.

Yufuin has avoided many of the pitfalls of modern tourism, and it wasn't an accident. City planners and investors went to Europe and came back with ideas about how to set up a quaint and lovely spa town. The center of town can become crowded with visitors in the middle of the day, but the outer edges with their ryokan and galleries are quiet and sedate. Relatively unadorned natural baths with great views can be found here, as can a thriving arts-and-crafts industry and fantastic food.

### GETTING HERE AND AROUND

The closest airport is Oita Airport. Flights from Tokyo's Haneda or Narita airports to Oita take 1½ hours. There are also direct

There are several public bathhouses along the shores of Yufuin's Kinrin-ko thermal lake.

flights from Nagoya and Osaka. Buses run from Oita Airport to Yufuin six times a day (55 minutes, ¥1,550).

You can reach Yufuin by train from Oita City (1 hour, ¥950). From Fukuoka's Hakata Station reserve a seat on the Limited Express train "Yufuin No Mori" for a scenic ride (2 hours, 13 minutes; ¥4,640). It is cheaper and a little faster to take the highway buses. The Nishitetsu bus from Hakata Station via Fukuoka Airport International Terminal to Yufuin takes 2 hours (¥3,250). Kyushu Sanko Kotsu buses make the 3 hour 20 minute trip between Kumamoto and Yufuin twice a day, departing at 8:29 am and 1:09 pm. The one-way fare is ¥4,600.

**AIRPORT INFORMATION Oita Airport.**
⊠ *Shimobaru, Aki-machi, Kunisaki*
☏ *0978/67–1174* ⊕ *www.oita-airport.jp/
en.*

**AIRPORT TRANSFER Kyushu-Sanko Buses.**
☏ *096/354–4845* ⊕ *kyushubusbooking.
com.*

**TRAIN STATION Yufuin Station.** ⊠ *8–2
Kawakita* ☏ *0977/84–2021.*

## VISITOR INFORMATION

To enjoy the best of Yufuin in a day, start by picking up an English map at the beautifully designed Yufu Tourist Information Office located just outside the train station.

**CONTACT Yufu Tourist Information.**
⊠ *Yufuin Station, 8–2 Kawakita, Yufuin*
☏ *0977/84–2446* ⊕ *yufu-tic.com.*

 **Sights**

**Artejio Museum** (アルテジオ ミュージアム)
**ART MUSEUM** | From Yufuin Station, take a five-minute taxi ride north to Kuuso-no-Mori, a hamlet in the forest that is home to a community of art galleries along the foot of Mt. Yufu. The Artejio Museum is a small modern art museum with a musical theme and minimalist vibe. The second floor has a library with books on art and music. Close by is the excellent Sansou Murata ryokan, the Yutaka Isozaki Gallery, and several cafés. ⊠ *1272–175 Kawakami,*

*Yufuin* ☎ *0977/28–8686* 🌐 *www.artegio.com* 🎫 *¥600* ⏲ *Closed Wed.*

**Lake Kinrin** (金鱗湖; *Kinrin-ko*)
**BODY OF WATER** | In winter, steam rises from the surface of this small thermal lake on the east end of town. Take a relaxing 10-minute stroll around the lake, before you sample the various cake and coffee sets at the local cafés. ✉ *1561–1 Yufuincho Kawakami, Yufuin.*

**Usa Shrine** (宇佐神宮; *Usa Jingu*)
**RELIGIOUS BUILDING** | The most important Hachiman shrine in Japan is about an hour from Yufuin and makes an easy day trip, Usa Jingu has lovely ponds dotted with lotus plants. Allot an hour to see the shrine and stroll the expansive grounds. There was a long tradition in Japan of building temples and shrines in the same precinct (abolished in the Meiji period), and this is said to be the first place to do so. ✉ *2859 Minamiusa, Usa* ✥ *From Yufuin take the 1-hr train to Oita, then board a 40-min limited express train to Usa. From Usa, it's a short taxi or bus ride to the shrine. If you take the bus, get on the one bound for Yotsukaichi and get off at the stop Usa Hachiman. From Fukuoka take the direct train to Usa (98 min, ¥4,110)* ☎ *0978/37–0001* 🌐 *www.usajinguu.com* 🎫 *Free.*

**Yunotsubokaido Street** (湯の坪街道・たけもと通り; *Yunotsubokaido Takemoto-dori*)
**STREET** | A short walk from the train station, this neighborhood is a long shopping street lined with traditional Japanese wooden buildings. You can wander in and out of artsy craft shops and souvenir stalls, or relax in one of the many coffee shops or tearooms. The southwestern end of the street is known as Yunotsubokiado, the north-eastern end of the street is called Takemoto Street. ✉ *Yunotsubokaido Takemoto, Yufuin.*

**Yutaka Isozaki Gallery** (由夛加磯崎ギャラリー)
**ART GALLERY** | Artist Yutaka Isozaki is happy to show visitors his varied artwork in various media, including pottery, paintings, and photography. You can buy small cards with inspirational messages and illustrations such as persimmons and wildflowers that make original souvenirs. Isozaki-san is now in his 70s but is always excited to meet new visitors. ✉ *1266–21 Kawakami, Yufuin* ☎ *0977/85–4750* ⏲ *Closed Wed.*

## 🍴 Restaurants

**BudouYa** (葡萄屋)
**$$$$** | **JAPANESE** | Part of the Yufuin Tamanoyu hotel, which until 1975 was a lodging for Zen Buddhist monks, this restaurant retains an air of solemnity. Multicourse menus include dishes such as salt-grilled fish, seasonal vegetables, and homemade *kabosu* (lime) sherbet, while vegetarian or vegan options can be prepared if given advanced notice. **Known for:** a tranquil atmosphere; impeccable service; fine local ingredients. [$] *Average main: ¥9,072* ✉ *Yunotsubo, Yufuin-cho, Yufu, Yufuin* ☎ *0977/84–2158* 🌐 *www.tamanoyu.co.jp/english.html* ⏲ *No lunch.*

## ☕ Coffee and Quick Bites

**thé théo, Theomurata Tea Room** (テテオ テオムラタ)
**$** | **CAFÉ** | Located in the forest beside the Artejio gallery, the Sansou Murata ryokan, and a small chocolate factory, the Theomurata Tea Room provides the perfect place to relax. Sample the exquisite handmade chocolates or the delicate roll cakes. **Known for:** fine chocolates; serene atmosphere; luxurious hot chocolate drinks. [$] *Average main: ¥1,280* ✉ *1272–175 Yufuin-cho Kawakami, Yufuin* ☎ *0977/28–8686* 🌐 *www.artegio.com.*

## Hotels

**Sansou Murata** (山荘無量塔)
**$$$$ | B&B/INN** | This unique and special place mixes the best of Western and Japanese accommodations, with rooms mostly in freestanding houses in a wooded setting, making autumn one of the best times to visit. **Pros:** incredible food; marvelous staff; real taste and atmosphere. **Cons:** expensive; fixed price for rooms all year; no wheelchair-accessible rooms. [$] *Rooms from: ¥111,620* ✉ *1264–2 Yufuin-cho Kawakami, Yufu* ☎ *0977/84–5000* 🌐 *www.sansou-murata.com* 🛏 *12 rooms* 🍴 *All-Inclusive.*

★ **Yufu Ryochiku** (御宿由布両築; *Onjuku Yufu Ryochiku*)
**$$$$ | B&B/INN** | When not submerged in the mineral waters at this relaxing lodging that dates from 1925, you can warm yourself by the glowing coals in the *irori* (sunken hearth) in the lobby and enjoy the delicious included meals. **Pros:** tranquil atmosphere; private mineral baths; excellent service. **Cons:** only toilets are private (all baths are shared); only eight rooms, so it books up quickly; car access can be crowded by tourists on Takemoto St.. [$] *Rooms from: ¥60,000* ✉ *1097–1 Kawakami, Yufuin-cho, Yufuin* ☎ *0977/85–2526* 🌐 *hpdsp.jp/yufuin-ryoutiku/en* 🛏 *8 rooms* 🍴 *All-Inclusive.*

# Takachiho (高千穂)

*80 km (49 miles) southeast of Kumamoto.*

Deep in the sacred mountains, a spiritual place full of atmosphere, Takachiho is the birthplace of Japanese mythology. A visit to the region takes you to the places where the gods first alighted on Earth, hid in caves, and created the first water spring.

More than one million Japanese visit Takachiho every year, yet few foreigners are aware of this magical and mysterious region that remains not unlike how it was generations ago. See the wonderful Kagura dances to the gods that have been performed since ancient times. Take a walk in the mountains, imbibe the sacred waters of mountain springs, and find your own path. You'll marvel at how the people of ancient times in these parts could create myths that so perfectly matched their environment. You'll marvel even more at the sense that these myths are still a part of everyday life in the region. An overnight stay is recommended to see the many sights and soak up the atmosphere. A day trip, while possible, doesn't really give you a full enough sense of the place.

## Takachiho, the Cradle of Myth

Both Takachiho and Takachiho-no-Mine (the latter in Kirishima-Kinkowan National Park) claim to be the places where the grandson of the sun goddess Amaterasu descended to Earth to establish the Japanese imperial family. Many years ago officials from both towns went to court to argue their respective points, but the judge demurred, ruling that each town had the right to believe it was the actual place where the gods descended to Earth. Both places are very spiritual and worthy of a visit.

### GETTING HERE AND AROUND

Reaching Takachiho is not easy, and that has kept the town from becoming an overdeveloped tourist trap. In the most northerly part of Miyazaki Prefecture, the town is a three-hour bus ride from Kumamoto. The "Takachiho-go bus" travels twice-daily from Kumamoto to Nobeoka on the west coast. It leaves from Kumamoto Train Station, stopping at the Kumamoto Sakuramachi Bus Terminal and Aso Kumamoto Airport before traveling to Takachiho and then on to Noboeka Station. Kumamoto to Takachiho is ¥2,700.

Renting a car and driving is a much more flexible option. Takachiho is approximately two hours by car east of Kumamoto, 90 minutes south 0f Kurokawa Onsen, or 50 minutes from the pensions around the south side of Mt. Aso. Takachiho. The town has limited public transportation, so a rental car will also serve you well once you're there.

## VISITOR INFORMATION

Get a guidebook and a map from the Takachiho Tourist Office, or download them from its website. The office can also connect you with an English-speaking guide. But go to some places on your own to enjoy the atmosphere.

**CONTACT Takachiho Tourist Office.** ⊠ Mitai ☎ 0982/73–1213 ⊕ takachiho-kanko.info.

#  Sights

**Amanoiwato Shrine** (天岩戸神社; Amanoi-wato Jinja)

RELIGIOUS BUILDING | This shrine is located near the cave where the sun goddess Amaterasu hid until Ame-no-Uzume managed to lure her out. If you apply at the entrance, a Shinto priest will take you into the sacred precinct from where you can look across the valley towards the cave. ⊠ 1073–1 Iwato, Takachiho-cho, Nishiusuki-gun ☎ 0982/74–8239 ⊕ amanoiwato-jinja.jp ☜ Free.

**Ama-no-Yasukawara Cave** (天安河原)

CAVE | A dark but deeply spiritual place, this huge cave faces onto a small river. According to the local legends, the gods gathered here to figure out how to get Amaterasu out of her cave. Although not a Shinto practice, visitors now pile stones on top of each other to leave their wishes, with little stone piles creating an otherworldly atmosphere. ⊠ Iwato, Takachiho-cho, Nishiusuki-gun ☜ Free.

**Takachiho Gorge**
(高千穂峡; Takachiho-kyo)

CANYON | One of Kyushu's most famous sights, this photogenic narrow gorge has several small waterfalls cascading into the Gokase River. You can walk along a hiking path at the edge or rent a rowboat from the riverside jetty below the parking lot (from ¥4,000). ⊠ Mitai, Takachiho-cho, Nishiusuki-gun ☜ Free.

**Takachiho Shrine** (高千穂神社; Takachiho Jinja)

RELIGIOUS BUILDING | The shrine is surrounded by a grove of old cedars. A pair of trees, that stand side by side, are known as the Wedded Cedars. A sacred shimenawa (twisted straw rope) hangs between the two trees. The presence of this romantic tree couple has made the shrine popular with those praying from match-making. Kagura is an ancient ritual dance to give thanks to the gods that has been performed since ancient times. These days it is performed throughout the night in homes between December and January. An excellent one-hour performance can be seen nightly at 8 pm at Kagura Hozonkan, on the grounds of Takachiho Shrine. ⊠ 1037 Mitai, Takachiho-cho, Nishiusuki-gun ☎ 0982/72–2413 ☜ Shrine free; ¥1,000 for Kagura dance.

# 🍴 Restaurants

**Nagomi** (和)

$$ | JAPANESE | This restaurant serves the famous local beef, which I can be cooked in the teppan style, table-side. The most popular menu is steak, but they also have yakiniku (Japanese beef BBQ), beef on rice, and beef hamburger steak. **Known for:** wide selection of steak dishes; beef and more beef; yakiniku. $ Average main: ¥2,000 ⊠ 1099–1 Mitai, Mitai ☎ 0982/73–1109 ⊙ Closed Wed.

**Sobadokoro Ten'an** (そば処天庵)

$ | JAPANESE | Stop for lunch at the wonderful soba shop run by Sayoko Kojima. The delicious soba and soup are served with different kinds of tempura and other dishes made with Kojima's own organic vegetables. **Known for:** family-run restaurant; delicious, crunchy tempura; fresh ingredients. $\boxed{\$}$ *Average main: ¥1,400* ⊠ *1180–25 Takachiho, Takachiho* ☎ *0982/72–3023.*

## 🛏 Hotels

★ **Shinsen** (神仙)

$$$$ | **B&B/INN** | Shinsen is the best ryokan in Takachiho, and one of Kyushu's finest (it's also quite expensive) since more than half the rooms have an open-air bath. **Pros:** private open-air bath in many rooms; excellent service; superb food. **Cons:** limited public transportation access; strict mealtimes, so no late arrivals; availability of rooms in high season. $\boxed{\$}$ *Rooms from: ¥110,000* ⊠ *1127–5 Mitai, Takachiho-cho, Nishiusuki-gun* ☎ *0982/72–2257* ⊕ *www.takachiho-shinsen.co.jp* ⤳ *15 rooms* ❗ *All-Inclusive.*

# Kirishima-Kinkowan National Park (霧島屋久国立公園)

*43 km (27 miles) northeast of Kagoshima.*

According to Japanese myth, the mountainous, volcanic Kirishima is one of two possible places where Amaterasu's grandson descended to Earth (the other is Takachiho). The national park, northeast of Kagoshima City, has good hiking trails and interesting shrines in addition to the sacred mountain Takachiho-no-mine. The fall foliage is particularly spectacular in the national park.

### GETTING HERE AND AROUND

From Kagoshima, take a local (one-hour) or express (50-minute) train to Kirishima Jingu Station. However, it's much easier to get around the national park if you have your own wheels. Consider renting a car in Kagoshima City and head northeast, or in Miyazaki City and head southwest.

## 👁 Sights

### Kirishima Shrine (霧島神宮; *Kirishima Jingu*)

**RELIGIOUS BUILDING** | The original shrine was established in the 6th century, but the present imposing structure was built under the patronage of the Shimazu clan in 1715. Wonderfully appointed and occupying an incredible setting, it has views as far away as Sakura-jima. The shrine, well worth a visit, is dedicated to Ninigi-no-mikoto, the legendary god who landed on the peak of Takachiho-no-mine nearby. ⊠ *2608–5 Kirishima-taguchi, Kirishima* ☎ *0995/57–0001* ⊕ *www.kirishimajingu.or.jp* ⌁ *Free.*

### Mt. Takachiho (高千穂峰; *Takachiho-no-mine*)

**MOUNTAIN** | This mountain is said to be where the goddess Amaterasu's grandson descended to Earth to establish the Japanese imperial family. Trouble is, the distant *town* of Takachiho also claims that honor. The dispute has never been settled, either legally or spiritually. Mt. Takachiho is at the southern end of the Kirishima range, and a hike to the summit takes about three hours. On a clear day you can see the surrounding mountains in Kirishima National Park. Due to volcanic activity, particularly of Shinmoe-dake, some trails may be closed. Ask ahead of time at the Takachiho-gawara Visitor Center. ⊠ *Takachiho-gawara Visitor Center, 2583–12 Kirishimataguchi, Kirishima* ☎ *0995/57–2505 visitor center* ⌁ *Free.*

## 🍴 Restaurants

### Ichi Nii San (いちにいさん)

$$$ | **JAPANESE** | The novel idea behind this restaurant is to serve pork shabu-shabu in soba broth. The broth imparts a delicate flavor to the thinly sliced pork, which is served with seasonal vegetables. **Known**

**for:** popularity with the locals; elegant interior; shabu-shabu dishes. $ *Average main: ¥3,500* ✉ *540–3 Kokubunoguchinishi, Kirishima* ☏ *0995/48–8123* ⊕ *ichiniisan.jp/access/kagoshima/kokubu.*

##  Hotels

### ★ Myoken Ishiharaso (妙見石原荘)

$$$$ | **B&B/INN** | Situated amongst the trees beside a river, Myoken Ishiharaso is the perfect rural escape. **Pros:** beautiful hot springs; incredible food; fantastic staff. **Cons:** higher rates on weekends and holidays; cheaper moutain view rooms do not overlook the river; more accessible by car than public transport. $ *Rooms from: ¥100,300* ✉ *4376–Kareigawa, Hayatocho, Kirishima* ☏ *0995/77–2111* ⊕ *www.m-ishiharaso.com/en* ⤴ *18 rooms* ❖ *All-Inclusive.*

# Kagoshima (鹿児島)

*171 km (106 miles) south of Kumamoto, 289 km (180 miles) south of Hakata/Fukuoka.*

Kagoshima is a laid-back, flowery, palm-lined southern getaway on the Satsuma Peninsula with mild weather, outgoing people, and a smoking volcano out in the bay. Ancient relics believed to date back to 9,000 BCE indicate that humans have been in the area a long time indeed. Kagoshima became a center of trade with Korea and China and was an important fortress town from the mid-16th century until the Meiji Restoration. Saigo Takamori and his rebel followers—reduced to a few hundred from 40,000—made their last stand in Kagoshima against the new emperor on September 24, 1877, chased here after having sacked Kumamoto Castle. Facing 300,000 well-supplied troops, they had no chance, and Takamori was injured in the fight. Rather than face capture, he ordered one of his own men to cut off his head. Reviled and vilified during the rush to modernization, he was posthumously pardoned and honored as a national hero.

Today the area is famous for growing the world's smallest mandarin oranges (only an inch across) and the largest white daikon radishes. Grown in the rich volcanic soil, these radishes can span 3 feet and weigh in at more than 100 pounds. There's also *kurobuta,* a special breed of black pig that locals convert into breaded, fried cutlets called *tonkatsu* (*ton* is pork; *katsu* means cutlet).

**GETTING HERE AND AROUND**
The flight between Tokyo's Haneda Airport and Kagoshima Airport takes 1¾ hours. There are also direct flights from cities including Kobe, Osaka, Fukuoka, Nagoya, and Okinawa. The Airport Limousine picks up passengers every 20 minutes until 9:30 pm at Bus Stop No. 8 outside Kagoshima Airport. From downtown, catch it in the Kagoshima Chuo Ferry Terminal, across the street from the East (Sakura-jima) Exit from JR Kagoshima Chuo Station. The 45-minute trip costs ¥1,300.

Frequent buses make the 4½-hour trip (¥5,000) from Fukuoka (departing from Hakata Kotsu Bus Center and Tenjin Bus Center) to Kagoshima Chuo Station. You can shrink your travel time to as little as 86 minutes by taking the Shinkansen bullet train from Hakata to Kagoshima Chuo Station (¥10,110).

For the past hundred years the easiest way to get around Kagoshima has been by streetcar. A ¥170 fare will take you anywhere on the trusty network. One-day travel passes for unlimited rides on streetcars and buses cost ¥600. You can buy one at the Kagoshima-Chuo Station Tourist Information Center, or on any streetcar or bus. Buses get around, but are run by five competing outfits on a complicated system.

To visit Sakura-jima, you must take a ferry from Kagoshima Port; it runs 24 hours a day. Ferries run every 15 minutes and

You can be buried in hot, black volcanic sand at the sand baths of Ibusuki Tennen Sunamushi Onsen.

the fare is ¥200. To get to the pier from Kagoshima Chuo Station, take Bus 16 or 24 for the short ¥190 ride.

**AIRPORT INFORMATION Kagoshima Airport.** ⊠ *822 Mizobechofumoto, Kirishima* ☎ *0995/73–3638 tourist and information office* ⊕ *www.koj-ab.co.jp/en.*

**AIRPORT TRANSFER Airport Limousine.** ⊠ *Kagoshima* ☎ *099/247–2341.*

**FERRY PORTS Kagoshima Port.** ⊠ *4–1 Shin-machi, Hon-ko, Kagoshima* ☎ *099/223–7271.*

## VISITOR INFORMATION

The Kagoshima Chuo Station Tourist Information Center is on the second floor of the station's Sakura-jima Exit. An English-speaking person is on hand to arm you with maps and advice or help you make hotel reservations.

**CONTACT Kagoshima-Chuo Station Tourist Information Center.** ⊠ *1–1 Chuo-cho, Kagoshima* ☎ *099/253–2500* ⊕ *www. kagoshima-kankou.com/for.*

#  Sights

**Ibusuki Sunamushi Onsen Natural Sand Bath** (指宿砂むし会館 砂楽; *Ibusuki Sunamushi Kaikan Saraku*)

**BEACH** | This laid-back seaside resort is at the southern tip of the Satsuma Peninsula and may provide your one chance to try a therapeutic hot-sand bath. At the Sand Bath Hall "SARAKU", you buy your ticket and rent a *yukata*, or cotton robe—the small towel is yours to keep—on the second floor of the main hall. In the locker room you change into your robe before heading to the beach. Stand in line and wait for an assistant to call you over. You'll be buried in hot, mildly sulfur-smelling sand. Aside from providing a powerful dose of joint-penetrating heat, the stimulating, sweaty experience is guaranteed to cleanse your pores and soften your skin. ⊠ *5–25–18 Yu-no-hama, Ibusuki, Kagoshima* ✛ *This onsen is a highly scenic 1-hr trip south of Kagoshima on the Ibusuki Nanohana local train line. Exit Ibusuki Station and follow the signs—it's a 20-min walk or a 5-min cab* *ride* ☎ *0993/23–3900* 🌐 *sa-raku.sakura.ne.jp/en* 🎟 *¥1,100, plus ¥200 for a small towel rental.*

**Sakura-jima Volcano** (桜島)
**VOLCANO** | Sakurajima is one of the world's most active volcanoes. Visible from Kagoshima City, across Kinko Bay, it is spews thick plumes of ash and smoke almost daily. The last big eruption was in 1955, but the far side of the cone sometimes lets loose with explosive belching that lights the night sky red and covers the island of Sakurajima in a blanket of ash. There are scattered lodgings and hot springs at the base of the volcano, as well as winding paths up to old lava plateaus with great views over the crater or back toward town. There are usually four ferries per hour from Kagoshima City to the Sakurajima. The one-way adult fare for the 10- to 15-minute trip is ¥200. ✉ *Sakura-jima Port, 61–4 Yokoyama-cho, Sakura-jima, Kagoshima* ☎ *099/293–2525.*

## 🍴 Restaurants

**Kumasotei: Traditional Satsuma Cuisine** (熊襲亭)
**$$** | **JAPANESE** | This restaurant offers the best of Kumamoto specialties in a maze of private and semiprivate Japanese-style rooms. There's an English-language menu with helpful photos, and staff can give recommendations for dishes. **Known for:** kurobuta tonkotsu (breaded, fried pork cutlets from locally bred black pigs); multicourse menus with a selection of local dishes; satsuma-age (fish cakes filled with potato or burdock root). [$] *Average main: ¥1,980* ✉ *6–10 Higashi Sengoku-cho, Kagoshima* ✥ *From Tenmonkan-dori tram stop walk 4 blocks north through covered arcade and turn left* ☎ *099/222–6356* 🌐 *www.kumasotei.com.*

## Mall Break

The Amu Plaza complex attached to Kagoshima Chuo Station will keep you busy with shopping and food opportunities. If you get bored, there's a cineplex. For one of the best views in town, ride the giant Ferris wheel (¥500) atop the mall.

## 🛏 Hotels

**Shiroyama Hotel Kagoshima** (城山ホテル鹿児島)
**$$$$** | **HOTEL** | On the site of the rebellious Saigo Takamori's last stand against the emperor in 1877, this hotel sits high enough to provide enviable views but not too far away to be inconvenient. **Pros:** lofty position with stunning views; great baths; excellent service. **Cons:** can be very busy with events; rooms with Sakura-jima view are expensive; not convenient for the city. [$] *Rooms from: ¥44,000* ✉ *41–1 Shinshoin-cho, Kagoshima* ☎ *099/224–2211* 🌐 *www.shiroyama-g.co.jp* 🛏 *355 rooms* 🍽 *Free Breakfast.*

# Chapter 13

# OKINAWA

Updated by
Chris Willson

| ⊙ Sights | 🍴 Restaurants | 🛏 Hotels | 💼 Shopping | 🍸 Nightlife |
|----------|---------------|-----------|-------------|-------------|
| ★★★★☆ | ★★★★★ | ★★★★★ | ★★☆☆☆ | ★★☆☆☆ |

# WELCOME TO OKINAWA

## TOP REASONS TO GO

★ **Local flavors:** Okinawa's food, music, art, and local spirit combine powerful influences from all over Asia with funky, homegrown flavors.

★ **War memorials:** Moving memorials tell the poignant story of the chaos that ravaged this idyllic landscape during World War II's fierce final battle.

★ **Outdoor adventures:** Snorkeling, diving, trekking, sailing, fishing, whale-watching, and kayaking are in your reach in Japan's most pristine and enticing natural vistas.

★ **Dazzling reefs:** Okinawa's abundant reefs are home to varied marine life thriving in clear, warm seas. Dive with manta rays and hammerhead sharks or simply glide over gardens of hard and soft corals.

Island-hopping outside Okinawa Main Island means traveling among several disparate clusters of islands; Okinawa Prefecture is a conflation of smaller archipelagos clustered together, not a steady string of pearls. Traverse the long distances by plane and use ferries to get from one nearby island to another; on the islands themselves you'll enjoy the most freedom with your own transportation, but whether a bicycle or an automobile is more appropriate depends on the size of the island.

**1 Okinawa Main Island.** Naha's Kokusai Street and Shurijo Castle are a great introduction to the area. More captivating are the war memorials on the southern peninsula, and the diving and snorkeling spots, active artisan workshops, and wild scenery to the north.

**2 Kerama Islands.** Dazzling coral reefs and white beaches are only a stone's throw away from Naha's Tomari Port. Though close to Okinawa Main Island, infrequent ferry times make planning ahead essential, but the vivid blue ocean makes these islands well worth the hassle.

**3 Miyako Islands.** A 45-minute flight from Naha, Miyako Island has arguably the best beaches in Japan. Along with snorkeling, diving, and great waterfront accommodations, Miyako offers a whole lot of R&R.

**4 Yaeyama Islands.** An hour flight from Naha, Ishigaki Island is a great place to visit and a launch point for the surrounding sights including time-forgotten villages on Taketomi Island and the reefs and forests of untamed Iriomote Island. It's the perfect mixture of developed getaways and seriously off-the-map adventure.

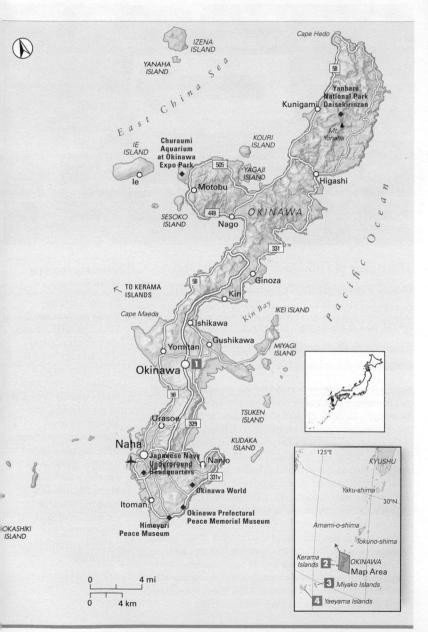

- Cape Hedo
- IZENA ISLAND
- YANAHA ISLAND
- East China Sea
- Yanbaru National Park
- Kunigami Daisekirinzan
- Mt. Yonaha
- IE ISLAND
- KOURI ISLAND
- Churaumi Aquarium at Okinawa Expo Park
- 505
- Ie
- YAGAJI ISLAND
- Motobu
- Higashi
- SESOKO ISLAND
- 449
- Nago
- OKINAWA
- 331
- TO KERAMA ISLANDS
- 58
- Ginoza
- Kin
- Cape Maeda
- Kin Bay
- IKEI ISLAND
- Ishikawa
- Gushikawa
- Yomitan
- MIYAGI ISLAND
- Okinawa
- 1
- Pacific Ocean
- TSUKEN ISLAND
- 56
- Urasoe
- 329
- KUDAKA ISLAND
- Naha
- Japanese Navy Underground Headquarters
- Nanjo
- 331v
- Okinawa World
- Itoman
- Okinawa Prefectural Peace Memorial Museum
- Himeyuri Peace Museum
- OKASHIKI ISLAND

0    4 mi
0    4 km

- 125°E
- KYUSHU
- Yaku-shima
- 30°N
- Amami-o-shima
- Tokuno-shima
- Kerama Islands 2
- OKINAWA Map Area
- 3 Miyako Islands
- 4 Yaeyama Islands

# OKINAWA'S WORLD WAR II SIGHTS

Himeyuri Peace Museum

The Battle of Okinawa is one of the most tragic events in modern history. Caught between two warring nations, the people of Okinawa were killed by a "Typhoon of Steel" and the brutal inhumanity of war.

By late March 1945, American forces began the assault on Okinawa, a pivotal stepping-stone to attacking the Japanese mainland. Japan's strategy was to drag out the conflict and force a war of attrition. Every sector of Okinawa's civilian population was mobilized into the front lines of the fighting. The initial bombardment by the United States was described as a "Typhoon of Steel." Artillery rained down so heavily that the bombs changed the very topography of the island. Horrific losses were followed by an awful land war. Okinawans who survived the shelling and flame throwers succumbed to starvation, disease, suicide, or the brutality of retreating Japanese troops. The final battle of the war claimed roughly 240,000 lives—over half of them civilian—more than a quarter of Okinawa's population. The memorials commemorating these events and the quest for world peace are Okinawa's most poignant landmarks.

## THE FUTENMA ISSUE

The U.S. Marine Corps Air Station Futenma is Okinawa's most controversial U.S. military base. It is surrounded by a residential area, and locals want it closed. In 1996 the U.S. and Japanese governments agreed to close the base, but expand Camp Schwab in northern Okinawa. Many Okinawans have opposed the expansion of Schwab into Henoko Bay, citing environmental concerns.

## MAIN ISLAND SIGHTS

In Naha City, **Sugar Loaf Hill** was a heavily defended strategic point on General Mitsuru Ushijima's Shuri Line. American Marines made repeated frontal assaults, losing thousands of men before capturing the hill on May 18, 1945. The hill is now dwarfed by the DFS Building (Duty-Free Store) just west of Omoro-machi Monorail Station. A plaque marks the spot where so many men died.

Just south of Naha City is the **Underground Headquarters of the Japanese Imperial Navy.** Visitors can explore the tunnels in which Imperial Navy Vice Admiral Minoru Ota lived with 4,000 men. You can see the various rooms, including the commander's office, but perhaps the most unnerving sights are the gouges in the walls and roof from grenades when the officers took their own lives.

Farther south, **Himeyuri Peace Museum** tells the tragic story of Okinawan schoolgirls who were mobilized as field nurses during the conflict. Harrowing accounts of their experiences convey the horrors of war.

**Peace Memorial Park** is at Mabuni Hill, and it's here where the final acts of the Battle of Okinawa took place. There are three main areas to the park. The Peace

Okinawa Peace Memorial Park

Memorial Museum tells the history of the Battle of Okinawa and the resulting desire of Okinawans for world peace. Outside is the Cornerstone of Peace, line after line of low, black, granite walls are inscribed with the names of more than 240,000 Okinawans, Japanese, Americans, Koreans, North Koreans, British, and Taiwanese who perished during the conflict. The Peace Memorial Hall houses a 32-foot statue of a person praying. The artist, Shinzan Yamada, began the project when he was 72, and the work took him 18 years. The statue sits on a six-petal flower representing the six continents to symbolize the global search for peace.

## AN UNDERWATER MEMORIAL

The USS *Emmons* was a U.S. destroyer that was hit by five kamikaze planes on April 6, 1945. The following day the ship was sunk before it drifted into enemy-controlled territory. In 2000 the Japanese Coast Guard discovered the wreck, and then in early 2001 it was found by local American divers. The *Emmons* lies at a depth of around 130 feet, just off Kouri Island. A few dive shops on Okinawa do offer recreational dives to view the wreck, but the depth and strong currents mean this is only an option for advanced divers.

Okinawa Peace Memorial Park

Tropical climate, sun-kissed beaches and crystal-blue waters, deserted islands ringed by rainbow-hued coral reefs, verdant jungle trails, and funky port towns full of laid-back, fun-loving islanders will welcome you to Okinawa, Japan's most diverse and exciting destination.

Naha, Okinawa's capital, is geographically closer to Taiwan than to any of Japan's main islands, but deeper distinctions of culture and history are what really set the islands apart. Okinawa's indigenous population comprises an ethnic group independent from the mainland Japanese, and local pride lays much heavier with Okinawa's bygone Ryukyu Kingdom than it ever will with the Empire of the Rising Sun. Island culture today forms an identity around its Ryukyu roots but also reflects the centuries of cross-cultural influence brought to Okinawa on successive tides of imperialism. Ships from ancient Polynesia, Ming China, Edo Japan, and most recently wartime America brought the ravages of conquest and the joys of new traditions (snakeskin instruments, the stir-fry, and Spam). Okinawa's melting pot is sharply different from mainland Japan's commercial culture of appropriation and pastiche, touching every element of island life and lending flavor to the music, language, cuisine, architecture, arts, and lifestyle that define the archipelago.

The Okinawan archipelago spans about 700 km (435 miles) of ocean, reaching from south of Kyushu's Kagoshima Prefecture to just east of Taiwan. Of the hundreds of islands only a handful are inhabited, and even the settled ones sport more jungle and beach than they do road and city. More than 90% of the population, numbering about 1.3 million, lives on Okinawa Main Island, the largest and most developed island of the chain. Okinawa Main Island is notorious for also housing the bulk of Japan's American military presence, though unless you're here visiting a friend in uniform, your focus will be the island's beaches, moving war memorials, natural escapes, and UNESCO World Heritage castles and monuments of the Ryukyu Kingdom.

With limited time to spend in Okinawa, we recommend you choose one of the three main island groups to explore instead of trying to cram it all in. It would be a missed opportunity to not venture beyond Okinawa Main Island. While its sights are terrific, you'll find more diverse adventure and welcoming islander hospitality as you get farther away from Naha City. Okinawa rewards a traveler's intrepid spirit, so head out into the wild blue yonder.

# Planning

## Getting Here and Around

Naha is the most common entry point to Okinawa, with flights taking roughly two hours and departing regularly from most major airports in Japan. A new international terminal and a growth in tourism means there are now direct flights from nearby international hubs (including Hong Kong, Taipei, Seoul, Pusan, Shanghai, Beijing, and Tenjin). Most odysseys through Okinawa begin here before moving farther into the archipelago, but there's no reason not to start farther out and work your way back: domestic flights connect directly to Miyako Airport from Osaka-Itami and Tokyo-Haneda, and to Ishigaki from Osaka-Kansai, Kobe, and Tokyo-Haneda. Flying from Naha to Miyako or Ishigaki takes around an hour. Travel agents anywhere in the country can arrange tickets for you, or or you can book them via airline websites. Booking early can get you a significant discount. It is also worth checking on the prices of flight-hotel packages that, if booked more than two weeks in advance, can be cheaper than the flight alone.

Public transportation in Okinawa leaves a lot to be desired. Naha is serviced by a handy monorail running from the airport through the city, out to Shurijo Castle, and terminating at Tedako Uranishi, with trains running about every 10 minutes. Outside the city things are less promising. The story is the same on each of the islands: yes, buses link to urban centers and popular tourist destinations, but schedules are inconvenient, hard to decipher, and confining. Budget for rental cars to make the most of your time on the larger islands.

# Hotels

Lodgings range from no-frills beach shacks to lavish resorts. Most Japanese tourists visiting Okinawa purchase packages that combine flights, a rental car, and hotel accommodations. Some choose to remain in Naha, but the majority stay at one of the large resort hotels on the west coast, many of which are on the Yomitan Peninsula, Onna Village, or Motobu Town. The high-end resorts often have their own golf courses, fine restaurants, and even wedding chapels. You don't have to spend large amounts of money to find paradise, however. You'll also get friendly service, meet interesting locals, and receive knowledgeable recommendations for tours when staying at smaller, locally run hotels and inns.

*For a short course on accommodations in Japan, see Lodging in the Travel Smart chapter.*

# Restaurants

Okinawa's culinary history doesn't have the same pedigree as the haute cuisine of Kyoto or Tokyo. A similar aristocratic tradition hasn't prevailed here, and prized local ingredients like soba, pork, and mozuku seaweed aren't necessarily expensive or hard to produce. This isn't to say that Okinawan cuisine falls short on rare delicacies or delicious cooking, but rather that great, true-blue Okinawan food can be had on the cheap, anywhere. Greasy-spoon joints will have fare as traditional and as tasty as the fancy gourmet establishments, so go enjoy!

■TIP→ **One effect of the American military presence has been to increase English-language proficiency throughout Okinawa. Most restaurants and hotels will have some English-speaking staff, so feel confident about going into any establishment for a meal or to inquire about a stay.**

## RESTAURANT AND HOTEL PRICES

Restaurant prices are the average cost of a main course at dinner or, if dinner is not served, at lunch. Hotel prices are the lowest cost of a standard double room in high season. Restaurant and hotel reviews have been shortened. For full information, visit Fodors.com.

### What It Costs in Yen

| $ | $$ | $$$ | $$$$ |
|---|---|---|---|
| **RESTAURANTS** | | | |
| under ¥1,500 | ¥1,500– ¥3,000 | ¥3,001– ¥5,000 | over ¥5,000 |
| **HOTELS** | | | |
| under ¥12,000 | ¥12,000– ¥18,000 | ¥18,001– ¥22,000 | over ¥22,000 |

# When to Go

The best time to visit Okinawa will depend on your goals. Avoid mid-May to mid-June, which is the rainy season. The subtropical climate means the temperatures in winter rarely drop below 15°C (59°F), and because of this Okinawa celebrates the arrival of cherry blossoms in January. For marine sports including scuba diving, July to October is the best time since the water temperature is around 25°C–28°C (77°F–82°F) and the southerly breezes are not strong. Nevertheless, July to September is also typhoon season, so the fantastic weather can be interrupted by several days of heavy rains and ferocious winds.

For those interested in Okinawan culture, try to schedule your trip to coincide with one of the many festivals, such as the Shuri Castle Festival (New Year), Naha dragon-boat races (March), Eisa festivals (August), or Karate Day and the Naha Tug of War Festival (October).

# Okinawa Main Island (沖縄島)

*Okinawa Main Island is 1,558 km (968 miles) southwest of Tokyo, and 1,145 km (711 miles) southwest of Osaka. By air: 2½ hours from Tokyo, 2 hours from Osaka. Weekly or daily connections with most major domestic airports.*

On arrival at Okinawa Main Island, you may be struck by the island's multicultural feel. There are obvious influences of American culture, but Okinawa, and the Ryukyu Kingdom before that, has long embraced a philosophy of "champuru" that mixes traditions from across the Indo-Pacific with the local way of life. In Naha City you'll find many connections to Okinawa's position as a tributary of China; Central Okinawa Main Island is where you'll see the main presence of the U.S. military; while Northern Mainland Okinawa has tourist-focused resorts, funky dive shops and a laid-back, tropical vibe.

Naha City makes for a fascinating day or two with great restaurants and numerous cultural sights. Naha also provides easy access to Southern Okinawa Main Island's moving war memorials that document the region's tragic history in World War II.

Central Okinawa Main Island is home to the bulk of American forces in Japan. Their presence has many pros and cons, but one positive is that areas around the bases such as Chatan have a vibrant cosmopolitan atmosphere in a country that is famously homogeneous. The west coast of central Okinawa has great entertainment options and better beaches than in Naha.

Northern Okinawa Main Island has smaller towns along the coast, interspersed by

# Planning Your Time

A journey to the tropics means relaxation is your top priority, so plan well to avoid the travel stresses Okinawa can throw at you. Two factors make getting around challenging: it's easy to forget just how vast an area the prefecture covers; and you're competing with "Okinawa Time," a relaxed island philosophy that is both endearing and frustrating. Minimize tension and maximize your fun by choosing one or two places to explore instead of trying to see it all—but don't spend your whole vacation on Okinawa Main Island. The farther you get from the beaten track, the more richly rewarding your time here will be.

Follow up a day devoted to Naha's sights with another day each for the northern and southern sights of Okinawa Main Island. After that, pick an island chain and head out. Adventure activities like scuba diving, sea kayaking, trekking, and snorkeling are readily available. Remember, though, that these sports take up energy and time, so if you plan to try a range of activities consider lingering around one locale for a few days rather than pinballing around the archipelago.

■ TIP→ You can't fly the same day you scuba dive.

We recommend Ishigaki Island and its neighbors Iriomote Island and Taketomi Island for a week away from it all; you'll find reliable guides for the gamut of adventure activities throughout the region's diverse natural environments, and sights ranging from homey city to jungle wilderness. The area has remained largely sheltered from the tourist industry, so this frontier is yours to claim.

resort hotels and some great treasures: active artisan enclaves, sweet diving spots, and the phenomenal Churaumi Aquarium. The northern peninsula, now designated as the Yambaru National Park, has overviews, rocky karsts, mangrove forests, and waterfalls.

If you rent a car you can see the highlights of Okinawa Main Island in about three or four days. A one-night stay in Naha lets you see the city then circle the southern peninsula. Staying a night or two up north on the Motobu Peninsula would let you hit the sights along the coast on your way there. Check out the sites of Motobu, Nakijin, and Yambaru National Park, then head back to Naha for a night out before the flight or ferry to your next destination.

# Naha (那覇)

Okinawa's capital city is the center of commerce, tourism, and youthful enterprise in the region. People here are more laid-back than elsewhere in Japan, with business suits replaced by brightly colored Kariyushi shirts, and you'll probably have an easy time feeling relaxed and energized by the city's verve as you tour the sights. Naha's appeal has a short half-life, however, and you may quickly tire of the students on school trips swarming the sidewalks, the kitschy souvenir shops and arcades, and the traffic congestion.

## GETTING HERE AND AROUND
Japan Airlines and All Nippon Airways fly to Naha from most major Japanese destinations, with tickets usually running between ¥20,000 and ¥30,000, but

discounts for booking in advance can bring the price as low as ¥9,000. Ferries between Naha and Kansai, Tokyo and southern Kyushu have fares expensive enough to make flying worthwhile, especially in light of the time you save: compare a two-hour flight from Tokyo versus a four-day boat ride with at best a ¥10,000 difference in price. Naha also has flights to Miyako, Ishigaki, and Yonaguni, all farther out in the archipelago. Several low-cost carriers fly between mainland Japan and Okinawa, including Skymark, Jetstar, and Peach Aviation.

Getting to the city is easy thanks to the clean, convenient monorail. The line begins at the airport, Naha Kuko, and weaves through the city before terminating at the castle Shuri-jo. Shopping, accommodations, and activities are all centered around bustling Kokusai Street in the middle of town. Depending on which end your hotel is closest to, you'll get off at the Kencho-mae, Miebashi, or Makishi Station. Everything you need is in within walking distance or a few monorail stops away. Trains run about every 10 minutes from 6 am until about 11:30 pm, and fares are ¥220 to ¥320 per trip.

When it's time to leave the city, ask your hotel for the closest rental-car place; Naha is denser with these than with noodle shops. It is also easy to rent a car from the airport on arrival. Most companies offer a similar selection of sensible subcompact cars, but if you want to cruise in style check out the vehicles at Celeb Rent-a-Car. Okinawa RV rents camping cars, and has international staff to give you advice on where to go. You will need to show an international driver's license or a Japanese driver's license to rent a vehicle.

### AIRLINE INFORMATION
**ANA.** ☎ 03/6741–6685 ⊕ www.ana.co.jp. **JAL.** ☎ 0570/025–121 ⊕ www.jal.co.jp/en.

### CAR RENTALS Celeb Rent-a-Car.
✉ Yamashita-cho 1–11, Naha ☎ 098/859–3337 ⊕ www.celeb-r.com. **Nippon Rent-a-Car.** ☎ 03/6859–6234 ⊕ www.nrgroup-global.com/en. **ORIX Rent-A-Car.** ☎ 098/851–0543 ⊕ car.orix. co.jp/eng. **OTS Rent-a-Car.** ✉ Toyosaki 3–37, Tomigusuku ☎ 098/856–8877 ⊕ www.otsinternational.jp/otsrentacar/ en/okinawa.

### VISITOR INFORMATION
Before you leave the airport, equip yourself with good local maps, time schedules, and service information at the tourist information desk in the main lobby of the airport. In the city, stop by Naha City Tourist Information Center inside the Tenbusu Building on Kokusai Street.

### CONTACT Naha City Tourist Information Center. 
✉ Okiei-dori, 3–2–10 Makishi, Tenbusu Bldg., 1st fl., Naha ☎ 098/868–4887.

## ◉ Sights

### Chindami Sanshinten (ちんだみ 三線店)
STORE/MALL | Don't leave Okinawa without hearing the unique sound of *sanshin* music made from the three-stringed, snakeskin-covered instrument native to Okinawa and the Amami Islands. And you shouldn't leave Naha without taking a peek into one of the most highly regarded sanshin-maker's shops in the country. Higa-san will give you a free lesson, and several ranks of beginner-oriented sets let you choose a good arrangement if you want to take one home. (Buy one made with fake snakeskin, as real snakeskin is illegal in many countries.) Chindami Sanshinten is on the side street off Kokusai-dori. ✉ 1–2–18 Makishi, Naha ☎ 098/869–2055 ⊕ chindami.com.

### Kiyomasa Touki (清正陶器)
STORE/MALL | This kiln was started by a distant forebear of the current master, Takashi Kobashikawa, himself a government-designated Master of Traditional Crafts. Mugs and tankards are around ¥5,000, cup and saucer sets from around ¥6,500, and larger bowls

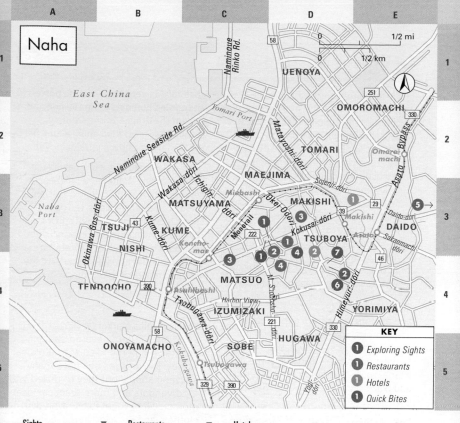

# Naha

East China Sea

Naminoue Rinko Rd.

58

UENOYA

251

OMOROMACHI

330

Yomari Port

Naminoue Seaside Rd.

Matayoshi-dōri

TOMARI

Omaro-
machi

Asato Bypass

Wakasa-dōri

WAKASA

Ichigin-dōri

MAEJIMA

Sotenji-dōri

5

Daito-dōri

Naba Port

MATSUYAMA

Kume-dōri

Miebashi

Okei Odori

MAKISHI

1

29

Makishi

Wakasa Gas-dōri

Okinawa Gas-dōri

TSUJI

43

KUME

Monorail

222

Kokusai-dōri

39

3

Asato

46

DAIDO

Sakaemachi-dōri

NISHI

Kencho-
mae

3

1

1

2

4

2

7

TSUBOYA

TENDOCHO

390

Asahibashi

MATSUO

M. Shōtengai

1

5

4

2

6

Himeyuri-dōri

Tsubogawa-dōri

Harbor View

IZUMIZAKI

221

330

YORIMIYA

58

ONOYAMACHO

Kokuba-gawa

SOBE

HUGAWA

Tsubogawa

Yogi-dōri

329

390

## KEY

1 Exploring Sights

1 Restaurants

1 Hotels

1 Quick Bites

## Sights ▼

1 Chindami Sanshinten.... **C3**
2 Kiyomasa Touki ........ **D4**
3 Kokusai Street .......... **C4**
4 Kosetsu Ichiba Market ................. **D3**
5 Shurijo Castle .......... **E3**
6 Tsuboya Pottery District .................. **D4**
7 Tsuboya Pottery Museum ................ **D4**

## Restaurants ▼

1 Bacchus no Ibukuro.... **D3**
2 Hateruma ................ **C3**
3 Kintiti soba Kokusaidori Mutsumi Shokudoten............. **D3**
4 Ukishima Garden ....... **D4**

## Quick Bites ▼

1 Blue Seal ................ **C3**

## Hotels ▼

1 Hotel Royal Orion ........ **E3**
2 Hyatt Regency Naha, Okinawa ................ **D3**

# Legend of the Shisa

*Shisa*, lionlike talismans, can be seen protecting doorways and adorning rooftops throughout the islands. It's said that during the reign of one of the ancient Ryukyu kings a dragon was terrorizing Naha, destroying settlements and devouring townsfolk. When the king encountered the dragon, a local shaman and his boy gave the king some advice they had received in dreams. The boy took hold of a pendant the king wore around his neck, a lionlike figurine that had been a gift from a Chinese emissary. Held aloft toward the dragon, the figure produced a ferocious roar, so powerful it toppled boulders from the heavens to pin the dragon to the shallow seabed, where it died and became part of the islands, now a park near Naha.

These days, shisa are Okinawa's most iconic image. Homes and businesses display them in pairs, one on either side of their entryways, the open-mouth one scaring off evil spirits, the closed-mouth partner keeping in good spirits. These good-luck totems are popular souvenirs and come in many shapes, materials, and colors.

and platters range from affordable to astronomical. Wrapping and domestic shipping services are available. From the Heiwa-dori arcade, head 200 yards until a small incline leads you up to the red-and-black sign. ✉ *Tsuboya 1–16–7, Naha* ☎ *098/862–3654.*

**Kokusai Street** (国際通り; *Kokusai-dori*)
**NEIGHBORHOOD** | You're sure to get caught up in the buzz of Kokusai Street, Naha's central hub for dining, shopping, and people-watching. It's an eye-popping introduction to Okinawa's varied demographics, from the crew-cut military personnel, Japanese teenagers on high school trips, honeymooning couples, and excited families, all while the local octogenarians do their daily shop at the market. You'll find many similarly laden souvenir shops filled with the local spirit *awamori*, *shisa* (lion-dog) figurines, purple sweet potato tarts, brown sugar, and Kariyushi shirts. However, amongst these you'll also find the stores of local craftsman selling traditional lacquerware, fabrics, and ceramics. The street is pedestrian-only on Sunday, making it the best time to visit. ✉ *Naha.*

**Kosetsu Ichiba Market** (那覇公設市場)
**STORE/MALL** | Three covered shopping arcades run perpendicular to Kokusai Street. The arcades still have many souvenir shops, but they're mixed with food vendors and more practical local stores selling vegetables, everyday clothes, and recycled items. Sample deep-fried doughnuts, leaf-wrapped mochi, and tropical fruit drinks on your way to the Kosetsu Ichiba Market, a five-minute walk from Kokusai Street. Passing between outdoor fruit stalls into an unassuming doorway leads you to a carnival of delightful and grotesque butcher counters, fishmongers, and pickle sellers. Pig faces stare ghoulishly down from racks displaying every other part of the animal (including some you likely never thought anyone could eat). Multicolor shellfish, neon eels, and giant crustaceans are so shockingly exotic they seem like they were pinched from the Okinawa Churaumi Aquarium. ✉ *Naha.*

Kosetsu Ichiba Market is filled with produce and food stands, including this fishmonger.

## ★ Shuri-jo Castle (首里城)

CASTLE/PALACE | The Seiden (central hall) of the royal castle Shurijo was destroyed by fire in October 2019; however, the castle walls, gateways, and many buildings still remain of the sprawling, grandiose seat of the ancient Ryukyu Kingdom. The castle, far more reminiscent of Beijing's Forbidden City than Kyoto's Imperial Palace, is still a marvel for the eyes. The original 16th century castle was once part of an even more extensive property, but was mostly leveled during World War II when the Japanese Imperial Army made the complex its local headquarters. After reconstruction in 1992, Shurijo was named a UNESCO World Heritage site. Once again Shurijo will rise like a phoenix from the destruction, supported by both local government and donations from around the world. Reconstruction of the Seiden is underway and is expected to be completed in 2026. It's a 10-minute walk from the Shuri monorail station. ✉ *1–2 Kinjo-cho, Shuri, Shuri-ikehatacho* ☎ *098/886–2020* ⊕ *oki-park.jp/shurijo/en* ✉ *¥400.*

## Tsuboya Pottery District
(壺屋焼; *Tsuboya-yaki*)

STORE/MALL | Over 300 years of ceramic tradition are celebrated in this area just a five-minute walk from Kokusai Street. More than 20 workshops produce Okinawa's distinctive pottery, ranging from affordable souvenirs to special pieces for wealthy collectors. The famous Japanese potter Shoji Hamada came here in the 1920s and left with the inspiration for his notable works. The limited space and minimalist design of Japanese homes means that buyers are more likely to invest in a single exquisite piece, and this can be shown in the pricing. Some potters specialize in creating elegant cups and teapots for Japanese tea ceremonies, while others produce more functional coffee mugs. A couple of the workshops have the option for you to try throwing your own pots, which they will fire, glaze, and ship to you. If you're looking for active wood-fired kilns, also check out the Yomitan Pottery Village (Yachimun No Sato) in Central Okinawa Main Island. ✉ *Tsuboya.*

**Tsuboya Pottery Museum** (壺屋焼物博物館; *Tsuboya Yakimono Hakubutsukan*)
**OTHER MUSEUM** | The small but heartfelt Tsuboya Pottery Museum has exhibits illustrating the history of the region's earthenware production, including representative pieces from all periods, and a reproduction of a traditional Okinawan house, showing Tsubo-yaki tableware and kitchen utensils. Next to the museum is an intact 19th-century climbing kiln, called a *nobori-gama.* Detailed English explanations make the experience more exciting and informative. Located at the edge of the Tsuboya Pottery District, where the cobbled streets begin. ✉ *1–9–32 Tsuboya, Naha* ☎ *098/862–3761* 🌐 *www.edu.city.naha.okinawa.jp/tsuboya* 🎫 *¥350* 🕒 *Closed Mon.*

## Okinawa Pottery

Walking through stalls of nearly identical terra-cotta shisa statues in the Tsuboya district, you may think that Okinawa's pottery tradition is a newfangled tourist gimmick—don't be fooled. Stop into Kiyomasa Touki for a look at 320 years of unbroken tradition. Take home a keepsake and you'll be in good company: visiting dignitaries often receive a plate as a gift from the city.

## 🍴 Restaurants

**Bacchus no Ibukuro** (バッカスの胃袋)
**$** | **ECLECTIC** | Still known to the locals as the Helios Pub, this microbrewery and restaurant serves up six tasty home brews along with hearty snacks like Okinawan-style seafood salads and herb-seasoned bratwurst sausages. They also have a selection of *awamori* from the Helios distillery in Nago including some excellent 18-year single cask bottles. **Known for:** tasty craft beers; German-style sausages; selection of local awamori. [$] *Average main: ¥1,100* ✉ *1–2–25 Makishi, Naha* ☎ *098/863–7227.*

**Hateruma** (波照間)
**$** | **JAPANESE** | **FAMILY** | In a traditional house with a tile roof, this lively izakaya-style restaurant has a helpful picture menu. On the second floor there are Okinawan music and dance performances most nights at 6, 7, and 8 (with an additional ¥550 service charge). **Known for:** traditional Okinawan dishes such as goya champuru (a stir-fried dish); lively atmosphere in the evenings; live music. [$] *Average main: ¥1,200* ✉ *1–2–30 Makishi, Naha* ☎ *098/863–8859* 🌐 *hateruma.jcc-okinawa.net.*

**Kintiti soba Kokusaidori Mutsumi Shokudoten** (金月そば 国際通りむつみ食堂店)
**$** | **JAPANESE** | This greasy spoon has been serving some of the island's best fare since 1958; locals know it simply as Mutsumi. Everything is twice as big and three times as filling as it looks, with soup and rice included. **Known for:** homey atmosphere; all parts of the pig including the squeal; big bowls of Okinawa soba. [$] *Average main: ¥750* ✉ *2–1–16 Makishi, Naha* ☎ *098/867–0862* 🌐 *kintitisoba.com* 💳 *No credit cards* 🕒 *Closed Mon.*

**Ukishima Garden** (浮島ガーデン)
**$** | **VEGETARIAN** | The longevity of Okinawans has gained worldwide attention, and Ukishima Garden provides the health conscious with delicious meat-free dishes and organic wines. The grain burger is tasty, but on a hot summer's day the cold noodles with crunchy veggies hit the spot. **Known for:** local organic ingredients; organic wines; delicious vegan and vegetarian food. [$] *Average main: ¥1,400* ✉ *2–12–3 Matsuo, Naha* ☎ *098/943–2100* 🌐 *www.ukishima-garden.com* 🕒 *Closed Mon.–Thurs. No dinner.*

The sanshin is covered by snakeskin (sometimes fake).

#  Coffee and Quick Bites

**Blue Seal** (ブルーシール)

$ | CAFÉ | While strolling down Naha's Kokusai-dori, stop by one of the island's iconic Blue Seal ice cream shops. "Born in America, Raised in Okinawa," Blue Seal combines American soft serve with Okinawan flavors such as *beni imo* (purple sweet potato), *ube* (mountain yam), or sugar cane. If you're desperate for a midnight snack you can also find Blue Seal ice creams at any 24-hour convenience store. **Known for:** beni imo ice cream; soft serve ice cream; flavors unique to Okinawa. $ *Average main:* ¥330 ✉ 1–3–63 Makishi, Naha ☎ 098/864–0105 ⊕ en.blueseal.co.jp ▭ *No credit cards.*

# 🛏 Hotels

**Hotel Royal Orion**
(ホテルロイヤルオリオン)

$$$$ | HOTEL | You couldn't ask for a better in-town lodging than this elegant, nicely furnished hotel. **Pros:** great location; good rates; selection of restaurants, café and bakery. **Cons:** no minibar or room service; only some staff speak English; traffic noise from Kokusai Street. $ *Rooms from:* ¥25,000 ✉ 1–2–21 Asato, Naha ☎ 098/866–5533 ⊕ www.royal-orion.co.jp ⮠ *209 rooms* ⦿ *No Meals.*

**Hyatt Regency Naha, Okinawa**
(ハイアットリージェンシー那覇 沖縄)

$$$$ | HOTEL | The Hyatt is elegant but without a stratospheric price tag. **Pros:** located close to Kokusai Street, but away from traffic noise; some suites have double beds; excellent buffet. **Cons:** far from beaches or marine sports; lacks the island feel; not as luxurious as other hotels in the Hyatt chain. $ *Rooms from:* ¥33,800 ✉ 3–6–21 Maikishi, Naha City,

*Naha ☎ 098/866–8888 ⊕ naha.regency. hyatt.com ➷ 294 rooms ✲ No Meals.*

##  Nightlife

You can't visit Okinawa without hearing the entrancing, energetic sound of the sanshin, a three-stringed musical instrument native to the Okinawa and the Amami Islands that is covered with snakeskin. Many liken its sound to that of a banjo. Hateruma on Kokusai Street has live shows of Okinawan music most nights. The nightlife scene in Okinawa is usually based around eating and drinking with friends at a restaurant or traditional izakaya. On bigger nights, locals may follow this with a *nijikai* or second stage, where they go for drinks or karaoke at one of the many small bars.

##  Shopping

**Jahana Kippan** (謝花きっぱん店)

CANDY | Not far from Kokusai Street is a shop fit for a king. In fact, the traditional sweets that Jahana Kippan produce were once made for the royal court of the Ryukyu Kingdom. The secret recipes have been passed down from generation to generation, and the ingredients are all natural, mainly based on sugarcane, winter melon, and *kippan*, a citrus fruit. Hisano speaks excellent English and can explain the different delicacies. The green-tea-covered sweets are popular, but the coconut-covered *tougan* (winter melon) is sublime. ⊠ *1–5–14 Matsuo, Naha* ☎ *098/867–3687* ⊕ *www.jahanakippan.com.*

##  Activities

**Marine House Seasir**
(マリンハウスシーサー)

WILDLIFE-WATCHING | FAMILY | From January to March, humpback whales visit the warm shallow waters around Okinawa to breed and to raise their young. Marine House Seasir runs day-trips from Naha out to the Kerama Islands. It can get choppy, particularly when crossing between Okinawa Main Island to the Keramas, so prepare sea-sickness remedies if needed. Marine House Seasir also offers diving excursions throughout the year. Credit cards are accepted. ⊠ *2–3–13 Minato-machi, Naha* ☎ *098/869–6329* ⊕ *www.seasir.com/ lang/en/naha* ✍ *Whale-watching half-day trip from ¥4,980.*

# South of Naha

The cultural park Okinawa World is an interactive trip through the islands' Ryukyu past, with restored houses, a large limestone cave, and traditional performances. More than the ancient Ryukyu culture, however, it is Okinawa's history during World War II that will resonate most with visitors. Himeyuri Peace Museum and Okinawa Peace Memorial Museum trace Okinawa's tragic story. Caught between American and Japanese militaries during the last months of the war, Okinawa suffered an astronomical toll in lost lives and resources. Like Hiroshima's Atomic Bomb Dome, these sights are important not only to local history, but also for their message teaching the value of peace to all.

### GETTING HERE AND AROUND

Bus routes will take you past all the sights, but infrequent schedules will rush you or leave you bored. It's an easy drive from the city, though—every sight is on Route 331—so renting a car is highly advisable. Bus schedules change year to year.

##  Sights

**Himeyuri Peace Museum**
(ひめゆり平和祈念資料館;
*Himeyuri heiwa kinen shiryokan*)

HISTORY MUSEUM | This moving museum tells the story of 240 girls from a high school near Naha. Mobilized as field nurses in the war's final months, their hellish experiences tending to wounded Japanese soldiers in hidden caves near the city are retold in an intensely poignant series of dioramas, textual explanations, and displays. Photographs and journals show the girls' innocence and hope before the war, providing a moving counterpoint to the ghastly conditions they endured during the fighting. Photographs of each girl drive home the war's tragic effects. The museum is an hour from Naha via Bus 34 or 89 (¥590), with a change in Itoman to Bus 82, 107 or 108 (¥330). Buses depart hourly and continue on to the Peace Memorial. ✉ 671–1 Aza-Ihara, Itoman ☎ 098/997–2100 ⊕ www.himeyuri.or.jp ⏱ ¥450.

### Japanese Navy Underground Headquarters (旧海軍司令部壕; Kyu Kaigun Shireibu-go)

MILITARY SIGHT | In these cold, clammy tunnels Admiral Ota and 174 of his men came to a dramatic end on June 13, 1945. He and six of his top officers killed themselves to escape capture or death by American forces. The grenade blasts that killed the rest of Ota's men left visible shrapnel damage on the walls. An information desk has pamphlets in English, but staff are unlikely to speak anything but Japanese. It's 25 minutes from the Naha Bus Terminal Asahibashi Mae via Bus 55, 88, or 98. Get off at the the Uebaru danchi-mae stop, and walk 10 minutes uphill to the ticket gate. ✉ 236 Aza Tomishiro, Tomishiro-shi, Tomigusuku ☎ 098/850–4055 ⊕ kaigungou.ocvb.or.jp/english/index.html ⏱ ¥600.

### Okinawa Karate Kaikan (沖縄空手会館)

SPORTS VENUE | Okinawa is the birthplace of karate, and it's definitely worth visiting the new Okinawa Karate Kaikan if you've come to the islands inspired by *The Karate Kid* or *Cobra Kai*. The main hall is used for seminars and competitions, while smaller rooms are available for training. The Reference Room is a small museum documenting the history of karate

and *kobudo* (Okinawan weapon-based fighting), with many fascinating insights into the legendary sensei. Karate Café AGARI has Okinawa Soba, and Okinawa *zenzai* (shaved ice with sweet beans). The Okinawa Karate Information Center (OKIC) is located with the Karate Kaikan and provides visitors to Okinawa with multilingual support on how to connect with individual karate masters and train at local dojos. ✉ 854–1 Tomigusku, Tomigusuku ☎ 098/851–1025 ⊕ karatekaikan.jp/en ⏱ ¥310 Reference Room ⊘ Closed Wed.

### ★ Okinawa Prefectural Peace Memorial Museum (沖縄県平和祈念資料館; Okinawa kenritsu heiwa kinen shiryokan)

HISTORY MUSEUM | Rows of black granite blocks inscribed with the names of the thousands who lost their lives in World War II cover the rolling, green hills around this excellent museum. Exhibits, some designed specifically for children, provide a rare opportunity to contemplate global issues. Focusing on the brutal Battle of Okinawa, interesting exhibits highlight each side's tactical perspective and the progress of the fighting. More personal displays reveal what life was like on the ground during the chaos and include testimonies of survivors (unfortunately, only a few of these are translated). A diorama portrays life in American-occupied postwar Okinawa. The museum is 80 minutes from Naha via bus; change from Bus 89 to 82 at Itoman Terminal. The total cost is ¥1,070. ✉ 614–1 Aza-Mabuni, Itoman ☎ 098/997–3844 ⊕ www.peace-museum.okinawa.jp/english ⏱ ¥300.

### Okinawa World (おきなわワールド)

CAVE | FAMILY | It's worth spending a few hours at Okinawa World to get a quick overview of local culture. There are tropical fruit orchards and workshops for textile weaving, glassblowing, pottery, dyeing, and printing. Traditional Eisa dance performances take place several times a day. The main attraction is Gyokusendo Cave, the second-longest limestone cave in Japan. You can walk through an 890-meter (2,920-foot) cavern and marvel at the giant stalactites and stalagmites. From Naha Bus Terminal, take Bus 54 or 83 and get off at Gyokusendo-mae. ✉ *1336 Maekawa, Nanjo* ☎ *098/949–7421* ⊕ *www.gyokusendo.co.jp/okinawaworld/ en* 💲 *¥2,000 (includes cave).*

# Central Okinawa

Central Okinawa Main Island is where you find the bulk of American forces in Japan. It can be a little surreal when your rental car is suddenly dwarfed by a Humvee or the even bigger JLTV. Just as likely is that during your day at a tranquil beach, castle, or picnic spot you'll be given an unexpected airshow as F-15 fighters, KC-135 Stratotankers, and AWACS make their way back to Kadena Air Base. The west coast of central Okinawa Main Island is still however a great place to visit. Chatan Town has a lively multicultural feel, varied restaurants, and great shopping opportunities, while the Yomitan Peninsula has excellent beaches, dive spots, clifftop walks, and a pottery community. Chatan is easily accessible by public transportation, but exploring Yomitan is best done by car.

## ◉ Sights

**Bokunen Art Museum** (ボクネン美術館; *Bokunen Bijutsukan*)
**ART MUSEUM** | Naka Bokunen is one of Okinawa's most celebrated artists. The Bokunen Art Museum, a stunning tile-clad building Bokunen designed, showcases his work, including huge woodblock prints of Okinawan landscapes using a reverse-coloring technique known as *uratesaishoku*. His work has been compared to Hokusai and Chagall, but he credits his true inspiration as the beauty of the Okinawan Islands. ✉ *9–20 Mihama, Chatan-cho* ☎ *098/926–2764* ⊕ *museum.bokunen.com* 💲 *¥800* ⊗ *Closed Tues.*

**Cape Maeda** (真栄田岬; *Maeda Misaki*)
**SCUBA DIVING** | Cape Maeda is one of Okinawa Main Island's most popular diving and snorkeling spots. During summer it gets packed by around 11 am, so it is usually best to arrive as early as possible. As with nearly all dive sites on Okinawa, early in the morning is most likely to give you calmer water for your entry and exit. Many of Okinawa's dive shops use this as a base for teaching. Cape Maeda has toilets, hot showers, vending machines, a cafe, and a large pay carpark. Great for convenience, but some will prefer quieter, more remote dive sites. ✉ *Cape Maeda, Yomitan-son* ⊕ *www.maedamisaki.jp/en.*

**Cape Zanpa Park**
(残波岬公園; *Zanpa Misaki Koen*)
**LIGHTHOUSE | FAMILY** | Cape Zanpa's lighthouse is set atop impressive cliffs. The Cape Zanpa Park is great place for a refreshing clifftop walk, plus there's a beach and a children's play area. In winter, it is one of the best locations to spot whales from the coast, while in summer it is a popular advanced level diving spot. You'll find various monuments including Okinawa's largest shisa statue, a statue of the diplomat Taiki who set up trade with China, and a mural to those who lost their lives during WWII's Battle of Okinawa. During and just after typhoons the cliff tops can be dangerous due to high winds and huge waves. ✉ *675 Uza, Yomitan-son.*

## 🍴 Restaurants

**Vongo & Anchor**
**$$ | FUSION** | Vongo & Anchor serves great coffee, pastries, and light meals in a relaxed atmosphere. Located on the sunset walk promenade, it's the perfect place to chill and recharge. **Known for:** great coffee; ocean views; vegan options. 💲 *Average main: ¥1,500* ✉ *Mihama 9–21, Chatan-cho* ⊕ *www.vongoandanchor. coffee.*

## Hotels

**Vessel Hotel Campana Okinawa**
(ベッセルホテルカンパーナ沖縄)
$$$$ | **HOTEL** | **FAMILY** | Overlooking Sunset Beach, the Pacific Ocean, and the shopping district of Chatan's American Village, the Vessel Hotel Campana Okinawa has the perfect location for those who wish to explore Chatan. **Pros:** ocean views; central location; family friendly. **Cons:** not all rooms have the ocean view; noise from planes; not as many facilities as the larger resorts. [$] *Rooms from: ¥44,400* ✉ *Mihama 9–22, Chatan-cho* ☎ *098/926–1188* 🌐 *www.vessel-hotel.jp/campana/okinawa* 🛏 *332 Rooms* 🍴 *No Meals.*

# Northern Okinawa

The north of Okinawa Main Island is where you find deserted beaches and ancient tropical forests. The Motobu Peninsula west of Nago City has several resorts and family-focused attractions, the highlight of which is the Ocean Expo Park and its Okinawa Churaumi Aquarium. Bridges now connect the peninsula to Sesoko Island and Kouri Island, both of which have their own idyllic beaches and cafes. In 2016, a large section of northern Okinawa Main Island became the Yambaru National Park, Japan's 33rd National Park. The area's most famous resident is the Okinawa rail, an endangered flightless bird that was only officially described in 1981.

## Sights

**Okinawa Churaumi Aquarium at Ocean Expo Park** (沖縄美ら海水族館; *Okinawa Churaumi Suizokukan*)
**AQUARIUM** | **FAMILY** | With one of the biggest saltwater tanks in the world, this is the most impressive aquarium in Japan. A pioneering coral-breeding experiment explains the fragile tropical ecosystem, while tanks hold sharks, freaky deep-water species, and thousands of other sea creatures. The star attraction is the 30-foot-deep tank holding a majestic whale shark, a dozen manta rays, and fish native to Okinawa. Additionally Ocean Expo Park includes an Oceanic Culture Museum with a planetarium (¥190), the Tropical Dream Center (¥760) that houses a vast number of orchid species, and a reconstruction of a traditional Okinawan village. A short stroll north of the park is the idyllic village of Bise with its narrow roads lined by fukugi trees. You can get to Ocean Expo Park by car or via the Yanbaru Express bus service that runs from Naha Airport, via central Naha to the aquarium (two hours, 20 minutes). Up-to-date bus schedules are on the park website. ✉ *424 Ishikawa, Motobu-cho, Kunigami gun, Motobu* ☎ *0980/48–3748* 🌐 *churaumi.okinawa/en* 🎟 *¥1,880.*

**Daisekirinzan**
(やんばる国立公園 大石林山)
**NATIONAL PARK** | Set in the very north of the Yambaru National Park, Daisekirinzan is a family friendly park where you can wander among giant banyan trees and the limestone spires of Japan's only tropical karst landscape. Many of the unusual formations are considered power spots by the islanders. Of the four trails, the longer Wonder of Rocks Trail, marked in yellow, makes for a very interesting 1-km (½-mile) scramble. Daisekirinzan was one of the shooting locations for the TV series *Cobra Kai*. After visiting the park, it's just a few kilometers further to Cape Hedo, Okinawa's northernmost tip, for more otherworldly rock formations. ✉ *1241 Ginama, Kunigami Village* ☎ *0980/41–8117* 🌐 *www.sekirinzan.com/en* 🎟 *¥1,200.*

**Nakijin Castle**
(今帰仁城跡; *Nakijin Joseki*)
**CASTLE/PALACE** | **FAMILY** | Nakijin Castle is the northernmost of Okinawa's UNESCO World Heritage sites. The hilltop castle ruins provide beautiful views over the forest and ocean to the islands of Izena and Iheya. In the 14th century, when

Okinawa was split into three principalities, Nakijin Castle was the fortress of the northern Hokuzan region. Nakijin Castle and nearby Mount Yae are the two most famous spots for cherry blossom viewing in Okinawa. The castle grounds contain hundreds of cherry trees which bloom in late January. Access is easiest by rental car, but is also accessible by either the #65 bus from Nago (plus a 15-minute walk uphill) or the Yanbaru express bus which stops at the Nakijin Castle entrance. Both buses also stop in front of Okinawan Churaumi Aquarium/ Ocean Expo Park. ✉ *5101 Imadomari, Nakijin, Motobu* 🌐 *www.nakijinjoseki-osi.jp* 🎫 *¥400.*

**Yambaru Art Gallery** (菊田一朗山原屛風; *Ichiro Kikuta Yambaru Byobu*)
**ART GALLERY** | A real hidden gem, Ichiro Kikuta is a wildlife artist and nature guide who lives in the remote village of Ada. His gallery is located inside the Ada Garden Hotel Okinawa and is themed around the plants and animals that surround him in the Yambaru National Park. Kikuta's work varies in scale from delicate watercolors in his notepad to traditional Japanese room dividers with scenes of the forest printed on the washi paper. His gallery is open to the public, but you need to call in advance, as he divides his time between working in his gallery, and guiding nature lovers in the local area. ✉ *1285–95 Ada, Kunigami Village* 📧 *byobu.japan@gmail.com* 🌐 *kikutaichiro.com* 🎫 *Free admission to museum* 🕒 *Closed weekends* ☞ *Ichiro Kikuta also offers nature guiding from ¥6,000 per person.*

## 🍴 Restaurants

**The British Wine and Tea Shop** (ザ・ブリティッシュ・ワイン・アンド・ティー・ショップ)
**$** | **BRITISH** | Warm scones with homemade jams and lashings of clotted cream, cucumber sandwiches, and quiches with buttery crusts—to find these British culinary icons hidden in the subtropical forest of northern Okinawa would seem almost impossible, until you find out that the tea shop's chef Maki once worked at London's Savoy restaurant. On her return to Japan, she brought her very particular set of skills to the town of Motobu, and since then local residents have been able to take afternoon tea like Her Majesty the Queen. **Known for:** fresh scones; afternoon tea sets; quiche. [$] *Average main: ¥1,400* ✉ *2490 Izumi, Motobu* ☎ *0980/47–7133* 🌐 *british.ti-da.net/e2559468.html* 💳 *No credit cards* 🕒 *Closed Fri.*

**Cafe Kokuu**
**$** | **JAPANESE** | Perched on the Hope Hills area of Nakijin, Cafe Kokuu serves delicious Japanese and Okinawan cuisine in an elegant wooden building with stunning views of the countryside and ocean. All dishes are created with organic wild and farm-grown vegetables from the Yambaru region. **Known for:** organic vegetables; vegan lunch set; ocean views. [$] *Average main: ¥1,200* ✉ *2031–138 Shoshi, Kunigami Village* ☎ *0980/56–1231* 🌐 *www.instagram.com/cafe_koku_okinawa* 💳 *No credit cards* 🕒 *Closed Sun. and Mon. No dinner.*

## 🛏 Hotels

**Hotel Orion Motobu Resort & Spa** (ホテル オリオン モトブ リゾート&スパ)
**$$$$** | **HOTEL** | **FAMILY** | This hotel is an oasis on the coast of Motobu located next to Ocean Expo Park and the Okinawa Churaumi Aquarium. **Pros:** beautiful view in every room; walking distance to the beach and Ocean Expo Park; thermal onsen (¥1,650). **Cons:** expensive; limited number of double rooms; far from Naha Airport. [$] *Rooms from: ¥85,000* ✉ *148–1 Bise, Motobu* ☎ *098/051–7300* 🌐 *www.okinawaresort-orion.com/english* 🛏 *238 rooms* 🍴 *Free Breakfast.*

**On the Beach Lue** (オン・ザ・ビーチ・ルー)
**$$** | **HOTEL** | This bungalow hideaway 15 minutes south of the Churaumi Aquarium is a laid-back alternative to the bigger

resorts. **Pros:** cheaper than the big resorts; lovely beach; good access for northern Okinawa. **Cons:** no double beds; spartan rooms; slim menu. $ *Rooms from: ¥17,400* ✉ *2626–1 Sakimotobu, Motobu* ☎ *0980/47–3535* ⊕ *www.luenet. com* ⤳ *36 rooms* ❖️ *No Meals.*

 ## Activities

### DIVING AND SNORKELING
#### Happy Surfing Okinawa
(ハッピーサーフィン)
**SURFING** | Okinawa is not an easy place to surf; because of the hidden reefs and frequently changing weather conditions, you really need to know what you're doing. Both novice and seasoned surfers should head to Danny Melhado at Happy Surfing Okinawa. Danny competed in the world championship tour, and now shares his passion for surfing and stand-up paddleboarding. It is also possible to stay at his guesthouse next to a prime surf spot. ✉ *431–3 Toya, Yomitan-son* ☎ *090/1943–8654* ⊕ *happysurfingokina-wa.com* ✉ *Group lessons from ¥12,500; private lessons from ¥15,000.*

#### Natural Blue Diving Company
(ナチュラルブルー)
**SCUBA DIVING** | There are many Japa-nese diving shops in Okinawa, but few instructors speak English. This can make it difficult to go on fun dives, and almost impossible to do a certification course. Natural Blue Diving Company, however, is run by Yasu, a bilingual diving instructor who studied marine biology in Florida. He bases his diving and snorkeling trips around Cape Maeda, one of Okinawa's most popular dive spots. Reservations are essential. ✉ *469–1 Maeda, Yomi-tan-son* ☎ *090/9497–7374* ⊕ *www. natural-blue.net* ✉ *Dives from ¥5,000.*

#### North of Nago Boat Charters
**SCUBA DIVING** | If you're an experienced diver and want to explore some of mainland Okinawa's more remote dive spots, this is a great option. One of the sites the company regularly dives is the wreck of the USS *Emmons* located near Kouri Island. It's close to 131 feet down, and there can be strong currents so this is only for advanced divers. Other spots include Ie Island, Sesoko Island, and Hedo Point. ■ **TIP→ You need to bring your own gear or rent it elsewhere.** ✉ *Motobu* ☎ *090/3790–2924* ⊕ *www. divebumoki.com/North%20of%20Nago. htm* ✉ *US$65 for a two-dive trip; US$85 for a three-dive trip.*

#### Reef Encounters International
**SCUBA DIVING** | Dive instructor Doug Bennett has been teaching classes on Okinawa since 1995. His shop offers NAUI certification courses at all levels. He also offers day trips to the Keramas and longer tours to Ishigaki, Iriomote, and Yonaguni. Friendly, reliable, and highly recommended, Bennett has become the guide of choice for those looking for an English-speaking dive company. ✉ *1–493 Miyagi, Chatan-cho* ☎ *098/995–9414* ⊕ *www.reefencounters. org* ✉ *Beach dives from ¥7,000; boat dives from ¥14,000.*

### KAYAKING
#### Moove
**CANOEING & ROWING** | **FAMILY** | Okinawa has plenty of tiny uninhabited islands just a stone's throw from Okinawan Main Island. Your guide Nik, a British expat, will get you out on the water in a kayak, and can guide you to some of those picture-postcard deserted beaches. Moove also offers paddle boarding, tide pooling, and river trekking, so there are family-friendly options whatever the season or ocean conditions. ✉ *Naki-jin, Kunigami Village* ☎ *70/4324–0550* ⊕ *moove.earth.*

### WHALE-WATCHING
#### Okinawa Island Crew
(沖縄アイランドクルー)
**WILDLIFE-WATCHING** | **FAMILY** | Okinawa Island Crew runs half-day humpback whale-watching tours from January to March. The shallow waters off of

the Motobu Peninsula are particularly suitable for mother and calf pairs. Whale-watching trips from Motobu are a good option for families as the ocean is usually calmer than trips that leave from Naha and cross over to the Kerama Islands. Okinawa Island Crew also offers various marine sports activities throughout the year and accepts credit cards. ⊠ *Sakimotobu 671–1, Motobu, Kunigami Village* ☎ *098/047–6140* ⊕ *oi-crew.com* 🖅 *Half-day whale-watching tours from ¥4,800.*

# Kerama Islands (慶良間諸島)

*35 km (22 miles) west of Naha by ferry.*

The Kerama Islands have many pristine beaches, and divers and snorkelers will be impressed by the diversity and health of the coral and the water clarity. There are two main islands, Tokashiki and Zamami, along with many smaller, uninhabited islets. You can experience the best of the Keramas in a day trip or two from Naha. Eating and drinking establishments are scattered over the two islands, so you won't lack for sustenance.

## GETTING HERE AND AROUND

From Naha's Tomari Port you can catch ferries to both Tokashiki and Zamami. The daily ferry *Kerama* reaches Tokashiki Island in 70 minutes. Marine Liner *Tokashiki* is the express ferry running twice daily. Call ahead as the schedules change frequently.

To get to Zamami you have two choices: the high-speed *Queen Zamami* ferry reaches the island in 50 minutes, sometimes stopping at Aka Island along the way. There are two or three departures daily. The slower *Zamami-maru* ferry reaches the island in two hours and makes only one daily run.

Once you're on one of the islands, you can rent bicycles or scooters from vendors at the piers. Zamami Island also has a small car-rental service.

**CAR RENTAL Asagi Rent-a-Car.** ☎ *098/896–4135.*

**FERRY INFORMATION Tokashiki-son Naha Renrakusho.** ☎ *098/868–7541 info for Ferry Tokashiki and Marine Liner Tokashiki* ⊕ *www.tomarin.com.* **Zamami-son Renrakusho.** ☎ *098/868–4567 info for Ferry Zamami and Queen Zamami* ⊕ *www. tomarin.com.*

### VISITOR INFORMATION

At Zamami's harbor you can duck into the tourist information office in the cluster of buildings to the left of the ferry exit for information in English on boat tours, bike rentals, and marine sports.

**CONTACT Zamami Tourist Information Office.** ⊠ *1–1 Chisaki, Zamami* ☎ *098/987–2277.*

 Sights

**Tokashiki-jima** (渡嘉敷島)

ISLAND | The largest of the Kerama Islands, Tokashiki Island gets the most tourist traffic from Naha. Two lovely beaches with clean, white sand are on the west side: Tokashiki Beach, in the center of the coast, and Aharen Beach, toward the south. ⊠ *Tokashiki.*

**Zamami-jima** (座間味島)

ISLAND | This little island paradise offers wonderful beaches, snorkeling, diving, and sea kayaking. From late January through March is prime whale-watching season, and during those months you can join two-hour boat tours from Naha. From land, the north shore gives you the best chance of seeing whale tails and fin-slapping humpback antics—but bring your best binoculars.

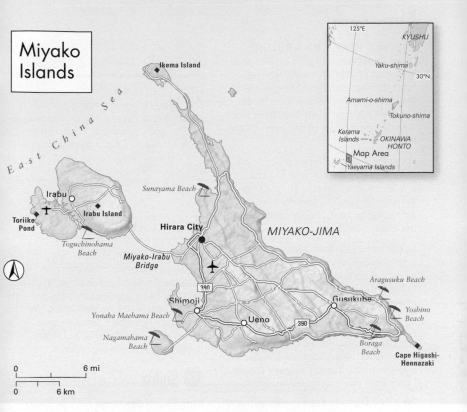

## Miyako Islands

East China Sea

Ikema Island

Sunayama Beach

Irabu

Irabu Island

Toriike
Pond

Toguchinohama
Beach

**Hirara City**

*MIYAKO-JIMA*

Miyako-Irabu
Bridge

390

Shimoji

Aragusuku Beach

Gusukube

Yoshino
Beach

Yonaha Maehama Beach

Ueno

390

Nagamahama
Beach

Boraga
Beach

**Cape Higashi-
Hennazaki**

0        6 mi

0        6 km

### Inset map

125°E

*KYUSHU*

*Yaku-shima*

30°N

*Amami-o-shima*

*Tokuno-shima*

*Kerama
Islands*  *OKINAWA
HONTO*

**Map Area**

*Yaeyama Islands*

---

For great snorkeling, try Furuzamami Beach, a short walk south of the harbor and village. In summer, there are snorkel rentals and showers. There's also a restaurant, and shuttle buses run to and from the pier. ✉ *Zamami.*

### 🏃 Activities

**Zamami Whale-Watching Association**
(座間味村ホエールウォッチング協会;
*Zamami-mura Eru Occhingu Kyokai*)
**WILDLIFE-WATCHING** | Weather permitting, from late December to early April, boats head out from Zamami port daily at 10:30 am and 1:00 pm. You can arrange these tours from Zamami Island or, more commonly and conveniently, from Tomari Port in Naha. Small boats and choppy seas can make whale-watching tough for those with weak stomachs. ✉ *Zamami* ☎ *080/8370–1084* ⊕ *zwwa.okinawa.*

# Miyako Islands (宮古諸島)

*300 km (186 miles) southwest of Okinawa Honto.*

Some intensive beach therapy can be engaged in here. In the southwest corner of the main island, Miyako Island, is Yonaha Maehama Beach, perhaps Japan's finest beach, and across the bridge on tiny Kurima Island lies the gorgeous Nagamahama Beach. Throughout the Miyako Islands you can find bright white sand and emerald, turquoise, and cobalt waters. If you're traveling to the Miyako Islands in July or August or during a Japanese holiday, book in advance.

## GETTING HERE AND AROUND

Japan TransOcean Air (part of JAL) and ANK (part of ANA) fly to Miyako-shoto from Naha (45 minutes, 13 flights daily). From the airport to Hirara, a taxi costs about ¥1,500. There are also direct flights with JTA from Tokyo Haneda and Osaka Itami.

Hirara Port, Miyako ferries make short trips to nearby Shimoji-jima, Tarama-jima, and Minna-jima. Tickets can be bought in the ferry terminal. Irabu-jima, once only accessible by boat, is now connected to the main island by bridge.

Buses on Miyako-jima depart from two terminals in Hirara and travel the coastal roads around the island. Buses to the north of the island and Ikema-jima (35 minutes from Hirara) depart from the Yachiyo bus station. Those heading south to Maehama (25 minutes from Hirara) and Cape Higashi-henna (50 minutes from Hirara) depart from the Miyako Kyoei terminal. Buses run every couple of hours from morning to early evening.

Taxis on Miyako-jima are convenient and reasonable. A taxi for the 10-km (6-mile) trip to Maehama Beach should cost no more than ¥5,000. Most drivers speak limited English but will be able to get you to the major sights without any problems.

For car rentals, reserving in advance is advisable. Nippon Rent-a-Car and most other companies will pick you up at the airport or ferry terminal. Rates vary, beginning at around ¥8,000 per day. Another option for getting around the island is by scooter or motorbike (from around ¥2,000 for a scooter per day).

**CAR RENTAL Nippon Rent-a-Car.**
☎ *03/6859–6234 English service desk in Tokyo* ⊕ *www.nrgroup-global.com/en.*

## Caution

Although following coastal roads is straightforward, driving in the interior of Miyako Island requires time and patience, and should not be attempted after dark. Signposting is confusing, and the endless sugarcane fields look identical.

# Hirara City (平良)

Hirara Port is the main urban area of Miyakojima City which technically extends across several islands. Miyako-jima City has a population of around 55,000, much smaller than cities on Okinawa Main Island. The port area doesn't have much to see but offers some budget accommodation.

## 👁 Sights

**Cape Higashi-Hennazaki** (東平安名崎)
VIEWPOINT | If you have a couple of hours to spare, take a leisurely walk out to see Cape Higashi-Hennazaki's rugged landscape. A twisty, narrow road atop a spine of rock leads through a thatch of green grass out to a lonely, perfectly lovely lighthouse. The 2-km (1-mile) peninsula retains an impressive, end-of-the-earth feeling, and in spring the ground is covered with trumpet lilies. The multicolored coral can be viewed from above. Allow about one hour to walk from the Bora bus stop at Boraga Beach. If you rent a scooter in Hirara, you can ride to the end of the road next to the lighthouse. ✉ *Miyako.*

**Ikema Island** (池間島; *Ikema-jima*)
ISLAND | Connected to the northwestern corner of Miyako Island by a bridge, this small island, ringed by a scenic coastal road, has fine views above and below the sea. The Ikema Wetlands in the center

Maehama Beach on Miyako-jima may very well be Japan's best beach.

of the island is a wildlife protection area, and home to a variety of ducks, egrets, and waders. The island is 35 minutes by bus from Hirara Port. ⊠ *Ikema-jima.*

**Irabu Island** (伊良部島; *Irabu-jima*)
ISLAND | This small island has two gorgeous and secluded beaches: Toguchi-no-hama Beach and Sawada-no-hama Beach. Irabu Island is connected to the main island by the longest toll-free bridge in Japan. ⊠ *Irabu Island, Miyako.*

**Tooriike Pond** (通り池)
NATURE SIGHT | If you travel across one of the several small bridges from Irabu-jima to Shimoji-jima, you can check out Tooriike Pond, a deep, mysteriously dark limestone-ringed pool connected by underwater caverns to the sea. It's a justly celebrated spot for diving.

##  Beaches

**Boraga Beach** (保良泉ビーチ)
BEACH | FAMILY | On the southern shore of the island, a swimming pool filled with water from a cold natural spring sits next to a picturesque stretch of sand. Snorkel gear and kayak rentals can be arranged through the pool complex, which includes a refreshment stand. Many of the local dive shops offer snorkeling excursions, or multisport packages that include a visit to the pumpkin-shape rock formation. **Amenities:** food and drink; lifeguards; parking (free); showers; toilets; water sports. **Best for:** snorkeling. ⊠ *Miyako.*

**Nagamahama Beach** (長間浜ビーチ)
BEACH | FAMILY | A lovely and often deserted beach on the west side of tiny Kurima Island, Nagamahama Beach can be reached via the bridge just southeast of Yonaha Maehama Beach. This is a fantastic place to spend the day snorkeling and

picnicking on the fine white sand. **Amenities:** parking (free). **Best for:** snorkeling; solitude; sunrise; swimming; walking; windsurfing. ✉ *Kurima-jima, Miyako.*

★ **Yonaha Maehama Beach** (前浜ビーチ)
**BEACH** | **FAMILY** | Yonaha Maehama Beach is regarded by many as Japan's best beach, and it lives up to its reputation. White sand stretches for miles on a smooth, shallow shelf extending far into the warm, clear water. In front of the Tokyu Resort there's a section of water that is netted off to protect swimmers from jellyfish, and a lifeguard on duty from 9 to 6. Water-sports equipment rentals, showers, refreshments, toilets, and showers are available at a beach shack. Take on your friends or the locals at beach volleyball—this is an amazing place to play a game. The beach is 25 minutes by taxi, 40 mins by bus from Hirara Port area. **Amenities:** food and drink; lifeguards; parking; showers; toilets; water sports. **Best for:** sunset; swimming. ✉ *914 Yonaha, Shimoji-aza, Miyako.*

**Yoshino Beach** (吉野ビーチ)
**BEACH** | **FAMILY** | The water here is said to have the highest concentration of colorful fish in all of the Miyako Islands; it's an awesome spot to snorkel. The beach is just north of Cape Higashi-Hennazaki. If Yoshino Beach is packed with busloads of tourists, try Aragusuku Beach a little farther north. Bathrooms, showers, vending machines and parking (¥500) are up on the clifftop; a shuttle bus transports visitors half a kilometer down the winding road to the beach. **Amenities:** parking (fee); showers; toilets; water sports. **Best for:** snorkeling; solitude; sunrise. ✉ *Yoshino, Miyako.*

## 🍴 Restaurants

**Chuzan** (中山)
**$** | **ASIAN** | This simple tavern serves inexpensive Okinawa favorites such as *goya champuru* (a stir-fry using bitter melon); Korean-style *bibimbap* (a delicious, tangy, healthful dish of kimchi, bean sprouts, spinach, and other vegetables stirred into rice); and a plate of *katsuo* (bonito) sashimi big enough for two or three people. There's live music on weekends. **Known for:** fresh seafood; goya (bitter melon) dishes; traditional Okinawan flavors. [$] *Average main: ¥800* ✉ *1–10 Nishizato, Hirara* ☎ *0980/73–1959* 🕒 *Closed Mon. No lunch.*

**Goya** (郷家)
**$** | **ASIAN** | The wooden walls of this rustic establishment are full of alcoves holding everything from dolls to farm implements to ancient jugs full of *awamori* (rice liquor). Partially enclosed tatami-style rooms offer intimate experiences, while the beer hall-style dining area in front of the stage makes socializing easy. **Known for:** benimo (purple potato) croquettes; large mugs of icy cold Orion (pronounced "oh-ree-yon") beer; rafute (bacon slow-cooked in a mix of awamori, soy sauce, brown sugar, and ginger root). [$] *Average main: ¥800* ✉ *570–2 Nishizato, Hirara* ✣ *10 min from downtown Hirara by taxi* ☎ *0980/74–2358* 🕒 *Closed Thurs.*

## 🛏 Hotels

**Central Resort Miyakojima**
(セントラルリゾート宮古島)
**$$$** | **HOTEL** | Renewed and renamed in 2021, this hotel provides a good central base. **Pros:** stylish rooms in new part of building; good location for bars; clean rooms. **Cons:** staff speak limited English; not close to the best beaches; less stylish rooms in the older business section. [$] *Rooms from: ¥22,000* ✉ *228–1 Nishizato, Miyako-jima, Hirara* ☎ *0980/73–2002* 🌐 *central-resort-miyakojima.com* 🛏 *135 rooms* 🍴 *No Meals.*

**Hotel Atoll Emerald**
(ホテルアトールエメラルド宮古島)
**$$$$** | **HOTEL** | This is the nicest and most convenient hotel in downtown Hirara, and every room at this contemporary high-rise hotel next to Hirara Wharf

boasts ocean views. **Pros:** friendly staff; lovely sea views; easy access to town. **Cons:** no rooms with double beds; staff speak limited English; the nearby beach is not one of Miyako's best. $ *Rooms from: ¥42,000* ✉ *108–7 Shimozato, Miyako-jima, Hirara* ☎ *0980/73–9800* ⊕ *www.atollemerald.jp* ↝ *137 rooms* ⦿ *Free Breakfast.*

★ **Miyakojima Tokyu Hotel & Resorts** (宮古島東急リゾート)

$$$$ | **RESORT** | One of Okinawa's finest resorts, the Miyakojima Tokyu Resort delivers everything you could want from a tropical vacation. **Pros:** unbeatable location; magnificent rooms; friendly staff. **Cons:** twin beds rather than a single queen or king; limited room service; swimming pool is unheated and closed midwinter. $ *Rooms from: ¥97,240* ✉ *914 Yonaha, Shimoji, Miyako-jima, Miyako* ☎ *0980/76–2109* ⊕ *www.tokyuhotels. co.jp* ↝ *248 rooms* ⦿ *Free Breakfast.*

### 🏃 Activities

**DIVING AND SNORKELING**

**Penguin Divers** (ペンギンダイバーズ)

**SCUBA DIVING** | Fijian Joe will show you the best of underwater Miyako as you explore the beautiful reefs off the coast of Irabu Island on either boat dives or shore dives. The company caters to both English and Japanese speakers. ✉ *40 Shimosato, Hirara* ☎ *090/8231–7161* ⊕ *diving-penguin.com/english.htm* ↝ *2-tank boat dive ¥15,000; gear rental ¥6,600.*

# Yaeyama Islands (八重山諸島)

*430 km (267 miles) southwest of Okinawa Honto.*

This is Japan's final frontier. For a country so famous for its high-tech, modern urban centers, Japan's remote islands are a dramatic incongruity. The difference is like day and night, even between Ishigaki-jima, the most developed island, and Okinawa Main Island. Ishigaki Island sports a tiny, funky port city, a few beaches, and picturesque lighthouses. Ishigaki Island is considered by many to be the best dive spot in Japan, and it's even possible to dive or snorkel with manta rays during the summer. The sandy lanes of its neighbor Taketomi Island have more talismanic shisa statues than actual people. You're unlikely to make it to Yonaguni Island, Japan's farthest shore, to dive the bizarre underwater "ruins," but the more easily accessible Iriomote Island promises plenty of adventure: practically the entire island is protected national parkland, from the lush jungles and mangrove-lined rivers to the glittering, shimmering coral under the waves.

# Ishigaki-jima (石垣島)

*1 hour by plane from Naha.*

A day of beachside R&R and a night in Ishigaki City's fun bars and cheap restaurants may be all it takes to make you want to move here. You wouldn't be alone: many of Ishigaki's residents are either escapees seeking asylum from Japan's business-driven culture or descendants of islanders repatriating themselves into their forebears' homeland.

### GETTING HERE AND AROUND

In 2013, Painushima Ishigaki Airport opened around 20 km (12 miles) northeast of the city. Buses run every 15 minutes into town. The 45-minute journey costs ¥540. A taxi costs ¥3,000. Both JTA (part of JAL) and ANK (part of ANA) airlines make the 55-minute flight from Naha to Ishigaki-jima. JTA also has direct flights from Ishigaki to Nagoya, Osaka, and Tokyo. Low-cost carrier Skymark also has flights to Ishigaki from Naha and Narita.

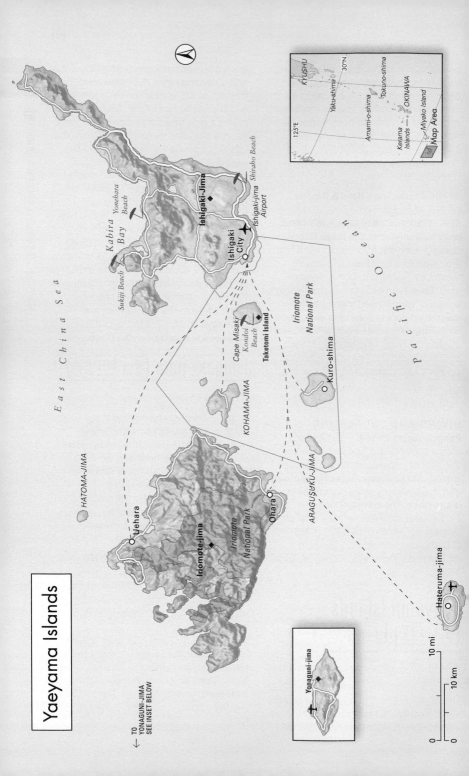

# Yaeyama Islands

East China Sea

Pacific Ocean

KYUSHU
30°N
Yaku-shima
Amami-o-shima
Tokuno-shima
OKINAWA
125°E
Kerama
Islands
OKINAWA Island
Miyako Island
Map Area

Kabira Bay
Yonehara Beach
Sukuji Beach
Ishigaki-Jima
Ishigaki City
Ishigaki-jima Airport
Shiraho Beach

HATOMA-JIMA
Uehara
Iriomote-jima
Iriomote National Park
Ohara
ARAGUSUKU-JIMA
KOHAMA-JIMA
Cape Misaki
Kondoi Beach
Taketomi Island
Iriomote National Park
Kuro-shima

Hateruma-jima

Yonaguni-jima

← TO
YONAGUNI-JIMA
SEE INSET BELOW

10 mi
0
10 km
0

Unless you're planning on leaving right away for Taketomi or Iriomote, it's well worth booking a rental car. From Ishigaki City, ferries connect to the surrounding islands. Only far-off Yonaguni-jima requires another flight.

Ishigaki City is small and walkable; pick up a map at your hotel or the bus center across from the port, where you'll also find pamphlets on attractions and vital ferry and bus schedules. Getting around the island by car or motor scooter is a snap—there's really no traffic and only a few roads—and rental places litter the town like sandal shops. Driving after dark can be an unnerving experience as you will probably find yourself swerving around trying to miss a wide range of frogs, crabs, snakes, and turtles as they hop, scuttle, slither, and crawl across the road.

**AIRLINE INFORMATION**

**ANA.** ☎ *0570/029–709* 🌐 *www.ana.co.jp.* **JAL.** ☎ *0570/025–121, 03/6733–3062 in Tokyo* 🌐 *www.jal.co.jp/en.*

**CAR RENTALS Nippon Rent-a-Car.** ☎ *03/6859–6234 National English Service Desk in Tokyo* 🌐 *www.nrgroup-global.com/en.* **TOYOTA Rent a Car.** ☎ *092/577–0091 national call center with English* 🌐 *rent.toyota.co.jp/eng.*

**VISITOR INFORMATION**

**CONTACT Painushima Ishigaki Airport Information Counter.** ✉ *Shiraho, Ishigaki* ☎ *0980/87–0468.*

## Sights

**Taketomi Island** (竹富島; *Taketomi-jima*)
**ISLAND** | It's a 15-minute ferry trip from Ishigaki City to the quaint terra-cotta-roofed cottages, sleepy lanes, and empty beaches of Taketomi Island. The cute little town is easily navigable by bicycle. Another fun option is the "old-fashioned" tour—meander between the narrow rock walls in a water buffalo-drawn cart while you're serenaded by a three-stringed *sanshin* and the soaring voice of the driver. Kondoi Beach, about 15 minutes by bicycle from the center of town, has good swimming with showers and changing facilities. Hoshizuna Beach is famous for its star sand, which is, depending on who you ask, either the tiny exoskeletons of marine protozoa or the children of stars. ✉ *Taketomi, Ishigaki.*

## Beaches

**Yonehara Beach** (米原ビーチ)
**BEACH** | **FAMILY** | Great swimming and snorkeling are yours at the sparkling Yonehara Beach. Watch out for strong currents during tidal changes and various types of critters that can sting or bite. There are several places to rent masks, fins, and snorkels, including the beach shack next to the main parking area. On the island's northern shore, Yonehara is about an hour from Ishigaki City by bus, or half an hour by car. You'll know you've found the right area when you see the giant multicolor shisas of Yoneko-yaki pottery on Route 79. **Amenities:** food and drink; parking (free); showers; toilets; water sports. **Best for:** snorkeling; swimming; walking. ✉ *Yonehara, Ishigaki.*

## Restaurants

★ **Usagi-Ya** (うさぎや)
**$** | **JAPANESE** | This spot serves Ishigaki's finest example of Okinawan izakaya cooking. Be sure to try something with delicious *kurumafu*, a chewy wheat gluten, and if the crunchy pig's ears are too much for you, try washing it down with golden Orion beer. **Known for:** tebichi-style pork legs; fresh mango drinks; the local classic goya champuru. [$] *Average main: ¥800* ✉ *Nakamura Heights 102, 1–1 Ishigaki, Ishigaki* ☎ *0980/88–5014* 🌐 *usagiya-ishigaki.com* 🕒 *No lunch.*

## Hotels

★ **ANA Intercontinental Ishigaki Resort**
**$$$$** | **RESORT** | Come for luxury, impeccable service, and stunning views across

Tamatorizaki Observation Point is on Ishigaki-jima's hilly northern peninsula.

the hotel's pools and gardens to Maesato Beach, and the azure waters beyond. **Pros:** excellent service; spa treatments; beachfront location. **Cons:** luxury comes at a cost; poolside bar depends on the season; far from diving locations around Kabira Bay. $ *Rooms from: ¥90,000* ✉ *354–1 Maesato, Ishigaki* ☎ *980/887111* 🌐 *www.anaintercontinental-ishigaki.jp/en* 🛏 *458 rooms* 🍴 *No Meals.*

**APA Hotel (Ishigakijima)**
(アパホテル 石垣島)
**$$$** | **HOTEL** | Unusually large beds and a central location—it's a block east of the ferry dock—make APA Hotel a great choice. **Pros:** reasonable prices; central location; all the amenities covered. **Cons:** breakfast not included; business hotel functionality rather than luxury; not within walking distance of beaches. $ *Rooms from: ¥19,440* ✉ *1–2–3 Yashima-cho, Ishigaki* ☎ *0980/82–2000* 🌐 *www.apahotel.com* 🛏 *89 rooms* 🍴 *No Meals.*

## Activities

### DIVING AND SNORKELING

The scuba diving and snorkeling around Ishigaki Island is superb. Dive spots include the coral reefs near Kabira Bay, Yonehara Beach, and Cape Hirakubo. Lunch-inclusive outings cost around ¥6,500 for snorkeling or ¥20,000 for diving (plus an additional ¥5,400 for gear rental). The most famous diving spot on the island (and perhaps in Japan) is Manta Scramble, near Kabira Bay. In autumn you can sit on the ocean floor and watch manta rays circle above you.

**Pushynushima** (ぷしぃぬしま)
**SCUBA DIVING** | This great dive company is by the port in Ishigaki City. Tanaka-san and the other dive instructors speak some English, and offer both half-day and full-day snorkeling or scuba diving tours, plus romantic sunset cruises. Diving is offered all year, but it's at its best August to October. ✉ *2 Misaki-cho, Ishigaki* ☎ *0980/88–6363* 🌐 *www.ishigaki-diving.*

*net* 🎫 *Half-day snorkeling ¥6,500; 3-tank dive ¥20,000, plus gear rental (¥5,400).*

**Tom Sawyer** (トムソーヤ)
**SCUBA DIVING** | The shop operates all year round, but ideally you want to visit in late summer so that you can see the manta rays. If you'd like to check out the ocean but don't fancy getting wet, there's also a glass-bottom-boat and a sunset cruise BBQ. Some instructors speak English. ✉ *2–41 Tonoshiro, Ishigaki* ☎ *0980/83–4677* 🌐 *ishigaki-tomsawyer.jp* 🎫 *Half-day dive trips from ¥11,500; snorkeling from ¥11,500.*

# Iriomote-jima (西表島)

*31 km (19 miles) west of Ishigaki Island, 50 minutes by ferry.*

Surging brown rivers, dense green forests, and crystal-blue seas are Iriomote's essential draws, and there's a surprising amount of helpful infrastructure in place to help you get the most fun out of it all. Skilled guides and tour companies make it easy and safe to explore the wilds of this pocket of primordial wilderness, and a few extremely nice lodging options let you enjoy some refined relaxation while you do. You'll want at least two nights—preferably three or four—to get the most out of Iriomote's varied landscapes, depending on what you want to try. After a few days' jungle trekking, sea-kayaking, sailing, snorkeling, scuba diving, or river cruising, returning to Ishigaki Island will feel like reemerging into civilization.

**TIP→ The post office ATM may be working, but bring enough cash for your entire stay.**

## GETTING HERE AND AROUND

Ferries from Ishigaki Island connect to two ports on Iriomote Island, southeastern Ohara (¥1,830) and northern Uehara (¥2,360), in just under an hour. Uehara is more convenient for Urauchi River and Hoshinosuna Beach. When seas are choppy the ferry to Uehara is canceled, but the ferry to Ohara will still run. The ferry company then provides a bus to transport passengers from Ohara to Uehara by bus. If the seas get very rough, usually during typhoons, boats will be canceled so plan your trip with some breathing room.

The long road ringing Iriomote's northern half terminates in the west at Shirahama and the east in Ohara and although infrequent buses connect them, tour companies will take care of transporting you to and from your hotel or port of call at the time of your excursion. Rental scooters and cars are available, but there are not many places to go; rely on your tour guides to get you around, and center your meals on your lodging.

## Hotels

**Hotel Irifune** (ホテル入船)
**$$** | **HOTEL** | In the main village of Sonai, Yonaguni's Hotel Irifune is the place to stay for divers visiting Yonaguni. **Pros:** knowledgeable staff; good value; diving instructors on site. **Cons:** hostel rather than hotel feel; spartan rooms; can be empty in the off season. [$] *Rooms from: ¥12,000* ✉ *59–6 Aza Yonaguni, Sonai* ☎ *0980/87–2311* 🌐 *yonaguni.jp/en* 🛏 *11 rooms (three without bath)* 🍴 *Free Breakfast.*

**Nilaina Resort** (ニライナリゾート)
**$$$$** | **HOTEL** | "Resort" is a misnomer for this small lodge, but the Nilaina has a perfect location, wooden decks where you can kick back, and a hot tub with an ocean view. **Pros:** friendly staff; great location; plenty of outdoor activities. **Cons:** often fully booked in summer; limited English spoken by staff; no double rooms. [$] *Rooms from: ¥25,300* ✉ *10–425 Uehara, Taketomi* ☎ *0980/85–6400* 🌐 *www.nilaina.com* 🛏 *4 rooms* 🍴 *Free Breakfast.*

**Pension Hoshinosuna** (ペンション星の砂)
**$$** | **HOTEL** | The exterior may look worn, but the rooms have possibly the best

## Did You Know?

A 16-km (10-mile) walking trail cuts directly through the dense interior jungle of Iriomote-jima. Local trekking companies can lead you on a guided hike through the bush.

view in Japan. **Pros:** tropical paradise views; near Uehara Port; quiet relaxation once the beach traffic has gone. **Cons:** no double beds; food selection limited; rooms aren't plush. $ *Rooms from: ¥17,600* ✉ *289–1 Uehara, Taketomi-cho* ☎ *0980/85–6448* ⊕ *www.hoshinosuna. ne.jp* ⤴ *11 rooms* ❙❍❙ *Free Breakfast.*

## 🏃 Activities

### BOAT TOURS

**Urauchigawa Cruises**

(浦内川観光; *Urauchigawa Kanko*)

**BOATING | FAMILY |** The Urauchi River, Iriomote's Amazon, is the reason many day-trippers come to the island. Boats navigate up the broad, coffee-colored water that is lined by mangroves and terns. It's a pretty magical place, almost as if you're about to enter Jurassic World. Rather than just float up and down on the river, get off the boat at the lower reaches station and then hike for an hour up to the Mariyudu and Kanbire waterfalls. Trek for another hour from the waterfalls and you are at the upper reaches station from where you can catch the boat back down the river. Kayak rentals are available if you want to go for it on your own, or you can opt for a guided kayak tour. Some companies tow the kayaks upstream so you can enjoy a leisurely paddle back down. ✉ *Iriomote* ☎ *0980/85–6154* ⊕ *www. urauchigawa.com* ✉ *¥2,200 round-trip* ☞ *First boat departs 9 am; last boat leaves 3:30 pm.*

### DIVING

**Waterman Tours** (ウォーターマン)

**SCUBA DIVING |** Diving instructor Tokuo-ka-san takes guests to the pristine reefs around Iriomote. Two dives cost between ¥13,000 and ¥18,000 plus ¥5,500 for full gear rental. For those without a diver's license he also offers half-day snorkeling

tours for ¥8,000. Stand-up paddleboarding tours are also available. ✉ *538–1 Uehara, Taketomi-cho* ☎ *0980/85–6005* ⊕ *www.i-waterman.com/english-page.*

### HIKING

★ **Simamariasibi** (島廻遊)

**HIKING & WALKING |** Trekking tours through Iriomote's verdant jungle are fun and exotic, especially with a tour guide so thoroughly knowledgeable about the island's trails and conscientious about his customer's safety and enjoyment. Nagasawa-san learned the ins and outs of Iriomote's interior by going boar-hunting with locals during the winter off-season, and leads his tours away from the regular tour spots to really immerse you in nature. Along the way he'll provide a surprising amount of information about the jungle and reveal some special overlooks and locations. Nagasawa-san offers a variety of packages starting at ¥8,200 for a half-day tour, and ¥12,100 for a full day tour including lunch, insurance, and transportation. ∎**TIP→ Canyoning trips are particularly fun in the hot summer months.** ✉ *984–1 Taketomi-cho, Iriomote* ☎ *0980/84–8408* ⊕ *www.simamariasibi. com.*

### KAYAKING

**Good Outdoor** (グッドアウトドア)

**KAYAKING | FAMILY |** This company offers adults and kids a wide range of outdoor sports activities. Spend a day or two exploring the ocean and rivers via kayak, or combine kayaking with trekking or snorkeling. All options are from ¥7,700 for a half day and from ¥11,000 for a full day. ✉ *607 Taketomi-cho Iriomote, Iriomote* ☎ *0980/84–8116* ⊕ *goodoutdoor.jp.*

**Mansaku Tour Service**
(まんさくツアーサービス)

KAYAKING | FAMILY | These sea kayaking
tours set off where the road ends at Shirahama; from there it's into the waves.
After navigating some shore points
and smaller straights and islets, you'll
weave in and out of the mangrove-lined
estuaries along the coast. The difficulty of
your tour will depend on the fitness and
experience of the participants along with
the weather. Your guide Mansaku-san
can speak some English and is skilled at
creating a fun atmosphere. If the weather is good, you can snorkel in the crystal
clear bay. Longer camping and fishing
tours are available. ✉ *Iriomote 1499–24,
Taketomi-cho, Iriomote* ☏ *0980/85–6222*
⊕ *mansaku.okinawa.*

**Yonaguni Island** (与那国島; *Yonaguni-jima*)

ISLAND | Underneath the waters off Yona-
guni Island, Japan's westernmost point,
is an enormous series of ancient stone
structures believed to have been a settlement that dates back to 8,000-10,000
BC, which would make it the oldest—by
5,000 years—human structure of this
sort. The site has become popular among
divers, especially because schools of
photogenic hammerhead sharks migrate
through the area in winter. Marlin fishing
here is also highly rated. Yonaguni Island
is also known for the enormous Yonaguni
atlas moth, and the wild Yonaguni ponies
that roam the blustery cliff tops. To get
to Yonaguni Island, you can fly via JAL
operated by Ryukyu Air Commuter from
Ishigaki Island or Okinawa Main Island.
✉ *Yonaguni-Jima.*

Chapter 14

# TOHOKU

Updated by
Jay Farris

👁 **Sights** ★★★★★  🍴 **Restaurants** ★★★★★  🛏 **Hotels** ★★★★☆  🛍 **Shopping** ★★★☆☆  🍸 **Nightlife** ★★☆☆☆

# WELCOME TO TOHOKU

## TOP REASONS TO GO

★ **Summer festivals:** Tohoku hosts a number of raucous, tumultuous, and exciting festivals every summer, the Tanabata Matsuri being the top draw.

★ **Coastal beauty:** Matsushima Bay's 250 islands near Sendai are beautiful, but the coast is postcard-pretty virtually anywhere.

★ **Seafood and vegetables:** The freshest seafood you'll ever eat is presented in many ways, all of them tasty. *Sansai* (wild mountain vegetables) are a specialty of the region.

★ **Country life:** Thatched-roof farmhouses, rice terraces, orchards, and rugged fishing villages usher you into a world where change is slow and traditions live on.

★ **Mountain adventures:** The many fine mountain playgrounds are made all the more appealing by the relative absence of people using them.

Tohoku, like the rest of Honshu, is divided by a dramatic series of densely forested mountains chains. Not only will their rugged beauty take your breath away, they can also make travel difficult.

**1 Sendai.** The livable, navigable city of fun-loving, stylish people within easy reach of both mountains and sea.

**2 Matsushima.** Just a short jaunt from Sendai, the town offers fascinating historical sights among spectacular scenery.

**3 Yamadera.** The temple complex built into a mountainside offers spectacular views that change with the seasons.

**4 Hiraizumi.** History buffs will love this compact town of well-preserved temple complexes.

**5 Yamagata.** The friendly city with a small-town feel can offer a quiet respite or quick access to excellent skiing.

**6 Morioka.** The funky city that's both a good jumping-off point to nearby destinations and a destination on its own for shopping for local wares like the famed cast-iron kettles.

**7 Tazawa-ko.** The lake's astonishingly blue waters provide a perfect backdrop for a quiet bike ride through nature.

**8 Kakunodate.** The samurai town comes alive in spring, and then is vibrant once again in fall, but is worth a visit in any season for its well-preserved, historic structures.

**9 Towada-Hachimantai National Park.** Preserving spectacular scenery within Tohoku's main mountain range, the park's natural areas offer breathtaking beauty compared to Japan's urban areas.

**10 Hirosaki.** The slightly out-of-the-way town is, nevertheless, worth a visit for its castle grounds and local color.

**11 Aomori.** The often overlooked, busy port town is an excellent place to stop for a meal of the freshest seafood.

**12 Akita.** Area southwest of Aomori known for its rice and sake.

**13 Tsuruoka and Dewa-Sanzan.** Fishing villages offering access to the three sacred mountains of Dewa-Sanzan.

The name Tohoku translates as "east–north," and it is an area less traveled by tourists from abroad. Though the addition of bullet trains stretching all the way to Hokkaido has made getting up here easier, Tohoku is still a world away from the crowded south. The mountain villages are more remote, the forests more untamed, and the people more reserved and wary of outsiders. But don't be fooled—they are extremely friendly if you show them you appreciate the pace, look, and feel of things.

Wild as the northeastern territory can be, Sendai (less than two hours away from Tokyo by bullet train) sets things in balance, right on the doorstep of the great wilderness. This attractive modern city of a million with wide, shady boulevards and covered shopping arcades, puts on one of Japan's biggest festivals, Tanabata, every summer in early August to honor an ancient legend of star-crossed lovers. It attracts more than 3 million people. Since the 2011 earthquake and tsunami, foreign visitors are particularly welcome here and throughout Tohoku.

The countryside, however, is one of Tohoku's greatest attractions. In comfort and convenience, you can ride the Tohoku Shinkansen to places like Lake Tazawa, Japan's deepest lake—a powder-blue reflection of sky that sits nestled in a caldera surrounded by virgin stands of beech trees draped in sweet-smelling vines, and steep hills studded with blue-green pines preside over all. Samurai history lives on virtually everywhere in the region, but especially in the well-preserved dwellings and warehouses that now play host to curious tourists in Kakunodate, a town also famous for its hundreds of lovely, ancient *shidare-zakura*, or dangling-branch cherry trees.

Tohoku cherishes its forever-frontier status, and has plenty of low-key cities and timeless small towns full of folks who work hard in the cool summers and somehow bide their time through the long winters, breaking the slow rhythm of rural life with countless energetic festivals. Many ski areas collect neck-high powder snow, making for great skiing and snowboarding. The fertile plains yield a bounty of treats, from the sweetest apples (Fuji apples, now found in supermarkets worldwide, originated in Tohoku) and tastiest tomatoes, to the perfect rice and purest water used to make some of the best *karakuchi* (crisp, dry) sake in the land. As a bonus, you're sure never to be far from an onsen.

## MAJOR REGIONS

Tohoku comprises six prefectures, and stretches from Fukushima, just a short train ride from Tokyo, to the remote and rugged Aomori, the northernmost tip of Honshu, within easy striking distance of Hokkaido. This broad swath of territory encompasses mountain ranges, primitive forests, stunning seacoasts, well-preserved feudal villages, sacred glaciated peaks and secluded temples, relaxing hot springs, and seemingly bottomless lakes in the craters of volcanoes.

The main city is **Sendai,** a cosmopolitan city that hosts the immense and colorful Tanabata Matsuri, a four-night, three-day festival that swells the town to three times its normal size.

Within easy striking distance are several destinations, including Matsushima, Yamadera, Hiraizumi, and Yamagata, that make easy side trips or even day trips.

By branching out from the Shinkansen hub of Morioka in **Northern Tohoku,** you'll come across traditional ironware teakettles, grand old castles, lovingly preserved samurai houses, sparkling lakes, and huge national parks with mountains to climb, hiking trails for all abilities, large virgin forests, and hot springs galore.

On **Tohoku's West Coast,** mountains give way to fertile plains that extend to the Sea of Japan. While you will find an occasional castle, everywhere you explore you'll encounter the best food, local women nationally celebrated for their legendary beauty, mountains often buried in powder snow, and countless onsen.

# Planning

To enjoy Tohoku to the fullest, travel lightly, tack on a day or two for the unexpected, and pack jackets or sweaters for the cold weather. People rarely speak fluent English, so drop into the tourist information offices (located within nearly every major train station) when you arrive, and you'll save yourself a lot of frustration later. One of the best features of the region is the incredible friendliness of those who live here, particularly older women. Even if they can't say much, they will be eager to help, and one or two words of Japanese in return will go a long way.

# Getting Here and Around

Most of the island's trains and buses ply north–south routes on either side of the mountains. Though trains are a viable means of getting around up here, in some cases a bus will save time. The most important travel routes fan out from Sendai and Morioka in the east, and from Yamagata and Tsuruoka on the coast of the Sea of Japan in the west. Routes are often highly scenic, but there are also many tunnels and occasional boring stretches where the road or track cuts away from the coast or into a steep ravine. A journey in Tohoku is all about life at a different pace, so expect those out-of-the-way places to be hard to reach.

## BUS

Buses take over where trains do not run, and they usually depart from and return to JR train stations. From Morioka to Hirosaki, highway buses are more convenient (and twice as fast) for getting to Akita than trains. From Tsuruoka to Yamagata, it's the same story (but it's a private bus line, not JR, and one of the terminals is in a shopping mall).

■TIP→ Overhead space is so severely limited that nothing bigger than a briefcase or handbag will fit. Store your bigger bags below.

## CAR

Driving in Tohoku may be a good way for getting to the remote spots but presents much of the same problems as driving in other parts of Japan, and then some: absence of proper signposting (especially in English); inclement weather; following tour buses on narrow, winding, one-lane roads; and getting nearly run off the highways by big trucks driven by daredevils. Although gas, tolls, and car rentals make driving expensive, some areas, such as Hachiman-tai, are more enjoyable by car.

Most rental cars are equipped with a car navigation system (which is in Japanese but with English handbooks), and that can make navigation easier than you expect. Nevertheless, the speeds are limited to 80–100 kph (50–62 mph) on expressways, 30–40 kph (19–25 mph) on secondary roads and in urban areas, making travel considerably slower than the Shinkansen. The approximate driving times from Tokyo (assuming you can clear the metropolitan area in two hours) are six hours to Sendai, 8–10 hours to Morioka, and 10–11 hours to Aomori. It may make sense if you are renting to wait until you get to Sendai.

All major towns have car-rental agencies. Nippon Rent-A-Car is the one most frequently represented. Other car-rental companies include JR Rent-A-Car, Toyota, and Nissan Rent-A-Car. These outfits usually have offices in or near major train stations, and even smaller ones. All you need is a valid International Driver's License (available from AAA in the United States) and your home state or country's license.

■ TIP→ Note that maps are not provided by car-rental agencies; be sure to obtain bilingual maps in Tokyo or Sendai.

CONTACTS Nippon Rent-a-Car. ✉ Sendai ☎ 03/6859–6234 English service desk ⊕ www.nrgroup-global.com/en.

Toyota Rent-a-Car. ✉ Sendai ☎ 0800/7000–815 toll-free, 92/577–0091 when calling from outside Japan ⊕ rent.toyota.co.jp/eng.

## TRAIN

The best way to get to Tohoku from Tokyo is on the Tohoku Shinkansen trains, all of which are included in the JR Pass. The fastest Hayabusa pass through Aomori and on to Hakunodate in Hokkaido, the slightly slower Yamabiko run to Morioka, the Tsubasa run to Yamagata, and the Komachi go to Akita. Elsewhere in Tohoku, JR local trains are slower and often less frequent on less-used lines when they cross the region's mountainous spine. Most trains and many buses are owned by Japan Railways, so a JR Rail Pass will be a worthwhile purchase. Be aware that most trains stop running before midnight. Overhead racks are adequate for small packs, but you should stow larger items in spaces at the ends of cars. In Japan no one is likely to touch your bags, even if left unattended.

# Hotels

Hotels in Tohoku run the gamut from minuscule to behemoth, and often reflect local character. Make advance lodging reservations for the busy summer season, or you may find yourself paying a premium for a leftover room. Hotels and Japanese inns have the standard amenities, and, as is common in Japan, provide free toothbrushes, hair articles, robes, slippers, plentiful towels, hair dryers, and more. Most large hotels offer a choice of Japanese or Western breakfast; though it is not often included in the rates, it's seldom more than ¥1,500–¥2,000 per person.

# Restaurants

Tohoku is a great place for fresh food, whether from the fields, mountains, forests, or seas. Restaurants range from

# On the Menu

Visitors seeking culinary excellence and diversity will not be disappointed in Tohoku. Restaurants in the region serve the freshest assortment of seafood, in sushi, sashimi, grilled, broiled, and boiled versions, as well as a bounty of seaweed and generous offerings of wild mountain vegetables (*sansai*) and mushrooms (*kinoko*) in season. *Tsukemono*, or pickled vegetables, are another Tohoku specialty. *Hinaijidori*, or special local chicken, is a year-round treat and so is the marbled, exquisitely tender beef known as *Yonezawa-gyu*—sometimes expensive but well worth it.

In Sendai don't be afraid to try the local delicacy—grilled or braised beef tongue, *gyutan*, which tastes like a juicy and less chewy version of well-seasoned beef jerky. In Morioka try the *wanko soba* challenge—eat as many bowls of cold buckwheat noodles as you can. In Akita locals are fond of *ina-niwa* udon noodles that are flatter, whiter, and more tender than the usual udon. In Kakunodate *sakura*, or cherry blossoms, are mixed into the flour, and the result is a mildly sweet noodle, as edible as it is pink. Don't miss the truly unique *kiritanpo* (hot pot) made with chicken, local vegetables, and distinctive tubular rice cakes that have been formed and cooked onto sticks of bamboo or cedar. Yamagata has its distinctive rounded, chewy soba and incomparable beef. The local sake is excellent throughout the region, thanks to the quality water and rice.

local sake shacks to upscale sushi bars and steak houses, and dress may be street-casual to office attire. Rarely will it be formal. Menus may not always be in English, but you can often find window displays full of plastic representations of the menu. Credit cards are fine in cities, but they are not always accepted in the countryside, so bring along enough cash. In some restaurants you'll take your shoes off at the entry and place them in a cubicle. If there is a step up and you don't know what to do, just wait and the staff will help. Often even locals are unsure.

## RESTAURANT AND HOTEL PRICES

Restaurant prices are the average cost of a main course at dinner or, if dinner is not served, at lunch. Hotel prices are the lowest cost of a standard double room in high season. Restaurant and hotel reviews have been shortened. For full information, visit Fodors.com.

## What It Costs in Yen

| | $ | $$ | $$$ | $$$$ |
|---|---|---|---|---|
| **RESTAURANTS** | | | | |
| | under ¥1,500 | ¥1,500–¥3,000 | ¥3,001–¥5,000 | over ¥5,000 |
| **HOTELS** | | | | |
| | under ¥12,000 | ¥12,000–¥18,000 | ¥18,001–¥22,000 | over ¥22,000 |

## Safety

Given the nuclear incident in Fukushima Prefecture in 2011, some people worry about lingering radiation in the water table or food chain, but longtime residents can assure you that it's not a concern, as it is very easy to detect. If you are worried at all, ask your hotel staff about the precautions they take.

# Visitor Information

Individual towns have tourist offices that provide local information. The largest and most helpful tourist center, which provides multilingual information on all of Tohoku, is at JR Sendai Station. Within Tokyo each prefecture has an information center with English brochures and maps. In summer the local Japan Travel Bureau can make arrangements for scenic tours by train, bus, or even taxi. The offices in Tokyo, Kyoto, and Sendai arrange tours, some in English.

**CONTACT Sendai Tourist Information Center.** ✉ *Aoba-ku Chuo 1–1–1, Sendai Station, 2nd fl., Aoba-ku* ☎ *022/222–4069* ⊕ *www.i-sendai.jp.*

# When to Go

The north and west have Japan's fiercest winters; transportation slows down significantly, even grinding to a halt during prolonged sieges of snowfall. Along the Pacific and around Sendai, however, things are decidedly milder. Fall colors in the region are fantastic, and spring brings spectacular blossoms of cherry trees. Summer is cooler with less humidity than in most of Japan, but don't be surprised by occasional heat when inland.

True festival enthusiasts could see all of Tohoku's big summer festivals in a single whirlwind visit, starting with Hirosaki's Neputa Matsuri (August 1–7), Aomori's Nebuta Matsuri (August 2–7), Goshogawara's Tachi Neputa (August 4–8), Akita's Kanto Matsuri (August 3–6), Yamagata's Hanagasa Festival (August 5–7), and the granddaddy of them all, Sendai's Tanabata Matsuri (August 6–8). Things do get fully booked well ahead (often as early as three to four months), so secure both your train and hotel reservations well in advance. Reserved seats on the Shinkansen can sell out up to a month before the date of travel.

# Sendai (仙台)

*352 km (219 miles) north of Tokyo.*

Sendai is Tohoku's largest city, and its million residents enjoy the big-city amenities coupled with the easygoing vibe of a small town. Devastated by World War II, Sendai has since become a thoroughly modern and well-planned city, with wide boulevards and a surprising amount and variety of greenery. It's the economic and educational capital of the region, hosting a broad range of industries and institutions, such as prestigious Tohoku University. In recent decades the city has become a magnet for international students, teachers, and workers, and this has helped foster Sendai's energetic and affable atmosphere.

The city's origins can largely be traced to the story of the "one-eyed dragon," local warlord Masamune Date (1567–1636). Affectionately nicknamed for both his one working eye (he was blinded in the other during a childhood bout with smallpox) and his valor in battle, Date established a dynasty in Sendai that maintained its position as one of the three most powerful *daimyo* (feudal lord) families during the shogun eras (his crescent-moon helmet is still found in popular samurai-battle imagery). In later life his talents expanded: he engineered a canal linking two rivers, improving the transport of rice; and in an effort to further trade with Europe, he dispatched an emissary to Rome and the Vatican. He remained to his death a closet patron of Christianity, and encouraged Japanese exploration of the outside world (even after both were formally outlawed by the Tokugawa Shogunate).

## GETTING HERE AND AROUND

Sendai Airport is well connected, with numerous daily flights to and from every major airport in Japan, and destinations in Asia and the Pacific as well.

But the easiest way to get to Sendai from Tokyo is the Shinkansen. From Tokyo the Hayabusa Shinkansen rockets to Sendai in only one hour, 30 minutes, for ¥11,000.

If you have time, the JR Express bus from Tokyo to Sendai is inexpensive (¥3,200–¥7,400) and takes just under six hours; departures leaving Tokyo from JR Shinjuku Station bus terminal at just before midnight arrive in Sendai around 5:30 am. There are also daytime departures, but allow at least six hours for the trip.

The Willer Express bus also runs from Tokyo to Sendai and takes approximately five hours in the daytime, six hours in the evening (around ¥2,500–¥6,500). Fourteen departures leave Tokyo's Shinjuku Bus Terminal with some passing through Sunshine Bus Terminal near Ikebukuro Station between 7:30 am and midnight. Willer Express buses have a larger choice of comfortable seats. On many routes you can choose from different classes of service.

Returning to Tokyo from Sendai, all night buses depart from the east side of JR Sendai Station between 10:30 pm and 12:30 am and arrive in Tokyo between 4:50 am and 8 am. Reservations are required.

Once you get to the city, take Sendai Loople, a limited access bus that stops at Zuihoden (15 minutes from the station) and Osaki Hachiman-gu (43 minutes) and other major sights. A full-day pass costs ¥630 and also gives you discounts to some sights, including Zuihoden; single rides cost ¥260. Buses depart from the West Exit of JR Sendai Station (Stop #16 where you can also find a ticket window) every 15–20 minutes from 9 am to 4 pm. There is a ¥920 Loople–subway combo ticket, but the Sendai subway, with only two lines, is of limited use to tourists. Check where you want to go before buying the combo ticket. It is probably only

of use if you need to cross town faster than the Loople will take you.

**CONTACTS JR Express Bus.** ☎ 022/256–6646 ⊕ www.jrbustohoku.co.jp/en. **Willer Express.** ☎ 050/5805–0383 national reservations ⊕ willerexpress.com/en.

## VISITOR INFORMATION
The Sendai City Tourist Information Center on the second floor of Sendai JR Station has English speakers who will gladly recommend hotels and restaurants. They also provide essential maps with walking and bus routes.

**CONTACT Sendai City Tourist Information Center.** ✉ Sendai Station Bldg. 2F, Aoba-ku ☎ 022/222–4069 ⊕ www.sentia-sendai.jp/english-guide.

#  Sights

Walkers and people-watchers will love Sendai; it seems as if the whole city is within a quick stroll. Thousands of shops, bars, restaurants, and cafés line glittering arcades. Not far from the station, and slicing cleanly through the central entertainment area, are three broad avenues: Aoba-dori, Hirose-dori, and Jozen-ji-dori. These main roads are conveniently intersected by the large Clis Road and Ichibancho covered shopping streets.

### Osaki Hachiman Shrine
(大崎八幡宮; Osaki Hachiman-gu)
**RELIGIOUS BUILDING** | One of the few structures left standing in Sendai after World War II, this shrine houses the guardian deity of military families. As such, the *shintai* (the object of worship in a Shinto shrine that is believed to contain the spirit of a deity) has a history of being passed among Tohoku's ruling families. In 1607, local daimyo Masamune Date had it brought to Sendai. Nestled among trees is the elegant wooden structure, with bright-metal ornamentation over subdued black lacquer. The main building has been designated a National Treasure. It's in the northwest section of the city, about 45

# Tanabata Matsuri (Tanabata Festival)

Tohoku's Tanabata festival, one of the largest in Japan, is held every year from August 6 to 8. On the eve of the festival, 16,000 fireworks are set off just to the west of the central part of the city near the site of Sendai Castle. The festival is believed to have evolved from a Chinese legend of a weaver girl (the star Vega, in her afterlife) and her cowherd boyfriend (the star Altair, in his). As lovers tend to do, they slowly went mad, and began to spend their time idly, living as if in a dream. A jealous ruler became irate and banished them to the far sides of his kingdom (the Milky Way). But he relented, perhaps remembering some foolish love affair of his own, and allowed them to meet on one day a year: the seventh day of the seventh month (of an old calendar).

The festival held here annually in their honor creates a great reservoir of energy. Colorful streamers flutter from every perch in town. Walking along the arcades with the endless streamers brushing down against your face, neck, and shoulders—as you bump against and smile back at other enraptured souls also seduced by the whole grand pageant—will make you feel glad to be alive and in Sendai at such a magical time.

Beginning on the evening of the sixth, parades, dances, events, and demonstrations of festival spirit are held nightly through the eighth, along a short stretch of Jozen-ji-dori between Kotodai Park and Bansui-dori. The tourist information office in JR Sendai Station can help with more details, also contained in countless pamphlets.

minutes from the station by the Loople and 30 minutes from the Zuihoden area. ⊠ 4–6–1 Hachiman, Aoba-ku ☎ 022/234–3606 ⊕ www.oosaki-hachiman.or.jp/pop ⚑ Free.

### Rinno-ji Temple (輪王寺)

TEMPLE | Interested in Zen meditation? This temple, with a quintessentially Japanese garden, holds free *zazen-kai* (seated meditation class) on Saturday evenings after the temple has closed to visitors. In early summer, the garden is a blaze of color as the various flowers come into bloom. During the blooming season, visit in the early evening when the crowds leave. From JR Sendai Station, take the JR train to Kita-Sendai Station and walk 10 minutes. ⊠ 1–14–1 Kitayama, Aoba-ku ☎ 022/234–5327 ⚑ ¥300.

### Sendai Castle (仙台城跡; *Sendaijo-ato*)

CASTLE/PALACE | Sendai Castle (or more accurately the ruins of Sendai Castle) offers views of the city. A restored

guardhouse is all that remains of what was the residence of the Date dynasty for three centuries. Sadly, it was all pulled down during the Meiji Restoration. The Aobajo Museum, located on the grounds, displays armor and weapons used by Masamune Date, as well as a CG reconstruction of the castle in its heyday. Nearby Gokoku Jinja (Gokoku Shrine) is now the area's main attraction. To get here by bus, take the Sendai Loople and get off at the Sendai-jo Ato/Site of Sendai Castle. ⊠ 1 Kawauchi, Aoba-ku ☎ 022/222–0218 Aoba Castle Museum ⚑ Grounds free; museum ¥700.

### SS-30 Observation Deck
(住友生命仙台中央ビル; *Sumitomo Seimei Sendai Chuo Building*)

VIEWPOINT | View the city of Sendai and the mountains for free from the observatory deck on the top floor of this 30-story skyscraper. Just follow the signs to the Sky Lounge. The northern side of

Sendai's colorful Tanabata Matsuri is one of Japan's biggest festivals.

the building is a wedding facility. ⊠ *4–6–1 Chuo, Aoba-ku* ⊡ *Free.*

### ★ Zuihoden (瑞鳳殿)

**TOMB** | The grand mausoleum of Masamune Date, the most revered daimyo of ancient Sendai, was made in the style of the Momoyama Period (16th century), where figures of people, birds, and flowers are carved and inlaid in natural colors. Looking like the world's fanciest one-story pagoda, there is so much gold leaf that in the right light it practically glows. Having burned during the firebombing in 1945, Zuihoden was reconstructed beginning in 1974. During the excavation, Date's well-preserved remains were found and have been reinterred in what appears to be a perfect replica of the original hall. The mausoleum is a 10-minute walk uphill from the Zuihoden stop; it's well worth it as it's a delightful change from other ancient architecture. ⊠ *23–2 Otamaya-shita, Aoba-ku* ☎ *022/262–6250* ⊕ *www.zuihoden.com/ en* ⊡ *¥570.*

##  Restaurants

### Aji Tasuke Honten (味太助)

**$$** | **JAPANESE** | This birthplace of Sendai's famous *gyutan* (grilled beef tongue) proudly serves excellent and inexpensive meals. It is a very casual environment but can get crowded with lines forming before opening. **Known for:** inexpensive lunch sets; oxtail soup; grilled beef tongue. $ *Average main: ¥1,700* ⊠ *4–4–13 Ichiban cho, Aoba-ku* ⊕ *From the Ichib-an-cho Exit of the Mitsukoshi department store, turn left, walk to the first narrow street, turn right, then go left at the next corner; Aji Tasuke is just before the torii gate on the left.* ☎ *022/225–4641* ⊟ *No credit cards* ⊗ *Closed Tues.*

### Go Shu In Sen (御酒印船)

**$$** | **SEAFOOD** | This good spot for cheap seafood and sake offers can't-beat lunch deals. Very casual, it's also a great place to sit at the counter and watch chefs at work. **Known for:** fresh fish; good-value lunch sets; lively atmosphere. $ *Average main: ¥1,500* ⊠ *3–1–24 Chuo, Aoba-ku*

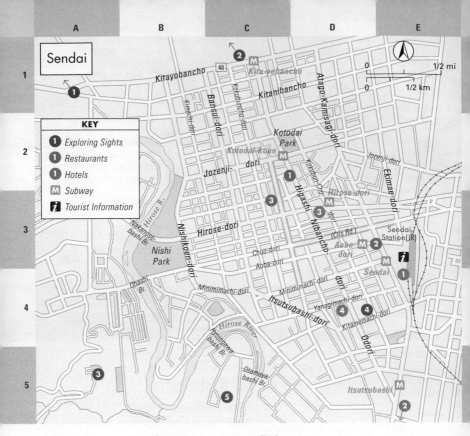

## Sendai

**1** Exploring Sights
**1** Restaurants
**1** Hotels
**M** Subway
**i** Tourist Information

### Sights ▼

1 Osaki Hachiman
  Shrine...................... **A1**
2 Rinno-ji Temple........... **C1**
3 Sendai Castle ........... **A5**
4 SS-30 Observation
  Deck...................... **D4**
5 Zuihoden................. **C5**

### Restaurants ▼

1 Aji Tasuke Honten ....... **C2**
2 Go Shu In Sen........... **D3**
3 Jiraiya.................... **C3**

### Hotels ▼

1 Hotel Metropolitan
  Sendai..................... **E4**
2 Ichijoh Ryokan ........... **E5**
3 Super Hotel Sendai
  Hirose Dori .............. **D3**
4 The Westin Sendai ..... **D4**

⚓ *Go Shu In Sen is on the basement level, so look for the entrance just across from a subway entrance a couple of mins from JR Sendai Station* ☎ *022/225–6868.*

### Jiraiya (地雷也)

**$$$$ | JAPANESE |** In its lively neighborhood, a curtain next to a big red paper lantern leads to this inviting eatery where *kinki* (deepwater white fish) are carefully grilled on a charcoal fire and other delectables are served. The interior is quaint and inviting and the walls are plastered with signed posters and artifacts from celebrities. **Known for:** grilled dishes; seasonal specialties; fresh seafood. Ⓢ *Average main: ¥6,000* ✉ *Inomata Bldg. B1, 2–1–15 Kokubun-cho, Aoba-ku* ⚓ *In the basement of a rundown corner building just off Ichiban-cho near Hiroso Dori* ☎ *022/261–2164* ⊕ *www.jiraiya.com/bk/english/origin_name.htm* 🕙 *Closed Sun. No lunch.*

 ## Hotels

### Hotel Metropolitan Sendai
(ホテルメトロポリタン仙台)

**$$$ | HOTEL |** This upscale hotel adjacent to the railway station is a great value, with spacious, tastefully furnished rooms. **Pros:** unbeatably convenient; comfy rooms; 10% discount with a rail pass. **Cons:** some rooms are a little dark; a bit of a cold atmosphere; traffic noise might disturb light sleepers. Ⓢ *Rooms from: ¥22,000* ✉ *1–1–1 Chuo, Aoba-ku* ☎ *022/268–2525* ⊕ *https://sendai.hotel-metropolitan.com* 🛏 *295 rooms* ⦿ *No Meals.*

### Ichijoh Ryokan (湯主一條; *Yunushi Ichijō*)

**$$$$ | B&B/INN |** The old and new are elegantly juxtaposed in this upscale ryokan, where a century-old four-story wooden building stands next to a newly built luxury lodging. **Pros:** impeccable service; excellent meals; some rooms have private hot spring baths. **Cons:** can feel isolated; not much going on nearby; remote location well away from Sendai. Ⓢ *Rooms from: ¥40,000* ✉ *1–48 Kamasaki, Shiroishi* ⚓ *Shirioshi is 27 km (17 miles) south of Sendai (about 15 mins by Shinkansen from Sendai Station)* ☎ *0224/26–2151* ⊕ *www.ichijoh.co.jp/english* 🛏 *24 rooms* ⦿ *All-Inclusive.*

### Super Hotel Sendai Hirose Dori
(スーパーホテル仙台・広瀬通り)

**$$ | HOTEL |** This budget hotel chain has a welcome bar where you can make your own drinks until 8 pm, but you might not want to spend too much time in the small but functional rooms. **Pros:** central location; natural hot spring bath; discounts for seniors and students (on certain days). **Cons:** reception not staffed after midnight; audible beeping noises from neighbors entering their room codes; small bathrooms. Ⓢ *Rooms from: ¥12,000* ✉ *2–9–23 Chuo, Aoba-ku* ⚓ *To get here from JR Sendai Station, walk on Hirose Dori toward the Hirose Dori Subway Station* ☎ *022/224–9000* ⊕ *www.superhoteljapan.com/en/s-hotels/hirose* 🛏 *180 rooms* ⦿ *Free Breakfast.*

### The Westin Sendai (ウェスティン仙台)

**$$$$ | HOTEL |** The sleek lobby on the 26th floor leads to the modern lounge with huge wall-to-wall windows overlooking the city, mountains, and distant ocean; the guest rooms share these gorgeous views. **Pros:** impeccable, sky-high rooms; endless views; friendly staff. **Cons:** feels far from the liveliness of downtown; entry in and out of the hotel can take some time; some rooms have lingering cigarette smell. Ⓢ *Rooms from: ¥30,000* ✉ *1–9–1 Ichiban-cho, Aoba-ku* ☎ *022/722–1234* ⊕ *www.marriott.com* 🛏 *292 rooms* ⦿ *No Meals.*

 ## Shopping

Sendai is the largest city in the Tohoku region, and you can find many well-known regional crafts of Miyagi Prefecture here: traditional wooden *kokeshi* dolls, handmade *washi* paper, and Sendai's *tansu* chests. Heading west out of the station, follow the elevated walkways across the busy street below to where the main shopping begins in earnest. The best variety of shops can be found along the popular Clis Road arcade.

The Asa-Ichi, or Morning Market (even though each store keeps different hours), is an east–west alley positioned midway in the big block that sits near the Hotel Green Well, a five-minute walk from JR Sendai Station's West Exit. It's busy from early morning to night, and you'll be able to see, hear, smell, and taste it all.

### Ekichika Souvenir
(おみやげ通り; *Omiyage-dori*)

**SHOPPING CENTER** | Below Sendai Station, this shopping area carries all kinds of souvenirs and will save you time if you're looking for local knickknacks. Follow the signs to S-PAL and head to the basement, but if you like shopping, then be sure to give yourself plenty of time to wander around. There is even an area full of a variety of restaurants. ⊠ *B1F Sendai Station, 1–1–1 Chuo, Aoba-ku.*

### Shimanuki (こけしのしまぬき本店; *Kokeshi Shinanuki Honten*)

**CRAFTS** | This store is tops for folk crafts and creative wares from around Tohoku, such as kokeshi dolls, Nambu ironware, and cherry-bark crafts, jewelry resembling red caviar, and even a unique blue lacquer they have developed. The store is about a 10-minute walk from Sendai Station. Follow the covered Clis Road and continue into the next covered arcade named Marble Road. Look for the kokeshi dolls on display out front on the left. ⊠ *3–1–17 Ichibancho, Aoba-ku* ☎ *022/223–2370* ⊕ *www.shimanuki.co.jp* ⊗ *Closed second Wed. of each month.*

### Takasho Kanamono Honten
(たかしょう金物本店)

**OTHER SPECIALTY STORE** | This store carries a whole variety of handsome cooking knives, wasabi grinders, lacquered chopsticks, teapots, and other useful items. It also has unique pet supplies. Why not

## Kokeshi Dolls

These simple wooden cylinders painted with striking red and green patterns are actually an indigenous Tohoku craft, first made during the long, snowy winters and sold to tourists at onsen resorts. You can still find them on sale there, as well as at shops selling traditional crafts; at Hirosaki's Tsugaru-han Neputa Mura, you can even paint your own.

get your dog some Sendai *gyutan* treats? ⊠ *2–1–22 Chuo, Aoba-ku* ✦ *On Clis Rd. shopping arcade. Look for the pet supplies outside* ☎ *022/263–3411* ⊗ *Closed Thurs.*

# Morioka (盛岡)

*184 km (114 miles) north of Sendai.*

Morioka is a busy commercial and industrial city ringed by mountains, and serves as a great travel hub; for that reason a one-day stopover is usually sufficient to give travelers a glimpse of the city's greenery and attractions. A nice, expansive park surrounds a ruined castle, a riverside collection of shipping containers turned into drinking and dining spots, and an ancient cherry tree has proven it belongs here by rooting itself into the crack of a huge granite slab in front of the district courthouse. But the city's major draw is the locally produced *Nanbu-tetsu*, a special type of cast iron forged into functional and highly ornamental wares. The most popular are heavy iron kettles. They are expensive, because they're specially tempered not to rust. As tea connoisseurs know, once conditioned, these pots soften the water by leeching out unwanted minerals and chemicals while adding the taste and health benefits of elemental iron. They will go on doing it forever, too, if properly cared for. Many locals are still using kettles from centuries past. Dozens of shops throughout the city sell Nanbu-tetsu, but the main shopping streets are Saien-dori and O-dori, which pass right by Iwate Koen (Iwate Park).

## GETTING HERE AND AROUND

From Sendai, the quickest way to reach Morioka is the Hayabusa Shinkansen (39 minutes, ¥6,590); the cheapest way to get there is the express bus (two hours, 40 minutes; ¥3,100). Both run many times a day from Sendai. If you want to fly from Osaka or Sapporo, Morioka (whose Hanamaki Airport is 45 minutes by bus, ¥1,430, from Morioka Station) has two or three flights daily from Osaka's Itami Airport (one hour, 30 minutes; ¥39,000) and also hour-long flights from Sapporo's Shin-Chitose Airport for around ¥28,000 on JAL.

To get to downtown Morioka from JR Morioka Station, you can walk or take the convenient loop bus, called Denden-mushi, which goes to the shopping area on the far side of the river past the park; the bus departs every 20 minutes between the hours of 9 and 4:45 pm from Bus Stop 15 or 16 in front of JR Morioka Station (¥120 for one ride, ¥350 for the day pass). You can also use IC cards for subway systems from other cities such as Suica or Pasmo (tap the card once to get on and once to get off). The reason you would use the Denden-mushi is because it's easy to spot and goes to all the areas you'll probably want to see. However, pay close attention to where your stop is and maybe count the stops since the announcements will likely be unhelpful.

## VISITOR INFORMATION

The Iwate/Morioka Regional Tourist Information Center is on the second floor of JR Morioka Station, and the English-speaking staff can give you maps and other information on the three prefectures of Iwate, Akita, and Aomori. The office can also help arrange accommodations with members of a ryokan union in Iwate.

**CONTACT Iwate/Morioka Regional Tourist Information Center.** ✉ *JR Morioka Station 2F, Morioka Ekimae Dori 1–48, Morioka* ☎ *019/625–2090* ⊕ *hellomorioka.jp.*

# ◉ Sights

### Hanamaki Onsenkyo (花巻温泉郷)

HOT SPRING | Among 12 onsen that collectively make up these gorges of hot water gushers, Osawa and Namari stand out for their quality and well-kept ryokan, offering comfort and long-cherished histories. Osawa is known as poet Miyazawa Kenji's favorite, and Namari is famous for Japan's 600-year-old deepest standing bath. Osawa is 30 minutes by bus from Iwate's Hanamaki Station (not the airport of the same name), Namari 50 minutes. From Morioka the easiest way is to take a train to Hanamaki Station and then use the bus to reach the onsen, which are on the outskirts of town. There is an information center at the station that can help you with bus connections, but be advised that it's a very quiet place, so you might be waiting. It's also possible to get to the area from Shin-Hanamaki Station (which is a different station than "Hanamaki") on a bus operated by the onsen association that stops at several different ryokan in town. If you are staying over, check with your ryokan for free shuttle times (usually only twice a day) and note from which train station and ask about pickup services from the onsen-area bus station. ⌂ *Yuguchi Aza Ōsawa 181, Hanamaki* ✛ *Hanamaki is 42 km (26 miles) from Morioka and is reachable from Morioka by train; it's easier to reach if you have a car, but there is bus service to the local onsen from both Hanamaki and Shin-Hanamaki train stations* ☎ *019/825–2021 Osawa Onsen, 019/825–2311 Namari Onsen Fujisan Ryokan* ⊕ *www.kanko-hanamaki. ne.jp/en/spa/index.html* ✉ *¥700 for a day visit to either onsen.*

★ **Hoon-ji Temple** (報恩寺)
**TEMPLE** | On the outskirts of Mt. Atago-yama is a temple district where a dozen temples are clustered. This one houses 499 statues of Buddha's disciples that were carved between 1731 and 1735, in a time of severe famine and increased religious devotion. Each is unique, and if you look hard, you will see disciples laughing, chatting with their neighbors, eating, drinking, and even napping. Behind Ho-Onji are a small cemetery and a tranquil Japanese garden. Monks ring a bell periodically; the sounds echo through the premises and the city. It is a bit out of the way, but if you enjoy wooden architecture, you will not be disappointed. ✉ *31–5 Nasukawacho, Morioka* ☎ *019/651–4415* 🌐 *visitiwate.com/article/4796* 🎫 *¥300.*

**Iwate Park** (岩手公園; *Iwate Koen*)
**CITY PARK** | This park is large enough to get lost in, with varied landscapes, an astonishing variety of artfully placed flowers and trees, shady groves, streams, and colors in every season. It's a good place for a romantic walk. In 1597 the 26th Lord of Nambu had a fine castle built here, but all that remains are ruined walls. Even so, the walls themselves are fascinating enough. ✉ *Morioka Shiroato Koen, Morioka* ✥ *Take the DenDen Mushi bus to the Morioka Joato Koen stop. Walking from the station takes about 20 mins* 🌐 *www.japan.travel/en/spot/1812* 🎫 *Free.*

**Kamasada Iron Casting Studio**
(釜定本店; *Kamasada Honten*)
**STORE/MALL** | The six casters here create the fine ironwork, and their products are as authentic and beautiful as Nanbu-tekki can be. Depending on the time of day, you can peer into the workshop to watch them at work. Attractive teakettles come in all sizes and prices. If you want to place a special order, you'll have to be patient: your piece will be produced and shipped to you in up to two years for the kettles and two or three months for other items. ✉ *2–5 Konyacho, Morioka* ☎ *019/622–3911* ⏲ *Closed Sun.*

## Tohoku Snacks 🍴

*Tsukemono*, or pickled vegetables, are the traditional snack of choice in Tohoku, where the growing season is short. You may well be offered some by a fellow passenger on a local train or a group of guests at an onsen. You can find local pickled things at souvenir shops all over the region. One excellent spot is on the 2nd floor of S-PAL connected to Yamagata Station.

## 🍴 Restaurants

★ **Azuma-ya Soba** (東家 わんこそば)
**$$** | **JAPANESE** | Hearty soba is made from plentiful northern buckwheat, and Azuma-ya is easily Morioka's most famous place to eat these healthful noodles. The second level is devoted to the courageous and hearty of appetite, where *wanko* soba courses—all you could possibly want to eat—are served. **Known for:** lively atmosphere; sets of seasonal local dishes; continuous bowls of soba. [$] *Average main: ¥2,920* ✉ *1–08–3 Nakanohashi Dori, Morioka* ✥ *Look for the indigo-colored cloth draped outside the shop* ☎ *0120/733–130 for all locations* 🌐 *www.wankosoba.jp/en/wankosoba.*

**Banya Nagasawa** (番屋ながさわ)
**$$$$** | **SEAFOOD** | When you slide open the door to what looks like a little house, you may notice the fish tanks and the freezer packed with flounder, sea bream, and sea creatures you might not recognize. But you'll instantly know what you'll be served here: all manner of seasonal grilled shellfish and fish, crisp and brown on the outside but white and tender inside. **Known for:** an excellent sake selection; dishes to match the

season; the freshest seafood. $ *Average main: ¥6,000* ✉ *2–6–1 Saien, Morioka* ☎ *019/622–2646* 🕙 *Closed Sun. and a few days in mid-Aug. No lunch.*

### Pyon Pyon Sha Morioka Ekimae Ten (ぴょんぴょん舎盛岡駅前店)

$$ | **KOREAN** | *Reimen*—a dish of clear noodles served cold with spicy kimchi, hard-boiled egg, watermelon, and a slice of beef—is a Korean delicacy that has become one of Morioka's signature dishes. It is served in a set with another Korean item such as *bibimbap* (rice in a hot stone bowl, topped with pickled vegetables, mincemeat, and egg) in this airy modern restaurant near Morioka Station. **Known for:** yaki-niku (grilled meat); creative noodle dishes; Morioka reimen (a cold noodle dish). $ *Average main: ¥2,000* ✉ *9–3 Morioka Ekimaedori, Morioka* ☎ *019/606–1067.*

 ## Hotels

### Fujisan Ryokan (藤三旅館)

$$$$ | **B&B/INN** | The main reason to stay here is to have the opportunity to steep in the venerable Namari Onsen, which has a high ceiling and a round shape that resembles nothing so much as a giant inkwell. **Pros:** storied history; good meals; charm to spare. **Cons:** not convenient to Morioka; the baths can be crowded in high season; loud announcements break the peaceful moments. $ *Rooms from: ¥30,000* ✉ *75–1 Namari, Hanamaki* ✛ *A free shuttle bus operates from Shin-Hanamaki station, or you will be picked up (depending on the number in your party), so ask when you make your reservation* ☎ *019/825–2311* ⊕ *namari-onsen-ryokan.com* 🛏 *36 rooms, 6 with private toilets* 🍴 *All-Inclusive.*

### Hotel Metropolitan Morioka New Wing (ホテルメトロポリタン盛岡ニューウイング)

$$$ | **HOTEL** | Tastefully furnished, spacious rooms and English-speaking staff make this hotel—run by the same group as the Hotel Metropolitan Morioka (original

branch)—a safe choice for visitors to Morioka. **Pros:** large, attractive rooms; various interesting packages on offer; central location. **Cons:** somewhat dull breakfast; corporate feel; plumbing can be erratic. $ *Rooms from: ¥20,000* ✉ *2–27 Morioka Ekimae-kitadori, Morioka* ☎ *019/625–1211* ⊕ *morioka.metropolitan.jp* 🛏 *121 rooms* 🍴 *No Meals.*

### Morioka Grand Hotel (盛岡グランドホテル)

$$$$ | **HOTEL** | This pleasingly secluded hotel sits near the top of a wooded hill, with a breezy view over the rolling green hills that surround the city. **Pros:** a tranquil location; great views; spacious rooms. **Cons:** far from the action; a bit difficult to find; dated decor. $ *Rooms from: ¥26,000* ✉ *1–10 Atagoshita, Morioka* ✛ *The hotel is a 10-min taxi ride from JR Morioka* ☎ *019/625–2111* ⊕ *www.m-grand.jp* 🛏 *27 rooms* 🍴 *No Meals.*

### Ryokan Kumagai (旅館熊ヶ井)

$ | **B&B/INN** | This friendly and cozy Japanese inn attracts budget-minded travelers, and it is a lot like visiting someone's grandmother's house. **Pros:** homey atmosphere; reasonable rates; festive atmosphere. **Cons:** smoking is allowed in the rooms and the smell can waft into corridors; can be a bit noisy; a bit rustic. $ *Rooms from: ¥10,000* ✉ *3–2–6 Osawakawara, Morioka* ✛ *Signs on the main street coming from the station lead you to a small alleyway that leads to the ryokan on the right* ☎ *019/651–3020* ⊕ *www.kumagairyokan.com* 🛏 *8 rooms without bath* 🍴 *No Meals.*

### Shikitei Hotel (四季亭)

$$$$ | **B&B/INN** | A half-hour bus ride from JR Morioka Station takes you to this quiet hot-spring town and upscale (and expensive), traditional ryokan, which serves two meals a day in your tatami room. **Pros:** excellent meals; pure relaxation; free Wi-Fi. **Cons:** not all rooms have a private bath; isolated from town; feels a bit claustrophobic. $ *Rooms from: ¥50,000* ✉ *137 Yunotate, Morioka* ✛ *Take the Iwateken Kotsu bus from Morioka*

Station bound for Tsunagi Onsen, Oshu-ku Onsen, or Hotto Yuda Station and get off at the Tsunagi Onsen stop (about 30 mins). Contact the hotel before you leave and they will meet you at the bus stop. The hotel is an 8-min walk from there ☎ 019/689–2021 ⊕ www.shikitei.jp/en ⤵ 22 rooms, 16 with bath ⦿I All-Inclusive.

## 🛍 Shopping

**Gozaku Store** (ござ九 森九商店; *Gozaku-Moriku Shoten*)
**CRAFTS** | This wealthy merchant's house was built sometime between the Edo and Meiji periods (1600–1868) and has a distinguished historical presence. It is now a miscellaneous store carrying lots of bamboo baskets, straw sandals, and other local wares. It's in a great area to wander around. Behind the store is a willow tree and the river—quite a scenic view. ✉ 1–31 Konyacho, Morioka ☎ 019/622–7129 ⊗ Closed Sun.

**Kogensha** (光原社)
**CRAFTS** | Specializing in quality folk crafts like lacquerware, dyed fabrics, kites, and pottery, this shop is composed of several small buildings around a courtyard. You can walk through the charming courtyard to a small café, where cold water is available to everyone. The buildings are interesting and there is an even a little lacquerware-making area. ✉ 2–18 Zaimo-ku-cho, Morioka ♣ Cross the river on Asahibashi bridge and turn left at the first light and follow the stone sidewalk until it narrows and the shop and its courtyard are on the left ☎ 019/622–2894 ⊗ Closed the 15th of each month. When the 15th is a weekend or holiday, it is closed the following weekday.

# Matsushima (松島)

*30 km (19 miles) northeast of Sendai.*

Matsushima and its bay are the most popular coastal resort destinations in Tohoku, and they owe this distinction to an infatuation in Japan with oddly shaped rocks, which the bay has in abundance. Hordes come to see the 250 small, pine-clad islands scattered about the bay. Long ago it was such a sublime and tranquil scene that it was fondly written of by the 17th-century haiku poet Basho. Its popularity aside, the bay is still beautiful, and it makes for a worthwhile side trip from Sendai.

## GETTING HERE AND AROUND

Avoid weekends or holidays and take in the view of the islands—consider renting a bicycle from one of the shops near the station and pedaling up into the hills. The key sights are within easy walking distance of each other. To get here take JR from Sendai (35 minutes northeast, ¥420). For maps and info, visit the tourist office about a five-minute walk from JR Matsushimakaigan Station toward the water and near the open plaza and sightseeing boat pier on the way to Godaido.

## VISITOR INFORMATION

**CONTACT Matsushima Tourist Information.** ✉ 98-1 Azachonai, Matsu-shima ☎ 022/354–2618 ⊕ www.matsushi-ma-kanko.com/en.

##  Sights

**Fuku-ura Island** (福浦島; *Fuku-ura Jima*)
**BEACH | FAMILY** | From Godaido Temple it's a short walk across a pedestrian bridge to the islet of Fuku-ura Jima. For the ¥200 toll you can break away from the crowds and enjoy a walk around this natural area with views across the bay. A stroll around the entire island should

Matsushima's Godaido temple is on a tiny islet connected to the mainland via two small bridges.

take less than an hour. ✉ *39–1 Senzui, Matsu-shima* ☎ *022/354–2618 Matsushima Tourist Information* 🎫 *¥200.*

### Godaido Temple (五大堂)

TEMPLE | Just beyond the plaza and boat pier in Matsushima is a small temple constructed in 1609 at the behest of daimyo Masamune Date. The temple is on a tiny islet connected to the shore by two small arched bridges. Animals representing the zodiac are carved in the timbers and facing each sign's corresponding direction. ✉ *111 Azamachinai, Matsu-shima* ⊕ *www.matsushima-kanko.com/en/sightseeing* 🎫 *Free.*

### Zuigan-ji Temple (瑞巌寺)

TEMPLE | Matsushima's main temple dates from AD 828, but the present structure was rebuilt to meet Masamune Date's tastes in 1609. Zuiganji is perhaps the most representative Zen temple in the Tohoku region. The museum, filled with the temple's treasures including a statue of the warlord, is also well worth

visiting. The natural caves surrounding the temple are filled with Buddhist statues that novices carved from the rock face as part of their training. ■ TIP→ **Tours in English are available if you call ahead.** ✉ *91 Azamachinai, Matsu-shima* ☎ *022/354-2023, 022/354-3218 English tours* ⊕ *www.matsushima-kanko.com/en* 🎫 *¥700.*

 **Hotels**

Although most travelers come to Matsushima on a day trip, spending the night is well worth the expense if you can afford the locally expensive hotel rates. There are also many good restaurants in the town, though they, too, are a bit overpriced and often full of pushy tour-bus groups. For this reason many people just wait to have a good meal when they return to Sendai; however, if you do stay, the hotels also have good restaurants.

**Matsushima Century Hotel** (松島センチュリーホテル)
$$$ | **HOTEL** | This large old-fashioned hotel sits on the island-studded bay near tourist attractions such as Zuigan-ji. **Pros:** great views abound; free pickup from station; a variety of rooms to choose from. **Cons:** ocean views in Japanese-style rooms or suites only; can attract large groups due to its size; busy and noisy tourist area. [$] *Rooms from: ¥22,000* ✉ *8 Senzui, Matsushima-aza, Matsu-shima* ☎ *022/354–4111* 🌐 *ssl.centuryhotel.co.jp/lg_en* 🛏 *130 rooms* 🍴 *No Meals.*

**Matsushima Ichinobo** (松島一の坊)
$$$$ | **HOTEL** | This posh resort hotel has a gorgeous garden that stays illuminated at night. **Pros:** luxurious touches from top to bottom; helpful staff; panoramic views. **Cons:** price can be prohibitive; food choices a bit limited for nonadventurous eaters; tourist sites not within walking distance. [$] *Rooms from: ¥44,000* ✉ *1–4 Hama, Takagi, Matsu-shima* ☎ *0570/05–0240 reservations line* 🌐 *www.ichinobo.com/matsushima* 🛏 *80 rooms* 🍴 *Free Breakfast.*

★ **Shoan Ryokan** (松庵)
$$$$ | **RESORT** | This plush, sedate ryokan sits quietly on the edge of a peninsula called Oku-Matsushima. **Pros:** peaceful hideaway; impeccable personal attention; great natural surroundings. **Cons:** Matsushima tourist sights are not within walking distance; single travelers might not be given a room at busy times; very expensive rates. [$] *Rooms from: ¥65,000* ✉ *1 Umeki, Tetaru* ☎ *022/354–3111* 🌐 *shoan-umine.com/en* 🛏 *11 rooms* 🍴 *Free Breakfast* ☞ *Call 1 day in advance if you want pickup from Matsushima Station.*

# Yamadera (山寺)

*49 km (30 miles) west of Sendai.*

If you'd like to see one of Japan's most revered—and scenic—temple complexes, come up here on an easy day trip from Sendai or Yamagata.

### GETTING HERE AND AROUND

Reach Yamadera from Sendai on the JR Senzan Line (¥860), or from Yamagata City on the same line (¥240). Once you leave the station, you'll find a tourist information office near the bridge, but it's likely that no English is spoken there. They do have pamphlets in a variety of languages and will be as helpful as possible.

## Sights

★ **Ginzan Onsen** (銀山温泉)
**HOT SPRING** | Ginzan is another relaxing hot spring close to both Yamagata and Sendai, but this one is more isolated than Sakunami. It's about two to three hours from Sendai by bus, but probably more accessible from JR Oishida Station using the Hanagasa-Go bus, which takes about 45 minutes depending on the season. ✉ *Ginzan Onsen, Obanazawa.*

★ **Risshaku-ji Temple** (立石寺)
**TRAIL** | **FAMILY** | Yamadera is like something conjured out of the ethereal mists of an ancient Japanese charcoal painting. Built in the year AD 860, Yamadera's complex of temples including Risshaku-ji, is perched high on the upper slopes of Mt. Hoju (Hoju-san), from where you can enjoy divine vistas. Just inside the temple-complex entrance is Konpon Chudo, the temple where the sacred Flame of Belief has burned constantly for 1,100 years. Near Konpon Chudo is a statue of the Japanese poet Matsuo

Basho (1644–94), whose pithy and colorful haiku related his extensive wanderings throughout Japan. During a visit to the temple, he wrote, "Stillness … the sound of cicadas sinks into the rocks" and buried the poem on the spot.

The path continues up many steps—nearly 1,100 of them, well-tended though they may be. At the summit is Oku no In, the hall dedicated to the temple founder, Jikaku Daishi. But if you've come this far, keep going. Of all the temples hanging out over the valley, the view from Godaido is the best. The path becomes crowded in summer and slippery in winter. ✉ *4456–1 Yamadera, Yamagata* ⊹ *To get to the temple complex from Yamadera's JR Station, walk through the village, cross the bridge, and turn right. The temple entrances are up some stairs on the left* ☎ *023/695–2843* ⊕ *www. rissyakuji.jp* ✍ *¥300.*

### Sakunami Onsen (作並温泉)

**HOT SPRING** | If you're looking for a stopover between Yamadera and Sendai, this hot spring area (with five hotels) is five minutes by free bus from JR Sakunami Station. Sakunami is only 39 minutes (¥500) by local express from Sendai Station, close enough to be an alternative spot to spend the night, but not convenient. There are also free tours (in Japanese only) at the nearby Nikka Whisky distillery here. ✉ *16 Sakunami Azamotoki, Aoba-ku* ☎ *022/395–2211 Iwamatsu Ryokan* ✍ *¥1,270 weekdays, ¥1,570 weekends for entry to Iwamatsu ryokan's baths* ☞ *Entry to the baths after about 3 pm is restricted to the ryokan's guests.*

 **Hotels**

### Iwamatsu Ryokan (岩松旅館)

**$$$$** | **RESORT** | Along the Hirose River, this large ryokan has rooms that peer out over the stream and mountains. **Pros:** local specialties served at dinner; secluded setting; free shuttle bus to Sakunami

Station. **Cons:** caters to large groups of business travelers, who can be rowdy at night; a bit far from everything; food gets mixed reviews. **$** *Rooms from: ¥30,000* ✉ *Sakunami Onsen Motoyu, Aoba-ku* ☎ *022/395–2211* ⊕ *ssl.iwamatu-ryokan. com* ⇌ *91 rooms* ⦿ *All-Inclusive.*

# Hiraizumi (平泉)

*120 km (75 miles) north of Sendai.*

A culture of gold flourished in Hiraizumi in the late 11th and 12th centuries, when the Oshu Fujiwara family, a then-powerful clan, chose to move here. Massive temple-building projects were carried out so as to create a peaceful society based on the principles of Buddhism. Hiraizumi evokes Kyoto in many ways, especially in its similar topography. In its heyday the city served as a convenient base to transport gold, fine horses, and other materials by land and sea, and trading it made the Oshu Fujiwara family prosper. Hiraizumi, then called Mutsu, supplied much of the gold to decorate images of the Buddha and tactfully traded with the capital Kyoto and even China.

For its magnificent Golden Hall and its lovely Buddhist Jodo Garden, Hiraizumi is a worthwhile day trip from Sendai or a stopover on your way to other destinations in the north.

## GETTING HERE AND AROUND

The nearest station is JR Hiraizumi Station. From Sendai the Yamabiko Shinkansen speeds to Ichinoseki Station (31 minutes), then you hop on the local train one stop for Hiraizumi (¥3,780 in total). It's also accessible by local trains (two hours, ¥1,980) and by express buses (100 minutes, ¥1,600 or ¥1800 directly to Chuson-ji). Within the small town, the bus is easy and useful. Ask at the tourist information office about the bus and about the nearby locations where you can rent bicycles.

### VISITOR INFORMATION

Ask about the multilingual audio guide pens you can rent for ¥500 that give information about the various sites in the city. Call ahead and ask about arranging a guide for the temple sites. Private guides may be available from April through November for an additional fee.

**CONTACT Hiraizumi Tourist Information Office.** ✉ *61–7 Izumiya, Hiraizumi* ✥ *Just outside Hiraizumi Station* ☎ *0191/46–2110* 🌐 *www.hiraizumi.or.jp/en/info/guide.*

## Sights

**★ Chuson-ji Temple** (中尊寺)

**TEMPLE** | Founded in AD 850, this temple's highlight is its Konjikido (Golden Hall), which was completed in 1124. The first Ou Fujiwara lord, Kiyohara, commissioned many temples and pagodas during his reign, perhaps as many as 40, not to mention residences for 300 priests. Nearly all were destroyed by fire except for Konjikido, and it is the only structure in Chuson-ji that remains unchanged. More than 3,000 objects have survived and are now kept in the treasure house (Sankozo Museum). It's a 20-minute walk from JR Hiraizumi Station or a 10-minute bus ride. ✉ *202 Koromonoseki, Hiraizumi* ☎ *019/146–2211* 🌐 *www.chusonji.or.jp/language_en/index.html* 🎫 *¥800.*

**Geibikei Gorge** (猊鼻渓・舟下り; *Geibikei Funa-kudari*)

**BODY OF WATER** | **FAMILY** | The surreal Geibikei Gorge is a slightly decrepit, definitely kitschy tourist attraction. You board a gondola at the local river, and your gondolier will sing in classic Japanese style as he maneuvers farther into the echoey gorge. Your destination is an upriver sandbar, where you disembark for a stroll, and for a nominal fee you can throw kiln-fired clay divots (*undama*) into a crack in a cliff across the river (each divot has a character on it, and if you chuck it in the hole, that fate is in store for you). Bring bread to feed the river fish—they aggressively follow the boat and jump for joy at handouts. Those fish are also available roasted and fried where you disembark. The trip takes 90 minutes, and boats depart approximately once an hour from 8:30 to 3 most days. ✉ *Nagasaka Asamachi 467, Higashiyama-cho* ✥ *Take JR train from Hiraizumi to Ichinoseki (20 mins), then change to Ofunato Line to Geibikei (30 mins) or check the seasonal bus schedule in Hiraizumi.* ☎ *019/147–2341* 🌐 *www.geibikei.co.jp/en* 🎫 *¥1,800.*

**Motsu-ji Temple** (毛越寺)

**GARDEN** | A UNESCO World Heritage site, Motsu Temple's main buildings were destroyed by the fire that consumed much of the area in 1226. Nevertheless, its remaining Heian-Period Jodo Garden still provides a beautiful scenery, as it was landscaped to depict the Amida Buddha's "Pure Land." Even the new (1989) main hall was built to reflect the Heian roots of the temple. ✉ *Osawa 58, Hiraizumi* ☎ *019/146–2331* 🌐 *www.motsuji.or.jp/en* 🎫 *¥500.*

## Hotels

**Shizukatei** (しづか亭)

**$$$$** | **B&B/INN** | The sounds of nature will lull you to sleep at this hot-spring inn set among the rice paddies outside Hiraizumi. **Pros:** peaceful rural location; delicious, plentiful food; free pickup from the station. **Cons:** not much to do; can feel a bit plain; very far from town. [$] *Rooms from: ¥42,000* ✉ *10–5 Hiraizumi Nagakura, Hiraizumi* ☎ *019/134–2211* 🌐 *shizukatei-hiraizumi.com* 🛏 *10 rooms* 🍴 *All-Inclusive.*

In summer hiking is a popular pastime in the mountains around Yamagata, which host skiers in the winter.

# Yamagata (山形)

*63 km (39 miles) west of Sendai, 120 km (75 miles) southeast of Tsuruoka.*

Yamagata, or literally "mountain shape," is the capital of the prefecture of the same name (and the sister city of Boulder, Colorado). It's a community of around a quarter-million people who enjoy one of the most visually stunning locations in Japan. Everywhere you look there are arrayed lovely mountains, a play of light and shadow shifting across their sculpted flanks and lofty summits. Connoisseurs of soba and mountain vegetables (*sansai*) will be delighted, as will fans of sweet, perfectly marbled beef. Yamagata Prefecture is the only prefecture to be 100% thermal—having at least one onsen, or hot spring, in each of its 35 municipalities. Mt. Zao is popular among visitors for its "ice monsters," trees that become pillars of frozen snow shaped into mysterious forms by the blizzards, as well as its hot springs.

During the **Hanagasa Festival** (August 5–7), some 10,000 dancers from the region dance through the streets in traditional costume and *hanagasa,* hats so named for the safflowers (thistle-like orange-red flowers, locally called *benibana*) decorating them. It is said to be based on an old ritual to promote fertility and ensure a rich harvest. Floats are interspersed among the dancers, and stalls provide food and refreshments.

## GETTING HERE AND AROUND

From Sendai, you have the choice of the JR Senzan Line, which takes about one hour (¥1,140 or buy a W-ticket for ¥1,540, which allows one person to make a round trip or two people a one-way trip from Sendai) or regular buses from the station (¥930). It's 2½ hours from Tokyo via the Tsubasa Shinkansen (¥11,000). If you're coming from Tsuruoka, you can take the non–JR bus from the S-mall (two hours; ¥2,470). Yamagata City is easy to navigate, so walking is the way to go unless you need to head farther afield.

### VISITOR INFORMATION

You can pick up free maps and brochures from the Yamagata Tourist Information Office opposite the ticket turnstiles inside Yamagata JR Station. There is also a larger information center on the ground floor of Kajo Central just outside the West Exit of Yamagata Station. Don't strain your eyes too much trying to see the very small English printed on the signs directing you there.

**CONTACT Yamagata Tourism Information Center.** ✉ *Kajo Central Bldg. 1F, 1–1–1 Jonanmachi, Yamagata* ☎ *023/647–2333* 🌐 *yamagatakanko.com/en.*

## 👁 Sights

**★ Ginzan Onsen** (銀山温泉)
**HOT SPRING** | Ginzan Onsen is known for its unique landscape and distinguished Taisho period (1912–26) architectural design. A flood once destroyed the village in the valley, but it sprung back up with 14 ryokan. A magnificent wooden four-story ryokan from there is depicted in Miyazaki's animated film *Spirited Away.* The Hanagasa dance shows take place Saturday evenings from May to October. From Yamagata, take a train to JR Oishida Station, then hop on the Hanagasa-Go bus bound for Ginzan Onsen (45 minutes). ✉ *Ginzan Onsen, Obanazawa.*

**Hirashimizu Pottery Village** (平清水焼きの窯元; *Hirashimizu Yaki no Kamamoto*)
**STORE/MALL** | If you're interested in pottery, go to this pottery village on the outskirts of Yamagata. It's a bit out of the way but definitely worth a visit if you are spending time in Yamagata. This small enclave of traditional buildings and farmhouses is a step back in time. About six pottery families each specialize in a particular style. You can take pottery lessons and have your handiwork fired, glazed, and, two to four weeks later, mailed back home. ■ **TIP→ The potteries are generally open daily, but the actual hours can be erratic, so definitely check ahead with the tourist information office at JR Yamagata Station before heading out.** ✉ *153 Hirashimizu, Yamagata* ✥ *From Bus Stop 5, in front of JR Yamagata Station, board bus bound for Geijutsu Koka Daigaku (sometimes called Geikodai) for 15-min ride (¥270). A taxi is about ¥2,000* ☎ *023/642–7777 Shichiemon kiln.*

## 🍴 Restaurants

**Sagoro Steakhouse** (佐五郎)
**$$$$** | **JAPANESE** | Sagoro will serve you a full dose of some outstanding Yonezawa and Yamagata beef. It will be difficult to forget the beef's impossible tenderness. **Known for:** reasonably priced lunches; local flavor; delectable, locally sourced beef. [$] *Average main: ¥9,000* ✉ *1–6–10 Kasumicho, Yamagata* ✥ *Head 3 blocks east from the station and turn left. Look for the meat shop, and you'll see the black bull on the sign above the street* ☎ *023/631–3560* ⏲ *Closed Sun. (unless the following Mon. is a holiday).*

**Shojiya** (庄司屋)
**$$** | **JAPANESE** | Yamagata is famous for soba, and Shojiya is the oldest soba restaurant in Yamagata. Go for lunch and then wander around the neighborhood. **Known for:** Yamagata's famous chewy soba; cold soba and tempura; friendly atmosphere. [$] *Average main: ¥1,500* ✉ *Nanokamachi 2–7–6, Yamagata* ☎ *023/673–9639.*

## 🛏 Hotels

**Ginzan Onsen Fujiya** (銀山温泉 藤屋)
**$$$$** | **B&B/INN** | Modern luxury permeates Fujiya Ryokan, which has the ambiance of an art gallery. **Pros:** excellent service; fabulous food; the pinnacle of modern ryokan experiences. **Cons:** only two rooms have beds and they're both king-size; the rest are futon-only; quite far from Yamagata; too expensive and contemporary for some. [$] *Rooms from: ¥79,000* ✉ *433 Shinpata, Obanazawa* ✥ *Oishida Station is 30 mins north of*

Yamagata. Call ahead to arrange pickup ☎ 023/728–2141 ⊕ www.fujiya-ginzan. com/english ⊷ 8 rooms ⦿ All-Inclusive.

### Hotel Metropolitan Yamagata
(ホテルメトロポリタン山形)

$$$ | HOTEL | Yamagata's most centrally located upscale hotel caters to many busy corporate travelers from Tokyo and other big cities. **Pros:** close to great eateries; nice views out front; perfect location for day trips out of town. **Cons:** plain for the price; mostly geared toward business travelers; breakfast is rather pricey. $ Rooms from: ¥20,000 ⊠ 1–1–1 Kasumicho, Yamagata ☎ 023/628–1111 ⊕ www.yamagatametropolitan.jp ⊷ 224 rooms ⦿ No Meals.

### Richmond Hotel Yamagata Ekimae
(リッチモンドホテル山形駅前)

$$ | HOTEL | Two minutes from JR Yamagata Station, this sleek 12-story hotel offers reasonable rates and comfortable rooms with many amenities: bath salts, skin-care products, and special packages for kids. **Pros:** pristine rooms; cheap and varied breakfast; there is a car rental place just downstairs. **Cons:** not much going on nearby; a bit plain; a bit far from the main attractions. $ Rooms from: ¥18,000 ⊠ 1–3–11 Futabacho, Yamagata ☎ 023/647–6277 ⊕ www.richmondhotel. jp/yamagata ⊷ 220 rooms ⦿ No Meals.

### Takamiya Ryokan Miyamaso
(深山荘高見屋; Miyamaso Takamiya)

$$$$ | D&B/INN | This more-than-300-year-old Japanese inn has an inviting yet sophisticated atmosphere and offers soft thermal waters, very attentive staff, and in winter, the chance to see Zao's famous "ice monsters"—those fabulous frozen pillars sculpted by blizzards. **Pros:** historic setting; famous hot spring; close to the ski slope. **Cons:** staff a bit cold and standoffish; no elevators, but lots of steps; far from the center of Yamagata City. $ Rooms from: ¥60,000 ⊠ 54 Zao Onsen, Yamagata ⊹ Buses for Zao Onsen (35 mins, ¥1,000) leave from Stop 1, Yamagata Station; from Zao's bus

terminal, follow the stone-paved street until you reach some steps that lead you slightly right and up to the ryokan ☎ 023/694–9333 ⊕ www.zao.co.jp/ lang/en/takamiya ⊷ 19 rooms ⦿ Free Breakfast.

### Yoshidaya Ryokan (吉田屋旅館)

$$ | B&B/INN | FAMILY | If you are looking for a casual ryokan experience as a stepping off point for skiing or hiking trips, this maze of interconnected hallways and varied rooms with English-speaking staff might be the place for you. **Pros:** delicious, hearty meals; convenient location from bus terminal; private showers in addition to the onsen. **Cons:** can get loud at busy times; the building is a bit of a maze; strong onsen smells. $ Rooms from: ¥18,000 ⊠ Zao Onsen 13, Yamagata ☎ 023/694–9223 ⊕ zao-yoshidaya.com ⊷ 20 rooms ⦿ All-Inclusive.

# Tazawa-ko (田沢湖)

_40 km (25 miles) west of Morioka, 87 km (54 miles) east of Akita._

The beautiful azure waters of Tazawa-ko, an almost perfectly round crater lake, can be enjoyed from the paths along the shore, a rented paddleboat, or the motorboat trip across to the statue of Princess Tatsuko and back. Nearby are several traditional hot-spring inns.

## GETTING HERE AND AROUND

A 12-minute bus ride (¥360) from the JR Tazawa-ko Station gets you to the Tazawa-ko Han center (the bus stop and rest area) on the eastern lakeshore. The buses typically leave soon after train arrivals. Once you arrive, a small and shallow swimming area is a short distance to the northwest along the road. A 30-minute bus ride from JR Tazawa-ko Station via Tazawa-ko Han takes you to Tazawa-ko Kogen (Tazawa-ko Plateau) for ¥620. The journey offers spectacular views of the lake. Once there you can rent your own paddleboat or rowboat.

Tazawa-ko is the deepest lake in Japan.

You'll want sunscreen and a hat or sunshade in summer. There's also regular bus service around the lake and bicycles available for rent (¥500 to ¥800 per hour, with two hours usually sufficient for the loop) at two places at the Tazawa-ko Han bus terminal and at many lodgings in the area. If you cycle around the lake, make sure you don't miss the lakefront bypass of a large hill on the southern side of the lake.

## VISITOR INFORMATION
The Tazawa-ko Tourist Information Office inside the JR Tazawa-ko Station has maps and bus schedules; it's open daily from 8:30 to 5:15.

**CONTACT Tazawa-ko Tourist Information Center.** ⊠ *JR Tazawako Station 1F, 68 Aza-Osaka, Obonai, Semboku* ☎ *0187/43–2111* ⊕ *tazawako-kakunodate. com/en/.*

 **Sights**

**Lake Tazawa** (田沢湖; *Tazawa-ko*)
BODY OF WATER | The clear waters and forested slopes of Tazawa-ko, Japan's deepest lake, create a breathtaking, mystical quality. According to legend, the great beauty from Akita, Tatsuko Hime, sleeps in the water's deep, disguised as a dragon. The lake never freezes over in winter because Tatsuko Hime and her dragon husband churn the water with their passionate lovemaking. The less romantic, scientific reason is that Tazawa-ko has been measured to a depth of 1,397 feet, which prevents it from freezing. Though clear enough to allow you to see a startling 300 feet or more down into it, the mineral-blue water is too acidic to support anything but a few hardy fish (you can buy food to feed them near the statue of Tatsuko Hime).

# Tohoku's Hinabita Onsen

The Tohoku region has some 650 onsen (thermal spas) that are mostly located or "hidden" in remote mountain villages. Traveling here (particularly in winter) is not always easy, but soaking in a relaxing onsen while you are surrounded by snow will remind you why it was worth the trouble to visit.

When you hear Japanese talk about Tohoku's onsen, there is one word you cannot miss: *hinabita*. The word means "rustic," redolent of a simpler past, and for many it's this simple charm that makes the onsen here so enjoyable. Tohoku's hinabita onsen are a magnet for connoisseurs. To enjoy it fully, an overnight stay is recommended. Nearly all onsen have adjoining lodgings, and most will pick you up at a nearby train station or bus stop. Many ryokan in the region welcome not only visitors but also long-term guests, who stay for months for *toji* (therapeutic purposes). *Toji* has been practiced since the 17th century and is still popular, particularly among cancer patients as an alternative medicine.

A scenic 20-km-long (12-mile-long) two-lane road is perfect for biking. Bicycles can be rented at the bus station near JR Tazawako Station, but you can also take a bus (timed with the arrivals of trains) to the lake and rent bicycles there for a relaxing ride around lake. In winter the Tazawa area is a popular downhill-skiing destination, and the deep blue of the lake is dazzling from the lifts and trails. ⊠ *Semboku* ⊕ *www.city.semboku.akita. jp/en/sightseeing/spot/04.*

## Tamagawa Onsen (玉川温泉)
**HOT SPRING** | The highlight is the strong, acidic water (which has a minor amount of radium): gushing out at almost 2,400 gallons per minute, it's Japan's swiftest flow from a single spring. In the vicinity is another geothermal area in a national park where many enjoy a hot-rock bath. Take worn-out T-shirts and towels because they will get stained by the waters or even the steam (be careful also of reactive jewelry, such as copper or silver). ⊠ *Tazawako Tamagawa, Semboku* ⊹ *From JR Tazawa-ko Station, take the Ugokotsu bus bound for Tamagawa Onsen. The trip takes 75 mins* ☎ *018/758–3000* ⊕ *www.tamaga-wa-onsen.jp* ⊒ *Onsen ¥600, hot rock baths free.*

##  Hotels

### Kuroyu Onsen (黒湯温泉)
**$$ | B&B/INN** | One of seven rustic ryokan in the Nyuto area, this one is the coziest, but no rooms have a private bath, though several categories (including the Western-style rooms) have private toilets in the room. **Pros:** great retreat; great service; wonderful pools. **Cons:** can be noisy; a bit out-of-the-way; no private bathrooms. $ *Rooms from: ¥13,500* ⊠ *2–1 Tazawa-ko Obonai, Semboku* ☎ *018/746–2214* ⊕ *www.kuroyu.com* ⊗ *Closed mid-Nov.–mid-Apr.* ⊐ *42 rooms (all without bath but most with private toilets)* ⊖ *All-Inclusive.*

# Kakunodate (角館)

*19 km (12 miles) southwest of Tazawa-ko,*
*59 km (37 miles) southwest of Morioka,*
*69 km (43 miles) east of Akita City.*

The little samurai town of Kakunodate, sometimes called "Little Kyoto," was founded in 1620 by Yoshikatsu Ashina, the local lord, who chose it for its defensible position and reliable water sources. An outpost of traditional Japan, Kakunodate is consistently regarded as one of the very best places for seeing cherry blossoms in spring. The whole town is full of *shidare-zakura* (weeping cherry trees), descended from the same trees that adorn Kyoto, and their pink flowers grace the dark-wood gates, walls, and roofs of ancient samurai houses. Along the banks of Hinokinai-gawa (Hinokinai River), these living jewel factories dangle a mile-long pink curtain. The town is also home to several samurai and merchant houses with eclectic collections of family treasures, many not at all crowded with visitors. From September 7 to 9, a loud town festival involving floats, drums, and dancing takes place here.

## GETTING HERE AND AROUND

On the JR Komachi Shinkansen Line, Kakunodate can be reached from Tazawa-ko (¥1,420) or Morioka (¥2,630). Akita City is about 45 minutes away on the Komachi Shinkansen Line (¥2,800). On local trains, the trip to Akita City takes 90 minutes to two hours because some trains halt at Oomagari Station for a half hour or so, and you might have to change trains there.

## VISITOR INFORMATION

The Kakunodate Tourist Information Center is in an old, white *kura*-style (warehouse) building, visible from the station. The might not all speak English, but have maps and information about the samurai houses and walks in town and

# Bark Shopping

Shops in Kakunodate are the best places in Tohoku to pick up the locally made *kabazaiku*, or cherry-bark-veneer items—everything from warmly translucent maroon lamp shades to tiny, intricate business-card holders. If you're looking to find unique souvenirs and crafts in Japan, give Kakunodate's shops a looking-over, since anything you're likely to find in the hokey souvenir shops in the big cities will be more kitschy and overpriced.

can recommend nearby lunch or dinner options. There are places to rest and lockers are also located inside.

**CONTACT Kakunodate Tourist Information Center.** ✉ *394–2 Kami Sugasawa, Kakunodatemachi* ☎ *018/754–2700* ⊕ *tazawako-kakunodate.com/en.*

##  Sights

**Ando House** (安藤醸造; *Ando Jyozo*)
**STORE/MALL | FAMILY |** A visit to this miso and soy sauce business, still located in the historic home of the Ando merchant family, is a treat for both the eyes and the taste buds. Beautiful seasonal flower arrangements and artifacts decorate the tatami rooms, while the unusual redbrick storehouse houses some fine painted screens. And don't miss the inner storehouse, where you can find free miso soup and pickles. ✉ *27 Shimoshinmachi, Kakunodate, Semboku* ☎ *018/753–2008* ⊕ *www.andojyozo.co.jp* 🎫 *Free* 🕐 *Closed Sun.*

## Aoyagi Samurai Manor Museum (武家屋敷 青柳家; *Bukeyashiki Aoyagi-ke*)

**NOTABLE BUILDING | FAMILY** | Several well-preserved samurai houses date from the founding of Kakunodate. The most renowned is Aoyagi-ke, which functions as a museum and even a bit of a shopping center (there are many restaurants and gift shops located here). The house displays an extensive collection of swords, armor, guns, and silk kimono wedding gowns as well as all kinds of historical artifacts to pore over, such as farm implements and household items. There are even some weapons and feel their weight. It also exhibits a large number of war documents, photos, and uniforms from the Sino-Japanese War (1894–95) to the Pacific War (1941–45). History buffs will love it, especially when you can see how much wealth these feudal bureaucrats could accumulate. The museum is a 15-minute walk northwest from JR Kakunodate Station. ⊠ *3 Shimo-cho, Araya-omotemachi* ☎ *018/754–3257* ⊕ *www.samuraiworld. com/english* 🗐 *¥500.*

## Kakunodate Cherry Bark Work Museum (樺細工伝承館; *Kabazaiku Denshokan*)

**OTHER MUSEUM** | A hall in front of a cluster of samurai houses serves as a museum and a workshop for the local cherry-bark veneer handicrafts that became the new source of income for samurai when they suddenly found themselves unemployed. Don't be put off by the imposing exterior of the Densho House—go right on in and watch a master craftsman at work. You can buy the products—often one of a kind—here, rather than from the shops on the street. The Satake-Kita family armor and heavily Kyoto-influenced ancient heirlooms are exhibited in adjacent parts of the building. You can also learn about life in old-time winters, with displays of plaited-maple sleighs and some truly inventive and adaptive tools and togs for coping with snow. ⊠ *10–1 Shimocho, Araya-omotemachi* ☎ *018/754–1700* ⊕ *www.city.semboku. akita.jp/en/sightseeing/spot/07_kabazaiku. html* 🗐 *¥300* ⊘ *Closed Dec. 28–Jan. 4.*

## Ishiguro Samurai House (武家屋敷 石黒家; *Bukeyashiki Ishiguro-ke*)

**HISTORIC HOME** | Direct descendents of the Ishiguro family open part of their residence to let people in to observe the oldest samurai house in Kakunodate. They lead tours around the house explaining the ornamented doors and the vestibule. The family's 12th-generation successor, Naonobu, explains them with English handouts. In the rear, the armory and historical documents, such as a German text on anatomy, are exhibited. The beautiful cherry tree in the garden is nearly three centuries old. This place can draw fairly dense crowds. ⊠ *1 Shimocho, Araya-omotemachi* ☎ *018/755–1496* ⊕ *www.city.semboku.akita.jp/en/sightseeing/spot/07_buke.html* 🗐 *¥300.*

#  Hotels

## Hotel Folkloro Kakunodate (ホテルフォルクローロ角館)

**$$ | HOTEL** | This low-rise hotel next to the train station has Western-style standard twin rooms with private baths; larger deluxe twins with sofas are worth the extra ¥2,000 or so per night. **Pros:** clean rooms; very convenient if arriving by train; breakfast is included. **Cons:** rooms are uninspiring; quiet neighborhood after dark; far from samurai houses. 🟢 *Rooms from: ¥16,000* ⊠ *14 Nakasuga-sawa, Kakunodatemachi* ☎ *018/753–2070* ⊕ *familio-folkloro.com/kakunodate/en* ⤳ *26 rooms* 🍴 *Free Breakfast.*

## Machiyado Neko no Suzu (町宿ねこの鈴)

**$$ | B&B/INN** | Smiling staff welcome you to this charming small inn that adjoins the town baths. **Pros:** local atmosphere in the baths; friendly staff; value for money. **Cons:** no individual baths; twin rooms can feel a bit cramped; little soundproofing of the rooms. 🟢 *Rooms from: ¥15,000* ⊠ *28 Shimonakamachi, Kakunodate, Semboku* ☎ *018/742–8105* ⤳ *13 rooms* 🍴 *No Meals.*

# Towada–Hachimantai National Park (十和田八幡平国立公園)

*158 km (98 miles) northwest of Morioka.*

Including the windswept expanse of Hachimantai Plateau, scenic Lake Towada, beech forests, marshes of wild flowers, and many hot springs, this national park offers many opportunities to get away from it all.

## GETTING HERE AND AROUND

The easiest way to reach Towada-ko by public transport is to take a JR bus from Aomori Station or Hachinohe Station. Mizuumi-Go's route travels between Aomori and Towada-ko in about three hours (¥3,090). JR Oirase-Go departs from Hachinohe Station (two hours, 15 minutes; ¥2,720). If you don't have a Japan Rail Pass, there is a two-day pass that covers the route from Aomori to Towada (¥5,000; check the Aomori Station bus terminal for information); it also lets you stop at other interesting sights such as Oirase Gorge. Local buses run along a network that links all the main spots, but service is frequently suspended during winter storms. There is no bus service from Morioka. If you rent a car, driving in Hachimantai is especially beautiful in early summer and fall.

## ◉ Sights

**Oirase Gorge** (奥入瀬渓流; *Oirase Keiryu*)
TRAIL | An excellent—if a bit crowded—choice for a walk is this gorge northeast of the lake at Nenokuchi. The carefully tended trail follows a river and a series of waterfalls for a total of 9 km (5½ miles; about two hours 40 minutes). A two-lane road parallels the river, so if you get tired you can catch buses north to Aomori and south to Nenokuchi and Yasumiya. Be prepared for cold mist or rain, pack ample snacks and water, and find out the bus schedule before you start out. ⊠ *Towada.*

★ **Osore-zan Mountain** (恐山)
HOT SPRING | FAMILY | If you have a car, a day trip to the uppermost "hook" of the Mutsu/Shimokita Peninsula is highly recommended. A 30-minute drive north of Mutsu takes you to Osore-zan, which literally means "Scary Mountain." On the ash-gray shores of the Lake Usori caldera, an otherworldly landscape awaits, with boardwalks that lead over sulfur pools and past shrines to the dead. There's even an enclosed onsen where you can shuck your clothes and bathe in the water. At festivals held in July and October, *itako* (traditionally blind female shamans, but most who do this are not blind now) open stalls to tell your fortune and communicate with your deceased loved ones. It's a memorable day at the end of the world. ⊠ *Mutsu* ⊕ *ao-mori-tourism.com/en/feature/detail_76.html* ⊠ *¥500 for the onsen* ⊗ *Closed Nov.–Apr.*

★ **Towada-Hachimantai National Park** (十和田八幡平国立公園; *Towada Hachimantai Kokuritsu Koen*)
NATIONAL PARK | For walking among the splendid and vast virgin beech, pine, and cedar forests deep in the heart of Tohoku, you could not pick a better destination than Towada-Hachimantai National Park. The mountains afford sweeping panoramas over the park's gorges and valleys, crystal clear lakes like Towada-ko, gnarled and windswept trees, and volcanic cones. The park straddles Aomori, Iwate, and Akita prefectures, and sprawls over 330 square miles (855 square km). Hot springs and tiny villages lost in time are secreted here, and the fresh tree-scented air promotes a feeling of true wilderness. Most facilities are closed between mid-November and April. ⊠ *Towada* ⊕ *www.env.go.jp/en/nature/nps/park/towada/guide/view.html* ⊗ *Closed mid-Nov.–Apr.*

**Towada-ko** (十和田湖; *Lake Towada*)
**BODY OF WATER** | Thanks to its famous
fall colors, Lake Towada welcomes a
rumbling fleet of packed tour buses
when the leaves begin to change. The
lake fills a volcanic crater to a depth of
1,096 feet, making it the third deepest in
Japan. The crater is held aloft like a giant
goblet above the surrounding topography,
giving it a dramatic illusory aspect.
Boat tours let you float by the lovely
landscape. ⊠ *Towada* ⊕ *towadako.or.jp/
en/experience-lake-towada*.

## 🛏 Hotels

### Hoshino Resorts Oirase Keiryu Hotel
(星野リゾート奥入瀬渓流ホテル)
**$$$$ | HOTEL** | Once a ryokan, this resort
hotel combines the best of both worlds:
there are great mountain views, two
meals are served each day, and yukata
robes are provided (and you are encouraged to walk around in them). **Pros:** lots
of activities; pleasant riverside stroll;
several dining options. **Cons:** fees for all
the extra programs; breakfast on the
terrace costs has a high extra charge;
boxy rooms. $ *Rooms from: ¥40,000*
⊠ *231 Tochikubo, Okuse, Towada, Towada*
☎ *0570/073–022 main hotel number
for Oirase Keiryu Hotel, 50/3786–1144
English line for when calling from abroad*
⊕ *hoshinoresorts.com/en/hotels/oirase-
keiryu* ⇩ *189 rooms* ⊙I *Free Breakfast*.

# Hirosaki (弘前)

*47 km (30 miles) south of Aomori, 230
km (143 miles) northwest of Morioka.*

Hirosaki is one of northern Tohoku's most
attractive cities. It's most famous for its
sweet apples, and its only real cultural
attraction is a small but photogenic
reconstructed castle. The town has a very
appealing, easygoing nature, and this is
suitably reflected in a local slang word,
*azumashii* (a feeling of coziness and

---

## Follow the Parade

In the first week of August, Hirosaki
outdoes itself with the **Neputa Festival** (ねぷた祭り). Each night, following
various routes, internally illuminated
fan-shaped floats brightly painted
with mythological scenes and characters (apparently borrowed from
Chinese legends) parade through
town. The festival is thought to
have its origins in the preparation
of a terrible battle and a send-off for
the warriors some 400 years ago.
Goshogawara, Hirosaki's neighboring town, has its own festival called
**Tachineputa** (五所川原立倭武多) with
spectacularly high floats.

---

comfort). It's a perfect town for wandering and discovering new things.

### GETTING HERE AND AROUND
The easiest way to approach Hirosaki is
to take a local train from Aomori (38–48
minutes, depending on the time; ¥680).
Express trains are slightly faster (34 minutes, ¥1,200). From Morioka, the fastest
and cheapest way is to take the JR
express highway bus (two hours, 15 minutes; ¥5,700 round-trip, ¥3,200 one-way).
If you're interested in cycling around
town, you can rent a bicycle for the day
(¥500 or ¥1,000 for an electric-assisted
bike) from April through November at the
Hirosaki Visitor Information Center, at
Neputa Mura, and three other locations
around the city. Ask at the information
center, but be ready to return your bicycle
by 5 pm. Alternatively, there is a ¥100
bus that loops around the main area of
the city.

### VISITOR INFORMATION
Hirosaki is compact and walkable, but
finding your bearings in this ancient castle town can prove difficult, as the streets

Hirosaki-jo is surrounded by cherry blossoms each spring.

were designed to disorient invaders before they could get to the battlements. Pick up a map at the Hirosaki City Tourist Information Center before setting out, on the right side of the train station as you exit. South of the castle grounds, the large Hirosaki Sightseeing Information Center has displays of local crafts and regional art, and provides tourist information.

**CONTACT Hirosaki City Sightseeing Information Center.** ⊠ *2–1 Shimo-Shiroganemachi, Hirosaki Koen Mae, Hirosaki* ✢ *Just south of Hirosaki Castle* ☎ *0172/37–5501* ⊕ *www.hirosaki-kanko. or.jp/en.*

 Sights

### Chosho-ji Temple (長勝寺)

TEMPLE | Thirty-three of the Soto Sect's Zen temples line up along Zenrin-gai (Zen Forest Street), at the end of which Chosho-ji temple stands with great dignity. The Tsugaru clan's family temple was originally built in Ajigasawa in 1528

but was moved here in 1610 to protect Hirosaki Castle. You'll see an elaborate gate meant to shake off greediness and complaining and 500 statues depicting Buddha's disciples. ⊠ *1–23–8 Nishi Shigemori, Hirosaki* ☎ *0172/32–0813* ⊕ *www.tsugarunavi.jp/en/detail/01_002_ hirosaki_a.html* ⊠ *Free.*

### Hirosaki Castle (弘前城)

CASTLE/PALACE | Guarded by deep moats, over which a red wooden bridge crosses in a picturesque curve, Hirosaki-jo is atop a high stone base. The original castle, completed in 1611, was set ablaze 16 years later by a lightning bolt. The present one, of a smaller scale, dates back to 1810. In spring the more than 5,000 *somei-yoshino* cherry trees blossom, while in fall the changing maples are also gorgeous. A snow-lantern festival with illuminated ice sculptures is held in early February. The castle is a 30-minute walk from JR Hirosaki Station. Take the ¥100 bus from the bus pool and get off at the Shiyakusho-mae stop. ⊠ *1 Shimo Shirogane-cho, Hirosaki* ☎ *0172/33–8733*

🌐 *www.hirosakipark.jp/en* 🎫 *¥310*
🕐 *Closed Nov. 24–Mar. 31.*

**Tsugaru Neputa Village** (津軽藩ねぷた村;
*Tsugaru-han Neputa Mura*)

**MUSEUM VILLAGE** | **FAMILY** | On the north-east corner of the castle grounds, this museum exhibits the giant drums and floats used in the annual Neputa Festival. If you miss the real thing, come here to see the 40-foot fan-shaped floats as they sleep off their hangovers from the mad midsummer revelry. In the work-shop you can paint your own traditional *kingyo-neputa* (bamboo-framed paper goldfish) or kokeshi (traditional wooden dolls) to take home as souvenirs. There is a cute Japanese garden within the complex where you can appreciate a few different architectural styles among the garden's scenery. Craftspeople are working inside one of the larger structures where you can see their wares and how they're made as well as take part. A food court on the premises providing inexpensive hearty Japanese meals. ⊠ *61 Kaminoko Machi, Hirosaki* ☎ *0172/39–1511* 🌐 *www.neputamura. com/en* 🎫 *¥550.*

# Restaurants

**Anzu** (杏)

**$$$** | **JAPANESE** | Avant-garde performances of live *shamisen*—an instrument similar to the banjo—by promising young performers and seasoned experts are the main attraction here. Arrive early to sit on cushions on the floor and enjoy the regional fare. **Known for:** local cuisine from Aomori's Tsugaru Penninsula area; shamisen performances; lively atmosphere. **$** *Average main: ¥4,000* ⊠ *44–1 Oyakata Machi, Hirosaki* ☎ *0172/32–6684* 🕐 *Often closed Sun. (call in advance). No lunch.*

**Kikufuji** (菊富士)

**$$** | **JAPANESE** | Tasty, healthful, and authentic dishes from the region are Kikufuji's specialty. Excellent local

# Shamisen

*Shamisen* is a three-stringed instrument that sounds somewhat like the American banjo. The sound-amplification board is traditionally made of tightly stretched dog or cat skin, and it is usually played with a large comblike plectrum made of tortoiseshell or ivory. The shamisen has more recently been exposed to young Japanese audiences—and to Westerners—by bands like the Yoshida Brothers, who forgo tradition and play the instrument with the ferocity of a rock guitar.

varieties of sake are available. **Known for:** local vegetable stews; local sake; very fresh seafood. **$** *Average main: ¥2,500* ⊠ *1 Sakamoto-cho, Hirosaki* ☎ *0172/36– 3300* 🕐 *Closed Thurs. and two other days per month (call to check).*

**Restaurant Yamazaki** (レストラン山崎)

**$$$$** | **FRENCH** | Try it for yourself and you'll see why people come here from all over Honshu for a cup of the *ringo no reisei supu* (cold apple soup topped with crust-ed baked apple skins). The totally organic "miracle" apples that farmer Kimura raises and the dishes chef Yamazaki pre-pares keep attracting customers. **Known for:** a prix-fixe menu; Hirosaki-based French courses; creative dishes with apples. **$** *Average main: ¥6,000* ⊠ *41 Oyakata Machi, Hirosaki* ☎ *0172/00 5515* 🕐 *Closed Mon.*

# Hotels

**Art Hotel Hirosaki City** (アートホテル弘前シティ)

**$$$** | **HOTEL** | One of the most pleasant modern lodgings in Hirosaki, the Art Hotel Hirosaki is next to the JR Hirosaki Station. **Pros:** well situated for travel in and out of town; tasty meals; easy online reservations. **Cons:** hot water can be unreliable; a little far from most of the attractions; a bit impersonal. Ⓢ *Rooms from: ¥20,520* ✉ *1–1–2 Omachi, Hirosaki* ☎ *0172/37–1229* ⊕ *www.art-hirosaki-city.com/english* ⤳ *134 rooms* ⦿| *No Meals.*

**Hotel New Castle** (ホテルニューキャッスル)

$$ | **HOTEL** | The biggest advantage to this hotel is its location, a block and a half from Hirosaki Castle. **Pros:** close to the castle; free Wi-Fi; three restaurants in the building. **Cons:** wedding receptions and other events might cause disruptions; far walk from JR Hirosaki Station; rooms are dated. Ⓢ *Rooms from: ¥13,000* ✉ *24–1 Kamisayashi Machi, Hirosaki* ☎ *0172/36–1211* ⊕ *www.newcastle.co.jp* ⤳ *47 rooms* ⦿| *No Meals.*

# Aomori (青森)

*37 km (23 miles) northeast of Hirosaki.*

Throughout the year you can enjoy delicious seafood from Aomori Bay, including *Oma no Maguro* (Oma tuna), as well as delicious fruits and vegetables (particularly garlic). And every summer (August 2–7), the town cuts loose during the decidedly wild Nebuta Matsuri festival, a frenzied, utterly unaccountable period when normal gets thrown to the wind. People come to see illuminated floats of gigantic samurai figures paraded through the streets at night. Aomori's festival, one of Japan's largest, is said to celebrate the euphoria of post-battle victory and is thus noisier and livelier than you may have experienced at other Japanese festivals. Dancers called *heneto* run alongside the floats, dancing and hopping crazily, and you're encouraged to join in— all you need is to buy or rent a *yukata* (a summer kimono).

## GETTING HERE AND AROUND

Despite the long winters, JR Shin-Aomori Station's connection to the Hayabusa Shinkansen line makes the journey from Tokyo and elsewhere on Honshu easy.

You can also continue on to Hokkaido from that same station, which is less central to the similarly named Aomori Station. The Hayabusa Shikansen runs more or less hourly from Tokyo (three hours, ¥17,470). By JR local train it's 45 minutes (¥680) from Hirosaki.

Aomori Airport has six daily flights from Tokyo's Haneda Airport on JAL. Aomori also has three JAL flights and three ANA flights from Osaka's Itami Airport, as well as three JAL flights and two ANA flights from Sapporo's Chitose Airport as well as some international connections.

The JR highway express bus departing from Tokyo Station's Yaesu Bus Terminal at 9 pm arrives at Aomori at 8:42 am (¥7,900 one-way).

**CONTACT Aomori Airport.** ✉ *1–5 Kotani, Aomori* ☎ *017/739–2121* ⊕ *www.aomori-airport.co.jp/en.*

## VISITOR INFORMATION

The Aomori City Tourist Information Center is outside the East Exit of Aomori Station, offering English maps and brochures for the city and prefecture.

**CONTACT Aomori City Tourist Information Center.** ✉ *JR Aomori Station, 1–1–25 Shinmachi, Aomori* ☎ *017/723–4670* ⊕ *www.en-aomori.com.*

 **Sights**

**Aomori Museum of Art** (青森県立美術館; *Aomori Kenritsu Bijutsukan*)

**ART MUSEUM** | This contemporary arts museum houses a collection of works by Munakata Shiko (1903–75), Nara Yoshitomo (1959–), and Terayama Shuji (1935–83). Another highlight is three of Marc Chagall's backdrops created for the ballet *Aleko* (the fourth belongs to the Philadelphia Museum of Art). Unlike many museums in which gift shops are near the entrance and packed with people, the gift shop here sits quietly in a corner upstairs, seemingly asking visitors to enjoy art first before shopping.

## Did You Know?

Aomori's Nebuta Matsuri, held annually August 2–7, is dominated by illuminated figures of giant samurai that are paraded through the streets at night. It's one of the country's largest and most raucous celebrations.

Outside, don't miss the statue of Aomori-ken (ken sounds like both the words for prefecture and dog) waits in front of his food dish. ⊠ 185 Chikano, Yasuta, Aomori ☎ 017/783–3000 ⊕ www.aomori-museum.jp/en ⊠ ¥510.

### Auga Market (アウガ)

MARKET | FAMILY | Fish, shellfish, preserved seaweed, and fish eggs—in short, all manner of marine organisms—are hawked by hundreds of vendors in this seafood market. It's one block east of JR Aomori Station, in the basement level of a modern building with distinctive crimson pillars. ⊠ 1–3–7 Shinmachi Dori, Aomori ☎ 017/718–0151.

### Nebuta Museum Wa-Rasse (ねぶたの家 ワ・ラッセ; Nebuta no Ie Wa-Rasse)

OTHER MUSEUM | FAMILY | If you can't visit Aomori during the Nebuta Festival, you can see the glowing papier-mâché sculptures painted with the fierce countenances of warriors from the past year's festival at this museum, right by Aomori Station. There are floats on display, but you can also learn how they are made and interact with a variety of exhibits. ⊠ 1–1–1 Yasukata, Aomori ☎ 017/752–1311 ⊕ www.nebuta.jp/warase/foreign/english.html ⊠ ¥600 ⊘ Closed Aug. 9–10 and Dec. 31–Jan. 1.

### Sannai Maruyama Site (三内丸山遺跡; Sannai Maruyama Iseki)

RUINS | FAMILY | Want to know what it was like to live in this area 5,500 years ago? One of the country's largest archaeological sites, this features a reconstruction of a Jomon settlement that lasted for roughly 1,500 years, from 3500 to 2000 BC. After an extensive excavation, it was opened to the public and has attracted crowds of children on school outings, tourists from all over, and, of course, archaeology buffs. Its interactive approach encourages visitors to try their hands at making crafts and cuisine. Free English-language tours can be arranged if you call in advance. ⊠ 305 Murayama, Sannai, Aomori ☎ 017/766–8282 ⊕ sannaimaruyama.pref.aomori.jp/english ⊠ ¥410 ⊘ Closed Dec. 30–Jan. 1.

### ★ Shirakami Mountains (白神山地; Shirakami Sanchi)

FOREST | South of Mt. Iwaki are the Shirakami Mountains, a UNESCO World Heritage site that is home to the world's largest virgin beech forest. The area is truly pristine and great for hiking. If you don't have a car, take the Konan bus from Hirosaki Bus Terminal or Hirosaki Station bound for Tsugaru Touge from June to October, getting off at Tashiro (55 minutes) and walking about five minutes to the visitor center or at Aqua Green Village, Anmon (90 minutes) to see get to the Anmon Falls. If you want to see the Mother Tree—the forest's largest, and presumably oldest tree—get off at the last stop, Tsugaru Toge (two hours, 10 minutes); the tree is a five-minute walk from there. Only a few buses run daily and only at certain times of the year, so check with the visitor's center or your hotel to be sure of departure times and bus stops. Also note that the road beyond Aqua Green Village only opens around July each year. ⊠ 61–1 Kanda Tashiro, Nishimeya-mura, Nakatsugaru-gun ☎ 0172/85–2810 Shirakami Visitor Center ⊕ www.experience-shirakami.com.

### Sukayu Onsen (酸ヶ湯温泉)

HOT SPRING | FAMILY | Milky, highly acidic water floods into the large cedar bathhouse known as a sennin-buro, a 1,000-person bath. Designated as a national health resort, Sukayu draws many travelers to its curative waters. It has a reputation for the best mixed-bathing in the nation. Several hours are reserved for women only. The trip is one hour from Oirase Gorge and 70 minutes from Aomori. From JR Aomori Station East Exit, take the bus bound for Towada-ko. If you are going to stay the night at the onsen's hotel, you can take the free shuttle bus from Auga's parking lot at 10:15 am or 2 pm daily.

✉ *50 Sukayuzawa, Minamiarakawayama Kokuyurin, Arakawa, Aomori* ☎ *017/738–6400* 🌐 *sukayu.jp* 🎫 *¥600.*

## 🍴 Restaurants

**Hide-zushi** (秀寿司)
$$$$ | **SEAFOOD** | You're in a major seafood city, and if you want some of the best of what is available in these cold waters, this is the place to get it. Dinner is not cheap, but lunches are more reasonably priced. **Known for:** seasonal fresh fish; affordable lunches; skillful plating. [$] *Average main: ¥6,000* ✉ *1–5–12 Tsutsumi Machi, Aomori* ☎ *017/722–8888.*

**Ippachi-zushi** (一八寿司)
$$$ | **SEAFOOD** | What was once an early 20th-century warehouse is now a modern sushi restaurant. The fish here is fresh, and the price is right (and a clear price list is hung on the wall). **Known for:** interesting architecture; lively atmosphere; fresh seasonal fish. [$] *Average main: ¥4,000* ✉ *1–10–11 Shinmachi, Aomori* ☎ *017/722–2639* 🕒 *Closed 2nd and 4th Sun. every month.*

**Mitsu-ishi** (酒肴旬 三ッ石; *Sake Sakana Shun Mitsuishi*)
$$$ | **JAPANESE** | Crowded with locals, Mitsu-ishi has a convivial atmosphere and dishes that appeal to everyone. If you're in the mood for drinks and some finger food, take a seat at the bar where you can watch the action. **Known for:** set menus with a variety of dishes; grilled shellfish; variety of sake. [$] *Average main: ¥4,000* ✉ *2–7–33 Yasukata, Aomori* ☎ *017/735–3314* 🕒 *Closed Sun.*

**Michinoku Nishimura**
(みちのく料理西むら)
$$ | **JAPANESE** | It would be hard to walk out of this restaurant hungry. The restaurant has mostly seating on tatami mats on the floor, but there are areas with tables. **Known for:** teishoku set meals at good prices; sea views; abalone and sea-urchin soup. [$] *Average main: ¥3,000* ✉ *ASPAM 10F, 1–1–40 Yasukata, Aomori* ☎ *017/734–5353* 🕒 *Closed when the ASPAM building is closed. Call ahead.*

## 🛏 Hotels

**Hotel JAL City Aomori**
(ホテルJALシティ青森)
$$ | **HOTEL** | This nine-story art deco–style hotel curves around a corner just up from the ASPAM building as if it belonged in a periodically snowbound Miami Beach. **Pros:** clean facilities; good location; comfortable rooms. **Cons:** dated interior; a bit of a cold atmosphere; chain-hotel service. [$] *Rooms from: ¥14,000* ✉ *2–4–12 Yasukata, Aomori* ☎ *017/732–2580* 🌐 *www.aomori-jalcity.co.jp/en* 🛏 *167 rooms* 🍴 *No Meals.*

**Richmond Hotel Aomori**
(リッチモンドホテル青森)
$ | **HOTEL** | A central location on a busy corner with bus connections and comfortably furnished rooms make this moderately priced hotel a good choice in Aomori. **Pros:** great rates; speedy automated check-in; free Wi-Fi. **Cons:** service in the restaurant can be slow; not a lot of character; a long walk from JR Aomori Station. [$] *Rooms from: ¥10,000* ✉ *1–6–6 Nagashima, Aomori* ☎ *017/732–7655* 🌐 *richmondhotel.jp* 🛏 *177 rooms* 🍴 *Free Breakfast.*

# Akita (秋田)

*186 km (116 miles) southwest of Aomori City, 148 km (92 miles) southwest of Hirosaki.*

In the scenic, faraway realm of Akita, the peaks of the Dewa Sanchi (Dewa Range), marked by Mt. Taihei, march off to the east, and the Sea of Japan lies at the edge of the fertile plains that extend to the west. The region's history began in the year AD 733, during the turbulent Nara period, with the establishment of Dewa-no-saku, a fortress built on a hill in Takashimizu by the powerful Yamato clan.

The area, set up to guard trade routes, soon gained strategic importance, and during the Heian era, soldiers and their families began spreading outward. The Ando and Satake families each built major bastions in the Yuwa and Kawabe districts after the Battle of Sekigahara in 1600. These municipalities, now merged, are considered to be the foundations of modern Akita City. Today the prefectural capital (population 300,000) is a lively, likable city full of delicious food from the mountains, plains, rivers, and sea.

The countryside is devoted to producing what locals feel is the best rice in Japan, and they certainly do make good sake with it. Additionally, the seasonal fruits and vegetables grown here are cheap and flavorful.

### GETTING HERE AND AROUND

ANA and JAL fly to Akita Airport up to nine times daily from Tokyo's Haneda Airport (65 minutes, ¥17,000). JAL and ANA both fly three times daily from Osaka's Itami Airport and two flights each from Sapporo's Shin-Chitose Airport. ANA flies twice daily from Nagoya's Chubu International Airport.

If you're traveling regionally by rail, the Komachi Shinkansen from Tazawa-ko (one hour, ¥3,550); JR express Tsugaru-go Aomori City (two hours, 40 minutes; ¥5,900), or from Hirosaki (2½ hours, ¥2,640) are the most convenient trains. From Tokyo the JR Komachi Shinkansen will spirit you off to Akita in about four hours (¥17,800).

By bus, the JR Express bus Dream-Akita departs daily from JR Tokyo Station at 10:30 pm, arriving in JR Akita Station at 7:10 am (¥6,900–¥8,000), while the Willer Express leaves Shinjuku Bus Terminal at 9:55 pm, arriving at JR Akita Station at 7:55 am (¥6,500–¥7,800).

**CONTACT Akita Airport.** ⊠ *Aza Yamakago, Tsubakigawa, Yuwa, Akita* ☎ *018/886–3366* ⊕ *www.akita-airport.com/en.*

# Big Bamboo

Akita's **Kanto Festival** (August 3–6) celebrates ancient fertility rites with young men balancing 36-foot-long bamboo poles (*kanto*) hung with as many as 46 lighted paper lanterns on its eight crossbars—and weighing up to 110 pounds—against a special pouched strap on their waist, hip, back, or shoulder. The lanterns represent sacks full of rice, and a bountiful harvest is fervently prayed for and celebrated in anticipation of its arrival.

### VISITOR INFORMATION

The Akita City Tourist Information Center is on the second floor at the station, just across from the exit from the Shinkansen tracks, and supplies many colorful English-language pamphlets and lots of friendly advice.

**CONTACT Akita City Tourist Information Center.** ⊠ *JR Akita Station 2F, 7–1–2 Naka Dori, Akita* ☎ *018/832–7941* ⊕ *www.akita-yulala.jp/en.*

## ⊙ Sights

**Akita City Folklore and Performing Arts Center** (秋田市民族芸能伝承館 ねぶり流し館; *Akita-shi Minzoku Geino Densho-kan Neburi Nagashikan*)

**NOTABLE BUILDING** | If you are not in town for Akita's famous Kanto Festival, this museum is the next best thing. Try balancing one of the poles topped with paper lanterns on your palm—local veterans will coach you, but it's more difficult than it looks. There is also an informative video about this and other Akita festivals. Your ticket also includes entry to the former residence and kimono-fabric shop of the Kaneko family, along a corridor beside the entrance. Don't miss the bats carved above the sliding doors. ⊠ *Oomachi*

1–3–30, Akita ☎ 018/866–7091 🚇 ¥100 🕙 Closed Dec. 29–Jan. 3.

## Akita Museum of Art (秋田県立美術館; *Akita Kenritsu Bijutsukan*)

**ART MUSEUM** | One of the best reasons to visit this museum is the building, designed by renowned architect Tadao Ando. The museum's highlight is the enormous *Annual Events in Akita,* painted by local artist Fujita Tsuguharu (1886–1968) in just 15 days. The painting of three local festivals merged into a single scene was rendered on one of the world's largest canvases at the time, measuring 11 feet by 66 feet. The museum also hosts temporary exhibitions relating to Akita life and art. ✉ 1–4–2 *Naka Dori, Akita* ✛ *From the northwest corner of JR Akita Station, head west on Akita Chuo Dori. After four blocks the museum will be on your left, just before the Castle Hotel* ☎ 018/853–8686 ⊕ www.akita-museum-of-art.jp 🚇 ¥310 (some exhibits are extra) 🕙 Check in advance for closures.

 Restaurants

Kawabata Dori is where people come in the evening to sample the regional hot-pot dishes, *shottsuru-nabe* (a salty fermented sandfish stew) and *kiritanpo-nabe* (a chicken stew), drink *ji-zake* (locally brewed sake), and to enjoy the lively bars. It's six blocks west of the Atorion Building, across the Asahi River and slightly south.

## 🍴 Akita Kawabata Isariya Sakaba (秋田川反漁屋酒場)

**$$$** | **JAPANESE** | **FAMILY** | This restaurant lives up to its promise of "All of Akita in one building." Delicious, unique regional dishes such as the highly recommended pickle selection topped with a tiny paper scarecrow, are served on antique plates by friendly staff. Look for the statue of the *namahage* (a fearsome monster from Akita's mountains) outside the entrance. **Known for:** excellent pickle selection;

popular statue of the namahage out front; seafood-focused menu. 🔲 *Average main:* ¥4,000 ✉ 4–2–35 Omachi, Akita ☎ 018/865–8888 ⊕ marutomisuisan.jpn. com/isariya-akita 🕙 No lunch.

## Inaniwa Sato Yosuke (稲庭佐藤養助)

**$$** | **JAPANESE** | Noodles can only be called Inaniwa Udon if they are produced in Inaniwa. Established in 1860, this noodle empire has many branches across the Tohoku region, but this one is for connoisseurs who want to sample regional foods and locally brewed sake. **Known for:** large lunch sets; creative takes on local dishes; a chewy type of noodle particular to Akita. 🔲 *Average main:* ¥2,000 ✉ *Seibu Building B1, 2–6–1 Nakadori, Akita* ✛ *In a collection of restaurants in the basement of the Seibu Building* ☎ 018/834–1720 🕙 Closed only when the Seibu Building is closed.

## 🛏 Hotels

## Akita Castle Hotel (秋田キャッスルホテル)

**$$** | **HOTEL** | Akita Castle Hotel has bright and airy rooms overlooking the moats of Senshu Park, with those on the fifth or sixth floor offering the better views, as do the window seats at the Japanese restaurant for breakfast. **Pros:** fine location for sightseeing; convenience store and shops on the ground floor; good views. **Cons:** impersonal feel; rooms can be noisy; a bit far from the station. 🔲 *Rooms from:* ¥17,000 ✉ 1–3–5 Naka Dori, Akita ☎ 018/834–1141 ⊕ www.castle-hotel.jp 🚇 150 rooms 🍽 No Meals.

## ANA Crowne Plaza Hotel Akita (ANAクラウンプラザホテル秋田)

**$$$** | **HOTEL** | The largest hotel in town, formerly the Akita View but now a member of the Crowne Plaza group, sits beside the Seibu Department Store right in the thick of all the shops that line the arcade extending out from the station, with many eateries located nearby. **Pros:** exciting location; varied on-site facilities; good value. **Cons:** a bit of a corporate feel;

some of the fixtures and furnishings are dated; wedding-related events might be troublesome. $ *Rooms from: ¥19,000* ✉ *2–6–1 Naka Dori, Akita* ☎ *018/832–1111* ⊕ *www.ihg.com* ⇄ *187 rooms* ⊙ *No Meals.*

### Hotel Metropolitan Akita
(メトロポリタンホテル秋田)

$$$$ | HOTEL | Adjacent to the JR Akita Station and ALS shopping mall, this hotel's location makes it a perfect choice for shopping and exploring the sights. **Pros:** sleek and modern setting; excellent location; discount for rail pass holders. **Cons:** service can be slow at busy times; wedding events can sometimes crowd the lobby; the large facility can be a bit impersonal. $ *Rooms from: ¥26,000* ✉ *7–2–1 Naka Dori, Akita* ☎ *018/831– 2222* ⊕ *https://akita.hotel-metropolitan. com* ⇄ *247 rooms* ⊙ *No Meals.*

# Tsuruoka and Dewa-Sanzan (鶴岡と出羽三山)

*132 km (82 miles) south of Akita.*

South of Akita along the Nihon-kai (Sea of Japan) coast are small fishing villages where nets hang to dry only inches from train windows, vast plains of rice fields lead to faraway hills, rushing rivers and clear streams are full of fish, and, closer to Atsumi Onsen, you will be confronted with lofty forested mountains coming down to the endless crashing waves. Along the way is the town of Tsuruoka, once a castle stronghold of the Sakai family, which serves as a gateway to the three mountains of Dewa Sanzan that are held sacred by members of the nature-loving Shugendo sect of "mountain warrior" Buddhists.

## GETTING HERE AND AROUND

If you are considering visiting Tsuruoka from Tokyo, the most inexpensive way is by overnight highway bus. Buses leave from Shinjuku Bus Terminal and make stops at Tokyo and Akihabara stations between 10 pm and midnight, and arrive in Tsuruoka in the early morning (between ¥5,000 and ¥8000 depending on your dates). Tsuruoka is 2½ hours south of Akita by JR Uetsu Line (¥2,310) or less than two hours on the Inaho express (¥4,400).

From Tsuruoka, it's easiest to get to the base of Haguro by bus (35 minutes), either from Bus Stop 1 in front of JR Tsuruoka Station, or from Stop 1 at the nearby S-Mall (Shonai Kotsu Mall). There are four departures in winter and at least hourly departures in summer; it's not a JR bus. A fare of ¥840 will take you from the station to the Zuishin-mon Stop at the entrance to the trail to the peak. Most buses from Tsuruoka toward Haguro continue to the summit, Haguro-san-cho, which is not much farther, but the fare jumps to ¥1,210. Plus, you would miss all the steps and things to see on the climb up.

## VISITOR INFORMATION

The Tsuruoka Tourist Information Office is across from the station in the building housing Foodever—the complex of local culinary delights related to Tsuruoka's designation by UNESCO as a City of Gastronomy. The staff at the visitor information desk speak some English, though most pamphlets about Dewa-Sanzan are in Japanese. They will help with bus schedules and lodging arrangements.

**CONTACT Tsuruoka Tourist Information Center.** ✉ *3–1 Suehiro Machi, Marika Higashi-kan 1st fl., Tsuruoka* ⊹ *From Tsuruoka Station, walk left around the bus stop area and you'll see the sign* ☎ *0235/25–7678* ⊕ *tsuruokacity.com.*

This wooden Five-Storied Pagoda on Mt. Haguro was built without a single nail.

# Sights

Of the three holy mountains of Dewa-Sanzan, only Haguro-san has year-round access, but you can reach the others during the summer months. In summer only, Shonai Kotsu buses depart from Tsuruoka, with stops at all three sacred mountains. Check the schedule before you go; some bus companies are not affiliated with JR, but they are generally not expensive and do connect to JR stations. Buses run between Yamagata City and Tsuruoka all year round. The city is also connected to Akita and Niigata by JR express and local trains.

## Mt. Gas-san (月山)

MOUNTAIN | Buses leave JR Tsuruoka Station and S-Mall in summer for the nearly two-hour trip (¥2,100) to the Gas-san Hachigo-me stop. Check schedules with the tourist information center as they change seasonally. From there you can hike three hours past the glaciers and wildflowers to the 6,500-foot summit of Gas-san, literally Moon Mountain—the highest of the three holy Dewa mountains. From the top you can see the whole gorgeous gallery of mountains that is Yamagata, including one called Mt. Chokai (also known as Dewa Fuji) for its perfect shape. There is even a temple at the top should the spirit take you. It's not possible to climb without snowshoes and winter gear from November to late April or May. ✉ Mt. Gassan, Haguromachi Kawadai, Tsuruoka ⊕ www.japan-guide.com/e/e7903.html ⊡ Free ⊗ Closed late Nov.–late Apr. or early May.

## Mt. Haguro (羽黒山; Haguro-san)

MOUNTAIN | The climb up Mt. Haguro begins at the red Zuishin Gate (Zuishin-mon), then goes up 2,446 or so stone steps to the summit. The strenuous ascent cuts through ancient cedar trees that rise to dominate the sky. You'll pass a 14th-century pagoda sitting alone in the forest. A tea shop is open from late April through October. The trail is just over 1.7 km (about 1 mile) in all, and it may take you an hour to reach the 1,400-foot summit with its thatched-roof shrine, Dewa-Sanzan Jinja. Up to 12 buses a day make the 35-minute trip to Zuishin Gate and up to the peak of Haguro from JR Tsuroka Station. It is possible to stay overnight on the mountain at the temple-lodge of Sai-kan, which is attached by a long stairway to the Dewa-Sanzan Jinja. ✉ *Mt. Haguro, Haguromachi Touge, Tsuruoka* ☎ *023/562–2355* 🌐 *www.japan-guide.com/e/e7902.html* 🎟 *Free.*

**Yudono-san** (湯殿山)
**MOUNTAIN** | One of the trio of Dewa peaks, 5,000-foot Yudono-san is generally the last on pilgrims' rounds. You can descend on foot in a few hours from Gas-san, but it involves interpreting signs in Japanese, a bit of exertion, and slippery metal ladders, and you'll want to check with the tourist information folks about current conditions and the bus schedule. Seasonal buses make the 80-minute (¥2,000) run between Tsuruoka and Sen-nin-Zawa, a trailhead for a short climb to the summit, where you make a small monetary donation and be purified in a secret ritual that you are forbidden to photograph or tell anyone about. Once cleansed, don't miss the last bus back down to Tsuruoka, which leaves at 5:20 pm. The Shonai Kotsu buses have an erratic holiday schedule to Yudono-san, so make sure to check the schedule in advance as the bus is the only way back apart from hiking; of the three mountains, ascending this one takes the most advance planning since the bus schedule is so erratic. ✉ *Mt. Yudono, Tamugimata, Tsuruoka* 🌐 *tohokukanko.jp/en/attractions/detail_1623.html.*

## 🍴 Restaurants

If you are staying overnight in Tsuruoka, you can stay in town or up on Haguro-san itself.

**Al-ché-cciano** (アル・ケッチァーノ)
**$$$$** | **ITALIAN** | Acclaimed executive chef and owner Okuda Masayuki prepares Italian dishes that are totally original and unique and reflect the region. The style of Italian comes with a commitment to the freshest ingredients, including the produce, fish, and meat. **Known for:** fresh local ingredients; courses divided up by price; delicious and creative interpretations of seasonal dishes. [$] *Average main: ¥5,940* ✉ *83 Ichirizuka, Shimoyama-zoe, Tsuruoka* ✥ *15 mins by taxi from JR Tsuruoka Station* ☎ *0235/78–7230* 🕒 *Closed Mon.*

## 🛏 Hotels

**Dewa Sanzan Jinja Saikan Shrine Lodge** (出羽三山神社斎館; *Dewa Sanzan Jinja Saikan*)
**$** | **B&B/INN** | This spartan lodge connected to Dewa-Sanzan Jinja by a long stairway allows you to enjoy the shrine and scenery at the summit after most tourists have gone home. **Pros:** healthful vegetarian food; tranquil garden; easy mountain access. **Cons:** no privacy at night; all the luxuries of a monastery; uphill walk from bus stop. [$] *Rooms from: ¥11,000* ✉ *Haguromachi Temukai, 7 Aza-Temukai, Haguro-cho, Tsuruoka* ☎ *0235/62–2357* 🌐 *www.dewasanzan.jp* 🛏 *200 futons* 🍽 *Free Breakfast.*

**Route Inn Tsuruoka Ekimae** (ルートイン鶴岡駅前)
**$** | **HOTEL** | This simple, well-kept hotel's location makes it a good base for visiting Dewa Sanzan or exploring other cities in Yamagata Prefecture. **Pros:** 30-second walk from the station; complimentary breakfast; free Wi-Fi. **Cons:** rooms are boxy; the area is quiet at night; not a lot of character. [$] *Rooms from: ¥11,100* ✉ *1–17 Suehiro Machi, Tsuruoka* ☎ *0235/28–2055* 🌐 *www.route-inn.co.jp/en/pref/yamagata/index_hotel_id_572* 🛏 *152 rooms* 🍽 *Free Breakfast.*

# Chapter 15

# HOKKAIDO

Updated by
Chris Willson

| ◉ Sights | 🍴 Restaurants | 🧳 Hotels | 🛍 Shopping | 🍸 Nightlife |
|:---:|:---:|:---:|:---:|:---:|
| ★★★★☆ | ★★★★★ | ★★★★☆ | ★★☆☆☆ | ★★☆☆☆ |

# WELCOME TO HOKKAIDO

## TOP REASONS TO GO

★ **The food:** Hokkaido has some of Japan's heartiest and most addictive regional dishes, from miso ramen and soup curry to lamb barbecue and fine seafood.

★ **The slopes:** Deep powder and uncrowded lift lines are hallmarks of Hokkaido's ski resorts at Niseko, Rusutsu, and Furano.

★ **The volcanoes:** At sulfur-spewing springs at Noboribetsu, Toya, Akan, and Shiretoko volcanoes burst forth into vents and craters. Check out the ash flow from the eruption of Toya's Mt. Usu.

★ **The last frontier:** Salmon-fishing bears and crested cranes, alpine flowers, and vast forests hold modern Japan at bay. Although the most convenient way to see Hokkaido in summer is by car, the vistas of mountains and plains are best viewed on foot or bike.

★ **Winter wonderland:** Frigid winter nights are brightened by festivals. Out east, icebreakers cut through Arctic ice floes, and passengers spy seals and eagles.

**1** **Hakodate.** Bustling, historic port.

**2** **Sapporo.** Hokkaido's capital.

**3** **Otaru.** Historic harbor town known.

**4** **Niseko.** Fantastic skiing, snowboarding, golf, rafting, and hiking.

**5** **Rusutsu.** A mammoth ski resort with smaller crowds.

**6** **Toyako.** Lakeside relaxation, and onsen bathing.

**7** **Noboribetsu Onsen.** Volcanism, onsen, and the occasional ninja.

**8** **Shiraoi.** Home to Upopoy National Ainu Museum and Park.

**9** **Daisetsuzan National Park.** Excellent hiking and camping.

**10** **Furano.** Lavender fields in the summer, epic snowboarding and skiing in winter.

**11** **Abashiri.** Explore the winter sea ice.

**12** **Shiretoko National Park.** Mountains, lakes, bears, and really big owls.

**13** **Akan Mashu National Park.** Lakes, forests, and magnificent swans.

**14** **Kushiro Shitsugen National Park.** Coastal wetlands with iconic red-crowned cranes.

Soya-misaki
Wakkanai
Sarufutsu
oronobe
*Shanai-san*
eshio
Esashi
betsu
Omu
*ISHIRI-IMA*
Okoppe
Bifuka
Monbetsu
Nayoro
Yubetsu
Tomamae
Shibetsu
Tokoro
bira
Wassamu
Engaru
moi
Kamikawa
Mashike
Asahikawa
Soun-kyo
Kuzure
*Shokanabetsu*
Fukagawa
*Mt. Daisetsu*
Kawashimo
Biei
*Ishikari-San*
Takikawa
*Furano ski resort*
Atsuta
Bibai
Furano
Daisetsuzan National Park
Tobetsu
Ikutora
Ebetsu
Shimizu
Yuni
Otofuke
apporo
Eniwa
Ikoda
Hayakita
*Mt. Poroshin*
Taisha
Mukawa
Nibutani
Churui
Shiraoi
Hidaka
*Shikotsu-Toya National Park*
Taiki
Shinhidaka
Hiroo
*Noboribetsu Onsen*
Urakawa
Samani
Erimo

Sea of Okhotsk

Shiretoko National Park
Aidomari
Utoro
KUNASHIRI ISLAND
Abashiri
Rausu
Shari
*Mt. Shari*
Kussharo-ko
Rubeshibe
Fujimi
Bihoro Toge
Mashū ko
Teshikaga
Akan Nat'l Park
Odaito
Akankohan
Bekkai
Ashoro
*Kushiro Shitsugen Nat'l Park*
Nemuro
Kushiro Marsh
Attoko
Hamanaka
Akkeshi
Onbetsu
Kushiro
Urahoro

RUSSIA

PACIFIC OCEAN

0          30 mi
0          30 km

# WINTER SPORTS IN HOKKAIDO

Scenic skiing at Niseko

Hokkaido is a land of wondrous winters. Ridiculous amounts of powder and great resorts delight skiers and boarders from both Japan and overseas.

Hokkaido is the northernmost of Japan's four main islands. In winter cold Siberian winds bring tons of snow for six months. For those who have to live with it, the half year of white shroud is a curse (driving, once you've dug out your car, is slow and treacherous), but for businesses appealing to skiers and boarders it is white gold. Those used to marginal pistes in other parts of the world let out whoops of joy as they float over the deep powder. Hokkaido has a quarter of Japan's landmass but only one-twentieth of its population. The resorts are nowhere near as crowded as on mainland Japan, and although the Hokkaido secret is out and Aussies, Chinese, and Koreans are scaling the slopes, there's more than enough powder for everybody. One of the great joys of winter sports in Japan is the special après-ski: after a long day on the slopes, you can soak your aching muscles in a local onsen (thermal spa).

## DOGSLEDDING

Although not a traditional method of transportation in Hokkaido, several dogsled races take place here during the winter months. Major events include the Japan Cup Dogsled Competition held in Wakkanai (February) and the JFSS Cup International Dogsled Race held in Sapporo (March). If you'd like to get up close and personal with man's best friend, you can give dogsledding a try at the Rusutsu resort area.

## HOKKAIDO'S SKI RESORTS

Hokkaido has more than 100 ski slopes, some with limited facilities that are used almost exclusively by locals, while others are vast resorts that attract and cater to international visitors. Hokkaido's big three are Niseko, Rusutsu, and Furano.

### FURANO

Furano, located in the center of island, is famous for its fields of purple lavender in summer, and creamy skiing in winter. Heavy snowfalls provide plenty of light powder while the local town has found a good balance between welcoming visitors and maintaining its traditional charm. Furano is about an hour from Asahikawa Airport, or three hours from Chitose Airport.

### RUSUTSU

Rusutsu is a large resort stretching out over East Mountain, West Mountain, and Mount Isola, with 37 courses provide everything from smooth groomed runs to steep and deep off-piste powder. Numerous gondolas, quads, and pair lifts mean you shouldn't have to wait in line. The resort also offers everything from snowshoeing to horseback riding. Rusutsu is about 90 minutes from Chitose Airport.

Gondola lifts are numerous at Rusutsu.

Huge snowfalls make for great downhill skiing in Hokkaido.

### NISEKO

The Niseko ski area is made up of four resorts, which when combined make it arguably the best place for skiing and snowboarding in Japan. Grand Hirafu, Hanazono, Niseko Village, and Niseko Annupuri are collectively known as Niseko United and can be skied on a single pass. This gives you access to dozens upon dozens of official ski runs, but locals and powder hounds know many more unofficial runs that make the most of the huge snowfalls. The chairlifts at nearby Niseko Weiss closed many years ago and have been replaced by a surprisingly inexpensive snowcat service. The tracked vehicles shuttle you up the mountain and let you enjoy the powder on the way down.

Over the last decade, Niseko has gone through an amazing boom, with a large increase in the number of foreign visitors, which allows you to get by with limited or no Japanese-language ability; rental equipment includes a bigger selection of large sizes; and there's a lively international scene with varied bars, accommodations, restaurants, and clientele. For those looking for a more traditional Japanese experience, it is worth spending at least some time exploring the more remote corners of Hokkaido.

Hokkaido is Japan with breathing space. People here don't put on the air-conditioning in summer—they open the windows. Outside, fragrant air, wild mountains, virgin forests, pristine lakes, and surf-beaten shores are all within easy reach of cities and towns.

Hokkaido's Japanese history is, compared to the mainland, relatively short. Born during the Meiji Restoration (1868–1912), Hokkaido was developed by Japan to keep Russia from getting to it. Until then this large northern island, comprising 20% of Japan's current landmass, had largely been left to the indigenous Ainu people, hunter-gatherers who had traded with the Japanese and Russians for centuries.

In the 1870s, after researching American and European agriculture, city design, and mining, Japan sent 63 foreign experts to harness Hokkaido's resources, introducing a soldier-farmer system to spur mainlanders north to clear and settle the land. Hokkaido was replete with coal and gold, herring shoals, and fertile soil conducive to dairy farming, potato growing, horse breeding, and even cold-climate rice planting. The legacy lives on—small holdings with silos and barns still anchor the rolling farmland, while flat landscapes with mountains on the horizon give stretches of Hokkaido a frontier flavor.

On the losing end of this colonization were the Ainu, who died by the thousands from disease, forced labor, and conflict with the Japanese. Forced assimilation and intermarriage have largely eliminated their way of life (although recent decades of activism have given the Ainu a modicum of public acceptance as Japan's only officially recognized distinct ethnic minority).

Hokkaido's people—who call themselves *Dosanko*—can be quite open-minded. Many readily come to the rescue of foreign travelers with a warmth and directness that make up for language barriers. Japanese tourists visit here for a less-traditional view of Japan, while others still settle here to seek an alternative way of life as farmers, artists, outdoor adventure guides, and guesthouse owners.

However, because Hokkaido consists more of countryside than culture-rich cities, the number of non-Japanese visitors has traditionally been small, and many locally promoted attractions—such as flower fields and dairy farms—may be of less interest to people from Western countries than the mountain scenery, wildlife, and volcanically active areas. Recently, visitors from China, Hong Kong, Taiwan, South Korea, Singapore, and Australia have started to drop by in the hundreds of thousands to enjoy the snow and escape the summer swelter.

Hokkaido remains a frontier in terms of geopolitics. In prominent places are signboards demanding the return of the southern four Kuril Islands, Japan-administered territory that the Soviet Union invaded in the final days of World War II. Japanese Self-Defense Force bases still dot the map as a Cold War–era deterrent, and travel to neighboring Russian air- and seaports is quite restricted. Nevertheless, a Russian business presence is noticeable in Hokkaido's northern and eastern fishing ports, where road signs in Wakkanai and Nemuro are in Japanese and Cyrillic; locals in Monbetsu, Abashiri, and Kushiro might first address Caucasians in Russian.

It's easy to romanticize Japan's Great White North as largely wild and untamed, but Hokkaido also has large cities (Sapporo's growing population is nearly 2 million, and eight other places have populations greater than 100,000), along with decent public transportation and urban lifestyles. Beyond the cities, though, small-town life in Hokkaido is quiet, and a tad cumbersome to experience without a car, but for the adventurous visitor, wild beauty and open spaces abound.

The island is a geological wonderland: lava-seared mountains hide deeply carved ravines; hot springs, gushers, and steaming mud pools boil out of the ground; and crystal clear lakes fill the seemingly bottomless cones of volcanoes. Wild, rugged coastlines hold back the sea, and all around the prefecture, islands surface offshore. Half of Hokkaido is covered in forest, home to bears, owls, hawks, cranes, foxes, and other wildlife you would have trouble finding elsewhere in Japan.

## MAJOR REGIONS

The port city of **Hakodate** is known for its fresh seafood, brick warehouses, and historic clapboard buildings. Mt. Hakodate, accessed by cable car, provides one of the best night views in Japan.

**Sapporo,** Japan's fifth-largest city, is the economic, academic, and transport hub for Hokkaido. The Sapporo Snow Festival attracts millions of visitors each year. The city is a good place to get oriented for a couple of days before moving on to explore the island.

West of Sapporo, **Otaru** is a medium-sized port city facing the Sea of Japan. Meiji-era stone warehouses line a canal illuminated at night by glowing lamps and filled by day with sightseers. Its herring-fishing heyday between the 1870s and 1930s created the riches that built the banks, warehouses, and grand houses that give the city its historical visage.

Southwest from Sapporo, you encounter majestic mountains which spend nearly half the year covered in meters of powder snow. The perfect cone of Mt. Yotei, known as the Ezo (Hokkaido) Fuji, rises up over fertile land offering up fruit, potatoes, pumpkins, corn, and hot springs. In winter this is one of Japan's leading ski areas with world-class resorts such as **Niseko** and **Rusutsu.** From May to October outdoor enthusiasts enjoy golf, mountain biking, river rafting and hiking. In summer the area is best experienced by car or bicycle over two or three days, in winter use the ski buses and let the professional drivers deal with the ice and snow.

Mountains, forests, hot springs, caldera lakes, and volcanoes are just a couple of hours south of Sapporo in **Shikotsu-Toya National Park.** The hotels around Lake Toya provide alpine relaxation, while at Noboribetsu Onsen enjoy the hot springs as the earth steams, rumbles, and erupts.

Breathtaking and often snowy, the Daisetsuzan National Park in Central Hokkaido is Japan's largest national park and home to Mt. Asahidake, Hokkaido's highest peak at 7,311 feet. Roads in the region skirt through farmland and flower fields to circle the mountains north and south, and cable cars lift visitors onto mountain plateaus with steaming volcanic vents, alpine flower meadows, and awe-inspiring views. Allow at least two days for reaching the area and enjoying its grandeur. **Asahikawa** is the area's largest city and the transport gateway to the park. **Furano** is best known in Japan for its lavender field, but known globally as having some of the softest driest powder snow.

Bears and eagles rule the mountains of **Shiretoko National Park** in Eastern Hokkaido. Farther inland are the mysterious lakes of **Akan Mashu National Park,** where Ainu people hold on to their pre-Japanese culture with spirit worship, music, and dance. South is the **Kushiro Shitsugen National Park** the vast wetland breeding grounds of the striking *tancho-zuru* (red-crested crane). On the eastern coast around **Abashiri** flowers carpet the land in summer, while in winter creaking ice floes nudge against the shore, providing a temporary home to seals and seabirds. Unfortunately, the ice is getting thinner and the viewing season shorter—this is the front line of global warming.

# Planning

## Getting Here and Around

In summer, the best way to explore Hokkaido is by train or car. Most car-rental companies allow different pickup and drop-off locations, and will meet customers at trains, ferries, and local flights. If you are staying at resort area hotels, free shuttle buses are often available. In winter, driving can be treacherous even for the locals. Ski buses and trains are usually reliable even in mid-winter.

### AIR

JAL and ANA link Hokkaido to Honshu by direct flights from Tokyo's Haneda Airport to Hakodate, Sapporo (New Chitose Airport), Asahikawa Airport, Abashiri (Memanbetsu Airport), Nemuro (Nakashibetsu Airport), and Kushiro Airport. Several direct flights a day depart from Tokyo's Narita International Airport (with many of the low-cost carriers serving Narita's no-frills Terminal 3). Budget carriers such as SkyMark, Jetstar, Peach, and the Hokkaido-based AirDo also fly into Sapporo. Other major cities on Honshu have flights to Sapporo, as do several places in the Asia and Pacific region, but flights to the smaller airports

are much less common. The cost by air from Tokyo to Sapporo can be as low as ¥10,000 compared with ¥29,020 by train, but be aware that the budget airlines can be inflexible when it comes to schedule changes with their cheapest deals. Some air travelers arriving in Japan on European flights can, with a change of planes in Tokyo, fly at no extra charge to Sapporo. If you're flying from overseas to Sapporo via Tokyo or Osaka, book the domestic portion when you buy your international ticket to save money.

Hokkaido's smaller airports in Asahikawa, Hakodate, Abashiri (Memanbetsu), Obihiro, Nemuro (Nakashibetsu), and Kushiro can be reached by quick flights from Sapporo. Flying across Hokkaido is a good way to cross the distances, particularly the far-flung eastern and northern regions. In winter, sudden changes in weather can divert or cancel flights, though, so plan adequate time for connections.

### AIRLINE INFORMATION All Nippon
**Airways.** ☎ *03/6741–6685* ⊕ *www.ana. co.jp*. **AirDo.** ☎ *0120/057–333* ⊕ *www. airdo.jp*. **Japan Airlines.** ☎ *03/6733–3062* ⊕ *www.jal.co.jp/en*. **Skymark Airlines.** ☎ *050/3786–0283* ⊕ *www.skymark.co.jp/ en*. **Peach.** ⊕ *www.flypeach.com/en*. **Jetstar Japan.** ⊕ *www.jetstar.com/jp/en*.

### BOAT AND FERRY
Ferries from Honshu connecting to Tomakomai, Hakodate, and Otaru offer a leisurely way to arrive, while in Hokkaido boats connect the islands of Rebun and Rishiri to the northern tip of Japan. In eastern Hokkaido, ferries offer the best bear-viewing off the Shiretoko Peninsula.

The ferries are the cheapest way to travel to Hokkaido on paper, but for roughly the same price you can fly there within two hours from the mainland. Of course, a night on the ferry does save you money on a hotel. If slow travel is your style, there are ferries from Niigata, Akita, Maizuru, and Tsuruga into Otaru or Tomakomai, and services starting on the Pacific side (Nagoya, Oarai, Sendai, Hachinohe, and Aomori) connect to Hakodate or Tomakomai. Other routes include Shin Nihon-kai Ferry's Niigata to Otaru (18 hours, from ¥7,300); Taiheiyo Ferry's Sendai to Tomakomai (14 hours, from ¥9,000); Shosen Mitsui's Oarai to Tomakomai (18 hours, from ¥10,740, although there are often online promotions that make it far cheaper); Taiheiyo Ferry's mammoth nearly 40-hour Nagoya-Sendai-Tomakomai (from ¥11,700); Kawasaki Kinkai Kisen's Hachinohe to Tomakomai (eight hours, from ¥5,600); and Tsugaru Kaikyo Ferry's service that crosses between Aomori and Hakodate (four hours, ¥2,460). Aside from winter, the Sea of Japan tends to be calmer than the Pacific. However, if you're worried about getting seasick, perhaps a plane or a train is a better option.

First-class is usually double the second-class price, but the premium buys you privacy and comfort, as most regular passengers stretch out on communal carpeted areas with no beds. Outside the summer holiday season, the ferries are mostly used by long-distance truck drivers and the occasional budget backpacker, cyclist, or motorcyclist.

The most budget-conscious, if you don't mind a roughly 24-hour journey, can book Shosen Mitsui's Pacific Story package. This is a bus-ferry-bus service which connects Tokyo to Sapporo from only ¥9,900, departing Tokyo mid-afternoon and reaching Sapporo the following afternoon. Reserve tickets at the Tokyo Yaesu Exit or Shinjuku Station JR Highway bus terminals, or via Shosen Mitsui's website.

**BOAT AND FERRY CONTACTS Kawasaki Kinkai Kisen Ferry.** ☎ 0120/539–468 ⊕ www.silverferry.jp. **Seikan Ferry.** ☎ 017/782–3671 Aomori, 0138/42–5561 Hakodate ⊕ www.seikan-ferry.co.jp. **Shin Nihon-kai Ferry.** ☎ 06/6345–2921 ⊕ www.snf.jp. **Shosen Mitsui Ferry.** ☎ 0144/34–3121 Tomakomai Reservation Center, 029/267–4133 Oarai Reservation Center, 0120/489-850 free dial (domestic) ⊕ www.sunflower.co.jp/en. **Taiheiyo Ferry.** ☎ 03/3564–4161 Tokyo, 011/281–3311 Sapporo ⊕ www.taiheiyo-ferry.co.jp/english.

### BUS

Buses cover most of the major routes through the scenic areas. There is, however, no English-language telephone service for buses in Hokkaido. The Sapporo International Communication Plaza opposite the clock tower will supply bus-route and schedule information and make telephone bookings if required. Alternatively, you can show up at a bus terminal and make arrangements in person.

### CAR

Driving in Hokkaido is made easier, despite mountain bends and snow, by wide roads and English-language signage that helps guide you to wilder places. Toll highways at this writing link Sapporo only with Otaru, Asahikawa, Rumoi, and Obihiro, but nearly complete (and recently cheapened) stretches can take you close to Hakodate and Abashiri. Otherwise, two-lane roads are the norm, and untimed stoplights can slow travel.

Most major auto-rental companies have offices at Sapporo's New Chitose Airport, in major cities, and in smaller tourist areas. Nevertheless, we recommend you make automotive plans around JR Sapporo Station. JR Hokkaido arranges very good-value travel packages, but service is available in English only at major stations such as Sapporo and Hakodate. Car rentals, depending on the season, can cost as little as ¥5,000 per day, but budget at least ¥10,000; reservations are best made through the ToCoo website for Orix, Times Car, Budget, Nissan, Toyota, MMC, and J-Net. August is peak holiday driving season, so book early. You can request an English-language navigation system called Carnavi.

Japanese are cautious drivers, and Hokkaido is the best place in Japan for driving, even though wide, straight roads, treacherous winter weather conditions, and most visitors' unfamiliarity with all of the above gives Hokkaido the worst traffic fatality figures in Japan. Beware of speed traps, especially in holiday periods: in apparently rural areas a hidden village can dictate urban speed limits of 40 to 60 kph (25 to 37 mph).

**CONTACTS JR Hokkaido Rent-a-Car.** ⊠ *1 Kita 6 Nishi 1, Kita-ku* ✛ *Just by railway overpass to east side of station across street from JR Tower Hotel* ☎ *011/742–8211* ⊕ *www.jrh-rentacar.jp.* **Nippon Rent-a-Car Hokkaido.** ⊠ *Kita 7 1–1–1* ✛ *North East exits from the station, near Toyoko Inn Kita-guchi hotel.* ☎ *011/733–0919 Sapporo Station North Exit Branch* ⊕ *www.nrgroup-global.com/en.* **ToCoo Car Rental!.** ⊕ *www2.tocoo.jp/en.* **Toyota Rent-a-Car.** ☎ *011/281–0100* ⊕ *rent.toyota.co.jp/eng.*

### TRAIN

Japan Railways Hokkaido helps visitors enjoy the big country in comfort, with a five-, or seven-day Hokkaido Rail Pass and good English-language information at major stations. Although there are no Shinkasen bullet trains yet, super-express trains connect Sapporo south to Hakodate (and on to Honshu), and north and east to Asahikawa, Kushiro, Abashiri, and Wakkanai. A five-day pass costs ¥20,000, and seven-day pass costs ¥26,000. There are also more limited four-day passes that cover the Sapporo-Noboribetsu area, and the Sapporo-Furano area.

The train journey from Tokyo to Sapporo can take as little as eight hours with good connections. This trip involves a combination of the Shinkansen train to Hakodate (Shin-Hakodate-Hokuto station; four hours, 15 minutes), currently the northernmost point on the new Hokkadio Shinkansen Line extension, and a change to the Ltd express Hokuto train for the remaining journey to Sapporo (three hours, 40 minutes). The JR Pass covers this route.

**TRAIN INFORMATION JR Travel Service Center.** ⊠ *JR Sapporo Station West Exit, Kita 6 Nishi 4, Kita-ku* ☎ *011/231–9908* ⊕ *www.jrhokkaido.co.jp.* **East Japan Railway Information Line.** ☎ *050/2016–1603 info services in English, Chinese, and Korean* ⊕ *www.jreast.co.jp/e.*

# Hotels

Accommodations that are easily booked in English tend to be modern, characterless hotels built for Japanese tour groups. Gorgeous lobbies and sterile, cookie-cutter rooms are the norm, although more attractive hotels are appearing as Japanese seek out lodging with more personality. Guesthouses or pensions are a cheaper and friendlier option, with welcoming owners who strive to impress guests with the catch of the day or wild vegetables on the dinner menu. Many (but not all) guesthouses have Western-style beds and regular sit-down toilets. Although booking in Japanese is the norm, simple emails via a website can work, too, and many hotels and inns now list on sites such as booking.com, hotels.com, and Japanican.com. A youth hostel is also a decent alternative in Hokkaido, both for price and for the sense of spirit and camaraderie. Some do not allow male-female couples to sleep in the same room. Hostels in towns and cities are usually clean and modern, and in the national parks, although in older buildings, they can be excellent touring bases.

Outside Sapporo, most hot-spring hotels (onsen) charge on a per-person basis and include two meals, excluding service and tax, in their rates. Increasingly, some also offer no meal plans. If they don't and you really don't want meals, you can possibly renegotiate the price (the word in Japanese is *sudomari*). Just remember that those hot-spring hotels and guesthouses are your best bet for dinner in remote areas.

■ **TIP** → Some onsen offer combination rooms, a Western-style room with a tatami section where you could also sleep on futon. If you're interested in trying out a Japanese-style room but still want to sleep in a Western-style bed, this is the perfect option.

## RESTAURANT AND HOTEL PRICES

Hotel reviews have been shortened. For full information, visit Fodors.com. Restaurant prices are the average cost of a main course at dinner or, if dinner is not served, at lunch. Hotel prices are the lowest cost of a standard double room in high season.

| What It Costs in Yen | | | |
|---|---|---|---|
| $ | $$ | $$$ | $$$$ |
| **RESTAURANTS** | | | |
| under ¥1,500 | ¥1,500–¥3,000 | ¥3,001–¥5,000 | over ¥5,000 |
| **HOTELS** | | | |
| under ¥12,000 | ¥12,000–¥18,000 | ¥18,001–¥22,000 | over ¥22,000 |

## Money

Outside major cities there are no foreign exchange services. Local banks in Hokkaido towns are not user-friendly for foreign visitors. Sapporo, Hakodate, Asahikawa, and Kushiro have banks with exchange counters and automatic teller machines. Banks in Sapporo are concentrated on Eki-mae Dori, the wide main street linking Sapporo Station and the Odori shopping area. Banking hours are weekdays 10–3.

Many establishments will not take credit cards, apart from large hotels, some restaurants, and gas stations. Outside of Sapporo in particular, we recommend you get yen cash (Japan is largely a cash-based society) from a post office (郵便局; *yubinkyoku*) ATMs, found in every settlement, or from the increasingly abundant Seven Bank ATMs associated with 7-Elevens. Post offices

are open until 6 pm every day, and most 7-Elevens are open 24 hours.

## Planning Your Time

You'll need at least a week to experience Hokkaido. If you are limited on time, start with a day or two in Sapporo, then spend several days touring the local area including Otaru, Niseko, Toyako, Noboribetsu, Shiraoi and back to Sapporo.

Hokkaido is a large island, and a train or road trip from west to east takes most of a day. Flying from Sapporo to Kushiro or Memanbetsu in the east will significantly cut travel time. Check on access and weather for each destination when planning a winter trip, when road conditions can be unpredictable and treacherous. In winter, ski buses are usually the best option to get to the major resorts.

## Restaurants

Hokkaido's regional food includes excellent seafood, beef, lamb, corn on the cob, and potatoes. Dining out is generally much cheaper than in Tokyo and Osaka. Look for lunch and dinner *tabehodai* (all-you-can-eat) smorgasbords (called *baikingu*, from the Japanese word for "Viking") ranging from ¥1,000 to ¥3,000. Many restaurants have picture menus or a visual display made of plastic in the window. Lead the waiter outside to the window display and point if necessary.

Outside the cities there may not be many dining choices in the evening, and many resort towns (where meals are included in hotel stays) may offer nothing but noodles and booze. Further, dinner reservations at guesthouses are required, and if you arrive without a reservation and are able to secure a room, you will generally have to eat elsewhere. Not to worry—you won't starve: There are 24-hour convenience stores (*konbini*) in any Hokkaido settlement, where you can pick up a bento box lunch, sandwiches, or just about any amenity necessary. While large hot-spring hotels often have huge buffet dinners, the smaller guesthouses excel in food that is locally caught, raised, and picked. Given the overall high quality of dining throughout Japan, you probably won't even need to leave your hotel to get a decent meal, though it's still worth making the effort to get out and eat in local restaurants.

## Visitor Information

The Japan National Tourist Organization's Tourist Information Center (TIC) in Tokyo has free Hokkaido maps and brochures. It's the best place for travel information in English. In Hokkaido, pick up multilingual brochures at the tourist information center found at the North Exit (北口; *kita guchi)* of JR Sapporo Station.

## When to Go

Hokkaido has Japan's most dramatic seasons. Summer lasts from May to September; January to March means lots of snowfall. From late April to mid-May, Hokkaido offers Japan's last *sakura* (cherry blossoms), as well as a fireworks display of spring flowers all at once. May to September offers perfectly temperate summer weather (except for a sometimes wet July). Hotel rooms can be more difficult to book in summer, and many scenic areas get crowded with tour groups and Japanese families. Sapporo and Otaru will be extremely busy in early February during peak ski season, and the Sapporo Snow Festival.

■ TIP→ Avoid the middle of August, when Hokkaido and the rest of Japan celebrates Obon homecoming and travel prices spike.

Late September ushers in brief but spectacular golden foliage, peaking in early October. The periods from November to December and late March to April

offer predominately chilly drizzle. Winter makes travel much more difficult (some minor roads and attractions are closed), but Hokkaido is no less beautiful, with snow covering everything in ever-freshened mounds of white. Early February offers the unmissable Sapporo Snow Festival.

## Hakodate (函館)

*318 km (198 miles) south of Sapporo.*

Facing out on two bays, Hakodate is a 19th-century port town, with clapboard buildings on sloping streets, a dockside tourist zone, streetcars, and fresh fish on every menu. In the downtown historic quarter, a mountain rises 1,100 feet above the city on the southern point of the narrow peninsula. Russians, Americans, Chinese, and Europeans have all left their mark; this was one of the first three Japanese ports the Meiji government opened up to international trade in 1859.

### GETTING HERE AND AROUND
Hakodate is 3½ hours south of Sapporo by express train and 4½ hours north of Tokyo by Shinkansen.

Streetcars cost ¥210 to ¥260, and municipal buses cost ¥210 to ¥320. The sightseeing area is hilly, so save foot power by using a one-day bus pass (¥800), a streetcar pass (¥600), or a combo pass (¥1,000). The tourist center can also direct you to electric-assisted bicycle rentals.

For sightseeing, hotel, and travel information in English stop at the Hakodate City Tourist Information Center inside the station building.

CONTACT Times Car Rental. ☎ 0138/27–4547 ⊕ www.timescar-rental.com.

Hakodate's Russian Orthodox Church dates back to 1916.

## VISITOR INFORMATION

**CONTACT Hakodate City Tourist Information Center.** ✉ *12–13 Wakamatsu-cho, Hakodate* ✛ *Located inside JR Hakodate Station* ☎ *0138/23 5440* ⊕ *www.hakodate.travel/en.*

 **Sights**

The main sights around the foot of Mt. Hakodate can be done in a day, but the city is best appreciated with an overnight stay for the illumination in the historic area, the night views from either the mountain or the fort tower, and the fish market at dawn. City transport is easy to navigate and English information is readily available.

**Hakodate Morning Market** (朝市; *Asa-ichi*) **BUSINESS DISTRICT** | Bright-red crabs wave giant claws from old fishing boats filled with water, squid dart furiously around restaurant tanks, and samples of dried octopus parts are piled high—it's all at Hokkaido's largest public fish market,

located one block from Hakodate Station. It opens at dawn; if you can stomach it, try a fish-on-rice breakfast. Asa-ichi, which also has a fruit-and-vegetable section, stays active until 2 pm. ✉ *9–19 Wakamatsu-cho, Hakodate* ⊕ *www.hakodate-asaichi.com.*

**Hakodate Orthodox Church** (函館ハリスト ス正教会; *Harisutosu Sei Kyokai*) **CHURCH** | A green Byzantine dome and tower rise above this beautiful white Hakodate Russian Orthodox Church. The present building dates from 1916, and donations help with the upkeep of one of the city's most exotic attractions. If you're less orthodox, the Episcopal and Catholic churches sit on either side. Extensive renovations took place until the end of 2022. Services are held Saturday at 5 pm, Sunday at 10 am. ✉ *3–13 Motomachi, Hakodate* ☎ *0138/23–7387* ⊕ *orthodox-hakodate.jp.*

**Sights** ▼

1 Hakodate Morning Market...... **C2**

2 Hakodate Orthodox Church...... **B4**

3 Kanemori Red Brick Warehouses...... **B3**

4 Motomachi Historic Area......... **B4**

5 Mt. Hakodate Observatory **A5**

**Restaurants** ▼

1 Meiji Hakodate Beer Hall.... **B3**

2 Yamasan Michishita Shouten..... **C2**

**Hotels** ▼

1 Hakodate Kokusai Hotel......... **C2**

2 Pension Puppy Tail... **D1**

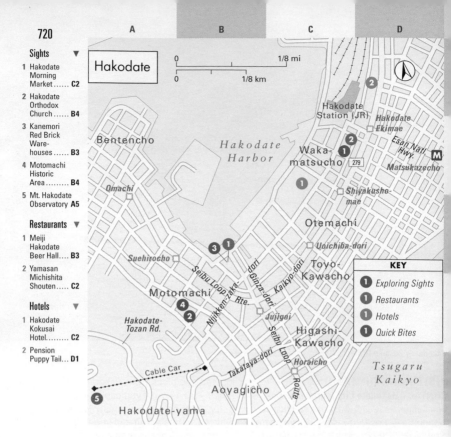

**Kanemori Red Brick Warehouses**

(金森赤レンガ; *Kanemori Akarenga*)

**BUSINESS DISTRICT | FAMILY |** On the cobbled waterfront of Motomachi, the Kanemori Red Brick Warehouses now bustle with shops, bars, and restaurants. Enjoy harbor cruises, cheer on street entertainers, or poke your head into glassblowing studios. In December there's a giant Canadian Christmas tree and nightly fireworks. The place is a 1½-km (1-mile) walk from Hakodate Station. ✉ *14–12 Suehiro-cho, Hakodate* ☎ *0138/27–5530 general info* ⊕ *hakodate-kanemori.com/en.*

**Mt. Hakodate Observatory**

(函館山展望台; *Hakodate-san Tenbodai*)

**VIEWPOINT | FAMILY |** Rated as one of Japan's three finest night views, the Mount Hakodate Observatory delivers sweeping views of urban Hakodate and the surrounding mountains and ocean after dark. The easiest way to get to the viewpoint is to take the cable car from the base of the mountain. Depending on the season, it operates until 9 or 10 pm daily. ✉ *19–7 Motomachi, Hakodate* ⊕ *334.co.jp* 🚠 *Cable car ¥1,500 round-trip.*

**Motomachi Historic Area** (元町)

**NOTABLE BUILDING |** Overlooking the western bay at the foot of Mt. Hakodate is a 2-square-km (1-square-mile) area of wide, sloping brick- and stone-paved streets lined with the 19th-century churches, stately consulates, interesting shops, and homes of the Japanese and other nationalities who first opened up this part of Japan to commerce. Return here at night when the illuminated buildings show why Hakodate is a favorite filming location for romantic movies and TV shows.

## On the Menu 🍴

Hokkaido is known for its seafood—the prefecture's name means "the Road to the Northern Sea." *Shakě* or *sakě* (salmon), *ika* (squid), *uni* (sea urchin), *nishin* (herring), and *kai* (shellfish) are abundant, but the real treat is the fat, sweet scallop (*kai-bashira*) collected from northernmost Wakkanai. The other great favorite is crab, which comes in three varieties: *ke-gani* (hairy crab), *taraba-gani* (king crab), and Nemuro's celebrated *hanasaki-gani* (spiny king crab)—often to be had for a reasonable price.

As for meat dishes, Hokkaido's most famous concoction, *jingisukan*, is thinly sliced mutton cooked on a dome-shape griddle. The name apparently comes from the griddle's resemblance to helmets worn by Mongolian cavalry under Genghis Khan. Vegetables—usually onions, green peppers, and cabbage—are added to the sizzling mutton, and the whole mix is dipped in a tangy brown sauce.

As for Japanese "soul food," ramen is extremely popular and inexpensive; get some *gyoza* (pot stickers) or *chahan* (fried rice) with it. Local residents favor miso ramen, which uses a less delicate variety of fermented soybean paste than miso soup. Ramen with *shio* (salt) or *shoyu* (soy sauce) soup base is also widely available. And on a chilly day, nothing is better than soup curry, Hokkaido's spicy mulligatawny-like concoction.

The most interesting historic buildings and museums are the Old Public Hall (旧函館区公会堂; Kyu Hakodate-ku Kokaido), with the Emperor's Toilet; the Old British Consulate (旧イギリス領事館; Kyu Igirisu Ryojikan), a nice place for tea and scones; and the Hakodate City Museum of Northern Peoples (函館市北方民族資料館; Hakodate Hoppo Minzoku Shiryokan). They can be visited with combined tickets. To visit Motomachi, get off the streetcar at the Suehiro-cho stop. ✉ *Motomachi, Hakodate* 🌐 *www.hakodate.travel/en/top7/motomachi* 🎫 *¥300 for 1 site, ¥500 for 2, ¥720 for all 3.*

## 🍴 Restaurants

**Meiji Hakodate Beer Hall**
(函館ビヤホール)

$$ | **JAPANESE FUSION** | This seaside hall serves seafood as well as a huge variety of other foods from pastas to salads that can keep just about anyone satisfied. The soaring rafters are beautiful and the atmosphere is lively. **Known for:** Hakodate's specialty ika somen (raw squid thinly sliced and resembling noodles); superfresh sashimi sets; local craft brews on tap. [$] *Average main: ¥3,000* ✉ *14–12 Suehiro-cho, Hakodate* ☎ *0138/27–1010* 🌐 *www.hkumaiyo.com.*

**Yamasan Michishita-Shoten**
(朝市お食事処 山三道下商店)

$$ | **JAPANESE** | Although squid is not the only thing on the menu, it is fresh—your squid is pulled flapping from the tank and might return minutes later sliced, with squid-ink black rice, delicious slivers of still-twitching flesh, soup, and pickles. If squid isn't your thing, don't fret, the restaurant has plenty of other seafood, and a picture menu for easy selection. **Known for:** crab-cream croquette; squid in many ways, including raw; reasonably priced rice bowl topped with uni (sea urchin), awabi (abalone) and ikura (salmon roe). [$] *Average main: ¥2,000* ✉ *Donburi Yokocho Ichiba, Asa-ichi, 9–15 Wakamatsu-cho, Hakodate* ✥ *It can be entered from inside market or from outside of*

market at its easternmost corner near main station ☎ 0138/22–6086 ⊕ map. uu-hokkaido.jp/e/michishita.

## 🛏 Hotels

**Hakodate Kokusai Hotel** (函館国際ホテル)
$$$$ | HOTEL | This bustling, modern hotel occupies three buildings a short walk from the station, the Morning Market, and the Kanemori Red Brick Warehouses. **Pros:** walking distance from train station; comfortably furnished rooms; good online deals. **Cons:** not all rooms have great views; tour-group central; modern box hotel. $ *Rooms from: ¥45,100* ⊠ *5–10 Otemachi, Hakodate* ☎ *0138/23–0591* ⊕ *www.hakodate-kokusai.jp* ⇗ *435 rooms* ℗ *Free Breakfast.*

**Pension Puppy Tail**
(ペンションパピィーテール)
$ | B&B/INN | The welcoming Fukui family will greet you at the train station, though it's just a 10-minute walk away from this inn named after their red setter's tail (they thought it looked like the Hakodate part of the Hokkaido map). **Pros:** genuine family welcome; walking distance to station; free Wi-Fi in lobby. **Cons:** some rooms very small and with dated decor; no credit cards; in the opposite direction from the sights. $ *Rooms from: ¥11,000* ⊠ *30–16 Wakamatsu-cho, Hakodate* ☎ *0138/23–5858* ▭ *No credit cards* ⇗ *19 rooms* ℗ *No Meals.*

## ▼ Nightlife

**Hakodate Beer** (はこだてビール)
PUBS | This brewpub serves the best locally made beer in the area, with five year-round brews and the occasional seasonal special on tap. On a chilly day, the 10% ABV *Shacho no yoku nomu biiru* (literally, "the beer the president often drinks") is guaranteed to warm the bones. They also do beer sampler sets if you want to try their less heady weizen, alt, ale or kolsch. There's basic izakaya fare on the menu, too. ⊠ *5–22 Otemachi,*

*Hakodate* ⊕ *www.hakodate-factory.com/ english* ⊙ *Closed Wed.*

# Sapporo (札幌)

*318 km (197 miles) north of Hakodate.*

Modern, open-hearted Sapporo is a good base for any trip to Hokkaido's wilder regions. Hokkaido's capital itself is also worth a few days' stay for its major snow (February), dance (June), and beer (July and August) festivals.

With 1.9 million inhabitants, it's four times larger than Asahikawa, the prefecture's next-largest city, but the downtown area can be crossed on foot in 25 minutes. Centered on the 11-block-long Odori Koen (park), an ideal people-watching place, it has wide streets and sidewalks and bustling shopping complexes. There is limited sightseeing, but there's enough to fill a day or two at a holiday's start or finish. Products from all over Hokkaido can be found, and the dining-out standards are high and relatively cheap.

### GETTING HERE AND AROUND
### AIR
Sapporo's New Chitose Airport is 40 km (25 miles) south of the city. International flights arrive from cities including Beijing, Hong Kong, Seoul, Taipei, Bangkok, Honolulu, and Helsinki. If you are purchasing an international flight with All Nippon Airways (ANA) or Japan Airlines (JAL) to Tokyo Narita or Haneda, Kansai, or Nagoya Centrair airports they can often add a discounted domestic connections to Sapporo's New Chitose Airport. More than 30 domestic routes link New Chitose, to the rest of Japan.

Along with ANA and JAL, budget domestic commuter airlines such as AirDo, Skymark, and Jetstar may have cheaper flights from Tokyo's Haneda or Narita airports and Nagoya, Kobe, Fukuoka, and Sendai.

Japan Railways (JR) runs every 15 minutes or so between New Chitose Airport

# Sapporo

**TO OTARU**

**JR Sapporo Station**

**JR HAKODATE LINE**

*Kitagojo* · *Teine-dori*

*Ishiyama-dori*

**Botanical Gardens**

*Ekr-mae loop*

**TOHO LINE**

*Rte. 5*

*Kita-Ichijo*

*Rte. 12*

**NISHI-11-CHOME**

**O-dori** **Koen**

**ODORI**

**TOZAI LINE**

*Soser-gawa*

**NISHI-4-CHOME**

**STREET CAR**

**CHUO-KUYAKUSHO-MAE**

**NISHI-8-CHOME**

**SOSEI-SHOGAKKO-MAE**

**SUSUKINO**

**STREET CAR**

**NAMBOKU LINE**

**HOSUI SUSUKINO**

*Rte. 36*

**TO NEW CHITOSE AIRPORT**

*Toyohira-gawa*

**HIGASHI HOGANJI-MAE**

## KEY

- **1** *Exploring Sights*
- **1** *Restaurants*
- **1** *Hotels*
- **1** *Quick Bites*

## Sights ▼

1 Botanic Garden
   Hokkaido University .... **B2**

2 Historical Village
   of Hokkaido.............. **E1**

3 Hokkaido-jingu
   Shrine ................... **A3**

4 Hokkaido Museum .... **E1**

5 Nakajima Koen........... **C5**

6 Sapporo Beer Museum
   and Beer Garden ........ **E1**

7 Sapporo Clock Tower .. **D2**

8 Sapporo Odori Park .... **B3**

9 Sapporo Olympic
   Museum ................. **A3**

## Restaurants ▼

1 Daruma .................. **C5**

2 Ebi-Ten Bun-Ten ......... **C4**

3 Kani Honke
   Sapporo Station......... **D2**

4 Keyaki ................... **C5**

5 Soup Curry Garaku ..... **D4**

6 Sushizen ................. **E3**

## Quick Bites ▼

1 Zazi ...................... **C4**

## Hotels ▼

1 Cross Hotel Sapporo ... **D2**

2 JR Tower Hotel
   Nikko Sapporo .......... **D1**

3 Sapporo Grand Hotel.... **C2**

4 Toyoko Inn
   Hokkaido Sapporo-eki
   Kita-guchi............... **D1**

# On the Calendar

One of Japan's best-known annual events, held for a week in early February, is the **Sapporo Snow Festival** (Sapporo Yuki Matsuri). More than 300 lifelike ice sculptures as large as 130 feet high by 50 feet deep by 80 feet wide are created each year by teams from around Japan and overseas. Memorable statues include baseball star Hideki Matsui, cavorting whales, dinosaurs, and the Taj Mahal.

The festival began in 1950 with six statues commissioned by the local government to entertain Sapporo citizens depressed by the war and the long winter nights. Now the event is so large that the sculptures are spread around three different sections of the city: Odori Koen, Susukino, and the suburban Tsudome site (at this site the event runs for almost two weeks). You'll also find ice slides for children. One highlight is the international teams of amateur and professional ice sculptors (some from countries without snow, such as Singapore), hired by major local businesses, who spend four days sculpting their creations. Although statues are roped off, taking photographs is no problem. The festival attracts more than 2 million visitors each year, so book your stay well in advance.

During the **Yosakoi Soran Festival** every second week of June, Sapporo's streets stage Japan's version of Carnival. Based on the festival of the same name in Kochi, Shikoku, close to 30,000 performers go wild in brightly colored costumes and face paint as they run, jump, and chant "*soran soran*" (a Hokkaido fishermen's folk song) through the city streets. A boisterous Japanese take on hip-hop crossed with aerobics, Yosakoi is far more exciting than the traditional *bon odori* community dancing. Dance teams wave enormous flags and snap *naruko* (wooden clappers) in the wake of giant trucks, mounted with powerful sound systems and *taiko* drummers in loincloths. Ticketed seats are available in the stands along the route in Odori Koen and at an outdoor stage, but they aren't necessary—most people just perch wherever they can get a vantage point. Dance teams also perform in Susukino at night.

and downtown Sapporo. The trip into Sapporo is usually made by rapid-transit train (39 minutes, ¥1,150). Hokuto Bus and Chuo Bus run shuttle buses (¥1,100) that connect the airport with downtown hotels and JR Sapporo Station, two or three times every hour. The trip takes about 70 minutes but can be significantly slower in winter. Train service is recommended.

■TIP➔ **Don't make the mistake of getting off the train at the suburban JR Shin-Sapporo Station.**

### CAR

Public transportation makes renting a car for Sapporo sightseeing unnecessary. However, in summer, Sapporo is a good place to rent a car before for setting out into the southern and western national parks. All major car companies are clustered around JR Sapporo Station, so rent your car there and take the newly opened expressways heading north, south, and east.

### PUBLIC TRANSIT

Two circular bus routes connect many of the main sites. The Factory Line—bus stops are confusingly marked "Sapporo

Walk"—connects downtown shops, the train station, the fish market, the Sapporo Factory, and the Sapporo Beer Garden. The *Sansaku,* or Stroller Bus (May to October only), connects downtown with Maruyama Park and Okurayama Jump Hill. Both cost ¥210 per trip or ¥750 for a day pass. Tickets are available on the buses or from Chuo Bus counter at the JR Station or bus terminal.

Most of Sapporo's subway signs include English. There are three lines: the Namboku Line, the Tozai Line, and the Toho Line. They all intersect at Odori Station. The basic fare, covering a distance of about three stations, is ¥210. A one-day pass costing ¥830 provides unlimited subway rides. Tickets are available at subway stations, and the machines have English instructions. The easiest way to use all the transport is with a rechargeable IC card. JR IC cards (Suica from Tokyo or Kitaca from Sapporo), Tokyo's Pasmo and Sapporo Subway's Sapica will work on subways, buses, streetcars, and JR trains. There is a deposit for the cards that varies by type, but you can get it refunded at an appropriate ticket desk.

## TAXI

Taxi meters start at ¥670 for the first 1463 meters. An average fare, such as from the JR Station to Susukino, runs about ¥850, but be aware the meter ticks up fast, especially after 10 pm. In winter most taxis are fitted with ski and board roof racks, and drivers are adept at stowing even the bulkiest winter gear. You don't tip taxi drivers in Japan.

## VISITOR INFORMATION

Your first stop after arriving in bustling JR Sapporo Station should be the Hokkaido-Sapporo Food and Tourism Information Center, a treasure trove of free multilingual pamphlets. The helpful staff are eager to please. Sapporo International Communication Plaza is a great place for information on sightseeing in and around Sapporo. Pick up a free copy of *What's on in Sapporo,* published by Hokkaido

International Women's Association, in a salon stocked with English-language books, newspapers, and brochures that's meant to encourage socializing and also has free Wi-Fi.

**Hokkaido-Sapporo Tourism Information Center.** ✉ *JR Sapporo Station, Western Concourse, North Exit, Kita 6 Nishi 4, Chuo-ku* ☎ *011/213–5088* ⊕ *www.tourist-information-center.jp/hokkaido/sapporo/en.* **Sapporo International Communication Plaza.** ✉ *MN Bldg. 3F, Kita 1 Nishi 3 Chuo-ku, Odori* ☎ *011/211–3670* ⊕ *www.plaza-sapporo.or.jp/en.*

## ◉ Sights

The name "Sapporo" is derived from a combination of Ainu words meaning "a river running along a reed-filled plain." In 1870 the governor of Hokkaido visited President Grant in the United States and requested that American advisers visit Hokkaido to help design the capital on the site of an Ainu village. As a result, Sapporo was built on a grid system with wide avenues and parks. Today the downtown area has uncluttered streets and English signs. It's distinctly lacking in pre-Meiji historic sights.

Sapporo is easy to navigate. Eki-mae Dori (Station Front Street) runs south of the station, crossed east–west by Odori Koen (Big Street Park), then continues south through the shopping district to the nightlife area Susukino and beyond to Nakajima Park. Addresses in Sapporo take advantage of a grid pattern, laid out north (*kita*), south (*minami*), east (*higashi*), and west (*nishi*). Every address has a coordinate followed by a number (for example, Kita 1 Nishi 1) to indicate a city block. So for an address of 5-29 Kita 1 Nishi 1, look for a building with a small blue metal chip on it reading 5-29 within the North 1 West 1 city block. Downtown sights are easily covered on foot in a few hours, using Odori subway station as the center point. Underground shopping

# Drinking Beer in Sapporo

"Sapporo" effectively means "beer" to drinkers around the world.

Head to the Sapporo Beer Museum, 2 km (1 mile) northeast of Sapporo Station for a cursory history lesson in the redbrick former factory, and then to the neighboring biergarten, where waiters in a cavernous noisy hall will rush to get a glass of the golden brew into your hands. Raise your glass—*Kampai* (Bottoms up)!

If you are in town in July and early August, join Sapporo Beer and other breweries at the Sapporo Beer Garden festival in Odori Park in the city center: every night for three weeks thousands of revelers sit out under the trees with beer steins and snacks.

Brewmaster Seibei Nakagawa spent two years at the Berliner Brauerei studying German know-how and returned ready to put it all into practice. The first brewery was at the current Sapporo Factory shopping mall, and Sapporo *Reisi* (cold) Beer, with a red-and-black label bearing the red star symbol, first went on sale in 1877 (Sapporo's cold climate was a competitive advantage in the era before refrigeration).

*Toriaezu biiru!* (For the time being, beer!) is still the first order of business at parties, beer-hall barbecues, and campsite cookouts. Sapporo Beer dominates the market up here, but microbreweries offer interesting alternatives. Look for local brews, *ji-biiru*, particularly Otaru Beer (factory tour available), Hakodate, and Taisetsu.

malls linking the subway station with Susukino, JR Sapporo Station, and the TV Tower are bustling thoroughfares, especially in winter.

**Botanic Garden Hokkaido University** (北海道植物園; *Hokudai Shokubutsu-en*)
GARDEN | FAMILY | With more than 5,000 plant varieties, these gardens are a cool summer retreat. Highlights include a small Northern Peoples Museum with a grisly but fascinating 13-minute film of an Ainu bear-killing ceremony in Asahikawa in 1935, and a stuffed husky sharing a room with bears and an Ezo wolf. This glassy-eyed hound in Hokkaido's oldest museum in the center of the park is Taro, one of the canine survivors abandoned in a 1958 Antarctic expedition—a story brought to non-Japanese audiences in the Disney movie *Eight Below* (2006). After his ordeal, Taro retired to Hokkaido University, died in 1970, and remains here in dusty, shaggy glory. ⊠ *Kita 3 Nishi 8, Sapporo* ☎ *011/221–0066* ⊕ *www.hokudai.ac.jp/fsc/bg* ✉ *May–Oct.* ¥420; *Nov.–Apr. greenhouse* ¥120 ⊙ *Closed Mon. Nov.–Apr., only greenhouse open.*

**Historical Village of Hokkaido** (北海道開拓の村; *Hokkaido Kaitaku no Mura*)
MUSEUM VILLAGE | FAMILY | Step back into 19th-century Hokkaido and see the herring-fleet dormitory, where 60 fishermen appear to have just folded up their futons and left for a day's work, or the village clinic where a Dr. Kondo seems to have vanished, leaving his scary-looking birthing table and books behind. It's easy to spend a few hours walking in and out of 60 historic homes, shops, farms, and offices brought here from all over Hokkaido. This park museum very effectively depicts how ordinary Japanese lived and worked under Japan's policy to develop Ezo into Hokkaido before the

Sapporo is famous for its beer.

Russians could. You can ride down the main street in a horse-drawn trolley (in summer) or sleigh (in winter). ■**TIP→ Ask for the excellent free English guide at the ticket counter.** ⊠ *1–50–1 Konopporo, Atsubetsu-cho, Atsubetsu-ku ✛ About 10 km (6 miles) outside Sapporo; easiest access is via 15-min bus ride (¥210) from Shin-Sapporo Station (Bus 22 heading to Kaitakunomura) or 10-min taxi ride from same station* ☎ *011/898–2692* ⊕ *www. kaitaku.or.jp* ✉ *¥800; trolley or sleigh ride (both seasonal) ¥250* ⊗ *Closed Mon.*

★ **Hokkaido-jingu Shrine** (北海道神宮)
RELIGIOUS BUILDING | Follow the long gravel paths under Maruyama Park's tall cypress trees until you come to the main gate of what looks like a fortress. Before entering, wash your hands and rinse your mouth at the stone basin, then climb the stone steps to Hokkaido's loveliest Shinto shrine. Hokkaido Jingu, originally built in 1871, honors the gods of land and nature, of land development, and of healing. To this day, families with babies, anxious students facing exams, and young engaged couples seek blessings under Shinto ceremonies. In May this is the city's main viewing spot for cherry blossoms, and as the year comes to a close it's coin-tossing central for those wishing for a better future. ⊠ *Maruyama Koen, 474 Miyagaoka, Chuo-ku ✛ 15-min walk from Maruyama Koen Subway Station* ⊕ *www.hokkaidojingu.or.jp* ✉ *Free.*

**Hokkaido Museum**
(北海道博物館; *Hokkaido Hakubutsukan*)
HISTORY MUSEUM | From woolly mammoth molars to bulky 1950s home electronics, the history of Hokkaido is meticulously exhibited here in glass-topped cases—it's all a tad dry compared to the vivid history lesson at the nearby Hokkaido Historical Village, but much more thorough. The building houses an overview of Hokkaido's natural history, how Meiji-era Japan realized that this northern island had coal, fish, and agricultural opportunities ripe for the picking, and also portrays Hokkaido's story in modern times in a newly renovated building.
■**TIP→ Basic audio guides are available**

in English. ✉ 53–2 Konopporo, Atsubet-su-cho, Atsubetsu-ku ☎ 011/898–0466 🌐 www.hm.pref.hokkaido.lg.jp 💴 ¥600 🕐 Closed Mon.

**Nakajima Park** (中島公園; Nakajima Koen)

CITY PARK | This green oasis is a 10-min-ute walk beyond Susukino's lights and contains Hoheikan, a white-and-blue Russian-influenced 19th-century imperial guesthouse; Hasso-an Teahouse, an Edo-era teahouse moved here in 1919 and located in a Japanese garden; a boating lake; and the Kitara concert hall, home of the Pacific Music Festival, started in 1990 by Leonard Bernstein. It's a pleasant stroll during the day. ✉ 1 Nakajimakoen, Chuo-ku ✛ To get here, take Nanboku subway line to Nakajima Koen Station 🌐 www.sapporo.travel/en/spot/facility/nakajima_park.

**Sapporo Beer Museum and Beer Garden** (サッポロビール博物館;

Sapporo Biru-en to Hakubutsukan)

OTHER MUSEUM | Quaint brick build-ings adjacent to a giant shopping mall make up the public face of Sapporo's most famous export. Here you'll find a small museum with signage mostly in Japanese that reveals the development of bottle and label designs and depicts decades of cheesecake shots from advertising posters.

■ TIP→ **Pick up an English-language guide at the counter for explanations of all the different things on display in the museum.**

For ¥300 you can taste any of the brews: Black Label is most popular, but the Classic and Kaitoku are only available in Hokkaido. Taste all three for ¥800. Also available are tea and soft drinks for ¥100.

In the evening the cavernous Sapporo Biergarten is filled with serious drinkers tackling the tabe-nomi-hodai (all-you-can-eat-and-drink) feast of lamb barbecue and beer (about ¥4,400 per person). The catch: You have to finish within 100 minutes. To get here, take a 15-minute Factory Line circular bus from the train station. It's a ¥1,000 taxi ride. ✉ Kita 7 Higashi 9, Higashi-ku ☎ 011/742–1531 for reservations at Beer Garden 🌐 www.sapporobeer.jp/brewery/s_museum 💴 Free 🕐 Closed Mon.

**Sapporo Clock Tower** (時計台; Tokeidai)

CLOCK | For millions of Japanese, this little white-clapboard Russian-style meeting-house defines Sapporo. Built in 1878 as the drill hall for students of Sapporo Agri-cultural College (now Hokkaido Univer-sity), it has become the city's symbol on souvenir packaging. A bit underwhelm-ing, Tokeidai contains photographs and documents telling the region's history and a clock from Boston. ✉ Kita 1 Nishi 2, Chuo-ku 🌐 www.sapporoshi-tokeidai.jp/english 💴 ¥200.

★ **Sapporo Odori Park**
(大通公園; Odori Koen)

CITY PARK | Stretching for more than a mile through the center of the city, Odori Park is one of the defining landmarks of Sapporo. Buy roasted corn on the cob and potatoes from food vendors and feast on them as you watch the skateboarders and street performers. In winter, enjoy the famous Sapporo Snow Festival with its massive snow sculp-tures. There's the energetic and loud Yosokoi Soran Festival every spring, and for three weeks in July and August the park hosts a bacchanal called the Sappo-ro Beer Festival. Every block becomes a biergarten for a major Japanese beer manufacturer (the foreign and micro-brews, naturally, are the farthest walk away), with Sapporo Beer smack in the middle of it all. Last orders at 9 pm, then everyone stumbles home or out for more partying in Susukino. Not to be missed if you're in town. ✉ Odori Nishi 2, Odori 🌐 www.sapporo.travel/en/spot/facility/odori_park.

**Sapporo Olympic Museum**
(札幌オリンピックミュージアム)

OTHER MUSEUM | FAMILY | Leap off a ski jump into the freezing air and land like a pro—or not. In this museum at the base of the Olympic Okura Jump, a realistic simulator lets you comparing jump distances. The 1972 Winter Olympics and other Japanese sporting successes in skating, curling, and many forms of skiing are celebrated with displays interesting even to nonsporting types. Outside the museum, take the chairlift to the top of the real ski jump for a chilling view of what athletes face before takeoff. From the Maruyama Koen Subway Station it is a 10-minute taxi ride, or take Bus No. 14 from Maruyama Bus Terminal to Okurayama Kyogijyo Iriguchi bus stop (10 minutes) then walk a further 10 minutes. Sapporo hopes to host the 2030 Winter Olympics, which will bring more attention to the island's great resorts. ✉ *1274 Miyanomori, Chuo-ku* ☎ *011/641–8585* ⊕ *www.sapporo-olympicmuseum.jp/english* 🎫 *¥600.*

## 🍴 Restaurants

The greatest concentration of restaurants for nighttime dining is in the entertainment district of Susukino; good daytime choices are in the downtown department stores and the shopping complex around JR Sapporo Station. Hokkaido is known for its ramen, and Sapporo for its miso ramen. The city has more than 1,000 ramen shops, so it's not hard to find a noodle lunch. To track down the current ramen star shack look for the lines of enthusiastic youths outside otherwise unassuming restaurants; young Japanese use their mobile phones and the Internet to research the newest hot spot.

Soup curry—similar to a mulligatawny soup—is a warming and moreish Sapporo creation, but if you want a conventional curry, the curry restaurants run by Indian and Nepali expats in the city are a better bet.

### Daruma (だるま本店)

**$$ | JAPANESE |** Below the red sign depicting a roly-poly mustachioed doll, this establishment founded in 1954 serves

the city's freshest barbecued lamb *jingisukan*. The slices of lamb are served steaming atop heaps of vegetables. **Known for:** local Sapporo atmosphere; good-value lamb plates; popular (can be a line in the evening). $ *Average main: ¥2,500* ✉ *Crystal Bldg., Minami 5 Nishi 4, 1st fl., Chuo-ku* ☎ *011/552–6013* 🕐 *No lunch.*

### Ebi-Ten Bun-Ten (蛯天分店)

**$$ | JAPANESE |** On a narrow street near the Mitsukoshi department store, Ebi-Ten Bun-Ten is as friendly a tempura place as you're likely to find in Hokkaido. The sliding doors behind a blue banner reveal a quiet, homey restaurant, managed for two generations by the friendly Yamada family. **Known for:** decadent king crab tempura (¥3,000); à la carte options; tendon sets (tempura served on rice) from ¥800. $ *Average main: ¥1,800* ✉ *Minami 2 Nishi 4, Chuo-ku* ☎ *011/271–2867* ⊕ *www.ebiten.co.jp/english.*

### Kani Honke Sapporo Station (かに本家)

**$$$$ | JAPANESE |** There are two branches of Kani Honke, one in Susukino, and the other in front of Sapporo Station. In business for more than 50 years, these crab-eating havens serves raw, steamed, boiled, and baked crustaceans—the waitress will tell you whether the *ke-gani* (hairy crab), *taraba-gani* (king crab), or *zuwai-kani* (snow crab) is in season. **Known for:** courses centered on crab shabu-shabu or crab sukiyaki; sides such as sashimi of tuna belly; local icon. $ *Average main: ¥6,000* ✉ *2–1–18 Kitasanjo-Nishi, Chuo-ku* ☎ *011/222–0018* ⊕ *www.kani-honke.jp/en.*

### Keyaki (けやき)

**$ | RAMEN |** This ordinary-looking 10-stools-at-the-plastic-counter joint in Susukino has had lines of faithful slurpers outside since the year 2000 (a lifetime for a ramen shop) and is still chopping, boiling, and serving its succinct seven-item ramen menu. Order from the vending machine at the door then wait on the bench or stand around the corner; once seated wait for the cook to hand down a steaming bowl topped generously with vegetables from the raised and hidden kitchen. **Known for:** garlic (ninniku) ramen; cha-shu (seasoned pork) ramen; corn and butter ramen. $ *Average main: ¥930* ✉ *Minami 6 Nishi 3, Susukino* ☎ *011/552–4601* ▭ *No credit cards.*

### Soup Curry Garaku (スープカレーGaraku)

$ | **JAPANESE** | In a city with no shortage of soup-curry restaurants, the long lines outside this place just south of Odori Park tell you how much the locals rate Garaku. There are eight basic soup curries on the menu to which you can add more toppings and tweak spice levels. **Known for:** rice topped with grilled cheese; classic chicken leg and vegetable soup curry; customizable spice levels from 1 to 40. $ *Average main: ¥1,200* ✉ *Minami 2, Nishi 2, Chuo-ku* ☎ *011/233–5568* ⊕ *www.s-garaku.com* ▭ *No credit cards.*

### Sushizen (すし善)

$$$$ | **SUSHI** | Hokkaido sushi is famed throughout Japan, and this is probably the best of the best. It's where locals take guests when they want to impress them with a pure sushi experience. **Known for:** fixed-price omakase course; elegant atmosphere; excellent service. $ *Average main: ¥22,000* ✉ *Kita 1 Nishi 27, Maruyama, Chuo-ku* ☎ *011/612–0068* ⊕ *www.sushizen.co.jp* ⊙ *Closed Wed.*

## ☕ Coffee and Quick Bites

### Zazi (ザジ)

$ | **CAFÉ** | A casual downtown coffee shop with an English menu, this hangout is popular with students and expats. Only one busy cook works in the kitchen, so don't expect a speedy lunch, but come in when you're peckish and you'll eventually leave feeling full. **Known for:** generous pasta portions; homemade cakes; one-pot stews. $ *Average main: ¥110* ✉ *Minami 2 Nishi 5, Susukino, Chuo-ku* ☎ *011/221–0074* ▭ *No credit cards.*

##  Hotels

### Cross Hotel Sapporo (クロスホテル)

$$$$ | **HOTEL** | At this hip-design hotel in central Sapporo rooms tend to mix natural or dark woods with neutral tones and artistic accents for a much more youthful vibe than many of the larger Western-style hotels nearby. **Pros:** helpful, English-speaking staff; laid-back bar and lounge; communal hot-spring baths with city views. **Cons:** books up quickly; rooms could be bigger for the price; not geared to families. $ *Rooms from: ¥26,000* ✉ *Kita 2, Nishi 2–23, Chuo-ku* ☎ *011/272–0010* ⊕ *www.crosshotel.com* ⮑ *181 rooms* ⦿ *No Meals.*

### ★ JR Tower Hotel Nikko Sapporo (JRタワーホテル日航札幌)

$$$$ | **HOTEL** | In a skyscraper looming high over the main train station, this hotel puts the city at your feet. **Pros:** part of the JR Sapporo Station complex; city views; soothing spa. **Cons:** onsen is an additional fee for guests; limited English of some staff; cheapest rooms a little cramped. $ *Rooms from: ¥41,494* ✉ *JR Sapporo Station Tower, Kita 5 Nishi 2, Chuo-ku* ☎ *011/251–2222, 011/251–2510 for reservations 9–6* ⊕ *www.jrhotels.co.jp/tower/english* ⮑ *342 rooms* ⦿ *No Meals.*

### Sapporo Grand Hotel (札幌グランドホテル)

$$ | **HOTEL** | With classic European style, white-gloved bellhops, and conveniences like in-room refrigerators tastefully hidden away in wooden cabinets, Sapporo's grand dame has welcomed guests since 1934. **Pros:** convenient location; long history; high-end service in a city full of business hotels. **Cons:** certain parts have a mall-like feel; limited English of some staff; small windows in main building. $ *Rooms from: ¥17,100* ✉ *Kita 1 Nishi 4, Chuo-ku* ☎ *011/261–3311* ⊕ *www.grand1934.com/en* ⮑ *494 rooms* ⦿ *No Meals.*

### Toyoko Inn Hokkaido Sapporo-eki Kitaguchi (東横イン北海道札幌駅北口)

$ | **HOTEL** | A no-frills business hotel with a great location next to the east exit of

Susukino is Sapporo's busy entertainment district.

Sapporo Station. **Pros:** value for money; great access to JR Sapporo Station; simple online booking. **Cons:** claustrophobic bathrooms; noise from the roads; small rooms. $ *Rooms from: ¥8,300* ✉ *1–4–3 Kita 6-jo, Nishi, Kita-ku, Sapporo* ☎ *011/728–1045* 🌐 *www.toyoko-inn.com* 🛏 *356 rooms* 🍴 *Free Breakfast.*

## Nightlife

Stretching for seven blocks in every direction, Sapporo's entertainment district of **Susukino** (すすきの) is a mind-boggling cluster of more than 4,000 bars, nightclubs, and eateries. Bars and clubs stay open late, some until 5 am. The seedier places are mostly west of Ekimae Dori, but all of Susukino is safe; just avoid places that don't list prices or are recommended by smooth-talking touts. Susukino can be cheap, too, if you ask for a *tabe-nomi hodai,* which might get you up to two hours of all you can eat and drink for a reasonable sum.

**Bar Yamazaki** (BARやまざき)
**COCKTAIL LOUNGES** | Tatsuro Yamazaki opened this cocktail bar in Susukino in the late 1950s and was still serving well into his nineties, before passing a few years ago. In that time, his bar established itself as one of Japan's classics; he became a legend on the drinks scene, winning international awards with concoctions like the sweet, vodka-based Sapporo, one of 200 original cocktails on the menu. The staff keep the traditions going in old-school fashion, with plaid waistcoats, white shirts and ties, and can also mix up standards or suggest a good whiskey. It's closed Sunday, and there's a ¥770 seating charge, as well as 10% service charge. ✉ *Katsumi Bdg 4F, Minami 3, Nishi 3, Chuo-ku* ☎ *011/221–7363* 🌐 *www.bar-yamazaki.com* 🕐 *Closed Sun.*

**The Craft** (ザ クラフト)
**BARS** | This Susukino bar with brick walls has 33 domestic craft beers on tap, ranging from crisp pilsners to hop-heavy IPAs, all listed on a chalkboard above the main

bar, where you can take a stool at the counter. Alternatively, take a seat by the window for a view of the nightlife outside and enjoy some bar food; the menu includes good pastas and grilled meats. It's about 30 meters west of Susukino's main crossing. ⊠ *Minami 4, Nishi 4, Susukino* ☏ *011/241–5555.*

### Half Note Jazz Bar (ハーフ ノート)

PIANO BARS | Even if you're not a fan of jazz, a night at the classy Half Note might make you into a convert. The impressive caliber of the musicians will keep you hanging on for drink after drink to see what gets played next. The cover charge and curtain time differ by night and artist, so stop by this basement spot to see if the groove going on is what you're into tonight. Wednesday is vocals night. ⊠ *Sanjo Mimatsu Bldg. B1, Minami 3 Nishi 5, Susukino* ⊹ *You can get in from Tanuki Koji side or next street. Look for white sign with outline of a piano* ☏ *011/261–5880* ⊕ *halfnote.zero-city.com* ⊙ *Closed Sun.*

## 🛍 Shopping

Sapporo Station is the hub for shopping in the city. Connected to the station are the huge department stores Sapporo Stella Place, Daimaru, and Esta. If you're looking for cameras or any other electronics, visit Yodobashi Camera just west of the station or Bic Camera just east of the station. Near Odori Park you'll find the high-end Mitsukoshi department store, and the Burton Flagship Store. Just south of Odori Park you'll find Tanukikoji shopping street a covered arcade that stretches east–west for seven blocks; however, its popularity and the quality of shops have waned over the years. A much better option is Sapporo Factory, a shopping mall with a large number of outdoor sports brands.

### Sapporo Factory (サッポロファクトリー)

MALL | FAMILY | If you're in Hokkaido to ski, snowboard, hike, climb, or bike then the Sapporo Factory mall is the best place to stock up on any missing gear. Within the mall you'll find specialist stores for Arc'teryx, Descente, Mont-bell, Columbia, Mammut, Rossignol, and The North Face. The food court has a wide range of vendors, and there's a cinema complex with IMAX on the second floor. Sapporo Factory is a 15-minute walk southeast from Sapporo Station. ⊠ *4-chome 1–2 Kita 2 Johigashi, Sapporo* ☏ *011/207–5000* ⊕ *sapporofactory.jp.*

# Teine (サッポロテイネ)

*23 km (14 miles) west of Sapporo.*

Teine is technically one of Sapporo's wards, but in reality is a coastal town set in between the cities of Sapporo and Otaru. Teine does have its own accommodation and restaurants, but it's easier to base yourself in the nearby cities and visit Teine as a day-trip. The main reason to visit is the Sapporo Teine ski resort, which is the most convenient large ski resort for those in Sapporo and Otaru. In summer, Sapporo Teine Golf Club has three challenging nine-hole courses with panoramic views.

### GETTING HERE AND AROUND

It is just a 10-minute train ride from JR Sapporo Station to JR Teine Station (¥340), and 20 minutes from JR Otaru (¥540).

**Activities**

## GOLF

### Sapporo Teine Golf Club
(札幌テイネゴルフ倶楽部)

**GOLF** | Changes in elevation and fast greens make these three challenging nine-hole courses fun. Add in fantastic views of Mt. Teine, the Sea of Japan, and Sapporo City. Each nine-hole course is around 3,000 yards. Prices are for 18 holes and include a cart, but a caddy is extra (you choose which two of the three courses to play). The cheapest rates are on weekdays. Green fees range from ¥7,900 to ¥12,800 for 18 holes with cart, but a caddy is extra. (You choose which two of three courses to play.) ⊠ 593–3 Teinehoncho, Teine Ward, Sapporo ☎ 011/688–1112 ⊕ golf.sapporo-teine.com 🎫 From ¥7,900 🎿 3 courses (Uguisu, Kitsuksuki, Raicho): 9 holes, 3000 yd, par 36.

## SKIING AND SNOWBOARDING

### Sapporo Teine (札幌テイネ)

**SKIING & SNOWBOARDING | FAMILY** | A fantastic location for skiing and boarding with easy access from both Sapporo and Otaru, Sapporo Teine is the perfect spot for a day of skiing when the conditions are right. The ski hill sits on the side of the 1,023-m (3,356-foot) Mt. Teine with the upper lifts reaching near the summit. The runs have great views looking down over the city of Sapporo and along the coast to Otaru. The resort is divided into two zones, the upper Highland Zone which has the steeper runs and powder, and the lower Olympia Zone which is better for beginners. The lift ticket covers both areas, and the zones are connected by a long winding green run. Two of the black runs in the Highland Zone were used for the Women's Giant Slalom, and Men's and Women's Slalom at the 1972 Sapporo Winter Olympics. If you're looking for deep powder head down the steep Kitakabe (North Face) black run.

There are discounts early and late in the season. 1-day rental of skis or a snowboard and boots is available at the Teine Highland rental shop, which has higher-level skis and snowboards including Burton's Step On system.

Ski buses run from major hotels in Sapporo and Otaru, but it is almost as easy to go by train to JR Teine, take the south exit, then jump on the number 70 bus to the ski hill (16 minutes). ⊠ 593 Teinehonco, Teine-ku, Sapporo ☎ 011/682–6000 ⊕ sapporo-teine.com/snow/lang/en 🎫 Lift pass from ¥5,500; ski and gear rentals from ¥5,700 ⊙ Ski season runs late Nov.–early May.

# Otaru (小樽)

*40 km (25 miles) west of Sapporo.*

Otaru nets its wealth in tourists these days, but the canal where barges used to land the catch of the day is still the center of action for thousands of domestic and Asian visitors reeled in by images of a romantic weekend retreat. Visitors from countries with 19th-century stone buildings of their own may be less impressed by the tourist strip along the canal, but rent a bike or walk away from the main drag and you can explore quaint neighborhoods and interesting buildings. Otaru also makes a good base for touring around Hokkaido by car. The tourist office or your hotel can help you make reservations.

The **Otaru Snow Lantern Festival** (whose official English name is "Otaru Snow Light Path") happens around the second week of February, when thousands of snow lanterns light up the canal area and old buildings. It is a quieter concurrent alternative to the blockbuster Sapporo Snow Festival.

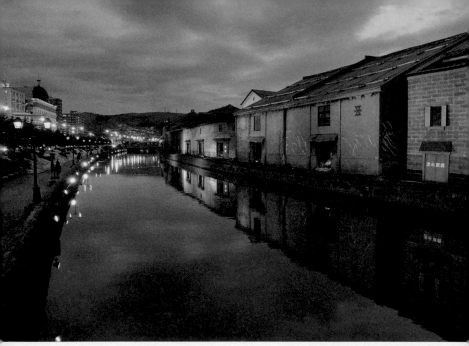

Otaru's canal is lined with 19th-century stone buildings.

## GETTING HERE AND AROUND

Otaru is an easy day trip from Sapporo. Trains depart every 20 minutes and take 33 minutes (express) or 45 minutes (local) for ¥750. On the way to Otaru, sit on the right facing forward for the best ocean views.

A one-day pass (¥750) on the local bus (some of them look like old trolleys) is a useful energy-saver; during the summer, but is relatively easy to cover central Otaru on foot.

If you're ready to leave Hokkaido the slow way, there are ferries from Otaru Port to Akita, Niigata, Maizuru, and Tsuruga.

## VISITOR INFORMATION

There is an Otaru Tourist Office inside the station, but the one at Otaru Canal Plaza directly down the street from the station has free Wi-Fi, helpful English-speaking staff, lots of guides and pamphlets, and a place to sit down and plan your stay.

**CONTACTS Charinko Otaru.** チャリンコ 小樽 ⊠ 2–7–9 Inaho, Otaru ☎ 0134/32– 6861. **Canal Plaza Tourist Information Center.** ⊠ 2–1–20 Ironai, Otaru ⊹ Head out of station and directly down hill to the canal. The building is on left ☎ 0134/33–1661 ⊕ otaru.gr.jp.

##  Sights

### Otaru Canal Area

(小樽運河周辺; Otaru Unga Shuhen)
**HISTORIC DISTRICT | FAMILY |** Otaru Canal is the town's most famous attraction, located eight blocks downhill from JR Otaru Station. The canal is pretty in winter and is at its most photogenic during the "Otaru Snow Light Path," when the walkways beside the canal are illuminated by flickering candles. The Otaru Snow Light Path is held around the same time as the Sapporo Snow Festival due to the huge increase in visitors coming to the area. Next to the canal you'll find Sakaemachi Street Historic District,

which is charming year-round: old banks and trading houses have been converted into boutiques and shops. Don't miss the music-box collection and the musical steam clock at Marchen Square on the eastern end of the district. ⊠ *Ironai and Sakaemachi, Otaru.*

## 🍴 Restaurants

### Ajidokoro Takeda (味処たけだ / 武田鮮魚店; *Takeda Sengyoten*)

**$$ | JAPANESE |** Claws emerging from a bed of fresh-cut crab and darkly gleaming red salmon eggs piled high on a bowl of rice are just two of the famous raw-fish options at this 50-year-old family restaurant in the middle of the noisy fish market. They also have lighter options like fresh shellfish and simple grilled fish, rice, and miso lunch sets. **Known for:** the well-priced omakase-don; fresh crab; half-shell oysters. $ *Average main: ¥2,000* ⊠ *3–10–16 Inaho, Otaru* ✚ *100 yd from Otaru Station* ☎ *0134/22–9652* ⊕ *www.otaru-takeda.com* ⊟ *No credit cards* ⊗ *No dinner.*

### Otaru Beer Otaru Warehouse No.1 (小樽ビール・小樽倉庫No.1; *Otaru Soko Namba Wan*)

**$ | INTERNATIONAL |** Located in one of the warehouses beside the Otaru Canal, Otaru Beer a great place to try the local Weiss, Pilsner, and Dunkel. The food is also international with a menu that includes such wildly differing foods as pizza, paella, german sausage, and roast pork. **Known for:** great house-brewed beer selections; fun atmosphere that draws locals and tourists; good pizza. $ *Average main: ¥1,000* ⊠ *Minato Machi 5–4, Otaru* ☎ *0134/21–2323* ⊕ *otarubeer.com.*

### Otaru Kita Togarashi Restaurant (北とうがらし)

**$$ | JAPANESE |** Standing apart from all the sushi joints in Otaru is this lamb barbecue heaven at the easy-to-find branch of a famous *jingisukan* restaurant. Purchase a plate of tender, succulent lamb, which you cook tyourself on a dome-shaped griddle with side orders of alfalfa sprouts (*moyashi*) and leeks (*negi*). **Known for:** lamb steaks; charcoal cooking; bustling vibe. $ *Average main: ¥3,000* ⊠ *Denuki Koji, 1–1–17 Ironai, Otaru* ☎ *0134/33–0015.*

### Otaru Masazushi (政寿司)

**$$$ | SUSHI |** In the middle of Otaru's famous strip of sushi restaurants, Masazushi serves up the morning's catch of herring, tuna, abalone, salmon, and more perched on quality vinegared rice. The staff will check your wasabi horseradish tolerance levels when taking your order. **Known for:** good-value lunch sets and children's meals; indulgent evening courses like the super-expensive omakase; uni-ikura don (donburi of sea urchin and salmon roe). $ *Average main: ¥3,300* ⊠ *1–1–1 Hanazono, Otaru* ☎ *0134/23–0011* ⊕ *www.masazushi.co.jp* ⊗ *Closed Wed.*

## 🛏 Hotels

### Authent Hotel (オーセントホテル)

**$$ | HOTEL |** This former department store in the heart of the downtown shopping area was remade into an elegant hotel. **Pros:** central location; sunset views from piano bar; on site bakery is a cheap breakfast option. **Cons:** crowded with tour groups; decor in the bar and some public spaces is a 1980s throwback; less-expensive rooms are boxlike. $ *Rooms from: ¥26,400* ⊠ *2–15–1 Inaho, Otaru* ☎ *0134/27–8100* ⊕ *www.authent.co.jp/th/english* ⌁ *195 rooms* ⑩ *No Meals.*

### Grand Park Otaru (グランドパーク小樽)

**$$$$ | HOTEL |** Overlooking Otaru Marina, this 18-story hotel sits atop the huge WingBay shopping complex, giving easy access to outlet stores, restaurants, and a movie theater; inside is a reliable, familiar chain hotel with an English-speaking staff. **Pros:** reliable service; train access, and ski bus connections in winter; shop without leaving the building.

**Cons:** shopping-mall atmosphere; lots of tour groups; out-of-the-way location for Otaru Town. $ *Rooms from: ¥23,450* ✉ *11–3 Chikko, Otaru* ☎ *0134/21–3111* ⊕ *www.parkhotelgroup.com/en/otaru* ⌁ *296 rooms* ❙❍❙ *No Meals.*

### Otaru Furukawa Hotel (運河の宿 小樽ふる川)

$$$$ | HOTEL | Dark wooden beams, shadowy corridors, and well-chosen antiques transform a modern canal-side building into a comfortable, old-fashioned Japanese inn—a rarity in Otaru. **Pros:** old-fashioned atmosphere; beside the canal; impressive baths. **Cons:** overlooks main road; staff speak limited English; tobacco smell in some rooms. $ *Rooms from: ¥35,400* ✉ *1-2-15 Ironai, Otaru* ☎ *0134/29–2345* ⊕ *www.otaru-furuka-wa.com/english* ⌁ *38 rooms* ❙❍❙ *Free Breakfast.*

## 🛍 Shopping

### Otaru Orgel Doh (オルゴール党)

ANTIQUES & COLLECTIBLES | FAMILY | With a selection of 25,000 music boxes, Otaru Orgel Doh is Japan's biggest music box emporium. It is also Otaru's most famous store, housed in a beautiful brick building, with an iconic 5½-meter bronze steam clock standing outside its doors. The giant clock chimes and steams every 15 minutes, and is a sibling to the steam clock found in Vancouver's Gas Town. The music boxes range from cute toys for just a few thousand yen, to the fine craftsmanship of movements such as the 72-note Sankyo Orpheus. The melodies played by the music boxes vary from classics such as Pachelbel's Canon to the latest anime and Disney tunes. ✉ *4–1 Sumiyoshi-cho, Otaru* ☎ *0134/22–1108* ⊕ *www.otaru-orgel.co.jp.*

## 🏃 Activities

### BIKING

#### Charinko Otaru (チャリンコ小樽)

BIKING | If you are looking for a bicycle rental, Charinko Otaru (*charinko* is a slang word for bicycle) will rent you a road bike by the hour, for a half-day, or for up to two days. Mountain bikes, electric-assisted bikes, strollers, wheelchairs, and children's bicycles are also available, and they have a luggage storage service (costs vary depending on the size). ✉ *2–7–9 Inaho, Otaru* ☎ *0134/32–6861* ⌁ *Hourly rentals ¥600; half-day rentals ¥1300; luggage storage from ¥300 per bag.*

### CANAL CRUISES

#### Otaru Canal Cruise (小樽運河クルーズ; *Otaru unga kuruuzu*)

BOAT TOURS | FAMILY | Take a 40-minute Canal cruise and view Otaru's famous stone and brick warehouses from a different perspective. The cruise will take you up and down the main canal with a little jaunt under Tsukimi and Asahi bridges into the port area. The boarding platform is just across the canal from the Otaru Tourist Office at Unga Plaza. In summer the daytime cruises run 10 times per day (11 at the height of summer) and two or three at night (after 7 pm), but check their schedule as it changes with the seasons. At the height of the season, reservations are recommended for the night cruise. Reservations can be made by phone or at the platform. ✉ *5–4 Minato Machi, Otaru* ☎ *0134/31–1733 for reservations* ⊕ *otaru.cc/en* ⌁ *¥1,500; ¥1,800 at night.*

# Niseko (ニセコ)

*73 km (45 miles) southwest of Otaru.*

For the best skiing in Hokkaido, head for Niseko's Grand Hirafu, Annupuri, Niseko Village, and Hanazono resorts. Popular with Japanese skiers in the 1970s, Niseko had another major boom three decades later when Australian tourists made this a favorite winter destination. Asia's economic downturn and the high exchange rate cut the number of foreign travelers, but international tourists from across Asia have now discovered this fantastic destination.

## GETTING HERE AND AROUND

Niseko is really a collection of villages near the town of Kutchan, a 2½-hour drive both from JR Sapporo Station and New Chitose Airport. From December to April public buses go from the airport to the Niseko ski resorts almost hourly until early afternoon. In the summer season, Chuo Bus Company has two buses a day. A one-way trip costs ¥2,650, but a return ticket is ¥1,680.

From Sapporo you can drive to the Niseko area in two hours, up and over Nakayama Pass. Trains from Sapporo to Kutchan depart every 90 minutes or so; the trip takes two hours and costs ¥2,100. You will probably have to switch trains in Otaru. From Kutchan seven trains a day go to the Hirafu and Niseko villages at the heart of the scenic area. Hotels and pensions pick up guests at these two stations. Travelers with no pick-up arranged should go a little farther to JR Niseko Station because Hirafu is tiny and deserted once the train has gone. In ski season there are shuttle buses connecting Kutchan, the villages, and the lift stations. Out-of-season, though, public transport is limited.

## VISITOR INFORMATION

Niseko-specific skiing information can be found online at ⊕ *www.niseko.ne.jp/en.* For up-to-date information on skiing and snowboarding in Niseko and elsewhere in Japan, check out the website ⊕ *snow-japan.com.*

Down the street from Kutchan Station is the excellent Michi no Eki Niseko, run by the Kutchan Tourist Association, which has information, Wi-Fi, hotel-booking help, and event listings. In Niseko go to the Grand Hirafu Welcome Center for accommodations help, tourist information, and to stay warm while waiting for the bus. It's next to the bus arrival/departure area at the top of Hirafu Village, near the Hotel Niseko Alpen.

**SKIING INFORMATION Niseko United.** ⊕ *www.niseko.ne.jp/en.* **Snow Japan.** ⊕ *www.snowjapan.com.*

**VISITOR INFORMATION Michi no Eki Niseko View Plaza.** ✉ *77–10 Motomachi, Abuta-gun, Niseko* ☎ *0136/43–2051.* **Grand Hirafu Welcome Center.** ✉ *204 Aza-Yamada, Abuta-gun, Niseko* ☎ *0136/22–0109* ⊕ *www.grand-hirafu.jp.*

## 🍴 Restaurants

**Izakaya Bang Bang** (居酒屋ばんばん)
$$$$ | ASIAN FUSION | Sizzling *yakitori* (meat on wood skewers) and other local favorites like grilled salmon and herring accompany imports like spareribs and tacos at this place in Hirafu Village. The folks at the nearby tables could become tomorrow's skiing or whitewater rafting buddies, and your hotel's staffers probably enjoy their evenings off here. **Known for:** chicken, skewered meats, and vegetable yakitori; fun vibe; international crowd. $ *Average main: ¥7,000* ✉ *188–24 Aza-Yamada, Abuta-gun, Kutchan* ☎ *0136/22–4292* ⊕ *www.niseko.or.jp/bangbang* 🕒 *Closed end of the ski season till July. No lunch.*

**Jo-Jo's** (ジョジョズ)

$$ | AMERICAN | FAMILY | This spacious, laid-back restaurant—all soaring beams and wide windows overlooking Mt. Yotei—on the second floor of Niseko Adventure Center is busy all day with guides and their nervous or elated customers. The platters here overflow with nourishing meals for adventurers, including an all-Hokkaido burger with only local ingredients. Jo-Jo's sells drinks from 9:30, but doesn't start serving food until 11. **Known for:** homemade cakes; fresh salads; juicy burgers. $ *Average main: ¥1,500* ✉ *179–53 Aza-Yamada, Abuta-gun, Niseko* ☎ *0136/23–2220.*

 ## Hotels

**Hilton Niseko Village** (ヒルトンニセコビレッジ)

$$$$ | RESORT | With wonderful views of Mt. Yotei and the slopes of Mt. Niseko Annupuri, this hotel has a ski-in, ski-out location beside the Niseko gondola—it's a nine-minute ride to powder heaven. **Pros:** awesome views; reasonable prices in summer; multilingual staff providing great service. **Cons:** expensive dining; standard rooms are small for the price; a 20-minute shuttle bus ride to Hirafu Village. $ *Rooms from: ¥29,189* ✉ *Higashiyama Onsen, Abuta-gun, Niseko* ☎ *0136/44–1111* ⊕ *www.hilton.com* 🛏 *506 rooms* ⵏ⃝ *No Meals.*

**Hotel Niseko Alpen** (ホテル ニセコ アルペン)

$$$$ | HOTEL | At the base of the Niseko Tokyu Grand Hirafu ski slopes (right beside the quad lift and ticket office) sits this modern hotel. **Pros:** ski-in, ski-out location; close to village life; two-min walk to the Hirafu bus terminal. **Cons:** crowded public areas during ski season; attracts tour groups; bland basic rooms with worn furnishings. $ *Rooms from: ¥22,400* ✉ *204 Aza Yamada, Abuta-gun, Kutchan* ☎ *0136/22–1105* ⊕ *www.hotel-nisekoalpen.jp/en* 🛏 *125 rooms* ⵏ⃝ *No Meals.*

**Park Hyatt Niseko Hanazono** (パーク ハイアット ニセコ HANAZONO)

$$$$ | HOTEL | This luxurious mountain retreat offers ski-in ski-out access to the Niseko Hanazono Resort as well as a wide range of restaurants and bars should you be lucky enough to spend several days here. **Pros:** luxurious accommodation; fine dining; ski-in ski-out location. **Cons:** minimum length of stay policy in winter; requires shuttle bus or taxi to visit restaurants/bars in Hirafu; some language limitations. $ *Rooms from: ¥67,300* ✉ *328–47 Aza Iwaobetsu, Kutchan-cho, Abuta-gun, Niseko* ☎ *0136/27–1234* ⊕ *www.hyatt.com* 🛏 *170 rooms* ⵏ⃝ *Free Breakfast* ⌖ *3-night min. during ski season.*

## Activities

Between the skier paradise of Mt. Annupuri and gorgeous Mt. Yotei is a gentle landscape of hot springs, dairy and vegetable farms, and hiking trails. For most international visitors the many adventure sports are the reason to visit. Australian and Canadian expats offer year-round thrills, including white-water rafting (best from April to May), backcountry skiing (December to April), mountain biking, and hiking.

### HIKING

**Mt. Yotei** (羊蹄山 *Yotei-san*)

HIKING & WALKING | Climbing this beautiful cousin of Mt. Fuji takes four to six hours—it's like a staircase that never ends. Two trails lead up the mountain: the more-challenging Hirafu Course and the easier but still arduous Makkari Course. It's a trudge without switchbacks all the way up. Regardless of your approach, you'll find wildflowers and bamboo shoots that grow wild on the hills in summer. A hut at the top provides simple lodging. To get to the trails, take the bus from JR Kutchan Station 20 minutes to Yotei Tozan Guchi (hiking trail entrance) for the Hirafu Course, or 40 minutes to the Yotei Shinzan Koen stop for the Makkari Course.

## SKIING AND SNOWBOARDING

Mt. Niseko Annupuri is one of the world's top skiing and snowboarding destinations. Niseko is well known for huge amounts of powdery snow, a great network of trails across four resorts, fast lifts and gondolas, excellent hotels, and a welcoming family-friendly international atmosphere.

From November to May, skiers and snowboarders can enjoy 61 courses covering 47 km (30 miles) of powder in the Niseko area. The 1,308-m (4,291-foot) Mt. Niseko Annupuri is divided into four separate but interlinked resorts: Niseko Annupuri, Niseko Village Ski Resort, Niseko Tokyu Grand Hirafu, and Niseko Hanazono Resort. You can buy lift passes that cover just one of the resorts, and this is a good option for beginners who are sticking to just one or two green runs. Most visitors, however, should purchase the Niseko United All-Mountain Pass, which in high season is ¥8,100 for an adult one-day pass. Lift passes are cheaper at the start and end of the season, if you book online, or if you're purchasing a multi-day pass.

Each resort has rentals of ski and snowboard gear including helmets. A one-day rental of skis/snowboard and boots is usually around ¥7,500. Rental of other skiwear, gloves, goggles, etc. is also available. Unlike some smaller resorts, Niseko rental shops have larger sizes of snowboard and ski boots suitable for most Americans. There are also several places to purchase gear, most in Hirafu. Rhythm Japan has a wide selection as well as helpful English-speaking staff.

In winter you can access the ski areas by train to Kutchan and then bus to the resorts, but ski buses operate directly between New Chitose Airport, Sapporo Station, major Sapporo hotels, Otaru, and other hubs. Some of the ski bus companies have special day-trip packages that combine the bus and lift ticket.

Renting a car and driving to Niseko in winter is not advisable for visitors to Hokkaido due to heavy snow, blizzard conditions, ice, and disappearing road markings.

### Niseko Annupuri (ニセコアンヌプリ)

SKIING & SNOWBOARDING | FAMILY | The wide, gently sloping runs that are kind to beginners and shaky intermediates keep people coming to this, the quieter of the Niseko resorts. Beginners will enjoy practicing on Niseko's famous powder, but practiced skiers will also enjoy the more challenging runs. Private lessons are available for children. Unfortunately, it's also less convenient than Niseko Tokyu Grand Hirafu, since Annupuri is the final stop on the bus. ⊠ *Aza Niseko 485, Niseko* 🕾 *0136/58–2080* ⊕ *annupuri.info/winter/english* 🎿 *1-day adult lift pass high season ¥5,600.*

### Niseko Hanazono Resort (ニセコHANAZO-NOリゾート)

SKIING & SNOWBOARDING | FAMILY | The Niseko Hanazono Resort is a great family area with easier runs. The new 10-person Hanazono Symphony Gondola, and a six-seater hooded chairlift with heated seats, mean you'll ascend the slopes with style. Facilities are limited at the base of the resort except for the luxurious and expensive Park Hyatt Niseko Hanazono. ⊠ *328–47 Iwaobetsu, Niseko* ⊕ *hanazononiseko.com/en* 🎿 *1-day adult lift pass high season ¥5,000 (Hanazono and Hirafu ¥6,600).*

### Niseko Tokyu Grand Hirafu (ニセコ東急 グラン・ヒラフ)

SKIING & SNOWBOARDING | FAMILY | The largest of the Niseko ski resorts has something for everyone, though most come for the deep powder. Being the biggest, however, does have its drawbacks and the slopes can get crowded, particularly on weekends. The trails are divided evenly between the beginner, intermediate, and advanced courses. This is the most convenient ski resort as ski buses first arrive at the Hirafu Welcome Center beside the ticket office and the Ace Quad Lift #2. ✉ *204 Aza Yamada, Abuta-gun, Niseko* ☎ *0136/22–0109* ⊕ *www.grand-hirafu.jp/winter/en* ✉ *1-day adult lift pass high season ¥6,300 (Hanazono and Hirafu ¥6,600).*

**Niseko Village Ski Resort** (ニセコビレッジ)
SKIING & SNOWBOARDING | FAMILY | Situated around the Hilton Niseko Village, this resort has a fast gondola that takes you to beautifully designed courses through the forested slopes. If you didn't get enough day skiing, the compact area is lit until 8 pm. Due to its orientation, much of the slopes stay in shadow for part of the season, keeping the powder dry and cold. There are two designated kids' play areas and a day-care center, plus options to try snowshoeing, snowmobiling, and reindeer sledding. ✉ *Higashiyama Onsen, Abuta-gun, Niseko* ☎ *0136/44–2211* ⊕ *www.niseko-village.com* ✉ *1-day adult lift pass high season ¥6,200.*

## SPORTS OUTFITTERS

**Niseko Adventure Centre** (ニセコアドベンチャーセンター)
HIKING & WALKING | This longtime favorite arranges guided river-rafting, mountain-biking, and winter sport outings. There's also an indoor rock-climbing wall at its village-center base. On the second floor of NAC is the popular Jo-Jo's café. ✉ *179–53 Aza-Yamada, Niseko* ☎ *0136/23–2093* ⊕ *www.nacadventures.jp.*

**Niseko Outdoor Adventure Sports Club** (ノーアスクアドベンチャーツアー; *Noasuku Adobencha Tsua*)
SNOW SPORTS | This activity center in Hirafu offers ski lessons in winter and leads rafting trips in the summer as well as guided backcountry tours that last either half a day, or a full day. ✉ *20–6 Aza Yamada, Abuta-gun, Niseko* ☎ *0136/23–1688* ⊕ *www.noasc.com.*

**Rhythm Base**
(リズムジャパン; *Rizumu Japan*)
SNOW SPORTS | The Rhythm Base team offers lessons and backcountry guiding in both Japanese and English. Friendly international staff have plenty of mountain experience and can give advice on the places to ski, board, bike, hike, eat, and drink in the region. It's also houses a popular rental and retail store on Koen Ave not far from the Hirafu Ski lifts. Along with sales and rentals, they provide ski and snowboard servicing, and have their own coffee shop. Rhythm Base is closed during the summer. Nearby, Rhythm Main St. is the original smaller retail outlet, but also has a coffee shop and international staff, and it is open year-round. ✉ *184–10 Aza Yamada, Niseko* ☎ *0136/23–0164* ⊕ *www.rhythmjapan. com* ⊙ *Closed June–Nov.*

# Rusutsu (留寿都村)

*20 km (12 miles) southeast of Niseko, 17 km (11 miles) north of Lake Toya.*

Located 30 minutes southeast of Niseko, and 30 minutes north of Lake Toya, Rusutsu is a small village with a large ski resort. In summer there is mountain biking, rafting, hiking, and golf, but Rusutsu is best known for getting over 42 feet of light, fluffy dry powder each year, and it is noticeably less crowded than Niseko, making it one of Japan's top winter resorts.

## GETTING HERE AND AROUND

In winter you can access Rusutsu by ski bus from Chitose Airport, Sapporo, Niseko, and Lake Toya. The schedules for buses vary during the season, and it is advisable to check with your Rusutsu accommodation on what bus services they offer, and how early you need to reserve.

In summer, when renting a car is a good option, Rusutsu is one hour, 30 minutes from Sapporo, 30 minutes from Niseko, and 30 minutes from Lake Toya.

 # Activities

## SKIING AND SNOWBOARDING

**Rusutsu Resort** (ルスツリゾート)

SKIING & SNOWBOARDING | FAMILY | Huge amounts of powder snow, 37 trails, 42 km (26 miles) of piste, limited crowds, and great facilities make Rusutsu one of the best winter destinations in Japan. The resort covers three mountains: Mt. Isola (994 m/3,264 feet), East Mt. (868 m/2,847 feet), and West Mt. (715 m/2,345 feet) with four gondolas, seven quad lifts, and seven pair lifts getting you quickly to the top of your next run. Luxurious ski-in ski-out accommodation can be found at the Rusutsu Resort Hotel, the Vale Rusutsu, and the Westin Rusutsu Resort. ✉ *13 Izumikawa, Rusutsu-mura, Abuta-gun* ☎ *0136/46–3331* ⊕ *rusutsu. com* 🚟 *1-day lift tickets are ¥6,500 for adults; 1-day rental of snowboard/skis and boots from ¥6,200.*

# Toyako (洞爺湖)

*179 km (111 miles) southwest of Sapporo.*

Mountains, forests, hot springs, caldera lakes, and volcanoes are not too far from the bright lights of Sapporo in Shikotsu-Toya National Park. Route 230 passes the large hot-spring village of Jozankei, then the mountains close in and the road climbs 2,742 feet to Nakayama Pass. On a clear day the view from the top is classic Hokkaido: farmland with the majestic Mt. Yotei in its midst, and on the southern horizon lie Lake Toya's volcanic crater and Noboribetsu hot springs, where the earth steams, rumbles, and erupts.

World leaders met here for the G8 Summit in 2008, but Lake Toya is best known for its geothermal events. In March of 2000, Mt. Usu exploded for the first time in 23 years, shooting a 10,500-foot-high cloud of ash and smoke over the quiet resort towns of Toyako Onsen and Sobetsu Onsen. About 16,000 people were evacuated. Amazingly, by July the towns were opened for business with the still-smoking craters in their midst. Volcanic eruptions are merely an occupational hazard for residents of hot-springs towns and residents pride themselves on living with nature.

Usu-san is one of several peaks on Lake Toya's crater, a huge volcanic rim that dominates the landscape. Route 230 from Sapporo drops over the northern edge, and Route 453 from Lake Shikotsu and Noboribetsu and roads from the coast come in from the south. Volcanic activity is centered on the small town of Toyako Onsen, and a few kilometers around the lake at Showa Shin-san. A road rings the water, dotted with campsites and hot springs; pleasure boats go out to three small islands where deer beg for snacks.

## GETTING HERE AND AROUND

Direct buses from Sapporo to Toyako Onsen via Nakayama Toge Pass take 2½ hours (¥2,830). Donan Bus makes that Sapporo to Toyako Onsen trip four times daily and reservations can be made by phone. Toyako Onsen is accessible by JR from Sapporo. Disembark from the train at JR Toya Station for a 20-minute bus ride to the lake. The bus departs throughout the day and is ¥340. Sightseeing boats leave the pier for the 20-minute crossing to the islands. Bike rentals are available near the bus station for ¥700 per hour or ¥2,000 per day, but check with your hotel or with the tourist information desk for the best deals. Some hotels have bicycles on hand for their guests. It takes about three hours to cycle the circumference of the lake.

## VISITOR INFORMATION

The tourist information center, inside the bus terminal, has English-speaking staff, and although officially unable to make hotel reservations, the website has access to online booking for some hotels. Toya Guide Center provides English-speaking guides for year-round excursions such as Canadian canoeing on the lake, walking the volcano, deer spotting, and waterfall walking, but be sure to make arrangements in advance.

**TOUR INFORMATION Toya Guide Center.**
⊠ *193–8 Toyako-cho, Abuta-gun, Toyama* ☎ *0142/82–5002* ⊕ *www.toya-guide.com.*

**VISITOR INFORMATION Toyako Onsen Visitor Center.** ⊠ *142–5 Toyako Onsen, Abuta-gun, Toyako-onsemmachi* ☎ *0142/75–2555* ⊕ *www.toyako-vc.jp/en.*

 Sights

**Nishiyama Crater Trail** (西山火口群散策路; *Nishiyama Kakogun Sansakuro*)
TRAIL | A fire station, a school, and houses stand at crazy angles amid the solidified ash flows where the 2000 eruption reached the edges of Toyako Onsen. See it all from boardwalks that wind up into the still-steaming hills. It's an impressive scene of what can happen when you live next to a volcano. As a bonus, there are views both of the lake to the north and the ocean to the south. There's also a whole series of boardwalks, mountain trails, and short stretches of roads that were cut off after the eruption. Access is from just behind the Toyako Onsen Visitor Center. ⊠ *3–4–5 Takashaga-dori, Toyako-cho* ✛ *Between Toya and Toyako Onsen* ⊠ *Free.*

**Showa Shinzan** (昭和新山)
MOUNTAIN | During an earthquake in 1943, Showa Shinsan rose suddenly from a farmer's wheat field. Kept secret during the Pacific War as a potentially unlucky sign, it continued growing to its present height of 1,306 feet by 1945. It's on private land, but a cable-car ride (¥1,800 round-trip) up the eastern flank of Mt. Usu provides great views of the mountain, Lake Toya, and Funka Bay. Avoid the Showa Shinza Bear Ranch near

the base—a depressing tourist attraction. ⊠ *184–5 Aza Showa Shinzan, Sobetsu-cho, Usu Gun, Toyako-cho* ☎ *0142/75–2401* ⊕ *usuzan.hokkaido.jp/en.*

**Toyako Onsen** (洞爺湖温泉)
HOT SPRING | Gazing up at the town-sponsored fireworks from a rooftop hot spring after a relaxing soak in the thermal waters and a pleasant dinner of local specialties—this is why thousands of Japanese come to this small lakeside town throughout the year. From April 28 to October 31, the 20-minute fireworks display is likely to be the highlight of your stay. A waterside walk in front of the wall of hotels is relaxing before the bus tours arrive in late afternoon. ⊠ *Toyako-cho.*

**Volcanic Science Museum**
(火山科学館; *Kazan Kagaku-kan*)
SCIENCE MUSEUM | FAMILY | A rumbling sound track and shaking floors recreate the area's 1977 and 2000 volcanic eruptions in this small information center. Although there's a good explanation of the science involved in this place where eruptions happen roughly every 30 years, the museum is less useful in describing the impact on the lives of locals. This museum shares a building with the Toyako Onsen Visitor Center. ⊠ *142–5 Toyako-Onsen, Toyako-cho* ☎ *0142/75–2555* ⊕ *www. toyako-vc.jp/en/volcano* ⊠ *¥600.*

🍴 Restaurants

**Boyotei** (望羊蹄)
$$ | EUROPEAN | A European-style restaurant set in a tranquil garden, with very friendly staff, Boyotei (which literally means "View of Mt. Yotei") charms with its stone floor, low beams, long-legged tables, and family photos dating back for decades. There are English menus available. **Known for:** hamburger steak platters; various macaroni gratins; Hokkaido onion gratin soup. $ *Average main: ¥1,900* ⊠ *36–12 Toyako Onsen, Abuta-gun, Toyako-cho* ☎ *0142/75–2311.*

##  Hotels

### ★ The Windsor Hotel Toya Resort and Spa
(ザ・ウィンザーホテル洞爺 リゾート&スパ)

$$$$ | **RESORT** | Visible for miles around—it looks like a giant cruise ship perched on the rim of the Toya Volcano—the Windsor is Hokkaido's best hotel for location and service. **Pros:** top service; stunning views; chance to spot Asian celebs on vacation. **Cons:** hours from major cities; some restaurants close unexpectedly during quiet season; expensive. $ *Rooms from: ¥80,600* ⊠ *Shimizu, Abuta-Gun, Toyako-cho* ☎ *0570/056–510 for reservations only, 0142/73–1111* ⮕ *386 rooms* ⏺ *No Meals.*

# Noboribetsu Onsen (登別温泉)

*53 km (32 miles) east of Toyako, 100 km (62 miles) south of Sapporo.*

If you want to see how many Japanese people prefer to relax and soak while on vacation, this is the place to go. Noboribetsu Onsen is Hokkaido's most famous spa destination. The town claims that some 34,300 gallons of geothermally heated water are pumped out every hour, making it the most prodigious hot spring in Asia. Not a quaint little hot spring town, Noboribetsu caters to Japanese-style onsen tourism (i.e., soak, eat, soak, get drunk, soak, sleep, soak), meaning services are limited once you step outside your hotel. The hotels are good, but the rest of the town is mainly shops just selling souvenirs.

## GETTING HERE AND AROUND
Noboribetsu City is one hour south of Sapporo by JR Limited Express. From the JR Station a local bus travels the 13 km (8 miles) up hill to Noboribetsu Onsen (¥350). If you are coming from Sapporo, it is possible to arrange a tour through your hotel, JR Sapporo Station or the Sapporo International Communication Plaza.

Donan Bus travels from Sapporo to Noboribetsu Onsen; the trip takes one hour, 50 minutes (¥2,200; reservations advised).

##  Sights

### Hell Valley (地獄谷; *Jigokudani*)
**HOT SPRING** | **FAMILY** | A volcanic crater in a bow-shaped valley, Jigokudani has hundreds of multicolored geysers pulsing like the heartbeat of Earth itself. Not to worry, though; the walkways to photo-ops have handrails and are very safe. It's a short walk from all Noboribetsu hotels and well worth a look. There's no admission fee or formal open hours, but parking is ¥500 during the day. ⊠ *Noboribetsu Onsen, Noboribetsu* ⭐ *Free.*

### Noboribetsu Date Jidaimura (登別伊達時代村)
**MUSEUM VILLAGE** | **FAMILY** | Noboribetsu Date Jidaimura is a touristy, culture park that's a good year round option for families with budding ninjas. There's a village of merchant houses, samurai residences, and shrines that are manned by numerous staff dressed as geisha, samurai, merchants, innkeepers, and ninjas. The shows are in Japanese, but international families will enjoy many of the activities including a disorienting ninja maze house, and posing for photos with the performers. If you'd like to dress up in Edo period costumes then stop by the Utsuro-kan to embrace your warrior spirit. The park is located just off the main road connecting Noboribetsu Station with Noboribetsu Onsen and is easily accessible by bus from the Noboribetsu Station (¥190) or taxi. ⊠ *53–1 Naka, Noboribets-cho, Noboribetsu* ☎ *0143/83–3311* ⊕ *www.edo-trip.jp* ⭐ *¥1,900.*

## Hotels

**Ryotei Hanayura** (旅亭花ゆら)
$$$$ | **HOTEL** | The Ryotei Hanayura hot-spring hotel has floor-to-ceiling lobby windows that look out on a small canyon and river and hot springs that bubble gently among rocks and trees. **Pros:** peaceful, dignified environment; great views; good dinners. **Cons:** not all rooms nonsmoking; meals not optional; no single-occupancy room pricing. [$] *Rooms from: ¥60,000* ✉ *100 Noboribetsu Onsen, Noboribetsu* ☎ *0143/84–2322* 🌐 *www.hanayura.com* 🛏 *43 rooms* 🍴 *All-Inclusive.*

**Takimotokan Hokkaido** (第一滝本館)
$$$$ | **RESORT** | Contemplate the Hell Valley while soaking in one of the 35 different baths at Takimotokan Hokkaido. **Pros:** a wide range of onsen; views of Hell Valley from the baths; recently renovated. **Cons:** noisy with groups; baths can be busy as they are open to nonguests; tobacco smell in some rooms. [$] *Rooms from: ¥33,600* ✉ *55 Noboribetsu Onsen, Noboribetsu* ☎ *0143/84–2111* 🌐 *takimotokan.co.jp/en* 🛏 *393 rooms* 🍴 *No Meals.*

# Shiraoi (白老町)

*90 km (56 miles) south of Sapporo, 27 km (17 miles) northeast of Noribetsu Onsen.*

Shiraoi is a small coastal town located due south of Sapporo. It has a significant Ainu population, and is home to the Upopoy National Ainu Museum and Park. With only one major attraction (albeit a notable one), it's more of a side-trip destination (and often visited by travelers staying over in Sapporo or Noribetsu Onsen).

### GETTING HERE AND AROUND

Shiraoi is easily accessible by train (one hour from Sapporo, 12 minutes from Noboribetsu, and 50 minutes from Toyako).

## Sights

★ **Upopoy National Ainu Museum and Park**
(ウポポイ(民族共生象徴空間); *Upopoi Minzoku Kyosei Shocho Kukan*)
**MUSEUM VILLAGE** | **FAMILY** | Upopoy, meaning "singing in a large group" in the Ainu language, is the National Ainu Museum and Park. Opened in 2020, this impressive facility "aims to build a society where Ainu pride is recognized, raise awareness of Ainu history and culture, and help to forge a future for the Ainu people." The large permanent exhibition in the museum covers aspects of Ainu culture including language, farming, fishing, and migration. Exhibits have explanations in both Japanese and English, and there are sections especially designed for children. Performances of Ainu singing and dancing take place year-round inside the cultural exchange hall, and also outdoors during the summer months. The *kotan*, traditional village, has demonstrations of archery and canoeing, plus several traditional houses with thatched roofs. It's a great day-trip from Sapporo, or a stopping-off point on the way to Noboribetsu Onsen. ✉ *2-3-2 Wakakusa-cho, Shiraoi Town* ☎ *0144/82–3914* 🌐 *ainu-upopoy.jp* 🎟 *¥1,200.*

# Daisetsuzan National Park (大雪山国立公園)

*50 km (31 miles) east of Asahikawa.*

The country's largest nature preserve, Daisetsuzan National Park contains the very essence of rugged Hokkaido: vast plains, soaring mountain peaks, hidden gorges, cascading waterfalls, thick forests, and steaming hot springs.

Daisetsuzan National Park has some of Hokkaido's most rugged scenery.

## GETTING HERE AND AROUND

Sounkyo village and canyon are 90 minutes east of Asahikawa by car on Route 39. The highway skirts the northern side of the park, and Sounkyo is the gateway. You can catch a bus directly to Sounkyo Onsen (¥2,140) from in front of Asahikawa's JR Station. If you are using a JR Pass, you can save money and time by taking the train to Kamikawa Station and transferring to the Dohoku Bus for the 35-minute run to Sounkyo (¥890).

Bicycles can be rented for ¥1,000 a day in the village, and a short cycling trail along the old road by the river is a peaceful way to enjoy the gorge. From July to September a ¥440 bus ride connects the village with the Daisetsu dam and lake, but there is only one bus each day. Ask at the visitor's center.

## VISITOR INFORMATION

The Sounkyo Tourist Information, beside the Kamikawa Station, provides hiking maps and information on sightseeing and lodging. English is spoken.

The Sounkyo Visitor Center is located at the base of the Kurodake Ropeway.

**CONTACT Soun-kyo Visitor Center.** ✉ *Sounkyo Gorge* ☎ *01658/94–400* ⊕ *www. sounkyovc.net.*

#  Sights

★ **Daisetsuzan National Park** (大雪山国立公園; *Daisetsuzan Kokuritsu Koen*)
NATIONAL PARK | Daisetsuzan, which means "great snow mountain," refers to the park's five major peaks, whose altitudes approach 7,560 feet. They are climbable even by moderately experienced hikers, with a ring trail that is best done in summer. But you can also catch a bus or train or even drive just south of Asahikawa and simply enjoy the picturesque region.

On the park's east side is Soun-kyo, but on its unconnected west side, two spa towns serve as summer hiking centers and winter ski resorts. Shirogane Onsen, at 2,461 feet, has had especially good skiing since its mountain, Tokachi-dake, erupted in 1962 and 1988, creating a superb ski bowl. At Asahidake Onsen you can take a cable car (¥2,000 one way, ¥3,200 round trip) up Asahi-dake to an altitude of 5,250 feet and hike for two hours to the 7,513-foot summit. In late spring and early summer the slopes are carpeted with alpine flowers. Serious skiers come for Japan's longest ski season. ✉ *Sounkyo Gorge* 🌐 *www.daisetsuzan.or.jp/english* 🎫 *Free.*

**Sounkyo Gorge** (層雲峡)

**CANYON** | Running through a 15-mile-long ravine, Route 39 cuts through the northeast entrance of Daisetsuzan National Park. For 5 miles, sheer cliff walls rise on both sides of the canyon as the road drills into the mountains. In winter and early spring, forbidding stone spires loom as if in judgment; in other seasons they thrust through glorious foliage. On the way there are a couple of river-carved gorges called Obako and Kobako. Go see Momijidani (Maple Tree Valley) if you're here in autumn.

Sounkyo Onsen village is halfway through the ravine. In summer, the pedestrian-friendly main street is lined with flower boxes, and guesthouses and souvenir shops add charm to what is basically a concrete version of an alpine village. From Late January to March, the frozen river and its ice cliffs are illuminated for the Sounkyo Onsen Ice Fall Festival, which is breathtaking. If you're driving, watch your gas tank, as there is no gas station in town. ✉ *Sounkyo Gorge.*

## Hotels

There's no lodging within the township of Sounkyo Onsen if you want to stay in the northern part of the park. Because Sounkyo's hotels are almost exclusively ryokan, where meals are included in your lodging cost, other dining opportunities in town are severely limited. Rates tend to be 20% lower in winter.

**Resort Pension Yamanoue** (ペンション山の上)

**$** | **B&B/INN** | This modern guesthouse sits in the center of the village's flower-filled pedestrian area. **Pros:** in village center; expansive Japanese or Italian dinners; butterflies in late June and early July. **Cons:** shared bathrooms; limited English, must book by phone, and cash-only; must go next door for hot springs. [$] *Rooms from: ¥11,600* ✉ *Soun-kyo Onsen, Kamikawa* ☎ *0165/85–3206* 🌐 *www.pen-yamanoue.com* 💳 *No credit cards* 🛏 *12 rooms* 🍴 *No Meals.*

**Sounkyo Choyotei** (層雲峡朝陽亭)

**$$$$** | **RESORT** | Perched on a bluff halfway up one side of the gorge, this hotel has the best views in the park. **Pros:** quality on par with other large hotels; large onsen baths; feels close to nature despite its size. **Cons:** busy meal times; not the most attractive hotel; full of tour groups. [$] *Rooms from: ¥35,700* ✉ *Soun-kyo Onsen, Kamikawa* ☎ *01658/5–3241* 🌐 *www.choyotei.com/en* 🛏 *200 rooms* 🍴 *Free Breakfast.*

## Activities

### HIKING

**Kurodake Ropeway** (黒岳ロープウェイ)

**HIKING & WALKING** | **FAMILY** | Technology helps even the most reluctant hikers up the mountains: a cable car and chairlift rise up the side of the gorge to 4,264 feet. Intrepid hikers can march one more hour to the top of Kurodake, 2,244 feet higher. From here, numerous well-marked trails lead either across volcanic gravel or shrubby plateaus. Crimson foliage sets the slopes ablaze in September. Daisetsuzan's beauty is best enjoyed slowly, as along with the breathtaking views you may encounter deer, foxes, and bears. Take care early in the season when bear cubs are being watched by their mothers. ✉ *Sounkyo, Kamikawa Cho, Sounkyo Gorge* ☎ *01658/5–3031* 🌐 *www.rinyu.co.jp/kurokdake* 🎫 *¥2,400 round-trip* 🕒 *Closed Jan.*

# Furano (富良野市)

*113 km (70 miles) northeast of Sapporo, 56 km due (35 miles) south of Asahikawa.*

This small town is famous throughout Japan for its lavender farms (when in bloom) and its ski resort. Flower fields and small farms at the base of the Daisetsuzan mountain range attract thousands of domestic and international visitors hoping to get a taste of the simple country life. For those who spend all their time in an Asian metropolis the flowers, potato fields, art galleries, and cute coffee shops are a breath of lavender-scented fresh air. The small town makes an attractive stopover area while driving to central or east Hokkaido between late May and September.

If you are traveling south from Asahikawa to Furano you'll pass through Biei, a small modern village with neighboring rolling hills and a patchwork of crop fields (potato, corn, soba, sunflowers).

## GETTING HERE AND AROUND

In July and August there are special trains, sightseeing buses, and bus or train packages from Sapporo, which combine Biei and Furano flowers with the Asahiyama Zoo in Asahikawa City. In winter, ski buses run from Sapporo Station, and New Chitose Airport to Furano Resort.

Trains from Asahikawa depart every hour and reach Biei in 35 minutes (¥640) and Furano in 70 minutes (¥1,290).

## VISITOR INFORMATION

Outside Furano Station, flower farm information, shuttle buses, and help with hotel searches are available at the Furano Tourist Association.

**CONTACT Furano-Biei Tourism Center.** ⊠ *JR Furano Station, Hinode Machi 1–30, Furano* ☎ *0167/23–3388* ⊕ *www.furanotourism.com/en.*

##  Sights

### Farm Tomita (ファーム富田)

**FARM/RANCH | FAMILY** | For many Japanese, lavender is one of the favorite souvenirs Hokkaido, and this is the farm where it all started—back in 1903. Now thousands of visitors come to see fields of lavender, poppies, cosmos, herbs, and marigolds. Irodori is the field with flowers planted in seven strips, each a different color. Lavender peak season is early July to early August. During this time, the JR Lavender Farm Station—seven minutes closer than JR Nakafurano Station—is open. This is worth a look if you're a flower aficionado. ⊠ *Hokusei, Sorachi-gun, Naka-furano* ☎ *0167/39–3939* ⊕ *www.farm-tomita.co.jp/en* ⊠ *Free.*

##  Activities

### ★ Furano Ski Resort (富良野スキー場; *Furano Sukii-jo*)

**SKIING & SNOWBOARDING | FAMILY** | Furano Ski Resort, also called Furano Ski Area, is one of Hokkaido's and Japan's best places to ski and snowboard. Central Hokkaido gets large amounts of light dry powder, and Furano Ski Resort with 28 trails gives skiers and boarders plenty of great options. The ski season is longer than other resorts running from late November to early May, and children under 12 get free lift tickets, so a great option for families. ⊠ *Nakagoryo, Furano* ☎ *0167/22–01111* ⊕ *www.princehotels.com/en/ski/furano/#tickets* ⊠ *1-day adult lift ticket is ¥6,000 (discounted to ¥4,500 at the start and end of the season), 1-day gear rental (boots, skis, and board) from ¥5,800.*

# Abashiri (網走)

*517 km (321 miles) east of Sapporo.*

A good touring base for eastern Hokkaido, Abashiri is a small town in the shadow of Mt. Tento. On the town outskirts are shallow coastal lakes with flowers and seabirds. Bicycles can be rented for slow sightseeing. The whaling fleet sets out from here on research trips ("research" is the official word, common parlance would call it "hunting") under Japan's interpretation of IWC rules, which keeps Japan at loggerheads with conservationists. Winters are harsh: visitors bundle up for boat tours through the *ryuhyo* (ice floes) that jam up on its shores and stretch out to sea as far as the eye can see.

## GETTING HERE AND AROUND

From Sapporo to Abashiri, the fastest option is to fly from New Chitose Airport to Memanbetsu Airport (40 minutes), then it is a 30-minute bus ride to Abashiri. By rail, you can take the limited express to Asahikawa (85 minutes) then switch to the limited express to Abashiri (four hours). The total train fare will be around ¥10,000.

Abashiri has enough sights for a day or more. In summer you could cycle the 27-km (17-mile) lakeside cycling road or the equally easy 40-km (25-mile) one-way cycle along Lake Notoro to Tokoro town. There are five buses a day from the station, circling the sights on Tento-san.

Abashiri is a good starting point to explore eastern Hokkaido. There a several car rental agencies in town, which is a great option, particularly in summer. From Abashiri you can go by train almost due south to Kushiro via Shrietoko-Shari, and Kawayu-Onsen.

## VISITOR INFORMATION

The Abashiri Tourist Association, adjoining the JR Station is where to find information about transportation and lodging in the area.

**CONTACT Abashiri City Tourism Association.** ⊠ *Minami 3 Higashi 4, Abashiri* ☏ *0152/44–5849* ⊕ *www.abakanko.jp/en.*

## ◉ Sights

**Abashiri Prison Museum** (博物館 網走監獄; *Abashiri Kangoku Hakubutsukan*)

**JAIL/PRISON | FAMILY** | Spartan cells line the central corridors in five wooden prison blocks, showing how the convicts who built much of early Hokkaido lived out their years. Used between 1912 and 1984, the prison is now a museum with cell blocks, watchtowers, and farm buildings. Only the most heinous criminals were banished to this forbidding northern outpost, the Alcatraz of Japan. Anguished-looking mannequins illustrate the grimness of life behind bars, and how for those who did escape it could be even worse. If you're in the mood, try out a prison meal—a tray with a bowl of rice, a piece of fish, miso soup, and a few pickles. ⊠ *1-1 Aza-Yobito, Abashiri* ☏ *0152/45–2411* ⊕ *www.kangoku.jp/multilingual_english* ▧ *¥1,500.*

**★ Hokkaido Museum of Northern Peoples** (北海道立 北方民族博物館; *Hoppo Minzoku Hakubutsukan*)

**HISTORY MUSEUM** | Hokkaido is the southernmost point of the northern community of the Ainu. This museum's delightful exhibits link the polar indigenous people, such as the Ainu, Inuits, and Sami (or Lapps) in a way that shows surprising similarities over wide spaces. Displays compare and contrast the kitchen implements, clothing, and hunting tools of various cultures from northern Japan, the neighboring Russian island of Sakhalin, and the northern parts of America and Eurasia. English-language pamphlets are available. Of particular interest are videos depicting life in the frozen north, such as building igloos. The museum is 5 km (3 miles) from JR Abashiri Station inside Okhotsk Park. ⊠ *309–1 Shiomi, Abashiri* ☎ *0152/45–3888* ⊕ *www.hoppohm.org/ english* 🎟 *¥550.*

## 🍴 Restaurants

### Nakazushi (中鮨)

**$$** | **JAPANESE** | Nakano-san presides over the catch of the day in a small restaurant, run since the 1970s by the same family. Take a seat at the wooden counter, over which Nakano-san offers you whatever seafood is in season. **Known for:** sushi sets; seafood donburi, a bowl of rice topped with sea urchin (uni), salmon roe (ikura), or other in-season produce; grilled seafood such as plump scallops (hotate). $ *Average main: ¥3,000* ⊠ *Minami 2 Nishi 2, Abashiri* ✛ *Near Abashiri Central Hotel* ☎ *0152/43–3447.*

## 🛏 Hotels

### Abashiri Central Hotel
### (網走セントラルホテル)

**$$$$** | **HOTEL** | Creature comforts await you at this downtown hotel, which seems a world away from rugged outback seaport city of Abashiri. **Pros:** in the town center; caters to foreign visitors; Japanese style rooms are especially good value. **Cons:** can get busy with weddings; boring views; cookie-cutter hotel design. $ *Rooms from: ¥26,000* ⊠ *Minami 2 Nishi 3–7, Abashiri* ☎ *0152/44–5151* ⊕ *www.abashirich.com* 🛏 *96 rooms* ❑ *No Meals.*

### Hotel Abashirikoso (ホテル網走湖荘)

**$$$$** | **RESORT** | Waterbirds drift by the windows of the big but friendly hotel on the shore of Lake Abashiri, a few miles from town. **Pros:** lakeside location; ideal for bird-watching; impressive menu. **Cons:** popular with tour groups; nowhere else nearby to eat or drink; out of town. $ *Rooms from: ¥28,600* ⊠ *78 Yobito, Abashiri* ☎ *0152/48–2245*

⊕ *www.abashirikoso.com* 🛏 *157 rooms* ❑ *All-Inclusive.*

## 🏃 Activities

### Aurora Icebreakers
(網走流氷観光砕氷船 おーろら; *Ryuhyo Kanko Saihyosen Orora*)
**BOAT TOURS** | If you really want to break the ice in future conversations about Hokkaido and you're in Abashiri between late January and early April, take in some ocean-drift icebergs (with some bird- and seal-watching). Weather permitting, icebreakers *Aurora 1* and *Aurora 2* depart from Aurora Terminal at the east end of Abashiri Port, letting you inspect winter *ryuhyo* (drift ice) at close range. Drift ice is unpredictable, so check local conditions before you sail.

Or go in the summer between late April and late October when you can board the same boats from Utoro Port (80 km [50 miles] away from Abashiri) for a cruise around the uninhabited peninsula of Shiretoko National Park. ■**TIP➜** Travel agencies in Tokyo and Sapporo offer package tours for both seasons ⊠ *Aurora Port, Minami 3 Nishi 4, Abashiri* ☎ *0152/24–2147 summer, 0152/43–6000 winter* ⊕ *ms-aurora.com/abashiri/en* 🎟 *From ¥3,500.*

# Shiretoko National Park (知床国立公園)

*76 km (47 miles) east of Abishiri.*

A highlight of any trip to Hokkaido, the spectacular and miraculously uninhabited Shiretoko National Park is a UNESCO World Heritage site. On the Shiretoko Peninsula, it's worlds away from modern Japan: brown bears hook salmon out of tumbling rivers, Blackiston's fish owls and Steller's sea eagles glide through the skies, and a steaming hot spring river tumbles to the sea at Kamuiwakka.

With the park's protected status came mass tourism. Efforts to preserve the area's natural beauty have resulted in strict rules, and limited shuttle-bus access to the last few kilometers of peninsula road—no longer close to Kamuiwakka—makes the experience more challenging. But it's worth the effort: the charming Ezo-shika deer stare at you with as much wonder as you do them. If you visit outside the summer crush—June and September are good times—Shiretoko is a remarkable, untouched pocket of wilderness in a heavily industrialized and technologically advanced nation.

Most tour buses whisk you in and out in 24 hours—with an overnight stay in a resort, quick photo stops along the way, and maybe a boat tour. If you're traveling on your own, it's best to visit the popular destinations at noon or at the end of the day when buses are headed out. Shiretoko is lovely, but the weather, even in summer, is fickle. A Shiretoko stay (and hiking plans) can be marred by mists and rain.

## GETTING HERE AND AROUND

From Sapporo to Abashiri it's a five-hour express train, then a local train to Shari, and finally a one-hour bus ride to Utoro. With connections the trip takes seven hours. Depending on the season, about seven daily bus connections go from Shari to Utoro. Buses from Abashiri and the airports in Kushiro and Memanbetsu also connect to Utoro. Coming from Kushiro it's a two-hour drive to the fishing village of Rausu on the south side of the peninsula, and then a 30-minute drive over the Shiretoko Pass (closed November–April) to Utoro.

From Sapporo the daily overnight Eagle Liner bus takes seven hours (¥8,400 one way, ¥15,700 round-trip to Utoro), departing Sapporo Chuo Bus Terminal at 11:15 pm (the return trip leaves Hotel Shiretoko at 9 am and drops by Utoro Bus Terminal at 9:20 am). Reservations with Chuo Bus are necessary and can be made at the terminal behind the TV Tower in Sapporo, where the bus departs. Utoro and Shiretoko Shari JR Station are also connected by six buses daily in summer.

From the end of April to the end of October, shuttle-bus trips link Utoro Bus Terminal with the Nature Center and Shiretoko Five Lakes. If you are coming by car, park at the Nature Center and board the shuttle. The 12-km (7-mile) dirt road to Kamuiwakka Onsen waterfall is open to shuttle buses only between July 13 and September 20 (closed in winter). Be careful of wildlife when driving; Shiretoko is full of grazing deer that favor cleared roadside verges and are largely unperturbed by vehicles.

Apart from hiking, a boat is the best way to see the wildest parts. From late April to October, several boat companies in Utoro harbor offer one- to three-hour trips (¥3,000–¥8,000) out along the peninsula, beneath soaring 600-foot cliffs to the tip of the cape. Early-morning and late-afternoon trips on a small boat offer the best chances to see bears come down to the beaches to forage. On the Rausu side, boats head out into the Nemuro Straits along Russia's Kunashiri Island, and summer is the best time for whale-watching. A stay of at least one night is recommended for hiking, hot springs, wildlife spotting, and silence. Look for the green sign with white lettering. Shiretoko Nature Cruise is a mom-and-pop operation offering summer and winter cruises from the Rausu side of Shiretoko Peninsula.

Shiretoko Naturalist's Association is a nonprofit offering nature walks, guided tours, and lots of local lore.

## TOURS
### BOAT TOURS
**Shiretoko Sightseeing Ship Aurora** (知床観光船おーろら; *Shiretoko Kanko Fune Oorora*)
**BOAT TOURS** | The same company that does the icebreaker tours off Abashiri run a couple of cruises off the cape from

Utoro. From June to September there's a three-hour Cape of Shiretoko cruise, and from the end of April to October a 1½-hour Mount Lo cruise. ✉ *Utoro Higashi 107, Utoro, Shari* ☎ *0152/24–2146* ⊕ *ms-aurora.com/shiretoko/en* 🚢 *90-min cruises ¥3,300, 3-hr cruises ¥6,800.*

### Shiretoko Nature Cruise (知床ネイチャークルーズ)

**BOAT TOURS** | Contact this company for sea cruises to see whales, sea lions, and birds along the coast on a much smaller boat than the Aurora. From late April to October they do a 2½-hour cruise of the cape; from January to mid-March there are one-hour ice tours. In February and early March, you can also take a 2½-hour tour. ✉ *27–1 Honcho, Menashi Gun, Rausu Cho* ☎ *0153/87–4001* ⊕ *www.e-shiretoko.com* 🚢 *Summer cape cruises from ¥8,800; winter ice tours from ¥4,400.*

### PARK TOURS

### Shiretoko Naturalist's Association (知床ナチュラリスト協会; *Shiretoko Nachurarisu-to Kyokai*)

**PRIVATE GUIDES** | The association's guides lead guided walks around the Shiretoko Goko (Shiretoko Five Lakes) (three hours, ¥5,100), but everything is in Japanese. ✉ *187–8 Utoro Nishi, Shari* ☎ *0152/22–5522* ⊕ *shinra.or.jp.*

### VISITOR INFORMATION

In Utoro, pick up information about the park, its sights, and access at Utoro-Shiretoko Rest Area, a two-minute walk from the bus terminal on the waterfront. On the Rausu side, information can be found at the Shiretoko Rausu Visitor Center. Don't forget to check out the hourly 26-foot-high geyser in the woods out back.

### CONTACTS Rausu Visitor Center.

✉ *6–27 Yunosawa, Rausu, Shiretoko* ☎ *0153/87–2828.*

## 👁 Sights

### Kamuiwakka Onsen (カムイワッカ湯の滝)

**WATERFALL** | *Kamui* means "spirit" or "god" in the Ainu language, and there's something wondrous, almost otherworldly, about this tumbling hot waterfall on the north shore under Io-zan (Mt. Io, as in Sulphur Mountain). Hot water rushes down the mountain through a series of multicolor falls and pools. Wear shoes that can get wet as you will scramble up over slippery rocks to a couple of pools higher upstream; the park staff are there to help you up and down and caution you not to go much farther than the roped-off third pool. Access is by car or bus only (at certain times of the year) from early June to early November. ✉ *Onnebetsumara, Shiretoko* ⊕ *www.shiretoko.asia/world/kamuiwakka.html.*

### Mt. Rausu (羅臼岳; *Rausu-dake*)

**MOUNTAIN** | Towering 5,448 feet along the spine of the peninsula, Mt. Rausu is snow-covered from October to June. The most accessible trailhead is 5 km (3 miles) east of Utoro behind the Hotel Chi-no-hate; if you are a fast hiker, you can walk for one hour, 20 minutes to a 1,920-foot rocky outcrop, then another two hours to the top. From there trails head west (two hours) to meet the Utoro-Rausu highway at Shiretoko Pass, or go over the ridge and down to Rausu (three hours). Check weather conditions before hiking, sign the trailhead books, and fix a bear bell to your backpack.

Aching muscles can be soaked in open-air hot springs waiting at the end of the hike: Iwaobetsu Onsen, just below the Hotel Chi-no-hate parking lot, has four steaming rocky pools. Near the trailhead and campsite on the Rausu side, look for Kuma-no-yu, two boiling pools areas for men and women separated by some unfortunate concrete and rusty pipes, but fenced in for privacy. ✉ *Yunosawacho, Shiretoko.*

Kamuiwakka Onsen is filled by a series of waterfalls.

### ★ Shiretoko Five Lakes
(知床五湖; *Shiretoko Goko*)

**BODY OF WATER** | **FAMILY** | A stop for every tour bus route in the region, this collection of small lakes sits on a forested precipice above the ocean. It takes just over an hour to walk around all five lakes on boardwalk paths, and there are some newer boardwalks for the city slickers who don't want to get their shoes dusty. The lakes are lovely reflecting pools for the mountains, but crowds do disturb the idyll a bit. Luckily, most tour groups only circle the first two lakes. Park at the Nature Center, and get bus tickets for the 20-minute drive Shiretoko Goko and beyond. Guided tours off the boardwalk paths are also available depending on the season. Check their website for available guides. During certain times (bear season or times when the ecosystem is particularly sensitive), you might have to pay for a guide or pay to attend a lecture before setting out. ⊠ *Shiretoko Goko Park Service Center, Shiretoko* ☏ *0152/24–2125 Shiretoko Shari Tourist Association* ⊕ *www. shiretoko.asia/world/shiretoko_goko.html* ⊠ *¥500 per car for parking.*

### ★ Shiretoko National Park Nature Center
(知床自然センター; *Shiretoko Shizen Center*)

**VISITOR CENTER** | Crowds swarm to this nature center for film screenings, souvenir shopping, and dining, but you might be more interested in the latest information about animal sightings. The mile-long trail behind the center offers a peaceful trek to the Furepe Waterfall that's even better because the day-trippers hardly venture here. Bears have been spotted on this trail in the early morning. The Nature Center is about 4 km (2 miles) from Utoro. ⊠ *531 Iwaobetsu, Utoro, Shari* ☏ *0152/24–2114* ⊕ *center.shiretoko. or.jp* ⊠ *Center free; film screenings ¥600.*

##  Hotels

**Iruka Hotel** (いるかホテル)

**$$** | **HOTEL** | Owned by a diver–wildlife photographer (*iruka* means dolphin), this well-kept guesthouse sits by the water in Utoro. **Pros:** personal welcome; great food; nature-spotting advice. **Cons:** small rooms; not much to do nearby; slow to respond to email reservation inquiries. $ *Rooms from: ¥15,000* ⊠ *Utoro Nishi 5, Shari, Shiretoko* ☎ *0152/24–2888* ⊕ *www.iruka-hotel.com* ⤳ *13 rooms* ⦿ *No Meals.*

**Shiretoko Daiichi Hotel** (知床第一ホテル) **$$$$ | RESORT | FAMILY |** Plush interiors, hot-spring baths, pool, play area for kids, excellent dining options—as far as Japanese resort hotels go, it doesn't get much better than this. **Pros:** luxurious digs; best place for sunset view; delicious dining. **Cons:** nature can oddly feel a bit distant; tour group frenzy in the lobby; Western rooms are plain and boxy. $ *Rooms from: ¥39,900* ⊠ *306 Utoro Onsen, Shari* ☎ *0152/24–2334* ⊕ *www shiretoko-1.com/en* ⤳ *199 rooms* ⦿ *Free Breakfast.*

# Akan National Park (阿寒国立公園)

*58 km (36 miles) southeast of Abashiri.*

This national park is sometimes overlooked in favor of Daisetsuzan and Shiretoko, but offers great fishing, hiking, and wildlife-watching opportunities.

## GETTING HERE AND AROUND
There are about three buses (75 minutes, ¥2,750) a day to Akanko from Kushiro Station via Kushiro Airport. You can also catch a bus from Akanko to Abashiri if you change buses in Bihoro. Two buses a day also connects Akan to Soun-kyo.

## TOURS
Akan Bus Co. (⊕ *akanbus.co.jp/foreign/ en*) has escorted bus tours (in Japanese only) from May to the end of October, departing from Kushiro Station for Akanko, Lake Mashuko, and Kawayu Onsen. Since there are so few options to see this part of Japan, such tours may be unavoidable for those who don't want to drive themselves. Reservations are required.

## Smelt Fishing

In winter, fishermen crouch in subzero temperatures to hook *wakasagi* (pond smelt) from the depths of Lake Akan. Visitors can slide across the lake and try their luck, fortified with *amasaké*, a delicious—and slightly alcoholic— drink made from sweetened brown rice. The successful can head back to the shore, where stall holders are on hand to mince the catch for a raw meal or fry or grill it. Wakasagi fishing costs ¥1,500 per person at Ice Land Akan, including a chair and your own personal ice hole.

Wildlife-expedition leader Dr. Mark Brazil literally wrote the book(s) on discovering Japanese wildlife from Western Okinawa to Eastern Hokkaido. Based near Teshikaga Town inside the Akan-Mashu National Park he can be hired for individual or group tours of Hokkaido from a day to a week or more. Contact Japan Nature Guides (⊕ *www.japannatureguides. com* ✉ *enquiries@japannatureguides. com*) to discuss rates and availability.

## ⊙ Sights

**Akan International Crane Center** (阿寒国際 ツル・センター; *Akan Kokusai Tsuru Senta*) **WILDLIFE REFUGE | FAMILY |** In the middle of winter, Akan International Crane Center is one of the key locations for viewing the stately red crowned cranes. The museum teachers visitors about the anatomy of the cranes, their courtship behaviors, and the kindness of Yamazaki-san who began feeding corn to cranes in winter and helped their population grow. The center is 60 minutes from Kushiro Station by bus. ⊠ *23–36 Akan-cho, Shiretoko* ☎ *0154/66–4011* ⊕ *aiccgrus.wixsite.com/ aiccgrus/english-page* ✑ *¥470.*

Smelt-fishing through holes chopped in the ice is a popular wintertime activity at Lake Akan.

**Akan-Mashu National Park** (阿寒摩周国立公園; *Akan-Mashu Kokuritsu Koen*)
**NATIONAL PARK** | Volcanoes rise from primeval forests and lakeside beaches bubble with hot springs in this national park, unfairly overshadowed by neighboring Daisetsu and Shiretoko. In Akan's northern forests, strange, cylindrical algae called *marimo* bob to the surface of the namesake lake. Elsewhere Ainu men pluck and blow eerie music from traditional instruments, while women dancers duck and weave in honor of the red-crested *tancho* white cranes that fly in every winter, breeding on the wetland on the park's southern border. In summer it's a hiker's heaven of trails and hot springs; in winter the lakes freeze over and ice festivals spill out onto the frozen expanses. ⊠ *2–6–20 Akanko Onsen, Akan-cho, Akan National Park* ☎ *0154/67–3200* ⊕ *en.kushiro-lakeakan.com.*

**Akanko Onsen** (阿寒湖温泉)
**TOWN** | A major stop on bus tours, this small town on the lakeshore has giant hotels blocking the views from the main road. Kitschy souvenir shops sell endless rows of carved Ainu-style bears, and bottles of marimo algae balls line the shelves. At the western end of the town is the one cobbled street of the Ainu village, lined by shops and restaurants and home to a small museum and a performance center. ⊠ *Ankanko Onsen, Akan National Park* ⊕ *en.kushiro-lakeakan.com.*

**Lake Akan** (阿寒湖; *Akan-ko*)
**BODY OF WATER** | Out on Churui Island, silence is green among Akanko's strangest inhabitants, marimo, as they nestle peacefully in display tanks. Marimo are spherical colonies of green algae that may be as small as a ping-pong ball or as large as a soccer ball (the latter taking up to 500 years to form). Rare life forms, marimo can only be found in Lake

Yamanaka, near Fuji-san, and in a few lakes in North America, Siberia, and Switzerland. These strange algae act much like submarines, bobbing to the lake surface when bright sunshine increases their photosynthesis, then diving below during inclement weather when light levels drop. Nearby shops offer them in bottles.

Northeast of Lake Akan you will find Lake Kussharo the largest caldera lake in Japan. In winter, hot springs keep sections of the lake free of ice, and these steamy areas attract large numbers of whooper swans. Sunayu, on the east edge of the lake, is the best place to find the swans in winter. You can even strip off and enjoy the hot spring waters at several outdoor onsen along on the lakeshore. ✉ *Ankanko Onsen, Akan-cho, Kushiro* 🌐 *en.kushiro-lakeakan.com.*

## Hotels

**Onsen Minshuku Yamaguchi**
(温泉民宿 山口)
**$ | B&B/INN** | A warm welcome is assured when you enter this small home, which is just past the Ainu village end of the town. **Pros:** good value; friendly service; great food. **Cons:** no lake views; no private baths; well-worn rooms with thin walls. [$] *Rooms from: ¥10,900* ✉ *5–3–2 Akanko Onsen, Akan-gun* ☎ *0154/67–2555* 🌐 *en.kushiro-lakeakan.com/stay/4502* 💳 *No credit cards* 🛏 *10 rooms* 🍴 *No Meals.*

## Performing Arts

**Lake Akan Ainu Theater Ikor** (阿寒湖アイヌコタン; *Akan-ko Ainu Kotan*)
**FOLK/TRADITIONAL DANCE | FAMILY** | From late April to November there are excellent traditional dance performances such as "The Epic Story of the Fire God." Unfortunately, the puppet theatre is only available for group bookings and doesn't have daily performances for general visitors. The venue's seating faces a wall that's open to the outside, which gives the performances a dynamic natural background. During the day, there are also craft workshops available. ✉ *4–7–84 Akanko Onsen, Akan-cho, Kushiro* ☎ *0154/67–2727* 🌐 *www.akanainu.jp* 🎟 *Performances ¥2,000.*

## Activities

**Akan Nature Center**
(阿寒ネイチャーセンター)
**BOATING** | Between May and October you can enjoy the lake from a canoe with the help of the Akan Nature Center, which offers two- or eight-person Canadian canoes for a 45-minute beginner course, a two-hour adventure course, or a three-hour early morning private tour. Reserve at least one day in advance. The center is in Akanko Han, near the Ainu village and next to Onsen Minshuku Yamaguchi on the north end of the main town street. Ask about their camping and mountain climbing trips, as well. If you are impervious to cold, it also has winter snowshoeing programs. Staff have limited English. ✉ *5–3–3 Akanko Onsen, Akan-cho, Akan National Park* ☎ *0154/67–2801* 🌐 *akan.co.jp* 🎟 *From ¥2,100.*

**Ice Land Akan** (あいすランド阿寒)
**ICE-SKATING | FAMILY** | Between January and March, Ice Land (which becomes Fishing Land from May through November) occupies the southern corner of Lake Akan and is used for a variety of outdoor activities such as ice-skating, Nordic skiing, snowmobiling, and ice fishing; activities are run by the tourist agency Koudai. There are four access points to Ice Land from around the hot spring area: one on either side of Hotel Gozensui (the access point on the

western side is the dock used during fishing season), one through an outdoor passage under the New Akan Hotel, and one just to the northeast of Akan no Mori Tsuruga Resort Hanayuuka. ⊠ *Akanko Onsen 2, Akan-cho, Kushiro* ☎ *0154/67–2057* ⊕ *www.koudai-akan.com* 💰 *From ¥1,000.*

# Kushiro-Shitsugen National Park (釧路湿原国立公園)

Graceful red-crested cranes preen and breed in protected Kushiro Wetlands, which constitutes 60% of Japan's remaining marshes. These rare cranes, whose feathers were thought to bring good luck, were ruthlessly hunted at the beginning of the 20th century and were even believed to be extinct until a handful of survivors were discovered in 1924. They now number about 650. The crane—long-legged and long-billed, with a white body trimmed in black and a scarlet cap—is a symbol of long life and happiness. Legends hold that the birds live 1,000 years, and indeed, in captivity some have made it to a rather impressive 80 years of age. They pair for life, making them the symbol of an ideal couple and are frequently seen decorating bridal kimonos.

November to March is the best season for wild-crane watching. This is when the birds fly in from Russia, China, and Korea and gather at feeding stations such as Tsurumidai, off Route 53. In summer, nesting birds retreat deep into the swamps to raise their chicks and can only be spotted with binoculars.

Canoe paddlers on the Kushiro River have a chance to see cranes and other birds: canoe rental companies are at Lake Toro, off Route 391, and by the Norroko-go, a slow sightseeing train from Kushiro (July and August only). The marshland comprises 71 square miles and viewing areas with wooden walkways and observation towers are located off Routes 53 and 359.

##  Activities

### Tsurui Ito Tancho Sanctuary
(鶴居・伊藤タンチョウサンクチュアリ)
**BIRD WATCHING | FAMILY |** Established by Wild Bird Society of Japan, the Tsurui Ito Tancho Sanctuary is possibly the best and easiest place to photograph the red-crowned cranes in winter. You'll want to bring a long telephoto lens with you, and wrap up warm because it can be bitterly cold. A small nature centre overlooks the field where the cranes gather, you can warm up, grab a hot drink, and learn more about the local flora and fauna. Wildlife tours such as those led by Dr. Mark Brazil (*see Akan National Park*) often visit here in winter. ⊠ *Aza Naka-setsuri Minami, Tsurui-mura, Akan-gun* ☎ *0154/64–2620* ⊕ *www.wbsj.org/en/tsurui* 💰 *Free* ⊙ *Close Apr.–Sept. Closed Tues. and Wed.*

### GETTING HERE AND AROUND
Kushiro City can be accessed by limited express train from Sapporo in four hours (¥9,460). Buses from Sapporo take around 5½ hours. Direct flights from Sapporo, Tokyo, Osaka, and Nagoya arrive at Tancho Kushiro Airport. Shuttle buses from the airport to the Kushiro city center are scheduled to depart shortly after the arrival of incoming planes (45 minutes, ¥950).

# Index

## A

**Abashiri,** *714, 747–749*
**Abashiri Prison Museum,** *748*
**A-Bomb Dome,** *533, 538, 540*
**A-bombed Gravestone,** *538*
**Ad Museum Tokyo,** *166*
**Adachi Museum of Art,** *554*
**Adashino Nembutsu-ji Temple,** *445*
**Addresses,** *58*
**Ainu theater,** *755*
**Aioibashi Bridge,** *538*
**Air Station Futenma,** *634*
**Air travel and airports,** *48–50, 68*
*Hokkaido, 714*
*Japan Alps and the North Chubu Coast, 341*
*Kansai region, 463*
*Kobe, 503–504*
*Kyoto, 385*
*Kyushu, 605*
*Nagoya, Ise-Shima, and the Kii Peninsula, 307–308*
*Nara, 489*
*Osaka, 466*
*Shikoku, 563*
*Tokyo, 132–133*
*Western Honshu, 526*
**Akan International Crane Center,** *753*
**Akan-Mashu National Park,** *714, 753–754*
**Akan National Park,** *753–755*
**Akanko Onsen,** *754*
**Akechi-daira Ropeway,** *299*
**Akihabara (Tokyo),** *207 210*
**Akita,** *701–704*
**Akita City Folklore and Performing Arts Center,** *702–703*
**Akita Kawabata Isariya Sakaba** ✕, *703*
**Akita Museum of Art,** *703*
**Akiyoshido Cave,** *540*
**Aman Kyoto** 🔲, *443*
**Aman Tokyo** 🔲, *144–145*
**Amanoiwato Shrine,** *626*
**Amano-Yasugawara Cave,** *626*
**Amerika-mura** (Osaka), *479*
**Ameya Yokocho Market Street** (Tokyo), *211*
**Amusement parks and centers,** *219, 227, 230, 248, 274, 293, 313–314, 472–473, 507*
**ANA Crowne Plaza Hotel Kobe** 🔲, *516–517*
**ANA Intercontinental Ishigaki Resort** 🔲, *659–660*
**Andaz Tokyo Toranomon Hills** 🔲, *144*
**Ando House** (shop), *692*
**Andy's Shin Hinomoto** ✕, *144*
**Anime,** *109*
**Anraku-ji Temple,** *391*

**Antique Nanae** (shop), *518*
**Antiques,** *171, 414, 415, 431, 518, 736*
**Aomori,** *698–701*
**Aomori Museum of Art,** *698, 700*
**Aoyagi Samurai Manor Museum,** *693*
**Aoyama and Harajuku** (Tokyo), *169–178*
**Aquariums.** ⇨ *See Zoos and aquariums*
**Aragawa** ✕, *508, 515*
**Arashiyama,** *443–449*
**Arashiyama Monkey Park,** *445*
**Archaeological sites,** *700*
**Architecture,** *338–339*
**Arimatsu-Narumi Tie-Dyeing Museum,** *313*
**Art House Project,** *577*
**Artejio Museum,** *623–624*
**Artizon Museum,** *150*
**Arts.** ⇨ *See Nightlife and the arts*
**Asahikawa,** *713*
**Asahiyama Zoo,** *33*
**Asakusa** (Tokyo), *218–226*
**Asakusa Jinja Shrine,** *219*
**Aso Volcano Museum,** *620*
**Aso-san (Mt. Aso),** *619–621*
**Atagawa,** *204*
**Atami,** *282–283*
**Atami Plum Garden,** *282*
**ATMs,** *61*
**Atomic Bomb Dome,** *533, 538, 540*
**Atomic Memorial Mound,** *538*
**Atsuta Shrine,** *313*
**Auga Market,** *700*
**Awa Odori** (festival), *580*
**Awa Odori Kaikan,** *582*
**Azuma-ya Soba** ✕, *680*

## B

**Baird Beer Taproom Harajuku** ✕, *176*
**Bamboo Forest,** *445*
**Banks,** *61*
**Bars**
*Kyoto, 430*
*Matsumoto, 354*
*Matsuyama, 595–596*
*Nagoya, 318*
*Osaka, 477, 487*
*Sapporo, 731–732*
*Takayama, 363*
*Tokyo, 149, 156, 160, 166, 170, 181, 191, 201–203, 224–225*
**Baseball,** *110–111, 318, 478*
**Bashamichi Street** (Yokohama), *241–242*
**Beaches,** *286, 590, 629–630, 652–653, 655–656, 659*
**Beams** (shops), *177–178*
**Beer halls and pubs,** *156, 184, 224–225, 354, 371, 430, 518, 722, 726, 728*
**Belfry** (Asakusa), *223*
**Bento,** *92*
**Beverages,** *93*
**Bicycling,** *64, 568, 599–600, 736*
**Boat and ferry travel,** *50, 68*
*Hokkaido, 714–715*

*Shikoku, 563*
*Western Honshu, 527*
**Boat tours**
*Abashiri, 749*
*Akan National Park, 755*
*Gifu, 319–320*
*Izu Peninsula, 281, 288*
*Okinawa, 663*
*Sado Island, 379–380*
*Shingu, 330*
*Shiretoko National Park, 750–751*
*Tokyo, 165*
*Tokushima, 581*
**Bokumen Art Museum,** *648*
**Books and movies about Japan,** *34–35*
**Bookstores,** *149, 152, 186, 204*
**Boraga Beach,** *655*
**Botanic Garden Hokkaido University,** *726*
**Breweries,** *376, 508, 576, 580*
**Buddhism,** *123–126, 263, 501*
**Bunraku theater,** *101, 487*
**Bus travel,** *51, 68*
*Hokkaido, 715*
*Japan Alps and the North Chubu Coast, 341*
*Kansai region, 463*
*Kyoto, 385*
*Kyushu, 605*
*Nagoya, Ise-Shima, and the Kii Peninsula, 308*
*Nara, 489*
*Shikoku, 563*
*Tohoku, 669–670*
*Western Honshu, 527*
**Byodo-in Temple,** *434–435*

## C

**Calligraphy,** *95–96*
**Canal cruises,** *736*
**Candy shops,** *646*
**Cape Higashi-Hennazaki,** *654*
**Cape Maeda,** *648*
**Cape Zanpa Park,** *648*
**Car rental and travel,** *51–52, 68*
*Hokkaido, 715 716*
*Japan Alps and the North Chubu Coast, 341*
*Kyushu, 605*
*Nagoya, Ise-Shima, and the Kii Peninsula, 308*
*Shikoku, 563–564*
*Tohoku, 670*
*Western Honshu, 527*
**Cemeteries,** *139, 248, 333*
**Cenotaph,** *538, 542–543*
**Central Kyoto,** *417–434*
**Central Nara,** *492*
**Central Okinawa,** *648–649*
**Central Shikoku,** *562*
**Ceramics,** *96–97, 171, 195, 414–415, 416, 510–511, 518*
**Chichu Art Museum,** *577–578*
**Chidorigafuchi National Cemetery,** *139*
**Chiiori House** 🔲, *585, 586*
**Chikurin-ji Temple,** *590*

Children, travel with, *32–33*
Children's Peace Monument, *533, 538*
Chinatown (Kobe), *506*
Chinatown (Yokohama), *242*
Chindami Sanshinten (shop), *640*
Chinese Parasol Tree, *539*
Chion-in Temple, *394*
Chishaku-in Temple, *394*
Choraku-ji Temple, *394*
Chosho-ji Temple, *696*
Christians, *435*
Chugen Mantoro (Midyear Lantern Festival), *494*
Chugu-ji Temple, *500*
Churches, *207, 614, 719*
Chuson-ji Temple, *686*
Chuzenji Temple, *299, 301*
Chuzenji-ko, *299–302*
Cicada ✕, *177*
Climate, *53*
Climbing, *270–271*
Clothing, *157, 171, 174, 177–178, 195, 225–226, 433, 596*
Comme des Garçons (shop), *174*
Confucius Shrine and Museum, *611*
Consulates, *59, 69*
Contacts, *69.* ⇨ *See also Visitor information*
Convenience stores, *130–131*
Crafts, *28–29, 94–97, 174, 204, 209, 226, 361, 405, 415, 416, 417, 431–433, 470, 492, 509–514, 531, 597, 619, 640, 642, 678, 692*
Credit cards, *61–62*
Cruises, *736.* ⇨ *See also Boat tours*
Cuisine, *24–25, 85–93, 182, 347, 411, 473, 515, 671, 680, 721*
Culture, *84–126*
Cup Noodles Museum Yokohama, *242*

**D**

Daibutsu (Great Buddha), *495–497*
Daigo-ji Temple, *435*
Daikanyama T-Site (shop), *186*
Dai-mon Gate, *332*
Daio, *329*
Daio Wasabi Farm, *351, 353*
Daisekirinzan (park), *649*
Daisen-in (garden), *438, 440*
Daisetsuzan National Park, *744–746*
Daitoku-ji Temple, *407, 438*
Dance, *387, 431, 755*
Dance clubs, *184, 318*
Deer, *458–459, 493*
Dejima (Nagasaki), *611*
Dembo-in Temple, *219*
Department stores, *152, 157–158, 162–163, 204–206, 431, 477–478, 487, 609*

Depato, *162–163*
Dewa-Sanzan, *704–706*
Dining, *32, 58–59, 82.* ⇨ *See also Restaurants under specific cities*
prices, *137, 238, 310, 342, 388, 465, 528, 565, 606, 638, 671, 717*
Disk Union (shop), *206*
Diving, *64, 648, 651, 657, 660–661, 663*
Dogashima, *287–288*
Dogo Onsen Bathhouse, *592*
Dogsledding, *710*
Dolls, *210, 248, 415, 416, 512, 518, 678*
Domannaka (festival), *309*
Doro-kyo, *330*
Dotombori (Osaka), *479*
Dover Street Market (Tokyo), *157*
Downtown Kamakura, *256–259*
Downtown Kobe, *506–508, 515–518*
Downtown Kochi, *588–589*
Dutch Slope (Nagasaki), *611*

**E**

East Hongan-ji Temple, *417*
Eastern Kyoto, *391–417*
Eastern Shikoku, *562*
Ecotours, *64–65*
Edo Wonderland (theme park), *293*
Ehime Museum of Art, *593*
Eikan-do (Zenrin-ji) Temple, *394–395*
Electronics, *158, 206, 210, 478*
Embassies and consulates, *59, 69*
Emergencies, *52*
Engaku-ji Temple, *253*
English House, *519*
Enno-ji Temple, *253*
Enoshima (island), *259–260*
Enryaku-ji Temple, *449*
Etiquette and behavior, *70–71, 87, 104–105, 107, 287*

**F**

Fans, *416*
Farm Tomita, *747*
Ferry travel.* ⇨ *See Boat and ferry travel*
Festivals and national holidays, *80–81, 125*
Hokkaido, *724, 733*
Japan Alps and the North Chubu Coast, *343*
Kansai region, *459, 494*
Kyoto, *402*
Nagoya, Ise-Shima, and the Kii Peninsula, *309*
Nara, *494*
Shikoku, *588*
Tohoku, *674, 687, 695, 702*
Tokyo, *140, 221*
Film, *148–149, 186*
Fire Festivals, *494*

Fishing, *753*
5 Days Children's Museum, *533*
Five-Story Pagoda, *545*
Flame of Peace, *533, 535, 538*
Food shops, *152, 225, 616, 692*
Former Residence of Ogai Mori, *551*
Four Seasons Hotel Tokyo at Marunouchi 🏨, *145*
Fuji Go-ko (Fuji Five Lakes), *236–237, 265, 274–275*
Fuji-Hakone-Izu National Park, *269*
Fuji-Q Highland, *274*
Fuji-san (Mt. Fuji), *236, 263, 265, 266–273*
Fukuoka, *606–609*
Fuku-ura Island, *682–693*
Furano, *711, 713, 746–747*
Furano Ski Resort, *747*
Fushimi-Inari Shrine, *435*
Futarasan-jinja shrine, *293*

**G**

Gardens and parks, *120–121*
Hokkaido, *713, 714, 726, 728, 744–746, 749–756*
Izu Peninsula, *282, 285*
Japan Alps and the North Chubu Coast, *344, 356, 367–368*
Kobe, *507*
Kyoto, *395, 397, 406–407, 408, 438, 440, 442, 445, 447, 452*
Kyushu, *607, 611, 613, 614, 618, 627–628*
Nagoya, Ise-Shima, and the Kii Peninsula, *307, 314–315*
Okinawa, *635, 648, 649*
Osaka, *469–470, 471, 479, 483*
Shikoku, *568, 590*
Tohoku, *680, 694–695*
Tokyo *139–140, 166, 168, 176, 197*
Tokyo side trips, *269*
Western Honshu, *529, 535, 536–539, 543, 546, 549–550*
Yokohama, *242, 246, 247*
Gassho-Zukuri Farmhouses, *338–339*
Gassho-zukuri Minkaen Outdoor Museum, *364*
Gate Hotel Asakusa Kaminarimon by HULIC 🏨, *224*
Gay bars, *202*
Geibikei Gorge, *686*
Geisha, *116–117, 397*
Gekkeikan Okura Sake Museum, *437*
Ghibli Park, *314*
Gifu, *307, 319–322*
Gifu Castle, *320*
Gifu City Museum of History, *320*
Ginkaku-ji Temple, *395*
Ginza (Tokyo), *153–158, 164*
Ginza Natsuno (shop), *174*
Ginzan Onsen (Yamadera), *684*
Ginzan Onsen (Yamagata), *688*
Gion, *397*

Gion Corner Theater, *414*
Giro Giro Hitoshina ✕ , *424*
Glover Garden, *611, 613*
Godaido Temple, *683*
Gohoten-do (shrine), *293*
Golf, *65, 733*
Gora, *277*
Grand Shrines of Ise, *325, 327*
Grass-Burning Festival, *494*
Great Buddha statue (Hase), *261*
Great Buddha statue (Nara), *495–497*
Great Hanshin-Awaji Earthquake Memorial, *506–507*
Greater Tokyo, *226–232*
Guided tours, *63–65.* ⇨ *See also under specific cities*
Gyokusen Garden, *367*

**H**

Hachiko, statue of, *179*
Hadaka (Naked) Festival, *309*
Hagi, *548–550*
Hagi Tamachi Shopping Arcade, *549*
Hakata Salt Company Omishima Factory, *598–599*
Hakodate, *713, 718–722*
Hakodate Morning Market, *719*
Hakodate Museum of Northern Peoples, *748*
Hakodate Orthodox Church, *719*
Hakone, *237, 275–280*
Hakone Checkpoint Museum, *279*
Hakone Free Pass, *275*
Hakone Kowakien Yunessun, *277*
Hakone Museum of Art, *277–278*
Hakone Open-Air Museum, *278*
Hakone Ropeway, *278–279*
Hakuba, *354–357*
Hakusa Son-so Garden, *395, 397*
Hakutsuru Sake Brewery Museum, *507*
Hall of Awa Japanese Handmade Paper, *582*
Hama Rikyu Garden, *166, 168*
Hanagasa Festival, *687*
Hanamaki Onsenkyo, *679*
Hanayashiki (amusement park), *219*
Happo-one Ski Resort, *355–356*
Happy Raft, *588*
Harajuku (Tokyo), *169–170, 175–178*
Harbor View Park, *242*
Harborland and Meriken Park, *507*
Harimaya Bridge, *588*
Hase, *259–263*
Hase-dera Temple, *260–261*
Hashima Island, *613*
Hatsu-shima Island, *282*
Hattori Ryokuchi Park, *469–470*
Hayatama Shrine, *329*

Health, *32, 59–60*
Heian Jingu Shrine, *397, 407*
Hell Valley, *743*
Henro, *569–573*
Hida Folk Village, *360*
Higashi Chaya District (Kanazawa), *367*
*Hikawa-maru* (ship), *242*
Hiking, *65, 272, 323, 359–360, 663, 738, 746*
Himejo, *520–522*
Himeji Castle, *521–522*
Himeyuri Peace Museum, *635, 646–647*
Hinabita Onsen, *691*
Hiraizumi, *685–686*
Hirano Shrine, *440*
Hirara City, *654–657*
Hirashimizu Pottery Village, *688*
Hirosaki, *695–698*
Hirosaki Castle, *696–697*
Hiroshi Sugimoto Gallery: Time Corridors, *578*
Hiroshima, *532–544*
Hiroshima Castle, *535, 542*
Hiroshima National Peace Memorial Hall for the Atomic Bomb Victims, *539, 542*
Hiroshima Peace Memorial Museum, *542*
Hiroshima Prefectural Art Museum, *542*
Historical Village of Hokkaido, *726–727*
History of Japan, *39–44, 115, 258, 277, 297, 390, 405, 467, 501, 572, 613*
Hufuku-ji Temple, *285–286*
Hokkaido, *23, 708–756*
cuisine, *721*
festivals, *724, 733*
guided tours, *749, 750–751, 753, 755*
lodging, *716–717, 722, 730–731, 735–736, 738, 742–744, 746, 749, 752–753, 755*
money matters, *717*
nightlife and the arts, *722, 731–732, 755*
outdoor activities and sports, *710–711, 733, 736, 738–741, 746, 747, 749, 753, 755, 756*
prices, *717*
restaurants, *717–718, 721–722, 729–730, 735, 737–738, 742, 748–749*
shopping, *719, 732, 736*
timing the visit, *717, 718*
transportation, *714–716*
visitor information, *718*
Hokkaido-jingu Shrine, *727*
Hokkaido Museum, *727–728*
Hokoku-ji Temple, *256–257*
Hondori Shopping Street (Hiroshima), *542*
Honen Festival, *309*
Honen-in Temple, *397, 404*
Hongu Shrine, *330*

Hoon-ji Temple, *680*
Horiuchi (Hagi), *549*
Horyu-ji Temple, *500–501*
Hot springs. ⇨ *See Onsen (thermal baths)*
Hotel Benesse House 🏨 , *579*
Hotel Granvia Kyoto 🏨 , *426–427*
Hotel Ryumeikan Tokyo 🏨 , *151*
Hotels
prices, *135, 238, 310, 342, 386, 465, 528, 565, 606, 638, 671, 717*
Housewares, *186–187, 415, 434, 678*
Hyatt Regency Kyoto 🏨 , *413*
Hyuka-man-goku Matsuri (festival), *343*
Hyogo Prefectural Museum of Art, *507*

**I**

Ibusuki Sunamushi Onsen Natural Sand Bath, *629–630*
Ice-skating, *755*
Idemitsu Museum of Art, *143*
Ieyasu Tokugawa, *297*
Iga Ueno, *307, 324*
Iga Ueno Castle, *324*
Iga-Ryu Ninja Museum, *324*
Ikeda 20th-Century Art Museum, *284*
Ikema Island, *654–655*
Ikuta Shrine, *507*
Imayo Tsukasa Sake Brewery, *376*
Immunizations, *60*
Imperial Hotel 🏨 , *359*
Imperial Palace (Tokyo), *138–142*
Imperial Palace East Garden, *139–140*
Imperial Palace Outer Garden, *140*
Inakaya East ✕ , *191*
Incense, *433*
InterContinental Osaka 🏨 , *477*
Internet, *60, 69*
Inuyama, *307, 322–323*
Inuyama Castle, *322*
Irabu Island, *655*
Iriomote-jima, *661–664*
Ironwork, *680*
Isamu Noguchi Garden Museum, *567*
Ise, *324–328*
Ise-Shima National Park, *20, 307.* ⇨ *See also Nagoya, Ise-Shima, and the Kii Peninsula*
Iseyama Kodai Jingu Shrine, *242–243*
Ishigaki-jima, *657, 659–661*
Ishiguro Samurai House, *693*
Ishikawa Local Products Center, *367*
Ishikawa Prefectural Museum of Art, *367*
Ishite-ji Temple, *593–594*
Issey Miyake (shop), *174*
Isshin-ji Temple, *479*

Itami Juzo Memorial Museum, *594*
Itineraries, *72–79*
Ito, *283–285*
Itsukushima Shrine, *545*
Iwakuni, *547–548*
Iwakuni Castle, *547*
Iwate Park, *680*
Iya Onsen 🏨, *586*
Iya Valley and Oboke-Koboke Gorges, *583–586*
Izakaya, *184, 185*
Izu Peninsula, *237, 280–288*
Izu Shaboten Zoo, *284*
Izumo Taisha (shrine), *557–558*

**J**

Jakko Falls, *301*
Jakko-in Temple, *451*
Japan Alps and the North Chubu Coast, *21, 336–380*
cuisine, *347*
festivals, *343*
guided tours, *378, 379–380*
lodging, *342, 345, 348, 349, 353–354, 356–357, 358, 359, 363, 370–371, 374, 377, 380*
nightlife and the arts, *354, 363, 371*
outdoor activities and sports, *355–356, 359–360*
prices, *342*
restaurants, *342, 344, 348, 353, 362, 369–370, 373–374, 377, 380*
shopping, *367, 369, 373, 376–377*
timing the visit, *342–343*
transportation, *341, 375*
visitor information, *342*
Japan Folk Crafts Museum Osaka, *470*
Japan Wood-Block Print Museum, *351*
Japanese Navy Underground Head-quarters, *635, 647*
Japanese Sword Museum, *219, 221*
Japanese Wax Museum and Kami-haga Residence, *596–597*
Jazz clubs, *148, 171, 195, 203, 477*
Jewelry, *158, 518*
Jigoku-dani Monkey Park, *348*
Jikko-in Temple, *451*
Jo-an Teahouse, *322*
Jochi-ji Temple, *253, 255*
Jomyo-ji Temple, *257*
J-pop idols, *109*
JR Tower Hotel Nikko Sapporo 🏨, *730*

**K**

Kabuki-cho (Tokyo), *205*
Kabuki theater, *99–100, 149, 156–157, 387, 414, 597*
Kagawa Prefectural Museum, *567–568*

Kagoshima, *628–630*
Kakunodate, *692–693*
Kakunodate Cherry Bark Work Museum, *693*
Kakusho ✕, *362*
Kamakura, *236, 250–263*
Kamakura Great Buddha, *261*
Kamakura Kokuhokan Museum, *257*
Kamakura-gu Shrine, *257*
Kamasada Iron Casting Studio, *680*
Kamigamo Shrine, *451–452*
Kamikochi, *341, 358–360*
Kaminarimon Gate, *221*
Kamuiwakka Onsen, *751*
Kanagawa Prefectural Museum of Cultural History, *243*
Kanazawa, *340, 364–371*
Kanazawa Castle Park, *367*
Kanda Myojin Shrine, *207*
Kanemori Red Brick Warehouses, *720*
Kankaso 🏨, *498*
Kansai region, *21, 456–522.* ⇨ See also Kobe; Nara; Osaka
festivals, *459, 494*
lodging, *464, 468, 476–477, 485–487, 489, 492, 498, 499, 504, 516–517*
nightlife and the arts, *468, 477, 487, 504, 517–518*
outdoor activities and sports, *478–479, 488*
prices, *465*
restaurants, *464, 468, 473, 476, 484–485, 489, 492, 497, 499, 502, 504, 508, 515–516*
shopping, *468–469, 477–478, 487, 492, 499, 504, 506, 518*
timing the visit, *464, 465*
transportation, *463–464*
visitor information, *465, 469, 506*
Kanto Festival, *702*
Kappabashi Kitchenware Street (Tokyo), *221*
Kappo Chiyo ✕, *550*
Karaoke, *185, 195*
Karate, *647*
Karuizawa, *343–344*
Karuizawa Wild Bird Forest, *344*
Kashikojima, *307, 328–329*
Kasuga Shrine, *493*
Katsura Imperial Villa, *445*
Katsurahama Beach, *590*
Kawai Kanjiro Memorial House, *404*
Kawaii, *109*
Kawakyo ✕, *556*
Kawasaki Merchant Warehouses, *327*
Kayaking, *546, 651, 663–664*
Kegon Falls, *301*
Keitaku-en Garden, *479*
Kencho-ji Temple, *255*
Kenroku Garden, *367–368*
Kerama Islands, *652–653*
Kiddy Land (shop), *178*

Kii Peninsula, *20, 307.* ⇨ See also Nagoya, Ise-Shima, and the Kii Peninsula
Kikunoi ✕, *410–411*
Kimonos, *158, 433, 513*
Kinkaku-ji Temple, *440*
Kinryo Sake Museum and Brewery, *580*
Kintaikyo Bridge, *548*
Kirishima Shrine, *627*
Kirishima-Kinkowan National Park, *627–628*
Kiso Valley, *357–358*
Kita (Osaka), *469–479*
Kita-Kamakura, *251–256*
Kitano Tenman-gu Shrine, *440*
Kitano-cho, *519*
Kite Museum, *150*
Kiyomasa Touki (shop), *640, 642*
Kiyomizu-dera Temple, *404*
Kiyomizu Kannon-do Temple, *211–212*
Knives. ⇨ See Swords and knives
Kobaien, *498*
Kobe, *503–520*
cuisine, *515*
Downtown Kobe. *506–508, 515–518*
Kitano-cho, *519*
lodging, *504, 516–517*
nightlife and the arts, *504, 517–518*
north of Kobe, *519–520*
restaurants, *504, 508, 515–516*
shopping, *504, 506, 518*
transportation, *503–504*
visitor information, *506*
Kobe beef, *515*
Kobe City Museum, *507–508*
Kobe Maritime Museum, *508*
Kobe Shu-Shin-Kan Brewery, *508*
Kobo Daishi, *571*
Kochi, *570–571, 586–591*
Kochi Castle, *588*
Kodai-ji Temple, *405*
Kofuku-ji Temple, *493–495*
Koinzan Saiho-ji (temple), *407*
Kokeshi dolls, *678*
Kokubun-ji Temple, *360–361*
Kokusai Street (Okinawa), *642*
Komuroyama Park, *285*
Konchi-in (garden), *407, 408*
Kongobu-ji Temple, *332*
Konpira Shrine, *580*
Korakuen Garden, *529*
Koryu-ji Temple, *446*
Kosetsu Ichiba Market, *642*
Kosho-ji Temple, *437*
Koshi-no-ei (Edo period house), *499*
Kotohira, *579–580*
Koto-in (garden), *440*
Koya-san, *307, 331–334*
Kumamoto, *616–619*
Kumamoto Castle, *617–618*

Kurashiki, 530–532
Kurashiki Museum of Folkcraft, 531
Kurobe Gorge Railway, 375
Kurokawa Onsen, 621–622
Kusakabe Folk Craft Museum, 361
Kusasenri-ga-hama, 620–621
Kusatsu, 344–345
Kushiro Shitsugen National Park, 714, 756
Kushiyaki Ganchan ✕, 191
Kutani Pottery Kiln, 368
Kyoto, 21, 382–454
Arashiyama, 443–449
Central Kyoto, 417–434
children, attractions for, 33
cuisine, 411
Eastern Kyoto, 391–417
festivals, 402
Gion, 397
guided tours, 389
history, 390
lodging, 386, 412–413, 426–428, 443, 448–449, 454
nightlife and the arts, 386–387, 413–414, 430–431
Northern Kyoto, 449–454
Philosopher's Path, 399–403
prices, 386, 388
restaurants, 388, 403, 410–412, 423–426, 442–443, 448, 453–454
shopping, 388–389, 414–417, 431–434
Southern Kyoto, 434–437
timing the visit, 387, 391, 403
transportation, 385–386, 403
visitor information, 389–391
Western Kyoto, 438–443
Kyoto Aquarium, 417
Kyoto Botanical Gardens, 452
Kyoto Brighton Hotel 🛏, 427
Kyoto Imperial Palace, 417, 420
Kyoto International Manga Museum, 420
Kyoto Museum of Crafts and Design, 405
Kyoto National Museum, 406
Kyoto Railway Museum, 420
Kyoto Seishu Netsuke Art Museum, 420
Kyoto Station, 420
Kyoto University Museum, 406
Kyushu, 22, 602–630
history, 613
guided tours, 610
lodging, 605, 608–609, 615, 618–619, 621, 622, 625, 627, 628, 630
nightlife and the arts, 609
prices, 606
restaurants, 606, 608, 614–615, 618, 624, 626–628, 630
shopping, 609, 615–616, 619, 630
timing the visit, 605–606
transportation, 605
visitor information, 606

L

La Baie ✕, 476
Lacquerware, 95, 187, 373, 416, 513, 518
Lafcadio Hearn Former Residence, 554
Lafcadio Hearn Memorial Museum, 554
Lake Akan, 754–755
Lake Ashi, 276
Lake Kawaguchi, 274
Lake Kinrin, 624
Lake Motosu, 274
Lake Saiko, 274
Lake Shinji, 554
Lake Shoji, 274
Lake Tazawa, 699–691
Lake Yamanaka, 274
Lake Yunoko, 301
Landmark Tower, 243
Language, 66–67
Language programs, 65
Lantern Festival, 494
Lavender farms, 747
Lee Ufan Museum, 578
Legoland Japan Resort, 313–314
Lighthouses, 648
Light-up Promenade, 494
Live houses, 185
Lodging, 32, 60–61. ⇨ See also under specific cities
money-saving tips for, 82
prices, 135, 238, 310, 342, 386, 465, 528, 565, 606, 638, 671, 717
ryokan, 106–107, 287
in temples, 61, 69

M

Makino Botanical Garden, 590
Malls and shopping centers, 149, 152, 174–175, 178, 187, 195–196, 247, 248, 478, 518, 549, 575–576, 609, 630, 678, 732
Mandarin Oriental, Tokyo 🛏, 151
Manga, 109, 420, 588
Mankamero ✕, 425
Mantoro (Lantern Festival), 494
Mare Gracia Omishima Baths, 599
Marine Tower, 243
Marishiten Tokudai-ji Temple, 212
Martial arts, 112–113
Markets, 164–165, 168, 211, 369, 373, 417, 434, 589, 642, 700, 719
Marui 0101 Main Building (shop), 205
Marunouchi (Tokyo), 142–149
Maruyama Park, 406
Matsue, 553–557
Matsue Castle, 554–555
Matsue History Museum, 555
Matsumoto, 341, 349–354

Matsumoto Castle, 350–351
Matsumoto City Museum of Art, 351
Matsumoto History Village, 351
Matsushima, 682–684
Matsuya (department store), 157
Matsuyama, 591–596
Matsuyama Castle, 594
Mausoleums, 297, 333, 435, 483–484, 675
Megijima and Ogijima Islands, 574
Meigetsu-in Temple, 255
Meiji Jingu Shrine, 175
Meiji-mura Museum, 322–323
Meimei-an Tea House, 556
Memorial Cenotaph, 538, 542–543
Memorial Tower for Mobilized Students, 539
Meriken Park, 507
Mido-suji Boulevard (Osaka), 482
Midyear Lantern Festival, 494
Miho Museum, 452
Mikimoto Ginza Main Store, 158
Mikimoto Pearl Museum, 327
Minami (Usaka), 479–488
Minamoto Yoritomo's tomb, 257–258
Minato Mirai 21 (Yokohama), 243
Miroku-in Temple, 406
Mitsubishi Minatomirai Industrial Museum, 246
Mitsuke Island, 372
Mitsuke-ji Temple, 372
Mitsukoshi Main Store, 152
Miyajima, 544–546
Miyako Islands, 653–657
Miyakojima Tokyu Hotel & Resorts 🛏, 657
Miyanoshita, 279
Mizuna ✕, 484
MOA Museum of Art, 282
Momijidani Park, 546
Money matters, 61–62, 82, 275, 717
Monozukuri, 509–514
Monument dedicated to Sankichi Toge, 539
Monument for the Korean A-Bomb Victims, 538
Mori Art Museum, 188
Morioka, 678–682
Motomachi Historic Area (Hakodate), 720–721
Moto-machi (Yokohama), 246
Motsu-ji Temple, 686
Mt. Asama Overlook, 344
Mt. Aso, 619–621
Mt. Fuji, 236, 263, 265, 266–273
Mt. Gas-san, 705
Mt. Haguro, 705–706
Mt. Hakodate Observatory, 720
Mt. Inasa Observatory, 613
Mt. Rausu, 751

**Mt. Rokko,** *519–520*
**Mt. Shirouma,** *356*
**Mt. Soun,** *279*
**Mt. Takachiho,** *627*
**Mt. Takao,** *237, 289–290*
**Mt. Tenjo,** *274*
**Muji** (department store), *157*
**Murin-an Garden,** *406–407*
**Muroto Cape,** *590*
**Museum of Modern Art, Kamakura Annex,** *258*
**Museums and galleries**
Hakone, *277–278, 279*
Hokkaido, *726–729, 743, 744, 748, 753*
Izu Peninsula, *282, 284*
Japan Alps and the North Chubu Coast, *351, 353, 360, 361, 362, 364, 367, 369, 373, 376*
Kamakura, *257, 258*
Kobe, *507–508*
Kyoto, *404, 405–406, 408–409, 420, 422, 437, 452*
Kyushu, *611, 613–614, 620, 623–624*
Nagoya, Ise-Shima, and the Kii Peninsula, *313, 314, 315–316, 320, 322–323, 324, 327, 333*
Nara, *495, 499*
Nikko, *293*
Okinawa, *635, 644, 646–647, 648, 650*
Osaka, *470, 472, 482*
Shikoku, *567–568, 574, 577–578, 580, 582–583, 585, 588, 590–591, 593, 594, 596–597*
Tohoku, *693, 697, 698, 700, 702–703*
Tokyo, *143, 150, 166, 170, 176, 179, 188–189, 212, 213, 216, 219, 221, 230*
Western Honshu, *530, 531, 533, 539, 542, 554, 555, 556*
Yokohama, *242, 243, 246–248*
Music
Kanazawa, *371*
Kobe, *517–518*
Kyoto, *413–414, 430*
Nagoya, *318*
Okinawa, *646*
Osaka, *477*
Tokyo, *148, 171, 186, 195, 196, 203–204, 210, 218*
**Music shops,** *187, 206, 640*
**Myoken Ishiharaso** ⌃ , *628*
**Myoryu-ji Temple,** *368*
**Myoshin-ji Temple,** *442*
**Myth of Tomorrow** (mural), *179*

# N

**Nachi,** *330–331*
**Nachi Shrine,** *330–331*
**Naga-machi Samurai District** (Kanazawa), *368*
**Nagamahama Beach,** *655–656*
**Nagano,** *341, 345–346, 348–349*
**Nagara River Ukai Museum,** *320*

**Nagasaki,** *610–616*
**Nagasaki Atomic Bomb Museum,** *613–614*
**Nagoya, Ise-Shima, and the Kii Peninsula,** *20, 304–334*
festivals, *309*
guided tours, *319–320, 322, 330*
lodging, *308, 317–318, 321–322, 323, 328, 329, 330, 333–334*
nightlife and the arts, *318*
outdoor activities and sports, *318–319, 323*
prices, *310*
restaurants, *310, 316–317, 321, 323, 328*
timing the visit, *310*
transportation, *307–308*
visitor information, *310*
**Nagoya City Science Museum,** *314*
**Nagoya Kanko Hotel** ⌃ , *317*
**Nagoya Castle,** *314*
**Naha and environs,** *639–643*
**Naka-dake** (volcano), *621*
**Nakajima Park,** *728*
**Nakamachi District** (Matsumoto), *351*
**Nakijin Castle,** *649–650*
**Nanzen-in** (garden), *408*
**Nanzen-ji Temple,** *407–408*
**Naoshima,** *576–579*
**Naoshima Bath I ♥ Yu,** *578*
**Nara,** *458–459, 488–502*
Central Nara, *492*
festivals, *494*
history, *501*
lodging, *489, 492, 498, 499*
Nara Koen, *493–498*
Naramachi, *498–499*
restaurants, *489, 492, 497, 499, 502*
shopping, *492, 499*
transportation, *489*
Western Nara, *500–502*
**Nara Hotel** ⌃ , *498*
**Nara Koen,** *493–498*
**Nara National Museum,** *495*
**Naramachi,** *498–499*
**Naramachi Museum,** *499*
**Nara's sacred deer,** *458–459, 493*
**Narita Airport area,** *232*
**Naruto Whirlpools,** *582*
**National Art Center, Tokyo,** *188*
**National Diet Building,** *140*
**National Museum of Ethnology,** *470*
**National Museum of Modern Art, Kyoto,** *408–409*
**National Museum of Western Art,** *212*
**Nawa Insect Museum,** *320*
**Nebuta Museum Wa-Rasse,** *700*
**Neputa Festival,** *695*
**Netsu-no-yu Bath,** *345*
**New York Bar,** *201*
**New York Grill** ✕ , *200*
**Nezu Museum,** *170*
**Nightlife and the arts**

Hokkaido, *722, 731–732, 755*
Japan Alps and the North Chubu Coast, *354, 363, 371*
Kobe, *504, 517–518*
Kyoto, *386–387, 413–414, 430–431*
Kyushu, *609*
Nagoya, *318*
Okinawa, *646*
Osaka, *468, 477, 487*
Shikoku, *582, 595–596*
Tokyo, *135–136, 148–149, 156–157, 168–169, 170–171, 184–186, 194–195, 196, 201–204, 210, 218, 224–225*
**Nihonbashi** (Tokyo), *150–153*
**Nihonbashi Bridge,** *150*
**Nihonbashi Yukari** ✕ , *150–151*
**Niigata,** *341, 375–377*
**Nijo Castle,** *421–422*
**Nijo Encampment,** *420–421*
**Ni-ju-bashi Bridge,** *140*
**Nikko,** *237, 290–302*
guided tours, *299*
lodging, *299, 302*
restaurants, *298–299, 302*
transportation, *290–291*
visitor information, *292*
**Nikko Futarasan Jinja Shrine Chugushi,** *301*
**Nikko Toshogu Museum,** *293*
**Nikolai-do Holy Resurrection Cathedral,** *207*
**Ninen-zaka** (Kyoto), *409*
**Ninna-ji Temple,** *442*
**Nintoku's tomb,** *483–484*
**Nippon Maru Memorial Park,** *246*
**Nipponbashi Den Den Town** (Osaka), *482*
**Niseko,** *711, 713, 736–740*
**Nishijin-ori Textile Center,** *422*
**Nishiyama Crater Trail,** *742*
**Noboribetsu Date Jidaimura,** *743*
**Noboribetsu Onsen,** *743–744*
**Noh theater,** *100–101, 157, 186, 387, 414, 430–431*
**Nomura-ke Samurai Residence,** *368–369*
**Noritake Garden,** *314–315*
**North Chubu Coast,** *21, 336.* ⇨ *See also* Japan Alps and the North Chubu Coast
**North of Kobe,** *519–520*
**Northern Culture Museum,** *376*
**Northern Kyoto,** *449–454*
**Northern Okinawa,** *649–652*
**Northern Tohoku,** *669*
**Noto Seacoast,** *372–373*
**Noto-hanto,** *340–341*
**Noto Peninsula,** *372–374*
**Nunobiki Falls,** *520*

# O

**Oboke-Koboke Gorges,** *583–586*
**Ogi,** *378–379*
**Ogijima Island,** *574*
**Ohara Art Museum,** *531*
**Ohori Park,** *607*
**Oirase Gorge,** *694*
**Okayama,** *528–530*
**Okayama Castle,** *529*
**Okayama Orient Museum,** *530*
**Okinawa,** *23, 632–664*
beaches, *648, 652–653, 655–656, 659*
guided tours, *663*
lodging, *637, 645–646, 649, 650–651, 656–657, 659–660, 661, 663*
nightlife and the arts, *646*
outdoor activities and sports, *646, 647, 648, 651–652, 653, 657, 660–661, 663–664*
prices, *638*
restaurants, *637, 644–645, 648, 650, 656, 659*
shopping, *640, 642, 646*
timing the visit, *638, 639*
transportation, *637*
Okinawa Churaumi Aquarium at Ocean Expo Park, *649*
**Okinawa Karate Kaikan,** *647*
**Okinawa Main Island,** *638–652*
**Okinawa pottery,** *644*
**Okinawa Prefectural Peace Memorial Museum,** *647*
**Okinawa World,** *647–648*
**Okuno-in Cemetery,** *333*
**Old Town** (Matsumoto), *350–351*
**Omi-cho Market,** *369*
**Onsen (thermal baths),** *102–105, 284*
Hakone, *277*
Hokkaido, *742, 743–744, 751, 754*
Japan Alps and the North Chubu Coast, *345, 348–349, 356*
Kyushu, *621–622, 629–630*
Nagoya, Ise-Shima, and Kii Peninsula, *331*
Shikoku, *578, 592, 599*
Tohoku, *679, 684, 685 688, 691, 694, 700–701*
Western Honshu, *551*
**Osado Skyline Drive,** *379*
**Osaka,** *465–488*
children, attractions for, *33*
cuisine, *473*
history, *467*
Kita, *469–479*
lodging, *468, 476–477, 485–487*
Minami, *479–488*
nightlife and the arts, *468, 477, 487*
outdoor activities and sports, *478–479, 488*
restaurants, *468, 473, 476, 484–485*
shopping, *468–469, 477–478, 487*
transportation, *466, 468*
visitor information, *469*
**Osaka Aquarium Kaiyukan,** *470–471*

**Osaka Castle,** *471*
**Osaka City Museum of Fine Arts,** *482*
**Osaka Expo Park,** *471*
**Osaka Marriott Miyako Hotel** ⌧, *485–486*
**Osaka Museum of History,** *472*
**Osaki Hachiman Shrine,** *673–674*
**Osore-zan Mountain,** *694*
**Ota Memorial Museum of Art,** *176*
**Otaru,** *713, 733–736*
**Otaru Canal,** *734–735*
**Otaru Snow Lantern Festival,** *733*
**Ote-mon Gate,** *140*
**O-torii Gate,** *546*
**Otoyo Shrine,** *409*
**Otsuka Museum of Art,** *582–583*
**Oura Church,** *614*
**Outdoor activities and sports,** *110–115.* ⇨ See also under specific cities
**Owari Tsushima Tenno Festival,** *309*
**Oyama Shrine,** *369*
**Oyamazumi Shrine,** *599*
**Oyu Geyser,** *282*
**Ozu Washi** (shop), *153*

# P

**Packing,** *62*
**Palace Hotel Tokyo** ⌧, *145*
**Papermaking,** *95, 153, 158, 164, 206, 514, 582*
**Park Hotel Tokyo** ⌧, *168*
**Park Hyatt Tokyo** ⌧, *201*
**Parks.** ⇨ See Gardens and parks
**Passports and visas,** *62*
**Peace Bell,** *538*
**Peace Clock Tower,** *538*
**Peace Flame,** *533, 535, 538*
**Peace Memorial Park** (Hiroshima), *535, 536–539*
**Peace Memorial Park** (Okinawa), *635*
**Peace Museum** (Hiroshima), *538–539*
**Peace Park** (Nagasaki), *614*
**Pearls,** *327*
**Philosopher's Path** (Kyoto), *399–403*
**Pond for Peace,** *538*
**Ponshukan** (shop), *376–377*
**Pop culture,** *108–109*
**Pottery,** *368, 549, 643–644, 688*
**Prada** (shop), *174*
**Prices**
Hokkaido, *717*
Japan Alps and the North Chubu Coast, *342*
Kansai region, *465*
Kyoto, *386, 388*
Kyushu, *606*

Nagoya, Ise-Shima, and the Kii Peninsula, *310*
Okinawa, *638*
Shikoku, *565*
Tohoku, *671*
Tokyo, *135, 137*
Tokyo side trips, *238*
Western Honshu, *528*
**Printed fabrics,** *512*
**Pubs,** *156, 184, 224–225, 354, 371, 430, 518, 722, 726, 728*
**Puppet theater,** *101, 487*

# R

**Rafting,** *586*
**Raku Museum,** *422*
**Ramen,** *89*
**Reihokan Treasure Hall,** *333*
**Religion,** *122–126*
**Rest House,** *539*
**Restaurants,** *32, 58–59, 82.* ⇨ See also under specific cities
prices, *137, 238, 310, 342, 388, 465, 528, 565, 606, 638, 671, 717*
**Rideshares,** *52–53*
**Rinno-ji Temple** (Sendai), *674*
**Rinno-ji Temple** (Nikko), *293, 295*
**Risshaku-ji Temple,** *684–685*
**Ritsurin Garden,** *568*
**Ritz-Carlton, Kyoto** ⌧, *413*
**Ritz-Carlton, Osaka** ⌧, *477*
**Ritz-Carlton, Tokyo** ⌧, *194*
**Roadside Station Tsuwano Onsen,** *551*
**Robata Honten** ✕, *144*
**Robatayaki,** *90*
**Rock clubs,** *477*
**Rokuzan Art Museum,** *353*
**Roppongi** (Tokyo), *187–196*
**Rusutsu,** *711, 713, 740–741*
**Ryoan-ji** (rock garden), *407*
**Ryoan-ji Temple,** *442*
**Ryogen-in** (garden), *440*
**Ryokan,** *106–107, 287*
**Ryokan Kurashiki** ⌧, *532*
**Ryosen-ji Temple,** *286*
**Ryotsu,** *378*
**Ryugaeshi Waterfall,** *344*
**Ryuko-ji Temple,** *261, 262*
**Ryuzu Falls,** *301*

# S

**Sacred Precinct,** *333*
**Sacred Stable,** *295*
**Sado Gold Mine,** *379*
**Sado Island,** *341, 377–380*
**Safety,** *32, 59–60, 671*
**Saiho-ji Temple,** *447*

Sai-no-Kawara Open-Air Bath, *345*
Saitou Family Villa, *376*
Sakamoto Ryoma Memorial Museum, *590–591*
Sake, *376–377, 437, 460–461, 507, 508, 580*
Sakino-yu Hot Spring, *331*
Sakunami Onsen, *685*
Sakura-jima Volcano, *630*
San'in Region (Western Honshu), *526, 547*
Sanja Festival, *221*
Sanjusangen-do Hall, *409*
Sankei-en (garden), *246*
Sanmachi Suji District (Takayama), *361–362*
Sannai Maruyama Site, *700*
Sannen-zaka and Ninen-zaka (Kyoto), *409*
Sanrio Puroland (amusement park), *227*
Sanyo Region (Western Honshu), *526*
Sanzen-in Temple, *452*
Sapporo, *713, 722–732*
Sapporo Beer Museum and Beer Garden, *728*
Sapporo Clock Tower, *728*
Sapporo Odori Park, *728*
Sapporo Olympic Museum, *728–729*
Sapporo Snow Festival, *724*
Seihakusai Dekayama festival, *343*
Seki Traditional Swordsmith Museum, *320*
Sendai, *669, 672–678*
Sendai Castle, *674*
Sengaku-ji Temple, *227, 230*
Senkaku Bay, *379–380*
Sen-oku Hakuko Kan Museum, *409*
Senshunraku Jōzan Pottery Studio, *549*
Senso-ji Temple Complex, *222–223*
Shamisen, *697*
Shibu Onsen, *348–349*
Shibu Onsen's Nine Baths, *349*
Shibuya (Tokyo), *178–187*
Shikoku, *22, 560–600*
  festivals, *580*
  guided tours, *565, 573, 581*
  history, *572*
  lodging, *564, 575, 579, 583, 586, 589, 595, 597, 600*
  nightlife and the arts, *582, 595–596*
  outdoor activities and sports, *568, 586, 599–600*
  prices, *565*
  restaurants, *564–565, 574–575, 578–579, 583, 588–589, 594–595*
  shopping, *575–576, 589, 596, 597*
  timing the visit, *564, 565*
  transportation, *563–564*
  visitor information, *565*
Shikoku Mura Mura Village, *568, 574*
Shikoku Temple Pilgrimage, *569–573*
Shikotsu-Toya National Park, *713*

Shima Hospital, *538–539*
Shima Teahouse, *369*
Shimanami Kaido, *598–600*
Shimanami Kaido Cycling Route, *599–600*
Shimoda, *285–289*
Shin Sekai (Osaka), *482*
Shinagawa Aquarium, *230*
Shingu, *329–330*
Shini-e-Omizutori (Water-Drawing Festival), *494*
Shinjuku (Tokyo), *196–206*
Shinjuku Gyoen National Garden, *197*
Shinkyo Bridge, *295*
Shinobazu Pond, *212–213*
Shinobazu Pond Bentendo Temple, *213*
Shinsen 🗺 , *627*
Shinto, *123, 126*
Shin-Yakushi-ji Temple, *495*
Shiodome (Tokyo), *165–169*
Shiomi Samurai Residence, *556*
Shirahama, *331*
Shiraito and Ryugaeshi Waterfalls, *344*
Shirakami Mountains, *700*
Shirakawa-go, *341, 363–364*
Shiraoi, *744*
Shirara-yu Hot Spring, *331*
Shiretoko Five Lakes, *751–752*
Shiretoko National Park, *714, 749–753*
Shiretoko National Park Nature Center, *752*
Shisa, *642*
Shitamachi Museum, *213*
Shitennoji Temple, *482–483*
Shizuki Park, *549–550*
Shoan Ryokan 🗺 , *684*
Shofukuji Temple, *607–608*
Shoho-ji Temple, *320–321*
Shopping, *26–29, 82.* ➪ *See also under specific cities*
Shopping streets and arcades (Tokyo), *225*
Shoren-in Temple, *409–410*
Shoren-ji Temple, *362*
Showa Shinsan, *742*
Shrines and temples, *30–31, 125–126, 290*
  Hokkaido, *727*
  Japan Alps and the North Chubu Coast, *346, 348, 360–361, 362, 368, 369, 372, 373*
  Kamakura, *253, 255–257, 258–259, 260–263*
  Kobe, *507*
  Kyoto, *391, 394–395, 397–405, 406, 407–408, 409–410, 417, 422–423, 434–435, 437–438 440 442, 445, 446–447, 449, 451–452*
  Kyushu, *607–608, 611, 624, 626, 627*
  lodging, *61, 69*

  Nagoya, Ise-Shima, and the Kii Peninsula, *313, 320–321, 325, 327, 329–331, 332*
  Nara, *493–497, 500–502*
  Nikko, *293, 295–298, 299, 301*
  Osaka, *472, 479, 482–483*
  Shikoku, *569–573, 580, 590, 593–594, 598, 599*
  Shimoda, *285–286*
  Tohoku, *673–674, 680, 683, 684–685, 686, 696*
  Tokyo, *141, 164, 175, 207, 211–212, 213, 216–217, 219, 222–223, 227, 230*
  Western Honshu, *545, 551–552, 557–558*
  Yokohama, *242–243, 247*
Shugaku-in Imperial Villa, *453*
Shuincho, *415*
Shukkeien Garden, *543*
Shukunegi, *380*
Shuri-jo Castle, *643*
Shuzenji, *288–289*
Silk, *246–247, 369, 416*
Silk Museum, *246–247*
Simamariasibi (tours), *663*
Skiing, *355–356, 711, 733, 738–741, 747*
Snorkeling, *651, 657, 660–661*
Snowboarding, *733, 738–741*
Soccer, *318–319, 478–479*
Soji-ji (temple), *247*
Soji-ji Soin Temple, *373*
Sounkyo Gorge, *745–746*
South Gifu-ken, *307*
Southern Kyoto, *434–437*
Souvenirs, *218, 225, 434*
Spas. ➪ *See Onsen (thermal baths)*
Sports and outdoor activities, *110–115.* ➪ *See also under specific cities*
Sports outfitters, *740*
SS-30 Observation Deck, *674–675*
Subway travel
  Kobe, *504*
  Kyoto, *385*
  Osaka, *466*
  Tokyo, *133–135*
Sugar Loaf Hill, *635*
Suizenji Jojuen Garden, *618*
Sukayu Onsen, *700–701*
Sumiyoshi Taisha Grand Shrine, *483*
Sumo, *114–115, 230, 319*
Sumo Museum, *230*
Suntory Museum of Art, *188–189*
Sushi, *88*
Swissôtel Nankai Osaka 🗺 , *486–487*
Swords and knives, *153, 164, 196, 219, 221, 225, 320, 514*

**T**

Taga Shrine, *598*
Taiho-an Teahouse, *437*
Taikodani Inari-jinja Shrine, *551–552*
Taimeiken Kite Museum, *150*
Taiyu-in Temple, *295–296*

Takachiho, *625–627*
Takachiho Gorge, *626*
Takachiho-no mine, *625*
Takachiho Shrine, *626*
Takamatsu, *565–576*
Takaoka City, *373*
Takayama, *341, 360–363*
Takayama Float Exhibition Hall, *362*
Takayama Jinya Historical Government House, *362*
Taketomi Island, *659*
Tale of Genji Museum, *437*
Tamagawa Onsen, *691*
Tanabata Festival (Tanabata Matsuri), *674*
Tawaraya Ryokan ⊤ , *428*
Taxes, *62–63*
Taxis, *52–53*
   Kyoto, *386*
   Nara, *489*
   Osaka, *466, 468*
   Tokyo, *133*
Tazawako-ko (lake), *699–691*
Tea, *155*
Tea ceremony, *118–119*
Teahouses, *322, 369, 437, 556*
Telephones, *63, 69*
Temple markets, *417, 434*
Temple Pilgrimage, *569–573*
Temples, lodging in, *61, 69.* ⇨ *See also Shrines and temples*
Tempura, *91*
Teine, *732–733*
Tenman-gu Shrine, *472*
Tenno-ji Park, *483*
Tenryu-ji Temple, *447*
Textiles, *97, 226, 422*
Theater
   Ainu, *755*
   Bunraku (puppet), *101, 487*
   Kabuki, *99–100, 149, 156–157, 387, 414, 597*
   Kyoto, *387, 414, 430–431*
   modern, *148*
   Noh, *100–101, 157, 186, 387, 414, 430–431*
   Osaka, *487*
   Shikoku, *582, 597*
   Tokyo, *148–149, 156–157*
Thermal baths. ⇨ *See Onsen (thermal baths)*
Tickets, *56–57, 111*
Timing the visit, *53.* ⇨ *See also under specific cities*
Tipping, *63*
Todai-ji Temple, *495–497*
Tofuku-ji Temple, *437*
Tohoku, *23, 666–706*
   cuisine, *671, 680*
   festivals, *674, 687, 695, 702*
   lodging, *670, 677, 681–683, 685, 686, 688–689, 691, 693, 695, 697–698, 701, 703–704, 706*
   prices, *671*

restaurants, *670–671, 675, 677, 680–681, 688, 697, 701, 703, 706*
   safety, *671*
   shopping, *677–678, 680, 682, 688, 692*
   timing the visit, *672*
   transportation, *669–670*
   visitor information, *672*
Tohoku's West Coast, *669*
To-ji Temple, *422–423*
Toka-e (festival), *494*
Tokashiki-jima (island), *652*
Tokei-ji Temple, *255256*
Toki no Kane Belfry, *223*
Tokugawa Art Museum, *315–316*
Tokushima, *580–583*
Tokyo, *20, 128–232*
   Akihabara, *207–210*
   Aoyama and Harajuku, *169–178*
   Asakusa, *218–226*
   children, attractions for, *33*
   cuisine, *182*
   festivals, *140, 221*
   Ginza, *153–158, 164*
   Greater Tokyo, *226–232*
   guided tours, *165*
   Imperial Palace, *138–142*
   Kabuki-cho, *205*
   lodging, *135, 142, 144–145, 148, 151–152, 156, 168, 183, 193–194, 200–201, 209, 217, 223–224, 231–232*
   Marunouchi, *142–149*
   Narita Airport area, *232*
   nightlife and the arts, *135–136, 148–149, 156–157, 168–169, 170–171, 184–186, 194–195, 196, 201–204, 210, 218, 224–225*
   Nihonbashi, *150–153*
   prices, *135, 137*
   restaurants, *136–137, 141–142, 144, 150–151, 153, 155, 165, 170, 176–177, 182–183, 191, 193, 200, 207, 209, 217, 223, 231*
   Roppongi, *187–196*
   Shibuya, *178–187*
   Shinjuku, *196–206*
   Shiodome, *158–160*
   shopping, *130–131, 137–138, 142, 149, 152–153, 157–165, 168, 171, 174–175, 177–178, 186–187, 195196, 204, 206, 209–210, 218, 225–226*
   timing the visit, *138*
   transportation, *133–135*
   Tsukiji, *164–165*
   Ueno, *211–218*
   visitor information, *138*
Tokyo Disney Resort, *230*
Tokyo International Forum, *143*
Tokyo Marathon, *140*
Tokyo Metropolitan Art Museum, *213, 216*
Tokyo Metropolitan Government Office, *197*
Tokyo Metropolitan Teien Art Museum, *179*
Tokyo National Museum, *216*
Tokyo Sea Life Park, *230–231*
Tokyo side trips, *20, 234–302*

Tokyo Sky Tree, *223*
Tokyo Station, *144*
Tokyo Tower, *189*
Tokyu Hands (shop), *186*
Tomb of Emperor Nintoku, *483–484*
Tooriike Pond, *655*
Torii, *290*
Toshodai-ji Temple, *501, 502*
Toshogu, *292–293, 295–299*
Toshogu Nikko Shrine, *296–298*
Toshogu Shrine, *295*
Tour de Château ✕, *618*
Towada-Hachimantai National Park, *694–695*
Towada-ko (lake), *695*
Toyako, *741–743*
Toyako Onsen, *742*
Toyama, *341, 374–375*
Toyosu Market, *168*
Toyota Commemorative Museum of Industry and Technology, *316*
Toyotomi Hideyoshi, *405*
Toys, *178*
Traditional wares, *225–226*
Train travel, *53–57, 69*
   Hokkaido, *716*
   Japan Alps and the North Chubu Coast, *341, 375*
   Kansai region, *463–464*
   Kobe, *504*
   Kyoto, *386*
   Kyushu, *605*
   Nagoya, Ise-Shima, and the Kii Peninsula, *308*
   Nara, *489*
   Osaka, *468*
   Shikoku, *564*
   Tohoku, *670*
   Tokyo, *133–135*
   Western Honshu, *527*
Transportation, *32, 48–57, 68, 69, 82.* ⇨ *See also under specific cities*
Travel agencies, *69*
Tsuboya Pottery District (Naha), *643*
Tsuboya Pottery Museum, *644*
Tsugaike Nature Garden, *356*
Tsugaru Neputa Village, *697*
Tsukiji (Tokyo), *164–165*
Tsukiji Hongan-ji Temple, *164*
Tsukiji Outer Market, *164–165*
Tsuruoka Hachimangu Shrine, *258–259*
Tsurui Ito Tancho Sanctuary, *756*
Tsuruoka and Dewa-Sanzan, *704–706*
Tsutenkaku Tower, *484*
Tsuwano, *550–553*
Tsuwano Castle Ruins, *552*
21st Century Museum of Contemporary Art, *369*
21_21 Design Sight, *189*

# U

Uchiko, *596–597*
Uchiko Townhouse Museum, *597*
Uchiko-za Kabuki Theater, *597*
Ueno (Tokyo), *211–218*
Ueno Tosho-gu Shrine, *216–217*
Ueno Zoo, *217*
Uji Shrine, *438*
Umagaeshi, *301–302*
Underground Headquarters of the Japanese Imperial Navy, *635, 647*
Underwater Memorial (Okinawa), *635*
Universal Studios Japan, *472–473*
Upopoy National Ainu Museum and Park, *744*
Urami Falls, *302*
Usa Shrine, *624*
Usagi-Ya ✕ , *659*
USS *Emmons*, *635*
Uwajima, *597–598*
Uwajima Castle, *598*

# V

Vending machines, *130–131*
Video games, *109*
Vine Bridges, *585–586*
Visas, *62*
Visitor information, *65, 69*
*Hokkaido, 718*
*Japan Alps and the North Chubu Coast, 342*
*Kamakura, 251*
*Kansai region, 465, 469, 506*
*Kobe, 506*
*Kyoto, 389–391*
*Kyushu, 606*
*Nagoya, Ise-Shima, and the Kii Peninsula, 310*
*Nikko, 292*
*Osaka, 469*
*Shikoku, 565*
*Tohoku, 672*
*Tokyo, 138*
*Western Honshu, 528*
Volcanic Science Museum, *742*
Volcanoes, *620–621, 630, 742*

# W

Wajima Lacquerware Museum, *373*
Wajima Morning Market, *373*
Wakakusa-yama Yaki (Grass-Burning Festival), *494*
Wakkoqu ✕ , *516*
Water-Drawing Festival, *494*
Waterfalls, *301, 302, 344, 520, 751*
Weather, *53*

Weathercock House, *519*
West Hongan-ji Temple, *423*
Western Honshu, *21–22, 524–558*
*lodging, 527, 530, 531–532, 543–544, 546, 550, 553, 556–557*
*outdoor activities and sports, 546*
*prices, 528*
*restaurants, 527, 530, 531, 543, 550, 552, 556*
*shopping, 542, 549*
*timing the visit, 528*
*transportation, 526–527*
*visitor information, 528*
Western Kyoto, *438–443*
Western Nara, *500–502*
Western Shikoku, *562–563*
Whale-watching, *646, 651–652, 653*
Windsor Hotel Toya Resort and Spa, The 🍽 , *742–743*
Workshop of Kaga-Yuzen, *369*
World Porters (shopping center), *247*
World War II sights (Okinawa), *634–635*

# Y

Yaeyama Islands, *657–664*
Yakushi-ji Temple, *502*
Yamada Heiando (shop), *187*
Yamadera, *684–685*
Yamagata, *687–689*
Yamaguchi, *547*
Yamashita Park, *247*
Yambaru Art Gallery, *650*
Yari Onsen, *356*
Yasaka Shrine, *410*
Yasukuni Jinja, *141*
Yokohama, *236, 238–250*
*restaurants, 249–250*
*shopping, 247, 248*
*transportation, 239–240*
Yokohama Archives of History Museum, *247–248*
Yokohama Cosmo World, *248*
Yokohama Doll Museum, *248*
Yokohama Foreign General Cemetery, *248*
Yokohama Red Brick Warehouses, *248*
Yokoyama Memorial Manga Museum, *588*
Yonaha Maehama Beach, *656*
Yonehara Beach, *659*
Yoritomo's tomb, *257–258*
Yosakoi Soran Festival, *724*
Yoshikawa 🍽 , *428*
Yoshino Beach, *656*
Yoyogi Park, *176*
Yudanaka Onsen, *348–349*

Yudono-san, *706*
Yufu Ryochiku 🍽 , *625*
Yufuin, *622–625*
Yumigahana Beach, *286*
Yunotsubokaido Street (Yufuin), *624*
Yutaka Isozaki Gallery, *624*
Yuuki ✕ , *552*

# Z

Zamami-jima (island), *652–653*
Zenko-ji Temple, *346, 348*
Zoos and aquariums, *33*
*Izu Peninsula, 284*
*Kyoto, 417, 445*
*Okinawa, 649*
*Osaka, 470–471*
*Tokyo, 217, 230–231*
Zuigan-ji Temple, *683*
Zuihoden (mausoleum), *675*
Zuiho-in (garden), *440*

# Photo Credits

**Front Cover:** Sean Pavone / Alamy Stock Photo [Description: DRJJJB Ginkaku-ji Silver Pavilion during the autumn season in Kyoto, Japan]. **Back cover, from left to right:** Shutterstock / NH; Martin Mette/Shutterstock; Sepavo | Dreamstime.com **Spine:** Shutterstock / Justin Lancaster **Interior, from left to right:** Moustache Girl/Shutterstock (1) Patryk Kosmider/Shutterstock (2) Pigprox/Shutterstock (5) **Chapter 1: Experience Japan:** apiguide/Shutterstock (8) Sepavo | Dreamstime.com (10) NavinTar/Shutterstock (11) Aduldej | Dreamstime.com (11) Romrodinka | Dreamstime.com (12) Pigprox / Shutterstock (12) Sepavo | Dreamstime.com (12) Prakobkit | Dreamstime.com (13) Eyeblink | Dreamstime.com (13) Bennymarty | Dreamstime.com (14) Phuong D. Nguyen / Shutterstock (14) Suab1977 | Dreamstime.com (14) Mengtianhan | Dreamstime.com (14) NH / Shutterstock (15) Matee Nuserm / Shutterstock (16) Checco | Dreamstime.com (16) Tktkttk | Dreamstime.com (16) J. Henning Buchholz/Shutterstock (16) Sepavo | Dreamstime.com (17) Sepavo | Dreamstime.com (17) Michaelmou85 | Dreamstime.com (17) Narongsak Nagadhana / Shutterstock (17) rayints / Shutterstock (18) Nachosuch | Dreamstime.com (18) f11photo / Shutterstock (18) Shootdiem | Dreamstime.com (19) Tommyakky/iStockphoto (24) Hideo Kurihara / Alamy Stock Photo (24) 2nix/iStockphoto (24) Tokyo Convention & Visitors Bureau. (24) gyro/iStockphoto (25) Pablo Hidalgo/Dreamstime (26) Phurinee Chinakathum/Shutterstock (26) image_vulture/Shutterstock (26) Walter Lim (26) Anutr Yossundara/Shutterstock (27) Mint Images Limited / Alamy Stock Photo (28) Fuminari Yoshitsugu (29) Luciano Mortula _LGM/Shutterstock (30) Nishitap/Shutterstock (30) orpheus26/iStockphoto (30) ItzaVU/Shutterstock (31) SeanPavonePhoto/iStockphoto (31) FOTOGRIN/Shutterstock (39) Luciano Mortula - LGM/Shutterstock (40) public domain (40) Sean Pavone/ Shutterstock (40) Razvan Radu-Razvan Photography/iStockphoto (41) Rachelle Burnside/Shutterstock (41) Fedor Selivanov/Shutterstock (41) CAN BALCIOGLU/Shutterstock (41) Ilya D. Gridnev/Shutterstock (42) Wikimedia Commons (42) Neale Cousland/Shutterstock (42) Yasufumi Nishi/JNTO (43) Dr_Flash/Shutterstock (43) Tataroko/Wikimedia Commons (43) KenSoftTH/Shutterstock (44) Lokyo Multimedia JP/ Shutterstock (44) Sueddeutsche Zeitung Photo / Alamy Stock Photo (44) **Chapter 2: Travel Smart:** Ned Snowman/Shutterstock (57) retirementbonus/Shutterstock (57) **Chapter 3: A Japan Culture Primer:** Sergii Rudiuk / Shutterstock (83) Stockmelnyk/Shutterstock (85) kezoka/Shutterstock (88) Payless Images/Shutterstock (87) Saga Prefecture/JNTO (88) JNTO (88) Hokkaido Tourism Organization/ JNTO (89) Hokkaido Tourism Organization/JNTO (89) Hokkaido Tourism Organization/ JNTO (89) Nagano Prefecture/ JNTO (90) Nagano Prefecture/ JNTO (90) JNTO (91)Jill Battaglia/iStockphoto (91) svry/Shutterstock (92) Tondo Soesanto Soegondo/Shutterstock (92) Kanazawa City/© JNTO (93) JNTO (94) gorosan/Shutterstock (95) JNTO (95) Muhammad Mahfuzh Huda/Shutterstock (96) Ishikawa Prefecture/JNTO (97) Ishikawa Prefecture Tourist Association and Kanazawa Convention Bureau/JNTO (98) su.bo, [CC BY-ND 2.0]/Flickr (99) Nagano Prefecture/ JNTO (99) Jim Epler,[CC BY-ND 2.0]/Flickr (100) Iwate Prefecture/JNTO (101) onemu/Shutterstock (102) JNTO (103) Nagano Prefecture/ JNTO (103) Narongsak Nagadhana/Shutterstock (104) kai keisuke/Shutterstock (105) Antonina Polushkina/Shutterstock (106) Ekaterina McCIaud/Shutterstock (107) julianne.hide/Shutterstock (107) Hannari_eli/Shutterstock (108) enchanted_fairy/Shutterstock (109) spatuletail/ Shutterstock (109) Sean Pavone/Shutterstock (110) Mirko Kuzmanovic/Shutterstock (111) picture cells/Shutterstock (111) oneinchpunch/ Shutterstock (112) Alexander Gatsenko/Shutterstock (113) Vladimir Vasiltvich/Shutterstock (113) J. Henning Buchholz/Shutterstock (114) J. Henning Buchholz/Shutterstock (115) bluehand/Shutterstock (115) Osaze Cuomo/Shutterstock (116) Juri Pozzi/Shutterstock (117) Patrick Foto/ Shutterstock (117) dach_chan/Shutterstock (118) Jose1971 | Dreamstime.com (119) Kajohnwit Boonsom/Shutterstock (119) CHEN MIN CHUN/ Shutterstock (120) Pxhidalgo | Dreamstime.com (121) Cambo01 | Dreamstime.com (121) Nyiragongo70 | Dreamstime.com (122) Viocara | Dreamstime.com (123) Nikitu | Dreamstime.com (123) PSno7/Shutterstock (124) Warapong Noituptim/Shutterstock (125) GAOP INTUCH/ Shutterstock (126) **Chapter 4: Tokyo:** Tokyo Visionary Room/Shutterstock (127) Kristi Blokhin/Shutterstock (130) Ned Snowman/ Shutterstock (131) Morumotto/Shutterstock (131) Leonid Andronov/Shutterstock (139) cowardlion/Shutterstock (143) 2p2play/Shutterstock (159) everyday polkadot/Shutterstock (160) idealisms/Flickr (160) Andrew Currie/Flickr (160) Mie Prefecture. JINTO (161) bptakoma/Flickr (161) robcocquyt/Shutterstock (161) Naruto4836 | Dreamstime.com (161) Kimtaro/Flickr (162) dichohecho/Flickr (163) JNTO (163) Iifonimages/ Shutterstock (166) Osugi/Shutterstock (189) f11photo/Shutterstock (190) Richie Chan/Shutterstock (204) Travel Stock/Shutterstock (212) MeeRok/Shutterstock (222) asiangrandkid/Shutterstock (227) **Chapter 5: Side Trips From Tokyo:** Yujiro/Dreamstime (233) kazu0/ Shutterstock (237) Cowardlion | Dreamstime.com (241) Aschaf,[CC BY-ND 2.0]/Flickr (252) engineer story/Shutterstock (260) Samuel Ponce/ Shutterstock (262) Banzai Hiroaki/Flickr, [CC BY-ND 2.0] (266) warasit phothisuk/Shutterstock (266) diloz/Flickr, [CC BY-ND 2.0] (267) Wikimedia Commons (268) Wikimedia Commons (268) Odakyu Electric Railway/JNTO (269) Blanscape/Shutterstock (269) diloz/Flickr, [CC BY-ND 2.0] (270) jetalone/Hajime NAKANO/Flickr, [CC BY-ND 2.0] (270) jetalone/Hajime NAKANO/Flickr [CC BY-ND 2.0] (270) jetalone/ Hajime NAKANO/Flickr, [CC BY-ND 2.0] (270) imgdive/Banzai Hiroaki/Flickr, [CC BY-ND 2.0] (270) skyseeker/Flickr, [CC BY-ND 2.0] (270) Azlan DuPree/Flickr, [CC BY-ND 2.0] (271) By imgdive/Banzai Hiroaki/Flickr, [CC BY-ND 2.0] (272) diloz/Flickr, [CC BY-ND 2.0] (272) jetalone/Hajime NAKANO/Flickr, [CC BY-ND 2.0] (272) Getty Images/iStockphoto (273) Aleksandar Todorovic/Shutterstock (278) Stray Toki/Shutterstock (292) Vladimir Khirman/iStockphoto (296) Taweep Tang/Shutterstock (300) **Chapter 6: Nagoya, Ise-Shima, and the Kii Peninsula:** satoshinpi/Shutterstock (303) Kuzmire | Dreamstime.com (315) Photoerngo/Shutterstock (321) Sepavo/Dreamstime (325) smshoot/ Shutterstock (332) **Chapter 7: The Japan Alps and the North Chubu Coast:** Tearswept/Dreamstime (335) Yupgi/Shutterstock (338) Puripat Lertpunyaroj/Shutterstock (339) Jayson_Photography/Shutterstock (339) b-hide the scene/Shutterstock (346) Photo_J/Shutterstock (350) Hiro1775/Dreamstime (355) leochachaume24/Shutterstock (357) Andreas H/Shutterstock (366) popcatter/Shutterstock (375) Wissuta. on/Shutterstock (379) **Chapter 8: Kyoto:** Luciano Mortula-LGM/Shutterstock (381) Matt Comeaux/iStockphoto (395) S35ktmo | Dreamstime. com (396) takuya kanzaki/Shutterstock (398) HardebeckMedia/Shutterstock (399) PlusMinus/Wikimedia Commons (400) rudiuk/Shutterstock (400) rudiuk/Shutterstock (401) whitefield_d/whity/Flickr (401) Pigprox/Shutterstock (401) Wikimedia Commons (401) Sean Pavone/ Shutterstock (402) anju901/Shutterstock (402) CYC/Shutterstock (402) Taromon/Shutterstock (402) Sanga Park/Shutterstock (403) Bossiema | Dreamstime.com (421) J Marshall - Tribaleye Images / Alamy Stock Photo (429) Cowardlion | Dreamstime.com (432) Prapstock | Dreamstime. com (438) Sepavo | Dreamstime.com (441) Khunta | Dreamstime.com (446) Kobby_dagan | Dreamstime.com (451) Taras Vyshnya/Shutterstock (453) **Chapter 9: The Kansai Region:** cowardlion/Shutterstock (455) Benny Marty/Shutterstock (458) saryanto yanto/Shutterstock (459) brinlietravels/Shutterstock (459) Getty Images/iStockphoto (460) Carolyne Parent/Shutterstock (461) Jamo Images/Shutterstock (470)

# Photo Credits

# Notes

# Notes

# Notes

# Notes

# Notes

# Notes

# Notes

# Notes

# Notes

# Notes

# Notes

# Notes

# Notes

# Notes

# Fodor's ESSENTIAL JAPAN

**Publisher:** Stephen Horowitz, *General Manager*

**Editorial:** Douglas Stallings, *Editorial Director;* Jill Fergus, Amanda Sadlowski, *Senior Editors;* Kayla Becker, Brian Eschrich, Alexis Kelly, *Editors;* Angelique Kennedy-Chavannes, *Assistant Editor*

**Design:** Tina Malaney, *Director of Design and Production;* Jessica Gonzalez, Senior *Graphic Designer;* Erin Caceres, *Graphic Design Associate*

**Production:** Jennifer DePrima, *Editorial Production Manager;* Elyse Rozelle, *Senior Production Editor;* Monica White, *Production Editor*

**Maps:** Rebecca Baer, *Senior Map Editor;* David Lindroth, Mark Stroud (Moon Street Cartography), *Cartographers*

**Photography:** Viviane Teles, *Senior Photo Editor;* Namrata Aggarwal, Neha Gupta, Payal Gupta, Ashok Kumar, *Photo Editors;* Eddie Aldrete, *Photo Production Intern;* Kadeem McPherson, *Photo Production Associate Intern*

**Business and Operations:** Chuck Hoover, *Chief Marketing Officer;* Robert Ames, *Group General Manager;* Devin Duckworth, *Director of Print Publishing*

**Public Relations and Marketing:** Joe Ewaskiw, *Senior Director of Communications and Public Relations*

**Fodors.com:** Jeremy Tarr, *Editorial Director;* Rachael Levitt, *Managing Editor*

**Technology:** Jon Atkinson, *Director of Technology;* Rudresh Teotia, *Lead Developer*

**Writers:** Jay Farris, Tom Fay, Rob Goss, Robert Morel, Chris Willson

**Editor:** Douglas Stallings

**Production Editor:** Monica White

2nd Edition

ISBN 978-1-64097-543-9

ISSN 2578-305X

All details in this book are based on information supplied to us at press time. Always confirm information when it matters, especially if you're making a detour to visit a specific place. Fodor's expressly disclaims any liability, loss, or risk, personal or otherwise, that is incurred as a consequence of the use of any of the contents of this book.

## SPECIAL SALES

This book is available at special discounts for bulk purchases for sales promotions or premiums. For more information, e-mail SpecialMarkets@fodors.com.

PRINTED IN THE UNITED STATES OF AMERICA

10 9 8 7 6 5 4 3 2 1

# About Our Writers

 **Jay Farris** has spent more than 20 years getting acquainted with Japan and now calls Tokyo home after a few years of living in Yamagata. He works as a translator and, having graduated from the University of Tokyo with a master's degree in urban engineering, as a lecturer for curious people interested in urban history and Tokyo's rich backstory. Jay updated the Experience, Culture Primer, and Tohoku chapters for this edition.

 **Tom Fay** is a British travel and outdoors writer who spent 15 years in Osaka, but now lives in a renovated farmhouse in southern Kyoto. He is the main author of a hiking guide to the Japan Alps and Mt. Fuji and is working on the first English-language guidebook to Hokkaido. Tom updated the Kyoto and Kansai Region chapters.

 Nagoya, Japan Alps, and Shikoku updater **Rob Goss** has lived in Tokyo since 1999. In that time, Rob has worked with more than 100 publications around the globe, including *Time, National Geographic,* and BBC Travel. He is also the author of seven occasionally award-winning books on Japan.

 **Robert Morel** has been exploring Japan since 2003 and still thinks the best way to get from Hokkaido to Okinawa is by bicycle. He currently writes about, photographs, and lives in Tokyo's Shitamachi neighborhood. He updated the Tokyo, Side Trips from Tokyo, and Travel Smart chapters.

 **Chris Willson** is a travel writer and photographer based in Motobu, Okinawa. Since 1999, he has lived in Honshu, Hokkaido, and Okinawa. He loves to snowboard in winter and scuba dive in summer. In recent years he has focused on documenting Japanese festivals, martial arts, and Ryukyu culture. His website is ⊕ *www.travel67. com.* He updated the Hokkaido, Western Honshu, Kyushu, and Okinawa chapters.